THE SANTA FE RING VERSUS Billy The Kid: The Making of an American Monster

BY GALE COOPER

GELCOUR BOOKS

COVER ART AND BOOK DESIGN BY GALE COOPER
Cover illustration inspired by a 19th century
Tammany Hall Ring cartoon by Thomas Nast

The Santa Fe Ring in Action: 'TWAS HIM!

OTHER BILLY THE KID BOOKS BY GALE COOPER:

BILLY AND PAULITA: THE SAGA OF BILLY THE KID, PAULITA MAXWELL, AND THE SANTA FE RING

BILLY THE KID'S WRITINGS, WORDS, AND WIT

THE LOST PARDON OF BILLY THE KID: AN ANALYSIS FACTORING IN THE SANTA FE RING, GOVERNOR LEW WALLACE'S DILEMMA, AND A TERRITORY IN REBELLION

BILLY THE KID'S PRETENDERS, BRUSHY BILL & JOHN MILLER

CRACKING THE BILLY THE KID CASE HOAX: THE STRANGE PLOT TO EXHUME BILLY THE KID, CONVICT SHERIFF PAT GARRETT OF MURDER, AND BECOME PRESIDENT OF THE UNITED STATES

BLANDINA SEGALE, THE NUN WHO RODE ON BILLY THE KID: SLEUTHING A FOISTED FRONTIER FABLE

THE COLD CASE BILLY THE KID MEGAHOAX: A RASCALLY REPLAY OF BILLY THE KID CASE'S FORENSIC FLIMFLAM AND BRUSHY BILL'S BILLY THE KID BAMBOOZLE

For Billy Bonney,
who won the Ring's prize
for its mightiest foes: a bullet

And
for the Ring's murdered opponents
before and after Billy Bonney:

John P. Slough, Franklin Tolby, Robert Casey, unnamed Maxwell Land Grant settlers, John Henry Tunstall, Dick Brewer, Frank MacNab, unnamed San Patricio massacre victims, Alexander McSween, Harvey Morris, Vincente Romero, Francisco Zamora, unnamed Lincoln County War fighters, Huston Chapman, Tom O'Folliard, Charlie Bowdre, Alexis Grossetete, Robert Elsinger, and Francisco Chavez

And
for the Ring's almost murdered opponents:

Raymond Morley, Clay Allison, Henry M. Porter, Oscar P. McMains, Juan Patrón, Ygenio Salazar, Jose Chávez y Chávez, Ignacio Gonzales, Florencio Chávez, Jim French, Ira Leonard, Montegue Leverson, Oliver Lee, and James Gilliland

COPYRIGHT © 2018 Gale Cooper

ALL RIGHTS RESERVED
*Reproductions, excerpts, or transmittals
of the author's original cover art or text in this book
are prohibited in any form whatsoever
without written permission of the author.
Infringers will be prosecuted
to the fullest extent of the law.*

FIRST EDITION

ISBN: 978-0-9860707-4-7 HARDCOVER
ISBN: 978-0-9860707-5-4 PAPERBACK
LCCN: 2016913770

GELCOUR BOOKS
2270D Wyoming Boulevard NE
Suite 217
Albuquerque, NM 87112

WEBSITE:
GaleCooperBillyTheKidBooks.com

YOUTUBE:
Gale Cooper's Real Billy the Kid

ORDERING THIS BOOK:
Amazon.com, BarnesandNoble.com, bookstores

Printed in the United States of America
on acid free paper

CONTENTS

PREFACE..xvii
AUTHOR'S FOREWORD xviii
METHODOLOGY xxii
ACKNOWLEDGMENTS xxiii

CHAPTER 1:
THE CONSPIRACY
TO KILL LADY LIBERTY

INTRODUCTION..3
THE ORGANIZED CRIME MODEL 4
THE PERFECT CRIME..6
A TERRITORY IN REBELLION 7

CHAPTER 2:
THE BOY WHO COULD
BREAK THE SANTA FE RING

HISTORY OF BILLY BONNEY...11
BILLY BONNEY'S CHAMPIONS.....................................30

CHAPTER 3:
HISTORY WRITTEN FOR VICTORS

HISTORY ROOTED IN MYTH 39
PAT GARRETT'S PROFITEERING
    BILLY THE KID DIME NOVEL..................................40
WALTER NOBLE BURNS'S PULP FICTION 41
RALPH EMERSON TWITCHELL'S
    RINGITE RENDITION..41
BLANDINA SEGALE, THE
    HISTORY HOAXING NUN 42
SILENCE OF THE REAL HISTORIANS............................42
FRUITS OF BANDWAGON HISTORIANS 48

CHAPTER 4:
A RING GROWS IN
NEW MEXICO TERRITORY

UNMASKING THE SANTA FE RING 51
EXISTENCE OF THE SANTA FE RING 54
CONTEMPORARY REPORTERS......................................61
A RING INSIDER'S EXPOSÉS..66
THE SANTA FE RING'S FORMULA 72

CHAPTER 5:
TERRITORIAL RING BOSS, THOMAS BENTON CATRON

THOMAS BENTON CATRON 75
EARLY YEARS 75
IMPLEMENTING SECRECY 81
CRUSHING ANTI-RING REVOLTS 85
ANGEL'S CATRON REPORT AND
    U.S. ATTORNEY RESIGNATION 86
DUDLEY COURT OF INQUIRY AND RING RISK 89
KILLING BILLY BONNEY 90
AMERICAN VALLEY MURDERS 91
FIXING ELECTIONS 92
TERRITORIAL LEGISLATURE 96
AN "ASSASSINATION ATTEMPT" 96
TERRITORIAL DELEGATE FAILURE OF 1892 98
MORE DELEGATE RUNS AND
    DEFENDING THE BORREGOS 101
FACING DISBARMENT 105
BEING MADE PRESIDENT OF THE NEW MEXICO BAR 129
REVENGE FOR DISBARMENT CASE 130
REVENGE AGAINST GOVERNOR THORNTON 132
FAILED DELEGATE RE-ELECTION 141
FAILURE TO SAVE THE BORREGOS 142
REUSING PAT GARRETT 144
ATTACKING MIGUEL A. OTERO 146
SEEKING RE-APPOINTMENT AS U.S. ATTORNEY 149
REWRITING HISTORY 150
STATEHOOD AND SENATORSHIP 151
DEATH AND LEGACY 153

CHAPTER 6:
WASHINGTON RING BOSS, STEPHEN BENTON ELKINS

STEPHEN BENTON ELKINS 157

CHAPTER 7:
THE CIRCLE OF "FRIENDS"

CORRUPT CRONIES 167
WILLIAM BREEDEN: FIRST FRIEND 167
COLFAX COUNTY KILLERS 168
LINCOLN COUNTY AGENTS 171

RING ENFORCERS 182
THUG ASSASSINS..196
PROPAGANDA PRESS 201
KEY CORONER'S JURY PRESIDENT 205
HISTORIAN FOR THEM ALL 205
WASHINGTON, D.C. FACILITATORS 206
THE ANTI-RING REBELLIONS...206

CHAPTER 8:
LEGISLATURE REVOLT
AGAINST THE SANTA FE RING

THE FIRST ANTI-RING FREEDOM FIGHT 209
THE 1872 LEGISLATURE REVOLT 210
AFTERMATH OF LEGISLATURE REVOLT 215
CREATING THE OUTLAW MYTH 225
DEAD GIDDINGS REPLACED 230

CHAPTER 9:
GRANT COUNTY REBELLION
AGAINST THE SANTA FE RING

THE GRANT COUNTY REBELLION 233
DEFLATED MISSION..237

CHAPTER 10:
COLFAX COUNTY WAR
AGAINST THE SANTA FE RING

COLFAX COUNTY WAR OVERVIEW 241
THE BEAUBIEN-MIRANDA AND
    MAXWELL LAND GRANT 242
AND MAXWELL LAND GRANT
    AND RAILWAY COMPANY..244
SETTLERS' REVOLTS..247
MALICIOUS PROSECUTION OF ADA MORLEY 248
ASSASSINATION OF FRANKLIN J. TOLBY 251
OSCAR P. McMAINS'S PURSUIT
    OF TOLBY'S KILLERS 253
EXPOSÉS AND RING RETALIATIONS..................................255
REMOVAL OF COLFAX COUNTY COURTS..........................261
THE "DEAR BEN" ASSASSINATION PLOT............................262
RING-CONTROLLED TAOS COURTS 264
McMAINS'S MURDER TRIALS...271
ADA MORLEY'S TERRIFIED LETTER...................................272

THE McPHERSON EXPOSÉS 275
COLLUDING PRESIDENT HAYES 311
CAPITULATING FRANK SPRINGER 312
COLFAX COUNTY WAR OUTCOME.. 325

CHAPTER 11:
LINCOLN COUNTY'S
SANTA FE RING "TROUBLES"

THE RING'S MOST GRUESOME LAND-GRAB 329
LINCOLN COUNTY "TROUBLES" 332
HERO IN WAITING... 334
LINCOLN COUNTY SUB-BOSSES... 335
ABOUT JOHN HENRY TUNSTALL 336
THE RING' STRIKES BACK.. 340
MALICIOUS PROSECUTION OF ALEXANDER McSWEEN .. 342
TUNSTALL EXPOSES THE RING... 344
TUNSTALL'S MALICIOUS PROSECUTION 347
McSWEEN'S ANTI-RING CRUSADE 349
RYNERSON BACKS MURDER 349
TUNSTALL'S ASSASSINATION 351
A COLFAX COUNTY RESPONSE 353

CHAPTER 12:
LINCOLN COUNTY GALVANIZES
AGAINST THE SANTA FE RING

CHOOSING REVOLUTION 357
HISTORY OF THE REGULATORS 358
POLITICIZING OF BILLY BONNEY.. 360
LEGAL PURSUIT OF TUNSTALL'S KILLERS........................... 365
RING RESPONSES 367
CITIZENS RESIST THE RING 369
THE LINCOLN COUNTY GRAND JURY................................... 375
MORE HOPE IN LINCOLN COUNTY 378
THE RING OBSTRUCTS JUSTICE 380

CHAPTER 13:
LINCOLN COUNTY WAR
AGAINST THE SANTA FE RING:

THE UNSUNG FREEDOM FIGHT 385
THE RING'S MURDEROUS RESPONSES 386
INVESTIGATOR ANGEL BRINGS HOPE................................. 389
CATRON'S FEDERAL INDICTMENT PLOT 411

CITIZENS REQUEST PRESIDENTIAL AID 415
THE POSSE COMITATUS ACT 422
RING MASSACRE AT SAN PATRICIO 422
BILLY BONNEY'S "REGULATOR MANIFESTO" 423
LOST LINCOLN COUNTY WAR BATTLE 425
AFTERMATH 430

CHAPTER 14:
REACTIONS TO THE LINCOLN COUNTY WAR

STILL SEEKING JUSTICE 433
BRAVE WIDOW SUSAN McSWEEN 439
FIRST FAME OF BILLY BONNEY 440

CHAPTER 15:
INVESTIGATOR ANGEL'S CAPITULATION

ANGEL'S RING COVER-UP 443
REPORT ON TUNSTALL'S MURDER 444
REPORT ON THE "TROUBLES" 446
PRESSURE ABOUT AXTELL 448
REPORT ON AXTELL 450
REPORT ON CATRON 458
CATRON'S RESIGNATION 461
AFTERMATH OF THE ANGEL REPORTS 464

CHAPTER 16:
LEW WALLACE ARRIVES FOR A GOVERNORSHIP

A STRANGE MAN FOR A STRANGE JOB 467
A RELUCTANT GOVERNOR 470
OUTLAW MYTH PROPAGANDA 475
WALLACE WARS ON OUTLAWS 476
A PRESIDENTIAL PROCLAMATION 478
WALLACE'S SHAM ACTION 480
HUSTON CHAPMAN WRITES TO WALLACE 480
WALLACE'S AMNESTY PROCLAMATION 482
WAR DEPARTMENT REJECTION 483
WALLACE'S SECRET RING LETTER 483
TRYING TO ESCAPE 484
RING REMOVAL RUMORS 484

CHAPTER 17:
THE RING STRIKES AGAIN

THE DUDLEY TIME-BOMB 487
HUSTON CHAPMAN'S ONSLAUGHT 489
DUDLEY ATTACKS WALLACE 493
THE RING RESPONDS TO CHAPMAN 498
ASSASSINATION OF CHAPMAN 500
AFTERMATH OF CHAPMAN'S MURDER 500
GRANT COUNTY CONDEMNS WALLACE 502
VOICES OF CONSCIENCE 503

CHAPTER 18:
LEW WALLACE CHASES OUTLAWS

COMING OF A "SAVIOR" 509
IRA LEONARD FILES CHARGES AGAINST DUDLEY 509
WALLACE GETS DUDLEY'S REMOVAL 517
ARRESTING CHAPMAN'S MURDERERS 518
DOLAN'S THREATS 518
ESCAPE OF THE PRISONERS 520
PURSUING MYTHICAL OUTLAWS 520
WALLACE FEIGNS FACT-FINDING 522
DUDLEY REQUESTS A COURT OF INQUIRY 526

CHAPTER 19:
BILLY BONNEY'S PARDON THREAT TO THE RING

THE PARDON PLAN 529
THE FIRST PARDON LETTER 530
WALLACE'S RESPONSE 531
THE SECRET MEETING 532
A HECTIC MARCH 20TH DAY 532
WALLACE'S WORRISOME REPORT 534
WALLACE INTERVIEWS BILLY 537
THE "BILLIE" LETTER 539
HERALDING WALLACE'S BETRAYAL 544
WALLACE ENLISTS LEONARD FOR PROSECUTIONS 546
MORE PRISONERS ESCAPE 546
WALLACE REPORTS PROGRESS 546

CHAPTER 20:
PARDON BARGAIN FULFILLED BY BILLY BONNEY AND AFTERMATH

BILLY TESTIFIES FOR THE PARDON 549
VENUE CHANGE FOR BILLY BONNEY 553
ATTEMPTED ASSASSINATION OF IRA LEONARD 555
GRAND JURY INDICTMENTS AND PARDONS 556
WALLACE BLAMES "OUTLAWS" 558

CHAPTER 21:
BILLY BONNEY ALMOST BREAKS THE SANTA FE RING

THE RING'S LAST LIABILITY 561
WALLACE'S PROGRESS REPORT 561
LEONARD PREPARES FOR THE COURT OF INQUIRY 562
LEW WALLACE TESTIFIES..562
LEONARD EXPOSES THE RING TO WALLACE 568
SUSAN McSWEEN TESTIFIES 576
BILLY BONNEY TESTIFIES 586
DUDLEY'S CAVALRYMEN TESTIFY 592
LEONARD'S RAGE AND DESPAIR..592
WALLACE'S DAMAGE CONTROL...593
LEONARD'S "OLD SCOUNDREL" LETTER..............................596
BILLY DEPARTS JAIL 599
DUDLEY TESTIFIES 599
WALLACE ADMITS THE RING TO SCHURZ 603
WALDO'S CLOSING ARGUMENT 603
PROSECUTOR'S CLOSING ARGUMENT 609
FINAL JUDGMENT OF THE COURT..611
WALLACE'S DAMAGE CONTROL...614
SUSAN McSWEEN'S CIVIL SUIT 614

CHAPTER 22:
HUNTING THE IMAGINARY KID GANG

GUERRILLA RUSTLING..617
WALLACE REPORTS ON THE RING 617
ENTER SECRET SERVICE OPERATIVE AZARIAH WILD 620
FIRST FOCUS ON BILLY BONNEY 625
A SECRET SERVICE PARDON 627
WILD'S IMAGINARY OUTLAW GANG......................................633
ENTER PAT GARRETT 637
WITCH-HUNTING BILLY...638

COYOTE SPRING AND GREATHOUSE AMBUSHES 640
AFTERMATH OF AZARIAH WILD 643
BILLY THE KID OUTLAW MYTH PRESS 643
WALLACE BACKS OUTLAW MYTH TO SCHURZ 645
BILLY RESPONDS TO NOTORIETY 645
WALLACE PLANS ESCAPE 648
BILLY GETS NATIONAL OUTLAW MYTH PRESS 648

CHAPTER 23:
BILLY BONNEY CAPTURED AND JAILED

CAPTURE AT STINKING SPRINGS 657
THE RINGITE MEDIA CIRCUS 657
BILLY'S LAST PARDON PLEA LETTERS 664

CHAPTER 24:
BILLY BONNEY'S TRIALS
BY THE SANTA FE RING

HANGING TRIALS IN MESILLA 669
SURPRISE QUASHING OF CATRON'S
    FEDERAL INDICTMENT 671
PREJUDICIAL PRESS 671
TRIAL FOR THE BRADY KILLING 672
BILLY'S RESPONSE TO SENTENCING 680
TRANSPORT TO LINCOLN COUNTY COURTHOUSE-JAIL . 682

CHAPTER 25:
BILLY BONNEY'S
GREAT ESCAPE AND KILLING

THE GREAT ESCAPE 685
BILLY ON THE RUN 686
WALLACE OVERTLY REJECTS PARDON 687
RING PRESS SWINGS INTO ACTION 689
PRESS FAME OF THE GREAT ESCAPE 690
WALLACE'S FIRST BILLY THE KID
    OUTLAW MYTH ARTICLE 691
LEW WALLACE EXITS 694
KISTLER'S *DAILY OPTIC* OUTLAW MYTH 694
WALLACE'S NEXT CERTAIN BILLY THE KID ARTICLE 695
KILLING BILLY IN FORT SUMNER 699

CHAPTER 26:
LEW WALLACE'S RING-INSPIRED BILLY THE KID MYTH

THE RING AND WALLACE IN SYNC 703

CHAPTER 27:
THE SANTA FE RING REGROUPS

THE SANTA FE RING UNCHECKED 725
LEW WALLACE ON CATRON 727
SANTA FE RING FIGHTER IN THE 20TH CENTURY 728

CHAPTER 28:
SUMMARY AND CONCLUSION

THE SANTA FE RING VERSUS BILLY BONNEY 731

SOURCES

ANNOTATED BIBLIOGRAPHY 735

INDEX

INDEX 821

PREFACE

Howdy. I'm the old-timer who gets in the first word for this here author's books. I tell you what: she's still fighting to get out the truth bout Billy Bonney - whose enemies made up that Billy the Kid name. Anyways, this here book is her showdown with them enemies: the Santa Fe Ring. From when it begun in 1866, to right now, it's a good ol' boys and gals club of New Mexico politicians and lawmen, lining their pockets by taking from yours.

People here learned you pay a damn big price - excuse the French - to rile up the Ring: like your life in Billy's day. It's pretty much the same nowadays. Ain't many that want to stand bare-assed in a nest of rattlers. If you're not sent to the pearly gates, you're run out of town. Only difference is nowadays you're called "troublemaker;" back then it was "outlaw."

So it comes down to: what fool would take on them varmints? Well, you got you two names on the front of this here book: Billy the Kid and this here author.

Now me, being a fictional character, I can look brave easy. So I says: "Give it to them sonsobitches Ringites - excuse the French - with double barrels."

Then you got you this here author. Ever since she got wind of the Santa Fe Ring, the Lincoln County War freedom fight against it, and Billy Bonney ending up fighting it alone, she's chose her side: it's Billy's. So you could say that all her books on him - and by now there's a pile big enough to hide behind if some Ringman was shooting at you - basicly take up the fight against the Ring where it hurts most: dragging it into the light of day. Cause the only way these varmints survive is underground - meaning if you accuse them, they say there ain't no such thing as the Ring. They don't sign up for no membership like some country club; they's just loyal to their pals right up to Hell's door - and probly in Hell itself. And them and their pals is all crooks. And when their pal is a judge or a legislator, or the Governor, the law's their pal too. So putting a Ringite in the hoosegow is hard as finding hair on a frog. You ain't gonna. So now you know all bout New Mexico when Billy lived there, and now. The difference is in his day people fought back. Then he fought back by hisself. Now it's basicly this here author taking them on.

      Vern Blanton Johnson, Jr.
      Lincoln, Lincoln County, New Mexico

AUTHOR'S FOREWORD

Today, the recorded history of Billy Bonney, aka Billy the Kid, and the Lincoln County War is comparable to recounting the Civil War while omitting slavery.

The atrocity of slavery had its counterpart in New Mexico Territory in the 1870's, when inhabitants lost their freedom to a murderous plutocratic cabal known as the Santa Fe Ring. A form of organized crime, it controlled politics, law enforcement, and commerce. It achieved riches by land-grabs of millions of acres. It suppressed opposition by malicious prosecutions and murders of hundreds, by military interventions, by complicit press, and by power reaching to Washington, D.C. It achieved the victors' reward of writing the history, which hid its crimes by denying its existence.

Myths, created first by Ringite press, outlawed opponents and omitted anti-Ring uprisings. Billy Bonney was transmogrified to uber-outlaw "Billy the Kid," and the Lincoln County War freedom fight, in which he participated, was reduced to a local mercantile conflict.

The 19th century quasi-historical writers embellished that mythology. More scholarly chroniclers of the 20th century merely plastered researched facts onto the armature of antique fictions. The reason was simple: to avoid confronting the Santa Fe Ring, whose menace has remained unbroken to the present.

Added to avoidance, was historians' naivety. One needed to experience the terror and desperation of Ring victims - denied protection or justice or a voice - to grasp those Old West events.

Fate gave me the chance for first-hand learning. As a Harvard Medical School educated M.D. and a forensic psychiatrist, I had moved to New Mexico in 1999 to write about Billy Bonney as a freedom fighter, and about the Santa Fe Ring that killed him. In 2003, after researching the historic sites and 40,000 pages of archival documents and books, I was writing my novel, *Billy and Paulita: The Saga of Billy the Kid, Paulita Maxwell, and the Santa Fe Ring*, when the Ring attacked Billy again!

The attack was a hoax for attention-grabbing profit. New Mexico's corrupt Governor, with colluding lawmen, sought to hijack the history by a "cold case" murder investigation against Pat Garrett, called "the Billy the Kid Case." They claimed Pat had shot dead an innocent victim, not the Kid; and that Billy survived as a Texan named Oliver "Brushy Bill" Roberts. Proof was to be from DNA matchings verifying that the innocent victim was in Billy's grave. Participating were a publicity hound DNA consultant, a state-paid history professor, a political donor lawyer and "Brushy" believer, the Lincoln County Attorney, a U.S. Marshal, District Court judges appointed by the Governor, and the press. So my first lesson was seeing the creation of a sheltered scam. Lesson two was learning New Mexicans' fear of backlash from the Ring by opposing it.

It was left to me to fight this cabal to save the true history. My expertise in the history and DNA forensics made me their nightmare. I hired attorneys to use local mayors to stop the exhumations of Billy and his mother based on there being no DNA to exhume! Their graves are just tourist markers. The mother's, in Silver City, has no remains. Billy's location in the Fort Sumner cemetery is unknown. Plus, there is no historic doubt that Pat Garrett killed him. And "Brushy" was a long-discredited imposter. So I won. But I was too fearful to reveal my role.

The hoaxers did not stop. They simply faked DNA from other sources. Revamping their hoax, they claimed Billy *was* shot, and they got his blood DNA from an old carpenter's bench (on which he had been laid out). This necessitated ridiculously claiming he "played dead," since their hoax needed his survival as "Brushy." Based on this fake DNA, they illegally exhumed some old-timers in Arizona, while churning out articles and a TV documentary.

I was forced to abandon my safe anonymity. In 2006, as a whistleblower, I demanded their DNA documents under the open records act. So I met the Santa Fe Ring head-on.

To force my retreat, the colluding County Attorney, with the lawmen, reported me as a terrorist for my request! Instead, I complained to the Bar Association. It refused action, saying no unprofessional conduct was shown. Next the lawmen denied having any DNA records to give me; though they had been used to justify the Arizona exhumations for DNA matchings. So my next lesson was in the expanding circle of mutual protection.

In 2007, I hired lawyers to litigate for the records. But five sets of them tried to throw my case, while the lawmen stonewalled and forged DNA records to trick the court. So I went *pro se*, and won by myself in 2014 - after *seven years*.

There was a catch: the Ring protects its own. Open records law awarded requesters who won litigation a per day penalty from the officials hiding records. In my long case, that added up to about a million dollars. Meanwhile, another open records case was lost by the state's crooked Attorney General, who had concealed his own incriminating records, and also faced a big pay-out penalty.

So the Ring responded by attacking troublemaking citizens. The state Court of Appeals accepted the Attorney General's appeal in which he rewrote the law to block penalties *unless the requester proved personal injury from not getting the records*! (This violated all Americans' right to get public records, and ignored that the Attorney General could not write any law - only legislators can). So my lesson was in the Ring's obstruction of justice to shield compatriots.

My District Court judge then used the Attorney General's case to punish me by denying all penalties, because, as a whistleblower, I had no personal injury. So he freed my law-breaking lawmen of any legal retribution; having already rewarded their stonewalling attorneys by a half-million dollars in unquestioned tax-payer funded fees (when the requested DNA records were available at day one at tax-payer's cost of postage). So I experienced the Ring's rigged system.

I took my case to the Court of Appeals. But, in preparing my District Court record for it, I discovered that my key exhibits from the litigation were gone. That was my lesson in Ring expurgations. But since I had kept copies, that trick failed.

Next, the Court of Appeals (the same judges who backed the Attorney General) denied my correct arguments against removing penalties. So I appealed to the state Supreme Court, arguing that the Attorney General's rewrite removed the law's intent for a time-based penalty to force corrupt officials' compliance. I added that, if they did not overrule the Court of Appeals, they could give citizens' realistic expectations by merely changing the law's acronym of IPRA (for Inspection of Public Records Act) to mean Ignoring of Public Rackets Act. My lesson was that my anger outweighed my fear. I now knew I could walk the path to the end.

The Supreme Court refused to hear my appeal. Its Chief Justice had been appointed by the corrupt Governor doing the hoax, was one of his major political donors, and his attorney wife had participated in the hoax with the Governor! And this was the same court that backed the corrupt Attorney General's rewrite.

During this crisis of democracy, when all New Mexicans, including me, were robbed of their right to open records access, the Ring-compliant state press refused to expose the scandal.

Back in District Court, my last step was to get a hearing for my judge's final written Judgment. But it was scheduled without informing me, and the judge let the losing lawmen's attorneys write it! I filed an objection and got a hearing; but the judge refused my Final Judgment summarizing the case's injustices, and still used the lawmen's version, which hid the issues for the final record. I objected in the courtroom. The judge took my version, but labeled it an exhibit. Since it was not an exhibit attached to anything, I then filed with the court an explanatory document for it. My judge stole my document from the clerk's office before its filing - an illegal act! I protested to his Chief Judge in District Court, and was stonewalled by him. There was no where else to turn. So my lesson was in rage and helplessness, identical to that of victims of the same illegal, immoral, and all-pervasive tactics in the 19th century's Santa Fe Ring take-over.

To stymie the Ring's strategy of total expurgation, I put my filings on my website: GaleCooperBillytheKidBooks.com. And I published two exposé books: *Cracking the Billy the Kid Case Hoax: The Strange Plot to Exhume Billy the Kid, Convict Sheriff Pat Garrett of Murder, and Become President of the United States;* and *Billy the Kid's Pretenders, Brushy Bill and John Miller.*

Since I am still alive, all this merely proves that the Ring did not consider me a powerful enough adversary. A bullet is reserved only for its greatest risks: like Billy the Kid.

What I did get was a priceless education about the workings of a criminal system that is beyond any layman's conception. If I omitted the dates and personal references in my story, you would be in 1870's New Mexico Territory, when democracy was obliterated, justice was unattainable, and rule was by the Santa Fe Ring's tyranny of fear and favor.

But fate works inscrutably. Billy Bonney had kept alive the memory of the people's freedom fight against the Santa Fe Ring; and he had inspired me. After my own fight against the Ring to save his history, and my fight against my own fears to endure its force field of inescapable criminality, I was finally ready to strike the Ring where it is most vulnerable: exposing it to the truth.

So here is the real history of Billy the Kid, when the original Ring well knew that its life-or-death fight was them versus him.

                              Gale Cooper, M.D.
                              Sandia Park, New Mexico

METHODOLOGY

OVERVIEW:

Since little has been written on the Santa Fe Ring, I presented it origins, members, and criminal organization. Its expurgation of incriminating documents for 1870's period of anti-Ring uprisings required demonstration of its conduct before and after the Lincoln County War period to extrapolate to the days of Billy the Kid.

I also felt obligated to analyze how and why historians of the Lincoln County War perpetuated the Ring's outlaw myths of Billy the Kid, and omitted the Santa Fe Ring.

Presented also are lives of key Ringites, to show how all prospered from their crimes, with none successfully prosecuted.

The attempted pardon of Billy Bonney, though covered, is more extensively treated in my 2017 book, *The Lost Pardon of Billy the Kid: An Analysis Factoring in the Santa Fe Ring, Governor Lew Wallace's Dilemma, and a Territory in Rebellion.*

PRIMARY DOCUMENTS:

Primary documents have italics for handwriting, two column newsprint for articles, and in distinctive font for published books. Retained are the misspellings, punctuation errors (usually no periods at end of sentences, missing capitalizations of the first word of the next sentence; or unmarked contractions like "dont"), underlinings, and cross-outs. Notably, the word "country" is used in them as "local area," not necessarily "America."

COMMENTARY:

Highlighted "Summaries" are provided throughout, author's boldface accentuates key points, bracketed "Author's Notes" are inserted, and the "Bibliography" is annotated. Missing information and corrections are added to documents in brackets.

FACILITATIONS:

"Santa Fe Ring" is often shortened to "Ring" and its members are often identified by the contemporary word: "Ringites." Bibliography entries are arranged chronologically. For navigation within the book, internal page references are provided. To spare Notes, page numbers for citations are inserted in the text.

ACKNOWLEDGMENTS

Overriding is my debt to Billy Bonney, whose cause, courage, intelligence, and joie de vivre are my inspiration.

Historical bedrock is from books by Frederick Nolan on Billy the Kid, the Lincoln County War, and John Henry Tunstall. As valuable is Leon Metz's Pat Garrett biography and Jerry Weddle's book on Billy Bonney's adolescence. Period military consultation was by Steven Alley, curator at the Kansas Fort Leavenworth Army Museum; historians Jim Minor and Tim Smith at the Shiloh National Military Park; and Bill Gwaltney, a General Miles Marching and Chowder Society re-enactor.

National Archive collections, with helpful a curators, were used in the Justice Department; Department of the Interior; the Secret Service Library Counterfeit Division; and the Department of War, Old Military and Civil Branch.

Other collections used, with helpful curators, were at the Las Cruces, New Mexico State University Library's Rio Grande Historical Collections' Herman B. Weisner Papers, ca. 1957-1992; the Albuquerque, University of New Mexico Center for Southwest Research's Thomas B. Catron Papers; the New Mexico State Library in Santa Fe; the Santa Fe, New Mexico, Fray Angélico Chávez Historical Library; the Roswell, Chavez County Historical Center for Southeast New Mexico; the State of New Mexico Office of Cultural Affairs Historic Preservation Division; the Office of the New Mexico State Historian; the Silver City Museum and Library; the Midland, Texas Nita Stewart and J. Evetts Haley Memorial Library and Historical Center; the Canyon, Texas Panhandle-Plains Historical Museum; the Austin, Texas, University of Texas Center for American History's Earle Vandale Collection, 1813-946; the Morgantown, West Virginia and Regional History Center at West Virginia University Libraries' Stephen B. Elkins Papers; and the Freemont, Ohio, Memorial Library's Rutherford B. Hayes papers; and the Indianapolis, Indiana, Historical Society's Lew and Susan Wallace Collection. Some New Mexico Territory newspaper articles were from the Library of Congress's "Chronicling America" database or NewspaperArchive.com.

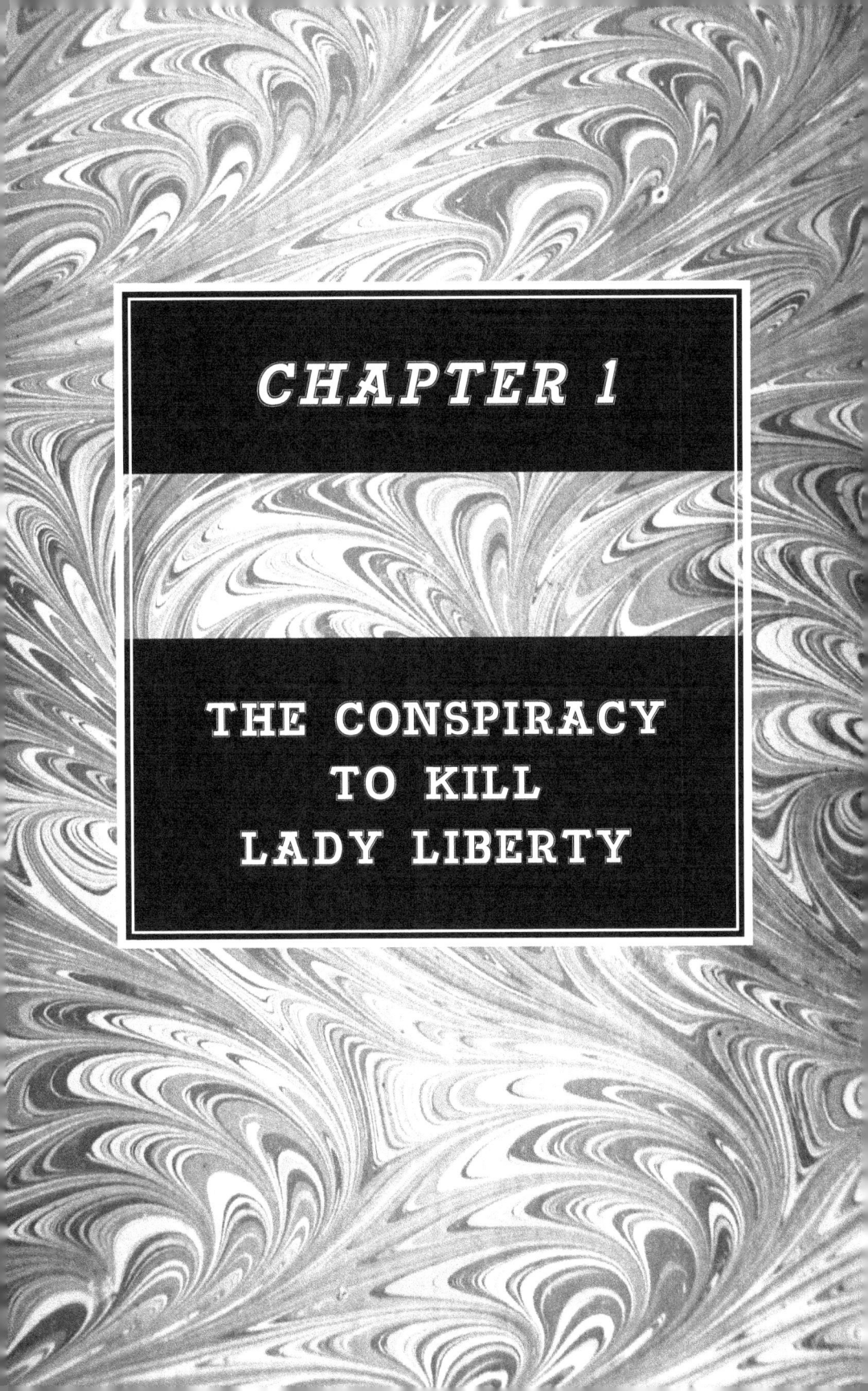

CHAPTER 1

THE CONSPIRACY TO KILL LADY LIBERTY

INTRODUCTION

SUMMARY: New Mexico Territory's corrupt Santa Fe Ring political cabal forced citizens to fight for freedoms guaranteed to them by the Founding Fathers.

Agnes Morley Cleaveland, named her 1952 book about New Mexico Territory *Satan's Paradise*. When her parents lived in Cimarron, it was a utopia for the making of an American monster: the Santa Fe Ring. That Ring, in turn, created a fictional monster, the outlaw "Billy the Kid," as cover-up for its malignant cronyism that killed hundreds, stole vast tracts of land, terrorized thousands, and debased America's democracy to a tyranny.

FOUNDING FATHERS' BALANCE OF POWERS

America's Founding Fathers knew that lust to dominate was human nature. So they created a balance of powers by dividing government into executive, legislative, and judicial branches; able to overrule each other. As James Madison stated in Federalist Papers No. 51 of 1788: *"The accumulation of all powers, legislative, executive and judicial in the same hands, whether of one, a few, or many, and whether hereditary, self-appointed, or elective, may justly be pronounced the very definition of tyranny ... The great security against a gradual concentration of the several powers in the same [branch], consists in giving those who administer each [branch], the necessary constitutional means, and personal motives, to resist encroachments of the others ... Ambition must be made to counteract ambition.*

CIRCUMVENTING CHECKS AND BALANCES

It took about a century for two men to sabotage the Founding Fathers' checks and balances. The vulnerability was assuming that separated power-holders would not collude for venal ends.

The history of Billy the Kid and the Lincoln County War is a story of those two, insatiably gluttonous, conniving law partners, Thomas Benton Catron and Stephen Benton Elkins, who infiltrated the three branches with cronies to gain absolute power and absolute immunity. Their opponents named the collusion the Santa Fe Ring. Another name for that system is organized crime.

THE ORGANIZED CRIME MODEL

In 19th century New Mexico Territory the lawmakers were the law breakers. There were no checks. There were no balances. All citizens were disempowered by the Santa Fe Ring's tyranny.

A model for that Ring is the American Mafia. As a crime group, the 19th century American Mafia, originating in Sicily, was characterized by rigid structure, retaliative tactics, fierce loyalty to members, and a code of silence. Its units were euphemistically called "families." The regionally isolated Santa Fe Ring was like one Mafia "family;" with members called "friends."

The American Mafia family tiered as "boss," "underboss," advisor, "captains" or "capos," "soldiers" and "associates." This layering shielded top-ranks from direct responsibility for crimes. Until laws in 1970 against conspiracies, bosses evaded prosecution by claiming "plausible deniability" of their involvement.

The Santa Fe Ring, likewise, had fixed structure, with most being initiated Masons. Territorial "boss," Thomas Benton Catron, ran the syndicate with Washington, D.C. co-boss, Stephen Benton Elkins. Sub-bosses exercised local power; as in Lincoln County's mercantile and cattle ranching monopolies. "Soldiers," enforcing Ring will, were lawmen, judges, and district attorneys. And "associates" were hired thugs for rustling, terrorism, and assassinations. Secrecy was by cipher-code communication and expurgation of incriminating records. Mafia-style layering shielded the upper echelon by plausible deniability.

The Mafia's boost was Prohibition Era take-over of illegal alcohol activities; with post-prohibition expansion to labor unions, construction, sanitation, drug trafficking, and fencing stolen merchandise, as it laundered money in legitimate businesses.

The Santa Fe Ring's comparable growth spurt involved mid-19th century theft of millions of acres of Hispanic land grants; added to loan-sharking, voter fraud, malicious prosecutions, witness intimidation, arson, and murder; as it diversified into mercantile monopolies, mining, railroads, and cattle ranching.

The Mafia lost its secrecy in 1951, when a U.S. Senate special committee, chaired by Senator Estes Kefauver, declared it "a sinister criminal organization" and empowered the FBI by the "Organized Crime Task Force" and "Top Hoodlum Program." In 1963, a Joe Valachi became the first Mafioso to reveal inner workings to a Senate Committee. In 1970, Congress defeated the "plausible deniability" defense tactic by passing the Racketeer Influenced and Corrupt Organizations Act (RICO) to enable prosecution of all members in a criminal organization. It attacked conspiracy for the same criminal objective; stating: "If conspirators have a plan which calls for some conspirators to commit the crime and others to provide support, the supporters are as guilty as the perpetrators."

The Santa Fe Ring retained its secrecy and immunity. No insider broke ranks. But the modern concept of conspiracy - that "supporters are as guilty as the perpetrators" - is the crux of this book's condemnations of these American monsters.

RING SYSTEMS

Other rings of colluding corrupt exploiters grew in 19th century America. During President Ulysses S. Grant's ring-supporting administration, his Secretary of War was bribed by merchants at army forts, post office contracts were bought from government officials, and tax money was embezzled for the St. Louis Whiskey Ring. And Grant made the Santa Fe Ring's first high-ranking New Mexico Territory appointments, including "boss" T.B. Catron.

THE "BOSS" TWEED RING EXAMPLE

Tammany Hall was a New York City patronage system controlling local and state government from the 1780's to the 1960's. It attained fame in the 1870's as the "Tweed Ring" under Democrat William Magear "Boss" Tweed. From 1858, he put cronies in political and judicial offices and bribed opponents. His ring controlled city government and property, ultimately embezzling $200 million tax dollars. Tweed became one of New York City's largest landowners; heading banks, public utility companies, a railroad, and was the city's official printer.

In 1871, his power weakened with rioting Irish immigrant workers and Thomas Nast's political cartoons in *Harper's Weekly*. And ring insider, Sheriff James O'Brien, gave information to the

New York Times, which also published Tweed's deceased bookkeeper's records as "Gigantic Frauds of the Ring Exposed."

Chairman of the New York State Democratic Committee, Ring-busting Samuel J. Tilden, audited city records, revealing Tweed's graft. Tilden was elected Governor of New York in 1874. (As an aside, Tilden overlapped the Santa Fe Ring and Billy the Kid history when he ran for President in 1876 against Republican Rutherford B. Hayes. Hayes, a Santa Fe Ring friend, lost the popular vote, but won by one Florida electoral vote, amidst accusation of election-box tampering by election monitor, Civil War General, Lew Wallace. Wallace's reward, in 1878, was New Mexico Territory's Governorship, in which he betrayed Billy Bonney's pardon and yielded the tragic saga of Billy's life.)

Tweed was arrested in 1871, and successfully criminally prosecuted in 1873. His civil embezzling suit landed him in the Ludlow Street Jail, though he escaped. Rearrested in 1876, he testified about workings of his ring in exchange for freedom; but Governor Tilden blocked his release. He died on April 12, 1878 in jail. Tweed had obviously not committed the perfect crime. The Santa Fe Ring did just that.

THE PERFECT CRIME

The difference between the Santa Fe Ring, and the American Mafia and the Tammany Hall Ring, is that latter two were the underworld. The Santa Fe Ring was the world. Tweed's Ring controlled city politics. The Santa Fe Ring controlled a whole Territory, under an umbrella of Washington, D.C. protection!

The Mafia was in an adversarial relationship with law enforcement and legislators. The Santa Fe Ring, once empowered in the 1870's, had its friends as governors, legislators, judges, sheriffs, district attorneys, lawyers, and the military. Presidents, Cabinetmen, and Senators were allies. Prosecution of members was impossible. "Boss" Tweed's Ring had powerful opponents to destroy it. "Boss" Catron eliminated all adversaries by favor, fear, malicious prosecution, and assassination. As Richard Maxwell Brown stated in his 1975 book, *Strain of Violence: Historical Studies of American Violence and Vigilantism*: "[New Mexico is] apparently the only place in America where assassination became an integral part of the political system."

Tweed was convicted. No Ringite of power has ever been convicted from 1866 to the present. Theirs was not aggressive capitalism; it was organized crime. And all their crimes became perfect crimes. The Ring's sole risk was from its oppressed victims. But they were defeated by rigged elections, malicious prosecutions, terrorist threats, forced flight, troops, biased press, and murder. The only option was rebellion.

A TERRITORY IN REBELLION

SUMMARY: In the 1870's, the rapaciously rising Santa Fe Ring met citizens' democratic idealism engendered by the Revolutionary and Civil Wars, and the frontier's promise of freedom. Popular uprisings flared in different counties; 1878's Lincoln County War Battle being the final brutal defeat. Finally, with all its criminals shielded from deserved punishment, only persistent bi-cultural rebel, Billy Bonney, was left between the Ring and its complete victory.

REVOLUTIONARY SPIRIT

The United States was born in revolution and declaration of its independence from England on July 4, 1776. Still fettered by slavery, it was further liberated by revolution in its Civil War, almost a hundred years later.

Thomas Jefferson, as an author of the "Declaration of Independence" had opined in a January 30, 1787 letter to fellow freedom fighter, James Madison, that a revolution *"at least once every 20 years [is] a medicine necessary for the sound health of government."* And Jefferson's words of rebellion in that first "Declaration" had led British citizens of the 13 colonies into war fervor and victory. He wrote: *"That whenever any form of government becomes destructive of these ends [that all men are created equal endowed with certain unalienable rights], it is the right of the people to alter or abolish it."*

In his "Emancipation Proclamation," President Abraham Lincoln completed that declaration, declaring: *"That on the first day of January, in the year of our Lord one thousand eight hundred and sixty-three, all persons held as slaves within any State ... shall be then, thenceforward, and forever free."*

Slightly over a decade after slavery's defeat, revolutionary spirit in New Mexico Territory led to fighting the Santa Fe Ring's despotism. Jefferson, in his January 30, 1787 letter to James

Madison had anticipated such a crisis by characterizing United States government *"wherein the will of every one has a just influence;"* as opposed to *"governments of force: as is the case in all other monarchies [which] is a government of wolves over sheep."*

By the 1870's, the wolves of force were unchecked in New Mexico Territory. But freedom and liberty were still enlivened by recent memory. To common people, democracy held the vigor of its revolutionary victory of 1776, with sacrifice of 50,000 dead and wounded, and celebrating its centenary. And the Civil War, spilling blood of over 646,000 dead and wounded to make all people free, had touched the lives of those now living.

So the people rose up in 1872, 1876, 1877, and 1878 against Santa Fe Ring tyranny. And when Billy' Bonney's group chose its name for its 1878 escalation to war, it was the "Regulators." That harked back to the first Regulators of 1771: pre-Revolutionary War, North Carolina farmers who opposed, and died fighting, corrupt and colluding Crown sheriffs and governors in haunting replication of Lincoln County's identically titled oppressors.

And the western frontier, the vast continental expanse symbolizing never-ending resources and resourcefulness, was still America's reality; then birthing anti-Ring opponents as varied as Cimarron grandmother, Mary McPherson; Lincoln community leader, Juan Patrón; British merchant and rancher, John Tunstall; Attorney and devout Presbyterian Alexander McSween; Lincoln County War widow and litigant, Susan McSween; teenaged ranch hand, Billy Bonney; and many others.

But dark clouds of despair were massing. Ring opposition would eventually be crushed in a reign of terror, with troops backing the Ring against citizens, and thugs assassinating opponents. And the Hayes administration was complicit.

The aftermath was the victorious Ring's re-writing of history and concealing or expurgating evidence to achieve the ultimate goal of organized crime: invisibility. So that period was the making of American monsters. A monster was the Santa Fe Ring itself. A monster was its Territorial boss, Thomas Benton Catron. And a "monster" was their creation, "Billy the Kid": the mythological outlaw, rustler, counterfeiter, gang leader and senseless serial killer of a man for each of his twenty-one years. But the real Billy Bonney, the unrelenting freedom fighter against their corrupt might, was the one person who could have broken the Santa Fe Ring. And the Ringites fully comprehended the risk.

CHAPTER 2

THE BOY WHO COULD BREAK THE SANTA FE RING

HISTORY OF BILLY BONNEY

SUMMARY: Born into a hardscrabble life of illegitimacy, and homeless at 14½ after his mother's death, William Henry Antrim turned to delinquency, becoming a killer at 17½ in a cantina altercation. Renaming himself Billy Bonney, he was converted to a freedom fighter by the Ring murder of his employer, John Tunstall. As the charismatic hero of the resulting Lincoln County War, and possible leader of a new uprising, he was outlawed by the Ring for hanging. His jailbreak left him victim of Pat Garrett's killing, and yielded a reality greater than any myth.

 In a hot, full-mooned, New Mexico Territory night as bright as day, the 21 year old, homeless youth, Billy Bonney, with trusting stockinged feet, approached the porticoed, two story, Fort Sumner mansion of the Maxwell family, at about a quarter to mid-night.
 That day, July 14, 1881, was the third anniversary of the Lincoln County War's start, which had left him branded as the outlaw, "Billy the Kid;" though, to himself, he was a freedom fighter: the last Regulator and that War's only participant to be convicted and sentenced to hanging.
 That July night, he intended to cut a dinner steak from the side of beef hanging, at the patrón's generosity, on the mansion's north porch. But first he would check in, as requested, with that patrón and town owner, Peter Maxwell, at his south porch's corner bedroom.
 Asleep in that mansion was Billy's secret lover, Maxwell's sister, Paulita, seventeen, and just pregnant with Billy's child. Also there, lived a never-emancipated Navajo slave, Deluvina; purchased, as a child, by Peter's and Paulita's fabulously wealthy, deceased father, Lucien Bonaparte Maxwell. Then, the family lived in Cimarron, a New Mexico Territory town in Colfax County, which Lucien had created on his and his wife's almost two million acre land grant; later named after himself.

That was before Lucien was cheated in the sale of that Maxwell Land Grant by unscrupulous lawyers, Thomas Benton Catron and Stephen Benton Elkins, who used their profits to propel their Santa Fe Ring. As Billy knew, that corrupt collusion of public officials still held New Mexico Territory in a stranglehold. As a hero in the failed Lincoln County War of 1878, Billy had fought that Ring. If Billy was thinking about his mortal danger, he knew its source was the Ring. If he thought about injustice, its focus would have been his promised pardon withheld by departed Territorial Governor Lew Wallace.

That July of 1881 day was 2½ months since Billy's jailbreak escape from his scheduled hanging on May 13th. He knew that Lincoln County Sheriff Pat Garrett would be in pursuit. Garrett had captured him on December 22, 1880 at Stinking Springs for his hanging trial. And in Billy's April 28, 1881 escape from Garrett's Lincoln jail, he had shot dead his deputy guards: James Bell and Robert Olinger. Garrett would kill him on sight.

When first tracking Billy in late 1880, Garrett had killed Billy's friends, Tom O'Folliard and Charlie Bowdre - missing Billy only by accident in two consecutive ambushes: at Fort Sumner and Stinking Springs. In fact, at the Stinking Springs capture of Billy and his companions, Garrett killed Bowdre by mistaking him for Billy: the prize for which the Ring had made Garrett a Sheriff.

To be near Paulita, Billy had recklessly chosen return to Fort Sumner, instead of fleeing to Old Mexico, the natural choice given his bi-culturalism. But he relied on the Maxwell family's protection, as well affection of the townspeople he had known since late 1877. It would take betrayal to bring his death.

Billy's life had been traumatic. Illegitimate, he was a second son, born on November 23, 1859, in New York City, as William Henry McCarty. Raised in Indiana with his brother, Josie, by his mother, Catherine, he became "Henry Antrim" after she married an Indiana man, William Henry Harrison Antrim, in 1873, after they relocated to New Mexico Territory. Antrim became a miner; and the family lived in Silver City. He was a rejecting father, evicting Billy at 14½ to homelessness when Catherine died of tuberculosis in 1874. But Billy's longing for a father remained, and he sometimes used the name "Antrim" for himself.

In Silver City's school, he learned Spencerian script. He also became fluent in Spanish; and, atypically, was equally comfortable in Anglo and Hispanic sub-cultures in those racist times.

By 1975, 15½ year old Billy spent his last year in Silver City doing petty thievery, and butcher shop and hotel work; while altercations with local boys revealed his violent temperament. By September, Silver City Sheriff, Harvey Whitehill arrested him for burglary, and laundry and revolver robbery; his adult accomplice having escaped. Facing ten years hard labor - the statutes making no provision for juveniles - he achieved his first dramatic escape: through the jail's chimney. He fled across the border to Arizona Territory's little town of Bonita.

In Arizona, as Henry Antrim, Billy again combined work - as a cook at a small hotel - with crime: stealing military blankets, saddles, and horses; while fatefully developing shootist skills. In 1876, incarcerated at local Fort Grant's guardhouse with his older, thieving accomplice, John Mackie, he escaped through a roof ventilation space. But he defiantly stayed in Bonita, relying on his rustling charges being dropped on a technicality, demonstrating risky behavior for his wish to have a "home."

On August 17, 1877, Billy's life again changed horrifically. His argument at Bonita's Atkins Cantina with a bullying blacksmith, Frank "Windy" Cahill, escalated to his fatally shooting that unknowably unarmed man. Billy escaped on a stolen horse. The Coroner's Jury declared him - as Henry Antrim - guilty of homicide, though in absentia; ignoring self-defense. So at 17½, Billy was almost hanged for murder. He escaped back to New Mexico Territory with an alias: William Henry Bonney - Billy Bonney. "Bonney" was likely his mother's maiden name.

In New Mexico Territory, by the next month of September, 1877, Billy attached himself to familiar sociopaths in Jessie Evans's murderous and rustling Santa Fe Ring-affiliated gang. And since all Ringites ended up immune to prosecution and profited financially, intelligent and energetic Billy, unknown to history, would have likely had a wealthy and long life.

But Billy had a conversion. He met kind, wealthy Englishman, John Henry Tunstall, a Ring competitor. By the next month, October of 1877, he left Jessie Evans's gang to become a Tunstall ranch hand. Tunstall's men affectionately nick-named him "Kid." Tunstall was the lost father found; even gifting him, under the Homestead Act, with a ranch on the Peñasco River in partnership with another employee, half-Chickasaw Fred Waite. That was likely Billy's proudest and most optimistic moment.

Billy had stumbled into a noble cause: ending Ring oppression. His gunman skill now elevated him as a protector of the good. His hair-trigger temper became vehemence for justice. And the town of Lincoln, as well as Tunstall's ranch on the Feliz River, became home. But Billy's tragic destiny was unrelenting. After only 4½ months, this idyllic time ended with Tunstall's Ring murder.

Lincoln, site of the future Lincoln County War, had already sustained Ring abuses through mercantile monopoly of "The House": a huge, two-story adobe, general store run by its Ring sub-bosses, Emil Fritz, Lawrence Murphy, James Dolan, and John Riley for secret partner, Ring boss, Thomas Benton Catron. They bled cash-poor Mexicans and Anglo homesteaders with usurious credit. Redress was impossible, since law enforcement and courts were Ring-controlled. Terror reigned. In 1875, when rancher, Robert Casey, defeated Murphy in a Lincoln election, he was assassinated the same day. Three weeks later, Lincoln's anti-Ring, Mexican community leader, Juan Patrón, was shot by Riley; though accidentally surviving as a limping cripple.

Hope for change began in late 1876 with arrival in Lincoln of English merchant, John Henry Tunstall; persuaded to settle there by a resident attorney, Alexander McSween, a Ring opponent, but once legal counsel to "The House." Tunstall planned to defeat the Ring by fair mercantile and ranching competition.

But Tunstall's plans coincided with boss Catron's monopolistic thrust into Lincoln County: secretly owning a Pecos River cow camp fronted by "The House," and making his Carrizozo Land and Cattle Company after getting dying Murphy's ranch in 1878.

By 1877, Tunstall built, just a quarter mile northeast of "The House," a general store and bank. And he began two cattle ranches to wrest from "The House" its beef and flour contracts to local Fort Stanton and Mescalero Indian Reservation. He even exposed Ringite Lincoln County Sheriff William Brady's embezzlement of tax money to buy rustled cattle for Catron's ranches. So Tunstall and McSween entered the Ring's hit list.

Ringmen preferred to kill with guise of legality. So they entangled Tunstall in fabricated criminality, starting with false prosecution of McSween, who was then attorney for the estate of "The House's" partner, Emil Fritz, who died intestate in 1874, but had two local siblings and a life insurance policy. The Ring seized on that policy. In 1877, McSween had successfully litigated to get its $10,000 proceeds from its withholding New York City insurance company, minus $3,000 to the collections firm - leaving $7,000 minus his fees. Knowing that the House faced bankruptcy from Tunstall's competition, and would extort that sum from Fritz's local heirs, he retained it while seeking heirs in Germany.

In December of 1877, McSween left on business to St. Louis with his wife and with Tunstall's business associate, the cattle king, John Chisum, then also president of the bank in Tunstall's store. The Ring pounced, declaring McSween an absconding embezzler of the Fritz insurance money. Ring boss Catron, then U.S. Attorney, issued an arrest warrant for capture. Chisum was also jailed in retaliation for backing Tunstall. On February 4, 1878, McSween had his hearing in Mesilla under Ringite District Judge Warren Bristol (later Billy's hanging judge), who indicted him for embezzling; intending his incarceration and killing in Lincoln by its Ringite Sheriff, William Brady. McSween was saved by the honest Deputy Sheriff, Adolph Barrier, from his Las Vegas, New Mexico, arrest site, who kept him in personal custody.

But Judge Bristol had set the Ring's traps for assassination of McSween and Tunstall. His indictment did two things. First, he set the bail at $8,000, with approval only by Ringite District Attorney William Rynerson; who refused all bondsmen to leave McSween open to Sheriff Brady's fatal custody at any time.

The second was Tunstall's trap. Bristol ordered attachment of McSween's property for $10,000 - falsely deemed the embezzled total - to ensure the money if he was convicted at that April's Grand Jury. Then Bristol lied that Tunstall was in partnership with McSween, to attach Tunstall's property also. And Bristol empowered Sheriff Brady to do attachment inventories at their properties. Intended was harassment to provoke Tunstall and his men to violence to justify his killing in "self-defense."

But Tunstall merely said that any man's life was worth more than all he owned. Billy, with Tunstall three months, must have been overwhelmed by this surprising idealism.

Tunstall's endeavors had bankrupted "The House," making boss Catron emerge from the shadows as its mortgage owner. And the April Grand Jury would likely acquit McSween. So the Ring acted, using the embezzlement case's property attachment.

On February 18, 1878, when Tunstall sought to transfer his fine horses, which were immune to the attachment, from his Feliz River Ranch to Lincoln, Brady called it theft of attached property and sent a large posse of Deputies, Ring rustlers, and Jessie Evans's outlaw gang after him and his men, including Billy. Tunstall, becoming isolated, was murdered, his horse slain; with both corpses mutilated.

This martyrdom of John Tunstall, coupled with more Ring outrages, triggered the Lincoln County War.

Sheriff Brady refused to arrest the murderers. So anti-Ring Justice of the Peace John "Squire" Wilson issued warrants for James Dolan, Jessie Evans, and his other possemen. For service, he appointed, as Deputy Constables under Town Constable Atanacio Martinez, Billy and Fred Waite. Billy had already given Wilson an affidavit as to eye-witness knowledge of the murderers. But Brady shielded them by illegally putting Billy, Waite, and Martinez in Lincoln's pit jail. And he confiscated Billy's Winchester '73 carbine - likely a gift from Tunstall.

Next, "Squire" Wilson defied the Ring by deputizing Tunstall's foreman, Dick Brewer; who, in turn, made Tunstall's men - including now-released Billy - his possemen to serve those murder warrants. Billy, then 18, was still a lawman.

Meanwhile, Attorney Alexander McSween, in mortal danger from Brady and the Ring, went into hiding with Deputy Sheriff Barrier; mostly in the nearby Hispanic town of San Patricio.

By March of 1878, Dick Brewer's posse had captured Tunstall murderers, William "Buck" Morton and Frank Baker, who were shot attempting escape. Billy was in the firing group.

At that point, including Frank "Windy" Cahill, Billy Bonney was now involved in three killings.

The Ring hit back. Ringite Governor Samuel Beach Axtell, by illegal proclamation, removed Wilson's Justice of the Peace powers to retroactively outlaw Dick Brewer's posse; then declared Sheriff William Brady to be Lincoln County's only law enforcer.

Enraged, Tunstall's men named themselves "Regulators" after pre-Revolutionary War freedom fighters. Included were Tunstall men - Billy; Fred Waite; John Middleton; Jim "Frenchie" French; farmer cousins, George and Frank Coe; and homesteader, Charlie Bowdre - and a John Chisum cattle detective, Frank MacNab. Dick Brewer was chosen as leader. Only one month after Tunstall's death, Billy was being schooled in politics of revolution.

The Ring's next chance to kill McSween was April 1, 1878, when he returned to Lincoln for his Grand Jury embezzlement trial. That morning, to save him, Regulators with carbines, and Billy with only a revolver, ambushed Brady and his deputies, George Hindman, Billy Matthews, and George Peppin, from the corral wall at Tunstall's store. Brady and Hindman died.

Recklessly, Billy, with Jim French, ran to retrieve his confiscated Winchester '73 carbine from Brady's body. Both got leg wounds from firing deputy, Jacob Basil "Billy" Matthews. But Billy regained his symbol of father-figure Tunstall. (It is likely the carbine held in Billy's famous tintype two years hence.)

Three days later, on April 4, 1878, Deputy Dick Brewer, seeking stolen Tunstall horses, led Billy, John Middleton, Fred Waite, Frank Coe, George Coe, and Charlie Bowdre to Blazer's Mill - a privately owned, way station and grist mill within the Mescalero Indian Reservation. Accidently encountered was Tunstall murder posseman, Andrew "Buckshot" Roberts, for whom they had a warrant. Roberts fired his Winchester carbine at Bowdre, who shot him in the belly. Roberts's bullet hit Bowdre's belt buckle, ricocheted, and wrenched George Coe's revolver, mutilating his trigger finger. Another Roberts shot hit Middleton's chest, though Middleton survived. Then Roberts killed Brewer, later dying himself from Bowdre's wound. Billy had not fired a shot. Roberts had demonstrably resisted arrest murderously, necessitating self-defense response. But Ring boss Catron, as U.S. Attorney, seized on this killing to file his federal indictment against the Regulators, including Billy, claiming the murder site was the Mescalero Reservation, under federal control.

Billy's murder involvement now totaled six men; though only "Windy" Cahill was demonstrably by his hand.

At the April, 1878, Lincoln County Grand Jury, McSween was acquitted of embezzling. He continued his anti-Ring fight, backed by the Regulators, though they had never been paid; John Chisum having dishonestly reneged. Revolutionary fervor sufficed. And Billy, their hot-headed fearless zealot, was becoming an inspiration - with McSween as his new father substitute.

McSween's lawful tactic was seeking high-level intervention, since murder of a foreign citizen could elicit a Washington, D.C. investigation. He filed a complaint with the British ambassador and to President Rutherford B. Hayes, accusing U.S. officials of murdering Tunstall. In response, investigating attorney, Frank Warner Angel, was sent by the Departments of the Interior and Justice. Arriving May 4, 1878, he took multiple depositions. Billy, volunteering for one, entered the national stage.

Public optimism of Ring defeat further grew when the Lincoln County Commissioners appointed neutral John Copeland, as

Sheriff replacing Brady. He even deputized Regulator, Josiah "Doc" Scurlock, to recover Tunstall's horses, stolen by the Ring. Still a lawman, Billy was on Scurlock's posse. And Wilson, ignoring Axtell's proclamation, continued as Justice of the Peace.

Optimism was short-lived. New Regulator leader, Frank MacNab, was killed in ambush on April 28, 1878 by Ringite Seven Rivers rustlers. By May 28th, because John Copeland forgot to post his tax collecting bond, Governor Axtell, by another proclamation, removed him and appointed as Sheriff, Ringite George Peppin, Brady's deputy, present at Brady's killing.

War fervor built, with furious Regulators and Mexicans calling themselves "McSweens." Billy's affiliation with local, firebrand youth, Yginio Salazar, and Billy's closeness to Hispanic residents of nearby San Patricio and Picacho, had arguably brought them all into the McSween alliance. By April 30, 1878, McSweens were skirmishing with Ring partisans, known as "Murphy-Dolans."

McSween again hid, often in San Patricio. In revenge, Sheriff George Peppin, with John Kinney's Ring-rustler gang from Mesilla, on July 3, 1878 massacred residents and destroyed property there. On July 13th, the "Regulator Manifesto" was sent to Catron's brother-in-law, then managing his Carrizozo cattle ranch, threatening retaliation against Catron himself. Signed only "Regulator," it was likely created by Billy.

The Lincoln County War's culminating battle began the next day: July 14, 1878. McSween, with 60 men - Regulators and Hispanic residents of San Patricio and Picacho - occupied Lincoln. Reflecting McSween's intended peaceful victory was that his wife, Susan, and her sister with five children, remained in his double-winged house; along with the sister's attorney husband's law intern, Harvey Morris.

McSween's men took strategic positions in houses throughout the mile-long town, most of whose inhabitants had fled. When Seven Rivers and John Kinney outlaws joined James Dolan and Sheriff George Peppin, Billy; his friends, Yginio Salazar and Tom O'Folliard; and San Patricio men - José Chávez y Chávez, Ignacio Gonzales, Florencio Chávez, Francisco Zamora, and Vincente Romero - rushed to McSween's house, joining guard, Jim French.

Though Ring men occupied foothills south of Lincoln, they were held at bay for five days by shooting McSweens. Regulators were about to win. But McSween did not realize that Fort Stanton's new Commander, Lieutenant Colonel N.A.M. Dudley, was beholden to the Ring. McSween was also reassured by the Posse Comitatus Act, passed the month before in Washington, baring military intervention in civilian disputes.

On July 16th, Commander Dudley began his invention by sending to Lincoln, for "fact-finding," 9th Cavalry Private Berry Robinson, who was almost hit in the mutual gunfire. Next, on July 18th, James Dolan used Ringite Lincolnite, Saturnino Baca, to claim his wife and children were at risk from the McSweens.

The next day, July 19th, violating the Posse Comitatus Act, Dudley marched on Lincoln with 39 troops - white infantry, black 9th Cavalry, and white officers - two ambulances; a mountain howitzer cannon; and a Gatling machine-gun, that period's most awesome weapon. Panicked McSweens - except for those in his besieged house - fled north across the nearby Bonito River. Dudley himself threatened McSween with razing his house if any soldier was shot. He then left three soldiers there to inhibit its defenders' shooting from it, and ordered three more to accompany Sheriff Peppin as a shield. Next, by death threats, he forced Justice of the Peace Wilson to write arrest warrants for McSween and his men as attempting murder of Private Robinson to feign a reason for his intervention. Then he encamped at the east side of Lincoln.

Backed by the participating troops, Sheriff Peppin's outlaw posseman set fire to McSween's house's west wing. His family was evacuated after Dudley refused his wife's plea to save him.

By nightfall, the McSween house conflagration - worsened by an exploding keg of gunpowder for bullet-making - left all trapped in the east wing. At about 9 p.m., escape was attempted into fire-lit shooting Ringites. With Billy was law intern, Harvey Morris, whom he saw fatally shot. And before Billy escaped across the Bonito River, at the property's rear - to rescue by fellow Regulators - he witnessed Dudley's treasonous crime: three of his white soldiers, imbedded with the assailants, fired a volley at those escaping. Arguably, they had killed Harvey Morris.

Shot dead were Alexander McSween, Francisco Zamora, and Vincente Romero. Yginio Salazar survived with two bullets in his back. Symbolizing horror, McSween's starving, yard chickens ate the eyeballs of his corpse. Again was Ring murder and mutilation in Lincoln County to gain treacherous victory.

No one knew that Ring influence extended to Washington, D.C. Investigator Frank Warner Angel, after documenting crimes of Governor S.B. Axtell, U.S. Attorney Catron, and Sheriff Brady's posse, nevertheless concluded falsely in his report - likely under duress - that no U.S. officials were involved in Tunstall's murder. As part of the cover-up, Catron resigned as U.S. Attorney. And President Hayes scapegoated Governor Axtell, replacing him with Civil War General Lew Wallace. But Angel secretly tried to help by writing for Wallace a notebook listing Ringites, and sending him a long exposé of the Santa Fe Ring, printed in 1877.

Though most Regulators fled the Territory, Billy stayed and carried out the "Regulator Manifesto's" guerrilla stock rustling with Tom O'Folliard and Charlie Bowdre - who had relocated to Fort Sumner with his wife Manuela. For his stolen stock, Billy used non-Ring outlets: Pat Coghlan in the western part of the Territory; and Dan Dedrick. Dedrick was a counterfeiter and rustler owner of Bosque Grande, a ranch 12 miles south of Fort Sumner. With his two brothers, he also owned a livery stable in White Oaks, a town about 45 miles northwest of Lincoln. Those brothers were another stock outlet for Billy. Billy also sold rustled horses in Tascosa, Texas; where he wrote a subsequently famous, bill of sale to a friendly doctor, Henry Hoyt, for an expensive sorrel horse - likely Sheriff Brady's. He also got money by gambling. He was again a homeless drifter. That would now be permanent.

Amidst public hope, on October 1, 1878, new Governor, Lew Wallace took office. A high-achieving elitist, he was the son of an Indiana governor; a Civil War Major General; an Abraham Lincoln murder trial prosecutor; author of a best-selling novel, *The Fair God*; and was writing *Ben-Hur A Tale of the Christ*. He had sought an exotic ambassadorship, like to Turkey, not governorship of backwater New Mexico Territory. So, to dispatch quickly with Lincoln County "troubles" without confronting the Santa Fe Ring, he issued, a month after arriving, an Amnesty Proclamation; though excluding those already indicted. Billy had been indicted for the Brady, Hindman, and Roberts murders.

There were more sources of hope. The new Sheriff, George Kimbrell - having been appointed to replace Sheriff George Peppin who resigned - was anti-Ring. And McSween's intrepid widow, Susan, had brought to Lincoln Attorney Huston Chapman to charge Commander N.A.M. Dudley with the Lincoln County War Battle's murder of her husband and arson of her home.

In that atmosphere of legal scrutiny, James Dolan made peace overtures, first to Susan McSween, then to Billy - a proof of that teenager's Ring threat. Billy and his Hispanic compatriots could yield another uprising - as Catron's feared.

The Billy-Dolan peace meeting was fatefully scheduled on the February 18, 1879 anniversary of Tunstall's murder. It ended in calamity. As James Dolan; Billy; Jessie Evans and Jessie's new gang member, Billy Campbell; and Billy's Regulator friends, Tom O'Folliard and Josiah "Doc" Scurlock, walked Lincoln's dark street after the meeting, they encountered Chapman. Dolan and Campbell fired at point-blank range, killing him, then igniting his clothing. Billy was again an eye-witness. And again there was murder and mutilation in Lincoln County.

Chapman's murder forced Governor Wallace to go to Lincoln - after procrastinating for five months after arriving. Once there, he avoided Ring confrontation, using the Ring's own concoction of vague "outlaws and rustlers" causing trouble. The Ring had given him a list of Regulators as "outlaws;" with Billy on it as "the Kid."

Focus on Billy - likely through Dolan - made Wallace put the astronomical reward of $1,000 on his head. Billy responded with his pardon plea, writing on March 13, 1879, to offer Wallace his eye-witness testimony against Chapman's murderers in exchange for annulling his Lincoln County War indictments. It was Billy's bold and calculated risk to negate Ring power over himself.

His articulate pardon plea letter, in fine Spencerian script, led to his March 17, 1879, nighttime meeting with Wallace in Justice of the Peace Wilson's Lincoln house. Evidence indicates that Wilson was covertly backing Billy's plea. And Billy believed Wallace agreed to his pardon bargain.

To avoid assassination before testifying, Billy requested from Wallace a sham arrest. (He had already seen Ring assassinations of John Tunstall, Alexander McSween, Harvey Morris, Francisco Zamora, Vincente Romero, and Huston Chapman.) He was kept in the home of his Lincoln friend, Juan Patrón, the town Jailer. Wallace, housed next door, interviewed Billy, and received his additional letter about Lincoln County War issues.

The next month, Billy fulfilled his pardon bargain by Grand Jury testimony, getting James Dolan and Billy Campbell indicted for first degree murder, and Jessie Evans as an accessory. But Ringite District Attorney William Rynerson, colluding with Judge Bristol, had his trial venue switched from Lincoln to Doña Ana County to guarantee a hanging verdict. Still Wallace issued him no pardon, while allowing pardon of the War's indicted Ringites.

By that April of 1879, Alexander McSween's widow, Susan, retained Attorney Ira Leonard, Chapman's office-mate from Las Vegas, to prosecute Dudley. So Dudley, under likely advisement from Catron - who had represented him for past court martials - got defamatory affidavits to diminish her credibility. And he requested a military Court of Inquiry, where judges would be biased, and where he would be defended by Catron's past law firm member, Henry Waldo. And on April 25th, the Ring tried unsuccessfully to assassinate Ira Leonard to stop the case.

Wallace, having removed Dudley as Commander, testified against him in the 1879 Court of Inquiry, though without confronting the Ring. Billy testified also, for his own anti-Ring agenda. He devastatingly reported the three white soldiers firing a volley at him and escaping others: meaning officers; meaning under Dudley's orders; meaning violating the Posse Comitatus Act and justifying court martial, and even hanging. Billy's courage made Ira Leonard take him as client.

By July of 1879, the biased Court of Inquiry acquitted Dudley. And Billy, with no pardon and imminent transport to Mesilla for a hanging trial, exited his bogus jailing.

The Ring recouped. By October of 1879, Susan McSween lost her civil trial against Dudley in Mesilla, to which her venue had been changed by Judge Bristol. That month, Bristol also voided James Dolan's Chapman murder indictment based on no witnesses daring to appear for a trial. Dolan, certain of immunity, had even taken over Tunstall's store. Tunstall's ranch property was given by the Ring to Dolan, Riley, and Rynerson; and Billy's Peñasco River ranch went to Jacob Basil "Billy" Matthews, head posseman for Tunstall's murder. And there was a more subtle Ring victory: Lew Wallace's humiliation in the Court of Inquiry made him shun Lincoln County "troubles" and Billy's pardon.

Billy's future killer, Patrick "Pat" Floyd Garrett, had arrived in New Mexico Territory's Fort Sumner in 1878. Born to an Alabama plantation family, relocated to Claiborne Parrish, Louisiana, when 9½ - and Billy was just born - he had even been willed a slave. After the Civil War, he drifted to Texas, where he possibly murdered a black man, before becoming a buffalo hunter from 1876 to 1878 with two partners and a kid named Joe Briscoe. Garrett murdered Briscoe, but claimed self-defense. He never met fellow buffalo hunter, John William Poe; but later, his, Poe's, and Billy's histories would merge on the night of July 14, 1881.

In Fort Sumner, tall Garrett met transient kid, Billy Bonney, gambling at Hargrove's or Beaver Smith's Saloons. They were given townspeople's nicknames, "Big Casino" and "Little Casino," for their poker playing and height discrepancies.

The original Fort Sumner was built in 1865 by the U.S. government on desert flatlands east of the Pecos River for soldiers guarding Bosque Redondo: a concentration camp for 3,500 Navajos and 400 Apaches, until their scandalous starvation caused release of the Navajos to their homeland in 1868; the Apaches having already escaped. In 1870, Fort Sumner was purchased by Lucien Bonaparte Maxwell, one of the Territory's richest men. Converting it into a town around its parade ground, and using its thousands of acres for sheep raising, he settled there with his wife, Luz Beaubien; daughters, including Paulita; and son, Peter. Retained was the military cemetery for his family. Eventually it received Billy's body, to lie beside Pat Garrett's earlier shooting victims: Billy's Regulator pals, Tom O'Folliard and Charlie Bowdre. Maxwell died in 1875, leaving the town to his wife and son, Peter; who became the family's ruin through mismanagement. But when Pat Garrett and Billy Bonney gambled there, Fort Sumner was still thriving.

Before buying Fort Sumner, Maxwell's wealth came from his marriage to Luz Beaubien, an heiress of the almost two million acre Beaubien-Miranda Land Grant, buying its shares from her siblings. In 1870, he then sold it as the Maxwell Land Grant. But he was cheated by his robber baron attorneys, Thomas Benton Catron and Steven Benton Elkins, who resold it for double the money. That profit fortified their Santa Fe Ring, as they enriched themselves with railroads, banks, and mines. Catron eventually owned six million acres - more than anyone in U.S. history. In the Lincoln County War period, he was Billy's lethal enemy, with the Ring branding him as the murderous outlaw "Billy the Kid" to justify killing him. By 1912's New Mexico statehood, Catron became one of the two first senators.

By 1878, before the Lincoln County War, Pat Garrett and Billy Bonney led separate lives, though connected by Fort Sumner's Gutierrez sisters: Juanita, Apolinaria, and Celsa. Billy befriended Celsa, married to her cousin, Saval Gutierrez, a Maxwell sheep herder. Billy's July 14, 1881 death walk would start at their house. Garrett married Juanita, who died soon after of a possible miscarriage. Two years later, in 1880, he married Apolinaria, with whom he would father eight children. It was a double marriage with his Fort Sumner, best friend, Peter Maxwell's foreman, Barney Mason, later a spy assisting Garrett's capture of Billy.

In 1878, Garrett had been desperate for employment. At Fort Sumner, he drove a wagon for Peter Maxwell; helped a local hog raiser, Thomas "Kip" McKinney; and bartended at Hargrove's Saloon. Then came 1880 and the opportunity of his life. For Lincoln County's November election, the Ring needed a compatible Sheriff. To qualify, Garrett moved with his wife, Apolinaria, to that county's town of Roswell; adding, as a boarder, an unemployed journalist named Ashmun "Ash" Upson. In 1882, Upson would ghostwrite Garrett's book about killing Billy the Kid.

By 1880, the Ring's outlaw myth propaganda had advertised Billy's gunman reputation. That almost succeeded in his killing on January 3, 1880 at Fort Sumner's Hargrove's Saloon. A Texan bounty hunter named Joe Grant tried to shoot him in the back. Saved by Grant's gun's misfiring, Billy retaliated fatally. Obvious self-defense, that killing was not legally pursued.

Billy was now linked to murders of seven men: Frank "Windy" Cahill, William "Buck" Morton, Frank Baker, William Brady, George Hindman, Andrew "Buckshot" Roberts, and Joe Grant.

That 1880, when his now-famous tintype photograph was taken, Billy may have heard first mythological whispers of his outlawry. The Ring was setting its legal trap for eliminating him. In addition to murderer and rustler, he would be declared a counterfeiter to bring in the Secret Service, a branch of the U.S. Treasury Department with funding and power to track him down. Catron's Lincoln County agent, James Dolan, initiated the investigation by reporting receipt of a counterfeit $100 bill in his Lincoln store. And Catron or Elkins were the likely contact to Secret Service Chief, James Brooks.

By September 11, 1880, Secret Service Special Operative Azariah Wild was sent to Lincoln. Dolan's counterfeit bill, falsely linked to Billy, actually came from two youths, Billy Wilson and Tom Cooper, employed by the real counterfeiter, Dan Dedrick. But they occasionally rustled with Billy and his regulars: Tom O'Folliard, Charlie Bowdre, and a "Dirty Dave" Rudabaugh. Billy himself used Dedrick as an outlet for rustled stock, along with Dedrick's brothers at their White Oaks livery.

Gullible Operative Azariah Wild was led to believe by James Dolan and Catron's brother-in-law, Edgar Walz - then managing Catron's Carrizozo ranch - that Billy was in the country's largest counterfeiting and rustling gang. In December of 1880, the *New York Sun* featured Billy in "Outlaws of New Mexico. The Exploits of a band headed by a New York Youth, War Against a Gang of Cattle Thieves, Murderers, and Counterfeiters." He was alias "the Kid." The Ring had launched his national outlaw myth.

The Ring's plot almost backfired when Wild was told by Ira Leonard that his client, Billy Bonney, would testify against the counterfeiters. On October 8, 1880, Wild wrote in his daily report to Chief James Brooks that he himself would arrange a pardon for Billy in exchange for that testimony. But Wild confided that pardon plan to his Ringite minders, who convinced him that Billy, staying in Fort Sumner, was the gang's leader! In his report for October 11, 1880, Wild wrote that he intended to arrest those desperados. By then, Billy was cautious. He held up the stagecoach with Wild's mail, read that report, and avoided apprehension by avoiding the meeting with Leonard and Wild. But another pardon chance was lost.

The Ring was determined to eliminate Billy. The next option was getting a Lincoln County Sheriff willing do it. The current Sheriff, George Kimbrell, who had assisted in Billy's sham arrest, was a McSween-side sympathizer. The Ring chose Pat Garrett. Secretly, Wild worked with him to form a dragnet to capture Billy and his "rustler-counterfeiter gang;" while, for the upcoming sheriff's election, Garrett was advertised as a law-and-order man to new gold-rush settlers in White Oaks, unaware of Lincoln County War issues, but a third of Lincoln County's voters.

In the November 2, 1880 election, Pat Garrett got 358 votes to Kimbrell's 141. Wild, convinced by his Ring contacts that Kimbrell protected the "Kid gang," also gave Garrett immediate Territorial power for the capture by appointing him Deputy U.S. Marshall. Unaware, Billy would have wrongly thought that Garret's lawman authority was limited to Lincoln County, not Fort Sumner's San Miguel County, where he stayed.

And unaware of his locally publicized "outlawry," Billy still brought stolen horses to the Dedrick's White Oaks livery. On November 22, 1880, a White Oaks posse ambushed him, Tom O'Folliard, Billy Wilson, Tom Pickett, and "Dirty" Dave Rudabaugh at nearby Coyote Spring, shooting dead two of their horses before Billy's group escaped. Five days later, that posse attacked them again at the way station ranch of "Whiskey" Jim Greathouse, 45 miles northeast of White Oaks; accidentally killing one of their own men, Jim Carlyle, but blaming Billy.

That accusation prompted Billy's only letter of 1880 to Governor Lew Wallace. On December 12th, he wrote, denying his outlawry and murdering of Jim Carlyle. He even described his Robin Hood role of seeking justice for the downtrodden. Wallace never answered. Instead, on December 22nd, he placed a Las Vegas *Daily Gazette* notice: "Billy the Kid: $500 Reward." He would repeat it in the *Daily New Mexican* on May 3, 1881, after Billy's jailbreak. His betrayal of the pardon bargain was complete.

By December of 1880, dreadful days began for Billy. U.S. Marshall Pat Garrett, backed by Azariah Wild, had assembled Texan posses to ride after Billy, since New Mexicans, to whom he was a hero, refused. Garrett's first ambush was on December 19, 1880, when Billy, Tom O'Folliard, Charlie Bowdre, Billy Wilson, Tom Pickett, and Dave Rudabaugh rode into Fort Sumner. O'Folliard was shot dead. The rest escaped.

Billy's group tried to flee the Territory in a snowstorm; but stopped, about 16 miles from Fort Sumner, on December 21, 1880, at a rock-walled, windowless, shepherds' line cabin at Stinking Springs. There Garrett ambushed them the next morning, killing Charlie Bowdre, whom he mistook for Billy, his intended victim. The rest surrendered. It would be seven months before Garrett succeeded in his mission to kill Billy.

Garrett transported his prisoners by train, via Las Vegas, New Mexico, to the Santa Fe jail. Billy remained there from December 27, 1880 to March 28, 1881, because the Ring awaited completion of the railroad to Mesilla to impede any rescue. But he almost escaped by tunneling out with fellow prisoners.

From his cell, Billy wrote four unanswered letters to Wallace, in 1881, pleading for his pardon: writing on March 4th: "*I have done everything that I promised you I would, and you have done nothing that you promised me.*" On March 2nd, he had threatened: "*I have some letters which date back two years and there are Parties who are very anxious to get them but I will not dispose of them until I see you.*" Wallace never got over that audacity or his own guilt, reworking the pardon obsessively till the end of his life in vindictive fictionalized articles on the outlaw "Billy the Kid."

Billy's Mesilla murder trial, under Judge Warren Bristol, began on March 30, 1881, with jurors unaware of Lincoln County War's issues, and without any Lincolnites daring to be witnesses for his defense. Attorney Ira Leonard represented him for past U.S. Attorney Catron's 1878 federal indictment, Case Number 411, the United States versus Charles Bowdre, Josiah Scurlock, Henry Brown, William Bonney alias Henry Antrim alias the Kid, John Middleton, Frederick Waite, Jim French, and George Coe for the murder of Andrew "Buckshot" Roberts. Surprising everyone, Leonard got it quashed as invalid, since the federal government had no jurisdiction over Blazer's Mill, the murder site, because private property, like it, was under Territorial jurisdiction. Its being surrounded by the federally-controlled Mescalero Reservation was irrelevant.

Remaining were only the Brady and Hindman Territorial indictments; and, though Billy been firing in the group of Regulators, he had only a revolver lacking accurate range. But, suddenly, Leonard withdrew, likely after a Ring threat. That was disastrous for Billy. He got Ring-biased, court appointed attorney, Albert Jennings Fountain, who considered him an outlaw, with Catron friend, Ringite John D. Bail, as co-counsel.

On April 8th and 9th of 1881, was Billy's Brady murder trial. His Spanish-speaking jury, given no translator, heard only prosecution witnesses - including James Dolan. After Judge Bristol's biased instructions (with translator) made Billy's mere presence equal to firing the fatal shot, the jury found him guilty of first degree murder; its sole punishment being hanging. On April 13th, Judge Bristol set Billy's hanging date for May 13th, to limit time for appeal. Billy was to be hanged in Lincoln by its Sheriff: Pat Garrett.

From the Mesilla jail, Billy wrote to Attorney Edgar Caypless - conducting his replevin case against Stinking Springs posseman, Frank Stewart for stealing his racing mare at Stinking Springs - hoping to get money from her sale to pay for an appeal.

Ironically, the new Lincoln jail, where Billy was incarcerated to await hanging, was in the past "House," which Catron had sold to Lincoln County for its courthouse, with second floor jail.

On April 21, 1881, Billy arrived to Sheriff Garrett's custody. For his 24 hour guard, Garrett deputized a White Oaks man, James Bell, and a Seven Rivers man, Bob Olinger. Garrett's further precaution was shackling Billy at wrists and ankles, with securing to a floor ring - all to guarantee his hanging death.

But on April 28th, with Garrett away collecting White Oaks's taxes, Billy escaped. He used a revolver from an accomplice's putting it in the outhouse, or by seizing Bell's. A likely accomplice was caretaker, Gottfried Gauss: Tunstall's past cook, and witness to Ring's Lincoln County War atrocities. Billy shot Bell dead as the man fled down the jail's stairway to sound alarm.

Deputy Bob Olinger, across the street at the Wortley Hotel with jail prisoners, either heard the shot or was directed to the ambush. Billy was at the second-floor window, and killed him with Olinger's own Whitney double-barrel shotgun.

Billy then spent hours using a miner's pick, supplied by Gauss, to break his leg chain to enable riding; while gathered loyalist Lincoln townspeople, in passive resistance, did nothing to stop him. He finally rode away on a pony supplied by Gauss.

As of that April 28, 1881 escape, Billy was involved in the murder of nine men; James Bell and Robert Olinger adding to Frank "Windy" Cahill and Joe Grant as Billy's only provable killings.

Of the dead, Billy would have said that that Cahill's and Grant's killings were in self-defense; that he was a legal posseman in the group's self-defense shooting of escaping and firing, arrested Tunstall murderers, William "Buck" Morton and Frank Baker; that his gun lacked range to hit Sheriff William Brady or Deputy George Hindman, and their killings by the Regulators were to save Alexander McSween from murder by them; that he had not shot Andrew "Buckshot" Roberts, a Tunstall murderer firing at his group and killing Dick Brewer, and being killed solely by Charlie Bowdre in self-defense; and that Deputy James Bell, after refusing to be tied, had tried to run for help, so was killed to save himself from unjust hanging (and Bell had been on the White Oaks posse, and possibly killed Jim Carlyle, then falsely accused him).

Only Seven Rivers rustler, Bob Olinger, would have been admittedly hated as being in each Lincoln County War period crime - Tunstall's murder, Frank MacNab's ambush murder, and the War's skirmishes and Battle. Billy's rage was so great, that he smashed apart Olinger's shotgun to throw it on his corpse, delaying his own escape.

That count of nine killed men - with only four certain - remained as Billy's final true tally.

Billy's escape route was across the Capitan Mountains to the Las Tablas home of his friend, Yginio Salazar; then to Fort Sumner and Paulita, where he hid in the Maxwell's sheep camps, confident of protection by the Maxwells and townspeople. He was unaware that Pat Garrett was paying Maxwell's foreman, Barney Mason, as a spy, through Secret Service Agent Azariah Wild.

Garrett's two deputies for the pursuit of Billy to Fort Sumner - John William Poe and Thomas "Kip" McKinney - did not know Billy. Poe, a buffalo hunter, past Deputy U.S. Marshall in Texas, cattle detective, and recent White Oaks settler, had met Garrett during the Wild-assisted tracking of the "Kid gang." McKinney knew Garrett from their 1878, hog farming days.

Once in Fort Sumner, Garrett, doubting Billy's presence, was urged by Poe to stay. On July 14, 1881, Poe searched the town and also checked with Sunnyside postmaster, Milnor Rudulph, seven miles to its north. That night, convinced Billy was nearby, he, Garrett, and McKinney planned an ambush in Peter Maxwell's bedroom, with Maxwell as traitor. Unknown accomplices likely directed Billy to Maxwell's bedroom, where Garrett waited, with Poe and McKinney outside to kill Billy if he escaped.

Near midnight, Billy proceeded from the converted barracks house of Celsa and Saval Gutierrez, carrying their butcher knife across the parade ground to cut a dinner steak in light of the almost-full huge moon. He first went toward Maxwell's bedroom; but seeing Poe, asked in Spanish who he was, then entered. Inside, to Maxwell in bed as decoy, Billy asked again in Spanish who was there, possibly sensing Garrett in the darkness. Garrett then fired. Next, he fired wild. But Billy was already dead.

The townspeople held a night vigil for Billy in their carpenter's shop. The Coroner's Jury, the next day, on July 15, 1881, had as President, Sunnyside Postmaster, Milnor Rudulph, a loyal Ringite who had helped take over the Legislature in 1872 to block anti-Ring bills. Bi-lingual, Rudulph wrote the Coroner's Jury Report in Spanish. The frightened juryman had no alternative but to sign his conclusion: *"[O]ur verdict is that the deed of said Garrett was justifiable homicide and we are unanimous in the opinion that the gratitude of all the community is due to the said Garrett for his deed and he is worthy of being rewarded."*

Ring terrorism was now complete. Silence fell for a generation before any dared contradict the Santa Fe Ring's outlaw mythology of Billy the Kid.

BILLY BONNEY'S CHAMPIONS

SUMMARY: Contradicting Billy Bonney's Santa Fe Ring outlaw myth began in the 20th century, when his aging contemporaries praised him in autobiographies which rode on his posthumous fame.

It took until the 20th century for Billy Bonney's aging contemporaries and fellow freedom fighters to feel safe enough to contradict the Santa Fe Ring's outlaw myth and praise him in print. They recorded his charismatic, bi-cultural, brilliance. But none dared mention the Ring.

FRANK AND GEORGE COE

John Tunstall's employees, local Homestead Act farmers, cousins Frank and George Coe, affectionately nick-named new ranch hand, teenaged Billy Bonney, as "Kid." They were 26 and 21 respectively when Billy met them in late 1877, when he was 17.

By 1878, after Tunstall's murder, the Coes became his fellow Regulators. After the lost Lincoln County War Battle, they fled to the Territory's northwest, near Farmington.

FRANK COE

As an old-timer, Frank Coe wrote about Billy in an unpublished letter to a William Steele Dean, dated August 3, 1926. He emphasized Billy's multi-culturalism, and above-average height (5'6" was average), belying his mythologized "shortness": "[He was] 5ft 8in, weight 138 lb stood straight as an Indian, fine looking a lad as I ever met. He was a lady's man, the Mex girls were all crazy about him. He spoke their language well. He was a fine dancer, could go all their gaits and was one of them. He was a wonder, you would have been proud to know him."

On September 16, 1923, Frank Coe - like Billy, considering himself a Regulator soldier - gave a quote to the *El Paso Times*: "[Billy] was brave and reliable, one of the best soldiers we had. He never pushed his advice or opinions, but he had a wonderful presence of mind; the tighter the place the more he showed his cool nerve and quick brain."

Frank Coe also related Billy's shootist preoccupation: "He never seemed to care for money, except to buy cartridges with ... and he always used about 10 times as many as any one else."

GEORGE COE

In 1934, George Coe published *Frontier Fighter: The Autobiography of George Coe Who Fought and Rode With Billy the Kid*. He confirmed Sheriff William Brady as dangerously brutal - even before John Tunstall's arrival - abusing him and fellow farmer and future Regulator, Josiah "Doc" Scurlock, by false arrest. And he described Tunstall's paternal affection for Billy:

> Tunstall seemed really devoted to the Kid. One day I was in Lincoln and I asked him about Billy.
> "George, that's the finest lad I ever met," he said. "He's a revelation to me every day and would do anything to please me. I'm going to make a man out of that boy yet. He has it in him."

George Coe also emphasized Billy's charisma:

> Billy came down to the Dick Brewer Ranch on the Ruidoso. He was the center of interest everywhere he went, and though heavily armed, he seemed as gentlemanly as a college-bred youth. He quickly became acquainted with everybody, and because of his humorous and pleasing personality grew to be a community favorite. In fact, Billy was so popular there wasn't enough of him to go around. He had a beautiful voice and sang like a bird. One of our special amusements was to get together every few nights and have singing. The thrill of those happy evenings still lingers – a pleasant memory – and tonight I would give a lot to live through one again. Frank Coe and I played the fiddles, and all of us danced, and here Billy, too, was in demand.

About Lincoln County War fighting, George Coe quoted Billy to show the boy's militant fervor in its freedom fighting: "As for ... giving up to that outfit, we'll die first."

Billy himself exhibited that brave bellicosity in his March 20, 1879 pardon bargain letter to Governor Lew Wallace; writing: *"I am not afraid to die like a man fighting but I would not like to be killed like a dog unarmed."*

George Coe gave a telling anecdote about Billy's teasing bravado which occurred around April 3, 1878 in the lead-up to the Lincoln County War. It shows how this teenager inspired grown men, and foreshadowed Billy's undaunted and ironic press interviews after his capture and after his unjust hanging trial:

> We made a big bonfire, and sat around swapping lies and bragging ... Then we talked about riding into Lincoln and setting in short order all the difficulties that were troubling the people there. We were a brave band as we told it.
>
> Our guns, which formed the most important part of our possessions, had been placed carelessly around against nearby trees. **Billy sized up the situation and, looking for a little fun and excitement with an inexperienced bunch of greenhorns, he slipped about five or six cartridges out of his belt and tossed them into the fire. In less than a minute they began to go off, and such a mad dash for tall timber you have never seen ... I looked back as I ran, and there stood the Kid with his arms folded, perfectly unconcerned ...**
>
> "Well, you're a damn fine bunch of soldiers. Run like a bunch of coyotes and forget to take your guns. I just wanted to break you in a little before we met the enemy, and, boys, I'm sure proud of your nerve."

YGENIO SALAZAR

Quoted in Walter Noble Burn's 1926 *The Saga of Billy the Kid*, Billy's good friend, Ygenio Salazar stated: " 'Billy the Kid' ... was the bravest fellow I ever knew. All through the three-days' battle [sic – six day Lincoln County War Battle] he was as cool and cheerful as if he were playing a game instead of fighting for his life." (Burns, p. 144)

GOTTFRIED GAUSS

German-born Gottfried Gauss, 56 at Billy's great escape from Lincoln's courthouse-jail, was part of Billy's Lincoln County history from that teenager's October of 1877 arrival as a John Tunstall ranch hand - when Gauss was Tunstall's cook - through the Lincoln County War period, and to Billy's 1881 jailbreak, when Gauss was the Lincoln courthouse-jail's caretaker and likely supplier of Billy's escape revolver. Gauss's anti-Ring stance went back to 1876 when he was employed in the Ring's store called "The House," and was cheated out of his wages and profits from its brewery, which he ran.

Billy himself mentioned Gauss, in his June 8, 1878 deposition to Washington Investigator Frank Warner Angel, as being at Tunstall's Feliz River ranch before Tunstall's ambush-murder, as well as during an earlier intimidation of its ranch hands by Sheriff William Brady's possemen. Billy's transcriptionist wrote: *"The persons at the ranch were R. M. Brewer, John Middleton,* ***G. Gauss****, M. Martz, R.A. Widenmann, Henry Brown, F.T. Waite, W$^{\underline{m}}$ McClosky and this deponent."* The night before Tunstall made his fatal return ride with his men and horses to Lincoln from that ranch, he assigned Gauss to stay. Thus, Gauss witnessed Brady's arriving murder posse.

On March 1, 1890, in an interview with the *Lincoln County Leader* about Billy's 1881 jailbreak, Gauss implied enabling by non-intervening Lincolnites, as well as his own sympathy for him. Gauss may have directed Deputy Bob Olinger to the courthouse's east side, where Billy shot him. Gauss stated:

I was crossing the yard behind the courthouse, when I heard a shot fired then a tussle upstairs in the courthouse, somebody hurrying downstairs, and deputy sheriff Bell emerging from the door running toward me. He ran right into my arms, expired the same moment, and I laid him down, dead. That I was in a hurry to secure assistance, or perhaps to save myself, everybody will believe.

When I arrived at the garden gate leading to the street, in front of the courthouse, I saw the other deputy sheriff Olinger, coming out of the hotel opposite, with the four or five other county prisoners, where they had taken their dinner. I called to him to come quick. He did so, leaving his prisoners in front of the hotel. When he had come up close to me, and while I was standing not a yard apart, I told him that I was just after laying Bell dead on the ground in the yard behind. Before he could reply, he was struck by a well-directed shot fired from a window above us, and fell dead at my feet. I ran for my life to reach my room and safety, when Billy the Kid called to me: "Don't run, I wouldn't hurt you – I am alone, and master not only of the courthouse, but also of the town, for I will allow nobody to come near us." "You go," he said, "and saddle one of Judge (Ira) Leonard's horses, and I will clear out as soon as I have the shackles loosened from my legs." With a little prospecting pick I had thrown to him through the window he was working for at least an hour, and could not accomplish more than to free one leg. He came to the conclusion to wait a better chance, tie one shackle to his waistbelt, and start out. Meanwhile I had saddled a small skittish pony belonging to Billy Burt (the county clerk), as there was no other horse available, and had also, by Billy's command, tied a pair of red blankets behind the saddle ...

When Billy went down the stairs at last, on passing the body of Bell he said, "I'm sorry I had to kill him but I couldn't help it."

On passing the body of Olinger he gave him a tip with his boot, saying, "You are not going to round me up again." And so Billy the Kid started out that evening, after he had shaken hands with everybody around and after having a little difficulty in mounting on account of the shackle on his leg, he went on his way rejoicing.

IRA LEONARD

Billy's best friend in a high place, Attorney Ira Leonard, bravely took Susan McSween's case against Commander N.A.M. Dudley right after the Ring murdered his office-mate predecessor: Attorney Huston Chapman. Leonard met Billy in Lincoln in 1879, when the boy was risking his life to testify against Chapman's killers in Lincoln County's April Grand Jury; followed by Billy's assisting Leonard in the prosecution by testifying in Dudley's Court of Inquiry. Aware of Lew Wallace's pardon bargain, Ira Leonard kept Wallace informed about Billy's Grand Jury testimony: that bargain's crux. In an April 20, 1879 letter to Wallace, he described Billy's courtroom pressure: *"I will tell you Gov. that the prosecuting officer of this Dist. [William Rynerson] is no friend to the enforcement of the law. He is bent on going for the Kid & ... is proposed to destroy his testimony & influence. He is bent on pushing him to the wall. He is a Dolan man and is defending him by his conduct all he can."*

Just before Leonard's 1879 litigation against Commander N.A.M. Dudley, he sustained a near assassination by the Ring. And in his 1881 representation at Billy's Mesilla hanging trial, he abruptly withdrew after a likely assassination threat.

HENRY HOYT

Henry Hoyt was a 24 year old medical doctor, working as a mail rider, when he met Billy Bonney in Tascosa, Texas, three months after the lost Lincoln County War Battle. Billy and fellow Regulators, Charlie Bowdre and Tom O'Folliard, were selling horses, rustled in retaliation from Ringmen, as forewarned in Billy's "Regulator Manifesto" letter of July 13, 1878 to Catron's Carrizozo cattle ranch manager and brother-in-law, Edgar Walz.

Billy became attached to intellectual Hoyt, and gifted him with an expensive sorrel horse, which may have belonged to killed Sheriff William Brady. Billy prudently gave Hoyt a legal bill of sale, dated October 24, 1878. Teenaged Billy, then 18, impressed Hoyt enough to save it. Hoyt admired his intelligence and bi-culturalism. In his autobiographical, 1829 book, *A Frontier Doctor*, he wrote about Billy:

> After learning his history directly from himself and recognizing his many superior natural qualifications, I often urged him, while he was free and the going was good, to leave the country, settle in Mexico or South America, and begin all over again. He spoke Spanish like a native and although only a beardless boy was nevertheless a natural leader of men. With his poise, iron nerve, and all-around efficiency properly applied, he could have made a success anywhere.

JOHN P. MEADOWS

A cattle rancher living in New Mexico from early 1880, John P. Meadows, when an old-timer, gave interviews to historians about having known Billy, and performed about it in an historical pageant called "Days of Billy the Kid in Story, Song and Dance" on February 26, 1931 in Roswell, New Mexico. Subsequently, he used his "Days of Billy the Kid" act for serialized newspaper accounts in the *Roswell Daily Record* on March 2nd, 3rd, and 4th of 1931. That year, Meadows also typed a 78 page manuscript with information about Billy. And from August 8, 1935 to June 25, 1936, the *Alamogordo News* printed almost forty reminiscence articles by him. These recollections are assembled in a 2004 book titled *Pat Garrett and Billy the Kid as I Knew Them: Reminiscences of John P. Meadows*. It gives insight into how Billy inspired the older men. Meadows stated: "When he was rough, he was as rough as men ever get to be, yet he had a good streak in him."

E.C. "TEDDY BLUE" ABBOTT

E.C. "Teddy Blue" Abbott, a cowboy about Billy's age, roving through New Mexico Territory in 1878, and having merely heard of him, recorded Billy's atypical multi-culturalism.
That implied Billy could instigate a Hispanic revolt against the land-grabbing, Anglo, Santa Fe Ring minority. "Boss" Thomas Benton Catron himself confirmed that fear of uprisings in a February 10, 1913 *Washington Times* article stating, "Mexicans ... were perfectly equal to starting five new revolutions in five days." As will be seen, Catron's anxiety fueled the Ring's mission to eliminate Billy by fabricating his outlaw myth.
In 1955, as an old-timer, "Teddy Blue" Abbott published *We Pointed Them North: Recollections of a Cowpuncher*. Open about his own racism, Abbott reported, as common knowledge, the existence of two sides, with Billy as the Mexican's hero, writing: "The Lincoln County troubles was still going on, and you had to be either for Billy the Kid or against him. It wasn't my fight ... it was the Mexicans that made a hero of him.

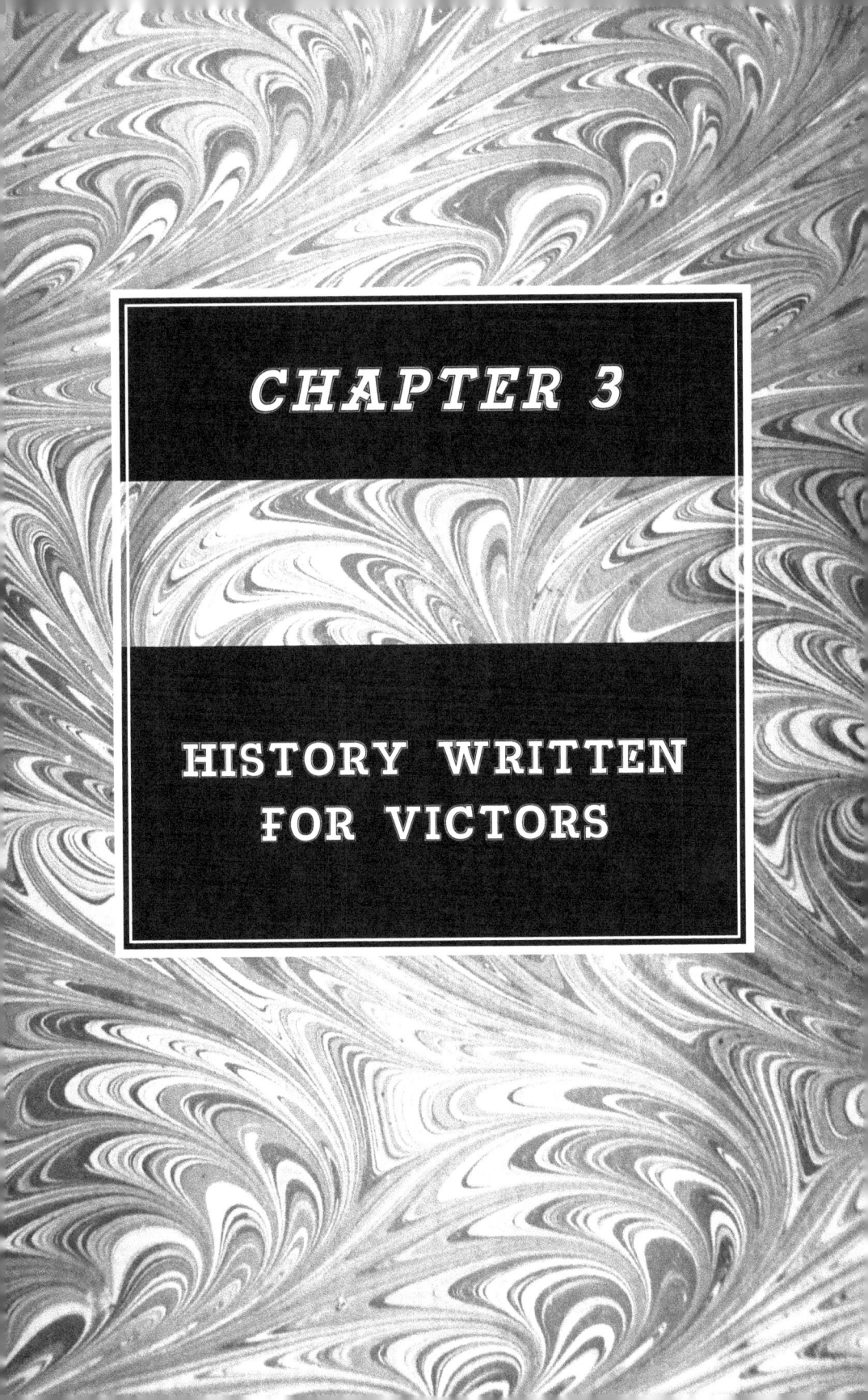

CHAPTER 3

HISTORY WRITTEN FOR VICTORS

HISTORY ROOTED IN MYTH

SUMMARY: Billy the Kid history has never escaped Santa Fe Ring outlaw myths, created to hide its crimes and the Lincoln County War freedom fight against its tyranny.

As will be seen, the history of Billy Bonney as "Billy the Kid" began in his lifetime; giving him the chance to comment on its fictions to Governor Lew Wallace on December 12, 1880; writing:

> *I noticed in the Las Vegas Gazette a piece which stated that, Billy "the" Kid, the name by which I am known in the Country was the captain of a Band of Outlaws who hold Forth at the Portales. There is no such Organization in Existence. So the Gentleman must have drawn very heavily on his Imagination.*

The situation was not destined to improve, with lies fueled by the Santa Fe Ring's outlaw myth propaganda, which created the moniker, "Billy the Kid." Back then, there existed just two sides in New Mexico Territory: Ringite minority and oppressed majority. By the time the last anti-Ring resistance was defeated in the Lincoln County War Battle, with surviving Regulators fleeing the Territory and Billy Bonney's pardon being refused by Governor Lew Wallace, no one dared publicly to take his side as the last anti-Ring fighter. And the Ring-controlled press, using leaked reports of the Ring-beholden Secret Service - brought in to kill him and the last resistance - poured forth its fables. That press was joined by hypocritical Lew Wallace, publishing his own articles of deadly desperado Billy the Kid, to hide his own moral failure at yielding to Ring pressure by denying Billy his deserved pardon for his Lincoln County War indictments.

That lurid press, was followed by dime novel-style books, with ambitious writers cashing in on Billy's burgeoning fame.

PAT GARRETT'S PROFITEERING BILLY THE KID DIME NOVEL

SUMMARY: Pat Garrett's 1882, ghostwritten book, The Authentic Life of Billy the Kid, concealed the Santa Fe Ring and set the tone - to the present - of a depraved, murdering, outlaw boy who had to be killed to get law and order.

Ring-beholden Sheriff, Pat Garrett sought profit from the incredible fame of killing Billy Bonney. Minimally literate, he used a journalist ghostwriter, Ashmun "Ash" Upson. In the popular, dime novel style, Upson created 1882's *The Authentic Life of Billy the Kid The Noted Desperado of the Southwest, Whose Deeds of Daring and Blood Made His Name a Terror in New Mexico, Arizona, and Northern Mexico by Pat F. Garrett, Sheriff of Lincoln County, N.M., by Whom He was Finally Hunted Down and Captured by Killing Him, A Faithful and Interesting Narrative.* Limited by both men's missing knowledge of Billy's life history and Lincoln County War issues, it compensated by fictional dramatizing. But it set the hysterically hyperbolic tone of the outlaw myth which plagued Billy's history ever since.

Since Billy's childhood was unknown until Jerry Weddle's 1993 book, *Antrim is My Stepfather's Name,* Upson simply made up a demonic boy in frothing prose: "When young Billy was about twelve years of age, he first imbrued his hand in human blood [stabbing to death a man who insulted his mother] ... [H]e went out into the night, and outcast and a wanderer, a murderer self-baptized in blood ... His hand was now against every man, and every man's hand against him."

Both Upson and Garrett would have been aware of the Santa Fe Ring, but *The Authentic Life's* thrust was to create a criminal boy leading a senselessly rampaging gang. Upson wrote: "The Kid had **a devil lurking in him.** It was a good-humored jovial imp, or a cruel and bloodthirsty fiend, as circumstances prompted. Circumstances favored the worser angel, and the Kid fell. [After the killing of Sheriff Brady] [t]he Kid and his desperate gang were now outlawed in Lincoln ... [After the lost Lincoln County War] the Kid gathered together such of his gang as were fit for duty and took to the mountains south of Lincoln."

WALTER NOBLE BURNS'S PULP FICTION

Walter Noble Burns, a flowery-penned journalist, like Ash Upson, is called Billy Bonney's first historian because he wrote his 1926 *The Saga of Billy the Kid* with interviews of surviving old-timer participants. In fact, his ignorance and motives matched Pat Garrett's, with no Santa Fe Ring present, and with its hook being the villain, Billy the Kid. Burns furthermore cribbed Garrett's book's fakery. Burns wrote: "[Billy] placed no value on human life ... He put a bullet through a man's heart as coolly as he perforated a tin can set upon a fence post. He had no remorse ... After him came the great change for which he involuntarily had cleared the way. Law and order came in on the flash and smoke of the six-shooter that with one bullet put an end to the outlaw and to outlawry."

RALPH EMERSON TWITCHELL'S RINGITE RENDITION

Ringite politician and attorney, Ralph Emerson Twitchell, authored 1911's five volume *Leading Facts in New Mexico History*. Hiding the Ring and uprisings against it, he made the Lincoln County War an outlaw depredation featuring "Billy the Kid."

In [Lincoln county] a feud was begun which, in the annals of New Mexico, is known as the 'Lincoln County War.' The cause of this trouble and era of crime can be traced to the rivalry existing between prominent cattlemen at the time living in Lincoln and the Pecos valley, respectively. Both were furnishing cattle to the Mescalero Indian reservation agent and each accused the other of stealing from their respective herds. This was the basis for the war ... Others believe ... that **the turbulence that terrorized the entire community, was the result of the outlawry established by such desperadoes as Billy the Kid** ...

The beginning of the so-called Lincoln County War occurred when John H. Tunstel [sic -Tunstall] was killed by a sheriff's posse seeking to levy an attachment upon property belonging to Tunstel [sic]. The latter had a friend and employe [sic], William H. Bonney, later famous as "Billy the Kid" ... **After the killing of Tunstel [sic] his sympathizers organized themselves into a party known as the McSwain [sic] faction and a sort of guerrilla warfare continued for the following eighteen months until finally broken up by the civil authorities with the aid of the military.**

BLANDINA SEGALE, THE HISTORY HOAXING NUN

A peculiar Billy the Kid history writer was Blandina Segale, a Sisters of Charity of Cincinnati missionary nun in the frontier southwest. I exposed her hoaxed relationship with Billy in my 2017 book, *Blandina Segale, The Nun Who Rode on Billy the Kid: Sleuthing a Foisted Frontier Fable.* Her 1932 book, *At the End of the Santa Fe Trial,* (in reprints to 2014), shows her ignorance of all events - lifting from Garrett's, Burns's, and Twitchell's books - and her own fantasies of interceding with a gang-leading homicidal Billy, about to scalp Colorado victims. Relying on the outlaw myth, she called Billy "the greatest murderer of the southwest." Her lies epitomized the profiteering pseudo-history of Billy the Kid through the early 20th century.

SILENCE OF THE REAL HISTORIANS

SUMMARY: The scholarly historians of the second half of the 20th century failed, as badly as the pseudo-historians that preceded them, because their omission of the central role of the Santa Fe Ring left them with only the antique outlaw myth to explain events.

Modern Billy the Kid history evolved by its writers retaining the antique armature of outlaw mythology, plastering on primary document research, and avoiding the Santa Fe Ring. But that merely continued the Ring's fable, as epitomized in Robert Utley's 1987 *High Noon in Lincoln: Violence on the Western Frontier,* calling the Lincoln County uprisings "a war without heroes."

PHILIP J. RASCH

Early historian, Philip J. Rasch, whose articles from 1949 to 1970 were compiled the 1997 book, *Gunsmoke in Lincoln County*, though mentioning the Ring, outlawed its opponents. Rasch's Ring is only a Masonicly dominated, political power. He wrote: "The dominant political power in New Mexico at this time was the Santa Fe Ring, led by Thomas B. Catron, U.S. district attorney and president of the First National Bank of Santa Fe. Practically all members of this Ring were Masons. District Attorney William L. Rynerson, Lieutenant Colonel N.A.M. Dudley, Emil Fritz, the Spiegelberg brothers, John Riley, John Kinney, and Morris Bernstein were lodge members. Catron, Murphy, Dolan and Brady were among those who organized the first Grand Lodge in New Mexico [and had] common desire for power." (Rasch, p. 11)

For Rasch, the Ring's opponents are outlaws. Billy was a "psychopathic young rustler" (Rasch, p. 18); and a greedy Tunstall was making a "new ring." (Rasch, p. 49) Rasch vilified Alexander McSween as an embezzler, and John Chisum as a deadbeat debtor to T.B. Catron. (Rasch, p. 56) The Regulators are called "the McSween gang." (Rasch, p. 94) And the Lincoln County War was a triumph of law: "[Tunstall's and McSween's] failure to recognize that the society of Lincoln County was one that would respond to the symbols of legal chicanery with gunfire resulted in their own destruction and that of many of their followers." (Rasch, pp. 131-132)

WILLIAM KELEHER

Early researcher and attorney, William Keleher, knew the Santa Fe Ring existed, but minimized it in his 1962 book, *The Fabulous Frontier*, as merely "the political ring of the Republican party" (Keleher, p. 214); writing: "The original 'Santa Fe Ring' was composed of T.B. Catron, Robert H. Longwill [doctor], H.L. Waldo [lawyer], Frank Springer [lawyer], and A. [Adolph] Staab [merchant]." (Keleher, p. 125)

Keleher's 1957 book on the Lincoln County War and Billy Bonney's history, *Violence in Lincoln County 1869-1881*, did not mention the Santa Fe Ring. And his denigration of Billy Bonney is willfully misleading. For the pardon bargain, he called Billy "almost illiterate," though having Billy's literate pardon letters; writing: "One correspondent [Lew Wallace] was a man of great prestige; the governor of a Territory; a man of acknowledged pre-eminence in letters and literature; a gallant soldier ... The other party to the correspondence was scarcely of legal voting age; **almost illiterate**; acquainted with comparatively few people; a desperado, gunman and outlaw; a man who had not hesitated to take human life on more than one occasion."

Keleher misstated Billy's Dudley Court of Inquiry testimony as "brief and failed to throw much light during the period July 14 to July 20;" even though he provides Billy's devastating courtroom testimony - "Three soldiers fired at me" - which was the crime that should have yielded Dudley's court martial.

Concealing the Lincoln County freedom fight, he attributes Lincolnites' inaction during Billy's hours-long jailbreak to watching some form of "exciting drama." Missed was their revelation that one person could defeat the juggernaut; and that the Lincoln County War could finally be won that way - as I portrayed in my 2012 docufiction book, *Billy and Paulita*: "But the crowd waited, looking at "The House": monument to greed, corruption, hubris, and oppression, conquered in hours and transformed into a symbol of freedom. George Washington, tears in his eyes, murmured, "So David prevailed over Goliath. And no jail could hold him, no hand of man could shackle him. Billy of Lincoln town."

ROBERT UTLEY

Popularizer of Billy the Kid history, Robert M. Utley, in his 1987 book, *High Noon in Lincoln: Violence on the Western Frontier*, has only four Santa Fe Ring references, and attributes its contemporary mention to "ring mania" following President Grant's administration. (Utley, pp. 24-25) He presents what he calls a "balanced view," citing Howard R. Lamar's 1966 book, *The Far Southwest, 1846-1912*: "No one has [shown] that [the Santa Fe Ring] existed as an entity rather than as a group of men individually pursuing similar ends in similar ways."

(Lamar, pp. 187-188) So Utley merely calls Catron the *"reputed head of the Santa Fe Ring."* (Utley, p. 28)

Utley's bad guy, like Philip Rasch's, is John Tunstall: "He made [a ring] for himself" (Utley, p. 26)

So Utley continues the Ring's myth of the Lincoln County War as an outlaw uprising. And, for him, Billy Bonney is a non-entity, inexplicably elevated to a icon. Utley concluded: "By July of 1878, [Billy's] values closely resembled those of the other regulators, ambiguously reflecting both the noble and ignoble ... Some of the Regulators turned toward good. The Kid turned the other way ... As for Billy the Kid's contribution to the Lincoln County War ... [h]ad he never found his way to Lincoln County – the course of the War would have almost certainly remained essentially as history has recorded it." (Utley, p. 165)

FREDERICK NOLAN

By 1992 came *The Lincoln County War: A Documentary History* by the greatest 20th century historian of that period: Frederick Nolan. But he had even greater antipathy for Billy than his predecessors, and a preference for establishment power, which matched the old outlaw myths.

His tome has only 22 Santa Fe Ring indexed references, with it seen as a vague patronage machine: "With Republican presidents occupying the White House since 1860, a well-entrenched Republican machine, feeding on the beneficence of Washington, controlled New Mexico. At its head was Thomas Benton Catron, U.S. district attorney and president of the First National Bank of Santa Fe. This loosely knit freemasonry of lawyers, soldiers, and Republican leaders with influential ties in Washington maintained a ruthless domination over federal patronage and the territorial capital in Santa Fe." (Nolan, p. 47)

Most of Nolan's 22 references are passing quotes made by contemporaries, without the Ring having a causal role in events. As examples, Ring agent, Governor S.B. Axtell, is described as having "a smear campaign ... launched by his opponents, alleging he was a Mormon bishop ... [and] was removed from office subsequent to the Angel investigation." (Nolan, p. 443) Omitted is that this accusation was a tiny part of an 1877 complaint to

President Hayes by a Mary McPherson, linking Axtell to the murderous Santa Fe Ring as the reason for his removal. (See pages 296-310) For Ringite District Attorney William Rynerson, who obstructed prosecution of Tunstall's assassins and backed Catron's malicious prosecutions of McSween and Tunstall, Nolan merely stated that he was "a prominent participant of the legal ramifications of the Lincoln County War."

Missing are the anti-Ring uprisings. And the Lincoln County Regulators' motivation is reduced to meaningless blather: "What prompted the men to take up arms? There can be little doubt that they were motivated by the complex mixture of emotion and rationalization that military historian John Keegan calls 'the will to combat,' a mixture made up in varying degrees of personal loyalties and resentments, the pressure of unavoidable compulsion, the prospect of personal enrichment, the endorsement of religion ... and not at all the least, drink, which we have already seen as a major factor in the violence of the times. Fueled in greater or lesser part by 'the will to combat,' inured by upbringing and experience to the commonplace character of violence in frontier life, decent men could - and would - justify to themselves actions they would - and did - condemn outright in other circumstances." (Nolan, p. 219)

And the grand Lincoln County War freedom fight is concluded to have been meaningless "self-deceptions": "Fueled by greed, propelled by religious and racial prejudice, by liquor, by firearms, and by some powerful American misbeliefs, the Lincoln County War was based on a whole catalog of self-deceptions. Each side believed it was 'us' against 'them' ... The Lincoln County War was a false premise pursued to an illogical conclusion. (Nolan, p. 439)

Nolan's Billy is as a "callow youngster" (Nolan, p. 124): a bit player caught up in events and accidentally celebrated: "Indeed, those who savor the ironies of history may find a certain sweet justice in the fact that today, of all the powerful, rich, and famous men of his era, **it is the Kid who is remembered best - and at that, for the things he never did.**" (Nolan, p. 3)

So about Billy's first pardon bargain letters - offering to put his life on the line to convict, by his testimony, the Ringite murderers of Attorney Huston Chapman in exchange for annulling his War indictments - unmoved Nolan wrote: "These two letters were the beginning of a correspondence unique in the **annals of outlawry**." (Nolan, p. 382)

Astoundingly, to justify the Ring-instigated Secret Service's 1880 hunting of Billy using Pat Garrett, Nolan reverted to none other than the original dime novel outlaw myth of Pat Garrett's ghost-writer, Ash Upson, as an authority: "Upson's catalogue of the Kid's thievery is likely to be accurate as any other. It paints a believable picture of his activities, and confirms why he and his *compadres* were soon to be considered as big a menace as the original gang whose name they now bore - the Rustlers ... But the times at last were changing, and a cold new wind of law and order was beginning to blow." (Nolan, p. 397)

In "Finale," Nolan did not comprehend that the New Mexican generation of silence that followed Billy's killing was the culmination of the Ring's terrorist victory. Nolan wrote: "With the death of Billy the Kid it was as if every one of the men who had participated in the years of bloodshed took a vow of silence. Thus, nowhere in the literature of the Lincoln County troubles is there any article, any memoir, any reminiscence of the times written between 1882 and the middle 1920's by someone who was actually there." (Nolan, p. 427)

JOEL JACOBSEN

New Mexican political insider, Assistant Attorney General Joel Jacobsen, published his 1994 book, *Such Men as Billy the Kid: The Lincoln County War Reconsidered.* It descends to even greater Santa Fe Ring denial and minimizing of Billy Bonney.

His title is a give-away, being a snide quote about outlawry of "such men as Billy the Kid" made by Ringite Lincoln County War Commander N.A.M. Dudley, and presented in his military Court of Inquiry for possible court martial by the widow of Ring-murdered Alexander McSween. She stated that when she told him he was being partisan, he said *"that he would send his soldiers where he pleased, that I have no such business to have* **such men as Billy the Kid** *... and others of like character in my house."*

Jacobson's index has just five mentions of the Ring, minimized as "an informal confederation of businessmen/politicians swapping favors and telling no tales." (Jacobson, pp. 44-45)

As to Billy Bonney, Jacobson saw him as a press creation. Citing a [December 3] 1880 *Las Vegas Gazette* article ["Desperadoe's Stronghold"] calling him "Billy the Kid," Jacobson concluded that the catchy name caused the fame: "The use of 'the' before such a common word [as kid] made the description iconic: a killer called Kid with a child's diminutive name." Then the Las Vegas *Gazette* joined in to call him " 'the best known man in New Mexico.' The Kid was a star." (Jacobson, p. 223)

VICTOR WESTPHALL

If other historians of the Lincoln County War period were Ring minimizers, Victor Westphall, was like a holocaust denier writing a Hitler biography. He is used herein as Ring's voice, from his 1873 book, *Thomas Benton Catron and His Era.* That hagiography was the outlaw myth's flip side: the Ringites were good, but maligned. After thanking the Catron family's help in preparing his book, he wrote unconvincingly: "[S]ome have already expressed suspicion that this is a biography arbitrarily designed to present only Catron's better side, thereby pleasing family and friends. Emphatically, such is not the case!" (Pages ix-x)

FRUITS OF BANDWAGON HISTORIANS

Billy the Kid bandwagon historians of the 20th century failed the brave 19th century Hispanic and Anglo New Mexicans who fought and died to protect America's promised freedoms. They failed their readers entitled to know inspiring and true events. They shielded the criminal and treasonous Santa Fe Ring victors. Concealed by them all was a Territory in revolutionary upheaval against tyranny throughout the 1870's, and the magnificent freedom fight of the Lincoln County War itself. Lost was the opportunity to condemn Santa Fe Ring criminals, and to credit the spectacular individual who made it all worth remembering: Billy Bonney. Yielded was meaningless mythology benefiting undeserving victors.

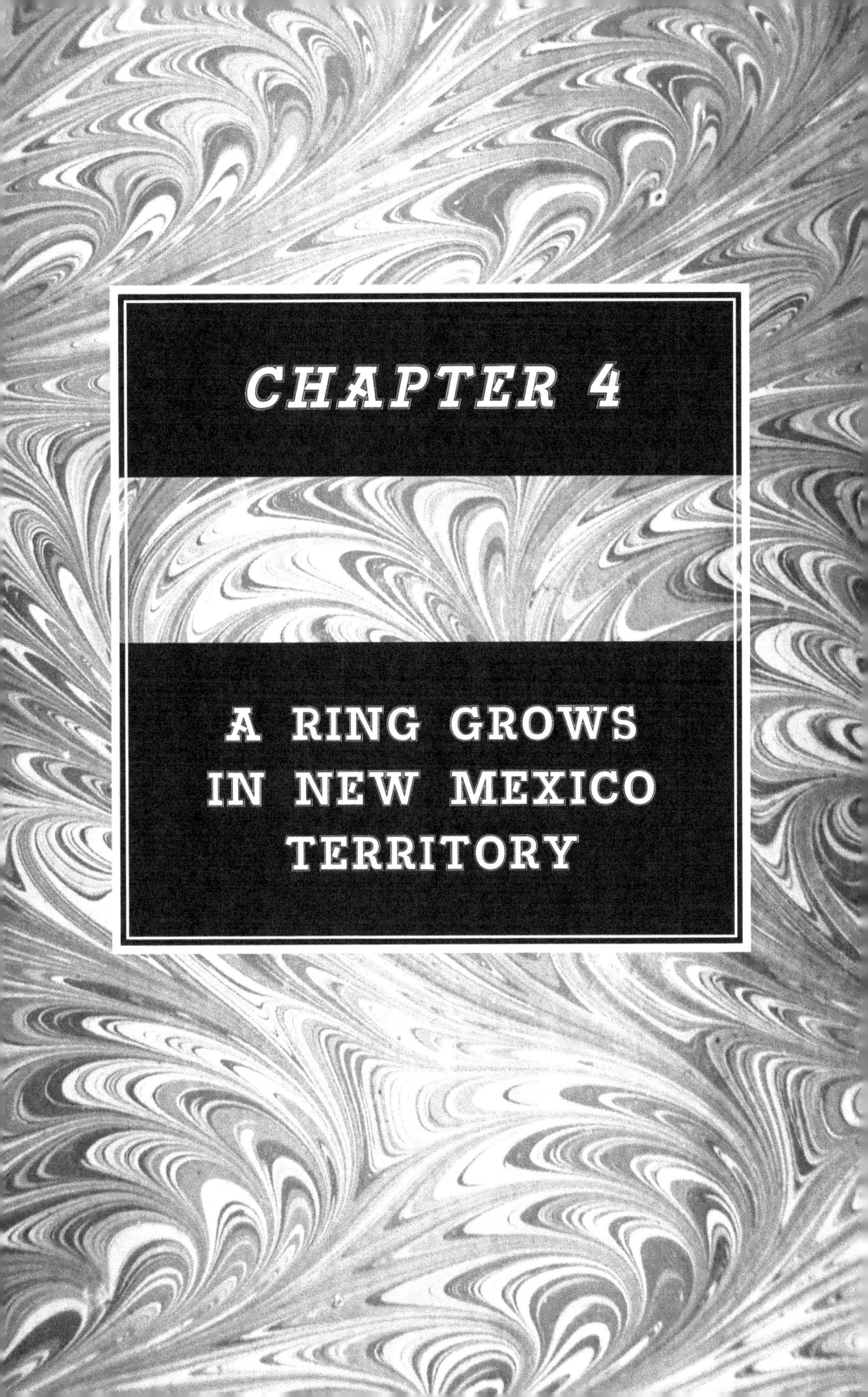

UNMASKING THE SANTA FE RING

SUMMARY: The Santa Fe Ring is a form of organized crime by malignant cronyism; which infiltrated New Mexico Territory's executive, judicial, legislative, and law enforcement branches. It sought profit, power, and secrecy. Opponents faced rigged elections, malicious prosecutions, obstructed justice, military suppression, and assassination. But the Ring was almost destroyed by a teenager: Billy Bonney, whom it outlawed for hanging as "Billy the Kid."

BACKGROUND

The Hispanic and Native American people living on the 525,000 square miles of future New Mexico, Arizona, Colorado, Nevada, Utah, Wyoming, and California, joined the United States after its 1848 Mexican-American War victory and Treaty of Guadalupe Hidalgo.

With Old Mexico losing its northern half and about 75,000 inhabitants, the Treaty promised protection of citizenship and land ownership for those remaining. Boundary disputes for New Mexico Territory yielded the Congressional Compromise of 1850. And the 1854 Gadsden Purchase sliced from Old Mexico the southwestern Mesilla Valley for New Mexico, and the southern portion of Arizona. The resulting almost square New Mexico Territory had an area of 121,697 square miles; of which about 15,000,000 acres were land grants.

Slightly more than a decade later, in 1866, the Santa Fe Ring arose to defraud the grant holders - in parallel with the federal government's genocide of Native Americans, also to get their land. The Ring was a scheme of Missourians, Stephen Benton Elkins and Thomas Benton Catron, past college friends and attorneys, seeking riches after the Civil War by exploiting a legal loophole in the Treaty of Guadalupe Hidalgo: grant holders had to prove ownership. Their titles were reviewed by a Surveyor General, then approved by Congress. Catron and Elkins could represent them as lawyers, buy their land far below value; then re-survey it with cronies for maximal boundaries, to keep or to sell to friends.

To shield that theft of millions of acres, a compliant political and judicial system were needed. So both men obtained legislative and judicial positions; first Territorial, then national. Their vast profits yielded diversification into banks, loans, railroads, mining, mercantile enterprises, and ranching. And their core strategies of loyalty to accomplices, impenetrable secrecy, and elimination of opponents never changed; yielding atrocities and immunity to prosecution, since all legal redress was obstructed by compatriots.

Billy Bonney's history intersected that period of Ring expansion. Its first growth spurt came by defrauding the Maxwell Land Grant's owner of his two million acres. Billy's history was entwined with that Maxwell family, and paralleled them in tragedy. By the time he re-entered New Mexico Territory from Arizona Territory in 1877, the Ring had crushed an 1872 revolt of the legislature, and grass-roots rebellions in 1876 and 1877. By the next year, he would fight that Ring in the Lincoln County War. And a year later, in 1879, new Governor Lew Wallace would face a dilemma of Billy's pardon being linked to defying that Ring.

Historian, D.W. Meinig, in his 1998 book, *The Shaping of America, A Geographical Perspective on 500 Years of History, Volume. 3, Transcontinental America 1850 - 1915* regarded the Santa Fe Ring an economic phenomenon imperiling democracy:

In the 1870's anticipation of railroad connections to the East began to alter the prospects [in New Mexico] for profits and position. Slowly forming over the years, the "Santa Fe Ring" now emerged into full notoriety: "it was essentially a set of lawyers, politicians, and businessmen who united to run the territory and to make money off this particular region. Although located on the frontier, the ring reflected the corporative, monopolistic, and multiple enterprise tendencies of all American business after the Civil War. Its uniqueness lay in the fact that, rather than dealing with some manufactured item, they regarded land as their first medium of currency." "Land" meant litigation, and "down the trail from the states came ... an amazing number of lawyers" who ... would build their own political and economic empire out of the tangled heritage of land grants." And so ... "eventually over 80 per cent of the Spanish grants went to American lawyers and settlers." Important differences were the presence in New Mexico of a much greater number of Hispanic peasants and communities well rooted on the land, the considerable resistance and violence generated by this American assault, and the sullen resentment created in an increasingly constricted and impoverished people who felt they had been cheated out of much of their lands ... In contrast to common representations it was not a case of vigorous, expanding society moving upon "a static culture," for "the Hispanos were still settling and conquering New Mexico, ever-extending their control" when the Anglos arrived. To the Anglos land was a commodity to buy and sell, to exploit as quickly as possible, a means of profit and propellant of one's personal progress. Furthermore, "American land policy featured precise measurement and documentation, assumed individual ownership, and came out of a tradition that expected western land to be open for settlement. ... This process of Anglo encroachment went through several phases over several decades but reached an important victory in an early court approval of the Maxwell Grant ... the invasion of New Mexico had taken on a new momentum.

By 1873, Catron and Elkins extended Ring reach by a division of "boss" roles, with Catron in the Territory and Elkins politically based in Washington, D.C. By the time of Billy the Kid, President Rutherford B. Hayes covered-up the Ring so successfully that his, and his complicit cabinetmen's, reputations were unscathed. But it was Catron's meganomaniacal, conscienceless, and vindictive nature which shaped Santa Fe Ring style. Like other tyrants, his domination relied on extermination and terror.

Catron and Elkins ultimately created a fiefdom controlling New Mexico Territory by fear and favor. It was the Ring's destruction of opposition in the days of Billy the Kid that gave it the victor's option of writing the history to vilify its adversaries. The fabrications were so successful, that the pre-Lincoln County War uprisings against it are largely unknown; the Lincoln County War is unrecognized as a freedom fight; and Billy Bonney is mythologized as an outlaw, instead of the Ring's most dangerous, freedom fighting opponent.

Conrad Keeler Naegle, historian of 1976's anti-Ring Grant County Rebellion, stated in a 1968 *Arizona and the West* article:

> Catron, [the Ring's] long-term leader, probably wielded more power in New Mexico, for almost half a century, than any other single individual. The Ring was composed of a majority of the legal profession, a number of probate and supreme court judges, governors, and other prominent men in the Territory. Although basically Anglo-Republican, it also included a few Spanish-Americans and Democrats among its adherents. (Naegle, *Arizona and the West*, pp. 226-227)

Naegle, in his 1943 *The History of Silver City, New Mexico 1870-1886* doctoral thesis, concluded that the Ring had "retarded progress in New Mexico." It parasitized an entire population.

EXISTENCE OF THE SANTA FE RING

SUMMARY: The Santa Fe Ring's first line of defense, and greatest achievement, was keeping secret its own existence.

MAKING VISIBLE THE INVISIBLE RING

Ring-biased historian, Victor Westphall, in his 1973 *Thomas Benton Catron and His Era*, hid contemporary exposés and anti-Ring Territorial uprisings in the 1870's. He called the Ring a fantasy: "romantic imagination [of] ... a sinister organization with members dedicated to unqualified promotion of their own selfish interests ... accompanied by connotations of violence, deception, deceit, fraud, and other nefarious implications." (Westphall, pp. 98-99) He blamed Democrats and fate for claims of Ring existence:

> Thomas Benton Catron was present when the Republican party in New Mexico was organized in the winter of 1867 and when the epithet "Santa Fe Ring" was applied to its leaders. It was Catron's fate to become the

acknowledged head of both party and ring ... (p. 97) While Catron was often assailed as leader of the Ring, he held that position by virtue of ability as a common spokesman for others interested in common goals. (Westphall, p. 201)

But in the Ring's earliest days, even national press reported its existence, and compared it to "Boss" Tweed's Ring. An editorial in March 13, 1876's *The Boston Daily Globe* was titled: "New Mexico, A Sorry Showing for a Would-be State, Tweed's Disciples Preying on the Populace." It stated:

NEW MEXICO.

A Sorry Showing for a Would-be State.

Tweed's Disciples Preying on the Ignorant Populace.

HOW THE TERRITORIAL RING IS RUN.

Why the Territory Should Not Be Made a State.

To the Editor of The Globe –
SIR: The New Mexico State question is again looming up ... In view of the fact that but little is known of New Mexico in the East, I propose to give a short sketch upon its social and political aspects, and **showing what a clique of Tweedian disciples are doing in that section** ... The majority of the legislators are elected, not for their worth or intelligence but because, for the emoluments of office, they are willing to become the tools of their superiors, elect the territorial officers and control the local appointments as directed.

The Territorial Government,

executive and judicial, is as closely an allied ring as ever inflicted itself upon a people. Its headquarters is at Santa Fé, and it includes among its members public officials of every grade, and is ably assisted in its operations by the judicial element of the Government and its official organ, the Santa Fe New Mexican ...

Justice in the Territory

is a sad delusion. The probate judges always have a hand in the election of the juries, and completely control the cases before the courts ... A.C.L.

Westphall himself revealed public awareness, quoting October 27, 1880's Las Cruces *Thirty-Four* newspaper's urging voters who desire "an honest administration of public affairs in this Territory [to] assist to overthrow the Santa Fe Ring by depositing his ballot against its [Catron-backed] candidate [Tranquilino Luna for Delegate to Congress]." It stated:

> The Santa Fe Ring is the most corrupt combination that ever cursed any country or community. It has controlled the machinery of the Republican party in the Territory for the past twelve years. It has vilified, oppressed or otherwise sought to ruin every man who had the independence and hardihood to oppose its corrupt schemes. It has grown fat upon the prostitution of the party it controls. It has used its power in the courts to defend its criminal tools from merited punishment. It has retained its power by wholesale bribery and intimidation of voters. It has threatened innocent men with prosecution in the courts, should they dare to oppose it. It has promised indicted criminals immunity from punishment if they would assist it to retain its power. The people of this county and every county will be benefited by its overthrow. (Westphall, p. 186)

Luna won. Westphall said those voting "three or four times" for him had "zeal for his candidacy" (Westphall, p. 188) - not fraud. But his opponent, Miguel Otero, wrote: "[Luna] was well groomed by the 'Santa Fe Ring,' the real machine controlling the political situation in New Mexico." (Westphall, p. 188)

In the 1880's, with the Ring ascendant, press reported controlled juries, fraudulent votes, and bribed legislators. (Westphall, p. 192) The March 4, 1884 *Albuquerque Daily Democrat* declared:

> The Ring must soon discover that the time has passed in New Mexico when men can be herded like so many sheep and be made to move at the wave of the hand in violation of law, and every precedent known to the laws governing free people. (Westphall, p. 191)

That 1884, a Reverend Oscar P. McMains (unidentified by Westphall as the Colfax County War's anti-Ring successor to Ring-murdered Franklin Tolby), introduced a later defeated, legislative memorial censuring Catron and Elkins for their land grant thefts. The March 15, 1884 *Albuquerque Daily Democrat* reported:

> [McMains's] reference to Tom Catron and the territorial courts, which aided and abetted the land steals that have been going on the last twenty years, was received with deafening applause and showed ... that the house is becoming deeply interested in putting a stop to the disgraceful and dishonest work of the ring. (Westphall, p. 193)

Also in 1884, when anti-Ring Edmund G. Ross was appointed Governor by President Grover Cleveland, "he learned that important people within his own party were tainted with what he considered the stigma of Ring association." (Westphall, p. 199) The bar association of 1886 then stymied Ross by its having approval power over legislative bills; which Westphall admits "meant that the bar association - which was essentially the Santa Fe Ring - effectively controlled the legislature." (Westphall, p. 201) Westphall conceded:

> This dual [party] relationship more than anything else explains the enigma of the Santa Fe Ring. It was groupings in constant flux of persons whose common interests brought them together for mutual action on specific problems that arose from time to time. Thoroughly democratic in its way, it was a devilish thing to fight for those who wanted to lash out at something they could get hold of. (Westphall, p. 202)

Without naming the Ring, but calling Catron "chief of this class of politicians," an August 18, 1890 *Las Vegas Democrat* article by the anti-land grab The Knights of Labor, exposed the machine. Titled "Scorching Letter," it was addressed to the organization's founder, Terence V. Powderly, and rightly claimed boldness in that time when assassinations were still a Ring retaliation. By members Jose Valdez and Enrique Mares, it stated:

SCORCHING LETTER

The Knights of Labor

SEND A COMMUNICATION TO POWDERLY!

Politicians Arraigned!

THE BOLDEST DOCUMENT EVER ISSUED IN THE TERRITORY!

Las Vegas, N.M. Aug. 18, 1890.

Hon. T.V. Powderly,
                Scranton, Pa.

DEAR SIR AND BRO.: [Responding to letters forwarded from Messrs. Butler and Barrett] In reference to the insinuations of Mr. Barrett that the K. of L., in this [San Miguel] county, have encouraged the lawless destructions of property ... this committee has only this to say, that all such insinuations ... are entirely false ... On the contrary, the K. of L., in this county, have, while taking a public and outspoken position in opposition to the attempts of this man, Barrett, his associates, **Catron,** Butler and a host of other would-be [swallowing up] land cormorants, to entrench themselves behind technical forms of law, in the possession of vast tracts of land ... have at the same time taken an equally open stand against clandestine and violent resistance on the part of individuals, **to the lawless and tyrannical aggessions of these community land thieves and public corruptionists** ...

Our order regards the excesses that have been committed in some parts of the county, as only a result of the corrupt and tyrannical political practices long continued in connection with the land-robbing acts of many of the leading lawyers, prominent politicians and business men of this county and Territory for years past.

In order that the situation here, at the present time, may be well understood, it is necessary to refer to a few historical and political facts. The Old Mexican patronage system prevailed here until slavery was abolished in the United States. A few large Spanish-Mexican families, up to that time, controlled the masses of the people in servile condition ...

But what has been the sequel after forty years for New Mexico in this condition? Following slowly, an Anglo-Saxon people pushed into the territory – first a few lawyers and sharp traders. These at once saw that money and political honors were to be had by cultivating close relations in the all-powerful ruling classes. The lawyers saw that under the treaty of Guadalupe Hidalgo there was an immense field wherein to enrich themselves by securing some kind of title to the princely land grants, scattered over the best location in the territory. They soon found means to do this. Playing on the ignorance of the poor people as to their rights, and stimulating the greed of the wealthy and outside friends **until their technical dragnet had scooped in ... a large part of the 15,000,000 acres embraced within these grants in the territory.** These men grew in influence, and their greed and political ambition have known no bounds. **They have for years controlled the legislatures, courts and county affairs, and prostituted all of these sources to power to gratify their venal mercenary propensities and vain ambitions**. Party names in this territory have never been anything but leaders of personal clan followings ... The mass of the poor people have been bull-dozed, cajoled and their votes bought directly and indirectly, and after having been secured by such means, the laws passed by these leaders appear purposely designed to ... systematically rob them by means of the courts and legal processes ... **Such political practices have not been confined to San Miguel alone, but have been practiced in all parts of the territory, and, in instances, murder has been committed from purely political motives**.

The poor class of people have been helpless to remedy the evils which have followed from the long period of political tyranny which has followed the train of such political practices. Among these evils may be mentioned (bearing in mind that these corrupting, mercenary politicians have controlled the enactment of laws and ... their administration), the enactment of laws designed to prompt district attorneys to secure indictments on frivolous pretexts against hundreds of poor people and dragging them instances from fifty to five hundred miles before the courts, and then dismissing their cases on pledges that they would vote for this or that political aspirant. Laws are frequently passed which are plainly intended to aid these public plunderers to retain a firm grip on lands within Mexican grants ... of which they are trying to rob the public. **As an example of this, a law was passed at the insistence of Tom Catron (the chief of this class of politicians) ... to enable large grant claimants to drag poor and small occupants of land before the courts and compel them to show by what title they held their homes** ... These political and land cormorants have not been satisfied in securing to themselves the class of old Mexican land grants ... [and] in the surveys stretching their boundaries long beyond what the Mexican government intended they should be, but they have invaded the purely community land grants ... fencing in and claiming large areas of land within their boundaries, thereby depriving the poor people who have lived on such grants for generations ...

This state of affairs exist in greater or lesser degree all over the Territory... **[I]t is well understood that Mr.

Barrett, in conjunction with Catron and others, has long been scheming through some legal technicalities to secure a large portion of the [Mora grant] land ... much of which has been occupied for generations by industrious people. In the past, on some of these grants, the people have been induced through their ignorance and confidence to deed away their rights, for a dollar or so, without knowing the effect of the paper they signed.

What is herein stated can be proven, and much more, if necessary. **In view of this situation, is it at all singular that now, when a large number of poorer people are pinched by poverty, and all are being deprived of the means of subsistence for their families ... and their tyrannical unjust treatment by these political and moneyed magnates, that some excesses should have been committed, in an endeavor to stop such lawless aggressions and public corruptions**.

You may be assured that the influence of the K. of L. here will always be directed to the course of true justice and equality, and that in the end right will prevail.

We do not apprehend any serious troubles, unless they are precipitated by the monopolistic class, in arbitrary efforts to crush the people back into the old servile condition where they have so long held them.

Very respectfully submitted, as adopted by the general committee on correspondence of the K. of L. and approved by the order in general meeting.

Jose Valdez
Master Workman, K. of L.
Enrique Mares
Secretary.

Ring accusations against Catron continued into the 20th century as shown by December 11, 1911 letter of a Bronson Cutting to a James Roger Addison: "Catron was the boss of the Territory from 1865 [sic – 1866] to 1900 and is probably still the most unscrupulous man in the Southwest. His methods of wholesale assassination and blackmail are [notorious]. [H]e still runs the gang in this country." (Westphall, p. 98)

Westphall used the Ring's own cover-up that it was not a formal organization: "There was no network of control in an organized sense; there was mutual cooperation ... for particular events or projects." (Westphall, p. 99) Such evaded culpability of plausible deniability was satirized by 19th century cartoonist, Thomas Nast, who drew "Boss" Tweed's Tammany Hall Ring as a circle of men, each pointing to the other, saying, " 'Twas Him."

CONTEMPORARY REPORTERS

Contemporary reports of the Ring are profuse - as in the Colfax County War period - though they are from its victims.

BILLY BONNEY

Billy Bonney knew the Ring existed, writing the "Regulator Manifesto" of July 13, 1878 to Edgar Walz: *"We are all aware that your brother-in-law, T.B. Catron sustains the Murphy-Kinney party ... Steal from the poorest or richest American or Mexican, and the full measure of the injury you do, shall be visited upon the property of Mr. Catron."*

JOHN HENRY TUNSTALL

John Henry Tunstall's letters to his British family documented, though underestimated, the Ring. His biographer is Frederick Nolan, in his 1965 *The Life and Death of John Henry Tunstall*. On April 27, 1877, to "Much Beloved Father," Tunstall prattled about *"rings."* As *"Adventurer,"* he naively thought a "ring" was a way to do business, so presented his own plan:

Everything in New Mexico, that pays at all (you may say) is worked by a "ring," there is the "Indian ring," the "army ring," "the political ring," the "legal ring," the "Roman Catholic ring," the "cattle ring," the "horsethieves ring," the "land ring," and half a dozen other rings; **now to make things stick "to do any good," it is necessary to either get into a ring or to make one out for yourself. I am at work at present making a ring & have succeeded admirably so far**; *you see, an adventurer like myself does not present a very formidable aspect when "in the ring," but anyone as well posted as myself can very nearly break up an incipient ring single-handed, by skirmishing on the outskirts ...*

I propose to confine my operations to Lincoln County, but I intend to handle it in such a way as to get the half of every dollar that is made in the county by anyone; & with our means we could get things in that shape in three years if we only used two thirds of our capital in the undertaking. (Nolan, *Life and Death*, p. 213)

ALEXANDER McSWEEN

Alexander McSween's February 23, 1878 letter to the father, John Partridge, of just-murdered Tunstall, stated: "J.J. Dolan & Co entertained fearful malice toward [John Tunstall] and me on account of business ... **[Tunstall] understood well from the U.S. Attorney [Catron] to the lowest magistrate that there was a combination and determination to keep down independence. This combination is known as the "Santa Fe Ring."** To the branch of the Ring down here he had become particularly obnoxious owing to the fact that he was acquiring so much land, and because I aided him." (Nolan, *Documentary History*, pp. 206-207)

LILLY KLASNER

Engaged to Bob Olinger when he was killed on April 28, 1881 by Billy Bonney in his famous jailbreak, Lilly Klasner, daughter of Robert and Ellen Casey, whose posthumous manuscript was edited by Eve Ball in 1972 as *My Girlhood Among Outlaws*, wrote:

Uncle John [Chisum] suffered at the hands of the **powerful Santa Fe Ring of those days. This ring, a group of politicians and businessmen, sought to control the courts and everything else in the state [sic] and to get their hands on as much resources of the state as possible to exploit in their own interests. In other words, they were greedy for personal gain and sought to obtain it by fair means or foul, most frequently the latter.** Some members viewed with jealousy the success of Uncle John's cattle running venture ...

Hostility reached a climax in the latter part of 1877 and the early part of 1878. **Thomas B. Catron - then United States District Attorney and commonly regarded as one of the most influential members of the Santa Fe ring, if not its guiding spirit** - instituted trouble for Uncle John in connection with some notes which had fallen into the hands of certain tools of the ring. Rather than submit to what he considered high-handed injustice, Uncle John spent several weeks of January and February 1878 in jail in Las Vegas. (Klasner, p. 260)

JOHN SIMPSON CHISUM

While jailed in Las Vegas in 1878 under Catron's malicious prosecution, cattle king, John Chisum, wrote a sarcastic account of the Santa Fe Ring. Lilly Klasner included it in her manuscript, which became 1972's Eve Ball-edited book: *My Girlhood Among Outlaws*. Chisum dated his piece to January 16, 1878. He also documented the anti-Ring uprisings in Grant and Colfax Counties (the Lincoln County War then being six months in the future), as well as Ring assassination (of Colfax County's Reverend Franklin Tolby) followed by illegal removal of Colfax County courts to block prosecution of Tolby's murderers. He wrote:

I know it is said by many of the citizens that there is a Ring at Santa Fe but as the Governor [Axtell] said in his last message there was no ring and I am of his opinion. If there was a ring there would be some show for the people as a Ring is not solid and there would be some show to get through it, or to get on the outside or inside of it but the thing they have got there is perfectly solid it cannot be penetrated from neither side or end and it is perfectly hard & solid and when this solid substance strikes a citizen it goes right through him and leaves him in such a condition that he never recovers from it. It is so powerful that it don't only ruin citizens but sometimes it strikes whole counties. This substance whatever it is struck and killed a good Methodist preacher [Franklin Tolby] up in my old county of Colfax. Some of the citizens of that county made some remark about it & this same something then struck the whole county of Colfax & set it clear over the mountain into Mora county. And it took the whole of our Legislature two years to get it back in the old place ... So you can see that it is worse than any Ring. No Ring could do that you know and the Governor [Axtell] lives right there in Santa Fe and he knows there is no Ring there.

[As to the "solid substance"] [i]t is what we call a Substance of light. Santa Fe is The City of Light and that is what furnishes light for ... our legislators ... [a]nd for our County officers all over the Territory ... It at one time reflected its light upon Grant County and the light was so dazzling to the Eyes of the citizens that they prayed to be spared from this great light and be attached to Arizona [in attempted secession]. (Klasner, pp. 268-269)

ROBERT WIDENMANN

Frederick Nolan, in his 1992 *Documentary History of the Lincoln County War* quoted John Tunstall's friend, Robert Widenmann, about the Ring. His February 23, 1878 letter to murdered Tunstall's father stated that the litigation against Tunstall and McSween "was in the hands of the New Mexican ring." (Nolan, pp. 208-206) His March 30, 1878 letter to a Tunstall relative stated: "The murderers will never be punished if an investigation is left to the U.S. officials in this Territory, since all or most of them are members of the ring. The persons Dolan & Riley mentioned in my statement as well as the Governor are the tools of the ring whose head Thos. B. Catron U.S. District Atty. at Santa Fe is." (Nolan, pp. 230-231) His letter of May 27, 1878 to Tunstall's father about Investigator Angel stated: "He gives me to understand that, no sooner had he reached Santa Fe, than the ring there offered to bribe him ... Mr. Angel says that if we will give him the testimony, he will have every U.S. officer from the Governor down removed providing the testimony will warrant." (Nolan, p. 294)

MONTEGUE LEVERSON

Montegue Leverson, a Colorado friend of John Chisum, wrote to Secretary of the Interior Carl Schurz about secret "charges leveled against [Governor Axtell] in 1877" being known "to Stephen B. Elkins, 'the brains of the Santa Fe ring.'" (Nolan, p. 303)

DAVID SHIELD

Murdered Alexander McSween's brother-in-law, David Shield, writing on July 30, 1878 to Montegue Leverson for a loan, said: "I do not wish to place myself under any obligation to the ring or their clique & they control everything here." (Nolan, p. 337)

SAM CORBET

A September 23, 1878 letter to murdered Tunstall's father from John Tunstall's shopkeeper, Sam Corbet, stated:

"[T]he latest and best news I have to tell you is the removal of Gov. Axtell, United States Attorney, T.B. Catron, Judge Bristol, United States Marshall Sherman, and Indian Agent Godfroy. All belong to the Santa [Fe] Ring." (Nolan, p. 348)

PAT GARRETT'S 1927 EDITOR: MAURICE GARLAND FULTON

Wary Pat Garrett did not name the Ring in his 1882 book, *The Authentic Life of Billy the Kid*; but he stated: "It is not the intention here to discuss the merits of the imbroglio or to censure or uphold either one faction or the other, but merely to detail such events of the [Lincoln County] war as ... [Billy the Kid] took part in. The principles in this difficulty were on one side John S. Chisum, called the Cattle King of New Mexico, with Alexander A. McSween and John H. Tunstall as important allies. On the other side were the firm of Murphy & Dolan, merchants in Lincoln, the county seat, backed by nearly every small cattle owner in the Pecos Valley. **This latter faction was supported by Thomas B. Catron, United States Attorney for the Territory, a resident of Santa Fe, one of the eminent lawyers of the Territory, and a considerable owner in the Pecos region.**" (Garrett, Page 52)

Early Billy the Kid historian, Maurice Garland Fulton, annotating the 1927 reprint of Garrett's book, added the Ring: "Garrett is one of the few writers of the Lincoln County War who has had the frankness and courage to mention Catron's name in connection with it. [Catron] is the figure that looms up behind the Murphy and Dolan faction. As the president of the powerful First National Bank at Santa Fe, he furnished the money needed by Murphy and Dolan in their business, of course taking mortgages which at the close of the War gave him possession of their store and its stock of goods. Catron was also a cattle raiser, and in some sense a dominating figure in that industry in the western part of the county. **Besides all this he was a powerful member of the clique of politicians and business men called in those days the "Santa Fe Ring," which largely controlled the Territory of New Mexico.**" (Fulton Note, p. 59)

A RING INSIDER'S EXPOSÉS

To the present, no Ring insider has turned state's evidence against compatriots. Closest was a politically active, Republican, attorney-judge named William B. Sloan in the 1880's. In the September 26, 1889 *Santa Fe Daily New Mexican*, he advertised himself as: "Lawyer, Notary Public and United States Commissioner, Dealer in real estate and mines, Special attention given to examining, buying, selling or capitalizing mines or Corporations in New Mexico, Arizona and Old Mexico. Have good large Ranches and Ranges, with and without stock, for sale. Santa Fe, New Mexico." Earlier ads, in 1885 and 1886, said he was New Mexico Commissioner for fair exhibits in Albuquerque and New Orleans.

Living in Santa Fe, in the Territory which descendent of Ring fighters, Agnes Morley Cleaveland, named *Satan's Paradise*, Sloan used the pseudonym "Ithurial." An angel in John Milton's *Paradise Lost*, his mission was to expose the Garden of Eden's serpent by poking him with his spear to force him to manifest his true form as the Devil. Sloan's spear was pen and press.

Ominously, Catron obtained Sloan's secret notes (they are in his collected papers) by unknown means. Sloan's stimulus was the 1884 Republican convention in which Ringite William Rynerson competed with L. Bradford Prince for Delegate to Congress. Sloan's multi-page exposé, apparently dated July 25, 1884, without addressee or signature, was written on stationery of the elegant Palace Hotel, near Santa Fe's central plaza. It began with: *"The situation is as follows."*

Also in Catron's possession was Sloan's penciled list of Ringites. Apparently coerced, on its right margin, was added: *"This is the original memoranda made by me as Prince talked, which forms part of the Ithurial letter of the 31st July W.B.S."* At the list's end, Sloan had written: *"These men in the past have all been found in bed with the ring. Col Rynerson pretended to get his back up, on account of the forming of the New County of Luna, but since his candidacy for delegate, he and Catron and have made friends, and D.M. [David] Easton is to visit Santa Fe to fix the balance of the ring for Rynerson."*

Sloan's reveal appeared in print under "Ithurial," in July 31, 1884's *Las Vegas Daily Optic*. It was an insider poking the Devil so the public could recognize him. It stated:

THE SANTA FE POLITICIAN.

He is not a Backward Individual in Religion, Politics or Society – The Ring and the Next Delegate to Congress.

To the Editor of the Optic.
DOWN THE LINE, July 29, 1884. –
Your invitation to Col. Breeden to give you a rest on Axtell and use his pen on other topics, was by the Colonel accepted with an avidity that is truly refreshing. The subject matter of his letter of the 25th was head-lined "Politicians of Santa Fe , and how backward they have been in asserting their claims on the party." Artemeus Ward [early 19th century humorist], if living, would say that this is "sarcasm." The idea of a Santa Fe politician being backward! You might as well look for a calf that will not suck ... as for a Santa Fe ring politician who does not think that the offices all belong to their clique. Great God, how they beg to have a cessation of hostilities on the old hoary-headed chief of the sinners – how they beg not to have a word said about capitol and penitentiary jobs, or about their little games of trying to outwit the outside counties on delegate to congress. They are working night and day to again out-general the republican party ... A deeper game than that is now afoot. The point is to have outside counties put up a man the ring want. I will explain this farther on. I wish to notice a part of the statement which Colonel Breeden starts out. It is susceptible to three divisions, and I will try and answer the second one, viz:
**** "And it has been persistently asserted that the Santa Fe ring was selfish, proscriptive, arbitrary and tyrannical, ruling and using the party for the interest of its members." **** "Now, what foundation is there for the assertion that Santa Fe (ring) is unfair and self-seeking in her relations to and connections with the republican party?"

I put the word "ring" in the sentence so as to complete the sense, as it is only in that light the public and the press make their attacks. As to the city of Santa Fe
DOING ALL IN HER POWER
to vie with other cities in the Territory to lead them in industries, size and commercial wealth, no one will gainsay ... I wish to say that it is not the city of Santa Fe that I attack, but what is known as the ring.

The ring proper is accredited with being composed of the following persons: T.B. Catron, S.B. Elkins, W.W. Griffin, **H.M. Atkinson, Max Frost, Gov. Sheldon,** Gen. Bartlett**, W.G. Ritch,** Judge Manderfield, **Colonel [William] Breeden,** Major [Marshall] Breeden, C.B. Hayward, Colonel Fisher, W.H. Bailhache, **R.H. Longwill, Judge [S.B.] Axtell**, C.M. Phillips, Trinidad Alarid, Antonio Ortiz y Salazar, Bert M. Read, **Colonel Rynerson, of Las Cruces**, and quite a following of second fiddlers and henchmen. Among those accredited with having co-operation with the ring in the past, I can name Gailes, Hillsboro; Mariano S. Otero, Bernalillo; **D.M. Easton, ex-Indian trader**; C.C. McComas, Albuquerque; W.H. Llewellyn, Las Cruces; J.A. Miller, Silver City; Waltah C. Hadley, Las Vegas; Sylvester Davis, Gallisteo; Antonio y Abeytia, Socorro. **Colonel Rynerson** got on his ear about the Sierra county bill, for awhile, but, since his candidacy for delegate, he has forgiven **Catron**, and the two lions grasp paws cordially. **Easton's** trip to the east is a splendid *blind* to fix things for Colonel **Rynerson**. That Colonel Breeden should back the ring is not to be wondered at ... Did not **Tom Catron, the acknowledged leader of the ring**, secure the passage of a bill by which Major Breeden, the brother of the Colonel, would be appointed assistant attorney general? ... Did it ever occur to readers of THE OPTIC that twenty of the twenty-one members of the ring proper have got a public teat to suck, and did you ever see a teat pulled from a baby's mouth when it did not cry? It is certainly very natural for the ring to want to control the nominations of the Territory,

LEST SOME OF THEM would have to surrender the lacteal gland. Now I come to the "milk in the coconut." What the ring cannot accomplish openly, they do covertly ... Only a few days ago, when the capitol commission met, a meeting of the ring was held in Catron's office, at which Mariano S. Otero was present. Catron and Antonio Ortiz y Salazar made use of every effort to induce Otero to become a candidate ... He has been a delegate once, which satisfied his ambition ... A part of the ringsters are continually importuning him, and they may yet succeed in getting him to agree to accept the nomination ... The question may arise as to the motive prompting the urging of Otero ... The answer is plain. If a weak democrat is run, they calculate that Otero could get in by the use of money. **In that case the ring would have a delegate entirely under their control. They care nothing for the general progress of the Territory, but only for their own selfish plans, or spoils** ... Whether elected or not, Otero's money would help elect local ring candidates,

FOR THE "FILTHY LUCRE" WOULD

be handled by the "old guard" ... A well-formed ring embraces men of both political parties, and the New Mexico one is remarkably well favored in that respect, for they put on the external appearance of fighting, when, in reality, they are pulling together ... if the ring fail to get Otero, they will next favor Rynerson, who, it turns out is making great efforts to secure the nomination ... **Rynerson** has got pledges from Lincoln County that will give him the delegates from that quarter ... One part of the program on the Colonel's behalf was for **D.M. Easton, ex-Indian trader**, to look after the Colonel's "cattle" in the northern counties. He had a long conference with Catron at Santa Fe last Saturday. Easton went east and Catron to Bernalillo ... **Colonel Rynerson has been one of the ring for some twenty years, and it is but his just dues that he have the support of the ring, especially Axtell and his friends, for did not Axtell when he was governor, appoint Rynerson district attorney, which appointment was one of the charges against Axtell when he was removed? Rynerson has always been true to the ring, and as part and pay for his services, did not the ring have passed for his benefit the bill removing the Doña Ana court house from Mesilla to Las Cruces, where it was located on property belonging to Colonel Rynerson ... The Colonel was taken under the care and protection of the ring at the time he shot and killed Chief Justice Slough in the Exchange Hotel in Santa Fe, from which affair they extricated him and since which time he has faithfully done their bidding. Did the Colonel not resign his place on the national committee to let Elkins, another of the ring, get on the committee, and, by so doing will**

have Elkins' influence when the time comes, to help him get the nomination? I have gone INTO ALL THESE DETAILS, historical in part, to show the motives of the ring in behalf of certain men whom they want nominated, but manipulate in the dark, to force outside counties to nominate a man to suit them ... **I hope this warning to the many good people of Santa Fe will be duly heeded, for the writer has nothing but the best wishes for the growth and prosperity of Santa Fe. I would like to see some of the ring's plans frustrated. ITHURIAL.**

Of course, the Ring attacked Sloan, forcing his confession as author. He was found out by Attorney Albert Jennings Fountain, who had been Billy Bonney's court-appointed lawyer guaranteeing his hanging sentence. To the September 27, 1884 *Rio Grande Republican*, Fountain, blaming L. Bradford Prince, wrote:

The "Ithurial" Letters

The following communication explains itself. The fact that [L. Bradford] Prince furnished the memoranda for the famous, or rather infamous letter, is easy of proof, the said memoranda having been seen by more than one gentleman well acquainted with Prince's handwriting:

Las Cruces, N.M., Sept. 23, '84
Editor Rio Grande Republican:

W.B. Sloan, in a communication which appeared in the *Gazette* of the 21st inst., admits that he is the author of the "Ithurial" letters and says that Judge Prince did not see these letters until after publication. This is probably true, but is no denial of the charge I made, that Prince inspired the letter signed "Ithurial," published in the *Optic* July 31. In an interview with Sloan at Santa Fe, August 26, he acknowledged to me that he was the author of said letter, but that in writing it he acted as the paid amanuensis of Prince, and that the letter was based upon data furnished him by Prince. In a later interview with Sloan, at Santa Fe, on September 15th, he, Sloan, repeated the above statements, and satisfied me that the original data, in Prince's handwriting, was in his, Sloan's, possession. A.J. FOUNTAIN [Notarized]

(It is worthy of remark, as showing the character of the man, that while Prince was inspiring the communication to the Optic, he was writing friendly letters to both Rynerson and his friends! "Put not your trust in Prince." – ED. REPUBLICAN.)

Adding credibility to Ithurial's claim of Catron backing Rynerson, Victor Westphall wrote: "Prince declared that everyone knew Catron was secretly the life of the Rynerson movement." (Westphall, p. 197) Ithurial succeeded. Repulsed voters saw the Devil and backed Democrat Antonio Joseph for Delegate.

Sloan did not stop. In the September 14, 1889 *Las Vegas Daily Optic* under "Telegraphic Tidings," and in apparently unpublished Dispatches to its Editor, he still anonymously attacked the Ring. In their Republican constitutional convention, Ringites attacked him again in a September 17, 1889 *Daily New Mexican* as "Affairs of State, The Optic Man Barred Out for Misrepresentation."

It presented their September 16, 1889 meeting in which Ringite Frank Springer warned about more anonymous editorials in the September 14, 1889 *Las Vegas Optic*; which he paraphrased: "That this convention sits here under the control of monopolies and trusts ... [and] we are here at the bidding of bosses, corruptionalists, monopolists, rings." A committee with Springer, Rynerson, and others, backed by Catron, was made to examine it.

Springer went himself to the *Optic* office, demanding to know if the author was Sloan. Springer was quoted: "I was informed by the editor that the dispatches also came from him."

That *Optic* editor was fired. But Sloan may have been untouchable because L. Bradford Prince was by then Governor. Catron, trying to set up his usual malicious prosecution stated: "Whoever wrote that dispatch wrote what he knew to be deliberate falsehood." The Ringite committee concluded:

Whereas, After being given full opportunity ... the said correspondent has failed to offer satisfactory explanation of his action, thus leaving no other reference than that the said dispatch was the result of deliberate intention to misrepresent the action of the convention, and to bring upon certain members thereof the condemnation of the people of the territory ... therefore be it

Resolved, That the statements contained in the special dispatch to the Las Vegas Optic of date September 14, 1889, purporting to give an account of certain proceedings of this convention ... are false in fact and scandalous in innuendo, and are made with the transparent intent to bring this convention into public disrepute ... and be it further

Resolved, That the privileges of the floor of this convention usually accorded to reporters are henceforth denied to W.B. Sloan as a newspaper correspondent or reporter.

Eccentric and brave William Sloan also evinced compassion for his enemy. On October 28, 1890, he wrote Catron a letter marked "Strictly confidential," to save Catron's life. It stated:

> Hon. T.B. Catron
> Although not a member of your lodge, yet as a <u>Mason</u>, I give you notice of approaching danger, & to that end, my advice to you is not to be in the street after dark next Saturday evening, any where.
> Yours paternally
> W.B. Sloan

And unlike other major Ring adversaries, Sloan began his journey to the great beyond without their assistance. The January 9, 1909 *Las Vegas Daily Optic* wrote that he died "Sitting in his chair as if asleep but cold in death." Ithurial was called home.

THE SANTA FE RING'S FORMULA

The Santa Fe Ring's formula for success was as follows:

- Have silent complicit "friends" with ironclad loyalty;
- infiltrate all Territorial public offices and law enforcement by cronyism, bribery, intimidation, and election rigging - with reach to Washington, D.C. - for mutual profit and protection from prosecutions;
- block legal redress by removing courts or adversarial public officials;
- engage in schemes like land-grabs, usurious loans, rustled beef for military and Indian Reservation contracts; and launder profits in monopolies of general stores, banking, railroads, mining, and ranching;
- eliminate all opponents and competitors by intimidation, malicious prosecution, outlawing, or murder;
- shield bosses by using use hired thugs to kill;
- conceal activities by denying Ring existence, writing in cipher-codes, and expurgating incriminatory evidence;
- control the press; and
- write self-serving cover-up history.

CHAPTER 5

TERRITORIAL RING BOSS, THOMAS BENTON CATRON

THOMAS BENTON CATRON

SUMMARY: T.B. Catron, a robber baron land-grabber, with fellow lawyer and politician, S.B. Elkins, founded New Mexico Territory's Santa Fe Ring. Working with Elkins in Washington, D.C., he linked profiteering public officials, and crushed opponents by malicious prosecutions and assassination. His criminality was rewarded by becoming America's largest landowner and a New Mexico Senator.

Thomas Benton Catron, a gluttonously bloated facsimile of robber baron cartoons by 19th century artist Thomas Nast, in 1866 co-founded the Santa Fe Ring, translating his brutal and vindictive personality into its operating style, and setting into motion New Mexico's malignant cronyism infiltrating government, law enforcement, and business. In his deadly force field, lives were warped by fear or favor; and opponents fled or were murdered. His fulfilled hope, like any criminal's, was hiding his crimes till death gave him immunity.

Catron's biographer, Victor Westphall, in his 1973 book, *Thomas Benton Catron and His Era*, replicates Catron's cover-ups, while providing accidental incriminations.

EARLY YEARS

Thomas Benton Catron, born on October 6, 1840, was 26 at the 1866 start of his Santa Fe Ring. He was fourth of nine children in a Lexington, Missouri, farm family with original German surname "Kettenring" - not Hispanic "Catrón," as sometimes misstated in New Mexico. His "Thomas Benton" honored Missouri Senator Thomas Hart Benton, coiner of the racist and genocidal "manifest destiny" doctrine rationalizing Anglo's continental take-over.

In 1857, at Lexington's Masonic College, Catron met Stephen Benton Elkins, a year younger. In 1859, they roomed together in the University of Missouri, with Catron graduating in 1860. In the

Civil War, Catron, then a Democrat, was a Confederate Second Lieutenant in the Missouri State Guard for four years. Elkins, had brief Union service, then settled in New Mexico Territory. In 1864, Elkins was admitted to the law bar, with practice in Doña Ana County's Mesilla. In 1865, elected to the Territorial legislature's House of Representatives, he moved to Santa Fe.

In 1866, Elkins convinced Catron, studying law in Missouri for the past year, to join him. Elkins accompanied Catron in his cross-country trip as both schemed. Biographer Westphall states: "Oral tradition indicates that on their journey Catron and Elkins mutually resolved to seek a seat in the United States Senate [and to create] economic empires." (Westphall, pp. 21, 25) Elkins also encouraged Catron to learn Spanish, like himself. (Westphall, p. 22) Premeditated was land-grab from Hispanic grant owners.

Catron arrived in Santa Fe on July 27, 1866. In 12 years, his and Elkins's Ring would completely control the Territory. Working first as a legal assistant and scrivener, Catron switched parties to befriend the Territory's Republican Party founder: attorney, William Breeden. With Breeden's backing, in December of 1866, five months after Catron's arriving, - with touring Governor Robert Byington Mitchell absent till 1867 - Acting Governor William F.M. Arney, a Territorial Republican big-wig since 1864, appointed Catron District Attorney for the Third Judicial District. And he made Elkins Attorney General. Catron's appointment was protested by the legislature's Council; but returned Governor Mitchell merely upheld it, and promoted Elkins to Territorial U.S. Attorney. (Westphall, p. 28)

Catron began law practice in Las Cruces, and was admitted to the bar on June 15, 1867. So by 1867, the year after he arrived, the infant Ring thrived with accumulating friends.

In late 1868, Catron was elected to the Territorial House of Representatives. In 1869, Governor Robert Mitchell, on Elkins's recommendation, appointed Catron Attorney General, as well as District Attorney for the dominant First Judicial District of Santa Fe. So Catron relocated there, partnering with Elkins in a law firm. As Attorney General, Catron was the Territorial prosecuting attorney in counties of Santa Fe, San Miguel, Santa Aña, Mora, Taos, Rio Arriba, and Colfax; and advised legislators and the Governor. As District Attorney of the First Judicial District, he was Chief Justice of the Supreme Court. And Elkins, as U.S. Attorney, was chief federal prosecutor. So by 1868, the Ring's potential for unimpeded malicious prosecution was in place.

In 1870, William Anderson Pile, the first Ringite Governor, took office. He retained Catron as Attorney General on recommendations of Elkins and Ringite Chief Justice Joseph G. Palen. In Pile's scandal-filled administration, he and Catron were accused of destroying Territorial archives and conspiring to split future state offices with Democrats. (Westphall, pp. 31-32)

In March of 1872, President Grant promoted Catron to Territorial U.S. Attorney, an office he held until his forced resignation in 1878 from Lincoln County War fall-out.

In 1872, President Grant had appointed another Ringite Governor, Marsh Giddings. In 1873, Elkins was elected Territorial Delegate to Congress, extending Santa Fe Ring influence federally. And Catron was accused of fixing Elkins's election by malicious prosecution to force votes. Westphall wrote:

> Following the 1873 election, charges were also leveled at [U.S. Attorney] Catron. It was alleged that many persons in San Miguel and Mora Counties were arrested and accused [by Catron] of illegal trading with Comanche Indians and were placed under bond and forced to appear for trial in Santa Fe. Upon payment of fees to ... Catron, and agreement on their part to vote for Elkins, they were released. Again, it was claimed that 600 suits were brought by Catron against persons living in Taos County for living on Indian lands. All but two of the suits were dismissed. It was charged that the suits were brought for the twofold purpose of getting fees for the prosecution and whipping in votes for Elkins. (Westphall, pp. 113-114; 132)

In 1875, Elkins was again elected Delegate, again with contested votes. (Westphall, p. 113) Colfax County citizens also accused the Ring of assassinating their anti-Ring, exposé writing leader, Reverend Franklin Tolby.

That 1875, Governor Marsh Giddings died in office, and President Grant repositioned Utah Territory Republican Governor Samuel Beach Axtell to the office. Axtell immediately became a major Ring agent, shielding Reverend Tolby's Ringite assassins by illegally removing Colfax County courts to obstruct their prosecution. Later, Axtell became a pro-Ring actor in the Lincoln County War history of Billy Bonney and the Regulator movement.

EARLY PROFITEERING

On arrival in 1866, Catron sought wealth. "While [Catron and Elkins] enjoyed politics, the political career of each was motivated ... by the part that politics could play in developing their respective economic empires." (Westphall, p. 25) That translated into Ringite "friends" profiting by cash or kind.

ACQUIRING LAND GRANTS

By early 1869, Catron and Elkins "turned their attention to acquiring large amounts of land in New Mexico by dealing in land grants." (Westphall, p. 34) Catron ultimately owned "at least thirty four [land grants and] property in Mexico, California, Oregon, Colorado, Arizona, Kansas and Missouri;" though it may have been more, since his records were "fragmentary." (Westphall, pp. 71-72) This "empire building" ... made Catron "the largest individual landowner in the history of the United States" (Westphall, p. ix), with up to six million acres.

Westphall, omitting Catron, blamed nameless " 'speculators' [who] coveted the large grants made by former Spanish and Mexican governments. New arrivals saw an opportunity for rapid gains ... centered around traffic in these grants." (Westphall, p. 35) These nameless attorney "Yankee newcomers," feigned complexity in getting titles, then took land as payment from grant holders (Westphall, pp. 35-36) - the Ring's own ploy.

As to Catron, Westphall states: "[He] has been accused of immoral, if not illegal, practices in connection with land grants he acquired." (Westphall, p. 41) Westphall denies proof; omitting Catron's canny expurgations and an 1888 office fire. "Another claim is that Catron took advantage of the ignorance of grantees in negotiating purchases and paid only a fraction of what land was worth." (Westphall, p. 42) Westphall rationalizes that land was cheap. For example: "[I]n 1871, Jesus Lujan sold the Eaton grant of 81,032.67 acres to Nicholas Pino for eighteen dollars cash." (Westphall, p. 42) In fact, that merely demonstrates why the land grant scam worked so well.

Catron himself revealed his scheme in a July 30, 1896 letter to a Don Matais Contreras, stating that he rarely purchased grants outright, but took a percentage of the land in lieu of his fee as a grant holder's attorney. Westphall reveals that Catron also kept his shares in the Mora Grant under Elkins's name (Westphall, p. 40); gave a fifth of the shares to Surveyor General T. Rush Spencer in return for trying to sell the grant; got the grant holders to deed the land to him in exchange for his doing the partitioning; and, in 1909, gave the grant to one of his sons. (Westphall, pp. 40-45) Westphall also describes how, in 1885, Catron's Tierra Amarilla Grant, surveyed by his business partner, Surveyor General Henry M. Atkinson, was found to have exaggerated extent (Westphall, p. 51); and later admits Atkinson's "outright malfeasance in office [of Surveyor]." (Westphall, p. 151)

Omitted in Westphall's fraud discussion is the 1870 grant sale that arguably fueled the infant Santa Fe Ring: the Maxwell Land Grant; acquired by Catron and Elkins by cheating its owner, Lucien Maxwell, then immediately reselling it to speculators for double the money paid to Maxwell. And omitted is their 1876, fraudulent, 500,000 acre Uña de Gato Grant sale to Arkansas Senator Stephen Wallace Dorsey, transacted by Governor Axtell.

Furthermore, Westphall hid that the cause of the Colfax County War was evicting of Maxwell Land Grant settlers as "squatters" by Elkins and Catron by malicious prosecutions and troops. Instead, he fabricates Catron's benevolence: "[Catron] was also accused of driving people from their homes who had settled on land he had acquired ... In fact ... he arranged for squatters ... to retain the land on which they lived." (Westphall, p. 71)

BRANCHING OUT

RAILROADS AND MINING

Catron had railroad connections; serving as attorney for the Atchison, Topeka, and Santa Fe railroad through the Maxwell Land Grant; as well as for the Southern Pacific; El Paso and South Western; and Denver and Rio Grande Railroads.

His mines partnered with "friends;" Elkins, Lehman Spiegelberg (Santa Fe dry goods supplier to "The House"), and William A. Pile (the Governor, who in 1870 made Catron Attorney General). Omitted by Westphall is that the Aztec gold mine - merely listed among his holdings (Westphall, p. 66) - was retained by Catron from the Maxwell Land Grant' sale, and was then the world's richest. Catron kept it till 1914, writing to his son, Charles, on September 30, 1914: "I have disposed of the Aztec mine."

BANKING

Westphall states: "Another facet of Catron's varied career in New Mexico was that of a banker. He participated in the sale of the First National Bank in Santa Fe from Lucien B. Maxwell." (Westphall, p. 67) Omitted is that bank was founded by Catron's and Elkins's tricking Maxwell into investing from his $650,000 land grant sale to be its president. They then made the competing Second National Bank of New Mexico to force him out; taking control, with Elkins as president and Catron as its major stockholder, till he passed the stock in 1907 to his son, Charles.

MONEY-LENDING AND MERCANTILE ENDEAVORS

Westphall admits that Catron's money-lending yielded "tradition that he habitually placed persons politically in his debt by loaning them money and making no effort to collect." (Westphall, p. 267) He began money-lending at his 1866 arrival. Given cattle as collateral, he first sold them as beef to Fort Bayard, near Grant County's Silver City. (Westphall, p. 33) By the early date of 1868, receipts show him allied to Lincoln County sutler store partner, Lawrence Murphy (Westphall, p. 74), who held, with Emil Fritz, beef contracts for Fort Stanton and the Mescalero Indian Reservation. They became his agents, along with the firm's later partners, James Dolan and John Riley, in Catron's secret Lincoln County mercantile monopoly: "The House."

Loans were also bribes, as with new Governor, Samuel Beach Axtell, getting a $1,800 "loan" in 1876 (the sum representing half his salary), and becoming a major and recklessly unprincipled Ring agent. Catron's loans yielded services. One recipient was Pat Garrett, Billy Bonney's killer. And lawyer-politician, Ralph Emerson Twitchell's, 1901 loan involved Catron's covering money Twitchell had embezzled as District Attorney. (Westphall, p. 390) Omitted by Westphall is that Twitchell's loan replicated Catron's 1878 cover-up payment for Sheriff William Brady, who had embezzled Lincoln County tax money to buy rustled cattle for the Ring - as John Tunstall had publicly exposed. Omitted also by Westphall, was that when Twitchell wrote his 1912, multi-volume, *The Leading Facts of New Mexico History*, he compliantly denied the Santa Fe Ring's existence.

CATTLE RANCHING

Catron's cattle ranching included the early 1870's Pecos River Cow Camp, fronted by "The House" in Lincoln, and called "Dolan's cow camp;" and the Carrizozo Land and Cattle Company ranch, from 1878 to 1882, run by Catron's brother-in-law, Edgar Walz. They were stocked by the Ring's Seven Rivers rustlers' stealing from cattle king, John Chisum. And they were a motive for murdering John Tunstall, as a competitor for the same beef contracts to Fort Stanton and the Mescalero Indian Reservation.

In 1878, Catron was also supplying beef for a San Carlos Indian Reservation contract. (Westphall, p. 132) For his 1882 incorporated Boston and New Mexico Cattle Company, Catron partnered with Ring friend and land grant acreage inflator, Surveyor General Henry M. Atkinson. Catron's 1885 Tularosa Land and Cattle Company rewarded with partnership his murderous Lincoln County War period friends: past "House" partner John H. Riley and past District Attorney William L. Rynerson. It controlled water rights along both sides of the Tularosa River, and from the Mescalero Indian Reservation to 10 miles west of the town of Tularosa. (Westphall, p. 69) Omitted by Westphall is that, in 1880, Catron eliminated future competition for that Tularosa Cattle Company by malicious prosecution of rancher, Pat Coghlan, in Tularosa valley's Three Rivers, by accusing him to the Secret Service of being a member of the fabricated "Billy the Kid gang."

Catron's 1878 elimination of Tunstall had also resulted in taking his ranch land as spoils, and giving them to James Dolan and William Rynerson, who named them the Feliz Land and Cattle Company, with Catron as a likely silent partner. In 1886, Catron started the American Valley Company ranch, also with Atkinson, which involved murdering its two owners; with Catron suspected, but never prosecuted. (Westphall, pp. 163, 324-325)

IMPLEMENTING SECRECY

From the start, Catron and Elkins knew their machinations had to be secret. Used were cipher-codes for letters and telegrams. And when incriminatory evidence from the period of Territorial anti-Ring revolts became too dangerous, Catron had an 1888 expurgating fire in his office.

THE CIPHER-CODES

The Lincoln County anti-Ring faction accidentally discovered the Ring's cipher-codes on the night of John Tunstall's assassination, when a panicked John Riley came to the Lincoln house of Alexander McSween to proclaim his innocence, but accidentally left his incriminatory pocket notebook containing cipher-codes. Westfall wrote that "codes were used in communications intended to be private ... [and used by Catron] on numerous occasions." (Westphall, p. 84) On June 6, 1878, McSween presented the Riley code in his deposition to Investigator Angel, 43 days before the Ring killed him too:

> *[Riley] threw out a memorandum book and after asking the men in [my] house ... if they wanted to kill him and receiving a reply in the negative took his departure leaving said memorandum book ...*
>
> *Deponent says that he examined said book with great care, that he found a letter in it in the handwriting of said W.L. Rynerson addressed to Dolan & Riley [the February 14, 1878 Friends Dolan and Riley letter anticipating Tunstall's murder] ... there was also a memorandum of cattle received by said Dolan & Riley from notorious cattle thieves whose names were given.* **That it also contained a list of names of persons well known in this county for their friendship for or opposition to said Dolan & Riley opposite each name was a <u>nome de plume.</u>**
>
> *Catron being "<u>Grapes</u>" Godfroy "<u>Hampton</u>" Burnstein (Indian agent clerk) "<u>soapweed</u>" Indians "<u>Tree</u>" Delaney (First Lieutenant at Fort Stanton) "<u>Warwick</u>" Murphy ... "<u>Box</u>" Rynerson ... "<u>Oyster</u>" Dowling [sic] (Post Trader at Fort Stanton) "<u>Pimp</u>" and McSween (the deponent) "<u>Diablo</u>" – Devil &c &c*

In going through all the Catron papers in the University of New Mexico Center for Southwest Research, I discovered two more, undated, cipher-code keys enclosed in Catron's personal notebooks. One was from Elkins, labeled in pseudo-calligraphy "Elkins – Telegraph Cipher." Since it coded "Angel" as "stick" and had codes about "resignation," I dated it as September to October of 1878 when Frank Warner Angel's report on Catron forced his resignation as U.S. Attorney. The page, in pencil, stated:

Cipher with Catron

Attorney General - - - - - - - - - - - - - - - - - - String
Resignation sent - - - - - - - - - - - - - - - - - - - Cold
Angel - stick
President- --- ox
Petitions ---- stale
Telegraph me - Hope
Secretary of War - - - - - - - - - - - - - - - - - - Inquire
Secretary of Treasury- - - - - - - - - - - - - - - - Easy
Fiske - House
I am satisfied - - - - - - - - - - - - - - - - - - - Grand
To-day - High
Your letter received - - - - - - - - - - - - - - - - Lou
Springer - jump
Your resignation
accepted - jump
Cabinet - Fringe
Removed - Force
It is better to - - - - - - - - - - - - - - - - - - - Reward
Impossible - Box
successor - Citizen
Dist. Atty - Cordial
There has been
appointed as
your successor - - - - - - - - - - - - - - - - - - - Kin

The second cipher-code I found listed major Ringite players - Catron firm member Henry Waldo, U.S. Attorney Simon Newcomb, District Judge Warren Bristol, and Attorney Albert Jennings Fountain - all of whom participated in trials involving Billy Bonney. It stated:

Waldo   *Robinson*
Newcomb   *Turner*
Bristol   *Tibbits*
Fountain   *Destiny*
Lhuff or
Lumbuck   *Martins*
S.P. RR   *Atchison*
T.B. RR   *Central*

Victor Westphall gave a Catron coded communication - simply to show his cleverness, with its translation. Omitted is that it seems to be a pay-off. And the name "Dame" is in Catron's papers in the early 1900's, with a W.E. Dame being his lackey attacking his rival, Miguel Otero. The code given by Westphall stated:

Claudicant Dame Saveloy Frache Fiveate Dollars Drawcansir Gravey and Fowling Drawcansir himself Dame Walloon Gravey Wareful Warily peeress Fowling capitulary Bacchanal Your Niece Acerous ...

[Translated as,] I have telegraphic communication with Dame in which he says one thousand four hundred dollars is due Gravey and five hundred dollars is due himself Dame will wait as long as possible Gravey in want of money Wants you if possible to pay five hundred dollars cash balance Your note will be accepted. (Westphall, p. 84)

In Catron's papers, I also found his letters to Ringite attorney-politician, Ralph Emerson Twitchell, about a transaction. Catron wrote on August 11, 1908: "I never contributed Two Hundred Dollars ... I agreed to contribute One Hundred Dollars, and that amount I will pay." Responding to Twitchell's disagreement, on August 14, 1908, Catron apparently used cipher-code to conceal the object of the payment as a "display of apples." The letter stated:

```
R.E. Twitchell
        Secty.[Irrigation Convention],
        Albuquerque, N.M.
Dear Sir:-
        Yours of the 13th at hand. I remember exactly
what I offered. It was One Hundred Dollars for the
best display of apples. Afterwards you, or someone
else, added the other to it. I did not authorize
it. I do not care about obligating myself for
anything more, but could say that should my means
be satisfactory at that time, I may be willing to
contribute as much more.
                    Very truly yours,
```

T.B. Catron

EXPURGATING OFFICE FIRE OF 1888

By 1888, Catron possessed incriminating documents going back to his arrival in 1866. Examples cited above were 1868 receipts to Lawrence Murphy (Westphall, p. 74), which proved his involvement with L.G. Murphy and Company began in their Fort Stanton sutler store phase. If revealed, his papers could ruin his ambitions, at a time when rumors of Ring corruption were rife.

So, conveniently, on July 20, 1888, he had a fire in his office, destroying almost all his papers. Arson was not questioned, and letters of condolence poured in to him and this then partners, John H. Knaebel and Frank W. Clancy. A Derwent H. Smith, writing on July 29, 1888, mentions *"the destruction of your office,"* and is the source for its date. On July 30, 1888, the law firm of Beatty, Denson & Oatman wrote: *"[W]e infer the loss of your papers, books and references must be almost irreparable. We desire to express sympathy with you."*

Another records-destroying fire occurred four years later, in 1892, in the Santa Fe Archives in the Territorial capitol building, though its expurgating function is unknown.

CRUSHING ANTI-RING REVOLTS

The anti-Ring revolts of the 1870's are covered below, and were first exposed by me as a pattern and named in my 2017 book, *The Lost Pardon of Billy the Kid: Factoring in the Santa Fe Ring, Lew Wallace's Dilemma, and a Territory in Rebellion.* They are the 1872 Legislature Revolt, 1876 Grant County Rebellion, the Colfax County War, and the Lincoln County War.

Those anti-Ring uprisings occurred from 1872 to 1878, in response to land-grabs, malicious prosecutions, defamatory affidavits, obstruction of Ringites' prosecutions, military interventions, and assassinations. The last to be stamped out was the Lincoln County War, which left Billy Bonney alone to fight by giving depositions and court testimonies, and by guerrilla rustling.

Victor Westphall hides pre-Lincoln County War anti-Ring uprisings by omitting their cause; by non-chronological placement after the later 1878 Lincoln County War; by leaving out the 1876 Grant County Rebellion; and by excluding these revolts' written exposés of Catron, Elkins, Axtell, Bristol, and the Santa Fe Ring.

The Lincoln County War period, following on the heels of prolific anti-Ring complaints to President Rutherford B. Hayes from Colfax County War fighters, resulted in the investigation for the Departments of Justice and the Interior for damage control, before the truth downed the Ring and the Hayes's administration for backing it - like the ring scandals of his predecessor, President Grant. Nevertheless, generated by the astute and ambivalent federal investigator, Frank Warner Angel, was a damaging, October of 1878 report on Catron, in answer to whether U.S. officials were involved in the murder of John Henry Tunstall. It was Catron's and the Ring's highest risk moment to date.

ANGEL'S CATRON REPORT AND U.S. ATTORNEY RESIGNATION

Westphall's responses to Frank Warner Angel's report to the Department of Justice on Catron, conceals its likely linking of him as Territorial U.S. Attorney, to Tunstall's murder; and conceals the report's necessitating Catron's October 10, 1878 resignation as U.S. Attorney. Instead, Westphall uses the outlaw myth for smoke-screen; writing: "Conditions of crime and lawlessness prompting the investigation by Frank Warner Angel and his report on conduct of officials in New Mexico had their genesis in the years following the Civil war. The situation had become serious by the time Samuel B. Axtell became governor of New Mexico on July 30, 1875." (Westphall, p. 122)

Westphall obscures Catron's resignation. He blames a Mary McPherson's "letter" [to Attorney General Alphonso Taft] as "the beginning of circumstances eventually resulting in Catron's resignation as United States attorney." (Westphall, p. 121) He blames Democrats' anti-Santa Fe Ring press making Catron want "to be free of public office to more effectively combat their attacks." (Westphall, p. 125) He blames "Boss" Tweed's April, 1878 death - seven months earlier - as reminding people about "ringleaders." (Westphall, p. 126) He blames Republicans' political power causing accusation for "chaotic conditions" in Colfax and Lincoln Counties. (Westphall, p. 126) He blames "national and international repercussions" of Tunstall's murder. (Westphall, p. 125) He blames Governor Axtell: "His approach, weak and vacillating, was not adequate; law and order gave way to open rebellion against authority." (Westphall, p. 124) (In fact, Axtell was an aggressive Ring agent, who removed Colfax County's courts by proclamation to obstruct prosecution of Franklin Tolby's Ringite murderers; fronted the Ring's fraudulent sale of the Uña de Gato Land Grant; used the "Dear Ben plot" for attempted assassination of Raymond Morley and others; shielded Tunstall's murderers by proclamations outlawing arresting lawmen - including Billy Bonney; and appointed Ringite Lincoln County Sheriff George Peppin after unjust removal of anti-Ring Sheriff John Copeland.)

Westphall admits that the "attorney general" [Charles Devens] had ordered Catron, as U.S. Attorney, to investigate if U.S. officials caused Tunstall's murder; but Catron had not, as Angel complained to Washington, D.C. So Westphall finessed: "No record has been found that Catron immediately replied." (Westphall, p. 125)

Westphall does reveal that Catron pressured Commander N.A.M. Dudley to give perjured affidavits for that Angel report. Dudley refused: "[Dudley] said he had refused to comply with Catron's insulting written demand at the time Catron's official conduct [as U.S. Attorney] was being investigated by Frank Warner Angel, that he go blind and certify to the United States attorney general [Charles Devens] that certain parties who had made affidavits against Catron were unreliable and unprincipled men ... Dudley characterized Catron as an all-powerful unscrupulous lawyer." (Westphall, p. 95)

Omitted was Catron's desperation. His Angel report forced him resign to stop criminal exposures. Westphall cites Elkins's incriminatory August 15, 1879 letter to Catron about having intervened with the Hayes administration to save Catron from indictment or dismissal (See pages 462-463 for letter), but minimizes it as just nasty business conflicts. (Westphall, p. 133)

Westphall adds that Catron was replaced as U.S. Attorney by Sidney Barnes. (Westphall, p. 134) Omitted is that in 1879 Ringite Barnes defended Dudley in Susan McSween's civil trial; in 1880, he helped Secret Service Agent Azariah Wild track down Billy Bonney; and, in 1881, was a prosecutor in Billy's hanging trials. With Catron stepping back, the Ring was still unbroken.

Westphall repeats Angel's arguably coerced conclusion that U.S. officials were not responsible for Tunstall's murder (Westphall, p. 127) - belied by Angel's evidence from depositions and secret interventions with new Governor Lew Wallace.

Westphall also claimed that Angel's report did not exist: "One of the unanswered, and apparently unanswerable, questions of history is whether Angel ever made a formal report of charges against Catron. A careful search of the National Archives discloses no report. Likewise, there is no record of the affidavits submitted to Catron for answer, nor of those in his defense. The interrogatories, though, are at hand." (Westphall, p. 130)

By 1892, it was clear that the report existed. On September 20, 1892, Catron's past law partner, Frank W. Clancy, worried about it during Catron's (ultimately lost) campaign for Delegate to Congress, warning him:

Dear Catron: -

From something I have heard, I believe the Democratic management is making an effort to get from Washington everything they can against you as U.S. Attorney and prepare to revive all the things urged against you before you resigned. I think you will better try to prevent their getting the information if you can, as there is no need of having more things to fight than we are compelled to. **Get Elkins to have obstacles put in their way.** *I fear they might spring the thing at so late a day in the campaign as to give you no chance to make effective answer. Don't fail to attend to this at once.*

Yours truly, F.W. Clancy

In addressing Catron's Delegate election crisis with his Angel report, Westphall contradicts his claim that it did not exist, and admits that Catron ordered Elkins to destroy it: "In 1892, Catron was running for delegate to the United States Congress. Word came to him that his political opponents intended to secure a copy of Angel's report on charges against him to use for political mudslinging. Catron wrote to S.B. Elkins, then secretary of war, requesting him to see that the attorney general did not issue a copy of the report to anyone ... Elkins assured Catron that the attorney general would comply with the wish. **The following year Catron requested that Elkins secure the report and destroy it.** Elkins replied that he had caused diligent search to be made in the attorney general's department for Angel's report but that it could not be found."

(Westphall, p. 130) More likely wily cipher-code writer Elkins's stating "it could not be found," tacitly confirmed its destruction - instead of foolishly confessing to expurgation in writing.

DUDLEY COURT OF INQUIRY AND RING RISK

The 1879 military and civil trials of Ringite Commander N.A.M. Dudley, for murder of Alexander McSween and arson of his house in the Lincoln County War Battle, are covered below.

Westphall's response was to belittle Susan McSween's charges against Dudley as money-seeking for her burned-down house and for defamation (Westphall, p. 94); omitting her charge of murder of her husband. He admits that Dudley's defense by Henry Waldo yielded "accusations of acting in concert with the Santa Fe Ring." (Westphall, p. 126) At stake, if Dudley lost, was exposing the Ring and its Lincoln County War crimes. So Westphall minimized the military Court for possible court martial as a "board" briefly investigating Dudley's conduct as commander; but he does add that Catron's law partner participated in the defense: "Catron's law partner [William T.] Thornton had assisted Henry L. Waldo in April 1879 [sic – May to July 1879] to successfully defend Dudley before a board [sic – military court] of inquiry which had investigated his conduct [sic- alleged crimes] as commanding officer at Fort Stanton." (Westphall, p. 95)

Westphall then misstates Susan McSween's civil case against Dudley, omitting that Judge Warren Bristol changed its venue from knowledgeable Lincoln County to Doña Ana County's Mesilla, that her attendance was blocked by Ring death threats, and that Dudley's acquittal in the military court swayed that civil court's not guilty verdict. But Westphall reveals another Ring lawyer, Sidney Barnes, as defending Dudley in Mesilla. He wrote: "On December 6, 1879, Susan McSween's case charging Dudley with arson and libel [by defamatory affidavits] was tried in Mesilla. United States Attorney Sidney M. Barnes was assigned to defend Dudley, while Ira E. Leonard presented the case for the prosecution. Catron, despite Dudley's earlier intimation, had no part in the trial during which Susan McSween, the leading prosecution witness, failed to appear. Dudley was acquitted by a jury that deliberated only a few minutes." (Westphall, p. 95)

KILLING BILLY BONNEY

Covered below, is the Ring's tracking down and eventual killing of Billy Bonney following the Lincoln County War Battle.

Catron had masterminded destruction of the last of the anti-Ring rebels by using his U.S. Attorney power to issue federal indictment No. 411 against Billy and the rest of the Regulators for the 1878 killing of Tunstall murder posseman, Andrew "Buckshot" Roberts; claiming its location was the federally-controlled Mescalero Indian Reservation. Concomitantly, prosecution of John Tunstall's Ringite murders had been obstructed by Ringites, Judge Warren Bristol and District Attorney William Rynerson.

But some Regulators, including Billy, could not be captured. In 1879, the Ring had intended to transport him to Mesilla for a hanging trial during his sham Lincoln jailing for his Lew Wallace pardon bargain; but Billy left before that was achieved.

So Catron, using "The House's" James Dolan as local spy, sabotaged the pardon bargain - which would have left Billy free to testify or lead another anti-Ring uprising. Then, brought in was a the Secret Service to track him down as the fabricated leader of a huge counterfeiting and rustling gang, while it paid possemen led by the Ring's selected future Lincoln County Sheriff: Pat Garrett.

The Secret Service reports were leaked to the press to start the outlaw myth of Ring-named "Billy the Kid," to justify his killing or apprehension for a hanging trial. Once captured by Garrett, Billy was tried in Mesilla by Judge Bristol, with major Ring lawyers doing the prosecution. Sentenced to hang, he escaped the courthouse-jail in Lincoln on April 28, 1881. His ambush killing by Pat Garrett on July 14, 1881, was a likely source of Ring celebration. A key assassination was completed.

Catron would continue his tactic of murdering, unaware that his killing of unforgettable Billy had planted the seed for the eventual destruction of his secret Ring and his smug immunity.

The relentless, federally backed tracking of Billy Bonney, with his 1881 killing, eliminated the last person likely to inspire an anti-Ring Hispanic and Anglo revolt. By then, the Ring had murdered, terrified, forced flight, paid-off, or politically engulfed all opponents. Ringite Governor Lionel Sheldon - Governor Lew Wallace's 1881 replacement - wrote sanctimoniously: "The desperado and thieving element has substantially disappeared, and nothing more is heard of vigilantes or lynch law."

(Westphall, p. 184) And in July of 1888, Catron's office fire conveniently destroyed evidence. That left Victor Westphall less cautious about presenting post-1870's documentation of the Ring by press, adversaries, and Catron himself.

So the rest of Westphall's biography inadvertently records Catron's sociopathic pattern of vindictive brutality, malicious prosecutions, attempted murders, and murders. Public naming of Catron as Ring "boss," makes Westphall blame Democrats: "Catron came to be singled out as the leader of [the Santa Fe Ring]." (Westphall, p. 185) And "boss" Catron's acts were no different from his vindictive brutality, malicious prosecutions, attempted murders, and murders in the 1870's period of anti-Ring uprisings, including the Lincoln County War.

AMERICAN VALLEY MURDERS

In 1886, Catron returned to the cattle business, partnering to form the American Valley Company with past corrupt Surveyor General Henry M. Atkinson (who helped inflate the Maxwell Land Grant's acreage, and was Catron's partner in another cattle company: the 1882 Boston and New Mexico Cattle Company). Through water rights, the American Valley Company controlled three million acres of grazing land, which Catron and Elkins had assisted in legally confirming in 1882. (Westphall, p. 151-152)

The formation of the American Valley Company replicated murdering of Tunstall to get his land (which became the Feliz Land and Cattle Company for Ringites James Dolan and William Rynerson; possibly with Catron as a silent partner).

In 1883, when an Alexis Grossetete and his partner Robert Elsinger said the land intended for the American Valley Company belonged to them, they were murdered on May 6th by "employees" of that company. Two of those "employees" were gunmen hired days earlier (Westphall, pp. 154-155, 163) (reminiscent of the assassins of Franklin Tolby being hired days before by Ringites, Melvin Mills and Robert Longwill; and of Jessie Evans and his boys being on Sheriff William Brady's Tunstall murder posse to carry out Tunstall's slaughter). Another of the "employees" was the brother of a one-third share owner, John P. Casey. Catron was entangled with the killings as being the company's attorney since 1882 (Westphall, p. 153); and, after the murders, by buying company cattle from one of the alleged killers, and "loaning" John Casey the huge sum of $6,000. (Westphall, p. 156)

The alleged killers were not convicted, and Westphall admits that Catron was suspected: "A whispering campaign started by John P. Casey ... insinuating that Catron was implicated in the murders was an important factor in Catron's defeat in the ... election [of 1892 for Delegate to Congress] ... Innuendo continues to the present." (Westphall, p. 163)

John Casey subsequently mortgaged his company interest to Henry Atkinson that May (Westphall, p. 157); and in April of 1885 Catron bought Casey's interest, becoming Atkinson's partner at the company's 1886 incorporation. (Westphall, p. 159) Atkinson died that year, so Catron got the American Valley Company for himself thanks to the demises of Grossetete and Elsinger.

FIXING ELECTIONS

Catron was elected to the Territorial legislature's Council in 1884, 1888, 1890, 1899, 1905, and 1909; often with accusations of election rigging. His and Elkins's vote buying in cash or kind, along with voter intimidation, had been exposed in Colfax County since Elkins's 1873 Delegate election. Catron's papers imply that activity. It should be noted that elections often had just hundreds of voters; every vote counted. A few examples of many follow.

BUYING VOTES

On October 25, 1888, Catron was sent a letter from his later political rival, future governor Miguel Otero; but here acting for him. Otero stated: *"At the time of the Rep. Convention in this City, Don Lorenzo Lopez claims that in making the settlement between the two factions,* **you agreed to pay him 500^{\underline{00}}$ provide he withdrew the name of Epifanio Baca for the clerkship.**"

On July 23, 1890, Catron received a letter from a vote buying Ring lackey named Francisco Gonzales y Borrego, his fellow member in the violent secret society of the Knights of Liberty. Borregos's name, in two years, would become famous throughout New Mexico Territory as one of the murderers - and Catron's possible hired assassin - of Catron's vocal political opponent: Santa Fe Sheriff Francisco Chavez. Borrego wrote:

Honorable T.B. Catron
dear Sir I have the honor to Report to you that **I have two men** ~~du~~ **that they have agreed to come to the Republican party but you know that they always want some money they want $10.00 each** ~~but~~ *they say that they will* ~~sigen~~ *sign you a promissory note for a sertain time for to pay it to you. I will tell you that each one of them is worth 2 votes and I am sure that they will be onest with us and to our party   now if you want to come and talk with them your* ~~sl~~ *self you must do it by coming up to my house* ~~to~~ *this afternoon and you wil see them but if you do not want to come and you want to believe me send me the money and send* ~~sm~~ *some note. Planks and I will make them sign the notes and for you   give me an answer   Respectfully*
Yours
Francisco Gonzales y Borrego

The October 29, 1890 letter from a Jose Anado Lucero, alluding to following orders, wrote to *"My Dear T.B. Catron"* not only asking for money to get Democrats' votes, but emphasizing its secrecy. Lucero wrote ingratiatingly: *"The Democrats are making a desperate fight and I been oblige to meet them in every way. I been suply the necessary money for what ever been presicelly necessary to be done instantly and as per your order I shall meet all Requirements - from here after, until election day ...* **I wish to say you that I been obliged to use good deal more money then which I was willing to expend but the circumstances did oblige me to do so**.*"*

On November 5, 1890, an intermediary got a letter from a R.M. Carley about evading residency requirements; stating: *"Rafael Lopes and Paulin Lopes only resided here four days prior to election and they had to swear that have live here the time prescribed by law before they were allow to vote. Any other information that you may need in as of contest I would be glad to give to you.* **Also I will say that I managed the matter in the most private way that possible could be done because if our friends find anything of our way of turning Democrats to our part a great deal of our work will be spoiled**.*"*

For that Delegate campaign, Catron got an August 30, 1892 letter from a D. Martinez Jr., in Velarde, to get votes by paying voters' poll tax. Martinez wrote: *"I have seen good many democrats in this precint of 350 voters, and they promise me to carry your name in their ticket,* **all they want is some help in paying up**

the poll tax ... *I will do my share in paying this tax for some of our loyal friends to qualify them to vote ... I would like to hear from you how to proceed in this respect, as you know this is the essential part in politics this year."*

On October 22, 1892, politically active Ringite, Ralph Emerson Twitchell, got a letter - later provided to Catron - from George W. Gregg, Chairman of the Republican Central Committee, about possible vote fixing: "The democratic majority ... are Mexicans and a party will be sent there on the day of the election to change it. A little money will be necessary on the day of election in 2 or 3 precincts."

On October 29, 1892, Second Judicial District Court Judge Charles R. Hunt, from Albuquerque, wrote about deals for votes; writing": *"I returned from Colfax County Wednesday last; I think we have made some trades there on the Vermejo, Cimarron and Ponil as well as in Raton and Springer that will materially aid us in reducing [Antonio] Joseph's former majority [in the election for Delegate] ...* ***I have authorized [another candidate on the Republican ticket] to say that I will furnish certificates of naturalization free of charge to those who vote our way.****"*

On November 4, 1892, Catron received a letter from a Cimarron couple, asking for money for getting votes; and citing that he had used their acquaintance for similar help. It stated:

Hon T.B. Catron
I write you a short letter to let you know that myself and hisband are in the field of Political and are working the best for you. we are verry Poor and all that we have got is our wagon and pair of horses to make a living with, and if you could help us in every way, we will be ever so muchoblige to you, we have our teem bet on you that you will beat Antonio Joseph ... So now pleas do not forget us, then you forget good Friend ... We have a great meney votes for you, and will have a great meney more before the Election comes off. all that we ask of you is that Help us all that you can. and we will do the same for you.
De tu apreciablo Amiga y Amigo.
Jesucita Amires
y Andres Amires

In 1896, for his ultimately failed re-election bid for Delegate to Congress against Harvey B. Fergusson, Catron received a letter from Taos, from a T.P. Martin, who wanted money to buy votes: *"The American miners are going to vote for Ferguson and the county republican ticket – The only way we can counteract this vote and prevent [Harvey B.] Ferguson from carrying the county by 200 is to get about $250 by next Sunday from the Territorial committee – I will take Geo. Miller and go into the Rincones and speed the Election there – **I am sure if I have the money I can buy enough votes there to carry the county**."*

Catron's political ally, Pedro Perea, wrote to him on November 1, 1896 about dismissing a law suit in exchange for a vote for Catron as Delegate: *"Mr. Joe Badaraco had a law suit in your county. He is a good republican, and he is working very hard for the ticket. I want you to fix his business for him if possible."*

LOANS FOR LOYALTY

Catron's money lending, often tied by mortgage to property - like to "The House" in Lincoln - left his papers filled with desperate pleas, and gave him control over land or resources, as well as votes. For example, on November 8, 1893, a loan holder named Emiterio Rivera wrote:

Mr T B Catron –
Dear Sir
As the time of my morght [mortgage] is coming I went to the ofes to spik with you of it to see if you can write for me for another length of time Mr Victor say that ther is hope of selling the land and then I will setel with you just as soon as I sell it. I hope you will do this for me.

As my wife dide I have veing [being] very sick since then I have my right side that I cannot do any thing with it. You know that with the lomber of the N.R.G. I can not do any thing they have not setel yet. I can not get the lomber for the N.R.G. vecause [because] ther is not the kind they want.

I hop in your kind hert you will wite [wait] for me

I remain very truly
Emiterio Rivera

TERRITORIAL LEGISLATURE

Catron had a long Territorial legislature career: elected in 1868 to its House; and in 1884, 1888, and 1890, to its Council. He was defeated in 1880 amidst backing removed Governor Axtell for Chief Justice, with rivals calling him "leader of the 'thirty-third degree ringsters.' " (Westphall, p. 189) His 1884 election to the Council, contested as voter fraud, resulted in take-over of the legislature by his opponents as a "Rump Council;" with his "Catron Council" linked to the Ring. (Westphall, pp. 190-191). The March 13, 1884 *Santa Fe Weekly New Mexican Review* accused him and his Ring of controlling grand juries and attempting to bribe the Clerk of the Rump Council. And Colfax County War anti-Ring hero, Oscar McMains, introduced a subsequently defeated memorial accusing him of land grant "steals." (Westphall, p. 193)

AN "ASSASSINATION ATTEMPT"

On February 5, 1891, shots were fired into a Council meeting. No one was hit. Catron declared it an assassination attempt against himself, though it mimicked his own pattern of killing opponents; like the April 25, 1879 assassination attempt on Susan McSween's attorney, Ira Leonard, likely by James Dolan.

Westphall accused "political intrigues," but provided the contemporary counter-claim that intended victims were legislators voting "against the Santa Fe Ring." (Westphall, pp. 208, 215)

On February 7, 1891, Stephen Benton Elkins wrote to Catron: "I was shocked this morning on reading of the attempted assassination of you and your friends, which I am so happy failed ... I hope the parties will be captured and punished. This was a close call, and you must take more care in the future."

Garnering fodder for malicious prosecutions, Catron accused a group called Las Gorras Blancas, or White Caps, of the assassination attempt. Westphall, applying the outlaw myth, calls them "as tough a bunch of badmen as could likely be found outside a penitentiary." (Westphall, p. 209)

In fact, these Mexican-American White Caps (adopting the French Revolution's Phrygian liberty cap), were dispossessed farmers and ranchers who fought to block Ring land-grabs. Westphall confirms that the *Las Vegas Optic* backed them by "calling Catron a land grabber." (Westphall, p. 211) Their movement resembled the Lincoln County Regulators. March 12, 1880's *Las Vegas Optic* published their "Proclamation" - reminiscent of 1878's "Regulator Manifesto - stating:

Our purpose is to protect the rights and interests of the people in general; especially those of the helpless classes ... We want no "land grabbers" or obstructionists to interfere. We will watch them ... There is a wide difference between New Mexico's "law" and "justice." And justice is God's law, and that we must have at all hazards ... The People are suffering from the effects of partisan "bossism" and these bosses had better quietly hold their peace. The people have been persecuted and hacked about in every which way to satisfy their caprice. If they persist in their usual methods retribution will be their reward.

So Catron may have tried to frame their leaders, Rallos Archuleta and Refugio Martinez. By February 9, 1891, he obtained an accusatory letter from the agent for his Tierra Amarilla Land Grant, W.E. Broad. (Earlier, on January 21, 1891, Broad heralded attacking White Caps by informing Catron that their ditch-making and fencing on that Grant was meeting settler's opposition; and stated: *"Some decisive action should be taken with these people which may avoid lots of future trouble."* Among the settlers named, was Refugio Martinez. Broad now wrote: *"Refugio Martinez declines to allow me to build a house on the premises he claims – and says I will have to do any work that I do there over his corpse."* This puts in context the likely staged "Catron assassination attempt," since Broad now used it to initiate malicious prosecution of Refugio Martinez. However, Catron failed to get any White Caps indicted. (Westphall, p. 215) But Broad had written:

Dear Catron.
*Since reading the account of the attempted assassination at Santa Fe, I have been informed that **Refugio Martinez**, and his brother in law, Rallos Archuleta, who are sworn enemies of yours, were in Santa Fe ... People here are very much gratified that the result was not serious.*
Yours truly
W.E. Broad

P.S.
Rallos Archuleta is said to be the leader of the White Cap organization here, and Refugio seems to be loco and dangerous.

The "assassination" incident was also used by syncophants to pledge allegiance to Catron. So, on February 7, 1891, parish priest at Rio Arriba's Parroquia de Santa Cruz, J.B. Francolon, wrote:

My Dear Friend,
Please accept my hearty congratulations on your happy escape of last night [sic]. Cheer up! Assassins, be they political ones are always contemptible; their despicable and wicked attempt will only add to your fame.
If God saved you, in this bloody case, no doubt that He thinks you have yet to work, hard and without fear, for the good and the welfare of New Mexico.
Again my friend, thanks be to God and to Him alone.
Very sincerely yours
J.B. Francolon

But on September 12, 1892, during Catron's first run for Territorial Delegate, a John M. Wright revealingly reported from the Silver City Republican Central Committee Headquarters to Ringite Ralph Emerson Twitchell that a district Attorney Ancheta *"is taking very hard about Catron. He is claiming to have gotten recent information showing that Catron instigated the conspiracy to assassinate him."*

TERRITORIAL DELEGATE FAILURE OF 1892

For his ultimately failed 1892 bid for Delegate to Congress, Catron faced accusations of murdering Alexis Grossetete and Robert Elsinger, and the sought Angel report; causing him to use Elkins for its destruction. On August 2, 1892, accused Tolby murderer, Melvin Mills, coached Catron on his campaigning, writing: *"First make Peace with all these people you are fighting with and quit this foolish resentment and ugly resentful demeanor. I believe you are man big enough to do it ... [I]mitate Elkins a little in flattery. You was not born with any of this thing but you can rake up a little deceit and cultivate it."*

As Catron anticipated, he was opposed by the White Caps. Mills continued his August 2, 1892 letter, writing from Springer, and wishing for the "good old days" of Judge Joseph Palen; and Governor S.B. Axtell, who declared anarchy and called in the military to crush civilians. He wrote: *"The White Caps are very threatening up here now, they are defying the law already. I am afraid that they would be hard to direct your way if you run, they seem to be against every body in the past authority, they are so deadly against the Grant that they would also be against you – they are increasing both in Mora and Colfax counties – They are an unknown quantity so I cannot guess [election] results with the cussed element in the field if you cannot work with them then my advice is to stay out of the race ... [I]f we do not get judges that will charge as the law and the facts command and* **run these courts more themselves like Palen and Axtell then New Mexico will fall into Anarchy. Also something must be done to aid the civil authorities in working arrests.**"

Unbeknownst to Mills, Catron may have already taken action on May 29, 1892, by the ambush murder of his political opponent, Sheriff Francisco Chavez, a reputed White Cap sympathizer. By 1895, that crime would be known as the Borrego murder case, named after two of Catron's thug killers. And for the election, Catron likely engaged in vote buying.

But a September, 1892 ad exposed his power and privilege:

CATRON AND THE LABORING MEN.

It is claimed by Catron's friends that the laboring men of the Territory will support him this fall for Delegate to Congress. This cannot be believed when it is remembered that he is the biggest corporation man and lawyer in New Mexico.

He is the attorney of the Southern Pacific Railroad, the biggest monopoly in the west.

He is the attorney for New Mexico of the Western Union Telegraph Company, another huge and ringing monopoly, and uses a frank for all his telegraphing.

He is the attorney for New Mexico of the Pullman Palace Car Company and rides in their cars on a pass.

He is the vice-president and attorney of the Santa Fe Southern Railroad and rides on a pass on all the railroads of the United States.

He is the attorney of many other corporations in all parts of the Territory.

He has never in all his different terms in the Legislature fathered or supported any measures in the interests of labor ...

He owns over 1,000,000 acres of land grants individually, and he partly owns over 4,000,000 acres more. He is interested in, as owner, part owner, or as attorney for the owners, seventy-five land grants in New Mexico ... He has never given employment to labor on any of his vast property interests in New Mexico.

How then, can laboring men support the biggest corporation man in New Mexico?

Catron responded by a front page ad in *The Daily New Mexican* of September 8, 1892;" stating:

One of the Ablest and Most Brainy Men in New Mexico.

The Republican territorial convention has nominated Thomas B. Catron, of Santa Fe, as delegate to congress. Mr. Catron is justly considered, even by his enemies, to be one of the ablest and most brainy men in the territory, consequently, he has been the most abused. There is not much doubt that he will be opposed by **Antonio Joseph, a perennial candidate of Democratic proclivities and Castilian antecedents. The Argus believes that the American voters of New Mexico will elect an American this fall to represent them** and the welfare of the territory in the halls of congress.
– Eddy Argus
He Should Be Elected.

At Las Vegas last Thursday the Republican Territorial convention nominated the candidate of the party for delegate to congress, Hon. Thomas B. Catron, of Santa Fe. Mr. Catron is without a doubt one of the ablest and most capable men in the Republican party. In the past the Index has felt constrained to oppose and criticize Mr. Catron. But that was on issues now most happily settled; and this journal now gives the gentleman a most cordial and earnest support, believing that he will be a most capable and efficient representative and that his professional standing at Washington will give the territory a prestige never heretofore enjoyed. He should be elected, and the Index believes he will be. – San Juan County Index

MORE DELEGATE RUNS AND DEFENDING THE BORREGOS

In 1894, Catron ran successfully for Territorial Delegate to Congress, serving from March 4, 1895 to March 4, 1897. But rumored was his 1892 instigation of the murder of Santa Fe Sheriff Francisco Chavez. *Daily New Mexican* president, Ringite Max Frost, on September 26, 1892, had written a long confidential letter to a Judge A.L. Morrison; stating: "In his [campaign] speech in Cerrillos Catron should refute ... charges which insinuate and somewhat strongly that Catron and [Santa Fe County Sheriff Charles] Conklin put up Frank Chavez's assassination."

Chavez's murder caught up with Catron in his failed 1895 campaign for Delegate, with the publicized trial of the four killers - including Catron's known lackey, Francisco Gonzales y Borrego, earning the public name as the "Borrego Case" - after it was filed in 1895 in the First Judicial District Court as "Case No. 2754, Territory of New Mexico vs Francisco Gonzales y Borrego, et al."

The Borrego case arose from the May 29, 1892 night-time murder of Francisco Chavez, when Catron was planning his 1892 run for Delegate to Congress and Chavez voiced opposition.

Chavez's political power at the time was made clear in a December 20, 1895 Supreme Court legal opinion by Judge Napoleon Bonaparte Laughlin, who had also been co-counsel for the prosecution in the Borrego murder trial. Laughlin wrote: "Chavez, by reason of his personal presence, his goodness of heart, and his kind and generous disposition, had attracted many followers, not only of his political faith, but of the opposite faith as well, so that the time of his assassination, and for a number of years prior, he was the acknowledged leader of his party, and much the strongest man politically in the county, and it was well known that he could elect or defeat any man he desired in local politics; and the testimony given at the preliminary hearing and on the trial on the indictment tended strongly to show that the primary motive for his assassination was political jealousy, and a fear of his popularity and power, and an inordinate desire to remove him from the road of political preferment."

Francisco Chavez was Catron's known, powerful, vocal, and dangerous opponent; and known associates of Catron murdered him: Francisco Gonzales y Borrego, his brother, Antonio Gonzales y Borrego, Laurencio Alarid, Patricio Valencia, and Hipolito Vigil (killed during apprehension). Furthermore, Chavez had told people that he feared assassination. So Catron himself was accused as instigating the murder.

Westphall, however, accused the unrelated White Cap movement for "malignant influence on receptive element in Santa Fe" (Westphall, p. 212) - presumably victim, Francisco Chavez. Westphall even opined disingenuously that Chavez might have been the Council chamber shooter trying to assassinate Catron on February 5, 1891. (Westphall, p. 213) Westphall, however, admitted that the subsequent murder trial against Chavez's four killers - where Catron was their defense lawyer - sought Catron's indictment: "More effort was being spent by the prosecution, including the entire Democratic party in the Territory, in trying to link [Catron] to the murder than in attempting to convict the defendants." (Westphall, p. 242)

Westphall used Catron's own alibi of not being in town at the murder time (the same one Westphall used to excuse him from Lincoln County War guilt); and called his accusers outlaws.

But Westphall does disclose how Catron was connected to the killers. With them, he and his law partner, Charles Spiess - also Catron's co-counsel in the Borrego case trial – belonged to a secret Republican organization called the Knights of Liberty (not to be confused with the anti-Ring Knights of Labor). That organization's known violence - compatible with Catron's usual *modus operandi* - is blamed by Westphall on members "of limited privilege in social attainments." Indeed, Francisco Gonzales y Borrego had himself murdered twice before, and had been defended successfully by Catron with self-defense claims. (Westphall, pp. 209, 225)

Westphall adds that the killers "had worked actively with [Catron] in ... recruitment for loyal Republicans." (Westphall, p. 267) For an example, Westphall selectively quotes from Francisco Gonzales y Borrego's July 23, 1890 letter to Catron (see page 93), claiming it proved Catron's loyalty to a "friend" by later defending him. (Westphall, p. 268) In fact, it showed that Francisco was a lackey used for vote buying, and implies unsavory Ringite services of all four of Chavez's murderers.

A crucial point, however, is loyalty - but not in the sentimental sense Westphall seeks. The Borrego case, and Catron's persistence with it, demonstrated Ring loyalty to its members. Catron knew the case signaled that he would shield all from their crimes, especially assassinations. That was confirmed by Ringite Santa Fe County Sheriff Charles M. Conklin doing nothing to arrest the killers; himself Catron's rumored murder accomplice of Chavez. (This repeated Lincoln County Sheriff William Brady's refusing to arrest John Tunstall's Ringite assassins, and being complicit in it.)

But Catron's opponents massed. In June of 1893, Democrat Jacob H. Crist was appointed District Attorney of the First Judicial District in Santa Fe, and would be the Borrego case prosecutor in two years. And Catron's past law partner, Democrat William Thornton, now Governor, had bought the *Santa Fe New Mexican* and merged it with Crist's *Santa Fe Weekly Sun* as the *Santa Fe Weekly New Mexican*. So Westphall claims that paper's accusations of Catron as Chavez's murderer were motivated by Democrats' bias. He quotes headlines like: "Ex-Sheriff Chavez Assassinated Because of his Political Influence." (Westphall, pp. 220-221, 224) But he omits Thornton's knowledge, as his law partner, of Catron's lethality. In fact, the articles were like 1877's Colfax County War exposés by the *Cimarron News and Press*.

Then Governor Thornton removed Ringite Sheriff Conklin for embezzling public funds (Westphall, p. 219) (like Sheriff Brady's embezzling Lincoln County tax money for the Ring); replacing him with a William P. Cunningham, a Democrat, to get arrests.

So on January 10, 1895, 591 days after the murder, Sheriff Cunningham arrested Francisco Gonzales y Borrego; his brother, Antonio Gonzales y Borrego; Laurencio Alarid; and Patricio Valencia for Sheriff Chavez's murder. (Westphall, p. 222)

Pre-trial evidentiary hearings began on January 14, 1894, with assistant prosecutor Napoleon B. Laughlin. Westphall discounted the *Santa Fe Weekly New Mexican*'s reporting that a prosecution witness, Juan Gallegos, had been told by the one of the five accused murderers - who was killed at capture of the other four - that Catron had offered him $700 to kill Francisco Chavez plus legal defense by Catron himself. (Westphall, p. 225) (Omitted is that, in 1875, gunslinger, Clay Allison, of Colfax County had also claimed that Catron had offered *him* $700 to kill anti-Ring activist, Franklin Tolby.) Despite evidence, the judge refused to charge Catron, but sent the other four to trial.

Westphall quotes Francisco Chavez's mother, who accused Catron in a letter, reprinted in March 8, 1894's *Santa Fe Weekly New Mexican* - which Westphall calls a forgery. She stated: "Mr. Catron, you are not above suspicion of knowing more about the assassination of my son than you have found it convenient to reveal, this suspicion is a natural one, the murderers as far as discovered are political partisans of yours, they frequented your office, were members of the same society, sworn with you to mutually protect each other, you have always defended them in their commissions of crimes, you have gone on their bail bonds and thus turned them loose on the community to commit other murders, and now in order to justify your conduct and the assassinations, you attempt to slander the memory of my dead son." (Westphall, p. 226)

The 37 day trial of Francisco Chavez's murderers was from April 23, 1895 to May 30, 1895, under Fifth Judicial District Judge Humphrey B. Hamilton; with District Attorney Jacob H. Crist as prosecutor. Catron, with law partner, Charles A. Spiess, unethically bribed, intimidated, and slandered prosecution witnesses. Catron also attacked arresting Sheriff William Cunningham with a May 14, 1895 defamatory letter from a Ring crony named Richard Hudson of the Board of Penitentiary Commissioners of New Mexico, accusing him of plotting to kill the defendants if they were acquitted. Hudson wrote to him as *"Friend Catron"*: *"In talking with a Santa Fe man a few days ago in regard to the trial of the men you are defending at present, I told him I thought they might get acquitted; "he then said if they get acquitted, I believe they will be mobbed & murdered the very night they were let out of jail" ~ intimated that Cunningham would be the leader with his Deputies to back him ... I thought it best to post you on the subject."*

"Friend" Hudson reappeared in 1897 to aid Catron's attempt to stop President William McKinley's appointment of Catron's enemy, Miguel Ortega, as governor. (Westphall, p. 273)

On May 29, 1895, the defendants were convicted of first degree murder and sentenced to hang. Catron had lost. He responded with his usual defamatory affidavits - here from jurors - claiming prosecution violations by Jacob Crist. But the judge rejected them.

And in plea bargaining, in July of 1895, to escape their death sentences, defendants Laurencio Alarid and Patricio Valencia confessed that they and the Borrego brothers murdered Chavez.

(Westphall, p. 229) An appeal by Catron and Spiess to the state Supreme Court failed. (Westphall, pp. 228-229)

But Catron, the likely accomplice, emerged untouched.

And that 1895, Elkins became West Virginia's U.S. Senator, and was positioned to use his Washington influence in this case, as well as backing the Ring overall until his death in 1911.

FACING DISBARMENT

Borrego trial fall-out made a major crisis for Catron. His unethical conduct to shield Chavez's killers - enhanced to counter claims that he was their accomplice - left him and the Ring as vulnerable as in the Lincoln County War period investigation by Frank Warner Angel. So Westphall white-washed: "[Catron] feared that it was the purpose of his antagonists to conduct a protracted investigation that would keep his name constantly in the public attention and thus hamper his effectiveness as a public leader." (Westphall, p. 248)

On August 20, 1895, the Borrego trial's angry prosecutor, District Attorney Jacob H. Crist, bravely filed incriminatory information with the New Mexico Supreme Court as Case No. 637, for unprofessional conduct in conducting the defense by Catron and his co-counsel partner, Charles A. Spiess. Crist petitioned for action to be taken against them. At stake was disbarment.

Crist asserted that: 1) prosecution witness and penitentiary inmate, Ike Nowell, was visited by Catron, to induce him to change his testimony; 2) prosecution witness Dominga Apodaca was visited by Spiess to induce her not to testify against Francisco Gonzales y Borrego; 3) prosecution witness Luiz Gonzales was offered money by Spiess to claim that Governor Thornton paid him for his testimony; 4) prosecution witness Porfilia Martinez de Strong stated that she had been forced to give false testimony shielding the defendants after being threatened by Catron and his agents; 5) prosecution witness Max Knodt changed his testimony in exchange for Catron promising him free railway passes; 6) after the trial, Catron used a Bernadino B. Baca as a spy at Crist's office to ascertain how much information on the witness tampering was possessed by Crist, Judge Laughlin, Governor Thornton, and Sheriff Cunningham; 7) before the trial started, Catron tried to bribe a Rosa Gonzales y Baca to force her two prosecution witness sons to testify falsely; and 8) prosecution witness Mauricio Gonzales was offered bribes by both Catron and Spiess to deny his eye-witness information.

Crist concluded "[that the acts] were not in accord with their duties and obligations as officers of this court, were destructive to the confidence of the people in the integrity of the bar, and hence were derogatory to the administration of justice [and] informant brings them to the attention of this honorable court for such action as it may seem just and proper in the premises."

The Supreme Court appointed a committee of five (Solicitor General J.P. Victory, A.A. Jones, P.S. Rodey, W. Childers, and S.B. Newcomb) to evaluate Crist's information, and conduct the prosecution. On August 31, 1895, it presented five charges for disbarment based on prosecution witness tampering as: "In the Supreme Court of New Mexico, In the Matter of the Information Concerning Thomas B. Catron and Charles A. Spiess." Ominous was omission of some of Crist's complaint. But the chilling charges were as follows:

First. The said Thomas B. Catron was guilty of unprofessional conduct in this: That one Ike Nowell had been and was a material witness for the Territory at the preliminary examination ... and before said [Borrego] trial the said Ike Nowell had been convicted of a violation ... and was confined in the Territorial Penitentiary in Santa Fe ... and while confined, the said Catron ... went out to the Penitentiary and ... endeavored to persuade said Nowell to give entirely different testimony [at the trial] ... from that which he had given in preliminary examination and suggested that he the said witness might avoid testifying to the facts ... by declining to answer upon the ground that the answer might criminate him.

Second: The said Thomas B. Catron was guilty of unprofessional conduct in this: That one Porfilia Martinez de Strong was ... examined on the said preliminary examination ... and then and there testified to material facts on behalf of the said defendants ... and was afterwards introduced upon the trial ... afterwards upon the cross examination ...

stated ... she had so testified falsely because she was afraid, meaning thereby that she had been induced to give said testimony ... in part as follows:

One Roman Garcia claiming to be sent for that purpose by the said Thomas B. Catron and one Carlos Conklin [the fired Sheriff], together with one Jose Dominguez, visited said witness ... and there falsely personating an officer pretended to serve a subpoena on the said witness ... when ... in fact the said Dominguez had no subpoena and thereby induced the witness to come with them [to a house] where the said Charles Conklin ... stated to the witness that he wanted her to testify ... for the purpose of contradicting ... Luis Gonzales, he having claimed to have seen the defendants or some of them near the place of the killing a very short time before the killing occurred. It is further represented that afterwards and upon the [ongoing] trial of said defendants ... one Fred Thayer also falsely personating an officer, pretending to have a writ for the arrest of said witness, took her into custody ... and brought said witness to the office of said Thomas B. Catron and Charles A. Spiess ... where the said Thomas B. Catron and Charles A. Spiess caused said witness to be kept and detained all of the balance of the night ... she having [then] been taken directly from said office to the court house and placed upon the witness stand ... all of which conduct tended to intimidate the witness, and, as she testified afterwards, caused her to testify falsely ... she being then and there an ignorant friendless woman.

Third: The said Thomas B. Catron was guilty of unprofessional conduct in this: That one Max Knodt had been a material witness for the Territory at [a] preliminary examination ... testifying that he saw and recognized the said defendant, Francisco Gonzales y Borrego going down Water street ... towards the place where said killing occurred and within and hour and a half of the time when said killing ... was alleged to have taken place and said

Max Knodt on the subsequent trial ... testified differently ... and not remembering facts ... thus rendering his testimony comparatively useless ... [He admitted] in cross examination, that the said Catron had promised him to procure a railroad pass to and from Fort Wingate at any time he ... desired ... the obtaining and [subsequent] giving [of said passes] was for the purpose and had the effect of inducing him to change his testimony.

Fourth: That the said Thomas B. Catron was guilty of unprofessional conduct in this: That he ... offered money and other indictments to one Rosa Gonzales y Baca, mother of Luis Gonzales and Mauricio Gonzales, both very material witnesses for the Territory ... and sought such offers to procure her ... to induce her sons to testify falsely in the said cause.

Fifth: That the said Thomas B. Catron was guilty of unprofessional conduct in this: That on a certain day between the 29th of December, 1894, and the 28th of February, 1895, he ... offered one Mauricio Gonzales money and otherwise attempted to induce the said Gonzales to make an affidavit falsely stating that he ... was not near ... the place of the killing.

Westphall demonized Catron's opponents and blamed vague "enmities and intrigues" for the procedure. He outlawed Prosecutor Jacob Crist for an 1884 murderer - for which Crist was not charged - at a mining company Catron owned, when he was Superintendant. (Westphall, p. 230) He vilified Supreme Court Judge, Napoleon B. Laughlin, (who would later back disbarment), by calling him a biased Democrat business partner of Crist, whom Catron had accused of being "controlled by the smallest kind of men ... [and] committed deliberate perjury." (Westphall, p. 239)

Catron himself, filing his response to the Supreme Court, denied the charges and "outlawed" the witnesses "whose testimony is so unreasonable, improbable and contradictory that it is insufficient to support a finding of guilty." On August 24, 1895, with usual defamation, he had written to Elkins in Washington:

"[Prosecution witnesses are] penitentiary convicts ... and disreputable characters, unworthy of credit or belief." (Westphall, p. 242) Spiess followed suit, likewise claiming to the Supreme Court that there was no valid evidence against himself.

SUPREME COURT TESTIMONY BY AGGRIEVED BORREGO TRIAL PROSECUTION WITNESSES

The transcript of the Supreme Court of New Mexico as "Case No. 637, In re Catron and Spiess, Unprofessional Conduct," gave witness testimonies that Catron could not expurgate; and are a horrifying window into his intimidation of vulnerable people in both the Borrego trial and this case disbarment against him.

Their words echo the experiences, 17 years earlier, of Catron's Lincoln County victims, like John Tunstall, Alexander McSween, Susan McSween, John "Squire" Wilson, and Billy Bonney, who faced his wrath.

Astoundingly, one of Catron's and Spiess's defense attorneys was Frank Springer, passing as anti-Ring in the Colfax County War, but who, as will be seen, secretly covered up the Ring's Lincoln County War atrocities in his August 9, 1878 deposition to Investigator Frank Warner Angel, earning massive Ring rewards.

On October 17, 1895, prosecution witness in the Borrego trial, Porfilia Martinez de Strong, testified to hearing from her house Francisco Chavez's fatal shots, and to a witness who came to her door. But she described being pressured by Catron to make an affidavit denying that for this Supreme Court case. Attorney Springer objected to stop testimony by calling it irrelevant as occurring after the Borrego trial at issue; but the Court denied the objection and responded to show extremity of Catron's criminality:

> **We propose to prove that one man at least went to [Porfilia Martinez] and demanded that she should make an affidavit contradictory to the testimony she now gives and contradictory to the specifications and charges in this case, and that she refused to do so, and that he beat her – blacked her eyes.** We also propose to prove that Mr. Catron prepared the affidavit, utterly at variance with the charges here, and we propose to introduce that affidavit in evidence, and that it was given to the [next] witness Ramon

Garcia, on the 20th or 21st day of September, with instructions to go and see this woman and get her to make this affidavit, and stated to this Ramon Garcia that unless he procured such affidavit that he would go to the penitentiary; that he so stated to Garcia, and gave Garcia the affidavit which [Catron] himself prepared in his own office on his own typewriter, and instructed him to get this woman [witness] to make this affidavit, and gave him five dollars to pay his expenses.

On October 18, 1895, prosecution witness, Dominga Apodaca, described being intimidated by a Catron thug, Gus O'Brien, about her disbarment case testimony. She stated: "I turned around and looked at him and he says if we cant get you here we will get you some other place. I turned around and look at him and made a face to him … [H]e said to me I was a son of a bitch and called me every name and said Cunningham [the sheriff] was paying me to come to testify against Catron and Spiess … that I was nothing but a bad woman."

On October 19, 1895, prosecution witness for the Borrego trial, Ike Nowell, stated Catron came to the penitentiary where he was locked up, to try to block his potentially devastating testimony of seeing Frank Borrego near the Francisco Chavez murder site on the night of the crime. Nowell stated: "[Mr. Catron came to the penitentiary] and sent for me to come to his private office … and he says … I don't want you to testify in this case, the Borregos killing Chavez, and I told him I didn't see how I could get around it; I says I gave my evidence in the preliminary investigation and I says to refuse to testify they would get me for perjury … he says I will tell you what to do … when they ask you if you know the Borrego boys you can tell them yes, and he says if they ask you if you know how Chavez was killed, you refuse to answer the question, just say it would incriminate you … I says … I have had enough of this trouble … and he says I will defend you." Nowell added that after he got out, Catron's people offered him money not to testify in the disbarment case, and go to Texas. He stated that Colonel [William] Breeden met with him and told him he "would hurt Catron ... [and] "to do [Catron] this favor [and not testify]." Nowell stated: "[Breeden] says if you will testify ... you go up and testify ... that you was drunk when you made this statement about Catron in the trial before, and I said … I was not drunk ... and he says if you will do this I will promise that I will give you half interest in a mine and fifty or seventy five dollars besides."

RESPONSES OF CATRON AND SPIESS

With turncoat lawyer, Frank Springer, for defense, Catron and Spiess declared all opposing witness to be of low moral character; thus, lacking credibility. And they denied all allegations, requesting the Court to find them not guilty of each charge.

CATRON'S CORRUPT COERCION OF HIS SUPREME COURT JUDGES

By October 5, 1895, Jacob Crist was feeling pressure from the disbarment case, and responded in a Letter to the Editor of the *Santa Fe Daily New Mexican* titled "Mr. Crist Speaks Out" to clarify that the Supreme Court itself formulated the charges against Catron and Spiess, not him; and he would not be testifying since he stated his objections on record during the Borrego trial.

Catron himself shamelessly coerced his five Supreme Court judges on the case: Chief Justice Thomas Smith, Needham Collier, Gideon B. Bantz, Humphrey B. Hamilton, and Napoleon B. Laughlin. Westphall provided Catron's October 25, 1895 letter to his friend, *Socorro Chieftain* publisher W.S. Williams, urging influencing his judges. Ignoring that this request alone merited Catron's disbarment and proved Ring obstruction of justice, Westphall presented the outrageous missive: "Catron requested that Williams confer with Judge Humphrey B. Hamilton ... and see that, if [Judge] Laughlin filed a dissenting opinion, the court prepare a finding absolutely vindicating himself and Spiess ... He wished Hamilton to prepare a ... positive opinion in the case that would take the guts out of anything that Laughlin wrote. [Catron wrote,] 'Hamilton should ... see that the decision is an absolute, complete, unconditional vindication. This is what I ask him. He can afford to give it.' " (Westphall, pp. 253-254)

By September 9, 1895, S.B. Elkins assisted long-distance to influence his wife's cousin, Justice Gideon Bantz; writing: "*Mr. Catron's prominence in the capital territory and his leadership together with his positive character has aroused not only opposition, but antagonism from certain quarters, and no doubt there are many people in the capital territory who would like to break him down, and this may cut some figure in the proceedings to disbar him.*"

CATRON'S ATTACK ON CHIEF JUSTICE THOMAS SMITH IN THE *ALBUQUERQUE DAILY CITIZEN ANONYMOUS LETTER PLOT*

Catron knew he could not manipulate Supreme Court Chief Justice Thomas J. Smith. And gone were the 1867 days when Ringite William Rynerson simply slaughtered Chief Justice John P. Slough. So Catron devised a smear campaign to destroy Smith professionally and personally. For his plot, Catron used *Albuquerque Daily Citizen* Editor, Thomas Hughes, to publish a fabricated anonymous letter, since, as Westphall states, Catron knew that Smith "was very tender in regard to newspaper articles." (Westphall, p 249) That Hughes had been under Catron's control for three years is shown by a September 26, 1892 letter to Catron by Ringite Ralph Emerson Twitchell, then Chairman of the New Mexico Republican Central Committee, stating that to get Hughes's paper's support, he needed to be bribed: "From Mr. Hughes reply you will see that the great trouble is in his not having received any favors from you in times past. The day after this letter was written the Citizen came out with a very pronounced editorial favoring your candidacy and campaign [for Delegate to Congress], and it seems to me that you should see Mr. Hughes when you go to Albuquerque."

The relationship having been sweetened, on October 9, 1895, Catron gave complicit *Albuquerque Daily Citizen* editor, Thomas Hughes, an anonymous "Letter to the Editor," written by himself, defaming Smith under the title: "Is It Honesty or Partisanship?" Westphall, not providing the letter-article, but covering for Catron, misleadingly paraphrased it as: "Smith had cast himself in the role of prosecutor and, therefore, disqualified himself from judging the case [and] was also accused of selecting members of the investigating committee ... hostile to Catron." (Westphall, p. 246)

In fact, Catron's published, anonymous, "Is It Honesty or Partisanship?" letter of October 9, 1895 demonstrated his conscienceless sociopathy and Machiavellian evil, as he defamed Judge Smith as corrupt by fabricated events, manipulated the Bar Association into an adversarial relationship with the Supreme Court to oppose Smith, promoted himself as victim of "partisan effort to ruin the character of an attorney [himself] whose only crime is that he was, at the last election, selected by a majority of about 3,000 votes to represent New Mexico in congress," and portrayed himself as an attacked champion of the common man by Smith's "zeal to cripple the influence of Catron [himself] to aid New Mexico and her people." And in just 16 days, this despicable ploy was rewarded, not excoriated. As "Anonymous," Catron wrote:

IS IT HONESTY OR PARTISANSHIP?

Last Sunday evening Chief Justice Smith, of the supreme court of this territory, wired W.B. Childers that he intended to spend the night with him in this city.

It has been reliably ascertained that the object of this visit to Albuquerque, outside of his own district, and away from Santa Fe, the seat of the supreme court, was to consult with Childers, one of the attorneys designated to "formulate" charges against T.B. Catron, based on information in the nature of affidavits and copies of a part of the evidence in the First Judicial District Court in the case for murder of Chavez, presented by J.H. Crist. Judge Smith notwithstanding the fact that he is a member of the supreme court, and as such one of the judges to hear and try such charges, has contrary to all precedent, delicacy and the ethics pertaining to the judicial action, descended from the high position which he should have commanded, so as to appear in the **partisan effort to ruin the character of an attorney whose only crime is that he was, at the last election, selected by a majority of about 3,000 votes to represent New Mexico in congress. In his zeal to cripple the influence of Catron to aid New Mexico and her people**, Judge Smith has made this visit to Albuquerque, and at the residence of Childers took up nearly the whole night in delivering the case and its merits. It is well understood that prior to any action taken in the supreme court in this matter Judge Smith also met and had a full consultation with Childers, Crist and other attorneys who were at enmity with Catron, in regard to the propriety and feasibility of pushing the cause against Catron; that it was there determined that it was necessary to push them for political and personal reasons; that Judge Smith would see that they were referred to a special committee of the bar, composed of a majority who would be hostile to Catron either politically or personally or both, but that it should be so done that it should be made to appear to the other members of the supreme court that it was intended to be non-partisan.

They should formulate the charges with the affidavits and parts of the evidence of persons who were ex-penitentiary convicts and jail birds, confessed prostitutes, and vagrants. It seems that this information was given out before any announcement came from the court as to what would be done.

At least one of the attorneys so consulted by Judge Smith let out enough to show that a consultation had been had and partly what had been agreed upon.

We are happy to say that we have no information that more than one member of the court participated in this conference nor do we believe the others would have done so, if requested even by the chief justice.

It is worthy of notice that the committee appointed was made up of three democrats, two of them were hostile to Catron, one of them W.H. Childers, and the only republican lawyer in New Mexico who is at enmity with Catron, that he, E.A. Fiske, stated his enmity in the court and asked to be excused from sitting on the committee, but the request was promptly denied by Judge Smith, acting apparently for the court, but without any consultation with any of the members thereof.

The court, however, a day or two afterwards, when Judge Smith had attended the meeting and gone away on one of his periodical absences as a non-resident judge, being composed of the remaining four members, still in session and attending to their duties, unanimously excused Fiske from sitting on the committee on the ground that he was an improper person and appointed B.S. Rodney in his stead.

We do not desire or intend to reflect on the supreme court or any member of it, only to state the facts as we have heard them, for the information of the public. We do think, however, that the meeting of Judge Smith was most reprehensible. He had no more occasion to consult with a member of that committee in advance than he had to become the prosecutor in that or any other cause which might come before him in the supreme court or the district court. He sits as a juror, having taken an active part in advising in regard to the cause, having manifested his prejudice, if we are correctly informed, he is no longer qualified in that case. Yet if appearance and reports are true, he has not dignified himself as a fair, upright and manly judge should have done.

No judge having any regard for his office or for the esteem of his fellows since the time of Bacon and Jeffreys has ever allowed himself to be consulted or to take part in advising the course to be pursued in a given case. The management of causes and the propriety of the course to be pursued and the accusation to be presented in any case should be left to the legal profession and in a case like this to the Bar Association of New Mexico, to which Catron and Spiess are both members, and where such matters properly belong.

It cannot scarcely be considered that Judge Smith has acted fairly and impartially in this cause if the facts as we learned them be true. The other members of that court should see that the judicial ermine is not dragged in the mud of politics and of personal enmity and should properly check any partisan zeal or political hostility which may be manifested in that cause if there be any display thereof. The cutting off of a member of the bar from practice of his profession is the destruction of property; it cuts off his income and materially injures his character and standing with his constituents. **Mr. Catron, as we learn, has for more than twenty-eight years practiced his profession in the courts of this territory. His character as an attorney has never before been assailed. He stands as an honest, upright and pure attorney.** Such record cannot be brushed aside or wiped out by such testimony as is sought to be presented against him. Catron and Spiess are both members of the Bar Association of New Mexico, which has been in existence for the last ten years. All of the most energetic, able and upright members of the bar belong to it. Since its organization, no charges have ever been entertained by any court against a member of that association, unless it first came from the association or the grievance committee thereof, or was referred by the court to the same for its consideration or action. In this way the best results have been reached. Why should a different course be pursued now? **Is it because there is a want of confidence in the Bar Association that the supreme court cannot trust three-fourths of the members of the association?**

Is it not pretended that a single act enlarged against Catron or Spiess occurred before the supreme court or in connection with the business before the supreme court. On the contrary it appears that if such acts occurred at all they occurred in the district court on a trial before Judge Hamilton. **The Bar Association is amply capable to assume control in this matter and to inquire into the correctness and probable truth of the charges**. In this way an attorney's character, business and standing would not be jeopardized or injured by an untrue consideration of facts and of their character.

Why does the supreme court assume to take control and ignore the Bar Association of which each member of the court is a member? Why is the grievance committee of that association, composed of such men as N.B. Field, George W. Knaebel, S.B. Newcomb, Frank Springer and A.A. Jones, ignored? Are not these men capable of looking into the truth and reasonableness of the charges? These are men whose integrity, ability and fairness cannot be questioned, unless it be by those who seek to perpetrate a wrong. It is no partisan committee. Three of its members are democrats, and two republicans. Two of them, Newcomb and Jones, have been placed on the committee to formulate these charges, but Field, Knaebel and Springer have been shoved aside, Field being chairman. Instead of three such men as Field, Knaebel and Springer, Victory, Childers and Fiske, persons either politically or personally hostile to T.B. Catron were placed with the committee. Why was this? Was it fair, or was it that they did not believe in the honesty, integrity and fairness of Springer and Knaebel and Field? Or was it possibly in order that the advocates of certain peculiar ideas should go upon the committee to besmirch the character of other members of the bar? We hope the latter is not the case. We believe it is not; but if it is such, then to what a low, contemptible, degraded and insignificant place can the judiciary descend?

It is said that after the conference between Smith and Childers on Sunday night, which lasted until 5 o'clock next morning, the conclusion reached was that the charges must be prosecuted most rigorously, that the Democrat, a newspaper under the control and management of Childers, should be brought to their aid; therefore an article either written or inspired by Childers was published influencing the public of the fact that although Crist, the district attorney of Santa Fe and the man who preferred the charges against Catron and Spiess had been detected in unprofessional conduct, yet the same could not be considered in connection with the charges against Catron. We never understood or thought they should, and we understand that Catron objects to the same also. That article says, in substance, that the full bench, after considering the charges, determined them of sufficient gravity to be examined into and had appointed a committee to consider them and present charges if found sufficient, and that the committee had so found them and presented the charges, and then draws the conclusion therefrom that the charges should be considered well founded and proper.

The individual who penned or inspired that article, or both, and everyone else who knows anything, knows that the members of the supreme court individually never read over the alleged charges and annexed papers, presented by Crist, nor have they heard them read over, but without reading or hearing them read referred them on the representation of someone to the committee with instructions simply to formulate charges based thereon; but not to examine into the truth of the facts or the probability of their correctness. It is further well known that Catron's attorneys applied to the court on motion and asked to have the charges investigated by the committee and their powers enlarged for that purpose, so that they might determine whether there was any reasonable foundation for preferring charges. The supreme court refused to accede to this motion; that thereafter the committee itself applied to the court and requested to be informed as to their duties, and most if not all the committee stated that if they were required to examine the facts of the charges or do anything except to act ministerially in formulating charges upon the supposed facts before them, that they declined to act upon the committee; they were therefore informed by the court that they were to formulate charges based upon the matters presented to them and stand between the court and wrong. What that meant does not seem very clear.

These facts, although done in private with closed doors, none present but four members of the court and the committee, have reached the light of day.

How can it be said that the court or any committee has any manner passed upon the correctness of the charges or the possibility of sustaining them. No investigation had been made by either.

Why were not these charges preferred in the district court, where the facts complained of are said to have happened, if at all? And that also before Judge Hamilton?

They were in fact, as we learn, presented to Judge Hamilton, in fact he was present and heard the testimony of each of the witnesses, also the cross-examination and other evidence contradictory and explanatory thereof, and in impeachment thereof, which cross-examination and other evidence contradictory and explanatory, has not yet been presented to the supreme court. Yet, in view of all the facts, which were virtually known to Judge Hamilton, he declined to entertain the charges. So they are taken to another court whose dignity or character was not in any manner trenched upon, if the charges be true and are even sustainable. None of the cross-examination, none of the contradictory evidence, none of the explanatory evidence or impeaching is brought before the supreme court, although Judge Hamilton had it all.

The facts before the supreme court are simply garbled. None of the testimony showing the character of the witnesses by whom it is sought to establish the charges is presented to the supreme court, so that they could pass upon the reliability of the proposed evidence. Why has that been omitted? Why has that not been called to the attention of the supreme court? Why has the committee not been allowed to look into these facts? We do not believe the supreme court desires to do wrong, but we think it should be more careful and cautious in attacking the reputation of a lawyer of more than a quarter century's standing, of the chosen representative of the people, of one against whom there has never been a scintilla proven regarding his integrity or standing. All the facts, at least those which have been made public, pro and con, touching upon them, should have been testified to, and the character of the witnesses should have been looked into, either by the supreme court or the committee, before they undertook to plaster the character of anyone with stigma, as is now sought to be done.

We believe that in the view of the fact that the testimony produced by the prosecution from penitentiary convicts, incumbents of the jails, notorious and confessed prostitutes, thieves and vagrants as they all are, the good standing of Mr. Catron as manifested by the confidence of three-fourths of the members of the Bar Association, men who have associated with him for years, who have enjoyed his hospitality, have been favored by him with every courtesy and every kindness, who have always been treated with the greatest of consideration and who esteemed him sufficiently to make him the representative of their numbers at the head of that association, which they have formed for their individual guide and government, should have some weight. The judge or the juror who would refuse to give such endorsement weight and take that of a penitentiary convict, of a public prostitute or of a petty thief instead, can hardly expect to go down to future generations possessing a reputation for the greatest amount of integrity and wisdom.

We do not write these facts to influence the supreme court, we expect it to be guided wisely and entirely by the merits of the case; we do demand, however, that the case shall be tried according to law, that a proper weight be given in view of all the facts and surroundings to the testimony of each witness; we do demand that politics shall be eliminated, that personal hostility and enmity shall be set aside and nothing but the strictest kind of justice and honesty shall prevail.

The next day, October 10, 1895, conscienceless Catron responded as himself to "Is It Honesty or Partisanship?" to complicit Editor Thomas Hughes, who printed it with Catron's pre-written response for him - putting Hughes in position of perjury. Catron's letter - with its Hughes response - stated:

Editor of the Citizen:

I have noticed an article in the Citizen of the 9th inst., which seems to reflect on Chief Justice Smith, and have learned that it is claimed by some of my political and personal enemies that I inspired the article or wrote it. As you are aware I had nothing to do with it. I cannot believe that a gentleman occupying the high and responsible position of Chief Justice of this Territory has been guilty of the great impropriety of counseling in regard to the conduct or merit of any cause to come before him. I suggest that you make this communication public, as an attempt is being made, as I understand, to prejudice me in the case pending against me in the supreme court.

Respectfully, T.B. Catron

We publish the foregoing as requested and state that **our information came from other sources than that of Mr. Catron.** He is not in any manner responsible for that article and we gladly print what Mr. Catron says, so as to put him right, as also the Chief Justice, to whom we desire to do no wrong.

The editorial in this paper of the 9th inst., entitled "is it honesty or partisanship", was published on what we deemed reliable authority, gathered from various sources. We are now informed that Mr. Childers and Judge [Thomas] Smith disclaim any idea that they were in consultation at any time Sunday night in the [disbarment] matter against Catron, but Mr. Childers says Judge Smith's visit to him was on other matters. Of course Mr. Childers and Judge Smith know best and we are willing to give them the benefit of a denial and of all reasonable doubts. We are glad to be informed that the statements made by us to the visit of Judge Smith last Sunday was not for the purpose and object we had been informed it was made for, and we are glad to have the public so to understand, and on this make the amende honorable, as we have heretofore and greatest confidence in the integrity of the Chief Justice. We hope hereafter to be able to entertain the same confidence.

That same October 10, 1895, abandoning his fake persona of his *Albuquerque Daily Citizen* response, Catron wrote a cajoling and threatening letter to Editor Hughes. It reveals Catron's psychopathic use of an accomplice, bribery, and expurgation of evidence by requesting its destruction. He wrote:

Dear Hughes:
   The editorial in your paper came to hand today and the democrats and members of the supreme court are very indignant. Some people seem to think that it may cause them to be vindictive against me. I have just wired you that I would meet you at your office, but on reflection, I have concluded that the best thing would be to have some one else see you, so I have requested Mr. Fort to go down. It may be the fiery and untamed chief justice [Thomas Smith] may wish to take out a writ of contempt against you, so I have reflected on the matter, and **should they get a contempt on you you must absolutely stand pat and not give away any information that will injure me.** If you should have to undergo any punishment I will undertake to make up the difference in any event. What I was thinking was that it might be well, if you do not desire to be brought up for contempt, for you to take a short trip to Arizona on some business which you have there, and go at once, as they may issue their warrant secretly. However, if you are willing to stand the proceeding, it might be a good thing, as it will advertise your paper all over the territory and probably do more to bring in the united Republican Party to your assistance than anything else. **I wish you would not however in any manner connect me with the [anonymous] article.** Simply say that it was based on information gathered by you from various sources and the public. ~~thought~~ Tell McCreight [Hughes's partner] to say nothing about it, as I mentioned that I left it with the merchant next door to be handed to you and told McCreight to say nothing. If they take steps against you, it will be the best thing on earth for your paper. **It will do no good to have me implicated with you.** If you should go to Arizona to stave off any proceedings for contempt till the July term, and by that time I expect to have a new supreme court for

the three territories, I shall bend every effort to that end.

A little thing which they could connect me with now might turn the entire [Supreme] court against me and cause them to believe thieves, whores and convicts. I think everything is all right, however.

This will be handed to you by Mr. Fort; do not let it get into anyone else's hands. **Better destroy it at once.**

Very truly yours,
T.B. Catron

Catron's plot backfired when he was recognized as the anonymous letter author; as warned in an October 14, 1895 letter by a Silver City broker named D.C. Hobart, who wrote:

Dear Sir: As I was returning home yesterday (on the train) I met Ferguson (of Albuquerque) and from him I learned that he is the party delegated by the Committee appointed to investigate the source of the article recently published in the "Albuquerque Citizen" for which Hughes and McCreight are apparently in contempt of the Supreme Court, attachments have issued &c.

In discussing the matter Ferguson told me, among other things that he had <u>positive evidence</u> that Catron wrote the "published article", also that if the Court did not disbar Catron at the hearing coming on Monday (which he thought they would) there was no question but that they had him on the "Citizen" article.

I suggested the idea that "my opinion was that Hughes was on a business trip and that when he returned he would state <u>under oath</u> that Catron had nothing whatever to with it (the article). His reply was that "if he (Hughes) has written the article, he would be sent to the penitentiary for perjury, as they had discovered <u>positive</u> evidence Saturday, that Catron wrote the article in question, and further that Catron had advised Hughes to skip out until the present hearing that would come up Monday was over.

He also said that "Hughes could not escape, or if he kept out of the way until the present term of

the Supreme Court was over, the Court could, or would, adjourn from month to month, so as to get action on Hughes as soon as found."
   If I can be of service in any way, advise me.
Very truly, yours
D.C. Hobart

Though Westphall dismisses this diabolical plot as merely Catron's "fit of uncontrollable pique," he admits Hughes was fined and jailed for 60 days for perjury and contempt. (Westphall, pp. 254-255) He uses the saga to prove Catron's loyalty; writing: "Tom Catron did not forget his promise to 'make up the difference' for Thomas Hughes forbearance in accepting quietly the jail sentence on behalf of Catron and the Republican Party in New Mexico ... Catron responded with financial aid." (Westphall, p. 260) On July 11, 1896, Catron wrote a pay-off check for $350 from the First National Bank of Santa Fe (equivalent to $9,226.77 today). Hughes endorsed it with his *Albuquerque Daily Citizen* co-owner William T. McCreight on July 28, 1896.

Catron did not stop. He continued attempts "to embarrass Judge Thomas J. Smith at every turn." (Westphall, p. 250) He got his usual defamatory affidavits to claim Smith had accepted bribes to reverse another judge's decision. (Westphall, p. 252) He then sent for publication the anonymous, raving, homophobic "Extra Billy Smith" letter of October 25, 1895 to his friend, W.S. Williams, publisher of the *Socorro Chieftain*. It unmasks Catron as an obscene, slandering, jeering, degenerate monster. He wrote:

Tom Smith, son of "Extra Billy" Smith, brother of ... the embezzler, who fled from justice in Arizona, and brother of the other Smith who took a prominent part in the murder of Dave Broderick ... says he washes his hands of the Catron & Spiess case. If he does he ought to do so near the Rio Grande, as the filth he has personally injected into it from his own hands would pollute the waters of that stream to such an extent that it would cause an epidemic along the whole course of that river ...

Who is Tom Smith anyhow ? ... Is he the same Tom Smith who has frequently been found drunk in Las Vegas and after having befouled himself been carried home by his companions to avoid scandal? Is he the same doubting Thomas, who was drunk on the bench at Vegas and was kindly advised to adjourn court because he was sick ...

The Citizen article surely had some effect. It knocked the saw-dust out of Smith five times in five minutes and then gave him a congestive chill, by which he was confined to bed ... Thomas, keep cool, or you will lose all your saw-dust and have another chill.

Some hard things are said about Tom Smith, and his moral character, but it is whispered that his physical manhood is even more a myth than his morality, for instance ... he smothers his poor rotting physique with musk and perfume. Is it true that in reality the chief justice is physically that which his lady-like manners indicate. We might cite his "domestic bliss" as another proof, but that isn't necessary.

The chief justice of New Mexico wears a cape overcoat. The cape has a delicate white silk lining. No matter whether the wind blows ... this "man" keeps his pretty little silk cape folded neatly back, so as to expose the captivating lining. How proud we ought to be of our lady-like chief justice? Everyone will anxiously await the appearance of the "manly" creature with his new spring bonnet next Easter.
(Westphall, pp. 251-253)

Catron's deranged malice continued in a November 11, 1895 sneering letter to a T.W. Collier about Chief Justice Smith: "His skin is so thin that the slightest attack punctures him. I think the papers should now puncture him so much that his skin will be too open for a first class sieve." (Westphall, p. 249)

PREVAILING AGAINST DISBARMENT

The pressured and manipulated Supreme Court judges, on October 25, 1895, vindicated Catron and his law partner, Charles A. Spiess. Traumatized Chief Justice Thomas J. Smith was absent, claiming illness. The majority opinion was given by Judge Humphrey H. Hamilton as: "In the Matter of the Charges and

Specifications Against Thomas B. Catron and Charles A. Spiess, Remarks and Observations." Catron's corrupt influence was evident. Judge Hamilton, the month before, had been the judge for his Supreme Court appeal on the Borrego case, and had upheld its guilty conviction *based on credibility of the same witnesses he now called lacking credibility in this disbarment case*! Hamilton essentially copied Catron's *Albuquerque Daily Citizen* letter, concluding that "the low moral character and poor reputation for veracity of the prosecution witnesses rendered their testimony beyond belief." (Westphall, p. 257) So the Court concluded:

> The ability and high professional standing of at least one of the respondents [Catron], the vast importance of this proceeding, in its results, both to them, and to the bench and bar of the Territory, the great public interest manifested in this investigation and the anxiety felt at its final determination, have rendered it proper, as I conceive, that I should individually express my views, and give the reason which, I think, furnish a sufficient justification for the conclusion at which I arrived ...
>
> The charges contain five ... specifications ... Testimony has been offered, which, if accepted as credible tends to the establishment of these charges. The respondents have each taken the stand and have positively, specifically and in detail denied all of the material allegations set forth ... [As to Ike Nowell, he was] a penitentiary convict ... abandoned his home, deserted his family, disavowed his marriage, dishonored his children, and became the companion of disreputable characters ... Take the testimony of this witness weigh it on the scales of impartial justice as against the testimony of [Catron] ... We therefore are irresistibly led to the conclusion that this charge is not sustained ...
>
> [As to Porfilia Martinez de Strong's testimony, it was denied by Spies, Catron, Thayer, and ... there is only one conclusion to which the court can come ... that is the innocence of the respondents ...
>
> [As to Max Knott, who wanted to visit a lady] and Mr. Catron told him he could not, probably get

him a [railroad] pass on that ground ... [W]e must accept the statement of the respondent as true with reference to this fact, and ... the third charge ... is not sustained in any particular.

[As to Mrs. Baca, mother of two prosecution witness sons] [W]e have , so far as this charge is concerned, the testimony of the woman, Mrs. Baca, and on the other side, and the testimony of the respondent [Catron], on the other... We hold, under our views ... that the amount of evidence which should be required to establish and maintain a charge of this kind [the prosecution] have wholly failed to sustain the allegations made.

[As to Mauricio Gonzales], [t]his charge stands upon ... the same character of testimony [as the other disreputable witnesses]. Catron denies absolutely, that anything of the kind [of bribing] was done ... Therefore, we say that under this testimony this charge cannot be sustained.

The testimony [on Catron's behalf] is that the woman, Mrs. Baca, ... was a woman whose character was such as to render her unworthy of credit. The testimony shows, too, that the witness[s] Luiz Gonzales ... [and] Muricio Gonzales, were of such a character as rendering them unworthy of belief. Prominent citizens of this community, officials in high standing, prominent members of the bar, reputable business men, in large numbers, have come upon the stand and have testified ... that they would not believe these witnesses under oath ... The witness, Porfilia Martinez ne Strong [admitted that she lied when giving her testimony in the trail]. [T]he testimony which has been introduced with reference to character applies to her as well. The testimony of Mauricio Gonzalez shows that he has been willing to make an affidavit on both sides of the case ... [So in weighing his testimony], we must conclude that these charges are not sustained.

Judge Hamilton added that Catron's subpoenaing de Strong and bringing her to trial was just being helpful.

As to Charles Spiess, Hamilton threw out his attempted influence of witness, Dominga Apodeca, because he denied it!

Hamilton called her a "public prostitute," whose testimony was without weight. As to his bribing Luis Gonzales for false testimony, Spiess denied it; so Hamilton denied the complaint!

Hamilton presented the Supreme Court's disgraceful decision to dismiss all charges for disbarment; stating:

> If any one of these charges was sustained by testimony, which could commend itself to the favorable consideration of the court, we would not hesitate one instant in proclaiming a judgment which might result in the disbarment of one or both of these respondents. But in the light in which we view this evidence, the character of the witnesses, the circumstances surrounding this cause ... **taking into consideration the frank, candid and unqualified manner in which the respondents have both testified in this case, as compared with the testimony offered against them ... we are led inevitably to the conclusion that these charges, in no particular, have been sustained against the respondents.**

But as Catron had worried, Judge Napoleon Bonaparte Laughlin proved uncorruptable. On December 20, 1895, he filed his long and honorable "Dissenting Opinion" in the disbarment case. For it, he reviewed complaint witnesses' testimonies, and Catron's and Spiess's responses denying them; and found no problem agreeing with disbarment.

Laughlin's clever argument pointed out that Catron and Spiess had relied on eliminating all the witnesses' testimony by alleging that they lacked moral character. But - implying fellow judges' hypocrisy - he reminded that the Borrego case's jury had sentenced Francisco Chavez's assassins to death *based on unquestioned credibility of those same witnesses; and this Supreme Court itself had upheld those convictions based on witness credibility - with Judge Humphey Hamilton himself presenting that verdict.* But now, in an obviously self-serving defense by Catron and Spiess, the Court suddenly reversed trust in those same witnesses.

He contended that, in fact, the complaint witnesses' testimony showed that Catron and Spiess had so believed in and feared their credibility that they made extreme efforts to stop their condemning testimony in the Borrego trial. Furthermore, even if the witnesses had bad moral character, it would not negate their ability to give truthful testimony.

He added that it is preposterous to expect people having first-hand knowledge of heinous criminals to be themselves necessarily respectable citizens; writing: "People whose moral character and standing for truth and veracity are unimpeachable do not, as a rule, frequent the haunts of the prostitute, "procuress," and petty thief, the very homes and comforters of crime; and if criminals shall go unwhipped of justice until reputable citizens be found by whose testimony they may be convicted, then the law of the vigilante must be invoked, and the laws established by the wisdom and experience of the past for the protection of life, liberty, and the pursuit of happiness must be abandoned."

Laughlin even contradicted that the witnesses had bad moral character; calling them merely destitute and uneducated, and the class of people who often furnish testimony in criminal cases.

He further pointed out that the coercions described by the witnesses in the five complaints had occurred in the presence of other people, but Catron and Spiess had suspiciously never used any for corroboration. So the only so-called evidence was Catron's and Spiess's own denials.

Laughlin further exposed his fellow justices' duplicitous argument as pretending there were five separate charges, instead of just one charge: "[T]hat Catron was guilty of unprofessional conduct as a lawyer in defense of the Borrego case." That meant that "all the evidence both direct and circumstantial [from all witnesses], must be considered together."

He even contested the claim that prominent citizens had testified for Catron and Spiess, adding that they were simply their friends. He added sarcastically, that, given their conclusion about the prosecution witnesses having bad character, his fellow judges should now free the Borrego case murderers - convicted by them!

He added that Catron's counsel [Frank Springer] had wrongly blocked admitting his *Albuquerque Daily Citizen* attack on Chief Justice Thomas Smith, which was needed to assess disbarment [implying common knowledge that Catron was its defamatory author].

As to the complaint witnesses' claims, he condemned Catron's and Spiess's criminality which debased the legal profession: "If such acts are to be passed over unnoticed by the courts, then the [legal] profession will be reduced, from the high and honorable place to which it belongs, to the level of the trickster and charlatan." He concluded his dissenting opinion:

> After a careful observation of the witnesses, the manner of their testifying while upon the stand, their interest or noninterest in the results, and a conscious consideration of all the testimony involved in the hearing, I am irresistibly driven to the conclusion, however unpleasant it may be, that the legal evidence contained in the record sufficiently sustains the charge of unprofessional conduct on the part of the respondent [Catron] during the progress of the trial of the said Borrego case, and I so find. The charge against respondent Spiess consists of four specifications; and, as the greater part of the facts are set out in the opinion of the court, it is sufficient for me to say that I cannot concur in the conclusions therein reached, for the reasons hereinbefore stated.

But for Ring-biased response on the disbarment and on honest Chief Justice Thomas Smith, one can turn to William Keleher in his 1962 *The Fabulous Frontier*: "If forced to come up with an 'equal opportunity political hack,' I might nominate Chief Justice Thomas Smith appointed by Democrat Grover Cleveland. Smith had served as a county judge and a state legislator in Virginia, as well as a N.M. U.S. Attorney during Cleveland's first term. **Smith made the history books by allegedly orchestrating a case against (republican) lawyer Thomas B. Catron, with the intent of sitting on the case as a judge.**"

And Victor Westphall concluded that Catron was a martyr: "[T]he tribulations he encountered brought him the fame that helped overcome adversities." (Westphall, p. 268)

In truth, Catron's shielding from his own indictment for murdering Francisco Chavez in the Borrego case, followed by the defeat of his justified disbarment for his illegal and unethical conduct in that trial and his further unethical behavior influencing and intimidating the Supreme Court Judges, marked his and his Santa Fe Ring's unassailable criminal ascendancy.

EXULTATION OF EVIL

With pseudo-religiosity, and with his *Albuquerque Daily Citizen* plot not yet fully exposed, Catron gloated in a letter of October 29, 1895 to a Walter C. Hadley; writing: "[Thomas Smith], thank heaven, took the diarrhoea from the article published in the "Citizen" and was soon after thrown into a congestive chill, from which doubtless under the interposition of divine providence he was not allowed to recover in time to take part in the nefarious transaction." (Westphall, p. 259)

Besides from Elkins, Catron received an outpouring of syncophants' congratulatory letters and telegrams lapping at the feet of his power.

One named T.J. Helm, from the Denver and Rio Grande Railroad Company, who apparently was also one of his anti-disbarment witnesses; wrote on October 28, 1895: "*Will you allow me to extend my harty congratulations. I even feel that I have myself been vindicated from the decision rendered, after the remarks of would be friends about my testimony on the witness stand. Thanking you for past manifestations of confidence.*"

Ring-beholden newspaper owner, Singleton Ashenfelter wrote on November 1, 1895: "*I congratulate you on the result of the Supreme Court Inquiry.*"

Another toady was Charles Rudulph, son of Ringite Milnor Rudulph, President of Billy Bonney's Coroner's Jury. Charles wrote on November 5, 1895: "*Allow me to congratulate you on your recent great victory. Let it be followed up by the humiliation of your persecutors.*"

BEING MADE PRESIDENT OF THE NEW MEXICO BAR

The disgraceful sequel to Catron's disbarment case was his immediate election as President of the New Mexico Bar Association: the group he had flattered in his *Albuquerque Daily Citizen* anonymous letter plot! He served from 1895 to 1896.

REVENGE FOR DISBARMENT CASE

Unleashed by the acquittal, was Catron's venomous vindictiveness against his perceived enemies: District Court Prosecutor Jacob Crist, dissenting Supreme Court Justice Napoleon Bonaparte Laughlin, Supreme Court Chief Justice Thomas Smith, and Governor William Thornton; each of whom he sought to destroy professionally. The actual assassinations he must have craved - like in the good old blood-soaked days of the Lincoln County War and slaughtering Billy Bonney - would have been too obviously incriminating of himself. Murdering Sheriff Francisco Chavez by his Borrego case henchmen had been too close a call. But his rabid rage against his Borrego case opponents gives a window into his past state of mind when ordering his atrocities in the 1870's, then blaming outlaw myths.

Catron revealed revenge plots in an October 25, 1895 letter to his *Socorro Chieftain* publisher friend, W.S. Williams: "Catron believed that newspapers from one end of the country to the other should 'open up like a line of sharp-shooters against Smith, Crist, and Thornton.'" (Westphall, p. 251)

ATTACKING JACOB CRIST

Westphall admits Catron's "punitive impulse," against Borrego case Prosecutor Jacob Crist, but outlaws Crist as a "tormenter" for attempting Catron's disbarment: "By October 25 [1895] the Supreme Court had rendered a verdict in favor of Catron. The protective motive in securing Crist's arrest was removed, and **punitive impulse was the remaining factor.** By this time the desire to punish Crist was sufficiently strong for Catron to press for capture of his tormentor." (Westphall, p. 240)

Westphall calls Catron's insanely barbarous pursuit of Crist "vigor and determination." (Westphall, p. 239) For his usual malicious prosecution, character assassination affidavits, and spying, Catron used investigators and sheriffs to get legal dirt on Crist, which yielded his over decade old, dormant, petty Colorado indictment for "larceny of household furniture." (Westphall, p. 234) On October 3, 1895, Catron's investigator, Charles A. Johnson, in Durango, Colorado, reported that the Sheriff there wanted to be paid arrest fees, since the county commissioners refused. So Catron himself paid the $100 costs to guarantee Crist's arrest. (Westphall, pp. 234-235)

On November 4, 1895, investigator Johnson nervously communicated from Durango, Colorado, about lack of witnesses against Crist, though he had gathered defamatory affidavits.

Then, learning of Crist's traveling plans into Arizona, Catron wanted Johnson to have him arrested by a Hinsdale County Sheriff. (This replicated his 1877 malicious prosecution arrest of Alexander McSween in Las Vegas on his fake embezzling charge. It also points to Catron's using an investigator in 1880 to uncover Billy's Arizona indictment for the killing of Frank "Windy" Cahill, to give to Secret Service Agent Azariah Wild for the fabricated case of Billy as a major murderer, counterfeiter, and rustler.)

This was risky business. Catron had just evaded justified disbarment. As Westphall wrote: "[Catron] realized the risk involved in having Crist incarcerated and then not sustaining a conviction." The next disbarment trial could be for malicious prosecution. So Catron backed down. As Westphall wrote: "Despite Catron's desire to see Crist brought to justice, the difficulty of gathering witnesses precluded further efforts to see him behind bars." (Westphall, p. 240) And even crazed Catron could realize that it was a bad time for another assassination.

NAPOLEON BONAPARTE LAUGHLIN

By November 4, 1895, Catron learned from Colorado investigator, Charles Johnson, that his Supreme Court judge, Napoleon Bonaparte Laughlin, was dissenting his vindication. Lackey Johnson wrote mockingly: "`[I]f he does so he would only give an exhibition of what an ass can do.`"

Catron's revenge against honest Judge Laughlin was to destroy his reputation in Washington by a defamatory letter, sent on July 18, 1896, to his politically powerful Ringite ally, William J. Mills (later New Mexico Territorial Chief Justice and last Territorial governor). Catron wrote: "This man Laughlin is trying to hamstring all of us here. He tried to disbar me and when he could not do it he wrote a filthy, dirty, dissenting opinion, had it published and caused his clerk to send a copy to every member of Congress and every head of Department in Washington, with the idea of breaking down my influence." (Westphall, p. 258)

REVENGE AGAINST GOVERNOR THORNTON

On September 5, 1896, Catron attacked Governor William T. Thornton for implicating him in Francisco Chavez's murder and backing hanging of his murderers in his *Santa Fe Weekly New Mexican*. To the Editors" of the *Albuquerque Daily Citizen* - meaning past co-conspirator Thomas Hughes - Catron, as "XXX," ran an anonymous letter in a convoluted scheme to discredit Thornton and the hanging sentence, in a re-run of his plot against Chief Justice Thomas Smith, in the same paper, the year before.

He attacked Thornton as dissolute "Poker Bill." Repeated was his outlawing of adversaries, here calling arresting Sheriff William Cunningham's men: "**[a] gang of deputies composed of people like those who testified against the Borregos**" (whom he had called penitentiary criminals). His motive, besides revenge, was fabricating a legal error that the Borregos were never "arraigned" (informed before a judge of the charges, and asked for their plea), and that Thornton himself had tampered with the court record by inserting a "**scrap of paper.**" It stated:

SEVERE CRITICISM.
Gov. Thornton Charged With Prostituting His Office.

Editors Citizen:

Santa Fe. Sept 4. – "Poker Bill" is now engaged in playing a game in which the lives of four men are at stake. He wants to have the two Borrego brothers hung, and agrees that should they be hung he will see that Lauriano Alarid and Patricio Valencia are sentenced to the penitentiary for life, provided they make a confession which will hurt Hon. T.B. Catron in the campaign [for Delegate] this fall.

Yesterday without any notice to the attorneys for the defendants, an armed gang of six-shooter deputies driven at break neck speed in a closed carriage, and with other deputies on horseback guarding the Borregos, dashed through the streets to the court house. The doors at the court house were locked, and it was with great difficulty that the attorneys managed to get inside. **A gang of deputies composed of people like those who testified against the Borregos**, were on hand insulting and threatening people. A person named King, who came here as some kind of a clerk in the surveyor general's office, but who some time ago was discharged by Mr Easley, and who has since been kept by Cunningham and fed at the county jail, was so abusive that he endeavored to stop Mr. Catron from entering the court room where is clients were, and threatened to kill Gus O'Brien, because he being the first to arrive on the scene told Francisco Gonzales y Borrego to answer no questions until Mr. Catron came.

Renahan, the stenographer who made an affidavit, states that the notes used to correct the record are on a separate piece of paper and do not run consecutively as the balance of the pages do. It seems strange to an uninterested party that this transcript of Renahan's should run page to page – full minutes and proceedings of the trial – until this all important part is reached, **and that that part, the part upon which the lives of the four men stands, should be tacked on at the last – a mere scrap of paper.**

The notes of Robert C. Gortner, who acted as stenographer during the trial and whose notes were accepted by Judge Hamilton as correct, do not show any arraignment on the day that Renahan claims that his scrap of paper shows that an arraignment took place.

Judge Hamilton stated before four witnesses on the day before yesterday that he had not arraigned the Borregos, because he had understood that they had been arraigned before he came.

Mr. Wyllys, the clerk of the court, states in his affidavit, that the failure of the record to show the arraignment and plea of the defendants was "due to clerical omission and oversight" on the part of H.S. Clancy, who was at that time employed by him in his office, and who wrote the records of the proceedings in the case. Clancy, before seeing the affidavit of Wyllys, made affidavit that he wrote the record of the case from day to day, from notes, or verbal information given him by Wyllys, and that he was never informed by Wyllys that the defendants had been arraigned. Clancy states to your correspondent that he was not present in the court room on the day it is alleged the defendants were arraigned, ands therefore knows nothing whatever on the subject, but is very positive that if he had been present he would never have over looked such an important proceeding, and would have noted the fact on the record. He resents the statement that he is in any manner to blame for the blunder, and says that when he first discovered the defect in the transcript on file in the supreme court, he made a search of the records of the district court, expecting to find the arraignment and plea had been entered by Mr. Goshorn, the former clerk of the court under Judge Seeds.

XXX.

On Thursday, September 10, 1896, Thornton, as rough as Catron - and privy to his secret Lincoln County War crimes as his then law partner - sent Catron a letter on his official gubernatorial stationery. He then reprinted it on the front page, top center, of his September 11, 1896 *Santa Fe Daily New Mexican* under the huge headline: "Open Letter to T.B. Catron." It called Catron a "poltroon" - meaning "dastardly coward" for the anonymity - and exposed him as the author of the *Albuquerque Daily Citizen* letter defaming Chief Justice Smith the year before. Thornton's letter to Catron stated:

```
Sir;
        The following is an extract from a
communication from Santa Fé which appeared in last
Saturday's issue of the Albuquerque Citizen under
the nom de plume of XXXX:

              -: Severe Criticism :-
  - Gov. Thornton charged with prostituting his
                    office -
Editor Citizen.
   Santa Fe, Sept. 4. [it was published on
Saturday, September 5th] "Poker Bill" is now engaged
in playing a game in which the lives of four men
are at stake. He wants to have the two Borrego
brothers hung, and agrees that they should be hung
he will see that Laurencio Alarid and Patricio
Valencia are sentenced to the Penitentiary for life
- provided that they will make a confession that
will hurt Hon. T.B. Catron in the campaign [for
Territorial Delegate] this Fall.
   [Contrary to the "poker Bill" letter] "Judge
Hamilton stated before witnesses on the day before
```

yesterday [September 8, 1896] that he had not arraigned the Borregos, because he had understood that they had been arraigned before he came."

This communication was prepared in your office, and at your dictation. In keeping with your well-known character, you were too much of a poltroon to assume the responsibility therefor by affixing your name thereto.

You knew you were lying when you said that I "had agreed Laurencio Alarid and Patricio Valencia had been promised a commutation of sentence to life imprisonment as an inducement to make a confession which would hurt you in the campaign this Fall." You had but recently perjured yourself in open Court to save these assassins; **You have been shown to be closely connected with this crime** and are so filled with fear that they may confess something connecting you therewith, that you are attempting to forestall public opinion, by spreading in advance, a report that such statements as they might make, were procured by a personal reward offered to them, just as you are trying to forestall the effect of your having falsely sworn that "They had not been arraigned" by publishing what I believe to be false when you assert that "Judge Hamilton had stated in the presence of four witnesses that he had not arraigned the Borregos."

Your accusations against me are on the par with the slanderous charges which you prepared and caused to be published against the Chief Justice of this Territory last year, when you permitted the Editor of the *Albuquerque Citizen*, in whose paper you had it published, to go to prison and suffer your act. Then, as now, you sent out your slanderous shaft under a nom de plume. Now, as then, you will show yourself to be too much of a poltroon and coward to assume personal responsibility for a communication which you know, and knew when you sent it out, to be false and slanderous, **but will attempt to throw the responsibility upon some of your willing tools that you keep around you.**

W.T. Thornton

Westphall wrote, "Thornton's letter provoked Catron mightily; in fact, it appears to have been one of the few times in his political life that he considered using bodily violence." (Westphall, p. 263) (This omits Catron's years of assassinating opponents like Franklin Tolby, Robert Casey, John Tunstall, Alexander McSween, Francisco Zamora, Harvey Morris, Vincente Romero, Billy Bonney; likely murders of Alexis Grossetete, Robert Elsinger, and Francisco Chavez; and failed killings of Raymond Morley, Frank Springer, Oscar P. McMains, and Ira Leonard.)

Thornton's come-back precipitated Catron's frenzied letters of September 16, 1896. They expose Catron's insane mind, as his paranoia projects onto Thornton his own violent wishes, while he pathologically denies his "Poker Bill" attack. Catron wrote:

Dear Sir:
... As a citizen of New Mexico, of over thirty years standing, interested in her welfare, I deplore sincerely that you, as her Chief Executive, have so far forgotten the dignity and obligations of the office you hold as to write such a letter as the one you addressed to me and published in your newspaper on the 11th inst. It has the appearance of **being designed to provoke me to some act of violence, which might give your adherents an opportunity to injure me physically** ... I prefer to consider your act that of one smarting under some fancied injury, to such a degree as to render you temporarily insane. I shall try to avoid your example ...

I am surprised that you could imagine that I would write an anonymous letter about you or anyone else ...

It ought not be necessary for me to assure you, of all men living, in view of our long and intimate association --- much of the time when you were my "willing" law partner, in which the most intimidate and confidential relations existed, -- that I have not written and will not write any anonymous attack upon you or anyone else ...

I shall not attempt to reply to your scandalous insinuations, believing them to be the effects of mental aberrations, -- except to say that they are untrue in substance and intent ...

I can not notice your scurrilous and slanderous statements. They are unworthy of your high official position and do not elevate your character as a gentleman, and it would degrade me to otherwise notice them. I leave them, with a simple denial, declining to follow your precedent, and will let the people who know us judge.

       Respectfully, &c.,
  T.B. Catron

That September 16th, Catron next tried unsuccessfully to get Thornton removed as Governor (and replaced by one of Billy Bonney's killers: Pat Garrett's Deputy, John William Poe (Westphall, p. 270), showing his loyalty to all who did his dirty-work). He wrote to President Grover Cleveland with his usual outlawing: here accusing Thornton of inciting "blood-shed." It is terrifying ranting of monster Catron, frothing with rage:

I enclose for your consideration copies of two letters, one written by W.T. Thornton, who is at present Governor of New Mexico, to me; the other by me to him, in reply. I wish to call your attention to the character of the communication written by Governor Thornton and the manner in which he is degrading and debasing the office he holds .He is the head of the newspaper called the "New Mexican" published in this city, and controls its policy. He caused this letter to me to be printed in this paper. You will observe that he copies therein a communication which was previously published in the "Albuquerque Citizen" and charges that I dictated the same. I simply wish to say … that I neither wrote inspired or dictated that article … **The letter of Gov. Thornton [in the September 11, 1896 of the** *Santa Fe Daily New Mexican* **and exposing his "Poker Bill" defamation plot] is regarded here by all good citizens as being … calculated to bring about a state of unrest and possible blood-shed. It is calculated to lower the character of our territory … He is insane in his desire to hold office and exercise power … I have no doubt that Thornton's letter to me was written with the design of getting me into some kind of broil and having me killed.**

The good people of this territory have lost all respect for Mr. Thornton. If he is allowed to continue as Governor and pursue his present course, he will bring about a state of anarchy and destruction of property. This I am anxious to avoid ... I believe that Gov. Thornton should be removed from office ...

I recommend his removal as Governor and the appointment of John W. Poe ... He ... is law-abiding in every particular, and full of courage. I have no great personal acquaintance with him but have met him. ... I hope you will feel it your duty to look into this matter carefully and make this change.

Still fuming on that September 16, 1896 day, Catron wrote to Elkins to get Thornton replaced with John William Poe; stating:

Dear Elkins:
Enclosed I send you copies of two letters, one written by Gov. Thornton to me and one written by me to him. Thornton's letter to me you will perceive the character of it; it is a low / foul; villainous letter, written by him in heat of passion, when he merely guessed that I had written or dictated the letter which he quotes. As a matter of fact I had nothing to do with the letter ...

This is purely of a political nature. **The intention was to provoke me into some kind of broil and have me killed, so as to get me out of the political fight.** The federal officials who are in the territory ... expect that ... New Mexico will be admitted to statehood, and that if I am out of the way, they can have things as they like.

I write this to you in order that you may see Mr. Francis ... and through him have Mr. Cleveland remove Gov. Thornton ... This letter of Thornton's ... is calculated to stir up strife, create feelings of enmity and to bring about bloodshed. **Thornton removed the sheriff of this county for nothing and appointed one of his henchmen to the place.**

[AUTHOR'S NOTE: Catron lies about removal of Ringite Sheriff Conklin - who was shielding the murderers of Sheriff Francisco Chavez - for embezzling tax money, and replacing him with William Cunningham, who was willing to arrest those murderers.]

This sheriff ... has imported a lot of persons from the outside [for his deputies] who are known to be shooters and killers. They do not regard the law, but violate it every day.

[AUTHOR'S NOTE: This is the outlaw myth against adversaries, used by the Ring since the days of Governor Marsh Giddings.]

Mr. Thornton is no friend of the administration. He and his friends are the most violent adherents of the anti-administration democrats, in the whole country ... As this whole action of Thorntons has been taken evidently to get me killed or injured in some way, I believe we ought to take such steps as will relieve us of him as Governor ... **There is a gentleman in Lincoln Country, named John W. Poe ... who stands well throughout the territory and who is a democrat – who would make an excellent governor. You can safely recommend him** ...

[AUTHOR'S NOTE: Catron is promoting Billy Bonney's killer for replacement Governor.]

I think you ought to push this matter for me and get this man out. You can certainly find some good democrat who will do it. Very likely ex-senator Davis [Elkins's father-in-law] would be willing to present the matter. Try &c   *T.B. Catron*

It should be remembered that 27 years earlier, if Governor Lew Wallace had pardoned Ring enemy, Billy the Kid, he would have faced the same ferociously insane Catron assault - and Wallace knew it. And it also repeats the press onslaught and Secret Service action used by Catron to destroy his outlaw creation and last of the anti-Ring Regulators: "Billy the Kid."

On September 16, 1896 Thornton got Catron's letter of that day (they were both in Santa Fe), and on September 17, 1896 published, in his *Santa Fe Daily New Mexican*, "Catron Begs the Question - Replies to Gov. Thornton's Open Letter - But Does Not

Deny That the Anonymous Screed Emanated From His Office." "Screed" meant "tedious speech," and scornful Thornton added:

In the above it will be observed by the discriminating reading public that Delegate Catron makes no denial of the direct allegations in the governors open letter that the venomous and malicious anonymous communication, appearing in the Albuquerque Citizen of the 4th [sic – 5th] instant, emanated from Catron's office. The governor says he is perfectly willing to rest the case with the people of New Mexico.

Thornton's revenge worked better than Catron's, since their fellow Masons took note. Unfortunately, Thornton stopped short of becoming a Ring-insider informer.

UN-MASONIC CHARGES

Thornton's September 17, 1896 publishing of Catron's defamatory letter, resulted in Catron's February 1, 1897 charge of un-Masonic conduct by his Montezuma Lodge No. 1, as "calculated to injure Brother W.T. Thornton, in violation of his duty as a Mason. It is therefore demanded that the said T.B. Catron, be tried for said offence according to Masonic law and usage."

On February 17, 1897, Catron responded glibly, with usual victim blaming, and threats to decimate the Lodge; writing:

[The conduct violations] simply charge that I wrote and published in the "New Mexican" the letter to Thornton, and that by doing so I was guilty of un-Masonic conduct. I did write the letter but I did not publish it in the "New Mexican". I gave sent it to Thornton, and he gave it to the paper himself.

Of course I had nothing to do with the communications which were written to the "Citizen". I never heard of them until Thornton, in his letter to me, called my attention to them.

I shall make no effort to hunt up a defense in the Lodge. My letter speaks for itself and is a pure Masonic letter in spirit, and if any Lodge can find reason for disciplining me for writing such a letter as that, I do not wish to belong to it ...

> I do not know what you mean by writing a "disclaimer" of the "Citizen's" letter, to the Lodge. I am not charged with writing any letters to the "Citizen," and if I was it would require proof to establish that fact. All I would do would be simply to deny it ...
> I care nothing about what Thornton prepares against m, or does. If the Masonic Order desires to disrupt itself ... I am inclined to think they will lose a great deal of standing, and it may result in having two Lodges in the Territory.

Catron continued to obsess, with a guilty person's tendency to protest too much. On February 23, 1897, he wrote to *Daily New Mexican* president, Ringite Max Frost, to deny the Masonic charges and his anonymous *Albuquerque Daily Citizen* "Poker Bill" letter: "As for my part, I care little about the matter, and shall certainly give little attention to the charges made against me; I shall simply make a denial of them, and defy any man on earth to establish my un-Masonic conduct in my letter [sent to Thornton]."

FAILED DELEGATE RE-ELECTION

Thornton's retaliatory response may have cost Catron his 1896 re-election as Delegate to Congress. Also, September 30, 1896's *The Las Vegas Daily Optic* had written about his first term: "Mr. Catron has shown his incompetency to serve."

Catron had tried to throw the election using Richard C. Kerens, a Republican operative instrumental in Benjamin Harrison's Presidential election, and doing railroad investing with Elkins. (Westphall, p. 55) Catron wrote, on August 31, 1896, asking him to implement vote-fixing by moving miners hostile to him to another locality before the election, so they would lose residency qualification to vote. (Sluga thesis, p. 19)

And there may have been vote buying. On October 12, 1896 a P.Y. Santistevan wrote to him: "*I am doing the possible for your Election as delegate to Congress. I hope you will send me about one hundred dollars to invest it in working for your Election ... Hoping you will ... keep this as a private affair of Friends.*"

FAILURE TO SAVE THE BORREGOS

By 1897, Catron tried to call in Ring favors to halt the Borrego case murderers imminent hangings. At stake was his perfect record in shielding his hired assassins from consequences. On January 22, 1897, he wrote on his House of Representatives stationery to his law partner and Borrego case co-counsel, Charles Spiess, stating:

> I wrote you a short time ago that I thought arrangements ought to be made to have the Gonzales [y Borrego] boys removed from the penitentiary to the jail. I learned from Gus [O'Brien] that, on the contrary, the other two [Laurencio Alarid and Patricio Valencia] have been taken to the penitentiary; that Kinsell is keeping in office a Democratic jailer ... This is not right. **Mr. Kinsell owes his election to the means I furnished in that county. The county election would never have gone Republican had I not put up at least $2000.00 for that purpose, and therefore I think I am entitled to some consideration.** I wish that you would see to it that the boys are very quietly moved back to the jail as soon as possible; that as soon as they get back there they should take matters into their own hands and see that the time is extended beyond the 4th of March before they can be executed. Now I ask you to treat this as entirely confidential, to look into the matter, and to **see that Kinsell acts with me. He must remember that I spent in that county the money which carried it.**

On February 16, 1897, Catron sent a long letter to President Grover Cleveland, claiming the defendants were innocent, and requesting that he "commute their sentence to imprisonment for life, or grant them at least a respite of sixty or ninety days." Catron rolled out his usual salacious outlawing of adversaries, claiming: "The evidence upon which they were convicted was entirely circumstantial and given by persons who were alleged accomplices, or were ex-penitentiary convicts, or petty larceny thieves, or perpetrators of small crimes, or were common prostitutes." Catron also lied that Governor Thornton conducted "political persecution" by replacing the Republican county sheriff with a Democrat sheriff to secure the defendants' arrests, because the victim, Francisco Chavez, was a Democrat (omitting the removal was for embezzling public money). Despite the Borrego case judge having already rejected his lying claims, Catron stated that prejudiced Democrat jurors were chosen, and Sheriff Cunningham tampered with them. He claimed hostile Democrats manipulated public opinion to influence the judge. He even projected his own long history of malicious prosecutions by carping that New Mexico courts have a "political character" and judges work "behind the scenes" and "the present executive officials ... are determined to execute the defendants."

President Cleveland granted a respite till March 23, 1897; giving hope that incoming President, William McKinley, could assist.

A press clipping from an unknown paper sent to Catron had scrawled on it: "Congratulations You're a dandy," titled "The Borregos Respited," it paraphrased a penitentiary speech by Francisco Gonzales y Borrego in which he stated that he and his fellow prisoners "respected Mr. Catron and Mr. Spiess for the noble work they had done for them, and he told his friends and relatives to stand by Catron and Spiess always ... and he further advised his relatives to lay down their lives in their service, if necessary."

Catron's agent and spy, Melvin W. Mills, accused killer of Franklin Tolby, reported to him on February 22, 1897 that in the Santa Fe court there was dissention about the President's power to grant the respite. Mills stated: "I think they are urging Thornton to have them hung notwithstanding." And Catron's law partner, Robert C. Gortner wrote to him on March 3, 1897 that he was trying to get beneficial affidavits from jurymen and the defendants' families.

Catron himself wrote to Melvin Mills on March 8, 1897, rationalizing defeat: "The Democrats may take all the consolation they wish from the President refusing to pardon the Borregos ... All I wished was a reprieve, and I got what I wanted."

The executions took place on April 2, 1897. So one can say that Francisco Chavez is the only Ring victim whose murderers (excluding Catron) got the full penalty of the law, and was the last known person to die in Catron's 25 year reign of terror; having been preceded by: John Potts Slough, Franklin Tolby, Robert

Casey, anti-Ring Maxwell Land Grant settlers, John H. Tunstall, Dick Brewer, Frank MacNab, San Patricio massacre victims, Alexander McSween, Harvey Morris, Vincente Romero, Francisco Zamora, Lincoln County War McSweens, Tom O'Folliard, Charlie Bowdre, Billy Bonney, Alexis Grossetete, and Robert Elsinger. But that does not mean that Catron stopped trying.

REUSING PAT GARRETT

The relationship between T.B. Catron and Pat Garrett is covered by Garrett's biographer, Leon Metz, in his 1974 book, *Pat Garrett: The Story of a Western Lawman.*

By 1896, Catron - after avoiding prosecution for Francisco Chavez's murder, and being acquitted in his disbarment case - seemed to feel untouchable. So he apparently returned to eliminating another rival: Tularosa Valley rancher, Oliver Lee. He first attacked Lee by likely malicious prosecution, after outlawing him as a rustler. Using Billy Bonney's betraying court-appointed Attorney, Albert Jennings Fountain, while himself acting as his special counsel, Catron pursued Case Numbers 1489 and 1890 as "Territory of New Mexico v. William McNew and Oliver Lee" for rustling and defacing brands. (Metz, p. 171) Bill McNew, as well as a James Gilliland were employed by Lee as ranch hands. (Metz, pp. 168, 220) Furthermore, convicting Lee would politically damage Fountain's and Catron's political rival, Albert B. Fall: in the Territory since 1887, founder of the *Independent Democrat*, and friend and legal counsel to Lee since 1889. (Metz, pp. 166-169)

Lee had come from Texas to New Mexico Territory's Tularosa Valley in 1884, buying land in Dog Canyon in 1893, after having founded his Sacramento Cattle Company. He was fearless and rough, had a local power base and gunmen ranch hands, and was arguably the most substantial adversary yet to face Catron's assassins.

On January 30, 1896, Fountain and Catron achieved Lee's and McNew's indictments in the Lincoln County courthouse. There, Fountain was apparently given a threatening note, later found in his abandoned buggy. With his eight year old son, Henry, he spent the night at Blazer's Mill, on the way to his Mesilla home. (Metz, p. 171) The next day, he and his son departed. On February 1, 1896, he encountered mail carriers, and expressed concern about being followed. He and his son were never seen again. Though their bodies were never found, murder seemed obvious. Governor

William T. Thornton, offered a $2,000 reward (Metz, p. 175) and turned to the outlaw tracker, Pat Garrett - by then famous for killing Billy the Kid - to solve the sensational crime.

To Catron, it was an opportunity to recycle his outlaw myth of Lee, with him as the murderer, so he could be killed under guise of law: by hanging. And, from his Billy the Kid hunt, Catron already knew that Garrett was ideal for killing without questioning.

Garrett, on hard times because of his alcoholism, abrasive personality, and business failures, was brought from Uvalde, Texas. As Garrett wrote to his wife on February 25, 1896, it was an "opportunity for me to make money, and a chance to get the Sheriff's office of Doña Ana County ... and $8,000 in case I succeed in arresting and convicting the murderers." (Metz, p. 179). This gives a glimpse of how the Ring may also have hired him as Billy's Sheriff-assassin (or how Sheriff William Brady likewise was a beholden murderer under guise of law). After political wrangling, Garrett was made Sheriff of Doña Ana County by his Ring promoters.

On the night of July 12, 1898, at Wildy Well, after having accused employee, James Gilliland, as Lee's accomplice, Garrett ambushed seemingly sleeping Lee and Gilliland on an adobe house rooftop. But they were awake. One posseman was fatally shot. Metz quotes Lee as saying to Garrett, "I've heard you intend to kill me." (Metz, p. 210) And Garrett was forced to retreat. Lee and his fellow accused, James Gilliland, later surrendered.

To prosecute Lee and Gilliland, Catron used a complicit District Attorney, John D. Bryan - as he had used William Rynerson in 1878 in the Lincoln County War period for malicious prosecutions. On October 1, 1898, Bryan reported to Catron from Las Cruces on his official stationery: "On yesterday indictments were returned by our Grand Jury against Oliver M. Lee, William McNew and James R. Gilliland for the murder of Col. A.J. Fountain and his son Henry Fountain ... **our court is progressing very satisfactorily**."

On May 21, 1899, Catron got a report from Ringite Sidney Barnes's Las Cruces law office, about convicting (meaning hanging) Oliver Lee. It even included witnesses *"afraid to speak before this on account of their own crime"* - for Catron's usual fake defamatory affidavits in exchange for protection. The letter stated:

> *I have a couple of days down here on the Fountain cases ... I believe we can safely announce ready for trial, with excellent chances for conviction ...*
>
> *Garrett is also following a clue that is almost a certainty and which will bring in the evidence of three Mexicans resident here who had a dead beef in an arroyo near the road about two miles west of Chalk Hill and who saw the murders [sic] pass with Fountain and his son. [They] have been afraid to speak before this on account of their own crime – they were stealing Cox's cattle. But we have worked it all up through an old Indian to whom they had confessed ... and we are prepared to force the truth out of the Mexicans.*

In their 1901 trial, Lee and Gilliland were declared innocent. Garrett's dead posseman was considered a self-defense killing. Lee subsequently had extensive business dealings, and was twice elected to the legislature. He was one of Catron's few victims to not only escape his lethal clutches, but to prosper afterwards.

ATTACKING MIGUEL A. OTERO

Having failed to remove opponent Governor William Thornton, Catron tried to control the next appointment. Westphall states that on May 2, 1897, among others, Attorney Henry Waldo (Catron's past law firm member and Commander Dudley's defense lawyer) and John Riley (past partner in "The House" and Catron's business partner and agent) met with new president, William McKinley, to block appointment of Catron's enemy, Miguel A. Otero. (Westphall, p. 273) But Otero was confirmed June 2, 1897.

Of Catron, Otero wrote: "It was inevitable that we should conflict. He was dictatorial and absolutely ruthless in his methods." (Westphall, p. 276) "[He used] his brains and energy to crushing opposition to himself with no thought of public welfare." (Westphall, p. 283)

Catron then let loose his usual vengeance. He filed charges against Governor Otero to President McKinley and Vice-president Theodore Roosevelt to block his reappointment. On April 4, 1901, Catron mailed Otero accusations to ally, Richard C. Kerens. They bizarrely project himself, and repeat his perverted sexual slanders as in the 1878 Susan McSween affidavits and his October 25, 1895 *Socorro Chieftain* rant about Judge Thomas Smith. Catron wrote:

"*[Otero's] administration has been guilty of the most wholesale plunder of the resources of this territory ... This man is vicious and venal to the core . **A few years ago he ... lived with a Public Prostitute ... Otero has surrounded himself generally with the most disreputable class of men** ... We wish to help New Mexico, to protect us from outrage, wrong, robbery and plunder.*"

But Otero was reappointed. Elkins, who had tried to carry out Catron's will, wrote on June 14, 1901 to him: "Otero was appointed Governor today. There was no way on earth to defeat him; he seemed to have all the railroads behind him, 45 out of 47 members of the Republican Committee and the leading businessmen of the Territory, besides a powerful lobby here in his behalf."

After President McKinley's September 14, 1901 assassination, Catron again enlisted Elkins on November 11, 1901, writing: "*You must see that Otero is not reappointed – that some other name is sent to the senate, and if his name should be sent to the senate, you must fight him and reject it.*"

Humorless Catron even accused Otero to new President Theodore Roosevelt of having a "ring!" Westphall quoted him: "This appointment [of Otero for a second term] ... is going to injure the Territory very much and hold it down. If the ring rule which now prevails here is to continue, I am of the opinion that many of our best people will pull out." (Westphall, p. 288)

Catron next attacked an Otero backer, past Rough Rider, W.H.H. Llewellyn, by resurrecting his attempted murder case, dismissed in his boyhood as self-defense. Catron's plot failed with Rough Rider loyalist Roosevelt.

Catron then tried for a third time to have Otero removed, in what Westphall calls a "fight for control of the Republican party in New Mexico." (Westphall, p. 290). Omitted is that Catron's accusations continued weirdly to mirror his own dirty dealings. In his September 20, 1902 letter to a Dave Winters, he wrote: "[Otero backers] have made a very villainous, mean ugly fight against me ... by means of lying, by the expenditure of money, by threatening individuals ... [by] threatening to prosecute ... they have worked a great many people to change them over." (Westphall, p. 291)

Westphall tried to sweeten Catron's chillingly obsessive vindictiveness: "[Catron's] lifelong habit of persistent attention to detail finally paid off. He had been quietly adding details to a considerable body of charges against the governor." (Westphall, p. 293) Catron claimed that Otero stole military equipment. And in May of 1905, a Fred Miller, wrote to President Theodore Roosevelt on Catron's behalf, with a confirmatory postscript by W.E. Dame (possibly Dame of Catron's cipher-code on page 84 above), accusing Otero of having a ring: "The impression prevails ... that a corrupt partisan machine has been built up [by Otero] by the use of patronage and public funds ... These matters can and will be fully presented to you by Mr. Catron, if you will only give him a hearing."

All that fakery finally worked. Catron met with President Roosevelt on June 14, 1905, and ended Otero's tenure (though Otero said he refused reappointment). (Westphall, pp. 295-296)

Catron next got Herbert J. Hagerman appointed Governor. He then contacted his father, James J. Hagerman - involved in "investigating" Otero for him - to make his son appoint him Attorney General, seeking *"immediate control of all prosecutions and investigations"* - implying intended malicious prosecutions - including Otero. On November 22, 1905, he wrote:

> *[If your son] is to be appointed, I shall be very pleased ... if he will take immediate steps to have the "Augean stables" cleaned ... as Hercules was required to clean the ancient ones; to do this he should appoint a new Attorney General, a new District Attorney at this place and new Territorial officials ... Criminal prosecution should be vigorously carried out against these plunderers of the Public Funds; I know upon investigation, that the grossest rottenness will be found everywhere. What I wish ... is to be appointed Attorney General ...* **I will want, if I am appointed Attorney General, a new District Attorney at Santa Fe; one with whom I Could work in absolute harmony; he would have immediate control of all prosecutions and investigations, which should be pushed through rapidly and with energy** *...*
>
> *I write you this letter in confidence, except so far as I request to act in the matter, I would ask in that case that it go no further than what I have indicated.* (Sluga thesis, pp. 87-88)

Catron was not appointed. Governor Herbert Hagerman's administration was so corrupt anyway that President Roosevelt removed him the next year, on April 20, 1907; replacing him with George Curry, a Catron friend. So Catron did prevail.

On April 6, 1906, Catron was elected Mayor of Santa Fe, serving till 1908. In 1908, he had Elkins successfully influence the Senate for Curry's reconfirmation as Governor. (Westphall, p. 303) Curry resigned on February 25, 1909, being replaced as governor with another Catron friend, William J. Mills.

SEEKING RE-APPOINTMENT AS U.S. ATTORNEY

During Miguel Otero's governorship, having failed in his 1896 Delegate re-election, conscienceless Catron sought reappointment as Territorial U.S. Attorney - despite his forced resignation in 1878 for his Lincoln County War atrocities. This prompted a December 2, 1896 warning by his past law partner, Frank W. Clancy, who stated: "I am much surprised at what you say in your letter of the 30th of November as to the office of United States Attorney. I do not think that your refusal to do what I want in the matter is at all justified by the suggestion that you may want the place yourself ... If I cannot get your support the probabilities are great that I cannot get the place ... Moreover, it is possible that your ceasing to participate actively in local [New Mexico] affairs might have the effect of allowing a good deal of the bitterness of your political *and personal* enemies in New Mexico to subside, - to some extent at least, - a feeling which clearly led to your recent defeat."

Elkins tried to pull strings for Catron in Washington, writing to him, in a letter marked "confidential," on December 4, 1897: "At first there was no doubt in the mind of the President nor of the Attorney-General as to your appointment ... but as time went on it became apparent that somebody here or elsewhere overcame the good things I had said for you in the mind of the president. I have been to see him frequently in your behalf, more than you have any idea; also the Attorney General ... My idea is that these people in

New Mexico have represented to the President that I wanted you appointed and certain Judges in order to control litigation, especially about grants. I am satisfied something of this kind has been said."

Catron also called in past bribes for this as payback, writing on December 16, 1897, to a Joshua S. Reynolds in Albuquerque: *"I am entitled to same from a political standpoint ... having made the race paying all the expenses of the territorial committee."*

Opposition to Catron's appointment came from past Governor Lew Wallace, then safely out of the Ring clutches, and aware of Catron's Ringite abuse of power during his own administration. On August 4, 1897, Catron wrote with understatement to Elkins about Wallace: *"He and I were not on friendly terms while he was governor."* Westphall's spin is that the rejected appointment was "prejudiced by his enemies in Washington." (Westphall, p. 281)

REWRITING HISTORY

In his speech on October 26, 1898 at the Bernalillo County Republican Convention at Albuquerque in support of his Ringite lackey Pedro Perea, running for Delegate to Congress against Harvey B. Fergusson - against whom Catron had lost in 1896 - Catron flaunted the Ring's rewritten history to his apparently Hispanic audience, concealing its land-grabbing, water stealing of his Tularosa Land and Cattle Company, oppression and murder of opponents, election fixing, and even Sheriff William Brady's embezzlement of Lincoln County taxes for Ring cattle; stating:

Pedro Perea ... says that he and his ancestors, you and your ancestors, have lived in this country for the last two hundred years; you have occupied the soils cultivated the lands and used the waters of the Rio Grande, you have obtained the property rights in those waters. The democratic [Democrats] idea of progression gentlemen, is that you ought to give up all you have to some capitalists, who may come here from the States, and allow them to appropriate, for instance, all this water, and have you buy it from them ...
If you put it into the hands of these old fossils ... you will have a repetition of the record of Santa Fe county, where the Democratic sheriff

who was collector for eight consecutive years
appropriated to himself and party the entire
revenue of the county ... In every instance from
Taos to Dona Ana and from Union to Grant the
democratic party has stood for fraud and
oppression.

Delegate Fergusson's speech, on October 29, 1898 in Santa Fe, cited Ring tactics, stating: " The Republican party to-day is the party that ... now proposes to disfranchise [sic] the Spanish-Americans of New Mexico."

STATEHOOD AND SENATORSHIP

Westphall dates Catron's goal of being New Mexico's first senator to his original cross-country trip with Elkins: "This consideration [of being a state senator] is so extensively indicated in [Catron's] correspondence as to give credence to the tradition that he and Elkins first mutually agreed to aspire to this lofty station when traveling to New Mexico in 1866." (Westphall, p. 311)

He adds monetary motive from Catron's February 3, 1894 letter to Richard C. Kerens: "If I can get New Mexico a state ... my property will be doubled in value." (Westphall, p. 312)

By 1892, Catron was actively strategizing with Elkins a senatorship for himself, writing on August 15, 1892 to him:
"If I should run for [Territorial] delegate this
fall and be elected, I would never take the seat
because the State would be admitted and Senators
elected before December 1893. In that event, the
candidate who runs for delegate, if successful,
would have plain sailing to become one of the
Senators. If I should refuse to run[for delegate],
I fear it would cause considerable dissatisfaction,
and render it very difficult to secure an election
as Senator myself."

By February 1, 1910, with statehood likely, Catron worried about changes to its bill - which he had helped to draft - which infringed on his and the Ring's cash cows - land and water. So he wrote to Elkins to intervene and argue states' rights. By September 19, 1910, Catron was optimistic, writing to Elkins:

"I think my chances [for senatorship] are very good, but there are a number of aspirants and they might all combine against me. I do not think they can however. Everything looks well here."

Elkins died on January 4, 1911, missing the statehood resolution signed by President Taft on August 21, 1911. New Mexico became the 47th state on January 6, 1912; with its Santa Fe Ring intact.

On November 15, 1911, Catron wrote from Republican Central Committee Headquarters to get legislators' backing, and omitting his vicious and bloody road to the top; stated: "I have been a resident of New Mexico for the last 45 years; all of my interests are identified with New Mexico: I believe I understand the wants of the people and have as good ideas for their welfare as any other citizen, and I believe that I can do as much as any other citizen towards accomplishing something in Congress for the benefit of the state. I, therefore, hope that I may receive your support."

U.S. SENATOR CATRON

When Catron ran for senator, past Franklin Tolby murder accomplice, Melvin Mills, his "confidant in crucial political matters" (Westphall, p. 349), wrote to him on September 12, 1911: "There are a few men who are candidates that I guess have some money ... some of this filthy stuff to scatter about. If so, they will likely be able to work up a combination that will lay us one side; not withstanding all our service in behalf of New Mexico." (Westphall, p. 350)

Westphall ignores Mills's bribery hint, as well as denying contemporary press accounts that Catron did bribe legislators to get their votes for him as senator. (Westphall, p. 354) But Westphall quotes Catron's son and law partner, Charles C. Catron, implying legislators' bribery. On June 3, 1921, Charles wrote to a Major Harry F. Cameron after his father's death: "My father probably spent over a million dollars in following up his hobby [of politics]. I in turn have learned to detest it ... and have conducted all of my father's business in [law]." (Westphall, p. 387)

On April 2, 1912, Catron was sworn in as New Mexico's Senator, along with Albert Fall. Catron held office from March 27, 1912 to March 3, 1917. He did not seek re-election.

As Senator, Catron's attitude about the Spanish-American War is revealing. Westphall paraphrases a *Washington Times* article of February 10, 1913 to present Catron's fear" about Mexican uprisings. Catron believed that: "Mexicans ... were perfectly equal to starting five new revolutions in five days ... He was convinced that intervention was inevitable and should have been carried out earlier." (Westphall, p. 375) And on May 28, 1911, Catron had written to his son Thom: *"[I]t is the disposition of most all of the Spanish-American people to indulge in revolutions."* (Hefferan, thesis, p. 111)

Catron's fear of Hispanic "revolutions" dovetails as motive for his massive military intervention in the 1878 Lincoln County War Battle - with Fort Stanton Commander N.A.M. Dudley bringing in a Gatling machine gun and howitzer cannon capable of leveling Lincoln - where opponents were primarily Hispanic; and for his comparable overkill in 1880 by using the highest echelon Secret Service Operative to eliminate the possible future instigator of another Hispanic revolt: Billy Bonney.

DEATH AND LEGACY

At 80, Catron died in bed on May 15, 1921, 79 days after still-existing Catron County was carved out in New Mexico on February 25, 1921, as a disgraceful memorial to the perpetrator of so much wickedness.

A George W. Prichard, for Catron's eulogy, effused and lied: "Hypocrisy was never laid at his door ... No man had a bigger kinder heart than he ... Thomas Benton Catron had his faults. Who has not? But they were the faults of a gladiator. He punished his enemies while the combat was on, but like a true fighter, he laid aside his weapon when the battle was over. He did not cherish animosity toward an enemy. Sometimes he tried to make himself think so, but his friends knew better. He never had an enemy that he would not take by the hand and help when appealed to. His enemies were generally self-constituted enemies, either from jealously or fancied wrongs. Those who had the hardest things to say of him knew the least about him ... The last half-century of the state would be incomplete with the work of his life left out ... Not only those of this generation, but those that will follow us will share a knowledge of the life and fame of this great man."

An E. Dana Johnson of the *Santa Fe New Mexican* skirted truth: "He was frankly a 'practical politician;' the appellation 'boss' complimented instead of offending him." (Westphall, p. 395) And Victor Westphall added his own flattery: "As Confederate, as Unionist, and as an American, [Catron] had faith in the land and its people and gave unstintingly of his time, his fortune, and his energy in a personal demonstration of that faith." (Westphall, p. 383)

Omitted by all were Thomas Benton Catron's real achievements: he was a murdering criminal who never got caught; and he invented a form of organized crime in which conspiring cronies created a fiefdom, insulated from exposure or prosecution; so that his perfect machine of corrupt and colluding public officials continues untouched, unchanged, and hidden to the present day.

CHAPTER 6

WASHINGTON RING BOSS, STEPHEN BENTON ELKINS

STEPHEN BENTON ELKINS

SUMMARY: Attorney and politician, Stephen Benton Elkins, was Thomas Benton Catron's co-founder of the Santa Fe Ring. Arriving first in New Mexico Territory, he brought in Catron as a law partner, before leaving in 1873 to a Washington, D.C. career exerting Ring influence. Like Catron, he was never prosecuted for crimes which left him rich and powerful in the Territory as a legislator, Attorney General, U.S. Attorney, and Delegate to Congress; then as U.S. Senator from West Virginia and Secretary of War.

Like Thomas Benton Catron, Stephen Benton Elkins had a loyalist biographer: Oscar Doane Lambert, author of the 1955 *Stephen Benton Elkins: American Foursquare*. As Lambert gushed: "Nature had endowed [Elkins] with those rare qualities which prepare one for unusual service ... which humanity receives from its greatest souls." (Lambert, p. 26) And the Santa Fe Ring has no mention. Even so, as with Catron's hagiographer, Victor Westphall, the devil emerges in Lambert's details.

Elkins, named, like Catron, after Missouri's racist "manifest destiny" Senator, Thomas Benton, was born in Perry County, Ohio, on September 26, 1841 to a slave-trader father, and moved at age three to Westport, Missouri. At the Masonic School in Lexington, Missouri, he met Catron. They attended the University of Missouri together, with Elkins graduating its law department in 1860. Serving two years in the Civil War, he was a Union captain in the 77th Missouri Infantry; mustering out in 1863.

That 1863, Elkins met a Henry Connelly, a Santa Fe Trail trader appointed governor of Arizona Territory by President Abraham Lincoln; and a Richard C. McCormick, appointed its Secretary. In 1864, Elkins joined a Connelly wagon train to New Mexico Territory, studying Spanish on the trip, and settled in Doña Ana County's Mesilla. There he read law with another new friend, Chief Justice Kirby Benedict, who backed him for the law bar that year; when Elkins was also appointed District Attorney of the Third Judicial District, serving until 1867.

In 1864 Elkins was elected to the Territorial legislature for Doña Ana County, serving until 1865, and moving his law practice to Santa Fe. There he specialized in land grant titles and apparently conceived the land grab scheme which birthed the Santa Fe Ring.

In June of 1866, Elkins returned to Missouri to marry a Sarah Jacobs, and traveled back with her and Catron by wagon train. (Lambert, p. 32) Lambert addressed the men's planned scheme with racism, likely shared by Elkins, whom he called "all in all, Anglo-Saxon." (Lambert, p. 55) "Spaniards and Mexicans had millions of acres ... but little interest in retaining it. They were too indolent to cultivate the soil and gave no attention to speculating it." (Lambert, p. 36) Lambert emphasized Elkins's grant lands focus: "[He] possessed a keen insight into the enormous possibilities of timber, minerals, coal and the fertile lands that remained hidden in the region." (Lambert, p. 49)

Lambert, unashamed by the speculation, stated: "A number of speculators, among whom [Elkins] was the master spirit, resolved to acquire legal titles to some of the old Spanish grants that showed prospects of becoming valuable property ... In order to clear these cases he set to work in the office of the Surveyor General of the Territory whose duties came under the supervision of the Department of the Interior of the United States. As he cleared case after case, Elkins would buy the title from alleged Mexican owners, have surveys made, pay off the delinquent claims and taxes and have the titles confirmed by the Commissioner of the General Land Office in Washington. The Surveyor General of the Territory made the surveys and filed his reports in the office of the Secretary of the Interior. In this manner Elkins and his coworkers validated their [own] claims." (Lambert, p. 34)

Lambert confirms that speculation was how Elkins acquired about two million acres; becoming, like Catron, one of America's largest land holders. (Lambert, pp. 34, 50) As to their decisive victim, Lambert states that Lucien Maxwell hired Elkins to secure the title to his land grant, paying him the huge retainer of $7,000. (Lambert, p. 31) Omitting Elkins's and Catron's initial 1870 purchase from Maxwell, Lambert confirms Elkins as negotiating the subsequent 1870 sale, with Colorado Senator Jerome Bunty Chaffe, to a Dutch syndicate for about $1,400,000. (Lambert, p. 31) Omitted is the additional manipulation of their dupe, Lucien Maxwell, into using his profit to found the First National Bank of Santa Fe; followed by Elkins supplanting him as its president, and serving till 1883. Lambert confirms Elkins's intended use of the Maxwell Land Grant for railroad development, and using his 1873 Delegate election to Congress to implement confirmation of the Maxwell Land Grant's title. (Lambert, p. 35)

Santa Fe Ring-exposing author, Norman Cleaveland, in his 1971 book, *The Morleys: Young Upstarts on the Southwest Frontier*, quotes a September 14, 1892 speech by a past New Mexico Territorial Surveyor General about Elkins and his land grant abuses: "Elkins dealings were mainly in Spanish grants, which he bought for a very small price. Elkins became a member of the land ring of the Territory, and largely through his influence the survey of these grants was made to contain hundreds of thousands of acres that did not belong to them. He thus became a great land holder, for through the manipulation of committees in Congress, grants thus illegally surveyed were confirmed with their factitious boundaries." (Cleaveland, p. 74)

Elkins was appointed as Territorial Attorney General in 1867 by Ringite Governor Marsh Giddings. Lambert notes that Elkins's serving under federal U.S. Attorney General William M. Evarts, made "a lifelong friendship" with him. (Lambert, p. 39) Omitted is that Evarts, as Secretary of State, became a valuable Ring loyalist in President Rutherford B. Hayes's cabinet during the Lincoln County War period's Washington, D.C. Ring cover-ups.

In 1867, Elkins was promoted to Territorial U.S. Attorney, first by President Andrew Johnson, then by President Ulysses S. Grant; serving till 1870. In 1872, he was elected Delegate to Congress, and re-elected in 1874; serving from March 4, 1873 to March 3, 1877. That gave him the Washington foothold for Ring influence. His Delegate elections were called fraudulent. Norman Cleaveland stated in *The Morleys*: "Elkins ... received a certificate of election, though he actually had not received a majority of votes. He was counted in ... by the leaders of the Republican Party ... This is a rather graphic example of how the Santa Fe Ring controlled the election machinery as well as the agencies of government in New Mexico." (Cleaveland, p. 77)

In Congress, Elkins added powerful friends: Speaker of the House James Blaine (whom he backed in failed bids for president); President Grant; President Hayes; and future President, Garfield. And after Elkins's wife died in 1872, he made a life-changing alliance. On April 14, 1875, he married Hallie Davis, daughter of rich and powerful West Virginia Senator Henry Gassaway Davis. Davis owned West Virginia land rich in timber and minerals - especially coal for railroads - and made Elkins his business partner. (Lambert, p. 53)

Elkins's second election as Territorial Delegate to Congress was also accused of fraud. By then, he was nationally accused as a Ringite. On March 13, 1876, *The Boston Daily Globe's* editorial was: "New Mexico, A Sorry Showing for a Would-be State, Tweed's Disciples Preying on the Populace, How the Territorial Ring is Run, Why the Territory Should Not Be Made a State." It stated:

The recent election furnishes some examples of political fraud and corruption almost unparalleled. A.B. [sic] Elkins, the Republican nominee for Delegate, had the wires laid, as he and his friends supposed, to carry the Territory by a tremendous majority, which result would have given them further opportunities to secure passage through Congress of the bill admitting New Mexico as a state, and elect themselves into office long enough to complete some enormous land robberies which are under way. At the eleventh hour however, Pedro Valdez, an almost unknown man, appeared for delegate on the Anti-Ring ticket ... [T]he popular vote for him ... showed defeat for Elkins. Not to be thwarted, however, word was immediately sent out to several of the counties, where the officials were in intrigue, to hold the returns until it was known how many votes were needed to elect the Republican ticket ... in one of the counties with less than 600 population and 125 voters, 1700 majority was given for Elkins ... The fraudulent ballots and tally sheets were all in the handwriting of a well known politician, and several instances prominent officials openly stuffed ballot boxes with perfect impunity.

Delegate Elkins's 1876 backing of Rutherford B. Hayes for president became key to the Ring's crime cover-ups in its rapacious 1870's growth. As Lambert stated: "[Hayes] manifested considerable reliance" on Elkins's counsel. (Lambert, p. 132)

When Elkins's second term as Delegate to Congress expired in 1877, he opened a Washington, D.C. "lucrative [law] practice ... buying and selling land in New Mexico ... [and] shares in his mining stock." (Lambert, pp. 53-54) In 1878, Elkins moved his law practice to New York. (Lambert, pp. 53-54, 88) Omitted is that Catron did much of that land dealing for their New Mexico Territory Ring, while Elkins got the titles with his Washington contacts. Lambert did admit: "Atchison, Chaffee, Catron and others had become railroad architects of the Southwest, all of whom were now on intimate business terms with Stephen B. Elkins." (Lambert, p. 57) In 1878, Elkins, Henry Davis, Davis's two brothers, and a political ally of Catron's, R.C. Kerens, formed the West Virginia Central and Pittsburg Railway. In addition, were other Elkins-Davis enterprises, like Davis Coal & Coke.

By 1880, " Elkins ... gave his attention to selling land in New Mexico, buying coal and timber in West Virginia, and operating silver mines in Colorado." (Lambert, p. 88) He also backed Garfield's presidential run, and was considered for Secretary of the Interior; as recommended by his fellow Missourian, Henry L. Waldo (Lambert, p. 89) - the Catron law firm attorney who had defended Commander N.A.M. Dudley and was then Chief Justice.

In 1884, Elkins was elected Executive Chairman of the National Republican Committee, and became a political force. He then backed James Gillespie Blaine for President, uniting with Illinois Senator John A. Logan, who traveled with him to Santa Fe to view his lands and visit ex-Senator Gerome B. Chaffee in Colorado. (Lambert, p. 93) Lambert does note that the Massachusetts Reform Club, which included William Evarts and past Hayes administration Secretary of the Interior Carl Schurz, "denounced Blaine and Logan as corrupt men dealing in corrupt practices," and favored Democrat Grover Cleveland. (Lambert, p. 99) Elkins, by Ring-style defamatory affidavits, then accused Cleveland of "being a grossly dissipated man who indulged in debauchery." (Lambert, p. 100) And when Cleveland won, Elkins claimed vote miscount. (Lambert, p. 102)

Lambert states: "[I]n a great measure Stephen B. Elkins named the President of the United States from 1889 to 1893." (Lambert, p. 119) In 1888, Blaine, then not running, schemed with Elkins in a March 1, 1888 letter to elect Benjamin Harrison. Blaine wrote: "Sherman ought not to be nominated ... [H]e is not in sympathy with our friends ... The one ... who in my judgment can make the best run is Ben Harrison ... Keep this letter sacredly-private." (Lambert, p. 120)

As to Elkins's New Mexico Territory interests, by 1884, he owned 26,026 gold and coal-rich acres of the Cerrillos Coal and Iron Company in Santa Fe County; which he sold for $1,000,000 in 1891, to the Atchison, Topeka and Santa Fe Railway Company.

Lambert wrote about a land deal of Elkins with Catron: "Thomas B. Catron, Elkins' friend of long standing ... bought and sold land, took part in mining adventures and railroad building [in New Mexico Territory]. On June 20, 1902, Catron offered to Elkins a half-interest in the Tierra Amarilla Land Grant, containing about 500,000 acres, and located in New Mexico and Colorado ... Catron added, 'I also authorize you to sell all my interest in said tract of land on such terms as to you may appear best.'" (Lambert, pp. 77-78)

Lambert stated that President Benjamin Harrison relied on Elkins as "one of his confidential advisors," writing jokingly, for example, to Elkins on February 22, 1889, after putting James Blaine on his cabinet: "I cannot put all your friends on the Cabinet, for they are more than eight." (Lambert, pp. 130)

Elkins also recommended ousted Ringite Governor Samuel Beach Axtell for New Mexico Territory Chief Justice. Harrison refused on June 30, 1891, writing: "I found that he would be attacked in the committee of the judiciary." (Lambert, p. 133)

Lambert states that, in 1891, Elkins was lending money to Russell B. Harrison, President Harrison's son, who let him know on August 15, 1891 that the Cabinet position of Secretary of War would be available. (Lambert, p. 135) By December of 1891, President Harrison appointed Elkins; and he served till 1893.

Elkins was even rumored to be Harrison's Vice-President pick if he ran in 1892. (Lambert, p. 141) But the next President was Grover Cleveland.

After Elkins resigned as Secretary of War in 1893, he returned to running "the largest [coal] mines and the nearest deposits of steam-making coal to the Atlantic coast." (Lambert, p. 160)

In 1894, Elkins was elected by the West Virginia legislature as U.S. Senator. He served until his death.

As Senator, Elkins influenced President William McKinley; stating: "I have introduced a thousand men to [him]." (Lambert, p. 225)

During McKinley's administration, a scandal revealed Elkins's protected status. On June 8, 1897, his tax evasion was exposed by the Cincinnati *Commercial Tribune*. Lambert paraphrased:

It seems that Senator Elkins was one of the five stockholders in the North American Commercial Company that had leased from the United States the sea Islands of Alaska. While carrying on the business of taking seals and selling the pelts, the company had failed to pay the legal taxes or rentals. In view of this default, the Government instituted a suit against the North American Commercial Company and secured a judgment of $1,188,000. The defendants appealed. While the case was pending in the courts, the Company continued to slaughter seals. Consequently, if the case could be held in the courts several years for final adjudication, the Company could have time to complete the destruction of the herds, give up its contracts and forfeit its bond guarantee of $500,000 to the Government. (Lambert, pp. 224-225)

While the government feigned action (like suggesting branding of seals), in 1898, Elkins got West Virginian, George M. Bowers, appointed U.S. Fish Commissioner. Bowers took over the Bering Sea fisheries, and left Elkins unimpeded and unprosecuted. (Lambert, p. 225)

By the turn of the century, Elkins was robber baron rich. He lived in his Deer Park, Maryland, Halliehurst mansion - named after his wife - with "the general appearance of a medieval castle," adjacent to his father-in-law's Graceland mansion. (Lambert, p. 72) In the valley below, he founded his town of Elkins. He owned 100,000 West Virginia acres with coal and timber rights, had New Mexico Territory grant lands and mines with Catron, and was building railroads. In 1890, he organized, and became president of, the Elk Garden Coal Company, joining the Davis Coal and Coke Company. It got its charter in 1906 as the West Virginia Coal Company, with stock of $6,000,000. (Lambert, p. 75)

By 1900, with McKinley's Vice-President dead, Elkins lost in a bid for the job to Theodore Roosevelt. McKinley died in office in 1901, making Roosevelt President (and letting one contemplate how close America had come to having a Ring boss president).

By 1904, for Roosevelt's re-election, Elkins was again a possible Vice-President. (Lambert p. 252) Despite his seal killing tax problems, he was made Chairman of the Interstate Commerce committee. (Lambert, p. 285) In 1908, he was a possible presidential candidate, but Roosevelt backed William H. Taft. (Lambert, p. 295) As a Jae Spears wrote for Elkins's biography in

2016's *The West Virginia Encyclopedia*: "For many years he operated a formidable machine within the [Republican] party."

By mid-1910, Elkins was ill. Brutish Catron wrote him on December 21, 1910: "I hear you are suffering from cancer of the stomach ... and you are starving to death." (Lambert, p. 327) On November 8, 1910, for the December 1910 Congressional session, Elkins traveled in his private railway car on the Baltimore and Ohio Railroad to Washington, D.C. He died on January 5, 1911.

Oscar Doane Lambert eulogized: "Big ideas [like his] ... compose the substance that made America great." (Lambert p. 78) In truth, as Elkins's extensive communications with T.B. Catron show, he shielded, nurtured, and plotted for their Santa Fe Ring, enabling its legal immunity, power ascendency, and tactics of terrorism and murder.

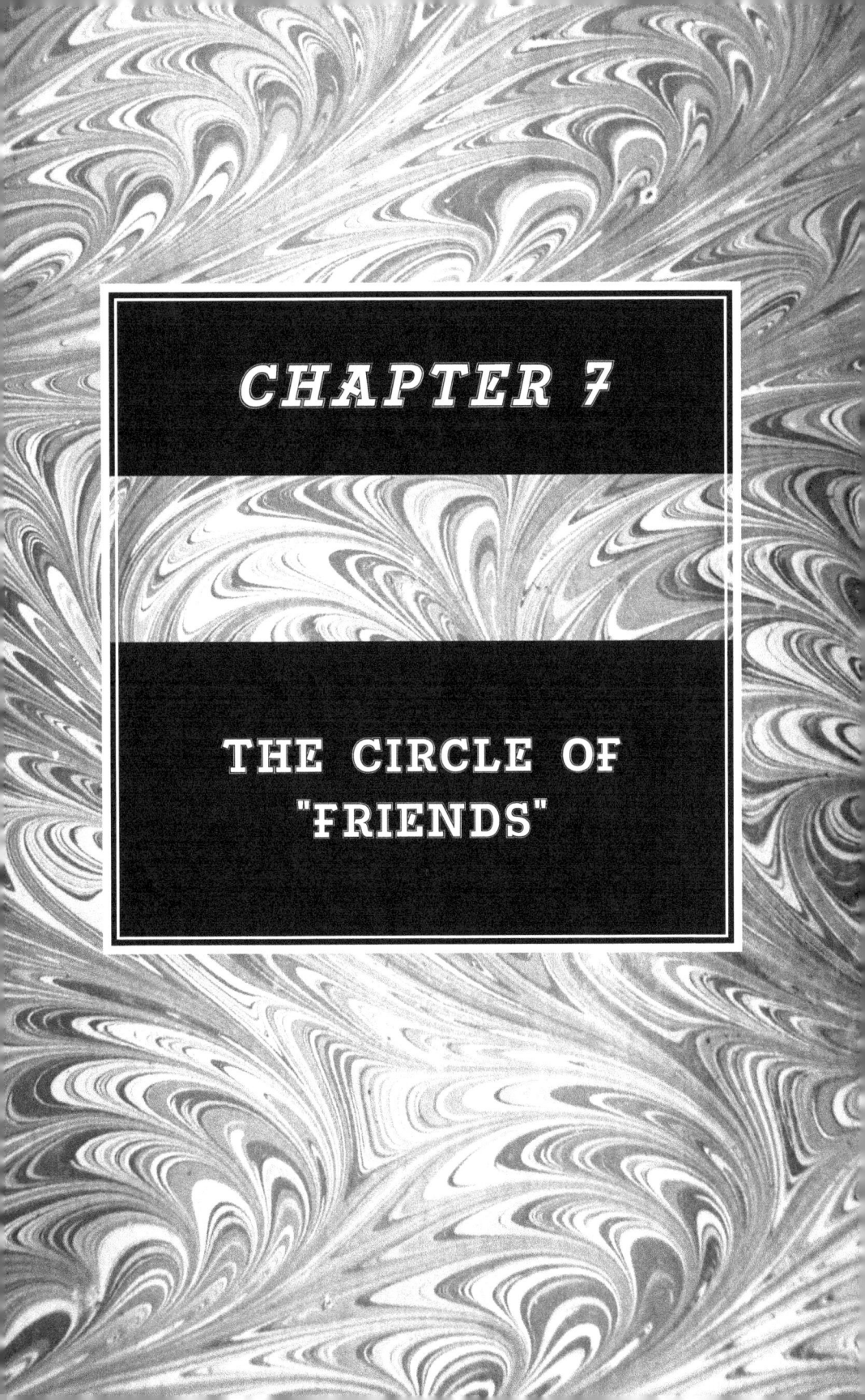

CHAPTER 7

THE CIRCLE OF "FRIENDS"

CORRUPT CRONIES

SUMMARY: Demonstrating the Santa Fe Ring's loyal patronage, is the continuity of players before, during, and after the Lincoln County War period. Every Ringite got life-long profit and legal immunity for their crimes.

One can grasp the Santa Fe Ring's pervasive power by tracking its corrupt "friends," who spawned the 1870's anti-Ring uprisings. Many were murderers. All profited. All were immune to successful prosecution. All died in old age, in bed.

WILLIAM BREEDEN: FIRST FRIEND

SUMMARY: Attorney and the Territory's Republican party founder, William Breeden, began Ring domination by backing T.B. Catron from his 1866 arrival; and likely influenced Acting Governor W.F.M. Arney to appoint him District Attorney for the Third Judicial District, and to appoint S.B. Elkins as Attorney General the next year.

Catron and Elkins gave birth to the Santa Fe Ring with William Breeden as mid-wife.
He was born in Mason County, Kentucky, on February 18, 1841, and was related to President James Madison on his paternal grandmother's side. When he was 12, his family moved to Keokuk, Iowa. After briefly attending the Lexington Masonic College in Lexington, Missouri, he went west in search of Pike's Peak gold. Returning to Missouri in 1860, he taught school until his Union Civil War service; interestingly participating in Brigadier General Lew Wallace's disastrous Battle of Shiloh. After that war and administrative work in Washington, D.C., he was appointed, in 1867, by President Andrew Johnson as assessor of internal revenue for New Mexico Territory; and served to 1869.

In 1867, he founded the New Mexico Republican party. In July of 1870, he was made clerk of the First Judicial District Court and the Supreme Court. In 1872, he began law practice in Santa Fe, and in 1874 was appointed Territorial Attorney General by Ringite Governor Marsh Giddings. And in 1876 and 1878, he was reappointed by Ringite Governor S.B. Axtell.

In 1875, he was elected to the legislature's Council from Santa Fe County, and was re-elected in 1878. In 1881, he was re-appointed as Attorney General by Lew Wallace's replacement, Ringite Governor Lionel Sheldon. He was also U.S. Attorney for a total of 14 years. In 1881, he was President of the New Mexican Printing and Publishing Company (which published the Ringite *Santa Fe New Mexican*) and Vice-President of Catron's and Elkins's Second National Bank of Santa Fe. He was then in law partnership in Santa Fe with Henry Waldo, originally in Catron's law firm. He died on January 28, 1913, with a laudatory death notice in *The New York Times*.

On May 31, 1874, Breeden wrote as Chairman of the Republican Committee to Elkins, newly elected as Delegate to Congress (in an allegedly rigged election): "*We all feel proud of you – You have distinguished yourself and the Territory ... Catron was well when I left him ... **Ben Stevens** has been very ill but is recovering.*" **[AUTHOR'S NOTE: In March of 1876, Second Judicial District Judge Benjamin Stevens plotted with Governor S.B. Axtell, to kill Colfax County anti-Ring activists]**

COLFAX COUNTY KILLERS

SUMMARY: In the 1870's Colfax County War, local Ringites were accused of murdering anti-Ring leader, Franklin Tolby, then colluding with Governor S.B. Axtell to kill others. All were shielded by T.B. Catron from prosecution.

MELVIN WHITSON MILLS

Attorney and Territorial legislator, Melvin Whitson Mills, was an accused assassin, with others, of Colfax County's anti-Ring Reverend Franklin Tolby. He was shielded from prosecution by Catron, then profited greatly as his business and political agent.

Mills was born in Sparta, Ontario, Canada on October 11, 1845. He attended Michigan State University law department, graduating in 1868; and moving to New Mexico Territory's Elizabethtown to seek gold in the pre-sale Maxwell Land Grant. As a Ringite knowing Lucien Maxwell, he may have set up Maxwell's ruinous contact with Catron and Elkins.

In 1870, he settled in Cimarron, then the county seat. In 1872, he began multiple legislature terms, amid accusations of voting fraud. In September of 1875, he was accused of murdering Franklin Tolby, with fellow Ringite, Robert Longwill, using thugs, Cruz Vega and Manuel Cardenas. Catron blocked his prosecution via Governor S.B. Axtell's illegal transfer of Colfax County courts to Taos County. In 1876, Mills was front-man for Catron's failed scheme to buy the Maxwell Land Grant for himself for back taxes.

In 1879, in the legislature, Mills rewarded fellow Ringite, Frank Springer, by moving Colfax County's seat to his town named Springer. Mills was appointed District Attorney by Ringite Governor Lionel Sheldon, then by Governor Edmund G. Ross. He owned a 6,000 acre ranch in the Canadian River canyon, 5,000 acres in Aquaje Ranch near Springer, extensive fruit orchards, and a 20 room, three story mansion in Springer.

Mills died in Springer on August 19, 1825. His biography and obituary in 1926's *The New Mexico Historical Review* called him "one of the makers of history in the Southwest."

Mills's prolific advising of Catron, in co-ordination with Elkins, is seen in his February 1, 1889 letter from New York City:

Would you take in a little of the political situation as we have it here ... There are several applicants and aspirants for Governor, the leading being Prince, Dwyer & Harrison & Otero with Chavez standing in my judgment in order named – **I hear even here that Lew Wallace will exert a felt influence for or against us** *– Col. D. [Dwyer] I saw yesterday, he did not unfold many of his plans to me as he tacks me on to you and he is not looking for much support from you I guess ... I could if it was desired smooth over differences and leave you and he running smooth ... But you know best what you prefer done and I will not patch up old clothes if the fellows who want to wear them would rather run around with their Asses out themselves –* **Elkins seems to favor Moriano but has not got much faith in his appointment and I guess it will be one of the other 3 or some dark horse** *–*

I was going to say to you a number of times that if any suit could be commenced by me for Rio Arriba Co for your Tierra Amarilla

Grant & that by filing a stipulation all signed by us now the taxes could be adjusted I would do it ... As we arranged I will do anything I can to adjust that for you..

On September 6, 1892, electioneering for Catron with Ringite, Ralph Emerson Twitchell, Mills spelled out Catron's enemies, grudge-holding, vote buying, and apparent bribes; writing:

My Dear Sir [R.E. Twitchell]:
I have all your communications ... I have written to every one of our friends to urge all our friends if any body will support Mr. Catron to pay their poll tax **and if any body be to poor to do so, to pay it for them and draw on me &c.** ... **Also I am stirring up the County Committee and getting all prospective candidates and our friends to subscribe to a fund for that and other election purposes** ... We must make Mr. Catron make all the peace he can with his enimies ... We shall of course lose Colfax and Mora Counties ... **We have a White Cap organization [anti-Ring and anti-land grabbing] up here we did not have to contend with before last election. Then we have got a few devils who hate Catron, who think their time has come now and they are whetting their scythes. All the [Maxwell land] Grant settlers swear vengeance against us this time and I do not know what I am to do with them.**
I enclose a list of fellows to send documents to and if Mr. Catron would write each and every one of them it would make votes for us.
Yours very respectfully,
MWMills

ROBERT LONGWILL

William Keleher considered Dr. Robert Longwill a central Ringite, writing: "The original 'Santa Fe Ring' was composed of T.B. Catron, Robert H. Longwill, H.L. Waldo, Frank Springer, and A. Staab." (Keleher, *The Fabulous Frontier* p. 125) Longwill was prominent in Colfax County history, when Catron was assassinating anti-Ring opponents there. In 1873, he was sent to the Territorial legislature from Colfax County, while his companion Ringite, Melvin W. Mills, was elected to the Territorial legislature in elections allegedly fixed by local Ringite, Francisco "Pancho" Griego.

In 1875, at Catron's apparent instigation, he and fellow Ringite, Melvin Mills, hired thugs, Manuel Cardenas and Cruz Vega, to murder anti-Ring activist Franklin Tolby. When he and Mills were accused, Catron intervened, giving him safe harbor in Santa Fe, where he was hired by missionary nun, Blandina Segale, to head her hospital. Since Catron was her attorney, he may have made the connection. When she left the Territory in 1889, Longwill advertised in the September 26, 1889 *Santa Fe Daily New Mexican*, with premises connected to Ringite Attorney Sidney Barnes and Sheriff Romulo Martinez (a Billy Bonney hanging trial prosecutor, and the Sheriff who jailed him in Santa Fe awaiting his hanging trial). Longwill announced: "R.H. Longwill, M.D. has moved to the east end of Palace avenue, to the Romulo Martinez house, formerly occupied by Col. Barnes."

Longwill's March 1, 1895 *Santa Fe Daily New Mexican* obituary called him a Director of the First National Bank of Santa Fe (Catron's and Elkins's stronghold since 1870) and "an active figure in the development of the Cimarron mining district." Added truthfully was: "He made lots of money ... He never let his right hand know what his left was doing. Dr. Longwill had his faults."

Catron stayed in contact with Longwill. On May 12, 1891, an Alice Moore McComas used Catron to locate him. After he died, a W.C. Roy contacted Catron on April 4, 1895 to settle his sheep-grazing dispute on land claimed by Longwill in Colfax and Mora Counties. In fact, Melvin Mills, managed the estate. On April 1, 1895, had tried to evict settlers like Roy; threatening to sue them.

LINCOLN COUNTY AGENTS

SUMMARY: Catron's earliest businesses of money-lending and military beef contracts yielded a relationship with the Fort Stanton sutler store of L.G. Murphy and Company. Its partners and associates all became key Ringites in the Lincoln County War period, when Catron sought mercantile and cattle monopoly by murdering merchant-rancher John Tunstall. Shielded by the Ring from prosecution, these criminal agents profited immensely for life.

EMIL FRITZ

Emil Christian Adolf Fritz founded "The House" with Lawrence Murphy. His 1874 intestate death initiated a dispute for his life insurance money, which the Ring used for malicious prosecution of Alexander McSween and John Tunstall.

Fritz was born on March 3, 1832 near Stuttgart, Germany, and had 10 siblings. (So Attorney McSween properly insisted on contacting his German heirs - besides his local siblings, before distributing his life insurance policy assets.)

He emigrated to America in the 1840's, and enlisted in the U.S. First Dragoons in 1851. In 1861, he was discharged in California as a Sergeant. He re-enlisted as a Captain, Company B, First California Cavalry at Camp Merchant, California, coming to New Mexico with Carleton's Column. He re-enlisted in 1864 at Fort Sumner, serving there and at Fort Stanton as commander, exiting on June 7, 1865 as a Lieutenant Colonel. He then made a sutler store at Fort Stanton with fellow soldier, Lawrence Murphy. By 1866, both were involved in Catron's ventures of beef and hay contracts to forts. Fritz died at his father's home in Stuttgart, Germany, on June 26, 1874.

LAWRENCE GUSTAV MURPHY

Lawrence Gustav Murphy's company was the front for T.B. Catron's local monopolistic goals.

Born about 1831 in County Wexford, Ireland, Murphy graduated from St. Patrick's College in Maynooth, coming to America as an adult. In 1861, he enlisted in the Army at Fort Union, New Mexico Territory, as a first lieutenant and quartermaster of the first Regiment of New Mexico Infantry; next serving under Kit Carson in the Navajo Wars. In 1865, General James H. Carleton made him a brevet major of volunteers at Bosque Redondo: the concentration camp for Apaches and Navajos connected to Fort Sumner. That year, Carleton also brevetted Navajo fighter William Brady and Kiowa and Comanche fighter Emil Fritz. They mustered out in 1866, knowing each other.

Going to Fort Stanton, nine miles from Lincoln, Murphy and Fritz made a sutler store as L.G. Murphy & Co., employing Brady, and James Dolan, and supplying the Mescalero Indian Reservation as quasi-Indian Agents and befriending officers by loans. Murphy also became a probate judge.

In 1873, after Dolan tried to murder a soldier, the firm was expelled from Fort Stanton. Relocating in Lincoln, they built a huge store, nicknamed "The House." Fritz died in the next year.

On April 1, 1874, Murphy made Dolan his partner. And, on April 20th, as Probate Judge, he appointed William Brady as Fritz's administrator. Machinations of Fritz's life insurance policy, were later used to attack "House" competitor, John Tunstall.

In 1875, Murphy likely instigated the murder of political rival and rancher, Robert Casey. Murphy had declared: "You might as well stop the waves of the ocean with a fork as to try and oppose me." But his embezzlement of Lincoln County taxes caused his withdrawal from politics - though without prosecution.

In 1876, for his Mescalero Reservation beef, hay, and flour contracts - met by defective goods and rustled beef - Murphy got the Indian Agent replaced with complicit Frederick C. Godfroy.

In December of 1876, Murphy became president of the Lincoln County Farmers Club. On March 14, 1877, he retired to his ranch, dying of cancer and alcoholism on October 20, 1878; without being active in the Lincoln County War. Catron, repossessing his huge ranch for mortgage debts, was his estate's administrator.

JAMES JOSEPH DOLAN

Violent sociopath and multiple murderer, "House" partner, James Joseph Dolan, functioned as Ring sub-boss with John Riley, and gained lifelong rewards.

He was born on May 22, 1848, in Loughrea County Galway, Ireland. His family came to New York when he was a child. In the Civil War, he served in the Union Army in the New York Zouaves then the Thirty-seventh Regiment, U.S. Infantry, until his 1869 discharge at Fort Stanton.

There he clerked in L.G. Murphy Company's sutler store. His attempted 1873 murder Cavalryman Captain James F. Randlett, got the group evicted. They relocated to Lincoln, building the two-story "House," which continued to supply rustled beef to the Mescalero Indian Reservation by replacing its legitimate Agent with Ring ally, Frederick Godfroy. On May 9, 1877, Dolan murdered a Hilario Jaramillo as a possible favor to "The House's" builder, George Peppin, who then married the widow; becoming a crucial Ring ally in the Lincoln County War as Sheriff.

In 1877, after Murphy retired, Dolan partnered with Catron-linked cattle broker, John H. Riley, to form J.J. Dolan & Co.

Bankrupted by John Tunstall's competition in 1877, Dolan mortgaged "The House" and its 40 acres to Catron. In 1878, Catron foreclosed on the property.

In the 1878 Lincoln County War period and aftermath, Dolan was indicted with others for murdering John Tunstall, was involved in the battle killing of Alexander McSween, was indicted for the 1879 murder of Attorney Huston Chapman, and likely attempted the 1879 assassination of Attorney Ira Leonard.

Probably the first to recognize Billy Bonney's threat to the Ring, Dolan tried to enlist him in a February 18, 1879 "peace meeting," which failed after Dolan murdered Chapman that night, with Billy as a witness. That left Billy to testify against him; while Dolan became a spy sabotaging Billy's governor's pardon.

As reward, Dolan got much of Tunstall's property - his Lincoln store and ranchland, which was renamed the Feliz River Cattle Company, in partnership with other paid-off Ringites, John Riley and William Rynerson; and with Dolan as president and general manager. In 1883, he was elected Lincoln County Treasurer; and in 1888 was elected to the Territorial Senate for the 1889 term. In 1889, he became receiver of the U.S. Land Office in Las Cruces.

Dolan died on February 26, 1898. His lying obituary in the March 2, 1898 *Santa Fe New Mexican*, titled "Death of the Hon. James J. Dolan, Has Been Engaged in Cattle Business in New Mexico for 30 Years - Faithful to Every Trust," declared: "He was a man whose personal integrity was without blemish, whose word was as good as his bond, and whose geniality, generosity and other manly qualities attracted to him many friends. His death is generally deplored as a loss to the territory." He was buried on the ranch of Charles Fritz (who enabled the malicious prosecution of Tunstall and McSween, and where the Seven Rivers rustlers ambush-murdered Regulator leader, Frank MacNab, in 1878).

Dolan's pre-1888 fire letters are lost, but his later ones, mostly about loans and political spying, are to "Dear Catron." On October 15, 1891, giving Fort Stanton as his address, he even accessed Elkins through Catron, seeking influence: *"Will you do me the kindness to send me a personal letter to S.B. Elkins, asking him to assist in getting the appointment of J.C. Watson as Postmaster at Deming, N.M. **[He is] a good friend of ours**."*

On November 26, 1892, Dolan reported on Catron's losing the Delegate election: *"[T]he result in this County is different from the time in which Johnny [Riley] and I carried the County for our friend S.B.E.[Elkins]* <u>Tom</u>, *[Catron] [illegible] with renewed force."*

On October 6, 1894, on his Feliz Land and Cattle Co. stationery, he reported spying: *"I met with [George] Curry in the street this evening and in speaking about Yourself and [Antonio] Joseph, he offered, before a large crowd, to bet $5,000 – (certified check) against $2,500 – that You would be defeated ... at the Coming Election ... I think it is a bluff, and only wish that I was able to call it myself."*

Dolan also used Catron as his attack dog, writing on Charles Fritz's son, Emil's, D.+D. Ranch stationery, on June 11, 1895: *"You no doubt have noticed that cowardly slanderous article against me, published in the Santa Fe [Daily] New Mexican of the 3rd inst. and their more than cowardly Excuse, in their issue of the 4th inst. Please examine into the matter .... **if there is any way to punish the outfit, I want you to do it**."*

That June 5, 1895 article was a mix-up with another Dolan by the *Santa Fe Daily New Mexican* quoting the *White Oaks Eagle*:

J.A. DOLAN MISSING

A Well Known Lincoln
County Politician
Said to Have Fled
the Country

The example set by Frank Lesnett, formerly receiver of the U.S. land office at Roswell, and Lucas, postmaster at Silver City under the Harrison administration, seems to have been adopted by the Hon. **James A. Dolan, also of Lincoln. "Jimmy," who in his day was a smooth manipulator of Republican political methods in his neck of the woods, is missing. Perhaps he has gone to South America to join his friend Lesnett** who was recently seen there and recognized by a former resident of New Mexico. The White Oaks Eagle says:

"It is reported that James A. Dolan is in Los Angeles. He suddenly disappeared from Gold Hill some months ago and it was thought for a time he was murdered. The country surrounding Gold Hill was thoroughly searched for him, but no trace could be found except a track leading to the Southern Pacific Railroad.

This "error" was too close to the terrible truths about himself, so justly uneasy Dolan also elicited the help of politician, George Curry, for a reply in the *Santa Fe New Mexican* on June 4, 1895; stating:

NOT JAMES J. DOLAN MISSING

Senator Curry Corrects a Misleading Paragraph – James A. Not James J. Dolan Missing ...

Hon. Geo. Curry, who represented Lincoln, Chaves, and Eddy counties in the last territorial council and recently appointed clerk of the district courts in the 5th judicial district by Judge Hamilton ... calls the NEW MEXICAN'S attention to the fact that the account of the disappearance of James A. Dolan from Gold Hill, Grant county ... is liable to do a serious wrong to James J. Dolan, of Lincoln, who holds no public office, possesses ample wealth and enjoys the respect and confidence of a large circle of acquaintances in southern and southeastern New Mexico. He is in no way related to James A. Dolan; is the trusted manager of the Feliz Cattle company; and Mr. Curry says he saw him and talked with him in Lincoln about a week ago. It seems strange that the White Oaks, Eddy and other papers let this matter slip into their columns without explanation.

On February 23, 1897, vengeful Dolan wrote to Catron attacking Florencio Gonzales, the anti-Ring, San Patricio Probate Judge who, in 1878, blocked his fraudulent claim for "The House" for $76,000 on the Fritz life insurance policy, and may have sheltered Billy during the 1879 pardon bargaining with Lew Wallace. Using his Feliz Cattle Co. stationery, Dolan stated:

My Dear Sir:

Your favor of the 2nd inst received, I have delayed answering it, until after my trip to Lincoln, returned last evening, while there, **I made it my business to Enquire from responsible men, both Mexicans and Americans, as to the force and influence of Florencio Gonzales, politically, over his people.** *The verdict is entirely against him, he has no influence whatever among his neighbors, or in fact any place within or outside this County. One of our representative Mexicans, and a good Republican, answers me in this way: "It is a well known fact that the Mexican people in this County are very much against Mr Gonzales receiving any recognition from the party ...*

I feel safe in saying to you, that Mr Henry Lutz can control 10 Mexican votes to Florencio's one ... He can fill either office, Register or Receiver ... **This man [Florencio] is entitled to no recognition by you or any of our friends** *– he was a candidate for Sheriff, last election, and defeated. He tried to gain his election* *by fighting the large cattle owners, Corporations &c, and worked in harmony with the Populist element of this county, and I ask of you to ignore his Petition ... With best wishes from self and family, I am as ever*

*Yours truly
Jas. J. Dolan*

JOHN HENRY RILEY

John Henry Riley was an attempted murderer, partner in "The House," and Catron's bridge to Lincoln County War events. After the War, he engaged in multiple businesses with Catron.

Born on May 12, 1850, in County Kerry, Ireland, John Henry Riley immigrated to America with his family in 1862, and in 1865 worked as a Colorado railroad contractor. In New Mexico Territory, he clerked for a beef contractor near the Mescalero Indian Reservation, had a ranch near Fort Stanton, and may have met Catron by 1866 through such businesses. In November of 1876, he became a partner in the Catron-backed L.G. Murphy and Co.'s "House" in Lincoln. In 1875 he failed his assassination of anti-Ring Juan Patrón, leaving him partially paralyzed.

On the February 18, 1878 night of the Ring's murder of John Tunstall, he went to Alexander McSween's house to proclaim his innocence, but accidently dropped his pocket notebook with rustled cattle deals and Catron's cipher-code. Enclosed was William Rynerson's February 14, 1878 "Friends Riley and Dolan" letter heralding killing Tunstall and McSween. During the Lincoln County War, he appears to have coordinated efforts with Catron.

After the War, he was rewarded - along with James Dolan and William Rynerson - by getting Tunstall's stolen Feliz River Ranch, named by them the Feliz Cattle Co. He also partnered with Charles Fritz's son, Emil Fritz, in the D+D Ranch. He was Assessor of Doña Ana County. Furthermore, he co-owned with Catron the American Cattle Company, Tularosa Land and Cattle Company, the Terra Amarilla Land Grant, and the Santa Teresa Land Grant. Moving back to Colorado, he had a hog ranch.

He died in 1916. His deceptive obituary, titled "John H. Riley Dead," in February 25, 1916's *The Deming Graphic*, stated: "John H. Riley, a pioneer of the Southwest and early resident of Las Cruces died in Colorado Springs, Colo. last week ... Mr. Riley was the owner of large cattle interests in Lincoln county in the early eighties and through the receiving a large beef contract from the government he became the butt of a bitter feud and figured prominently in what is remembered as the Lincoln County War, in which he and his friends were victors. His fortune is estimated at $250,000."

Riley's letters to Catron document their profuse business and political endeavors. His ruthless letter of February 5, 1890 about destroying opponent Eugene Fiske, implies usual defamatory affidavits and harassment. Riley wrote: *"I today mailed Senator Edmunds my affidavit corroborated by Dolan against Fiske – Rynerson writes me he is making it <u>hot</u> for him ... Do all you can to down him but do not let it appear as coming from you."*

On December 19, 1891, Riley coordinated a meeting with himself, Rynerson, and Catron *"on political matters affecting the future."* Tellingly, he used Ring secrecy: *"There are several matters we wish to consult with you about and we cannot write them."*

On December 8, 1900, he wrote to Catron on stationery listing himself as having "Ranches at Colorado Springs, Fowler and Rocky Ford, Colorado." He coordinated their selling the Tularosa Land and Cattle Company, defining their ownership after William Rynerson's 1893 death; stating: *"On my arrival here today I found your letter enclosing the contract and* ~~agreem~~ *copy of same in connection with the sale of The Tularosa Land & Cattle Co's land – The contract is perfectly satisfactory and your understanding of the agreement is mine. You and I own the stock equally. The property was bonded and all the bonds are held by the First National Bank of Santa Fe to secure the indebtedness – which now only amounts to the amount due the Bank."*

EDGAR A. WALZ

Edgar A. Walz, was a brother of Catron's wife, Julia Walz. He was born in Owatanna, Minnesota, on March 3, 1859. In 1876, he moved to New Mexico Territory. In 1878, Catron made him manager of his 12,800 acre Lincoln County Carrizozo Land and Cattle Company, and then of "The House."

After the Lincoln County War period, Walz had multiple jobs, while frequently begging Catron for money. He managed life insurance companies and was president and general manager of hotel services for check cashing, debt reporting, and sales.

His death was reported in *The New York Times* as "Edgar A. Walz Dead: Expert on credit, Founder of The Travelers Hotel Credit Corporation – Managed New Mexico Ranch in Youth." It stated :"[H]e left home as a lad to seek his fortune in the

Southwest. He established himself in the cattle business and for years managed a large ranch in New Mexico."

Through Catron, Walz gained access to Ringite heights of power, writing on June 8, 1897 to Catron from New York City, from The Hotel Men's Confidential Agency, of which he was President, to get S.B. Elkins as an investor. It gives insight into both Ring bosses' style. Flatterer Walz wrote:

Dear Mr. Catron: -
I have often while in New Mexico heard it said that if one asked Mr. Elkins for a favor, he would shake you by the hand, smile on you, pat you on the back and ask you to come again, but he would never grant your wish; that if you asked Catron for a favor, he would bluster, take your head nearly off, but give you what you asked for if it was a reasonable request.
If Elkins had said [to me] no I will not do anything, it would have ended it, but he led me to believe he would invest $15,000. And at one time stated in plain English that he would do so, if I could guarantee him his money if I died within the year. I then insured my life for $15,000 and sent to him the policy. I went on with my plans feeling sure he would go in ... and I used it to carry out certain arrangements I had made pending the carrying out of his promise. Before I was brought up for examination [for the debt by him] I was scared to death. I had read in the papers accounts of people being examined and I knew if such an account was published of my condition, it would simply kill my business. I pleaded with E. [Elkins] not to have me examined, telling him why. He referred me to his Attorney. The Attorney demanded security; I sent him all my 10,000 shares of ship cleaner stock and then he had me examined in a private office and no notice was made in the papers ...
[Elkins] getting a judgment has injured my business very much. If times do not improve this year and I don't make some money in some other way, I cannot pay him ... I hope to God the good times we have been so long looking for will arrive.
Yours truly, *Ed*

DAVID M. EASTON

David M. Easton, was Catron's agent in Lincoln County, stationed in the Mescalero Indian Reservation and colluding with corrupt Indian Agent Frederick Godfroy to defraud government contracts. Historian Philip Rasch called him "the local business manager of Catron." (Rasch, *Gunsmoke in Lincoln County*, p. 129) During the Lincoln County War period, as a Justice of the Peace, he was enlisted by James Dolan to write false arrest warrants against Alexander McSween, Billy Bonney, and other Regulators to feign legality for malicious prosecutions and physical attacks.

Easton's communications with Catron after the 1888 expurgating fire, exemplify the type of desperate and deceitful puppet Catron preferred for his criminal ends. Easton also was entangled with other Ringites, and gave false affidavits.

On April 8, 1889, Easton wrote from Mescalero to Catron:

As I told you I would like your assistance in obtaining for me some employment by which I can be able in time to pay you what I owe. *I would have liked the position of Indian Agent at this place [Mescalero Indian Reservation] but if I could not get that I would be content with the position of Clerk ... If I can't get either of these I would like some work in Santa Fe ... In fact ... I would be glad of any employment by which myself and my wife could live and have something over to pay my debts.*

I have tried every means in my power to sell my property here ... I have even offered it for but little more than would pay my note to you, but without success ...

Riley and Rynerson both promised me that they would see that I "was taken care of". *I have letters from both of them to that effect ...*

As to the Affidavit I gave regarding their Desert Land Entries, it was in their favor ... [I]t directly and flatly contradicted every witness [a Ring adversary] had ... Dolan spoke to me in Santa Fe ... I explained to him what I have explained in this ...

To conclude, I can only repeat what I have said before, that I earnestly ask your assistance in obtaining some paying employment, now no matter what or where.
              Very Respectfully
              D.M. Easton

SATURNINO BACA

Saturnino Baca, a Ringite Lincoln resident, betrayed the Hispanic cause of the Lincoln County War by implementing intervention by Commander N.A.M. Dudley by deceitful request of protection for his wife and children from McSween men.

Baca was born on November 11, 1830, in Cebolleta, Valencia County. An unsavory man, on September 15, 1855, he notoriously married a 14 year old girl, with whom he fathered five children, with two more adopted. In the Civil War, he was a First Lieutenant in Company E, First New Mexico Cavalry under Colonel Kit Carson. On March 20, 1864, he was made Captain. Fort Stanton was among the forts at which he served for attacking Apaches and Navajos.

After discharge in 1867, he settled in Lincoln; likely allying with its Ringite veterans at its sutler store. By 1868, he used Catron - as well as Lawrence Murphy, William Brady, and Joseph Blazer - to pass a bill forming Lincoln County, with Lincoln as seat. Brady became its first Sheriff, and Ring-backing Governor Robert Byington Mitchell made Baca a Probate Judge.

In 1878, Baca was caught stealing 12,000 pounds of coffee, sugar, and other supplies from the Mescalero Indian Reservation, in likely collusion with Agent Frederick Godfroy and "The House." In 1882, he murdered black Lincoln resident, George Washington, who had eloped with one of his daughters. In 1889, he lost an arm to a gunshot in an altercation about grazing his sheep. In 1897, he was on the New Mexico Board of Prison Directors. In 1909 he was Master at Arms of the New Mexico legislature.

Baca died on March 7, 1925 in Lincoln. In 1961, a Tom Charles, in an essay, "The Father of Lincoln County," called him "one of Lincoln County's most loved citizens;" stating that he, Murphy, and Brady were "citizens seeking establishment of better law and order in southeastern New Mexico."

Baca's Ring dealt with the early "House;" with some records spared in the 1888 fire revealing his apparent collusion with Emil Fritz and Lawrence Murphy to control hay supply. On July 19, 1871, he wrote to Chief Quartermaster Captain A.J. McGonigle, about not meeting his contract for four hundred tons of grama grass hay for Fort Stanton. On July 20, 1871, he refused to sign a contract obligating delivery. That day, Fort Stanton Commander Lieutenant Colonel August V. Kantz wrote to McGonigle about being pressured to accept inferior bottom hay by sutler store partner, Emil Fritz, based on Vaca [sic] saying grama was not available. Kantz added that *"Fritz & Murphy have the control of the whole matter,"* and recommended seeking hay elsewhere; adding: *"If this is not done Fritz and Murphy will be the owners of all the hay in the country and we shall be obliged to buy at their prices."* On September 24, 1871, angry Chief Quartermaster McGonigle wrote that he wanted Baca barred from getting future contracts. Instead, the future "House," was establishing a monopoly, with Saturnino Baca as one supplier.

Like other Ringites, Saturnino Baca, secure in loyalty, contacted Catron with when he needed influence. On March 28, 1892, writing from Fort Stanton (showing privileged access), he requested help for a possible relative named Francisco Baca for his claim *"against the government for Indian depredations."* Saturnino added imperiously: *"Please let me know if the claim has been allowed, or what shape it is in."*

RING ENFORCERS

SUMMARY: Only by having friends in enforcer positions could the Santa Fe Ring exercise its malicious prosecutions and terrorism with guise of legality and with impunity by obstructing justice. The Lincoln County War period demonstrated the enforcers' unchecked barbarity.

GOVERNOR SAMUEL BEACH AXTELL

Samuel Beach Axtell, a Ring-bribed Governor, was a key in crushing the anti-Ring uprisings in Colfax and Lincoln Counties.

Born on October 14, 1819, in Franklin County, Ohio, Axtell attended Oberlin College; was admitted to the Ohio bar; became a District Attorney in Amador County, California; served in Congress as a Democrat; as a Republican was appointed in 1874 by President Ulysses S. Grant as Governor of Utah; and was transferred to New Mexico Territory in 1875 to replace deceased Marsh Giddings as Governor. He was almost immediately bribed by the Ring, getting a $1,800 "loan" in 1876 from John Riley, as Catron's agent, (that being half of Axtell's salary).

He became a major Ring enforcer in the period of anti-Ring uprisings, issuing illegal proclamations outlawing opponents.

From 1875 to 1878 in the Colfax and Lincoln County Wars, to shield Ring murderers, he removed Colfax County's courts and Lincoln County's Justice of the Peace, Deputies, and Constables. Scapegoated in 1878 to cover up the Santa Fe Ring by Frank Warner Angel's report blaming him for the "troubles," he was removed from office and replaced by Lew Wallace.

In 1882, after efforts by Elkins and Catron, he was made Chief Justice of New Mexico Territory; serving to 1885. He resided in Santa Fe until his death on August 6, 1891.

JUDGE WARREN HENRY BRISTOL

Judge Warren Henry Bristol, was in earliest Ring plots to outlaw opponents, and was exposed during the Colfax County War to President Hayes. In the Lincoln County War period, conspiring with District Attorney William Rynerson, he implemented malicious prosecutions of John Tunstall, Alexander McSween, and the Regulators. Later he was Billy Bonney's hanging judge. Unsurprisingly, Ringite attorney and historian, Ralph Emerson Twitchell, in his 1912 *The Leading Facts of New Mexico History* wrote that Bristol performed "with great honor and credit."

Born on March 19, 1823, in Stafford, New York, Bristol was educated at Yates Academy, Lima Seminary, Wilson Collegiate Institute, and Fowler State and National Law School; joining the bar in Lockport, New York. In 1850, he moved to Minnesota to practice law, becoming a District Attorney in the 1850's in Hennepin and Goodhue Counties. In 1855, he was elected Chairman of the Republican Party Convention. From 1866 to 1870, he served three terms in the Minnesota legislature.

In 1872, he was appointed by President Ulysses S. Grant as Associate Justice of the New Mexico Supreme Court and District Attorney of the Third Judicial District, encompassing Lincoln, Doña Ana, and Grant Counties. He served for a little over 12 years, and resigned on July 26, 1884 to practice law in Deming. Bristol died in Deming, New Mexico, on January 12, 1890.

DISTRICT ATTORNEY WILLIAM RYNERSON

William Logan Rynerson was a key Ringite, implementing Catron's Lincoln County War crimes, and gaining life-long profit.

Born on February 22, 1828 in Mercer County, Kentucky, Rynerson attended Franklin College in Indiana. In 1852, he went to California for the gold rush; remaining to study law, in Amador County, along with future Governor, S.B. Beach Axtell. In Union service, he came to Las Cruces in General James Carleton's California Column. Mustering out in November of 1866, as a Lieutenant Colonel, he stayed there, making local mining claims.

In 1867, he was elected to the legislature's Council. But John Potts Slough, irascible Supreme Court Chief Justice since 1865, jury reformer, opponent of peonage and Indian slavery, and the General who saved the West from Confederates in the 1862 Battle of Glorieta, called it rigged. Ringite Territorial Secretary William F. Arney provocatively berated Slough, and got accosted. Rynerson then got a legislative resolution to remove him as Chief Justice. Democrats called it malicious prosecution. (Notable is that the year before, Arney, as acting Governor, appointed Catron District Attorney for the Third Judicial District, and Elkins Attorney General.) Then, in the Exchange Hotel, on December 15, 1867, seven foot tall Rynerson met Slough, demanded his retraction of insults, was refused, and fatally shot him. So Slough became the first anti-Ring opponent as well as its first assassination. Represented by then Territorial U.S. Attorney S.B. Elkins, Rynerson was acquitted for "self-defense." He served in the legislature till 1870. And provoking violent responses to attain a "self-defense" killing became a mainstay of Ring assassinations.

In 1869, Rynerson was trader at Grant County's Fort Bayard, recipient of Catron's beef since 1866; and may have had ties with him. In 1870, he was admitted to the bar; and Ringite Governor William Pile made him Territorial Adjutant General. He also developed Silver City mining claims, and was a customs inspector.

In 1871, he campaigned, with others, for a Republican ticket; but they were accused of violence and attempted assassination of Democrat candidates' relatives - in the emerging pattern of Ring terrorism. The climax was the Mesilla Riot of clashing groups, with nine killed. And the Democrats won the election.

In 1872, he joined Catron and Ringite John D. Bail (Billy Bonney's future hanging trial co-attorney) in a Silver City mining law suit. In 1874, he litigated to get the Mesilla Land Grant, and to evict its settlers. Elkins, then Delegate to Congress, got him appointed receiver of the Mesilla land office. But he lost the suit.

In January of 1876, his friend from California days, Governor S.B. Axtell appointed him District Attorney for the Third Judicial District, covering Doña Ana, Grant, and Lincoln Counties; and reappointed him in 1878 for the Lincoln County War period.

As District Attorney, Rynerson authored the "Friends Riley and Dolan" letter of February 14, 1878, encouraging murder of Tunstall and McSween. He assisted Axtell on the improper proclamation to remove Lincoln County Sheriff John Copeland, and recommended Ringite replacement: George Peppin. He was District Attorney for the 1878 Lincoln County Grand Jury that indicted Tunstall's killers - whose arrests he blocked - while pursuing arrests of Regulators, including Billy, for murders of Brady, Hindman, and Roberts. He colluded with Judge Warren Bristol to change Billy's trial venues to Doña County's Mesilla to ensure hanging juries. For the 1879 Lincoln County Grand Jury, with Judge Bristol, he blocked arrest of Attorney Huston Chapman's Ringite killers, while trying unsuccessfully to discount Billy Bonney's eye-witness testimony against them.

In the late 1870's and early 1880's, he assisted then District Attorney Simon Newcomb (his law partner) and Judge Bristol in Billy's 1881 Mesilla hanging trial. He, or James Dolan, likely threatened Billy's lawyer, Ira Leonard, causing his withdrawal and replacement by Rynerson's friend - and Billy's enemy - Attorney Albert Jennings Fountain.

In the 1880's, he ranched near Las Cruces, becoming a hog breeder; joining the Doña Ana Stock Association with John Riley and Ringite Max Frost. In 1882, with Attorney Simon Newcomb, he got the county seat transferred from Mesilla to Las Cruces, so his land there could be bought for its courthouse and jail.

The 1880's also marked Rynerson's sharing in spoils of Tunstall's murder and theft of his property. In 1884, he became a partner in the Feliz River Land and Cattle Company with Catron, John Riley, James Dolan, Numa Raymond and John Lemon on Tunstall's past Feliz River Ranch. The year before he had claimed land along both sides of the Tularosa River under the Desert Land Act, prevailing against its settlers with likely Ring influence.

In 1884, he, and future Governor, L. Bradford Prince, competed to be the Republican candidate for Delegate. Rynerson hypocritically accused his opponents of being Ringites (though Judge William B. "Ithurial" Sloan showed that Rynerson was the Ringite). Billy's hanging trial lawyer, A.J. Fountain backed Rynerson. But Democrat, Antonio Joseph won the election.

In 1889, Rynerson joined Catron and Riley in the Tularosa Land and Cattle Company, but suffered a debilitating stroke. After he died, on September 26, 1893, they assumed his stock. The September 30, 1893 *Rio Grande Republican* eulogized him under

"Local Items": "Expressions of regret are heard on every side on account of this sudden death of one of our best citizens." He was buried in the Las Cruces Masonic Cemetery.

Rynerson benefited from Catron's expurgating July of 1888, office fire. But his later letters to Catron show his loans and close work with John Riley (whom he calls "our Friend Riley") as a political agent for Catron, and as connected with them in the Feliz Cattle Company and Tularosa Land and Cattle Company.

From Las Cruces, on November 11, 1888, he wrote to Catron, making clear his work for the Ring "friends" and alliance with Riley, as well as working for election of Billy's betraying lawyer, Albert Jennings Fountain. He wrote:

Dear Catron -

I notice what you say ~~in~~ in relation to having mutual understanding in regard to appointments in this Territory – Riley and I were talking over this at the time of receipt of your favor of the 8th inst. Some of us will come up and confer with you and other friends at an early day – There must be no clashing as to applications for office. If we are united we will succeed – otherwise not.

I am sorry you have that one vote majority against you but it will be all right, as we will have a majority in the Council and if you have been fairly elected will get the seat. We have elected both the councilors for this District by majorities not less than two hundred – Doña Ana, Grant and Sierra each giving a majority for us aggregating over five hundred majority.

*In next House we have elected all three of the members of these two Districts (Grant and Sierra) – <u>Foster</u>, (and Dona Ana and Lincoln) Lesnet and **Fountain** ...*

We have elected best part of our ticket in the county. Sheriff, Assessor, and the County Commissioners – losing the clerk Probate Judge and School Superintendent.

We have lost the county on delegate by about 200 – perhaps a little over as the whole eastern part of the county which formerly was in Lincoln gave about 150 against us –

We have like you had a hard fight against the enemy.

Let me hear from you and if you will be in Santa Fe middle or latter part of this week – Answer right away. –

Yours &c
W.L. Rynerson

From Glorieta, Rynerson, on December 28, 1888, wrote to Catron, as "Confidential" and "Your friend," exhibiting his connections to Russell Kistler of the *Las Vegas Optic*, S.B. Elkins, President Benjamin Harrison, and influence on the New York press: *"My Dear Catron = I was close after you – I learned from Kistler of the Optic that you got in last night. I will ... be home tomorrow – I saw Mrs. Catron. She was well. Saw Elkins and Gov. [Richard] McCormick [past Governor of Arizona Territory, then living in New York City, and holding presidency or directorship of mining companies and a bank]. Had a very satisfactory talk with both of them.* **They will help us all they can and will see that the N.Y. Tribune gets right** *... Let me hear from you – I hope you had a glorious Christmas with your folks at your old home."*

SHERIFF WILLIAM BRADY

A Ringite from his Fort Stanton days, Sheriff William Brady was a valuable and murderous Ring enforcer in the Lincoln County War period.

He was born on August 16, 1829 in County Cavan, Ireland; emigrating to America in 1851, joining the Army, serving in Texas until discharge in 1856, and re-enlisting in the First Regiment of Mounted Rifles till 1861. That year, he joined the Second New Mexico Volunteer Infantry as a First Lieutenant. Serving as a Major at Fort Stanton, he met Ringite sutler store proprietors, Emil Fritz and Lawrence Murphy, working for them before becoming Lincoln County Sheriff. As Sheriff, he was exposed by John Tunstall for embezzling county taxes to buy rustled cattle for "The House." He implemented Catron's malicious prosecution of John Tunstall - whom he successfully murdered - and of Attorney Alexander McSween. He was killed by the Regulators on April 1, 1878 to protect McSween as his next assassination victim.

CHIEF DEPUTY JACOB BASIL MATTHEWS

Jacob Basil "Billy" Matthews was Chief Deputy in Sheriff Brady's Tunstall murder posse.

He was born on May 5, 1847 in Woodbury, Tennessee. Serving in the Union Army, he was discharged in 1865. He mined in Colorado, then moved to New Mexico Territory in 1867. In 1874, he made a Peñasco River ranch without having full title, but sold it to John Tunstall in 1877, using the money to buy into

"The House." In 1878, Sheriff William Brady made him Chief Deputy to harass Tunstall, then to lead the posse to murder him.

When Brady was killed by the Regulators on April 1, 1878, Matthews was with him, on the way to murder Alexander McSween when he entered Lincoln for the upcoming Grand Jury. He participated in Lincoln County War period skirmishes, and tried to kill Billy Bonney and Charlie Bowdre. He was in the Lincoln County War Battle in Peppin's outlaw posse. Indicted for Tunstall and Lincoln County War murders, he was represented by Catron who got him, and other indicted Ringites, pardoned in 1879 by abuse of Governor Lew Wallace's Amnesty Proclamation.

He was rewarded by the Ring, by gift of John Tunstall's Peñasco River ranch; which he named the Peñasco Cattle Company. In 1892, he and James Dolan became directors of the Peñasco Reservoir and Irrigation Company. In 1894, he moved to Roswell, becoming manager of the Pecos Irrigation and Improvement Company. In 1898, with past Seven Rivers rustler, Buck Powell, he unsuccessfully made an Arizona ranch. He then became Roswell postmaster, dying there on June 3, 1904.

Matthews, like the other Lincoln County War criminals, stayed in contact with Catron. On August 31, 1892, he wrote:

> *My Dear Sir and friend.*
> *I congratulate you upon your nomination [for Territorial Delegate], and you can rest assured that I will give you all the support that is in my power from now until the 8th of November when you will be elected by at least 5000 maj. I know that you have other true friends in this county, as well as many enemys ...*
> *Yours sincerely &c*
> *J.B. Matthews*

SHERIFF GEORGE WARDEN PEPPIN

As Lincoln County Sheriff, George Warden Peppin was the murderous leader against Lincoln County War freedom fighters.

Born in Ohio in 1843, he served in Company A, Fifth Regiment California Infantry, came to New Mexico Territory with Carleton's column, and mustered out in Mesilla in 1864. Settling in Lincoln, he built "The House." He was Sheriff William Brady's Deputy for John Tunstall's murder, and was in Brady's fatal ambush by

Regulators. He became Sheriff by proclamation of Ringite Governor S.B. Axtell to replace non-Ring Sheriff John Copeland.

As Sheriff, Peppin led John Kinney's outlaw gang for July 3, 1878's massacre at San Patricio, and conducted the Lincoln County War Battle. He, thus, murdered San Patricio residents, Alexander McSween, Harvey Morris, Francisco Zamora, and Vincente Romero by his outlaw posses of Seven Rivers rustlers and John Kinney's gang; and enabled Commander N.A.M. Dudley's attack on Lincoln with murder, arson, and looting. He later gave a false affidavit defaming Susan McSween for Dudley.

In 1885, he was director of a school board; and in 1893 a Lincoln jailor. He was a Deputy to Sheriff George Curry. His being a mass murderer was no deterrent in this Ring-dominated land.

He died at home on September 18, 1904. The *Capitan News* of September 23, 1904, under "Old Citizen Gone" reported tersely: "The history of Lincoln county would be extremely partial that did not give the deceased the important role in the conduct of its affairs, for Mr. Peppin was one of the oldest settlers in the county ... Mr. Peppin was a good citizen, a true friend and kind husband and father."

DEPUTY U.S. MARSHAL TONY NEIS

Tony Neis, as Deputy U.S. Marshal, was one of Billy Bonney's guards at the Santa Fe jail; then, on March 28, 1881, transporting him to his Mesilla hanging trials, with Deputy U.S. Marshals Francisco Chávez and Bob Olinger (the Seven Rivers rustler-murderer). Neis remained as Billy's guard during the trials.

After being an enabler of Billy's hanging sentence, Neis, continued to assist "boss" Catron. On November 12, 1892, from Cerrillos, he acted as vindictive spy during Catron's bid for Territorial Delegate; writing: *"Friend Catron you have seen by this time how this town went at the Election the other day as W.H. Kennedy told you I had only the Democrats to fight but some of your republican friends I have them all down on my list that Dutchman Holam Landinslaugher worked hard against you and I want to remind you that the house he owns and lives in is 10 feet on one of your lots I think Lot 7 you sold 8x9 to Reaser ... he was told the day before the Election about his house being on your property but he seemed not to care I hope you are Elected and if there should be a contest I can furnish you plenty of material from here call on me at any time you will always find me your friend."*

ATTORNEY HENRY L. WALDO

An inner circle Ringite, Henry L. Waldo was important in shielding Commander N.A.M. Dudley in his Court of Inquiry from conviction for his Lincoln County War crimes.

He was born on January 16, 1844 in Jackson County, Missouri, and grew up with S.B. Elkins. From 1859 to 1861, he went to Missouri State University at Columbia and West Virginia's Bethany College. In 1864 he studied law in Amador County, California; and was admitted to the California bar in 1866. In 1867, he was elected District Attorney in Amador County.

In July of 1873, he moved to Santa Fe to join the Elkins & Catron law firm after Elkins went to Washington as Delegate. In 1875, he made his own firm with Ringite William Breeden; though from 1876 to 1878 he was appointed Chief Justice by President Grant. In 1878, he resumed the Breeden partnership, specializing in land and mining laws. Governor S.B. Axtell appointed him Territorial Attorney General, with his serving to 1881.

In the 1880's, he was a Director of the New Mexican Printing and Publishing Company (publishing the Ringite *Santa Fe New Mexican*), with his partner, William Breeden, as President.

Waldo was also Director and attorney for the Rio Grande, Mexico and Pacific Railroad Company, and of the New Mexico and Southern Pacific Railroad Company; and was President of the New Mexico and Arizona Railroad Company.

He died on July 10, 1915, being eulogized in August, 1915's *The Santa Fe Magazine* by an unnamed reporter: "[W]e see the staunch qualities of heart and mind which enabled this man to rise to be one of New Mexico's most honored citizens ... [H]is great dignity, integrity of purpose and unimpeachable character enabled him to deal with political officials and bosses of whatever party without fear or favor." For his sanitized biography, the reporter quoted Ring historian R.E. Twitchell.

Waldo's communications show youthful adulation of S.B. Elkins, calling him "My most loved friend." On February 18, 1866, from Ione City, Amador County, California, he foreshadowed his future corruption: "*I am much hampered in my undertakings by <u>poverty</u> ... I am starting at the ground ... I am stimulated by your example –* **I do not expect to emulate it in all aspects, but I can feebly imitate it.**"

ATTORNEY FRANK SPRINGER

Turn-coat attorney, Frank Springer, switched from the anti-Ring cause, to profit for life in Catron's inner circle. William Keleher wrote: "The original 'Santa Fe Ring' was composed of T.B. Catron, Robert H. Longwill, H.L. Waldo, **Frank Springer**, and A. Staab." (Keleher, *The Fabulous Frontier*, p. 125)

Born on June 17, 1848 in Wapello, Iowa, Springer was lured from Iowa to Cimarron, New Mexico, by his railroad engineer friend, Raymond Morley, who sought an ally against the Santa Fe Ring. Admitted to the New Mexico bar in 1876, Springer joined Morley's and the Maxwell Land Grant's settler's anti-Ring uprising of the Colfax County War, publishing Ring exposés in 1877 in their *Cimarron News and Press*. After Morley's forced flight after near assassination by the Ring, and the lost Lincoln County War, Springer opportunistically switched sides.

Springer could have broken the Santa Fe Ring with his August 9, 1878 deposition to Investigator Frank Warner Angel. Instead, he hid the Ring's and Catron's involvement in killing John Tunstall, and in the Lincoln County War.

As apparent Ring reward, he got a 320 acre tract of valuable land within the Maxwell Land Grant. In 1879, it was named Springer in his honor, when the intended tracks of the Atchison, Topeka, and Santa Fe Railroad arrived. And to punish anti-Ring Cimarron, it was made the county seat; until Raton got the designation in 1887. In 1901, Springer was elected to the legislature's Council.

His obituary in the September 23, 1927 *Albuquerque Journal* was titled: "Frank Springer, Pioneer of the State, is Dead, Was prominent in Early Affairs of New Mexico." It called him "a lawyer, a scientist and philanthropist [and a] pioneer resident of northern New Mexico ... largely interested in the land and cattle business." In memorial to his hypocrisy, it listed one of his heirs as named Lew Wallace (whom he had refused to back in Ring opposition)!

Springer worked with Catron as a Maxwell Land Grant and Railway Company attorney. Missing are letters before the 1888 expurgating fire, which would have shown how he fell. By 1895, he proved his degradation by defending Catron and Charles Spiess in their disbarment trial for witness intimidations and bribery.

That Springer litigated for Catron is shown by his September 6, 1888 letter to Catron's partner, Frank Clancy, when Springer was the Assistant Attorney for the Atchison, Topeka &

Santa Fe Railroad Company along with past Catron firm member, Henry Waldo as New Mexico Solicitor. Springer wrote, calling it confidential *"between you & Catron & me"*: *"In the winter of 1885,* **I obtained for Mr Catron, as a result of the litigation I carried out for his benefit as well as my own, $15,500** – *for his services up to that time. As he knows I was instrumental in getting the amount calculated at double the rate it was under his original understanding."*

An October 24, 1888 letter to the Catron firm showed that he now called the Maxwell Land Grant settlers *"squatters,"* whom he was fighting in the Supreme Court to block their ownership claims going back to 1869.

On March 14, 1889, Catron's law partner, Frank Clancy, shared political gossip with Springer, who was in Las Vegas, and urged him to get a judgeship for Ring friend, Van der Veer, that was being opposed by Lew Wallace with Republican President Benjamin Harrison. Clancy wrote: "Van der Veer is now in Washington trying to look after the chances of his being appointed Judge. Mr. Fiske has gone there with an avowed intention of doing all he could to beat Van der Veer, on the ground that Van der Veer is "Catron's man", and also for the purpose of fighting everybody and everything that Catron has any interest in. **It has recently been reported to me that Fiske says Gen. Wallace has promised him to go to the President against Van der Veer, and Sulzbacher** ... Now, cannot you do something with Gen. Wallace or somebody else, to counteract the mischief which Mr. Fiske is working against Van der Veer and Sulzbacher? ... If you can do anything, we wish you would, and that you would advise us by telegraph tomorrow of what you do, so that we may do something in harmony with you."

On May 8, 1889, Frank Clancy showed the Ring's political boosting of him; writing: "Have you done anything about the U.S. Attorney business ... I believe it is important that you should be a candidate."

Springer responded on May 10, 1889, to Clancy, apparently blasé with the glut of Ring favors: *"I have done nothing about U.S. Atty business, because I really do not want the office."* Than, after consulting with Catron, he was tempted – conniving with Clancy on May 30, 1889: *"I said to Catron that if a quiet movement could be started in the Territory in my favor, by which, without direct solicitation from me ... I would go in and pull the wires at the other end of the line."* Ultimately, Ringite William Breeden got the job.

Springer even assisted Robert Longwill, alleged murderer of anti-Ring Franklin Tolby, then practicing medicine in Santa Fe. On August 1, 1889, he wrote to Catron's firm to help Longwill collect fees: *"Downs claims to have paid out $125 to Longwill & Sloan for medical attendance to fix up a dislocation which Gorden overlooked. Longwill says he has never been paid anything."*

On August 24, 1892, Springer, as a delegate to the Republican Convention in Las Vegas, strategized Catron's run for Delegate with alleged Tolby killer, Melvin Mills. On October 13, 1892, Mills conveyed Springer's advice to Catron: "I was taking with Springer to day, he thinks you are too much on the defensive, that you are answering charges instead of making charges. This makes us look as if we were on the run … [W]e should have [Democrat opponent, Antonio Joseph] presented as an object of petty disgust and derision at Washington and get articles of that kind published."

ATTORNEY JOHN D. BAIL

After coerced departure of Billy Bonney's lawyer, Ira Leonard, from Mesilla in April of 1881, Ringite John D. Bail was appointed co-counsel to Albert Jennings Fountain to get Billy hanged.

Bail was born in Ross County, Ohio, on July 4, 1825. He entered the army in 1844, serving in the Mexican-American War. In 1849, he studied law in Springfield, Illinois, and was admitted to the bar in 1852. He moved to California for mining, before returning to practice law in Springfield. He fought on the Union side, locating afterwards to St. Louis, Missouri, then New Mexico Territory, living in Doña Ana and Grant Counties. His law practice was in Mesilla, then Silver City. He twice served in the legislature's House of Representatives, and once on the Council. He died on June 20, 1903. His obituary in the 1904 *Minutes of the New Mexico Bar Association* claimed: "[He] was personally recognized as a man of sterling honor and uprightness."

Bail's post-1888 fire documents demonstrate his Ringite loyalty to Catron, and their extensive legal and political work together. He also spied for the Ring. On December 28, 1888, Catron's firm requested: "Can you give us any information in regard to A.M. Connor, whom we are informed is living in Silver City? As to whether he has any property subject to execution."

On August 21, 1889, he coordinated a Southern Pacific Rail Road case for Catron. Proving their pre-1888 fire relationship, Bail alluded to papers sent before it: "*I will attend to the Hughes case [Hughes vs. S. Pacific referred to in his earlier letter to Catron of June 8, 1889], and I think beat it. As to the tax cases – there are two of them – Bantz informs me that you have been furnished with copies – over a year ago – **Maybe it was before you were burned out, and have in this way lost them**. I will furnish them again ... Bantz – who represents the County – is very anxious to have these cases personally disposed of and I might suggest that you do something, or advise me what to do.*"

Bail also did convoluted money-lending with Catron, with one case involving a Catron debt to be settled in sheep by a "Prado and wife." It went back "*several years*" before 1885, dating Bail's working with Catron to Bail's 1881 appointment time as Billy Bonney's case's co-counsel. In his letter of May 14, 1890, Bail reviewed the sheep debt: "*Thornton [when Catron's partner] told me in my office that my share of the sheep was 600 head, and that you had sold them ... I am of course, satisfied that you would not retain a dollar belonging to me [but someone else might have].*"

SHERIFF PAT GARRETT

Best known of Ring-beholden participants in Billy the Kid history, Billy Bonney's killer, Pat Garrett, bridged the Ring's enforcers and its thug assassins, by getting a lawman's title.

Born on June 5, 1850 (almost a decade before Billy Bonney) in Chambers County, Alabama, he moved with his family to a Claiborne Parish, Louisiana, plantation when he was three. His father died in 1868, and Garrett headed west. He may have had an illegitimate child in Texas, and killed a black man there. In 1876, as a buffalo hunter, he murdered a teenager named Joe Briscoe, who was part of their group. Though one of the partners claimed it was malicious, Garrett got off on self-defense.

Depressive, alcoholic, lacking in skills besides killing animals and people, and poorly literate, he went to Fort Sumner, New Mexico Territory, where he worked as a wagon driver for town owner, Peter Maxwell, a bartender in the town's Hargrove Saloon, and as a helper in a hog farm of a Thomas "Kip" McKinney.

His was the right profile for the Ring's choice to kill its foe, Billy Bonney. Promoted for Lincoln County Sheriff, he won on November 2, 1880. He then joined Secret Service Agent Azariah Wild - also engaged by the Ring for that task - who made him a Deputy U.S. Marshall, with money to pay spies and a Texas posse.

Garrett tried hard to kill. He ambushed Billy, first on December 19, 1880 (killing Tom O'Folliard instead); then on December 22, 1880 (killing Charlie Bowdre instead). He settled on capturing Billy at Stinking Springs. After sentence in Mesilla, Billy, however, escaped Garrett's Lincoln jail, 15 days the before the hanging date. Garrett finally succeeded in killing him in a Fort Sumner ambush, 77 days later.

To profit from that famous killing, Garrett used ghostwriter Ash Upson for his dime novel-style 1882 book, *The Authentic Life of Billy the Kid*, to advance the outlaw myth and to conceal his own Ringite participation.

Likely not reelected as Lincoln County Sheriff because of killing Billy, his employment woes continued. In 1896, living in Uvalde, Texas, with his large family, he was brought back to New Mexico Territory to find the February 2, 1896 killers of Attorney Albert Jennings Fountain and his son, Henry near White Sands; and was made Doña Ana County Sheriff for arrests. Much like his Billy the Kid task, its intent was eliminating a Ring enemy – now Catron's political and ranching rival, Oliver Lee. Garrett, accusing Lee and his ranch associate, James Gilliland, of the murder, tried his usual ambush tactic, but got his posseman killed instead by Lee and his ranch hands. And when Lee and Gilliland were tried for the Fountain and deputy murders, they were acquitted.

Garrett killed again on October 7, 1899, assisting a Sheriff George Blalock of Greer County Oklahoma, in New Mexico. The victim was an accused murderer named Norman Newman.

In 1901, based on his Billy the Kid killing fame, he was made El Paso Customs Collector by President Theodore Roosevelt. But his apparent incompetence led to his removal in 1906. He bought a New Mexico ranch, but its near bankruptcy forced his return to El Paso for real estate company work. His accusation of living with a prostitute there, made Governor-elect George Curry withdraw on offer of a prison superintendent job.

His destitute family had rented his New Mexico ranch to a goat raiser named Wayne Brazel. On February 29, 1908, on a road near Las Cruces, during Garrett's and Brazel's heated dispute about the upcoming sale of the goats, Brazel shot him dead. A jury later cleared Brazel based on self-defense, since Garrett was armed with a shotgun and had behaved in a threatening manner. Oliver Lee, who had cause to resent Garrett, was never charged as involved with the killing. Garrett was buried in the Las Cruces Masonic Cemetery.

Like other Ring-beholden enforcers, chronically indebted Garrett was on Catron's loan payroll. Garrett's biographer, Leon Metz, in his 1874 book, *Pat Garrett: The Story of a Western Lawman*, described Garrett being pressured by Catron for an unpaid $500 note signed on February 20, 1901. On May 31, 1904, Catron's collector wrote back that local banks told him that Garrett "was no good and that the endorser would have to pay. They did not even want to take it for collection as they had plenty of their own against him." (Metz, p. 260) By June 1, 1904, Catron wrote to Garrett with paternal benevolence reserved for his minions: "The time will come when there will be a reappointment, and then all these businessmen [to whom you are indebted] will turn loose against you, and you may find it somewhat difficult to get a party to stand by you." (Metz, p. 260) There was no record that Garrett paid Catron. He may have considered it a bonus fee for his services.

THUG ASSASSINS

SUMMARY: For the legal cover of plausible deniability, the Ring often murdered by hired thugs, whose connection to higher-up instigators could then be denied. Thus, Robert Casey was killed by a Willie Wilson, instead of by Lawrence Murphy. Franklin Tolby was killed by Cruz Vega and Manuel Cardenas, beholden to Melvin Mills and Robert Longwill. Tunstall was killed by Jessie Evans and his boys, while responsible Sheriff, William Brady, denied using them for his posse. Alexander McSween, Harvey Morris, Francisco Zamora, and Vincente Romero were murdered by Ringite Seven Rivers rustlers and John Kinney's gang, brought in by Sheriff George Peppin. And when thugs had inadequate power, soldiers were used, like in the Colfax County "Dear Ben" assassination plot of anti-Ring opponents; or the use of Commander N.A.M. Dudley and troops to enable Lincoln County War Battle murders, with three of his officers ordered by him to participate in the killings. And behind it all was the instigator: Ring "boss," Thomas Benton Catron.

RUSTLER-MURDERER GANGS

SEVEN RIVERS RUSTLERS

In the 1870's, drifters from Texas formed minimalist cow camps, with dug-out sod houses and corrals, in the Seven Rivers area of the north-to-south Pecos River, to exploit the 80,000 strong herd of John Simpson Chisum. Their customer was T.B. Catron, to stock his Pecos Cow Camp (fronted by James Dolan, with foreman William "Buck" Morton) and Carrizozo Land and Cattle Company to meet beef contracts for Fort Stanton and the Mescalero Indian Reservation (fronted by "The House" in Lincoln).

These Seven Rivers rustlers, became pro-Ring fighters in the Lincoln County War: Andrew Boyle; Milo Pierce; Marion Turner; Louis Paxton; "Dutch" Charlie Kruling; Bob and John Beckwith; Wallace and Bob Olinger; John, Jim, and Bill Jones; William "Buck" Powell, Josiah "Joe" Nash; and Nathan Underwood.

Underwood and Nash were the subject of John Tunstall's January 16, 1878 "A Tax-Payer's Complaint" Ring exposé in *The Mesilla Valley Independent*, accusing them of being paid for cattle by Sheriff William Brady's embezzled county taxes.

All were rewarded. Indicted in the April, 1879 Lincoln County Grand Jury for murder and arson in the Lincoln County War Battle, by May 1st, Catron and colleagues got them all pardoned by colluding with Judge Warren Bristol and misstating Governor Lew Wallace's Amnesty Proclamation, which excluded those indicted. And by 1881, killer Bob Olinger was made a Deputy U.S. Marshal by the Secret Service to guard Billy Bonney.

Perpetual Ring loyalty to these "friends" was demonstrated in a January 16, 1886 letter from Catron's firm about Joe Nash, by then elevated to enforcer of Lincoln County's quarantine law, and conducting malicious prosecution through the Stock Association to eliminate competitors. It stated: "Enclosed I send you a memorandum, or rather, a letter from J.H. Nash to Edward C. Wade Esq., giving a list of persons who have violated the quarantine law in Lincoln County. This letter was forwarded to the Stock Association, and the Stock Association have instructed me to bring suit, wherever I thought proof could be obtained sufficient to insure a judgment."

JOHN KINNEY GANG

Rustler and killer of Regulator leader, Frank MacNab, and victims in San Patricio and the Lincoln County War, Mesilla-based John Kinney was accused in Billy Bonney's July 13, 1878 "Regulator Manifesto": "*Mr. Walz. Sir: - We are all aware that your brother-in-law, T.B. Catron sustains the Murphy-**Kinney** party.*"

Kinney was born in about 1847 in Massachusetts, fought on the Union side, and came to New Mexico Territory in 1868 in the 3rd U.S. Cavalry. Mustering out in 1873, in Las Cruces he developed a major rustling operation. After his Lincoln County War service, he was made a Deputy Sheriff to guard Billy in his transport from his Mesilla hanging trial to Lincoln's courthouse-jail. In 1883, he was briefly imprisoned in Leavenworth for rustling. He then lived in Texas and Arizona. On August 29, 1919, his lying obituary was in *The Daily Arizona Silver Belt* as "Captain Kinney Dead." It called him a "Pioneer of the border;" stating: "He started a civil career in New Mexico and came to be a deputy sheriff where he soon became known for his daring in running down bandits. Captain Kinney stepped aside to give Sheriff Pat Garrett of Lincoln county, this honor, but he kept in the saddle and performed equally daring deeds to wipe out the large criminal element."

Victor Westphall linked Kinney to Catron (Westphall, p. 90), though calling it a "legend ... that Catron was responsible for Kinney's participation in Lincoln County troubles." But he gives Catron's then law partner, William Thornton, as defending Kinney for rustling. He blames William Rynerson: "If any Territorial official is to be charged with recruitment of the outlaw element, it must be District Attorney Rynerson." Westphall does admit that Sheriff George Peppin used Kinney and his gang for posses - but omits that they were for the April 29, 1878 murder of Regulator leader Frank MacNab, the July 3, 1878 San Patricio massacre, and the Lincoln County War Battle.

JESSIE EVANS AND HIS GANG

Murderer of John Tunstall and Huston Chapman in the Lincoln County War and aftermath, Jessie Evans was born in 1853, in Missouri or Texas, into a criminal family. On June 26, 1871, they were arrested in Elk City, Kansas, for passing counterfeit money. In 1872, coming to New Mexico Territory, he rustled with John Kinney; then made his own gang with Tom Hill, George Davis (Graham), William "Buck" Morton, and Frank Baker as a Ring supplier of rustled beef for "The House's" contracts.

Billy Bonney, after escaping Bonita, Arizona, on August 17, 1877, joined Jessie's gang. Billy was identified on October 1, 1877, in a stagecoach robbery with them. But by the end of the month, Billy changed direction, being hired by Tunstall as a ranch hand.

Jessie's direction was with the Ring, and he played an active part in the Lincoln County War. On February 18, 1878, he was in Sheriff Brady's posse to kill Tunstall. The Regulators subsequently arrested Jessie's gang members, Morton and Baker, killing them while they attempted escape. Jessie was present in the Lincoln County War Battle, along with the rest of Sheriff George Peppin's outlaw posse.

On February 18, 1879, with his gang member, Billy Campbell, and James Dolan, he killed Huston Chapman in Lincoln. Arrested by Lew Wallace on March 8, 1879, and held at Fort Stanton, he and Campbell escaped on March 15th, with likely Ring assistance.

Relocating to Texas, on July 4, 1880, he and his gang killed a Texas Ranger named George Bingham during their capture. On October 9, 1880, Jessie was indicted for Bingham's murder.

In his October 15th trial, its District Attorney, T.A. Falvey, reduced his charge to second degree murder, because he was in a shooting group, and could not be proven to be the actual killer **(opposite to Billy's first degree murder charge in his Ring-controlled court, though he too was in a group shooting at Brady and Hindman and could not be the proven killer)**.

Given a 20 year sentence at Texas State Penitentiary, Jessie escaped on May 23, 1882, disappearing from history.

COMMANDER N.A.M. DUDLEY

Nathan Augustus Monroe Dudley had a dishonorable military career, and treasonously intervened in the Lincoln County War Battle. His apologist biographer is E. Donald Kaye, in his 1997 *Nathan Augustus Monroe Dudley, 1825-1910: Rogue, Hero, or Both?* There is no mention of the Santa Fe Ring.

Born on August 20, 1825 in Lexington, Massachusetts, Dudley began his army career in 1855, as a First Lieutenant in the 10th Infantry, where he was involved in massacring Sioux in Nebraska and plundering their village for artifacts for the Smithsonian Museum. In 1857 to 1858, as acting Commander of

Company E, he was in Utah's Mormon War against Brigham Young. There, a Jesse A. Grove wrote: "As a soldier he is not considered equal to most of the others." In 1861, he was promoted to Captain, and had his first court martial trial for unbecoming conduct of lying to another officer. He was found not guilty.

In March of 1862, he was made a Colonel, but was never promoted above brevet brigadier general of volunteers in the Civil War; during which he was in no major battles, but became known as "Gold Lace Dudley" for embellishing his uniform. In June of 1862, with his 30th Massachusetts Infantry regiment, he burned down the plantation of a suspected Rebel fighter, George Keller, around women and children - an atrocity he repeated 16 years later at the McSween home in the Lincoln County War Battle.

After the Civil War, he was transferred to the 3rd Cavalry. In 1871, he was court martialed and found guilty of drunkenness on duty at Arizona Territory's Camp McDowell, and was confined for two months in Camp Bowie. General Edward Hatch tried unsuccessfully to remove him from service for alcoholism.

In 1877, he was court martialed again. Having been made Lieutenant Colonel of the 9th Cavalry on July 1, 1876, and Commander of Fort Union in 1877, he was arrested for drunkenness on duty, disrespect to his superior officer, and trying to force a marriage between the raped post chaplain's daughter and her rapist. Catron and his law partner, William T. Thornton, represented him, yielding no punishment.

A year later, on April 5, 1878, he was given command of Fort Stanton, after removal of George Purington. He may have been Ring bribed, since his wife's estate had expensive jewelry, beyond his means. Doing Ring service, on June 28, 1878, he raided San Patricio with Sheriff George Peppin in failed attempt to murder Alexander McSween. And on July 19, 1878, he violated the Posse Comitatus Act by intervening for the Ring in the Lincoln County War Battle. On February 18, 1879, he was a co-conspirator in murdering Huston Chapman. New Governor Lew Wallace had him removed as Commander for upsetting Lincolnites. He faced a 1879 military court of inquiry for his Lincoln County War intervention, being represented by Ringite Henry Waldo and in a corrupt court. So he was cleared despite Billy Bonney's eye-witness testimony of his officers firing a volley at civilians.

Dudley was returned to Command at Fort Union on January 14, 1880. That year, he was in Colonel George Buell's campaign against Mimbres Apache Chief Victorio, which drove him and his tribe to Mexico where they were massacred. In 1887, transferred to the Midwest as a 1st Cavalry Colonel, Dudley fought in Montana's Crow War. In 1889, he retired. On April 29, 1910, he died in Roxbury, Massachusetts; being buried in Arlington National Cemetery, his treasonous murders in Lincoln and his genocide of Native Americans without retribution.

PROPAGANDA PRESS

SUMMARY: Ring victory was helped by the press, providing outlaw scapegoats and blocking the voice of the oppressed. And Catron used newspapers for anonymous defamatory letter plots to destroy adversaries. Ringite press was responsible for the first outlaw myths of Billy the Kid.

JOHN H. KOOGLER: LAS VEGAS GAZETTE

Catron kept pocket notebooks with payment records. In one, he recorded: "*Paid Koogler for Paper & advertisement for April 18, 1881, 13$\underline{00}$.*" Whether real advertising or Ring ""advertising," Koogler helped create the Billy the Kid outlaw myth during the Ring's lethal pursuit of Billy Bonney. Billy himself wrote in vain to Governor Lew Wallace on December 12, 1880; stating: "*I noticed in the Las Vegas Gazette a piece which stated that, Billy "the" Kid, the name by which I am known in the Country was the captain of a Band of Outlaws who hold Forth at the Portales. There is no such Organization in Existence. So the Gentleman must have drawn very heavily on his Imagination.*"

Also using city editor Lucius "Lute" M. Wilcox, the *Las Vegas Gazette* encouraged Billy's killing with articles like the following: "Desperadoe's Stronghold, An Organized Gang Assisted by Nature and Defiantly Reckless, Who Terrorize the Country to the East of Us" of December 3, 1880; "The Kid. Interview with Billy Bonney The Best Known Man in New Mexico" of December 27, 1880; Koogler's own "Interview with Lew Wallace on 'The Kid' " of April 28, 1881; "Billy 'the Kid' " of May 12, 1881; and "Billy 'the Kid' is in the vicinity of Sumner" of May 15, 1881. Its *Las Vegas Morning Gazette* ran: "A Bay-Mare. Everyone who has heard of Billy 'the Kid' has heard of his beautiful bay mare" of January 4, 1881; "The Kid. Billy 'the Kid' and Billy Wilson were on Monday taken to Mesilla for Trial" of March 15, 1881; "Billy the Kid Seems to be having a stormy journey on his trip Southward" of April 5, 1881; "Barney Mason at Fort Sumner states the 'Kid' is in Local Sheep Camps" of June 16, 1881.

Like other Ringites, John Koogler was a dependent beggar. On July 17, 1889, he wrote to Catron from Las Vegas: "I start for Kansas City to-morrow ... **I wish you would send the money expected from Marshall, Field & Co. to me at Kansas City ... It will be doing me a favor, as I will be quite short of funds unless I receive it.**" On July 29th, he implored: *"I had made confident calculations on getting [the money] by this time ... I need it, or part of it, badly."*

RUSSELL A. KISTLER: LAS VEGAS DAILY OPTIC

Ringite Russell A. Kistler, owner of *Las Vegas Daily Optic*, helped to demonize Billy Bonney as "Billy the Kid" in Catron's campaign with the Secret Service and Sheriff Pat Garrett to kill him. Published were: "A Big Haul! Billy Kid, Dave Rudabaugh, Billy Wilson and Tom Pickett in the Clutches of the Law" on December 27, 1880; "Billy Bonney. Advices from Lincoln bring the intelligence of the escape of 'Billy the Kid' " on May 2, 1881; "Dare Devil Desperado. Pursuit of 'Billy the Kid' has been abandoned" on May 4, 1881; "The question of how to deal with desperados who commit murder has but one solution - kill them" on May 10, 1881; " 'Billy the Kid' has been heard from again" on June 10, 1881; " 'Billy the Kid,' He is Reported to Have Been Seen on Our Streets Saturday Night" on June 13, 1881; "Billy the Kid would make an ideal newspaper-man in that he always endeavors to 'get even' with his enemies" on June 13, 1881; "Billy the Kid" on June 28, 1881; and " 'The Kid' Killed" on July 18, 1881.

The *Optic* also ran a June 15, 1881 article, possibly by Governor Lew Wallace for his own outlawing campaign, titled: "**Land of the Petulant Pistol**. 'Billy the Kid' as a Killer."

Catron was loyal to Kistler for decades. A December 12, 1891 letter from his law partner, William J. Mills, relates a Kistler visit about a boycott of the *Optic*. Kistler wanted Catron's retaliation. Mills wrote: "Kistler is also talking about suing the signers of the paper by which he is boycotted and I wish to consult with you about this also."

As shown by an August 19, 1899 letter from a George T. Gould to Catron, Frank Springer and others, in February of 1898 had bought the *Optic* with its lots from Kistler for $8,500. The Ring's hold could continue unbroken.

THOMAS HUGHES: THE ALBUQUERQUE DAILY CITIZEN

Thomas Hughes came to Albuquerque in 1881, from Marysville, Kansas, and bought the *Albuquerque Morning Journal*; selling it in about 1883. It later passed to the *Daily Democrat's* owner, and was mortgaged to Catron for $9,000, showing his bi-partisan control of Territorial press. In 1885, Hughes bought the *Albuquerque Daily Citizen*, then the *Evening Citizen*. In 1888, William T. McCreight, from Shelbyville, Kentucky, and in the Territory since 1880, bought half interest, and worked as its business manager and city editor.

It was with Hughes and McCreight that Catron conducted his 1895 anonymous defamatory letter plot against his Supreme Court Chief Justice, Thomas Smith, to sabotage his disbarment case. The resulting December 20, 1896 trial, in which Hughes was Catron's fall-guy, was filed in the Supreme Court as "In the Matter of Contempt vs. Thomas Hughes, Respondent."

Catron's $350.00 pay-off check of July 11, 1896 was signed by both Hughes and McCreight as recipients. In 1896, Hughes next participated in Catron's anonymous "Poker Bill" defamatory published letter against Governor William Thornton.

Hughes owned the *Albuquerque Daily Citizen* till April 1, 1905, selling it to a W.S. Strickler. He died on June 30, 1905.

SINGLETON M. ASHENFELTER: THE GRANT COUNTY HERALD, NEW SOUTHWEST, DAILY SOUTHWEST

Pennsylvania born and college educated, Singleton M. Ashenfelter was a world traveler, arriving in New Mexico Territory in 1870. He was appointed U.S. District Attorney by President Ulysses S. Grant, and was in office till 1872. He then settled in Mesilla, and ran the J.F. Bennett & Company stage coach line. In 1872, he made a law partnership with Ringite John D. Bail, moving to Silver City in 1877. He also published at different times the *Grant County Herald*, the *New Southwest*, and the *Daily Southwest*. In 1885, he was appointed District Attorney for the Third Judicial District by Governor Edmund G. Ross. He died in Silver City on January 23, 1906.

Catron bribed Ashenfelter by "renting" his printing office for his 1892 Delegate campaign. On October 26, 1892, Ashenfelter wrote: `"Johnny Riley writes me from Las Cruces, that I am to look to you for the $100 rental still due on the printing office used here at Deming."`

On April 10, 1893, Riley wrote to Ashenfelter that he would remind Catron about paying. He did so on May 13, 1894: "*About the $100⁰⁰ ... I have gone over the matter with you often –* **When you ran for [Delegate to] Congress your friends felt you should have a paper to support you at Deming ... [Ashenfelter's] paper was nearly entirely devoted to your interest.**"

There were no hard feelings. On April 14, 1898, Ashenfelter wrote to Catron about a possible land grant purchase opportunity. All Ring lackeys knew where their bread was ultimately buttered.

WILLIAM BREEDEN AND HENRY WALDO: THE SANTA FE NEW MEXICAN

As mentioned above, William Breeden and Henry Waldo, as President and Director respectively, published the Ringite *Santa Fe New Mexican*. It was downstairs on the two-story Catron block, bordering the east side of Santa Fe's central plaza; with Catron's office upstairs. A March 13, 1876 *The Boston Daily Globe* article, "New Mexico, A Sorry Showing for a Would-be State;" wrote: "[The Ring's] `official organ [is] the Santa Fe New Mexican."`

It ran Lew Wallace's reward notice on May 3, 1881 as "Billy the Kid. $500 Reward." It also used the outlaw myth with: "The Kid" on May 1, 1881; "The Kid's Escape" on May 3, 1881; "More Killing by Kid, When But a Short Distance From Lincoln, He Meets one of His Old Enemies, and Kills Him and His Companion. Two More Victims" on May 4, 1881; untitled articles about the escaped "Kid' being in Albuquerque" on May 5, 1881 and back in Stinking Springs on May 5,, 1881; "The Kid was in Chloride City" on May 13, 1881; "The Kid is believed to be in the Black Range" on May 19, 1881; "Billy the Kid was last seen in Lincoln County" on May 19, 1881; and "The Kid" on June 16, 1881.

KEY CORONER'S JURY PRESIDENT

SUMMARY: The oddity of Billy Bonney's Coroner's Jury Report praising Pat Garrett for killing him - opposite to Fort Sumner residents' sentiment - is explained by Ringite Sunnyside Postmaster, Milnor Rudulph, being its President.

Milnor Rudulph was born in Maryland on August 25, 1826. He became a teacher and merchant in Memphis, Tennessee. In 1849, he came to New Mexico Territory, joining the Third Regiment, New Mexico Volunteers in 1861. In 1870, he was elected to the Territorial legislature. On January 10, 1872, as the Ringite Speaker of the House he illegally halted the legislature to block anti-Ring bills; precipitating the Legislature Revolt. In 1878, he became postmaster as Sunnyside, near Fort Sumner. On July 15, 1881, he was made President of Billy Bonney's Coroner's jury. He likely pressured the Report's jurymen to praise Pat Garrett for killing Billy. In 1882, he returned to the Mora valley and teaching. He died there on November 8, 1887.

His son, Charles Rudulph, kept in touch with Catron, congratulating him in a November 5, 1895 letter for winning Delegate to Congress. (See page 129)

HISTORIAN FOR THEM ALL

SUMMARY: Attorney and politician, Ralph Emerson Twitchell, advanced Santa Fe Ring propaganda with his multi-volume Leading Facts in New Mexico History, which covered-up the Ring and outlawed opponents.

Ralph Emerson Twitchell was born in 1859, in Ann Arbor, Michigan, and lived in Jackson County, Missouri. In 1882, he got a law degree and moved to Santa Fe, joining Henry Waldo's firm, working there for life. In 1885, he became President of the Bar Association. From 1889 to 1892, he was District Attorney for the First Judicial District. In the 1890's, with Catron and Francisco Gonzales y Borrego (murderer of anti-Ring Francisco Chavez), he was in the Ring-associated Knights of Liberty. In 1893, he was Mayor of Santa Fe. In 1902 and 1903, he chaired New Mexico's Republican Central Committee. In 1911 and 1912, he published his Ring-denying *Leading Facts in New Mexico History*. In 1924, he was President of the Historical Society of New Mexico. He died in California on August 26, 1925.

Twitchell had profuse communication with Catron, often about borrowing money and Ringite election manipulations.

On October 16, 1892, campaigning for Delegate, Catron instructed him: "*I want this campaign to be lively for the next three weeks, so get me three or four parties & let them keep matters boiling. I will pay their expenses (necessary).*" On October 22nd, Chairman of the Republican Central Committee George W. Gregg, wrote to him about possible vote buying: "The democratic majority ... are Mexicans and a party will be sent there on the day of the election to change it. A little money will be necessary on the day of election." On October 24, 1892, John Riley, as President of the Doña Ana Republican Central Committee, helping Catron's campaign, wrote to Spanish-speaking Twitchell to "get out in Spanish a number of copies of your letter with [Democrat Antonio] Joseph's bill in reference to taking out water from Rio Grande ... to stir up our fellows over there."

As mentioned above, Catron may have also communicated with Twitchell in cipher-code.

WASHINGTON, D.C. FACILITATORS

SUMMARY: Santa Fe Ring enablers in Washington, D.C., colluding with S.B. Elkins - and at times with T.B. Catron directly - were presidents, cabinet members, and senators. Relevant to the Lincoln County War period were President Rutherford B. Hayes, Secretary of the Interior Carl Schurz, and Secretary of State William Evarts, as seen below.

THE ANTI-RING REBELLIONS

All these Ringites' fortunes were built on blood and terror. But they had to run the gauntlet of uprisings against them in the 1870's: the 1872 Legislature Revolt, 1876 Grant County Rebellion, 1877 Colfax County War, and 1878 Lincoln County War. That was when the people miscalculated the Ring's superhuman might, not realizing that martyrdom was the only possibility.

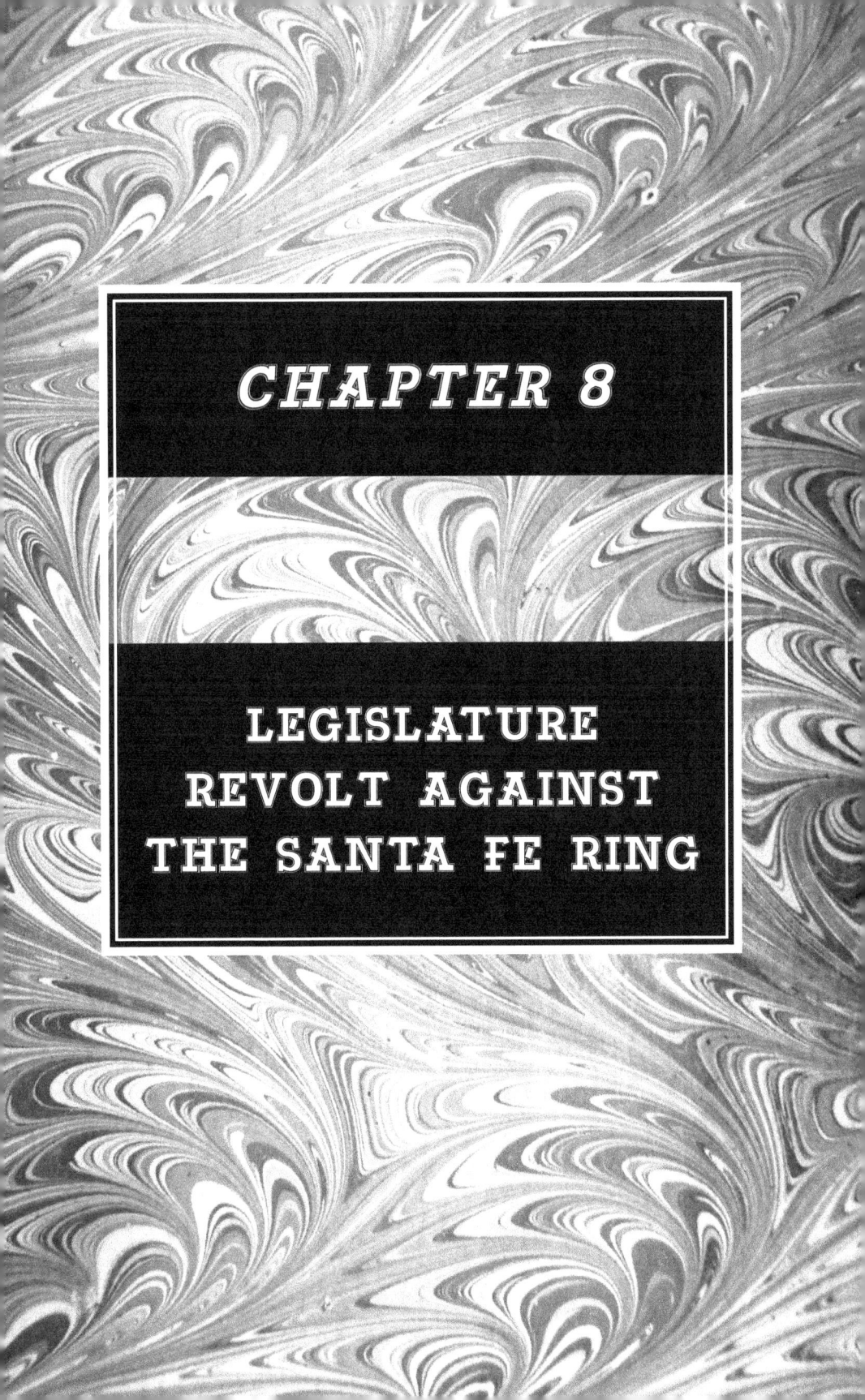

CHAPTER 8

LEGISLATURE REVOLT AGAINST THE SANTA FE RING

THE FIRST ANTI-RING FREEDOM FIGHT

SUMMARY: The first anti-Ring uprising occurred in the Territorial legislature. From the Ring's start, Elkins and Catron sought judicial power for malicious prosecutions. By 1871's, their corrupt control of courts met opposition. And the brutal Ringite response set its future pattern.

By 1872, the Santa Fe Ring had been expanding for six years, and beleaguered public officials were first to react to its abuses. Fittingly, it was in the seat of democratic power, the legislature, populated by elected representatives of the people, that the first stand was taken. And the issue was Ringite control of the courts for malicious prosecutions and shielding of cronies. I named the uprising the Legislature Revolt of 1872.

RINGITE GOVERNORS ROBERT MITCHELL, WILLIAM PILE, AND MARSH GIDDINGS

Almost immediately, the canny new Ring sought judicial power. In December of 1866, Thomas Benton Catron, only five months after his Territorial arrival, achieved appointment as District Attorney for the Third Judicial District; and Stephen Benton Elkins was made Territorial Attorney General. Backed by Ringite, William Breeden, they used acting Governor William F.M. Arney while Governor Robert Byington Mitchell was traveling. The legislature's House protested these power seizures; but returned Governor Mitchell merely promoted Elkins to Territorial U.S. Attorney and Catron to Attorney General.

On August 16, 1869, President Ulysses S. Grant appointed Republican William Anderson Pile from St. Louis, Missouri, as Governor. Pile kept Catron as Attorney General based on recommendations by Elkins and Chief Justice Joseph G. Palen whose Ringite corruption would precipitate the 1872 Legislature Revolt. In Pile's scandal-filled administration, he and Catron were accused - without consequences - of selling and destroying Territorial archives. Called "The Battle of the Archives," it was an anti-Ring protest to Catron's taking the archive room for his own office, and disposing of its records with Pile's permission. Pile was further accused of wrongly keeping Catron as Attorney General. Both were accused of conspiring to split state offices with Democrats if statehood occurred. (Westphall, pp. 31-32) Pile also quashed Maxwell Land Grant's settlers' anti-Ring Elizabethtown riot by a Proclamation of April 17, 1871 to assist Elkins's evicting them. Those riots led to the 1877 Colfax County War.

On August 4, 1871, President Grant appointed, as next Governor, Marsh Giddings of Michigan. His repressive actions in the 1871-1872 legislature further empowered the Ring and precipitated the Legislature Revolt. Giddings died in office in June 3, 1875; but in his three years he advanced the Ring, used troops against its adversaries, applied Ring-style patronage for political appointments, and taxed land grants to facilitate Ring's land-grabs from impecunious owners. And, with Catron, Giddings began the Ring pattern of vilifying opponents as "outlaws."

THE 1872 LEGISLATURE REVOLT

SUMMARY: In the legislative session of 1871 to 1872, Democratic legislators passed bills to block Ring control. In response, Ringite Governor Marsh Giddings attempted to veto them, precipitating the January 1872 Legislature Revolt. To suppress it, he brought in troops and the U.S. Marshal; Ringites usurped the legislature; and the anti-Ring bills were nullified by the Supreme Court. Giddings, by February of 1872 Proclamation, blocked future opposition by reapportioning the legislature to halve representation of anti-Ring Grant, Doña Ana, and Lincoln Counties.

Ironically, the first anti-Santa Fe Ring revolt was precipitated, in part, by thwarted interests of Grant County's Silver City; where Billy Bonney had spent early adolescence from 1873 to 1875, and may have heard residents' angry talk about Ring oppression.

Anti-Ring resistance began with Democrat legislators in the 1871 to 1872 session of the legislature, and led to overt revolt. Ringites, including Governor Marsh Giddings, recognized the threat to their control of Territorial politics, as evidenced by Giddings's writing, the next year, to the Department of Interior, calling the revolt *"that terrible war"* and *"one of the most reckless revolutionary efforts made any where."* And the Ring's successful suppression set its future patterns of bribery; abuse of executive, legislative and judicial power; and using troops for terrorism.

The 1872 Legislature Revolt was hidden by Ring-denier historians, like Victor Westphall and William Keleher, in their respective 1973, *Thomas Benton Catron and His Era,* and 1957, *Violence in Lincoln County.*

Exposing the Revolt as anti-Ring was Conrad Keeler Naegle, historian of the Grant County Rebellion, in his 1943 doctoral thesis and in his 1968 article in *Arizona and the West* journal. Naegle used the legislature's own transcripts in *Diario del Consejo* and *Journal of the House of Representatives.*

THE DANGEROUS BILLS

Precipitant to the 1872 Legislature Revolt was Democrat legislators' passing bills to limit the then largely Republican Ring's abuses. At the session's start, on December 7, 1871, Democrats controlled the Council, and seemed likely to gain the House of Representatives. That would have stifled the fledgling Ring. Ultimately, federal troops were used to crush them. Naegle, in his *Arizona and the West* article, quoted alarmed reporting: "In January 1872, the Denver *Rocky Mountain News* described a recent event in Santa Fe, New Mexico, which it called 'unparalled in the history of western politics.' Federal troops had been stationed in the halls of the Territorial legislature to assure control by the Santa Fe Ring, a political and economic clique." (Naegle, *Arizona and the West*, p. 225)

Naegle quoted Council President Don Diego Archuleta: "Before we submit to such despotic action on the part of the Executive, the Mexican people had better be placed upon reservations as the Indians are now. We had better resign our seats than to beg our rights of the newly fledged governor who seeks to overawe us, and force us to obedience to his despotic will by the presence of U.S. bayonets." (Naegle, thesis, p. 37)

Some legislation passed by the House had been mundane: for Silver City's incorporation and Grant County's making a public school system. But on December 30, 1871, the Council and House passed, by large majorities, redistricting of Ring-biased judges. It was a bull's eye attack on the Ring, intended to transfer Ringite Supreme Court Chief Justice Joseph G. Palen from Santa Fe's First Judicial District Court to remote Third Judicial District Courts. (Naegle, thesis, p. 32) That would end his Supreme Court position and his Ring-enabling tactic of malicious prosecutions. He was accused of issuing biased decisions for Catron and Elkins in exchange for "sharing plunder." (Westphall, p. 105)

RINGITE RESPONSES

Victor Westphall minimized the bills as an "attempt to humiliate" Palen (Westphall, p. 107); but confirmed Palen's clique: "[Palen] became a particular friend of [Republican Party head] William Breeden, and the two, along with Elkins and Catron, were repeatedly and vehemently accused by enemy newspapers of largely controlling the Territorial courts." (Westphall, p. 103)

Westphall outlawed Catron's opponents, Alexander P. Sullivan, editor of the *Santa Fe Post*, and Territorial Secretary Henry Wetter, by claiming they wanted Palen removed to prevent their own indictment for business dealings; and "Attorney General Catron was in a position to bring indictments and Judge Palen to sit in judgment." (Westphall, p. 104) Omitted was that such malicious prosecutions were the cause of the anti-Palen bill. Westphall also revealed that legislator, August Kirchner, on February 1, 1872, sent an affidavit to U.S. Senator Lyman Trunbull, Chairman of the Judiciary Committee, swearing "Catron and Elkins had approached him ... to buy legislative votes in an effort to leave Palen undisturbed." (Westphall, p. 107) Governor Giddings had countered by telegramming Attorney General George H. Williams, in Washington, to call Kirchner's affidavit "grossly false." (Westphall, p. 107)

On January 4, 1872, Governor Giddings vetoed all the Democrat's bill's, including the one for Palen's reassignment. The "Journal of the House of Representatives" stated: "Governor [Giddings] vetoed the act on the grounds that the assembly ... had no power to make changes without first gaining the consent of Congress." But Conrad Naegle retorted that the veto violated "U.S. Statutes at Large" adopted by New Mexico on September 9, 1850, which stated: "'L]egislative assemblies of New Mexico ...

may assign the judges ... in such manner as deems proper and convenient." (Naegle, thesis, p. 32)

On January 5th, to block Democrats votes over-riding Giddings's veto, Ringites added names of four absent Taos legislators to get a Republican majority. (Naegle, thesis, p. 34) Then, on January 9th, the Ring tried to end the session as null and void. (Naegle, thesis, p. 33)

On January 10th, the four Taos men arrived. But rather than risk a vote, Ringite Speaker Milnor Rudulph (later President of Billy Bonney's Coroner's Jury, creating the report praising Pat Garrett for killing him) illegally halted the legislature. After objection by the Democrat majority, Rudulph declared the House adjourned and left, taking ten legislators with him.

THE ANTI-RING LEGISLATURE REVOLT

The Legislature Revolt began the day Speaker Milnor Rudulph illegally stopped the legislature: January 10, 1872. Defiant legislators declared that no legal adjournment by vote had occurred; and stated that, with Speaker Rudulph departed, there was a vacancy. So they elected, as new Speaker, Silver City mine developer, John R. Johnson. (Naegle, thesis, p. 34) They then directed the Sergeant-at-Arms to get Santa Fe County Sheriff Carlos M. Conklin to arrest and bring back exited legislators for a quorum. Returned were arrested Milnor Rudulph and two others. (Naegle, thesis, p. 37) Westphall called all that: "lawless and revolutionary maneuvers [of the] legislative mob." (Westphall, pp. 104-105)

Ringites retaliated. On January 11th, Governor Giddings and Milnor Rudulph, still calling himself "Speaker," declared "anarchy and rebellion" to allow General Gordon Granger, Commanding the U.S. Military District for New Mexico, to send a squad from Fort Marcy into the legislature. (Keleher, *Violence in Lincoln County*, p. 12) Chief Justice Palen called in Santa Fe's U.S. Marshal John Pratt with deputies. Catron, as Attorney General, filed writs of *habeas corpus* in the Supreme Court to free Rudulph and the two other legislators as illegally detained and to get an emergency Supreme Court session to decide their case. (Westphall, p. 105)

But on January 11th, with Milnor Rudulph and John R. Johnson both claiming to be "Speaker," there were two competing Houses of Representatives; though the majority supported Johnson. He introduced the bill for Grant County's taxing to create a public school system. (Naegle thesis, p. 37) But Catron and Elkins allegedly then bribed his Councilmen - including a Candelario Garcia and original protester, Don Diego Archuleta - to vote for Rudulph's House. (Naegle, thesis, p. 37) A September 2, 1884 *Las Vegas Optic* article referenced that bribery in the 1895 disbarment attempt against Catron, stating:

> Catron and Elkins bought off a number of legislators including August Kirchner [to make him retract his affidavit to Trumbull about Catron trying to use him to bribe legislators to protect Palen]. Elkins promised [Kirchner] a favorable decision in a certain suit should Palen not be removed. Elkins also promised to cancel a $780 mortgage on the property of Pascual Baca for his vote.

The Ring's response was military suppression. On January 12, 1872, Speaker John Johnson was seized by Fort Marcy troops, and U.S. Marshal Pratt's lawmen escorted Milnor Rudulph to the Speaker's chair. Rudulph then suspended the legislature pending the Supreme Court's decision. (Kelleher, *Violence in Lincoln County*, p. 12)

But the Johnson House nevertheless tried to institute Silver City's incorporation - already passed by the House in December – and also passed by the Council. (Naegle, thesis, p. 28)

On January 22nd, to crush the Revolt, the emergency Supreme Court session, under Judge Hezekiah S. Johnson, - with troops and Ringite Santa Fe County Sheriff Carlos Conklin present for intimidation, wrongly exceeded the *habeas corpus* issue before them, to declare null and void all passed Democratic legislation of the session. The Democrats accused Judge Johnson of being "but a puppet of Judge Palen." (Kelleher, *Violence in Lincoln County*, p. 12) Westphall stated: "[The Supreme Court] ruled that the attempt to take over the House of Representatives was illegal and void. Forces of the United States marshal's office, reinforced by United States soldiers, stood by to see that there was no further interference. The Republican majority passed a resolution expunging from the record and nullifying all proceedings of the revolutionary Democratic minority." (Westphall, p. 105)

RUTHLESS RINGITE VICTORY

Thus, Ringite judges were kept in place, and legislative acts beneficial to Grant County and Silver City were voided. The 1872 Legislature Revolt ended with Ring victory, and tested use of complicit lawmen and troops for suppression.

Then the Ring, ever cognizant of its incriminating paper trails, expurgated the records of the 1872 Legislature Revolt. Naegle, in his *Arizona and the West* article, wrote: "[A] report titled *Diario del Consejo Legislativo del Territorio de Nuevo Mejico, Session de 1871-1872*, was made by a special committee of the Council concerning the stationing of federal troops in the legislative halls. The *Diario* is a scarce item, for **an attempt apparently was made to destroy or steal all copies.** A copy was found by this writer in 1942 in the basement of the old Supreme Court building [in Santa Fe]." (Naegle, p. 227)

AFTERMATH OF LEGISLATURE REVOLT

After January's 1872 Legislature Revolt, the Ring's stranglehold tightened. First, Governor Marsh Giddings issued a gerrymandering Proclamation on February 28, 1872, denying equal representation to Democratic counties by redistricting their legislative representation by combining Grant, Doña Ana, and Lincoln Counties, and halving their legislators to two, with just one senator. (Similar disempowerment tactics were used by the next Ringite governor, S.B. Axtell, who blocked prosecutions of Ringite murderers in 1876 in Colfax County by removing its courts; and in 1878 by removing Lincoln County's Justice of the Peace. The Colfax and Lincoln County Wars resulted.) Naegle wrote: "This [denial of equal representation] marked the beginning of gerrymandering in New Mexico and was the second factor [after illegal disposal of the Johnson House's legislation for Grant County] that served to crystallize the desire of the people of Silver City to be free from the domination of the Santa Fe 'ring.' " (Naegle, thesis, pp. 38-39)

By the next year, 1873, Governor Giddings used Ring-style patronage to appoint officials without proper legislative approval; even making his own son Adjutant General.

CHARGES AGAINST GOVERNOR GIDDINGS

Marsh Gidding's out-of-control Ringite patronage resulted in charges against him to the Department of the Interior and led to his son's withdrawal as Adjutant General. But, backed by Catron, William Breeden, and Judge Joseph Palen, he was not censured.

Giddings's charges exposed the class struggle against the plutocratic Ring. An example is Delegate to Congress Jose Gallegos's March 13, 1873 protest to President Ulysses S. Grant:

Washington March 13th 1873
To the President of the United States:
Sir.
My people are extremely anxious to have Governor Giddings removed as Governor; he are officious, meddling, disagreeable man to my peoples.

I will not ask the appoint of any particular man, but the names of W<u>m</u> L. McKnight of Ill, and that of Col Isaac S. Stewart late Paymaster in the Army have been presented for my considerations by their friends. The appointment of either of these gentlemen would be accepted by my people with great satisfaction and gratitude.

Very Truly Yours.
Jose M. Gallegos

On March 26, 1873, Giddings denied the charges to the Secretary of the Interior. Then, with possible input of Catron and Elkins, he initiated the Ring's tactic of outlawing and defaming opponents. On April 3, 1873, he scrawled a rambling, twenty-seven page letter, blaming his charges on the *"revolution"* of the legislature's Democrats, past corrupt officials, and *"vilest of the vile [Mexicans from] slums of vice"* in Santa Fe. He wrote:

To His Hon the Sec of the Interior
Washington D.C.
Sir – A transfer of Territorial officers from the State Dept. to the Dept of the interior of which I was just advised by the Secretary of State, and a renewal of charges heretofore made against me, to the Secretary of State, with some little additions thereto, force me to make a statement to your Dept. of my conduct ... I have not the charges, but an outline of them from Senator Ferry ...

The legislature convened about the first of December [1871] and everything looked well. It looked as if the recommendations of my message would be headed, and legislation made to correspond. But after a little time and before legislation had proceeded much there arose trouble. Party spirit came up. The democrats feared the republican party would gain something if the recommendations of the governor were carried out. Aside from this arose another serious difficulty. A most shameful and causeless attack was made upon Chief Justice Palen ...

[Palen's enemies] all combined to disgrace, and get rid of Chief Justice Palen ... [T]hese men conspiring together with the worst democrats, secured passage of a bill ... by the most wicked falsehood, whereby Chief Justice Palen was thrown out of the Santa Fe District ... so as to disgrace him & prevent his presiding in certain cases of interest to the parties who had joined the conspiracy ...

[AUTHOR'S NOTE: Giddings conceals that the opposition was to Ring control, and omits Palen's Ring-biased decisions.]

[AUTHOR'S NOTE: Giddings next vilified the 1872 Legislature Revolt to justify its crushing by him.]

This brought a terrible war. *The republican members saw they had been misled, and stood by the executive ... The democrats were determined to prevent a vote that would sustain me ...*

Upon my vetoing this measure to displace Judge Palen the House broke up and divided into two parts ... Two days before the close of the session, we succeeded in effecting a compromise ... ***Thos B. Catron now U.S. Attorney & then my Territorial Attorney learning that the Sec. of the Territory, as a part of this progression to break up my legislature, who refusing and neglecting to pay the members their per diem allowance, himself actually paid the republican members who could not remain without pay and with other friends provided for expenses of various kinds to hold the legislature together until we could defeat the revolution and secure needed laws. He has not yet been reimbursed.***

[AUTHOR'S NOTE: This is Catron's bribery of legislators.]

But the best evidence that my course was satisfactory is shown in the fact that all the public offices and the best citizens of the Territory stood by me with their money and their influence. And though this extraordinary aid ... we were enabled to keep the legislature together, and to pass more really valuable laws within the last two days of the session than had been secured before by many years of legislation.

The greatest excitement prevailed when the House divided & it continued for weeks. The Speaker was obliged for some days to call in the military to his aid.

[AUTHOR'S NOTE: This covers up that "The Speaker" was resigned Milnor Rudulph, not the newly elected Speaker, John Johnson; and covers up that Giddings himself called in troops.]

Outsiders were set on to crowd into the House, make noise & disturbance & bring on a riot ...

[AUTHOR'S NOTE: This begins the Ring's outlaw myth demonizing opponents. The "riot" was legislators' own response to Ringites illegal take-over of their legislature.]

For many days a fight seemed inevitable. Riot & bloodshed were imminent ... [E]very member was armed and at any moment a fight might occur. At last, I went into the House, took a seat by the side of the Speaker and remained there for hours for the passions to cool, and until the adjournment of the House for the day.

After all we secured the passage of some excellent measures, and it is universally conceded now by the best men here, that we have made more real progress within the last year and a half than has ever been accomplished within any six years prior to my coming ...

[AUTHOR'S NOTE: Giddings omits that troops were stationed for intimidation as Ringite legislation was passed.]

[AUTHOR'S NOTE: Giddings next addressed appointing his son as Adjutant General, by calling accusers bad people or enemies of Palen and himself; and that the two Special Agents sent to investigate him were wrong to support the accusations. He added that Catron, as U.S. Attorney (since that February), filed charges against one of those Agents (this being the malicious prosecution that the legislators were trying to stop).]

[AUTHOR'S NOTE: Next Giddings covered up his Ringite appointments without legislative approval by blaming the 1872 Legislature Revolt, omitting that they would have been blocked if subjected to proper legislative approval.]

The legislature was in a state of revolution and until within two days before the close of the session, we could do nothing, and therefore the whole legislature for two years had to be done. Appointments were not thought of - nor were they of any consequence compared to the passage of more important laws for taxation to run the Territorial government & other grave matters. And these matters occupied the entire & every moments attention of the legislature during these two days. Even the appointment of senators & representatives had to be neglected & *I was driven to make this appointment to stand for ten years in consequence of the neglect of the legislature.*

And worse than all during the last five days of the session, exhausted by the constant night and day effort to prevent riot revolution & bloodshed for so many weeks I was broken down by sickness so that my family nearly despaired of my recovery, and I had to trust nearly everything for a time to my Territorial Attorney [Catron] for examination of acts to be approved or otherwise.

[AUTHOR'S NOTE: Giddings let Catron take over the legislature! His proper substitute was the Territorial Secretary.]

On the last day of the session & just before its close & between eleven and twelve oclock noon the hour of closing, a democratic member of the council who had fought me all winter arose & introduced a resolution requiring the governor to send to the council the names of his appointees. Every member of that body knew my situation [having left as sick], and although it was a democratic trick & the resolution passed, yet no member ... or other person was authorized to notify me, as appears by the record, but from some source [likely Catron] I was informed of what had been done, and knowing it was a trick I endeavored to get up & go to my table & send in names at the same time remarking to those present that it was a trick & that the council should have advised me in time if any desired to bring up that business, but before I could get to my room and write a line the legislature had adjourned.

After the legislature had adjourned I had to apportion the Territory and to appoint the Attorney General, Auditor of Public Documents, Treasurer, Quartermaster General, **Adjutant General [his son, William]**, *Librarian, and attorneys for the several Judicial Districts & perhaps others.*

All these appointments were made upon the recommendations of the best citizens of the Territory including generally the Federal officers [like Catron as U.S. Attorney] ...

As to putting off nominations for fear they would not be confirmed, how senseless, and what if the council did not confirm ... & less than two days the council must by law adjourn & the same result would have been secured. This charge is rather thin ...

[AUTHOR'S NOTE: Giddings omits that "best men" meant Ringites; and that he was avoiding legislative approval.]

The men who are making & pushing charges against me are not the friends of Gen. Grant's Administration ... [and I assisted] in nominating president Lincoln and Grant ... ***[A]fter having broken down here the most wicked revolution against the government and this administration & maintained as by a miracle the perfect administration of that part of the public affairs entrusted to me****, and brought great credit here upon Gen Grant & his administration as it is understood I carry out his views ... I say I can not but feel that I am entitled from my experience to exercise somewhat my own discretion in the appointment of the little offices relating to Territorial affairs, and* <u>*entitled to be believed*</u> *after more than* <u>*thirty years*</u> *of public life, in which my statements have never before been called into question ...*

[AUTHOR'S NOTE: Giddings calls the revolt a "revolution."]

I seek to do the will of the government but first of all to do right. If I am in accord with the government I want to know it. If I am not I desire to know above all things wherein I am not.
     Very respectfully
      Your obt servt
       Marsh Giddings

Giddings enclosed a support letter of March 26, 1873, signed by Catron, other Ringites, and Judge Joseph Palen himself:

Hon Thomas W. Ferry
   U.S. Senate
Sir – We have just learned that the character of the Adjutant General of New Mexico has been attacked at Washington with the view evidently, not so much as to effect him as to injure his father the Governor [Marsh Giddings]. Therefore we desire today, to you and to all whom it may concern, that we have known William M. Giddings for more than a year last past, and are acquainted with his character - And we desire to say that he is a gentleman in his bearing and demeanor - that he is a man of good moral character -

that he is competent to fill the office he occupies, and we have heard no complaint that his duties of said office were not satisfactorily performed.

He was appointed to the place upon recommendation of nearly all the Federal and Territorial Officers in the Territory, as also of a large portion of the members of the legislature.

Very Respectfully

T.B. Catron Attorney of U.S. for New Mexico
M.A. Breeden Clerk 1$\underline{st}$ Jud. Dist Court N.M.
W$\underline{m}$ Breeden Attorney at Law
José D. Sena Attorney at Law
J.G. Palen Chief Justice Sup. Court N.M.
T.F. Conway Atty. Gen. New Mexico

On April 20, 1873, Giddings followed-up by a letter to the Department of the Interior, promoting his legislation on land grant surveying for taxation, omitting its enabling of the Ring's land-grab. It was the Ring's manifesto of power. He wrote:

By the enactment of these laws in the last two days of the session our securities doubled in value within six months, and our debt of 75,000 or 80,000 will be paid off within three years if the property is properly assessed & tax collected. We have now highway laws, railroad laws & the whole face of things material is changed and set ahead nearly a quarter of a century ...

In accomplishing these great results I have been sustained by **Chief Justice Palen and the other Judges. The U.S. Attorney Catron, the Attorney General Conway, Col. W$\underline{m}$ Breeden former Clerk Sup Court here, S.B. Elkins Prest First Nt Bk Santa Fe** *& his cashiers & Directors and in fact all the Federal & Territorial Officers ... & every prominent republican with some of the best democrats in the Territory.*

I should not have mentioned these things now lest in the course of events these facts so few as they were communicated went to the Sec. of State & I desired therefore to give just an out live view of the unexpected success we had met here in this apparently dead country & community, against **one of the most reckless revolutionary efforts made any where** *...*

The administration will never have a nobler set of men to aid it, then those who surrounded me [by protection] in our Territorial rebellion, and these men today stand as firm by me as stand the hills & mountains around us.

EXPOSING ELKINS, CATRON, AND THE RING

In February of 1872, following the Legislature Revolt, August Kirchner failed to block President Grant's appointment of Catron as U.S. Attorney by his affidavit to Chairman of the Judiciary Committee, Senator Lyman Trumball, about Catron and Elkins bribing him to shield Judge Palen. (Westphall, p. 107) Within a month of his appointment, Catron indicted the legislators of the anti-Palen bill (Westphall, p. 108) - conducting malicious prosecutions that the Legislature Revolt had tried to stop.

The Legislature revolt had been suppressed, but not forgotten. On September 2, 1884, the *Las Vegas Daily Optic* reprinted a *Omaha Herald* exposé, triggered by Elkins's growing power in Republican politics, titled: "Our Own Dear Steve, How Elkins Made His Influence Felt in New Mexico - The Ring in Which a Judge Figured - Politics in 1870." It resurfaced in an 1895 *Las Vegas Democrat* article during Catron's disbarment trial. The 1884 article stated:

OUR OWN DEAR STEVE.
How Elkins Made His Influence Felt in New Mexico – The Ring in Which a Judge Figured – Politics in 1870.

From the Omaha Herald.

The fact of Steve Elkins having been picked out by Mr. Blaine to manage the republican canvass this fall makes him an object of more than ordinary interest ... Twenty-five years ago Steve Elkins was a boy of 18 hanging about his father's groggery at Westport, Mo., with plenty of book learning ... Steve struck out for New Mexico. The next heard of him he was studying law in the office of Judge Ashurst. In three months Steve was talking Spanish as glibly as any of the native New Mexicans, and after six months apprenticeship, swung out a board with "Stephen B. Elkins, attorney-at-law." on it. Business poured in on him, and after a while **Thomas B. Catron found it profitable to go into partnership with him**. Steve turned out to be a rustler, but with the awakening of his dormant business faculties, came the death of all sense of honor and integrity. **In some unknown way he made himself a power in New Mexico politics, and with Thomas B. Catron, Wm. Breeden, and James [Joseph] Palen, formed a ring for the organized plunder of the Territory.** At first they contented themselves with gobbling all the land they could reach ...

THE NEW MEXICAN RING

About 1870 the New Mexican ring was in its prime. Thomas Benton Catron was attorney general for the Territory, James [Joseph] Palen was United States judge for the third [first] district, and Stephen B. Elkins was general manager of the deviltry. It was the open boast of Elkins and Catron that they had made a bargain with Judge Palen by which it was impossible for any other attorney to conduct a case successfully before him ... [But after Catron and Elkins lost a case before Palen after it was appealed] [t]he people took heart from this, and **at the meeting of the legislative assembly in December, 1871, they succeeded in having a bill passed assigning Judge Palen to another district** ... The governor [Marsh], at the request of the ring, vetoed the bill, and then the people organized a popular movement to secure its passage over the veto. Elkins and Catron bought up enough representatives, lacking two, to prevent the two-thirds vote, and of there efforts to secure these, the following affidavits will tell:

ELKINS ATTEMPTS AT BRIBERY.

TERRITORY OF)
NEW MEXICO,)
COUNTY OF SANTA FE)

Before me, a clerk of the probate court for the county and Territory aforesaid, personally appeared, this first day of February A.D. 1872, August Kirchner ... who, after being duly sworn, deposes and says:

"I am by occupation a butcher, business in Santa Fe since 1859 ... and am now the contractor to supply fresh beef to the United States troops in all the forts of this Territory.

On the --- day of December, 1871, the legislative assembly of New Mexico , then in session, passed a law ... to assign the chief justice and two associate justices to their respective districts, and by which Judge Palen of the first district, was assigned to the third district. Saturday, the 30th day of December, 1871, I went out to buy hogs on the public square [in Santa Fe]. In front of the Palace of the Governors I met S.B. Elkins, attorney at law, and a resident of this place. He said to me, "You are the man I need. The legislature want to remove Judge Palen; you have influence and you must help me, so they cannot remove the judge from his district. You will have a law suit in court to be brought against you by Samuel Ellison about your property. If you help us, and the judge is not removed, I promise you that you shall win that suit in this court."

I promised Mr. Elkins to do my best and went right to the house of representatives, but I found there was too large a majority in favor of the bill, and for that reason I did not speak to any of the members.

Monday, the first day of January, 1872, between the hours of three and four o'clock in the afternoon, Thomas B. Catron, attorney general for the Territory of New Mexico, entered my butcher shop, and asked me to go with him to my private room, to which I made no objection ... after which Catron spoke to me in the following manner:

"Look here, Kirchner, you must now help us; you know the legislature has passed the bill removing Judge Palen; and now we have the governor all right and he will veto the bill, but we want to be sure that the legislature may not pass the same with a two-thirds vote over the governor's veto ... [and we need two more representatives] and you are the only man who can fix that, because I have already spoken to them; you can pay them ($250) two hundred fifty dollars each, that is $500 together; go to the bank and get the money. I will leave orders there to pay you that amount.

After the above proposition was made to me by said Catron, I told him if he wanted to buy the members of the legislature with money he should do it himself, but that I would not bribe them under any circumstances. My answer to Catron made him very angry and he left. Next morning, January 2d, 1872, I received a letter from the before mentioned S.B. Elkins, asking me to come immediately to his office as he wished to see me on very particular business, but I refused to go ...
(signed) AUGUST KIRCHNER ... [followed by signees attesting to his veracity] ...

At the hour for the gathering of the assembly, the town was wild with excitement. The streets were filled with people from all parts of the Territory **and two companies of United States troops, under command of General Gorden Granger, surrounded the legislative hall, having been called out by the sheriff, who was afraid that he would not be able to keep the people from assassinating Catron, Elkins, Palen, and Breeden on the spot. The outlook was so threatening that Elkins was afraid to let the matter come to a vote, and instructed his tool, Speaker [Milnor] Rudulph, to address the house before a quorum was present. Rudulph did so, and wandered off outside the town, threatening to kill whoever pursued him**. The sheriff swore in [a deputy] and instructed him to bring Rudulph back ... [H]e led him back to the chamber [but the time was too late]. Before the body could be reconvened Judge Palen died, and it is general opinion to this day that he committed suicide to avoid the exposure and punishment that was sure to follow his transfer to another district.

This is the partial history of the man who is now entrusted with the management of the Blaine canvass ... [T]here are men in high authority at Washington who are in possession of money derived from the great land steals engineered by the distinguished Steve.

To excuse Catron in this exposé, Westphall cited Governor Giddings's 1872 cover-up telegram to Attorney General Williams, stating that he was backed "by the better classes of citizens," and that the Territory was saved from "anarchy [when] a minority had attempted to take over the legislature." (Westphall, p. 108)

In fact, the failed revolt yielded Catron's free rein for malicious prosecutions and his outlaw myth of opponents. That ploy would eventually cause the death of the last in line: Billy Bonney.

CREATING THE OUTLAW MYTH

The Ring learned from the 1872 Legislature Revolt. By 1873, Ringites would never again legitimize opposition as "revolution" or "rebellion." Only "outlaw" would label adversaries for malicious prosecution and assassination, as Territorial take-over advanced with complicit governors, lawyers, judges, lawmen, and troops.

By 1874, Catron and the Ring had sights on Lincoln County. On January 10, 1874, setting the stage for military suppression, Judge Warren Bristol wrote to Governor Giddings. In four years, the Ring would murder John Tunstall and Alexander McSween there, and troops would intervene. Importantly, Bristol here advanced the "outlaw" myth to justify Ring aggression:

To the Governor
Sir
From sources of information that I deem perfectly reliable I am satisfied that there are public disorders in Lincoln County that call for an extraordinary and vigorous remedy.

Since the beginning of last month these disturbances have culminated in a regular guerrilla warfare between the Mexicans and Texans and is being carried on very much in the same spirit that activates hostile Indian tribes. Hundreds are already implicated in an open breach of the laws ...

These disorders are so wide spread and the people of the County so generally implicated either openly or through sympathy that I deem it out of the question to obtain juries in that county who will find indictments or verdicts impartially and justly.

In fact all along at the several terms of the District Court that I have held in that county I have been exceedingly embarrassed for the want of reliable juries. The gravest crimes have been too often passed over unnoticed.

Previous to my advent to the Judicial District of which Lincoln county is a part little or no effort had been made to sustain the courts in that county - it being occupied mainly by Mexicans

Within the last two or three years the eastern and central portions of the county have been settled to a considerable extent by cattle dealers - herders and ranchmen mostly from the border of Texas including a number of what are commonly known as "Cowboys."

This population made up of these mixed elements has had but little or no schooling in the duties and responsibilities of self-government and are prone upon very slight or no provocation to use their weapons.

Our judicial system - as you are aware - applicable to that as well as every county in this Territory is precisely the same as that in the most civilized and orderly communities throughout the land. Under this judicial system the <u>people</u> through their juries perform an important part in the administration of the criminal laws. If through terror or sympathy or any other cause they fail to perform their duties as jurors faithfully and promptly under the instructions of the Court - then it follows that the Court to that extent must necessarily fail in the maintenance of public order.

Complaints growing out of these present disturbances in some instances I understand have been made to the local Magistrate and warrants issued but that no arrests have been made ...

[F]rom what I learn of the situation of affairs in that county **I have every reason to believe that the Sheriff will not and cannot make the arrests with any force in his command.**

The next term of the District Court for that county will not be held until the middle of April next - In the mean time prompt and vigorous measures ought to be adopted to quell the disturbances and disarm the contending parties - **At present I see no way whereby this can be done effectively except by a sufficient military force.**

I deem it my duty to lay this matter before you hoping that through your instrumentality the required aid may be obtained.

*I have the honor to be
Very respectfully
Warren Bristol,
Associate Justice*

Two days later, on January 12, 1874, Giddings passed this fabrication to Secretary of the Interior as: "In relation to disturbances in Lincoln County New Mexico." Its intent was to get permission for troop use to suppress citizens – a Ring tactic which would escalate to the 1878 treasonous Lincoln County War Battle. It was forwarded to the Secretary of War on January 28th; stating:

Hon. C. Delano
*   Secretary of the Interior*
Sir
* I have the honor to inform you that for a number of weeks just past there have been disturbances between the Mexicans and Texans living in the extreme southern part of New Mexico in Lincoln County. Sometime in December the military commandant here at Santa Fe was so kind as to furnish me copies of some letters he had received from that vicinity showing a bad state of feelings in that quarter ...*
  I think the <u>officers</u> generally seek to do right, and there is great need of the military if we can use them in aid of the civil authorities. *The difficulties & disorders in that county have been continually increasing until there is now a guerrilla war being carried on among the inhabitants of the county and no one however law abiding now feels safe. The Texan owners & herders of Stock Ranch men and "Cowboys" are generally well armed with the best of fire arms, while the Mexicans are generally but poorly armed ...*
  That there is wrong on both sides there can be no doubt but wholesale butchery of men women & children should be prevented if possible. ***We have no Territorial military force nor can we organize one ...***
  The legislature a few days since gave the executive power to offer a small reward in such cases and messengers from that county having been sent here for some aid, I made a proclamation offering a reward of $500 for the apprehension of certain criminals there, and at the same time Judge Bristol issued his warrant for the apprehension of the same parties.
  The most deplorable state of things exists there now as will be seen upon examining the statement of Judge Bristol & others herewith enclosed.
  Upon examining the papers and advising with Judge Bristol, and the Attorney of that District as well as the Attorney of the 2ᵈ District all of them well acquainted with the people and the

causes of the trouble, **all concur that it was my duty in order to prevent any further murders to ask the aid of the military forces nearby in keeping the peace, and to aid if necessary the civil authorities in the execution of civil process until we could receive instructions from the general government.**

And I therefore made a statement today of the facts substantially as given by Judge Bristol and others, to Col. John J. Gregg commanding the military forces here, and appended thereto a request that he "would furnish such military force as the exigencies of the case may require to <u>aid the civil</u> **authorities in executing the lawful processes of the civil courts and authorities, and to aid the officers and authorities in the arrest of criminal violators of the laws, and to aid in keeping the peace among and between people of said county of Lincoln until order shall be restored to the inhabitants of said county or until some further order or direction can be obtained from the general government."**

I could make no <u>order</u> *on such military officer, but it seemed to me that right & humanity dictated that I should make such* <u>request</u> *on him, and let him do so much, and as the law should direct under the circumstances.* **Last year I made a request for some military aid in the case of disturbances in Cimarron in the northern part of the Territory and was telegraphed I think by Gen Sheridan that a small force had been ordered to that point to aid the civil authorities.**

[AUTHOR'S NOTE: This was suppression of Maxwell Land Grant settlers, being evicted from their land as "squatters" by the Ring. The anti-Ring Colfax County War would follow.]

In this deplorable state of affairs and on the border where are more or less likely to have constant repetitions of like occurrences it becomes, it seems to me, an absolute necessity that we should have some instructions or directions of some kind for guidance in such emergencies. **The civil authorities are powerless to do anything in these remote parts - No Territorial military power in existence, and no power to create a military force, we are driven to the terrible necessity of seeing these murders committed where these border feuds exist unless we can have the aid of their military forces of the United States stationed in the Territory.** *And if we can have such aid we need instructions as to what necessities shall arise before the aid can be called for ...*

I have therefore laid the whole matter before you as far as I can learn the facts and shall be glad to carry out any directions or suggestions from your Department, in regard to this and like cases.

I have the honor to be
Very Respectfully
Your obt servt
Marsh Giddings
Gov. New Mexico

Since writing the foregoing I have received some additional information. I learn from Judge Bristol and others that there are really no civil authorities by way of courts through whom any demand can be made on the military for aid. - That the Justices of the peace, and they are not numerous, are themselves implicated in the disorders or if not [,] dare not issue papers for arrests - that the Judge of Probate having resigned and the Sheriff having put himself away from the scene of the disturbances, there are no civil authorities seeking to quiet the disorders by calling for military aid or otherwise. The District Judge 300 miles from the place & now in Santa Fe may issue his warrant but he is too far away from parties and witnesses to be of much service. The military authorities would undoubtedly go to the aid of the civil if there was any active civil authority in the county. There being none - what should be done. Judge Bristol is exceedingly anxious on the subject, not only for this occasion but for future occurrences.

On the other hand, from a letter just received from Lincoln County I learn that they are holding Peace meetings with good prospect of preventing further bloodshed for the present.

We are so differently situated from the people of the States away in the borders of a remote Territory that it seems improbable to keep order under the same rules & regulations <u>only</u>, which are sufficient for a well settled state. And the judge so desires me to seek some direction for the future.

Truly yours Giddings

[AUTHOR'S NOTE: Spelled out is the Ring's outlaw myth formula: criminalize opponents; use troops to kill them. In one year, Colfax County would be attacked; in four years, it would summarize Lincoln County War atrocities.]

DEAD GIDDINGS REPLACED

After Marsh Giddings died in office on June 5, 1875, President Ulysses S. Grant appointed Governor of Utah, Samuel Beach Axtell, to his position. Axtell's Governor's "Message" to the legislature's 22nd Session, provided for pro-Ring property assessment: "You can in no better way equalize taxation and prevent the crime of false assessments than by assessing the property of the Territory yourselves ... *[E]xempt nothing, and permit no deduction for debt.* You will thus render it impossible for fraud and cunning to escape the just and honorable burden of taxation."

So by 1875, the Santa Fe Ring fox was in charge of the Territorial hen coop. Land grant holders could now be taxed out of ownership as they turned futilely to attorneys like Thomas Benton Catron for protection.

By 1876, Axtell was the Ring's front for attempted murder and murder of its Colfax County opponents, while he facilitated land grant sales there and caused the 1877 Colfax County War by removing their courts. The next year he backed the Ring's reign of terror, murders, and blockade of justice in the Lincoln County War. And he would build on the outlaw myth created by the Ring in the aftermath of the 1872 Legislature Revolt. But first came the anti-Ring Grant County Rebellion in 1876.

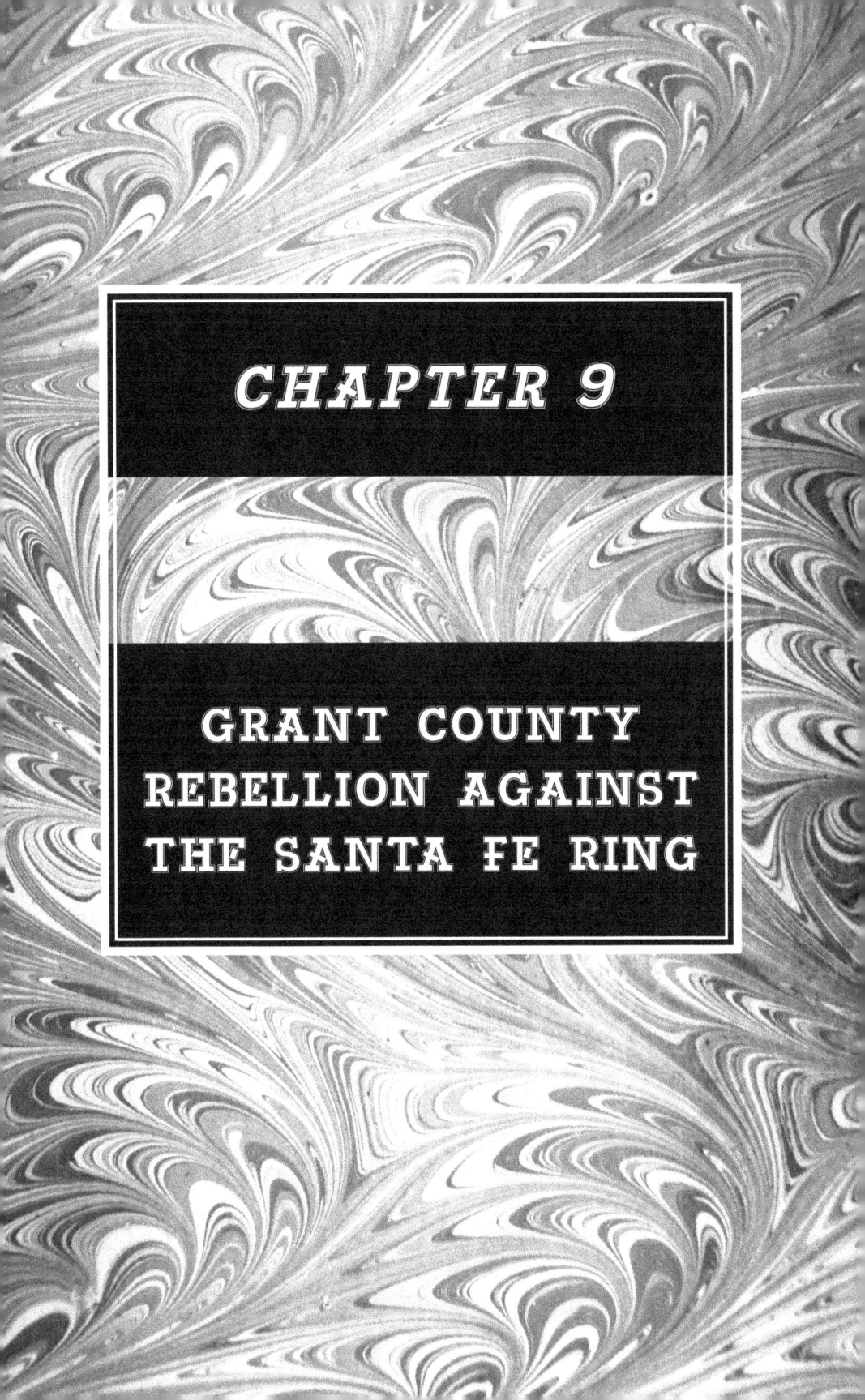

CHAPTER 9

GRANT COUNTY REBELLION AGAINST THE SANTA FE RING

THE GRANT COUNTY REBELLION

SUMMARY: Grant County citizens never forgot Ring injustices that caused and followed the 1872 Legislature Revolt. By 1876, they made the Grant County Rebellion, intending to secede and join Arizona Territory, and published a "Declaration of Independence" from the Ring. But, lacking leadership, they lost momentum; though were spared the Ring's violence in Colfax and Lincoln Counties.

RESURGENCE OF A GRANT COUNTY REVOLT

Grant County - site of the second anti-Ring rebellion - was named after Ulysses S. Grant, and was formed in 1868 by the Territorial legislature by division from Doña Ana County. It occupied the southwestern corner of New Mexico Territory, and bordered Arizona Territory on its west. That boundary was set in 1863 when the federal government divided western New Mexico Territory into Arizona Territory. Only fifty miles from that border was Silver City, its mining-rich county seat, founded in 1870.

As mentioned above, the historian for the 1876 Grant County Rebellion is Conrad Keeler Naegle, with his 1943 doctoral thesis titled *The History of Silver City, New Mexico 1870-1886*; and a 1968 article in *Arizona and the West: A Quarterly Journal of History*: "The Rebellion of Grant County, New Mexico in 1876." Naegle noted that the Ring was involved from Grant County's inception, with its first district court in 1868 having Thomas Benton Catron himself as District Attorney. (Naegle, thesis, p. 3)

Naegle wrote that the Grant County Rebellion grew from the 1872 Legislature Revolt, which he called an "unsuccessful attempt to oust the 'ring' from its control over the Territorial legislature in order to prevent it from obstructing further the will of the people." He noted that Grant County residents, especially in Silver City, were "well educated and of means"

(Naegle thesis, p. 29), and by 1871 wanted to escape Ring clutches. He quoted March 23, 1871's Las Cruces *Borderer*: "As early as 1871 these liberty-loving Americans had voiced their desire for annexation to Arizona, in order that they might be freed from domination by the Santa Fe 'ring' that had 'so faithfully and ably misrepresented' them." (Naegle, thesis, p. 31)

Grant County's "liberty-loving" people had contributed to the 1872 Legislature Revolt by seeking increased self-government through bills for incorporation of Silver City and for the right of taxation to create a public school system, and receiving Ring backlash. Naegle wrote: "These high-handed measures of the 'ring,' coupled with the forestalling of the incorporation of Silver City and the substitution of an inadequate school law ... were almost more than the people of Silver City and southwestern New Mexico could endure. On the other hand they had come so near to upsetting the 'apple-cart' [by the 1872 Legislature Revolt] that the 'ring' took steps to curb the rising power of ... those of southern New Mexico who had proved such virile opposition." Naegle, thesis, pp. 37-38)

SECESSION AND ANNEXATION

By August 8, 1875, the *Grant County Herald* reported that Grant County's citizens sought secession from the Territory to escape the Ring's "political vassalage." (Naegle, thesis, p. 39)

The Grant County Rebellion intentionally coincided with the American Revolution's centennial. On September 16, 1876, the *Grant County Herald* published "A Contemplated Political Change." Announced was a citizens' meeting to discuss annexation of Grant County to Arizona Territory to leave behind the "dictatorial and corrupt spirit" of men in Santa Fe. (Naegle, thesis, p. 40) Three causes were listed:

First: legislation by "Americans" would be more liberal and better suited to the progress of the county, for the primary interest of both Grant County and Arizona was mining.

Second: Grant County has been denied equal representation in the legislative assembly of the Territory ...

Third: that after attempts to procure remedial legislation they have been denied redress, and held in a state of vassalage without hope of relief.

Naegle noted: "[T]he people of Grant County seemed to be unanimously in favor of the measure." (Naegle, thesis, p. 41)

On September 30, 1876, the *Herald* announced that the "Annexation Meeting" would be in Silver City on October 4th at 2 o'clock p.m. in Burns Hall. Sixty-two citizens, mostly from Silver City, had pledged to approve secession. (Naegle, thesis, p. 41)

A DECLARATION OF INDEPENDENCE

At the October 4, 1876 Grant County Annexation Meeting, legislator John M. Ginn was elected Presiding Officer, and James Corbin as Secretary. A committee of five was elected to write resolutions: James Mullen, Peter Graves, William H. Eckles, Robert Metcalf, and D.B. Rhea as chairman. That day, they authored the "Grant County Declaration of Independence." The independence sought was from the Santa Fe Ring, called a "selfish oligarchy" functioning for "selfish interest." A committee of eight was chosen to write for Congress the memorial for annexation.

On Saturday, October 7, 1876 , the *Grant County Herald* printed in full the "Grant County Declaration of Independence":

Pursuant to call, a meeting of the citizens of Grant county, New Mexico, was held at Burns Hall, in Silver City, October 4, 1876, for the purpose of considering the propriety of severing our connections with New Mexico and annexing to the Territory of Arizona.

On motion, J.M. Ginn was called to the chair who explained the object of the meeting and forcibly set forth the advantages to be derived from such a union.

On motion of I.N. Stevens Jas. Corbin was elected Secretary. After which James Mullen was loudly called for who responded and gave most satisfactory reasons why Grant County should ally her destinies with Arizona.

Upon motion of D.B. Rea it was moved and carried that a committee of five be appointed on resolutions. Whereupon the Chair assigned as committeemen: D.B. Rea, CHAIRMAN, James Mullen, Peter Graves, W.H. Eckles, and Robert Metcalf.

During the absence of the committee, Colonel Ledbetter was called upon and entertained the meeting with some happy remarks, setting forth advantages of becoming a part of a progressive people, which were well timed and well received.

Mr. Rea, Chairman of the Committee on Resolutions, reported the following, which were read and unanimously adopted:

Whereas: Pursuant to a call published in the Grant County HERALD, signed by many prominent citizens of the said county, to make such steps as may be deemed necessary to sever our relations as a county from the Territory of New Mexico and annex to the Territory of Arizona; and we the citizens of Grant County here assembled, having met pursuant to said call, do hereby declare it is our earnest wish to join our political destinies with the neighboring Territory of Arizona and cease our political connection with the Territory of New Mexico, of which our county forms a part and for taking this important step we assign the following as some of the principal reasons for the desired change:

1. That we are geographically nearer the center of population and capital of said Territory of Arizona than that of the present Territory.

2. That we have a near community of interest with the said Territory of Arizona, in that our leading pursuit, which is mining, is identical with theirs.

3. That the laws enacted by our Territory are unsuited to our wants, and we consider those which govern our neighboring Territory better adapted to the exigencies of a mining community.

4. That we, as a community, are denied legal representation with the other counties of the Territory, and have little or no voice in the enactment of laws which are necessary to our welfare which we believe would be remedied by the liberal-minded people of Arizona.

5. That we consider the Territory of New Mexico badly governed owing to the fact that the chief power in the Territorial legislation rests in the hands of a selfish oligarchy, who designedly wield the same in their own selfish interest, and owing to the prevailing temper and habits of her people we see no hope for relief in the near future.

6. That our geographical situation in relation to the Southern Pacific Railroad is such as induces us to believe that material interests will be greatly advanced by joining on to Arizona.

7. That this portion of our Territory is subject to Indian depredations from the same Apache bands who have their homes in Southern Arizona, and consequently a means of common defense in the way of a militia system could be better integrated ... with said Territory, whose interests in that respect is identical with ours; therefore be it

Resolved: That it is the wish of the people of Grant County, as expressed through the persons here assembled, that the necessary steps to be taken at once to further that view herein expressed.

Resolved: That the Governor and all other officials of the Territory of Arizona and also all her influential citizens be requested to co-operate with us in this movement.

Upon motion of W.H. Eckles, annexation be voted upon at our county election in November next was carried.

Mr. Rea moved that a committee of correspondence consisting of eight persons be appointed by the Chair. Carried ...

Mr. Lucas moved that the proceedings of this meeting be published in the Grant County HERALD and copies of same be forwarded to the Arizona papers and publication requested. Carried.

Mr. Wilson moved that the Chairman authorize a sufficient number of extra copies of the proceedings of this meeting to be published by the HERALD and forwarded by the committee to each member of the U.S. Senate and House of Representatives. Carried.

DEFLATED MISSION

On November 7, 1876, Grant County citizens voted almost unanimously for annexation to Arizona Territory. On January 3, 1877, Arizona Territory's Governor A.P.K. Safford seconded Grant County's annexation. (Naegle, thesis, pp. 45-46)

Then national politics collided. November 1876's national election yielded Democratic control of the House. But anti-corruption Presidential candidate, Democrat Samuel J. Tilden, who had brought down William "Boss" Tweed's Tammany Hall Ring, lost by one electoral vote to Republican, Rutherford B. Hayes. So Republican victor, Hayes, opposed Democratic Arizona's benefiting by inclusion of mine-rich Grant County.

Into that hostile political climate, on October 29, 1877, Arizona representative R.S. Stevens introduced to Congress House Resolution 795 for Grant County's annexation. It was referred to the committee on Territories, where it was killed. No one realized that President Hayes was entangled with the Santa Fe Ring. And Grant County's escape from that Ring was blocked.

Historian Naegle saw the positive: "The Silver City [and Grant County] 'rebels' had failed in their attempted 'secession,' but they reaped a victory in defeat. The specter of House Resolution 794 hovered over that 'selfish oligarchy' ... and thus enabled the citizens of Silver City to have enacted almost any legislation they desired, for those 'political parasites' feared that the attempt might be repeated. They had no desire to lose New Mexico's richest county as a source of revenue." (Naegle, thesis, pp. 48-49)

Omitted is that the Grant County Rebellion ended with a whimper of accepting Ring concessions. Silver City was incorporated in 1878, enabling electing of their own public officials and assessing and collecting of their own taxes to create public schools. But there was no restoration of equal legislative representation, lost to Governor Marsh Giddings's 1872 gerrymandering. The rebellion of Grant County had deflated, lacking leadership and spirit for further fighting. Instead, Grant County retreated into silence and non-intervention as the Ring's rampages escalated in other parts of the Territory.

By the October 7, 1876 "Grant County Declaration of Independence," New Mexico Territory's Governor was Ringite Samuel Beach Axtell, who had been in office since the year before. He was gaining experience on crushing anti-Ring uprisings. In the future, concessions would be replaced by brutality.

And in Arizona Territory, a 16 year old, using the name Henry Antrim, having escaped Silver City's jail on September 23, 1775 for his burglary and robbery charges, and having fled New Mexico Territory in his own bid for freedom, was supporting himself as a cook at a small hotel; and as a thief of military horses, saddles, and blankets. And he was likely perfecting his hobby: gunmanship. But there was still no need for inventing his new name: William Henry "Billy" Bonney.

CHAPTER 10

COLFAX COUNTY WAR AGAINST THE SANTA FE RING

COLFAX COUNTY WAR OVERVIEW

SUMMARY: Peaking in 1877 with anti-Ring exposés, the Colfax County War uprisings pitted original Maxwell Land Grant settlers against the Santa Fe Ring-backed Maxwell Land Grant and Railway Company, which attempted their eviction. The Ring resorted to murder, then illegal removal of their courts to block redress. From 1873 to 1887, 200 people were killed; with the 1875 Ring murder of anti-Ring leader, Franklin Tolby, being its lightning rod.

The Colfax County War - actually warring, since its anti-Ring uprisings spanned 1873 to 1887 without a central battle - peaked in 1877 with anti-Ring exposés in the press and in complaints to the Hayes administration. While fighting back, the Ring perfected strategies for tyranny: assassination of opponents, malicious prosecution, shielding of its criminals, obstructing courts, and using troops against civilians. The Lincoln County War would be a more brutal re-run, made memorable with its hero: Billy Bonney.

COLFAX COUNTY WAR SOURCES

No historian has yet documented the Colfax County War's specific uprisings and 200 victims; or noted its place in the Territory's escalating, anti-Ring, freedom fights. But books do feature its major figures: Ring-murdered Revered Franklin J. Tolby, Ring-prosecuted Reverend Oscar P. McMains, anti-Ring gunslinger Clay Allison, railroadman Raymond Morley, and Attorney Frank Springer. Used here are: Norman Cleaveland's 1971 *The Morleys: Young Upstarts on the Southwest Frontier*; Morris F. Taylor's 1979 *O.P. McMains and the Maxwell Land Grant Conflict*; Agnes Morley Cleaveland's 1941 *No Life for a Lady* and 1952 *Satan's Paradise: From Lucien Maxwell to Fred Lambert*; and Jim Berry Pearson's 1961 *The Maxwell Land Grant*. Replicating Ring cover-ups, are Victor Westphall's 1973 *Thomas*

Benton Catron and His Era and William Kelleher's 1964 *The Maxwell Land Grant: A New Mexico Item*. The War is mentioned in David L. Caffey's 2007 *Frank Springer & New Mexico: From the Colfax County War to the Emergence of Modern Santa Fe*.

The Colfax County War itself generated a treasure-trove of contemporary sources documenting the Santa Fe Ring's existence, members, and crimes; and citizens' attempts to end its oppression. The *Cimarron News and Press*, under editors Raymond Morley and Attorney Frank Springer, published anti-Ring articles. Morley's mother-in-law, Mary Tibbles McPherson, became an anti-Ring fighter, who, in 1877, wrote extensive exposés for Washington, officials. She foreshadowed the Lincoln County War the following year by detailing crimes of T.B. Catron, S.B. Elkins, Governor S.B Axtell, Chief Justice Henry Waldo, and Third Judicial District Judge Warren Bristol. And her daughter, Ada Morley, wife of Raymond Morley, wrote letters revealing citizens' terror at Ring retributions.

COLFAX COUNTY WAR AND BILLY BONNEY

Billy Bonney was connected to the Colfax County War through love and death, because it involved the almost two million acre Maxwell Land Grant. Profit from its 1870 sale, arranged by Catron and Elkins, rocketed their Ring's power. The Grant's duped owner, Lucien Bonaparte Maxwell, then bought demilitarized Fort Sumner for his family, making it a town of that name. He died in 1875, but his daughter, Paulita, became Billy's secret lover. Maxwell's widow, Luz Beaubien Maxwell, protected Billy after his 1881 jailbreak. And in the Maxwell's Fort Sumner mansion, occurred Billy's fatal ambush by Pat Garrett.

THE BEAUBIEN-MIRANDA AND MAXWELL LAND GRANT

SUMMARY: By 1869, the Ring sought possession of Lucien Maxwell's 2 million acre Maxwell Land Grant, with its potential railroad route over the Raton Pass into New Mexico Territory; and its ranchland, mines, coal, and timber. Ignored in the land-grab was that it already had long-term settlers claiming tracts as their own.

The anti-Ring fight in Colfax County is rooted in the history of the Maxwell Land Grant and its settlers. Originally part of Mexico, occupying the future northern New Mexico and southern Colorado Territories, it was gifted by the last Mexican Governor, Manuel Armijo, on January 8, 1841, to Charles Hipolite Trotier de Beaubien, a French Canadian relocated to Taos. Beaubien, in 1823, had married Spanish heiress, María Paula Lovato, two years after Mexico won independence from Spain. Renaming himself Don Carlos Beaubien, he partnered with a Guadalupe Miranda, Armijo's secretary, for the Beaubien-Miranda Grant.
     That 1841, to Taos came Lucien Bonaparte Maxwell, a son of the wealthy, politically active, Illinois, Menard family, with his frontiersman friend, Kit Carson. Maxwell married Don Carlos Beaubien's daughter, Luz Trotier de Beaubien. Among their children were Paulita - who became Billy Bonney's sweetheart - and Peter, who betrayed Billy to Pat Garrett's ambush.
     In 1848, the Beaubien-Miranda Land Grant was impacted by the Treaty of Guadalupe Hidalgo, which ended the Mexican-American War and relinquished Mexico's northern half to the United States. It guaranteed grant holders ownership after Congressional approval of their titles and boundaries. Approval was by recommendation of the Surveyor General to the Commissioner of the General Land Grant Office, with submission to Congress for issuance of a patent to the claimants. The Santa Fe Ring was founded to exploit that approval process.
     The Beaubien-Miranda Grant's heir, Carlos Beaubien's only son, Narciso, was killed on January 18, 1847 in the Taos Rebellion in the Mexican-American War. Beaubien then made Lucien Maxwell his heir. When Beubien died in 1864, Maxwell bought all Grant shares from his wife's family and from Beaubien's partner, Guadalupe Miranda; making it the Maxwell Land Grant.
     Lucien Maxwell was larger than life. He ranched sheep; encouraged settlement; and founded Rayado, Elizabethtown, and Cimarron, where he built his gigantic mansion, a store, and a three story gristmill. But his beneficent control faltered as settlers flooded in for an 1866 gold rush near Mount Baldy; where he had his Aztec gold mine, the world's richest.
     By 1867, Elizabethtown had 7,000 settlers. Ignoring Maxwell, they petitioned the Territorial legislature to rename the Grant as Colfax County, after President Grant's Vice-President, Schyler Colfax. It was approved on January 15, 1869, with Elizabethtown as its county seat, legally empowering its settlers.

In 1869, Maxwell was told that the Grant was arbitrarily limited to 97,000 acres by Secretary of the Interior Jacob D. Cox. In 1870, longing to escape its management complexities, naïve Maxwell became prey to legal advice of Catron's and Elkins's land-grab, selling them the Grant for $650,000. Their resale and boundary inflation empowered their Ring.

Maxwell continued his bad choices by moving his family from the magnificent Grant to the Territory's southeastern bleak flatlands of demilitarized Fort Sumner, within Bosque Redondo, an abandoned Navajo and Apache concentration camp, which he bought for $5,000. There he ranched sheep, and planted corn and peaches. He refurbished its buildings skirting its old parade ground, making the officers' quarters his mansion.

Equally misguided were his investments through Elkins and Catron. By September of 1870, he gave them $150,000 from his sale to found the First National Bank of Santa Fe to become its President. The next year, they founded the competing Second National Bank of New Mexico to force his sale to them. Elkins then took over the First National Bank of Santa Fe's Presidency; and that bank became central to Ring finances. With Elkins's and Catron's advice, Maxwell also invested $150,000 into the Kansas Pacific Railroad; but quickly lost the money when it reorganized. Devastated, Maxwell died on July 25, 1875. His inadvertent revenge was the Colfax County War.

MAXWELL LAND GRANT AND RAILWAY COMPANY

SUMMARY: After buying the Maxwell Land Grant in 1870, Elkins, Catron and speculators resold it to British, then Dutch, buyers, with acreage inflation by Ring-beholden surveyors; followed by an audacious, brief, take-over by Catron himself, before repurchase by the Dutch investors.

From the time of Lucien Maxwell's 1870 sale of his Grant, its owners and officers were correctly linked in settlers' minds with the Santa Fe Ring. Immediately after its sale, the Grant was resold for $1,350,000 to speculator "friends" of Catron and Elkins: Colorado Senator and mine owner, Gerome Bunty Chaffee; Colorado congressman, George Chilcott; Cimarron lawyer and mine investor, Charles Holly; and entrepreneur, Wilson

Waddingham. Elkins acted as lawyer (Westphall, p. 100), along with William Evarts, past Attorney General and future Ring-biased Secretary of State under President Rutherford B. Hayes. The profits fueled the growing Ring, and added loyalists.

The Chaffe syndicate then resold the Grant to British investors, headed by a John Collinson, who, as foreigners, could not own New Mexico Territory land. So Catron and Elkins enlisted three "friends" to front for filing as the Maxwell Land Grant and Railway Company: Governor William Pile; Territorial Surveyor General T. Rush Spencer; and past Territorial Chief Justice John S. Watts. (Westphall, p. 101)

That 1870 was when Governor Pile favored Catron with reappointment as Attorney General, and colluded with him about Territorial archives and splitting offices with Democrats. And "friend" John Watts resurfaced for filing U.S. Attorney Catron's June 21, 1878 federal indictment Number 411 against Billy Bonney and other Regulators for "Buckshot" Roberts's killing. (That federal case prevented Territorial pardons.)

The Collinson syndicate took over the Grant in April of 1870, for subdivision sale to new settlers. Elkins was made President of their Board of Directors. Other Directors were H.M. Porter, J.B. Maingay, Attorney Melvin W. Mills, and Dr. Robert H. Longwill. (In 1875, Longwill and Mills were accused of murdering anti-Ring Franklin Tolby.) The company surveyed the Grant to yield about 2 million acres. This was unsurprisingly approved by Surveyor General T. Rush Spencer, a member of the company. (Westphall, p. 100)

In 1872, the British syndicate sold the Grant to Dutch investors for $5,000,000. They incorporated as the Maxwell Land Grant and Railway Company, with Elkins as President of their Board of Directors, and Catron as their attorney (serving into the 1900's). According to Norman Cleaveland, in his 1971 book *The Morleys*, Elkins was also an owner. (Cleaveland, p. 75) The plan was sale of mining claims, timber, coal, agricultural land, grazing land, and railroad passageway over its Raton Pass.

In 1873, the Dutch Company hired 26 year old William Raymond Morley from Iowa - a Chief Construction Engineer of the Atchison Topeka and Santa Fe Railroad - as their Vice-president, to develop its route into New Mexico. He brought his wife, Ada McPherson Morley. They were housed in the company's headquarters, the grand Maxwell mansion. And Morley became editor of the company's *Cimarron Press*.

In 1874, the Ring made a brash take-over move, with Elkins as Delegate to Congress exerting Washington influence. The Department of the Interior, ignoring the 1860 Congressional act, declared the Grant public domain. Then, with Catron having replaced Elkins as President of the Board of Directors (Westphall, p. 109), the company defaulted on its property tax bond. As Norman Cleaveland stated: "Morley blamed Elkins and Catron ... and felt the Santa Fe Ring was attempting to gain control of the Grant as they controlled almost everything else in New Mexico." (Cleaveland, *The Morleys*, p. 87)

Next, for the land-grab, in 1876, Ringite Melvin W. Mills, bought the entire Grant at public auction for its back taxes of $16,479! That left Catron poised to buy it from Mills for $20,000 – at one cent per acre! Westphall wrote:

> [T]he property was auctioned on December 16 [1876] to Melvin W. Mills for $16,479.46. The money for purchase of the tax deed was raised by a Santa Fe group headed by Catron. On July 19, 1877, Mills deeded the property to Catron for $20,000 ... There seems little doubt ... that this was a maneuver by Catron to acquire the property for himself and his group. (Westphall, p. 110)

But the stockholders redeemed it (Westphall, p. 110), presumably paying Catron.

In 1877, President Hayes's Secretary of the Interior, Carl Schurz, requested resurvey of the Grant for final Congressional confirmation. Ringite Surveyor General Henry M. Atkinson (Catron's later partner in the American Valley Company) awarded the contract to Elkins's brother, John T. Elkins, who, in an implausible twenty-one days, declared it as 1,714,764.94 acres. (Westphall, p. 111) On June 5, 1878, the Grant's patent was issued by Ring-friendly Schurz (who also helped that year to cover up the Ring's Tunstall's assassination in the Angel reports). That day, Catron's then law partner, William T. Thornton acted as the patent's receiver.

Norman Cleaveland addressed this Ringite surveying fraud by quoting a September 14, 1892 speech of past New Mexico Territorial Surveyor General. Cleaveland wrote:

[Elkins] made himself particularly conspicuous as the hero of the famous Maxwell Grant, which as Secretary [of the Interior Jacob D.] Cox decided in 1869, contained only about 96,000 acres, but which under the manipulation of Elkins, was surveyed and patented for 1,714,764 acres, of nearly 2,680 square miles. (Cleaveland, *The Morleys,* p. 74)

SETTLERS' REVOLTS

The Colfax County War was a prolonged revolt of Maxwell Land Grant settlers against eviction. Elkins and Catron had tried to outlaw them as illegal "squatters." By October 27, 1870, they were rioting in Elizabethtown. And Elkins got Governor Pile to send troops for suppression. For malicious prosecutions, on September 17, 1870, Elkins increased Catron's power by resigning as U.S. Attorney and recommending him to President Grant; achieving that appointment in March of 1872.

In 1872, Elkins' sent out ignored eviction notices, with Catron's legal back-up. Elizabethtown rioted again. In response, Ringite Governor Marsh Giddings, petitioned by Elkins, sent in local Fort Union troops; just as he had used Fort Marcy troops to suppress the Legislature Revolt earlier that year. (Noteworthy is that that Fort Union's future commander, Ringite Nathan Augustus Monroe Dudley, in 1878, would, with his new command at Fort Stanton, likewise use troops to crush the Lincoln County War Battle's freedom fighters.) To further curtail Elizabethtown's settlers' power, Giddings moved Colfax County's seat from Elizabethtown to Cimarron, where the Maxwell Land Grant Company was headquartered.

Westphall claimed Elkins's Grant connection ended in 1873 when he became Delegate to Congress; omitting that "Catron was made a director of the company so he could serve as their attorney." (Westphall, p. 109) Also, Elkins worked for the Grant by Congressional bills. (Westphall, p. 113) Westphall stated disingenuously: "As United States attorney [Catron] had no contact with eviction of settlers which was a district court matter involving the territorial attorney general: William Breeden" (Westphall, p. 109) - omitting that he was a Ringite too.

After 1873, Raymond Morley surprisingly became anti-Ring, bringing in his Iowa attorney friend, Attorney Frank Springer, to

Cimarron to negotiate with settlers in place of company lawyer, Catron. By 1874, Morley and Springer were opposing Catron, Elkins, and Directors Longwill, and Mills, as being Ringites.

In 1874, the settlers got a voice. Morley made Springer his co-editor for *Cimarron News*. That year, they opposed Elkins's re-election as Delegate to Congress, and consolidated the paper with unsuspected Ringite, Will Dawson's, Elizabethtown *Press and Telegraph* as the *Cimarron News and Press*. Cleaveland wrote: "[Morley and Singer] undoubtedly considered a newspaper a necessity in any effective opposition to the Santa Fe Ring which controlled most of the other newspapers in the Territory." (Cleaveland, *The Morleys*, p. 84)

By 1875, settlers' anti-Ring fervor increased when a known Ringite, Francisco "Pancho" Griego, murdered two soldiers in a gambling quarrel in Cimarron's St. James Hotel, but was not prosecuted. And Raymond Morley and Ring opponent, Methodist Minister Franklin J. Tolby, were, at the time, anonymously writing exposé articles for the *New York Sun* about the Ring's "stranglehold." (Cleaveland, *The Morleys*, p. 87). The Ring responded aggressively to save itself.

MALICIOUS PROSECUTION OF ADA MORLEY

While the murder of Franklin Tolby was likely being planned, Catron initiated malicious prosecution of Raymond Morley's wife, Ada. Laid bare was his megalomaniacal madness, full-blown by 1875. As U.S. Attorney, for revenge against her anti-Ring husband, and hoping to silence him and her anti-Ring mother, Mary Tibbles McPherson, he tortured her by fake litigation.

The triggering incident involved Mary McPherson. Inspired by Franklin Tolby, she mailed an anti-Ring letter to Washington, D.C. at Cimarron's post office. Ada, frightened by its ramifications to her family, retrieved it from the postal box. Ada's grandson, Norman Cleaveland, recounted: "It was a made-to-order situation for the Santa Fe Ring." (Cleaveland, *The Morleys*, p. 91)

Ringite Postmaster, John B. McCullich, reported Ada to Catron, who federally indicted her for mail theft, and issued an arrest warrant. Westphall claimed by 1876 "Catron dropped the case." (Westphall, p. 117) But her family attested that it was never dropped, and they lived in fear. Norman Cleaveland wrote:

And with practically all the courts and law enforcement agencies, including the U.S. Army, under [Catron's] control, the Morleys and Mother McPherson had real cause for concern. (Cleaveland, *The* Morleys, pp. 94-95)

To hide that wickedness, Westphall lied that Ada and Catron had merely argued about using the Grant Company's buggy, and that she was not indicted. But Ada's daughter, Agnes Morley Cleaveland, described her mother's anxiety in her 1941 book, *No Life for a Lady*: "When my mother told me this story in 1884, the statute of limitations had not yet taken effect. 'I'm still under indictment,' she said." (Agnes Cleaveland, p. 9)

Norman Cleaveland reported that Attorney Frank Springer tried to intervene with Ringite Probate Judge Robert Longwill to prevent Ada's indictment. But he tried to extort Springer into silencing his press. Springer then turned to Attorney Melvin W. Mills, who litigated for the Ring in Colfax County; and learned that Ada would be indicted. Springer then acquired a secret sadistic letter written on July 18, 1875 by Mills to Longwill, which he gave in his deposition to Investigator Angel on August 9, 1878. It stated:

Dear Doctor.

We are having great times here - the delegation from Cimarron is here and I think we have the best of everything. Springer gets a dam cold reception from every body. Mrs M- [Morley] will be indicted without fail ... the mission of S- [Springer] to keep Mrs M- from being indicted is a total failure.

Yours very truly
Mills

This arrogant and mocking voice of organized crime should be remembered. Its smug immunity was heard again in the Lincoln County War period's letters of Ringites James Dolan and District Attorney William Rynerson, and in the defense arguments of Attorney Henry Waldo in the Dudley Court of Inquiry.

It is also important to remember that this Mills-Longwill letter was written as they were arranging the murder of Franklin Tolby, two months away, on September 14, 1875.

Their criminal collusion is also shown in their December 5, 1873 letter used as "Exhibit A" by Springer in his August 9, 1878 deposition to investigator Angel. It stated:

> Santa Fe, N.M.
> Dec 5th 1873
>
> Dear Doctor [Robert H. Longwill].
>
> Thought I would write you how things are running. C. [Catron] is in good humor and said that your money had come, or rather that $18,000 would be paid in Smith & Humphreys judgment ...
>
> The legislature is doing well and we will pass more laws than there was ever passed before ... If you should think best to have it [the fence law] passed let me know ... **I can pass any law I want to in spite of anybody that is not here or most anybody that might come here.** I gave your compliments to Ben Stevens [later accomplice in Governor Axtell's 1876 "Dear Ben plot" to kill Frank Springer, Raymond Morley, and Clay Allison] and he said that he owed you a very great obligation for treating him. **I believe – I have got in with the big side by a little sharp figuring.**
>
> Destroy. <u>Strictly private</u>
> Mills

By the time Ada Morley was indicted by the Ring-controlled Taos Grand Jury in 1876, Catron had already murdered Tolby through his agents, Longwill and Mills; and had tried to kill Springer, Morley, Porter, and Allison. In two more years, Catron's despotic and unrelenting fury would be unleashed against John Tunstall, Alexander McSween, the Regulators, residents of San Patricio, and, finally, Billy Bonney himself.

Catron's viciousness is further shown in the actual buggy incident with Ada, as presented in a March 31, 1876 deposition by Asa F. Middaugh, partner in the banking firm of Porter and Middaugh. Ada's grandson, Norman Cleaveland, in his book, *The Morleys*, felt the buggy incident showed Catron's power obsession. He was in Cimarron as the Grant Company attorney, and wanted to use its buggy. But since her husband, Raymond Morley was the company's manager, she expressed anti-Ring spite by taking it herself. That made Catron furious. The Middaugh deposition was "Exhibit B" in Frank Springer's August 9, 1878 deposition to Angel. Middaugh stated:

Territory of Colorado)
County of Rio Grande)

Asa F. Middaugh, being duly sworn, on his oath deponent says, that on or about the fifth day of April AD 1875, at the town of Cimarron New Mexico, he had a conversation with Thomas B. Catron in reference to certain charges which had been or were being made against Mrs Ada M. Morley, wife of W.R. Morley, of taking a letter out of the Cimarron Post Office. That during said conversation Catron declared that Mrs Morley had insulted him by taking away a certain buggy at a time when said Catron wanted to use it, and that said Morley [in his Cimarron News and Press] had been throwing mud at him, **and that he - said Catron - had a chance to get even now, and he would be a fool if he did not take advantage of it. Said conversation being with reference to possible criminal proceedings against said Mrs Morley in the United States District Court, and said Catron being then the United States District Attorney.** *It was deponent's understanding from the language of said Catron that he, said Catron, meant that he had a chance to have said Ada M. Morley indicted and prosecuted for taking a letter out of the Post Office, and that he would be a fool not to do it in order to avenge himself for the real or fancied insult which had been offered him by said Ada M. Morley.*

Asa F. Middaugh

Subscribed and sworn to before me
this 31st day of March AD 1876

Thomas W. Smith
Notary Public

ASSASSINATION OF FRANKLIN J. TOLBY

The persistence of Colfax County settlers in the face of eviction notices, military interventions, malicious prosecutions, and bloodshed was unexpected to the Ring; at the time having weathered only the feeble 1872 Legislature Revolt and 1876 Grant County Rebellion. So it escalated to assassination of their leader. The accused killers were Melvin Mills and Robert Longwill, employing hired thugs for the deed. (That stratagem would be repeated in three years in Lincoln County with local Ringites James Dolan, John Riley, and Sheriff William Brady using outlaw Jessie Evans and his gang to murder John Tunstall.)

So Colfax County War settlers may have lacked a central battle, but they got a martyr: Methodist Reverend Franklin J. Tolby, a missionary circuit-rider to Colfax County's Cimarron and Elizabethtown. He had become an anti-Ring, anti-Land Grant Company, pro-settler activist. From Indiana, he had arrived in Cimarron on January 1, 1874. By July of 1875, an unsigned letter printed in the *New York Sun* - believed to be by him - accused Catron, Elkins, and Chief Justice Joseph P. Palen of being Ring leaders. (Palen had kept his judgeship after the defeated 1872 Legislature Revolt.)

In early September of 1875, Tolby and Palen were seen in public altercation in Cimarron. Tolby accused him, U.S. Attorney Catron, and Attorney William Breeden of obstructing indictment of Francisco "Pancho" Griego for murder. (And it was commonly believed that Griego rigged the 1872 elections for Mills and Longwill.) Palen attacked Tolby for criticizing his court. Defiantly, Tolby stated - according to Frank Springer's August 9, 1978 deposition to Presidential Investigator Frank Warner Angel - that he would "write up [Palen] so that 200,000 readers should see the record." This threat seemed to confirm Tolby's authorship of the anonymous *New York Sun* letters exposing Palen, Catron, Elkins, and their Ring. (Cleaveland, *The* Morleys, pp. 97-98) Tolby had also exposed Governor S.B. Beach Axtell. (Taylor, p. 39)

On September 14, 1875, Tolby, alone on horseback, was murdered on a remote canyon road to Cimarron, after preaching at Elizabethtown. He was 33, and married with three children. His concealed corpse had two bullets in its back, his horse was tethered, and there was no sign of robbery. His obvious Ring assassination added fuel to Colfax County's fighting.

Tolby's martyrdom switched Ring-backer, prior Confederate soldier, Clay Allison, to anti-Ring. A Grant settler since 1866, he was a cattle rancher, racist, drunk, and trigger-happy gunslinger; rumored to have refused $700 to kill Tolby himself. He ended up Colfax County's less charismatic - and, at 35, a much older - pale version of Billy the Kid; dying at 47 by a drunken fall from a wagon. For accusing Tolby's Ringite killers, he later earned Ring retaliation of murder indictments.

And there also emerged a new anti-Ring leader: Reverend Oscar P. McMains.

OSCAR P. McMAINS'S PURSUIT OF TOLBY'S KILLERS

From murdered Tolby's blood, sprang Reverend Oscar P. McMains, a more aggressive Ring opponent. A high-minded, hot-tempered, circuit riding Methodist missionary, he had come to Cimarron from Colorado in June of 1875, becoming Tolby's assistant, while working as a *Cimarron News and Press* printer.

After Tolby's September 14, 1875 murder, McMains took over his missionary circuit as well as assuming leadership of pro-settler opposition to the Maxwell Land Grant Company and the Santa Fe Ring. Importantly, he sought justice for Tolby.

Since the Ringite Colfax County Sheriff did nothing about the killing, McMains organized what he called the "Colfax County Ring" to arrest Tolby's murderers (as the Lincoln County Regulators would later try to arrest of John Tunstall's Ringite murderers when Ringite Sheriff Brady refused). McMains soon discovered the culprits, thus, becoming the Ring's next victim.

He exposed Ringite mail contractor, Florencio Donoghue, who admitted to hiring a new Cimarron Constable, Cruz Vega, to deliver mail for the murder day only, along the murder site canyon. But the Sheriff refused to arrest Vega, a nephew of local Ringite Francisco "Pancho" Griego.

So McMains took men to question Cruz Vega at the ranch where he worked. Vega's recalcitrance led to a feigned hanging and his confession of witnessing the murder, which he claimed was done by a Manuel Cardenas. He added that Cardenas had been hired by Florencio Donoghue to kill Tolby. When the violence escalated, McMains left. And masked Clay Allison was believed to have completed Cruz Vega's lynching.

So Cruz Vega's uncle, Francisco "Pancho" Griego, drunkenly accosted Allison, on November 1, 1875, at the St. James Hotel, across the street from the Maxwell mansion. Allison killed him with three shots, claiming self-defense.

As to Manuel Cardenas, an arrest warrant was issued based on Cruz Vega's accusation. Cardenas was arrested in Elizabethtown, and questioned by its Justice of the Peace on November 6th. He accused Vega of the murder, but confessed that they had both been hired to do the killing for $500 by Florencio Donoghue, Melvin Mills, Robert Longwill, and now-dead Francisco Griego.

Cimarron was in an uproar. Raymond Morley's wife, Ada, in her diary, called it *"The Week of the Reign of Terror."* (Cleaveland, *The* Morleys, p. 122) Now firmly anti-Ring, Clay Allison tried and failed to capture Dr. Robert Longwill, who escaped to Fort Union, then to Catron's protection in Santa Fe. Florencio Donoghue, Melvin Mills, and Manuel Cardenas were arrested.

On November 8, 1875, for intimidation, Governor Samuel Beach Axtell sent Fort Union's 9th Cavalry to Cimarron.

Norman Cleaveland wrote that his grandfather, Raymond Morley, fearing he would be murdered by the troops, fled town: "[I]n Colfax County the U.S. Army from Fort Union was at the service of the Santa Fe Ring. Grandfather knew the leaders of the Ring well enough to be convinced that they would not hesitate to use the Army to advance their political and financial interests." (Cleaveland, *The Morleys*, p. 102)

Ada wrote to her hiding husband that November 8, 1875, *"The revolution has begun in earnest."* And her fire-brand mother, Mary McPherson, updated him on him "news." (Cleaveland, *The Morleys*, p. 102)

On November 11, 1875, Manuel Cardenas, Melvin Mills, and Florencio Donoghue had a preliminary hearing in Cimarron under Justice of the Peace Trauer. They were represented by Catron's law firm member, Henry Waldo. (In 1879, Waldo would defend Ringite Commander N.A.M. Dudley for his Lincoln County War Battle atrocities.) At the hearing, Cardenas withdrew his confession, and Mills claimed innocence; but Donoghue's murder threat against Tolby had been witnessed. Only Mills was released for lack of evidence. And stool pigeon Cardenas was killed while being led back to jail. Masked men shot him in the head.

Oscar McMains then made a citizens' committee. It met on November 10, 1875, as reported in the *Cimarron News and Press*, to determine the Ring's role in Tolby's "murderous assassination." Already subjected to the Ring's "outlawing," they countered: "We are not a mob of lawless men as has been reported abroad, bent upon violence and defiance of law, but on the contrary have assembled legally and quietly for the purpose of the doing of justice and securing the punishment of crime." Mary McPherson enclosed that article in her complaint to Washington. It claimed that Cruz Vega and Manuel Cardinas were "the tools of other parties;" and that troops were illegally used obstruct justice. It stated:

Whereas; On the 14th day of September, A.D. 1875, the Rev F.J. Tolby, a minister of the gospel resident among us, and a man who for sterling qualities, both as a minister and a citizen, commanded the highest respect and esteem among all the people of this county, was foully assassinated, while traveling upon the public highway, and, Whereas the report of this murder ... has created an impression that the lives of peaceable citizens are not safe here, and has thereby worked a great detriment and injury to our county, deterring many persons from settling and making their homes here ...

That the facts disclosed revealed **deliberately planned assassination, in which the men Cruz Vega and Manuel Cardinas were the tools of other parties**, who from some motive, aside from plunder, planned the murder and procured the two men above named to perform the cowardly act.

That we regard those who procured the commission of the murder as far more guilty, if possible, than the duped and hired tools, and that if satisfactory evidence is found to discover and identify any such party or parties there should not be permitted to them any loophole to escape the extreme penalty of the law ...

That we regard the action of the United States authorities at Fort Union in concealing **R. [Robert] H. Longwill** [Ringman who hired Cruz Vega and Manuel Cardinas], and shielding him from arrest by properly authorized officers of the county, with warrants legally issued, and thereby enabling him to escape, and avoid an examination here, upon charges made against him, as **an unwarrantable obstruction of justice and an arbitrary and illegal use of power of the army** of the United States, and it deserves reprehension and condemnation of all citizens.

By 1878, John Tunstall's killing replicated Tolby's, with hired thugs. Tolby's Ring killers, like Tunstall's, would get no penalty.

EXPOSÉS AND RING RETALIATIONS

SUMMARY: After the Colfax County War's Ring murder of Reverend Tolby, the Ring's existence was imperiled in a new way: by citizens not only willing to fight, but having a public voice through press and whistleblowers. The Ring responded by malicious prosecutions, outlawing opponents, attempted assassinations, and removing Colfax County's courts.

Victor Westphall hides Colfax County's Ring exposés, claiming: "Catron acquired the role of villain in **oral tradition** surrounding Colfax County troubles." (Westphall, p. 115) In fact, the Ring faced exposés more than "oral" by Raymond Morley and Frank Springer in their *Cimarron News and Press*, and by Mary McPherson to Washington. But Westphall called the articles a "feud [with Catron about] little things." (Westphall, pp. 114-115) And he attacked McPherson: "While Catron's contretemps in Colfax County - and they were fundamental to his public career - started in disagreements with Morley and Springer, their culmination can be attributed to one person more than any other: Mary E. McPherson, mother-in-law of William R. Morley, and mother of Morley's wife, Ada." (Westphall, p. 116)

But Catron had failed to get rid of Raymond Morley by his malicious prosecution of Ada. The settlers did not stop rioting after Tolby's murder. And Mary McPherson was unfazed in her production of voluminous exposés of the Ring.

Westphall argued: "To do all these [bad] things would have required more official power on the part of Catron than he possibly could have possessed." (Westphall, p. 118) In truth, the Ring, in despotic control by 1875, did have that horrific power.

RING DECLARES COLFAX COUNTY IN ANARCHY

The Ring outlawed citizens, as November 16, 1875's *Santa Fe Weekly New Mexican* reported in "Anarchy in Cimarron":

The situation in Cimarron remains in many respects about as reported ... There seems to be an armed band of men in and about town bent on violence, lawlessness and ruling to suit themselves; they declare they are assisting civil authorities, but from all we can learn compel them to do as they see fit. The citizens are terrified and many of them have left to save their lives. **Mr. Mills and Donoghue who have been charged with complicity in the murder of Tolby (which we believe to be entirely unfounded) are in the hands of the mob**, and it is said they declare their intention not to surrender [to] them even on writ of habeas corpus. **U.S. troops are on the ground and they will prevent violence and bloodshed if they have notice in time**; but even their presence has not had the effect to disperse the mob who seem to have control of the prisoners and the administration of affairs.

"THE TERRITORY OF ELKINS" RING EXPOSÉ

Colfax County's response was fierce. On December 22, 1875, the *New York Sun* published an anti-Ring article about Tolby's murder: "The Territory of Elkins.' Assassination of Supposed Sun Correspondent. The Murder of the Rev. F.J. Tolby in New Mexico. A Probate Judge Accused of Complicity in the Crime. Indignation Meeting." Agnes Morley, daughter of Ada and Raymond, in her 1941 book *No Life for A Lady*, said her father wrote it. (Agnes Cleaveland, p. 7) And Mary McPherson included it in her 1877 anti-Ring complaint to Washington. It stated:

"THE TERRITORY OF ELKINS."
Assassination of Supposed Sun Correspondent. The Murder of the Rev. F.J. Tolby in New Mexico. A Probate Judge Accused of Complicity in the Crime. Indignation Meeting.

"Santa Fé, N.M., Nov. 26. - **The political revolution which has taken place and is still in progress in this Territory is mainly attributed to the exposures of the Santa Fé Ring which have appeared in the Sun, and which have created great consternation among our corrupt officials, the Sun having a wide circulation in this region.** By means of libel suits, and still more effectual measures, **the Ring** has succeeded in intimidating the local press, with one or two exceptions; **and so long as the courts are constituted as they are at present, it is absolutely unsafe for any man to actively oppose the corrupt scheme of the Ring**.

The nature of the means taken to harass those who show rebellious spirit has already been described in this correspondence, and events of recent occurrence, which will form the subject of this letter, will give the reader an idea of the difficulties which are encountered by those who are striving to effect a reform in the administration in our territorial affairs.

"On the 14th of September last, the Rev. F.J. Tolby, a minister of the gospel, generally respected and beloved, was brutally murdered on the highway while passing through a lonely canyon. The murder was involved in mystery for a time. Mr. Tolby was an active, bold, and outspoken man, who took much interest in public affairs, and did not hesitate to express his opinion. **He was not known to have an enemy in the world, save members of the Ring whom he had vigorously and publicly denounced for their offence against society.**

"It is said that a few days before his death Mr.

Tolby had a warm discussion with Judge Palen of the first Judicial District, one of the chiefs of the Ring, who tried to intimidate him without effect, for the preacher boldly announced his intention of writing of the Ring rascalities for the eastern press, and up to the time of his murder he exerted all his influence against the rogues in office.

"It was known that Mr. Tolby had threatened to make exposures through the press, and in some quarters he was suspected of having written the letter to the Sun which excited such commotion in the Federal Ring. These, and other circumstances, excited suspicion from the first that he had fallen a victim to the malevolence of the Ring, or of some of its members, but for a long time no direct proof of it could be obtained. At last, however, the actual murderers were hunted down, and when it was found that they implicated the principal members of the Colfax county branch of the Ring as the instigators of the crime, the indignation of the people knew no bounds. At one time it was feared that every one of the politicians named in the connection with the murder would be strung up by the neck without the intervention of judge or jury; but calmer counsel prevailed, and acting upon information gained from the murderers and other sources, warrants were issued for the arrest of the accused parties.

"The persons charged by the murderers as the planners and accessories to the murder are the recognized strikers of the Ring in Colfax county. Some of them were lately elected to office through the influence of the Ring. Their names are R. [Robert] H. Longwill, Probate Judge; M. [Melvin] W. Mills, member of the Legislature; F. [Florencio] Donoghue and F. [Francisco] Griego**. Longwill fled to this city [Santa Fe] where he still remains, protected by his Ring friends from arrest. Mills was discharged for want of evidence. Donoghue is in jail awaiting trial in default of $20,000 bail, and Griego is dead ... Although there was no legal evidence to prove that the recognized leaders of the Ring either had any connection with the assassination of Mr. Tolby, or knew that such an atrocious crime was in contemplation, yet it is impossible to make the majority of the people of Cimarron and vicinity believe that they are altogether guiltless, and the feeling against all persons who are supposed to be connected in any way to the operation of Elkins & Co. is bitter in the extreme ...

"On the 10th of November [1875] a mass meeting of the citizens of Colfax county was held in the court house in Cimarron, which was largely attended by the leading men from all parts of the county. **The Rev. O.P. McMains presided, and resolutions were adopted that the killing of Mr. Tolby was a deliberately planned assassination, in which the actual murderers were the tools of other parties, who aside from plunder, planned the murder; and those who procured the murder are far more guilty, if possible, than the duped and hired tools, and that, if satisfactory evidence is found to discover and identify any such party or parties, there should not be permitted to them any loophole to escape the extreme penalty of the law.

"If a new election for Delegate to Congress could be held for tomorrow, Elkins would be defeated by such a tremendous majority that not even the tools of the Santa Fé Ring would dare attempt the job of counting him in."

PRO-RING AND ANTI-RING BACKLASHES

On December 21, 1875, with Morley and Springer out of town, secret Ringite, Will Dawson, their co-editor, published a pro-Ring obituary of hated Judge Joseph Palen - whose judgeship was assumed by Catron's law firm member, Henry Waldo.

On December 31, 1875, Dawson, again inflamed settlers by attacking the "Territory of Elkins" *New York Sun* article; writing:

We find another one of those lying, brutal letters in the New York Weekly Sun of the 22d inst., without signature, and purporting to come out of Santa Fe. The writer, whoever he may be, will be looked upon as a coward, a disturber of the peace, as well as a slanderer upon the good name and fair fame of this portion of New Mexico ... There can be none but the worst imaginable motive in any one who will persist in keeping alive the bad condition of feeling in this county which has grown out of distressing crimes, ending in blood and death.

Over 150 Colfax County settlers, published a signed response letter to Dawson. Morley and Springer resigned the *Cimarron News and Press*s. Mary McPherson used it as "What the People of Colfax Say," in her August of 1877 booklet to the Departments of Interior and Justice as: "In the Matter of the Charges vs. Gov. S.B. Axtell and Other New Mexico Officials." Its point - prophetic for Lincoln County - was: "[T]he history of the past few years has shown that through the regular legal actions of the authorities in power, such cruel and bloodthirsty deeds [as Tolby's murder] are not likely to be punished." The response letter to Dawson stated:

Will. D. Dawson, Publisher News and Press:

"Sir, - In your issue of Dec. 31st, you take the occasion to depart from the former [Anti-Ring] course of your paper and to condemn in the strongest terms a certain article in the New York Sun, which gives an account of the recent troubles in Colfax County, growing out of the murder of Rev. F.J. Tolby.

"We the citizens of Colfax County, have read the account in the *Sun*, and notwithstanding your severe denunciation of it, declare that it is in substance true, and that your comments are unjust in the extreme, not only as regards the article in question, but also as regards to further articles in the *Sun* which have opened the eyes of the world to the corruptions which have and do exist in New Mexico politics, and we hope and trust that the *Sun* and the newspaper press generally will continue their efforts until a thorough investigation, from proper sources, is made, which will bring about a better state of things. Further than this, we consider, notwithstanding your insinuations to the contrary, that the action of the people in investigating the Tolby murderers and punishing such of them as were caught, was a public necessity, and for the public good, inasmuch as **the history of the past few years has shown that through the regular legal actions of the authorities in power, such cruel and bloodthirsty deeds are not likely to be punished.** We hereby request you to publish with this the *Sun* article referred to, with your criticism on the same, that all may see and know where the right is.

[153 signatures follow, including Raymond Morley's, Frank Springer's, Oscar McMains's, and Clay Allison's]

McPherson added the Ring's malicious prosecution; stating:

> An attempt to indict all the signers of the petition was made, but was abandoned from motives of policy, and indictments for other alleged offences instead, were secured against upward of fifty persons.

On January 19, 1876, Clay Allison took his own action. With others, he nocturnally raided the *Cimarron News and Press* office and typeset a red headline: "CLAY ALLISON'S EDITION." Then he threw the printing machinery into the Cimarron River. The next day, sobered-up, he reimbursed Morley's wife, Ada, for new equipment. Then Morley and Springer resumed editorships of the *Cimarron News and Press* without Dawson.

REMOVAL OF COLFAX COUNTY COURTS

With Colfax County not backing down, the Ring next chose suppression. On January 14, 1876, the Maxwell Land Grant Company, colluding with Governor Axtell, petitioned to force settlers to buy or rent their land, with eviction for refusal.

That day, Axtell abolished Colfax County's courts through a bill joining its judiciary to distant Taos County. (This mimicked Governor Giddings's 1872 disempowerment of legislators in the Legislature Revolt by cutting representation of Grant, Doña Ana, and Lincoln Counties.) Furthermore, Colfax County residents were barred from Taos juries; and Colfax County witnesses in litigation had to travel 55 miles over a mountain range to Taos. When Axtell was telegraphed to stop before meeting with a Cimarron delegation, he responded. "Bill Signed. S.B. Axtell."

Intended was blocking Tolby's murderers' trials, hanging McMains and Allison, and snuffing out the Colfax County War.

On January 19, 1876, Raymond Morley, Henry M. Porter, and Sheriff William Cunningham sent telegrams to Governor Axtell pleading for restoration of their courts. Axtell's answer was Ring totalitarianism, masked by the outlaw myth: "Law requires two terms be held in Taos. Should it appear that its objects have been accomplished, the Governor is authorized to restore courts to Colfax ... I see two sides. Broken laws, property wantonly destroyed and murdered men are on one side. I have no compromise to make." (Cleaveland, *The* Morleys, p. 113)

Springer, Morley, Porter, and Allison then asked Axtell to meet them in Cimarron. Their signatures became a Ring hit list.

Then Springer went to Santa Fe to meet with Axtell about the removed courts. In his deposition of August 9, 1978 to Frank Warner Angel, Springer stated: *"[Axtell] spoke with extreme bitterness about the people of Colfax county .... I asked and urged him to go to Cimarron and see the people and learn the facts for himself, but he positively refused ...* **He said there were bad men there and that he intended to have them punished or compelled to leave the county, if it took all the troops in New Mexico***. He spoke particularly and repeatedly of one [Clay] Allison and seemed very bitter towards him and mentioned him especially as one whom he intended to have indicted and punished, or compelled to leave the county."*

THE "DEAR BEN" ASSASSINATION PLOT

In 1876, to implement paralyzing Colfax County resistance, the Ring chose to murder more leaders. Again Governor Axtell was the agent. Victor Westphall called that a misunderstanding of Axtell's intent! (Westphall, p. 127)

By then, the Ring was habitually using troops to potentially kill citizens. Governor Marsh Giddings had sent Fort Marcy soldiers into the Catron and Palen Supreme Court nullifying the legislature's acts from the 1872 Legislature Revolt; Giddings had sent Fort Union troops against Elizabethtown settlers fighting evictions; and Governor Axtell had deployed Fort Union troops in November of 1875 to stop arrests of Franklin Tolby's murderers. And later in 1876, Fort Union troops would be positioned to impair dissent during the Ring-controlled Taos County Grand Jury's unjust trials clearing Tolby's killers. By 1878, Fort Stanton soldiers under Commander N.A.M. Dudley would facilitate murder and arson in the Lincoln County War Battle.

So it was predictable that, in 1876, Governor Axtell enlisted Fort Union troops to kill, under guise of law, Colfax County's anti-Ring leaders: Raymond Morley, Frank Springer, Clay Allison, and Henry Porter. It became known as the "Dear Ben plot."

The plot unfolded in March of 1876, when Ringite Second Judicial District Judge Benjamin Stevens arrived in Cimarron with a telegram to lure the victims, while also having secret telegraphed directions from Axtell. Stevens, knowing Morley, then invited him to his room at the St. James Hotel, giving him the lure telegram stating that Axtell was coming by that Saturday's coach for a secret meeting with him, Springer, Allison, and Porter about the Colfax County courts. In fact, Axtell was not coming. They were to be met by Fort Union's black 9th Cavalrymen, under a Captain F. Moore, who would kill them. The twisted logic was that racist Allison would react violently to black men, and justify the soldiers shooting all four men in self defense.

But Morley was warned of the plot, possibly by the telegraph operator, since he received Axtell's secret telegraph to Benjamin Stevens as *"Dear Ben."* It said: *"Do not hesitate at extreme measures. Your honor is at stake now and failure is fatal."* Axtell later denied authorship, but Captain F. Moore confirmed the plot. The telegram stated:

Dear Ben – The second telegram delivered to you at Fort Union, directed to Cimarron, was intended to leak, but the operator here says he cannot raise the Cimarron office. If I was expected, our friends would probably be on hand, as the guard is only a Government escort. I do not think your definite business is suspected. Wade [James F. Wade, Commander Fort Union] informed Hatch [General Edward S. Hatch, Commander, District of New Mexico] that he had been ready all the time to assist you, but could not find that you wanted to do it. Hatch says that their opinion is that you weakened and do not want to arrest the man. **Have your men placed to arrest him and to kill all the men who resist you or stand with those who do resist you. Our man signed the invitation with others who were at that meeting for me to visit Colfax – Porter, Morley, Springer, et. al.** *Now, if they expect me Saturday, they will be on hand.* **Send me letters by messenger, and do not hesitate at extreme measures. Your honor is at stake now, and a failure is fatal.** *If others resist or attempt murder, bring them also. Hatch is excited, and wishes, of course, to put all the blame on the civil officers. I am more anxious on your account than for any other reason. I clearly see that we have no friends in Colfax, and I have suspected all along that some of our pretended friends were traitors. Yours &c., S.B. Axtell*

To ensure success, Axtell removed Colfax County's elected Sheriff, O.K. Chittenden, by claiming he had not filed his tax bond. (Axtell repeated this tactic on May 28, 1878 to remove anti-Ring Lincoln County Sheriff John Copeland.) Axtell then appointed a Ringite and complicit sheriff named Rinehart.

Morley warned the others. So the plot failed when none were present when the fatal Saturday coach arrived.

But the Fort Union troops stayed in Cimarron for a week, accompanying Sheriff Rinehart to Clay Allison's ranch to arrest him for murders of Francisco Griego, Cruz Vega, and even Manuel Cardenas - still provoking violence to kill him. (Inciting of violence to justify murder was used in Lincoln County in 1878 by Sheriff William Brady to harass John Tunstall and Alexander McSween by property attachments during the Ring's malicious harassment embezzlement case; and using troops to attempt capture of McSween at John Chisum's ranch before the Lincoln County War.)

A year later, in 1877, Morley and Springer published that secret "Dear Ben plot" telegram in their *Cimarron News and Press*. Mary McPherson added it to her complaint to the Departments of Justice and the Interior about Axtell and other Ringites; and Frank Springer gave it in his August 9, 1878 deposition to Investigator Angel to justify Axtell's removal.

RING-CONTROLLED TAOS COURTS

After Governor S.B. Axtell's removal of Colfax County's courts by joining them to Taos County courts, everything was in place for obstruction of justice without recourse, since the Taos jurors were ignorant of Colfax County issues and could also be influenced by the Ring to shield Ringite criminals, while witnesses for anti-ring defendants were hindered from attending by distance and fear. (This manipulation was repeated to ensure conviction of Billy Bonney in 1881 by the change of his venue from knowledgeable Lincoln County to Mesilla, in Doña Ana County.)

TAOS GRAND JURY OF 1876

The April 1876 Taos County Grand Jury had Fort Union troops for intimidation. Its judge was Ringite Chief Justice Henry Waldo, having replaced deceased Judge Joseph Palen in 1875. Ringite Attorney General William Breeden was present to "assist" jurymen. Assured was Ada Morley's indictment for mail theft.

For the trial of Franklin Tolby's killers, Melvin Mills was represented by side-switching Frank Springer. McMains was the star witness, but refused to name Tolby's murderers with certainty because Judge Waldo reprehensibly instructed the jurymen to charge him with libel if he did.

Waldo gave the following prejudicial instructions to the jurymen, as reported in the *Daily New Mexican* of May 1, 1876, and quoted in the Pueblo, Colorado *Chieftain*, May 25, 1876:

"Your jurisdiction is extended over a district of county to whose inhabitants no doubt such annexation was and is somewhat obnoxious, and who may be disposed to resent such legislation, as a reproach to them as a community." In the same statement [Waldo] explained that the districts had been combined because Cimarron's reputation was notorious and the three killings [Tolby, Vega, and Cardenas] were only the more spectacular examples of lawlessness. Instructing the jurors to identify and indict the killers, he also directed them, **in the Tolby case, to return indictments for libel if certain men had been maliciously and falsely implicated**. (Taylor, p. 49)

Judge Waldo's decision was quoted by Norman Cleaveland:

The fullest investigation which the grand jury could make was given to the charges against Mills, Longwill and Donoghue; and all persons who were supposed to have any knowledge of the facts as far as the Grand Jury could learn, were brought before it and thoroughly examined, being permitted to tell what they knew. The Grand Jury was unable to discover the least evidence which implicated either of the persons above named in the assassination, the charges brought against them, as far as the jury could ascertain, being based solely on rumors and suspicion.

From the evidence placed before the Grand Jury it appears that the only persons that is responsible to suppose had knowledge of the assassination were themselves murdered [Vega and Cardenas] while in the custody of persons ostensibly engaged in an investigation to discover the facts about Mr. Tolby's murder [McMains and others]. (Cleaveland, p. 124)

So Ringites Melvin Mills and Robert Longwill were acquitted.

The May 13, 1876 Ringite *The Daily New Mexican's* editorial completed the cover-up of Mills's and Longwill's role in Tolby's assassination; writing:

Our readers will recollect that soon after the assassination of Rev. Mr. Tolby in the Cimarron cañon last September, Dr. R. H. Longwill and M. W. Mills were charged with being implicated in the terrible crime. To those who were acquainted with these gentlemen, and who were cognizant of the feelings and motives of the different factions or cliques existing in Colfax county, just prior to that sad event, these charges were looked upon as the fabrications of bitter, malignant personal and political enemies of Dr. Longwill and Mr. Mills; and others though not so well informed in these respects have readily surmised as much from the evidence brought to substantiate the charges and the proceedings thereon. All these two gentlemen desired was an opportunity for a full and impartial investigation of the charges before a competent tribunal.

Such an opportunity was afforded them at the last session of the district court for Taos county. During the entire session of that court the grand jury devoted its labors exclusively to a careful and patient investigation of crimes and offences committed in Colfax county, aided by the Attorney General [Breeden], who was untiring in his efforts to ferret out the perpetrators of crime, and worked steadily with the grand jury from an early hour in the morning till late at night. Every day of the term the grand jury carefully and patiently investigated all charges of crime brought to their knowledge or notice.

As a result of their labors we subjoin the following extract from their report presented to the court at the close of the term:

"We have carefully investigated in reference to the murder of Mr. Tolby committed in the county of Colfax last September, but were unable to find any evidence of importance relating to the commission of that crime. The fullest investigation which the grand jury could make was given to the charges made against Mills, Longwill and [Florencio] Donoghue; and all persons who were supposed to have any knowledge of the facts as far as the grand jury could learn were brought before and thoroughly examined being permitted to tell what they knew: and after a very careful examination the grand jury was unable to discover the least evidence which implicated either of the persons above named in the assassination: **the charges brought against them, as far as the grand jury could ascertain, being based solely on rumors and suspicions**. From the evidence placed before the grand jury it appears that the only persons who it is reasonable to suppose had any knowledge of the assassination. were themselves murdered while in the custody of persons ostensibly engaged in an investigation to discover the facts about Mr. Tolby's murder. About fifty witnesses residing in Colfax county, among them several prominent citizens of that county, were called before, and examined by, the grand jury.

This extract shows on how slight a basis these serious and terrible charges ere made against Dr. Longwill and Mr. Mills. People generally believe that they were invented and set afloat by malignant enemies of these gentlemen at a time when the populace, wrought up to a fever heat of excitement were ready to consign any man against whom the slightest suspicion was breathed to an ignominious death at the hands of a mob; and that they were so invented an circulated in the hope that thereby men who had successfully opposed and thwarted the schemes of the authors of these suspicions; might be removed from their path.

We congratulate Dr. Longwill and Mr. Mills on their complete vindication from these terrible charges, and we sincerely hope that this investigation will serve as a warning hereafter to people to be slow in giving credence to charges so serious when made on formulations so slight, against men of respectability and character, or participating in lawless organizations to murder innocent men for imaginary crimes.

And in this connection we cannot refrain from a word of caution to some eastern papers against the ready admission to their columns of wholesale denunciations of men and measures in New Mexico. Lying newspaper correspondents appear to be special nuisances amongst us just now and eastern papers ignorant of the true state of affairs here seem inclined to give them ready credence, however wild and farcical their diatribes. We caution them, as a result of the course of some of them in the Tolby murder, to hesitate in admitting to their columns so serious charges against gentlemen of character and reputation.

Then those who had opposed the Ring were attacked. Clay Allison was indicted for three murders: Francisco "Pancho" Griego, Cruz Vega, and Manuel Cardenas; and of libel for accusing Melvin Mills, Robert Longwill, and Florencio Donoghue of murdering Franklin Tolby. Oscar P. McMains was indicted for the lynch murder of Cruz Vega. He was jailed in Cimarron, at the impossibly high bail of $20,000 set by Judge Waldo, to await trial (or assassination). (This scenario, would be repeated with Alexander McSween in Lincoln County, by his fake embezzlement case arrest, then by Judge Warren Bristol setting a high bond with blocked bondsmen during harassing property attachments to give opportunities for his assassination.) The Pueblo, *Colorado Chieftain*, whose staff knew Oscar McMains, on May 25, 1876, denounced his indictment as Santa Fe Ring scapegoating.

McMains himself tried intervention by his politically powerful, Republican brother-in-law in Indiana, Attorney William Fishback, who got President Hayes to refer the case to non-Ring Attorney General Charles Devens. Devens ordered New Mexico's Attorney General William Breeden, a Ringman, to suspend McMains's case. Instead, the *Santa Fe Daily New Mexican* got a leak of those secret negotiations and accused Devens of meddling. The leaker was obvious: Catron via Elkins. According to Westphall, as U.S. Attorney, Catron notified Devens that jurisdiction was solely his. (Westphall, p. 125) Devens then telegraphed Governor Axtell to request suspension of McMains's case, but was, of course, refused by that colluding Ringite. (Taylor, p. 53) So Oscar McMains remained in Ring clutches, defended by fence-riding Attorney Frank Springer and a W.D Lee.

TAOS GRAND JURY OF 1877

The Taos trials of 1877 can be seen through Raymond Morley's eyes, since he wrote to Mary McPherson on March 6, 1877 - when she was in Washington presenting her complaints - and in the midst of his own crisis of Catron's malicious prosecution of Ada, and his fears of vindictive repercussions of Mary's exposés. She enclosed his letter in her addendum to her May 1877 anti-Ring complaint to President Hayes and the Department of the Interior. Morley wrote:

Cimarron, March 6th 1877
.... I was astonished beyond measure at your proceedings, and have fears as to the result: at the same time I will not throw a straw in your way, but will do what I can to help matters ...

Efforts have been made to get the Court back here, but failed. ***The Ring will not permit it, and say that the objects for which the Court was taken away have not been accomplished: Now you know what the objects were - to defeat the Tolby investigation, and to punish Colfax County for presuming to interfere in such matters.*** *I have to go to court the last of the month - and you know what a Taos court is.* ***The election of Hayes leads many to think that the old regime will hold over [the ring corruption of President Grant], and that other Tolby affairs will happen.***

[AUTHOR'S NOTE: This is prophetic. The next year were Ring murders of John Tunstall, Alexander McSween, and their followers; and the start of the Ring's lethal pursuit of the remaining Regulators and Billy Bonney.]

The people are badly discouraged, and many talk of leaving the county, as their only protection against the machinations of their enemies in power. ***New Mexico today is ruled by five of the Ring, supported as they have been by Federal authority; and the use of troops.***

[AUTHOR'S NOTE: This is prophetic. Troops under Fort Stanton Commander N.A.M. Dudley would defeat the Regulators at the next year's Lincoln County War Battle. Also, Morley understood Ring extension to the federal government.]

If you can affect any removals, you will certainly do good.

[AUTHOR'S NOTE: Morley seems unaware that President Hayes and Secretary of the Interior Schurz helped Ring cover-up.]

Four or five men run this Territory, and run it with unparalled desperation ... The removal of one or two, even, of these officials would remedy the great evil; provided men were in their places who could not be controlled by the Ring. If the office of Chief Justice alone could be filled by a new man with good motives and principles, a short time would defeat the rest.

[AUTHOR'S NOTE: The Chief Justice was then Ringite Henry Waldo, who would defend Dudley in military court in 1879.]

The Governor [Axtell], Chief Justice [Waldo], and U.S. Attorney [Catron] control New Mexico ... If you could remove any of these men, do so by all means. But to get evidence of the facts, which you and all of us are convinced, can only be done in one way, viz: If a secret agent were to come here <u>duly authorized</u> , he could get them – get evidence to astonish the world!

[AUTHOR'S NOTE: Morley is prophetic about Frank Warner Angel sent the next year by the Departments of Justice and the Interior to investigate; but cannot foresee Ring obstruction of his investigation on the Washington, D.C. level.]

But people are afraid to tell what they know in affidavits until they feel sure it will not pass into the hands of the enemy to be used against themselves ... But secrecy is all important - <u>publicity is dangerous in the extreme</u>. You must be cautious also what you do, or it will react on us here ...

[AUTHOR'S NOTE: By the 1890's Morley was shot dead in Mexico; the cause given as an accidental firing of a rifle.]

Remember that Elkins [sic - Union], Catron, and Waldo were all in the Rebel cause from and about Westport, Missouri, and all red hot Democrats up to their appointment for office, since when, they were radical of radicals ... I would urge that if you can effect any removal do so before the Taos court; or if a secret agent could be sent, let him get here to witness the performance.

As a specimen of the way New Mexico is governed, see in solicitor's Office, Treasury Dep't, in 1872, just prior to Elkins election – six hundred suits [in Taos County] brought by the U.S. Attorney [Catron setting up Elkin's election of Delegate to Congress] ... and only two or three tried – the rest dismissed. It is charged that this was for the double purpose of whipping in voters, and getting fees for prosecution [and Elkins won, becoming Delegate to Congress] ...

Effect one removal, - the Governor or Chief Justice, and if a Governor could be appointed who knew the circumstances here, it would be best, - <u>any good, square man would do.</u> *A removal or two would restore confidence, so that evidence and petitions could be gotten ... but as it is now people are disheartened.*

[AUTHOR'S NOTE: Morley is prophetic, and this letter may have influenced Lew Wallace's appointment as governor.]

Grant, the other American County [meaning Anglo like Colfax County], is likely to secede and join Arizona, to get away from the Ring.

[AUTHOR'S NOTE: Like his wife, Ada, Morley was aware of the Grant County Rebellion.]

W.R. Morley
Vice Prest & Executive Officer
Max. [Maxwell] Land Grant & R'wy Co.

Mary McPherson also tried to help Oscar McMains through her May 1, 1877 complaint to President Hayes, filed as "W.B. Matchett and Mary E. McPherson 'Make certain charges against the U.S. Officials in the Territory of New Mexico." It had an April 21, 1877 Pueblo, Colorado, *Enterprise and Chronicle* article titled: "At It Again" by a J.J. Lambert. She wrote: "*Upon the murder of Tolby, Mr. McMains, a printer by profession, and also a [Methodist] missionary, took an active part in ferreting out the perpetrators (Cruz Vega, Manuel Cardinas, Robert H. Longwill, M. [Melvin] W. Mills, and Florencio Donoghue), and drew upon him the wrath of the powers in Santa Fe, and from that period until the present, they have pursued him with a foolish persistency that is too apparent to be misinterpreted. He has ever been a true and unwavering friend of the [settlers of Land] Grants. The manner in which the Court at Taos has recently treated this subject upon argument before it, will not relieve it from an inexplicable suspicion.*"

[ENCLOSED ARTICLE]:

At It Again

The latest advices from New Mexico are to the effect that the "ring" are at their old tricks ...
One of our correspondents says: "People here are in constant fear and nobody dares to raise his voice against the terrible anarchy we are undergoing in this country. These gentlemen and their organ at Santa Fe, (The *New Mexican*) seem to have an absolute power in everything in New Mexico. They run our legislature and make this ignorant people pass such laws as will gratify their rapacious ambition. They control the courts to such an extent that respectable citizens regard them as a public calamity. They have juries appointed, who, instead of bringing peace to the community, will cause but alarm to the people. As a general thing thieves and murderers are turned loose."
The lawyers of New Mexico, with the exception of a very few honorable exceptions, are members of this corrupt ring ... **A defendant who has been prosecuted by the ringites has but little chance of being defended, and even if he does succeed in obtaining the services of an attorney, the rulings of the courts are always against him.**

In August of 1877, jailed Reverend Oscar McMains was tried before the Taos County Grand Jury for Catron's federal charge of the Cruz Vega killing; but, defended by Attorney Frank Springer and W.D. Lee, had his indictment quashed. So he was immediately re-indicted in "Territory vs. O.P. McMains" for that killing. But Springer and Lee got a venue change to Mora County.

MCMAINS'S MURDER TRIALS

Reverend Oscar McMains's Mora County trial for the killing of Cruz Vega was held on August 22nd and 23rd, 1877, still under Ringite Judge Henry Waldo, and with Ringite Attorney General William Breeden as prosecutor. Attorneys Frank Springer and W.D. Lee argued his innocence, since he left before Cruz Vega's lynching. The unprejudiced jurymen ruled murder in the "fifth degree," with penalty of a $300 fine. The Ring was foiled, despite Waldo's lying to the jury that the Taos jury had found him guilty - still trying to get him hanged.

But Oscar McMains refused to accept guilt or pay the fine! Springer and Lee got a new trial over Judge Waldo's objection.

It was in Colfax County, which had regained its courts by January of 1878. In that trial, McMains's murder indictment was thrown out by Judge L. Bradford Prince based on lack of evidence.

For the rest of his life, McMains continued his opposition to Ring control of the Maxwell Land Grant and Railway Company, as well as the Ring's fraudulent, 500,000 acre Uña de Gato Land Grant, sold through Governor Axtell as Ring frontmen to an Arkansas Senator, Stephen Wallace Dorsey.

McMains died of natural causes on April 15, 1899. His anti-Grant colleague, F.B. Chaplin eulogized in his obituary his fighting "crime and corruption, ever pleading for right in defense of the poor." But the *Raton Range* of April 20, 1899 did Ringite outlaw myth crowing: "O.P. McMains, the agitator, is dead."

ADA MORLEY'S TERRIFIED LETTER

Oddly present in Mary McPherson's official file in the Department of the Interior's National Archives is a private letter to her from her daughter, Ada Morley, dated March 7, 1877. It would have been mailed to Washington, D.C. while Mary was there vainly trying to meet with President Hayes and other officials about the Ring. It opens the questions of her mail being intercepted, and whether she even received it. Notwithstanding, it is the best contemporary rendition of the terror and hopelessness under "boss" Catron's Ring regime. Ada Morley wrote:

Cimarron New Mexico March 7th 1877
My dear Mother
Yes, we [with her husband, Raymond Morley] have received all your letters at Vermejo and here, but we have hesitated about replying for many reasons. I have little hope of your being able to cause any removals [of Governor Axtell, Judges Henry Waldo and Warren Bristol, and Thomas Benton Catron] for you know the Republicans have gained the day and our <u>ex-Rebels</u> here are the finest Republicans in New Mexico. Only this - Hayes and his friends will have friends to put in office and in the confusion and change we might get a new set of Officials. **I am really afraid to write on these matters.** *Elkins of course is there trying to keep his friends in their present positions and as I said I have little hope or faith that you can succeed. You ask <u>what</u> we want. You ought to know. You have been here and know how we are oppressed and persecuted - You know too how ~~you~~ the Court has been robbed from*

Colfax Co. This last is the worst. Had we our court we would be comparatively safe. The Citizens signed a petition to the Gov. asking him to give us back our court but he refused saying "it had been taken away for the purpose of accomplishing certain objects and that the objects <u>had not</u> yet been accomplished." You know what they have done and that McMains is to be tried in three weeks [this was written before his August trial] and <u>I'm sure</u> they will convict him though he is innocent as Agnes [her little daughter] of murder. I am half crazy too because Raym [her husband, Raymond] must go to be tried - it will cost a hundred dollars then he will likely be indicted again for something - and I often think they will manage to kill him in some way or other. If they do I'd be a second Mrs Tolby. They'd hear from me ...

[AUTHOR'S NOTE: Ada recognizes the Ring's malicious prosecution. Soon Susan McSween would join the growing ranks of Ring widows in 1878's Lincoln County War Battle.]

Every body here is discouraged and disheartened. All that I see you can do is to have an Agent sent but a secret one. He could see & hear and learn all – and such bloody work as has been done here is dreadful. Well, could we have our court back – and the Gov now has the power to annul the law we would be happy. Grant County by desperately fighting the Santa Fe Ring will probably join Arizona. That move will help us <u>for it will</u> cause an investigation and the public attention turned this way.

[AUTHOR'S NOTE: Ada Morley is aware of the anti-Ring 1876 Grant County Rebellion.]

Mother one thing worries me. You have not the means to carry you through and we have not money enough to pay <u>our</u> debts. O! and should you fail in this the Official here will torture Raym to death. He will have to take the blows here for your mistakes. I often wish you <u>had done</u> as you promised gone to <u>Iowa</u> and settled down quietly. Should you succeed what a glorious and great blessing it would be for this Godforsaken country. But I dont see how you can. People wont put in black & white what <u>they know</u>.

[AUTHOR'S NOTE: Ada is right about the silence. Hers is a rare document putting in writing the horror of Ring injustices.]

An Agent sent will be the only thing possible of good you can do. You spread your strength too much. Let Postmasters alone.
Get an investigation or an Agent or something to turn attention this way. That's all we need.

[AUTHOR'S NOTE: The tragedy of this statement will be apparent by the end of 1878, when Washington Investigator Frank Warner Angel merely submitted Ring cover-up reports for the Hayes administration.]

Who is ===/===? Maybe he is anything but what he pretends. We are afraid and cautious. Does he intend interesting himself in the Maxwell [Land Grant]? Fortunes have been made out of it and many more can be made. But tell me what is his object ...

[AUTHOR'S NOTE: Concealed is W.B. Matchett, Mary's attorney co-filer, as required in Washington for a layman's filing.]

I am so afraid for McMains. This term of court it makes me sick. If only we had a new Judge [replacing Henry Waldo] here or Governor or something. Well I get like everybody else when I commence writing and feel like giving up entirely. But Hayes may make changes if he will and when he learns these men have been rebels and are turncoat Republicans [Catron] he may in mercy do something, **but had Tilden been elected we would have been sure of new officials** ...

Later ~

Who is ===/===? Be careful lest hes some rogue. We are all afraid till we know more. I do pray you may succeed but I don't see how you can. I have no faith, none at all. I'm worried most about money matters. You'll spend all your money and to whom can you look for aid. If you can get a place in Washington to make a cent you better do it. Get a position of some kind. Indeed mother I fear you'll see the day you'll curse your present work and time you stay in Washington. Then I fear Raym and I will have all the blame here to bear. Had we known of your intention to go to Washington we would have opposed it to the bitter end. How will you ever get out of Washington ...

Rayms health is only fair. He has quit smoking. I think he is less nervous now. He has changed so much in some ways. Willie [older son, William Raymond Jr.] loves him and he can do as much with Agnes [their daughter] as I. Is in every way good and devoted to his family. I wish you could see him. We are a loving and happy family – All well.

Write often to your daughter
Ada

THE MCPHERSON EXPOSÉS

SUMMARY: Iowa resident, Mary Tibbles McPherson, became an unsung Colfax County War heroine when, visiting her daughter, Ada Morley, and son-in-law Raymond Morley, in Cimarron from early 1875 to the end of 1876, she was inspired by Reverend Franklin Tolby, then by his murder and efforts of Reverend Oscar McMains. So, in 1877, she exposed the Santa Fe Ring to Washington, D.C., leaving no doubt that President Rutherford B. Hayes and Secretary of the Interior Carl Schurz knew about its criminality before the next anti-Ring uprising - the Lincoln County War - and investigator Frank Warner Angel's 1878 reports. She was undaunted by Catron's malicious prosecution of her daughter, Ada; or by the Ring's "Dear Ben plot" to murder her son-in-law, Raymond Morley. Later, the Morley's daughter, Agnes Morley Cleaveland, and Agnes's son, Norman Cleaveland, continued this special family's Santa Fe Ring condemnation into the 20th century.

During the 1877 Colfax County War, Mary Tibbles McPherson documented Ring crimes against the Maxwell Land Grant's settlers; with sheriffs serving eviction notices, pastures set afire, cattle stolen, homes and ranches raided, and 200 killed.

She was born into a freedom fighting family in Ohio, which moved to Illinois then Iowa, where she married politician and judge, Marcus McPherson. Her brother, Thomas Henry Tibbles, was an abolitionist follower of John Brown; fighter for Native American rights; Methodist missionary; editor of the Omaha, Nebraska, *Daily Herald*; and eventual 1904 Populist Party vice-president nominee advocating for Native Americans and Blacks, and for income and inheritance taxation.

As told by her great-grandson, Norman Cleaveland in his 1971 book, *The Morleys: Young Upstarts of the* Southwest, she arrived in Cimarron from Iowa in the spring of 1875 to visit her daughter, Ada, and son-in-law, Raymond Morley, and to meet her year old granddaughter, Agnes (his mother).

Inspired by the anti-Ring mission of Reverend Franklin Tolby, she mailed her first Washington D.C. complaint letter. Frightened of repercussions, Ada retrieved it; thus, becoming victim of Catron's malicious prosecution of her for mail theft.

By 1877, after her daughter's torture and Tolby's murder, and with amassed evidence, she moved to Washington, to complain in person. Her goal was removal of Ringites from public offices. Her writings show a fearless, angry, articulate, unrelenting chronicler of Colfax County's oppression by T.B. Catron and S.B. Elkins as the Ring's heads, and Governor S.B. Axtell and Judge Warren Bristol. After her, the Ring had no secrets.

Her exposés went to Colfax County locals, to the Department of Interior's Secretary Carl Schurz, to Department of Justice's Attorney General Charles Devens, and to President Rutherford B. Hayes. Land-grabbing, voter bribery and intimidation, removal of Colfax County's courts, malicious prosecutions, attempted murder and murder, were her litany - and heralded the Ring's blueprint, the next year, for defeating Lincoln County War freedom fighters.

Her indirect homage was Victor Westphall's lying. Though her exposés are available in the National Archives, he minimized her devastating productions to just one complaint, which he called a letter of February 7, 1877 to Attorney General Alphonso Taft about Catron's buggy tiff with Ada. That was just her start!

Her actual anti-Ring complaints, from February to August of 1877, are 141 pages of letters; affidavits; petitions; newspaper articles; and printed charges against Ringites. Her focus was U.S. Attorney T.B. Catron, Delegate S.B. Elkins, Chief Justices Joseph Palen and Henry Waldo, and Judge Warren Bristol. Appropriately and bravely, she first exposed Catron himself.

EXPOSING T.B. CATRON AND ACCOMPLICES

On February 7, 1877, in Washington, D.C., Mary McPherson, began her crusade with Attorney General Alphonso Taft (about to be replaced by Charles Devens in the Hayes administration). She mailed him her handwritten "Charges against Thomas B. Catron, U.S. Attorney, and Others." It said it all: ***"I wish to bring to your attention the sufferings of the people of New Mexico ... In searching out the assassins, the evidence pointed strongly to U.S. officials ... all US officers out there are in league together, and the people are the sufferers."*** (The next year, it would be Investigator Frank Warner Angel's task to cover up her proof that U.S. officials committed murder.) She wrote:

Washington Feb 7th 1877

Atty Gen Taft
Sir.
I wish to bring to your attention the sufferings of the people of New Mexico, and especially of Colfax Co, where I ~~have~~ *resided from Feb 1975 until Oct 1976. I would ask you to investigate the situation of the people in that Territory and prove the truth and falsity of my statements.*

The county of Colfax is now "attached to Taos, for judicial purposes" that the U.S. officials may punish persons through the courts, who have boldly taken stand for their inalienable rights, that of life and liberty and the pursuit of their respective callings.

I think I shall be able to bring facts to establish the opinion freely spoken, that Thomas B Catron uses his official position to oppose the innocent instead of punishing the guilty *- "That court was dismissed" in Cimarron Colfax Co. in Aug '75 for several days and that Thomas B Catron took individuals in his pockets and went to districts which were for Valdez" and as the phrase there is "shook them over the heads of the parties wishing to vote thus, until they promised and did vote for Elkins" - that it was said "the court adjourned to go electioneering."*

It is always said that "feeing [paying off] Catron one will not be indicted" *- That this Catron was a member of the Maxwell Land Grant Co, whose Executive officer was WR Morley. This Co gave Morley use of a buggy and tram, aside from Co business. Court was in session. This buggy was taken to bring Catron and others to Cimarron. But during the court, the wife of WR Morley took this buggy, to which she had a right, and fulfilled a previous engagement. This was, when Mr Catron wished the buggy, in preference to "staging" [going by stagecoach]. Within a year, report said an indictment was found in Santa Fe against Mrs W.R. Morley for robbing the mails When it was found there was one, Catron was reported to have said, "Yes there is one, that woman insulted me and I intend to punish or repay her." He referred to her using her own buggy, given in her husbands salary and gave this as reason for bringing out this indictment. This indictment was seen by her husband WR Morley in the hands of U.S. Marshall John Pratt.* **This is only a case in point one out of a number occurring constantly.**

I was only visiting my daughter but remained to protect her ...

Forty men in Colfax Co have been dragged to court for near or quite two years, "to intimidate them," it is said and still their trial is postponed.

Rev F.J. Tolby remarked "that the Courts of N.M. were now for political purposes" and in a short time was assassinated, *when returning from an appointment to preach. He said he was going to inform parties at Washington.*

In searching out the assassins, the evidence pointed strongly to U.S. officials, *this was the impression of every good citizen ... The evidence pointed to the Rep. of the county [Melvin W. Mills]. He went to Santa Fe and had law enacted attaching Colfax to Taos Co.* **At this [Taos] court all suppond [sic - subpoenaed] to be implicated in the plot [to kill Tolby] were <u>set free</u> and all parties in Colfax searching out assassins were found [issued] <u>murder indictments</u>; until it was said "to be indicted was a work of respectability" – which it really was.** *Twenty five or more were to be arrested for murder, all living in Colfax. Two only were arrested, one of those the successor of Rev F.J. Tolby [Oscar P. McMains] who was instrumental in searching for the assassins.*

Indeed it is a matter patent to all good persons that they should fear the courts and all criminals feel safe to prosecute their wickedness, as not one has ever received their rewards [recompense]. They all escape justice.

It is said Thomas B Catron and his associates the present Judge, his name has escaped me [Henry Waldo], are pitted against Colfax Co and especially against those searching out the assassins of Rev FJ Tolby.

I do not know myself but it is prevalent among the people that **all US officers out there are in league together, and the people are the sufferers.**

Very Respectfully
Mrs Mary E. McPherson
1127 Thirteenth St

Catron responded to Attorney General Alphonso Taft on February 24, 1877 as "Answering Charges of Mary E. McPherson." It would test how far the new Hayes administration would go to cover-up the Ring, and how much S.B. Elkins could call in favors for its shielding. The outcome would be cover-up.

With smug sociopathic complacency, Catron denied everything, and called McPherson insane: *"such an idea could only emanate in the brain of a crazy person."* He used his time-tested outlawing and defaming of adversaries. He gave Ring mantras: *"[L]awlessness seemed to prevail in the county of Colfax ... It is absolutely false, that I have in any maneuver or at any time used my official position to oppress any one instead of punishing the guilty ... I simply know that the Courts of New Mexico are as free from politics as any Courts in the United States."* And about the Ring, he, as its head, hissed: *"It is utterly false that the U.S. officials in this Territory are in any manner engaged together so that the people <u>are sufferers</u>, or that there is any combination among them for any purpose whatever."* Catron wrote:

Office of
T.B. Catron,
Attorney at Law
& U.S. Attorney
Santa Fé, N.M. <u>*Feb 24*</u> *187<u>7</u>*

Alfonso Taft –
Attorney General
    Washington D.C.

Sir: I am just in possession of your communication of the 14th inst. enclosing the communication of Mrs Mary E McPherson, which I herewith return as requested. I will notice the charges made by Mrs McPherson in detail –
The county of Colfax is "attached to the county of Taos for Judicial Purposes," this was done by the last Legislature, for the reason that **lawlessness seemed to prevail in the county of Colfax at the time; several men had been taken and hung or shot, by armed bands of men, one from the hands of the authorities, and no effort was made to stop it by the people of Colfax, but in the contrary the same was encouraged by W.R. Morley the son-in-law of Mrs McPherson who, at the time, was editor of the news-paper in said county of Colfax.** *As I am informed it was believed that no grand-jury could be found to indict for these outrages, or petit jury to convict them, in Colfax Co. I was not a member of that Legislature nor had I any connection with it. The courts of both Taos & Colfax counties are courts in which no United States business was transacted, they were courts*

established by the Legislature under Section 1874 of the Revised Statutes of the United States, and I had no official connection with the same, except as <u>an</u> <u>Attorney</u> who practiced therein, all my official business as U.S. Attorney being at the time confined to the U.S. Branch of the court in said District held at Santa Fe. The Attorney General of the Territory William Breeden being the person who had charge of the prosecutions in those counties.

It is absolutely false, that I have in any maneuver or at any time used my official position to oppress any one instead of punishing the guilty. *It is absolutely untrue that Court was dismissed in Aug. 75 for several days or that I took any indictment or indictments and went to any district with them or took any indictments over the heads of any one whatsoever until they promised to vote for Elkins or any thing else to that effect, or that said court adjourned to go electioneering. As before stated I have nothing whatever to do with the indictments in said Court, they being all for the offenses against the laws of the Territory and not the United States. I may have been employed to defend some of the accused.*

It is absolutely untrue and false that any one can or ever has feed me to present an indictment and I deny that there is any suspicion that I ever received a fee to prevent an indictment, **such an idea could only emanate in the brain of a crazy person.**

Mrs. W.R. Morley was not indicted by the U.S. jury in Santa Fe for stealing a letter from the U.S. mail, the circumstances are as follows as detailed before the Grand Jury by the Post-master and his deputy; viz

The sister [sic – mother-in-law, Mary McPherson] of W.R. Morley went to the post-office and dropped a letter in the box, the deputy Miss Bishop was standing by the box and noticed the letter and address, in a few minutes Mrs Morley her sister-in-law [sic – daughter] went to the post office very hurriedly and said she Mrs Morley had made a mistake and dropped in the wrong letter, and without waiting she ran to the box picked up the letters selected one and left the office. Mrs Bishop then stepped to the box and examined and found the letter put in by Morley's sister [sic – mother-in-law] gone. She informed the Post-master Mr John B McCullich, who immediately called in Mrs Morley and accused her of taking the letter, she first admitted it then denied it. Some little talk was had about the matter when Mr Morley threatened to prosecute McCullich for neglect of his duties in reference to the letter. Mr McCullich then wrote to me at Santa Fe informing me of the facts and requested that he and his deputy Miss Bishop be summoned before the Grand Jury of the U.S. at Santa Fe which I caused to be done, and **on their testimony an indictment was presented.** *It is absolutely false that I ever said that Mrs. Morley had insulted me or that I intended to punish her, or that I refused to her use, of the buggy, referred to, or that I gave that as a reason for prosecuting the indictment. Some time before the indictment was framed I was approached by a friend of Mr Morley [Attorney Frank Springer] and requested to prevent an indictment where I answered that, that was a matter for Mr McCullich and the Grand Jury, that if Mr McCullich did not ask the matter to be pushed, that I would be governed by his wishes, that he had requested to be summoned before the jury and I had done so. And that in that matter neither Mr Morley nor his wife had the right to ask any favors of me, which is about all I ever said about the matter. It is absolutely untrue that Marshal Pratt ever had the indictment in his hands. He had a warrant for the arrest of Mrs Morley, but I requested him not to serve it, as I had learned Mrs Morley was in a state of pregnancy, and arresting her might result to her seriously; before the next term of Court Mrs Morley and her husband left the Territory and as Mr McCullich did not wish to follow the matter up any further, at his insistence, I discontinued the case. As to any indictment against Mrs McPherson for libel, I could have nothing to do with it, that being a Territorial offense, but I will say this is the first time I have heard of it. As Mrs McPherson has referred to the board of Missions of M.E. Church in New York City – I would refer you to the correspondence of Rev Thomas Warwood of that church, with said board of missions, to which she had preferred charges against him, they can probably tell who or what Mrs McPherson is.*

If any men had been dragged or taken to Court to intimidate them it has not been the United States side of the Court. Yet from my knowledge of the facts I pronounce Mrs McPhersons letter on that point, as to any court in this Territory untrue. Some 30 or 40 persons who committed the outrages which induced the Legislature to attach Colfax to Taos Co. for judicial purposes, have been indicted in Taos Co, some have been tried and convicted others have not been arrested others who have been arrested have applied for continuances which at their own insistence have been granted. I do not think a single trial has been delayed by the Territory.

I know nothing about what Mr Tolby said or thought, **I simply know that the Courts of New Mexico are as free from politics** *as any Courts in the United States. I have never before heard it intimated that any U.S. official was under the least suspicion of being implicated in the murder of Tolby,* the matter has been twice very thoroughly investigated and there was not a scintilla of evidence against a single U.S. official ... There was not a particle of evidence against the Representative of Colfax Co [Melvin Mills] with reference to the murder of Tolby, that representative instead of getting the law passed attaching Colfax to Taos Co. did, as I am informed, oppose the enactment of the law, very vigorously.

Several persons were arrested who were indicted for murders. Others are at large who are indicted as I am informed, but whom the officers have so far been unable to arrest others have left the country. **Mr FJ Tolbys successor is indicted for murder in being instrumental in lynching a man I am told the proofs are positive, given by a man whom he induced to entice the victim out into the hands of the mob who both hung and shot him.** The successor of Mr Tolby Mr McMains was present and assisted as I am told.

It is utterly false that either I or the present Judge [Henry] Waldo are in any manner pitted against Colfax Co or those searching out the assassins of Tolby but I assert on the contrary that we have both used our utmost endeavors to find the guilty parties and have them punished ...

It is utterly false that the U.S. officials in this Territory are in any manner leagued together so that the people are sufferers, or that there is any combination among them for any purpose whatever –

Thanking you for referring this communication of Mrs McPherson to me and giving me the opportunity to contradict the charges made.

    I am very respectfully,
        Thomas B. Catron, U.S. Atty

EXPOSING NEW MEXICAN OFFICIALS

For her next hand-written complaint, Mary McPherson added the Washington lawyer, W.B. Matchett, about whom her daughter, Ada Morley, had anxiously questioned in her March 7, 1877 letter. (See pages 272-274) Apparently Secretary of the Interior Carl Schurz had made the hurdle of her needing an attorney to get her complaints read. Matchett's added legalese did improve her layman effort of her complaint against Catron. On May 1, 1877, she and Matchett submitted "Charges Against New Mexican Officials, Together With Corroboration Evidence." It included "Petition to Remove Judge Bristol" and two lists of "Charges Against S.B. Axtell, Governor of New Mexico." Its format was a cover letter to Hayes, with inserted evidence and charges.

The Ring's organized crime was spelled out: *"[The named public officials] conspired together to corrupt and defraud justice and defeat the ends thereof, both by fraudulent and illegal practices in their respective Districts and offices; and by procuring the passage of insidious legislative enactments tending to dismemberment, confusion, and centralization of power and designed to protect infamy, legalize crime, deprive its citizens of personal liberty, and the right of trial by jury; compass the revenues of the Territory and the property of its citizens for purposes of private gain ... It is in evidence that for several years these parties have been in collusion in a general plan having for its aim the centralizing of power, the reduction of large and valuable private Grants of land within the Territory to their personal use and benefit, by corrupt Territorial and Congressional enactments, and by passage of bills of attainment & de facto laws depriving the citizens of due process of law ... To accomplish these purposes this Ring so formed appears to have paused at nothing however difficult or questionable."*

McPherson's and Matchett's goal was explicit: *"[T]hey therefore respectfully request their removal from office."* Named was the Santa Fe Ring and its members: U.S. Attorney Thomas Benton Catron, Delegate to Congress Stephen Benton Elkins, Governor Samuel Beach Axtell, Chief Justice Henry Waldo, and District Judge Warren Bristol. They wrote:

To the President:

The undersigned in behalf of the people of the Territory of New Mexico herewith present the following <u>charges</u> with evidence in support thereof against the persons named herein and ask your early consideration of the same:

They charge the United States District Attorney, Thomas B. Catron; Associate Justice Warren Bristol; Henry L. Waldo, Chief Justice; Samuel B. Axtell, Governor, and others of the said Territory, to them unknown, as having conspired together to corrupt and defraud justice and defeat the ends thereof, both by fraudulent and illegal practices in their respective Districts and offices; and by procuring the passage of insidious legislative enactments tending to dismemberment, confusion, and centralization of power and designed to protect infamy, legalize crime, deprive its citizens of personal liberty, and the right of trial by jury; compass the revenues of the Territory and the property of its citizens for purposes of private gain ... And they therefore respectfully request their removal from office:

It is in evidence that for several years these parties have been in collusion in a general plan having for its aim the centralizing of power, the reduction of large and valuable private Grants of land within the Territory to their personal use and benefit, by corrupt Territorial and Congressional enactments, and by passage of bills of attainment & de facto laws depriving the citizens of due process of law, legalizing crime and then punishing the criminal, and thereby making the Court a vehicle to compass their covert and vindictive designs, thus rendering its edicts a farce and bringing its judicial character into distrust and contempt.

To accomplish these purposes this Ring so formed appears to have paused at nothing however difficult or questionable. *This course has kept back the prosperity of the Territory and its people in a continued state of disquiet and insecurity both of persons and property – An inside view of this matter may be better obtained by a glance at its origin:*

Among the possessions acquired by the Treaty of 1848 with Mexico, were large private Grants of land, both to individuals and corporations – (about 150 in number) – which excited at once the cupidity and avarice of the of the unscrupulous adventurer and the wily politician.

The failure of the U.S. Government to afford the relief guaranteed by the Treaty and by the Confirmatory Act of 1860, June the 21st, left matters in an unsettled state as to titles, which fact was soon taken advantage of by the settlers and caused difficulties to arise between them and the holders of the Grants. Upon the influence of population these difficulties were increased and under the constant pressure they were compelled to take sides against the Grants.

The Ring perceiving their opportunity, forced themselves into power, and began a system of corrupt and compulsory legislation, oppressive in its exactions upon the grantees and those who sided with them, to worry them into submission, or by fraudulently depreciating their titles, compel them either to abandon their grants entirely, or sell at a sacrifice and quit the Territory. Many did this, - some did not. Under this compulsion the Ring or their friends became the purchasers ...

[INSERT] *"The Real Purpose of the New Mexico State Bill"*
[AUTHOR'S NOTE: Omitted here is her concern that the Ring's land-grab was for Mormon colonization.]

It is essential for them [the Ring] to get possession of most of the valuable land in the Territory; and for this purpose the situation is particularly favorable, since nearly all the good land is included in the old Spanish and Mexican Grants of which there are upwards of 150, ranging in size from a few thousands to one or more millions of acres.

At present these lands are chiefly owned by natives, who own little else, and with title as yet imperfected by the Federal Government ... In most cases however the grants are owned jointly by a number of people, the descendants of the original grantees, and agents have been at work and bought one or more interests on many of the grants.

The Legislature of New Mexico under the dictation of the Ring of speculators [Catron and Elkins], recently passed a law, by which the district court can order the whole of a grant, to be sold at public auction, upon such notice as it sees fit, upon the demand of any one of the parties in interest, no matter how small that interest may be. By this means all these grants are to be forced to sale, for cash, and as the titles are in an unsettled state, and most of the papers and records are in the hands of the Ring, there can be little petition in bidding, and the lands will be obtained at nominal figures ...

To make forced sale of these lands, as is contemplated, would not be easily accomplished without some show of force, as the owners, who have lived on them all their lives, and whose ancestors for generations occupied, cultivated, and defended them would rebel ... [But] supported by the whole power of the Grant administration, the natives will have little chance for a successful resistance to the atrocious.

[INSERT] *"Legislative Action on Land Partition"*

[AUTHOR'S NOTE: Attacked is the act partitioning land by court-appointed commissioners empowered to divide it as they saw fit to establish taxes. It enabled Ring take-over by crippling owners with onerous taxes.]

[A] delinquent tax payer became not only liable to a civil suit for unpaid taxes [and] to have his property sold summarily by the sheriff, but also to be arrested, convicted, and punished as a criminal ... Now, as taxation is a new thing to the Mexicans - the Territorial Government having been supported by licenses and special taxes prior to the accession of the Ring to power ... thousands became delinquent, and at present the courts are busy with indictments for their offence which will be held over the head of the unfortunates until after election when they will be dismissed with costs and attorney's fees ...

This law ... is peculiarly adapted to some of the larger Spanish grants consisting of hundreds of thousands of acres ... No one but a capitalist has the means to purchase the whole ... In brief they [grant holders] will be compelled to sell their home for a song, and be turned loose upon the face of the earth, all for the benefit of a few scheming speculators, who will then perfect the title with the general government and have a clear title to the property ...

[AUTHOR'S NOTE: This was the Ring's land-grab formula.]

[LETTER TO PRESIDENT HAYES CONTINUES]

It will be seen that immediately upon the passage of this law, <u>a move was made at both ends of the line</u> – the Delegate in Congress [Elkins] arose in his place and presented a bill providing for the confirmation of a large number of private claims in New Mexico ... and the U.S. District Attorney, Catron, of New Mexico (becoming solicitor for private parties in their prosecution) filed bills under the "Partition" Act versus the Maxwell Land Grant and Railway Company ...

Another convenient system of iniquity is that relating to Indictments: They are obtained with the greatest possible ease imaginable – and in <u>any numbers required for the emergency</u> – and for the <u>same offence</u> – in some cases <u>several indictments</u> for the same offence.

[AUTHOR'S NOTE: McPherson understood how Catron and Elkins worked the Ring from Territorial to federal levels, for land-grabs and malicious prosecutions.]

That Colfax County made the most diligent opposition to the attempts of the Ring to deprive them of their rights and subject them to their schemes. (In fact this is the only county that saved itself from their rapacity.)

Failing in this, the pretext soon came, upon the assassination of a Methodist Missionary, named Tolby, - a worthy man, - who at the first sympathized with the Ring, but, upon maturer reflection, abandoned them, when they hired two assassins to deliberately murder him, after they (the Ring) had publicly warned him to leave the country, - which he failed to do ...

[INSERTS] Tolby's Coroner's Jury Report; and articles about his September 14, 1875 murder, Ring complicity, and Governor Axtell's transfer of Colfax County's courts to Taos County to shield his Ringite murderers, Melvin Mills and Robert Longwill, and for malicious prosecution of Colfax County citizens for Ring opposition.]

[INSERT] November 10, 1875 *Cimarron News and Press* on citizens meeting on Tolby's murder. (See page 255)

[INSERT] December 22, 1875 *New York Sun* article, "*The Territory of Elkins*" about Ring complicity in Tolby's murder. (See pages 257-259)

[INSERT] "*Petition and Charges to Remove Judge Bristol*" (See pages 301-303)

[AUTHOR'S NOTE: This was a copy of a February 18, 1876 Grant County petition to President Hayes to remove Judge Warren Bristol, and reprinted in the *Cimarron News and Press* in 1877 from the *Grant County Herald*. McPherson and Matchett added that, in a subsequent Grant County citizens' meeting, "a long letter was read from U.S. Attorney T.B. Catron in which he denies the charges ... against Bristol." The charges were that Bristol used his court to benefit the Ring and to maliciously punish its opponents. By 1878, Bristol would repeat this abuse by malicious prosecution of McSween and Tunstall for a fake embezzlement case, leading to their murders and the Lincoln County War. He was also Billy Bonney's 1881 hanging judge in Mesilla for his Lincoln County War indictments.

[INSERT] April 21, 1877 *Enterprise and Chronicle* article from Pueblo, Colorado, by a J.J. Lambert titled "At It Again," about Oscar McMains's pursuit of Franklin Tolby's killers, and resulting Ring attack. (See page 271)

[INSERT] Affidavits [here excerpted] on Ring corruption.

[On August 6, 1877] I, John L. Taylor, a resident of San Miguel Co., N.M. do voluntarily make the following statements.

I have resided in said Territory and in said County for the past twenty-two (22) years – Am well informed as to the political history of the Territory. I have been credibly informed by various persons, all well known to me, **that during the first candidacy of Stephen B. Elkins for Representative in the U.S. Congress from this Territory, many persons in San Miguel and Moro Counties were arrested, charged with illegal trading with the Comanche Tribe of Indians ... They were placed under bonds, and when they appeared for trial at Santa Fe, they were released – as I am informed by them and verily believe – upon the payment of fees to prosecuting Attorney, and the agreement upon their part to cast their Ballots for said S.B. Elkins. The above-mentioned transactions took place about four years ago [in 1873].**

John L. Taylor

[AUTHOR'S NOTE: This documented Ringite vote fixing.]

****

[On August 30, 1877] Frank Springer [Colfax County resident], being duly sworn says ... upon information and local newspaper reports of the time, that said Axtell has made visits to every other county in the Territory [except Colfax] ... much of the time in company with Wilson Waddingham, Esq. a well-known speculator in land grants ... **and when he passed through [Colfax County], in company with Senator S. [Stephen] W. Dorsey, [it was] for the purposes as was generally understood, of selling to him the Una de Gato grant** *in the eastern part of Colfax County; and, to facilitate that sale, among other corrupt motives, the courts had been moved by Axtell from Colfax to Taos County.*

[AUTHOR'S NOTE: This documents Axtell as a Ring frontman in grant fraud. In 1878, Investigator Angel confirmed the Uña de Gato Land Grant used forged documents for boundary inflation, to the detriment of its Colfax County settlers/landowners.]

****

[On July 1, 1877] a Louis Kingman of Santa Fe gave his deposition and stated,] The new facts [of forged Uña de Gato Grant papers] combined with the statements of reputable citizens of Santa Fe lead me to the belief that the Une de Gato grant is fraudulent and I am informed by persons who are familiar with the Mexicans of Santa Fe Co. that the Mexicans who were brought before James K. Proudfit Surveyor of N.M. to prove up the title to the said Une de Gato grant bear a bad reputation and ... that for the sum of one dollar these particular witnesses would swear to anything that might be required of them –

Thomas B. Catron the United States District Attorney for New Mexico is generally understood to represent and to be interested in this grant.

[LETTER TO PRESIDENT HAYES CONCLUDES]

[AUTHOR'S NOTE: Not realizing that the Ring extended to Washington, D.C., they appeal to Hayes for investigation.]

It is requested that there be a thorough and rigid investigation of the matters herein charged, that crime shall not run riot, nor its perpetrators go unpunished; and, that the laws of the land be administered in such a manner as to command the respect and cheerful obedience of the people.

Respectfully

W.B. Matchett
Mary E. McPherson
In behalf of the people of New Mexico

Washington, April, 1877

[INSERT] "CHARGES AGAINST S.B. AXTELL" (March 1877)

<u>Charges</u>, against
S.B. Axtell, Governor of New Mexico:

<u>First</u>. – *His connection with a corrupt combination of men in procuring the enactment of laws inimical to the interests of the people of the Territory, and especially of Colfax County, having for their object the removal of their Courts ... thus depriving them of the right to a speedy and impartial trial by jury of their own countrymen in the district where the crimes charged were alleged to have been committed ...*

Through the operations of this combination, the Legislature of the Territory enacted a law authorizing the Governor ... to remove the Court from its proper locality, to any distant point. And in pursuance of this law, he did so cause the removal of the said Court from Cimarron, Colfax County, on or about March, 1876, to Taos, Taos County, a distance of about fifty-five miles [and over a mountain range], for the purpose of punishing the people of Colfax County for attempting to ferret out the perpetrators of a cold blooded murder of a Methodist preacher named Tolby, which the officers of the law had failed or declined to do. This removal of the Court compelled all persons charged with crime or as witnesses to leave their avocations and travel, some of them fifty to one hundred fifty miles over and beyond a range of mountains ten thousand feet in height and now covered with snow, encamping enroute to attend said court upon fine or imprisonment for refusal under this oppressive law.

It will be seen, by the following item clipped from the Santa Fe paper, that the Governor had been petitioned [by Colfax County citizens] on the subject of the return of the Court, but denied the petition, alleging that the "objects for which it had been removed had not yet been accomplished" – the real "purpose" being to drive the people from the country, or worry them into submission ...

Thus the designs of these men are apparent: The County of Colfax, the most covered by large private grants, being the most persistent in their opposition, are to be gotten rid of ...

They allege,

2<u>dly</u> *His (the Governor's) collusion with said combination having for their ultimate object the reduction of large private grants of land to public domain, with a view to private gain ...*

To show somewhat the "objects" of these men, which they affirm "had not yet been accomplished," it will be necessary to look a moment at the question of the system of "Grants," which affects the Territory of New Mexico, more than any other, and probably the County of Colfax, more than any other. Taking one, for instance, for example, the "Maxwell and Beaubien" Land Grant: under the laws of New Mexico, this grant was confirmed by "natural" metes and bounds, as "rivers and mountains" &c. Quite early, a party arose, who contested the validity of the claim so made, and contended that only about a tenth or twentieth of that amount of land was conveyed by Mexican Law, and further confirmed by the Treaty of Guadalupe Hidalgo, and by the law of the U.S. Congress of 1860. To this end, they [Ringites] have kept up a "running fire" against the [land] holders, and they have been in a constant state of unrest and insecurity ...

With this explanation, it is clear to see what the "object" is ... to pass laws prescribing the "Grants," – "run" all people from the Territory who differ with them, or who have differed with them, in the past - either by frightening them off by "indictments," or, impoverishing them by oppressive enactments ...

It is clear therefore from the foregoing statement of facts, that ... Governor S.B. Axtell [is] unfit to represent the people ... and we therefore ask for his removal.

Accompanying are letters and papers from citizens of the Territory, which we put in evidence, and request in behalf of the people of the Territory the earliest attention of the government to the matter.

Very respectfully
Your obdt serts.
W.B. Matchett
M.E. McPherson

Washington, March, 1877

[INSERT] "Charges, against S.B. Axtell, Governor of New Mexico"

[AUTHOR'S NOTE: This is another list of charges against Governor Axtell.]

Charges, against
S.B. Axtell, Governor of New Mexico:

First. – His refusal to execute properly the laws of the Territory by removing their Courts, and refusing to return the same upon petition.

Second . – His neglect to listen to the petitions of the people of the Territory, to either visit them or interest himself in, or redress their grievances.

Third . – His denial of justice in his refusal to give them a speedy trial by a jury of their peers, and within the District where the pretended crimes with which they stand charged were alleged to have been committed.

[AUTHOR'S NOTE: This Ring ploy of venue change to get an ignorant or Ring-compliant jury was used in 1881 for Billy Bonney's hanging trial in Doña Ana County.]

Fourth. His collusion with the "Rings," having for their direct object the reduction of the private Grants to public domain by a class legislation, with a view not only to enhance himself, but ... the driving out of all good citizens from the Territory.

ADDENDUM TO COMPLAINT: MAY 3, 1877

On May 3, 1877, McPherson and Matchett sent, via President Hayes, Raymond Morley's March 6, 1877 letter as an addendum to their March, April, 1877 complaint, for forwarding to Secretary of the Interior Carl Schurz as *"a part of the evidence in the case of "Charges against New Mexican Officials" together with the corroboration evidence filed at the Department of Interior."* (See pages 268-270 for the Morley letter.)

PUBLIC RECORDS REQUEST TO SECRETARY OF INTERIOR CARL SCHURZ

On July 26, 1877, Mary McPherson met corruptions' basic response: stonewalling (exactly like I met 130 years later when I fought the modern Santa Fe Ring)! She and W.B. Matchett made an ignored public records request to Secretary of the Interior Carl Schurz about the Ring; writing:

Washington, July 26th, 1877

To the Hon.
The Secretary of the Interior -
We have respectfully to request that the following named records, documents, papers, communications and correspondence be supplied in the case now pending before The Interior Department in the "Charges vs. Governor S.B. Axtell in connection with the Santa Fe Ring" of New Mexico; the same to be made a part thereof:

<u>First</u>: *The correspondence between Solicitor General Phillips, or, of the Department of Justice, with the Federal Judiciary of New Mexico concerning the Taos Court and its rulings.*

<u>Second</u>: *All papers, evidence, Petitions etc, in relation to the charges filed at same Department (and all such filed during a period of four years last past - especially the answer of U.S. Attorney Thomas B. Catron in answer to M.E. McPherson of New Mexico.*

<u>Third</u>: *All recent correspondence by and between S.B. Elkins, Ex-Delegate, and the other New Mexican Officials charged, in relation to the charges, and how they should be met.*

<u>Fourth</u>: *Gov. Axtell's application for the Office of Governor, and the letters and endorsements in support of the same.*

<u>Fifth</u> *Gov. Wm A. Pile's Public Proclamation in relation to New Mexico troubles, while Governor of said Territory.*

<u>Sixth</u>: *Dates of appointments and periods of service of S.B. Elkins, and Thomas B. Catron, as U.S. Attorneys of New Mexico, with their endorsements for same.*

<u>Seventh</u>: *Any letters, Statements, and evidence in the possession of the President, which he may see fit to communicate, not incompatible with the public interest.*

Very respy your obdt. serv'ts.
W.B. Matchett
& M.E. McPherson, For New Mexico

CHARGES PLACED WITH ATTORNEY GENERAL

With no answer from the Secretary of the Interior, on August 23, 1877, Mary McPherson tried to contact Attorney General Charles Devens. She was again stonewalled. She wrote:

> Washington D.C.
> Aug 23 1877
>
> To the President
> Please place before the Attorney General for immediate action "The Charges vs. New Mexican Officials" now on file, as evidence in the case of Gov Axtell of New Mexico.
> Respectfully
> Mary E. McPherson

REQUESTS TO BE HEARD IN PERSON

By September 30, 1877, McPherson sought audience with Secretary of the Interior Carl Schurz, and was stonewalled. She wrote:

> Sep 30th 1877.
>
> Hon Carl Schurz.
> Sir.
> I desire to know when I can be heard through the Attys employed in the case of the Charges vs Governor Axtell.
>
> During the progress of the case you refused to hear us "as it was ex parte," but at the same time the Solicitor, to whom you referred us promised to sit at the time for us to be heard, and we left the case open, for introduction of final evidence.
>
> This has not been complied with.
>
> Please send a reply. I read the note in the "Nation and Star" that the case was decided.
>
> I shall not accept newspaper reports as a decision in a case of the Interior.
>
> Most Respectfully
> M.E. McPherson

AXTELL RESPONDS TO DENY ALL CHARGES

Mary McPherson's charges were too dangerous to merely stonewall. So Secretary of the Interior Carl Schurz gave them to Governor S.B. Axtell, who, "immediately wired back that to couple his name with 'land rings was libel and slander' and he requested an investigation." On June 23, 1877, Axtell wrote to Schurz "denying all allegations and citing lawlessness as the reason for relocating courts to Taos for sole purpose of bringing justice to certain parties who seemed to overawe the juries in [Colfax] county." (Cleaveland, *The* Morleys, pp. 135-136)

While Axtell was bluffing, the Ring was in full swing. Elkins was planning resurvey of the Maxwell Land Grant that September by his brother, John, to confirm almost two million acres and massive profit from cheating Lucien Maxwell.

And that same fall of 1877, Axtell himself was fronting for the Ring for the fraudulent 500,000 acre Uña de Gato Land Grant sale in eastern Colfax County to Arkansas Senator Stephen Wallace Dorsey. According to Norman Cleaveland, that fraud was revealed to Raymond Morley by past New Mexico Surveyor Lewis Kingman who had surveyed that Grant's area. Kingman stated: "The tract was generally known and believed to be public lands until the spring of 1874 when papers purporting to be the original papers of the Grant were brought to the county clerk's office of Colfax County ... to be recorded - and contrary to the usual custom were recorded by someone other than the county clerk. Lewis Kingman, suspecting forgery, went to the Surveyor General's office in Santa Fe and examined the original papers, and found erasures and alterations that confirmed fraud. Frank Springer signed Kingman's affidavit, and confirmed that Axtell had passed through Cimarron with Senator Dorsey for the purpose as was generally understood of selling him the Una de Gato grant." (Cleaveland, pp. *The Morleys*, 142-143)

That Ring sale, exposed as fraud by Investigator Frank Warner Angel, led to a July, 1887 *North American Review* article titled "Land Stealing in New Mexico" by Surveyor General George W. Julian - which confirmed Mary McPherson. Julian wrote: "[T]he wholesale plunder of the public domain was carried on ... through extravagant and fraudulent surveys ... The influence of these claimants over the fortunes of New Mexico is perfectly notorious. They have hovered over the Territory like a pestilence. To a fearful extent they have dominated governors, judges, District Attorneys, Legislatures, surveyors general and their deputies, marshals, treasurers, county commissioners and the controlling business interests of the people. They have confounded political historians and subordinated everything to the greed for land." (Cleaveland, *The Morleys*, p. 143)

PRINTED CHARGES TO THE DEPARTMENTS OF THE INTERIOR AND JUSTICE

SUMMARY: In August of 1877, Mary McPherson wrote the best contemporary documentation of the Ring, titled: "In the Matter of Charges vs. Gov. S.B. Axtell and Other New Mexico Officials. It likely added impetus to the Frank Warner Angel investigation, and would have prevented the Lincoln County War, if acted upon.

Mary McPherson's 31 page, typeset booklet, "In the Matter of Charges vs. Gov. S.B. Axtell and Other New Mexico Officials; Submitted to the Departments of the Interior and Justice, August, 1877" fully exposed the Santa Fe Ring. (Future New Mexico Territory Governor Lew Wallace owned it; possibly given by Investigator Angel after his thwarted reports. It could have prevented the Lincoln County War; and it heralded its atrocities.

For it, McPherson distilled her past complaints, with intent to expose the Ring; its fraudulent land grant grabs; its murder of Franklin Tolby; its false indictments of Oscar McMains; and its suppression of Colfax County settlers by removing their courts. And she dispensed with lawyer, W.B. Matchett. She wrote:

IN THE MATTER OF THE CHARGES VS. GOV. S.B. AXTELL AND OTHER NEW MEXICO OFFICIALS; SUBMITTED TO THE DEPARTMENTS OF THE INTERIOR AND OF JUSTICE, AUGUST, 1877.

ARGUMENT:

In the matter of the Charges against Governor Samuel B. Axtell, of New Mexico, (in connection with other Federal Officials of said Territory,) we respectfully submit:

That it is clearly proven that he is a member of, and in full sympathy with, a **corrupt ring, at Santa Fé**; and that in collusion with them he has aided and abetted the consummation of Legislative, Congressional, and other acts, intended and designed for personal aggrandizement and the oppression of the people, and should therefore be removed from office.

WHAT ARE THE FACTS?

That there has existed in Santa Fé for several years past, a Ring, is now beyond question. That this Ring has, by its power and influence, controlled all the offices, revenues, and Courts of the Territory, - and that they have used this power to oppress, intimidate and plunder the people, cannot now be denied. And just what period it formed, it is not now possible to know; but it grew, and grew quietly. It existed when **Axtell** became Governor, they securing his appointment. It has even grown to such proportions that it has defied the power of the General Government, and has treated its mandates with contempt, - justifying its course, perhaps, by presuming on the slender tenure by which it is supposed to hold its own office; as well as taking advantage of the general upheavals threatening the nation ... - all tending and designed to render themselves secure from the national interference ...

THE LAND-GRANT INTEREST.

The private grants of the Territory, number among the hundreds, dating back, some of them, nearly 200 years; - some of them inchoate, and others with imperfect titles, and some of them with no titles at all. Here was the field of the **Ring's** speculations. Their object seems to have been in some cases to resuscitate old, dead claims; in others, to depreciate sound titles, buy in, or get in, and then procure territorial and congressional action rendering the titles valid! In this branch of the business, they also had the assistance and connivance of the Courts. **S.B. Elkins**, who appears to have emigrated thither the earliest of the party, occupied all the Federal offices in succession up to delegate in Congress; and during this *heigira*, seemed to have opened his "mine" in Grants, and became interested himself very largely, and interested others, placing that interest in hands that would be most effective. For, as early as June, 1872, he appears, together with the present U.S. Attorney, **Thos. B. Catron**, (what their offices were at that period, will appear,) as the managing firm of the "Sierra Mosca Grant," No. 75 - (date of Grant, 1846.) In 1873, he appears in the Martinez and Padilla Grant, No. 74, (date 1742.) And in the Bernalillo Grant, No. 83, the present Chief Justice, **H.L. Waldo**, appears, Feby. 20th, 1874, as he does also in the Angostura Grant, No. 94, Feby. 28, 1874.

Thos. B. Catron, also, is interested in the Ojo Caliente Grant, (Hot Springs,) No. 77; while the Governor of the Territory, **Samuel B. Axtell,** is, at this time, upon one of the Grants of his interest, the Una de Gata, No. 94, in Colfax Co., bargaining its sale to **U.S. Senator [Stephen W.] Dorsey** of Arkansas. How many more of these large grants these parties are interested in, may appear more fully below.

On the 28th of January, 1874, **Elkins** wrote the Com'r of the General Land Office, to "proceed with the surveys" of another Grant, the Maxwell, in Colfax Co., for the purpose of having the Government survey it into "sections" at its own expense, for their benefit.

On the 17th of December, 1875, however, **Mr. Elkins** arose in his place in the House of Representatives, (44th Cong., 1st Sess.,) and presented House Bill, No. 344, entitled "A Bill to confirm private land-claims in the Territory of New Mexico." This bill embraced claims numbered from "49" to "104," inclusive. In the latter clause of the 1st section, a provision inserted as follows, viz: "*Provided*, that such confirmation shall only be construed as a quit-claim, or relinquishment, of all title or claim on the part of the United States to any of the lands embraced in either of the said claims, and shall not affect the adverse rights of any person or persons, to the same or any part thereof." And, in the last clause of the 3d section, it is provided still further, "That no grant bearing date since the 18th day of August, 1824, shall be confirmed or patent issue for mere [more] than eleven leagues of land for each original claimant or grantee under said Mexican Government."

Now, the meaning is simply this: Take, for example, claim No. 75, the Sierra Mosca Grant, (one of the claims in which **"Elkins, Catron & Co."** are interested;[)] the "original claimant" may be one person: the first part of the bill provides that the Government shall divest itself of all claims on about 200,000 acres of land. While the last clause gives to this "one" "original claimant" about 49,000 acres only." What is to be done with the balance? Why, that belongs to **Elkins and Co.**! But suppose the Grant embraces less than "eleven square leagues?"

Why, the Government would have to make up the balance from other lands.

This is but a sample of the half a hundred claims sought to be confirmed by this bill. How many others they have an interest in is left for future development at the Land Office. That many of these claims were dead, and were only "revived" by this **Ring** is fully shown. And this Bill, No. 344, was reported back to the House without amendment, with a substantial report by the Committee favoring it.

Now for the sequel: When the Bill came up for debate, it was probed and killed ... [based on the argument that the grants were confirmed by the Treaty of Guadalupe Hidalgo, so it was superfluous to confirm them again.]

On January 12, '76, **Elkins** introduced another bill, entitled, "A Bill to enable claimants to lands within the limits of the Territories of New Mexico, Arizona and Colorado to institute proceedings to try the validity of their claims ... [The bill died in the House.] [I]t was to follow as a counterpart an act passed by the other end of the line in Santa Fé, entitled, "An act relating to partition of real estate and for other purposes," (passed about January 16, 1876,) and means one and the same thing, viz: **to go into the Courts of New Mexico, manipulated by the Ring, and get just such decisions as they wanted to complete this general land steal or "partition" of other men's property among themselves!**

Elkins, the Delegate, failed in his three Bills, but **Catron & Co.** at Santa Fé succeeded in theirs, and **Gov. S.B. Axtell** was a party to it and gave his signature. Immediately, **Catron & Co.** acted upon the Territorial "Partition Act," and filed Bills *vs.* The Maxwell Land Grant and other grants ... [the issue being an attempt to seize the land of Grant settlers – the cause of the Colfax County War.]

[T]he interest of these men in these grants is unaffected; it is still intact, and, in many instances, this interest is the result of the improper resuscitation of old claims that have been dead hundreds of years! It is held to be against the interests of public policy, if not improper, for persons holding official relations with the Government or Congress, to legislate or become interested in or prosecute claims to money or lands, when the Government is the most remotely interested ...

THE OFFICIAL "SLATE."

Now let us see how these men manage to get into office, and then help their friends in, in order to carry out their schemes: Elkins held the office of U.S. Attorney for a long time previous to 1872; at that time he gave place to his friend and partner, Catron, while he ran for Delegate to Congress. The record which he gives of himself is found in the Congressional Directory, 44th Congress, 1876. "Member of the Legislature, 1864-1865: Territorial, District, and then Attorney General and U.S. Attorney: was elected to 43d Congress and was re-elected to 44th, as a Republican, by 1580 majority over Pedro Valdez, Dem." **For the correctness of this latter statement we refer to the record; it is shown that in three precincts of Valencia county alone they report for Elkins in 1,500 majority, when there were but between 600 and 700 inhabitants, and Rio Arriba county gave Elkins a larger majority than there were votes cast, while Sweetwater precinct, Mora county, cast 13 votes, 10 of which were for Valdez, and when the ballot box arrived at Mora it was found to contain a majority of 80 votes for Elkins and none for Valdez!** ...

HOW IT WAS BROUGHT ABOUT.

In 1873 when Elkins ran for Congress, this Ring had about 600 persons indicted for living on Indian lands, and these indictments were hung over their heads until they voted for him – when they were all dismissed. **They were defended by the Ring counsel Elkins & Co.; Catron and he arranging it between them.** The fees and expenses in each case could not have cost the Government less than $20. If any one should speak out against their way of doing things, they would at once disbar them: such was the case with Judge Benedict, ex-Chief Justice of the Territory, and several others of almost equal note, among them the present editor of the Grant County *Herald* ...

The **Ring** had **Axtell** appointed Governor in 1875, and, when [Henry] **Waldo** (Chief Justice) was up for confirmation, he came near defeat by the opposition from the Territory.

(The Ring secured Waldo's appointment on the death of Palen, Chief Justice, in '75.)

In February, 1876, a petition was signed by 250 well known citizens of New Mexico for the removal of **Judge [Warren] Bristol** (associate Justice,) and **sent to Washington. They filed charges with affidavits, in support. So strong was the Ring influence, that no attention was paid to it.**

PETITION TO REMOVE JUDGE BRISTOL, (Feb. 18, '76.)

We the undersigned citizens of the Third Judicial District of the Territory of New Mexico, without regard to party, would respectfully request and petition for the removal of **Judge Warren Bristol** from the office of Judge of the District and Territory aforesaid, for the following special and general reasons.

1st. We charge that Warren Bristol has been guilty of secretly making known his opinions to attorneys engaged on the side of a cause pending before him, and informing them as to the nature and character of his decisions, several days before delivering them judicially from the bench.

2nd. We charge that in consequence of his secretly making known his opinions that great advantage thereby resulted to the parties employing said attorneys, and great loss and injury to the opposite party.

3d. We charge that Warren Bristol in an important mining suit, in which Martin W. Bremen and Silas Tidwell were plaintiffs, and Robert B. Wilson made defendant, secretly advised with an attorney of said plaintiffs, and informed and advised him as to the proper steps he should pursue in conducting the cause during the very time that the subject matter of his secret advice was under consideration by said Warren Bristol, as Judge.

4th. We charge Warren Bristol with writing out a full and complete form for re-locating a mine for one of the plaintiffs aforesaid, while the title to said mine was then a matter before his court for adjudication.

5th. We charge that Judge Bristol imprisoned an honorable and worthy citizen of Grant County, for contempt, during the pleasure of the court, for no other reason than that he availed himself of information communicated to him by his counsel, which had been prematurely and secretly revealed by the said Judge Bristol.

6th. We charge that Judge Bristol, during the July term of court 1875, held in Grant county, did in open court publicly confess that he had been guilty of revealing a secret opinion to one of the attorneys employed by said Bremen and Tidwell, but rendered no valid excuse for such injudicial conduct.

7th. We charge Judge Bristol with granting a writ of restitution to the plaintiff in a suit of ejectment after an appeal had been allowed and perfected to the Supreme Court, in the absence of any statutory provision authorizing such to issue.

8th. **We charge that Judge Bristol, acting as Judge aforesaid, actually refused in an important murder trial, after the prisoners arraignment at the first term, to grant continuance, although proper affidavits were filed according to law, for the procurement of absent material witnesses, and forced the prisoner to trial which resulted in his conviction and execution.**

9th. We charge that Judge Bristol in another important murder trial absolutely refused to the prisoner the right of compulsory process to procure witnesses in his behalf.

10th. We charge that Judge Bristol, as Judge aforesaid, willfully refused in two other important murder trials, to allow the defendants to exercise their right to the full number of peremptory challenges to jurors, given by the statutes in such cases, although his attention was repeatedly called to the statutory provision allowing the defendant the right to ten preemptory charges.

11th. We charge that the said Judge Bristol made a false accusation from the bench against the grand jurymen of Grant County, N.M. and that they, in proper justification of themselves, were forced to state publicly and in print that such accusation was false; and furthermore, that said public statement of the grand jurymen aforesaid has not, and cannot be denied by the said Judge Bristol.

12th. **We charge that Judge Bristol is guilty of manifest partiality, while acting in the trial of causes.**

13th. And generally we charge that Judge Bristol, as judge aforesaid, frequently consults and advises with attorneys about causes coming and pending before his court for adjudication, who are interested in the results of the suits as feed attorneys.

14th. We charge that Judge Bristol frequently makes rulings in important causes involving large amounts of property and the liberty of citizens, without proper thought and investigation; and that, in consequence of this, he constantly changes his rulings during the progress of important trials, and orders his clerk to expunge the records, in order to hide his indolence and ignorance, and thus deprives parties litigante of the proper recorded history of the causes.

15th. We charge that Judge Bristol is ignorant of the fundamental rules and principles of law with which every tyro should be conversant, and that he is indolent and not disposed to study, thus causing a universal feeling among the people of insecurity to life, liberty and property.

16th. We charge that Judge Bristol appointed a man clerk of his court, whom he knew all the time to be lewdly and publicly living with a kept mistress; and notwithstanding he is still so living, continues to retain him as clerk of his court.

17th. We aver that all of the foregoing statements and specifications can be substantiated on oath, by good, respectable citizens of this Territory irrespective of party predilections.

Here follows about 250 signatures among which are many of the most influential men in that section of the Territory.

THE REMOVAL OF THE COURTS.

We come now to the more serious part of this business. What the Ring failed to do in manipulating the Courts in one place, they assayed to do by removing them in another. **In January, 1876, they pushed through the Territorial Legislature an act to "annex the county of Colfax to that of Taos," the object of which was to punish the citizens of that county [Colfax] for charging the "Ring" with the assassination of Rev. F.J. Tolby.** Now, let us see what reason they had for this charge: Tolby was an outspoken man, became offensive to the **Ring,** and must be "got rid of." In going from Elizabethtown to Cimarron, his home, after filling an appointment, he was assassinated while passing through a lone canyon. Suspicion fell on a Mexican named Cruz Vega, who had been employed by one **Donoghue (of the Ring)** to carry the mail for two trips only, as the **Court Judge J.G. Palen, (also of the Ring,)** had taken possession of the stage, to carry itself around to his appointments. Tolby had had a disagreement with Palen on account of some evidence he, Tolby, had volunteered before the Grand Jury in Colfax against a Mexican named **Fran. Griego alias Pancho**, for the killing of three U.S. soldiers. **Pancho was a Ring man** and a deputy sheriff; the **Ring cleared him**. The office of Governor also being vacant [with the death of Governor Marsh Giddings], Tolby was working for Brooks of Arkansas for the appointment, while the Ring wanted Axtell. Tolby died, and the Ring elected their man.

THEIR GUILT.

Vegas [Vega] being questioned closely, admitted knowledge of the murder and finally his guilt was beyond question ... This man, in his confession, implicated one Cardenas, a worthless fellow; **stated that Cardenas did it for the sum of $500 paid him by the allies of this Ring. Soon after, Cardenas was arrested and corroborated the story of Vega, in that Vegas [Vega] did it for $500; that the money was paid by [M.W.] Mills, R.H. Longwill, Francisco Griego, (Pancho,) and F. Donoghue**, and before he knew of Vegas' confession ...

The following is in the record:

"City and county:

"In accordance with the confession of Manuel Cardenas, Justice Trauer issued warrants for the arrest of **R.H. Longwill, M.W. Mills, and F. Donoghue, - Pancho Griego** having been killed in attempting to assassinate Capt. R.C. Allison.

"Captain R.C. Allison, Jas. Allison and P. Burleson, were sent after **Longwill**, who had fled.

"**Cardenas** brought from Elizabethtown and lodged in jail at Cimarron, for protection, (as he had turned State's evidence.)

"Lieut. Cornish and 17 men [soldiers] arrived at Cimarron to do guard duty.

[AUTHOR'S NOTE: Use of troops for citizens' suppression.]

"R.C. Allison was examined for the shooting of Francisco Griego, and cleared on the ground of justifiable homicide ...

"United States vs. Mills, Donoghue, and Cardenas for the murder of Tolby." ...

DECISION.

"Nov. 11, '75. We find that Manuel Cardenas is guilty of murder of Rev. F.J. Tolby, and Florence Donoghue is guilty as accessory thereto, and it is ordered that they be committed to jail to await the action of the grand jury ... There is not sufficient evidence vs. M.N. Mills to bind him over: it is ordered that he be discharged. R.H. Longwill not having been arrested, [fleeing to Santa Fe] no decision is given as to him.

SAM'L S. Trauer, *Justice of the Peace*

MASS MEETING.

At a mass meeting it was resolved "That we regard those who procured the commission of murder as far more guilty, if possible, than the duped and hired tools, and that if satisfactory evidence is found to discover and identify such party or parties there should not be permitted to them any loop-hole to escape the extreme penalty of the law ...

The following also from the leading editorial of the Ring organ, the Santa Fé New Mexican ... speaks for itself, ([Judge Henry] Waldo was there defending the Ring's allies ...)

[AUTHOR'S NOTE: Below is typical Ring-biased press.]

"We had the pleasure of meeting Mr. Waldo on his return from Cimarron. There have been so many conflicting reports of the condition of affairs in the county of Colfax and so much uncertainty in regard thereto, that it is a relief to learn the particulars definitely. One thing we are very glad to learn, and of which we are assured by **Mr. Waldo**, and that is the quiet and order which he found existing among the people on his arrival there ... interrupted only by the unfortunate taking off of the man Cardenas. This occurrence we extremely regret, for whatever may have been his crimes, and there seems to have been little doubt that he was either the murderer or one of the murderers of Mr. Tolby – still it is far better for the cause of justice that the penalty of the law should be inflicted upon the violators thereof by the law. We gather from Mr. Waldo that the proceedings before the magistrates were of such a character that ... a full and thorough investigation of all the facts and circumstances that might be thought in any way connected with the killing of Mr. Tolby.

THE RING'S DEFENSE.

The Defense of the Ring and of Axtell, is managed by Catron and Waldo. They prepare his papers and swear each other through! The defense of Catron and Waldo in the Department of Justice, is the same in language, direction, and in some cases, the same handwriting of Axtell's defense, in the Interior Department! Axtell's statement is sworn to be before Waldo! ...

[AUTHOR'S NOTE: Omitted here is McPherson's accusing Axtell of using land-grabs for a Mormon settlement.]

THE "OTHER" LAW: COLFAX UNITED TO TAOS.

This law passed Febru'y, 1876, was gotten through the Legislature to "punish the people of Colfax county." It provided that the Court should be removed from Cimarron, Colfax county, to Taos, in Taos county, a distance of 55 miles, over a mountain range 10,000 feet high, at times impassable; that after two terms the Governor might at his option return it, which he has not yet done. This act was a trick to **repay the Colfax people for meddling [accusing the Ring] in the trial of the murderers of Tolby**, and demanding their arrest and punishment. The main provision was: "The Grand Jury empanelled in the district court of the county of Taos, shall be sworn and charged to inquire as to offences and other matters in said county of Colfax." The "other matters" may possibly have reference to the manly, intelligent and effective manner in which **the Colfax people opposed the aggression of what is known there as the "Santa Fe Ring" upon the system of Land Grants, the private property of persons who had received them from Mexico under the Treaty of Guadalupe Hidalgo.**

The Gov. says: "I deny being in a combination of men" to pass laws inimical, &c. The law annexing the County of Colfax to the county of Taos for judicial purposes, is the only one to which the people of Colfax county particularly objected, so far as I know; that law was passed with the concurrence of at least two-thirds of the members of the Legislature. **I understand that the course of the Legislature in that respect was approved by the Chief Justice" and "the U.S. Attorney,."** Of course the Chief Justice and the U.S. Attorney approved of it , for they drew it; had it presented and pressed to its passage! It was a Ring measure and intended for "Ring purposes" ...

The Gov. further says: "I had no objection to the 'measure' or part in its passage, except that I signed and approved the law" ...

And the refreshing part of all this is, the Gov. says, that "the course of the Legislature in that respect was approved by the Chief Justice (Waldo) and the U.S. Attorney" (Catron!) both Ring managers!

[AUTHOR'S NOTE: Next McPherson angrily exposes the Ring murder of Tolby and framing of Oscar McMains for Manuel Cardenas's murder to get him hanged by the Taos court.]

The Gov. says: "I transmit herewith a copy of the charge of the **Chief Justice (Waldo!)** to the Grand Jury at the Taos Court, on the facts which included the action of the Legislature," &c. Now what is this "charge" but a covert attempt to hide the true "cause" of the Colfax troubles and strike at somebody else over the corpse of the murdered Tolby? **It is a plain, transparent ruse to direct attention from the subject of the murder of Tolby to the lynching of his murderers [only Cruz Vega was lynched, Manuel Cardenas was shot] after the authorities had utterly failed or willfully neglected to do their duty, and arrest and bring to trial and punishment men [Donoghue, Mills, and Longwill] plainly implicated in the murder of Tolby! They had "got rid" of one preacher [Tolby]; they wanted to get rid of another [O.P. McMains]! besides others who were distasteful to them, and they supposed "two terms" would be sufficient.** "All was quiet and orderly in Cimarron!"

But, the Governor says: "I am informed that the grand-jury; and the **'Attorney General,' (Breeden!)** – made the most careful and thorough investigation, but we were unable to discover any evidence as to the murder of Mr. Tolby."

And immediately thereafter he adds: "Some of the persons engaged in the killing of the man Vega, are now under indictment (!) for that offence, amongst others, Rev. Oscar P. McMains, who is alleged to have been the leading spirit in the affair!" Here is a case of special pleading for you! **The "dead" Tolby is of no account. The "living" McMains is, – and the Ring wants him, dead or alive!** ...

It will be noticed that the troubles arose with the Ring in Santa Fé and were bruited about the country long before McMains arose, and it is straining a very nice point for these gentlemen to try to saddle their Colfax county indiscretions on him.

The Governor adds: "It is true that I refused to restore the District Court to Colfax County, and in this I am sustained by all the **Territorial and Federal officers here, 'including' the Chief Justice and Attorney General Breeden!" (Certainly!)** "That the 'time' has nor yet come for the return of the Court, is approved by 'its' officers!" **(of course, the same men, all through – the Chief Justice, the U.S. Attorney [Catron] and Attorney General [Breeden]!** ... Colfax has been "quiet" since Waldo spoke there! but the "Rev. Oscar P. McMains" – the opposer of the "Ring" – is not yet tried, or made to "leave" the county, although he has had hanging over his head for two years "several indictments" which the Ring organ in Santa Fé says, "can be secured at Taos, and are bad things to have lying around loose!" And although his counsel has repeatedly asked an appeal to the Supreme Court of the U.S., the Ring-Court have as often quashed the indictment to defeat the appeal, and then had him re-indicted again and imprisoned ...

[AUTHOR'S NOTE: This is the Ring pattern of malicious prosecution of opponents, to be repeated in Lincoln County.]

The following editorial from the *News and Press*, the organ of Colfax Co., Feb. 11, 1876, edited by W.R. Morley, Esq., is pertinent here:

"TAOS COUNTY', Nee COLFAX – A COUNTY THAT WAS, BUT IS NO MORE.

... "Now it is a notable fact, that no notice was taken by the powers that be, of any crime or disorder in the county, until the indignant populace got after the Tolby assassins ... and some of Elkins party charged in connection with the Tolby murder, it was discovered at Santa Fé that this county was in a state of rebellion, etc. In one sense they were right. It is a state of rebellion against Elkins and his combination, which no legislative act can subdue.

"As soon as the period of retribution in the Tolby case begun, sensational reports were spread abroad ... and the impression was sought to be created that the people of the county were in a state of anarchy and lawlessness, and that the lives of innocent persons were in jeopardy here. Every little scrap of the frontier history of the county was raked up and thrown into the scale to make the case, and every sort of false and ridiculous argument used to induce the legislature to pass the annexation [to Taos County] bill. Many of these charges are utterly false, and the argument deduced without an iota of truth ..."

[AUTHOR'S NOTE: This is the Ring's vilifying opponents by the outlaw myth, to be used next in Lincoln County.]

The following are the articles referred to in the above:

[INSERT] December 22, 1875 *New York Weekly Sun* article about that paper's commentator - likely Franklin Tolby - having been murdered for anti-Ring accusations.

[INSERT] August 2, 1877 *Cimarron News and Press's* notice titled "U.S. Attorney Catron and the Maxwell," stating: "Mr. M.W. Mills has conveyed his tax title to the Maxwell grant to Thomas B. Catron, of Santa Fé." [Catron's take-over of Grant]

[INSERTS] Letters from S.B. Elkins and other Ring backers to President Hayes and to the Department of the Interior backing Governor S.B. Axtell.

REVIEW.

TOLBY opposed the Ring's schemes of plunder and violations of law, and Tolby must fall!

ALLISON stood, with an iron hand, between their rapacity and the people of Colfax, and they struck at him with would-be assassins, - not daring to do it themselves!

MORLEY fought the battle of the Grants, and failing to reach him by their "system" [scheme] of "indictments" – they touch his family with the tongue of slander. [Catron's malicious prosecution of Ada Morley for mail theft.]

McMAINS – the successor of Tolby – would not bow to the "Ring," and, determining to ferret out the murderers of his brother [missionary], found them too near their doors, and he too must fall under their proscription.

Let these Ring managers – Axtell, Catron, Waldo, Breeden, Elkins & Co., - not imagine for a moment that they can "divert" the attention from their own crimes and thereby thwart justice, by attempting to hide behind the blood of the guilty Vega, while that of the murdered Tolby cries out from the canyon: There is "another" account to settle first! ... Let these gentlemen understand that they have

> "Sown the wind,
> "And have reaped the whirlwind!"

And they must not "wince" if they rest under the suspicion of "judicial murder!"

THE RESPONSIBILITY.

Now, what we say is that the Governor, S.B. Axtell, is responsible for all this. He should have "controlled" this Ring while it was his power to do it, and not let the Ring control him! He should be impeached. **And if the Government allow them [Ringites] to retain their place and power, in the face of this showing; it deserves to have its authority defied; and no one will wonder at the slow decay that will follow in the wake of the administration, and render the Republic itself unstable!**

Respectfully submitted, M.E. McPherson,
In behalf of the Citizens of Colfax Co., New Mexico

COLLUDING PRESIDENT HAYES

Unlike Mary McPherson, Ringites had easy access to President Hayes, and colluded with him to ignore and to cover-up Colfax County's exposés. Elkins, ending his second term as Delegate to Congress, and progressively gaining the immense, corrupt political power he would exert throughout his career, wrote to Hayes backing Governor Axtell. Noteworthy is that Elkins argued by using the Ring's outlawing of opponents, calling Axtell's critics *"irresponsible parties ... [and] a few bad people to whom ... the Governor gave offence in attempting to repress violence and murder."* Elkins wrote:

June 11, 1877

To the President:
I trouble you to say a word in behalf of Gov. Axtell of New Mexico whose removal I am informed is now under consideration.

During Gov. Axtell's administration in New Mexico he has given general satisfaction, and the bonafide citizens, property holders & good people without distinction of party heartily indorse him, and believe him to be a worthy and efficient officer.

The charges filed against him in the Interior Department are for the most part vague & indefinite and as far as certain are absolutely false. **They are proffered by irresponsible parties now residents who have no interest in the Territory & to satisfy a few bad people to whom I am informed the Governor gave offence in attempting to repress violence and murder.**

If the Administration should <u>remove Go. Axtell</u> on the charges proffered it will join hands with irresponsible parties who have no interest in New Mexico in doing a gross injustice to a good man a worthy officer and a republican.

<u>Against such action</u> as a citizen of New Mexico deeply interested in her welfare and as a friend of your administration I beg to record my <u>protest</u>.

Very respectfully
S.B. Elkins
Ex <u>Delegate</u> New Mexico

CAPITULATING FRANK SPRINGER

SUMMARY: Besides Mary McPherson, Attorney Frank Springer could have broken the Santa Fe Ring. But he was an opportunist, vacillating between anti-Ring exposés in his Cimarron News and Press, and legal defense of Ringites. By the time of his August 9, 1878 deposition to Frank Warner Angel, he had converted to the Ring side. Though providing evidence of Ring crimes, he concluded despicably and hypocritically by lying that U.S. officials were not behind the "troubles" and murders in Colfax and Lincoln Counties.

Author David L. Caffey is Frank Springer's uncritical biographer in his 2007 *Frank Springer & New Mexico: From the Colfax County War to the Emergence of Modern Santa Fe*.

Frank Springer was born 1848. As a 24 year old, ambitious Iowa attorney, he arrived in Cimarron in 1873, invited by his past Iowa classmate, William Raymond Morley, then Vice-President of the Maxwell Land Grant and Railway Company, to assist with settler conflicts. The Company's main attorney was T.B. Catron. So Springer arrived right in the middle of the Colfax County War.

Though Springer became co-editor with Raymond Morley of the *Cimarron News and Press*, wealth was his lure. Caffey quotes him: "When I have made my fortune, perhaps I may come back to Iowa to live. I would much prefer it, were money made as easily as here." (Caffee, p. 21)

As corrupting for Springer were his political ambitions. In 1875, he ran for the legislature. He lost to Ringite Attorney Melvin Mills - just before Mills arranged the murder of Franklin Tolby, and Governor S.B. Axtell relocated Colfax County's courts to Taos County to obstruct prosecution of Tolby's murderers.

In 1876, Springer was an intended victim of the Ring's "Dear Ben plot" to murder him, Raymond Morley, Henry Porter, and Clay Allison. Nevertheless, he later defended Tolby's killer, Melvin Mills, at the Taos Grand Jury, getting Mills's acquittal.

But Springer hedged his bets by also defending Colfax County's anti-Ring crusader, Oscar P. McMains. And he certainly knew anti-Ring fighter Mary Tibbles McPherson.

By April of 1878, with the death of Ringite District Attorney Benjamin Stevens - arranger with Governor Axtell of the "Dear Ben plot" - Springer chose a self-serving option of scapegoating Axtell, instead of exposing the Ring.

SCAPEGOATING AXTELL TO SPARE THE RING

On June 10, 1878, Springer wrote a cover letter to Secretary of the Interior Carl Schurz, accompanying a Colfax County petition to President Hayes charging Axtell with crimes. It was returned to him by direction of Hayes on July 12, 1878. But it may have inspired the administration's strategy after the Lincoln County War, and via the investigation by Frank Warner Angel, to scapegoat Axtell to spare the Ring. Springer wrote:

> FRANK SPRINGER,
> ATTORNEY AND COUNSELOR AT LAW,
>
> *Cimarron, New Mexico,* June 10, 1878
>
> Hon Carl Schurz,
>   Secretary of the Interior
>   Sir:
>   I endorse herewith, directed to the President charges against S.B. Axtell, Governor of New Mexico, supported by affidavits verifying the facts stated.
>   **As one whose life was jeopardized by the action of Mr. Axtell, whether through malevolence, stupidity, or blind partisanship matters little. I submit the facts and request you to present them to the President.**
>   Very respectfully
>   Frank Springer

[ENCLOSED: THE COMPLAINT]

To His Excellency, the President of the United States:
        The undersigned, a citizen of the County of Colfax, Territory of New Mexico, begs to call your attention to the official conduct of Samuel B. Axtell, Governor of New Mexico, which show that said Axtell has by false pretense and representation procured the use of United States troops, and employed them in the County of Colfax in a manner directly calculated to produce confusion and bloodshed, and to create disturbance of the public peace in a time of quiet.
    That under pretence of a desire to arrest a certain person for some pretended offence, not disclosed, said Axtell planned and conspired by falsehood and treachery to induce a number of peaceable citizens to assemble in a place and

under circumstances where under the instructions given by said Axtell for the occasion it was almost certain that most of them would be killed. That had not the plot of said Axtell been discovered in time, it is very probable that it would have resulted in the death of the undersigned, and several other law abiding citizens assembled for a peaceful purpose upon the strength of an invitation to meet the governor. And it is the belief of the undersigned that it was expected by said Axtell that such would be the result of the sending of U.S. troops to said Colfax County.

That the real object of said Axtell was not merely the arrest of a certain person is indicated by the fact that when afterwards arrested by the military this person was at once released and that said Axtell – while Governor of New Mexico – afterwards made an appointment with the person and traveled with him in a friendly way in the stage coach.

The undersigned respectfully submits that whether through ignorance or corrupt motive, the action of said Axtell is to keep many parts of the territory in a state of turmoil and confusion when intelligent and non partisan action on the part of the executive might end much of the difficulty. His use of the military force of the United States has been partisan in every instance and the undersigned submits that no person capable of forming such a letter of instructions as the one set forth in the accompanying affidavit is fit to be entrusted with any power whatever, and respectfully asks that he be removed from his position.
Very respectfully
Your obedient Servant, Frank Springer

FRANK SPRINGER'S DEPOSITION

On August 9, 1878, a month after the Lincoln County War's bloody final battle, and aware of Mary McPherson's exposés the year before, hypocritical Frank Springer gave a deposition to the Departments of Justice and the Interior's Investigator of the Lincoln County and Territorial "troubles," Frank Warner Angel. Of all Angel's deponents, Springer was arguably the only one with enough power and prestige to end cover-up of the Santa Fe Ring's crimes and force federal retribution. But he demonstrated only self-serving opportunism by alluding to the Ring, and crimes by Catron, Elkins, Axtell, and other Ringites; then denying knowledge of U.S. officials' involvement in "*any mismanagement, corruption, fraud, or improper action*" causing Territorial "troubles." So his toothless deposition documents Colfax County War struggles with Ring domination fear and favor - Springer being a recipient of both - while being a cover-up. He stated:

Deposition of Frank Springer, of Cimarron, New Mexico, given at the request of Frank Warner Angel Esq. upon interrogatories propounded by him.

Int 1. What is your name and occupation?
A. My name is Frank Springer and I am by profession an attorney of law.
Int 2. What do you know about troubles in Colfax County. When and how did they originate, and what was their character ...
A. I came to Colfax County in February 1873, and have no personal knowledge of affairs in New Mexico previous to that time. There had been some troubles in Colfax County before that, I learned, coming out of controversies between the Maxwell Land Grant and Railway Company and settlers in regard to title and possessions of portions of a large Mexican grant, claimed by the company. **I heard a great deal of talk at that time and afterwards about a so called "Ring" which it was alleged controlled to a large extent the courts in New Mexico. The names of Judge Palen, Mr. Elkins, Mr. Catron were mentioned most frequently in this connection** *and in regard to Colfax County the name of Dr. R. [Robert] H. Longwill was often spoken of as being connected with ... the so-called "Ring." He was probate judge in the county when I came here ... It was a frequent subject of comment that through the persons above mentioned the power of the courts were unfairly used to advance the interests of the said Maxwell Land Grant and Railway Company ...*
Int 3. You have spoken of a "Ring." What do you know of its existence?
A. The facts upon which its existence was predicated were not generally within my personal knowledge except as to the facts connected with subsequent troubles in Colfax County which impressed me with the belief that a few men had almost absolute control of affairs in the territory. *In 1873, Mr. M. [Melvin] W. Mills who had been a prominent opponent of the Maxwell Company and of the men who controlled it, was elected a member of the territorial legislature. Very soon*

after this he became very intimate with Dr. Longwill, whom he had before strongly opposed. And after he went to Santa Fe to attend the session of the legislature, he wrote to Longwill, in which he informed him that "by a little sharp figuring" he had got "in with the big side": a copy of the letter is hereto attached as "Exhibit A." From that time on [Melvin] Mills became and continued very intimate with [Robert] Longwill as well as with Messrs Elkins and Catron, and represented their business and political matters in the county to a very large extent ... And in 1875, when Mills was again a candidate for the legislature and Longwill for Probate Judge, all their powers were exerted to promote his election. A circumstance came under my observation during that election campaign which impressed this strongly in my mind. In June 1875, a man by the name of Francisco Griego murdered two soldiers in Cimarron in a gaming table quarrel, shooting and stabbing them in the back. He fled and was a fugitive for sometime. When at last he came in and gave himself up, he was at once taken before the Justice of the Peace who was a clerk in [Melvin] Mills office and examined and bound over to await the action of the Grand Jury, in $1,000- bail, this action of the Justice being taken after an hour recess and a consultation with Longwill and Mills ... The political campaign was then opening and some weeks afterward I had a conversation with one C. Lara, an especial friend of Griego, who was then actively working in the interest of the Longwill and Mills ticket, as was also Griego himself. Lara had previously been on the other side, and in my asking him the reason of his change of attitude he told me that his friend was in danger of prosecution for the killing of the soldiers and that he - **Lara – had been to Santa Fe and had talked with the gentlemen, and that they promised him that if he and Griego would use all their influence with the Mexicans in favor of the ticket of Elkins** *[running as* **Delegate to Congress]** *and* **[blacked out]** **his friend Griego should not suffer, and that for this reason he was obliged to work on such that he had always before opposed. Upon my asking him who the gentlemen were who had promised him, he mentioned with much reluctance Messrs Breeden and Catron** *... [Francisco] Griego was discharged without being indicted for anything, nor were any further proceedings taken against him in the matter.*

[AUTHOR'S NOTE: Killer thug Griego's Ringite immunity was repeated in 1878 by Jessie Evans's and John Kinney's gangs.]

Int 4. What was the cause of the troubles in Colfax County since you lived there?

A. The assassination of Rev. F.J. Tolby in September, 1875.

Int 5. State the circumstances connected with the death of Tolby, and what followed ...

A. F.J. Tolby was a minister of the Methodist church who had been stationed in Cimarron and had been doing missionary work in the county for nearly a year. He was a man of ability and rather free in talking about men and their acts. During the first weekend in September 1875, while the court was in session in Cimarron Judge Palen and Tolby had a rather spirited altercation, the judge denouncing him for some remarks he heard made about the court and its actions. Tolby immediately declared he would **"write up that judge so that 200,000 readers should see his record," which led some to suppose that he might have been the author of some letters which had appeared in the eastern press reflecting on Palen, Elkins and others.**

On the 16th of Sept, 1875, just after the election and the adjournment of District Court, Tolby was found murdered in the canyon between Cimarron and Elizabethtown. He had started from the latter place two days before, and had been dead two days apparently. He was shot from behind with two bullets and his watch and money were not taken. Mystery surrounded the affair for a time. When at last circumstantial evidence fixed the guilt upon two Mexicans, one of whom had been employed for that day only by [Florencio] Donoghue, the mail contractor, to carry the mail on horseback along that road.

[AUTHOR'S NOTE: This scenario was replicated in 1878's Lincoln County murder of John Tunstall using Jessie Evans and his boys in concert with Ringite Sheriff William Brady's posse.]

The county was intensely excited over the murder, and the people generally were fiercely indignant, and determined to punish the guilty if they could find them. The two Mexicans were arrested separately. one of them – [Cruz] Vega - after having a rope put around his neck and strung up a few seconds, made a statement to the effect that Tolby had been killed by the other Mexican – [Manuel] Cardenas – that he saw him do it, and **that they had been hired by [Francisco] Griego and [Florencio] Donoghue to do it.** *The other one – Cardenas – without any violence being used, stated that Vega had killed Tolby, that he saw* *him do it, and that they had been hired to do it by Longwill, Mills, Donoghue and Griego.* Vega was taken by a mob and hanged. Griego was killed by R.C. [Clay] Allison in self defense, Griego trying to kill him. **As soon as Longwill was informed of the statement Cardenas had made, he left the town and relocated to Santa Fe,** *after eluding a vigorous pursuit. Mills and Donoghue were arrested, and an examination had before magistrate, which resulted in the discharge of Mr. Mills for want of evidence, and the commitment of Donoghue and Cardenas. Previous to the examination Cardenas was visited in jail by three prominent friends of the parties accused ...* **The examination before the magistrate was concluded about ten o'clock at night and while Cardenas was being taken from the court room to the jail under a guard, a man sprang from behind a corner and shot Cardenas dead,** *and escaped out of sight ... This act always remained a mystery. It cannot be reasonably charged to the friends of Tolby, for it was clearly to their interest to keep him. During the pendency of these proceedings a detachment of U.S. troops arrived from Fort Union being sent in ... at the request of Gov. Axtell, it being declared that the town was in a state of riot and anarchy, and life and property in danger from a mob.*

[AUTHOR'S NOTE: This military suppression of civilian opponents would be escalated in the Lincoln County War to achieve murder and defeat of its freedom fighters.]

The troops remained several days & found nothing to do – found the people quiet and peaceable and the law taking its course, but very bitter and excited feeling among them on account of the murder of Tolby. Some minutes afterward [Florencio] Donoghue was taken to Santa Fe on a writ of <u>Habeas Corpus</u> *and released on $1000 bail. He and [Robert] Longwill have ever since remained there.*

[AUTHOR'S NOTE: The Ring's freeing of members was repeated after the 1879 Lincoln County murder of Attorney Huston Chapman, after Governor Lew Wallace arrested James Dolan, Billy Matthews, and Seven Rivers boys, imprisoning them in Fort Stanton. They were released by Ring attorneys using *habeas corpus*, and never prosecuted.]

At a term of court subsequently, in Taos, the Grand Jury ignored the charges against them ...

[AUTHOR'S NOTE: Axtell had moved courts from Colfax to Taos County, where the juries could be controlled by the Ring.]

Int 6. What action did the governor take to prevent the troubles in Colfax County?

A. He took no action in regard to the county until after the passage of the act [of attaching Colfax County to Taos County so as to move the courts from Colfax County to Taos County] except to send troops during ... the examination of the parties charged with complicity in the Tolby murder ...

Int 7. Was it necessary to attach Colfax to Taos Co. for judicial purposes?

A. No, not for any legitimate end.

Int 8. What was the object of attaching Colfax County to Taos?

A. The alleged reason was that lawlessness persisted in Colfax and the laws could not be enforced, but it was not true ... **In my opinion, judging by what occurred subsequently, as well as at the time, the real object of annexation of Colfax Co to Taos was to so intimidate and punish by means of indictments found by juries of Mexicans full of ignorance & prejudice [about Colfax County], the people who had taken an active part in the search for the Tolby murderers, and who had been strongly hostile to the suspected parties [Catron and Elkins and local Ring members], and thus enable these parties to regain control in the County which through these events they had lost ...**

[AUTHOR'S NOTE: This Ring tactic for shielding Ringite murderers from conviction was repeated in Lincoln County following John Tunstall's 1878 murder, by Governor Axtell's March 6, 1878 illegal Proclamation removing its Justice of the Peace, John Wilson, to block his warrants for apprehending Tunstall's killers; then by District Attorney William Rynerson's and Judge Warren Bristol's venue change to Mesilla of these murderers' cases to get jurors ignorant of the issues to guarantee acquittals. That manipulation was repeated in 1879, by Rynerson's and Bristol's transfer of venue of Billy Bonney's murder cases to Mesilla to avoid Lincoln County jurors aware of Lincoln County War issues behind his indictments, who might have freed him or refused a first degree murder verdict.]

Int 9. Could the laws at this time be enforced honestly and impartially in Colfax County?

A. ... So far as the people of the county were concerned, yes.

Int 10. Did the people take any action to prevent the change of the courts?

A. There was no time for any. The bill was introduced the day before the close of the session of the legislature ... Several gentlemen telegraphed Axtell requesting him to withhold his signature ... He telegraphed in reply "Bill signed. S.B. Axtell."

[AUTHOR'S NOTE: This was repeated by Governor Axtell by his illegal Lincoln County Proclamation invalidating Justice of the Peace Wilson's deputy appointments - including Billy Bonney.]

Int 11. What action did the Governor take to enforce the bill?
A. ... He said there were bad men there and that he intended to have them punished if or compelled to leave the county if it took all the troops in New Mexico ...

[AUTHOR'S NOTE: This is the Ring's outlaw myth tactic, later repeated in Lincoln County and against Billy Bonney.]

Int 12. Was there any resistance to the court [transfer] offered or threatened?
A. Not to my knowledge ...
Int 13. Was it a benefit or not to attach Colfax County to Taos? ...
A. ... It was a gross injury and injustice to the people of Colfax County ...
Int 14. Could the troubles in Colfax County have been quieted in any other way? ...
A. As I stated, there were no troubles calling for any outsider influence ...
Int 15. What was done, if anything, by the Governor, in regard to Colfax County after the passage of the act?

[AUTHOR'S NOTE: Springer gives the "Dear Ben plot." In 1878, its inducing violence tactic was repeated in Lincoln County by Sheriff Brady's harassing property attachments to justify killing Tunstall and McSween in "self defense."]

A. In the meantime Axtell had removed the Sheriff of Colfax County, who had been elected, and appointed in his place one of the strong partisans of Elkins, [Robert] Longwill et. al. [the Santa Fe Ring]... [District Attorney of the Second Judicial District Benjamin Stevens] went to Cimarron ... telling the people that he was going to try to induce the Governor to visit the county. Instead of going to Santa Fe, he went to Fort Union. Whence he returned to Cimarron in a few days, and followed by a company of U.S. soldiers of the 9th cavalry (colored) ... He exhibited a telegram from the Governor, which read as follows: "Do not let it be known that I will be in Cimarron in Saturday's coach. Body guard all right." Stevens ... said it now proved his efforts with the Governor had been successful and that the Governor was coming to visit the county and would expect to meet those who had signed the invitation to him, and that they must be on hand at the arrival of the coach on the following Saturday to meet with him. He especially mentioned [Clay] Allison, as one that ought to be on hand. He also urged on Mr [Raymond] Morley with whom he had been talking, to keep the matter quiet as the governor did not want a crowd, but only wanted to meet those who had invited him. The Governor did not intend to be present or to visit Colfax at the time, and did not in fact arrive on Saturdays coach, but the telegram and the action of Stevens made in furtherance of a plot which the details are set forth in a letter which the Governor wrote to Ben Stevens at the time of sending the telegram, and of which the following is a correct copy:

[INSERT] 1876 "Dear Ben plot" letter, published in 1877 in the *Cimarron News and Press*. (See page 263)

The plot disclosed in the foregoing letter was discovered, and none of the parties mentioned were on hand, so the scheme ended in failure. The Mr Porter mentioned in the forgoing letter was the leading banker and merchant in the county who possessed large influence and was a strong opponent of the party which had been controlling the county [the Santa Fe Ring]. Mr Morley and myself had actively opposed them politically, and were at the time owners and controllers of the newspaper in Cimarron which was vigorously attacking all parties concerned with removal of the courts, and exposing the violations thereof. The person referred to as "our man" was ... Mr R.C. [Clay] Allison ... He occupied a prominent place in the eyes of the public on account of his well known desperate courage and resolute character. He had never refused to face the legal consequences of his acts. He was ... a man of strong impulses and quick temper, prompt to react to any injury or to resist an indignity. His character was well known, and he was recognized as a leader among the cattle men of the county. **He had been on most friendly terms with [Robert] Longwill and his associates, and had, together with his friends, vigorously supported them during the election of Sept, 1875.** ~~He had~~ **When Tolby was murdered he had greatly invested himself in trying to discover the murderer, and took a leading part in the arrest and examination of those** *charged with complicity therein and had led a hot pursuit of Longwill on that occasion ... But whether there was or not [any grounds to arrest him], it is almost certain, that if when he had come to the coach upon the invitation of the Governor to meet and pay respect to him as the Executive of the Territory, he had found himself beset with negro soldiers seeking to arrest him [as a known racist], his first motion would have been resistance, and in that case, according to the instructions of Gov Axtell not only he, but those who stood with him, were to be killed, and among those ... were named "Porter, Morley, Springer." The character of Allison was well known to the Governor ... and it was well known to everybody that he would not quietly submit in the manner described and planned ... It is my belief that it was expected that Allison would resist, and that the soldiers would then fire on the party indiscriminately, in which the chances were that most of us would be killed. The result of which would have been 1ˢᵗ the parties named would have been out of the way & 2ⁿᵈ the people of the county would have been driven to desperation, and an excuse afforded for keeping troops in the county, and through these means it may have been hoped that control of the county could be regained by Axtell and the party in whose favor he has become partizan [the Ring] ...*

Int 16, 17, 18, 19, are answered in my last answer.

Int 20. Was there any law as to restoring the courts to Colfax County?

    A. Yes ... [T]he Governor might restore the courts to Colfax County by proclamation.

Int 21. Did the people try to induce the Governor to restore the courts?

    A. Yes. After two terms had been held in Taos, petitions were signed by many citizens, and presented to the Governor by Hon. W.L. South, member elect, of the Territorial House of Representatives of Colfax County. Mr South reported that the Governor promised to do so after certain objects had been accomplished, but he never did it.

[AUTHOR'S NOTE: What follows gives the Ring's land-grab scheme connected to Colfax County court's removal: make a new county for the Uña de Gato Land Grant there. This tactic was repeated after the Lincoln County War when the Ring grabbed dead Tunstall's store and his 4,000 acre ranches.]

In the summer of 1877, Gov Axtell came to Colfax County in company with Senator S.W. Dorsey to examine a tract of land in the eastern part of the county called the "Uña de Gato Grant' ... He met many citizens in the eastern part of the county, to whom he said that the courts would never be restored to the county at Cimarron ... but told them that they ought to cut loose from the Cimarron crowd and have a new county for themselves ...

Int 22. Have the courts been restored? ...

    A. Yes, by act of the legislature – January 1878.

Int 23. Had the Governor any reason for refusing the request of the people to have the courts restored to Colfax County?

    A. No legitimate reason ... A large number of indictments were formed against parties in Colfax County for crimes alleged to have been committed there, and with the exception of pleas of guilty to minor offences ... there have been but very few convictions ...

Int 24. Do you know anything about the indictment of Mrs W.R. Morley"

[AUTHOR'S NOTE: Springer next presented U.S. Attorney Catron's malicious prosecution of Ada Morley for mail theft, as well as giving supporting evidence by Exhibits, correctly attributing Catron's action to attacking her Ring opponent, husband, Raymond Morley: *"it was an unworthy way to fight a man by attacking his family."* **It should not be missed that Springer was here giving evidence of Catron, as a U.S. official, causing Colfax County "troubles."]**

    A. In July 1875, I learned that there was to be a prosecution commenced in the U.S. Dist Court in Santa Fe against Mrs Morley, the wife of W.R. Morley, on a charge of abstracting a letter from the Post Office at Cimarron [by her mother, Mary McPherson] ... I wrote to Dr [Robert] Longwill [a subsequent Tolby murderer] and appealed to him to use his influence to stop it as *it was an unworthy way to fight a man by attacking his family. He promised to do so, but said to me that "Morley ought to stop attacking Elkins through the newspaper." Mr Morley was then opposing the party of Elkins and his friends politically.* I went to Santa Fe ... and found that it was determined that Mrs Morley should be indicted, and my opinion was confirmed by a letter written by Mr [Melvin] Mills to Dr Longwill ... of which the following is a copy. [Given as Exhibit A] As bearing on the subject of the proceedings, I refer to the affidavit of A. [Asa] F. Middaugh of a conversation between him and Mr Catron of which I attach hereto as Exhibit B as a true copy. [Given as Exhibit B]

In August following I was present at a conversation between W.R. Morley and John Pratt, U.S. Marshall for New Mexico at Clifton in Colfax County ... Morley said to him to tell Mr Catron to crack ahead with it [serve arrest warrant on his wife], that what he had already done would cost Elkins 500 votes [for Delegate to Congress] ... Mrs Morley was never arrested.

Int 25. Do you know of any mismanagement, corruption, fraud, or improper action by any U.S. official in his official capacity or of any fact or facts which would render him an improper person to be such official, which the Departments of Justice and Interior should be informed of? If so state names or facts in detail!

[AUTHOR'S NOTE: This is the key question in Angel's investigation. But Springer folds and shields the Ring – to save his life and future. He obviously knew Angel's report could not be kept from Elkins in Washington, and doubletalks evasively, ending: "I have no personal knowledge further that I recall." And, equally self-serving Angel likely bet that Springer would balk, allowing Angel to save himself by demonstrating that a knowledgeable deponent swore under oath that "no U.S. officials were involved in Territorial mismanagement, corruption, fraud, or improper action."]

A. I know of a case in which four indictments were found in the U.S. Court against Dr Wm N. Michaels of this place, two in charges of selling liquor & two tobacco, without the U.S. license ... Whether any official is responsible for them I do not know ... I have no personal knowledge further that I recall.

[AUTHOR'S NOTE: This is Springer evasion and capitulation.]

Frank Springer

[EXHIBIT A] The December 5, 1873 letter of Attorney Melvin W. Mills to Dr. Robert H. Longwill gloating about Catron's indictment of Ada Morley for mail theft. (See page 250)

[EXHIBIT B] March 31, 1876 Deposition of Asa F. Middaugh about Catron's vindictive motive in prosecuting Ada Morley. (See page 251)

COLFAX COUNTY WAR OUTCOME

SUMMARY: Though settler skirmishes continued in Colfax County till the late 1880's, focused Ring opposition ended by stonewalling of Mary McPherson, by malicious prosecution of Oscar McMains, by Frank Springer's betrayal, and by Raymond and Ada Morley's fleeing the Territory. But settlers probably considered as victories regaining their courts and seeing Ringite Governor Axtell removed in 1878.

GOVERNOR AXTELL REMOVED

Governor S.B. Axtell was expelled in 1878 for his Lincoln County War crimes. Colfax County citizens, who hated him for removal of their courts, shared in feeling victory.

On September 6, 1878, Raymond Morley's and Frank Springer's *Cimarron News and Press*, celebrated with headlines: "Rejoicing at Cimarron," "Axtell's Head Falls at Last," and "General Lew. Wallace Appointed Governor." They jibed at Ringite presses: "It will now be in order for the [Santa Fe] New Mexican and Las Vegas Gazette to wear the usual badge of mourning for 30 days."

But those two papers, unruffled, merely praised Axtell on September 21st and October 19th, 1878.

THE MORLEY'S FORCED FLIGHT

By 1879, Raymond and Ada Morley, like most Ring victims, fled New Mexico Territory, according to their daughter, Agnes, in her 1941 book *No Life for a Lady*. Raymond worked in railroad construction in Mexico until 1882, when he died from an alleged accidental rifle discharge. (Agnes Cleaveland, pp. 14-16)

In her other book, *Satan's Paradise*, Agnes voiced the Ring's traumatic legacy: "[T]he Santa Fé Ring was a closely knit political organization exerting a powerful influence ... which left its impress upon its descendants even unto the third and fourth generation, and to which much of the turmoil that enveloped the Maxwell Grant was traceable." (Agnes Cleaveland, *Satan's Paradise*, p. 65)

RETURN OF THE RING TO COLFAX COUNTY

By 1878, Catron's and Elkins's land-grab vision was realized. The Raton Pass of the Maxwell Land Grant along the old Santa Fe Trail was bought by the Atchison, Topeka, and Santa Fe Railroad to run its tracks from Colorado into New Mexico Territory. And, by April 18, 1887, by federal Supreme Court decree, the Ring achieved eviction of all Maxwell Land Grant settlers.

All Colfax County Ringites prospered. Reverend Franklin Tolby's murderers, Melvin Mills and Dr. Robert Longwill lived lucrative lives under Ring protection and beneficence, with Mills staying in Colfax County, and Longwill heading a Santa Fe hospital. Converted Ringite and betrayer of the anti-Ring cause, Frank Springer, basked in his lifetime of profit. By 1878, he was gifted by the Ring with Land Grant acreage along the route of the Atchison, Topeka, and Santa Fe Railroad, which named it Springer in his honor. Tracks arrived there in 1879. By 1882, Colfax County's seat was relocated there from Cimarron.

The Colfax County War's achievement was clinching the Ring's blueprint for unbeatable organized crime: control the governor, legislature, courts, and law enforcement; conduct malicious prosecution; use the outlaw myth against adversaries; remove legal redress to shield members from prosecution; enlist troops for intimidation; hire thugs for assassinations; expurgate incriminating documents; and have Washington's protection. The upcoming Lincoln County War period would test that strategy with tragic results for democracy.

The flaw in this Ring scheme was its need for secrecy. Lacking charisma, the Colfax County War's anti-Ring fighters sank into historical oblivion. But the Ring was about to encounter a teenager - just renamed by himself as "Billy Bonney" - whom the world would not forget. He would thrust them into the glare of insatiable curiosity about his life and death, until their atrocities were common knowledge. And on August 17, 1877, his trajectory was a mad dash from Arizona Territory to New Mexico Territory on a stolen racehorse after his self-defense killing of Frank "Windy" Cahill. He may have heard of Jessie Evans and his boys: Santa Fe Ring thugs. By that September, he would be riding with them and for the Ring as just another gunman.

CHAPTER 11

LINCOLN COUNTY'S SANTA FE RING "TROUBLES"

THE RING'S MOST GRUESOME LAND-GRAB

SUMMARY: After emerging unscathed from Colfax County War exposés, Catron and his Ringite minions were emboldened for take-over of gigantic Lincoln County for cattle raising, mercantile monopoly, and supply contracts to Fort Stanton and the Mescalero Indian Reservation. In place were his agents at "The House," his Pecos Cow Camp, and the Reservation; as were rustlers supplying cattle for his beef contracts and for his new Carrizozo Land and Cattle Company. Competition from British mercantile and ranching settler, John Henry Tunstall, seemed insignificant given proven elimination tactics. That underestimation of citizens' resistance would make the Ring descend deeper into atrocities and treason to exert its will. And it would encounter its most dangerous adversary, Billy Bonney.

After weathering the 1877 Colfax County War exposures, and now confident of complicity of President Rutherford B. Hayes and Secretary of the Interior Carl Schurz, T.B. Catron's next land-grab was 30,000 square mile (19,200,000 acre) Lincoln County, then the largest in the United States and its Territories. It constituted the southeast quarter of the Territory, equaling a combined Massachusetts, Connecticut, Vermont, Rhode Island, and Delaware. Catron's Ring was evolving to from land-grab to land use for cattle, and to mercantile endeavors. But his gluttonous goal was still monopoly - owning and controlling everything.

To avoid incriminating Catron in horrors to come, his loyalist and deceptive biographer, Victor Westphall, fabricated that the upcoming strife was a mere local conflict of "McSween and his adherents" and "the Murphy-Dolan cause" with "[e]conomic considerations ... the determining factor in the factional alignments." (Westphall, p. 78)

CATRON'S LINCOLN COUNTY INVOLVEMENT

Victor Westphall inadvertently incriminates Catron in the next anti-Ring rebellion by providing his economic links to Lincoln County, which gave his motives for eliminating John Tunstall. As discussed, Catron, from his 1866 arrival, dealt in military beef contracts. Westphall dates his Lincoln County involvement to at least 1868 by receipts he kept, signed by Lawrence Murphy for merchandise from C. Brown & Co. of Santa Fe. (Westphall, p. 74) That linked Catron to Fort Stanton's beef suppliers, Emil Fritz and Lawrence Murphy, then operating their sutler store as L.G. Murphy and Company. At the Fort were also other future Ringites: store employee and future partner, James Dolan, and then-Major and future Lincoln County Sheriff, William Brady.

Catron was the likely silent partner in that company in 1873, when its partners were expelled from Fort Stanton and proceeded to build Lincoln County's biggest adobe structure nine miles away in the town of Lincoln, as a two-story general store and post office, nick-named "The House," on a 40 acre property. Philip Rasch, in the 1997 compilation, *Gunsmoke in Lincoln County*; stated: "U.S. district attorney Thomas B. Catron, head of the Santa Fe Ring and president of the First National Bank of Santa Fe, [was a] financial backer of Dolan and Company." (Rasch, p. 56) And the enriched Lincoln builder of "The House" was future Ringite Lincoln County War Sheriff, George Peppin.

Westphall was able to document Catron's loans to "The House" from 1876; writing: "Catron loaned money to the Murphy firm and to Lawrence G. Murphy personally." (Westphall, p. 79) That year, with Murphy ailing, John Riley became Dolan's partner and "cattle dealer" for "The House" - then renamed J.J. Dolan Co. (Westphall, p. 76)

Westphall also revealed Catron as silent owner of Dolan's supposed Pecos River Cow Camp (Westphall, p. 87), which held John Chisum's rustled cattle. Catron also controlled the Mescalero Indian Agent, Frederick Godfroy, for acceptance of "The House's" stolen cattle, shoddy hay, and mealy flour.

Connection to Godfroy was through Blazer's Mill-based David Easton, "Catron's agent, representing him in business interests in the area;" according to a complaint cited by Fort Stanton's Commander, N.A.M. Dudley, about Catron's and Easton's inferior supplies to Fort Stanton. (Westphall, p. 94)

David Easton was also an agent for Catron's other local "business interests": "a brewery located at Fort Stanton." (Westphall, p. 94) That "The House's" founders made that brewery when at their sutler store, again shows Catron's early connection. Intriguingly, the partners also ran a counterfeiting press in a nearby cave; making counterfeiting another possible early business of Catron's, and a possible inspiration for accusing Billy Bonney to the Secret Service in 1880 as a counterfeiter!

In the Lincoln County War, as a Justice of the Peace, David Easton served the Ring by writing false arrest warrants on May 30, 1878 outlawing McSweens for malicious prosecutions.

Westphall topped off Catron's local interests by stating that his brother-in-law, Edgar Walz, was also his agent there. Walz ran Catron's Carrizozo Land and Cattle Company ranch, which, Westphall relates, was obtained from dying Lawrence Murphy to settle his debt to Catron. (Westphall, p. 81) Implied is Catron's massive money-lending to "The House" and Murphy, since the ranch was 20 square miles (12,800 acres).

By January of 1878, Catron finally emerged from his shadowy relationship with "The House," then bankrupting from Tunstall's competition. Westphall states: "On January 12, 1878, James J. Dolan and John H. Riley executed a mortgage deed conveying to Catron forty acres of land in Lincoln together with their house, store [collectively "The House"], and all personal property, including a herd of about 2,000 cattle at Seven Rivers. The loan from Catron had been needed to pay Spiegelberg brothers [suppliers] in Santa Fe." (Westphall, p. 81)

That transaction further revealed Catron's presence. It was conducted in Lincoln by his law partner, William T. Thornton. (Westphall, p. 82) Catron then put Edgar Walz, in charge of "The House." (Westphall, p. 81) So when Tunstall was murdered on February 18, 1878, "The House" was Catron's! This was no local mercantile competition!

To protect his corrupt Lincoln County interests, Catron needed a Ring-beholden Governor. Westphall cites S.B. Axtell's May of 1876 "loan" of $1,800 as being from John Riley (Westphall, p. 78); omitting that as a "House" partner Riley was Catron's agent, it was half of Axtell's salary, and it yielded his illegal proclamations shielding of Tunstall's Ringite murderers from prosecution.

But Westphall, having inadvertently given Catron's Lincoln County holdings, agents, and motives, concluded unconvincingly:

"If one examines the record of [Catron's] affairs in that time and place objectively, it can be seen that he does not fit well the role of conniving manipulator that tradition has assessed to him. Furthermore, there is little reasonable basis for claiming in the pages of history that he supported partisan intervention in the quarrel. He owned property there and wanted it protected." (Westphall, p. 96)

And Catron-style protection was malicious prosecutions and murders, if needed. Enforcers were in place with Sheriff William Brady, District Attorney William Rynerson, and Judge Warren Bristol. The Seven Rivers rancher-rustlers were available for violence, as were rustling outlaw gangs of Jessie Evans and John Kinney. And only nine miles from Lincoln, the county seat, was Fort Stanton with its Ring-biased Commander, George Purington.

LINCOLN COUNTY "TROUBLES"

There existed no Lincoln County "troubles," if that meant generalized outlawry. Actual troubles were years of citizens' victimization by the Ring's monopolistic aggression. Catron-backed L.G. Murphy and Co. oppressed cash-strapped locals with supplies sold on usurious credit, while underpaying them for their farming produce. In 1875, Robert Casey, cattle ranching on the Hondo River, was murdered by Ring thug Willie Wilson in Lincoln immediately after he won an election against Lawrence Murphy. A month later, Juan Patrón, Lincoln's anti-Ring Hispanic leader, was crippled in attempted assassination by John Riley.

But, by 1877, it was Catron who had "troubles."

In Lincoln, near "The House," recent British settler, John Henry Tunstall, had built his own large general store and bank, whose fair dealings were bankrupting "The House." His two cattle ranches, watered by the west-to-east Feliz and Peñasco Rivers, controlled grazing land all the way to the north-to-south Pecos River. He had used his employees, like Billy Bonney, to homestead land on the Peñasco River, after buying another ranch there from Jacob Basil "Billy" Matthews. So by 1878, Catron's dream of mercantile and cattle monopolies for government contracts was vaporized.

And Tunstall was one of the few people in the Territory with considerable cash through his wealthy British father's investment plan; so he could compete aggressively. In a fair market, Tunstall would have won. Magnifying risk to Catron was high-minded Lincoln Attorney Alexander McSween, who knew Ring crimes after working for "The House" from 1875 to 1876, and was inspiring Tunstall's anti-Ring fervor.

Tunstall was also poised to take over the Ring's contracts, as he and McSween exposed "The House's" Fort Stanton and Mescalero Indian Reservation supply scams. In 1878, their complaint triggered Department of Interior Investigator E.C. Watkins's investigation, which showed that Indian Agent Godfroy was giving Reservation supplies, like blankets, to "The House;" and accepting rustled beef from John Kinney. Godfroy was also billing for 1,500 hundred Apaches, while a few hundred were present.

Catron was also having "troubles" with his cattle rustling victim, John Chisum. A cattle king, with herd of 80,000 along the Pecos River, he had been elevated to President of Tunstall's bank.

There was only one solution: eliminate Tunstall.

RINGITE OUTLAWING OF ADVERSARIES

So Catron's gave his Lincoln County competition "troubles." Westphall advanced Catron's outlaw myth, which would echo through time as pseudo-history. Besides trivializing conflict to local mercantile competition, Westphall claimed lawlessness: "Far removed from more settled sections of the Territory, law here became largely what the residents made it." (Westphall, p. 75)

So Alexander McSween becomes "ambitious and aggressive;" and his 1876 quitting as "The House's" attorney to reject its corruption, is called "conflict with Murphy." (Westphall, p. 77) Fabricated is his owning Tustall's store and bank: "But [McSween] was not content merely to practice law ... He started a bank and opened a store to challenge Murphy's trade monopoly. Chisum probably supplied the financial backing for the store. McSween was jealous of Murphy's economic and political power and sought to replace him as a leader in the community. His methods were contentious." (Westphall, p. 77)

John Chisum - Tunstall's ally, president of his bank, and Ring cattle ranching competitor - becomes an "outlaw," because Catron, as U.S. Attorney, had prosecuted Chisum since 1875. (Westphall, p. 77) Omitted is its being malicious prosecution; with Chisum being arrested for fictitious debts in 1877 - along with McSween - and put in the Las Vegas jail.

John Tunstall becomes an "outlaw," by Westphall fabricating a dishonest partnership with McSween. This repeated Catron's malicious prosecution plot to entangle Tunstall in the fake McSween embezzlement case. So Westphall lies: "[T]unstall had earlier met Alexander A. McSween in Santa Fe, and they now became closely allied in business. Tunstall furnished financial backing that enabled McSween to make more extensive inroads in the financial monopoly that had been enjoyed by L.G. Murphy & Co. Tunstall ... did not scruple at sharp business practices along the way ... [He] was a foreigner who even wrote home about his machinations." (Westphall, p. 79)

On Westphall's Lincoln County "outlaw" list, is, of course, "Billy the Kid," called leader of the "forces." Westphall wrote: "McSween, when the indictment for embezzlement was returned against him, hired gunmen to protect himself from arrest. Among those was Billy the Kid, who became the leader of the McSween forces." (Westphall, p. 80)

This, in Victor Westphall's fiction, Lincoln County divided along partisan lines with Chisum joining villain McSween, and good-hearted Murphy-Dolans using "smaller sheep and cattle growers to whom they had been generous in extending credit" (Westphall, p. 80); omitting that those "growers" were Catron's beholden and murderous Seven Rivers rancher-rustlers.

So, without their knowing, Lincoln County citizens' fight would not only be for freedom, but for truth. And they were destined to lose both.

HERO IN WAITING

Just a recent ranch hand for John Tunstall, and a homeless drifter on the run from an unresolved Arizona murder and earlier Silver City robbery, teenaged Billy Bonney would be converted to his and McSween's anti-Ring cause, while accidentally becoming the opponent able to break the Ring - in life, or after his killing.

When he began employment with Tunstall in October of 1877, 17 year old Billy likely exceeded his compatriots in appraising their enemy, since in the two months before hiring, he had befriended Ringite Seven Rivers men, had ridden with Ring outlaw Jessie Evans and his gang, and had likely encountered James Dolan: all future Lincoln County War adversaries.

There was more. By late 1877 or early 1878, Billy had met the Maxwell family in Fort Sumner; and the teenaged daughter of Lucien and Luz Maxwell, Paulita, became his secret sweetheart. So he must have heard first-hand from them about Catron's and Elkins's *de facto* theft of their Land Grant, their exile to desolate Fort Sumner, and Lucien's early death after his traumatic losses.

So Billy would have had a measure of Ring crimes exceeding other Lincoln County fighters. And, but for a quirk of fate - his meeting kind and honest John Tunstall - he would have fought for the Ring side in the ensuing conflict.

In fact, Billy was so charismatic and competent that the Ring tried to keep him. After the Lincoln County War, James Dolan courted him in a "peace meeting" in Lincoln. (It ended unexpectedly with the murder of anti-Ring Attorney Huston Chapman - with Billy as witness.) So even after the War, Billy could have returned to the Ring's fold where the prospects were prosperity and safety.

But Billy again rejected the Ring. Instead he would request a pardon from new Governor Lew Wallace to remove the Ring's prosecutory power over himself, and to continue his anti-Ring fight, becoming the Ring's most dangerous enemy.

LINCOLN COUNTY SUB-BOSSES

"The House" began in near murder. James Dolan, the savage hooligan clerk for Emil Fritz and Lawrence Murphy, had become enraged that 9th Cavalry Captain James F. Randlett had exposed their corruption as Mescalero Indian Reservation quasi-agents in a July 22, 1873 complaint to the Adjutant General; writing:

I came to this Post with my Troop in April 1872. I found the tradership of the Post in the hands of L.G. Murphy & Co. (Indian traders) and their prices for goods sold to enlisted men extortionate almost to robbery. These parties have also been engaged in supplying the Indians supposed to be on this [Mescalero] Reservation; I soon became convinced they were swindling the Government in the matter outrageously. As a Troop's Captain I complained of the prices for goods sold to my men. As an officer of the Government ... I have spoken freely of my condemnation of which I have every reason to believe of the dishonesty of their transactions connected to the supplies furnished to the Indians and I believe it is generally understood that I have no better opinion of their place than that it is a den of infamy ...

[O]ne officer of the Army told me that Murphy has said he would kill me, another that so mighty was the power of the firm that they could get false testimony enough to deprive me of my Commission as an officer. Murphy I am told ... has said that if he could not have his way in feeding the Indians [the beef contract] he would put them on the Warpath [likely with his supplying illegal whiskey to them from his brewery] ... [A]nd one of their employees 'Dolan' I believe said that he would put on a breech cloth and lead the Apaches against me." (Nolan, *Life and Death of John Henry Tunstall* p. 186)

Dolan and Murphy were arrested. But Randlett learned the hard way about the Ring's existence. Likely intervention by Catron as U.S. Attorney, got Dolan's and Murphy's charges dropped, and Randlett charged instead!

So Ringite tactics had procured the foothold in Lincoln. With addition of John Riley as a partner, the Ring's sub-bosses were ensconced. Their sutler store employee, Fort Stanton Major, William Brady, was soon their enforcer as Sheriff. And their store's builder, George Peppin, would get that office too, but by improper Proclamation of Ringite Governor S.B. Axtell.

ABOUT JOHN HENRY TUNSTALL

SUMMARY: John Tunstall was a new type of Ring opponent: an economic competitor with cash for investments in stores and ranches. His idealism and Ring murder martyrdom converted his teenaged delinquent ranch hand, Billy Bonney, to the anti-Ring cause in their 4½ month relationship. And that martyrdom would galvanize a war.

AN INNOCENT COMES TO SATAN'S PARADISE

In the fall of 1876, Lincoln attorney, Alexander McSween, convinced wealthy young Englishman, John Henry Tunstall, to come to Lincoln County to expand his family's mercantile business. McSween had his own agenda. Almost a Presbyterian minister, coming from St. Louis in 1875, he worked as

"The House's" attorney until quitting in 1876 because of their repellant corruption. He kept his legal practice in Lincoln, where he owned building plots. Like Colfax County's Reverend Franklin Tolby, he became anti-Ring. He realized that bringing rich Tunstall to cash-poor Lincoln, could break the Ring's monopoly.

By 1877, Tunstall had built, on the northeast side of Lincoln's only street, a single-story building housing his store, bank, and personal apartment; just a quarter mile from "The House." He had made John Chisum his bank's president. Under the Desert Land Act, he had gotten about 4,000 acres of ranchland along Lincoln County's Feliz and the Peñasco Rivers; thus controlling miles of grazing land by access to its only water. And McSween built a large house: a two-wing structure for himself and his wife, Susan, on one side; and the other side for his brother-in-law and law partner, David Shield, husband of Susan's sister, Elizabeth, with their five children. There, McSween and Shield also made their law office, with Shield's law student, Harvey Morris, added.

Tunstall planned to wrest from "The House" its beef and flour traderships; while, at the same time, waging a newspaper campaign starting with exposé of Lincoln County Sheriff William Brady's embezzlement of tax money to buy cattle for the Ring.

Historian Frederick Nolan's 1965 biography, *The Life and Death of John Henry Tunstall*, reprinted Tunstall's affectionate letters to his London family, revealing that he lacked cynicism to recognize the lethal evil in "Satan's Paradise."

Born March 6, 1853 in England to John Partridge Tunstall and Emily Ramie Tunstall, he adored his three sisters, Emily Frances, Lillian, and Mabel, whom he nicknamed his "Trinity": "Minnie," "Jack," and "Punch." And he whimsically addressed his father as "Beloved Governor." They lived at prosperous 7 Belsize Terrace in London; and owned the mercantile business Turner, Beeton and Tunstall in Victoria, British Columbia.

Though he did not mention Billy in his letters home, Tunstall, poignantly blind in his right eye, must have offered to that rough teenager a revelation of gentle and vulnerable goodness, becoming a father-figure and inspiration. One can experience the Tunstall, who inspired Billy, from his letters.

On June 12, 1876, Tunstall, seeking business opportunities, wrote home from California: "*My desire is for wealth, that I may have the means of smoothing the path of life for Old Min & our two pets, & in fact of doing for them, as you, my much Beloved Governor, would have them done by ... I look ahead & anticipate the hardships (as they are called) somewhat as a sailor does, but I have no fear, but that the ship will stand it alright; & I have great faith in the captain."* (Nolan, p. 133)

By June 17, 1876, Tunstall wrote from the San Louis Obispo, California, ranch of a Robert Flint, who pointed him toward New Mexico, but warned about dangers of "the ring": "*He says the American population is very small, that the people are very poor ...* **He says the politics are in the hands of a ring who control things as they like.** *According to his account, there are very few sheep & cattle there. He says that as soon as I go there, everyone will know my business, that it is 'a rare field full of razors' ... He ... advised me to get posted on cattle.*" (Nolan, pp. 137-138)

On August 15, 1876, Tunstall arrived in Santa Fe, and wrote home to "Much Beloved Governor" about investing seven thousand pounds of family money to be recovered future earnings. He misconstrued the "ring" as just political; and threat of "smelling powder" was as unreal and amusing as in a dime novel. He wrote: "*This is the first place I have been in which everyone goes armed, all the men have a great "six shooter" slung on their hip, & a knife on the other as counterpoise ... [But he did not see himself as having to use a gun.] That sort of experience & adventure depends somewhat upon a man's disposition & habits & the places he frequents; a man who gambles & drinks is very apt to be 'that, or thar abouts' when any shooting takes place, as he belongs to the shooting crowd & will be with his crowd;* **but a man who attends to his own business only & above everything else does not figure in politics may live in this country a great while without smelling powder.**" (Nolan, p. 155)

By October 28, 1876, to "Much Beloved Governor," Tunstall described his first meeting with Attorney Alexander McSween: "*There is a very nice young fellow here just now from Lincoln County, a lawyer by profession, who has the outward appearance of an honest man, (Herlow [owner of Santa Fe's Herlow Hotel, where Tunstall was staying in his New Mexico visit] speaks highly of him) he has been trying to persuade me to go into stock & not buy land but I have seen too much of California to do so unless I am obliged. But I must say his plan has a great deal to recommend it.*" (Nolan, p. 180)

Though it did not occur to Tunstall that the Ring tolerated no opposition, his family were more realistic. On March 9, 1877, to "Much Beloved Father," he responded to their concerns:

As regards my getting shot, I don't expect it. There are two very prolific causes for shooting in this country, viz., drink and jealousy. I don't frequent the locality of the former ... & I don't make myself an object for the excitement of the latter ... I have a presentment that I shall not get killed but that I shall live to accomplish my schemes & will give those three Pets such a time as will make their heads swim (as we say on the frontier).

[AUTHOR'S NOTE: Tunstall next blithely refers to the Ring, thinking their shenanigans mere humorous caricatures of greed.]

The whole of this country (New Mexico) is under the control of a ring composed of two or three lawyers ... & their practices & power throughout New Mexico are quite astonishing ... I will give you just an instance; they passed a law, in the legislature, allowing a man to defend himself in court through an attorney without appearing in person. At the sitting then, of all the courts, men who had been in the graves a dozen years or more were indicted, summoned for various causes, one of the ring defended the case, & another, who was the public prosecutor, received $20 for his services to the Territory, which of course, belonged to the ring. This is ... but a sample of their most innocent means of making money. (Nolan, pp. 200-201)

On March 23, 1877, he described putting money into the First National Bank at Santa Fe (leaving Catron privy to his plans):

I shall acquire property, which in the event of my death you could recover every cent of ...

[And] groceries in this country, realize a profit of 50 percent on the return & they are a cash item ... In the third place, the Mexican is a "borrowing" animal ... but unlike most borrowers, he will pay willingly as soon as it is in his power ... Now ... what scheme, if practicable, would catch the ready money of the Indian department & the Army, & avoid the dangers of too many debtors ... The first part of the question is simple to answer; by having hay, beef, corn or flour raised within the district, Uncle Sam is compelled to patronize you ... All the fixtures necessary to run my store will be a desk, a scale, & a safe, & I should need all of these if I had nothing but a cattle ranch. (Nolan, pp. 205-207)

Tunstall's 24th birthday was on March 6, 1877; he would not make his 25th. On April 27, 1877, to "Much Beloved Father," he prattled about "rings." As self-styled "adventurer," he called a "ring" a way to do business; so gave his own plan:

> [Y]ou would very likely think that I must be crazy to talk about making money in this country at all; Everything in New Mexico, that pays at all (you may say) is worked by a "ring," there is the "Indian ring," the "army ring," "the political ring," the "legal ring," the "Roman Catholic ring," the "cattle ring," the "horsethieves ring," the "land ring," and half a dozen other rings; **now to make things stick "to do any good," it is necessary to either get into a ring or to make one out for yourself. I am at work at present making a ring & have succeeded admirably so far;** you see, an adventurer like myself does not present a very formidable aspect when "in the ring," but anyone as well posted as myself can very nearly break up an incipient ring single-handed, by skirmishing on the outskirts ...
>
> I propose to confine my operations to Lincoln County, but I intend to handle it in such a way as to get the half of every dollar that is made in the county by anyone; & with our means we could get things in that shape in three years if we only used two thirds of our capital in the undertaking. (Nolan, p. 213)

So guilelessly, he overlapped Ring enterprises with his store, ranches, and plans. And with British proclivities as a gentleman, he also bought fine horses, and became attached to them. That last idiosyncrasy would be the immediate cause of his death.

THE RING STRIKES BACK

With stock harassment already employed in the Colfax County War to force flight of settlers, the Ring used Jessie Evans's gang to steal Tunstall's horses and mules. Tunstall described that in his letters home of November 29, 1877 and January 9, 1878, which go back to September 29, 1877. (Nolan, pp. 243-249) He responded with amusement to Jessie's calling him "The Englishman;" though he realized the gang was *"incited [by] some people we know very well ... & whose business I have very nearly taken away"*: i.e., the Ring. He tells of his men's post-theft capture of the gang; and that

"*Jesse Evans says he can't tell how he failed to hit Dick [Brewer, Tunstall's foreman] as he had three fair, square shots at him & he was saving his shots for him alone.*" As gaily, he quoted Lincoln County's Justice of the Peace John "Squire" Wilson: "*Well, Englishman, they seem bound to drive you out of the country.*" Having about a month left on earth, he had written:

> *My horses, 2 of them, & a pair of magnificent mules that I own had been stolen by some desperados named Jesse Evans & Frank Baker who belong to & are at the head of a very numerous band (100 men in all) that raid on stock in this country ... They had, it appears, threatened to kill McSween & Brewer & "That Englishman" on sight,* **they were incited to make these threats by some people we know very well, against whom McS[ween] is bringing a lawsuit [part of the Emil Fritz estate resolution], with whom Brewer has had difficulty about a ranch [Murphy and Dolan sold him his ranch without having its title, and McSween told Brewer], & whose business I have very nearly taken away.** (Nolan, p. 243)

[AUTHOR'S NOTE: Tunstall next describes giving his men carbines, one likely Billy's Winchester '73, which he later retrieved from Brady's body, after Brady's confiscation of it on February 20, 1878, and after Tunstall's murder.]

> *I had a case of carbines in just before they left [Brewer and his men, including Billy] & they each carried one of them, they are the finest weapon manufactured & you bet there was no discount on the way those boys could handle them.* (Nolan, p. 249)

By November 7, 1877, Tunstall faced usual Ringite obstruction of justice to shield members. Thus, Jessie Evans and his gang, arrested for his horse and mule theft and held in Lincoln's pit jail, were abetted in escape by Sheriff Brady. And Brady tried a "Dear Ben-style plot" to incite violence to justify killing by accusing Tunstall of aiding that escape - as told by McSween in his June 6, 1878 deposition to Investigator Angel (with McSween then only 44 days before his own Ring murder). McSween stated: "*A few days afterward [following the Evans gang's escape] Sheriff Brady came to Tunstalls store in a half intoxicated condition and indirectly accused Mr Tunstall of giving the credit of the arrest of said outlaws to R.M. Brewer (now deceased) and accused*

Mr Tunstall of having tried to aid Baker, Evans, Hill & Davis to escape. Mr. Tunstall told him you know their shackles are filed, & there are holes cut in the logs and take no pains to secure them, and do you dare to accuse me who have aided in the arrest of these persons, who have threatened my life, with assisting them to escape. Sheriff Brady thereupon put his hand on his revolver as though he was going to draw it and I stepped between them and placing my hand on his shoulder said it ill becomes you as a peace officer to violate the law by shooting. **Brady replied I won't shoot you now, you haven't long to run** ... and then left the store."

MALICIOUS PROSECUTION OF ALEXANDER McSWEEN

By late 1877, Catron ramped up his attacks to malicious prosecution. His diabolically convoluted plot used as its hook Tunstall's friend, Alexander McSween, as the attorney attempting collection of the $10,000 life insurance policy of "House" partner, Emil Fritz, who had died intestate in Germany in 1874. McSween represented the heirs, including Fritz's local siblings, Charles Fritz and Emilie Scholand. But the dishonest policy holder withheld payment, necessitating litigation in New York, and depleting the sum, after costs and his fees, to less than $7,000. But for due diligence, he delayed payment to seek German heirs. And he awaited the Probate Court's decision on James Dolan's fraudulent claim that Fritz's estate owed "The House" $76,000.

But McSween was unaware that Charles Fritz was under Ring control by mortgage of his ranch near Lincoln; or that Dolan, District Attorney William Rynerson, and Judge Warren Bristol were poised to attack him. On December 21, 1877, Charles Fritz's sister, Emilie Scholand, was manipulated by Dolan and Rynerson into filing an embezzlement complaint with Judge Bristol, claiming McSween had stolen their policy money.

Victor Westphall inadvertently removed Catron's frontmen, Rynerson and Bristol, to reveal him as that complaint's prime mover; though he garbled the case as the heirs contacting Lawrence Murphy about McSween's high collection fees: "Murphy **retained Catron** and William L. Rynerson to recover the money. These attorneys obtained a judgment against McSween ... McSween refused to pay the judgment, and his property was attached. Tunstall's holdings were also attached on the representation that he had an interest in McSween's affairs." (Westphall, p. 80)

On December 25, 1877, as U.S. Attorney, Catron advanced the malicious prosecution. Knowing that McSween and his wife, Susan, along John Chisum, were leaving to St. Louis, Missouri, for business, he alleged that McSween was absconding with the money, and got a warrant from Bristol to arrest him. He also got Chisum arrested as reneging on loans (as Chisum wrote in his Memoir from jail (see page 63).) Both were seized in Las Vegas by the San Miguel County Sheriff. McSween's arrest warrant stated:

Territory of New Mexico)
Third Judicial District)

The Territory of New Mexico to the Sheriff or any constable of the County of San Miguel in said Territory.
Whereas Emily Scholand has made complaint to me on oath that she is informed and verily believes that Alexander McSween has committed the crime of embezzlement by **embezzling and commuting to his own use the sum of ten thousand dollars** *belonging to the estate of Emil Fritz deceased at the County of Lincoln in said Territory on the tenth day of December in the year A.D. 1877. Now therefore you are hereby commanded to arrest the said Alexander McSween forthwith and bring him before me in the Third Judicial District of said Territory together with this writ that he may be dealt with according to law.*

Given under my hand at
Mesilla County of Dona Ana
Territory of New Mexico this 21st day of
December A.D. 1877.
Warren Bristol
District Judge

McSween and Chisum were jailed in Las Vegas. McSween was then transported to Lincoln by honest and brave Deputy Sheriff Adolph Barrier, who, knowing McSween risked Ring murder, kept him in personal custody as he awaited his hearing. But crafty John Chisum stayed in the remote Las Vegas jail to wait out the Ring's inevitable violence.

TUNSTALL EXPOSES THE RING

On January 18, 1878, Tunstall joined the fray as a "taxpayer's" "duty" by attacking the Ring in an editorial titled "A Tax-payer's Complaint," in January 26, 1878's *The Mesilla Valley Independent*. With his usual wry humor, he must have been amused that the real embezzler was local lawman: Sheriff Brady. Tunstall wrote:

FROM LINCOLN COUNTY:

A Tax-Payer's Complaint

Office of John H. Tunstall,
Lincoln, Lincoln Co., N.M.,
January 18, 1878

"THE PRESENT SHERIFF OF LINCOLN COUNTY HAS PAID NOTHING DURING HIS PRESENT TERM OF OFFICE"
Governor's Message for 1878

Editor of the Independent:
The above extract is a sad and unanswerable comment on the efficiency of Sheriff Brady, and cannot be charged upon "croakers." Major Brady, as the records of this County show, collected over *Twenty-five hundred dollars*, Territorial funds. Of this sum Alex. A. McSween Esq, of this place, paid him over *Fifteen hundred dollars* by cheque on the First National Bank of Santa Fe, August 23, 1877. Said cheque was presented for payment by John H. Riley, Esq, of the firm of J.J. Dolan & Co. This last amount was paid by the last named gentleman to Underwood and Nash for cattle. Thus passed away over *Fifteen hundred dollars* belonging to the Territory of New Mexico.

With the exception of thirty-nine dollars, all the taxes for Lincoln County for 1877 were promptly paid as due.

Let not Lincoln County suffer the delinquency of one, two or three men.

By the exercise of proper vigilance the tax payer can readily ascertain what has become of that he has paid for the implied protection of the commonwealth. It is not only his privilege but his duty. A delinquent tax-payer is bad; a delinquent tax collector is worse. J.H.T.

The potential danger to the Ring of Tunstall's complaint rested not as much in accusing a sheriff of tax money embezzling, but in identifying cattle rustlers, Underwood and Nash, as the recipients. Implied, thus, was input from his powerful anti-Ring ally, John Chisum, who knew about the Seven Rivers ranchers rustling from his giant herd. And Underwood and Nash were the end of an evidence chain which led to Catron, revealing his rustler-based sourcing of cattle, as fronted by "The House," his Carrizozo Land and Cattle Company, and his Pecos Cow Camp.

According to Patrick Dearen in his 2017 book, *A Cowboy of the Pecos*, Josiah "Joe" Nash was from Mississippi, then Texas, and had come to New Mexico Territory for the cattle business. He first partnered with relocated Texan, Nathan Underwood, near Seven Rivers. But by 1875, he had joined H.J. "Jim" Ramer in a cow camp with other Seven Rivers rustlers: Milo Pierce and Lewis Paxton. On April 10, 1877, Chisum's men had encountered Underwood with James Dolan herding Chisum cattle to Underwood's cow camp, presumably for "The House." (Nolan, *The West of Billy the Kid*. p. 74) Ringite Sheriff William Brady had refused to take action against them. So Tunstall (or Chisum) dated the Underwood-Nash partnership a bit late; even though they had revealed the big picture to the public.

Even Victor Westphall linked Catron to the "Tax-payers Complaint" scandal; writing: "Catron had paid the money on behalf of Brady with proceeds of Indian Department vouchers made out to John H. Riley and forwarded to the First National Bank in Santa Fe for deposit." (Westphall, p. 82)

Cover-up was needed. So James Dolan, on January 29, 1878, responded for the Ring in the Mesilla *Independent*. He stated:

Answer to a Tax-payer's Complaint.
Las Cruces, N.M.,
January 29, 1878
To the Editor of the Independent:

Dear Sir – In answer to a communication in reference to taxpayers of Lincoln County published in your issue of the 26th inst. and signed J.H.T., I wish to state that every thing contained therein is false. In reference to Sheriff Brady, I will state that he deposited with our house Territorial funds amounting to nearly $2,000 subject to his order and payable on demand. Owing to sickness in the family of Sheriff Brady he was unable to be in Santa Fe in time to settle his account with the Territory. This I hope will explain satisfactorily how the Gov. in his Message had our County (Lincoln) delinquent. If Mr. J.H.T. was recognized as a gentleman, and could be admitted into respectable circles in our community, he might be better posted on public affairs. For my part, I can't see the object of Mr. J.H.T.'s letter, unless it is to have the public believe that A.A. McSween is one of the largest tax-payers in our County, when in fact he is one of the smallest. Sheriff Brady is ready and willing at any time to show uneasy tax-payers what disposition he has made of the money paid by them; he can also show clean receipts from the Territorial treasurer of his account.

Respectfully,
J.J. Dolan.

Tunstall saw his "fight" as just an endurance game. On January 20, 1878, he asked for more money from home:

I have secured a beautiful cattle range & have it working on a most economical basis ... I have about 300 head [of cattle] & ought to get to work getting the rest as soon as possible, these would if bought right at cost about $12.00 per head, this foots up to $8,400.00. There are some lands yet that I want to buy & that we ought to have, as there is a fortune in them if secured in connection with what I have already got my claws into, that will cost something like 1500 (pounds) ... The longer I live & the more I see, the more I get confirmed in my land views. That I can make a fortune here I feel convinced if I only have strength enough to play the cards ... I won't give up or back down, as long as I can give another kick. (Nolan, p. 263)

On January 30th and 31st, 1878, Tunstall, with 18 days to live, he wrote his last letter to "Much Beloved Governor." He was then about to travel to Mesilla for the hearing under Judge Bristol for McSween's embezzlement case; not realizing it was a trap for him. But he was enjoying a new horse and learning Spanish. He wrote:

[Blind] Colonel, is, as I told you, a splendid saddle horse, I have got very much attached to him ... He will come when I call him, & follow me around as if he could see ...

I have of course by this time got well established, the Mexicans think that "El Englais" does not dress & put on quite as much style as they would do if they "Vale tanto" (were worth as much as he) "Perro es muy buen hombre, muy rico" (but he is a first rate man & very rich.) (Nolan, pp. 264-266)

TUNSTALL'S MALICIOUS PROSECUTION

Ignorant of Colfax County War exposés of corrupt Ringite Third Judicial District Judge Warren Bristol the year before, on February 4, 1878, Alexander McSween, with Deputy Adolph Barrier and law partner, David Shield, left for his embezzlement hearing with Bristol in Mesilla. Tunstall and Justice of the Peace John "Squire" Wilson accompanied them for support.

At the hearing, Bristol set the Ring's traps for assassination of McSween and Tunstall. To enable Sheriff Brady to take McSween into fatal custody, Bristol set bail of $8,000, with approval only by District Attorney Rynerson; who would refuse all bondsmen. To ensnare Tunstall, Bristol falsely declared him McSween's business partner, and, thus, also responsible for the debt.

He thereby ordered property attachment of both the allegedly embezzled sum of $10,000. Brady was to do the attachments - again in a "Dear Ben-style plot" to incite violence to justify murder.

Westphall revealed Catron as directly involved in the Bristol-Rynerson bondsman trap, by giving Catron's own intimidation of one of the bondsmen: José Montaño had "informed McSween of a threat made by Dolan - that, if Montano became surety for McSween's bond, he would have him persecuted by United States Attorney Catron for cutting timber on public land." (Westphall, p. 83) Westphall calls that Catron's duty, omitting that this obstruction would leave McSween in Brady's custody.

On February 8, 1878, Brady began attachments by ransacking McSween's Lincoln house. Tunstall's store, bank, apartment, and ranches were likewise invaded; though Brady's inventory sum far exceeded the required $10,000.

At the February 11, 1878 inventory at Tunstall's store, furious Billy Bonney almost tipped the balance to violence; though he was restrained by fellow Tunstall employee, Fred Waite, Billy's partner in his Peñasco River ranch.

McSween, to prove Rynerson's obstruction of his bondsmen, in his June 6, 1878 deposition to Frank Warner Angel, gave as Exhibit 15, Rynerson's outrageous rejection of a $35,500 bond for his $8,000 bail - Tunstall by then having been assassinated. McSween stated:

Territory of New Mexico)
County of Lincoln)

Before me the undersigned authority personally came and appeared on this the 9$\underline{th}$ day of February AD 1878 J.H. Tunstall, James West, John N. Copeland, Isaac Ellis, Francisco Romero y Valencia & Jose Montena [Montaño] whose names are signed to the above instrument of writing, who each having first by me duly sworn according to law upon his oath says that he is worth the amount set opposite to his name below in property situated within the Territory of New Mexico, over and above all his just debts and liabilities and property exempt by law from execution and forced sale.

J.H. Tunstall	20000\underline{00}$
James West	4000\underline{00}$
John N. Copeland	3000\underline{00}$
Isaac Ellis	4000\underline{00}$
Francisco Romero y Valencia	2000\underline{00}$
Jose Montena [Montaño]	1500\underline{00}$

Attest
Isaac Ellis
John B. Wilson

Sworn to and subscribed before me by [repeat of above names and sums].

Witness my hand and Notarial Seal
D.P. Shield
Notary Public

Endorsed

The within Bond is not approved for reasons as follows. Before approving the within Bond the surities must justify before the undersigned as I have reason to doubt that the surities for the most part are worth the amount set opposite their names ... Furthermore the death of one of the surities [Tunstall] who is a partner (said to be) of the principal somewhat complicates the matter.

W.L. Rynerson
Dist. Attny

McSWEEN'S ANTI-RING CRUSADE

McSween continued his anti-Ring crusade; and, knowing his innocence, assumed he would prevail in the upcoming Grand Jury. So on February 11, 1878, seven days before Tunstall's murder, he exposed "The House's" contracts to Secretary of the Interior Carl Schurz as Mescalero Indian Agent Frederick Godfroy's beef and flour frauds; thus, inadvertently exposing Catron, since Godfroy was his agent through David Easton, as discussed above. McSween wrote:

It looks as though the agent were the property of J.J. Dolan & J.H. Riley, known here as Dolan & Co. For the past two years these men have had the flour & beef contracts (as subcontractors I think) ... and have delivered articles unfit for use. Sprouted half rotten wheat has been mashed and turned in as first rate flour ... These fellows are also Indian traders. At their store they receive "surplus" by an underground railway process [selling the Indians' supplies in their store as received from Agent Godfroy].

The beef they furnish is of poorest quality ... They never kill the number reported nor do they feed the number of Indians they report ... I suggest you send a detective here who will ferret this matter; he'll find things as I have stated them. (Nolan, p. 266)

RYNERSON BACKS MURDER

Having failed to incite violence of Tunstall and McSween for "self-defense" murders (by Sheriff Brady), the Ring descended to an ambush murder mimicking Reverend Franklin Tolby's 2 years and 5 months earlier. The plot was given circumspectly by District Attorney William Rynerson in his secret, February 14, 1878 letter to John Riley and James Dolan, four days before Tunstall's murder. It was found by Alexander McSween, folded in Riley's pocket notebook, when Riley dropped it accidentally in his house after coming to proclaim innocence on the night of Tunstall's murder. To his fellow Ringites, Rynerson - the arrogant, sadistic, unpunished murderer of Chief Justice John P. Slough, 11 years earlier - had written:

LAW OFFICE OF
WILLIAM L. RYNERSON
District Attorney 3^d Judicial District, New Mexico

Las Cruces, N.M. Feby 14th 1878

Friends Riley & Dolan,
Lincoln N.M.

I have just received letters from you mailed 10th inst. Glad to know that you (Dolan) got home OK and that business was going on OK. If Mr Weidman [Tunstall employee Robert Widenmann] interfered with or resisted the Sheriff in Discharge of his duty Brady did right in arresting him, And any one else who does so must receive the same attention. Brady goes into the store in McS' place and takes his interest. Tunstall will have same right there he had heretofore but he neither must not obstruct the sheriff or resist him in the discharge of his duties. **If he tries to make trouble the Sheriff must meet the occasion <u>firmly</u> and legally.** *I believe Tunstall is in with the swindlers with the rogue McSween. They have the money belonging to the Fritz estate and they know it.* **It must be made hot for them all the hotter the better.** *Especially is this necessary now that it has been discovered that there is no hell.*

It may be that the villain <u>Green</u> "Juan Baptista" Wilson will play into their hands as Alcade. If so, he should be moved around a little. **Shake that McSween outfit up till it shells out and squares up, and then shake it out of Lincoln.** *I will aid to punish the scoundrels all I can. Get the people with you. Control Juan Patron if possible. You know how to do it. Have good men about to aid Sheriff Brady, and be assured that I shall help you all I can, for I believe there was never found a more scoundrely set than that outfit.*

Yours &c
W L Rynerson

TUNSTALL'S ASSASSINATION

On February 18, 1878, only 56 days after Catron began his malicious prosecution of McSween and Tunstall on December 25, 1877, he achieved Tunstall's murder by Sheriff Brady and his posse - including Jessie Evans's gang - by false claim that Tunstall was evading the embezzlement case attachment by herding his (actually exempt) horses to Lincoln from his Feliz River Ranch; though he was doing it simply to protect them. The Ring's urgency to kill likely resulted from the upcoming April 8, 1878 convening of the Lincoln County Grand jury, with likelihood of McSween's acquittal for embezzlement; thus, freeing Tunstall of legal harassments from the concocted "partnership." And it was obvious that intimidation had failed to force flight of him or McSween.

Separated from his fleeing men by Sheriff Brady's attackers, Tunstall died alone, just as had Franklin Tolby. It was an intentionally terrifying execution, with direct contact coupe de grâce exploding his skull with a circumferential fracture. In perverted mockery, his hat had been placed on his likewise murdered horse's head. Rumor later had the horse's severed tail rammed in his mouth; though, more plausibly, it was the horse's penis as desecration. And, like Tolby's corpse, Tunstall's was hidden to delay pursuit of his killers.

Westfall's fabricated murder version had Sheriff Brady's sending one deputy, William Morton. Omitted was that Morton was Catron's Pecos Cow Camp foreman; that the attachment was illegal; and that Brady's posse was actually huge, consisting of his deputies, and gangs of Seven Rivers men and Jessie Evans's boys. But Westphall admits that Catron was accused: "It was a cowardly murder probably planned by no one in advance, but it gave rise to much speculation, then and since, of a sinister plot involving not only Dolan and Riley, but also Sheriff Brady, United States Attorney Catron, and District Attorney Rynerson." (Westphall, p. 83)

The trauma to then 18 year old Billy Bonney was unimaginable. Collapsed after only 4½ months was his newfound "family" with its marvelous father figure and a future as a rancher on the Peñasco River. Ended forever was a life of normalcy.

Tunstall's Coroner's Jury Report was done on February 19, 1878. Billy began his testifying against the Ring that day, with an eye-witness affidavit, and likely evidence at the inquest also. The named murderers were Jessie Evans and his boys, Frank Baker and Thomas Hill; Deputy George Hindman; James Dolan, and William "Buck" Morton. From that list, Lincoln County Justice of the Peace John "Squire" Wilson generated arrest warrants.

But Catron was poised to repeat his 1875 obstruction of arrest of Franklin Tolby's Ringite killers. And for cover-up of motive, Ringite Fort Stanton surgeon, Dr. Daniel Appel, wrote a fraudulent autopsy report attributing Tunstall's split skull to thinning by venereal disease; which he fabricated as causing Tunstall's insane shooting first at posseman. But McSween countered that anticipated fakery by a legitimate autopsy by Lincoln's Dr. Taylor Ealy. The Coroner's Jury declared:

Territory of New Mexico)
County of Lincoln   )

We the undersigned Justice of the Peace and Coroners Jury who sat upon the inquest held this 19th day of February 1878 on the body of John H. Tunstall here found in precinct № 1 of the County of Lincoln, Territory of New Mexico find that the deceased came to his death on or about the 18th day of Feb'y 1878 by means of divers bullets shot and sent forth out of and from deadly weapons and upon the head and body of said John H. Tunstall which said deadly weapons were there and then held by one or more of the persons who are herewith written, to wit, Jessie Evans, Frank Baker, Thomas Hill, George Hindman, J.J. Dolan, William Morton, and others not identified before the Coroners Jury.

We the undersigned to the best of our knowledge & belief, from the evidence of the Coroners inquest believe the above statement to be a true and impartial verdict.

Geo B Barker
R.M. Gilbert
John Newcomb
Samuel Smith
Benj'n Ellis
John B. Wilson
    Justice of the Peace in and for precinct № 1,
        Lincoln County, Territory of New Mexico

A COLFAX COUNTY RESPONSE

Surprisingly, Colfax County turn-coat attorney, Frank Springer, sided with Lincoln County citizens, possibly reminded of his own near-murder in the 1876 "Dear Ben" plot. He attempted secret intervention with a new Lincoln resident.

Presbyterian missionary and doctor, Taylor Ealy, a nephew of Senator Rush Clark - likely attracted to living in Lincoln by McSween's plans to build a Presbyterian church and school there - had done Tunstall's autopsy and later moved his family into his apartment in the store. So Springer picked Rush Clark.

Springer's warning, written 51 days after Tunstall's homicide, prophetically describes immanent danger of "*the whole power of the Territorial government, strengthened by the active aid of the U.S. military forces,*" as he knew from Fort Union troops in his own murder attempt. And he called Tunstall's murder "*a deliberately planned assassination.*"

Sadly, by August 9, 1878, after the horrific Lincoln County War Battle (and possibly after being Ring-gifted the land for his future town of Springer), he retreated, denying to Investigator Angel knowledge of U.S. officials' guilt; thus, hiding his own statement to Rush Clark that: "***The republican party & a republican administration owes it to itself to see that such abuses are not perpetrated under its name.***" And a mystery remains: From whom was Springer getting his referenced "*mass of private information?*" And Rush Clark did nothing to stop the carnage to come anyway. Springer wrote:

<u>Confidential</u> Cimarron, N.M.
 Apr 9, 1878

Hon Rush Clark.
 My dear Sir:
 I hope you have received a full account of the Troubles in Lincoln County from your nephew [Taylor Ealy], whose statements, as a disinterested party, would be entitled to great weight. ***There is no doubt, in my mind, from a mass of private information I have received, that the whole power of the Territorial government, strengthened by the active aid of the U.S. military forces, has been either ignorantly or intentionally used to protect and assist a small***

combination of corrupt men – speculators in military and Indian contracts – against the best men in the county. That the men thus protected & aided by the govt. had in their employ members of a band of desperados, cattle thieves, highwaymen & murderers, who have infested that region for a long time to the terror of good citizens, and that J.H. Tunstall an estimable man, connected with a wealthy family in England, who has invested $15000 in business & proposed to invest $100,000 – was murdered by some of these very outlaws who were serving in the sheriffs <u>posse</u>, *attempting to seize Tunstall's private property for another man's debt. There is no doubt that the U.S. troops have been employed in a most illegal manner, to search private houses & arrest peaceable citizens without warrant.* **No effort has been made by the Territorial Governor, or the U.S. troops to arrest the murderers of Tunstall, but the governor by the President's authority, called upon the troops practically to protect them from arrest. Nobody doubts that his murder was a deliberately planned assassination.** *The people seem to be driven to desperation by these acts and scenes of violence have been enacted. I have no interest in the matter & no acquaintance with the principal actors, but I would like to see an end to wholesale crime in the Territory &* **would like to see the power of the U.S. Govt employed to punish & not to aid in protecting criminals.** *I believe the people there have done some wrong, but they have been crazed to see the murderers of Tunstall running at liberty under the protection of the authorities. I have sent you newspapers with reports of all the late doings there & most of it I believe to be reliable.* **The republican party & a republican administration owes it to itself to see that such abuses are not perpetrated under its name.**

Yours very truly
Frank Springer

CHAPTER 12

LINCOLN COUNTY GALVANIZES AGAINST THE SANTA FE RING

CHOOSING REVOLUTION

SUMMARY: Thomas Benton Catron had complacently believed Lincoln County would succumb to his Colfax County tactics of malicious prosecutions and assassination. The reverse happened, with the rise of the Regulator movement, which included the outraged Hispanic populace. Unexpected also was emergence of its charismatic symbol of militant zeal: Billy Bonney was entering the world stage.

T.B. Catron underestimated Lincoln County citizens and democracy's power when he had John Tunstall murdered. They recalled July 4, 1776's "Declaration of Independence": *"[W]hen a long train of abuses and usurpations, pursuing invariably the same Object evinces a design to reduce them under absolute Despotism, it is their right, it is their duty, to throw off such Government, and provide new Guards for their future security."*

So Tunstall's employees would unite for justice, calling themselves "Regulators." The long-exploited Mexican population identified with their cause, leaving the Ring to face an overdue Hispanic uprising, with San Patricio and Picacho men constituting most of the Lincoln County War Battle fighters. And Territory-wide, that Hispanic majority could have broken the Ring by votes or combat (as Ringite Governor Marsh Giddings had warned in 1872). Furthermore, a leader emerged: Alexander McSween.

Zealot Billy may have suggested the name from Edward L. Wheeler's dime novel: "The Deadwood Dick Library, A Tale of the Regulators and Road-Agents of the Black Hills, The Double Daggers; or, Deadwood Dick's Defiance" published by *Beadles Half Dime Library* in 1877. It proclaimed that "Regulators strike blows in defense of justice." It would be fitting if he got it from Tunstall's store in the brief 4½ months he worked for, and idolized, that man.

But a critical vulnerability was isolation. Residents knew about Catron's Ring, but not its power or past uprisings against it. They wrongly believed in protection from President Hayes, unaware of his Ring bias and S.B. Elkins's Washington influence. They never suspected local military alliance with the Ring. And they lacked a newspaper to give a voice to rebellion. But all was counterbalanced by their being the first New Mexico Territory citizens organizing to fight and to die for liberty and justice.

HISTORY OF THE REGULATORS

The original Regulators were 18th century American colonial, pre-Revolutionary War freedom fighters, extolled in song and dime novels. The Regulator movement began in North Carolina in 1771, five years before the "Declaration of Independence." Their fight, like Lincoln County's, was against corrupt public officials and lawmen.

The colonial Regulator movement's main historian is Marjoline Kars in her 2002's *Breaking Loose Together: The Regulator Rebellion in Pre-Revolutionary North Carolina*. There, public official elites conducted land-grabs. Poor homesteaders, working to purchase their land, relied on credit and payment by harvests, but were subjected to stolen titles and usurious interest. Pious pacifist activists first wrote the 1766 Sandy Creek Manifesto. By 1768, militant "Regulators" arose, inspired by 1765's Stamp Act protestors, the "Sons of Liberty," who opposed British taxation of stamped paper, including newspapers and legal documents.

North Carolina's counterpart of 1870's Ringite governors was Governor William Tryon, who dissolved the legislature's Assembly to block its delegates from attending New York City's Stamp Act Congress, which achieved the Act's repeal in 1766. Kars quotes Pauline Maier's 1991 book *From Resistance to Revolution*: "[There is] a particular strand of Anglo-American political thought which legitimated resistance by making it, like obedience, a cornerstone of the social contract. This contract rested on the notion that people could protect their liberties by transferring part of their power and sovereignty to government and abiding by that same government's just laws. When the authorities abused this trust and evaded the laws or passed oppressive ones, people were obliged to obtain relief by legal and peaceful means, such as petitions and elections. **But when such attempts were ignored, did not produce results, or were subverted by corrupt authorities, forceful popular resistance was deemed a civic duty crucial to the preservation of the public good.**" (Kars, p. 134)

Implicit in that democratic consciousness, was oppressed citizens' "expectation of freedom" (Kars, p. 120): seeing themselves as "Regulators ... not as enemies of government but as its true defenders." (Kars, p. 131) The Regulators' leader was Herman Husband, who wrote: "All we want is to be Governed by law, and not by the Will of officers, which to us is perfectly despotick and arbitrary." He added that such was merely "the iron hand of tyranny." (Kars, pp. 135, 152)

But North Carolina's injustice continued with tax collecting sheriffs repossessing property for resale at personal profit, with elections to the legislative Assembly corruptly controlled, and by courts threatening prosecution of contempt against protesters. And the despotic Assembly of 1768 appropriated 15,000 pounds to build a "palace" for Governor Tryon with poll and liquor taxes.

So, in 1768, the Regulators printed a public announcement that they would put their officials under "honester Regulation than they have been for some time past." (Kars, pp. 137-138)

Suppression by troops resulted. Colonel Edmund Fanning called Regulators outlaws in "defiance of law and contempt of authority." (Kars, p. 139) Governor Tryon wrote that the Regulators were "destroying the Peace of this Government, and the Security of its inhabitants" (Kars, p. 154), and briefly jailed their leader, Herman Husband. In trials, Fanning himself was convicted of extortion, but fined just one penny for each offense. (Kars, p. 159). And taxation to build Tryon's palace was approved.

In September, 1770, failure of peaceful redress yielded a Regulator skirmish in Hallborough. In response, Herman Husband was barred from the Assembly on fabricated libel charges. And the December 15, 1770 Johnston Riot Act was passed to allow military intervention if ten or more men refused to disperse in an hour after being ordered, making them chargeable as felons, with two charges punishable by execution. Herman Husband was imprisoned under that Riot Act and the libel charge, but was freed on February 7, 1771 by a grand jury.

The final fight was the May 16, 1771 Battle of Alamance where 2,000 leaderless Regulators, lacking ammunition, met 1,100 British troops with six swivel guns and two brass cannons. Three Regulators, sent to negotiate peace, were taken prisoner by Governor Tryon, who shot one dead in sight of the others. Then his army rampaged, destroying farms and crops of Regulators. Six prisoners were hanged at Hillsborough on June 19, 1771. A bounty was placed on Husband, dead or alive. And

Governor Tryon foreshadowed an Amnesty Proclamation over a century later by post-Lincoln County War Governor, Lew Wallace. It declared: "While the Piedmont population was thus intimidated and terrorized, Tryon issued a proclamation promising to pardon all Regulators who would ... promise to pay their taxes and obey all laws. He excluded outlawed Regulators and prisoners." (Kars, p. 204)

Some call the Battle of Alamance the American Revolution's first battle. Kars states: "**Regulators envisioned a world ... in which morality and economics would not be separate**." (Kars, p. 215)

Lincoln County Regulators may have heard the North Carolina Regulators' freedom song, eventually collected in 1947 in Arthur Palmer Hudson's "Songs of the Carolina Regulators":

> From Hillsborough town the first of May
> March'd those murdering traitors.
> They went to oppose the honest men
> That were called the Regulators. (Hudson, p. 146)

POLITICIZING OF BILLY BONNEY

After his mother's tuberculosis death in 1874, Billy Bonney had helplessly endured injustice of his stepfather's stealing their house and possessions, leaving him homeless at 14½. His rage manifested in a year of delinquency in Silver City, before he escaped jailing for robbery and burglary to flee to Arizona Territory. There, he escalated to stealing military horses and blankets; then to killing a man, likely in self defense, in a cantina altercation, resulting in his flight back to New Mexico Territory.

But John Tunstall's Ring murder crystallized a new identity for that teenager. Not only did he join the anti-Ring cause, but from the day after Tunstall's killing, he began risking his life to testify against Ringites; becoming the Ring's main gadfly; as epitomized in his pardon bargain with Lew Wallace *"as a witness against those that murdered Mr. Chapman."* By then, Billy could have galvanized another anti-Ring war.

FIRST LEGAL TESTIMONY

The day after Tunstall's February 18, 1878 murder, Billy's voice is first heard publicly. On February 19th, he gave an eye-witness affidavit to Justice of the Peace John "Squire" Wilson, along with Tunstall's foreman, Richard "Dick" Brewer, naming the killers as Sheriff Brady's possemen: "*James J. Dolan, Frank Baker, Jessie Evans, George Davis, A.H. Mills, W.S. Morton, [William] Moore, George Hindman, [Frank] Rivers, Pantaleon Gallegos, divers other persons unknown.*" It yielded Wilson's February 19th legal arrest warrants, stating:

> *Territory of New Mexico)*
> *County of Lincoln   )*
>
> *Be it remembered that before the undersigned Justice of the Peace in and for the County and Territory aforesaid, personally came R.M. Brewer & **W. Bonney** who being duly sworn according to law deposeth & saith that at the County and Territory aforesaid on the 18th day of February 1878 in and upon the [presence] of J.H. Tunstall, Robt A. Widenman[n], R.M. Brewer, **William Boney** [sic] & John Middleton, then and there in the Peace of the Territory an assault was made with divers deadly weapons to wit with Winchester Guns and Colts Revolvers, and divers other deadly weapons by James J. Dolan, Frank Baker, Jessie Evans, George Davis, A.H. Mills, W.S. Morton, [omitted first name] Moore, George Hindman, [Frank] Rivers, Pantaleon Gallegos, divers other persons unknown and did then and there as affiant believes wounded & killed J.H. Tunstall contrary to the statute in such case made and provided against the Peace & dignity of the Territory.*
>
> *R.M. Brewer*
William Bonney.

DEPOSITION ON TUNSTALL'S MURDER

On June 8, 1878, Billy next gave his eloquent deposition on John Tunstall's murder to Investigator Frank Warner Angel, with Justice of the Peace Wilson as witness. He was risking his life by coming to Lincoln after Governor Samuel Beach Axtell's outlawing of the Regulators, and after his own April Grand Jury indictments for the Brady, Hindman, and Roberts killings. He stated:

Territory of New Mexico)
County of Lincoln   )
)

    William H. Bonney was duly sworn, deposand says that he is a resident of said county, that on the 11th day of February A.D. 1878 he in company with Robt. A. Widenmann and Fred T. Waite went to the ranch of J. H. Tunstall on the Rio Feliz, that **he and said Fred T. Waite at the time intended to go to the Rio Peñasco to take up a ranch** *for the purpose of farming. That the cattle on the ranch of said J. H. Tunstall were throughout the County of Lincoln, known to be the property of said Tunstall; that on the 13th of February A.D. 1878 one J.B. Matthews claiming to be a Deputy Sheriff came to the ranch of said J.H. Tunstall in company with Jesse Evans, Frank Baker, Tom Hill and [Frank] Rivers, known outlaws who had been confined to the Lincoln County jail and had succeeded in making their escape, John Hurley, George Hindman, [Andrew] Roberts and an Indian aka Poncearo the latter said to be the murderer of Benaito Cruz, for the arrest of murderers of whom (Benaito Cruz) the Governor of this Territory offers a reward of $500. Before the arrival of said J.B. Matthews, deputy Sheriff, and his posse, having been informed that said deputy sheriff and posse were going to round up all the cattle and drive them off and kill the persons at the ranch, the persons at the ranch cut portholes into the walls of the house and filled sacks with earth, so that they, the persons at the ranch, should they be attacked or murder attempted, could defend themselves, this course being thought necessary* **as the sheriffs posse was composed of murderers, outlaws, and desperate characters none of whom has any interest at stake in the County, nor being residents of said County.** *That said Matthews when within about 50 yards of the house was called to stop and advance alone and state his business, that said Matthews after arriving at the ranch said that he had come to attach the cattle and property of A.A McSween, that* **said Matthews was informed that A.A. McSween had no cattle or property there**, *but that if he had he, said Matthews could take it. That said Matthews said that he thought some of the cattle belonging to R. M. Brewer whose cattle were also at the ranch of J.H. Tunstall, belonged to A.A. McSween, that said Matthews was told by said Brewer that he Matthews could round up the cattle and that he, Brewer, would help him. That said Matthews said that he would go back to Lincoln to get new instructions and if he came back to* the ranch he would come back with one man. That said Matthews and his posse were then invited by R.M. Brewer to come to the house to get something to eat.

Deponent further states that Robert A. Widenmann told R.M. Brewer and the others at the ranch, that he was going to arrest Frank Baker, Jesse Evans and Tom Hill said Widenmann having warrants for them. That said Widenmann was told by Brewer and the others at the ranch that the arrest could not be made because if it was made they, all the persons at the ranch would be killed and murdered by J.J. Dolan and their party. That said Evans advanced upon said Widenmann, said Evans swinging his gun and catching it cocked and pointed directly at said Widenmann. That said Jesse Evans asked said Widenmann whether he Widenmann, was hunting for him, Evans, to which Widenmann answered that if he was looking for him, he, Evans, would find it out. Evans also asked Widenmann whether he had a warrant for him; Widenmann answered that it was his (Widenmann's) business. Evans told Widenmann, that if he ever came to arrest him (Evans) he, Evans would pick Widenmann as the first man to shoot at, to which Widenmann answered that that was all right, that two could play at that game. That during the talking Frank Baker stood near said Widenmann, swinging his pistol on his finger, catching it full cocked pointed at said Widenmann.

The persons at the ranch were R. M. Brewer, John Middleton, G. Gayss [Gauss], M. Martz, R.A. Widenmann, Henry Brown, F.T. Waite, Wm McClosky and this deponent. J.B. Matthews after eating started for Lincoln with John Hurley and Ponceano the rest of the party or posse saying they were going to the Rio Peñasco. Deponent started to Lincoln with Robert A. Widenmann and F.T. Waite and arrived at Lincoln the same evening and again left Lincoln on the next day, February the 14th in company with the above named persons, having heard that said Matthews was going back to the ranch of said J.H. Tunstall with a large party of men to take the cattle and deponent and Widenmann and Waite arrived at said ranch the same day.

Deponent states that on the road to Lincoln he heard said Matthews ask said Widenmann whether any resistance would be offered if he Matthews returned to take the cattle, to which said Widenmann answered that no resistance would be offered if the cattle were left at the ranch but if an attempt was made to drive the cattle to the Indian Agency and kill them for beef as he, said Matthews had been heard to say would be done, he, said

Widenmann, would do all in his power to prevent this.

Deponent further says that on the night of the 17th of February A.D. 1878 J.H. Tunstall arrived at the ranch and informed all persons there that reliable information had reached him that J.B. Matthews was gathering a large party of outlaws and desperados as a posse and the said posse was coming to the ranch, the Mexicans in the party to gather up the cattle and the balance of the party to kill the persons at the ranch. It was thereupon decided that all persons at the ranch excepting G. Gauss, were to leave and Wm McClosky was that night sent to the Rio Peñasco to inform the posse who were camped there, that they could come over and round up the cattle, count them and leave a man there to take care of them and that Mr. Tunstall would also leave a man there to help round up and count the cattle and help take care of them, and said McClosky was also ordered to go to Martin Martz, who had left Tunstalls ranch when deponent, Widenmann and Waite returned to the town of Lincoln on the 13th of February and asked him said Martz to come to the ranch of said Tunstall and aid the sheriffs posse in rounding up and counting the cattle and to stay at the ranch and take care of the cattle.

Deponent left the ranch of said Tunstall in company with J.H. Tunstall, R.A. Widenmann, R.M. Brewer, John Middleton, F.T. Waite, said Tunstall, Widenmann, Brewer, Middleton and deponent driving the loose horses, Waite driving the wagon. Said Waite took the road for Lincoln with the wagon, the rest of the party taking the trail with the horses. **Deponent says that all the horses which he and the party were driving, excepting 3 had been released by sheriff Brady at Lincoln that one of these 3 horses belonged to R.M. Brewer, and the other was traded by Brewer to Tunstall for one of the released horses.**

Deponent further says, that when he and the party has traveled to within about 3 miles from the Rio Ruidoso he and John Middleton were in drag in the rear of the balance of the party as just upon reaching the brow of a hill they saw a large party of men coming towards them from the rear at full speed and that he and Middleton at once rode forward to inform the balance of the party of the fact. Deponent had not more than barely reached Brewer and Widenmann who were some 200 or 300 yards to the left of the trail when the attacking party cleared the brow of the hill and commenced firing at him, Widenmann and Brewer. Deponent, Widenmann and Brewer rode over a hill towards another which was covered with large rocks and trees in order to defend *themselves and make a stand. But the attacking party, undoubtedly seeing Tunstall, left off pursuing deponent and the two with him and turned back at the caño in which the trail was. Shortly afterwards we heard two or three separate and distinct shots and the remark was then made by Middleton that they, the attacking party must have killed Tunstall. Middleton had in the meantime joined deponent and Widenmann and Brewer. Deponent then made the rest of his way to Lincoln in company with Robt. A. Widenmann, Brewer, Waite and Middleton stopping on the Rio Ruidoso in order to get men to look for the body of J.H. Tunstall.*

Deponent further says that neither he nor any of the party fired off either rifle or pistol and that neither he nor the parties with him fired a shot.
William H. Bonney

LEGAL PURSUIT OF TUNSTALL'S KILLERS

A key factor in Lincoln County War history, is the lawman status of those pursuing Tunstall's killers - including Billy Bonney. That added urgency to the Ring's illegal outlawing of them to cover-up the legitimacy of their mission to apprehend the murderers, and the illegality of Sheriff Brady's refusal to do so.

DEPUTIZING OF TUNSTALL'S MEN

With Billy's and Brewer's affidavit, on February 20, 1878, Justice of the Peace Wilson made arrest warrants. After Sheriff Brady refused to serve them, Wilson concluded that *"there being then and there no officers to serve such warrant the undersigned as directed by law, in such cases specially empowered Richard H. Brewer to serve the same endorsing such deputation on said last mentioned warrant."* Wilson wrote:

The Territory of New Mexico)
County of Lincoln   )

I, John B. Wilson justice of the Peace in and for precinct N⁰ 1 Lincoln County, New Mexico, do hereby certify that on or about the 19th day of February 1878 **W. Boney** *[sic] and*

R.M. Brewer filed in my office affidavits charging John [James] J. Dolan, J. Conovair, Frank Baker, Jessie Evans, Tom Hill, George Davis, A. [Andrew] L. ["Buckshot"] Roberts, P. [Panteleon] Gallegos, T. Green, J. Awly, A.H. Mills, "Dutch Charley" proper name unknown, R.W. Beckwith, William Morton, [Deputy] George Hindman, J.B. Matthews and others with having murdered and killed one John H. Tunstall at the said County of Lincoln on or about the 18th day of February 1878, that on or about the 20th day of Feby 1878, I secured warrants on said affidavits for the arrest of the parties above named and directed the same to the Constable of for precinct № one in said County to wit: Antonacio Martines [Atanacio Martinez].

That on or about the 20th day of Feby 1878 said warrant was returned "not served" that on or about the said last mentioned day the undersigned issued an alias warrant for the apprehension of the above named persons, and there being then and there no officers to serve such warrant the undersigned as directed by law, in such cases specially empowered Richard H. Brewer to serve the same endorsing such deputation on said last mentioned warrant.

In testimony whereof I have hereinto set my hand at Lincoln Precinct № 1 Lincoln County, N. Mexico this 31st day of August 1878.

John Wilson
Justice of the Peace

This allowed Special Constable Dick Brewer to deputize Billy and Fred Waite as Deputy Constables under Lincoln Town Constable Atanacio Martinez to serve the arrest warrants.

COMPLAINT TO THE BRITISH AMBASSADOR

Probably the Ring's greatest mistake was assassinating a foreign citizen. To cover up that international crime, would sorely test its powers in Washington, D.C. and beyond.

On February 23, 1878, Alexander McSween, after determining that murder of a British subject, like Tunstall, triggered federal investigation, wrote a complaint to British Ambassador Sir Edward Thornton. And for the remainder of McSween's life - a mere 146 days before his own Ring assassination - he never lost his faith that legal justice would prevail.

KILLING OF MORTON AND BAKER

With Wilson's arrest warrants, Special Constable Brewer, with Tunstall's men - including Billy - as his posse, on March 6, 1878 apprehended Tunstall murder possemen William "Buck" Morton (Catron's Cow Camp foreman), and Jessie Evans's gang member, Frank Baker. On March 9th, they were fatally shot attempting escape en route to Lincoln's jail. Billy likely fired at them with the others. All claimed self-defense, since Morton grabbed the gun of Brewer's posseman, William McClosky, killing him first.

RING RESPONSES

SUMMARY: The unexpected resistance led the Ring to backlash by military intervention, obstructing of arrest warrants for Tunstall's murderers, and illegal Proclamation by Governor Axtell to remove Justice of the Peace Wilson and to make Sheriff Brady the sole law enforcer. The Ring had descend into blatant tyranny.

MILITARY INTERVENTION

Alexander McSween naively requested soldiers from Fort Stanton's Commander, George Purington, on February 19, 1878, the day after Tunstall's killing; unaware of his Ring loyalty and Sheriff Brady himself colluding with Governor Axtell to get troops approved by New Mexico's District Commander, General Edward Hatch, for suppression there. So Purington sent to Lincoln First Lieutenant Cyrus Delaney and a 9th Cavalry squad to "The House," facilitating the murderers' escape. Brady even led cavalrymen to dead Tunstall's store to get hay for their horses.

So McSween had Justice of the Peace Wilson issue an arrest warrant for hay theft against Brady, with a $200 bond. He and Wilson still believed there was legal recourse against the Ring.

OBSTRUCTING ARREST WARRANTS

On February 20, 1878, when Town Constable Atanacio Martinez and Deputy Constables, Billy Bonney and Fred Waite, accompanied by a Citizens' Committee led by Hispanic leader and Lincoln County jailor, Juan Patrón, went to "The House" to serve

Wilson's alias warrants for Tunstall's murderers, Sheriff Brady arrested Martinez, Bonney, and Waite. Having no legal basis, but with Ring hubris, Brady simply said he had the power. He also confiscated Billy's Winchester '73 carbine - his prized possession from Tunstall - and marched his captives in intimidating display through Lincoln to the pit jail. They were illegally held until February 22nd, demonstrating the likely motive of restraining them until Tunstall burial to the east of his store that day. And Brady did not return Billy's carbine.

GOVERNOR'S ILLEGAL PROCLAMATION

On March 9, 1878, with a Fort Stanton escort, Governor Axtell came to Lincoln to obstruct justice - as he had done in Colfax County by removing its courts to shield Tolby's Ringite killers.

That day, he issued an illegal Proclamation removing Justice of the Peace Wilson to make his deputizings illegal, and to make Sheriff Brady Lincoln County's only law enforcer. Axtell wrote:

Proclamation
To the Citizens of Lincoln County.
The disturbed condition of affairs at the County seat brings me to Lincoln County at this time; my only object is to assist good citizens to uphold the laws and to keep the peace, to enable that all act intelligently, it is important that the following facts should be clearly understood.

1st
John B. Wilson's appointment by the County Commissioners as a Justice of the Peace was illegal and void, and all processes issued by him were void, and said Wilson has no authority whatsoever to act as Justice of the Peace.

2nd
The appointment of Robt Wiedeman as U.S. Marshall has been revoked and said Wiedeman is not now a peace officer nor has he any power or authority whatever to act as such.

3rd
*The President of the United States upon an application made by me as Governor has directed the Post Commander Col. George A. Purington to assist Territorial civil officers in maintaining order and enforcing local process. It follows from the above statement that **there is no legal processes in this case to be enforced except the writs and processes issued out of***

the Third Judicial District Court by Judge Bristol and there are no Territorial Officers here to enforce them except Sheriff Brady and his Deputies.

Nor therefore in consideration of the premises I do hereby command all persons to disarm and return to their homes and usual occupations, under penalty of being arrested and confined in jail as disturbers of the Public peace.   *S.B. Axtell*
Governor of N.M.
Lincoln, March 9, 1878

As to this illegal proclamation that got Axtell fired as Governor by that October, Victor Westphall lied; stating: "From a standpoint of establishing jurisdiction, there was some logic in his proclamation of March 9 that only District Judge Warren H. Bristol and Sheriff Brady had the right to enforce law in Lincoln County." (Westphall, p. 85)

AXTELL SEEKS TROOPS

Westphall admitted that Sheriff William Brady immediately involved Catron as U.S. Attorney, and that he requested troops through Governor Axtell - with intent of subduing Lincoln County opposition. On March 3, 1878, Axtell telegrammed President Hayes, wielding usual outlawing of opponents; stating: *"I am unable to enforce the law and to protect life and property in this Territory, and request assistance from the President."* Then, on July 17, 1878, escaping personal risk, Axtell temporarily absconded the Territory *"to visit my family in Ohio."*

CITIZENS RESIST THE RING

SUMMARY: Again the Ring would be surprised by citizens' resistance, though they lacked adequate power.

LETTER TO DEPARTMENT OF INTERIOR

Montegue Leverson, a politically connected, eccentric, Colorado friend of John Chisum's, seeking a New Mexico Territory governorship, bravely went to Lincoln to intervene by providing the truth to Washington. On March 16, 1878, on Juan Patrón's crossed-out letterhead, he wrote to Secretary of the Interior Carl Schurz, enclosing a letter to President Hayes exposing the Ring; unaware that both men knew about its crimes since 1877 from Mary McPherson, whom they had stonewalled. Leverson wrote:

 LINCOLN, LINCOLN CO. N.M. __16 March__ __1878__

Hon Carl Schurz
 Secy of the Interior
Dear Sir.
 I earnestly entreat you to read the enclosed letter and to hand it to the president and beg his earnest attention to its contents. I refer you also to my former letters on the subject of the state of affairs here, sent by me to the president from Santa Fe ...
I expect to be back in Santa Fe in 10 or 12 days, and shall be ready to give my aid in any manner that may be desired for the purpose of putting an end to the <u>organized anarchy</u> prevailing in this Territory and to bring justice to the evil doers.
    Respectfully
    Montegue Leverson

[ENCLOSED LETTER]:
    Lincoln, Lincoln Co. New Mexico
    March 16<u>th</u> 1878.
His Excellency Rutherford B. Hayes
 President of the United States.
Excellency!
  Since my last letter to your Excellency on the state of affairs in this Territory, I have come here to select, in this garden of New Mexico, a suitable location for a colony from Old and New England. Whether such colony will be formed, will depend on the restoration of peace, and life and property being made secure in this distracted country; **<u>the insecurity of life and property</u> and the <u>disturbed condition</u> of affairs <u>being caused by the United States officials</u>!**
 I have made careful inquiry <u>from both sides</u> into the base and brutal murder of Mr. Tunstall ... and I solemnly assure you that a <u>real</u> investigation will prove conclusively that the murder was plotted and contrived by the District Attorney of the Third Judicial District [William Rynerson] by whom the District Judge [Warren Bristol] is used as a tool!

I deeply regret to add that the Governor [S.B. Axtell] has <u>illegally</u> and <u>despotically</u> exerted his favor to screen the murderers, as the document herewith will prove ...

When Mr. Tunstall was murdered ... sworn informations were presented to Mr. Wilson [Justice of the Peace], on which he issued <u>warrants for arrest of the actual murderers</u>.

"Paper C" [attached Axtell proclamation] will show your Excellency the conduct of the Governor thereupon, <u>for the purpose of screening the murderers from arrest</u>. Even if Mr. Wilson's appointment had been illegal (which it was not) I need not remind your Excellency that he (the Governor) had neither right nor power to pass upon it ...

But illegal as was the Governor's conduct, it has been none the less disastrous having served to discourage and demoralize the honest portion of the community ...

*The assassins assert that Mr. Tunstall was killed while in the act of resisting the Sheriff's posse. The statement is <u>wholly false, and will be proved to be so on the first inquiry</u>. [H]is murders were men who had escaped jail [Jessie Evans and his boys], but had been joined to the Sheriff's posse for the express purpose of the murder. <u>All this can be proved by irreproachable testimony</u>. Your Excellency! Mr. Tunstall was a British subject, and **it is not likely that the British Government will allow the murder of one of its subjects <u>by United States officials and their appointees</u>, to pass without a rigorous investigation, and a demand of indemnity for the family of the murdered man.***

[AUTHOR'S NOTE: This is the red flag that forced President Hayes's cover-up investigation using Angel.]

For the honor of the United States I entreat your Excellency to anticipate the action of the British Government by yourself causing an investigation to be made, not only into this matter but into the general state of affairs in New Mexico. Your Excellency will then find that the U.S. Attorney [Thomas Benton Catron] and the Surveyor General have been plundering and defrauding the United States, that the former has been in the habit of forging indictments which were never found by any grand jury, of purchasing testimony, and of other malfeasance too numerous to be here mentioned.

[AUTHOR'S NOTE: Condemnation of Catron and his Ring.]

> But to render life and property even temporarily secure pending such investigation, <u>as well as to prevent the destruction of evidences</u> of crime, I respectfully suggest that the following measures should be taken immediately and by telegraph:
>
> **1<u>st</u> The suspension of the Governor [Axtell].**
>
> **2<u>d</u> The suspension of the U.S. Attorney [Catron], and <u>immediate</u> appointment of some one to take possession of the books and papers of the office.**

[AUTHOR'S NOTE: By 1888, Catron had the expurgating fire in his law office to destroy incriminatory documents.]

> 3<u>d</u> Orders to the person to be appointed (pro tem) to act as Governor to remove the District Attorney of the 3<u>d</u> Judicial District [Rynerson], and by telegraph to appoint some person in his place to take possession of books and papers before they can be destroyed …
>
> Charges against the Judge of the 3<u>d</u> Judicial District were (I am informed) presented about two years since [Grant County petition], and are now on file in the Attorney General's office. Of these charges, if their nature be as stated to me, some are of a very serious nature, **but have never been investigated**, owing, it is alleged, to the influences brought … by the United States District Attorney for New Mexico [Catron], thro Mr. Elkins.

[AUTHOR'S NOTE: Leverson may have known about Mary McPherson's exposés, and knows how the Ring has Catron working New Mexico Territory and Elkins working Washington]

> <u>Fresh and still more serious charges</u> are ready to be presented the moment it is seen that there would be any hope of an impartial investigation.
>
> I have the honor to be your Excellency's most obedient servant.
>
> Montegue R. Leverson.

AMBUSH KILLING OF BRADY AND HINDMAN

Sheriff William Brady was the Ringite tasked with Tunstall's murder. His Deputy, George Hindman, was named in the Brewer-Bonney affidavit of February 19, 1878 as one of Tunstall's murderers. After Judge Bristol and District Attorney Rynerson obstructed McSween's bondsmen to get him jailed by Brady, and after Governor Axtell's Proclamation gave sole legal power to him, it was obvious that McSween's murder by Brady was being set up.

The Regulators knew that McSween, with his wife, had been hiding-out at John Chisum's South Spring River Ranch. On March 28, 1878, Sheriff Brady had already brought Fort Stanton troops there as his "posse" to arrest him for not filing his bail-bond, and likely to murder him in a "Dear Ben"-style plot. But Chisum had concealed McSween.

Brady's next chance to murder was at McSween's return to Lincoln for his Grand Jury embezzlement trial. McSween had even naively tried to arrange an escort by Fort Stanton soldiers; thus, revealing to them his day of return as April 1, 1878. The troops obviously never arrived. But Chisum, more canny, had apparently told the Regulators to be there to protect him, since body-guard, Deputy Sheriff Adolph Barrier, had returned to Las Vegas. As further precaution, Chisum himself, with Montegue Leverson, joined McSween and his wife in their buggy to Lincoln.

So on April 1, 1878, the Regulators, including Billy, were secretly in Lincoln, to foil Brady's killing McSween that day. They chose his death instead. Concealed in Tunstall's corral behind the long building of his combined store, bank, and personal apartment, they observed Brady walking eastward on Lincoln's single street, brandishing Billy's confiscated Winchester '73 carbine, and in the direction McSween was soon to arrive. With Brady were his armed Deputies: George Hindman, Jacob Basil "Billy" Matthews, George Peppin, and Jack Long.

At 9:00 a.m., the Regulators acted, firing from behind the corral's adobe wall. Matthews, Peppin, and Long escaped. Brady and Hindman did not. In the firing group, only Billy would have lacked a carbine, likely using a Colt .44 revolver, lacking range for the necessary 60 yards. After Brady's killing, Billy ran out, with Jim "Frenchie" French for cover, to retrieve his carbine from the corpse. He and French were wounded by Billy Matthews. The Regulators then fled, having ensured McSween's safe arrival.

KILLING OF "BUCKSHOT" ROBERTS

The Regulators ignored Governor Axtell's partisan March 9, 1878 Proclamation, and continued to serve Wilson's warrants. Dick Brewer had one for Andrew "Buckshot" Roberts, a murder posseman. The Regulators, seeking Tunstall's cattle, stolen by the Ring after his murder, chanced to meet Roberts, on April 4, 1878, at Blazer's Mill, a way station, post office, and grist mill of Dr. Joseph Blazer within the Mescalero Indian Reservation.

Refusing arrest, Roberts fired his carbine at them, hitting John Middleton and Charlie Bowdre's belt buckle, with a ricochet that wrenched George Coe's revolver, mutilating his trigger finger. Bowdre, in self-defense, shot him in the abdomen. From retreat in Blazer's office, Roberts fatally shot Brewer. So Roberts, a Tunstall murderer, had now killed another innocent man, and injured others. Billy fired no shot. Roberts died the next day.

McSween gave Investigator Angel the press report of Brewer's death as "Exhibit 17" in his June 6, 1878 deposition. It stated:

The following for the death of Brewer has been sent us for publication:

"We the undersigned residents of Lincoln county, in the Territory of New Mexico, deeply deplore the loss our county sustains by the death of Richard M. Brewer, a young man of irreproachable character, who commanded the respect and admiration of all who knew him ... He was a hard working, generous, sober, upright and noble minded young man. Cattle thieves and murderers and their "kid-gloved" friends ["The House"] hated him, and promised him a violent death years ago.

In good faith he went as special constable to arrest the murders of John H. Tunstall, by virtue of a warrant issued by John B. Wilson, a Justice of the peace in the town of Lincoln. Before he could make his return thereon, Governor Axtell issued a proclamation to the effect that Wilson as not a legal J.P., although the act of our legislature, by virtue of which said Wilson was appointed justice, was approved by his Excellency. Mr. Wilson had acted as such justice for over a year without having his authority questioned. Immediately after the issue of that proclamation, our late sheriff and those who were interested in screening the murderers, obtained warrants against Mr. Brewer and posse for having made an effort to execute the warrant issued by Wilson. Brewer and his posse knew well that if the late sheriff arrested them they would be murdered, so they took to the mountains.

We tender our heartfelt sympathy to the aged parents of the deceased Richard M. Brewer, and other relatives in Wisconsin, and we beg to assure them that whilst they have lost a good son and relative, we feel that our county has lost one of her best citizens.

(Signed) John S. Chisum. I. Ellis & Sons, Merchants. G.B. Barber, Surveyor and Civil Engineer. J.B. Patron, Speaker of the House of Representatives. Jose Montano, Merchant. McSween & Shield, Attorneys, J.N. Copeland, Sheriff. J. Newcomb. T.F. Ealy, M.D. Dow Brothers, Merchants. R.M. Gilbert. A. Wilson. W. Fields. C. Sampson, and ONE HUNDRED AND FIFTY OTHERS.

APPOINTMENT OF SHERIFF JOHN COPELAND

By April 9, 1878, citizens had hope. With Brady dead, their County Commissioners appointed local rancher, John Copeland, a Regulator sympathizer, as Sheriff. Victor Westphall fictionalized him as "outlaw" in a likewise apocryphal Regulator rustling incident from Catron's Pecos Cow Camp, reported by John Riley to Commander N.A.M. Dudley on May 19, 1878. (Westphall, p. 90)

THE LINCOLN COUNTY GRAND JURY

The Ring hurried to kill McSween before his Grand Jury trial and likely acquittal. On April 3, 1878, Ringite George Peppin, claiming to be a Deputy, arrested him and his brother-in-law, Attorney David Shield, for the Brady-Hindman killings, ignoring his proclaimed innocence and clarification that Peppin was not a Deputy once Brady was dead; thus, had no arresting power. Nevertheless, Peppin used Commander George Purington to illegally search McSween's house and Tunstall's store - in yet another "Dear Ben" plot-style to incite violence by harassment. Then both men were incarcerated at Fort Stanton (with Susan McSween insisting on staying there too with her husband).

Montegue Leverson, still in Lincoln, confronted Purington's Constitutional violations, and got his thuggish Ringite curse: "Damn the Constitution and you for an ass." Leverson then filed a complaint to President Rutherford B. Hayes, unaware that he was a co-conspirator. But Leverson probably saved McSween from murder at Fort Stanton by making intent too obvious.

The April 1878 Lincoln County Grand Jury, ignoring Ringite bias of Judge Bristol and District Attorney Rynerson, acquitted McSween of embezzling. It indicted Tunstall's murderers - including James Dolan and Billy Matthews - and also indicted Billy and other Regulators for the murders of Brady, Hindman, and Roberts (with these indictments later being the reason for his pardon proposal to Governor Lew Wallace). Presence of Fort Stanton soldiers was misconstrued by citizens as protection.

McSween had provided his July 19, 1877 accounting from the insurance policy recovery firm, Donnell Lawson & Company in New York, which he later gave to Investigator Angel as Exhibit 7 in his June 6, 1878 deposition to disprove embezzling. It stated:

Dear Sir

We credit you *$7,148.49* proceeds, Life Ins Policy Emil Fritz after deducting our com's [commissions] as per agreement with you which we mention here, that the parties for whom you are acting may see it was the best could be done under the circumstances & has resulted greatly to the interest of all concerned.

The settlement offered you was *$6500* less *$700^{00}* charges, reducing the amount to *$5800^{00}*.

Out proposition to you was *$6500* less the *$700^{00}* charges, reducing the amount to *$5800^{00}*.

Our proposition to you was to advance this the *$700^{00}* & and get possession of the policy & proof & guarantee you the *$5800^{00}* ourselves & prosecute the case in the courts.

In consideration of this advance & <u>guarantee</u> we were to receive one half the surplus after paying over to you the *$5800^{00}* & remembering ourselves for the outlay of *$700^{00}* attorneys fees, &c. Under the old arrangement *$5800^{00}* is all you could have obtained, whereas now you get *$7,148^{49}*.

The following statement shows the whole transaction.
Received from our lawyers
  From this deduct
        Advance $700.
Lawyers fees and telegrams 803.03
Out ½ net profit   1348.51
        To your Cr [credit]
Thus   10,000.
Less advance 700
Fees & Tel   803.03   1,503.03
                        $8,496.97
Am't Guaranteed   5800.00
½ of this net profit   ½ 2,696.97
To us _____   1,348.48 ½
The other ½ 1348, added to $5800 + 7,148.49.

This we think must surely give great satisfaction to you & more especially to the parties you represent.

Lincolnites, proud of justice, published that Grand Jury's outcome:

NEW MEXICO.
Report of the Grand Jury of Lincoln County.

Through the courtesy of Harry Wigham, editor of the Cimarron News and Press, we are enabled to give the following document to our readers at this date:

To the Hon. Warren Bristol, Associate Judge of the Supreme Court of the Territory of New Mexico, and Presiding Judge of the 3d Judicial District thereof:

The grand jury of the April, 1878, term of the District Court for the County of Lincoln, deeply deplore the present insecurity of life and property, though the revival and continuance of the troubles of past years.

The murder of John H. Tunstall, for brutality and malice, is without a parallel and without a shadow of justification. By this inhuman act our county has lost one of our BEST and most useful men, - one who brought intelligence, industry, and capital to the development of Lincoln county. We equally condemn the most brutal murder of our late sheriff, William Brady, and George Hindman. In each of the cases, where the evidence would warrant it, we have made presentments.

Had his Excellency, S.B. Axtell, when here, ascertained from the people the cause of our troubles, as he was requested, valuable lives would have been spared our community; especially do we condemn that portion of his proclamation relating to J.B. Wilson as J.P. Mr. Wilson acted in good faith as J.P. over a year. Mr. Brewer, deceased, arrested, as we are informed, some of the alleged murderers of Mr. Tunstall by virtue of warrants issued by Mr. Wilson. The part of the proclamation referred to virtually outlawed Mr. Brewer and posse. In fact, they were hunted to the mountains by our late sheriff with U.S. soldiers. We believe that had the governor done his duty whilst here, these unfortunate occurrences would have been spared us.

Under the impression that stealing the property of the United States was a crime against our territory, we heard evidence in regard to the administration of affairs at the Mescalero Apache Indian agency in the county; but we are now informed by the District Attorney [William Rynerson] that crimes of the character thus investigated by us are not indictable in this court. We have, however, ascertained by evidence that the Indians are systematically robbed by their agent [Frederick Godfroy] of a large and varied assortment of supplies. We mention this here for the reason that it will explain why the Indians arc migrating marauders and steal from and murder our citizens. The witnesses by whom these facts can be proven are residents of this town and neighborhood, and a list of them has been furnished by us to the United States District clerk.

Signed J.H. BLAZER. Foreman.

MORE HOPE IN LINCOLN COUNTY

Empowered with successes, Lincoln County citizens believed that the worst was over. But they continued to seek justice for Tunstall and to expose the Ring. All underestimated their risk.

CITIZENS PETITION PRESIDENT HAYES

Alexander McSween continued his anti-Ring campaigning by futile reporting to President Hayes; writing:

LAW OFFICE
OF
McSWEEN & SHIELD
Lincoln County Bank Building

Lincoln, New Mexico, *April 26, 1878*

To his Excellency Rutherford B. Hayes, President of the United States of America:
 Excellency! The undersigned have the Honor of transmitting you, as requested, a copy of the proceedings of a meeting held by the citizens of Lincoln County N.M., relative to the late troubles
 Respectfully
 A.A. McSween, B.H. Ellis, Secretaries

Its attached transcript was later published in the *Mesilla Independent* and the *Cimarron News and Press*. It stated:

Pursuant to an hours notice, after the adjournment of the District Court April 24th 1878, the citizens of Lincoln County, from every section thereof, assembled at the Court House to express their sentiments relative to the present troubles. The room was crowded.
 The Hon. J.B. Patron called the meeting to order, and nominated the Hon. Florencio Gonzales, Probate Judge, for President, and Capt. Saturnino Baca and Jose Montaño, County Treasurer, for Vice Presidents, with Alex. A. McSween and B.H. Ellis as secretaries.
 Judge Gonzales stated the object of the meeting to be the consideration of our present troubles. His speech was vociferously cheered, and interrupted by frequent applause.

Speeches were also made by Hon. J.B. Patron, Jose Montano and Mr. Herford. The latter gentleman closed with these significant remarks: "I trust that the pledges of friendship and good feeling made this evening in so solemn and appropriate a manner, may never be marred or broken."

The Chair appointed Hon. J.B. Patron, Messrs. John S. Chisum, and Avery M. Clenny a committee to draft and submit Resolutions. In due time they submitted the following, which were unanimously adopted:

Be it Resolved: That it is the sense of this meeting that our present troubles are only a continuance of old feuds dating back five or six years that will now cease as the cause has been removed.

Be it Resolved: That thanks of the people of Lincoln County are due, and are hereby tendered to Lieut. Col. Dudley U.S.A. Commanding Fort Stanton N.M. for his conduct as an officer and Gentleman. That we do and will consider the day he took command at Fort Stanton an important era in the history of our county. That we assure him of our appreciation of the intelligent, cautious and earnest manner in which he has applied himself in ferreting out the cause of our troubles. That his non-partisan conduct and frankness towards the people on the one hand and the men on the other, is a guarantee that he <u>alone</u> is the Commanding Officer at Fort Stanton, and that: therefore we tender him our heartfelt thanks in recognition of our appreciation of a man who discharges his duty <u>fully</u>.

[AUTHOR'S NOTE: Dudley's Ring bias was then unknown.]

That we condemn without qualification, the conduct of the Governor, S.B. Axtell, while here in March last. That his refusal to investigate our troubles stamps him as a little, one-sided partisan. That his conduct and proclamation of March 9, 1878, are unworthy of an officer filling his exalted station. That as a result of that proclamation, he is responsible for the loss of life that has occurred in this County since his visit.

Be it Resolved: That we recognize ... the good and united feeling that binds all our people, Mexicans and Americans, together! That we recognize our mutual dependence upon each other, and that we pledge our lives and our property to the protection of each other, and the maintenance of the laws.

Be it Resolved: That a vote of thanks be tendered the United States Soldiers, Non-commissioned Officers and Privates for their commendable conduct while here during Court.

Be it Resolved: That we tender our thanks to John N. Copeland for having accepted the office of Sheriff and for his important and efficient discharge of duty as such since he took charge.
Signed Florencio Gonzales President
Alex. A. McSween
B.H. Ellis   Secretaries

THE RING OBSTRUCTS JUSTICE

SUMMARY: Now desperate, the Ring rushed to protect its own, taking ever greater risks of exposure in the climate of mobilized citizens and an ongoing investigation of Tunstall's killing through the British ambassador.

RYNERSON REFUSES TO ARREST

After the April 1878 Grand Jury indicted Tunstall's killers, District Attorney William Rynerson refused to issue their arrest warrants. McSween intervened, and got Rynerson's insolent and mocking letter of May 2, 1878; which McSween gave to Investigator Angel as Exhibit 20 in his deposition of June 6, 1878. Rynerson, a Ring-shielded murderer himself, taunted, knowing McSween was a dead man walking. But he did issue arrest warrants for indicted Regulators. Rynerson wrote:

Las Cruces N.M.
May 2ᵈ 1878

A.A. McSween Esq
  Law office of McSween & Shield
Lincoln N.M.
Dear Sir: I am just in receipt of yours of the date of 2 of st ulto, directed to me in which you say "If parties have been indicted by the last Grand Jury for the murder of J.H. Tunstall, I wish to ask you to place warrants in the hands of our Sheriff for their arrest please reply." In reply I have to say that I shall discharge my duty, without let or hindrance from anyone, and when warrants are necessary in every case they will be issued and placed in the hands of the proper officer. Just whom you mean by "<u>our Sheriff</u>" is not clear to me, as in the past few months it is said you had some interest in more than one sheriff. You may mean Martines, you may

mean Barrier, or you may mean someone else whom I do not know that you have reduced to possession and are pleased to designate as our (your) Sheriff and since you have undertaken the task of directing me in my duties I may be permitted to suggest that you seem to have forgotten to dictate or direct as to what should be done as to the warrants. "If parties have been indicted by the last Grand Jury for the murder of" Sheriff Brady, George Hindman, A.L. Roberts, and others in Lincoln County."
Passing strange
Very Respt'y
W.L. Rynerson Dist. Atty

A NEW RINGITE FORT STANTON COMMANDER

SUMMARY: Fort Union's Commander Nathan Augustus Monroe Dudley was brought in to replace Fort Stanton's unpopular Commander George Purington. Ring-beholden Dudley was a career soldier, already three times court martialed, and represented by T.B. Catron. He was being positioned for potential intervention; but Lincoln County citizens, including Alexander McSween, believed he was their protector - until it was too late.

By April 5, 1878, unbeknownst to Lincoln County citizens, the fate of their anti-Ring struggle for justice against Tunstall's murderers was sealed. And more horrors awaited them. In the guise of conciliation, Fort Stanton's Commander, Lieutenant George Purington - whose Ring affiliation had been too obvious by his shielding of the Tunstall's murderers in "The House" on the night of his killing - was replaced by Fort Union's Commander, Nathan Augustus Monroe Dudley.

Ominously, but unknown by Lincolnites, it was from Fort Union that troops had been drawn by the Ring to suppress the Cimarron populace after Franklin Tolby's murder, as well as for intended murder of Ring opponents in the "Dear Ben plot." And McSween failed to recognize the danger, even though Fort Stanton soldiers had been used by Sheriff Brady as his "posse" in an attempt to take him captive at John Chisum's ranch.

In 3½ months, Dudley and his troops would commit far worse crimes against innocent citizens of Lincoln County than anyone in America could then imagine.

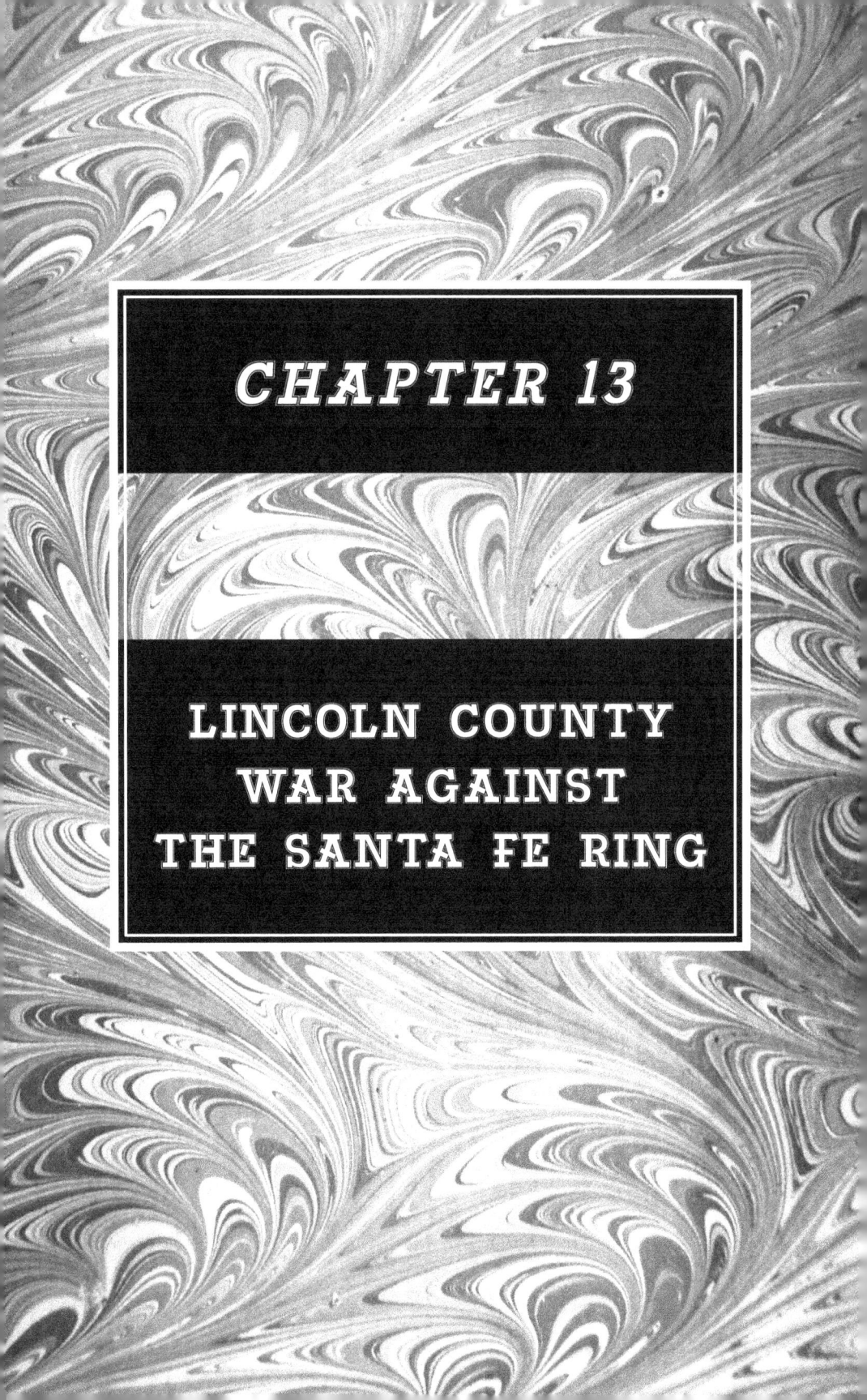

CHAPTER 13

LINCOLN COUNTY WAR AGAINST THE SANTA FE RING

THE UNSUNG FREEDOM FIGHT

SUMMARY: After exhausting all legal remedies to arrest John Tunstall's murderers, after Governor S.B. Axtell's petitions illegally removing their Justice of the Peace and replacing their newly-appointed Sheriff, after futilely petitioning President Hayes, and after more attempts to murder Alexander McSween, Lincoln County citizens took up arms against the Ring. And their brave fight would be hidden by the victorious Ring's smoke-screen of outlawing.

When did the Lincoln County War begin? Billy Bonney must have reflected contemporary consensus in his March 13, 1879 letter to new Governor, Lew Wallace, when he began his pardon request. He wrote: *"I have indictments against me for things that happened in the late Lincoln County War."*

Those indictments, considered by Billy "in the late Lincoln County War," were for the April of 1878 Regulator killings of Tunstall's murderers: William Brady, George Hindman, and Andrew "Buckshot" Roberts. He would likely have included the Regulator's self-defense killings, the month before, yielding no indictments, of Tunstall's murderers: Frank Baker and William "Buck" Morton. So the War began with Tunstall's murder.

As to their adversaries, Billy cites the Ring in his July 13, 1878 "Regulator Manifesto," stating: *"Mr. Walz. Sir: - We are all aware that your brother-in-law, T.B. Catron sustains the Murphy-Kinney party."* That "party" headed by Catron, included Lincoln County Sheriff George Peppin and his Deputies; and the rustler gangs of Jessie Evans, John Kinney, and Seven Rivers boys. It would take until July 19, 1878 for Regulators to realize that Commander N.A.M. Dudley was on that list of killers. But Billy later testified against him, on May 28th and 29th, 1879, in his military Court of Inquiry for potential court martial.

And everyone would have dated the War's end to the battle of July 14th to 19th, with the Regulators' defeat.

As to total deaths in the Lincoln County War, Billy gave a cheeky response for an April 3, 1881 Santa Fe *Daily New Mexican* article titled "Something About the Kid." Aware of his outlaw myth press, he was in custody awaiting his Mesilla hanging trial. He stated: "At least two hundred men have been killed in Lincoln County during the past three years, but I did not kill all of them."

THE RING'S MURDEROUS RESPONSES

The 1878 Lincoln County War represented Catron's and his Ring's greatest risk of exposure by crimes of assassination, massacre, and military treason. Victor Westphall's mission was to hide these terrible truths by calling the War an "imbroglio" - meaning "quarrel." Catron's role is called "shrouded with mystery" (Westphall, p. 74), with the spurious alibi that "at no time was he personally in the region" (Westphall, p. 78) – which ignores his "boss" role, local ownerships, and agents.

USE OF TROOPS AGAINST McSWEEN

After Tunstall's killing, Ringite troop use and citizens' resentment resulted in replacement of Commander George Purington with N.A.M. Dudley on April 5, 1878. But Dudley continued pro-Ring troop interventions, culminating in his July 19, 1878 intervention in the Lincoln County War Battle.

FIRST MAJOR SKIRMISHES

On April 29, 1878, Seven Rivers rustlers and John Kinney's gang, calling themselves a "posse" to arrest murderers of Brady, Hindman, and Roberts, rode to Lincoln, where Regulators waited secretly in Isaac Ellis's house. Frank MacNab, new Regulator leader after Dick Brewer's murder, departed with Frank Coe to do reconnaissance. Near Charles Fritz's ranch, they were ambushed by that "posse." MacNab was murdered. Coe was taken captive.

The next day, the "posse" came to Lincoln to kill McSween. Regulators in the Ellis house faced them. George Coe wounded Seven Rivers rustler, "Dutch Charlie" Kruling; and four other assailants were killed. Dudley, at overwhelmed Sheriff Copeland's request, sent Second Lieutenant George Smith with a squad to Lincoln. Twenty-seven Seven Rivers men were taken to Fort Stanton. And prisoner Frank Coe was released.

McSween then resumed hiding, largely in San Patricio, where the Ring would soon take revenge by massacre.

WARRANTS FOR McSWEEN AND "THE KID"

McSween reported Frank MacNab's murder to San Patricio Justice of the Peace Gregorio Trujillo to obtain arrest warrants for Sheriff John Copeland.

But James Dolan rode to Blazer's Mill, with George Peppin and Jacob Basil "Billy' Matthews, to swear out warrants to Catron's agent, David Easton - then a Justice of the Peace - against McSween, William Bonney alias Henry Antrim alias Kid, and others unknown, for the killing of the four MacNab murderers and injured "Dutch" Charlie Kruling. The Ring now saw Billy as enough risk for singling out. These warrants were key to continuing the attack on McSween after his Grand Jury acquittal.

But Easton, quit, fearing reprisal. That voided his warrants. So 80 days later, on July 19, 1878, Commander Dudley, in Lincoln with troops, learned there was nothing to rationalize his presence. So he forced Justice of the Peace Wilson to write false warrants against McSween and Regulators for allegedly shooting at his fact-finder, 9th Cavalryman, Private Berry Robinson three days earlier.

DUDLEY'S RING BIAS REVEALED

By May 4, 1878, Commander Dudley showed his Ring allegiance. That day, Sheriff George Copeland gave him Justice of the Peace Gregorio Trujillo's arrest warrants for MacNab's Seven Rivers murderers held at Fort Stanton, with hearing for May 6th. Instead, Dudley gave Copeland Easton's warrants for McSween and "the Kid," sending him with a "military escort" to San Patricio to arrest them. But they were not found. Dudley then released the Seven Rivers men. None ever stood trial. They would be part of Sheriff George Peppin's murderous posse by that July's battle.

Then, setting-up future military intervention, the Ring made a sham complaint. On May 19, 1878, John Riley sent Dudley a letter alleging that the Regulators had stolen 2,000 of Catron's Pecos Cow Camp cattle, and had murdered one of Catron's men there. (Westphall, p. 87) Westphall - hiding all Lincoln County War issues - says it was done "to hamper Riley in fulfilling his contract with Godfroy." (Westphall, p. 88) Of course, this reveals Catron as owner and contract supplier! Westphall completed Catron's link stating his "recovered" cattle were taken to his Carrizozo ranch. (Westphall, p. 88) Westphall then revealed that Catron authored Riley's fake Regulator rustling/murder letter by quoting Catron's May 30, 1878 letter to Axtell:

I also learn that all the stockmen on the lower Pecos living **near my cattle** have been compelled to abandon their stock and go to the mountains where they are awaiting an attack. There seems to be no authority in the county of Lincoln to compel people to keep the peace or obey the law, and there seems to be an utter disregard of all law in the county as well as life and private rights. **I would most respectfully request that some steps be taken to disarm all parties carrying arms, and that the military be instructed to see that they all keep the peace.**

I am informed that the sheriff [John Copeland] keeps with his deputies large posses armed who are one of the factions only and who take occasion at all time to kill persons and take the property of the other faction whenever they get an opportunity. **There is no power from what I can learn that can keep the peace in that county, except the military.** (Westphall, pp. 89-90)

AXTELL'S SECOND PROCLAMATION

On May 28, 1878, Governor Samuel Beach Axtell, by Proclamation, removed Sheriff John Copeland - in office only 49 days - giving questionable cause as his not having posted his tax collector bond in his first month in office (the same way he removed the non-Ring Colfax County Sheriff in 1876 before launching his "Dear Ben plot"). Axtell replaced him with George Peppin, Brady's deputy and Tunstall murder posseman. Westphall admitted that Peppin, was "a Dolan-Riley partisan." (Westphall, p. 90) Westphall, however, then used Peppin for the outlaw myth, writing that he "had no more success in controlling lawlessness than had his predecessor." (Westphall, p. 90) In truth, the only lawlessness in predecessor Sheriff Copeland's tenure was murderous attacks on McSween and Regulators by the Ring.

INVESTIGATOR ANGEL BRINGS HOPE

Unlike their Colfax County War predecessors, Lincolnites could force grievances on President Hayes because of the potential international incident, with British Ambassador Edward Thornton demanding investigation of Tunstall's murder.

So on May 4, 1878, by presidential order, Attorney Frank Warner Angel, reporting to the Departments of Justice and Interior, was sent to New Mexico Territory for investigations including the Lincoln County "troubles," Tunstall's murder, corruption in the Mescalero Indian Reservation Agency, and land grant frauds. But the question of U.S. officials' involvement, more closely matched Mary McPherson's exposés of the year before.

By the next month, on June 8, 1878, Billy would risk his life by coming to Lincoln to give Angel his own deposition on Tunstall's murder. (See pages 362-365)

ALEXANDER McSWEEN'S DEPOSITION

On June 6, 1878, Alexander McSween gave his deposition to Investigator Angel, 43 days before the Ring killed him. Though Angel took 39 depositions, McSween's was the best rendition of Lincoln County's "troubles." And it belies Angel's future, likely coerced, conclusion that U.S. officials did not murder Tunstall.

McSween's 69 page deposition, with 21 exhibits totaling 111 pages detailed the bogus embezzlement case to achieve Tunstall's murder by false property attachments; and documented murder attempts on himself. He recounted partisanship of Sheriffs William Brady and George Peppin and their Deputies; of District Attorney William Rynerson; and of Mescalero Indian Reservation Agent Frederick Godfroy. He documented the arrogance of power of "The House's" Lawrence Murphy, James Dolan, and John Riley; along with their using outlaws, Jessie Evans and his gang, as enforcers and rustlers. He makes clear partisan interventions of Governor S.B. Axtell, of Fort Stanton soldiers under Commander George Purington, and of U.S. Attorney Catron, who, by then, had taken possession of "The House" from Dolan and Riley.

McSween knew "The House's" partners were backed by *"all the power in Santa Fe;"* but unimaginable to him was that Commander Dudley would be the Ring's weapon against himself.

After Tunstall's death, he was Billy's next father figure; and Billy's subsequent acts and writings show his inspiration by both men; with McSween's deposition likely repeating what Billy had already heard himself. McSween stated:

Territory of New Mexico)
County of Lincoln   )
Alexander A. McSween being duly sworn says. I have resided in Lincoln County since the 3^d day of March 1875 and since that time am conversant with the state of affairs that has existed in that County ... I am a lawyer by profession and have been and now am engaged in the practice of my profession.

I have given the subject of what has caused the trouble in Lincoln County considerable attention and study, and have inquired and talked with a great number of persons as to the causes which has produced the state of affairs which has resulted in the death of John H. Tunstall and as to the general lawlessness that exists in said County.

From this examination and inquiry of the matter I am informed that Lawrence G. Murphy and Emil Fritz doing business under the style of L.G. Murphy & Co had the monopoly for sale of merchandise in this County, and used their power to oppress and grind out all they could from the farmers and force those who were opposed to them to leave the County. For instance the farmers would buy merchandise of them at exorbitant prices, and were compelled to turn in their produce in payment thereof that suited L.G. Murphy & Co, and if the farmers refused so to do, they were subjected to litigation and the whole judicial machinery was used ... [T]he result of these proceedings were that L.G. Murphy & Co were absolute monarchs of Lincoln County and ruled their subjects (the farmers and others) with oppressive iron heel. This state of affairs has existed for some time, at least ten years, and was carried out either by L.G. Murphy & Co or their successors.

The said L.G. Murphy & Co in carrying out their schemes would drive out a settler who had opposed them ... and without a particle of right title or claim take possession of such persons real estate and claim that it belonged to them, and then rent it to some other person who was led to believe that it belonged to them – and if such person should afterwards find out that they had no right title or interest in the property, and refused to pay them for the rental thereof, a system of persecution would be instituted which resulted in either the opposing party giving in or leaving the

County. This rule of Murphy & Co and their successors continued until the matter was precipitated by the event of the killing of John. H. Tunstall – and that in order to support this monarchy it is reported that L.G. Murphy & Co and their successors have latterly surrounded themselves, and were employing the most desperate characters in the County. And affairs were carried by such a high hand after deponent came to this County and Murphy desiring to regain lost power and obtain control over the people desired ... to organize a vigilance committee ostensibly to put down horse stealing but really as after facts show to kill persons who were opposed to him, and among other persons to be disposed of he named to me that he was going to have this vigilance committee kill Hon. J.B. Patron, Stephen Stanley and Richard M. Brewer since deceased and he informed me that in as much as I appeared to support them I would have to leave the County – **Deponent further says that he discountenanced in every way this measure and used his influence to prevent that state of affairs, wishing rather that the people would stand by and see the laws enforced, these facts and the further fact that the people were determined to throw off the burden of Murphy & Co found that the power to influence courts, juries, and even to kill persons was being lost ... compelled them to resort to more desperate measures which culminated in the death of John H. Tunstall.**

Deponent has heard L.G. Murphy assert that he controlled not only the courts and juries, but that he could cause the death of any person who opposed him ...

The foregoing facts I believe are the formative cause of the troubles in Lincoln County at the present time. The direct and immediate cause ... was the death of John H. Tunstall which occurred as herein stated.

In November of 1876 John H. Tunstall came to this County for the purpose as he said of going into the stock raising business, & took steps to secure four thousand acres of land for that purpose and invested about $2500 in his business of stock raising and in merchandise for a store which he opened in Lincoln. At this time the firm of J.J. Dolan and John H. Riley seemed to be friends of his, and knowing that he had considerable money to invest, they tried to have him as far away from Lincoln as they could and also to get his money away so that he would be financially crippled and for that purpose tried to have him purchase L.G. Murphy's ranch at Fairview about 35 miles from Lincoln and knowing that I was a *friend of Tunstall, they tried to induce me to use my influence with Tunstall to have him buy it and promised me if I would induce Tunstall to buy it, that they would give me $5000. I informed Tunstall of this offer and told him that they had no good title to the land and Tunstall refused to buy – this was the beginning of the enmity of Murphy, Dolan, & Riley against Tunstall.*

During the month of August 1877 horses were stolen from Tunstall and myself by Jessie Evans and Tom Hill ... They were afterwards arrested at Beckwiths on the Seven Rivers by Sheriff Brady and lodged in [the pit] jail at Lincoln under an indictment for stealing said horses. That on or about the [blank] day of November 1877 I was informed by J.B. Patron that Evans, Baker, Hill, and Davis had filed off their shackles and cut the logs in their cell and were ready to make their escape. I told him to inform Sherriff Brady ... whereupon Brady, Patron, & Shields went and examined the said prisoners and the jail and found the statement to be true and correct. The Sheriff however took no precautionary steps to better secure their confinement.

A few days afterward Sheriff Brady came to Tunstalls store in a half intoxicated condition and indirectly accused Mr Tunstall of giving the credit of the arrest of said outlaws to R.M. Brewer (now deceased) and ... accused Mr Tunstall of having tried to aid Baker, Evans, Hill & Davis to escape. Mr. Tunstall told him you know their shackles are filed, & there are holes cut in the logs and take no pains to secure them, and do you dare to accuse me who have aided in the arrest of these persons, who have threatened my life, with assisting them to escape. Sheriff Brady thereupon put his hand on his revolver as though he was going to draw it and I stepped between them and placing my hand on his shoulder said it ill becomes you as a peace officer to violate the law by shooting. **Brady replied I won't shoot you now, you haven't long to run** *... and then left the store ...*

A day or so after the prisoners referred above made their escape during the night ... Upon further investigation I found that no one had been left in charge of the jail that night, and that the doors [to the guardhouse above the pit, with its trap door opening up to the guardhouse] had not even been locked ... I am informed and verily believe that the augers and files ... [used to break the shackles] were packed in goods bought in the store of J.J. Dolan & Co where Murphy resided, and by one of their employees (Pantaleon Gallegos) delivered to the said prisoners I went to

Sheriff Brady and offered to raise twenty men to go and recapture the escaped prisoners. Brady replied I arrested them once and I will be d – if I am going to do it again ... Subsequently some of the escaped prisoners ... were seen at the store of J.J. Dolan ...

About this time it was reported that J.J. Dolan and Co were using the Territorial Tax money which Sheriff Brady had collected and not paid over to the Treasurer. In order to ... see if they were endeavoring to run the County in their own interests ... I enquired of them ... why they did not get the tax money from Brady, and Dolan said that Riley had already got it – [but Riley used that money to buy rustled cattle for "The House"].

About June 24, 1874 Emil Fritz died in Germany, at this time his partner L.G. Murphy was Probate Judge. No steps were taken to administer on the estate of Fritz until about April 20, 1875 when one William Brady the late Sheriff of Lincoln Co. was appointed Administrator by said Murphy. At that time Dolan who had been clerk for L.G. Murphy & Co and afterwards partner of L.G. Murphy, and the said L.G. Murphy admitted to me that according to the books of the firm the said Emil Fritz had an interest in the business at the time of his death to the amount of about $48000 ... and that they desired that Charles Fritz and Emilie Scholand, brother and sister of the deceased, should have whatever interest Emil Fritz had in the business.

***About that time I was employed by Brady administrator to make collections for the estate, and instructed by him that Dolan & Murphy should receive all money collected**, among the assets of the estate was a life insurance policy on the life of Fritz in the Merchants Life Insurance Company of New York City for $10000. Mr Brady, administrator, informed deponent that this policy had been placed in the hands of Levi Spiegelberg of New York City a member of the firm of Spiegelberg Brothers of Santa Fe New Mexico, by Mr L.G. Murphy without consulting him. (Brady)*

About the month of February 1876 I went in company with Mr Brady to Santa Fe, during our journey we became quite confidential with each other. Brady told me among other things that he was in the power of L.G. Murphy. After we got to Santa Fe he informed me that J.J. Dolan the junior partner of said Murphy had compelled him to give an order on Levi Spiegelberg, to place the money received on the Fritz policy to the credit of L.G. Murphy & Co with Spiegelberg & Bros of Santa Fe New Mexico, with whom at that time said L.G. Murphy & Co were greatly indebted for goods and merchandise.

In October 1876 Brady resigned his administratorship of the Fritz estate, and Emilie Scholand and Charles Fritz were appointed administratrix and administrator ... I was then employed by them on behalf of the estate [T]his policy among other things was placed in my hands to be attended to.

On that behalf I proceeded to St. Louis and consulted with parties as to the best course to be pursued in collecting the money, and also to obtain letters to some responsible part[ies] in New York City in order to collect the money on said policy. I received a letter of introduction to Donnell Lawson & Co Bankers of New York City. I proceeded to New York City – and after considerable trouble with Levi Spiegelberg ... who refused to deliver the papers in his possession belonging to the said estate ... I obtained the papers. I thereupon entered into an agreement with Donnell Lawson & Co under and in pursuance of a power of attorney ...

On my return to Lincoln I found J.H. Riley was exceedingly angry and was trying to create trouble, during my absence he had broken into my office and destroyed some of my furniture grossly insulted my wife and vowed that he would run me out of the County.

About December 21, 1876 I caused notice to be served on the administratrix and administrator of the Fritz estate, and such proceedings were thereupon had that my accounts were approved by the Probate Judge ...

During the month of May 1877 L.G. Murphy of the late firm of L.G. Murphy & Co petitioned the Probate Court that a commission be appointed to examine the books of said firm in order to find out if ... the said [Fritz] estate was indebted to him ...

By this report it will appear that L.G. Murphy was indebted to said estate in the sum of $23376.10.

On or about the 1ˢᵗ day of August 1877 I received a letter from Donnell Lawson & Co Dated 19 July 1877, [and] a bill from Stam & Ruggles attorneys ...

That thereupon and on or about the 1ˢᵗ day of August 1877 I sent a letter to Mrs Emilie Scholan[d] and Charles Fritz ... informing them of the fact that the policy of insurance on the life of Fritz had been collected ... which letter was subsequently acknowledged by them to have been received in Aug aforesaid.

Deponent further says that on the same day ... he sent a copy of the same to L.G. Murphy out of courtesy [H]e [deponent] claims about this time for the first time to have some claim against the estate.

That hereafter and on or about the month of November 1877 I was requested to go to St. Louis on professional business, making no secret of my proposed journey. I even wrote friendly letters to my friends, among others Judge Bristol Judge Newcomb, A.J. Fountain and J.D. Bail informing them in connection with other business of my proposed trip and of the length of time I expected to be absent which was not to exceed six months.

Deponent further says that on or about the 15th of December 1877 Charles Fritz ... was in the office of deponent, then well knowing that deponent intended to go to St. Louis as aforesaid, that deponent informed said Fritz then and there **that as soon as he or any other person was authorized by Emilie Scholand to receive and receipt deponent for the money [from the Fritz estate], the money would be paid.** *Deponent further informed said Fritz of the nature of his business to St. Louis, how long he expected to be absent and who would attend to his business during his absence. That said Fritz therefore expressed himself as satisfied with deponents statement of the affairs of the estate ... D.P. Shield [McSween's law partner and brother-in-law] was present during said interview.*

Deponent further says that he has always been ready and now is, to pay over to the administrator and the administratrix of said estate the amount of money in his hands over and above the allowances made him by the Probate Court ... and his commission per agreement.

During January (1878) term of the Probate Court in and for said Lincoln County, said L.G. Murphy filed a claim against said estate of Fritz deceased to the amount of $76000 every dollar of which was disapproved by said Court and from which decision there has been no appeal the proof being that said Murphy owed the said estate about $30000. **That deponent knows of his own knowledge that should he turn all the moneys in his hands over to said administrator and administratrix, without deducting his fees therefrom, he would never get a cent for his professional services to said estate** *... the administrator and administratrix aforesaid being completely in the power of Murphy Dolan and Riley aforesaid, that said Fritz as deponent has been informed and believes has been threatened with summary vengeance by said Murphy Dolan & Riley if he and the administratrix should settle with deponent upon any other terms than receiving all the money in my hands collected for the aforesaid estate without the deduction of my account ...*

they threatening him [Charles Fritz] with ruin on the ground that he is heavily indebted to them. In this matter they (Murphy Dolan & Riley) have threatened to run him out of the County without a shirt unless he does as they desire him to do.

I left Lincoln on the 18th of December 1877 in company with my wife and John S. Chisum my client and whose business I was then going to St. Louis to attend to.

On the 23rd of December 1877 we arrived at Las Vegas New Mexico. On the morning of the 24th I went to the office of Louis Salebasher a brother attorney. **He informed me that he had a telegram from T.B. Catron U.S. District Attorney inquiring if I was in Las Vegas. I told him to telegraph Mr Catron that I was, and then I determined and did wait to see what he wanted of me. [O]n the night of the 24 of December 1877 the Sheriff of San Miguel County called on my room at the hotel in Las Vegas and said he had a telegram from W.L. Rynerson Territorial District Attorney for the 3d Judicial District requesting him to arrest me for the crime of embezzlement** *and that the warrant would be sent on. The Sheriff left me at the hotel on my own parole and I waited until the warrant arrived, whereupon I & Mr Chisum were lodged in jail. I requested the Sheriff to take me before Judge Bristol for examination. [H]e refused. Whereupon I sent word to J.B. Patron to tell Sheriff Brady of Lincoln County who were both then in Santa Fe that I was a prisoner in jail and that I wanted him to take me down before Judge Bristol.*

Not hearing from Sheriff Brady and the Sheriff of San Miguel County refusing to take me before Judge Bristol I offered the said Sheriff of San Miguel County to give bonds in the quantity of $20000 to be approved by him for my appearance before Judge Bristol within ten days, at my own expense **to answer for the charge of embezzlement of $10000 realized from the aforementioned policy of insurance.** *He thereupon ... telegraphed to Santa Fe for instructions [from Catron] and refused to accept the said offer made by me ...*

On the 4th of January 1878 having been confined all this time in jail I proceeded to Mesilla by way of Lincoln in charge of Deputy Sheriff A.P. Barrier. I arrived at Mesilla on or about the 1st of February and thereafter I had an examination before Judge Bristol and after the evidence against me had been introduced, and it appeared that the testimony of Hon J.B. Patron who was in attendance at the session of the Legislature Hon Florencio

Gonzales Probate Judge of Lincoln County and certain papers and files in his office were necessary for my case and on the suggestion of Judge Bristol and the Territorial District Attorney [Rynerson] I consented to a continuance until the meeting of the Grand Jury at Lincoln County April term of the District Court of said County whereupon bail was fixed by Judge Bristol at $8000 to be approved by the Territorial District Attorney and I was delivered to the charge of Deputy Sheriff Barrier aforesaid to be taken to Lincoln County and delivered to and held by Sheriff Brady of said County until I should give the aforesaid bail.

On or about the 5th day of February 1878 I started for Lincoln in charge of Deputy Sheriff Barrier and in the company with D.P. Shield J.B. Wilson and J.H. Tunstall. On the evening of the same day we camped at St Augustine [Shedd's Ranch], and shortly after going into camp Jessie Evans, Frank Baker, Long alias "[Frank] Rivers" notorious outlaws came into our camp and inquired as if we had passed J.J. Dolan on the road, whereupon D.P. Shields [Shield] replied that we had not that he understood that Mr Dolan would not leave till tomorrow morning (the 6th) Baker said that they had found Jimmie meaning (J.J. Dolan) very punctual ... and that Dolan had made an appointment with them to meet them here and that they believed he would come.

Deponent further says that it was a notorious fact that this Evans, Baker, Rivers and others had determined to take J.H. Tunstalls and my life owing to our activity in having them previously arrested for horse stealing.

Deponent further says that about one or two o'clock of the morning of the 6th of February 1878 said J.J. Dolan reached San Augustine aforesaid.

About 8 or 9 oclock of the said day whilst Tunstall, D.P. Shield, J.B. Wilson and this deponent were eating breakfast at their camping place ... deponent saw J.J. Dolan with gun in hand and another man descending a house occupied by Mr. Shedd, said house being situated about 70 or 80 yards due south of where deponent, Tunstall, Wilson Shield and Barrier were camped said J.J. Dolan and the person accompanying him appeared to be going in a westerly direction thus hiding themselves from us by the southeast corner of said corral.

In a few minutes said J.J. Dolan and Jessie Evans came around the southeast corner of said corral. Mr. Dolan drew his Winchester carbine on Mr Tunstall and asked him if he was ready to fight and settle their difficulties. Mr Tunstall

asked him if he asked him to fight a duel. Mr. Dolan replied "You d – d coward. I want you to fight and settle our difficulties." Dolan drew his gun cocked, on Mr Tunstall three times. Mr Barrier placed himself between or in line with Dolan & Evans and saved as I believe the lives of Tunstall and myself. When Mr Dolan was leaving he used these words "you won't fight this morning, you d – d coward but I'll get you soon." After he had gone off about 20 yards he turned around and said to Tunstall "When you write to the "Independent" again say that I am with "The Boys." The term "The Boys" being used in Lincoln and neighborhood to denote notorious thieves and murderers such as Evans, Baker, Hill, and Davis – and the reason that he mentioned the "Independent" was because Tunstall had written said newspaper published at Mesilla New Mexico a letter dated January 18, 1878 which letter was published ... in its issue of the 26th January 1878 charging Wm Brady Sheriff as aforesaid with having allowed said J.J. Dolan& Co to use the Territorial funds collected by said Brady as Ex officio collector of said Lincoln County and the Governor of said Territory in his message to the Legislature having reported that said Brady was in default in payment of the money collected by him (said Brady) ...

Deponent further says that said letter elicited a reply from said J.J. Dolan, which was published in said Independent on or about the 2d of February 1878 ...

Deponent further says that after the occurrence of the attempted killing of Tunstall and myself related above we started for Lincoln, after traveling about 20 miles we were passed on the road by said J.J. Dolan, Evans, Baker, Hill and Long alias "Rivers.. Evans and Baker rode with Mr Dolan in his ambulance [military conveyance]. It was known to Mr Dolan at the time that all these men were highwaymen and escaped prisoners.

On or about the 7th we saw Baker Hill and Long alias "Rivers" at the Mescalero Indian Agency – at this place they appeared to be quite familiar with Maj. Godfroy the agent ...

Deponent further says that when he arrived at the town of Lincoln he was informed that a courier had proceeded me from Mesilla with a writ of attachment. That Riley, Dolan and Murphy and Sheriff Brady were in ecstasy over deponents prospective confinement in the County [pit] jail and I was informed that Sheriff Brady was making the occasion a subject of merriment by making contracts to grind corn in the mexican mills to make gruel for my maintenance that said Riley had swept out the jail in order that he might in future have it to say that he swept out the room in which I was incarcerated. [T]hat said Brady expressed himself in the presence of E.A. Dow and others to the effect that Tunstall and I had reported that he (Brady) was a defaulter to the Territory, but that he meant to show us that he would not make a default in confining this deponent in jail and taking the spirit out of him – that he may have allowed Baker Evans and Hill to escape but that he would not allow deponent to do so.

Deponent further says that he found a writ of attachment had been issued out of the Third Judicial District Court in which said Emilie Scholand and Charles Fritz were plaintiffs – that it was dated the 7th of February 1878 and that **the Sheriff commenced to attach thereunder on the 8th it having been sent a distance of about 154 miles in almost unprecedented short time for this Territory – that he [Brady] not only attached my personal property but also my real, together with the property of J.H. Tunstall ... He (the Sheriff) was commanded to attach and safely keep so much property as would secure the sum of $8000 but he attached property both real and personal worth over $40000. At this time I was not Mr Tunstalls partner though I was to become such by articles of agreement in May 1878.** *I was his attorney and took an active part in the management of his business ...*

Deponent further says that on or about the 14th of February 1878 Mr Tunstall was informed that one J.B. Matthews (who was in the employ of Murphy and attended to any thing that Dolan and Riley desired done) was at his (Tunstalls) Ranch with said Baker Evans Hill and Davis as Sheriffs posse to attach Tunstalls cattle and horses as the property of this deponent. That said J.B. Matthews as Sheriff Bradys Deputy was informed that deponent had neither cattle or horses there but that he could "round up" and if he found any he could take them, that he could not take Tunstalls property ... That said J.B. Matthews stated that he would return to Lincoln and report to Brady - that he would return in a day or so ... [and] would bring only one man with him.

R.M. Brewer who was Tunstalls foreman told him [Matthews] that when he came he would "round up" the cattle & horses & he could see if there were any of McSweens horses or cattle there. On or about the 14th of February 1878 Robert Widenman[n] came in from Tunstalls cattle ranch and informed Tunstall in my hearing ... that he was satisfied that Matthews intended to raise a large posse and take the cattle by force, that for that purpose said

Baker had gone down to Dolan & Companys cow camp on the Pecos with instructions to W$^{\underline{m}}$ *Morton their foreman to raise all the men he could and meet Matthews with his posse at Turkey Springs a few miles from Tunstalls cattle ranch on the evening of the 16*th *February 1878.* **Mr Tunstall was informed in my hearing by George Washington [a Lincoln resident] that Murphy, Riley & Dolan had helped Matthews to raise a force to the number of 43 men, that said Riley informed him (Washington) that there was no use in McSweens and Tunstalls trying to get away from them this time as they had them completely in their power that they could not possibly be beat as they had the District Attorney (meaning Rynerson) the Court and all the power in Santa Fe [Catron] to back them, that their plan was to take the cattle from Tunstalls ranch ... so as to draw the men in Tunstalls house out of it, then the balance of the posse were to take possession of the house and "get" Tunstalls men.** *[U]pon this information Mr Tunstall canceled to go to the ranch and induced his men to leave and allow Matthews and posse to take the property and seek his remedy in the courts, for the purpose as he informed me he left Lincoln on the night of the 16*th*. This was the last time I saw Tunstall alive.*

I have been informed by R.M. Brewer (deceased) John Middleton, **W Bonney***, R.A. Widenmann, F.T. Waite and Henry Brown that as Tunstall reached his cattle ranch on the night of the 17*$^{\underline{th}}$ *and commanded them all to leave the ranch and come to Lincoln which they did. McCloskey (deceased) informed me that Mr Tunstall [told him] to get one Martin ["Dutch" Martin Martz] who was a good cattle man to come to the ranch and turn the cattle over to Deputy Sheriff J.B. Matthews ...* **that he would not sacrifice the life of one of his men for all the cattle for they would all be killed if they remained at the ranch.** *Said McCloskey informed me further that he not only delivered that verbal message to said Martin but told the same to said J.B. Matthews and informed him that Mr Tunstall would offer no resistance to the taking of the property, though none of it belonged to this deponent.*

Deponent further says that on the night of the 18th *February 1878 he was informed by R.M. Brewer,* **W. Bonney***, J. Middleton and R.A. Widenmann that said J.H. Tunstall was murdered on the road to Lincoln about 30 miles from his cattle ranch by Jessie Evans, Frank Baker, J.J. Dolan, W. Morton, T. Cocoran,*

P. [Pantaleon] Gallegos, A. [Andrew] L. Roberts, Tom Hill, George Davis, Robert W. Beckwith, Tom Green, George Hindman, J. Hurley and others to the number of 18 men ... I am informed that Tom Green who was present when the murder was committed that Morton who was acting as Deputy under orders from said Deputy Matthews called out to Tunstall to stop that he wanted to see him and that they did not want to hurt him, and that thereupon Mr Tunstall dismounted and walked towards Morton and delivered him a Colts pistol carried by him (Tunstall) and that a few minutes thereafter Jessie Evans aforesaid took aim at Mr Tunstall and shot him the ball taking effect in his breast and that as he (Tunstall) fell on his face, said Morton fired another shot at Mr Tunstall out of Tunstalls revolver the ball entering the back of his head and coming out in the forehead and that **thereafter Morton walked to Tunstalls horse and shot another shot out of Tunstalls pistol at said horse whereupon the horse dropped dead and that the murderers carried the corpse of said Tunstall and laid him close to the said horse putting his hat under the dead horse's head.**

On the night last above this deponent wrote a note to John Newcomb requesting him to go to where Tunstalls corpse was and bring it into Lincoln that it might have a decent burial. That on the night of the 19th February 1878 said John Newcomb with others brought into Lincoln the lifeless body of said Tunstall ... That on the night of the day last mentioned a coroners inquest was held on the body of said Tunstall ... **That on or about the 20th I carried the body of said Tunstall to be embalmed and a post mortem examination made by Drs Ealy and Appel, that not only was the body shot as already stated but the skull was broken into pieces by a blow from some instrument after being shot as aforesaid,** that on the 19th day of February 1878 I caused affidavits to be filed before J.B. Wilson Justice of the Peace within the said town of Lincoln charging the murder of Mr Tunstall on the parties named upon which affidavits a warrant of arrest for such parties was duly issued and said affidavits placed in the hands of Atanacio Martinez constable in and for said town of Lincoln for execution ...

That upon the 20th day of February 1878 said constable Martinez called upon W. Bonney and F.T. Waite to help him serve said warrant. That it was well known that ten or twelve of the murderers of Mr Tunstall were then and there in the house ["The House"] of L.G. Murphy Dolan and Riley aforesaid – That as *this deponent is informed by said constable said constable proceeded to said house ... to make arrests ...* **[H]e met the said Sheriff Brady who without any warrant or authority of law took the said Bonney and Waite [and Constable Martinez] prisoners and refused to aid or allow them to arrest though the majority of said murderers were then and there with said Sheriff. [T]hat on the evening of the day last mentioned said Constable [Martinez] was released and Bonney and Waite retained for two days more.**

That after the burial of Mr Tunstall on the 22nd of February 1878 a meeting of the citizens of Lincoln County was held to prevent further bloodshed if possible – that at such meeting Hon Florencio Gonzales Probate Judge of said County, Isaac Ellis, merchant, Jose Montaño, merchant, and John Newcomb farmer were appointed a committee to wait for said Sheriff Brady to ascertain why he prevented the said constable from executing said warrant and making arrests as therein directed and took said constable and posse as aforesaid prisoners and still **held Bonney and Waite as such. [T]hey informed me on their return that Sheriff Brady said he held both the constable and posse prisoners because he had the power,** *they further informed me that ... he would not take a bond of any kind from the deponent for said property [in the embezzlement case].*

Deponent further says that five or six deputies were put by said Brady in charge of the store of J.H. Tunstall, decd. with its stock of general merchandise attached as the property of deponent ... [T]hat on or about the 18th day of February 1878 said Sheriff Brady had a detachment of United States soldiers from Fort Stanton stationed at the house of Murphy, Dolan & Riley aforesaid and that he caused to be issued for the horses belonging to such detachment the hay belonging to Mr Tunstall in his lifetime without authority or permission ... [T]hat on the 19th day of February 1878 an affidavit was filed with said J.B. Wilson Justice of the Peace charging said Deputy Brady deputies as aforesaid with appropriation of goods [the hay] ... and that as a result ... Brady was held to await the action of the Lincoln County Grand Jury for April 1878 ...

Deponent further says that on the 11th day of February 1878 he made and executed an appearance bond as required by Judge Bristol and sent the same by Registered Letter to W.L. Rynerson District Attorney ... Said bond was

refused ... Jose Montaño merchant in said town of Lincoln volunteered to become one of my bondsmen ... Subsequently he [Montaño] informed deponent that he was threatened with ruin by J.J. Dolan & Co if he became one of my bondsmen. The said Sheriff as said Montaño informed the deponent, used all his influence with said Montaño to prevent his becoming one of my surities ... so as to prevent me from giving bonds and to oblige me to go to jail. Joseph H. Blazer informed me that J.J. Dolan & Co had also threatened that if he became one of my bondsmen they would have him prosecuted for cutting timber in the Public Lands ... in the U.S. Courts by T.B. Catron U.S. District Attorney in Santa Fe.

A few days after the execution of said Bond said Sheriff Brady called upon said Jose Montaño as the latter informed me, with a letter purporting to be from said W.L. Rynerson to the effect that though a friend to said Montaño he could not accept him a bond of this amount and requesting that he draw his name from said bond. After such representations and coaxing by said Sheriff, said Montaño signed a letter complying with said request of withdrawal, written by said Brady. The surities on said bond justified in different sums amounting to the aggregate sum of $34500. **Deponent was informed by G. [George] Washington that he heard Brady and Riley aforesaid say that there was no use in deponent trying to give bonds as W.L. Rynerson aforesaid would not approve of any that he (deponent) would give & that he would have to go to jail.**

Deponent now learnt that J.J. Dolan went to Mesilla to get an alias warrant for this deponent [Note: Alias warrants are issued when a person fails to respond to a citation; here posting bond in lieu of going to jail. If there has been no final judgment - here by the Grand Jury - bond can be posted to lift that warrant; but here all bonds have been purposefully refused to justify Brady's jailing McSween], *said* **Deputy Sheriff Barrier having failed to deliver me to said Brady he having been induced to that course by the representations of the best citizens in said County that if he delivered this deponent to said Brady deponent would thereby lose his life** – *[T]hat this deponent informed the said Deputy Sheriff from Las Vegas that as a matter of law he would be guilty of contempt of court by failing to comply with his warrant, but that from that species of offences he could purge himself but at no time did I ask or request said Barrier not* *to comply with his warrant though* **I believed then as I do now that had I been delivered to Brady aforesaid I would have been murdered ...**

Deponent further says that on or about the 24<u>th</u> of February 1878 he was informed that said J.J. Dolan went to Mesilla to see W.L. Rynerson aforesaid for the purpose of obtaining an alias warrant for my arrest and another for the arrest of said Barrier and that though I was entreated by the citizens both American and Mexican to quit the town of Lincoln at once for a while, that I done so first remaining at one farm house and then another. That on or about the 9<u>th</u> day of March I returned to the town of Lincoln with the determination to remain there and submit to any order said Brady might get against me even if I lost my life. [U]pon my arrival at Lincoln about 2 pm of the day last mentioned I learnt that his Excellency S.B. Axtell Governor of New Mexico had been to Lincoln and had left a short time before my arrival and that he had removed J.B. Wilson Justice of the Peace aforesaid.

Everybody with whom I conversed appeared to be very much disheartened owing to the refusal of the Governor to hear them in relation to the troubles and in removing Wilson claiming that the Governor had espoused the cause of Murphy Dolan & Riley aforesaid and cited the fact ... that he had procured troops for said Brady by order of the President ....

Hon F. [Florencio] Gonsales [San Patricio Probate Judge], I. Ellis, J. Montaño and J. Newcomb aforesaid and many others insisted that I absent myself under the circumstances as hereinbefore stated until the meeting of the District Court to which I reluctantly consented.

On or about the [blank] day of [blank] 1878 R.M. Brewer was deputized by J.B. Wilson Justice of the Peace to serve a warrant for the arrest of W. Morton and Frank Baker two of the alleged murderers of Tunstall ...

That said Morton and Baker were then at the cow camp of J.J. Dolan & Co aforesaid on the Pecos River a distance of at least 150 miles. That on or about the night of the 10<u>th</u> of March 1878 R.M. Brewer came to see me before I should leave the town of Lincoln that then and there he informed me that he and posse arrested said Morton & Baker and that within 30 miles of Lincoln, W Morton snatched the pistol of one W. [William] McCloskey ... now one of Brewers posse and shot said McCloskey in the head and then put to the mountains ... that *thereupon the posse chased and killed said Morton & Baker. Said Brewer after relating the death of said three persons ... requested me to advise him as to how to make his return. Deponent then informed Mr Brewer of the Governors visit, his removal of J.B. Wilson, his forbading said Wilson in person not to exercise the functions of such Justice of the Peace any longer and that he was about to issue a proclamation ...* **I further informed Brewer that I understood that Murphy Dolan and Riley had taken steps to have him and posse arrested for undertaking to arrest Morton & Baker by virtue of warrants issued by said J.B. Wilson.** *I advised Mr Brewer to keep away from Lincoln and out of the way of Murphy, Dolan & Riley until the District Court convened when I was satisfied we would get justice. I parted with Brewer on the night last aforesaid and have not seen him since and am credibly informed that he is dead. I knew Mr Brewer since I came to the County of Lincoln. He was a man who never drank any kind of liquor nor quarreled with anyone and was thoroughly honest. He was a hardworking farmer and stockman. Our people ... considered him one of our best & most peaceful citizens. He was not on good terms with Murphy Dolan & Riley, he often expressed himself to the effect that he knew they wanted to kill him ... I know of my own knowledge that he paid them in two years $1000 rental for a piece of unsurveyed public lands and when he refused to continue to pay they wanted him killed or out of the way.*

Deponent further says that from the time he returned from Mesilla until he left Lincoln ... nearly every person who came to see him urged him to leave the town until Court met stating that unless deponent done so he would lose his life. [T]hat on or about 10 of March 1878 deponent left the town of Lincoln in company with G. Washington, G. Robinson and Deputy Sheriff A. P. Barrier aforesaid for [John Chisum's] South Spring River Ranch in said County of Lincoln a distance of 70 miles from said town of Lincoln where I remained until on or about the 29 of March 1878 when I left in company with J. Chisum, R.M. Gilbert Dr M.R. Leverson ... and my wife for the town of Lincoln to attend court.

On the 28th day of March 1878 said Sheriff Brady with a posse of soldiers went to South Spring River Ranch to summons jurors, John S. Chisum informed me that Brady then and there assured him that he did not want to arrest me ... as he knew I would be at court. By a clerical mistake the venire was made returnable on the 1st Monday of April whereas the term set by law for the holding of the District Court of said County of Lincoln is the second Monday of April ...

But for the fact that the Sheriff stated as I am informed that court was to have begun on the 1ˢᵗ Monday I should not have left South Spring River Ranch for another week, having no faith in the guarantees of Brady that he would not arrest me ... **On the 1ˢᵗ day of April 1878 in company with the aforementioned persons I went to the town of Lincoln and then and there learnt for the first time that said Brady and Geo Hindman had been killed on said day.** On said day in the evening at Lincoln one George W. Peppin, a tool of Murphy Dolan & Riley, with Lieut Smith and a few soldiers from the fort arrested me on the alias warrant already referred to said G.W. Peppin claiming to be acting as the Deputy of the dead Sheriff Brady.

Seeing that Peppin aforesaid, J.B. Matthews aforesaid and three of Tunstalls alleged murderers were endorsed in all they done by Col George Purington with U.S. soldiers I appealed to Col Purington for protection ... but he claimed that he had no place for me at the fort. My friends insisted that W. Dowling Post Trader at Fort Stanton had a room that I could secure ... After much entreaty he consented to take me up to the fort where subsequently he came near preventing me from securing a room aforesaid ...

Deponent further says that G.W. Peppin went to said Col Purington and asked him (Purington) if he would allow him (Peppin) to search the house of deponent for arms. Purington replied in the affirmative. Peppin and posse then went to the house to search, deponent forbade them to enter unless they had a warrant. I used these words on that occasion "Peppin you know that you are not an officer, but were you you can't search without a warrant for that purpose" whereupon Matthews aforesaid replied "We can't aye we'll show you what we can do" ... During all this Dr Leverson [McSween's guest] said to Purington that the constitution of the U.S. guaranteed a man immunity from search seizure &c **whereupon Col Purington used these words "Damn the constitution and you for a fool"** ...

Deponent further says that D.P. Shield G. Washington, Geo Robinson, and R.A. Widenmann were arrested by said G.W. Peppin & posse without warrant charging them with being implicated in the murder of Brady and Hindman. That Col Purington was appealed to by said persons for protection and that he consented to take them to the fort with the deponent ... Purington placed a guard at each door [of the custody rooms] ...

with orders to shoot any or all of us who left the rooms without permission ...

[AUTHOR'S NOTE: N.A.M. Dudley assumed Fort Stanton's Command on April 5, 1878, and granted them "the liberty of the Post until the District Court convened." So McSween wrongly thought that Dudley was unbiased.]

The District Court convened April 8, 1978 ...

Deponent further says that the Grand Jury for the April (1878) term of said District Court for the County of Lincoln examined the charges of embezzlement against this deponent and their findings [were that deponent was innocent of embezzling] ...

That on or about the 18th day of February 1878 JH Riley aforesaid came to the residence of the deponent in a drunken condition, that at this time Mr Riley was anxious to show that he had no weapons about his person and to convince persons in the room [gathered after Tunstall's murder] of that fact turned out his pockets, that in doing so he threw out a memorandum book and after asking the men in the house ... if they wanted to kill him and receiving a reply in the negative took his departure leaving said memorandum book on the table at the residence of the deponent.

Deponent says that he examined said book with great care, that he found a letter in it in the handwriting of said W.L. Rynerson addressed to Dolan & Riley [the February 14, 1878 Friends Dolan and Riley letter anticipating Tunstall's murder] ... there was also a memorandum of cattle received by said Dolan & Riley from notorious cattle thieves whose names were given. **That it also contained a list of names of persons well known in this county for their friendship for or opposition to said Dolan & Riley opposite each name was a <u>nome de plume.</u>**

Catron being "<u>Grapes</u>" Godfroy "<u>Hampton</u>" Burnstein (Indian agent clerk) "<u>soapweed</u>" Indians "<u>Tree</u>" Delaney (First Lieutenant at Fort Stanton) "<u>Warwick</u>" Murphy aforesaid "<u>Box</u>" Rynerson (District Attorney aforesaid) "<u>Oyster</u>" Dowling (Post Trader at Fort Stanton) "<u>Pimp</u>" and McSween (the deponent) "<u>Diablo</u>" – Devil &c &c

Deponent further says that he has often expressed himself to the effect that he was determined to use all lawful means to bring the murderers of Tunstall to justice if it cost him every dollar he possessed or could earn. That after the adjournment of the April 1878 term of the said District Court for Lincoln County deponent learnt from the Sheriff of said County [John Copeland] that the **Prosecuting Attorney said W.L. Rynerson had failed and refused to place warrants in his hands for the arrest of parties indicted for the murder of Tunstall, but had placed warrants in the Sheriff's hands for the arrest of all indicted persons supposed to sympathize with feeling against Murphy, Dolan and Riley**

[AUTHOR'S NOTE: These are the indictments of Billy and other Regulators for the murders of Brady, Hindman, and Roberts that would be the basis of Billy's pardon appeal in 1879.]

that thereupon and on or about the 27th day of April 1878 deponent addressed and sent a letter to W.L. Rynerson asking him to place warrants in the hands of said Sheriff for the arrest of all persons indicted by said Grand Jury for the murder of said Tunstall ... that afterwards to wit on or about the 4th day of May 1878 deponent received from said W.L. Rynerson and answer to said letter dated April 27 1878. [sic - May 2nd; see pages 380-382]

Deponent further says that from all he can gather the recent troubles in Lincoln County are owing to the determination of Murphy Dolan and Riley to prevent opposition to their business and that nothing else is the cause of Tunstalls death

[AUTHOR'S NOTE: McSween never fully conceptualized the Santa Fe Ring's power in the conflict, though he was aware of "The House's" connection to T.B. Catron, and of the Ring.]

that the deponent has been satisfied that the parties named (Murphy Dolan and Riley) have been working to take the life of this deponent for the last two years, and that to do that said Dolan offered one Stephen Stanley (as deponent is informed and believes) $1000. **This deponent declares in the most solemn manner that he knows of no reason for the hatred of Murphy Dolan and Riley towards him other than deponent has professionally and as a neighbor helped people to throw off the yoke of said Murphy, Dolan & Riley, informing parties of their rights when requested so to do, and by encouraging emigration [like Tunstall's] and helping those who were in the County to remain whether acceptable to Murphy Dolan & Riley or not. That I have done all in my power, a man and a citizen, to stimulate our people to energy and independence of action and character and that this course** *caused Murphy, Dolan & Riley together with their way of dealing with the people to lose their power, their loss of power having finally culminated in the death of Tunstall. That a petition ... was signed by every resident of Lincoln County to whom it was presented asking them to leave the County and giving as a reason that our people might have permanent peace.*

Deponent further says that on or about the 4th day of April 1878 Richard M. Brewer aforesaid and A.L. Roberts one of the alleged murderers of Tunstall was killed at Mescalero Apache Indian Agency in this county under the following circumstances as was related to me by one who was present and saw the shooting from beginning to end (Frank Coe) ... Brewer Coe and others [including Billy Bonney] went to the Agency – some to look for stolen stock – some for business – all to talk to the Indian Agent for harboring alleged murderers and thieves who were helping Murphy, Dolan & Riley against the people, **there they met A.L. Roberts one of Tunstalls alleged murderers who drew his gun on Chas Bowdre and fired as he [Bowdre] approached said Roberts**, *the bullet grazing Bowdres abdomen, whereupon Bowdre fired at Roberts, the bullet entering the stomach of Roberts. Roberts now shot Middleton & Coe not fatally, and killed Brewer aforesaid.*

That on or about the 1st day of May I was informed by Saturnino Baca that five men had wanted to enter his house & secrete themselves for the purpose of killing me and others – that they said they had killed a man or two [killed Frank MacNab] a few miles below belonging to the "Regulators." **We now received tidings to the effect that ten or twelve men were stationed at the house ["The House"] west of my house formerly occupied by Murphy, Dolan & Riley but now controlled by T.B. Catron U.S. District Attorney Santa Fe – being represented by his brother in law E.A. Walz** *... [and] that there were 20 more well armed men on the East of my residence – [U]pon this information the sheriff (Copeland) placed 4 or 5 men on my house for the protection of my life and property and done the same as he and others informed me in the centre and at the east end of the town. Learning that these men numbered 30 or more men said Copeland as I am informed sent for a detachment of soldiers to aid him in resisting said bands of men. From Frank Coe I learned that when on his way home from said Lincoln to wit on or about the 11th day of May 1878 [sic – April 29, 1878] in company with Frank McNab [MacNab] and James Sanders they were fired at by different* *parties of men in ambush in different directions, killed McNab [MacNab] and dangerously if not fatally wounded Sanders ... and holding said [Frank] Coe until next day as hostage – that the party after that came to the town of Lincoln and divided as already stated. [J]ust about noon of said day firing was commenced by the Sheriffs party or by the murderers ... About 3 o'clock in the afternoon of the same day Lieut Smith and a number of soldiers with Sheriff Copeland took about 22 men prisoners. Deponent has been informed that said 22 men after killing McNab [MacNab] and wounding Sanders as aforesaid desired to attack the store of I. Ellis but that after going near the building about daylight next day said posse found the doors and windows of said house were kept closed for the purpose they supposed of concealing armed men [Regulators] from their view and so abandoned the purpose.*

That on or about the 3rd day of May 1878 an affidavit was filed with J.G. Trujillo Justice of the Peace of Precinct No 2 in said Lincoln County charging R.[Robert] W. Beckwith, Johnson and 20 others with the murder of McNab [MacNab] and wounding of Sanders aforesaid – that a warrant was issued on said affidavit and was placed in the hands of Sheriff Copeland for execution. That on or about the 4th day of May 1878 this deponent with several others went to Precinct No 2 for the purpose of testifying against the 22 men aforesaid.

That on or about the 6th day of May 1878 Lieuts. Goodwin and Smith with about 25 soldiers in charge of the said Sheriff came to said Precinct No 2 with warrants for the arrest of all witnesses against said 22 men – **that the warrant on which affidavit and others were sought to be arrested was issued by D. Easton Justice of the Peace for Precinct No 3 and that the offence charged was assault with intent to kill** *based upon an affidavit before some military officer in Fort Stanton by said G.W. Peppin and J.B. Matthews - That this deponent was grossly insulted by Lieut Goodwin - That said Goodwin refused to obey the Sheriff and informed the Sheriff then and there that he would not allow any one to be arrested unless the Sheriff turned the deponent over to him (Goodwin) to be taken to Fort Stanton - That said Goodwin positively refused to obey the Sheriffs orders – That Goodwin by his words and acts showed himself to be a bitter partisan – That after reaching Fort Stanton this deponent with I. Ellis & Sons and others were put in the guardhouse in Fort Stanton – that we were kept in confinement for two days – that we were taken from the guard house to have an examination by a* *justice of the peace – that the 22 men [murderers of Frank MacNab] referred to as I am informed were turned loose and failed to be taken or go before a Justice of the Peace so the charge of murder still remains against them without examination.*

Deponent has been informed that said Johnson with the balance of the 22 men as posse, was acting as the Deputy of Sheriff Brady who had been dead at that time about two months a fact known to said Johnson & his party [thus, not a legal deputy].

Deponent has been informed that said 22 men started from the Pecos [Seven Rivers boys] for Lincoln for the purpose of killing I. Ellis, Sheriff and this deponent.

Deponent further says that nearly all of said 22 men were the persons and tools of said Murphy Dolan & Riley deriving their support chiefly from said Murphy Dolan & Riley ...

Deponent further says he has given a concrete statement of the troubles in said Lincoln Co that culminated in the death of Tunstall and of the discord and violence that has followed so far as the knowledge and information of the deponent extends – that he has given a true statement of events without regard as to the light in which the same may place him.

A.A. McSween

Read subscribed and sworn to before me this 6th day of June 1878 –

Rafael Sutienes, Probate Clerk
By Juan B. Patron, Deputy [Clerk]

CATRON'S FEDERAL INDICTMENT PLOT

On June 21, 1878, with Regulators holding ground, Catron, as U.S. Attorney, exposed himself by intervening to bolster his outlaw myth, take control of prosecutions, and prevent gubernatorial pardons. Among his accused would be Billy as "Kid": a local nickname Catron likely got from James Dolan. The Brady and Hindman killings had Territorial indictments, but Catron argued that the "Buckshot" Roberts killing at Blazer's Mill was under his federal jurisdiction, since it was located in the Mescalero Reservation, which was federal "Indian Country."

So he filed federal Case No. 411 against the Regulators as: "United States vs. Charles Bowdry [Bowdre], Doc Scurlock, Henry Brown, Henry Antrim - alias Kid - John Middleton, Stephen Stevens, John Scroggins, George Coe and Frederick Waite." He wrote:

The United States of America)
Territory of New Mexico   )
Third Judicial District   )

  In the United States District Court for the Third Judicial District of the June Term of 1878.
    The Grand Jury of the United States of America from the body of the good and lawful men of the Third Judicial District aforesaid – duly empanneled sworn and charged to the Term of aforesaid to inquire in and for the body of the Third Judicial District aforesaid upon their oaths do present that Charles Bowdry [sic - Bowdre throughout], Doc Scurlock, Henry Brown, **Henry Antrim – alias Kid** – John Middleton, Stephen Stevens, John Scroggins, George Coe and Frederick Waite, late of the Third Judicial District in the Territory of New Mexico on the fifth [sic - fourth] day of April in the year of our Lord Eighteen hundred and Seventy-eight **at and in this reservation of the Mescalero Apache Indians in the Said Third Judicial District, Said Reservation then and there being a part of the Indian country,** with force and armed in and upon one Andrew Roberts then and there being in the Said Reservation feloniously, willfully, unlawfully of this malice aforethought and from a premeditated design to effect the death of the Said Andrew Roberts, did make an assault, and that the Said Charles Bowdry, Doc Scurlock, Henry Brown, **Henry Antrim – alias Kid** – John Middleton, Stephen Stevens, John Scroggins, George Coe and Frederick Waite certain guns then and there loaded and charged with gunpowder and divers leaden bullets, which said guns the Said Charles Bowdry, Doc Scurlock, Henry Brown, **Henry Antrim (alias Kid)** John Middleton, Stephen Stevens, John Scroggins, George Coe and Frederick Waite in their hands then and there had and held to, against and upon the Said Andrew Roberts there and then within the Said Reservation feloniously, willfully, unlawfully of this malice aforethought and from a premeditated design to effect the death of the Said Andrew Roberts – did shoot and discharge, and that the Said Charles Bowdry, Doc Scurlock, Henry Brown, **Henry Antrim – alias Kid** – John Middleton, Stephen Stevens, John Scroggins, George Coe and Frederick Waite, with the leaden Bullets aforesaid, out of the guns aforesaid, then and there by force of the gunpowder that discharged and sent forth as aforesaid and on Roberts in and upon the right side of the belly of him the Said Andrew Roberts then and there within the Said Reservation

feloniously, willfully, unlawfully of this malice aforethought and from a premeditated design to effect the death of the Said Andrew Roberts, did strike, penetrate and wound, giving to the said Andrew Roberts then and there and within the said Reservation and with the leaden Bullets aforesaid, that discharged and sent forth out of the guns aforesaid by the said Andrew [Charles] Bowdry, Doc Scurlock, Henry Brown, **Henry Antrim – alias Kid** *– John Middleton, Stephen Stevens, John Scroggins, George Coe and Frederick Waite in and upon the right side of the belly of him the said Andrew Roberts one mortal wound of the depth of ten inches and of breadth of one half of an inch of which said mortal wound the Said Andrew Roberts then and there at the said Reservation instantly died and so the Jury aforesaid upon their oaths as aforesaid do say that the Said Charles Bowdry, Doc Scurlock, Henry Brown,* **Henry Antrim – alias Kid** *– John Middleton, Stephen Stevens, John Scroggins, George Coe and Frederick Waite the Said Andrew Roberts in manner and form aforesaid feloniously, willfully, unlawfully of this malice aforethought and from a premeditated design to effect the death of the Said Andrew Roberts, did kill and murder against the form of the Statute in such case made and provided against the Peace & dignity of the United States. And the Jurors aforesaid upon their oaths aforesaid do further present that Charles Bowdry late of the Third Judicial District in the Territory of New Mexico on the fifth day of April in the year AD Eighteen hundred and Seventy-eight at and within the Reservation of the Mescalero Apache Indians said Reservation being then and there situate in the Third Judicial District aforesaid and then and there being Indian Country in and upon Andrew Roberts then and there being in the Said Reservation in the Said District, feloniously, willfully, unlawfully of his malice aforethought and from a premeditated design to effect the death of the Said Andrew Roberts did make an assault and that the Said Charles Bowdry a certain gun then and there loaded and charged with gunpowder and one leaden Bullet which gun he the Said Charles Bowdry in his right hand then and there had and held to at against and upon the Said Andrew Roberts then and there within the Said Reservation feloniously, willfully, unlawfully of his malice aforethought and from a premeditated design to effect the death of the Said Andrew Roberts, did shoot and discharge and that the Said Charles Bowdry with the leaden Bullet aforesaid out of the gun aforesaid then and there by force of the gunpowder aforesaid shot and sent forth as aforesaid the Said Andrew Roberts* in and from the right side of the belly of him the Said Andrew Roberts then and there and in the Said Reservation feloniously, willfully, unlawfully of his malice aforethought and from a premeditated design to effect the death of the Said Andrew Roberts, did strike, penetrate and wound, giving to the Said Andrew Roberts then and there with the leaden Bullet aforesaid so as aforesaid that discharged and sent forth out of the gun aforesaid by the Said Charles Bowdry in and upon the right side of the belly of the Said Andrew Roberts one mortal wound of ten inches and of breadth of one half of an inch of which said mortal wound the Said Andrew Roberts then and there at the said Reservation instantly died and the Jury aforesaid upon their oaths aforesaid do further present that Doc Scurlock, Henry Brown, **Henry Antrim – alias Kid** – John Middleton, Stephen Stevens, John Scroggins, George Coe and Frederick Waite of the Third Judicial District aforesaid and on the day and year aforesaid with force and arms at the Said Reservation in the Said District aforesaid **feloniously was present aiding and abetting and assisting the [Said] Charles Bowdry the felony and murder aforesaid to do and commit against the form of the Statute in such case made and provided against the Peace & dignity of the United States and the Jurors aforesaid upon their oaths aforesaid do say that the Said Charles Bowdry Doc Scurlock, Henry Brown, Henry Antrim – alias Kid – John Middleton, Stephen Stevens, John Scroggins, George Coe and Frederick Waite in manner and form aforesaid feloniously, willfully, unlawfully of his malice aforethought and from a premeditated design to effect the death of him the Said Andrew Roberts, him the Said Roberts did kill and murder against the form of the Statute in such case made and provided and against the peace and dignity of the United States.**

Thomas B. Catron
United States Attorney
for New Mexico

<u>411</u>

The United States
vs)
)
Charles Bowdry, Doc Scurlock, Henry Brown, **Henry Antrim alias "Kid,"** John Middleton, Stephen Stevens, John Scroggins, George Coe and Frederick Waite

A true bill
   C.P. Crawford
   Foreman of the Grand Jury

Witnesses
Aurelius Wilson, John Pallen, John Watts, J.H. Blazer, Sam F. Mills, [missing first name] Howe, William Gentry

Filed in my Office
the 21 day of June 1878
   John S. Crouch, Clerk

CITIZENS REQUEST PRESIDENTIAL AID

SUMMARY: Inspired by Alexander McSween and Montegue Leverson, even the humblest Lincoln County citizens complained to President Rutherford B. Hayes. This onslaught of truth was likely relayed to T.B. Catron, because massacre and military retaliation stood ready to crush this unquenchable determination for justice.

LETTER OF GEORGE COE AND J. ISAACS

The voice of the Regulators can be heard in the June 22, 1878 letter of J. Isaacs and George Coe to President Hayes against *"the U.S. officials who are the head and front of all these thieves."* Accused is *"Mr. Catron the U.S. District Attorney having transferred to him the property of the Murphy Dolan & Reilly gang has got the U.S. troops to be sent [after alleged rustlers, and for disarming citizens]."* Focus was on Governor S.B. Axtell's proclamations shielding Tunstall's killers, and replacing Sheriff Copeland with murderous George Peppin. They got no answer. They wrote:

>Coes Ranch, Chicora Park,
>Colfax Co. New Mexico
>22 June, 1878.

To His Excellency R.B. Hayes President of the United States
Excellency
   We are two residents of Lincoln Co., who after incurring the greatest peril to life and property at the hands of thieves and murderers whom the

Governor and U.S. troops aid and abet in their crimes, have succeeded in bringing whole skins to this section where the brother of one of us possesses this ranch.

We respectfully desire to call to your attention the necessity of removing the present Governor of New Mexico, unless in your excellencys opinion the people of the territory are to be regarded as his charges.

Enough has already been laid before your Excellency with regard to Mr. Axtell's conduct to render it highly indecorous that he should be longer retained in office as Governor. **His proclamation in Lincoln Co. which he has never attempted to deny, was so palpable a usurpation and so evidently issued to secure the escape of Mr. Tunstall's murderers that nothing else should have been needed for his removal;** but an act which he has recently committed; which in fact induced us to quit the County, and is rapidly depopulating it is, if possible, still worse.

On the death of Sheriff Brady the county commissioners appointed Mr. John Copeland, a gentleman respected by all the honest men of Lincoln Co. to be sheriff in his place, the power of appointment to vacancies in county offices being by law vested in them. **Mr. Axtell set aside this appointment and appointed in his place one G.W. Peppin, a man not only totally unable to furnish the bonds required by law, but against whom <u>three warrants for three several murders committed by him, were in the hands</u> of the officers of the law, at the very time the Governor appointed him.**

Further – Mr. Catron the U.S. District Attorney having transferred to him the property of the Murphy Dolan & Reilly gang has got the U.S. troops to be sent to round up and collect, not really <u>his</u> cattle but the cattle stolen from Mr. Hunter by the man employed for that purpose by Murphy Dolan and Reilly and the U.S. troops are now being used for that purpose.

All who have seen Mr. Angel feel great confidence in his skill and integrity, but we feel assured of this, that if the U.S. officials who are the head and front of all these thieves fail in the efforts they will make to <u>buy up</u> Mr. Angel, they will proceed to steal his papers, and if necessary for that purpose will <u>murder</u> him.

Thus it is due to the safety of the commissioner your Excellency has appointed <u>as a security for his life</u> that Axtell be immediately removed. By the constitution of the United States – (which when brought to the notice of Col. Purington as forbidding his illegal acts, <u>was publicly damned by him.</u>) – the right to bear arms is secured to the citizens, **the U.S. troops in pursuance of orders from the Governor and Gen. Hatch are violently disarming all the honest citizens, leaving the thieves armed.**

We are informed that the mainstay and support of Mr. Axtell is General Garfield.

[AUTHOR'S NOTE: Republican James Abram Garfield became President after Hayes, and backed the Ring.]

Having every confidence in Gen. Garfields integrity, we presume his mind has been abused. We would therefore suggest that your Excellency cause to be laid before him all the papers the administration has received on the subject.

We believe he will be likely to place confidence in the statement by Dr. M. N. Leverson of Douglas Co. Colorado whom he will remember from several of his publications, and particularly on "the uses and functions of money" published in 1867.

Yours Respectfully
J Isaacs
G.N. Coe

MONTEGUE LEVERSON INTERVENES AGAIN

Montegue Leverson's June 28, 1878 letter to Secretary of the Interior Carl Schurz and President Hayes, titled "Affairs of New Mexico," was returned to him *"by direction of the President"* without action on July 12, 1878, two days before the Lincoln County War Battle's start. His major exposé of Catron, Elkins, Axtell, and the Santa Fe Ring was ignored by Ring-complicit Hayes and Schurz, but proves that, before Angel's reports, they fully knew that U.S. officials were involved in Tunstall's murder and Lincoln County "troubles." Furthermore, Leverson saw through the Angel investigation, stating *"that the present investigation is meant to be <u>a whitewashing one</u>."* Leverson wrote:

Post Office
Larkspur

Leverson Ranch.
Douglas Co., Colorado

28 June 1878

Dear Sir:

It is with the greatest reluctance that I yield to the solicitations which have reached me in great number by every main since my return, to address you once more upon the affairs of New Mexico. I have been the more reluctant again to intrude myself upon your notice because Mr. Angel, the gentleman charged to investigate & report to the administration has impressed me most favorably, and inspired me with great confidence both in his ability and integrity.

The unfortunate citizens of New Mexico – clinging to any hope of relief from the <u>very slavery in which they are held</u> – seem to attach a weight to such poor representations as I may make to the administration, which <u>unfortunately</u> for them I know too well they do not possess. I do honestly aver that I believe my representations <u>ought</u> to have the weight these citizens seem to think they do possess and that by reason of my services to the Union during the war (declared by the Hon C.F. Adams to have been "worth an army corps") & by my services to the Republican party since I have lived in this country: but I have no "political influence" being a single citizen whose only desire is <u>to see the right prevail</u>.

But I can no longer refuse the aid of my humble efforts to the heartrending entreaties made to me; and I write to point out to you the terrible wrong which is being daily done to the citizens of New Mexico by the president allowing that man Axtel [Axtell throughout] to remain governor of the Territory.

Surely the administration <u>must</u> feel that a governor should exist for the good of the people, <u>not</u> the people for the governor's benefit – Yet is the conduct of the administration such as would be rational, only on the contrary supposition!

During the whole time Mr. Axtel has been governor, robbery and murder and the blackmailing of respectable citizens by the law officers of the U.S. have been rife & common throughout the Territory, the governor has thus failed in his first duty of maintaining peace and order & seeing that the laws are executed, & surely whether his failure be owing to incompetency or to guilt, ought on <u>this account alone</u> to be removed.

His appointment of Rynerson, the murderer of C.J. [J.P.] Slough to be District Attorney in the 3rd Judicial Dist – is another sufficient reason for his removal.

His infamous proclamation made so evidently to ensure the escape of the murderers of Mr. Tunstall, is yet another, even tho' he were innocent of that motive; because of the Usurpation of Judicial authority palpable on the face of it needing no evidence but the document itself, which even the governor's effrontery has not attempted to deny.

But worse, if that be possible, has since happened

On the death of Sheriff Brady, the County Commissioners appointed a Mr. Copeland, a gentleman who had the confidence of all the good citizens of Lincoln Co, to be sheriff; the governor has set aside this appointment and appointed one G. Peppin to be sheriff of Lincoln Co; although at the very time of that appointment 3 warrants for 3 several murders committed by Peppin were in the hands of the proper law officers for his arrest!

Since then, by the desire of the Gov, and in express violation of the constitution of the United States, the military authorities have issued orders to the U.S. troops, which these troops are carrying out, to disarm all persons carrying arms except the Sheriff (!) & his posse; in other words, they disarm the honest men, leaving their arms to the thieves and murderers!

It is impossible for me to express to you in a letter, the mistrust & fear evinced by the people of the Territory, even in the bona fides of the present administration, and I must in all honesty acknowledge that the past and present course even of the present administration affords but too much ground for such mistrust; nothing indeed but the strong faith I have in you personally, in President Hayes and the very favorable impression produced upon me by Mr. Angel would have overcome like mistrust even in my part.

I will presently name to you some of the reasons which cause this mistrust on the part of the citizens, **meanwhile permit me to call attention to the consequences of it; viz: that much most important testimony will not be forthcoming because of the terror dominating those who should give it.**

[AUTHOR'S NOTE: In this dangerous atmosphere, Billy would give his deposition to Investigator Angel on June 8, 1878.]

The investigation on which Mr. Angel is embarked will necessarily occupy several months, **meanwhile the governed are subjected to all the oppression of [Santa Fe] Ring misrule, a misrule which that of the Tweed in New York was justice and truth in comparison!**

There is not one of the citizens but feels convinced that if the investigation is meant in real earnest, **and the Santa Fe ring fails to "buy up" Mr. Angel** – *which it is my belief registered through the past.*

Now as to some of the causes of the prevailing mistrust of the bona fides of even the present investigation.

1. The most weighty and alarming is the continuance of Mr. Axtel in office in the teeth of his usurpation (by the proclamation before mentioned) and of his appointment of the murderer Peppin to be sheriff, and after his own letter to "Ben Stevens" plotting the murder of the best citizens of Colfax Co: has been made public and brought to the notice of the administration.

2. **The continued employment of U.S. troops in the aid of unlawful and <u>criminal</u> acts of the "Santa Fe ring"** *and their continued and open violation of the Constitution of the U.S. as by disarming citizens & searching houses and making arrests without color of warrant or lawful authority.*

3. The total disregard by the administration of the charges proferred against Axtel in 1877; charges supported upon oath.

4. **The <u>betrayal</u>, aye the <u>immediate</u> betrayal of those affidavits to Hon S.B. Elkins, the brains of the 'Santa Fe ring" altho these affidavits had been obtained under pledge of confidence,** *until a public investigation should be had, made or at least authorized by yourself!*

5. **The immediate communication to Catron of the times appointed by Mr. Axtel for his departure from Santa Fe for Lincoln Co, and of the postponements made by him from time to time for the <u>express</u> purpose of avoiding the company of W. Thornton (Catron's law firm partner) who nevertheless, through the information promised him by the military at Santa Fe, actually traveled down to Ft. Stanton in Mr. Angel's company!**

6. The permission given by Lieut. Loud of Santa Fe to a man stated to be a noted cattle thief **and <u>known to be employed by Catron</u> (one McCabe)** *to ride down to <u>Stanton in the U.S. ambulance with Angel!</u>*

The foregoing are a few of the reasons which, not unreasonably, <u>you must admit</u>, have excited suspicion in the minds of the citizens that the present investigation is meant to be <u>a whitewashing one</u>, and I respectfully urge that some <u>proof</u> should be published to the people that it is meant in all honesty.

I do assure you, and Mr. Angel will bear witness to the fact that I have expended great efforts to conquer this suspicion, and to give all who put any confidence in me, confidence in the bona fides of the investigation; and I am in the daily receipt of letters tending to show that my efforts have had some success among parties who, but for my urgency and professions of belief, would have held aloof & even fled the county. And yet, it is my faith as I have before said in <u>you personally</u>, in President Hayes and in Mr. Angel which alone enable me to continue trustful, notwithstanding the evidence <u>apparently furnished</u> to the contrary by the facts and circumstances above detailed ...

I have, since I commenced this letter, received a letter from a Mr. Coe informing me of more citizen's on Lincoln Co. who have abandoned their all (himself being one) rather than continue subject to the oppression and the peril which daily beset them and their families while in Lincoln Co.

He also asks me in his own name and in that of a number of friends to proceed to Washington to lay before the President a fuller statement than can be made in writing of the oppression under which the honest and downtrodden citizens of New Mexico are laboring, offering that he and his friends would pay my expenses and liberal fee.

If I thought I could do good by going to Washington I would do so, (altho' just now, it would greatly derange my own affairs,) <u>without any fee</u>; but I feel that even my necessary expenses of transportation and subsistence (if worthy of being incurred at all,) should be defrayed by the U.S. and not by the victims of U.S. misrule, but I feel also that there would be nothing to be gained by my presence in Washington, unless I were there in consequence of the desire of the president to obtain a more accurate knowledge of the state of affairs in New Mex than could be obtained from written communications. Only then, on the invitation of the administration would I care to make the sacrifice of my private affairs which my going to Washington would entail, because only in the event of such invitation should I hope for any beneficial result.

   Apologizing for this lengthy intrusion which I hope may be the last. I have the honor to be

   Your obedient
           Montegue Leverson

THE POSSE COMITATUS ACT

A newly passed Congressional Act should have enabled the McSween-Regulator side to win the Lincoln County War, because it blocked military intervention. Before the new Act, the law of posse comitatus permitted a county sheriff to conscript soldiers for peace keeping or pursuit of a felon. Sheriff Brady had used that on March 24, 1878 to take Fort Stanton soldiers as his posse to arrest Alexander McSween at John Chisum's South Spring River Ranch.

But, on June 18, 1878, such use of soldiers was barred by Congress by "Article LVIX, Employment of Troops as a Posse Comitatus," known as the "Posse Comitatus Act;" stating: "It shall not be lawful to employ any part of the Army of the United States, as a posse comitatus, or otherwise, for the purpose of executing the laws, except in such cases and under such circumstances as such employment of said force be expressly authorized by the Constitution or by act of Congress ... [And] it shall be lawful for the President ... to take such measures, by the employment of the militia or the land and naval forces of the United States ... for suppression of such insurrection, domestic violence, or combinations .. [T]he president shall forthwith, by proclamation, command the insurgents to disperse and retire peaceably to their respective abodes, within a limited time."

So troops could not be used in civil disturbances, unless by Presidential proclamation. Its exception was military duty to protect women and children. Since Lincoln County citizens were unaware of Dudley's risk to them, this Act may have seemed irrelevant. But, just then, Catron was seeking ways for its evasion. And Ringite Lincoln resident, Saturnino Baca, may have been poised for his possible role in case of an actual battle.

RING MASSACRE AT SAN PATRICIO

Racism was central to the Santa Fe Ring's New Mexico Territory take-over. The Hispanic population, considered defenseless by Catron and Elkins in their land-grab formulation, bore the brunt of their plunder and intimidation. Governor Marsh Giddings used that racism in his April 3, 1873 response to the Department of Interior about his suppressing the 1872 Legislature Revolt, calling Mexicans *"vilest of the vile"* from *"slums of vice"* in Santa Fe. He complained: *"Nearly all the people of the Territory are Mexican 86,000 out of 93,000."*

Ringite racism and rage at opposition yielded the July 3, 1878 massacre at San Patricio, 12 miles east of Lincoln. Its citizens, likely inspired by bi-cultural Billy Bonney, who often stayed there, had protected McSween and Regulators before and after Tunstall's murder; and they hid McSween after his Grand Jury acquittal and heightened Ring attempts to kill him.

On June 28, 1878, Sheriff George Peppin used Fort Stanton's new Commander, N.A.M. Dudley and troops, in violation of the Posse Comitatus Act passed 10 days earlier, to invade San Patricio for intimidation and a last try to kill McSween there.

The actual retaliatory massacre occurred 8 days later, and 11 days before the Lincoln County War Battle started. Peppin used Mesilla's John Kinney and his gang for his "posse." Men, women, children, and farm animals were slaughtered; property was destroyed. No one was ever prosecuted. Fury remains to this day in the victims' descendants.

But like every prior Ringite terrorist act in Lincoln County, it failed. Instead of withdrawal, it yielded recruitment of fighting men. So most of Alexander McSween's 60 fighters were from San Patricio and Picacho, making the Lincoln County War Battle the Territory's largest Hispanic anti-Ring uprising.

BILLY BONNEY'S "REGULATOR MANIFESTO"

Billy Bonney must have been enraged by the San Patricio massacre. On July 13, 1878, 10 days after it, he took action: challenging the Ring, in what I named the "Regulator Manifesto." It is the anti-Ring declaration of the Lincoln County War Battle, starting the next day. It is signed only *"Regulator."*

Existing as a copy, it was first attributed to Charles Bowdre by early historian, Maurice Garland Fulton, who claimed implausibly that its recipient, Catron's brother-in-law, Edgar Walz, recognized his handwriting. It exists in Washington's National Archives of the Adjutant General's Office as only a rewritten copy.

But I believe it was Billy's production, either dictated to Bowdre, or wrongly attributed to him by Walz, as a Regulator name he knew. It has Billy's zealot's bellicosity, bi-cultural loyalties, and articulateness. It calls the Ring a *"murderous band,"* which includes Catron, his law partner, William Thornton, his brother-in-law, Walz, and "The House" as the *"Murphy party;"* and allies them with John Kinney's massacring gang. It shows Billy's literary skill, as evident the next year, on March 20, 1879, in one of his pardon bargain letters to Governor Lew Wallace, stating: *"I am not afraid to die like a man fighting but I would not like to be killed like a dog unarmed."* And Edgar Walz, by late 1878 and through 1880, became one target of Billy's retaliative guerrilla rustling - just what the Regulator Manifesto threatened.

Walz, as managing Catron's Carrizozo cattle ranch, found the "Manifesto" either sufficiently alarming or incriminating to give it to Fort Stanton's Post Adjutant: Ringite 9th Cavalry Second Lieutenant Millard Fillmore Goodwin. Goodwin, in turn, made its *"true copy"* - pointing to future incriminatory intent. He had it certified by Ringite David M. Easton, hiding that he was no longer a Justice of the Peace, having resigned after the "Buckshot" Roberts killing on April 4, 1878. The "Regulator Manifesto" stated:

In Camp, July 13, 1878.

Mr. Walz. Sir: - We are all aware that your brother-in-law, T.B. Catron sustains the Murphy-Kinney party, and take this method of informing you that if any property belonging to the residents of this county is stolen or destroyed, Mr. Catron's property will be dealt with as nearly as can be in the way in which the party he sustains deals with the property stolen or destroyed by them.

We returned Mr. Thornton the horses we took for the purpose of keeping the Murphy crowd from pursuing us with the promise that these horses should not again be used for that purpose. Now we know that the Tunstall estate cattle are pledged to Kinney and party. If they are taken, a similar number will be taken from your brother [in-law, Catron]. It is our object and efforts to protect property, but the man who plans destruction shall have destruction measured on him. Steal from the poorest or richest American or Mexican, and the full measure of the injury you do, shall be visited upon the property of Mr. Catron. This murderous band is harbored by you as your guest, and with the consent of Catron occupies your property.

Regulator

This grand document mobilized all Victor Westphall's deceit. He ante-dated it three months to John Riley's May 19, 1878 letter to Commander Dudley fabricating Regulator rustling and murder at Catron's Cow Camp. So Westphall called it a Regulator warning to the Cow Camp: "That same day, men in charge of Catron's cattle on the Pecos were warned by Regulators that unless they left the ranch and cattle they would be killed." (Westphall, p. 87)

Westphall quoted the whole Manifesto to prove Catron's property was threatened (Westphall, p. 91), but missed that it implicated Catron and his henchmen, and proved the anti-Ring thrust of the Lincoln County War Battle.

LOST LINCOLN COUNTY WAR BATTLE

SUMMARY: By July 19, 1878, after assassinating John Tunstall, issuing illegal proclamations shielding his killers, killing Regulator leader Frank MacNab in ambush, trying repeatedly to murder Alexander McSween, and massacring at San Patricio, the Ring escalated to full-blown extermination: using troops and weapons of war against civilians in Lincoln to crush the freedom fight of the Lincoln County War.

Catron and his minions responded to Lincoln County citizens' unbending defiance with make-or-break crimes in the final battle of the Lincoln County War from July 14th to 19th of 1878.

On July 13, 1878, Investigator Frank Warner Angel was in Las Vegas, New Mexico, taking the deposition of Deputy Sheriff Adolph Barrier, who had risked his life to save McSween from the Ring because, as he told Angel: *"justice should be meted out to everyone without fear or favor."* McSween, the Regulators, and San Patricio and Picacho men were about fight for that democratic ideal in that six day battle.

Lying Victor Westphall shrinks the battle to one day, fictionalized as a local "affray" from "violent emotions": "These emotions would soon result in the famous affray in Lincoln on July 19, 1878, when the McSween house was burned and several persons killed." (Westphall, p. 126)

But he revealed Catron's role in that battle's decisive and illegal military intervention by Commander N.A.M. Dudley. Catron set the stage by informing District Commander Edward

Hatch about need for troops; which Hatch relayed on April 23, 1878 to army headquarters at Fort Leavenworth. (Westphall, p. 86) Westphall confirmed that Dudley was beholden to Catron for defending him in his court martials of 1871 and 1877: "[I]t has been conjectured that Dudley was grateful for this ... [and] followed Catron's advice on how to proceed with his new command at Fort Stanton." (Westphall, p. 94) Indeed, Dudley risked court martial, and even hanging for treason, by violating the Posse Comitatus Act to attack Lincoln's civilians on July 19, 1878. His trepidation explains his death threat that day to coerce Justice of the Peace Wilson into writing false arrest warrants for McSween and others to give color of rightness to his intervention.

Westphall covers up that fiasco by writing: "Dudley's staff officers persuaded a reluctant justice of the peace." (Westphall, p. 93) Westphall calls Dudley's Posse Comitatus Act violation a need to protect women and children; ignoring that Dudley mortally endangered Susan McSween; her sister, Elizabeth Shield; the Shield's five children, Dr. Taylor Ealy's wife, the Ealy's two children; and José Montaño's wife.

DAY 1: JULY 14, 1878

Eminent battle was no secret. Most townspeople fled Lincoln. Present were Sheriff George Peppin, Deputies Billy Mathews and Jack Long, James Dolan, and Ring loyalist Saturnino Baca and his family. John Riley was in Santa Fe plotting with Catron about evasion of the month-old Posse Comitatus Act, blocking military intervention in civilian conflicts. Heading to Lincoln was an outlaw hoard of about 60 - Seven Rivers rustler-ranchers and Mesilla's John Kinney and his gang - to become Peppin's "posse." And outlaw, Jessie Evans, was likely with Dolan.

Reflecting Alexander McSween's optimism for peaceable victory, was that his family remained. In his house were his wife, Susan; her sister, Elizabeth Shield, with her five young children; and David Shield's law intern, Harvey Morris. Shield was away, giving more evidence that all were sure of an innocuous confrontation. In the Tunstall store's apartment were Dr. Taylor Ealy, his wife, and two children. Justice of the Peace "Squire" Wilson stayed resolutely at home, having ignored Governor Axtell's Proclamation removing his title.

After leaving the safe haven of John Chisum's South Spring River Ranch, McSween arrived in Lincoln with his men, including

Billy; and homesteader, Josiah "Doc" Scurlock, as new Regulator head, replacing murdered Frank MacNab.

McSween's men took strategic positions along Lincoln's single street to hold the town: occupying Tunstall's store, and houses of José Montaño, Juan Patrón, and Isaac Ellis. At the western end were only "The House" and the Ring hang-out, Wortley Hotel.

McSween's more realistic men had well provisioned his house, including a keg of gunpowder for reloading ammunition. But, initially, McSween only permitted Jim "Frenchie" French into his house as a guard.

Arrival of shooting Seven Rivers and Kinney men, convinced him to add, from the Montaño house, Billy, Yginio Salazar, Tom O'Folliard, Jose Chávez y Chávez, Francisco Zamora, and Vincente Romero from San Patricio; and Ignacio Gonzales and Florencio Chávez from Picacho. The terrain of Lincoln was ideal for McSween's intended defense. To the south were nearby, sparsely vegetated, high foothills, which would leave assailants exposed to gunfire. To the north, immediately behind his house, was the Bonito River, preventing positioning of adversaries.

DAY 2: JULY 15, 1878

In McSween's house, his men blockaded windows and cut defensive portholes in its adobe bricks. McSween, with his usual punctilious legality, sent by messenger an eviction letter to Saturnino Baca, his tenant in a house east of Tunstall's store, with grounds of Baca's giving aid to men threatening his life. Baca, the Ring stooge, relayed the letter to James Dolan at "The House" to claim that his wife and children were in danger from McSween and that he needed soldiers to protect them. Baca had likely earlier been coached to use his family as the excuse for a Posse Comitatus Act exception for military intervention by Fort Stanton Commander N.A.M. Dudley; who would also have been prompted.

But that day, the only aggression was Sheriff George Peppin's Deputy, Jack Long's, attempt to serve the invalid David Easton warrants on McSween and "the Kid" for the April 30, 1878 killings and wounding of the Seven Rivers attackers in Lincoln. But Long retreated at warning shots from inside. And McSween seemed realistically confident of no great threat to his victory.

DAY 3: JULY 16, 1878

Since Dudley apparently still did not feel safe to act, stymied Ringites resorted to the outlaw myth to offer him of another excuse for giving military aid. Sheriff George Peppin sent him a letter; stating: *"Sir. If you could loan me a howitzer, I am sure that parties for whom I have warrants would surrender. We are being attacked by a lawless mob."*

So Dudley took a tentative step: he sent to Lincoln a courier, 9th Cavalry Private Berry Robinson, for "fact finding." A staged shot at Berry Robinson, likely from "The House," caused his horse to throw him. Uninjured and remounted, he escaped back to the Fort.

But Alexander McSween was now set up for another malicious prosecution: attempted murder of a soldier; as the Ring attempted to maneuver around the Posse Comitatus Act's mine field of restrictions on intervention.

DAY 4: JULY 17, 1878

With Private Berry Robinson "attacked," Commander Dudley took action. By Fort Stanton's telegraph, he was likely receiving instructions from Catron on evading the Posse Comitatus Act. So, that day, Fort Stanton's Ringite Post Surgeon, Daniel Appel, writer of Tunstall's fraudulent autopsy report; Ringite Captain George Purington, still at the Fort; and five soldiers went to Lincoln for more "fact finding."

There they questioned McSween about the Private Robinson shooting, and ignored his denial. And Peppin used the cease-fire of troops' presence to position his men on the south foothills.

That day had first casualties. From the Montaño house, Fernando Herrera, Charlie Bowdre's brother-in-law, fatally shot, with his Sharps Big Fifty buffalo rifle, Seven Rivers posseman, Charlie Crawford, 915 yards away on those foothills. And Isaac Ellis's son, Ben, was wounded by Peppin's men shooting down from them. From then on, carnage would be solely by the Ring.

DAY 5: JULY 18, 1878

Since the south foothills were easily defended, McSween began to anticipate a near-bloodless victory. And charismatic Billy Bonney inspired all, with Susan McSween later describing him as "lively."

DAY 6: JULY 19, 1878

On July 19, 1878, Commander N.A.M. Dudley marched on Lincoln, treasonously violating the June 18, 1878 Posse Comitatus Act by was intervening as a partisan in a civilian conflict; and endangering women and children in the McSween, Ealy and Montaño houses. With terrorist intent, he brought into the tiny town 39 soldiers, a Gatling machine-gun, howitzer cannon - all sufficient to level it and kill everyone.

Dudley personally threatened McSween with annihilation if any of his soldiers were fired upon, and left three soldiers on his property for intimidation and besiegement. Furthermore, he placed three soldiers with Sheriff Peppin as guards.

In likely panic after learning that David Easton's warrants were invalid, Dudley forced refusing Justice of the Peace Wilson by death threat to write false arrest warrants for McSween and "the Kid," using the Private Berry Robinson shooting.

He next pointed his howitzer cannon at José Montaño's house, commencing its loading drill. Terrified McSween's fled from there, precipitating mass flight of their comrades throughout the town, except for those trapped in McSween's house. Dudley then berated Peppin for not capturing or killing them all.

After setting up camp in Lincoln, he scornfully refused Susan McSween's personal plea for protection. He then enabled the arson of the McSweens' house by inhibiting defensive response of its trapped defenders.

When the McSween house inmates, including Billy, attempted nighttime escape from the burning building, Dudley positioned three officers, with Peppin's outlaw possemen, to fire at least one volley, becoming accomplice to Peppin's posse's murder of Alexander McSween, Harvey Morris, Francisco Zamora; and Vincente Romero - or possibly even murdering Morris themselves.

Escaping Yginio Salazar was left with two bullets in his back for life. McSween's house was destroyed.

McSween's side injured no one that day. But Seven Rivers posseman, Robert Beckwith, was killed by friendly fire.

But that night, during Billy's escape with others, in the firelight, he had witnessed Dudley's three white soldiers firing at them. His cool-headed moment would impact his pardon bargain when he later took his own action against Dudley by testifying against him in a military Court of Inquiry for his illegal intervention and for his court martial.

AFTERMATH

The following day, July 20, 1878, Alexander McSween's corpse was found in his rear yard, with its eyeballs eaten by his starving chickens. Next door, Sheriff Peppin's outlaw possemen, with soldiers as enabling guards, looted Tunstall's store. For cover-up lies of that culminating crime, Westphall used Catron's brother-in-law agent, Edgar Walz, in town the next day, who blamed "Mexicans" and Susan McSween. (Westphall, p. 93)

Opposition to the Ring had been crushed by uninhibited atrocities of obstructed justice, malicious prosecutions, massacre, murders, military treason, arson, and terror. And soon to come was the shielding of all the responsible Ringites. For their criminal carnage at San Patricio and the Lincoln County War Battle, not a single Ringite would be punished, and their villainy would be muffled by the outlaw myth. Never again in New Mexico would people dare to rise up against the all-pervasive organized criminality of the Santa Fe Ring. So the Ring never ceased to exist or to control.

The immediate response was exodus from the Territory by most of the Regulators; and frightened silence in Lincoln County. The Lincoln County War was the Ring's greatest triumph, not only by exterminating mercantile, banking, and ranching competition; not only by crushing opposition; but by using the outlaw myth to hide it as a freedom fight. It would also be the Ring's potential historical undoing by creation of larger-than-life "Billy the Kid."

And there was a final surge for freedom. Its fighter was McSween's widow, Susan, seeking justice against Commander Dudley. But the hope of Lincoln, Colfax, and Grant Counties rested with a new governor: Lew Wallace. And Ringites braced for their next fight for complete hegemony.

CHAPTER 14

REACTIONS TO THE LINCOLN COUNTY WAR

STILL SEEKING JUSTICE

SUMMARY: After the Battle, the vanquished sought justice, well aware that their adversary was the Santa Fe Ring.

JOHN TUNSTALL'S FATHER

John Partridge Tunstall pursued reparations of $200,000 ($5,730,913.53 today) for his son's murder and property theft, filing charges with British Foreign Secretary Lord Salisbury and Prime Minister William Gladstone. But his accusing U.S. officials likely caused the Santa Fe Ring's blockade through then-Senator S.B. Elkins; until death in the late 1880's ended his pursuit.

DAVID SHIELD

On July 26, 1878, traumatized David Shield wrote to Montegue Leverson about the Ring and McSween's murder, asking for help. It was the only way Leverson got the news. The battle was missing from newspapers. Shield wrote on dead McSween's stationery: *"Your letter of the 23rd inst is at hand and content noted … I had read a letter about 2 hours previous hereto announcing the murder of A A McSween in his own house and the burning of his ~~his~~ & the house in which my family resides together with the contents thereof on the 20th [19th] inst. My family I learn are at Fort Stanton & will come here the first opportunity. The destitute condition in which they are in I trust will be sufficient apology to you for my asking of you a loan of One Hundred Dollars for ninety days …* **The ring element here … are jubilant over the news but their joy will be turned to grief. I would not have asked you for the loan but I do not wish to place myself under any obligations to the ring or their clique & they control everything here.***"*

MONTEGUE LEVERSON

On July 28, 1878, Montegue Leverson, using David Shield's news, wrote to President Hayes about the murders of Alexander McSween and Frank MacNab; with a copy to Secretary of the Interior Carl Schurz. He stated correctly: "*your Excellency's administration is accountable before God and man.*" He stated:

    Post Office   Leverson Ranch.
    Larkspur   Douglas Co., Colorado

                                   28 June [sic- July] 1878

His Excellency Rutherford B Hayes
       President of the U.S.
Excellency

    I enclose a letter I have just received [July 26, 1878 letter from David Shield] advising me of the murder of another admirable gentleman A.A. McSween. For this murder – as also for that of McNab [Frank MacNab] committed some weeks ago your Excellency's administration is accountable before God and man.

    You have now known long enough the character of the wretches appointed to office [Catron as U.S. Attorney] by your predecessor [President Ulysses S. Grant]. Your Excellency was warned that this would be the result of continuing them in office *and all you have done has been to send down an able and upright gentleman to investigate!! Meanwhile men equal to yourself in every quality of heart and mind are being daily murdered by procurement of the villains your predecessor appointed to office and you maintain there!*

    Excellency I have no way sought the office – dangerous indeed for a man who does his duty of governor of New Mexico, but I know my name has been mentioned in that connection to the administration.

    Tho' it would entail heavy pecuniary sacrifices on my part I would accept the office & pledge myself to restore peace and order to New Mexico within 60 days of my installation or perish in the attempt.

                                         Respectfully
                                    Montegue Leverson

Leverson's letter that day to Carl Schurz confirms common knowledge of the Ring, Catron, and assassinations. He even hints at the link of the Hayes administration to the Ring. He wrote:

𝔓ost 𝔒ffice   𝔏everson 𝔑anch.
𝔏arkspur   𝔇ouglas 𝔊o., 𝔊olorado

28 June [sic- July] 1878

Hon Carl Schurz
    Secy of the Interior
    Dear Sir.

I send you herewith copy of a letter I have published & I send it to you for several reasons. First to show you **how the possession of power has corrupted the Republican leaders [Catron and the Ring] in this State,** *as indeed might well have been judged by you by their endorsement of the execrable mal-administration of President Grant during his 2nd term & sneering condemnation of every good thing done by President Hayes;* **and secondly to suggest to the administration the impolicy and** **<u>positive wickedness</u>** **of submitting to the dictation or influence of the old and proved-to-be corrupt republican politicians [Catron and the Ring], which I greatly fear the president has lately shown signs of doing in various instances, of which his <u>non action</u> in New Mex ie his abstaining from affording the oppressed people of that Territory the relief they need, seems to me a very grave indication.**

My letter, of which the [newspaper published] copy is sent you, has led to my being requested to stump this State for the Democratic party this fall.

Altho' that party is by no means so purified by adversity as to command my hearty adherence, **the Republican leaders, <u>here and in New Mexico,</u> are so bad, that I shall probably comply with the request ...** **<u>if the administration should not anticipate my efforts by affording</u>** **the needed relief.**

In this connection I will add some remarks somewhat personal on a matter lately ... brought under my notice but <u>before</u> I published the enclosed letter.

I am told that my name has been urged on the administration as a fitting person to be appointed governor of New Mex <u>for the benefit of the people.</u>

I <u>do not seek, I have not sought, I do not desire</u> the appointment: not because I dread the danger (as you will presently *observe)* **although strongly persuaded I should not live 3 months in New Mexico for even now, further plots have been laid for my life by the ruffians now holding power one of which lately failed signally. They have laid their plans – of course neither Axtel [Axtell] nor Catron has appeared openly in the matter, to get hold of some 5 or 6000$\underline{00}$ worth of my property expecting I should go down in person to save it. The coach was stopped the day they expected me by two masked & armed ruffians who demanded the way bill & who cursed & swore when they found <u>I</u> was <u>not</u> in the coach but allowed it to proceed without robbing it!**

[AUTHOR'S NOTE: This Ringite attempted assassination of Leverson, repeats Axtell's "Dear Ben plot" in Colfax County.]

Nevertheless I <u>would cheerfully sacrifice my own private business & peril my life</u>, to furnish security for the lives and property of the citizens; the only purpose for which government should be tolerated at all!

Were I appointed governor my first act would be to request that the U.S. troops be ordered to confine their activities to protecting the citizens from the Indians & to aid the U.S. Marshall, instead of as heretofore, aiding the thieves and murderers to rob and murder, making searches and arrests without warrant, depriving the good citizens of their arms (all in violation of the constitution) & helping the U.S. Attorney of New Mex to steal J.H. Tunstalls cattle!

[AUTHOR'S NOTE: Leverson knows the Ring used troops in Cimarron, against McSween, and in the Lincoln County War. So he opposes it.]

Without the use of the U.S. army an efficient and <u>upright</u> governor would restore peace to New Mexico within 60 days relying on the people only to aid him.

I do not doubt that the [published] letter, a copy of which I enclose, will utterly extinguish such poor chance, if ever there were one, of my being chosen by the president for ~~the~~ governor of New Mex, tho it might be otherwise if appointment to office were determined only by the fitness of the appointee to benefit the people. In such case that letter would neither forward nor obstruct. Unhappily things are in such a state that sometimes I begin to almost "despair of the Republic."

Very respectfully
Montegue R. Leverson

[ENCLOSURE] Undated newspaper article.

INDIGNANT

A genuine Republican at the Lack of Truth in His Party Press

To the Editor of the Democrat
... And because in this state that [Republican] party has become the party of fraud, the party of illegality and usurpation, I now fall into line with the opponents of that party ... In order that the assault attempted upon constitutional liberty may be defeated and the breach effectively repaired, every honest citizen of this state, every lover of its liberties, whether he call himself democrat or republican, should, in the absence of a people's ticket, vote for the nominees of the democratic party to both branches of our state legislature. He who does otherwise will thereby prove that he cares more for party than for freedom.

CITIZEN JOHN G. HUBBARD

There were also New Mexico Territory still citizens bold enough to complain directly to President Hayes, as shown by this August 1, 1878 letter from a John G. Hubbard focused on Axtell's "Dear Ben plot." Hubbard correctly identified the Ring, and linked its use of the military to suppress or to murder citizens in both Colfax and Lincoln Counties. He wrote:

N.M. Aug 1 of 1878

To The Prest U.S.
  My Dear Sir:
      Herewith I hand you an extract from one of our N.M. papers relative to Gov Axtell of New Mexico to which I would draw your Especial attention, this man Axtell is a very dangerous one & calculated to do <u>any administration a great deal of harm</u>, & who certainly is void of moral honesty & steeped deeply in crime as well and has appeared by strict investigation of **the poor suffering New Mexicans, who from pure loyalty to the Govmt and an indisposition to create trouble, have quietly acquiesced to the Ring &c.**
With marked esteem Yours truly
      John G. Hubbard

[ENCLOSURE] Newspaper article dated July 31, 1878.

WHY AXTELL WANTED TROOPS

SANTA FE, July 31. The popular demand for a reduction of the regular army finds support in the history of its doings in New Mexico for the past few years. **The fact is, the United States troops, like everything else official and public in New Mexico, have been chiefly used to advance the interests of the Santa Fe Ring, headed by Elkins, Catron, Axtell, and the rest;** and the district commander, Col. Hatch of the Ninth Cavalry seems to be so entirely wrapped up in these men, and has employed his soldiers in such complete subservience to their wishes that the sinuous folds of the **Ring** have enveloped him also.

It is now something more than two years since Colfax county had an experience with these fellows not unlike that which Lincoln county has more recently gone through. The facts are worth recalling. The Rev. F.J. Tolby, a man respected and loved by the community, was murdered on the highway. His watch and money were not taken. It was clear that the motive of the murder was not robbery. He had made himself obnoxious to **the Ring** by bold public denunciations of its members and tools. Some of the latter prudently fled the county. One man who did not get away soon enough was hanged by the people, and others would have been if the people could have laid hands on them.

Gov. Axtell came to the rescue as usual. He removed the Sheriff whom the people had elected, and put in his place a man whom they detested, and who managed in the brief time he remained in office to steal $1000 of school money. He wrote on to Washington for authority to send troops into the county. He sent District Attorney Ben Stevens to superintend the military operations. A company of forty-five soldiers, under the command of Capt. F. Moore, marched into Colfax. Some twelve – or fifteen – leading citizens wrote to the governor asking him to visit the county and see for himself whether the alleged lawlessness really existed.

The troops remained two or three weeks, arrested one man [Clay Allison], immediately turned him loose, and finally marched back to Fort Union, having found no disorders to suppress, and no shadow of excuse for further stay.

The true design of this foray has lately been exposed in the Cimarron *News and Press* which publishes a telegram and letter sent at the time by Axtell to his agent, District Attorney Stevens. The plan was to create a disturbance, and kill off some persons who were in the way of **the Ring**. I give the documents; they are interesting reading coming from the Governor of a Territory. The telegram was sent to Stevens at Fort Union, and runs as follows:

Do not let it be known that I will be in Cimarron on Saturday's coach. Body guard all right. S.B. Axtell

The letter was as follows:

DEAR BEN: The second telegram delivered to you at Fort Union, directed to Cimarron, was intended to leak, but the operator here says he cannot raise the Cimarron office. If I was expected our friends would probably be on hand, as the guard is only a Government escort. I do not think your definite business is suspected. Wade informed Hatch that he had been ready all the time to assist you, but could not find that you wanted to do it. Hatch says their opinion is that you weakened and do not want to arrest the man. *Have your men placed to arrest him and to kill all the men who resist you, or stand with those who do resist you.* Our man signed the invitation with others who were at that meeting for me to visit Colfax – Porter, Morley, Springer, et al. Now, if they expect me Saturday, they will be on hand. Send me letters by messenger; and do not hesitate at extreme measures. Your honor is at stake now, and a failure is fatal. If others resist, or attempt murder, bring them also. Hatch is excited, and writes, of course, to put all the blame on the civil officers. I am more anxious on your account than for any other reason. I clearly see that we have no friends in Colfax, and I have suspected all along that some of our pretended friends were traitors.

Yours &c. S. B. Axtell

The Porter, Morley, and Springer here mentioned were among the leading citizens of the county, and strong opponents of **the Ring** and its defunct Colfax county branch ... That the troops were sent on an infamous bushwacking expedition nobody here doubts.

BRAVE WIDOW SUSAN MCSWEEN

Susan McSween, like Mary McPherson before her, took courageous action. Not only did she return to Lincoln the day after her husband's murder and her home's arson, but she tried to stop looting of Tunstall's store. Then, moving to Las Vegas to live with the Shield family, she hired an attorney there named Huston Chapman - presumably after refusal by David Shield. One-armed from a childhood shotgun accident, Chapman compensated by doughtiness. His father had founded Portland, Oregon's first newspaper: *The Oregonian*. He and Susan would have known that her intent to prosecute Commander Dudley risked their lives. And she would also have met his office-mate: Attorney Ira Leonard. Both men became intrinsic to Billy Bonney's fate.

Unbeknownst to Susan, Catron's law firm would be collecting

its usual defamatory affidavits against her veracity and chastity. Ring mouthpiece, Victor Westphall, lied snidely that she was not grieving that much after the War, since she was having sex with Regulator, Jim French. (Westphall, p. 93)

FIRST FAME OF BILLY BONNEY

By July 19, 1878's end of the Lincoln County War, Billy Bonney, 18 years 7 months and 27 days old, was locally famous. His youth, gunmanship, and fierceness against Ringites had earned affection and respect. As John P. Meadows had summed it up in his 1931 talks and articles about the "Days of Billy the Kid": "When he was rough, he was as rough as men ever get to be, yet he had a good streak in him." And Billy's bi-culturalism appealed to the majority of Lincoln County citizens, who were Hispanic.

But Billy's fame would be sealed by his literacy and audacious self-confidence; fueled by America's promise that he was the equal of any man. In 7 months and 22 days he would write his first letter to the Territory's highest official: Governor Lew Wallace.

But by October of 1878 - as he had warned in his "Regulator Manifesto" - he was revenge-rustling from Ringites. His outlets were a Dan Dedrick, with a Pecos River ranch and a White Oaks livery; and a Pat Coghlan, at Three Rivers.

Billy was also selling Ringites' horses in Tascosa, Texas. There, on October 24, 1878, he sold to a Dr. Henry Hoyt a sorrel horse - likely once Sheriff Brady's and likely stolen by Billy from Catron's Carrizozo ranch. Billy priced the horse high for its bill of sale, which showed that he had acquired legalese, possibly from Alexander McSween. It would be used in 132 days to write a pardon plea letter to Governor Lew Wallace. To Hoyt, Billy wrote:

Tascoso Texas
Thursday Oct 24th 1878

Know all persons by these presents that I do hereby Sell and deliver to Henry F. Hoyt one Sorrel Horse Branded BB on left hip and other indistinct Branded on Shoulders for the sum of Seventyfive $ dollars in hand received
W HBonney

CHAPTER 15

INVESTIGATOR ANGEL'S CAPITULATION

ANGEL'S RING COVER-UP

SUMMARY: The fate of New Mexico Territory and the Santa Fe Ring rested with Frank Warner Angel's October, 1878 reports on his five month investigation of murder and fraud by U.S. officials. He had damning evidence, but he knew his personal risk, so he became a reluctant actor in cover-up.

HISTORY PENNED BY VICTORS

Investigator for the Departments of Justice and the Interior Frank Warner Angel could have broken the Santa Fe Ring. But he would have destroyed himself. So, like Colfax County's Attorney Frank Springer, he capitulated. But Angel had generated proof of Ring illegalities. So, in likely moral indignation, he gave that raw incriminatory evidence to his superiors, while writing forced contradictory concluding reports absolving U.S. officials - thus, enabling someone in the future to break the Ring.

Angel's appointment was likely a mistake. President Hayes and Secretary of the Interior Schurz needed a simple cover-up for British Ambassador Sir Edward Thornton about John Tunstall's murder. Instead, by assigning superb sleuth Angel, they almost exposed the Ring. Angel had also been mistaken. He likely first thought he was assigned a legitimate investigation.

The result of his coercion was his contrived reports of October, 1878. Worse, to shield the Ring, he blamed fictional outlaws for Lincoln County's "troubles," conforming to the Ring's cover-up going back to the 1872 Legislature Revolt. And to feign action, he then scapegoated Governor S.B. Axtell. Angel's reward, the month after submitting his reports, was promotion to Assistant District Attorney of the Eastern District of New York State.

But Angel's conscience yielded covert anti-Ring action. Knowing Civil War General Lew Wallace was replacing Axtell, he secretly wrote for him a small red notebook naming Ringites. It was enough to make Wallace the one who could break the Ring.

REPORT ON TUNSTALL'S MURDER

Before he prepared the October 4, 1878 primary report of his New Mexico Territory assignment - "In the Matter of the Cause and Circumstances of the Death of John H. Tunstall, A British Subject" - Frank Warner Angel had taken 39 depositions, including ones from Alexander McSween, Deputy Sheriff Adolph Barrier, Frank Springer, and Billy Bonney. Since he also traveled throughout the Territory investigating land grant frauds and Indian Agency violations, he was exposed to additional facts about Ring members and crimes. His reports demonstrate his truncating of truth. For Tunstall's murder, he reported to the Justice Department's Attorney General Charles Devens; writing:

<u>Department of Justice</u>.

In the Matter
~ of the ~
cause and circumstances of the death
~ of ~
John H. Tunstall,
a British Subject.

<u>*To the Honorable*</u>
<u>*Charles Devens,*</u>
<u>*Attorney General*</u>

In compliance with your instructions to make careful inquiry into the cause and circumstances of the death of John H. Tunstall, a British subject, and whether the death of said Tunstall was brought about through the lawless and corrupt conduct of United States officials in the Territory of New Mexico, and to report thereon.

I have the honor to submit the following report in relation to the premises.

<u>*First:*</u> *- As to the cause of the death of John H. Tunstall.*

John H. Tunstall by his straight-forward and honest business transactions with the people of Lincoln County, New Mexico ... had been instrumental in the arrest of certain notorious horse thieves ... He had exposed embezzlement of Territorial officers ... He had incurred the anger of persons who had control of the County, and who used that control for private gain ... He had introduced honesty and square dealings in his business ... and to the enmity of those persons, can be attributed the only cause of his death ...

<u>Second:</u> - *As to the circumstances of his death.*

An attachment had been obtained against the property of one Alexander A. McSween ...

It was claimed that said Tunstall was McSween's partner ...

The Sheriff in order to attach certain property, viz; stock and horses, alleged to belong to McSween and Tunstall sent his deputy to Tunstall's ranch to attach the same ... - when said deputy visited said ranch and was informed that he could attach the stock and leave a person with it until the Courts could adjudicate to whom the stock belonged ... - he left without attaching said property, and immediately assembles a large posse among ... whom were the most desperate out-laws of the Territory ... They again started for Tunstall's ranch, in the mean-time Mr. Tunstall had been informed of the action of the Sheriff, and believing that the real purpose was to murder and not attach ... left his ranch, taking with him all the horses and started for Lincoln, the County seat ...

Directly after Tunstall had left his ranch, The Deputy Sheriff and said posse arrived there, and finding that Tunstall had left with the horses, deputized W. Morton ... who selected eighteen men and started out ostensibly to capture the horses. After riding about thirty miles, they came up to Tunstall and his party with the horses, and commenced firing on them ... - Immediately Tunstall and his party left the horses and attempted to escape ... were pursued and Tunstall was killed some hundred yards or more from the horses ...

Who shot Tunstall will never be known. But there is no doubt that W<u>m</u> S. Morton, Jesse [Jessie hereafter] Evans and [Tom] Hill were the only persons present and saw the shooting, and that two of those persons murdered him ... For Tunstall was shot in two places – in the head and breast ... Of these persons Morton and Hill were afterwards killed, and the only survivor is Jesse Evans a notorious out-law, murderer and horse-thief. Of these persons Evans and Hill had been arrested at the instigation of Tunstall.

They were at enmity with Tunstall, and enmity with them meant murder ...

There was no object for following after Tunstall – except to murder him, for they had the horses ... which they desired to attach before they commenced to pursue him and his party. These facts, together with the bitter feeling existing against Tunstall, by certain persons to whom he had become obnoxious ... and the deputy allowing those notorious out-laws to accompany him ... lead me to the conclusion that John H. Tunstall was murdered in cold blood ... and was not shot in attempting to resist an officer of the law ...

<u>Third:</u> - Was the death of John H. Tunstall brought about by the lawless and corrupt action of United States officials –

After diligent inquiry and examination of a great number of witnesses, I report that the death of John H. Tunstall was not brought about through the lawless and corrupt action of United States officials in the Territory of Ne Mexico.

All of which is respectfully submitted
         Frank Warner Angel
         Special Agent.

REPORT ON THE "TROUBLES"

To hide anti-Ring freedom fights, Angel used euphemistic "troubles" and the outlaw myth in his October 4, 1878 report: "In the Matter of the Lincoln County Troubles."

<u>Department of Justice</u>.

| In the Matter ~ of the ~ Lincoln County Troubles. | <u>To the Honorable</u> <u>Charles Devens</u>, <u>Attorney</u> <u>General</u> |

        The history of Lincoln County has been one of blood shed from the day of its organization.

These troubles have existed for years with occasional break-outs, each one being more severe than the other.

L.G. Murphy & Co. had the monopoly of all business in the County, controlled governmental contracts, and used their power to oppress and grind out all they could from the farmers, and force those who were opposed to them to leave the County.

This has resulted in the formation of two parties, one led by Murphy & Co., and the other by McSween (now dead). Both have done many things contrary to the law, both violated the law. McSween, I firmly believe acted conscientiously - Murphy & Co. for private gain and revenge.

Bands of desperate characters who are ever found on the frontier, particularly along the Texas border, who have no interest in Lincoln County, men who live by plunder, and who only flourish where they can evade the law, have naturally gravitated to one or the other of these parties, and are now in their pay, being hired for so much a day to fight their battles.

Gov. Axtell appoints Peppin a leader of the Murphy & Co. faction, as Sheriff, he comes to Lincoln accompanied by John Kinney and his notorious band of out-laws and murderers as a body guard to assist him in upholding law and order. McSween then collects around himself an equally distinguished body. The County becomes the Elysium for out-laws and murderers.

A battle is fought – for five days it rages – more desperate action than was seen in these unfortunate days, by both sides, is rarely witnessed. Both parties desire revenge and they are now reorganizing and collecting more desperate characters (if that were possible), than they previously had. Before I left Santa Fe, it was reported that there were two hundred armed men in the field.

Men are shot down "on sight" because they belong to one or the other party, and the residents of the County have been forced to take one side or the other from inclination or necessity. One day Murphy & Co. and his party of out-laws control the County – the next day McSween and his "out-fit" would be the masters.

When these men were not engaged in battle, and when the County seemingly was at peace, they were employed to steal cattle, either from the farmers or the Indians – a ready market and no questions asked, was found in the persons who held government contracts. If the people protested, they were persecuted and driven out the County.

This state of affairs would be carried to such an extent, that it would end in a fight or a war similar to the one now being waged in the County.

During these years the law-abiding citizens, or those who would be if they could, have been reduced to poverty by professional thieves, who have made the County their camping ground without the least fear of molestation.

The laws cannot be enforced, for the reason that if the Murphy party are in power then the law is all Murphy – and if the McSween party are in power then the law is all McSween.

The leaders of these parties have created a storm that they cannot control, and it has reached such proportions that the whole Territory cannot put it down. Lands go uncultivated; ranches are abandoned; merchants have closed their stores; citizens have left the homes they have occupied for years; business has ceased, and lawlessness and murder are the order of the day.

These out-laws who prowl the County with the avowed purpose of murder, who have no interests in the County or wrongs of their own to redress, no matter on which side they belong, should be hunted down, and made to answer for their crimes.

The Territory has no militia, and the County being in the hands of those armed out-laws, the laws and mandates of the Courts cannot be enforced or respected, nor lives or property protected. It is impossible for even the Courts to be held.

I would respectfully refer to my report to the Interior Department on the charges against Governor Axtell as to the additional causes for the existing troubles in Lincoln County.

I would most respectfully recommend that such assistance be given the Governor of New Mexico that the laws may be enforced and respected, and life and property protected.

Washington, October 4th 1878.

Frank Warner Angel
Special Agent.

PRESSURE ABOUT AXTELL

From his New York office, on August 24, 1878, Angel angrily documented Ringite pressure, indicating his ignorance that his conclusions had been pre-determined by the corrupt Hayes administration. To Secretary of the Interior Carl Schurz, he wrote:

No 62 Liberty Street
New York City Aug 24 1878

The Honorable
   C. Schurz
        Secretary of the Interior
             Sir:

I enclose copies of a letter received by me from Gov Axtell (marked A) and my reply thereto (marked B) – by which you will see that we did not part the best of friends on his part.

I have given him thirty days to reply subject to <u>your approval</u>.

He claims that the Interior Departments have no control over him – and that he will not be investi<u>gated by me.</u>

I have returned to N.Y. and with the counsel of the Honorable Attorney General [Charles Devens] I am to remain here until I index, & arrange my testimony & prepare my reports.

I have had a very difficult and dangerous mission, **and every obstacle thrown in my way by officials in New Mexico** *– and yet notwithstanding this I have accomplished a great deal.*

As soon as I receive the Governors reply, unless ordered sooner by you, will prepare and forward my reports –
 Very respectfully
  Your obedient Servant
   Frank Warner Angel, Special Agt.

[ENCLOSED: On August 12, 1878, Axtell had written]

A. *"Your communication of 11th Inst (Sunday) was duly received. You furnish me with a list of 31 interrogations which imply about as many charges of corrupt misconduct in office and ask that I should reply to them in 24 hours. Do you think this is reasonable?"*

[On August 13, 1878, Angel responded]:

B. *"I have found certain parts of this Territory in a terrible and deplorable state – some one is responsible for the same – and with a view to try and discover if you were responsible for the same I prepared and forwarded the interrogations to you ...You desire to know if I had given you a reasonable time to reply to said interrogations. I can only say that if I was the accused party I should not want desire or wish twenty four hours to answer same.*

On September 6, 1878, Angel complained to Schurz, that Rynerson was a biased Axtell appointee, implying the Ring:

 No 62 Liberty St
  New York Sept 6 1878

The Hon C. Schurz
 Secretary of the Interior
  Sir:

I have just been favored by a call from W.L. Rynerson <u>Territorial</u> *Dist. Attorney 3^d District New Mexico – in the interest of Gov. Axtel. I presume that he will pay you a visit.*

He desired to know on what grounds I reported in favor of the removal of Gov Axtel. I declined to answer without the permission of the Department –

He is an appointee of Gov Axtel – a strong partisan – and his conduct in the Lincoln County troubles is open to censure – He has not used his office for the punishment of all parties alike – He has been oppressive in the exercise of the functions of his office and due allowance must be taken of what he says – I do not believe he will willfully tell an untruth – but his interests are with the officials who have suffered the existing troubles to continue in New Mexico –

[AUTHOR'S NOTE: So, on September 6, 1878, Angel blamed New Mexico officials for the "troubles." By his October, 1878 reports, he hid that conclusion to shield the Santa Fe Ring.]

Your obedient servant
Frank Warner Angel
Special Apt- [Appointee]

REPORT ON AXTELL

By October, Angel stopped accusing the Ring and scapegoated Governor S.B. Axtell in his report: "In the Matter of Investigation of the Charges Against S.B. Axtell Governor of New Mexico." Noteworthy is his apparent use of Mary McPherson's complaints, while hiding her Ring exposé. Angel wrote:

<u>Interior Department</u>.

> *In the Matter of the investigation of the charges _____*
> *_____ against _____*
> <u>*S.B. Axtel*</u>
> *Governor of New Mexico*

To the Honorable
C. Schurz,
Secretary of the Interior

In compliance with your request made at the time I made my first report herein I herewith make my supplemental and final report as to the charges against said S.B. Axtel [Axtell throughout].

Since making said report I have found no reason for changing the same – but on the contrary believe as I did then that the best interests of New Mexico demanded the removal of S.B. Axtel as Governor.

A brief resuma of the facts laid before you at the time will be necessary to make this report complete.

Under your instructions I visited New Mexico for the purpose of ascertaining if there was any truth to the repeated complaints made to the Department as to fraud incompetency and corruption of United States officials. *I determined to see with my own eyes and hear with my own ears. I traveled over most of the Territory. I visited almost every important town and talked with the principal citizens thereof.*

I was met by every opposition possible by the United States civil officials and every obstacle thrown in my way by them to prevent a full and complete examination - *with one exception and that of the surveyor general who not only sought but insisted on a full and thorough examination as will more fully appear in my report submitted as to his office.*

I found universal complaint against the administration of affairs in the Territory and from facts coming under my observation and affidavits of the people the following charges in substance were made against the Governor of said Territory.

<u>First</u>

<u>That</u> the Governor had taken strictly partizan [partisan throughout] action as to the troubles in Lincoln County.

<u>Second</u>

<u>That</u> he refused to listen to the complaints of the people in that County.

<u>Third</u>

<u>That</u> he had been paid the sum of two thousand dollars to influence his action.

<u>Fourth</u>

<u>That</u> he arbitrarily removed Territorial officers thereby outlawing citizens, and usurping the functions of the Judiciary.

<u>Fifth</u>

<u>That</u> he removed officials and in their place appointed strong partizans.

<u>Sixth</u>

<u>That</u> all action taken by him has increased rather than quieted the troubles in Lincoln County.

Seventh

<u>That</u> he appointed officials to office and kept them there who were supported by the worst out-laws and murderers that the Territory could produce.

Eighth

<u>That</u> he knowingly appointed bad men to office.

Ninth

<u>That</u> he was a tool of designing men weak and arbitrary in exercising the functions of his office.

Tenth

<u>That</u> he was a Mormon and desired to turn the Territory into a Mormon settlement.

Eleventh

<u>That</u> he conspired to murder innocent and law abiding citizens because they opposed his wishes and were exerting their influence against him.

Twelfth

<u>That</u> he arbitrarily refused to restore the Courts to Colfax County and refused to listen to the petitions of the people of that County for the restoration thereof.

<u>The Governor</u> at first refused to be investigated preferring to ignore the complaints against him on the grounds that the Department of the Interior had no power to investigate him ... He has not even answered the charges by a sworn statement. I received just before making my first report a news paper article which was not even signed by him to reply to the charges against him.

<u>By</u> much care and patience I have investigated the above charges impartially, seeking to obtain the truth and punish the guilty.

<u>Many things</u> came to my notice and observation of which no affidavits could be obtained. Many suspicious circumstances existed which convinced me beyond a peradventure that Gov Axtel was an improper person for the place. He is a man of strong prejudices, impulsive, conceited and easily flattered – all these make a man easily influenced – **a complete tool in the hands of designing men**.

[AUTHOR'S NOTE: Angel hints about Ring control of Axtell]

<u>As to the charges one and two I found</u> Lincoln County convulsed by an internal war. I enquired the cause. Some one was responsible for the blood shed in that County. I found two parties in the field one headed by Murphy Dolan and Riley – the other lead

[led] by McSween – both had done many things contrary to the law – both were violating the law – McSween I firmly believe acted conscientious – Murphy Dolan & Riley for revenge and personal gain. The Governor came, heard the Murphy Dolan and Riley side, refused to hear the people who were with McSween or the residents of the County and acted strictly in advancing the Murphy Dolan and Riley party – Murder and unlawful acts followed instead of peace and quiet which could have been accomplished if the Governor had acted as he should have done and listened patiently to both sides. The opportunity presented itself to him to have quieted and stopped the trouble in Lincoln Co – by his partizan action he allowed it to pass and the continuations of **the troubles that exist today in Lincoln County are chargeable to him**. He was a partizan either through corruption or weakness and charges first and second have been sustained.

<u>Charge Third</u> – The facts are that in May 1876 Gov Axtel borrowed of Mr Riley $1800 and it is alleged that the same was paid in November ... I do not believe that Gov. Axtel received this money to directly influence his action. It was some time before the troubles actually commenced in Lincoln Co. – although they were brewing at the time.

[AUTHOR'S NOTE: Axtell removed the Colfax County Courts.]

The only influence this transaction could have on the action of Gov. Axtell was in as much as Riley had befriended him to return the compliment, and certainly his official action lays him open to serious suspicion that his friendship for Murphy Dolan and Riley was stronger than his duty to the people and the government he represented.

<u>Charge Fourth</u> – I find that this charge has been fully sustained.

By his proclamation of March 9, 1878 ... he usurped the functions of the Judiciary and in fact removed J.B. Wilson a Justice of the Peace, and thereby made certain persons who were in good faith enforcing the warrants issued by said Wilson out laws ...

[AUTHOR'S NOTE: This confirms legality of deputizings of Billy and Fred Waite under Town Constable Atanacio Martinez.]

What right had he to do this? He did not veto the bill under which Wilson was appointed – and suffered him to act some months before he arbitrarily removed him.

Charge Fifth – *John Copeland after the murder of Sheriff Brady was appointed Sheriff. He was an honest conscientious man, perhaps he was not the strongest man in character that ever existed – but I am yet to hear of any arbitrary act on his part any murder, robbery, arson in which he had been a party or of his being supported while in office by a band of notorious out laws and non residents. He was on the contrary surrounded by and had the confidence of a majority of the residents of the County – one of the County Commissioners was his bonds-man. By the laws of the Territory the Sheriff is ex-officio tax collector. The bonds as collector have to be fixed by the County Commissioners after they have ascertained the amount of taxes to be collected. Copeland had nothing to do with this – and owing to the troubled states of affairs in the county the County Commissioners could not find the amount of taxes to be collected.*

The Governor immediately seizes the opportunity to aid Murphy Dolan & Riley. He this time acts strictly within the letter of the law, and would that I could say the interest of the law and non-partizan. He removes Copeland and appoints G.W. Peppin, one of the leaders of the Murphy Dolan and Riley party – who comes from Mesilla accompanied by his murderous out fit of out laws, as a body guard to assist him in enforcing law and order. Again we have an unusual number of murders, robbery and accompanied with arson, and after Kinney and his party have accomplished their mission of murdering McSween and robbing and stealing all they can

[AUTHOR'S NOTE: Here is Angel's reprehensible cover-up of the Lincoln County War Battle, its military involvement, and the Ring murder of Alexander McSween. He dishonestly avoids blaming U.S. officials - instead blaming Peppin and Kinney! And hidden is that the "*stealing*" was looting of Tunstall's store.]

they retire on their laurels and return from whence they came, and Sheriff Peppin without the confidence in himself retreats to Fort Stanton at which place he is under the case and protection of the soldiers.

I find that Gov Axtel acted in the interests of the Murphy Dolan & Riley party and was strictly partisan and that the charge is sustained.

Charge Sixth – *I report that this charge has been sustained as already set forth.*

Charge Seventh – *I report that this charge has been sustained as appears by facts set forth under Charge Fifth.*

Charge Eighth – Under this charge is the appointment of Col Chaves and Peppin. It was rumored that Col Chaves had falsified the election returns as a reward he was nominated and appointed Territorial District Attorney. There is however no evidence of this fact and I accordingly report that as to this part of the charge the same is not sustained, But that as to Peppin the charge is sustained.

The Governor replies that he appointed Peppin under recommendation of W.L. Rynerson ... Rynerson is undoubtedly a good lawyer but he is nevertheless a strong partisan and his record in the Lincoln County troubles show that he has used his office for oppressive purposes. The Governor must have known this, therefore with knowledge of Peppin's character he acted again strictly partizan and appointed an improper man.

[AUTHOR'S NOTE: Angel fabricated Axtell's bias as from a Riley loan, but exposes Rynerson collusion - and almost the Ring.]

Charge Ninth: I find has been sustained as appears from the facts set forth herein.

Charge Tenth As to this charge there are no substantiated facts to show that he is a Mormon. I therefore report that the same is not sustained.

Charge Eleventh – On considering this charge we must go back in the Unwritten History of New Mexico to the time when Colfax County **by the arbitrary and unlawful acts of certain officials**, *became too hot for them, and they had to leave the County for the Countys good.*

[AUTHOR'S NOTE: This is another secret swipe at the Ring]

The plan was devised and carried out to join Colfax County & Taos County for judicial purposes and a bill was rushed through the Legislature and signed at once accomplishing this design. Immediately the people at Cimarron telegraphed Gov Axtell "Requesting him to withhold his signature until a delegation from Colfax could wait upon him." The reply came back "Bill signed S.B. Axtell." If there was trouble in Colfax County which could not be quieted – then there was a justification in having this bill. It would then have been an excellent measure.

But the facts show that when this bill was passed the troubles in Colfax Co had been quieted and stopped and that there was more lawlessness in other parts of the Territory than in Colfax ...

No benefit resulted from their change – but on the contrary it was a gross injury and injustice to the people of Colfax County. The two counties are separated by a range of high mountains, the lowest pass 9000 feet in altitude, which when the Court is in session are difficult and dangerous to cross. It required a journey over three mountains of 54 miles to reach Court. The juries were entirely taken from Taos County, manipulated by **Pedro Sanches** *a* **ringite***, and prejudiced by* **outside influence.**

[AUTHOR'S NOTE: Here Angel and reveals the Santa Fe Ring: "*ringite*" and "*outside influence;*" implying later editing out of his reporting, which accidentally missed this exposé!]

There never could be a fair trial in criminal proceedings and all most all civil business was suspended ... - it was a great expense to Colfax Co for witnesses and fees.

Is it surprising that opposition to the arbitrary Governor arose – and with opposition came murderousness and revenge on the part of the opposed.[?]

[AUTHOR'S NOTE: This double-talk obfuscates the Ring murder of Franklin Tolby and Colfax County Ring exposés.]

The Governor was visited at Santa Fe said he was hartily [heartily] in favor of the bill and spoke with extreme bitterness about the people of Colfax County – and refused to go to Colfax Co and investigate the facts for himself saying <u>"He was fully advised about matters in their County and didn't need further information"</u> ...

After this at a public meeting at Cimarron an invitation in courteous language was addressed to the Governor inviting him to visit Colfax County and make a thorough investigation and learn the facts for himself. This invitation was signed by ten or twelve prominent citizens. To this the Governor makes no reply or acknowledgment ...

At this stage Ben Stevens Territorial District Attorney, an appointee of the Governor appears.

He circulates the report that he is going to try and have the Governor visit Colfax, leaves Cimarron goes to Fort Union, and returns in a few days with a company of soldiers (colored), and exhibits a telegram from the Governor which reads as follows <u>"Do not let it be known that I will be in Cimarron on Saturdays coach. Body guard all right"</u> *and said it was proof that the Governor is coming to visit the County and would expect to meet those who had signed the invitation and that they must be on hand* on the arrival of the coach to meet him. He requested that the matter be kept quiet as the Governor did not want a crowd but only wanted to meet those who had invited him ...

The facts subsequently show that the Governor did not intend to visit Colfax Co. and that the action of Stevens was in furtherance of a plot as will appear by the following [pasted on] letter [as reprinted in the Cimarron News and Press] –

[INSERT] A reprint of the "Dear Ben" telegraph. (See page 263 for telegraph)

was there ever a cooler devised plot with a Governor as sponsor?

The Governor admits the letter in toto ... <u>"That it sounds like me."</u> and then subsequently attempts to explain away part of its terrible features ...

He makes no attempt as to the telegram. Nor why he wished it to "leak." But by a down right falsehood he attempts to assemble certain persons who are obnoxious to him so that in the event of resistance, to be arrested, of a person by the name of [Clay] Allison an excuse would be offered <u>"to kill all the men who resist or stand with those who resist you."</u> He does not explain this. He cannot.

Stevens and the soldiers were sent by Governor Axtel ostensibly to arrest a person by the name of [Clay] Allison – but reading the foregoing telegram and letter I do not believe that it was the real object, for Allison was afterwards arrested and at once set at liberty ... and Governor Axtel subsequently made an appointment and traveled with said Allison in a friendly way in the stage coach ...

Any man capable of framing and trying to enforce such a letter of instructions as the one set forth in this report is not fit to be entrusted with any power whatever – I therefore report that this charge has been sustained.

[AUTHOR'S NOTE: Angel's outrage at the "Dear Ben plot" is hypocritically disingenuous, since he is covering it up as a Ring tactic also used for murdering Tunstall and McSween.]

<u>Charge Twelfth :</u> On February 1876 a bill was passed through the Legislature providing that the Courts should be removed from Cimarron Colfax County to Taos, Taos County and that after two terms the Governor might at his option restore the Courts to Colfax County. For the reasons set forth under Charge Eleventh I find that this charge is sustained.

> *In conclusion* I respectfully submit that whether through ignorance or corrupt motives the action of said Axtel has been to keep many parts of the Territory of New Mexico in a state of turmoil and confusion, when intelligent and non-partizan action on his part might have avoided much of the difficulty, and that the removal of Governor Axtell viewed with the evidence and his reply received before my first report, was an absolute necessity, and it becomes more evident that such was the right course on receiving his subsequent replies.
>
> **It is seldom that history states more corruption, fraud, mismanagement, plots and murders than New Mexico has been the theatre under the administration of Governor Axtel –**

[AUTHOR'S NOTE: Angel lists the Ring's "*corruption, fraud, mismanagement, plots and murders*," but capitulates by blaming it all on Axtell.]

> *I transmit herewith the testimony herein –*
> *All of which is respectfully submitted -*
> <u>Dated Washington, October 3 1878.</u>
>
> Frank Warner Angel
> Special Agent
> Department Interior.

REPORT ON CATRON

Angel needed only his Catron Report to prove U.S. officials' role in murdering Tunstall. Catron's subsequent strategy was to claim no report was written. But contemporaries confirmed it.

"JOHN C. ROUTT" CONFIRMS THE REPORT

In August of 1878, Catron's worry was not the existence of Angel's report, but its forcing his removal - as well as removal of Axtell by the one on him. So on August 29, 1878, a John C. Routt - a lackey or Catron himself by nom de plume - wrote to President Hayes about *"effort being made to remove the said officers."* "Routt" floated the outlaw myth to warn that removals would encourage *"the lawless conduct that has caused so much trouble in the Territory."* Of course, that original damage control proved the existence of the reports on Catron and Axtell, which made the effort *"to remove the said officers!"* From Santa Fe, "Routt" wrote:

President Hayes.

Dear Sir.

*I am here on a visit to my daughter and have more by accident than otherwise heard statements pro and con in relation to the causes of the recent troubles in this Territory **and also in relation to the supposed misconduct of Gov Axtell and [U.S.] District Attorney Catron. I also learned that there is an effort being made to remove the said officers**, and from all I can learn, in my judgment the **charges against those officials have been made without good cause, and [without] the best people in and around Santa Fe**. I think it would be against the interest of the Territory to remove the said [without] the best people in and around Santa Fe. I think it would be against the interest of the Territory to remove the said officials or either of them ... It seems to me that this removal would have much influence to encourage the lawless conduct that has caused so much trouble in the Territory ... It would also encourage the unlawful conduct of persons who are responsible for the murder and killing that has recently taken place in this Territory ... This statement is also made at my own suggestion.*

John C. Routt

WALLACE CONFIRMS THE CATRON REPORT

Unaware that Catron claimed his Angel Report did not exist, Lew Wallace referenced it to Secretary of the Interior Carl Schurz, in a letter draft of February 16, 1880. (See pages 618-619 for full letter) Wallace wrote:

Mr. Catron is not unknown to fame in your department ... ~~He also figures largely, I am told in the report of Mr. Angel, in which, as late U.S. District Attorney, he was admitted to a kind of head-centership of the famous old Santa Fe ring.~~

ELKINS INTERVENES TO HIDE REPORT

Elkins intervened. He, like Catron, knew the Angel Report existed, and focused on the *"effort being made to remove [Catron]."* Like "Routt-Catron," he used the outlaw myth, writing on September 24, 1878 to the report's future recipient, non-Ringite

Attorney General Charles Devens, stating: *"I think it can be clearly established that only bitter political & personal enemies have assailed [Catron] & the charges are unfounded."* He also announced contact with President Hayes, and coming to Washington himself. He added that Catron was available too.

Elkins was negotiating with Ring-shielding Hayes and his Cabinetmen: Secretary of State William Evarts (who had worked as an attorney with him and Catron in 1870 to swindle Lucien Maxwell out of his Grant), and Secretary of the Interior Carl Schurz (who had stonewalled Mary McPherson's 1877 exposés). Elkins apparently succeeded in getting the report hidden from the public. (Years later, he would destroy it.) He wrote:

Deer Park, MD.
Sept. 24 1878

Hon Chas Devens,
 Attorney General
Sir:
 I have just received from Mr. Catron a telegraphic message informing me that his testimony & answer [to Angel] was delayed in being forwarded until the 19th inst. & requested me to ask that no action be taken until they should be received. I think they will reach the Department by the 26th – unless there is some unusual delay & I hope you will grant his request in this respect –
 Very Respectfully
 <u>S.B. Elkins</u>

N.B.
I will be in Washington on Monday next, & if it would be agreeable to you to hear me, I would like to make a statement in Mr. Catrons behalf. **With the testimony & his answer & the facts I know I think it can be clearly established that only bitter political & personal enemies have assailed him & the charges are unfounded.** *I have written the president today & hope the letter will be referred to you ...*

 If you desire him to appear a telegraph to him at Mesilla New Mexico will reach him in time – if not & you will kindly notify me. I will telegraph him.
 Very Respectfully
 <u>S.B. Elkins</u>

CATRON'S RESIGNATION

With his Angel Report hidden in a secret deal, Catron had no choice but to resign. From Albuquerque, on October 10, 1878, he wrote to Attorney General Charles Devens:

> *Sir: In accordance with a purpose long entertained, I hereby tender my resignation as United States Attorney for New Mexico, to take effect November 10th 1878.*
> *Very respectfully yours &c.*
> *T.B. Catron*

On October 19, 1878, Devens accepted without further ado.

But, apparently delayed in positioning the right Ringite successor, Catron telegraphed Devens on November 4, 1878: "*Please change my resignation so as to take effect as soon after the thirtieth inst as my successor may be appointed & qualified.*" On November 12th, Devens accepted. So Catron stayed in power until Sidney Barnes replaced him on January 20, 1879. (Later that year, Barnes defended Dudley in his civil trial by Susan McSween. By September of 1880, he directed Secret Service Agent Azariah Wild's pursuit of Billy Bonney. And he was the prosecutor for Billy's March 30, 1881 Mesilla hanging trial for the Roberts case.)

This completion of the Angel Report cover-up by staged resignation was spelled out by Elkins in his August 15, 1879 letter to Catron. Called "smooth Steve" by his enemies, he preferred cloying persuasion to Catron's brutish threats. In this important letter - discussed above as minimized by Victor Westphall (see page 87) - Elkins, while squabbling about their business dealings, reminded Catron about the rescue. It shows how close Catron's crimes had brought the Ring to destruction. Elkins had stated: "About 1 year ago when your enemies were fighting you both in New Mexico and Washington and your dismissal as U.S. Attorney was ordered and an indictment talked of strongly, I let every other matter drop and devoted myself to your defense. I never exerted myself more in my life, and I have been assured by the authorities that but for me and the fight I made you would have been dismissed."

On his Halliehurst mansion stationery, Elkins wrote:

Halliehurst,
Elkins, West Virginia

118 Broadway,
New York City.
Aug. 15, 1879

My dear Tom,

I have waited some time to reply to your lengthy letter of the 1st. inst. ...

About 1 year ago when your enemies were fighting you both in New Mexico and Washington and your dismissal as U.S. Attorney was ordered and an indictment talked of strongly, I let every other matter drop and devoted myself to your defense.

I never exerted myself more in my life, and I have been assured by the authorities that but for me and the fight I made you would have been dismissed. In this defense I incurred obligations that to this day I am discharging ...

If I had never known you before the contest I made for you and your honor I thought that of it self was sufficient to bind you to me forever and that nothing I might do could invoke your enmity, - but how deceived I have been when I read your letter before me I can but ask is there any one in whom one can trust, how weak is human friendship.

We have had out differences, - all men have, - but I never thought you would try to force my resignation as President [of the First National Bank of Santa Fe] ...

Ingratitude is a sin. I am not going to try and answer your letter in detail. I have fully written you about the bank and I will say now that I never wrote the officers anything but asking kindness and indulgence to you. I have repeatedly asked them so far as the interests of the Bank would permit it to help you and lend you all the money they could. <u>I stand squarely upon this record.</u> **If I had wanted to injure you I need not have hunted for ways and means** ...

Now as to the presidency of the bank, I don't care to hold the place a moment and particularly with even one stockholder opposed. I have told you repeatedly I wanted to resign, - and this is my purpose but I won't do it nor think of it if you undertake to compel me to do so. The Bank has never done me a service, I have never borrowed a dollar from it and hope I never may...

You call at once for deeds to all of your property in my name. You don't offer to make any deeds to me but I am willing to make a full settlement with you and interchange deeds. I made you a statement long ago about the interests I have in my name belonging to me and you have always been protected on my books, but for two years or more I have been urging and you have been promising to make me a statement of land you hold for me in your name.

Why don't you send me a statement? You always said I had an interest in the lands you own on the Puerco River and some grants near Santa Fe, also that I was interested with you in a fifth of the Aztec mine [world's richest gold mine]...

Now make me a statement and let us have a settlement...

As to my going to Washington for you I have made a great many journeys there for you and I should go now but I don't believe I could do anything with the Commissioner. Am afraid not but if you think you want me to do so I will try.

After reading this I wish you could get your consent to withdraw your letter before me. It may not do you any material service - but it is best to be friends when it is so easy. I am not angry at your action, I am only sorry and disappointed. **I don't think yet you would do me an injury and unless you compel me to open hostility I will always be ready to do you a kindness.**

If I were in New Mexico these differences and misunderstandings would not be, they ought not to be and if they continue the fault will not be mine.

        Very truly,
       signed S.B. Elkins

AFTERMATH OF THE ANGEL REPORTS

Unscathed by Angel's compromised reports, the Santa Fe Ring raced to exterminate their last adversaries. Colfax County anti-Ring fighter Raymond Morley had been prophetic, writing to his wife Ada on August 15, 1878, 27 days after the lost Lincoln County War Battle: *"In the meantime the Ring seems more and more desperate. If I am a good guesser, the War in Lincoln is far from over. The Murphy party say they mean to kill or drive every McSween man from Lincoln."* (Cleaveland, *The Morleys,* pp. 152-155) And the Ring most wanted to *"kill or drive"* away zealot Billy Bonney, who had just miraculously escaped being burned alive, executed by soldiers' volleys, or riddled with bullets of their Lincoln County Sheriff's outlaw gang posse.

An additional potential obstacle to the Ring's unmitigated success was Lew Wallace, the new Territorial Governor replacing S.B. Axtell. It must have confused one-dimensional Ringites - whose gluttonous goals were just money and power - to contemplate the romantic complexity of him: Civil War Major General; graphic artist; best-selling author of an historical novel, *The Fair God*, about conquistador Hernando Cortez; prosecuting attorney who hanged Abraham Lincoln's murderers; and, at the time, writing a novel called *Ben-Hur* about the coming of Jesus Christ. And unbeknownst to them, he came bearing Frank Warner Angel's secret notebook, made for him and cataloguing Ringites, and Mary McPherson's 1977 printed pamphlet Ring exposé: "In the Matter of Charges vs. Gov. S.B. Axtell and Other New Mexico Officials."

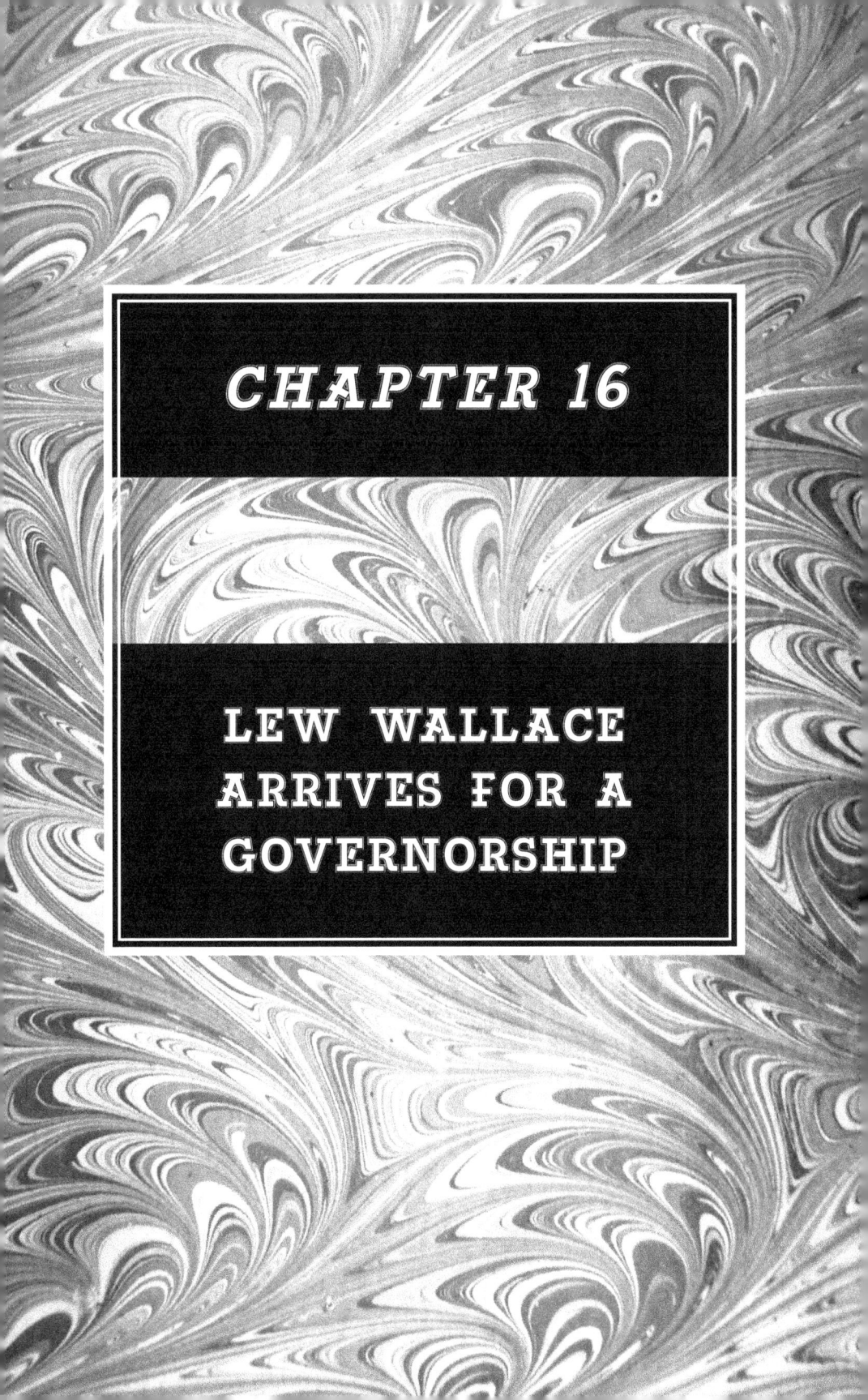

CHAPTER 16

LEW WALLACE ARRIVES FOR A GOVERNORSHIP

A STRANGE MAN FOR A STRANGE JOB

SUMMARY: The Ring and the Hayes administration dodged criminal exposures by scapegoating Governor S.B. Axtell. Their next challenge was whether his replacement, non-Ringite Lew Wallace, would get them through the aftermath of litigations and citizens' rage.

In late 1878, besides Billy Bonney, Lew Wallace was the most unusual man in New Mexico Territory. His complex psychology and creative talents were examined in my 2017 book: *The Lost Pardon of Billy the Kid: An Analysis Factoring in the Santa Fe Ring, Lew Wallace's Dilemma, and a Territory in Rebellion*. The coming together of Billy, as the last freedom fighter, and of this failed Civil War General still fighting his own demons, had implications for Billy's pardon and the future of the Ring.

LEW WALLACE'S BIOGRAPHY

SUMMARY: Lew Wallace's early years resulted in his personality of reality-escaping dreamer and authoritarian elitist, further complicated by his being blamed by Ulysses S. Grant for disastrous casualties in Shiloh's Battle.

Lew Wallace's affectionate biographers are Robert and Katherine Morsberger in 1980's *Lew Wallace: Militant Romantic*. And his autobiography in progress was edited and published posthumously by his wife, Susan, in 1906, a year after his death.

He was born a second son as Lewis Wallace, in Brookville, Indiana on April 10, 1827, with two brothers following. His mother died of T.B. when he was eight. His West Point educated, lawyer father, David, abandoned him to neighbors and relatives. In 1837, David became Indiana's Governor, and was party to massacring 150 Potawatomis Indians, refusing illegal relocation.

By 15, Louis, wrote his first novel, *The Man at Arms: A Tale of the Tenth Century*, set in Jerusalem in the Crusades. At 16, he ran away to join Texas's War of Independence. Brought back, he was punished by his angry father by being cut-off from the family.

Lewis apprenticed as a lawyer, then raised a company for the Mexican-American War, though saw no fighting. Back in Indiana, he got his law license in 1849, then married wealthy Susan Arnold Elston from Crawfordsville. They had a son, named Henry. In 1859 his father died.

In April 1861, he was made an Adjutant General by Indiana Governor Oliver P. Morton, becoming Colonel in the 11th Regiment of Indiana Volunteers. And he renamed himself as "Lew."

By June, Lew's regiment had a successful skirmish in Romney, West Virginia. In August of 1861, he was to report to Brigadier General Charles F. Smith as a Brigadier General of volunteers. But Smith died suddenly, being replaced by Ulysses S. Grant. In 1862, Wallace, then Commander of Fort Henry, without orders, joined Grant's winning battle at Fort Donnellson. The next month he was made Major General of volunteers.

Then came Grant's Battle of Shiloh, Tennessee, starting on April 6, 1862. That day, woolgathering Wallace got lost in the mile and a half to the battleground with his 7,500 troops. He arrived the next day and assisted Union victory. But the final casualties of 23,746 were the worst in America to that date. Grant publicly blamed him; removing him from command in June of 1862. Wallace returned to Crawfordsville, and would spend the rest of his life futilely seeking a pardon from Grant for Shiloh.

In August of 1862, Indiana Governor Morton got Lew sent alone to Cincinnati, Ohio, where coincidentally he won a battle with Confederate General Kirby Smith by conscripting citizens.

For Abraham Lincoln's 1864 reelection, Wallace was sent to Baltimore, Maryland, to "protect" poling places from rebels. But he hysterically decided to hang four, possibly innocent, men whom he called Confederate spies; though Lincoln stopped him.

In July of 1864, was the Maryland Battle of Monocacy, where Wallace, as the only Union officer available for command, was defeated by Jubal A. Early. But he praised himself as saving President Lincoln, because he delayed Early's advance long enough for Washington, D.C. to organize and repel him.

In 1864, he passed secret governmental aid to Mexico's President, Benito Juárez, to expel French colonizing forces. But, fantasizing a Confederate coalition with the French, he wrote an

Amnesty Proclamation for Confederates to reunite America. It was rejected by them. And by May 26, 1864, the Confederate Trans-Mississippi Department surrendered anyway.

Then, on April 15, 1865, President Lincoln was assassinated. Wallace was appointed prosecutor by new President, Andrew Johnson, for the conspirators' trial - the actual assassin, John Wilkes Booth having been killed. Wallace was subsequently accused of suppressing evidence to get Lewis Powell, David Herold, George Atzerodt, and Booth's innocent landlady, Mary Surratt, hanged. That year he also led the military commission which hanged Andersonville's Commander, Captain Henry Wirz.

On November 30, 1865, he left the army. To his killed battle adversaries, he had added five hangings, and almost hanged more. For him, sadistic power balanced Shiloh's failure.

After a brief and financially fruitless return to Mexico, he came back to Crawfordsville with fear of failure at 40. In 1868, he tried politics; losing a seat in Congress amidst press reviling his hanging of Mary Surratt. And his enemy, Grant, was by then President. In 1970, he tried again for a seat in Congress, losing to attacks about Shiloh and Surratt.

In 1871, he returned to writing, finishing two unsuccessful plays. In 1873, he completed *The Fair God: A Tale of the Conquest of Mexico*. It was a best-seller.

In 1876, he campaigned for Rutherford B. Hayes against Democrat Samuel Tilden. For that contested election, being on the canvassing board, he helped Hayes to win. So on March 9, 1877, he requested from Hayes an exotic ambassadorship to Italy, Brazil, Spain, or Mexico. And he was writing *Ben-Hur: A Tale of the Christ*. Hayes offered him a Bolivian ambassadorship. He declined. He was then offered Samuel Beach Axtell's remaining gubernatorial term. He accepted.

Wallace arrived in Santa Fe on September 30, 1878, and was sworn in as New Mexico Territory's 11th Governor on October 1st. His goal was rapid pacification, for rapid departure to an ambassadorship. So he sought martial law, adopted the Ring's simplistic outlaw myths against the Regulators, and made a November 13th Amnesty Proclamation for all non-indicted Lincoln County War participants. And he devoted himself to redecorating the Palace of the Governors and completing *Ben-Hur*.

Reality intruded with widow Susan McSween's planned litigation against Commander N.A.M. Dudley for arson and murder. The killing of her attorney, Huston Chapman, on February 18, 1879, forced Wallace to visit Lincoln.

By March of 1879, being seen as a savior, he heard from Billy Bonney, proposing a pardon in exchange for testimony against Chapman's killers. That left Wallace in a dilemma of honoring the bargain, or betraying it to save himself from Ring vengeance.

Next he testified in the corrupt Court of Inquiry for Commander Dudley. His efforts not to antagonize the Ring made him look incompetent. In response, he retreated to the Ring's outlaw myth to feign effort, betrayed his pardon bargain with Billy, and created outlaw myth articles on "Billy the Kid."

In January of 1880, he announced to the legislature that he had restored peace in Lincoln County, ignoring that he had reduced its citizenry to helplessness. That fall, he campaigned for James Garfield and finished *Ben-Hur*, an immediate best-seller. As President, Garfield made him Ambassador to Turkey. Before he left, he issued Billy's death warrant for Sheriff Pat Garrett.

From 1881 to 1885, Wallace was Ambassador to Turkey. In 1893, he published another best-seller: *The Prince of India: Or Why Constantinople Fell*. And he continued to write lying articles on the outlaw Billy the Kid, in which he was the hero and Billy betrayed the pardon bargain. He died on February 15, 1905, with his *Lew Wallace: An Autobiography*, completed in 1906 by his wife, Susan, who omitted his terrible flaws.

A RELUCTANT GOVERNOR

SUMMARY: Lew Wallace was uninterested in the Santa Fe Ring or recent conflicts. So the outlaw myth was appealing.

APPOINTMENT AND ARRIVAL

Lew Wallace's trip to assume his governorship was in the Ring's toxic embrace; being joined by Ringites Henry Waldo and U.S. Marshal John E. Sherman, as reported in the October 5, 1878 *Albuquerque Review*. They may have told him the Ring's outlaw myth. On October 1st, he was sworn in by Judge Warren Bristol. That day he wrote to Secretary of the Interior Carl Schurz about intending "extreme measures." On October 6th, Sherman gave him a list of "outlaws" (mostly past Regulators). He immediately used it for the outlaw myth, and was poised to hang them all.

WALLACE GETS SECRET ANGEL NOTEBOOK

Lew Wallace knew about the Ring from the start. Investigator Frank Warner Angel had written a secret notebook for him on Ringites. Dangerous Catron, with no entry, was referenced seven times; others were called his partner or *"tools."* On its red cover was: "Gov. Lew. Wallace/ Santa Fe, N.M." It stated:

<u>Newspapers</u>

Albuquerque Review, Independent
News & Press, Cimarron Ind – not a very high toned paper – It is agst. the gov.
Las Vegas Gazette, Republican – Favors the ring –
Santa Fe New Mexican, Ring paper, Republican
The Sentinal Santa Fe, Independent
Santa Fe News, Democratic
The Independent, Mesilla Independent, Mesilla News, Ring papers

Andrews Enos Santa Fe, reliable
Ayers John, Honest – Liquor his worst enemy
Axtel S.B. Santa Fe, conceited – egotistical, easily flattered, Tool unwittingly of the ring – goes off" half cocked"
Arney W.F.M. Santa Fe, The great American liar - Look out for him – No power or influence – Runs the Palace for Axtel
Atkinson Wm. Santa Fe, Surveyor Gen – Honest and very reliable, only official who courted investigation
Boyle Andrew, at present at Mesilla, Outlaw murderer
Blazer, Jos. H. Lincoln Co., Reliable – Knows a great deal – Will not tell what he knows -
Bartlett Chas H. Lincoln County, honest -
Barrier Adolph P. - Las Vegas, Dept. Sheriff – Favors McSween party – Has acted for the right so far –
Beardsley Ezra I Cimarron, not reliable – Ex Post Master ofc not correct – since been made all O.K.
Berillia Sheriff at Mesilla, Not reliable - Ring tool
Breeden M.A. Santa Fe, post master, weak ring man, can be lead with a string
Bruden Col Santa Fe, I do not think he is reliable
Bristol W. Mesilla, Ast. Justice – Honest and reliable outside of Lincoln troubles

Beckwiths [blank] Pecos, Look out for the old man, The boys are honest & reliable outside of Lincoln Co troubles –
Bail [blank] [John] Mesilla, reliable and square man
Carroll Henry Capt – Hatch man, Fort Stanton, Reliable outside of Hatch matters
Coghlan Pat, Honest great friend of Murphy party, Godfroy & that crowd – resides at Tulerosa
Cline – [blank] Lincoln, reliable – I do not think he is mixed up in the Lincoln troubles -
Copeland John M Sheriff, removed by Gov – Lincoln, McSween party, I think is reliable
Chaves A. Albuquerque, Territorial Dist. Atty, Strong ring man – Has reputation of altering election returns 1875
Crouch Jno [John] A. Mesilla U.S. Clerk – Editor Mesilla Independent Trickish not reliable in every respect
Conway Thos Santa Fe, Lawyer some ability – I think reliable
Coe boys Lincoln, I think are reliable especially Frank
Chisum John S. Pecos, Backbone of McSween party – Sharp be careful with him
D'Sena Jose D – Santa Fe, Politician considerable influence – not entirely reliable
Davis Geo Lincoln, outlaw murderer
Dorsey W. near Cimarron, Senator – be careful with him
Dolan J.J. Lincoln Leader in Lincoln Co, trouble, Murphy party, Brave sharp - determined fellow – Badly mixed up with ring &c
Dudley, N.A.M. Fort Stanton Post Commander – Honest mortal enemy of Hatch, Talks too much, rely on him rather than Hatch
Dowlin Will Post Trader, Fort Stanton, Honest reliable – is Co Commissioner
Delgado F. Santa Fe, I think reliable, great church man
Evans Jesse Lincoln Co – outlaw – murderer –
Ellis [Isaac and Ben] Lincoln – There are two of these persons – McSween men but I think they are good citizens and reliable -
Elkins S.B. "Silver tongued" further comment unnecessary -
Elkins John brother of S.B. Honest but dependent upon brother – strong ring man -
Eley Rev at Las Vegas, weak, not reliable, McSween man
Ellison Sam – Santa Fe, weak tool, of Catron
Fields Westley – Lincoln Co, I think is reliable
Farmer Jos H. Lincoln Co, honest –

Fiske E.A. Santa Fe, Lawyer – Shrewd – honest reliable – can be of great service to you. He controls the U.S. Marshal Has been of great service to me - Well posted as to the people and frauds in the Territory
Fisher   Santa Fe, of Fisher and Lucas, reliable -
Gallegos Panteleon, Not reliable in employ of Dolan – a tool -
Godfroy C.F. Indian Agent near Ft. Stanton, Badly mixed up
Gonsoles [Gonzales] F [Florencio] Probate Judge, Lincoln, reliable
Grace Fred Santa Fe Politician
Griffin W.W. Santa Fe, reliable & honest, in 1st Nat Bank & is influenced by Elkins
Howe Albert H. Lincoln Co, I think is reliable
Hurley John Lincoln – Easily influenced – Murphy party
Hubbel Judge Las Vegas, I think reliable, likes his toddy
Hill John Albuquerque, Under ring influence
Hatch E. Santa Dist Commander, Dudleys mortal enemy - Rumors- of his fraud and corruption To be handled with gloves
Hockradle Jerrie, Murphy man but honest & I think reliable
Jones   Mesilla, Catrons tool – not reliable
Kriling Chas Pecos, Honest but not reliable
Leverson M.R. Now on his ranch Larkspur Col – knows 6 times more than he can prove & 6 times more than anyone else – He can be of service to you <u>use him</u> Don't commit yourself – <u>Strong McSween man The Great American letters newspaper &c writer"</u>
Lee Wm D Cimarron, reliable but weak, under influence of Springer
Loud Lieut. Santa Fe, officious – Works for the ring – not reliable
Longwill Dr Santa Fe, Good Dr – but mixed up in Colfax Co trouble, Axtel man, ring man, do not rely on him -
Lucas   Santa Fe, of Fisher & Lucas – very reliable and a square man
Laudon "Judge" Santa Fe, reliable – but I think a democrat
Matthews J.B. Dept Sheriff Lincoln – Partisan Murphy party
Montaño Jose Lincoln, I think reliable –
Mattherson M. Socorro, Minister, Has done good work in Socorro & I think reliable
McPherson Mrs M.E. Washington D.C. Not reliable – Is interested or mixed up in Colfax Co troubles
McDaniels Jim [James] Lincoln, desperado

Murphy L.G. Santa Fe, Mixed up in Lincoln Co – now a drunkard, no reliability He believes himself a martyr & McSween the devil – Handle him with gloves –

McMullen Wm Santa Fe, not reliable

McSween Mrs – Lincoln now at Las Vegas – Sharp woman now that her husband is dead, a tiger <u>use her however ("molasses catches more flies than vinegar")</u>

McCandleis Chas Santa Fe, Sup. Judge <u>very</u> reliable, good man to work with

Michaels Dr Cimarron, Sharp fellow, Axtel man –

Newcomb John Lincoln, Honest, McSween party, I think reliable -

Patron J.B. – Lincoln, Has considerable influence with Mexicans – not entirely reliable

Perry S.R. Pecos – I think reliable – But of no standing

Probst   Santa Fe, Honest – reliable – but shallow -

Purington G.A. Fort Stanton Captain - Honest but is a Hatch man

Peppin G.W. Present Sheriff Lincoln Co – Weak Murphy man – Partisan, not reliable -

Romero J. Delegate, influenced by Elkins

Romero R. La Cueva, Smart young man, I think reliable –

"Roxey" Lincoln, Outlaw

Riley J.H. Las Cruces – Sharp cunning fellow also leader of Murphy party Lincoln – Very disapated, not reliable – interested with Catron in Gov Contracts

Ritch W.G. Santa Fe Sec Territory, Axtel man, otherwise reliable

Rynerson W.L. Territorial Dist Atty Mesilla – Strong partisan, Axtel man – Murphy man – has used his office oppressively – not reliable

Stanley Steph Lincoln D.B. dishonest drunkard

Sherman John Jr – U.S. Marshal Santa Fe (Bro of Secy) means to tell all he knows – reliable – but not much back bone unless "braced up" Use him through Fiske E.A.

Springer F. Cimarron, Reliable, educated – runs Cimarron – very hostile to Gov Axtel –

Shields D.P. Las Vegas, Brother in law McSween, I believe reliable

Smith G.A. Santa Fe U.S. Collector – Old foggy used by Catron, makes good returns to Government not reliable

Spiegelberg Bros Santa Fe, Not reliable, use them agst Z Staub Bros & visa versa

Staab Z & Bro Santa Fe Axes to grind not reliable, use them agst Speigelberg Bros & vice versa

Smith G. G. Santa Fe, Pastor Presp. Church, I do not believe he is reliable –

Strachan W.J. Santa Fe , A democrat but I think reliable, **Catrons enemy** *–*

Tompkins R.H. Santa Fe, honest - & I think reliable – Old age against him –

Thornton W.T. Santa Fe, Catrons partner

Thayer Chas Santa Fe, Gambler – honest & I think reliable

Upson M.A. Roswell, Smart but dishonest, not reliable –

Wilson Andrew Lincoln Co, Reliable

Wakefiels E.H. Las Cruces, has mail contract from there to Ft Stanton, easily influenced, Murphy party – I think he means to be honest

Widenmann R.A. Now at Mesilla, Great friend of McSween – given to boasting, veracity doubtful when he speaks of himself, well connected in the east & well educated

Whigham Henry Cimarron, Editor Cimarron News & Press – Not very reliable unless backed by Frank Springer, McSween man

Waldo H Santa Fe, Present Atty. Gen Honest good lawyer and reliable but great friend of Axtel

Wilson J.B. Lincoln Justice of Peace, "Old fox" and very <u>weak</u> – easily influenced On the fence

West Jos Lincoln, honest & I believe reliable

Watts J.H. Santa Fe, I think he is reliable

Walz E.A. Lincoln – a tool of Catron – a boy – not reliable

OUTLAW MYTH PROPAGANDA

SUMMARY: Protective of his political future, Lew Wallace adopted the outlaw myth to feign action by using U.S. Marshal John Sherman's "outlaw" list to jail or hang them, preferably by troops under martial law.

The Lincoln County troubles did involve "outlaws." They were Ring "boss" T.B. Catron; his judicial enforcers; local bosses, James Dolan and John Riley; Jessie Evans and his gang; Seven Rivers and John Kinney rustler-killers; and Commander N.A.M Dudley. But Lew Wallace preferred the simplistic outlaw myth for the simple solution of elimination. The Ring helpfully assisted.

DUDLEY DISTRACTS FROM HIS CRIMINALITY

Commander N.A.M. Dudley joined the "outlaw" chorus in a likely Catron-prompted letter of September 29, 1878 to his central command. His messenger was James Dolan! Its concocted *"gang of sixty to eighty strong"* would become the outlaw myth's statistic to exterminate the last Regulators. Likely miscopying his prompt letter's "rustlers" to "wrestlers," he wrote: *"The party of men styling themselves* **the "Wrestlers"** *made up of renegades from Texas especially, some of whom have been partisans with both of the leading factions here, since I assumed command, have renewed their raiding with almost unparalled vigor ... I have reliable information that the gang of which these men are a part, are from sixty to eighty strong ... I respectfully and earnestly ask in the name of God and humanity, that I may be allowed to use the Forces of my army command, to drive these murderers, horse-thieves, and escaped convicts out of the county. The wives and daughters of quiet and good citizens are being daily sullied by these desperados."*

BRISTOL BLOCKS THE GRAND JURY SESSION

Ringite Judge Warren Bristol joined in by telegramming U.S. Marshal Sherman on October 4, 1878, pretending that the fall Lincoln County Grand Jury could not be held because any jury would lack *"the better class of the population,"* and was *"tainted"* by *"gross partisanship."* Intended was blocking its indicting of July's San Patricio massacre perpetrators and Lincoln County War Battle arsonists and murderers of Alexander McSween, Harvey Morris, Francisco Zamora, and Vincente Romero.

WALLACE WARS ON OUTLAWS

The Ring may have failed to get a new recruit in Lew Wallace, but they got a dishonest fellow-traveler.

On October 4, 1878, in only his fourth day as governor, Wallace got Bristol's telegram via Sherman, and asked Secretary of the Interior Carl Schurz and Secretary of War George McCrary for martial law to hunt down "outlaws." For McCrary, fiction writer Wallace wrote fiction: *"Against Indians in out midst, and bands of outlaws on the borders, our people ... cannot make a show of resistance."*

477

By the next day, October 5, 1878, Wallace was in the foggy-headed hysteria that made him a liability at Shiloh. He deluged Schurz about his intended military campaign against "outlaws." He wrote: *"In my judgment nothing remains for me to do except to call upon the President to exercise his constitutional authority, and declare the existence of insurrection in the county of Lincoln,* **place the county without loss of time under martial law** *... and appoint a military commission to come and hold sessions there for the trial and punishment of offenders."* He also wanted Texas Rangers: *"Their combination with the regulars on this side will bring permanency of peace, by stamping out the robber element and breaking up their corrals and depots of plunder."*

SHERMAN'S OUTLAW LIST

On October 6, 1878, Sherman acted. He gave Wallace a list of the Territory's *"worst outlaws."* William Bonney, as "The Kid," was number 14. It stated:

1 John Slaughter	*(Murder)*
2 Andrew Boyle	*(Horse stealing)*
3 John Selman	*(Murder)*
4 _____ Selman, alias "Tom Cat."	*(Murder)*
5 Gus Gildey	"
6 _____ Irvin	"
7 Reese Gobles	*(Murder)*
8 "Rustling Bob" [Bryant]	*(Murder)*
9 Robert Speakes	"
10 "The Pilgrim"	"
11 John Beckwith	*(Horse stealing)*
Hugh M. Beckwith	*(Murder)*
12 Jim French	"
13 Joe [Josiah "Doc"] Scurlock	"
14 "The Kid" William Bonney	"
15 Tom Folliard [O'Folliard]	"
16 Charles Bowdrey [Bowdre]	"
17 Henry Brown	"
18 John Middleton	"
19 Fred Weight [Waite]	"
20 Jacob B. Matthews	"
21 Jesse [Jessie] Evans	"
22 James J. Dolan	"

23 George Davis, alias "Tom Jones"   "
24 _____ [Frank] Rivers   "
25 Injenio [Ygenio] Salazar   "
26 John Jones   "
27 William Jones   "
28 ~~William~~ James [Jim] Jones   "
29 Marion Turner   "
30 Caleb Hall (Collins)   "
31 Haskell [Heiskell] Jones   "
32 Joseph Hill, alias Olney   "
33 Buck Powell   "
34 James Hyson   "
35 Jake Owens   "
36 Frank Wheeler   "

WALLACE ACCUSES "WRESTLERS"

By Wallace's first week in office, it may be guessed that usually humorless Ringites rolled with laughter at his gullibility. On October 7, 1878, he relayed to Schurz his embellishment of Dudley's crazy "Wrestlers" story: *"The Wrestlers took the wives of these two [rancher] men, and forced them into the bush, stripped them naked and used them at their pleasure … [T]he people are flying in search of protection."*

WALLACE ACCUSES AN OUTLAW HOARD

On October 14, 1878, Wallace telegraphed Schurz, about *"outlaws;"* whose number had swelled to *"80 to 150"* *"Texans"* and *"Buffalo hunters."* Other than relief that he was not fighting the Ring, Schurz and Hayes must have wondered how out-of-control he would become.. Wallace wrote: *"[T]here is nothing to be done but make war upon murderous bands."*

A PRESIDENTIAL PROCLAMATION

Wallace's headlong rush was stopped. President Hayes refused martial law - and his own obvious involvement - and merely issued a Proclamation admonishing people to stop making trouble. It ran only from October 7th to 13th of 1878; stating:

BY THE PRESIDENT OF THE UNITED STATES OF AMERICA:

A PROCLAMATION.

WHEREAS, it is provided in the laws of the United States, that whenever by reason of unlawful obstructions, combinations or assemblages of persons, or rebellion against the authority of the government of the United States, it shall become impracticable in the judgment of the President to enforce by the ordinary course of judicial proceedings, the laws of the United States within any state or locality, it shall be lawful for the President to call forth the militia of any or all of the states, and to employ such parts of the land and naval forces of the United States as he may deem necessary to enforce the faithful execution of the laws of the United States, or to suppress such rebellion in whatever state or territory thereof the laws of the United States may be forcibly opposed or execution thereof forcibly obstructed; and

WHEREAS it has been made to appear to me, that by reason of unlawful combinations and assemblages of persons in arms, it has become impracticable to enforce by the ordinary course of judicial proceedings, the laws of the United States within the Territory of New Mexico, and especially within Lincoln County thereof, and that the laws of the United States have been forcibly opposed, and the execution thereof forcibly resisted; and

WHEREAS, the laws of the United States require that whenever it may be necessary in the judgment of the President to use the military force for the purpose of enforcing the faithful execution of the laws of the United States he shall forthwith by proclamation command such insurgents to disperse and retire peacefully to their respective abodes within a limited time. Now therefore, I RUTHERFORD B. HAYES, President of the United States, do hereby admonish all good citizens of the United States, and especially of the Territory of New Mexico, against aiding, countenancing, abetting or taking part in such unlawful proceedings, and I do hereby warn all persons engaged in or connected with said obstruction of the laws to disperse and return peaceably to their respective abodes on or before noon of the thirteenth day of October instant.

> IN WITNESS whereof I have hereto set my hand and caused the Seal of the United States to be affixed. Done in the City of Washington this seventh day of October the year of our Lord eighteen hundred seventy-eight, and of the Independence of the United States the one hundred and third.
>
> RUTHERFORD B. HAYES.

By the President:
F.W. SEWARD, Acting Secretary of State.

WALLACE'S SHAM ACTION

The President's inaction justified his own. On October 9th, Wallace wrote to Secretary of State William Evarts: "*I shall go down to Lincoln county immediately.*" He did not go. On October 23rd, he announced to Schurz that he was redecorating the Palace of the Governors. The day before, he had fabricated progress to Schurz; writing: "*In Lincoln and Doña Ana counties there has been no report of violence or wrong.*"

THE "PACIFICATION PLAN"

Wallace's outlaw war swelled to "*pacification.*" With his narcissistic insensitivity, he wanted troops sent to Lincoln, forgetting it was just three months since Dudley's military terrorism there. On October 26, 1878, he mailed this plan to General Edward Hatch, adding: "*I think it would be advisable to select … officers who are not accused of connection with such feuds or supposed to have had any part in them.*"

The next day, on October 27, 1878, his desire for soldiers was flattered. Army Headquarters in Santa Fe informed Commander Dudley by First Lieutenant and Adjutant of the 9th Cavalry John S. Loud (identified in Angel's secret notebook as "*Works for the ring*") to grant Wallace troops.

HUSTON CHAPMAN WRITES TO WALLACE

On October 24, 1878, reality intruded. Susan McSween's attorney, Huston Chapman, sent Wallace a letter. It is unlikely that Wallace remembered Frank Warner Angel's notebook entry: "*McSween Mrs – Lincoln now at Las Vegas – Sharp woman now that her husband is dead, a tiger <u>use her however ("molasses catches more flies than vinegar")</u>.*" That "tiger" wanted justice. She wanted to prosecute Commander N.A.M. Dudley.

On October 24, 1878, 3 months and 25 days before his Ring murder, from Las Vegas, Chapman mailed Wallace his complaint about Dudley, unaware that Dudley was a lynchpin in Wallace's military fantasies for suppressing Lincoln County, and unaware that conflict with an officer was Wallace's Achilles heel. He wrote:

Gov Lew Wallace,
Santa Fe, N.M.

  My Dear Sir -

   You will please pardon me for presuming so much upon your kindness, but knowing your earnest desire to protect the interest of any citizen of this Territory, and to see justice done all, I have made it my warrant for writing you in regard to affairs in Lincoln County.

  From advices received this morning from Lincoln, affairs there seem as unsettled as ever, and the people are expecting, really wishing for, martial law to be proclaimed by you. As such an event is very probably in the next few days, I desire to call your attention to one person whose actions have been offensive in the extreme to a large number of the best citizens of that County, and that man is Col. Dudley. I am in possession of facts which make Col Dudley criminally responsible for the killing of McSween and he has threatened that in case martial law was declared that he would arrest Mrs. McSween and her friends immediately. Through fear of his threat Mrs. McSween left Lincoln and is now visiting here, until such time as she may with safety return home. She has fears of harm only from Col Dudley and in case he has the power he will do all in his power to annoy and arrest her. Mrs. McSween has some interests in Lincoln County which really demands her presence there at the meeting of the Probate Court next month, but in view of the threats made by Col Dudley she is afraid to return there. As the attorney of Mrs. McSween I ask that should martial law be proclaimed in Lincoln County you will prevent Col. Dudley from exercising any authority that would enable him in any way to interfere with Mrs. McSween, or her affairs. Believe me that I do not wish to influence you in any action in regard to the affairs in that county and am sorry to be forced to lay these complaints before you, but owing to the very prominent and partisan manner in which Col Dudley has acted I think you will agree with me that he is not a fit man to act in so delicate and complicated a matter.

  There seems to be but one opinion entertained by the people and that is that you are determined to see that ample justice is had in Lincoln County.

  Hoping that you will pardon any liberty I have assumed in making these suggestions, I am

       Yours very truly
        H.I. Chapman

WALLACE'S AMNESTY PROCLAMATION

By November 13, 1878, Wallace expanded his strategy to be left alone by simply pardoning all these "feuding" people; and included soldiers with civilians to dispose of all possible complainers. The ploy would backfire badly. He wrote:

Proclamation by the Governor.

For information of the people of the United States, and of the citizens of the Territory of New Mexico in especial, the undersigned announces that the disorders lately prevalent in Lincoln County in said Territory, have been happily brought to an end. Persons having business and property interests therein, and who are themselves peaceably disposed, may go to and from the County without hindrance or molestation. Individuals resident there, but who have been driven away, or who, from choice, sought safety elsewhere, are invited to return, under assurance that ample measures have been taken and are now and will be continued in force, to make them secure in person and property. And that the people of Lincoln County may be helped more speedily to the management of their civil affairs, as contemplated by law, and to induce them to lay aside forever the divisions and feuds which, by national notoriety, have been so prejudicial to their locality and the whole Territory, the undersigned, by virtue of authority in him vested, further proclaims a general pardon for misdemeanors and offences committed in the said County of Lincoln against the laws of the said Territory in connection with the aforesaid disorders, between the first day of February, 1878, and the date of this proclamation.

And it is expressly understood that the foregoing pardon is upon the conditions and limitations following:

It shall not apply except to officers of the United States Army stationed in the said County during the said disorders, and to persons who, at the time of the commission of the offence or misdemeanor of which they may be accused were, with good intent, residents citizens of the said Territory, and who shall have hereafter kept the peace, and conducted themselves in all respects as becomes good citizens.

Neither shall it be pleaded by any person in bar of conviction under indictment now found and returned for any such crimes and misdemeanors, nor operate the release of any party undergoing pains and penalties consequent upon sentence heretofore had for any crime or misdemeanor.

In witness whereof I have hereunto set my hand and caused the seal of the Territory of New Mexico to be affixed.

{SEAL} Done at the city of Santa Fé, this 13th day of November, A.D. 1878
LEWIS WALLACE,
By the Governor,
W.G. Ritch, Secretary

WAR DEPARTMENT REJECTION

On November 23, 1878, Wallace's hope of again being a General in a war was rejected by Secretary of War George McCrary. He was aware of Shiloh; and likely was told the mission was keeping Wallace away from interfering with the Ring.

WALLACE'S SECRET RING LETTER

Lew Wallace was hiding how much he knew. He had Angel's secret input. He well realized how dangerous the Ring was. On November 14, 1878 - the day after his Amnesty Proclamation - he wrote in anxious confidence to his Civil War friend, Absalom Markland, that the Ring was trying to get him removed:

Santa Fe, N.M.
Nov. 14, 1878.

Col. A.H. Markland,
My dear Colonel:
Our mutual friend, Mr. Hinds, who will hand you this, goes to Washington tomorrow; and I write late at night.

Enclosed find a paper with markings which may interest you and Mrs. M., to whom please give my regards. They will tell you with what success I operate to finish the outlawry in this Territory, and how it was done.

After you have read them, a word as to my confirmation.

I came here, and found a "Ring" with a hand on the throat of the Territory. I refused to join them, and now they are proposing to fight me in the Senate. Ex Delegate Elkins is head-center in Washington. *He is the fellow who got the* <u>Washington Sunday Herald</u> *to publish the lie which the paper enclosed contradicts. The paper, by the way, is the Democratic organ of the Territory.*

Elkins will rely on Orth, in the House, and Davis, of Virginia, and Dorsey, of Arkansas ... Davis is Elkins' father-in-law. **Dorsey was an associate of the ring in land-grant speculation**, *which came to grief in New Mexico a few weeks ago. The paper upon which the grant was based was a forgery – and Dorsey knew the fact before he went into it – that is, before he went before the Surveyor General.*

[AUTHOR'S NOTE: This is the Uña de Gato Land Grant fraud exposed by Investigator F.W. Angel, saying Axtell was the Ring's agent to buyer, Senator Stephen W. Dorsey.]

Now can't you turn out and help me in the business? You know everybody, and just who to see, and how to get at them. Give me a little of your old time energy, and do me a little of the old style fighting. And write to me when you have looked the ground over.

Say to Mrs. Markland that this is singular country. Six sevenths of the population are Mexican, and so is society and the customs generally. I would like it, but I shrink from bringing my wife. After the Senate has pronounced on me, if unfavorably, of course I will go home – if yea, it is probable I'll go back any hour for my wife's sake.

Write me, Truly, your friend, Lew Wallace.

TRYING TO ESCAPE

By November 18, 1878, in office 48 days, Lew Wallace wanted out. On November 18, 1878 he floated, to no avail, a proposal to Secretary of State William Evarts stating that since *"the progress made in suppressing the insurrectionary troubles in Lincoln county [which was my] special mission here [is] accomplished, do you not think me entitled to promotion?"* He was ready for that exotic ambassadorship now!

RING REMOVAL RUMORS

Wallace also sought reassurance from Carl Schurz about Ring removal attempts. On December 9, 1878, Schurz answered: *"I have not heard of any intention on the part of anybody in the Senate to defeat your confirmation."* Though this was supportive, Lew Wallace was clearly factoring in Ring retaliation to protect his political future.

CHAPTER 17

THE RING STRIKES AGAIN

THE DUDLEY TIME-BOMB

SUMMARY: By his first month as Governor, Lew Wallace was aware of the enmity of Lincoln citizens to Commander Dudley; though he ignored it. The Ring was equally aware of that enmity endangering themselves. The situation would soon spin out of control.

In his first month in the Territory, Lew Wallace had gotten Attorney Huston Chapman's October 24, 1878 letter about Susan McSween's litigation against Commander Dudley. He failed to see the emerging crisis. But Catron knew that Chapman now was the Ring's greatest risk. It was time to strike again.

WALLACE RESPONDS

Unaware that he was beside a volcano about to erupt, Lew Wallace's response to Huston Chapman's October 24, 1878 complaint about N.A.M. Dudley was attempted placation of both, while staying clear of the fray. He had included Dudley in his Amnesty Proclamation so he would feel immune to prosecution. For Chapman, he would try to remove Dudley from Command as a local irritant. That way he could cleverly blame Lincolnites for the accusations. And he needed Dudley's help for outlaw scapegoating.

For his plan, on October 28, 1879, Wallace wrote to General Edward Hatch, calling *"incredible"* Chapman's *"accusations;"* but also granting Chapman's request for Susan McSween's safe-guard. He seemed to forget that if Dudley was found guilty of Posse Comitatus Act violation, Hatch would be blameworthy as his superior. Hatch realized. He stonewalled Wallace.

On November 9, 1878, Wallace tried again with Hatch, still appeasing: *"my object being to give [Dudley] an opportunity to be heard upon the subject."*

DUDLEY RESPONDS

After Hatch's apparent telegraphic order, Dudley responded the same November 9th to Wallace with bombastic snideness reeking of Ring shielding and dictation by Catron. Enclosed were already-prepared usual defamatory affidavits - here against Susan McSween's chastity - to devalue her credibility for court testimony. Dudley wrote:

*Headquarters.
Fort Stanton, N.M.
Nov. 9' 1878*

*To his Excellency,
    Lew. Wallace.
        Governor Territory of New Mexico*
  Sir:

I am in receipt of a copy of letter written by one H.I. Chapman, calling himself the Attorney of Mrs. A.A. McSween, widow of the late McSween, lawyer at Lincoln N.M., also your letter addressed to the District Commander, both having been referred to me for remark.

I have no comments to make upon either, except to respectfully invite your attention to the seven affidavits and one certificate sent to District Headquarters, from parties here, who know the facts in the case, and the woman equally as well, who asks for a safeguard.

I have requested that they be laid before you at once, for the reason that I believe you should know the character of some of your informants, regarding matters upon which you are to act.

If these papers do not satisfy you, any number of a similar kind can be forwarded. *I am prepared to defend myself from any and all attacks, coming from whatever source they may, and shall require no time to do it, and shall not need the services of an attorney either.*

[AUTHOR'S NOTE: The words "satisfy you" would become a Ring trap for Wallace in Dudley's Court of Inquiry.]

I have complete reports of every detachment, guard, posse and escort that has left this post, since I assumed command, at 12 PM, April 5th 1878.

Not an officer or soldier of my command has ever left the reservation on any duty appertaining to Lincoln County affairs, even as a simple courier, unless he went under carefully written orders, and a full report was required of the result of the tour, and which I have now in my possession, all of which are matters of record.

I am not here, quietly to submit, and allow such allegations against myself, as your Excellency has seen proper to forward to District Headquarters, without making an unqualified denial, and I defy proof to the contrary.

*Very Respectfully,
Your Obt. Servant
N.A.M. Dudley
Lieut Col 9' Cavalry, Comdg Post.*

WALLACE RESPONDS AGAIN

When Wallace pardoned Dudley in his Amnesty Proclamation, he missed the implication: that Dudley *needed pardoning*. Dudley - and the Ring waiting to pounce - did not. And after Dudley's reply of November 9th, Wallace blundered again - still trying to placate Dudley - by responding to Hatch on November 14th that Dudley's response was *"perfectly satisfactory."* That merely meant that Dudley had responded as to him as requested; not that Dudley's actions, or the enclosed defamatory affidavits about Susan McSween, were acceptable. But by May of 1879, in the military Court of Inquiry, he would face Dudley's Ringite lawyer accusing him of having already exonerated Dudley.

HUSTON CHAPMAN'S ONSLAUGHT

The flip side of Lew Wallace's emerging nightmare was Attorney Huston Chapman. By his November 25, 1878 letter, he was blaming Wallace; hissing:

> *You attach much importance to the awe-inspiring influence of the military, but it would pain you to see in what contempt they are held by the people whose confidence they have so shamefully abused. These depraved specimens of humanity who disgrace the name of soldier by the debauchery and immoral conduct are little to be relied upon in any matter where they are interested.*
>
> *It is a matter of surprise to me that a man like Col. Dudley, who is a whiskey barrel in the morning and a barrel of whiskey at night, is entrusted with so important a position, or even retained in the army where his debaucheries*

must work such a damaging influence upon younger and better officers, and thus destroy their usefulness.

Col. Dudley is continually under the influence of liquor and has used his position as commandant of Ft. Stanton to insult and abuse offending citizens until his conduct has become a reproach to the military service of the country and an insult to every officer who tries to maintain the dignity of his position. I desire particularly to call your attention to the conduct of this man Dudley to the end that in the future we may know upon whom to place the responsibility for his wrongdoings. (Nolan, *The Lincoln County War*, p. 359)

On November 29, 1878, Chapman sent Wallace another fierce letter which laid ruin to his outlaw myth subterfuge. He blamed the Ring for Lincoln County's crisis! He saw through Wallace's Amnesty Proclamation as shielding Ringites from murder indictments. And he repeated Shiloh: Wallace had failed by not showing up ... now in Lincoln! From Lincoln, Chapman wrote:

Dear Governor.

You must pardon me for so often presuming upon your kindness, but I write this letter to inform you of the true status of affairs in Lincoln County. To-day this town was thrown into a panic by two hundred deputy sheriffs charging into town on their horses with their guns cocked and directed at the house of Mrs. McSween. A few minutes afterwards a posse of soldiers under the command of one Lieut Goodwin came riding into town with three horse-thieves who had formerly been of Sheriff Peppin's posse, and were brought in for examination before the Justice of the Peace. What I have to complain of is the riotous manner in which the military, Sheriff and deputies charge about over the county giving unnecessary alarm and anxiety to peaceably disposed citizens. The Sheriff's deputies who were with the military were drunk and had with them a flask of whiskey from which they were continually drinking and their conduct was anything but that of a peace officer. One of the deputies, who accompanied the military, fired his gun into the street to the great danger of peaceable citizens, and in fact there was no disturbance except that made by the military and drunken deputies. I will tell you candidly that the people have more fear of outrages from the military and the quasi sheriff who is harbored and protected at Ft. Stanton than from any other source. The people have too painful a remembrance of the murder of

*McSween by order of that "<u>brave</u> <u>and</u> <u>accomplished</u>" soldier Col. Dudley, to rest quietly while he is permitted to continue his acts of rapine and murder ... Your own proclamation that peace had been restored in Lincoln County supersedes the necessity of further aid from the Government and prevents the use of the military to aid the civil authorities in Lincoln County, and I have advised the citizens here to shoot any officer who shall in any manner attempt their arrest, or interfere with their rights. I have counseled the people to observe your proclamation and will continue to do so as long as the military and Sheriff Peppin and his outlaws observe it, but while I counsel its observance I question your authority to grant amnesty before conviction in trial for offences against the laws. The McSween men are willing to stand their trial in the proper courts of the territory, or to observe your proclamation, **provided, the other side or "ring" observe it,** but they will never allow themselves to be arrested by murderers like Col. Dudley and Sheriff Peppin, but will peaceably surrender to any decent man who may be sent with a warrant for their arrest. When the courts are held in this county Dudley and Peppin will be arrested and tried for the murder of McSween and others and the legality of your amnesty proclamation will then be tested. I cannot but think that if you had visited Lincoln County, as you should have done, that you would have acted differently, and not have pardoned notorious outlaws and murderers. You have been grossly imposed upon by the military who have lied to you in order to shield themselves from the outrages they have committed in this county. There is not an honest man in Lincoln who would believe Col. Dudley on oath, yet you rely on him for all your information, and have pardoned him for the murder of an innocent man. **I can assure you that the people take no stock in your amnesty proclamation and they think you have been derelict in your sworn duty as Governor in not visiting Lincoln County and acquainting yourself with the true state of affairs.***

The people of Lincoln County are disgusted and tired of the neglect and indifference shown them by you, and next week they intend holding a mass-meeting to give expression to their sentiment, and unless you come here before that time you may expect to be severely denounced in language more forcible than polite.

To show you in what contempt and distrust the military are held by the people I will cite one instance: When your proclamation was received by at Ft. Stanton by Col. Dudley, he at once sent for the leading citizens of Lincoln to come to the Fort and with him, but not <u>one</u> man responded to his invitation. They had been treacherously betrayed once before, and they refused to be duped again. Yet this is your confidential advisor as to affairs in Lincoln County.

I have written this letter at the earnest solicitation of many prominent citizens in hopes that you might be induced to come to Lincoln County and inform yourself as to the affairs here. And I can assure you that I have written this letter with the best of motivation and the kindest wishes for your success as chief executive of the Territory; and in my feeble way I have tried to assure the people that you would yet come to Lincoln County and personally hear their grievance.

I am now preparing a statement of facts for publication, which, I am sorry to say will reflect upon you for not coming here in person, for no one can get a correct idea of the outrages that have been committed here by quietly sitting in Santa Fe and depending on drunken officers for information. A decent respect for the people of this county would have caused you to have come here in person and ascertained who was responsible for all the trouble, and then you should have seen that the guilty were punished. I am no believer in making the laws a convenience or prostituting them for the sake of peace, and the people of this county will not submit to it quietly.

Fort Stanton is to-day and has been during all the troubles, the rendezvous of the worst outlaws that have infested Lincoln County, and to-day the disreputable class who are harbored there is a disgrace to the Government. The horse and cattle thieves who are, and have been, depredating throughout the county [Seven Rivers and John Kinney's men] were deputies under that notorious murder[er] the <u>quasi</u> Sheriff, Peppin, and they have always been favored associates of the officers at the Fort.

I desire to retain your friendship but I owe a duty to the people of this county, and will discharge it to the very best of my ability, and without fear or favor. I earnestly desire to see your administration as chief executive of the territory made as popular as possible, but I believe that it can only be done by firmly upholding the supremacy of the law and punishing wrong-doing.

Hoping that upon receipt of this you may find it convenient to visit Lincoln County and confer with the people.
I remain as ever,   Yours very truly
                                    H.I. Chapman

DUDLEY ATTACKS WALLACE

Being caught between the devil and the deep blue sea of the Ring and the Lincolnites, with sole objective of protecting himself, Wallace had vacillated wildly. After writing, on November 30, 1878, to Dudley that he was trying to protect him; on December 7, 1878, he wrote to Edward Hatch asking for Dudley's removal as a "local irritant." Again Wallace missed the point: removal was an even worse accusation than need for pardon!

The Ring had taken a tremendous risk to use Dudley and his troops for assassinations. So Catron strategized his protection. On December 14, 1878, a supposed letter by Dudley was published in the Ringite Santa Fe *Weekly New Mexican* blaming Wallace and outlaws as: "An Open Letter, By Lieut. Col. N.A.M. Dudley, 9th Cavalry, to His Excellency Governor Lew Wallace." It was reprinted in the *Mesilla News* on December 21, 1878. Attached was a signed letter of support from Fort Stanton officers (who were participants in the Lincoln County War Battle).

Wallace folded. He made no counter-accusations. He refused to ruin his own future. The "Open Letter" stated:

**AN OPEN LETTER
By Lieut. Col. N.A.M. Dudley, 9th Cavalry, to his Excellency Governor Lew Wallace.**

Fort Stanton, New Mexico,
Nov. 30, 1878
To His Excellency,
Lewis Wallace,
Governor of the Territory of New Mexico

Sir: I have the honor to acknowledge the receipt of your communication of the 16th inst., wherein you state that my letter to District Headquarters and the several affidavits accompanying it, relating to the charges laid before you by H.I. Chapman of Las Vegas based upon representations of one Mrs. A.A. McSween, had been submitted to you by Act. Assist. Adjutant General of the District, and that you made the answer, that **the matter was "perfectly satisfactory."**

You further state: "I also requested that the application (which you had made) for a safe guard for Mrs. McSween be recalled."

You also stated: "The indignation (meaning the writer) showed was not at all displeasing to me, the same charge preferred against me, if untrue, would have certainly moved me the same way."

In the same letter you further state, referring to myself: "If you will examine the files at Headquarters here, you will find a communication over my hand, addressed to General Hatch, and of a date prior to the receipt of either of your replies, in which I stated explicitly, that I do not believe the charges against you." These statements are made three days after the date of your Proclamation.

Having permitted yourself to be the medium of forwarding to my senior such false, grave and slanderous charges, founded, as I have reason to believe, on the representations of a notoriously bad woman, it would, it seems to me, under the circumstances have been only justice, to have furnished myself, also, with a copy of your letter, setting forth your disbelief of the charges in question; but, instead, your Excellency promulgated an official Proclamation dated the 13th inst., granting a general pardon among others, to "officers of the United States Army stationed in the County of Lincoln, Territory of New Mexico, during the late disorders" for misdemeanors and offences committed in said County of Lincoln against the laws of said Territory, in connection with the aforesaid disorder, between the 1st day of February, 1878, and the 13th day of November, same year.

Not having any leniency for myself and well knowing that no officer serving in the country has, and as your Excellency cannot very consistently grant a pardon to an individual, or to a class or body of men who have not committed a crime, I am with other officers of my command, at a loss to correctly interpret this part of the Proclamation.

I am not aware of having done a single illegal act, one that be construed into a violation of law and order, neither do I know of any officer in the Army serving in Lincoln County, having done so since I assumed command at Fort Stanton, on the 5th day of April last.

Not an officer or soldier of my command, has ever left the Military reservation, on any duty appertaining to Lincoln County affairs, even as a simple courier, unless he went under carefully written orders, and a full written report required, of the result of the tour performed, all of which orders and reports are matters of official record, and in my personal possession at the present time.

I unqualifiedly assert, that neither your Excellency, or any official can find the first objectionable act of myself, or any member of my command, or one that can be construed, in any possible way, into a misdemeanor, offence, or violation of any single Territorial law of New Mexico, in any of these orders or reports.

On the contrary, if your Excellency had taken the trouble, as I respectfully invited you to do, when you first arrived in the Territory, and examined the official weekly reports, made by myself to the Headquarters of the District, you would have learned what kind of duty had been required of the officers and men serving here and how that duty has been performed.

It certainly is very singular, that neither Major General Pope, Commanding the

Department of Missouri, or General Hatch, Commanding the District of New Mexico, should have not discovered that the officers of the Army, serving in the County of Lincoln, were guilty of misdemeanors, and violation of Territorial laws, for they both have complete and full reports, on every movement made by the command, weekly, and neither of these officers has personally deemed it necessary to visit this region ever to send an officer to investigate the conduct of either myself or the officers serving under my command.

Your Excellency alone, without an investigation, except an exparte one without having given one of the parties thus accused, an opportunity to explain their position, are charged with acts seriously affecting their honor, and pardoned for the same in one document just promulgated by your Excellency.

The Proclamation in question grants a pardon to officers who have on repeated occasions risked their lives, under fire at times, to aid and protect the women and children of Lincoln County against the outrages of armed organized bands of murderers, horse thieves, and convicted as well as unconvicted felons ...

[AUTHOR'S NOTE: This is the Ring's outlaw myth: soldiers were protecting citizens against outlaws.]

There can be but one construction placed upon the language of the Proclamation. It virtually charges myself and officers of the Army who have been on duty here since the 1st of February last, with having violated the laws of the Territory, and then proceed to pardon us; classing one and all of us, with the murderers, cattle thieves, and outlaws who killed Sheriff Brady, Roberts, Bernstein, Beckwith, **Tunstall**, and a score of other citizens of the county.

[AUTHOR'S NOTE: Billy will need the Wallace pardon for the Brady, Hindman, and Roberts killings; but they are being advertised by the Ring as acts of outlawry alone. And do not miss that Ring-murdered Tunstall is slipped in as killed by vague "outlaws" too.]

I earnestly submit, that to warrant giving publicity to such defamatory charges in a public proclamation, against a body of officers of long service and good repute, it was but just to have allowed them a hearing first; not to come to a hasty conclusion, based on evidence on a solely exparte character not even submitting to them a synopsis of the charges for which they are pardoned.

I respectfully request to be informed of what offence I am charged, and who my accusers are. I shall have no trouble in exhibiting their characters in a similar light, that you have had of the woman who solicited and obtained a safe guard for herself [Susan McSween]. It is my right to be so informed, and until I am found guilty of any violations of the laws of the Territory, I respectfully decline accepting a pardon at the hands of your Excellency.

If this pardon is only to prevent further annoyance to myself and the officers of my command, in the nature of vexations, suits of the law, at the hands of evil disposed persons, then, in that case, I for myself and them sincerely thank you for the intervention.

From the extraordinary wording of your Excellency's Proclamation, its readers, scattered all over the country, will wonder what crimes the officers of the Army stationed in Lincoln County, N.M., have committed against the laws of the Territory they were employed to guard, protect and aid in executing, which brought forth a general pardon from the governor.

We, one and all, feel most painfully, to be published to the country in this manner, you Excellency have been a soldier, cannot on reflection blame those who are now, for most earnestly placing on record this solemn, but respectful protest against such allegations.

Without any intention of criticizing the official course of your Excellency, permit me to state that you have now been more than eight weeks in the Territory, and have never been during this period, within nearly 200 miles of the scene of the terrible death struggles, that have been enacted in this county, during this time.

Five innocent persons, natives, and residents of the County of Lincoln, have been inhumanely murdered in about the same number of hours, all within a few miles of each other, and without the slightest provocation. Women have been dragged from their private conveyances, from off the public mail highways and treated in a manner too disgusting to be related here. Whole bands of horses have been stolen and driven off, in the presence of their honest owners in broad daylight. Herds of cattle containing hundreds of head, have been taken in the same manner, their herders killed, and not a single arrest has ever been made by the civil authorities since I have been in the county.

[AUTHOR'S NOTE: Irrelevant description of crimes following anarchy after the War is used here to distract from Dudley's crimes in the War's Battle. As to no arrests since Dudley arrived in April of 1878, that was when Governor Axtell and Sheriff Brady had blocked arresting Tunstall's killers.]

Many of the facts have been laid before your Excellency, immediately after their occurring, and until the President's Proclamation dated on the 7th October, what steps, I ask have been taken by the Territorial officers to put a stop to such unlawful conduct? I answer None!

The occasional passing of troops over the public roads have had the effect to give the poor frightened settlers an opportunity of a few hours of seeming security. Where ever the colored cavalry have made their appearance, doors that have been for weeks or months barred, and barricaded windows, have been opened for a few hours. Husbands and sons have enjoyed the luxury of a night's rest at their homes when ever the troops have camped a single night near their ranches.

For weeks and months, they have been compelled to seek safety in the caverns, and mountain fastness against the very class of men included with the officers of the United States Army, in the pardon of your Excellency.

In coming to the Territory your Excellency passed through a section of the country, which has been the retreat and asylum for many of the class, who have raided and assisted in every way possible to bring upon Lincoln County the long train of crimes and disaster, which have almost depopulated it.

[AUTHOR'S NOTE: This may refer to Wallace's Cimarron meeting with Frank Springer and reported to Catron; adding credence to Catron's authoring this "Open Letter" to conceal the Ring's War crimes.]

Pardon me for saying, it is not to be wondered at, that you have received erroneous views of the exact state of affairs here. I most respectfully ask you to come to Lincoln County, and see and judge for yourself, from personal observation, of the facts.

I am aware that it is not within the province of an officer of the Army, to make such suggestions to a civil functionary, occupying the high position of yourself, much less criticize his official course; but when false and unjust accusations are made, against either myself, or the gallant officers of my command, it becomes my duty to demand for them and myself a hearing and not allow a general pardon to be promulgated for them or myself, for offences we know not of, and of which we feel wholly guiltless.

I am Sir, respectfully
Your obdt. Servant
N.A.M. Dudley
Lieut. Col. 9th Cavalry

Fort Stanton, New Mexico
November 30, 1878

General N.A.M. Dudley
Fort Stanton, New Mexico

Dear General – We, the undersigned officers of the U.S. Army, stationed at this Post during the recent troubles in Lincoln County, have heard and read an open letter addressed by you to His Excellency the Governor of New Mexico and desire to say that the said letter expresses most fully and explicitly our feelings upon the subject, in this publicly declining to accept for us the pardon rendered by His Excellency.

D.M. Appel, Asst. Surgeon, U.S.A. Post Surgeon; G.W. Smith, 2nd Lt. 9th Cav. Post

Adjutant; M.F. Goodwin, 2nd Lt. 9th Cavalry; Sam S. Pague, 2nd Lt. 15th Inf. And A.A.Q.M. and A.C.S.; J.H. French, 2nd Lt. 9th Cav. Comdg. Co. M.

[AUTHOR'S NOTE: Dudley's supporters include Ringites: Appel is the son-in-law of Mescalero Indian Reservation Agent Frederick Godfroy, exposed by McSween and Angel; and the officers had marched on Lincoln with Dudley, and three of them had fired at escaping McSweens. Goodwin was present when Susan McSween made her plea for protection at Dudley's camp while being ridiculed by obscenities.]

WALLACE ON THE DEFENSIVE

The Ring's "Open Letter" put Wallace on the defensive. On December 16, 1878, he responded to its signers - Lincoln County War Battle murderers - with deference. He wrote: *"I will take pleasure in showing you that the insertion in the Proclamation of the clause of which you complain was even more than a kindness to such of you that were on duty in Lincoln county during the disorders there."*

He also turned to Schurz, writing, on December 21, 1878, to discredit Chapman as a trouble-maker to save himself. In three months, Billy' Bonney's pardon would depend on this flawed man.

Wallace's removal request for Dudley also proved embarrassing. He had missed that by blaming Dudley, he accused not just Hatch, but his superior, Major General John Pope, Commanding the Department of Missouri. So Dudley's removal was refused up the line to Secretary of War George McCrary. On December 31, 1878, McCrary declined also.

THE RING RESPONDS TO CHAPMAN

From late October of 1878, the Ring had faced Huston Chapman and Susan McSween: both more threatening than John Tunstall and Alexander McSween, since they had monstrous crimes to prosecute. So Chapman now had a short life expectancy.

Savage James Dolan was enlisted. On December 31, 1878, he snarled to Wallace: *"I and many of our Citizens feel Confident that if this man was silenced, the troubles would End."* Unfortunately, Lew Wallace agreed, and did nothing. Dolan wrote:

<u>Confidential</u>   Lincoln, N.M.
                          Dec 31st 1878

Governor Lew Wallace
    Santa Fe, N.M.
My Dear Governor –

On my arrival at Fort Stanton, I reported Your Explanation to the Comdg Officer (Gen'l Dudley) – he seemed too much pleased, and said that if it was possible that You and him "Could meet and talk matters over with Each other for an hour" he was "satisfied that You would be fast friends." I also explained matters to Sheriff Peppin and many of our citizens all of whom were pleased. I am Convinced that the Explanation has Caused a very different feeling from that in Existence before I came down. Mr. Delany has also interested himself in giving Your Explanation both to the officers and citizens. Your [informant Chapman] appears to be the only man in this County who is trying to Continue the old feelings. **I and many of our Citizens feel Confident that if this man was silenced, the troubles would End.** I presume ere this you have heard of the trouble which Lieut French got into with Chapman and Mrs. McSween – from what I can learn about the affair it originated from an attempt to make arrests of men for whom the Deputy U.S. Marshal had warrants – It may be that Mr. French was over zealous in the attempt. Still I consider this all Can be said against him. I have learned enough since I returned here that should I remain in this County, my fate will be that of Major Brady and others. I only intend remaining until such time as I Can straighten up my business to the interests of the Creditors, and as per agreement with them. It makes me and my friends mighty sore, that we are compelled to leave our homes and businesses, which we are Compelled to do, or put ourselves on Equal footing with the outlaw and assassin. Hoping, Governor, that you wont Consider this letter presuming on Your Kindness, and with Kind regards   I remain
                    Yours Respectfully
                    Jas J. <u>Dolan</u>

P.S.
Should it ever be in my power to do anything in this section that would be of interest to you always Command me.
                    Dolan

ASSASSINATION OF CHAPMAN

On the night of February 18, 1879 - the first anniversary of Tunstall's murder - one armed Attorney Huston Chapman joined the growing list of eradicated Ring opponents. Though his murder was inevitable, it occurred that day by coincidences of his having accompanied his client, Susan McSween, back to Lincoln from Las Vegas; and of, earlier that evening, James Dolan and Catron's brother-in-law, Edgar Walz, having had a "peace meeting" with Billy Bonney in town. Present had been Billy Matthews and Ringite thugs, Jessie Evans and his gang member, Billy Campbell, as likely protection. That conciliatory gathering was a measure of Billy's growing local fame and power.

On about 8 p.m. that dark night, on Lincoln's single street, Chapman encountered the wandering "peace" group, after it exited Juan Patrón's house, where Campbell had drunkenly tried to kill Patrón. Recognizing Chapman, Dolan shot him point-blank; followed by Billy Campbell, who shouted revealingly that he did it for God and Dudley. Evans was their back-up, as Walz and Matthews watched. Dolan then doused Chapman's corpse with liquor from his pocket flask, and ignited it. Billy was eye-witness.

This crime would be Billy's bargaining chip for a pardon from Lew Wallace. Billy's peace-making with the Ring was over.

AFTERMATH OF CHAPMAN'S MURDER

SUMMARY: Lew Wallace's response to humiliation of Huston Chapman's murder was to retreat to the outlaw myth with Sherman's outlaw list and input from James Dolan. He was, thus, directed to eliminate murder witness, Billy Bonney. And Wallace forced that task on appalled Lincoln officials, and happily willing soldiers.

After Chapman's killing, Wallace was directed by Ringites to "outlaws" for elimination. Topping the list was Billy Bonney; not just an anti-Ring fighter, but now an eye-witness to a Ringite assassination. His friend, Ygenio Salazar, was included. Wallace had no idea what he was doing, but the Ring did: both teenagers were primed for more anti-Ring rebellion. Wallace, with usual wild hyperbole, put the astronomical award of $1,000 on "the Kid."

Avoiding going to Lincoln, Wallace forced Sheriff George Kimbrell to catch his chosen scapegoats: "the Kid" and Salazar. Non-Ringite Kimbrell was married to a Picacho townswoman, obviously knew about the massacre at San Patricio, and sympathized with the boys' Regulator mission. There were other ways he could, and would, aid them. But he had been forced by Wallace to request a detachment of soldiers for Lincoln.

SAN PATRICIO ATTACKED AGAIN

The Ring used Wallace's request for troops to conduct a terrorist raid under Second Lieutenant Millard Fillmore Goodwin on San Patricio on February 19, 1879, in case Chapman's murder tempted another uprising. To the residents, it was a flashback to Sheriff George Peppin's using the same soldiers on June 28, 1878 to pursue Alexander McSween and the Regulators, and to the July 3, 1878 massacre there by Peppin and John Kinney's gang. Even Dudley, the real outlaw, gleefully joined this "outlaw" pursuit, writing on February 24, 1879 to headquarters about Goodwin trying to *"aid in the arrest of Bonney, alias 'Kid.'"*

WALLACE REPORTS TO SCHURZ

Lew Wallace waited nine days, till February 27th, to report Chapman's murder to Schurz, and to admit his failed "pacification." And he blamed outlaws: *"I have further information that certain notorious characters, who have long been under indictment [this is Catron's federal indictment of Billy and other Regulators], but by skillful dodging, have managed to escape arrest, have formed an alliance which looks like preparation for raids when the spring opens."*

One should remember that Schurz and Hayes knew the Ring was systematically murdering opponents. They knew Colfax County's charges about Franklin Tolby's murder, and Axtell's "Dear Ben plot" to kill more adversaries there. They had just covered up Angel's reports almost exposing Ringite U.S. officials who killed John Tunstall. Alexander McSween's murder had followed, along with slaughter of his defenders. And Schurz and Hayes had covered up Catron as a criminal U.S. Attorney by letting him resign. So Wallace and Washington were merely conducting a charade to keep secret the Santa Fe Ring. And scapegoated for public consumption would be "outlaws."

GRANT COUNTY CONDEMNS WALLACE

Lew Wallace was fooling himself; but not rebellion-tempered Grant County citizens. On March 1, 1879, Silver City's *Grant County Herald* published "Wallace and Lincoln County" denouncing him; stating:

> A few weeks since, while Governor Wallace was at Trinidad, Col., he was interviewed by a reporter of the Denver *Tribune* and ... gave some very remarkable information in regard to the condition of affairs in this Territory – particularly those portions of it which he has never visited. Among other things, the Governor assured the reporter that, upon reaching his post of duty, "he found the Territory in a state of anarchy and confusion," that "by systematic management," etc. "he had brought about a state of prolonged peace," and furthermore that "lawless men" who previous to his advent, had "infested," "carried terror" and all that sort of thing, "have a wholesome fear of the present authorities."
>
> Had the story which Wallace told the single merit of truthfulness, it would still be open to criticism, because of the narrator's evident anxiety to secure to himself all credit for what had been accomplished; but unfortunately the entire statement is false: Governor Wallace did not find the Territory in a state of anarchy and confusion. Previous to his arrival, our most sparsely populated county had been the scene of bitter and deadly strife between contending factions, but throughout the rest of the Territory order prevailed ... Moreover, Governor Wallace, with all his "systematic management," has not "brought about a state of prolonged peace," even in the single county where disturbances had occurred; and it is unfortunately true that the "lawless men" of Lincoln are not imbued with a "wholesome fear of the present authorities."
>
> The Governor found the County of Lincoln in a greatly disturbed condition. Numerous murders had been committed ... At the time of his arrival the bloodiest part of the struggle was over, but lawless acts still frequent. He issued a proclamation. After the lapse of several weeks, we were granted with a companion document ... But ... the condition of affairs in Lincoln county was substantially the same, at the time of the second proclamation, announcing the restoration of order and proffering amnesty alike to innocent and guilty, was issued, as it had been weeks before when the Governor threatened a declaration of martial law.
>
> In our telegraphic columns today, we publish an account of another murder [Huston Chapman's] committed upon

the principal street of the town of Lincoln. The admirers of the Governor will doubtless receive the news with mingled feelings of surprise and chagrin ... **It is charitable to think that Governor Wallace himself supposed a good deal to have been accomplished ... but upon its face, the whole affair looks very much as though he had tried to manufacture capital from misrepresentation**.

VOICES OF CONSCIENCE

Lew Wallace still delayed going to Lincoln, as shown by his March 1, 1878 letter draft announcing his departure to Territorial Secretary William Ritch, his Santa Fe proxy. His crossed-out February 27th became March 1st. He did not want to go. But voices of conscience, that were not his own, would impel him.

ATTORNEY IRA LEONARD

SUMMARY: After Huston Chapman's killing, the man seeking justice in Lincoln County was his office-mate: Attorney Ira Leonard, hired by Susan McSween to continue her case against N.A.M. Dudley. He also became Billy Bonney's lawyer, and Lew Wallace's voice of conscience. His uncompromising morality and idealism would mark him for attempted assassination, then life-long revenge.

Ira E. Leonard was born on March 15, 1832 in Genesee County, New York. In his youth in Batavia, New York, and in Boston, his profession was printer; first at the Batavia *Republican Advocate*. Compatible with his later idealism, in 1852 he was typesetter for Harriett Beecher Stowe's *Uncle Tom's Cabin*. In the 1850's, he also studied law in Batavia with a Judge Moses Taggart, and attended Albany Law School, graduating in 1855. That year he married; and they had a daughter in 1857.

By 1859, he moved his family to Watertown, Wisconsin, to join a law practice; and had three more children. In 1865, they moved to Jefferson County, Missouri, where he practiced law, and had a fifth child. In 1867 he was appointed Circuit Prosecuting Attorney of the 18th Judicial District, keeping that position till 1870.

For his failed candidacy for state Supreme Court Judge, the September 7, 1872's *St. Louis Democrat* stated: "[He] won golden opinions as to being a fearless Circuit Judge in a district infested by desperate law-breakers." By 1874, his asthma necessitated his relocation to Boulder, Colorado. In 1878, again for his asthma, he moved to Las Vegas, New Mexico. There he befriended Attorneys David Shield - Susan McSween's brother-in-law - and new arrival, Huston Chapman, who became his office-mate.

Wallace may have met Leonard in September of 1878 in Las Vegas, as he traveled southward for his governorship in Santa Fe. He must have been more open to the Leonard's anti-Ring sentiment, because he recommended him, on November 13, 1878, to judgeship of the First Judicial District of Santa Fe County - a usurpation of its Ring control - or to the Third Judicial District, to replace Ringite Warren Bristol. The appointments were blocked by Secretary of the Interior Carl Schurz and Attorney General Charles Devens, though Leonard got a lesser judgeship.

After Chapman's February 18, 1879 murder, Leonard wrote to Wallace on February 24, 1879, seeing him as a savior, and urging him to go to Lincoln. He also proposed a Lincoln County newspaper for an anti-Ring voice. Leonard was the last thing Wallace wanted: a conscience. Leonard's sole weakness was his lack of brightness. And he would face very clever Ringite lawyers.

And by February of 1879, three months after Leonard's failed judgeship appointments, Wallace was in secret retreat; while Leonard had become the Ring's adversary by replacing Chapman as Susan McSween's *pro bono* lawyer against Commander Dudley.

Ultimately, Leonard's backing of her and Billy Bonney's pardon bargain with Wallace, led to the Ring's attempted assassination of him in April of 1879, and blockade of his career.

But in 1880, Leonard lived in Lincoln and White Oaks, where he tried unsuccessfully to get Billy a different pardon through Secret Service Operative Azariah Wild. After Billy's capture by Pat Garrett on March 22, 1881, Leonard protectively traveled with him by train and coach to Mesilla. He was Billy's defense attorney on March 30, 1881 for the "Buckshot" Roberts federal indictment, achieving its quashing. But a likely Ring death threat forced him to withdraw, leaving Billy to Ring-biased court-appointed Attorneys Albert Jennings Fountain and John D. Bail, with resultant hanging sentence for William Brady's killing.

He continued as Susan McSween's lawyer after she remarried, still settling the estates of Tunstall and McSween. With sad irony, he was paid by land, which he sold to James Dolan by 1883.

In 1882, he was postmaster at Socorro, New Mexico. Likely because of ill health, he failed in ownership of the *Socorro Sun*; a law partnership, a ranch, and mining investments. In 1888, he moved to San Bernadino, California, with his son, Ira, but his asthma worsened. On November 26, 1888, he contacted Lew Wallace for help in getting the Second Judicial District Judgeship; writing pathetically: "*I need the position because I am unable to engage in active practice and am very poor and the salary would enable me to live and support my family and save something.*" Wallace apparently recommended him to Attorney General W.H. Miller, but that failed because of Ringite defamatory affidavits discrediting his health and accusing him of being a mining fraudster and unethical lawyer.

Ira Leonard died on July 6, 1889, another unsung and heroic Lincoln County freedom fighter; with his Las Cruces *Rio Grande Republican* obituary merely stating: "[He] had been ailing for some time and his death was not unexpected." He was buried by his son William in Boulder, Colorado.

HUSTON CHAPMAN'S FATHER

On March 20, 1879, Ira Leonard got a heartbreaking letter from W.W. Chapman, Huston Chapman's father. He forwarded it to Lew Wallace. If Wallace's sole focus was not himself, he might have been moved to nobility by W.W. Chapman's ideals. That founder of *The Oregonian* newspaper had written: "*It is through the Executive and Judiciary that men are made to respect the laws. It is upon this theory that our institutions regard the Military subject to the civil powers, and is upon this theory alone that peace can be restored to your distracted Territory. Men must understand that the poorest and most humble citizen may seek with perfect safety through the judiciary a relief of grievances, and that the highest and most exalted must submit to judicial examination when charged with crimes or misdemeanors.*"

But W.W. Chapman was unaware that democracy's intended checks and balances had been destroyed under Ringite legislative and judicial control; and that Governor Lew Wallace had abnegated his executive power.

CHAPTER 18

LEW WALLACE CHASES OUTLAWS

COMING OF A "SAVIOR"

SUMMARY: Having been forced to go to Lincoln by Huston Chapman's murder, Lew Wallace intended to feign action by focus on the outlaw myth. But Ira Leonard's start of Susan McSween's litigation against Commander Dudley forced Wallace to try again to remove Dudley. That misled Lincolnites to see him a their savior; as he would soon convince Billy Bonney.

On March 1, 1879, Lew Wallace left Santa Fe for Fort Stanton with District Commander Edward Hatch. Hatch stayed there. Wallace did too until March 5th, when he finally went to Lincoln. To Lincolnites, a savior had come. But the only salvation Wallace sought was resurrecting his reputation. And the only demons he hoped to exorcise were mythical outlaws, not hellish Ringites. But reality of Susan McSween's case would trump his needs.

IRA LEONARD FILES CHARGES AGAINST DUDLEY

On March 4, 1879, Ira Leonard and Susan McSween continued Huston Chapman's litigation against N.A.M. Dudley. They were risking their lives. Buried to the east of Susan's burned-down house and looted Tunstall store now lay John Tunstall, Frank MacNab, Alexander McSween, Harvey Morris, and Huston Chapman. Leonard's charges were for the April Lincoln County Grand Jury, where Susan might also testify against Sheriff George Peppin as a murderer and arsonist accomplice of Dudley.

Leonard had already made the charges public in a March 1, 1879 *Las Vegas Gazette* article linking Dudley to Huston Chapman's murder. Leonard had written: *"I, the undersigned certify that I believe the ... charges and specifications to be true ... and if substantiated to have the officers named herein punished"*.

Charges and specifications against Lieutenant Colonel N.A.M. Dudley, Commander at Fort Stanton, New Mexico.

1st

That Lieutenant Colonel Dudley, Commander at Fort Stanton, New Mexico, on the 19th day of July A.D. 1878 without authority of law, or by any right vested in him so to be, did take a squad of armed soldiers, numbering around 60, also one cannon and one Gatling gun, and went to the town of Lincoln, and assigned and gave aid to an armed band of outlaws, and by reason of the aid furnished by said Dudley, and the soldiers under his command and direction, aided in killing one A.A. McSween, a citizen of said county; that at the same time and place the said Dudley aided in the crime of arson, by causing the house of said McSween to be set on fire, the lives of the inmates therein put in jeopardy, that at the same time the said Dudley caused said building to be fired, there were in the house two defenseless females, and five infant children; that his conduct on that occasion was most brutal and inhuman, and unbecoming a soldier and officer.

2nd

That at the same time and place as last above stated the said Lieutenant Colonel N.A.M. Dudley, did maliciously, and willfully, and corruptly for the purpose of giving a color of right to his wicked and unlawful action, compel one John B. Wilson, a Justice of the Peace of said town of Lincoln aforesaid and by threat of ironing and imprisonment, said John B. Wilson, if he refused to issue a warrant for the arrest of said A.A. McSween, and other citizens of said county, and that by reason of said threat and the fear of violence and imprisonment from said Dudley, the said John B. Wilson did issue the warrants demanded by the said Lieutenant Colonel N.A.M. Dudley for the apprehension of said A.A. McSween and others.

3rd

That on the 20th day of July A.A. 1878 at the town of Lincoln, in the County of Lincoln, in said Territory of New Mexico, the said Lieutenant Colonel N.A.M. Dudley, with his soldiers entered the store belonging to the estate of John H. Tunstall and plundered upwards of six thousand dollars worth of goods, and when the said Dudley was appealed to, to prevent the same, he aided the plunderers to consummate their objective.

4th

That sometime during the month of November or December A.D. 1878 the said Lieutenant Colonel N.A.M. Dudley, at the county of Lincoln aforesaid did procure base and wicked men to make false and slanderous charges and statements against the character and virtue of Mrs. S.E. McSween, the widow of said A.A. McSween murdered as aforesaid, and did cause the same to be filed in the military department of the government for the purpose of ruining her reputation, and destroying her influence in seeking redress for Lieutenant Colonel N.A.M. Dudley's gross outrages perpetrated by the said Dudley against her.

5th

That during the fall of 1878, one Easton (whose given name is unknown to me) had a contract for delivering corn at Fort Stanton aforesaid and that Lieutenant Colonel N.A.M. Dudley demanded of him an affidavit, testifying against the character of S.E. McSween for truth and chastity, and upon the refusal of said Easton to swear to the statements demanded, he ordered that no more corn should be received from him.

6th

That during the month of November or December A.D. 1878 the said Lieutenant Colonel N.A.M. Dudley, Commander of the post at Fort Stanton as aforesaid, in order to subvert the ends of justice, and to prevent Governor Lew Wallace from restoring peace in said county did maliciously and falsely publish an open letter, in the New Mexican, a newspaper published at Santa Fe, New Mexico, which letter was calculated and intended to foment the disturbances then rife in said county, and that he did in that open letter make false and malicious charges against the character of Mrs. S.E. McSween, and called attention to certain false and wicked affidavits which he had forwarded to District Headquarters concerning her.

7th

That on or about the 12th day of December A.D. 1878, Lieutenant Colonel N.A.M. Dudley, Commander of Fort Stanton as aforesaid, detailed a squad of soldiers under the command of Lieutenant J.H. French, one of the officers at said post, to go to the town of Lincoln to aid and assist the sheriff of said county in discharge of his duties at a Probate Court to be held in said county, that while the said French was at Lincoln as aforesaid, he became intoxicated, and while in a drunken debauch went with certain of the soldiers under his command to the house of a Mexican by the name of Maximo (surname unknown) and without any right or authority to interfere with said citizen, broke into his house and abused him in a shameful manner, and threatened to kill him, and on the same occasion, the said Lieutenant J.H. French as aforesaid did break and violently enter the house of one John Copeland, of Lincoln, Lincoln County aforesaid, and then and there use abusive, threatening, and insulting language to the wife of said Copeland, and that the said French had no authority or power to enter the house, but the same was a willful assault by him upon innocent an unoffending citizens, and that the said Lieutenant French at the same time and place without right or authority violently and being in a drunken and debauched condition entered the private dwelling of Mrs. S.E. McSween, with two or more armed soldiers, and did then and there, use towards the said Mrs. McSween, abusive and insulting language, did without any right place her under arrest, and treat her with violence, and he did then and there without authority, arrest one H.I. Chapmen who was endeavoring to protect the said Mrs. McSween from the violence and insult of said Lieutenant French, and he threatened the life of said Chapman, if he interfered to protect the said Mrs. McSween, that notwithstanding, the said Lieutenant Colonel N.A.M. Dudley was fully advised of the conduct of said Lieutenant French, on said occasion, and knew, and was fully cognizant of his violation of duty as a soldier, and of his drunken and disorderly conduct, took no measures to have the said French punished or brought to an account for the same, but on the contrary, when the said H.I. Chapman complained before J.B. Wilson, a Justice of the Peace of the town of Lincoln, against said French, he was held to bail by the said Justice to answer to the charge before the Grand Jury of the said county. For his said conduct as aforesaid, the said Lieutenant Colonel N.A.M. Dudley, in an act of retaliation against Chapman, corruptly, willfully, and maliciously caused the said Chapman to be classified as one of the outlaws, and breakers of the peace of Lincoln County and denied him the privilege of the post, and promulgated a military order to that effect.

That same March 4, 1878, Ira Leonard also suggested a military court of inquiry for Dudley's potential court martial to Secretary of War George McCrary. He enclosed the following March 1, 1879 *Las Vegas Gazette* article on Chapman's murder:

DEATH OF CHAPMAN.

The people of Las Vegas were greatly shocked on Sunday last to hear of the cold blooded murder, in Lincoln County: on the 18th of February of H.I. Chapman, Esq.

Mr. Chapman was a young lawyer from Portland, Oregon, and the son of the Honorable W.W. Chapman of that place. Immediately prior to his coming to Las Vegas, he was engaged as one of the civil engineers at the A.T.&S.F.R.R., and had charge of bridge construction.

In September last, he came to Las Vegas to commence the practice of his profession and remained here about two months, when he was employed by Mrs. McSween to go to Lincoln County, and assist her in the settlement of her husband's estate.

The citizens of this territory are pretty familiar with the lawlessness, and wholesale murders, and outrages that have perpetrated in that county within the last year. They have been carried on to such an extent that the President of the United States in September last, issued a proclamation directed to the insurgents and bandits, to disperse, and following the proclamation of the President was one of amnesty by Governor Lew Wallace, forgiving past offences and inviting the people to quiet and peace. Troops have been distributed in different parts of the country to maintain and prevent lawlessness.

When Mr. Chapman went to Lincoln it was supposed that life was reasonably secure, and that citizens could pursue their ordinary avocations without fear of assassination.

Those who are familiar with the disturbances that have left the county in a state of revolution and disorder for so long a time, knew that A.A. McSween, the husband of Mrs. McSween, was shot and killed on the 19th of July last, under circumstances that led her and his friends to believe that the murder of McSween was brought about, and in fact directly aided by Lieutenant Colonel Dudley, of the 9th U.S. Cavalry, and commander of the military post at Fort Stanton, in that county, and that a bitter feeling has existed and shown itself on the part of Col. Dudley towards Mrs. McSween since then, which was practically demonstrated in Col. Dudley's open letter published a few weeks hence in the Santa Fe papers and addressed to Governor Wallace, in which he characterizes Mrs. McSween as being everything except a good woman.

It had even extended so far that when the Probate Court was held in Lincoln County in December last, and a posse of soldiers had been detailed from the fort to aid the sheriff in performing his duties, which soldiers were in charge of Lieut. French, an officer under Col. Dudley: that French took a squad of soldiers at night and went to the house of Mrs. McSween and there greatly insulted her, made threats of violence, and directed the soldiers to arrest Mr. Chapman, and threatened to blow his brains out if he resisted. For this outrage a complaint was made before a Justice of the Peace in Lincoln by Mr. Chapman, and Lt. French was held to bail to await the action of the Grand Jury of that county, and as a matter of retaliation Mr. Chapman was, by order of the post commander, excluded from the privilege of the post and denounced as one of the outlaws of Lincoln County.

When the military become the perpetrators of outrages, when the houses of private citizens, in pursuit of their vocation, were invaded and lawlessly broken into by military officers and their squads of soldiers, and violence inflicted upon them, Mr. Chapman thought it was time to take steps to see if citizens had any rights that the military were bound to respect, and he left Lincoln about 20th January to go to Santa Fe to see what could be done towards protecting and securing the people against these continued outrages.

The following article which appeared in this paper Feb. 8th 1879 shows the results of Mr. Chapman's visit to Santa Fe.

Mr. H. I. Chapman has just returned from Santa Fe, where he went for the purpose of securing arrest of Col. Dudley who is charged with the murder of A.A. McSween, on the 19th day of July, 1878. Mr. Chapman was informed by the military at Santa Fe that he could not see any of the reports, orders, or affidavits that had been received from Col. Dudley except upon the express order of the Secretary of War, whereupon Mr. Chapman concluded that it was useless to attempt to do anything more here but will lay the whole matter before the Secretary of War, and ask an investigation of the charges against Col. Dudley.

The military are in possession of most of the testimony against Dudley and will do nothing to further it unless ordered by the Secretary of War.

Mr. Chapman will go to Lincoln to gather evidence to lay before the government, both as to the murder of McSween and Tunstall.

On the 12th of February Mr. Chapman left here to return to Lincoln and had been there but a very short time when he was assassinated, as will appear from the following article copied from the News and Press of Cimarron.

A gentleman in Lincoln County writes us this week the particulars of another atrocious deed in the blood stained town of Lincoln. The victim this time was H.I. Chapman, who but a short time since, was in the employ of the A.T.&SF Railway company as a civil engineer. He left the road and located in Las Vegas to practice law. Here he was employed by Mrs. A.A. McSween to settle up the estate of her late husband, and attend to other legal business in which she was interested.

These required his presence in Lincoln. He had been there but a very short time when he came in collision with Col. Dudley, the commander at Fort Stanton, who, throughout the troubles in that county, has shown a bitter partisan spirit against the McSween faction.

On the 18th inst. Mr. Chapman and Hon. Juan Patron had just arrived from Las Vegas and discovered that Dolan, Capt. Jesse Evans and others of that party were in town apparently bent on mischief, and in a short time they were called upon by some of the men, who were with some difficulty prevented from taking the life of Mr. Patron. A little later Mr. Chapman was walking down to his office when he was fired on by some of the Evans gang, who were running the town, and instantly killed, two balls striking him in the breast.

Not satisfied with killing this poor one armed man, they set fire to his clothing and left him to burn in the street. At the time of writing our correspondent says Sheriff Kimball [Kimbrell] and twenty four soldiers were in the town of Lincoln, but that no arrest had yet been made. The Coroner's inquest was to be held that day.

This comes from letting notorious desperados run at large. We shall expect to see Governor Wallace use all the power he may possess to hunt these infamous assassins down, and if there is any virtue in the laws, they should be disposed of so that it would be impossible for them again stealthily and in cold blood to take the life of a law abiding citizen. The honor of the territory demands that such cowardly scoundrels should not be permitted to run at large no matter what it may cost to arrest them. But unless there is a change made in the Commanding Officer at Fort Stanton we shall have little faith in the Governor receiving any substantial aid from the military.

The Dolan faction will be spared as much as possible by the present commandant of the post.

With General Pope rest the responsibility of continuing Col. Dudley in command, but rather making a change which the bitter feeling in that county engendered by the part he played in the McSween massacre alone, would permit the feud to continue, and the lives of good men to be sacrificed to his caprice. It will be almost impossible for the executive to restore order in Lincoln County until a change is made in some of the officers at Fort Stanton.

A more cold blooded and dastardly outrage could hardly be conceived of. If the policy of Governor Wallace had been carried out when he came to this territory and assumed the duties of his office, this gross murder would never have occurred. He saw the situation of matters in Lincoln County and that Col. Dudley was implicated in them, and was believed by one faction to be giving aid and assistance to the other, and in fact to have been instrumental in causing the death of A.A. McSween.

When the Governor issued the Proclamation of Amnesty and Pardon, he desired to have all the influence which could impair or retard speedy restoration, peace and order, thoroughly removed. Knowing this feeling against Dudley, he desired that a change in the post commanders should be made, but General Pope, Commander of this Military District, would not act, and treated his request with indifference, or paid no regard to it.

When Col. Dudley saw his advantage he became more overbearing and insolent, he paraded himself before the public in a bombastic letter addressed to the Governor attacking the Governor and his motives, and formulated a beastly tirade against Mrs. McSween, attacking her private character, and charging her with being a woman of bad reputation.

It may be from a military stand point regarded brave for a military officer shielded behind government barracks to attack a defenseless woman whose husband has been murdered in cold blood by aid and assistance furnished a lawless band of desperados by that officer, but to the outside world it looks like an act fit only to emanate from a cowardly poltroon.

Mr. Chapman determined to see justice done to the victims of Dudley's and French's caprice, they were in a fair way of having their conduct exposed and being brought to justice for their crimes, and it was essential that he should be disposed of to prevent their exposure and punishment. The act was accomplished, perhaps not by these men, but very evidently by those who had been shielded and protected at the government post and who had been mentioned in the outrages perpetrated in the county.

On the morning Mr. Chapman left here, the 12th of February, the writer had a long talk with him concerning the situation, and the danger his life was exposed to in consequence of the active part he took against Dudley and French. He frankly stated he did fear violence incited by them, but from no other source: he said that notwithstanding the danger that surrounded him, he should try and have them brought to justice.

We who knew Chapman in this county, know he was an earnest upright man, and that he met his death through his earnest and strong adherence to his friends, at the hands of as base a set of cowards and murderers as ever infested a civilized country.

The question now rears how long the people of this territory have got to submit to this state of things, and there is no adequate mode of reaching and punishing these assassins who render life and property so insecure in our territory.

We do hope that the government will be aroused to take such active measures as will afford protection and security to the lives of its citizens.

WALLACE GETS DUDLEY'S REMOVAL

At his March 5, 1879 Lincoln arrival, Wallace was diverted from pursuing his war on outlaws by locals' angry clamor about dead Chapman and dangerous Dudley, coupled with Ira Leonard's charges. So on March 7, 1879, he again requested General Hatch to remove Dudley from command. He likely hoped Dudley would quietly depart. But with his usual strategic disconnect, he had again passed the blame to Hatch. Possibly buoyed up by local's adulation, and Ira Leonard's noble charges, Wallace even presented the truth; writing in his draft: *"I will ~~also add~~ state in general terms that it is charged here that Lieut. Col. Dudley is responsible for the killing of McSween and the men who were shot with that person; that he was an influential participant in that affair, and yet is an active partisan. I have ~~also~~ information also connecting him with the more recent murder of H.I. Chapman: to the effect that he knew the man would be killed, and announced it the day of the night of the killing, and that one of the murderers stated publicly that he had promised Colonel Dudley to do the deed."*

That worked. General Hatch, still at Fort Stanton, removed Dudley from his command there the next day, March 8, 1879. Dudley's part in yet another Lincoln County murder was too risky for another simple cover-up.

DUDLEY'S RESPONSE

Thrice court martialed Dudley was no virgin to accusations; but Attorney Ira Leonard's were the worst. Nevertheless, he was confident of Catron's repeated protection. His service to the Ring had been elimination of two major opponents: Alexander McSween and Huston Chapman. So, under likely advisement from Catron, or his past firm member, Henry Waldo, Dudley responded by denials to Hatch on March 9, 1879, especially calling the murder charges *"based upon rumor solely."*

Unbeknownst to Dudley's handlers, in four days, Billy Bonney would present himself to Wallace for a pardon bargain as an eye-witness not only to Chapman's murder, but also to Dudley's guilt in ordering troops to fire on escaping McSweens, undoing the smoke-screen of "rumor solely."

ARRESTING CHAPMAN'S MURDERERS

Wallace was now forced to pursue real outlaws: Chapman's murderers. To achieve arrests, he turned to General Hatch, who told him it was Sheriff George Kimbrell's job; but by March 8, 1879, did catch Evans, Campbell, and Matthews; as well as some Seven Rivers rustlers. Worked-up Wallace reported to Justice of the Peace Wilson, in his fevered imagination as "the General;" exclaiming: *"Stand firm now, and we will win!"* It is unclear what he wanted to "win." He certainly was not fighting the Ring. But Wilson must have thought he was; especially after Dudley's removal. And, as will be seen, Wallace's progress was being communicated to Billy Bonney as his pardon plan was being hatched with Wilson and Juan Patrón. Its letter would be delivered to Wallace in five days.

Next Wallace fretted about his prisoners, writing multiple letters to Dudley's replacement Commander: Henry Carroll. On March 10, 1879, Wallace saw James Dolan in Lincoln, and wanted Carroll to apprehend him. Likely informed, Dolan simply went to Fort Stanton and surrendered, and was given free run there.

DOLAN'S THREATS

Wallace apparently stayed in contact with captured Dolan in a quixotic fantasy, revealed in his March 21, 1879 letter to Carl Schurz. (See pages 535-537 for letter) Knowing that Dolan had *"larger money interests in the county,"* he planned to make him *"pliant as a witness!"* Lethal local Ring boss Dolan, must have considered him an idiotic twit. But he may have played along to feed Wallace Regulators' names for his pursuits of "outlaws" - like Billy Bonney. And on March 14, 1879, Dolan tried to scare Wallace off; writing obviously from Fort Stanton:

Governor: -
I hear from reliable authority that it has been reported to you that I was one of a party who stopped Your Ambulance the other evening while en route to the plaza [of Lincoln]. Such report is basely false, and I feel confident that it is a ruse resorted to by my treacherous enemies with a view of prejudicing You against me. I Sincerely regret my action, which gave my Enemies the opportunity for the charge, and which they, so promptly, availed

themselves of. If You can afford me an opportunity of seeing You, You will please do so, as I am anxious to give You an explanation. This news causes me much uneasiness, and I ask that You give the matter a thorough investigation at Your earliest Convenience. Hoping that you will pardon me for the liberty I take in writing to You, and that I can still look to you as a friend. I remain
Your humble servant
Jas. J. <u>Dolan</u>

On March 29, 1879, Dolan made a more direct threat. And by April 25, 1879, he would also try to kill Ira Leonard - only 66 days after he killed Huston Chapman. Prisoner Dolan wrote:

My Dear Governor: -
Attorney [Ringite Sidney] Wilson told me yesterday that Your "life was threatened," and told it in such a manner that I was Compelled to believe that You Considered me the author; and that in Case it should happen, my "life would be taken in one hour after" &c. Governor, I cant believe for a moment that You would do me such an injustice, as to think that I was connected in any way with such threat – And won't, until I see, or hear from You – Still, this news, with my present Condition, and the many rumors about the underhanded work which is going on against me, makes me feel anything but happy.

I don't doubt in the least but what there are bad men roaming over this County that would kill any man, friend or Enemy, should Either be in their way, therefore, You can't be <u>too Careful</u>.

I have good reasons for believing that there are now men in the Plaza, who would kill You in a moment, providing they were certain they Could get away with it, and that I would suffer thereby.

I wish that I could be close to you when those making the threat intended carrying it out, I would try to Convince You that such was not my nature. I sincerely hope that the report will prove without foundation. I don't write this to you as Governor of New Mexico, or with the expectation of its influencing Your Official action toward me in any Manner, whatever. It is simply, because You have Commanded my respect, from the first time we met, that I look upon You as a friend. And it grieves me to think You would give such a report credence.

> *I learned Yesterday that my Pony had been stolen from the Carriso [Carrizozo] Ranch by the two men who Escaped from here. The Pony is known all through Southern New Mexico as being mine, and when seen with those men [Jessie Evans and Billy Campbell], another report will be circulated that I am aiding them. wishing You success in Your arduous undertaking, I remain*
> *Yours Respectfully*
> *Jas. J. <u>Dolan</u>*

ESCAPE OF THE PRISONERS

By March 18, 1879, 10 days after capture, likely surprising no one but Lew Wallace, Jessie Evans and Billy Campbell had "escaped" with help of a Fort Stanton soldier, "Texas Jack," who then deserted. Other likely helpers had real Ringite names: "Purington, "Goodwin," and "Smith;" implementing "boss" Catron's protection policy. Dolan stayed as a likely informant to Catron.

On March 19, 1879, Wallace offered a reward of $1,000 for the capture of Evans and Campbell - just as he had with Billy Bonney that February.

He also enlisted Ira Leonard, who tried to inject reality, answering by an April 9, 1879 letter: *"Dangerous diseases requite heroic treatment that's what is needed now."* Wallace answered that day, fantasizing his savior-like sacrifice: *"You have no idea how pleasant it is to have one hearty assistant and sympathizer with my work. To work trying to do a little good, but with all the world against you, requires the will of a martyr."*

PURSUING MYTHICAL OUTLAWS

In the midst of dealing with Chapman's assassins, Wallace never stopped his war on mythical outlaws. But he replaced killer-border-Texan-buffalo-hunting-desperado-rapist-rustler-wrestlers with Regulators on Sherman's outlaw list. He left unexplained these Regulators' connection to real Lincoln County War crimes: murdering John Tunstall and Frank MacNab, massacring at San Patricio, and slaughtering Alexander McSween, Harvey Morris, Francisco Zamora, and Vincente Romero.

For his ploy, Wallace outfitted his toy soldier Lincolnites against "outlaws" with flamboyant titles: like: "Cattle Keeper of the County" and "Captain of the Rangers."

In his second day in Lincoln, March 6th, Wallace had renewed his chase of Billy Bonney, as "the Kid," and Yginio Salazar in a letter to General Edward Hatch. And he accused them of being accessories to Chapman's murder! It was his sly fictional solution to sparing Ringites, and updating his war on outlaws to put Billy Bonney back in the bull's eye of his pursuit. He sent Hatch another letter that day, about pursuing Regulators Josiah "Doc" Scurlock and Charlie Bowdre. Hatch, answering on March 7, 1879, merely tried to switch the futile searching to Fort Union troops.

On March 11, 1879, undaunted, Wallace turned again to Fort Stanton Commander Henry Carroll, to whom he sent a copy of Sherman's outlaw" list, accompanied by manic fantasizing, including *"Indian trailers,"* and the outlaws as *"the "Black Knights" and their confederates [to be pushed] without rest, and regardless of boundary lines."*

With cruel narcissistic oblivion, he had also forced Lincoln officials - Justice of the Peace "Squire Wilson, Jailer Juan Patrón, and Sheriff George Kimbrell - to pursue Regulators. The first two were themselves victims of Ring murder attempts. Kimbrell was married to a woman in Picacho, from which some of McSween's fighters came. All considered Regulators as heroes. Wallace's acts may have driven these men's covert effort, discussed in the next chapter, to save Billy Bonney by a pardon.

In undated notes, Wilson tried to redirect Wallace to real outlaws: Seven Rivers Ring rustlers: *"Probable fighting men John Jones Jim Jones Bil Jones George Davis Mron Turner Bob Speaks Gunter John Smith or Silton & tom cat or Silvan & that is all I know about Seven Rivers that are Desperate men."* And on April 8, 1879, Wilson initialed a one-page letter assassination warning. But the intended victim was Ira Leonard. Wilson wrote:

> *Lincoln april 8th 79*
> *Dear Governer Wallace*
> <u>it is said that G Pepin told a mexican that the ~~of a~~ pimping</u> *Governer thought Himself safe at town. But the first thing He knew He would Be killed & then the other officers of such as sheriff & probate & Justices could easily Be Done away With So you can se what they are after Be very careful about yourself also said you Would not Be attacked on the Road when you had an escort But in town   confidential*
> *Yours in truth*
> *JBW*

Sheriff Kimbrell's deputy, Robert M. Gilbert, also got Wallace's "outlaw" assignment. Having been on Tunstall's coroner's jury, he knew Ring terrorism. In his June 1, 1879 letter to Wallace, he reported obstructed arrest of real Lincoln County War criminals by Ringite Henry Waldo, then defending Dudley in his Court of Inquiry. Gilbert wrote: *"Judge Waldo read some law stating very clearly that no arrest could be made on witnesses during their attendance on courts ... and that I had better releace the prisners that I had arrested ... so then I wrote out a releace and let them loos."* This was a reality. So Wallace ignored it.

By March 12, 1879, Lew Wallace's "outlaw" solution spun out to using Native Americans as trackers of outlaws. So he turned for referrals to Mescalero Indian Reservation Agent Frederick Godfroy, who, as Investigator Frank Warner Angel, in his October 2, 1878 "Examination of charges against F.C. Godfroy, Indian Agent, Mescalero, N.M." had already reported, was guilty of defrauding the U.S. government in collusion with "The House" by accepting bad flour and hay, and rustled beef. Godfroy must have been astounded by Wallace's absurdly telling him: *"I recognize, of course, that you are officially interested in putting a stop quickly as possible to the lawlessness now prevalent."*

WALLACE FEIGNS FACT-FINDING

Lew Wallace further misled and encouraged Lincolnites as to future action by doing fact-finding interviews. Billy himself, then in sham arrest for his pardon bargain, would volunteer for one on March 23, 1879. Some, set up as "affidavits," in fact, were not signed, dated, or notarized. It was more of Wallace's fiction.

"Squire" Wilson poured out his liturgy of Lincoln County War crimes; but when Wallace was questioned in the Dudley Court of Inquiry, he denied memory of his interviews. Wilson had stated:

> *Territory of New Mexico*
> *County of Lincoln*
> *Before me the undersigned authority personally came and appeared John Wilson who after being duly sworn according to law deposeth and saith*
> *That he is a duly elected Justice of the Peace in Precinct No. 1 in Lincoln County New Mexico and that he was ordered by Col Dudley Commanding Fort Stanton in New Mexico on or about the 19th of July 1878 to take the affidavits of*

Col Purington, Capt Blair and Dr Appel accusing A.A. McSween and others that was in his house on July 16th 1878 of having committed an assault on the person of one Berry Robinson a Soldier of Fort Stanton by having shot 4 or more shots at him with intent to kill as they had been informed and believed.

I told Col Dudley that I was not certain whether it was lawful for me to issue such an order or not and I thought it was the duty of a United States commissioner to issue it as there was a Soldier concerned in it and he got very angry at me for refusing to issue it on that ground and told me if I did not take the affidavits and issue the warrant forthwith that he would put me in double irons and would report me to the Governor and he called me a coward and said many other bad words to me

I then went to my office and took the affidavits of the above named Officers as aforesaid and after they signed and swore to it I issued the warrant to the Sheriff of Lincoln County for the arrest of A.A. McSween and others that was in the house on the 16th of July 1878 as per affidavit and gave it to George W. Peppin to serve returnable forthwith and said warrant has not been returned to my office up to this date by Peppin or any other person for him **I did not issue said warrant by my own will but by the preemptory order of Col Dudley** he Dudley coming in person to my office before I had it ready and told me I was not trying to issue the warrant in a hurry as it was my duty to do Col Dudley was the only person that appeared to be so much interested in the issue of the warrant I was not ordered or solicited by any other person but by Col Dudley to issue the warrant above mentioned for the arrest of McSween and others **to the best of my knowledge Col Dudley was sure desirous to have McSween and parties arrested than all the others.** Parties that was in Lincoln at the time not even the Sheriff asked me to issue the warrant I gave it to the Sheriff without him asking me for it I further state that Col Dudley camped ~~his~~ with his command about 30 yds north east of the house of Jose Montaño in Lincoln and planted a cannon about 15 yds from the front and pointing towards said house and **told a woman that understood English to tell the people in the house that if there was a shot fired out** *of the house over his Soldiers that he would fire on the house with the cannon which was pointed at the house at the time.*

Col Dudley stopped in Lincoln with his command until after McSween's house was burnt and McSween and others killed then left with his command for Fort Stanton leaving 3 soldiers at [Saturnino] Baca's house [Ringite resident of Lincoln] to protect Baca's family.

Minor merchant Isaac Ellis and his family lived at the far northeast side of Lincoln. In the Lincoln County War Battle, McSweens were stationed there, but fled when Dudley arrived. Ellis's "affidavit" described specific horrors. In the Court of Inquiry, cross-examined Wallace would deny all memory of it:

Territory of New Mexico
    County of Lincoln
        Before me the undersigned authority personally came and appeared Isaac Ellis personally known to me as such. Who being duly sworn according to law deposeth and saith to wit,
    That the deponent is a Merchant of the Town of Lincoln County of Lincoln Territory of New Mexico. That on or about the 17$\underline{th}$ of July 1878 Sheriff Peppins ~~and~~ Posse attacked the Town of Lincoln, and kept up firing from the neighboring hills until the morning of the 19th when Lieut Col N.A.M. Dudley with Capt George Purington Capt Blair Lieut Goodwin and Dr Appell [Appel] of Fort Stanton with a company of Soldiers and 2 pieces of Artillery [howitzer cannon and Gatling gun] arrived here, and went into camp about the center of Town, and sent for ~~the deponent~~ me, and when I arrived at his camp he seemed to be greatly excited.
    *When I was informed by said Col Dudley that **if a gun was fired out of mine or any house in Town he would immediately tear it to the ground regardless of women and children** and while [I was] at the camp of Col N.A.M. Dudley the socalled Sheriff George W. Peppin came riding into camp with 3 Soldiers … and after talking a short time with said Dudley, Dudley order[ed] the Soldiers to go back with sheriff Peppin. I then returned to my house. the said Dudley set one piece of artillery about 200 feet from and pointing towards my house **in a short time the Said Peppin together with about nine men came from the direction of the camp of said Dudley and came in**

my house and ordered me to give them coal oil [kerosene] for which they stated they intended to use in setting fire to the house of A.A. McSween. they further stated that they had him in the house and intended to burn him out They took the coal oil with them and went back, when opposite the camp Dudley came out and they Dudley and Peppin talked for some time. they went on towards the house of A.A. McSween and in a little while firing commenced around McSweens and we soon saw smoke arise and firing was kept up until about nine oclock at night

the following morning McSween with three others [Harvey Morris, Francisco Zamora, Vincente Romero] was found dead in the yard riddled with bullets and said house and contents totally destroyed by fire. And the same morning the store of John H. Tunstall decd was broke open and robed of about Six Thousand Dollars worth of Goods. after the Store was rob, Col Dudley broke up camp and returned to Fort Stanton

Sam Corbett, John Tunstall's shopkeeper, had experienced the illegal, harassing property attachment there by Sheriff Brady as prelude to Tunstall's murder. In his "affidavit," he described the next day's looting of the store, enabled by Sheriff Peppin and Commander Dudley. Wallace would later deny memory of this:

Territory of New Mexico
County of Lincoln
Before me the undersigned authority personally came and appeared Samuel R. Corbett well known to me to be such. That the deponent was clerking in the Store belonging to the Estate of John H. Tunstall until it was broken open and robbed of its entire contents, and since that time has been clerking for Isaac Ellis & Sons Merchants of the Town of Lincoln County of Lincoln Territory of New Mexico ... about 9 oclock in the morning [of July 20th, after the killing of McSween and others the day before] I went to the Store and found Sheriff Peppin and about eight of his posse in the Store. I spoke to Sheriff Peppin and asked him if he could not stop the men from taking the Goods out of the Store, and he told me that he was not responsible for nothing and went out. Col Dudley was in the store and saw men carrying out goods he walk out with Peppin and they talked a while in the street. the same day Col Dudley with his command went back to Ft Stanton.

DUDLEY REQUESTS A COURT OF INQUIRY

On March 13, 1879 - the day Billy Bonney sent his first pardon plea letter to Lew Wallace - a new crisis hit the that unhappy Governor. Removed Commander Dudley pre-empted a case against himself by requesting the Adjutant General in Washington, D.C. to grant him a military court of inquiry "*to clear his name*" from Wallace's besmirching. That meant Wallace would have to testify against Dudley to justify himself! And unbeknownst to Wallace, that Ring-arranged kangaroo Court would be delayed until May to ensure availability of its Chief Judge, Fort Union's Colonel Galusha Pennypacker, Dudley's best friend from his service there.

But by then, Wallace would have as his ally teenaged Billy, who could confound all the Ringites' plans and power.

CHAPTER 19

BILLY BONNEY'S PARDON THREAT TO THE RING

THE PARDON PLAN

SUMMARY: The pardon bargain Billy Bonney proposed to Lew Wallace had two goals: freeing himself from Lincoln County War murder indictments, and freeing himself to fight the Ring. And he knew that his offer to testify against Ringites would mark him for murder. But Wallace had his own agenda which would add to Billy's risk.

After Huston Chapman's murder, and encouraged by Lew Wallace's apparent anti-Ring interventions, Billy Bonney offered him a bold bargain: a pardon for his Lincoln County War indictments in exchange for his eye-witness testimony in April's Grand Jury against Chapman's killers. The indictments were for Regulator killings of Sheriff William Brady; Deputy Sheriff George Hindman; and posseman, Andrew "Buckshot" Roberts.

BILLY'S SECRET PARTISANS

Billy did not act alone. In my 2011 book, *Billy the Kid's Writings, Words, and Wit*, by authenticating a new letter of Billy's to Wallace, I discovered that his rare embossed Lady Liberty stationery was shared with Justice of the Peace John Wilson and Jailor Juan Patrón; indicating that they were helping him. Wilson provided his Lincoln house for Wallace to meet with Billy. Patrón took Billy into his home for the sham arrest. And Sheriff George Kimbrell, would do the sham arrest. As Billy wrote to Wallace: "[A]s to my Character I refer to any of the Citizens, for the majority of them are my Friends and have been helping me all they could."

Wilson and Patrón knew Billy's anti-Ring commitment. On February 19, 1878, he gave Wilson an affidavit about John Tunstall's murder. As Wilson's Deputy Town Constable, he tried to serve the Tunstall murder warrants in company of Patrón and a citizens' committee. He was on Dick Brewer's posse pursuing Tunstall's killers. He was on the posse of Sheriff John Copeland's

Deputy Josiah Scurlock to reclaim dead Tunstall's stolen horses. He risked his life on June 6, 1878 to give Investigator Frank Warner Angel a deposition about Tunstall's murder. And he was in all Regulator skirmishes in the Lincoln County War. He defended McSween in the Battle. Now he was an eye-witness against Huston Chapman's assassins for the Grand Jury; and he would later testify in the Court of Inquiry against N.A.M. Dudley.

Furthermore, Regulator killings were all Ringite murderers; hated by Wilson and Patrón. There was no doubt to men like them that freedom fighting Billy deserved a pardon.

BECOMING THE RING'S TARGET

Billy knew he was risking his life. As he wrote to Lew Wallace in his first pardon bargain letter of March 13, 1879: "*I ... am afraid to give up because my Enimies would Kill me.*" But, as his letter of March 20, 1879 showed, he just wanted arrangements to stay alive before testifying: "*I am not afraid to die like a man fighting but I would not like to be killed like a dog unarmed.*"

But he would have known that after his anti-Ring Lincoln County War heroics, and after his rejection of Dolan's "peace meeting" re-entry to the Ring's fold, the pardon attempt would be the final stroke in pitting the Ring against himself.

THE FIRST PARDON LETTER

Just 23 days after Huston Chapman's killing, on about March 13, 1879, Billy sent Lew Wallace his pardon proposal, because his indictments for Brady, Hindman, and Roberts excluded him from the Amnesty Proclamation. Noteworthy is that he asked to "*annuly*" - meaning annul - them. That was correct: a pardon is granted after a sentencing; annulment is before. That may have been input from Justice of the Peace Wilson.

Billy's letter is audacious and egalitarian. He felt Wallace's equal. As to Wallace's huge reward of $1,000 - presumably dead or alive - he airily dismissed it as negotiable; rewording it as, "*which as I can understand it means alive as a witness,*" to segue into his bargain: exchanging his testimony for the annulling! And his brilliance was obvious. He was no ordinary "outlaw." His fine Spencerian script, and correct spelling of even "*indictments*" must have surprised Wallace. And Wallace was suddenly offered a solution to his Chapman crisis wrapped in romance of an outlaw boy of the wild frontier. And the accused murderers were already captive at Fort Stanton. His luck seemed changing. Billy wrote:

> To his Excellency the Governor.
> General Lew. Wallace
> Dear Sir I have heard that You will give one thousand $ dollars for my body which as I can understand it means alive as a witness. I know it is as a witness against those that murdered Mr. Chapman. if it was so as that I could appear at Court, I could give the desired information. but I have indictments against me for things that happened in the late Lincoln County War and am afraid to give up because my Enimies would Kill me. the day Mr. Chapman was murderded I was in Lincoln, at the request of good citizens to meet Mr. J.J. Dolan to meet as Friends. So as to be able to lay aside our arms and go to Work. I was present when Mr. Chapman was murderded and know who did it and if it were not for these indictments I would have made it clear before now. if it is in your power to Annully those indictments I hope you will do so so as to give me a chance to explain. please send me an annser telling me what you can do. You can send annser by bearer.
>
> I have no wish to fight any more indeed I have not raised an arm since Your proclamation. as to my Character I refer to any of the Citizens, for the majority of them are my Friends and have been helping me all they could. I am called Kid Antrim but Antrim is my stepfathers name.
> Waiting for an annser I remain
> Your Obedient Servant
> W.H. Bonney

WALLACE'S RESPONSE

On March 15, 1879, Wallace responded to Billy as the wily attorney who had hanged John Wilkes Booth's innocent landlady, Mrs. Surratt: leaving open getting his testimony, then hanging him as a trophy in his war against "outlaws." And, reflecting Ringite input, he insultingly linked Billy to outlaw Jessie Evans: Tunstall's and Chapman's killer. Ominous was his lawyer's trick:

feigning a bargain by saying: *"I have the authority to exempt you from prosecution."* Wallace might *"have the authority,"* but he was not promising to use it to pardon Billy! Additionally, he *did not* have authority to pardon for Catron's federal indictment for the Roberts killing. Only President Hayes could. Wallace wrote:

> Lincoln, March 15, 1879.
> W.W. Bonney.
> Come to the house of Old Squire Wilson (not the lawyer [Sidney Wilson]) at nine (9) o'clock next Monday night alone. I don't mean his office, but his residence. Follow along the foot of the mountain south of the town, come in at that side, and knock on the east door. **I have the authority to exempt you from prosecution, if you will testify to what you say you know.**
> The object of the meeting at Squire Wilson's is to arrange the matter in a way to make your life safe. To do that the utmost secrecy is to be used. So come alone. Don't tell anybody - not a living soul - where you are coming or the object. If you could trust Jesse Evans, you can trust me.
> Lew Wallace

THE SECRET MEETING

The secret meeting of Wallace and Billy was on March 17, 1879 at 9 p.m., with Justice of the Peace "Squire" Wilson, in his house on Lincoln's single street's south side. Billy trusted the bargain; especially if Wallace had said, "Testify ... before the Grand Jury and the trial court and convict the murderer of Chapman and I will let you go scot-free with a pardon in your pocket for all your misdeeds;" as he claimed 23 years later, on June 8, 1902, for *New York World Magazine*, as: "General Lew Wallace Writes a Romance of 'Billy the Kid.' " Specifics of this meeting are unknown, but Wallace remained obsessed with reworking it and his betrayed pardon promise for the rest of his life.

A HECTIC MARCH 20TH DAY

The March 18, 1879 "escape" from Fort Stanton of Billy Campbell and Jessie Evans impacted the pardon bargain by loss of defendants against whom Billy could testify. Still "held" at the Fort by Wallace - besides James Dolan and Billy Matthews - were

20 Seven Rivers rustlers. Billy wanted assurance that the pardon deal still held. Then he wanted a sham arrest, so he would not be suspected as a witness and killed by the Ring before testifying.

Billy began March 20th's letters by writing to "Squire" Wilson to check on the feigned arrest plan with Wallace. He wrote:

> <u>San Patricio</u>
> Thursday 20th *1879*
> Friend Wilson.
> *Please tell You know who that I do not know what to do, now as those Prisoners have escaped. So send word by bearer. a note through You it may be he has made different arrangements if not and he still wants it the same to Send :William Hudgins [Hudgens]: as Deputy, to the Junction tomorrow at three Oclock with some men you know to be all right. Send a note telling me what to do*
> WHBonney
> P.S. *do not send Soldiers*

Wallace responded to Wilson with arrangements, wanting to know if Kimbrell was right for the sham arrest. And he enclosed a "note" for Billy. It exists as a draft, which further implies a trick, since Wallace crossed out the bargain's references: "*I will comply with my part if you will with yours*" and substituted "*arrangement*" for "*understanding;*" as if avoiding to promise a pardon in writing. Wallace wrote to Billy:

> *The escape makes no difference in arrangements.* ~~*I will comply with my part if you will with yours.*~~
> *To remove all suspicions of* ~~arrangement~~ *understanding, I think it better to put the arresting party in charge of Sheriff Kimball [Kimbrell], who will be instructed to see that no violence is used.*
> *This will go to you tonight.* ~~*If you still insist upon Hudgens, let me know*~~*. If I don't* ~~*get*~~ *receive other word from you the party (all citizens) will be at the junction by three o'clock* ~~*tomorrow*~~*.*

Billy responded with a precautionary scenario for his sham arrest:

> San Patricio
> Lincoln County
> Thursday 20th 1879
> General. Lew. Wallace:
> Sir. I will keep the appointment I made. but be Sure and have men come that You can depend on I am not afraid to die like a man fighting but I would not like to be killed like a dog unarmed. tell Kimbal [Kimbrell] to let his men be placed around the house and for him to come in alone: and he can arrest us. all I am afraid of is that in the Fort we might be poisoned or killed through a window at night. but You can arrange that all right. tell the Commanding Officer to watch)Let Goodwin(he would not hesitate to do anything there Will be danger on the road of Somebody Waylaying us to kill us on the road to the Fort. You will never catch those fellows on the road Watch Fritzes. Captain Bacas ranch and the Brewery they Will either go to Seven Rivers or to Jicarillo Mountains they will stay around close untill the scouting parties come in. give a spy a pair of glasses and let him get on the mountain back of Fritzes and watch and if they are there there will be provisions carried to them. it is not my place to advise you, but I am anxious to have them caught, and perhaps know how men hide from Soldiers, better than you. please excuse me for having so much to say
> and I still remain Yours Truly
> W H. Bonney
>
> P.S.
> I have changed my mind Send Kimbal [Kimbrell] to Gutieres just below San Patricio one mile, because Sanger and Ballard are or were great friends of Camels [Billy Campbell's] Ballard told me ~~today~~ yesterday to leave for you were doing everything to catch me. it was a blind to get me to leave tell Kimbal [Kimbrell] not to come before 3 oclock for I may not be there before

WALLACE'S WORRISOME REPORT

Wallace's drafted a progress report to Carl Schurz on March 21, 1879, the day of Billy's sham arrest. As usual, he feigned success. But he ominously omitted his star witness for Chapman's murder, and, instead, promoted his "outlaw" campaign as *"taking the head off the evil."* And he even enclosed Sherman's "outlaw" list with " *'The Kid' William Bonney.*" He wrote:

Lincoln, March 21, 1879.

Hon. C. Schurz,
Sec'y Dept. Interior.
Sir:

My time has been so constantly occupied in getting my work into operation and hearing people who have grievances and information, that I have had no opportunity to write you ~~in full~~ as might be desired. At last, however, ~~I can do so,~~ everything being in progress, I can send you a sufficient outline ...

A short interview with the leading citizens [in Lincoln] satisfied me that it would not be possible in the beginning to obtain affidavits against parties well known to be guilty of crimes; this on account of the terrorism so general after the brutal assassination of H.I. Chapman, the night of the 18th ~~March~~ February ... I decided to proceed immediately without warrants ... Accordingly the same evening ~~I sent~~ the following request was sent to the Fort, which is ten miles away.

[ENCLOSURE] Copy of a March 5, 1879 letter to Hatch telling him how to capture Chapman's killers

[AUTHOR'S NOTE: For his outlaw myth, Wallace focuses on outlaw Evans, who was merely present.]

General Hatch promptly complied, and next day the three – Campbell, Evans, and Matthews – were secured, and in due time lodged in the Fort. These men, you should understand, were all principals in the Chapman murder. Two of them are the most desperate of the outlaws. Evans ~~was~~ is one of the murderers of Tunstall. He and Campbell have to answer for several other lives feloniously taken. **Of the same gang is J.J. Dolan; but as I had hopes that his larger money interests in the county, amounting to $70,000 or $80,000, would make him pliant for use as a witness, he was not included in the order of arrest**. Two days afterwards he came and voluntarily surrendered himself to me; whereupon, with the same object in view, I took his parole & confining him to the limits of the Fort .... I set much store upon the moral effect of the prompt seizure of these men.

In course of my interviews with the people, both Mexican and American, of the town and county, it became apparent that ~~all~~ attempts to restore confidence would be ~~long defeated delayed~~ delayed if not wholly fruitless, while Lt. Col. N.A.M. Dudley, 9th Cavalry, was in command of Fort Stanton. I addressed the following communication to General Hatch:

[ENCLOSURE] Copy March 7, 1879 letter to Hatch requesting Dudley's removal (See page 517)

[AUTHOR'S NOTE: Next Wallace credits himself for Dudley's removal, unaware that Schurz and Hayes did not want to reopen the can of worms that Angel had just closed. The last thing they wanted was "*showing of ... misconduct and abuse of authority*" by public officials. But Wallace reassuringly ended with his "outlaw" solution.]

It is almost needless to say General Hatch relieved Col. Dudley upon the request as presented ... **It is my belief that the charges can be sustained; and that, in the** ~~same~~ **connection, there will be an astonishing showing of other incidental misconduct and abuse of authority, all tending to establish that the Colonel was a** ~~promoter of disorder and the hand~~ **most mischievous partizan if not actually a promoter of disorder ...**

Captain Henry Carroll was the successor in command of the Fort.

I next busied myself making a list of outlaws to proceed against. On the 11th March, I was able to send ~~Ca~~ *the following communication.*

[ENCLOSURE] Wallace's March 11, 1879 letter to Captain Carroll with Sherman's outlaw list. (See page 521)

[AUTHOR'S NOTE: Wallace's following outlaw fabrications are glaring lies, since he spent the past month talking to Lincolnites, and Billy himself. He knew the Lincoln County War freedom fighters were not random killers. But he makes clear his "*war*" is against those on Sherman's outlaw list.]

The list, I stop to remark, is by no means perfect; yet it was enough to begin with. Some of those named are guilty of double murders; some of triple ...

If, however, I should be fortunate enough to get all ~~that~~ *the list, it would be no more than* **taking the head off the evil.** ~~leaving it To accomplish end it permanent cure, it is necessary to get down to the paps the roots and dig them up.~~ **To dig up the roots, it is necessary to** ~~break up~~ **crush the number of cattle camps ...**

[AUTHOR'S NOTE: Next Wallace gave his absurd rustling solution, but slipped in that his *only* setback was escape of Chapman's killers, Evans and Campbell.]

Besides overhauling and breaking up the camps and depots alluded to, I hope, by bringing stolen cattle &c. to the county seat [Lincoln], to furnish every honest citizen an opportunity to reclaim his lost property ...

The only set back in my operation yet sustained was the escape a few nights ago of two of my prisoners, Campbell and Evans. They were helped out of the guard-house at the Fort by a faithless sentinel, who deserted with them. I have offered $1000 for their return, and hope to recapture them yet.

Having thus set my measures afoot, I am waiting here for Judge Ira Leonard; when he comes, I shall employ him as an attorney in behalf of the Territory in connection with this business; then I shall go to Mesilla, over in Doña Ana county, to concert action with the commandant of Fort Bliss, looking to thorough cleansing of that county. In probability the purification will take the whole summer.

With a hope that my action will meet your approval and that of the President, I am, most respectfully,

Your friend & servant,
Lew. Wallace, Gov. New Mexico

WALLACE INTERVIEWS BILLY

In Lincoln, Lew Wallace and Billy were housed next door to each other; with Billy in Juan Patrón's house, and Wallace at José Montaño's. On March 23, 1879, Wallace interviewed Billy, asking nothing about the Lincoln County War. But his notes show that Billy revealed Ringite rustlers and murderers; stating:

William Bonney ("Kid")
relative to arrangement
with him.

Notes:

3-23-1879

<u>Statements by Kid, made Sunday night March 23, 1879</u>

1. There is a cattle trail beginning about 5 miles above Yellow Lake in a cañon, running a little west of north to Cisneza del Matcho (Mule Spring) and continuing around the point of the Capitan Mountains down toward Carrizozo in the direction of the

Rio Grande. Frank Wheeler, Jake Owens and Dutch Chris are supposed to have used this trail taking a bunch of cattle over. Vansickle told K. so. They stopped and killed two beavers for Sam Corbett – hush money to Vansickle to whom they gave the beavers. Vansickle also said the Owens-Wheeler outfit mentioning "Chris" Ladbessor using this trail for about a year, but that lately their horses had given out, and of 140 head which they started to work they had only got through with 40. That now they were going to the Reservation to make a raid on the Indian horses to work on.

<u>The Rustlers.</u>

The "Rustlers," Kid says: were organized in Fort Stanton. Before they organized as "Rustlers" they had been with Peppin's posse. They came from Texas. Owens was conspicuous amongst them. **They were organized before the burning of McSween's house**, and after that they went on their first trip down the county as far as the Coe's ranch and **thence to the Feliz where they took the Tunstall cattle.** From the Feliz they went to the Pecos, where some of them deserted, Owens amongst them. (Martin [Martz], known to Sam Corbett) was in charge of the Tunstall cattle, and was taken prisoner, and saw them kill one of their own party. On the same trip they burnt Lola Wise's house, and took some horses. Coe at the time was ranching at the house. On this trip they moved behind a body of soldiers, one company, and a company of Navajo Scouts. They moved in sight of the soldiers, taking horses, insulting women. Lorenzo Trujillo (Jus. Peder) Juan Trujillo, Jose M. Gutierres, Pancho Sanchez, Santos Tafoya, are witnesses against them. They stopped on Pecos at Seven Rivers. Collins, now at Silver City, was one of the outfit – nick-named the Prowler by the cowboys. At Seven Rivers. There joined them Gus Gildey (wanted at San Antonio for killing Mexicans) Gildey is carrying the mail now from Stockton to Seven Rivers – James Irvin and Reese Gobles, (rumored that their bodies were found in a drift down the Pecos) – Rustling Bob (found dead in the Pecos, killed by his own party) – John Selman (whereabouts unknown) came to Roswell while [Captain] Carroll was there –

The R's [Rustlers] stayed at Seven Rivers; which they left on their second trip via the Berenda for Fort Stanton. On their return back they killed Chavez boys and the crazy boy, Lorenzo – and the Sanchez boy, 14 years old. They also committed many robberies. They broke up after reaching the Pecos, promising to return when some more horses got fat.

Shedd's Ranch

The trail used going from Seven Rivers to Shedd's was round the S.W. part of the Guadalupe Mts. by a tank on the right hand of trail: from Shedd's the drives would be over to Las Cruces Jesse [Jessie] Evans, Frank Baker (killed) Jim McDaniels (at Cruces, ranging between Cruces and El Paso) Reed at Shedd's bought cattle from them – also sold cattle to E.C. Priest, butcher in Cruces. "Big Mose" (at Cruces last heard from) and [blank], deserter from cavalry – (went to Arizona)

Mimbres

Used to be called Mormon City – situated 30 miles on the road to Cruces from Silver City south. A great many of what are known as "West Harden gang" are there. Among them Joe Olney, known in Mimbres as Joe Hill; he has a ranch in old Mexico somewheres near Coralitos. He makes trips up in this country: was at Penasco not long ago.

San Nicholas Spring

Is about 18 miles from Shedd's Ranch on the road to Tularosa, left hand road. There's a house at the spring and about 4 or 5 miles from it N.W. is another corral of brush and a spring, situated in a cañon. There Jim McDaniels used to keep stolen Indian horses. McD. one of the Rio Grande posse. Kid says the latter is still used.

The Jones Family

Came from Texas. Used to keep saloon at Fort Griffin. The family consists of the father, Jim Jones, John Jones, boy about 10 years old, a girl about 13, and the mother. Marion Turner lives with the family, and he killed a Mexican man at Blazers Mill "just to see him kick." He had no cattle **when the War started**. *The Jones, John and Jim, killed a man named Riley, a partner of theirs, on the Penasco 3 or 4 years ago.*

THE "BILLIE" LETTER

Billy next wrote to Wallace on March 24, 1879, to give Lincoln County War information. It is now a one-page fragment in Lew Wallace's papers, signed "Billie." I authenticated it in my 2011 book, *Billy the Kid's Writings, Words, and Wit*. For it, his "jailor," Juan Patrón, gave his embossed Lady Liberty stationery to write:

... on the Pecos. All that I can remember are the So Called Dolan Outfit but they are all up here now. and on the Rio <u>Grande</u> this man Cris Moten I believe his name is he drove a herd of 80 head one Year ago last December in Company with Frank Wheeler Frank <u>Baker</u> deceased Jesse Evans George Davis alias Tom Jones. Tom Hill, his name in Texas being Tom Chelson also deceased, they drove the cattle to the Indian Reservation and sold them to John Riley and JJ Dolan. and the cattle were turned in for Beef for the Indians the Beckwith family made their boasts that they came to Seven Rivers a little over four years ago with one Milch Cow borrowed from John Chisum they had when I was there Year ago one thousand six hundred head of cattle. the male members of the family are Henry beckwith and John Beckwith Robert <u>Beckwith</u> was killed the time McSween's house was burned. Charles [blank] Robert Olinger and Wallace Olinger are of the same gang. their cattle ranch is Situated at Rock Corral twelve miles below Seven Rivers on the Pecos. Paxton and Pierce are Still below them forty miles from Seven Rivers there are four of them Paxton: Pierce: Jim Raymers, and Buck Powel. they had when I seen them last about one thousand head of cattle: at Rocky Arroyo there is another Ranch belonging to [blank] Smith who Operated on the Penasco last year with the Jesse Evans gang those and the places I mentioned are all I know of this man Chris Moten at the time they stole those Cattle was in the employ of JJ <u>Dolan</u> and <u>Co.</u> I afterwards Seen Some of the cattle at the Rinconada Bonita on the reservation those were the men we were in search of when we went to the Agency. the Beckwith family were attending to their own Business when this War started but G.W. Peppin told them that this was John Chisums War. and so they took a hand thinking they would lose their Cattle in case that he Chisum won the fight. this is all the information I can give you on this point

Yours Respectfully Billie

"BILLIE" LETTER COMMENTARY

Analysis of the "Billie" letter demonstrates his risk to the Ring by his detailed knowledge of their murder and rustling operations. Commentary is added as follows:

on the Pecos.

[AUTHOR'S NOTE: The fragment starts with a sentence ending. But "*on the Pecos*" were Lincoln County War participants. On the Pecos was cattle king, John Chisum, who betrayed Tunstall and McSween, and reneged on his promise to pay Regulators' wages. Billy possibly shared his anger at Chisum in the missing page(s) here or in his Interview, and did blame Chisum in his December 12, 1880 letter to Wallace. Wallace later used that in his Billy the Kid fictions as Billy's "outlaw" revenge motive to hide Billy's anti-Ring cause. On the Pecos were Seven Rivers Ringite rustlers who murdered Regulator leader, Frank MacNab, and participated in the Lincoln County War Battle's killings. And on the Pecos was the Catron-Dolan cow-camp south of Seven Rivers, holding rustled stock for the Ring's military and Indian reservation contracts. Its foreman, William "Buck" Morton, was killed by the Regulators as a Tunstall murderer.]

all that I can remember are the So Called D<u>olan</u> Outfit but they are all up here now:

[AUTHOR'S NOTE: This is special information that Billy would know: that by 1879 Dolan did not have the Pecos Cow Camp after his bankruptcy in 1878 from mercantile competition with Tunstall. Intriguingly, Dolan's name is underlined for emphasis; and he was a Ring's boss in Lincoln County, being the one to call in Commander Dudley in the Lincoln County War Battle when the McSween side was winning.]

and on the Rio G<u>rande</u> this man Cris Moten I believe his name is he drove a herd of)80(head one Year ago last December in Company with Frank Wheeler Frank <u>Baker</u> deceased Jesse Evans George Davis alias Tom Jones. Tom Hill, his name in Texas being Tom Chelson also deceased.

[AUTHOR'S NOTE: Billy lists outlaw Jessie Evans's men: Frank Baker, George Davis, and Tom Hill. Billy knew them, and rode with them in September of 1877. They were involved in killing Tunstall. And Evans was at Chapman's killing. And Billy snidely calls Frank Baker "*deceased*." (Tunstall murderer Baker, was a Regulator victim on March 9, 1878. Billy was likely one of his assailants.) As intimate, is Billy's knowing about the death of Evans's gang member, Tom Hill, as well as his alias and place of origin. Though Billy again says "*deceased*," it was an obscure killing; implying that Billy kept track of erstwhile associates. (During an Evan's gang robbery, Hill was shot by a Cherokee partner of a German sheep herder named John Wagner near Shedd's Ranch, a Ringite outlet for rustled stock. In that shooting, Jessie was hit in the right wrist.)]

they drove the cattle to the Indian Reservation and sold them to John Riley and JJ Dolan. and the cattle were turned in for Beef for the Indians

[AUTHOR'S NOTE: This amazing statement shows Billy's insider's knowledge of Ring dynamics that led to Tunstall's murder and the Lincoln County War. It is also the key point which Wallace avoided in his "Interview": <u>that rustling was a Ring endeavor to meet beef contracts for the Mescalero Indian Reservation and for Fort Stanton.</u> Tunstall was working to supplant the Ring with his own contracts to both entities with his cattle ranches on the Feliz and Peñasco Rivers, where Billy and Fred Waite were Homestead Act owners. That Ring competition was why Tunstall had to die. So, here Billy is giving Wallace the dynamics he needed to really end the Lincoln County "troubles" - dynamics which Wallace concealed.]

the Beckwith family made their boasts that they came to Seven Rivers a little over four years ago with one Milch Cow borrowed from John Chisum they had when I was there Year ago one thousand six hundred head of cattle.

[AUTHOR'S NOTE: This is Billy's wry sense of humor, about the Beckwith family "borrowing" a cow from Chisum; but in four years acquiring almost 2000 head. This was the description of Seven Rivers rustling for the Ring. And it is insider information. (In September of 1877, when Billy first returned to New Mexico Territory from Arizona Territory, he stayed with the Jones family at Seven Rivers, and got to know the Beckwiths.) John and Robert Beckwith eventually fought for the Ring in the Lincoln County War.]

the male members of the family are Henry beckwith and John Beckwith Robert <u>Beckwith</u> was killed the time McSween's house was burned.

[AUTHOR'S NOTE: Billy not only elaborates on the Beckwith family members, but connects Robert Beckwith's death to the most dramatic event of the Lincoln County War Battle: the murder of Alexander McSween during attempted escape. Billy's reference to *"the time McSween's house was burned"* implies his assumption that Wallace knows he is referring to that arson. And they may have discussed it at the "Squire" Wilson house meeting on March 17th. Billy states that Bob Beckwith *"was killed,"* omitting here that it occurred when he was serving Justice of the Peace Wilson's coerced arrest warrants on McSween, and was caught in friendly fire during McSween's murder by Peppin's outlaw posse.]

Charles [blank] Robert Olinger and Wallace Olinger are of the same gang. their cattle ranch is situated at Rock Corral twelve miles below Seven Rivers on the Pecos.

[AUTHOR'S NOTE: Billy is clear on the Olinger brothers, Robert and Wallace as being in "*the same gang*," meaning the Seven Rivers rustlers.]

Paxton and Pierce are Still below them forty miles from Seven Rivers there are four of them Paxton: Pierce: Jim Raymen, and Buck Powel. they had when I seen them last about one thousand head of cattle: at Rocky Arroyo there is another Ranch belonging to Smith who Operated on the Penasco last year with the Jesse Evans gang

[AUTHOR'S NOTE: Billy is listing more Seven Rivers rustlers.]

those and the places I mentioned

[AUTHOR'S NOTE: Stating "*and the places I mentioned*" implies his Wallace "Interview," now with follow-up specifics.]

are all I know of this man Chris Moten at the time they stole those Cattle was in the employ of JJ Dolan *and* Co.

[AUTHOR'S NOTE: Billy knows that the rustling gangs he has described are "employed" for the beef contracts of J.J. Dolan and Company – thus giving Wallace the m.o. of real outlaws.]

I afterwards Seen Some of the cattle at the Rinconada Bonita on the reservation those were the men we were in search of when we went to the Agency.

[AUTHOR'S NOTE: This refers to "Buckshot" Roberts's Regulator killing on April 4, 1878 at Blazer's Mill in the Mescalero Indian Reservation. Billy calls it "the *Agency*" because Indian Agent, Frederick Godfroy, lived in its way station. Billy may be following up his "Interview" statement to Wallace as to "*those were the men we were in search of when we went to the Agency.*" That pertains to the pardon bargain, since Roberts's killing there was one of Billy's indictments - even though Billy did not know that Catron's federal indictment for it barred Territorial pardon.]

the Beckwith family were attending to their own Business when this War started but G.W. Peppin told them that this was John Chisums War and so they took a hand thinking they would loose their Cattle in case that he Chisum won the fight.

[AUTHOR'S NOTE: Billy is giving insider information about why the Seven Rivers men fought on the Ring side in the Lincoln County War: that Chisum had sided with Tunstall and McSween, and they were Murphy-Dolan Ringite rustlers.]

this is all the information I can give you on this point
Yours Respectfully Billie

HERALDING WALLACE'S BETRAYAL

By March of 1879's end, it was clear that the pardon bargain would have a tragic outcome, since Wallace's progress reports rely on the Ring's outlaw myth, while he faced testifying in the Dudley Court of Inquiry and hid the Ring to protect himself.

On March 31, 1879, he sent Secretary of the Interior Carl Schurz a letter to forward to President Hayes, asking again for martial law. The reason was the outlaw myth: *"The feuds recently in Lincoln county, New Mexico, left a large many thieves and murderers, who, with others of like class since added to their number, are now confederated for plunder."*

Even more ominous, was Wallace's not only omitting Billy as his upcoming star witness, but ridiculing him in as a *"precious specimen."* So just 18 days after Billy first contacted him, Wallace gave no indication of honoring the pardon. For Wallace, the way out was the outlaw myth; as he stated: *"The desperadoes include some of the most noted of their class in the United States."* Billy would never hear from him again. Wallace wrote:

> *Lincoln, N.M., March 31, 1879*
> *Hon. Carl Schurz*
> *Sec'y Dept Interior.*
> *Sir:*
> *Today I forward a telegram to you, with*

another to the President, requesting him to proceed under his October proclamation and place this county [Lincoln] and Doña Ana under martial law ...

To still further weaken my confidence in juries as instruments of the law in this county, I have been forced to take account of the fact that everybody of any force or character has in some way been committed to one side or the other in the **recent war***, and is yet all alive with prejudices and partialities.*

[AUTHOR'S NOTE: This is the only time that Wallace correctly calls the conflict a "war," but he conceals particulars.]

A precious specimen nick-named "The Kid," whom the Sheriff is holding here in the Plaza, as it is called, is an object of tender regard. I heard singing and music the other night; going to the door, I found the minstrels of the village actually serenading the fellow in his prison.

[AUTHOR'S NOTE: Every part is a lie: 1) implying real incarceration, 2) implying that Billy was an outlaw, 3) implying that citizens' affection was inexplicable. This despicable betrayal by Wallace was the turning point for Billy. Wallace was as much a moral monstrosity as was T.B. Catron himself.]

Enough is disclosed to put you in possession of the reasons underlying my clear conviction that coming session of the court will in the present situation be useful only to the wrong-doers; leaving, as I see now after nearly one months study and patient exertion upon the very ground, nothing to be hoped except from martial law.

[AUTHOR'S NOTE: Wallace is lying. Lincoln County's jurors knew the issues; and would correctly indict Ringites.]

The desperadoes include some of the most noted of their class in the United States, and they cannot be made to quit except by actual war – by guns and pistols, not with writs or lectures, and then only by co-operative action between the military of New Mexico, Texas, and Arizona ...

[AUTHOR'S NOTE: This is the outlaw myth.]

I hope the President will act upon my request. The expeditions to which I have alluded have not been entirely barren of good results; one is certain, the enemy have been driven to their hiding places, and will not re-appear before the preliminary measures essential to the proposed new regime can be taken.
I have the honor to be, Very respectfully,
Your friend & servant,
Lew. Wallace, Gov. New Mexico

Judge Bristol has been notified of my opinion as to the advisability of holding his court, and my intention to ask a declaration of martial law. His views coincide with mine.

WALLACE ENLISTS LEONARD FOR PROSECUTIONS

Ira Leonard arrived in Lincoln on April 1, 1879 for the Lincoln County Grand Jury. Wallace had asked him to aid prosecutions, as mentioned in Leonard's May 20, 1879 letter to Wallace. (See pages 570-575 for letter) That was another callous concoction: for anti-Ring Leonard to help Ringite District Attorney William Rynerson. And Leonard knew that Billy would be testifying against Chapman's murderers - thus, against the Ring. With his office-mate Chapman murdered just 91 days earlier, Leonard was also frightened; writing to Wallace that District Attorney Rynerson *"aroused among the friends of the [Ringite] outlaws here a feeing of antagonism against me."*

MORE PRISONERS ESCAPE

On April 13, 1879, the Ring acted again to protect their own. To Fort Stanton, were sent heavy-hitting attorneys - Simon Newcomb (who would be one of Billy's prosecuting attorneys in his Mesilla hanging trial), Sidney Wilson, and Albert Jennings Fountain (who would be one of Billy's court-appointed attorneys in his Mesilla hanging trial) - along with Judge Warren Bristol, to free Wallace's remaining prisoners: James Dolan, Billy Matthews, and Seven Rivers rustlers. They filed writs of *habeas corpus* - claiming no legal justification existed to hold them longer. Bristol rubber-stamped that. The upshot was that Billy was now the sole "outlaw" in Lew Wallace's "captivity."

WALLACE REPORTS PROGRESS

In the midst of chaos and failure, on April 18, 1879, Wallace proclaimed "progress" to Schurz; writing: *"I have the honor to inform you that affairs in Lincoln county are progressing favorably as could be expected. Court opened at the county seat Monday morning, having eighteen prisoners charged with murder and grand larcenies to occupy its time and attention."* He added: *"This morning I start for Santa Fe to make some preparation for Col. Dudley's court of inquiry, which begins on the 25 proximo."*

CHAPTER 20

PARDON BARGAIN FULFILLED BY BILLY BONNEY AND AFTERMATH

BILLY TESTIFIES FOR THE PARDON

SUMMARY: Billy Bonney fulfilled his side of the pardon bargain by testifying in the April 1879 Lincoln County Grand Jury against Huston Chapman's murderers. And he achieved indictments of James Dolan and Billy Campbell for first degree murder, and of Jessie Evans as accessory to that murder. But Wallace issued no pardon.

BILLY'S GRAND JURY TESTIMONY: APRIL, 1879

The transcript of the April, 1879 Lincoln County Grand Jury under District Judge Warren Bristol was likely expurgated. But Billy's testifying is confirmed by contemporary records.

Attorney Ira Leonard, aware of the pardon bargain, confirmed Billy's testifying to Lew Wallace on April 20, 1879, describing Ringite pressure; writing: "*[Rynerson] is bent on going for the Kid … to destroy his testimony & influence he is bent on pushing him to the wall. He is a Dolan man and is defending him by his conduct all he can.*" Billy's testimony also yielded Leonard's admiration and loyalty, and Ringites' hatred. Leonard wrote:

Sunday eve April 20th 1879
Lincoln Plaza
Dear Gov. The air is filled tonight with "rumors of wars" or rumors that the military force is to be immediately withdrawn from here. Lee Keyser came from the Fort this evening and brought the intelligence, and one of Col. Dudleys particular friends is offering to bet five to one that he will be commissioned out at the Post in twenty days I have suspicion that there may be something of the kind up, that is the withdrawal of the troops – The soldier you ordered to report to me and remain with me had orders last night to leave and report to the Fort so after one days duty he took his leave under orders

[AUTHOR'S NOTE: Guard removal may have been preparation for Leonard's planned Ring assassination in two days.]

I had made an arrangement with the Sheriff to take those Hudgens boys and Henry to Fort Stockton and deliver them over to the authorities there with their stolen plunder. It would be the best thing that could be done if they could be sent through the country where the outlaws congregate under a strong Military guard with their stolen property & returned to the field where they perpetrated their crimes. That would be a sort of comity worth something because we could then establish relations with Texas which would induce them to pick up thieves who plunder from here and bring them to us and vice versa and a very short time would induce these fiends to leave this field for one more healthy to operate in. My plan was to have him write to the officers at the Fort Stockton telling them that he would have these thieves at El Paso at a certain time and to be there ready to move property & secure them. I tell you Gov they shall not get away We have got to use extraordinary measures and I think my plan a good one to break up this plundering. What do you think of it. If the people have got to depend on themselves without aid a short course can be made of it. The only remains left is to take these parties by force & ask surrender to the authorities where they can be punished & have them bring our outlaws back to us and my word for it will be but a short time before they will skin out of this country –

Court is moving on have tried no more habeas corpus cases I stave them off – **I tell you Gov that the prosecuting officer of this Dist [William Rynerson] is no friend to the enforcement of the law. He is bent on going for the Kid & notwithstanding he knows how it is proposed to destroy his testimony & influence he is bent on pushing him to the wall He is a Dolan man and is defending him by his conduct all he can**

I am going to have the Sheriff demand a Military escort & then shove these prisoners into Texas – It may be he can't get it but we will try for it –

Be sure & send me Session laws if you have to borrow them of Judge Waldo for awhile –

Write me & keep me posted

Yours &c
Ira Leonard

BILLY ACHIEVES INDICTMENTS

District Attorney William Rynerson's filing on April 28, 1879 verified the Chapman case's indictments. It should be noted that he was not required to issue arrest warrants. Evans and Campbell had already escaped. And Dolan was never arrested or tried - a rerun of his shielding from murdering Tunstall. Rynerson wrote:

The Territory of New Mexico
County of Lincoln
In the District Court of the County of
Lincoln at the April A.D. 1879 Term Thereof
The Grand Jurors for the Territory of New Mexico taken from the body of the good and lawful men of the County of Lincoln in the Territory of New Mexico, duly elected, empanelled, sworn and charged at the term aforesaid, to inquiry in and for the body of the County of Lincoln aforesaid, upon the oaths do present that ***James J. Dolan and William Campbell*** *late of the County of Lincoln in the Territory aforesaid on the nineteenth [eighteenth] day of February in the year of our Lord one thousand eight hundred and seventy nine at the County and Territory aforesaid with force and arms in and upon one Huston I. Chapman then and there being of their malice aforethought, unlawfully, feloniously, willfully, and from a premeditated design to effect the death of him the said Huston I. Chapman, did make an assault. And that the said James J. Dolan and the said William Campbell certain pistols then and there loaded and charged with gunpowder and divers leaden bullets,* ***(which pistols they the said James J. Dolan and the said William Campbell in their right hands then and there had and held) to against and upon the said Huston I. Chapman then and there of their malice aforethought unlawfully, feloniously, willfully and from a premeditated design to effect the death of the said Huston I. Chapman did shoot and discharge****. And that they the said James J. Dolan and the said William Campbell with the leaden bullets aforesaid out of the pistols aforesaid then and there by force of the gunpowder shot and sent forth as aforesaid the said Huston I. Chapman in and upon the left breast of him the said Huston I. Chapman* ***then and there of their malice aforethought, unlawfully, feloniously, willfully, and from a premeditated design to effect the death of him the said Huston I. Chapman did strike, penetrate and wound, giving the said***

Huston I. Chapman then and there with leaden bullets aforesaid so as aforesaid shot discharged and sent forth out of the pistols aforesaid by the said James J. Dolan and the said William Campbell in and upon the left breast of him the said Huston I. Chapman one mortal wound the said Huston I. Chapman then and there instantly died. And so the jurors aforesaid upon their oaths aforesaid do say that the said James J. Dolan and the said William Campbell the said Huston I. Chapman in manner and form aforesaid and by the means aforesaid of their malice aforethought **unlawfully, feloniously, willfully, and from a premeditated design to effect the death of him the said Huston I. Chapman did kill and murder.**

And the jurors aforesaid upon their oaths aforesaid do further present that **Jessie Evans** late of the County and territory aforesaid before the said Huston I. Chapman was killed and murdered as aforesaid in form as aforesaid to wit on the nineteenth [eighteenth] day of February in the year aforesaid at the County aforesaid **did feloniously and maliciously unlawfully and from a premeditated design to effect the death of him the said Huston I. Chapman, incite move procure and counsel, hire and command the said James J. Dolan and the said William Campbell the said felony, to wit the murder of the said Huston I. Chapman as aforesaid in manner and form aforesaid to do and commit against the form of the statute in such case made and provided against the peace and dignity of the Territory of New Mexico.**

W.L. Rynerson
District Attorney
3rd Jud Dist N.M.

GRANT COUNTY HERALD REPORTS

Billy Bonney's Grand Jury testimony was also confirmed in May 10, 1879's *Grant County Herald*, as reprinted from the *Las Cruces Thirty-Four*. It also reported that Rynerson kept Billy in custody. Noteworthy were the indictments of Peppin and Dudley, the many Ringites granted pardons using the Amnesty Proclamation, and Billy Bonney's early publicity. It stated:

At the recent term of court in Lincoln, about 200 indictments were found. Among them, Col. Dudley and George W. Peppin for burning McSween's house, **Dolan and Campbell for the Chapman murder, in which the Kid is the principal witness**; about 25 persons for the murder of MacNab; Tom O'Folliard for stealing Fritz's horses. But two criminal cases were tried - that of Lucas Gallagos for the murder of his nephew. He was found guilty and sentenced to one year; and a case of assault in which the accused was acquitted. No civil case was tried. In nearly all of them, one or the other party was dead. O'Folliard, Jack Long, Marion Turner, and others, plead the governors [Amnesty] pardon and were discharged. Peppin, Dolan and Matthews took a change of venue to Socorro, and Dudley took a change of venue to Dona Ana county. **The District Attorney would not consent to the release of the Kid for turning State's evidence. His case comes to Dona Ana county**. The greater portion of persons indicted will probably come forward and plead the governor's [Amnesty] pardon. Dolan and Matthews, indicted in the last term for the Tunstall murder, also go to Socorro on change of venue. Opinion is divided as to what the result will be. Some think a fresh outbreak is imminent, and others that the trouble is over. The two opposing factions have about exhausted themselves and future troubles will only arise from bands passing through and plundering. Jesse Evans and Campbell have not been rearrested.

VENUE CHANGE FOR BILLY BONNEY

No pardon followed from Lew Wallace after Billy Bonney fulfilled his pardon bargain by testifying. So the Ring implemented its preferred style of killing: under guise of law. Judge Bristol changed Billy's trial venue to Doña Ana County's Mesilla court to guarantee hanging - repeating the 1876 tactic of Governor S.B. Axtell's moving Colfax County courts to Taos County to shield Tolby's killers. Though indicted also, John Middleton and Henry Brown had long escaped from the Territory.

On April 21, 1879, District Attorney Rynerson filed the order. It was witnessed by Ringite Lincoln County War accomplices to murder: John Long and Marion Turner. Rynerson wrote:

Territory of New Mexico
District Court 3d Judicial
District County of Lincoln
April Term A.D. 1881

In the Third Judicial
District Court April Term / 1879

Territory of New Mexico)
vs)
) *Murder*
John Middleton & Henry Brown)
William Bonney alias Kid)
Alias William Antrim)

Now comes the said Territory by her attorney W.L. Rynerson District attorney of the said Third Judicial District and moves the Court for a change of venue from said County of Lincoln in above titled cause as to the said defendant William Bonney alias "Kid" alias William Antrim for reasons set forth in the affidavit following and annexed.

W.L. Rynerson
Dist. Atty –

Territory of New Mexico) SS.
County of Lincoln)

W.L. Rynerson District Attorney of the Third Judicial District of the said Territory of New Mexico being first duly sworn deposes and says that justice cannot be done the said Territory on the trial of the said defendant William Bonney alias Kid alias William Antrim in the said County of Lincoln for the reason that jurors in attendance and all those liable to be summoned for the trial of said defendant, by reason of partisanship in the late and existing troubles and lawlessness in said County have so prejudiced the said jurors that they cannot fairly and impartially try the said defendant; and for the further reason that said jurors and the witnesses in said cause are so intimidated by lawless men in said Lincoln County by fear of violence and

lawlessness against their persons and property on the part of said lawless men that the said jurors and witnesses cannot fearlessly and justly perform their respective duties at said trial in said Lincoln County.
                                        W.L. Rynerson
Sworn & subscribed before me in open court April 21, 1879.
                                        Louis H. Baldy, Clerk

Territory of New Mexico   )
County of Lincoln   )

Marion Turner and John Long being each duly sworn depose and say severally that they have heard the Foregoing affidavit read and know the contents thereof and that the matters and things as therein stated are true.
                                        John Long
                                        Marian Turner

ATTEMPTED ASSASSINATION OF IRA LEONARD

Ira Leonard had been uneasy about his safety, as the next obvious Ring victim after Huston Chapmen, writing to Wallace on April 12, 1879 about rough characters arriving in town: *"There are some suspicious circumstances as that require vigilance ... for the last two or three days there have straggled in here from four to six hard looking characters a day ...* **I have an idea that the object is to rescue their friends if brought here for trial.***"*

The next day, April 13th, Wallace's remaining Fort Stanton prisoners were freed on the *habeas corpus* writ.

So it was likely James Dolan, who, on April 25, 1879, tried to kill Ira Leonard; though he was never charged. That day, Leonard's legal assistant in Lincoln, George Taylor, informed Wallace of the crime; writing: *"Last night two of those outlawed scoundrels who are so numerous around here made a dash through town horseback and fired into our building. Judge Leonard had changed the place of his bed and they seemed to be aware of the fact for the bullets were directed where he lay, fortunately the side of the house was struck and no damage done but had they not been going so rapidly* **when they fired they may have accomplished** *their purpose which was evidently to kill or injure the Judge so he cannot prosecute them.*"

GRAND JURY INDICTMENTS AND PARDONS

The Grand Jurymen proved their ability to charge Ringites for Lincoln County War crimes, with N.A.M. Dudley, past Sheriff George Peppin, and James Dolan indicted. But none would ever be prosecuted. And Wallace himself would pardon the rest of those indicted. After those latest obstructions of justice, Lincolnites withdrew permanently into learned helplessness.

REPORT OF CAPTAIN GEORGE PURINGTON

Fort Stanton's Captain George Purington reported bitterly on May 3, 1879 to Headquarters, that the April, 1879 Lincoln County Grand Jury made "*two hundred indictments against one of the factions [Murphy-Dolans], and none against the other [McSweens].*" Purington singled out Billy Bonney: "*Doc. Scurlock and the "Kid," the two most notorious murderers of the County, have been in custody of the Sheriff at Lincoln. The Grand Jury did not indict them.*" He wrote:

Sir. –

The District Court adjourned on Thursday the 1st inst. **The Grand Jury returned nearly two hundred indictments against one of the factions [Murphy-Dolans], and none against the other [McSweens].** *Lieut. Col. N.A.M. Dudley, U.S.A., was indicted for arson. He appeared in Court and took a change of venue to Doña Ana County, to appear on the 16th of June. He was held on his own recognizance, in two thousand dollars (2000\underline{\underline{00}}$) to so appear.* **Most of the citizen prisoners who were indicted by the Grand Jury were arraigned and pleaded the Governor's pardon. The Court held that the Governor's proclamation was a general amnesty for all offences coming within its provisions.** *The prisoners were discharged.* **Doc. Scurlock and the "Kid," the two most notorious murderers of the County, have been in custody of the Sheriff at Lincoln. The Grand Jury did not indict them.** *The Sheriff [George Kimbrell] who is Deputy U.S. Marshal released them although he* *knew that there were indictments against them for murder in the U.S. Court [past U.S. Attorney T.B. Catron's federal indictment No. 411 done in 1878], and the warrants for their arrest said to be in his hands.*

[AUTHOR'S NOTE: Billy stayed in jail after Grand Jury testifying to testify against Dudley in the Fort Stanton Court of Inquiry. "Doc" Scurlock eventually left the Territory.]

Mr. Dolan, and Ex-Sheriff did not avail themselves of the Governor's proclamation. They changed their venue to Socorro County. Mr. Dolan is still in confinement at the Post. Mr. Peppin is under bonds ...

The Judge Advocate [Galusha Pennypacker] arrived on April 24th, '79 and Major Osborn and Captain Brinkerhoff [the two other Judges] of the [Dudley] Court [of Inquiry] arrived on the 1st instant.   I am, Sir,
Very respectfully
Your obedient servant,
Geo. C. Purington
Capt. 9th Cavalry

WALLACE PARDONS INDICTED RINGITES

Lew Wallace was unwilling to pardon Billy, but was quite willing to pardon Ringites in his ongoing campaign for his own future. So, on May 1, 1879, in the Grand Jury, T.B. Catron; his law partner, William Thornton; and Ringite Attorneys Sidney Wilson and Simon B. Newcomb (in 1881, one of Billy's prosecuting attorneys in his Mesilla hanging trial) brazenly filed pardon requests for their *indicted* Ringite clients to bar any future prosecution, by simply ignoring Wallace's Amnesty Proclamation's exclusionary clause. Colluding Judge Bristol granted the pardons. So Ringite Tunstall killers and Lincoln County War Battle murderers and arsonists - "*Jacob B. Matthews, William B. Powell, John Long and John Hurlie et al Defets*" - got no punishment.

Theoretically, Billy could have claimed that amnesty too; but neither he nor Attorney Ira Leonard seemed to realize that. And, of course, that scam worked only for Ringites.

For Wallace, permitting his Amnesty Proclamation to be misused was Ring placation. But he later hypocritically rationalized it in a June 11, 1879 letter to Carl Schurz, as avoiding future costly trials. (See pages 593-596 for letter)

WALLACE BLAMES "OUTLAWS"

Having gone through the mockery of the 1879 Lincoln County Grand Jury which yielded indictments without consequences, Ringite pardons, and Billy Bonney's pardon bargain betrayed, on May 5, 1879, Wallace informed Schurz that *"Lincoln county is enjoying a term of peace ... That it is due to the active measures taken against the outlaws the last month or two cannot be doubted."* He added: *"I leave this afternoon to be present as a witness in the Court appointed for Lt. Col. N.A.M. Dudley."*

By May 7, 1879, Wallace's communication to Carl Schurz from Lincoln was leaked - likely by him - to the *Chicago Times*; leading to his *Santa Fe Sentinel* interview quoted that day in the Denver *Daily Tribune*. Wallace made Lincoln County an epicenter of outlawry; its freedom fight concealed. Soon he would single out one outlaw for literary impact: "Billy the Kid." Wallace was quoted:

"The article represents me describing the Territory of New Mexico as overrun by a hoard of thieves, murderers and banditti ... The letter in question had relation to the situation in Lincoln county exclusively, and was in no wise applicable to any other portion of the Territory. It gives me great pleasure to say that outside of that one county life and property are as safe as in any State in this Union."

CHAPTER 21

BILLY BONNEY ALMOST BREAKS THE SANTA FE RING

THE RING'S LAST LIABILITY

SUMMARY: Still trusting Wallace's pardon bargain, and in his sham custody, Billy Bonney volunteered for the Dudley Court of Inquiry as eye-witness to soldiers shooting at civilians. For Wallace, that Court would reveal his incompetence, and yield his humiliated retreat. For the Ring, that Court would test its power, and would yield its ultimate target for assassination: Billy Bonney.

After his 1879 County Grand Jury testimony, Billy still trusted Lew Wallace. With his sham jailing as cover, he next volunteered to testify in the Court of Inquiry as eye-witness to Dudley's soldiers firing on him and other civilians in the Lincoln County War Battle. That proved his anti-Ring commitment, since it was unrelated to his pardon bargain.

But for Wallace, that military court would repeat Shiloh's humiliation, making him retreat even more from Lincoln County and from his pardon promise to Billy. And, for the Santa Fe Ring, that court would test its ability to maintain complete cover-up of its War crimes and total shielding of its criminals.

WALLACE'S PROGRESS REPORT

By the time Lew Wallace wrote, on April 4, 1879, to Secretary of the Interior Carl Schurz, he and Schurz knew about the March 4, 1879 charges filed by Attorney Ira Leonard and Susan McSween with Secretary of War George McCrary against past Fort Stanton Commander N.A.M. Dudley, which likely incorporated legal work of Huston Chapman before his murder. So Wallace cautiously updated Schurz by minimizing the upcoming military court as an *"unfortunate"* intrusion on his attention for the April Grand Jury to start in 10 days. In fact, he was doing little preparation for either unpleasant confrontation.

LEONARD PREPARES FOR THE COURT OF INQUIRY

Attorney Ira Leonard, unaware of Wallace's Ring cover-ups, had made his charges against N.A.M. Dudley implying the Ring's role in his Lincoln County War Battle intervention. (See pages 510-512 for full charges). He accused Dudley of taking troops to Lincoln to aid an outlaw posse to kill McSween and burn down his house around women and children, getting false arrest warrants against McSweens by threatening Justice of the Peace Wilson, enabling Tunstall's store's looting, obtaining defamatory affidavits against Susan McSween to devalue her as a witness, publishing an open letter to sabotage Wallace's peace-making attempts, and sending a squad to Lincoln to intimidate Susan McSween and Huston Chapmen. On Leonard's side was truth. Against him was that the Court of Inquiry was rigged for the Ring.

LEW WALLACE TESTIFIES

Lew Wallace was in a bind. His request for Dudley's removal from Fort Stanton's command, merely to quiet Lincolnites, had allied him to the Court of Inquiry's prosecution. That meant attacking not just an officer, but the Ring. And his compatriots would be mediocre military prosecutor, Recorder/Judge Advocate Captain Henry H. Humphreys, 15th Infantry at Fort Bliss; assisted by asthmatic and not brilliant Ira Leonard. On May 10, 1879, Wallace even tried unsuccessfully to make Humphreys keep his testimony secret. So Wallace's reprehensible solution was to testify covertly to benefit the defense - meaning the Ring.

WALLACE'S TERRIBLE TESTIMONY

Wallace was in a no win situation as a prosecution witness in his testimony from May 12th to May 15th, 1879. His indifference to issues would haunt him when it emerged that he had done no real fact-finding. And, by attempting to placate the Ring, he would be unable to accuse Dudley. He would look incompetent.

He began testifying on May 12th, the court's fourth day, before its judges, Colonel Galusha Pennypacker 16th Infantry (Dudley's best friend from Fort Union), Major Nathan W. Osborne

15th Infantry, and Captain Henry R. Brinkerhoff 15th Infantry. Also present were prosecutor, Henry Humphreys, with consulting counsel, Ira Leonard; Lieutenant Colonel N.A.M. Dudley, and his counsel, Henry Waldo, then considered the best trial lawyer in the Territory. And the biased judges sustained Waldo's obstructions and objections.

By the third question of the first day, with Humphreys trying to get Wallace to substantiate the charges, Waldo attacked:

Q. by Recorder. In this letter [to Hatch on March 7, 1879] you use the expression, "and yet [Dudley] is an active partisan." Please state to the Court on what facts you have made such an allegation.

Answer. I beg to call your attention to the language of the letter, which is as follows: "I would state in general terms, it is charged here (meaning in Lincoln), that he, Lieutenant Colonel Dudley, is responsible for the killing of McSween."

Objected to by Lieutenant Colonel Dudley, through Counsel [Waldo]. The witness is asked a pointed and direct question, and it is asked that he give a pointed and categorical answer ...

Court cleared and closed ...

Court opened ... Objection sustained.

Q. by Recorder. It is charged here in your letter "and yet is an active partisan." On what do you base such an allegation?

Answer. The charge is based upon the conclusion drawn from a number of official dispatches from Colonel Dudley, to the Commander of the District, Colonel Hatch: from reports of different sources of the relation between Colonel Dudley and others of the so called leaders, or influential and active men, of one of the parties disturbing the country: also upon certain acts of Colonel Dudley towards certain individuals, or supposed members of the so called party, or the party rather, known as the McSween party.

Objection was here made by Lieutenant Colonel Dudley to the answer of the witness ... upon the ground that this [Court] is an investigation of elicit facts, and not to collect the conclusions of the witness ... and move to strike the same from the record.

Wallace's vagueness, without real evidence, came from his lack of preparation and fear of antagonizing the Ring. Next came attack of his "perfectly satisfactory" remark to Hatch:

Q. by Recorder. What do you mean by "perfectly satisfactory" in the letter that you wrote in answer to [Hatch to] the letter of Colonel Dudley of November 9, 1878?...

A. The words "perfectly satisfactory" have reference to Colonel Dudley's letter of November 9th which I had interpreted as a denial of the charges contained in the letter of Mr. Chapman, which at my instance had been referred to Colonel Hatch for remarks.

Q. by Recorder. Had it any reference to the enclosure contained in that letter embracing the affidavits?

A. ... The enclosures were not within the meaning of the words "perfectly satisfactory" ... The affidavits or enclosures are alluded to elsewhere in my letter ... I did not mean to say that I was satisfied that Mrs. McSween was a woman of bad repute.

Waldo cross-examined on "perfectly satisfactory" on May 14th. And he exposed that Wallace had never even reviewed Dudley's record. Wallace's incompetence was emerging on record:

Q. by Lieut. Col. Dudley. In your letter of Nov. 16th 1878 you used the words "Your former letter upon the same subject with the several affidavits accompanying it were submitted to me, etc." Why did you allude to the affidavits at all, if you did not intend to include them under the terms "perfectly satisfactory" to you?

Answer. Partly to identify the letter, and that he might understand that I read both the letter and the affidavits ...

Q. by Lieut. Col. Dudley. You state in your examination in Chief, that the words "perfectly satisfactory" had reference to the reply of Colonel Dudley, what do you mean by the word reply?

Answer. I mean the letter of Colonel Dudley of the date Nov. 7th ...

Q. by Lieut. Col. Dudley. Is any reference then made to the affidavits?

Answer. Yes Sir. Her [Mrs. McSween's] character was not a point of consideration in the correspondence ...

Q. by Lieut. Col. Dudley. In gathering information upon which to base your Proclamation did you examine all the reports from Colonel Dudley which had been received at District Headquarters in October, in the Lincoln County matters?

Answer. I think I examined all of them ...

Q. by Lieut. Col. Dudley. State if you can, what others you have read, and in what month they were made?

Answer. I cannot recall now any particular reports ...

By his second day, May 13th, Wallace was attacking his side to benefit the Ring! When Humphreys sought evidence that Dudley blocked peace efforts by his "Open Letter," Wallace blamed Chapman! He claimed Chapman's anger at his refusal to give him Dudley's affidavits against Susan McSween made Chapman litigate against Dudley. The right answer was to accuse Dudley of getting false affidavits to shield his crimes. Instead, Wallace said that trouble-making Chapman was stirring up Lincoln locals:

Q. by Recorder. State what facts, if any, occurred growing out of the open letter of Colonel Dudley's that embarrassed your efforts to restore peace in Lincoln County, and in what manner they promoted the disturbances then rife in the county? ...
Answer. Shortly after publication of the open letter, I was awaited upon at my office in Santa Fe, by two gentlemen who demanded of me inspection of the affidavits referred to in the open letter. Being refused inspection of the letter and affidavits, one of them, Mr. Chapmen, returned to Lincoln, where at the house he resided, in a high state of indignation and wrath against Colonel Dudley, and the military, and about that time he commenced some criminal proceedings against Colonel Dudley.

Humphreys tried again to get Wallace's evidence for Dudley agitating Lincolnites, to segue into his July 19, 1878 war crimes. Instead, Wallace lied, saying that Mrs. McSween's friends' anger at Dudley's "Open Letter" caused Chapman's murder - instead of the correct response that the "Open Letter" was irrelevant, and Chapman was murdered to stop his litigating against Dudley:

Q. by Recorder. What effect had the open letter of Colonel Dudley's in re-opening the difficulties in Lincoln County, if any?
Answer. ... After the publication of the open letter the indignation of Mrs. McSween's friends proceeded to action against Colonel Dudley, and went on until the affair finally culminated in the murder of Mr. Chapman in the streets of the town of Lincoln.

On the third day of testimony, May 14th, Wallace was still covering for the Ring, blaming *"the McSween faction,"* and saying his Amnesty Proclamation was to protect Dudley from their prosecuting him in a partisan Grand Jury! And, despicably, he omitted Dudley's crimes which caused the citizens' outrage:

> *Q. by Recorder. State what facts came to your knowledge, concerning the acts of the military which led you to include them in the Proclamation of Pardon?*
>
> *Answer.* **It came to my knowledge, that it was the intention of certain parties living in Lincoln, who I had reason to believe were endeavoring to revive the McSween faction, intending commencement of prosecution of a criminal nature against Colonel Dudley.** *Mr. Chapman waited upon me in my office at Santa Fe, stated to me that he, amongst others intended such a course, for which purpose it was his design to resort to the Grand Jury of the next Court. I remonstrated against such a course, but without effect.* **I then resolved that such should not be done if I could help it, or at least could furnish Colonel Dudley with a plea in case of such prosecution, if he chose in the event of his indictment to plead it.** *I did not stop to consider whether Colonel Dudley was guilty or not guilty: in connection with the McSween killing affair. I foresaw if he were indicted, he would be put at great cost, vexation and harassment, I foresaw he might be confronted by a partisan jury.*

When Humphreys tried to get Wallace to give proofs about the charges, after long digression, and giving no evidence, lawyer Wallace called them hearsay - meaning legally useless:

> *Q. by Recorder. State all that you know concerning the charges you made against Colonel Dudley in your letter to General Hatch, of March 7, 1879, asking his removal as Commandant of Fort Stanton?*
>
> *Answer.* **... It was not then pretended that the charges were anything more than hearsay accusations.**

By May 15th, Wallace's fifth and last day of testimony, Waldo must have realized that Wallace would betray his own side; so he used Wallace's lie that Dudley's "Open Letter" made Susan McSween's trouble-making friends cause Chapman's murder. It worked! When pressured, Wallace betrayed her case by claiming there was no real evidence against Dudley:

> *Q. by Lieut. Col. Dudley. You say after the publication of the open letter, the indignation of Mrs. McSween's friends proceeded to action against Colonel Dudley, and went on until the affair was culminated in the murder of Mr. Chapman in the streets of*

Lincoln. Now state to your knowledge, any instance of violence, or exhibition of agitation, or excitement occurring after the publication of the open letter.
Answer. My knowledge on that subject is derived solely upon information received from others [i.e. meaningless hearsay].

Since lack of evidence was Waldo's defense for Dudley, he used Wallace's as tacitly complicit. So under cross-examination, Wallace concealed having affidavits from "Squire Wilson, Isaac Ellis, and Sam Corbet. And having said citizens were in "dread" of Dudley, he gave no reasons - like Dudley's violating the Posse Comitatus Act to enter Lincoln and enable arson and murder:

Q. by Lieut. Col. Dudley. In your examination in chief you state you made an investigation as to the situation of affairs in Lincoln County, and as a consequence thereof, reached the conclusion that a considerable portion of the people were suffering from intimidation caused by dread they had of Colonel Dudley. How long were you in the making of that investigation, and what was its extent and nature?

Answer. I arrived in Lincoln, the afternoon as I recollect now, of March 5th last. Immediately I commenced informing myself of the state of affairs ... but they all declined, giving as a reason that it would endanger their lives. I argued with them there was now no room for fear, because ... they had the protection of the military. Their reply was in substance, they had no confidence in the military, because they believed the Commandant of the Fort, Colonel Dudley, was the friend of the alleged murderers, who he would assist rather than them, the citizens. **I found no one willing at that time to make the affidavits.**

And Waldo exposed Wallace's lack of diligent investigation:

Q. by Lieut. Col. Dudley. Did you call upon Colonel Dudley for any explanation of the charges contained in the letter of request for his removal, before writing such letter March 7th?
Answer. I did not.

Sly Waldo then linked the prosecution charges to Wallace's claim that they were hearsay, and that he had no sworn affidavits, little recall of informers' names, and had avoided Lincoln County -

all meaning that his action against Dudley had no substance. And Wallace did not try to vindicate himself, because he was unwilling to give information incriminating the Ring:

Q. by Lieut. Col. Dudley. You say that you contained in your letter of request of March 7th to the District Commander, a statement of the charges, **which you say were upon hearsay,** *in order from this statement he might form a proper judgment of the proper course to pursue. Was this your intent?*
Answer. It was.

For a re-direct, poor Prosecutor Humphreys tried to save this miserable testimony by asking about whether he had put Lincolnites' complaints in writing. So Wallace lied:

Q. by Recorder. Explain what you mean by not being able to answer yes or no to the question whether they were sworn to.
Answer. ... **I never reduced any of their statements to writing, or had them sworn to. These statements were given to me verbally and not in writing in any form.**

LEONARD EXPOSES THE RING TO WALLACE

Despite Lew Wallace's weak testimony, Ira Leonard sent him two encouraging letters about the Court's progress after Wallace had returned to Santa Fe. It was then just 26 days after Leonard's own near assassination. His letter of May 20th was enclosed in one of the 23rd. He crowed on the 23rd: *"I tell you we are pouring "hot shot" into Dudley so fiercely that his face for the last three days has strikingly resembled the wattles of an enraged turkey gobbler ... He is the most unmitigated old scoundrel that ever had an existence."* Leonard also exposed their real adversary - the Santa Fe Ring - unaware that Wallace well knew about it. But a faint note of doubt was creeping in. On the 23rd, Leonard also wrote: *"If when we get through with D here if his record is not black I shall be mistaken - but I believe the Court will stretch their powers a good ways to sustain him."* [Note also the debilitation of Leonard's asthma.] Leonard wrote:

Lincoln May 23rd 1879

Dear Governor

I write to you with pencil because I am laboring for breath and it is less labor than with a pen. We have been dragging along seven and eight hours a day in the Court ever since you left and **I tell you we are pouring "hot shot" into Dudley so fiercely that his face for the last three days has strikingly resembled the wattles of an enraged turkey gobbler.** *Today a little episode occurred in Court. Mrs. McSween was on the stand and old Dudley accused me of conveying to her by a shake of my head the answer she should make. I did not do it or think of it and in fact was not looking at her at all and I resented it as an insult and pitched into him and the Court read the riot act in the Articles of War for our mutual benefit.* **He is the most unmitigated old scoundrel that ever had an existence.** *The Court have taken a short turn on us and will not let us give any evidence except that which bears upon the charges ...*

[AUTHOR'S NOTE: Leonard still seems unaware of Court bias.]

If when we get through with D here if his record is not black I shall be mistaken – but I believe the Court will stretch their powers a good ways to sustain him ...

I will write you further Governor in a day or two and give you minutely the proceedings here ...

Let me hear from you and remember me kindly to Mrs. Wallace

Yours truly

Ira E. Leonard

[ENCLOSED LETTER: ABOUT THE RING]:

The enclosed letter of May 20, 1879, presenting to Wallace "*our secrets*" - as referred to in the cover letter - raises the question of whether Wallace, anticipating victory, had offered to replace "*Civil*" and "*Military*" officials connected to the "*Santa Fe Ring*." Also, it may have been intended by Leonard and Wallace for President Hayes, because it appears staged, since Wallace's testimony is not mentioned, and he would have known some of the information being "*provided.*"

Importantly, Leonard left no doubt about the Ring's existence. As to Murphy and Dolan he stated: "**They were a part and parcel of the Santa Fe Ring that has been so long an incubus on the government of this Territory.**" He wrote:

Lincoln, New Mexico
May 20, 1878 [1879]

Governor Lew Wallace
Santa Fe, N.M.

Dear Governor,
When you left here *I promised to write you concerning events transpiring here and I do so.* **as you will remember when I came here from Las Vegas about the 1st of April last with the intention of remaining if I considered it safe to do so, I had a conference with you, and you stated to me the situation in which you were placed in coming into this distracted county where lawlessness and disorder was the rule instead of the exception, you stated to me also that you had no one with whom to advise, and had no authority to employ counsel but desired me to assist in prosecuting, and bringing to justice the outlaws then under arrest [Chapman's murders and Seven Rivers rustlers] and who might be arrested. I promised to give you my best endeavors in that direction whether I was ever compensated for it or not.** *what I did while you were here you know, and of my earned endeavors to aid in that direction you are fully cognizant ... You know that the first few days proceedings were at Fort Stanton before the convening of the Court.* **Some fifteen or more writs of Habeas Corpus were issued by Judge Bristol upon the application of prisoners confined at the Fort prison for safe keeping, and you are fully aware of the flimsy technicalities upon which many of the desperate men were released** *... Now as to what succeeded after you left this County which I believe was on the day that Court convened for business, the first three or four days being occupied in procuring a Jury, one term having lapsed, it required the selecting and summoning a new panel of Jurors, and this County being so large, it took several days to procure them. The Grand Jury so far as I was able to judge of the men was composed of as good and intelligent men as any county would average and it was the same with the Petit jury. The Grand Jury went earnestly to work but labored under great difficulty in procuring witnesses, there had been no term of Court here for a year, and within that time, murders of the most atrocious character had been perpetrated by the score, and crimes of nearly all grades known to the criminal code had been of frequent occurrence. Officers were sent in every direction for witnesses ... When you consider that the County of Lincoln is as large*

as the states of New Hampshire, Vermont, Massachusetts, Connecticut, and New Jersey together, you can readily appreciate the difficulty in collecting from this large area, witnesses to appear before a Grand Jury and testify as to crimes committed in the various portions of it, and when you consider also that the Judge [Bristol] was ... was constantly hurrying the Grand Jury to expedite their business ... although they found a large number of indictments during their labors ...

Now Governor, I want to state to you the conduct of the District Attorney which I consider contemptible ... He was to my own knowledge in secret and open conference with Dolan the murderer of Chapman, and intends to defend him at Socorro, the place to which the venue is changed, it being out of his District and he connived to procure the change of venue from the District for that purpose.

[AUTHOR'S NOTE: This Dolan indictment for Chapman's murder was the achievement of Billy's testimony and the fulfilling of his pardon bargain with Wallace.]

He aroused among the friends of the outlaws [Ringites] here a feeing of antagonism against me that resulted in their posting a notice on a tree to which I had my horse hitched addressed to me, informing me that if I did not leave this country "they would take my scalp and send me to hell."

[AUTHOR'S NOTE: The assassination attempt on Leonard was on April 25, 1879 in Lincoln, as described next.]

A few nights after this notice was posted on the tree two desperados came riding by my office on a full run with their horses, and fired two shots arriving at the window and the bullets striking near it. Mr. Taylor a civil engineer who came down to this country with me and I believe a cousin of President Hayes, was rooming with me at the time, and you may be sure we were both ready for a fight in short order, and this is not all. McPherson the man I brought down with me, and who was taking care of my horses, was out looking for them in the foot hills of the Capitan Mts. And some unknown party fired on him, the ball entering his hat rim and grazing his forehead leaving the mark distinctly visible on his head for several days, their peculiar hostility to him grows out of the fact that the Sheriff of the county [Kimbrell] deputized him during the late term of the Court to serve process, and he in the exercise of his duties arrested quite a number of the outlaws. This is the condition of affairs here now.

[AUTHOR'S NOTE: Leonard is making clear that the "outlaws" attacking and frightening people are Ringites – who were arrested and indicted - and not Wallace's vague outlaw myth.]

Since the Court of Inquiry convened at Fort Stanton to inquire into the conduct of Lieut. Col. N.A.M. Dudley and his connection with civil matters in this County which Court is now in its thirteenth days session, **the most violent threats are made by the desperate men whom I am sorry to say for the honor of that branch of the public service have found a staunch friend in Col. Dudley. The evidence so far in his case discloses the most inexcusable conduct on the part of a Military Officer.** *I have been a constant attendant upon that Court assisting the Judge Advocate in the prosecution since it convened and if Col. Dudley can justify his conduct towards the people in this distracted district I shall be greatly astonished,* **without the slightest warrant of authority he went to Lincoln, and gave substantial aid and assistance to an armed band of outlaws who under pretence of executing writs against the McSween party, made their visit to his knowledge, one of theft, arson, and murder, and if justice is properly meted out to him, he will be dismissed [from] the service of his country in disgrace.**

From what I have seen of affairs in this County I am forced the following conclusions: that all of your efforts to restore peace here, and give security to the peaceable and law abiding citizens under the present existing status of affairs will prove unavailing, unless you are supported by the government in having effected a radical change of the administration of the civil and military authorities.

[AUTHOR'S NOTE: Leonard argues need to replace Ringites in power to get peace. If Dudley had been found guilty, Wallace might have even intervened. But Leonard is inadvertently calling Wallace's bluff about the outlaw myth solution. Next Leonard presents true Lincoln County War issues.]

My reasons for these conclusions are first as to the civil authorities. **Judge Warren Bristol at the April Term of the Court in 1878 made himself very obnoxious to the party known as the McSween party in his charge to the Grand Jury, when he instructed them as he did to find an indictment against A.A. McSween on the charge of** *embezzlement. McSween it seems had been brought before Judge Bristol upon that charge and the Judge had acted in the manner as an examining Magistrate to inquire into the charge made against McSween for embezzling some money he had collected on a Life Insurance Policy. It was very wrong in Judge Bristol, whatever his private conversations might have been to so instruct the Grand Jury, it was wrong for him to particularize this case, or give any directions to that body in his charge to them, in doing so he arrayed himself not only against the man charged with the offence, who had no opportunity to defend himself but he made himself the champion of the faction, that were pursuing McSween, and in my judgment Judge Bristol's action on that occasion was the immediate cause of all the great misfortunes and fatal results that have followed in this County. The Grand Jury did investigate the charge and honorably acquitted McSween and in a report made to the Court characterize the proceedings against McSween as being a persecution,*

[AUTHOR'S NOTE: Leonard, without knowing, is repeating Mary McPherson's complaint on Bristol – which Wallace owned.]

and it came from a Grand Jury too that had been selected by the officer and Sheriff [George Peppin] who has been so notorious in the difficulties in this County. **The result of Judge Bristol's conduct on this occasion caused the organization of the factions that are currently known here as the Dolan Murphy or Sheriffs party, and the McSween party, which has resulted in the killing of upwards of eighty persons in this County in a little over a years time, and created difficulties that will require many years to overcome,** *the results of that action also is not alone confined to the killing of so many persons but has had the further result in causing these desperate men to organize for plunder and theft ...*

[AUTHOR'S NOTE: Leonard identifies Ring-side outlaws, and gives one of the few body counts on the Lincoln County War - "*upwards of eighty persons.***" Billy later said 200.]**

I know that your own judgment about who are the peaceable and law abiding citizens of this County and that your views will correspond with my own from the long time you spent here in earnest inquiry into the difficulties and your endeavors to get at the truth and learn the exact situation, and you found as I have done that nearly all the men who belonged to and were sympathizers of the McSween party are the substantial peaceable and law abiding citizens of this County. And you found also that the Dolan Murphy party were determined to drive these men out of the Country because they had come into it to engage in business and were as that party imagined in their way securing government contracts and plunder. That party had for a long time uninterrupted sway in this County and could not brook opposition and they were determined either by fair or foul means to have no opposition and they resorted to every artifice in their power to accomplish that purpose. They were a part and parcel of the Santa Fe Ring that has been so long an incubus on the government of this Territory ...

[AUTHOR'S NOTE: This equation of the Murphy-Dolan party to the Santa Fe Ring is what Wallace knew and concealed in his Court of Inquiry testimony and in his outlaw myth.]

If the Court had sustained you as it ought to have done in your efforts to bring to justice those gross violators of the law and you had found hearty co-operation in the Military in your attempt to arrest and punish these bad and desperate men I am sure the future would have been less prolific in crime than it has been in the past, and there would have been much less than the future promises ...

[AUTHOR'S NOTE: Leonard is accidently hitting a painful point: Wallace failed to achieve a true solution. His outlaw myth did not convince honorable Leonard. And Leonard also suggested removal of Bristol, unaware that he had already been shielded by the Hayes administration from Mary McPherson's complaint the year before.]

In addition to a change in the Judiciary there is another change equally important to be made in the affairs of this section, before peace and good order can be restored and that is the Military. You saw while you were here what had been the conduct in the Military management at Fort Stanton, that since Col. N.A.M. Dudley has been in command at this Post the very worst characters in the country have been harbored and sustained about this Post and he has given aid to them in carrying out and furthering their wicked designs upon the innocent people of this County. **He became a very strong and active partizan in the struggles between the factions here, lending military aid** *when McSween and four others were killed his presence in Lincoln Plaza at that time with fifty or sixty soldiers without right or authority and the direct aid he rendered on that occasion to the outlaws resulted in the killing of these parties on that occasion, and the proof already elicited in the Court of Inquiry clearly shows his wicked and unwarranted action on that occasion. I say wicked because his action was most wicked and vile and if such conduct can be sustained by the authorities, every citizen has a right to fear, instead of to honor and respect the Military power of the Government. The proof shows that he went to Lincoln Plaza and by his intimidations and threats with his soldiers and guns, gave such aid to the band of outlaws that they killed McSween and four others on that day, and so put the people in fear that to this day they feel that the Military here are their enemies and the friends and supporters of the outlaws.* The action of Col Dudley has more or less implicated every officer at Fort Stanton save one Capt Carroll, and from their association and connection with the action of Col Dudley, there is no safety until there is an entire change at the Post. **No officer who has been here and been mixed up with the affairs and disturbances that have been rife here for the last two years ought to remain ...**

[AUTHOR'S NOTE: Leonard wants Wallace to remove officers implicated in Lincoln County War, unaware that Wallace was refusing to confront the Ring.]

[T]here may be occasions and I think this instance is one of them, where to remove the causes of such grave difficulties and disasters as have fallen on these people [in Lincoln] a change is absolutely necessary to a complete restoration of peace and good order.

I have endeavored Governor to give you a fair and unbiased statement of affairs here and what to my mind are the essentials to a return of peace and good order ...

I shall fulfill my promises to you [to aid prosecution] while I remain in the County and do all in my power to bring to punishment the outlaws but with little hope of good results under the present management in Civil and Military authority.

[AUTHOR'S NOTE: This is Leonard's polite denial of Wallace's dishonest outlaw myth solution]

> I am truly yours
> Ira E. Leonard

SUSAN McSWEEN TESTIFIES

Susan McSween's seeking justice was superhumanly brave in light of murders of John Tunstall, her husband, and Huston Chapman; arson of her home; and death threats and defamatory affidavits by N.A.M. Dudley. And Governor Wallace had given her no support. Her three day, star witness testimony - on May 23rd, 24th, and May 26th, starting on the Court's 14th day, was marred by incompetence of Prosecutor Henry Humphreys and Ira Leonard, who inadequately sought her evidence. But in a fair Court, her testimony would have been adequate to prove that Dudley's partisan aid to Peppin's side caused retreat of McSween's men, arson of her house, murder of civilians, and risked women and children - all Posse Comitatus Act violations. Her transcript, echoing terrified Colfax County's Ring victim, Ada Morley, in her March 7, 1877 letter to her mother (see pages 272-274), follows:

[On Friday, May 23, 1879] Mrs. Sue E. McSween, a witness being duly sworn, testified as follows.

   Q. by Recorder. State your name and place of residence?
   Answer. Mrs. Sue E. McSween, Lincoln, Lincoln County, New Mexico.
   Q. by Recorder. State whether you are the widow of A.A. McSween, deceased, who was killed at Lincoln on the 19th day of July last, if so state all about the circumstances of his being killed, and Col. Dudley's connection therewith, if any?

[AUTHOR'S NOTE: This is incompetent questioning, forcing her to structure too much information. Multiple questions should have been asked to help her organize facts.]

   Answer. Yes Sir, I am sure on the day that he was killed. That morning, about 10 o'clock, Col. Dudley came into Lincoln with about 40 or 50 soldiers ... Well, on his way he stopped at a place known as the hotel [Wortley] occupied by a band of men comprised, or known, as the sheriff's posse, or who called themselves the sheriff's posse. He stopped there about 5 or 10 minutes as near as I could tell, then passed on by our place and camped in what is the middle of town. A few minutes afterwards I saw three soldiers going up to the hotel. I went out to ask the soldiers why they were in town and why they had come here and what their intentions were.

Lt. Col. Dudley, by his Counsel, objects with witness stating any conversation or giving any statements made by the soldiers ... unless it was ... in the presence ...of Col. Dudley.
Recorder replied. The testimony is competent for the reason that the evidence already elicited has shown the soldiers escorted Peppin to Col. Dudley's camp ... [A]nything the soldiers may have said concerning Col. Dudley's purpose is competent as they are supposed to be carrying out the orders of their superior officer, Col. Dudley, and whatever they told of those intentions is competent. Objection is sustained.

[AUTHOR'S NOTE: Bias is obvious. Recorder Humphrey's argument is correct. Yet the objection is sustained to block her from giving evidence that the soldiers were used in a partisan manner - which caused defeat of then winning McSweens.]

(Witness resuming.) Now in a few minutes afterwards I saw the same three soldiers going back with Peppin. Now after seeing this we all became alarmed, who were in the house, seeing Peppin guarded by the soldiers. Then Mr. McSween wrote a note and sent it by a little girl [her sister's daughter] asking Col. Dudley ... well, I am afraid I am ahead of my story. Before sending this note we saw three soldiers ... standing back of our house and on the same side we saw these men of Mr. Peppins coming behind the house, some of them coming down the road after the soldiers, and broke into the house opposite ours, immediately afterwards they hung out the black flag [meaning no surrender, death]. After we had seen this Mr. McSween wrote the note.

[AUTHOR'S NOTE: This shows her problem organizing information; a fault of inadequate questioning. But she does describe soldiers guarding Peppin, occupying her property, and enabling his men to take offensive positions. She also describes her husband's letter questioning Dudley's intervention.]

Now, in a few minutes afterwards the little girl returned with the answer from Col. Dudley ... He says before "blowing up my house, I wish to know ..." [Dudley's Gatling gun and howitzer cannon panicked McSween, who clumsily wrote that before blowing up his house, he wanted to know why Dudley was in town. So with Ringite insolence, Dudley taunted his grammar by saying if he wanted to blow up his house he could.] The substance of the letter was to find out ... whether he intended to assist Peppin and his men ... Now before this letter was written Col. Dudley sent us word *that if a shot was fired from our house at his soldiers, or near them, that he would turn his cannon loose ... and tear the house to the ground, regardless of the inmates ... I then said to Mr. McSween that I believe that I would go down to his camp and talk with him myself ... I then started with Mr. McSween's consent on my way to his camp .... At the time I saw three of Murphy's men ... I then asked what they were doing,* **they said ... [t]hat Peppin and Col. Dudley had sent them to carry lumber to our house to set it on fire** ... *I then begged them not to do so ... I then started again for Col. Dudley's camp and met Mr. Peppin ... He then said that if I did not want my house burned down I must make those men who were in the house get out of it, that he was bound to have these men ... dead or alive ... I then started again for Col. Dudley's camp. Arriving there I told him ... that these men and Mr. Peppin intend to burn down the house, and to ask him if he would give me some protection and save our house from being burned. He said he ... did not intend to have anything to do with either party ... I then said it looked strange to me to see his men, or his soldiers I should say, guarding Peppin back and forth through town and sending soldiers around our house ... if he had nothing to do with it.* **He then got very angry and said it was none of my business, that he would send his soldiers where he pleased, that I have no such business to have such men as Billy the Kid, Jim French, and others of like character in my house. He then ... said that he had come to protect women and children. I then asked why he did not protect myself, my sister, and her children.** *He said I have no business, or we had no business, to be in that house, that he would not give us protection, and if a shot was fired from our house at any of his soldiers ... he would turn his cannon loose and tear the house to the ground regardless of women and children ...*

[AUTHOR'S NOTE: Though rambling, she confirms Dudley's partisanship and not protecting women and children. Note that by May 23, 1879, Billy is Ring-labeled as "Billy the Kid."]

I then said they were trying to kill McSween with the protection of having a warrant and we were sure they had none. He then said they had ... a U.S. warrant for him and we will have him. I then told him I did not see for what reason they could procure a U.S. warrant for him unless it was done falsely ... Col. Dudley then said that he was guilty of such crime and that his men had fired at his soldiers the evening before. I told him he must be mistaken ...

[AUTHOR'S NOTE: These warrants were for the July 16th Private Berry Robinson shooting, coerced by Dudley from Justice of the Peace Wilson after learning the Easton warrants were invalid.]

He then made sport of me being Mrs. McSween as though it was degrading to be called Mrs. McSween. I then told him I was proud to be his wife, that I know him to be a man of principle and far better principle than those men he was escorting.

Lt. Col. Dudley, by his Counsel [Henry Waldo], called the attention of the Court to the character of the testimony and suggests that he is unable to see even its relevancy and that it is occupying the time of the Court to no purpose..

Recorder made the following reply. The testimony is a narrative of the conduct of Col. Dudley on that occasion, and is material ... as to Col. Dudley's conduct on that occasion ...

[The Judges closed the court for discussion; then re-opened it.] The Court directs the Recorder to confine witness to more direct answers to his questions.

[AUTHOR'S NOTE: Waldo is outrageously objecting to her giving evidence. Ominously, the Court supports his objection.]

(Witness resuming.) I told him he was assisting men who I believed he knew to be known thieves and murderers, who have broken out of jail and [were] known by everybody [as a posse of Seven Rivers and John Kinney men]. I asked him why he could not understand these troubles and assist such men if he intended to do what was right. He then got very angry with me, used abusive language towards me and those with my husband. He said I was not a woman of good character.

[Waldo here repeats his objection of irrelevancy; and Humphreys and Leonard do not even counter that lie.]

Q. by Recorder. State what Col. Dudley said to you and how he treated you on the occasion ...

Answer. He treated me in a very abusive manner, then made slurs against my character. He said he wanted nothing to do with me or our party, **that we were the party of outlaws** *...*

[AUTHOR'S NOTE: Humphreys here missed the chance to address that the affidavits were untrue, that the McSween party were not outlaws, and that Dudley's arrest warrants were invalid since they were obtained by threatening Wilson.]

Q. by Recorder. State what conversation passed between you and Col. Dudley in reference to the letter you have said Mr. McSween had written ...

Answer. ... I asked him why he threatened to blow up our house. He said because McSween and others were in it and he was a man of no principle ... [She requested to see the letter to explain that McSween was afraid they would blow up their house, but Dudley told a soldier present, "I'll thank you to shoot this lady if she takes this letter."] He ... kept on abusing me and using language against me that was inappropriate and unbecoming of his kind. **He said he could not help such a man as McSween or I either, that he was trying to make all the disturbance in the county. I told him that he was not, that he was trying to be right by all good citizens, the other party was committing the crimes, and that they have commenced it. This all came ... because he was in opposition to them in business, that they had threatened his life for two years, and that then some were now publicly saying, or telling, everybody that they would kill McSween ... I said to Col. Dudley that I knew that if they ever caught sight of him they would kill him, and then asked if he would not protect him, send some of his soldiers to the house to rescue him, that I knew if he would do this McSween would give himself up willingly.**

[AUTHOR'S NOTE: Though Humphreys failed to add focus, she dramatically proved Dudley as a murderous partisan.]

Q. by Recorder. State what Col. Dudley replied to you?

Answer. He refused to send them and ordered me out of camp ...

Q. by Recorder. What did you see going on about your house by the parties who were outside when you got back, if anything?

Answer. **I saw three soldiers standing near the house, on the west side, and some of these Murphy men standing close up to the wall by the house ... I saw one man ... pouring coal oil on the floor of my sister's house [one of the two wings of her house] ... Jack Long threw something that popped ... it set the coal oil on fire. They then began to shoot into every door and window on that side of the house. I remained with Mr. McSween until 5 o'clock that afternoon.**

[AUTHOR'S NOTE: This arson risked the women and children.]

Q. by Recorder. Did you go to Col. Dudley's camp [again]?

Answer. I did not go to his camp, but went to a house near there, where I remained all night. During the evening I saw Col. Dudley and several other officers with an opera glass.

[AUTHOR'S NOTE: She was in the vacated house of their tenant, Saturnino Baca, east of Tunstall's store. Dudley was camped farther east. She was risking her life to collect evidence, while the attempted escape and murders took place at her house.]

Q. by Recorder. What did you see, if anything, of Col. Dudley's actions on that day with his troops?

Answer. ... I saw him ordering the soldiers to turn the cannon to a certain direction when ever he saw a man appear on the other side of the river ...

[AUTHOR'S NOTE: This is Dudley's obstructing return of fled McSweens. But Humphreys has not clarified by questioning either how Dudley caused their flight or blocked their returns.]

Q. by Recorder. What time of day was your husband and the others killed on that day?

Answer. About dark ...

On Saturday, May 24, 1879, she continued her testimony:

Q. by Recorder ... State whether you saw any parties taking goods from [Tunstall's store], if so who they were, on the day after the fight when Col. Dudley was in town, what you saw of their actions?

Answer. I was not in the store until the second day after Mr. McSween was killed, but I saw some of Peppins men in Col. Dudley's camp, dressed with old clothing in the morning, and then I saw them again with suits of new clothing that I recognized as clothing from the store ...

CROSS EXAMINATION.

Q. by Col. Dudley. How did you recognize that clothing as coming from the Tunstall store?

Answer. By the color .. I had seen the clothing many times before and handled them. I could say that I recognized them by the style of the check.

Q. by Col. Dudley. Was that style of check contained only in the Tunstall store and not in any other store in the town of Lincoln?

Answer. I don't know but I know at the time these men were taking goods.

Lt. Col. Dudley, by his Counsel [Henry Waldo], moves the Court to instruct the witness to confine her answers so as to be expressive of the questions propounded to her. If she desires to make explanations, this is not the time to make them ...

[AUTHOR'S NOTE: Waldo is now purposefully harassing to confuse her, here to conceal Dudley's enabling of looting. Since Humphreys did not object, Waldo then proceeded viciously.]

Q. by Col. Dudley. What was the first thing you said to Col. Dudley, or Col. Dudley to you, on that day on the occasion of the conversation [in his camp]?

Answer. I told him I had come there to see if he would not protect us. That we were having trouble with the Murphy party ...

Q. by Col. Dudley. In that conversation, I understood you to say you wanted him, Col. Dudley, to protect your house from the Murphy men. Did he not say to you in that conversation that he could not interfere with actions of the sheriff?

Answer. I don't remember him telling me.

Q. by Col. Dudley. Did he not give as a reason for not interfering in regard to your house that the men within are the men for whom the sheriff had warrants he was trying to serve and that he would not interfere with the sheriff nor take any part in the contest going on between the parties in any way whatsoever, or words to that effect?

Answer. He refused to give protection, he refused to give protection and said ... [She is here cut off by Waldo before she can complete her answer; and Humphreys does not object.]

Lt. Col. Dudley, by his Counsel, moves the Court to instruct the witness to answer the question in the manner which the form of the question calls for [and he wanted her to answer just yes or no].

[AUTHOR'S NOTE: Waldo is trying to put words in her mouth to make Dudley seem a non-participant. And his harassment is flustering her; though her answer was correct.]

Recorder made the following objection. The witness has the right to answer the question by stating just what Col. Dudley did say and not answer yes or no to the question. The Court can then determine the facts from the whole of the conversation ...

The Court [Judge Galusha Pennypacker] instructs the witness to answer yes or no.

[AUTHOR'S NOTE: Biased Pennypacker backs Waldo's abuse, and blocks her giving evidence to just saying "yes or no."]

Answer. I cannot answer that question yes or no intelligibly. A part of the conversation would infer that he would not assist us and a part of the conversation would infer that he was really helping them.

[AUTHOR'S NOTE: On her own without a competent prosecutor, she gives makes a come-back, refusing manipulation. It was with good reason that Frank Warner Angel called her "a tiger." But Waldo's badgering continued until he exhausted her, and her answers eventually became addled, as seen below. And Humphreys and Ira Leonard never protected or encouraged her by objecting properly or by correctly eliciting her evidence.]

Q. by Col. Dudley. Do you swear that Col. Dudley ever, at anytime, refused to furnish you protection?

Answer. He refused me on that day ... no, I do not remember that he had, for I never asked for it ...

[AUTHOR'S NOTE: All Humphreys needed to do was to ask for her earlier testimony to be read if she needed help to recall.]

Q. by Col. Dudley. Now Mrs. McSween, is not your feelings towards Col. Dudley quite bitter and harsh?

Answer. They are not.

Q. by Col. Dudley. Have you not been quite active in collecting testimony for the purpose of this investigation?

Answer. I have, but a great deal more has been told to me, most certainly more than I asked for.

Q. by Col. Dudley. Have you not said that you intended to have him indicted in the Territorial Courts for what you have said was his connection with the killing of your husband and burning of your house on the 19th of July last?

Answer. I did not, but I said I would await the action of the Grand Jury for the burning of my house and the killing of Mr. McSween, if the government would not do their duty before that time ...

Q. by Col. Dudley. You were a witness, were you not, before the last Grand Jury and gave testimony against him, did you not?

Answer. Yes Sir.

Q. by Col. Dudley. Have you not said, or did you say soon after the killing of your husband and the burning of your house, that you would spend thousands of dollars, or words to that effect, to have the shoulder straps stripped from him?

Answer. No Sir. I never used such language. But I have said I would try to bring him to justice.

Lt. Col. Dudley, by his Counsel, states he is finished with the witness.

REDIRECT

Q. by Recorder. Explain how you happened to be familiar with the clothing in the Tunstall store. How you happened to handle the clothing, and know that what you saw these men have on came from the store?

Answer. I was there when the goods were opened. I helped to mark them and was there daily, seen them handled by the clerks frequently and looked through them myself many times ...

[AUTHOR'S NOTE: Humphreys should then have asked if that was why she was sure of the looting the next day, but did not.]

Q. by Recorder. Explain how long it was, as near as you can remember, from the time Col. Dudley went into camp at Lincoln on that day, up to the time the house was set on fire?

Objected to by Lieut. Col. Dudley, by his Counsel.
Recorder withdrew the question ...
Recorder stated that he had finished with the witness.

[AUTHOR'S NOTE: Outrageously, Humphreys did not redirect questioning to get her evidence into the record. That let the Court (the three Judges) ask their own biased questions to shield Dudley's guilt.]

Q. by Court [one of the Judges]. Did Col. Dudley or any of his officers or soldiers commit any act which caused your house to be set on fire, if and what?

Answer. Nothing more than those three soldiers standing by the house and guarding Peppin which I suppose was done for the purpose of intimidating those who were in the house.

Q. by Court. Did you see Col. Dudley or any of his soldiers enter the store belonging to the estate of John Tunstall on the 20th day of July last, while the same was being robbed and plundered?

Answer. I cannot say ...

Q. by Court. What was said or done by Col. Dudley on the occasions of the firing of your house that was **most inhuman and unbecoming a soldier and officer,** *at any time during the day?*

Answer. His expression I cannot remember. He appeared to be very much angered and said many unkind things about Mr. McSween, said he was a mean man, and the parties with him were bad men, that I have no right to expect protection if I upheld such parties, that I was not a woman of good character. He ordered me out of the camp and ordered a soldier to shoot me if I took a letter from his hand. There was nothing done except his manner appeared very hostile.

[AUTHOR'S NOTE: She is so confused after Waldo's day of verbal assault, that she fails to state how Dudley's behavior was "*most inhuman and unbecoming a soldier and officer*": omitting his maligning her to her face, refusing her aid, and assisting Peppin to kill her husband and burn down her house around women and children - all things she had said earlier.]

Witness retired but will remain in Court.

The Court directed the Recorder to read the following.

[In Susan's hearing, the Court refused to hear the Prosecution's 120 listed witnesses, demanding a shortened list. It also limited presentation of evidence of Dudley's culpability, followed by near praise of him "during a very trying period," stating:] The Court is the judge of the sufficiency of evidence upon any and all allegations before it to enable it to make an intelligent conclusion. And not in reason be expected to follow every point which might be construed to be material by interested persons by such exhaustive examination as may be desired by them. **The military culpability of Col. Dudley in connection with the management of one affair during a very trying period is the only subject of examination.**

At 5.15 PM the Court adjourned ...

On Monday, May 26, 1879, Susan McSween completed her testimony, with questions asked by the Court:

Q. by Court. Did you on the 15th day of January last make an affidavit before John B. Wilson, Justice of the Peace, in and for the County of Lincoln, Territory of New Mexico, in which you swore that Alex. A. McSween was feloniously, willfully, and of malice aforethought, killed and murdered, on the 19th day of July last and that the said murder was committed by Lieut. Col. N.A.M. Dudley, George Peppin, and Jack Long, and also in the same affidavit did you swear that Lieut. Col. N.A.M. Dudley, George Peppin, and Jack Long, on the 19th day of July last, set fire to and burned the house of Alex. A. McSween, and did you ask in and upon said affidavit that the warrants might be issued for the arrest of the said Lieut. Col. N.A.M. Dudley, George Peppin, and Jack Long?

Answer. I made an affidavit but I cannot remember anything contained in it. It was made by my attorney and carelessly read to me, I did not pay much attention to it, I could not say as to the time. It was an affidavit made against Col. N.A.M. Dudley, Peppin, and Long.

[AUTHOR'S NOTE: After three days of defense abuse, inadequate prosecution, and a biased Court, she folded. But she had given enough evidence to convict Dudley. But like all Ring victims, she would never see justice.]

Witness then retired.

BILLY BONNEY TESTIFIES

Proof of Billy Bonney's anti-Ring commitment was his testifying against N.A.M. Dudley, since it was not part of his pardon bargain. And, as he had written to Lew Wallace on March 13, 1879, he knew his risk: *"[M]y Enimies would Kill me."* But he twice made the unprotected, nine mile trip from his Lincoln sham custody to the courtroom in the Fort Stanton Adjutant's office adjacent to the parade ground for his court appearances on May 28th and 29th, 1879.

His Regulator zeal, plus his courage and intellectual brilliance, made him unshakable under Henry Waldo's abusive cross-examination. His precise and devastating testimony alone should have gotten Dudley a court martial, after this interchange: *"How many soldiers fired at you? ... Three ... How many shots did those soldiers fire, that you say shot from the Tunstall building? ... I could not swear to that on account of firing on all sides, I could not hear. I seen them fire one volley ... Were the soldiers which you say fired at you as you escaped from the McSween house on the evening of July 19th last, colored or white? ... White troops."*

A volley meant the three soldiers fired in unison. That required Dudley's order. "White" meant they were officers. That directly linked Dudley to ordering his soldiers to murder civilians. That was his treasonous Posse Comitatus Act violation. So dangerous was this evidence, that Henry Waldo's closing argument devoted a large part to false discrediting of Billy.

And Billy's selfless testimony magnified Lew Wallace's perfidy and moral failure. For his fellow citizens, that teenager had testified against Chapman's Ringite killers and the Lincoln County War's arch-villain. He would now be in the Ring's lethal spotlight until his death was achieved. And, as Susan McSween's testimony had shown, the Ring had already bestowed his outlaw moniker: "Billy the Kid." His transcript stated:

WILLIAM BONNEY, a witness being duly sworn, testified as follows.

Q. by Recorder. What is your name and place of residence?

Answer. My name is William Bonney. I reside in Lincoln.

Q. by Recorder. Are you known or called Billy Kidd, also Antrim?

Answer. Yes Sir.

Q. by Recorder. Where were you on the 19th day of July last and what, if anything, did you see of the movements and actions of the troops in that city, state fully?

Answer. I was in the McSween house in Lincoln, and I saw soldiers come from the post with the sheriff's party, that is the sheriff's posse joined them a short distance below there, the McSween house. Soldiers passed on by and the men dropped off and surrounded the house, the sheriff's party. Shortly after, the soldiers came back with Peppin, passed the house twice afterwards. Three soldiers came and stood in front of the house, in front of the windows. Mr. McSween wrote a note to the officer in charge asking what the soldiers were placed there for. He replied saying that they had business there, that if a shot was fired over his camp, or at Peppin, or at any of his men, that he had no objection to blowing up, if he wanted, his own house. I read the note myself, he handed it to me to read. I saw nothing further of the soldiers until night. I was in the back part of the house. **When I escaped from the house three soldiers fired at me from the Tunstall store, outside corner of the store.** *That's all I know in regards to it.*

Q. by Recorder. Did the soldiers that stood in front of the windows have guns with them while there?

Answer. Yes Sir.

Q. by Recorder. Who escaped from the house with you and who was killed at the time, if you know, while attempting to make their escape?

Answer. Jose Chavez [Chávez y Chávez] escaped with me, Vincente Romero, Francisco Zamora and McSween.

Q. by Recorder. How many persons were killed in that fight that day, if you know, and who killed them, if you know?

Answer. I seen five killed, I could not swear to who killed them, I seen some of them that fired.

Q. by Recorder. Who did you see that fired?

Answer. Robt. Beckwith, John Hurley, John Jones, **those three soldiers, I don't know their names.**

Q. by Recorder. Did you see any persons setting fire to the McSween house that day, if so, state who it was, if you know?

Answer. I did, Jack Long, and there was another man I did not recognize.

Recorder stated he had finished with the witness.
Cross examination.

Q. By Col. Dudley. What were you, and the others there with you, doing in McSween's house that day?

Answer. We came here with McSween.

Q. By Col. Dudley. Did you know, or had you not heard, that the sheriff was endeavoring to arrest yourself and others there with you at the time?

Answer. Yes Sir. I had heard so, I did not know.

Q. By Col. Dudley. Then were you not engaged in resisting the sheriff at the time you were in the house?

Objected to by Recorder. The Court has already ruled that nothing extraneous from the actual occurrence that took place, and Col. Dudley's actions in connection therewith, should be further inquired into … it cannot be a matter of defense of Col. Dudley or justify his actions however much the parties may have been resisting the sheriff or civil authorities.

Lt. Col. Dudley, by his Counsel, states he does not deem it necessary to make reply to the objection.

Objection sustained.

Q. By Col. Dudley. In addition to the names you have given, are you also known as the "Kid?"

Answer. I have already answered that question, Yes Sir, I am, but not "Billy Kid" that I know of.

Q. By Col. Dudley. Were you not and were not the parties with you in the McSween house on the 19th day of July last and the days immediately preceding, engaged in firing at the sheriff's posse?

Court objects to the question.

Lt. Col. Dudley, by his Counsel, asks, does the Court intend to rule here, that after once gone into this matter of firing into the McSween house by the testimony of this witness, it is not permissible to show all the circumstances under which this firing took place ...

Court cleared and closed.

Court opened and its decision announced ...

The Court directs the case to proceed calling attention to its previous rulings which were deemed sufficient by explicit.

Q. By Col. Dudley. Whose name was signed to the note received by McSween in reply to the one previously sent by him to Col. Dudley?

Answer. Signed N.A.M. Dudley, did not say what rank, he received two notes, one had no name signed to it.

Q. By Col. Dudley. Are you as certain of everything else you have sworn to as you are to what you have sworn to in answer to the last proceeding question?

Answer. Yes Sir.

Q. By Col. Dudley. From which direction did Peppin come the first time the soldiers passed with him?

Answer. Passed up from the direction of where the soldiers camped, the first time I saw him.

Q. By Col. Dudley. What direction did he come from the second time?

Answer. From the direction of the [Wortley] hotel from the McSween house.

Q. By Col. Dudley. In what direction did you go upon your escape from the McSween house?

Answer. Ran towards the Tunstall store, was fired at, and there turned towards the river.

Q. By Col. Dudley. From what part of the McSween house did you make your escape?

Answer. The northeast corner of the house.

Q. By Col. Dudley. How many soldiers fired at you?
Answer. Three.

Q. By Col. Dudley. How many soldiers were with Peppin when he passed the McSween house each time, as you say?

Answer. Three.

Q. By Col. Dudley. The soldiers appeared to go in company of threes that day, did they not?

Answer. All that I ever saw appeared to be three in a crowd at a time after they passed the first time.

Q. By Col. Dudley. Who was killed first that day, Bob Beckwith or McSween men?

Answer. Harvey Morris, McSween man, was killed first.

Q. By Col. Dudley. How far is the Tunstall building from the McSween house?

Answer. I could not say how far, I never measured the distance. I should judge it to be 40 yards, between 30 and 40 yards.

Q. By Col. Dudley. How many shots did those soldiers fire, that you say shot from the Tunstall building?

Answer. I could not swear to that on account of firing on all sides, I could not hear. I seen them fire one volley.

Q. By Col. Dudley. What did they fire at?

Answer. Myself and Jose Chavez [Chávez y Chávez].

Q. By Col. Dudley. Did you not just now state in answer to the question who killed Zamora, Romero, Morris, and McSween that you did not know who killed them, but you saw Beckwith, John Jones, **and three soldiers fire at them***?*

Answer. Yes Sir. I did.

Q. By Col. Dudley. Were these men, the McSween men, there with you **when the volley was fired at you and Chavez by the soldiers***?*

Answer. Just a short ways behind us.

Q. By Col. Dudley. Were you looking back at them?

Answer. No Sir.

Q. By Col. Dudley. How then do you know they were just behind you then, or that they were in range of the volley?

Answer. Because there was a high fence behind, and a good many guns to keep them there. I could hear them speak.

Q. By Col. Dudley. How far were you from the soldiers when you saw them?

Answer. I could not swear exactly, between 30 and 40 yards.

Q. By Col. Dudley. Did you know either of the soldiers that were in front of the window of McSween's house that day? If so, give it.

Answer. No Sir, I am not acquainted with them.

Redirect.

Q. by Recorder. Explain whether all the men that were in the McSween house came out at the same time when McSween and the others were killed and the firing came from the soldiers and others?

Answer. Yes Sir, all came out at the same time. **The firing was done by the soldiers until some had escaped.**

Recorder stated that he had finished with the witness.

Q. by Col. Dudley. How do you know if you were making your escape at the time and the men Zamora, Morris and McSween were behind you that they were killed at that time, is it not true that you did not know of their death or the death of either of them until afterwards?
Answer. I knew of the death of some of them, I did know of the death of one of them. I saw him lying down there.
Q. by Col. Dudley. Did you see any of the men last mentioned killed?
Answer. Yes Sir, I did, I seen Harvey Morris killed first, he was out in front of me.
Q. by Col. Dudley. Did you not then a moment ago swear that he was among those who were behind you and Jose Chavez [Chávez y Chávez] when you saw the soldiers deliver the volley?
Answer. No Sir, I didn't think I did. I misunderstood the question if I did. I said he was among them that was killed not behind me.

Witness then withdrew ...

In Billy's second day of testimony on May 29th, the Court's 19th, he confirmed that Dudley's white officers had fired at escaping McSweens, including himself; and that visibility was distinct by the burning McSween house making the escape area *"almost light as day."* The transcript stated:

Q. by Court. Were the soldiers which you say fired at you as you escaped from the McSween house on the evening of July 19th last, colored or white?
Answer. White troops.
Q. by Court. Was it light enough so you could distinctly see the soldiers when they fired?
Answer. The house was burning. Made it almost light as day for a short distance all around.

Witness then retired.

DUDLEY'S CAVALRYMEN TESTIFY

Other prosecution witnesses, and unsung heroes, Private James Bush and Sergeant Huston Lusk, as brave and honest as Billy, also proved Dudley's guilt. They were black 9th Cavalrymen whom Dudley ordered treasonously to assist Sheriff George Peppin against McSweens, and to enable arson of McSween's house. By testifying, they risked their lives and futures, demonstrating the same post-Civil War democratic zeal that had inspired the Regulators. And their testimony supported Billy's.

LEONARD'S RAGE AND DESPAIR

By June 6, 1879, Ira Leonard realized he was in a kangaroo court, though unaware of Lew Wallace's abandonment. Thus, it was to Wallace's deaf ears that he wailed in his letter of June 6, 1879: *"This evidence against Dudley would hang a man in any country where right and justice prevailed."* He wrote:

> Fort Stanton N.M
> June 6th 1879

Gov Lew Wallace
   Santa Fe

Dear Gov: *Dudley commenced on the defense Thursday afternoon and our apprehensions as to what the Court intended to do are plainly visible, they mean to white-wash and excuse his glaring conduct. They have transcended all rules of evidence to allow hearsay coming through other channels than direct parties and are allowing liberally to Dudley what they peremptorily refused us* **I have no hope of any good results I am thoroughly and completely disgusted with their proceedings.** *They held yesterday that since the prosecution had closed we could not call out from the witnesses on the defense on cross-examination in matters they had testified to concerning Dudley's culpability. They had Dolan on the stand and cut off my examination of him by not allowing me to interrogate him even upon what he had testified to in chief. I had a good notion to show my disgust by abandoning the case and let them have it their own way -* **There is nothing to be looked or hoped from this tribunal it is a farce on judicial investigation and ought to be called and designated "The Mutual Admiration Inquiry"** *I hope the evidence may go to the War Department so that they can* *see how things are managed.* **The evidence against Dudley would hang a man [for treason] in any country where right and justice prevailed ...*

My health has much improved since you left. Remember me to Mrs. Wallace.

A little episode occurred here a few days ago. [Deputy Sheriff Robert] Gilbert endeavored to arrest the men for whom he had warrants that were here as witnesses [like James Dolan] and the Atty Genl [Henry Waldo, also Court of Inquiry's defense lawyer] who is a little less than a damned ass threatened to have him Gilbert arrested for taking the witnesses on a criminal warrant because he claimed they were privileged from arrest. [See page 522 for letter] That is the first time I ever heard that a criminal as a witness could not be arrested at any time under the laws of England as well as this Country witnesses are privileged from arrest on civil process but never criminal See Wharton on Evidence Sec 389.

Let me hear from you.
                Yours truly.
                Ira E. Leonard.

WALLACE'S DAMAGE CONTROL

Instead of responding to Ira Leonard's letter of excruciating injustices, five days earlier, Wallace drafted one to Schurz on June 11, 1879 for his own damage control. He did not mention the Court of Inquiry's prejudice. Instead, he promoted Catron's getting pardon's for indicted Ringites with his Amnesty Proclamation as saving future court time! And he covered up the ongoing turmoil of wretched and angry Lincoln County citizens with the outlaw myth: "[T]he only ~~remaining~~ disturbing element remaining to be grappled with is the <u>confederacy of outlaws</u>." He wrote:

Hon. C. Schurz,
Sec'y Dept. Interior.

Sir:
Enclosed please find a copy of the report of the commandant at Fort Stanton. As the statement of Capt. Purington is fully sustained by intelligence received privately, I think myself justified in informing you of a continuance in Lincoln county of the peace reported in my last letter. And in the connection, you will pardon

me, I think, for calling your attention and the President's to the fact, that for quite eight months now **there has been but one murder - Mr. Chapman's** *- with reference to which you know my procedure.*

[AUTHOR'S NOTE: Wallace chillingly minimizes Chapman's murder and his murderers' indictments. But to achieve that indicting Billy had risked his life by testifying against the Ring.]

This leaves me at liberty to repeat for your better understanding of the present situation there, that the old factions known respectively as the "Murphy-Dolan" and the "McSween" are as dead organizations; to which may be added now, that my amnesty proclamation has had exactly the effect intended; which was to shear the past off, and make present and future all questions which might require official action, pertinent to civil affairs in the locality. To illustrate, the grand jury empanelled for the recent county court was, with one or two exceptions, composed of men accounted of the McSween or anti-Dolan party, for it is undeniable that nearly all citizens eligible as grand-jurors are ~~inimical to the latter~~ *of that persuasion. They found nearly 200 indictments, the whole, with a few exceptions, against the Dolan people. Nearly 200 indictments in a county of a voting population of 150* ~~in all~~ *total!*

[AUTHOR'S NOTE: Wallace's narcissistic callousness leaves him blind to Lincoln County citizens' attempt to get justice.]

You cannot fail to see what would have come of trial of the accused - how long they would have lasted - the expenses to a county which has nothing in its treasury ... **As it was most of the indicted appeared in court and plead the amnesty in bar [of further prosecution].** <u>Hereafter the labors of grand juries will be confined strictly to offences subsequent to my proclamation</u> *...*

[AUTHOR'S NOTE: Ringites ignored the Amnesty Proclamation's exclusion of the indicted, and plead "*amnesty in bar*" of further prosecution. And Judge Bristol granted it. So Wallace rationalizes that outrage as less work for juries!]

You will see from this description that **the only** ~~remaining~~ **disturbing element remaining to be grappled with is the <u>confederacy of outlaws</u>** <u>and their friends.</u> *That done effectively, I believe a permanently healthful condition can be promised.*

The question is, how to best ~~can~~ *proceed.*

The method which seems to have met with most favor in the Territory is martial law. And I confess at one time I thought it the best and only method. Two months upon the ground, however, and much study and reflection there where the advantages and disadvantages, forecasting probabilities, were directly under eye, have changed my opinion ...

The restoration of civil authority, it is to be feared, would, in this case at least, be the signal for **the outlaws, over in Mexico, Texas, the Staked Plains, and for that matter, the contiguous counties of New Mexico***, to return and renew their operations, with the additional incentive of fresh victims to prey upon. To these objections, I have heard but one point in answer – that under military protection, the county would become settled, and able to take care of itself. Possibly* it would *so, though I doubt it, for the reason that, as a rule, people looking out for new homes find very little attraction in martial law;* on the contrary there is *the strongest ground for a belief is that its prevalence would be almost universally accepted as a warning to stay away. Under martial law contractors would multiply and flourish;* while *men* of means *with families would look elsewhere.*

[AUTHOR'S NOTE: This is Wallace's outlaw myth to use random outlawry to hide the Ring crimes and Lincoln County citizens' fears, since no Ringite had been successfully prosecuted, although citizens had indicted them.]

Instead of martial law, I recommend simply a transfer of all troops now at Fort Stanton, except Captain Carroll and Lieut. Dawson and their companies; substituting, in place of the transferred, officers and troops wholly disconnected with the past troubles and without bias one way or the other

I beg not to be required to support this recommendation with charges against anybody. They get me into personal quarrels for which life is too short .... Respectfully but frankly, it is very desirable to know ... if the support heretofore given me will be continued – ***for now I can retire without loss of credit*** *...*

[AUTHOR'S NOTE: Wallace's only concern is to avoid any more miserable Courts of Inquiry, and to protect his reputation.]

If, however, the President thinks better to resort to martial law, his decision will be cheerfully accepted.

Passing from Lincoln county, it gives me great satisfaction to report the Territory elsewhere in a prosperous state. The recent mineral discoveries and the resolution of the railroad companies (the Denver and Rio Grande and the Atchison, Topeka and ~~Rio Grande~~ Santa Fe) to extend their lines immediately, are at last drawing to New Mexico the attention she really deserves, and already we are feeling the effects. The hotels in this city are crowded, and a stream of miners is pouring along the roads from the east.

I have the honor to be
Very respectfully
Your friend,
Lew. Wallace, Governor New Mexico

LEONARD'S "OLD SCOUNDREL" LETTER

Two days after Wallace wrote glowingly to Schurz, on June 11th, Ira Leonard, on June 13, 1879, intruded reality about looming Court of Inquiry disaster: *"If you ever saw three men [the Judges] who strained every effort to protect & shield an old scoundrel this Court have done it."* From Fort Stanton, he wrote:

My dear Governor:
Yours of the 7th inst reached me in due time, and I was glad to hear from you … **A petition has been gotten up complaining of the action of Judge Bristol and begging his removal on account of his strong partisan feeling and forwarded also to the President and I think you ought to take your action at once if you have not done so yet.** *I had a conversation with Col Purington a few days ago and he informed me Judge B had advised him that after your Proclamation of Pardon and Amnesty the Proclamation had served the persons intended and that the General order made by the War Department was virtually abrogated … to call on the Military for assistance & he would not furnish aid to the officers without further instructions although he has since sent Capt Carroll down on the requisition made of him by the Sheriff of the Seven Rivers country to aid the Sheriff in making arrests but with* **strict orders not to assist him moving stolen stock**, *Capt Carroll informs me that for any practical purpose his hands have been absolutely tied by his orders …*

[AUTHOR'S NOTE: This was shielding of Ringite Seven Rivers rustler-murderers: real outlaws]

Now on to what perhaps to you will be more interesting the progress of the Dudley case. We closed on the part of the prosecution a week ago Monday and it is unnecessary for me to tell you how rigidly & particularly the Court ruled while you were still here, **and as we progressed in the case and we were pouring "hot shot" into him they tightened the reins to such an extent that they would not enter our objections of record some of them where the ruling of the Court would make them appear ridiculous and at one time I feared the Court would order me out of the case when I objected to the ruling of the Court ... If you ever saw three men who strained every effort to protect & shield an old scoundrel this Court have done it.** *After ruling us down in a shameful manner as soon as the defense commenced they opened every gate to Dudley and it makes no difference what he offers they receive it & allowed the most flagrant hearsay evidence anything and everything that will in the Court have a tendency to excuse his conduct they admit without stint reservation or objection.* **They would not allow into show any of the circumstances that brought about the difficulties or give an account of them and of their inception and progress and the character of the mob that murdered McSween and the others but confined as to Dudley's conduct on the day he went to Lincoln they would not allow us to show the conspiracy formed with Dolan beforehand to go the Lincoln and said that when we were trying to pose the conspiracy that that was a charge not incorporated either in your charges or mine but now everything near, remote, traditional guess, and thought and what this one said & that one said weeks & months before the events, of the fight is dragged in and allowed if it only has some show of making the McSween side look black & will give them an excuse to shield Dudley** *and the provoking part of it to me is when Waldo and I get together he will laugh and push me in the rib, at the fools the Court are making of themselves in their rulings. I never desire any more experience before a Military Court comprised of egotistical damned fools. All I wish in this matter is to have this case examined before some sensible officer at Washington if we have not enough evidence to send him out of this country I shall be greatly mistaken.* **I am more clearly convinced every day I remain here that there will never be peace and good order restored here until there is a radical change here at the Post and in fact there ought not to be one** *man left who can tell the tale of the outrages the Military have inflicted upon this people ...*

[Letter continues the next day]

Saturday Morning June 14th
The Court adjourned this morning until Monday morning at 10 AM on account of the illness of Col. Purington ...

[Edgar] Walz arrived here but too late for us unfortunately to make use of him I am so sorry we had not had him in time unless I am greatly mistaken we could have made a very strong circumstantial case against Col. D. in the Chapman murder –

[AUTHOR'S NOTE: The Court let key eye-witness to Chapman's murder, Edgar Walz, avoid prosecution questioning.]

Dolan has renewed his application before Judge Bristol for his release in Habeas Corpus. The venue was changed to Socorro County, but there was no Court held there and he was detained here as a witness for Col Dudley, and now he renews his application to be released on bail and I know that Rynerson will allow him to be released.

[AUTHOR'S NOTE: The Court concealed that Dolan was indicted for Chapman's murder, but Waldo used Billy's indictments.]

The whole outfit of the Seven River men have also made application to be released before Judge Bristol of course they will be. They are making preparations to start over at once. Turner, Pierce, the two Olingers [Bob and Wallace], Boyle, Buck Powell and a numbers of others.

I tell you Governor as long as the present incumbent occupies the bench all that Grand Juries may do to bring to justice these men every effort will be thwarted by him and the sympathizers of that [Ring] side.

I am going to Lincoln today to remain over Sunday and when anything further occurs of interest I will write you –

I have written to Senator Teller & Judge Belford M.C. from Colorado to aid me in seeking the appointment here in the place of Judge B. I received a letter from a Denver friend informing me that a change would certainly be made and to write then as he had already done to secure the appointment for me – I wish it might occur but I have no very strong hopes of it.

Remember me to Mrs. Wallace. My health is much improved.
Yours truly Ira E Leonard

BILLY DEPARTS JAIL

Billy had kept trust in Wallace, as had Ira Leonard, who had become Billy's loyalist and lawyer. So without pardon, and possibly aware from Leonard of the bad turn in the Court of Inquiry, on June 17, 1879, Billy decided his risk in custody was too great. So he simply left Juan Patrón's house to continue guerrilla rustling from Catron's and Charles Fritz's Lincoln County ranches, and to await the pardon. Later, conscienceless Wallace - knowing the arrest was a protective sham - would accuse Billy of escaping, as one of his many published lies for why he never pardoned the boy.

DUDLEY TESTIFIES

N.A.M. Dudley's lying testimony, beginning on the Court's 45th day, was from June 28th to 30th, 1879. Obviously coached, he, voiced the Ring's arrogance and certainty of immunity. By the time of his testimony, the corrupt judges were out-of-control: even blocking prosecution from using witnesses to prove defense witnesses' perjury, and not permitting cross-examinations. The judges stated: *"The Court declines to call the witnesses requested by the Recorder before it as it regards the testimony sought to be elicited is not material."* The transcript is as follows:

... Q. by Col. Dudley [Waldo]. Do you admit to having gone to Lincoln on the 19th day of July last, if so, state what induced you to go there at the time?

Answer. I did go to Lincoln on the 19th day of July last. I was induced to go to Lincoln being thoroughly convinced that it was my solemn duty to do so. I had been in command of the post. My object in going to Lincoln was to give protection to women and children and parties, and parties who were not engaged in the disturbances then existing in Lincoln.

Q. by Col. Dudley. State whether or not in going there it was done in pursuance of any promise by you, or of any agreement or understanding, direct or indirect, between you and Sheriff Peppin, or anyone on his behalf?

Answer. There was no agreement, no ...

Q. by Col. Dudley. State whether or not in any manner or to any extent you aided or assisted Sheriff Peppin or his posse on the 19th day of July last, or took part in any of the measures adopted by him that day, or whether any of the soldiers under your command by your order or with your knowledge or consent took part in any of the transactions that day connected with the contest going on between the two parties there that day?

Answer. I did not, they did not.

Q. by Col. Dudley. Did you hear of any soldiers being at or near the McSween house on the 19th day of July last whether taking any part with the sheriff's posse against the McSween party or standing about there doing nothing in the day or night time before it was mentioned before the Court?

Answer. I never did ...

Q. by Col. Dudley. State whether or not you had any conversation with Justice John B. Wilson at or near camp that morning of the 19th of July last ... that if he did not issue the warrant, referring to the warrant for McSween, you would put him in double irons ...

Answer. My recollection of the conversation was that there was nothing unpleasant said by Justice Wilson or myself ... I did not threaten to put him in irons ...

Q. by Col. Dudley. State whether or not you had a conversation with Mrs. McSween in or near your camp on the 19th day of July last, if so what the conversation was ... and whether or not in the conversation you said to her that if a shot was fired from the McSween house near any of your soldiers ... you would turn your cannon loose and tear it to the ground ...

Answer. I did have a conversation with Mrs. McSween near my camp ... I can simply give the general purport. When she first came up, I said good morning Madam. She returned the salutation. She appeared a good deal excited ... crying. To the best of my recollection, the conversation commenced by her saying, what are you doing with U.S. soldiers surrounding my husband's house. I assured her that there were no U.S. soldiers around her house to my knowledge ... I told her then of the object of my visit to Lincoln to the effect, that I have come to Lincoln with my small command for the purpose of giving protection to women and children and such other parties as may avail themselves of it ... I further remember her referring to the sheriff's posse burning or attempting to burn her house ... I did not credit her statement and told her at the time I had received a letter from her husband in which he stated he was going to burn up his own house ... I stepped inside my tent and produced the letter ... I told her she could not have the letter, she saying give me that letter ... I will say in this connection *that to the very best of my knowledge and recollection that nothing could be construed toward Mrs. McSween as showing anger or passion ...*

*Q. by Col. Dudley. You heard the testimony of **Bates** in which he attributed certain expressions to you in conversation stated to have taken place in or near your camp with Sheriff Peppin about ... Peppin's undertaking not proving successful if it had not been for you, state whether or not anything of this kind occurred ...*

Answer. I know nothing of such a conversation with Peppin ... as stated by the Negro Bates ...

[AUTHOR'S NOTE: Waldo is deviously garbling. The witness was not the McSween's black servant, Sebrian Bates, but black 9th Cavalrymen James Bush and Huston Lusk, ordered by Dudley to help Peppin capture of fleeing McSweens, and witnessed Dudley's anger at Peppin for allowing their escape.]

Q. by Col. Dudley. State whether or not you said to Sheriff Peppin out in the street between camp and Montano's house ... that if he came when word was sent he could have captured the men that were in the Montano house, or anything to that effect?

Answer. I never did ...

Q. by Col. Dudley. State whether or not you were notified that the [Tunstall] store was being robbed?

Answer. I was not.

Q. by Col. Dudley. State what passed between you and Mrs. Montano in the morning of the 19th of July last in regard to giving her protection ...

Answer. I could not say if any conversation occurred with Mrs. Montano and myself directly ... I told my interpreter ... to explain ... I was going to leave a guard with Capt. Baca ... and if anything occurred she could go over to Baca's or call upon the soldiers ...

[AUTHOR'S NOTE: Dudley is lying about protecting women and children. In truth, he ordered his howitzer cannon pointed at the Montaño house with her inside. He also endangered women and children in McSween's and the Ealy's. And Baca was a Ring stooge, faking family danger to bring Dudley to Lincoln.]

Dudley's testimony continued on June 30, 1879, as follows:

Q. by Col. Dudley. State whether or not you had any opportunity for explanation of the charges made against you by Governor Wallace before removal from the command of Fort Stanton ...

Answer. I did not have the slightest opportunity ... I was removed of command by Col. Edward Hatch, ordered to Fort Union at the time I was doing everything in my power ... to assist the civil authorities in the County of Lincoln in carrying out the laws of the Territory ...

Cross Examine.

Q. by Recorder. What induced you to think it was your solemn duty to go to Lincoln on the 19th day of July last, upon what authority did you base that action, and was your sole and only object that of humanitarian?

[AUTHOR'S NOTE: Humphreys fails to show Dudley's lying, or that the Posse Comitatus Act required Presidential order for intervention, or that he endangered women and children at McSween's, the Ealys in Tunstall's store, and Montaño's home.]

Answer. My knowledge of the situation of affairs in Lincoln, my sense of duty as an Officer of the Army. It was decidedly as I understood that word.

Q. by Recorder. If you went there in the capacity of an humanitarian why did you not carry out that purpose and prevent the bloodshed and destruction of property that was going on there instead of promoting the disturbance by allowing a warrant to be issued against McSween and others?

Objected to by Lieut. Col. Dudley, by his Counsel. Question objected to because it assumes that Col. Dudley was engaged in fomenting disturbances and assumes that he allowed a warrant to be issued by McSween.

Recorder stated he had no reply to make.

Objection sustained ...

[AUTHOR'S NOTE: This shows the Court's bias as well as Humphreys' inadequacy. Humphreys should have responded to Waldo by saying Dudley had admitted to intervening; and his claim of a "humanitarian" act was refuted by his brutal acts endangering women and children, backing the losing Peppin side, and causing murder and arson. And eye-witness account proved his ordering troops to fire a volley at McSweens.]

Q. by Recorder. You are charged with having acted in a brutal and inhumane manner on the 19th day of July last while in command of a portion of the garrison of Fort Stanton at Lincoln, N.M. ... What reply have you to make to this charge ...

Answer. Most emphatically no.

WALLACE ADMITS THE RING TO SCHURZ

In his July 3, 1879 progress report to Schurz, Wallace hinted at the Ring by referencing its plot (as he had reported to his friend, Absalom Markland). He wrote: *"The only thing worth attention is the development of the conspiracy of which I have had knowledge for some time, looking to removal of a number of federal appointees, including myself.* ***It is the expiring flurry of the old ring****."* So Wallace - knowing that he had left the Ring unchecked in Lincoln County - implied it was irrelevant, since it was "expiring!" And Schurz played along. For the complicit Hayes administration, Wallace was achieving with finesse what brutal Governor Axtell had failed: suppressing citizens without their recognizing the malice.

WALDO'S CLOSING ARGUMENT

On July 5, 1879, two days after Wallace told Schurz the Ring was expiring, it reared up in full potency on the Court of Inquiry's 49th day, in the hours-long closing argument by Henry Waldo. He defamed all prosecution witnesses to enable the corrupt Judges to disregard of their evidence - using "boss" Catron's well-worn ploy. And he despicably made a martyr of Dudley; stating: *"Nothing has been accomplished in the least that connects Col. Dudley with anything which transpired in the town of Lincoln on the occasion of his presence there on the 19th and 20th day of July last ... [But he] has been libeled and vilified ... He has been heralded forth as a house burner and a murderer from one end of the territory to the other."*

ATTACK ON WALLACE

Waldo sealed Wallace's humiliation and defeat, recycling Shiloh's. And he implied the spy system that Catron used to attack victims. He knew about Wallace's secret communications about the Ring to Absalom Markland and Carl Schurz about feared Ring attempts to remove him. So he mocked, with terrifying Ring power: *"[T]he Governor was in great alarm about the awful "bug bear" the "Santa Fe Ring" preventing his confirmation. He wanted to manufacture some political thunder whose reverberation would resound in the halls of the Senate chamber in Washington."*

Waldo's closing argument stated:

[Dudley] has been branded as a conspirator, a robber and a thief by no less a person than Governor Wallace, whose lips have blistered to a crisp and pealed to the bone when they uttered the foul malicious accusation. False and slanderous charges have been preferred by the crafty and designing old lawyer, Ira E. Leonard, to the Secretary of war, and by the wily and unscrupulous politician Governor Wallace, to the Commander of the District.

Look at this for a moment, here was this man Leonard when he made these charges and had never even been in Lincoln county. He resided in Las Vegas, two hundred miles away, and never had an opportunity of ... making an investigation into the truth of the charges formulated by him. **Governor Wallace had been in the county of Lincoln but one day, took no sworn or written testimony, never even inquired of the officers who were present with Col. Dudley, when he was in Lincoln at the time mentioned.**

Language strong enough and severe enough cannot be employed in denunciation of the hideous and monstrous wickedness of these bad men who united in their efforts to disgrace and ruin a man who had never harmed either of them, in thought, word, or deed, and that man an officer of high rank, and long and distinguished service in the Army of this country. *Here, has Col. Dudley been forced to submit to the humiliation and mortification of knowing that such charges had been lodged against him with the Department of War in Washington, and that he was the subject of comment and discussion of his superiors and among brother officers, besides the publicity which they necessarily obtained throughout the country, to the effect of which can never be obliterated, and compelled to seek the vindication of himself, and able to obtain only the poor and meager and inadequate redress, which this Court of Inquiry can afford ...* **Lew Wallace and Ira E. Leonard are alone responsible for this annoyance trouble and harassing case. By their act, this disgrace has been brought upon a pure, humane, and just man. By their act has the luster of a bright and honorable career been dimmed. Time does not remain to Col. Dudley to clear away the stain, by them**

placed upon his name and character. The best years of his life are passed and gone, spent in the service of his country ..

He [Wallace] did not come [to Lincoln] to learn the truth. He came bent on finding for which he could use to injure Col. Dudley. He came to accomplish the removal of Col. Dudley even if he had to manufacture the testimony which it would be necessary to have, in order to do it. To succeed, even if he had to write as evil and malicious a letter as that upon which the removal was effected. Did Gov. Wallace seek true knowledge of Col. Dudley's relations to Lincoln County matters? Why did he not come to officers of the post? Why did he not seek his information from all the parties, but no, he never came to the post, but went directly to Lincoln, and talked with a few rabid and malignant partisans, took a one sided version from prejudiced and irresponsible parties he knew he could get what he wanted from, and then tries to make it appear from the witness stand that this information was derived from persons who came from all parts of the county ...

For five days he attitudinized before this Court in a labored effort betwixt an harangue and a narrative, the object of which was plainly manifest to be an exculpation of, or apology for the errors and follies of his course in dealing with Lincoln County matters ...

It was after this purposely one sided investigation he comes to the post and wrote his letter of request, filling it with lying statements, which, with an hypocritical attempt at an apology, he states, he was cautious to say, were given upon information merely, and after he had accomplished, in this unjust and infamous manner, the removal of Col. Dudley ...

He [Wallace] wants somebody to lay the blame upon. It [Amnesty Proclamation] was a weak and ridiculous idea in the first place. What the villains who had made a hell of Lincoln County needed was a gallows, not a pardon. The whole truth about that proclamation, as we look at it, is that just about the time the Governor was in great alarm about the awful "bug bear" the "Santa Fe Ring" preventing his confirmation. He wanted to manufacture some political thunder whose reverberation would resound in the halls of the Senate chamber in Washington ... He had been sent specifically to pacify the troubles in New Mexico. To this, his official announcement of the complete success of his efforts to pacification in Lincoln County is promulgated.

ATTACK ON BILLY BONNEY

Waldo's lying attack on Billy Bonney culminated his Ring "outlawing," begun with U.S. Marshal John Sherman's October 6, 1878 outlaw list. A pardon now looked like backing an outlaw - obviously a path Wallace would reject, since it needed Ring exposé for justification. About Billy, Henry Waldo stated:

Then was brought forward William Bonney, alias "Antrim," alias "the Kid," a known criminal of the worst type although hardly up to his majority, murderer by profession, as records of this Court connect him with two atrocious murders, that of ["Buckshot"] Roberts and the other of Sheriff Brady. Both of them are cowardly and atrocious assassinations.

There were warrants enough for him to the 19th of July last to have plastered him from his head to his feet, yet he was engaged to do service as a witness and his testimony showed that his qualifications did not terminate with blood guiltiness. His testimony was brief, yet he signalized his opening sentences with a lie. He swears that members of the sheriff's posse fell in with the troops and came up to the McSween house, but I will quote his words. "I was in the McSween house in Lincoln, and I saw the soldiers come down from the fort with the sheriff's party, that is, the sheriff's posse joined them a short distance above there, the McSween house, soldiers passed on by, the men dropped right off and surrounded the house." It has been proven by competent and unimpeachable witnesses that this statement is without any foundation in fact. Sheriff Peppin, his Deputy Sheriff Powell, Deputy Sheriff Marion Turner, Milo Pierce, Robert Olinger, Joseph Nash, Andrew Boyle, J.B. Matthews, Lt. Goodwin, Captain Purington and Corporal Bugold, who brought up the rear of the column all swear that none of the posse was anywhere near the troops as they passed the Wortley Hotel and came up to the McSween house ...

[AUTHOR'S NOTE: These "*witnesses*" are Ringite Lincoln County War Battle murderers and arsonists.]

He also testified as to the note received by McSween in answer to one sent by Col. Dudley. He swears that the note was signed N.A.M. Dudley, "did not say what rank." About this he might have been mistaken, but it shows him to be a willing and reckless witness. But what is of importance is that he swears that letter contained the following, he is positive about it because he says he read it, he volunteers that statement. His testimony stated three soldiers came down and stood in front of McSween's building and McSween's wife wants to know why they are there ... and Col. Dudley replied saying, "They had business there, and if a shot was fired over his camp, or at Peppin or any of his men, that he had no objection to his blowing up, if he wanted to, his own house." That this note contained nothing about firing upon Peppin or any of his men is clear enough ... to say nothing of the contradiction given by Lt. Goodwin, who wrote the note and signed it.

He also swears that three soldiers fired at him when he was escaping from the McSween building. Attention will also be called to this part of the testimony further on. It is sufficient to say of this part of the testimony now that if he swears falsely about so material a fact as to the manner of the sheriff's posse surrounded the house, that is to say under cover by means of protection of the troops as they marched by, he would not hesitate to swear falsely about soldiers firing at him that night as he was escaping. "A liar once is a liar all the time."

As to seeing the soldiers about the Tunstall building, at the time of the escape of the men from the McSween house the evening of the 19th of July last, Jose Chavez [Chávez y Chávez] was also called. He was with the "Kid" according to both of them. "Kid" says that the soldiers stood at the outside corner of the Tunstall building ... Now this story comes with its own reputation. In the first place, in the intense excitement of the moment, these men could not have had the coolness to select from a number of shots delivered at them, the firing of certain particular shots, to fix it in their minds, the men who did the firing. Besides, in the deceptive glare of the fire, it is very doubtful if any of the parties who were looking upon the space between those two houses could identify with any degree of certainty, particularly at such a time, the kind of clothes anybody wore. This difficulty would be enhanced in the case of the "Kid" and Chavez because they were looking from the center of the light out against the darkness, which is a circumstance of the greatest importance. While from the darkness to the wall objects are plainly discernable, the direct opposite follows when the conditions are changed.

[AUTHOR'S NOTE: Lying Waldo even absurdly fabricates that Billy could not see soldiers because firelight from the building could light the building he left, but not people facing it!]

There is a considerable discrepancy between the two witnesses also as to the distance they say the three soldiers were from where they fired. "Kid" said 30 to forty yards, Chavez makes it only ten yards.

Another conclusive argument against the presence of soldiers there at the time is the extreme danger, the almost certain danger of death from such an exposed position, the witnesses testify that it would have been between cross fire at a time when everybody else was seeking and keeping cover. It is to be supposed for a moment that three soldiers, who had no interest in the contest would have been in such a place, for if they were at all they slipped out against orders and came there of their own choice.

[AUTHOR'S NOTE: Waldo hides a volley meaning under orders.]

Besides, it is clear the soldiers were not then present, the evidence of the Sergeant who testified that late roll call for the night was at dusk, or near as he can judge, about a quarter past eight, and that the men were then all there. This escape being among their first that was made must have been about that time ...

[AUTHOR'S NOTE: The escape was after: at 9 p.m.]

In addition to all this we have the evidence of Boyle, or Nash, or Olinger or of Hurley all who say they had a distance view of the space between the McSween house and the Tunstall building ... that there was nobody at the corner of the Tunstall building, where these soldiers were located. The evidence of Olinger and Hurley is especially valuable, each of them had distinct views of this particular corner. One, Olinger in the Stanley house, and the other, Hurley, to the southeast of it in the Wilson house ...

[AUTHOR'S NOTE: Ringite outlaws are used; and Olinger's and Hurley's locations were not near the shooting soldiers.]

Besides, we must take into consideration that some of these men were of the sheriff's posse ... were dressed with soldier jackets ..., and it was easy enough for these frightened fleeing men ... to mislocate the men they say shot at them. To all probability as they fled they may have seen some of these men who had soldiers' jackets and thought they were soldiers. It is more charitable to suppose this, than that they have come here and deliberately lied.

[AUTHOR'S NOTE: Waldo, still focused on attacking Billy's fatal testimony, after having fabricated that he lied, now lies wildly that the shooting soldiers Billy saw were actually Peppin's possemen dressed as soldiers!]

LYING CONCLUSION

In concluding, Henry Waldo was on a roll, victory ensured. He gloated: *"The foul conspiracy to disgrace and ruin Col. Dudley concocted by Lew Wallace, Ira E. Leonard, and Sue E. McSween has ended in utter and ignominious failure."* Lying, racist, and Ringite Waldo stated theatrically and revoltingly:

When we look at the strong manly forms, and honest, brave and resolute faces of the sheriff and those of his posse, who have appeared before this Court as witnesses, and think of the miserable hoard of Mexicans and cut throat Americans opposed to them, (some of whom you have seen on the witness stand) and when you reflect upon the skill and address shown by the sheriff's posse in isolating the house of McSween, cutting it off, and commanding all the approaches to it ... we know and everybody knows who at all understands the situation, that no power under heaven could have prevented the sheriff, and his posse from accomplishing what they started out to do, namely, to arrest the men in that house or kill them in the attempt or be killed themselves ...

The foul conspiracy to disgrace and ruin Col. Dudley concocted by Lew Wallace, Ira E. Leonard, and Sue E. McSween has ended in utter and ignominious failure. For them, and for all who had any share in contriving or promoting any portion of it, scorn and contempt alone remains as their portion. *Col. Dudley comes forth from this fiery ordeal unscathed. No blemish rest on his character, no cloud to darken his fame.*

All that remains is to return thanks to the Court for the attention given me, and at the same time, for the kind and considerate treatment I have uniformly received at its hands.

PROSECUTOR'S CLOSING ARGUMENT

Prosecutor Henry Humphreys, with Ira Leonard - instead of summarizing damning evidence, debunking Waldo's lying refutations, decrying Dudley's crimes, and asserting Posse Comitatus Act violation - relied on simple sincerity and brevity to appeal to moral fiber in the three judges. There was none. Humphreys stated:

To the Honorable Court of Inquiry convened at Fort Stanton, New Mexico.

This cause having occupied the Court in its investigation of the matters for over two months now has closed and the only remaining duty on the part of the Recorder is to present to the Court an argument upon the facts which have been elicited in the investigation ...

The motives which directs the actions of men are judged in what they do and not by what they say, and for the proof that Lieut. Col. Dudley took part in all the disturbances that existed in Lincoln County from nearly the beginning of his taking command of Fort Stanton to its termination shows him a strong and bitter partisan, I simply refer to the Court the proof that he alone has introduced in his defense ...

The fight between the factions had been, at most, unproductive, with no success to the sheriff's party between the 15th to the 19th of the month of July ... And not until Col. Dudley comes upon the field of combat as a pretended neutral party on the 19th did the sheriff and his posse have any apparent show of success, and can anyone believe that results would have been different than they had been prior to his coming if he had remained away? ...

If there is any proceedings during the occurrences of the 19th day of July that more palpably shows the malice which activated Col. Dudley in his proceedings on that occasion [it is the attack on the McSween house].

Let us look at that portion one moment. The proof discloses the fact that the house McSween occupied was a double house, and half of it belonged to Mrs. Shields [sic], the sister of Mrs. McSween, who was in possession with five children in the portion belonging to her ... Mrs. McSween went to the camp of Col. Dudley and begs in her own sister's behalf for him to save it from destruction, but Col. Dudley who was in Lincoln, as he told Mrs. McSween, but to prevent wanton destruction of property and to protect women and children instead says, "I understand he (meaning the sheriff) had warrants for several persons, among them, your husband, and he must be the judge of the means in carrying out his instructions." Col. Dudley goes to Lincoln on a pretended mission of mercy, but when he is sought to save the property of an innocent family, his ears are deaf to their appeal, and he refuses to protect the house that shelters the mother and her five children ...

We assert the fact that the killing of McSween with others of his party was murder and the burning of his house constituted the crime of arson, and every person engaged in it, formulated it, are equally criminal. There is no law, humane or otherwise, that will justify the measures adopted on that day to arrest persons charged with crimes.

FINAL JUDGMENT OF THE COURT

That same July 5th of 1879, the corrupt, three judge Court of Inquiry gave its foregone conclusion, with Final Judgment read by Chief Judge Galusha Pennypacker. He declared, *"After careful investigation and mature deliberation the court finds the following pertinent and material facts:*

FIRST: That Lieut. Col. N.A.M. Dudley, 9th Cavalry, had command of the post of Fort Stanton, N.M., on the 5th day of April 1878, that at the time of his taking command until relieved on the 8th day of March 1879, that at the time of his taking command and for a considerable period of time thereafter two factions of men known respectively as the McSween party and the Dolan and Riley (or Dolan and Murphy) party were engaged in contest against each other during which many lives were lost, that the peacefully disposed people of the town and county of Lincoln were kept in almost a constant state of apprehension and alarm during this period, and the lawful avocation of the people frequently suspended or altogether prevented through fear on one or the other or both of these factions.

SECOND: That warrants were issued early in the month of July 1878 for the arrest of McSween and others of his party for offences committed during the period of contest between the factions and placed in the hands of the sheriff of the county for service, that the sheriff anticipating resistance summoned a posse to his assistance including several persons who had been previously identified with the Dolan and Riley party.

THIRD: That on the 19th of July 1878 Lieut. Col. Dudley proceeded from Fort Stanton, N.M. to the town of Lincoln, Lincoln County, distance about 9 miles from the fort, with one howitzer and one Gatling gun and a detachment from the garrison consisting of four officers and thirty five men for the **purpose of giving protection to the lives and property of the citizens then in jeopardy by**

612

reason of resistance by arms made by McSween and his followers to the repeated attempts of the sheriff and his posse to serve the warrants that he held.

FOURTH: That on the arrival of Lieut. Col. Dudley in the town of Lincoln about 10 o'clock in the morning of July 19th 1878 the sheriff's posse numbering about 28 men and the McSween party numbering from 40 to 60 men occupied the street and houses in town, that shortly after the arrival of Lieut. Col. Dudley he personally stated to the sheriff and subsequently to a representative of the McSween party that **he had come to Lincoln for the purpose of affording protection to women and children** *and would give no aid or assistance to either party but if any officer or soldier of his command were either killed or wounded by shots from either party he would return fire.*

FIFTH: That within a short time after the arrival of. Col. Dudley in the town of Lincoln a warrant issued upon the affidavit of certain officers of the command for the arrest of McSween for an alleged assault upon the person of a United States soldier with intent to kill was obtained and placed in the hands of the sheriff for service by the civil officer issuing the same.

SIXTH: That shortly after the arrival of Lieut. Col. Dudley with his command into the town of Lincoln all of McSween's followers then present excepting only about nine men occupying the McSween house with their leaders and possibly two or more persons in a building known as the Tunstall building escaped from the several buildings and enclosures which they occupied and fled from the town, that the sheriff along with his posse made an assault the same day upon the McSween house, set it on fire and destroyed it and at last shot and killed McSween and three or more of the persons with him, **the said McSween and those with him resisting by force of arms until his death***.*

SEVENTH: That **Lieut. Col. Dudley did not intend any aid or assistance to either party** *and that Lieut. Col. Dudley and his officers and men of his command did all that could properly be done to protect the lives of peaceable and law abiding citizens.*

EIGHTH: That on the 7th day of November 1878 Lieut. Col. Dudley forwarded to the headquarters of the District of New Mexico certain affidavits which he procured from citizens of Lincoln County affecting the character and chastity of Mrs. McSween for the purpose of impairing the credibility of certain other allegations made by the said Mrs. McSween through her attorney against Lieut. Col. Dudley which said allegations had been forwarded to His Excellency the Governor of the territory and by him transmitted to the Commanding Officer, District of New Mexico.

NINTH: That Lieut. Col. Dudley caused an open letter dated Fort Stanton, N.M., November 30, 1878 and addressed to His Excellency Lewis Wallace, Governor of the Territory of New Mexico, to be published in the "New Mexican" a newspaper published in Santa Fe, New Mexico in its issue dated December 14, 1878 in which open letter Lieut. Col. Dudley defended his action in relation to civil affairs in Lincoln County and declined to accept for himself a pardon extended by His Excellency the Governor of New Mexico in a proclamation dated November 13, 1878 for misdemeanors and offences committed in the said county of Lincoln against the law of said territory in connection with the aforesaid disorder between the 1st day of February 1878 and the date of the proclamation and which pardon applied to the officers of the United States Army stationed in the said county during the said disorder.

TENTH: **That no evidence has been presented by the Recorder to sustain a statement made by His Excellency the Governor of New Mexico as follows: "That information also connecting him with the more recent murder of H.I. Chapman** *to the effect that he knew the man would be killed and announced he day of the night of the killing that one of the murderers stated publicly that he had promised Col. Dudley "to do the deed." And that no evidence from any source in this connection is before the Court.*

OPINION.

In view of the evidence adduced the Court is of the opinion that Lieut. Col. Dudley, 9th U.S. Cavalry, has not been guilty of any violation of law or orders, and that the act of proceeding to the town of Lincoln on the 19th day of July 1878 was prompted by the most humane and worthy motives and of good military judgment under exceptional circumstances.

The Court is of the opinion that none of the allegations made against Lieut. Col. Dudley by His Excellency the Governor of New Mexico or by Ira E. Leonard have been sustained and that proceedings before a court martial are therefore unnecessary.

WALLACE'S DAMAGE CONTROL

Dudley's acquittal made Wallace justify himself to men on whom his future depended: Secretary of the Interior Carl Schurz and Secretary of War George McCrary. He was unaware that he was a success to the Ring-backing Hayes administration as long as he left the Santa Fe Ring alone. So his July 30, 1879 letter to Schurz praises himself for Territorial pacification, and mentions the Court of Inquiry as a minor annoyance insulting himself. From McCrary he got reassurance on August 26, 1879: *"[T]here is nothing in the proceedings of the Court to reflect injuriously upon the course pursued by Governor Wallace."* So by September 15, 1879, to Schurz, he reduced the Lincoln County crisis to *"the killing of outlaws by outlaws"* by citing an irrelevant murder of Seven Rivers rustler, John Jones by fellow rustler, Bob Olinger (deputized in 1881 by Sheriff Pat Garrett as Billy's Lincoln guard).

Now Billy was the sole outlaw left for Wallace to attack.

SUSAN McSWEEN'S CIVIL SUIT

On the one year anniversary of the Lincoln County War Battle's start, on July 14, 1879, Ira Leonard filed Lincoln County Civil Cause No. 298 on behalf of Susan McSween and against N.A.M. Dudley for arson of her house, and Cause No. 176 for libel by defamatory affidavits. Judge Warren Bristol had changed its venue to the November 1879 Doña County's Grand Jury. Ring death threats made Leonard request a continuance. Instead, on November 18, 1879, Judge Bristol issued a warrant for her arrest on contempt, to force her life-threatening trip of 120 miles from Lincoln to Mesilla for a court appearance a week later.

There, represented by Catron's Ringite replacement as U.S. Attorney, Sidney Barnes, using his acquittal in military court, Dudley was found innocent of arson; and the libel charge was dropped. December 6, 1879's Ringite *Mesilla News* of wrote that after the verdict "outburst of applause came from the large audience which with difficulty was suppressed by the sheriff and court."

This would be the court, judge, and populace that Billy Bonney - the only Lincoln County War participant without amnesty, or pardon, or quashed prosecution, or willingness to flee - would face in 1 year, 3 months, and 24 days to receive his intended hanging sentence from the Ring.

CHAPTER 22

HUNTING THE IMAGINARY KID GANG

GUERRILLA RUSTLING

SUMMARY: After failure of all justice, and Lew Wallace's pardon inaction, Billy Bonney bided his time by petty retaliatory rustling of Ringites' stock. Wallace retreated to his imaginary world of Ben-Hur. And the Ring organized its last campaign to destroy resistance: using the Secret Service and complicit Sheriff Pat Garrett to kill "the Kid."

From Lew Wallace, Billy Bonney got, instead of a pardon, a gunslinger reputation. On January 3, 1880, that yielded his attempted killing by Texan bounty-hunter, Joe Grant, who aimed for his back in Fort Sumner's Hargrove's Saloon. Billy, however, heard the revolver's misfiring click, whirled, and shot Grant dead. As self-defense, it had no legal repercussions.

To earn money, Billy gambled a circuit from Fort Sumner to Las Vegas. And he did guerrilla rustling against Ringites as threatened in his July 13, 1878 "Regulator Manifesto" *"upon the property of Mr. Catron."* He sold stock to non-Ringites: Fort Sumner-area Dan Dedrick (also a counterfeiter) and Three Rivers rustler and slaughter house owner, Pat Coghlan. He also took rustled horses to Tascosa, Texas. His helpers were past Regulator friends Charlie Bowdre and Tom O'Folliard; and career thieves: Dave Rudabough, Tom Pickett, and Billy Wilson - likely met through counterfeiter, Dan Dedrick, who employed them to pass fake bills.

WALLACE REPORTS ON THE RING

On February 16, 1880, Lew Wallace surfaced from creating *Ben-Hur* to boast to Carl Schurz about his facing the Ring, ignorant of Schurz's and Hayes's Ring complicity, and feeing safe after appeasing it and foiling its opponents. He wrote:

Hon. C. Schurz.
Sec. Dept. Interior.
Sir.

I have the honor to inform you that the legislature of this Territory adjourned <u>sine die</u> Friday the 1st instant ...

My appointments were submitted the last day of the session. For Attorney General of the Territory, Eugene A. Fiske; for Treasurer, Juan Delgado; for Auditor, Trinidad Alarid; for District Attorney of the Second District, J. Francisco Chavez; **for District attorney of the Third District, Albert J. Fountain;** for Commissioners to revise the laws of this Territory, William Breeden, Frank Springer, and Simon B. Newcomb; for Librarian, Richard M. Tompkins ...

[AUTHOR'S NOTE: Wallace did not appoint Ira Leonard for a judgeship, instead appointing Ringites Alarid, Chavez, Fountain, Breeden, Springer, and Newcomb.]

The determined opposition was against Mr. Fiske, and of that a few words.

There were originally four applicants for the appointment, of whom the most prominent were Thomas B. Catron, William Breeden, and Eugene A. Fiske. Mr. Catron is not unknown to fame in your department. ~~I believe he has there a suspended payment on his accounts as a beef contractor. He also figures largely, I am told in the report of Mr. Angel, in which, as late U.S. District Attorney, he was admitted to a kind of head-centership of the famous old Santa Fe ring. Finding he was not likely to succeed in his aspiration owing to the very doubtful relations existing between us.~~ He retired from the contest early leaving the field to Mr. Breeden and Mr. Fiske.

[AUTHOR'S NOTE: In this draft's breath-taking cross-out, Wallace confirms Catron as Ring head, confirms Angel's Catron report (which Catron would later have Elkins destroy), confirms Catron's beef contracts, and confirms his own conflict with the Ring. Since Wallace crossed this out, it was not likely sent to Schurz – who knew anyway!]

Mr. Breeden is a gentleman of undoubtable merit, long resident of the Territory, in politics a Republican, and a leader of the party in this region. ~~In fact~~ I would have given <u>him</u> the appointment but for ~~three circumstances;~~ first that the adherents of the ring rallied unanimously to his support *after Mr. Catron's withdrawal;* ~~*second,*~~ *leaving a fear in my mind that his appointment would* ~~*have been*~~ *be received throughout the Territory as a "Ring" victory, and lose me all the results of a year and more of vigorous contest with that powerful faction.* ~~*Thirdly, it was of great*~~ *In addition to that I judged it important* ~~*at this time*~~ *to give some recognition to the incoming tide of immigration – all this, it must be observed, aside from the question whether Mr. Breeden was really a member of the "ring."*

[AUTHOR'S NOTE: Again Wallace confirms the Ring, and even lies that he made a *"vigorous contest"* against it for a *"year or more;"* when he had only pursued his outlaw myth.]

Mr. Fiske ... is of studious habits, fair ability, a Republican, and **has the merit of having made a sturdy fight against Mr. Catron and his combination, to which circumstance their** ~~*bitter fight made against*~~ *opposition to him may be chiefly attributable.*

[AUTHOR'S NOTE: Again Wallace confirms Catron's Ring.]

~~*This opposition to him in*~~ *The Council* ~~*was able to prevent his*~~ *refused to confirm*~~*ation*~~ *him ... Next morning I commissioned Mr. Fiske. He assented to his commission to the Court (Judge Prince's) and was qualified. The opposition* ~~*opposition*~~ *was carried from the Council into the Court. Argument was had as to the legality of his appointment, Col. Barnes and Mr. Fiske* **affirming and Mr. Catron and Judge denying** *... Mr. Catron's appearance in this case is significant of the meaning of the* ~~*opposition*~~ *fight in both court and council. Well informed people here accept it, so far as he is concerned, as a last struggle of the "Ring." And that you and the President may be posted as to the matter should it be brought to you in Washington, I have been thus particular ...*

[AUTHOR'S NOTE: Wallace must have seemed naïve to Ring-enablers Schurz and Hayes, who knew it would long outlast his stay, and was far from any *"last struggle."*]

The completion of the railroad [Atchison, Topeka, and Santa Fe] to this city was celebrated Monday, the 16th instant.
    I have the honor to be,
        Very respectfully, Your friend & s'v't,
        Lewis Wallace,
            Governor of New Mexico

ENTER SECRET SERVICE OPERATIVE AZARIAH WILD

SUMMARY: Billy Bonney was one of the first political assassinations aided by the Secret Service, here for the Ring. Ironically, its Operative, unaware of that plot, almost pardoned Billy himself - until the Ring intervened.

By late 1880, with Lew Wallace enabling Ring cover-ups, it seems that Catron hatched a plan to kill remaining Regulators - primarily Billy. In 1878, as U.S. Attorney, he had laid groundwork with his federal indictment Case No. 411: "The United States versus Charles Bowdre, Josiah Scurlock, Henry Brown, **William Bonney alias Henry Antrim alias the Kid**, John Middleton, Frederick Waite, Jim French, and George Coe for the murder of Andrew "Buckshot" Roberts."

Secret Service Chief, James Brooks, was recruited, likely by Elkins in Washington, to send one of his 40 Special Operatives to New Mexico Territory to investigate counterfeiting; his Department's duty as part of the U.S. Treasury Department. Pointing to ulterior motive, is that the Ring knew counterfeiting was minor, and that Regulators were not counterfeiters. But the convoluted plot involved linking counterfeiters to Billy's guerrilla rustling. Key was local Ringites duping of that Special Agent.

The chosen man, Azariah Wild, proved ideal. The actual counterfeiters were Dan Dedrick, located 12 miles south of Fort Sumner in his Bosque Grande Ranch, and his brothers, Mose and Sam, at the family livery stable in White Oaks, out of which operated their distributors of fake bills: Billy Wilson, Thomas Cooper, and Tom Pickett. Dedrick's *modus operandi* was to buy cattle with counterfeit bills, then resell them. And his men also made occasional local purchases with bills in Lincoln.

The hook was that Billy used Dedrick as one outlet for rustled stock. And Billy used Wilson and Pickett for rustling. So Wild would be led by Ringite informers to believe there was a huge counterfeiting and rustling gang headquartered in Fort Sumner, where Billy stayed. That rustling hook was also used to end Catron's ranching competition in the Tularosa Valley: Pat Coghlan. So in a report Wild described the "gang" as having "*two ranches. One seventy five miles [Coghlan's] the other twelve miles from Fort Sumner [Dedrick's].*"

ABOUT AZARIAH WILD

Azariah Faxton Wild was born on March 4, 1835 in West Fairlee, Vermont. In the Civil War, he fought for the Union until January of 1866, then settled in New Orleans with his wife and seven children. On June 15, 1877, he was hired as one of 40 Special Operatives by Secret Service Chief James Brooks. His territory was "the Gulf States." On September 26, 1877, Brooks described him as *"well posted man on Cotton and Whiskey matters."* That translated into total ignorance of the West.

Though the Secret Service dealt with counterfeiting, its agents could respond to related crimes. Thus, Wild would be led by Ring informers to link counterfeiting to rustling, so he could eliminate last Regulators too canny to catch - like Billy Bonney.

Wild was an ideal pick, being lazy, dull-witted, and gullible. From his September 10, 1880 assignment, to his December 23, 1880 departure, he did no investigating, remained with Ringites in Fort Stanton, Lincoln, White Oaks, and Roswell; and relied on Ringite contacts. He was bamboozled about a huge, murderous, counterfeiting-rustling gang; then persuaded that it was headed by Billy Bonney "the Kid" (whom he called "Antrom"). He even made the crackpot conclusion that it included Jesse James! In short, he became a farcical parody of Lew Wallace, as believing an outlaw myth, which Wallace merely fabricated.

To capture his imaginary gang, Wild helped elect Ring-complicit Pat Garrett as Lincoln County Sheriff - and also made him a Deputy U.S. Marshal. Garrett knew his mission was to eliminate Billy; but Wild had him pursue "the Kid gang."

Nevertheless, Wild got side-tracked by Ira Leonard's proposal that he give Billy a new pardon to testify against the counterfeiters. But Ringites redirected Wild, ending that chance.

And, perfidious Lew Wallace encouraged Wild's pursuit of "the Kid gang;" even offering a $500 reward on December 22, 1880.

Key is that without Wild and his puppet Sheriff, Garrett, using Secret Service-funded spies and Texas possemen, Billy would never have been captured for his Mesilla hanging trial. Wild sealed Billy's tragic and unjust fate.

Following Wild's Mexico Territory stay, he served as a Special Operative out of New Orleans until he resigned on June 10, 1893; possibly forced out after pursuit of corrupt New Orleans officials. Wild died of heart disease in New Orleans on June 10, 1920.

WILD'S DAILY SECRET SERVICE REPORTS

Azariah Wild followed Secret Service protocol of writing a daily report to his Chief, James Brooks; which, for his New Mexico Territory assignment, included paying spies. He got his assignment on September 10th, and responded to Chief Brooks on September 11th on his official report form, as follows:

U.S. Treasury Department,
SECRET-SERVICE DIVISION,

<u>New Orleans</u>   District

James J. Brooks,
  Chief U.S. Secret Service

Sir: I have the honor to submit the following, my report as <u>Special</u> Operative of this District for ___<u>Friday</u>___ the <u>10</u>th day of ___<u>September</u>___, 18<u>80</u>, written at <u>New Orleans, Louisiana</u>, and completed at <u>9</u> o'clock <u>A.</u> M on the <u>11</u>th day of _____<u>September</u>_____, 18<u>80</u>
In New Orleans La.

        Engaged in and about the city the entire day.
        I have the honor to acknowledge the receipt of your letter of the 7th instant relative to my trip to New Mexico with your letters received by the Department from citizens of New Mexico enclosed therewith.
        I expect to start for New Mexico next Wednesday Sept 15th. I will endeavor to carry out your wishes in the matter.
        I have made arrangements for several Winchester rifles to take along with me in case they are wanted they are at hand.
        I also have spoken to the U.S. Marshal [John Sherman] for such articles as I may want in the shape of "bracelets etc"...

Respectfully Submitted
Azariah F. Wild
Special Operative

Wild's early reports in New Mexico Territory show he first correctly identified counterfeit bill distributors - whom he calls *"passers of the queer"* - as William Wilson and a Thomas Cooper.

For September 20th, he reported from Santa Fe, after meeting with Ringite U.S. Attorney Sidney Barnes and James Dolan, who came as the victimized Lincoln merchant who got a counterfeit $100 bill. These "informants" set-up Wild by magnifying outlawry of counterfeiter, Dan Dedrick's, men. Wild wrote:

Engaged ... at the office of U.S. Attorney Barnes in consultation with him about the counterfeiting cases in White Oaks Lincoln County New Mexico ... [H]e will look more into the case, send for the U.S. Marshal [John Sherman] ... consult together and act in concert.

The men (Thomas Cooper and William Wilson) are amongst the worst characters in Lincoln County where there have been over forty murders committed within the past two years, and not an arrest made.

Judging from statements made by U.S. Attorney Barnes a bad state of affairs exists here in New Mexico. He informs me that there has not been a single arrest made here since last term of Court .... [and has] hopes of arresting Wilson and Cooper ...

I met the post trader [James Dolan] here this day from Fort Stanton on whom one [of] these notes was passed. He has offered to render me any assistance possible, *and has named several parties on whom I can rely to assist in making the arrests when we are ready to act.*

He repeats the information contained in the letters you sent me only a little more full in his details.

[AUTHOR'S NOTE: That Chief Brooks was the Ring's contact, sending his unaware Special Operative to do the Ring's bidding, is indicated by "merchant James Dolan" being one of the "citizens" who provided "letters" to the Secret Service to get Wild assigned.]

For September 22, 1880, Wild wrote from Santa Fe, revealing his Ring manipulation; though confusing Lincoln residents' refusal to arrest their hero Regulators with White Oaks residents, who were unaware of Lincoln County War issues. In fact, White Oaks men, later agitated by Wild, would form a rabid posse to capture "the Kid." Wild wrote dramatically:

> *I am going to have trouble in getting assistance to make arrests in White Oaks. The reputation of Lincoln County in which White Oaks is situated, that no one is willing to undertake the arrests or be known to have had anything to do with so far as I can find thus far, unless more money is paid than I believe the Division can afford to pay. I have come here to arrest or have these men arrested and am bound to do it if I have to attempt it by myself.*

For September 24, 1880, Wild, staying put in Santa Fe, met with Lincoln Ringites, vouched for as *"reliable"* by Ringite U.S. Attorney Barnes. Idiotically, Wild had disguised himself as a miner (presumably in denim); so he must have stood out like a sore thumb. He wrote:

> *I have this day seen and consulted in company with U.S. Attorney Barnes with several reliable men who are doing business in Lincoln County New Mexico [James Dolan; John Riley; Catron's brother-in-law, Edgar Walz] and who know the parties who I am after and all about them.*
>
> *The U.S. Attorney [Barnes] will meet with the U.S. Marshal [Sherman] on Monday at the Albuquerque Court and endeavor to get him to send 4 or six good Deputies down to make the arrests soon as he hears from me.*
>
> *I have purchased me a complete suit of miners clothes ... which was necessary to keep from being suspicioned.*

For September 25, 1880, writing from Santa Fe to get a free railroad pass - he stupidly revealed to the railroad company his secret mission about a *"band of Counterfeiters and passers of the queer [who] are operating in the Territory ... I have been directed by the Department to visit this section of the country with a view to breaking them up and bring them to justice."*

For October 3, 1880, Wild wrote from Fort Stanton after meeting in Lincoln with James Dolan to see the counterfeit bill. But straying from Ring control in town, he also met with Ira Leonard - someone who could set him straight.

For October 4, 1880, Wild wrote from Fort Stanton documenting William Wilson's also passing a $100 counterfeit bill to Lincoln merchant José Montaño, and another to post trader firm Dowlin and Delaney, describing the bills, and stating that he would use those victims as witnesses against suspects, William Wilson and Thomas Cooper (whom misnames as "*Sam*").

FIRST FOCUS ON BILLY BONNEY

For October 5, 1880, from Fort Stanton, Wild showed Ring manipulation, likely by Dolan, by expanding focus on Billy Wilson to rustling. Wild stated: *"[H]e is an American who has been here in Lincoln County for several years, and has the name of being engaged with others of his kind in stealing horses and cattle."* That segued into linking him to Billy Bonney, Charlie Bowdre, and Tom O'Folliard at Fort Sumner, with whom Wilson rustled. About Billy, he reported: *"William Antrom [Antrim] alias Wm Bonney alias Billy Kid"* is *"an outlaw in the mountains here who came here from Arizona after committing a murder there."* Using "Antrom" with an Arizona murder, implies Catron's ferreting out of past indictments - as he did in 1895 to attack his disbarment official, District Attorney Jacob H. Crist. So he had likely found Billy's 1877 Cahill killing as Henry "Antrim" - with Dolan telling Wild.

Thus, Wild, 28 days after case assignment, had been told by Barnes, Dolan, and Walz - with Catron's agent, David Easton, now added - that Billy was a murderous counterfeiter outlaw *"with whom these cattle thieves meet, and by many it is believed that they (the cattle thieves and shovers of the queer) receive the counterfeit money."* Though Wild still doubted, he inflated his investigation to men of *"notorious character [acting] in concert in their hellish deeds."* He wrote for that October 5th report:

> In tracing up the history and character of William Wilson known here as Billy Wilson I found that he is an American who has been here in Lincoln County for several years, and has the name of being engaged with others of his kind at stealing horses and cattle. A few weeks ago he and several of his clan stole 38 head of beef cattle from a ranch near Fort Bascom, and brought them here to Lincoln County where they found their way into the hands of the United States and are now on the Mescalero Indian Reservation **as I am informed by David Easton, one of the men in charge.** The evidence is conclusive against Wilson as being the party who stole them and sold them here ...

[AUTHOR'S NOTE: Ringite Easton conceals Catron's rustling for beef contracts by blaming it on what Wild calls the "clan" - which he soon updated to Western lingo of "gang." And citing rustling at Fort Bascom – at the Texas border - indicates that he was now blaming any Territorial rustling on this "clan."]

There is an outlaw in the mountains here who came here from Arizona after committing a murder there named William Antrom alias W<u>m</u> Bonney alias Billy Kid with whom these cattle thieves meet, and by many it is believed that they (the cattle thieves and shovers of the queer) receive the counterfeit money. I have found no evidence so far to support their suspicions. The people here as a general thing do not know good money from bad.

The following is a copy of a letter this day [October 5, 1880] written to U.S. Attorney Barnes ...

S.M. Barnes Esq.
    U.S. Attorney
        Santa Fe New Mexico
Dear Sir:

On or about the 5th day of August 1880 in the town of Lincoln (Lincoln County) New Mexico one William Wilson now residing at White Oaks did pass on James J. Dolin [sic] a $100 counterfeit national bank note on the Merchants National Bank of New Bedford Massachusetts dated February 14, 1865 ...

In connection with the passing of this note I will state that at the time William Wilson passed the note on Dolin he (Wilson) gave him (Dolin) three $100 notes of the same kind and as he believes of the same character with a $50 note ...

I will respectfully state from information that [Thomas] Cooper and [William] Wilson are both employed at a livery & sales stables at White Oaks [owned by counterfeiter, Dan Dedrick's brothers, Mose and Sam] kept by James West a notorious character recently from Texas.

When they go out they generally travel together, and are supposed to act in concert in their hellish deeds.

I have this far been unable to find only one man who is willing to step forward, and assist in the arrest of these men not out of any fear they have of their resistance but assassination afterwards ...

I expect to go to White Oaks the last of this week & expect to remain some days ...

        Very Respectfully Yours
            Azariah Wild
              Special Operative

The letter of which the foregoing is a copy has been written as per agreement with the U.S. Attorney [Ringite Sidney Barnes] before leaving Santa Fe.

He (the U.S. Attorney) there proposed that he would swear out warrants himself on information I would send him [from Ring informants], and have Deputy Marshals sent from Santa Fe provided men could not be found in Lincoln County to make the arrests.

I expect to go to Lincoln at 7 A.M. Wednesday the 6th to meet Judge Leonard and the Clerk of Court who went to White Oaks Sunday morning after which I will go to the Oaks myself - the first conveyance I can get.

[AUTHOR'S NOTE: Leonard was trying to counter Ring control. Though, with usual inadequate strategizing, he never explained the Ring to Wild or put Billy's Regulator role in perspective.]

A SECRET SERVICE PARDON

Since Azariah Wild was not intentionally aiding the Ring, he accepted Ira Leonard's help to investigate the counterfeiting. So Leonard, as Billy's lawyer, engineered a second pardon bargain in exchange for Billy's testimony against the real counterfeiters (like Dan Dedrick). He also disclosed the pardon bargain with Wallace, explaining Billy's exclusion in the Amnesty Proclamation; as Wild reported: "*Gov. Wallace has issued a proclamation granting immunity to those not indicted but as Antrom has been indicted the proclamation did not cover his (Antrom's) case.*" So Wild was now poised to save Billy's life by a pardon which Wallace might have backed, since it freed him of its responsibility.

Wild described the new pardon option in his report for October 8, 1880, written in Fort Stanton; stating:

I left Fort Stanton at 7 o'clock A.M. on the stage and reached Lincoln the County seat at 8:30 A.M. a distance of 9 miles.

The object of my visit to Lincoln was to see Judge Ira Leonard and the Clerk of the County Court who went to White Oaks Sunday and returned Tuesday.

They inform me that Tom Cooper is at White Oaks. That William Wilson left White Oaks some time since and was at Bosque Grande N.M. [counterfeiter Dan Dedrick's ranch] on the Rio Pecos above [sic- 12 miles below] Fort Sumner ...

> In my report of October 5th I spoke of an outlaw whose name was Antrom alias Billy Bonney. During the Lincoln Co. War he killed men on the Indian Reservation for which he has been indicted in the Territorial and the United States Court.

[AUTHOR'S NOTE: Wild, likely informed by Leonard, garbles Billy's "Buckshot" Roberts 1878 federal murder indictment by U.S. Attorney Catron as killing men on the Reservation.]

> Gov. Wallace has issued a proclamation granting immunity to those not indicted but as Antrom has been indicted the proclamation did not cover his (Antrom's) case and he (Antrom) has been in the mountains as an outlaw ever since a space of about two years time.
>
> Governor Wallace has since written Antrom's attorney on the subject saying he should be let go but has failed to put it on shape that satisfied Judge Leonard Antroms attorney.

[AUTHOR'S NOTE: This is Wild's garbling of Wallace's not filing Billy's pardon in a court of law.]

> It is believed, and in fact is almost known that he (Antrom) is one of the leading members of this gang.

[AUTHOR'S NOTE: Wild here entangles his Ringite input, and is clearly confused about Billy's counterfeiting role. And it seems that Leonard forgot to describe Billy's anti-Ring role or testimonies. In fact Wild, an honest man, might have been sympathetic, since he himself was likely forced into retirement in 1893 for exposing New Orleans political corruption. But the toxic seed had been planted in Wild's mind that Billy was *"one of the leading members of this gang."* And with increasing Ringite input, Wild would soon claim Billy as the gang's leader.]

> Antrom has recently written a letter to Judge Leonard which has been shown to me in confidence that leads me to believe that we can use Antrom in these cases provided Gov. Wallace will make good his written promises and the U.S. Attorney [Barnes] will allow the case pending in the U.S. Court to slumber and give him (Antrom) one more chance to reform.

[AUTHOR'S NOTE: Wild is prepared to get Billy's pardon granted. He is convinced Wallace made the pardon promise, and believes he could get Wallace to issue the pardon affidavit.

But Wild also realizes that Catron's federal indictment for the "Buckshot" Roberts killing would block Territorial gubernatorial pardon unless "*the U.S. Attorney [Barnes] will allow the case pending in the U.S. Court to slumber.*" In fact, Wild's identifying that federal indictment obstacle may have helped slow-witted Leonard formulate the most clever argument of his career to get it quashed in Billy's 1881 hanging trial.]

I have promised nothing and will not except to receive any propositions he (Leonard) and his client see fit to make and submit them to U.S. Attorney Barnes.

Judge Leonard has written Antrom to meet him (Leonard) at once for consultation.

The chances are that the conversation will take place within the next week when I will report fully to you and submit whatever propositions they see fit to make to US. Attorney Barnes for such action as he deems proper to take.

[AUTHOR'S NOTE: Leonard's pardon plan was doomed, since Wild naively planned to reveal it to the Ring via Barnes.]

While it may appear to you that I am working up this case slowly I will respectfully ask you to take into consideration that I am where there is no telegraphic communications with any point [apparently the Ring concealed the Fort Stanton telegraphic option], and the mail facilities next to nothing so that I have not received a letter since I left New Orleans even from my own family, also that I am in a place where the better citizens are afraid of their lives should they be known to give information against the gang, and the officers are more or less linked in and connected with the outlaws. **In my candid judgment I have struck the worst nest of counterfeiters in the United States, one that I believe will lead to the headquarters of the gang and the long looked for [money printing] plates if continuously worked.**

If you will have patience with me I am willing to remain here and will work these cases although the change of climate is great between this and that in my District proper [New Orleans]. We have had snow in the mountains since I arrived, and I have been compelled to get heavy clothing throughout.

[AUTHOR'S NOTE: Wild's anxiety about justifying his mission after collecting almost no counterfeit bills and apprehending no counterfeiters or printing plates made him exaggerate the magnitude of his quarry as "*the worst nest of counterfeiters in the United States.*" He was further befuddled by Ring input which isolated him by concealing the telegraphic option at Fort Stanton, declared citizens as afraid to give evidence against the "gang" (instead of against the Ring), and which accused Sheriff Kimbrell as in cahoots with the counterfeiters. Also, soft and miserable Wild was further curtailing his activities because of cold weather, leaving himself open to more Ring control. All these variables would add up to his lazy solution: the creation of "the gigantic Kid gang."]

For October 7, 1880, from Fort Stanton, Wild reported Ira Leonard's apparent attempt to also educate him on Ring frauds - here land grants - possibly as lead-in to explaining Billy's freedom fighting role. Wild was uninterested in the big picture, and Leonard did not pursue it. Instead, he informed Wild about counterfeiters - Dan Dedrick, James West, Billy Wilson, and Thomas Cooper - as a "gang." But he carelessly did not exclude Billy, leaving Wild open to Ringite's inclusion of Billy in it.

Wild's report for October 8, 1880, from Fort Stanton, made clear that Catron's brother-in-law, Edgar Walz, had been in Wild's first meeting with U.S. Attorney Barnes. Walz was now acting as Wild's minder (probably with James Dolan) by setting up "informers." One was a William Delaney. Wild wrote: *"Post Master and post trader here [with Will Dowlin], and he believes there is just such a gang working the frontier ...* **He also thinks Antrom alias Billy Bonney to be one of the gang**.*"* Demonstrated is a ricochet technique of Ringite cronies to trick Wild - with Delaney and Dowlin in with Walz and Dolan. Likely aware of a new pardon promise, they were linking Billy to the "gang" to end Wild's plan.

Reporting for October 9, 1880, still at Fort Stanton, in his letter to Ringite U.S. Attorney Sidney Barnes - recopied in his report - Wild revealed his new pardon bargain for Billy. He also revealed that Ira Leonard had given information about the counterfeiters in White Oaks and at Dan Dedrick's ranch - likely obtained by Leonard from Billy to advertise Billy's value to justify the new pardon bargain. In addition, Billy wrote himself. Wild stated: *"I have recently seen a letter written by him [Billy] in which he expresses himself as being tired of dodging the officers &c. The letter has been answered and the chances are that I will meet him."* But Wild added derogatory Ringite input about Billy, and located him at Fort Sumner, making clear that well-meaning but slow-witted Leonard, had failed to counteract Ring sabotage. So Wild had used the information to inform the Ring, via Barnes, about Billy's new possible pardon. Wild wrote:

The following is a copy of a letter written to U.S. Attorney Barnes this day: Fort Stanton NM Oct 9th 1880

Hon Sidney N Barnes
       U.S. Attorney Santa Fe N.M. –
Dear Sir.
       Since I wrote you last Judge Leonard and the Clerk of Court have been to White Oaks, and on their return inform me that West with whom Cooper and Wilson have been making their headquarters at White Oaks left there around the 24th of September to go to Deadwood to look after a drove of cattle supposed to have been stolen by the clan.
       William Wilson is reported to be at Bosque Grande at Dedrick's ranch. Dedrick is reported as being one of the leaders of the clan, and partners with West in the Corral at White Oaks.

[AUTHOR'S NOTE: Wild is on the right track for counterfeiting, likely getting the information from Ira Leonard via Billy.]

William Antrom alias Billy Kid is at Fort Sumner and is a member of the clan. I have recently seen a letter written by him in which he expresses himself as being tired of challenging the officers. The letter has been answered and the chances are that I will meet with him under circumstances which may bring about good results the particulars of which I will communicate should they be worthy of mention ...

While I am waiting for the necessary papers to arrest Wilson and Cooper I am working to catch other fish in my net, and if able to use Antrom alias Billy Kid on reasonable terms with the party referred to as being willing to give information for a consideration I am satisfied full fifty arrests will follow.

[AUTHOR'S NOTE: Leonard's careless strategy for a face-to-face meeting of Billy with Wild, left Billy open to capture; which Wild's revelation to Barnes now ensured. And Wild had inflated the "gang" to 50 strong!]

                              Respectfully Yours
                              Azariah F. Wild

At 2 o'clock P.M. I received through the mail a letter from Ira E. Leonard Esq. of Lincoln dated Oct 9th giving information relative to a meeting of 14 of the clan at [Beaver] Smith's Saloon at Fort Sumner ... I wrote out a copy of this letter and forwarded it to U.S. Attorney Barnes ...

I will respond to Judge Leonards request and go to Lincoln Monday A.M. [October 11, 1880].

[AUTHOR'S NOTE: Leonard's eagerness to help made Wild connect a "gang" to Fort Sumner, where he also located Billy.]

Reporting for October 11, 1880, Wild wrote from Lincoln, having followed Ira Leonard's misguided suggestion to appoint Bob Olinger as U.S. Deputy Marshal to catch the counterfeiters. Leonard was apparently unaware that Olinger was one of the Seven Rivers murderers of John Tunstall and a killer possemen in the Lincoln County War. Wild also requested from Barnes arrest warrants for Regulators. So Ringite input had scuttled Leonard's pardon plan: Wild intended to arrest Billy, Bowdre, Scurlock, and O'Folliard. To Barnes, Wild wrote: "*It may be well to send down warrants for the other parties who stand indicted in U.S. Court, and who are making Fort Sumner their headquarters.*"

For October 14, 1880, still in Lincoln, Wild demonstrated that he had merged counterfeiters with Billy's group in Fort Sumner. He wrote: "*William Wilson is at present with eighteen other desperados at Fort Sumner one hundred and sixty miles from here, and 125 miles from Las Vegas. He has with him three men who were indicted in the U.S. Court.* **They are a terror to the whole country** *... I think I will have trouble in making the arrests.*"

Since October 6, 1880, Billy's new pardon was in abeyance, awaiting the Wild meeting. But by October 16, 1880, Billy, far more canny than Leonard, having determined the mail route for Wild's reports, robbed the stagecoach to get them. He would have read Wild' report for October 11th stating: "*It may be well to send down warrants for the other parties who stand indicted in U.S. Court, and who are making Fort Sumner their headquarters.*" He decided that meeting with Wild would be a trap.

So the second pardon chance was lost because of Ira Leonard's failure to properly negotiate or to clarify Billy's anti-Ring role. Wild did not mention it again. Like Lew Wallace, having accomplished nothing in the Territory, Wild now needed "the Kid" to fake his own outlaw myth to feign action.

WILD'S IMAGINARY OUTLAW GANG

Wild was unaware of the mail theft for four days. Reporting on October 15, 1880, still from Lincoln, he gave inadvertent evidence of Catron as his mission's puppeteer. Writing a garbled rendition of Tom Cooper's helping John Chisum round up rustled cattle, Wild stopped calling the Carrizozo ranch Edgar Walz's, and correctly called it *"Catron's ranch."* Telling, is Wild's familiarity by omitting the full name, as required. And he even knew that Chisum's rustled cattle were at *"Catron's ranch!"* He wrote: *"I have received reliable information that Tom Cooper was in White Oaks Thursday morning and left to go to* **Catron's ranch ten miles distant to assist John Chisum 'round up' his cattle.***"*

Reporting for October 16, 1880, still in Lincoln, Wild blamed his inactivity on awaiting arrest warrants, and on lawmen not arresting men with federal indictments (like Billy). Ringite input is evident. Now Wild had a big gang in Fort Sumner, a Sheriff George Kimbrell playing cards with Billy, and Catron's brother-in-law, Edgar Walz, offering a "witness" about the gang. Also, Wild, was getting paranoid in his isolated situation, stating: *"I am led to believe that many people here mistrust my business."* He wrote:

These men (outlaws) have centered at and make Fort Sumner their headquarters, and at the present time there are about eighteen notorious characters there who are engaged in stealing stock, passing counterfeit money, and robbing the mails all of which they do with impunity and as I am told in open daylight.

There are four of the men who I number amongst the eighteen who are indicted in the U.S. Court (one for murdering the Indian Agent) [Billy with garbled Blazer's Mill killing of "Buckshot" Roberts] **and for whom warrants are out for and no attempt has been made to arrest them although I am reliably informed he** [Billy] **comes into the towns nearby and plays cards with the Sheriff of this county** [George Kimbrell]. *I have endeavored to get warrants of arrest from the territorial courts for these parties but find the witnesses unwilling to appear. I also find that should the arrests be made that the lives of the court officers would be in danger ... To place them in jail we could not do as we have none ...*

[AUTHOR'S NOTE: The refusal of the locals to help, would result in Pat Garrett's recruiting Texans to hunt Billy.]

> *I am led to believe that many people here mistrust my business ... I have traced up another $100 – note and trace it back to William Wilson ... I have not yet seen the note ...*
>
> *In a recent report I spoke of a man who claimed he could give valuable information who was in the employ of E.A. Waltz [Walz]. I have just received a note from Walz [about that].*

Wild's report for October 17, 1880, from Lincoln, focused on random "outlaws" and Regulators, whose histories he garbled:

> *As I have learned the names of several of the outlaws now congregated at and near Fort Sumner I will give them with their history so far as I have it which is about as follows:*
>
> *Charles Bowdre: Hails from Va. Indicted by the U.S. Grand Jury in 3rd Dist. of this Territory for murder.*
>
> **William Antrom alias Billie Bonnie alias "Billie Kid": Indicted in 3rd District of U.S. Court for the murder of the Indian Agent. Comes from Kansas here.**
>
> *Dr Joseph G. Scurlock [Josiah "Doc" Scurlock]: Indicted for same offense. He claims Georgia as his native place. He is indicted for murder in 3rd Dist. U.S. Court. He killed one man each in Louisiana and Texas ...*
>
> *James French: From Texas. Indicted in U.S. Court for murdering Maj Brady Sheriff of Lincoln County ...*
>
> *There are many more men connected with this gang whose names I have not learned but are making Fort Sumner and vicinity their headquarters.*

Wild's report for October 18, 1880, still from Lincoln, documents contact with Edgar Walz about his witness employee, a James DeVours, who, refused to *"make any written proposition"* but will *"tell you all he knows about the gang of counterfeiters."* DeVours, supposedly a ranch hand, was in the long Ring tradition of fake testifiers, adding, according to Walz, that he would *"leave it to your Chief to say what he shall receive [be paid] provided that his name can be kept secret."* So this supposed ranch hand knew about the Secret Service Chief! DeVours claimed, according to Walz, that *"their presses and plates are in this county ... [and] they have near $200,000 struck ... [T]here are a large number of persons engaged in passing [the counterfeit bills]."* Wild added officiously: *"I do not fully credit his story but I think enough of it to probe it to the bottom."*

For his report for October 20, 1880, still in Lincoln, Wild finally admitted to Chief Brooks Billy's mail theft. He muffled that fiasco by adding mail theft to his fabricated gang's crimes, and claiming need of a posse to seize them in Fort Sumner:

In this mail I had several reports which if taken and read as they must have been as both mail pouches were cut open and the contents scattered about the ground. If this is as I believe it must be the plans of our capture and my mission here is as well known to them as it is to myself.

I have respectfully notified the U.S. Attorney [Sidney Barnes] of this gang of men, and of their headquarters being at Fort Sumner. I have also asked for warrants to arrest these men and for Commissions for such men as are willing to assist me in the making of the arrests ...

I have organized secretly a "Posse Comitatus" of thirty men here to go and assist me in making these arrests. Not only those who are wanted for murder & robbing the U.S. mail and are indicted in the U.S. Courts ...

So far as having arrests made by the Territorial officers I have explained the many difficulties. **The Sheriff of this county [George Kimbrell] has since he had the warrants in his possession for their arrest for murder under the hand of the Territory played cards and drank with him [Billy] repeatedly** ...

The parties Kid, Wilson, O'Follier [O'Folliard] and Picket who are undoubtedly the ones who robbed the mail on the 17th [sic – 16th] are out at a ranch twelve miles from Fort Sumner. Tom Cooper and Dedrick are at White Oaks, and can be taken at any time unless my reports taken from the mail frighten them away.

[AUTHOR'S NOTE: Billy is now listed first, as Wild lumps Regulators with Dan Dedrick's few counterfeiters]

For October 22, 1880, still in Lincoln, Wild now accepted any Ringite input to inflate his "*Wilson and Kid gang*," and attributed to it any rustling in the Territory. He wrote:

Wilson and his gang have within the past four days stolen sixty-eight head of cattle from a man named Ellis – 400 head from another party and seven horses from John Chisum ...

The man who was driving the mail back at the time it was robbed says (so I am informed by the mail carrier who arrived at this post [Fort Stanton] this morning) recognized several of the gang as being **the Wilson and Kid gang** who done the robbing of the mail on the night of the 16th inst.

I am informed that the Sheriff of San Miguel County [including Fort Sumner] went to their headquarters near Fort Sumner to arrest some one of the gang and was repulsed and left without making arrests.

For October 27, 1880, still in Lincoln, Wild included a copy of his response letter to Edgar Walz's "ranch hand witness," James DeVours - who had written with suspiciously legal skill sounding like Catron - to confirm payment for information.

For October 28, 1880, still from Lincoln, Wild reported that he had told DeVours that he was "*at liberty to select for this purpose the men*" for spying. That meant that Wild had handed his investigation to the Ring! For Chief Brooks, Wild now inflated the gang to a "*force,*" writing:

I am now perfectly confident that there is a counterfeiting gang here who are making counterfeit $100 – and $50 – notes as I am of anything that I do not know absolutely certain, and that I have not seen with my own eyes ...
The force of desperados now at Fort Sumner the headquarters of the gang numbers twenty six. They openly say that they number sixty two in Lincoln County and defy the authorities.
Captain Conrad now commanding at Fort Stanton said to me "You might as well go. You never will be able to make the arrests. You have not, and in my judgment cannot get a sufficient force to handle the men you have to contend with."

[AUTHOR'S NOTE: Here gullible Wild reveals himself also being fed Ringite information by colluding Fort Stanton officers.]

I replied I believed I would but at the same time was in doubt.
I especially call your attention to the location: **All the outlaws or nearly all have been driven out of Texas and Arizona, and concentrated at Fort Sumner. They have two ranches. One seventy five miles the other twelve miles from Fort Sumner. They have a band of their men out stealing horses, cattle, robbing mails ... whilst the balance of their force remain at the ranch guarding stock they have stolen ...**

[AUTHOR'S NOTE: Wild has fused Dan Dedrick's counterfeiting to Billy's petty rustling and any other Territorial rustling, now in line with the Ring's and Lew Wallace's outlaw myth!]

This is a case that requires time to work but I candidly believe I can work it successfully by taking time. If I had a good man with me it would be of great service.

The leading man of the gang is W.H. West ... He is one of the proprietors of a coral or stable at White Oaks. He has as partners several brothers named Dedrick [Dan, Mose, Sam] who own a ranch near Fort Sumner. It is at this ranch that it is believed the plates and tools &c are at the present time.

I am informed this day by Judge Leonard that a lady passenger who was along at the time the stage was robbed near Fort Sumner that she recognized No. 80 and William Antrom alias "Billy Bony" as two of the robbers who robbed her and the mails.

By his October 31, 1880 report, still from Lincoln, Wild hysterically decided he was in another Lincoln County War! Additionally, he revealed his intent and power to "*kill.*" He wrote:

If things are not looked to [by arrests] ... **soon it will end in another "Lincoln County War."** *I have on two occasions stopped a disturbance between the stockmen and the outlaws by asking them to delay until I could get warrants for my parties when we would take the eleven warrants now here and* **arrest or kill the whole business.** *They now say as soon as the election is over they are going to delay no longer.*

[AUTHOR'S NOTE: Revealed is that Wild was agitating White Oaks miners (here called "stockmen") about "outlaws." And he had worked to get Ring-complicit Pat Garrett elected Sheriff to replace George Kimbrell to "*arrest or kill the whole business.*"]

ENTER PAT GARRETT

The person picked by the Ring to kill Billy was Patrick Floyd Garrett: a tall, 30 year old, depressive, alcoholic, past murderer and ex-buffalo hunter living in Fort Sumner. He would have met frequent visitor, Billy Bonney. Azariah Wild was proving inadequate for the task, and Sheriff, George Kimbrell, was anti-Ring. So Garrett was advertised as a law-and-order candidate to White Oaks men, misled by Wild's hunt for a rustling and counterfeiting gang headed by Billy Bonney and Billy Wilson.

Garrett was elected Sheriff on November 2, 1880. Wild immediately made him a Deputy U.S. Marshal to add Territorial jurisdiction, and forced Sheriff Kimbrell to deputize him.

Garrett likely knew that the "Kid gang" was a fabrication. But he also knew that killing Billy was a life-changing chance. He took it; and, as his outlaw myth book of 1882, *The Authentic Life of Billy the Kid*, showed, he had no intent to ever reveal the truth.

WITCH-HUNTING BILLY

Having recruited Sheriff-elect Garrett and mob-mentality White Oaks residents, Azariah Wild decided to attack Fort Sumner. For November 4, 1880, still in Lincoln, he wrote to Chief Brooks: *"I am now engaged in making preparations to get fifty men together to go to Fort Sumner and arrest this gang of men."*

Reporting for November 6, 1880, still in Lincoln, Wild was in a paranoid tizzy about his swelling "gang," with its "leaders": *"William Wilson and ... 'Billy Kid.'"* And Judge Bristol happily issued arrest warrants for their Secret Service dupe. Wild wrote:

From every indication there is no scare amongst this gang or they are calculating to make a stand at Fort Sumner and fight. They are known to be twenty nine in number ...

Judge Bristol is now here and in an interview with him yesterday he said he would issue warrants for parties who have been engaged in violating the United States law ...

I will soon be in readiness to go to Fort Sumner after certain parties ... The parties who robbed the mail or who were the leaders of it was William Wilson and **William Antrom alias "Billy Bony" alias "Billy Kid."**

Reporting for November 10, 1880, still in Lincoln, Wild had met with Garrett *"to make a raid on Fort Sumner to arrest the counterfeiters."* Wild, declared the "gang" *"the worst (organization) gang of men that this country has;"* writing:

[W]e have organized a force in the "Pan Handle" (Texas) to cooperate with us in this raid with a aim of acquiring a huge number of these outfits who are from that state. By doing this there will be but little chance of their escaping and if captured **will**

probably break up the worst (organization) gang of men that this country has. John Kinney has qualified as Deputy U.S. Marshal so I have a man to represent the U.S. Marshal [Garrett] while the other parties will act as a 'Posse Comitatus.'"

[AUTHOR'S NOTE: From Ringites' referrals, Wild appointed as a Deputy U.S. Marshal outlaw, John Kinney: Ringite rustler and San Patricio massacre perpetrator with Sheriff Peppin, and posseman in the Lincoln County War Battle! This added to making Seven Rivers rustler Robert Olinger a Deputy U.S. Marshal, as he reported on October 13, 1880. Even Lew Wallace had called Olinger *"amongst the most bloody of the "Bandits of the Pecos"* in a September 15, 1879 letter to Carl Schurz.]

For November 14, 1880, still in Lincoln, Wild described using a White Oaks man, James Bell, *"to make a deal with [a counterfeiter] if possible."* (Bell would be a posseman involved in killing Jim Carlyle in friendly fire at Greathouse's ranch, then blaming Billy. He was later deputized by Pat Garrett as Billy's pre-hanging guard, and was killed by Billy in his jailbreak.)

For November 18th and 20th, 1880, still in Lincoln, Wild reported hiring Garrett's friend, Barney Mason, Peter Maxwell's Fort Sumner foreman, to spy there. He Wild wrote:

It appears from the statements of Garrett and Mason that he (Mason) is an experienced stockman and is now and has been for some time past in the employ of a man named Maxwell who resides at Fort Sumner. He (Mason) states that a few days ago one Daniel Dedrick who resides at Bosque Grande, and who has an interest with his brother Samuel Dedrick & West in a livery stable at White Oaks came to him and proposed [to hire him to take $30,000 counterfeit money to Texas, buy cattle there, take them to a place near Mexico to Dedrick and West, then leave the country] ...

[And] Mason states that William Wilson boards at his house when at Fort Sumner ...

[And Mason states] [t]hat William Wilson and Billy Kid left about the 15th inst with sixty head of stolen horses and went down the Canadian River to be gone two or three weeks. That on their return they would probably return to his house when he would turn them over to Patrick F. Garrett Deputy U.S. Marshall and Sheriff.

[AUTHOR'S NOTE: Manipulated by Pat Garrett and Barney Mason, this is how Wild mingled Billy's petty rustling with a concocted Wilson-Kid gang to feign accomplishment to Chief Brooks for his failed mission.]

COYOTE SPRING AND GREATHOUSE AMBUSHES

Having elected Pat Garrett as Sheriff by their majority voting to eliminate "the Kid gang," White Oaks men were primed for action; though unaware Billy was still bringing rustled horses to the Dedrick's livery there. The residents formed the White Oaks posse, under Deputy Sheriff Will Hudgens, to capture him.

On November 22, 1880, they ambushed Billy and his companions near White Oaks at their Coyote Spring campsite; but firing wildly, they merely killed two of their quarry's horses.

Billy's group made it to "Whiskey Jim" Greathouse's ranch, about 40 miles to the north. There, at November 28, 1880's dawn, the posse attacked them again. When Billy offered to negotiate, they sent in Jim Carlyle. But Carlyle panicked, fleeing through a window, and being killed in friendly fire when mistaken for Billy. The posse then retreated. But Billy finally realized his danger.

The posse later burned down the that ranch, and blamed Carlyle's killing on Billy. The Ring, Wallace, and Wild had fanned flames of lies enough for a spreading conflagration.

From Pat Garrett's Roswell home, Azariah Wild reported his fables. For November 23, 1880, related to Chief Brooks the Coyote Spring ambush. His "Billy Kid" was now leader of the *"Kid force,"* magnified to outnumber White Oaks men, with exaggerated casualties of horses. He wrote: *"The [Deputy] Sheriff at White Oaks with his Posse went out ... and attempted to arrest Billy Kid, William Wilson and others on Monday the 22nd instant and have return to town empty handed.* **Kid force out numbered that of the Sheriffs***. Each party had several horses killed ... There is talk of "Judge Lynch" trying them at last account."*

Wrongly dating as November 26th, still at Garrett's house, excited Wild reported the Greathouse ranch attack of the 28th: *"Information has just reached me through a reliable source that Billy Kid had been driven out of the Canadian River country and was now at Greathouse's ranch with twenty five armed men and a bunch of stolen horses ...The citizens went out to capture them but they made their escape after about forty shots were exchanged."*

Reporting for that November 26th, still at Garrett's house, Wild invented a near-war, and described Garrett's posse; implying Garrett had lied about the "Kid gang" as being Texas rustlers to get the Panhandle Cattleman's Association involved. Wild wrote:

Information has reached me here this day that William Wilson with about twenty five others are near White Oaks, and that every man able to bear arms at that place is under arms to protect the place ... Barney Mason has not yet returned [from making his counterfeit money deal with Dan Dedrick]. We would start from here (Roswell) with a force only nearly every horse in this section of the country is sick at present with distemper.

Deputy U.S. Marshal [Frank] Stewart from Texas [actually a Panhandle Cattleman's Association detective] is reported to be at Puerta de Luna with 40 men and after several of the men who are in this gang for crimes committed in Texas. I shall communicate with him soon as I can get a reliable man to send, and then press the "Rustlers" from White Oaks back into Fort Sumner and then surround the place with forces from above and below.

Wild reported for November 27, 1880, still at Garrett's Roswell home, and by then in paranoid terror of his imaginary gang; though his sole fact was that his spy, Barney Mason, had related that Dedrick had backed out of the cattle-for-counterfeit-money deal. And Mason had given Dedrick's counterfeiting associates as only William Wilson, James West, and Tom Cooper. Apparently Mason, like Garrett, was just duping Wild for personal profit, knowing that no "gang" existed. Wild wrote: "*I will respectfully state that I am very impatient to get away from here but the shape things have taken I feel it my duty to remain ... At the present time I am entirely cut off from reaching the rail road by these outlaws and will have to employ a guard unless I remain until arrests are made and go along to Santa Fe with them.*"

For November 28, 1880, Wild wrote more misinformation from Garrett's Roswell house, stating that "*the Kid with seventeen men were [at the Greathouse ranch].*"

For November 29, 1880, Wild, still at Garrett's house, wrote that he was setting out with "*an armed and mounted force of twenty men under command of Deputy U.S. Marshals Olinger and Garrett.*" With feverish paranoia, he added certainty that "*there will be blood shed.*" He wrote: "*We have at the present time between one and two hundred armed men out scouting for this gang of outlaws and counterfeiters ... It is believed that there will be blood shed when ever our men come up with the main gang if ever we are able to do so.*"

For November 30, 1880, still at Garrett's house, Wild reported the Greathouse ranch ambush, with usual fabrications; writing:

"*Information has reached me this day that William Wilson et al of their gang numbering 17 were run into Greathouses Ranch. That the house was surrounded by a Deputy Sheriff [Will Hudgens] and a posse numbering in all 13. One of the posse named Carlisle [Jim Carlyle] ... was one of the leaders ... and after a little talk with the parties on the inside of the house he was induced to go in. Soon as he was inside of the house he was murdered. Soon after Carlisle was murdered William Wilson and his gang made a rush out of the house, and made their escape under cover of the night."*

For December 1, 1880, Wild reported that he had stayed in Roswell, but Garrett had left *"with a Posse to go to Fort Sumner."*

Writing for December 2, 1880, Wild hysterically decided that the gang had come to Roswell after him! He wrote: " *Several of Wm Wilson gang of men have been seen near this place this day. It is feared trouble is brewing near at this place and I am now writing my report in the post office of this place which is filled with men arrived to resist any attack that may be made ... I am unable to get out of this place with safety."*

On December 3, 1880, Wild, still in Garrett's house, reported ludicrously that Garrett *"had divided his force"* and was apparently arresting random people - like ones in *"a cave some twenty miles from Fort Sumner."* Lacking any real arrests - or even a real gang - Wild whined to his Chief: *"There has been cold weather and snow since the 20th of September to say nothing of being away from my family and almost severed from civilization. I have felt it my duty to do as I have and hope you will consider this and not place the blame of the delay on me."* Wild added that his work was appreciated locally, unaware that the appreciation was by the Ring, now poised to kill Billy Bonney.

For December 5, 1880, Wild, still in Garrett's house, reported his arrests of random murderers. For Chief Brooks, Wild rationalized failure as: *"The outlaws have divided up and have men on every road leading from Lincoln County to the Rail Road. You need not feel any anxiety as to my getting out of here safe as there are good citizens enough to protect me when I start."*

For December 7, 1880, Wild, still in Garrett's house, tracked his phantom and migratory gang to Lincoln. *"They left going in the direction of the Capitan Mountains where it is believed their main force is."*

For December 9, 1880, he wrote that Garrett had captured *"a large number of stolen horses and cattle."* This was his distortion of what Billy reported to Lew Wallace on December 12th:

that two of his mules had been robbed by Garrett from the Fort Sumner area ranch of a Thomas Yerby. Garrett, unlike Wild, knew his job was to hunt just one man.

For the same December 9th, still in Garrett's house, flagrantly paranoid Wild reported: *"I am very anxious to get away from here ... [T]he "rustlers" a (name given to Wilson and his band) have men on two out of three roads ... I am going to leave here for headquarters first occasion that presents itself to get away with safety."* By December 23, 1880, Wild was departing New Mexico Territory, and reporting from Santa Fe en route to New Orleans.

AFTERMATH OF AZARIAH WILD

In 3 months and 13 days from case assignment to departure from New Mexico Territory, Azariah Wild had collected a few apparently counterfeit bills and had captured no one in his imaginary counterfeiting-rustling mega-gang. Real counterfeiter, Dan Dedrick, had fled permanently to California. But Wild achieved the Ring's goal: empowering a lawman, Pat Garrett, to capture or kill Billy Bonney, and to give a gloss of legitimacy to murder.

BILLY THE KID
OUTLAW MYTH PRESS

By December 3, 1880, the Ring began its press campaign against Billy using leaked "secret" reports of Azariah Wild about the "Kid gang" as the largest counterfeiting-rustling group in the country, with Fort Sumner as its headquarters. That day, Ringite John H. Koogler, published in his *Las Vegas Gazette* an editorial titled "Desperadoe's Stronghold, An Organized Gang Assisted by Nature and Defiantly Reckless, Who Terrorize the Country to the East of Us." It replicated Catron's usual smear campaigns against adversaries, but it was unabashedly lethal: encouraging a lynch mob for "the army of vengeance." And Billy Bonney was now publicly "Billy the Kid."

Billy's reasonable response should have been to leave the Territory. However, nine days later, on December 12th, he would defiantly choose instead to write his corrective letter to Governor Lew Wallace. The article stated:

DESPERADOE'S STRONGHOLD.

An Organized Gang Assisted by Nature and Defiantly Reckless.

Who Terrorize the Country to the East of Us.

There is a duty which the people of San Miguel county should immediately discharge in the busting of a powerful gang of outlaws, who are continuously harassing the stock men in the Pecos and Panhandle country and terrorizing the people of Ft. Sumner and vicinity.

Between thirty and forty miles from Sumner is a place called the Portales, a lake on the edge of the Staked Plains, the shore of which is fringed with rocks, and is by nature and situation one of the wildest places in the country.

When the storms come, the herds are driven there for shelter, and no matter what direction the storm blows it is sue to carry with it a rich bovine tide.

Taking advantage of this, a gang of outlaws have made it their *rendezvous*, and building dugouts, have made for themselves a little camp, which with the natural advantages of the locality, they consider well nigh impregnable.

The gang includes forty to fifty men, all hard characters, the off scouring of society, fugitives from justice, and desperados by profession. Among them are men, with whose names and deeds the people of Las Vegas are perfectly familiar, such as "Billy the Kid," Dave Ruterbaugh [sic], Charles Bowdre, and others of equally unsavory reputation ...

The band is well armed and have plenty of ammunition, and as they have no hankering to be "pulled in" are very determined ...

Although the band has been organized for some time, it never was so strong as it is to-day, and the party of old offenders who have been obligated to change their quarters many times are the nucles of the present organization ....

Lincoln county people who have been made the victim of their depredations, at last rose in their might and making it too hot for them, flatly and forever drove them from their territory.

[AUTHOR'S NOTE: This is Koogler's Ring version of the Lincoln County War.]

The gang is under the leadership of "Billy the Kid," a desperate cuss, who is eligible for the post of captain of any crowd, no matter how mean and lawless. They spend considerable time in enjoying themselves at the Portales, keeping guards out and scouting the country for miles around before turning in for the night. Whenever there is a good opportunity to make a haul they split up in gangs and scour the country, always leaving behind a detachment to guard their roost and whatever plunder they may have stored there ...

Whenever the caprice seizes them, they flock to Ft. Sumner and take possession, running things to suit themselves, drinking, carousing, rowing and giving balls.

They run stock from the Panhandle country into the White Oaks and from the Pecos country into the Panhandle, equalizing the herds, but true middle-men style always make heavily by the transaction ...

Are the people of San Miguel county to stand this any longer? Shall we suffer this hoard of outcasts and the scum of society, who are outlawed by a multitude of crimes, to continue their way to the very border of our county?

We believe the citizens of San Miguel County to be order loving people, and call upon them to unite with little bands, scattered to the east of us, in forever wiping out this band. Now is the time to act, for every storm enriches them by driving to their *rendezvous* large herds from which they make their selection. If anything is done, reinforcements in plenty could be secured from the Panhandle country, and resolute men from the association of stockmen could **be drafted into the army of vengeance.**

WALLACE BACKS OUTLAW MYTH TO SCHURZ

By a December 7, 1880 letter to Secretary of the Interior Carl Schurz, Wallace was paralleling his own outlaw fabrication with Azariah Wild's, and concealing Billy's new pardon for testimony bargain with Wild. His reprehensible intent was to make Billy's pardon impossible, to spare himself its Ring repercussions; while making Billy the scapegoat for Territorial "troubles."

BILLY RESPONDS TO NOTORIETY

On December 12, 1880, when Billy wrote again to Governor Wallace to respond to J.H. Koogler's December 3, 1880 *Las Vegas Gazette's* "Desperadoe's Stronghold." His rebel glory would have been dimmed by injustice of outlaw notoriety. He had likely amazed Catron by not fleeing the Territory. But to self-centered Wallace it must have seemed brazen taunting of himself.

By that December 12th, Billy had endured Secret Service pursuit, another lost pardon, two White Oaks posse ambushes, and a false murder accusation for Jim Carlyle. Possibly his teenaged lover, Paulita Maxwell, in Fort Sumner had added to his determination to stay. His letter gives *"Fort Sumner"* for address.

Seven days later, Garrett's posse would ambush Billy's group at Fort Sumner, killing Tom O'Folliard, instead of Billy. Ten days away was Billy's Stinking Springs capture, where Garrett would shoot dead Charlie Bowdre when mistaking him for Billy.

But by that December 12th, and throughout his months of life remaining in 1881, Billy's writing and press interviews showed that, even hunted, even jailed after capture, even sentenced to hang, even held shackled and guarded, he had no doubt of escaping; and he had no diminution of his rebellious spirit.

His letter, rebutting Koogler's article nine days before, marks Billy's transformation: hardened by living with daily threat of death and raging at injustice, he is now famous, with a flashy sobriquet, "Billy the Kid." Unaware of Ring effort, he blamed John Chisum, who had refused Tunstall aid. And he addressed Wallace with bold familiarity and equality:

Fort Sumner
Dec. 12th 1880
Gov. Lew Wallace
Dear Sir

I noticed in the Las Vegas Gazette a piece which stated that, Billy "the" Kid, the name by which I am known in the Country was the captain of a Band of Outlaws who hold Forth at the Portales. There is no such Organization in Existence. So the Gentleman must have drawn very heavily on his Imagination. My business at the White Oaks at the time I was waylaid and my horse killed was to See Judge Leonard who has my case in hand. he had written me to come up, that he thought he could get Everything Straightened up I did not find him at the Oaks & Should have gone to Lincoln if I had met with no accident. After mine and Billie Wilsons horses were killed we both made our way to a Station, forty miles from the Oaks kept by Mr Greathouse. When I got up the next morning The house was Surrounded by an outfit led by one Carlyle, Who had come into the house and Demanded a Surrender. I asked for their Papers [warrants] and they had none. So I concluded that it amounted to nothing more than a mob and told Carlyle that he would have to Stay in the house and lead the way out that night. Soon after a note was brought in Stating that if Carlyle did not come out inside of five minutes they would Kill the Station Keeper)Greathouse) who had left the house and was with them. in a Short time a Shot was fired on the outside and Carlyle thinking Greathouse was Killed jumped through the window. breaking the Sash as he went and was killed by his own Party they think it was me trying to make my Escape. the Party then withdrew.

they returned the next day and burned an old man named Spencer's house and Greathouses also

I made my way to this Place afoot and During my absence Deputy Sheriff Garrett Acting under Chisum's orders went to the Portales and found Nothing. on his way back he went by Mr Yerby's ranch and took a pair of mules of mine which I had left with Mr Bowdre who is in Charge of mr Yerby's cattle. he (Garrett) claimed that they were stolen and even if they were not he had no right to Confiscate any Outlaws property.

I had been at Sumner Since I left Lincoln making my living Gambling the mules were bought by me the truth of which I can prove by the best citizens around Sumner. J.S. Chisum is the man who got me into Trouble and was benefited Thousands by it and is now doing all he can against me There is no Doubt but what there is a great deal of Stealing going on in the Territory. and a great deal of the Property is taken across the [Staked] Plains as it is a good outlet but so far as my being at the head of a Band there is nothing of it in Several Instances I have recovered Stolen Property when there was no chance to get an Officer to do it.

       one instance for Hugo Zuber Post office Puerto de Luna. another for Pablo Analla Same Place.

if Some impartial Party were to investigate this matter they would find it far Different from the impression put out by Chisum and his Tools.

                Yours Respect
                     William Bonney

CLIMAX OF PARDON BETRAYAL

Wallace did not answer Billy's letter. On December 13, 1880, he requested from Territorial Secretary William Ritch a reward notice. Nine days later, on December 22, 1880, the *Las Vegas Gazette* published Wallace's reward notice in a front page column:

BILLY THE KID
$500 REWARD
I will pay $500 reward to any person or persons who will capture William Bonney, alias The Kid, and deliver him to any sheriff of New Mexico. Satisfactory proofs of identity will be required.
    LEW. WALLACE,
       Governor of New Mexico

WALLACE PLANS ESCAPE

The day after Wallace requested the reward notice for Billy the Kid, he implemented his own escape. On December 14, 1880, he requested leave from Carl Schurz to promote his just-released *Ben-Hur: A Tale of the Christ*. For Schurz, he overlapped his outlaw myth with Operative Azariah Wild's fabricated "Billy Kid" outlaw gang. He wrote: "*I have intelligence to day from Lincoln County. The citizens are yet in the field under a very active and energetic deputy-sheriff [Pat Garrett], who has had several skirmishes, and made five important arrests; so that the authorities here are confident that they can take care of themselves.* ***To stimulate them, I have made proclamation of $500 reward for the capture and delivery of the leader of the outlaws [Billy the Kid].***"

BILLY GETS NATIONAL OUTLAW MYTH PRESS

On the same December 22, 1880 day of Wallace's reward notice, Azariah Wild's likely Ring-leaked and garbled Secret Service reports gave Billy and his "outlaw gang" national fame in the *New York Sun*. Dime-novel fodder, it would become Billy's history, distorting books and media to the present.

At this point, Billy had no hope of salvation; but he never accepted that; even to the moment of escaping his inescapable jail before hanging, or stepping into darkness of Peter Maxwell's bedroom before midnight a little less than seven months later.

The *New York Sun* article stated:

OUTLAWS OF NEW MEXICO.
THE EXPLOITS OF A BAND HEADED BY A NEW YORK YOUTH.

The Mountain fastness of the Kid and his Followers— War against a Gang of Cattle Thieves and Murderers — The Frontier Confederates of Brockway, the Counterfeiter.

LAS VEGAS, New Mexico, Dec. 20.—One hundred and twenty-seven miles southeast of Las Vegas, New Mexico, is Fort Sumner, once the base of operations against the Indians who committed depredations against the stockmen. The fort was abandoned some ten or twelve years ago, owing to the removal of troops further south, toward the border of Mexico. The property was condemned and sold to Pete Maxwell, a well-known ranchman of the section. Since then it has been a depot of supplies for stockmen and a stage station on the postal route to the Pecos Valley and Panhandle, Texas.

Until recently, on almost any fair day, there might have been seen lounging about the store or engaged in target practice four men, all of them young, neatly dressed, and of good appearance. A stranger riding in the little hamlet would have taken them to be a party of Eastern gentlemen who had come into that sparsely settled region in search of sport. Many who have gone into that country have struck up an acquaintance with these men and found them agreeable fellows. These men are the worst desperadoes in the West, and large parties of armed men are now scouring the country in pursuit of them.

For a number of years the people of eastern New Mexico and Panhandle, Texas, have been harassed by a gang who have run off stock, burned ranches, and committed acts of violence and murder. It was only recently that the leaders and organization of the band were discovered. The leaders are Billy the Kid, so called from his youth; Dave Rudabaugh, Billy Wilson, and Tom O'Phallier, the four loungers about Fort Sumner. The Kid is the captain of the gang. Their fastness is about thirty-five miles nearly due east from Fort Sumner, on the edge of the great Staked Plain. In that region there is a small lake called Las Portales. It is surrounded by steep hills, from which flow numerous streams that feed the little lake. This place the robbers selected for their resort partly on account of its hiding places, but mainly on account of the opportunities it afforded them for stock thieving. No matter from what direction the storm came, it drove to the lake the herds of cattle which roam at large in the rich grazing country. There the band built for themselves one of those rude dugouts so common on the Western frontier, two sides formed by the side of the hill, the other two constructed of sod and dirt plastered together, and the whole covered by a thatched roof. Stockades or corrals were built near by in which to put stolen stock. During pleasant weather the members of the gang lounged about Fort Sumner or other stations in that section. When the storm sent cattle scudding over the plains to the haven afforded by the hill-protected lake basin, the gang would hurry to their rendezvous and cut out from the herds the best cattle, driving them into their corral, whence they were later sent to market. Their booty was large, for they had a vast stock to select from, the whole country for a distance of one hundred and fifty miles either way being a rich, continuous pasture. Besides the active members of the band, there were many who had apparently some settled occupation and made themselves useful in disposing of the stolen cattle. In every town of any size within a radius of 150 miles there were butchers who dealt regularly in this stolen stock. When supplies from roving herds ran short the desperadoes would make a raid on herds that were guarded, attacking ranches and killing or diving off the inmates. Besides their station at Las Portales, they had one at Bosque Grande, fifty miles to the southwest, and another at Greathouse's rancho, fifty miles to the north. Whenever they were pursued when running of stock, they had the choice of three places to which to resort.

The people of the surrounding country finally found the existence of this band unendurable. After repeated searches, which failed, owing to the smallness of the pursuing parties, it was resolved to organize several bands, who should cooperate in a campaign, which should end only when the outlaws were driven out of the country, or their capture, dead or alive, was effected. The authorities of the several counties which bordered on the country ranged over by **the Kid's gang** had been repeatedly petitioned to send out a posse of men to hunt them down, but, as Las Portales was on disputed territory, the authorities were never able to settle upon any plan of action. At last the ranchmen took the matter into their own hands, and the first party they sent out succeeded in getting on the track of a detachment of the gang who were hauling material to Las Portales, where they were building large stock yards. Although the party was not successful in capturing the outlaws, they made the outlaws flit about the country in a more lively manner than had been their wont. This showed that nothing could be done by a small force. A guard was always kept out on the numerous peaks about Las Portales, from which outlook; the country for twenty miles either way could be scanned by the outlaws, so that they could easily elude a small party!

The Panhandle Transportation Company, an association

of stockmen of western Texas, banded together for mutual protection, commissioned their superintendent, Frank Stewart, a brave fellow, who was just the man for such work, to organize an expedition against the outlaws. The White Oaks, a flourishing mining camp, organized a band of rangers. Still another party of picked men, under the lead of Sheriff Pat Garrett of Lincoln County, who is considered one of the bravest and coolest men in the whole region, joined in the campaign. In the latter part of November Garrett, with a force of fourteen men, made a dash for Bosque Grande, riding all night, and there succeeded in capturing five of the outlaws. One of them was a condemned murderer who had escaped from jail; another of them was a murderer for whose arrest $1,500 had been offered. These are the sort of men who reinforce the band. Las Portales has long been an asylum for fugitives from justice. Bosque Grande (Great Forest) is situated in one of the most fertile regions of the West, and as the rich lands bordering on the Pecos River are the objective point of many who intend to settle in the Territory, it was thought best to rid that region of the outlaws first, in order that none might be deterred from settling there. Precautions have been taken which will prevent this refuge of the band from ever sheltering them again.

It was expected that the two other parties would work with Garrett's band, but the Panhandle party were delayed, owing to scarcity of feed, and the White Oaks Rangers had their hands full in another quarter. The latter party had a brush with the Kid, Rudabaugh, Wilson, and several others at Coyote Spring, near the Oaks camp, and the outlaws succeeded in escaping, although two had their horses shot from under them. The rangers started back for reinforcements and supplies, and then pressed on after the outlaws, coming upon them at their other station at Greathouse's ranch. It was night when the rangers reached the ranch. They threw up earthworks a few hundred yards from the stockade of the ranch, and when the outlaws rose up in the morning they found themselves hemmed in. The rangers sent a messenger to Jim Greathouse, the owner of this ranch, demanding the surrender of the outlaws. Greathouse replied in person. He came out to the camp of the rangers and stoutly asserted that the outlaws had taken possession of his ranch and that he had no power over them nor anything to do with them. It was considered best to hold Greathouse as a hostage, while Jim Carlyle, the leader of the rangers, heeded to the Kid's request for a conference. A long time elapsed and Carlyle did not return. His men began to feel uneasy about him, and dispatched a note to the renegade chief saying that unless Carlyle was given up in less than five minutes they would kill Greathouse. No reply was received.

Soon after the rangers saw Carlyle leap from the window and dash down the hill toward their entrenchments. He had not gone far, however, when they saw the Kid throw half his body through the window, and, taking deliberate aim, brought down poor Carlyle, killing him instantly. A sharp fight followed, but the outlaws succeeded in making their escape, Greathouse also getting away during the confusion. Before leaving for home with the dead body of their leader, the rangers fired everything about the place, and Greathouse concealed some miles away, saw the smoke of his burning property.

The three parties are now engaged in scouting the country, and will not give up the chase till the country is rid of every one of the outlaws. Money and outfits have been freely offered by men who have large interests in that section. Government officials are now interested in the campaign, for, in addition to their other crimes, the outlaws have put in circulation a large quantity of the counterfeit money manufactured by William Brockway, the forger. The bills were obtained by one of the gang named Doyle who formerly operated in Chicago, and counterfeit $100 bills in large numbers have been put in circulation among the stockmen and merchants in all that region. The information that enabled the Government officers to discover the handling of counterfeit money by the Kid's gang came from a freighter named Smith. Soon afterward, while Smith was on his way from Las Vegas to Fort Sumner with a load of freight, he was waylaid and murdered by some of the gang.

William Bonney, alias the Kid, the leader of the band, is scarcely over 20 years of age. He is handsome and dresses well. He has a fair complexion, smooth face, blue eyes, and light brown hair. He is about six feet tall and deceptively handsome. A beautiful bay mare, that he has carefully trained, is all that he seems to care for, unless he reserves some affection for his brace of six-shooters and Winchester rifle, which have helped him out of many a tight place. His care of the beautiful mare is well deserved, for many a time has her fleetness which surpasses that of any other horse in the Territory, saved his life. The Kid is an admirable rider, and as he is always expected to be obliged to take flight, he usually rides another horse, leading his pet behind, in order to make the best time possible on a fresh horse. **He is considered a dead shot and much of his time is spent in target practice. He was born in New York State, but his parents removed to Indiana when he was quite small, and thence to Arizona. There in the Tombstone District the Kid killed his first man when he was only 17 years old, and was obliged to leave the**

country. He came to New Mexico, where he has since lived.

About three years ago a difficulty arose in Lincoln County, New Mexico, between the stockmen and the Indian agent on the reservation. The trouble arose in regard to some cattle that had been purchased for the Indians. Nearly every man in the county was under arms, and the troops were called out by Gov. Wallace to quell the disturbance. The Kid was mixed up in the affair, and had some narrow escapes. On one occasion he was hotly pursued and was obliged to take refuge in a house in Lincoln, which was surrounded by sixty solders. To the demand to surrender, he only laughed and shot down a soldier just to show that he was game. The house was set on fire, when the Kid, after loading up his Winchester Rifle, leaped from the burning building and made a dash for liberty. All the while he was running he kept firing from his Winchester, bringing down a number of his pursuers. Bullets whistled over his head, but he made his escape, and leaping on a horse was soon laughing at his pursuers. There is no telling how many men he has killed. He sets no value on human life, and has never hesitated at murder when it would serve his purpose. Gov. Wallace a few days ago offered a reward of $500 for his capture, and prominent citizens would make up a handsome purse in addition.

Billy Wilson is much the same sort of good looking fellow as his chief. He is about the same build, with dark hair and a slight moustache. He left the Ohio home where his people, who are all highly esteemed, still reside, several years ago. After being engaged in the cattle business in Texas for some time, he came to New Mexico. When the excitement broke out over the new camp at White Oaks, he went there and was engaged in the butchering business. He was always considered a smart, energetic fellow, and was well thought of. In some way the Kid persuaded him to join his party, and it was by him that much of the forged paper was put into circulation.

Tom O'Phallier is a Texan and is also a man of good appearance. He has a ruddy, face, and can be an exceedingly agreeable companion. He has been with the band from the first, and has committed many crimes.

Dave Rudabaugh is 36 years old, and was born in New York city, where he lived until about eight years ago. He has raided over southern Kansas, the Indian nations, Texas, southern Colorado, and New Mexico. It would not be difficult to establish charges of murder against him in any or all of those States and Territories. In Colorado, a few years ago he ran off some Government stock, and, while pursued by a detachment of soldiers, he killed a Sergeant and two privates. He once headed an attack on the Las Vegas jail, in order to liberate one of his friends, and shot down a guard who interfered. He is a thorough desperado in look, word, and action, ready at all times for a fight. He thinks no more of putting a bullet through a human brain than through the bull's eyes of the target before which he is continually practicing. He is 5 feet 8 inches tall, and weighs about 180 pounds. He has a swarthy complexion, black hair and beard, and hazel eyes, whose cruel, defiant expression has often been noted.

The career of the band is about run, for they are hotly pursued, and the chances are that before long they will be killed or captured. **It is not expected that the Kid or Rudabaugh will be taken alive, as they will fight to the last**.

CHAPTER 23

BILLY BONNEY CAPTURED AND JAILED

CAPTURE AT STINKING SPRINGS

SUMMARY: Billy Bonney's capture at Stinking Springs united the loathsome individuals in his pursuit: Catron and his Ringites, Secret Service Agent Azariah Wild, and Deputy Sheriff and Deputy U.S. Marshal Pat Garrett.

There is no indication that Pat Garrett thought Billy Bonney was an outlaw king, or that a huge gang of counterfeiter-rustlers were in the Territory. But he knew his mission was to kill Billy. After failing to kill him in ambushes in Fort Sumner on December 19, 1880, and at Stinking Springs on December 22, 1880, he settled on capture there and an inevitable hanging trial.

On December 23, 1880, departing Azariah Wild met with Lew Wallace, delightedly piggy-backing on Wild's fakery. Wild wrote: *"I called on Gov. Wallace who was anxious to know the situation and stated such facts as I know. He at once said 'tell Mr Garrett to follow these men any place in the territory and tell him I say so.'"*

On January 1, 1881, back in New Orleans, Wild wrote about Stinking Springs for his report of December 24, 1880: *"I have this day received information of an almost positive nature, that Deputy U.S. Marshal P.F. Garrett has the Kid & Wilson gang of outlaws at his mercy and that he will either kill or arrest them."*

THE RINGITE MEDIA CIRCUS

SUMMARY: For the short remainder of his life, Billy was aware of outlaw myth propaganda, generated by the Ring and Lew Wallace; with the motive of both being cover-up of Ring crimes. But the sole outlaw was now "Billy the Kid."

On December 27, 1880, the Ringite *Las Vegas Daily Gazette*, published editor, Lucius "Lute" Wilcox's, article about the Stinking Springs capture and prisoner transport to Las Vegas, titled: 'The Kid. Interview with Billy Bonney The Best Known Man in New Mexico, The greatest excitement prevailed yesterday when the news was abroad that Pat Garrett and Frank Stewart had arrived in town bringing with them Billy 'the Kid.' "

Billy, with his increasingly famous moniker "Billy the Kid," was the prize catch. And Wilcox's interview showed that his spirit and insouciance were unabated. About the gathered crowd and his defamatory press, Billy said: "Well, perhaps some of them will think me half man now; everyone seems to think I was some sort of animal." And when Wilcox mentioned his dire fate, Billy reposited: "What's the use of looking on the gloomy side of everything. The laugh's on me this time." Wilcox wrote:

With its customary enterprise, the *Gazette* was the first paper to give the story of the capture of Billy Bonney, who has risen to notoriety under the sobriquet of "the Kid," Billy Wilson, Dave Rudabaugh and Tom Pickett. Just at this time everything of interest about the men is especially interesting, and after damning the men in general and "the Kid" in particular through the columns of this paper we considered it the correct thing to give them a show.

Through the kindness of [San Miguel County] Sheriff Romero, a representative of the *Gazette* was admitted to the jail yesterday morning.

Mike Cosgrove, the obliging mail contractor, who has met the boys frequently while on business down the Pecos, had just gone in with four large bundles. The doors at the entrance stood open, and the large crowd strained their necks to get a glimpse of the prisoners, who stood in the passageway like children waiting for a Christmas tree distribution. One by one the bundles were unpacked disclosing a good suit of clothes for each man. Mr. Cosgrove remarked that he wanted "to see the boys go away in style."

"Billy the Kid," and Billy Wilson who were shackled together stood patiently while a blacksmith took off their shackles and bracelets to allow them an opportunity to make a change of clothing. Both prisoners watched the operation which was to set them free for a short while, but Wilson scarcely raised his eyes, and spoke but once or twice to his compadres. **Bonney on the other hand, was light and chipper,** and was very communicative, laughing, joking and chatting with the bystanders.

"You appear to take it easy," the reporter said.

"Yes! What's the use of looking at the gloomy side of everything. The laugh's on me this time," he said. Then looking about the placita, he asked: "Is the jail at Santa Fe any better than this?"

This seemed to trouble him considerably, for as he explained, "this is a terrible place to put a fellow in." He put the same question to every one who came near him and when he learned that there was nothing better in store for him, he shrugged his shoulders and said something about putting up with what he had to.

He was the attraction of the show, and as he stood there, lightly kicking the toes of his boots on the stone pavement to keep his feet warm, one would scarcely mistrust that he was the hero of "Forty Thieves," romance which this paper has been running in serial form for six weeks or more.

"There was a big crowd gazing at me wasn't there?" he exclaimed, and then smiling continued: "Well perhaps some of them will think me half a man now; everyone seems to think I was some kind of an animal."

He did look human, indeed, but there was nothing very mannish about him in appearance, for he looked and acted like a mere boy. He is about five feet, eight or nine inches tall, slightly built and lithe, weighing about 140; a frank and open countenance, looking like a school boy, with the traditional silky fuzz on his upper lip, clear blue eyes, with a roguish snap about them, light hair and complexion. He is, in all, quite a handsome looking fellow, the only imperfection being two prominent front teeth, slightly protruding like a squirrels' teeth, and he has agreeable and winning ways.

Not to be outdone, Russell A. Kistler, published his equally Ring-biased news in his *Las Vegas Daily Optic* of December 27, 1880, as "A Big Haul! Billy the Kid, Dave Rudabaugh, Billy Wilson and Tom Pickett in the clutches of the law, Notorious Gang of Outlaws Broken up, and the County Breathes Easier." It stated:

A BIG HAUL

Billy the Kid, Dave Rudabaugh, Billy Wilson and Tom Pickett in the clutches of the law,

Notorious Gang of Outlaws Broken up, and the County Breathes Easier.

Our readers are familiar with the depredations committed in the lower country by a gang of daring desperados, under the leadership of Billy the Kid, and of the repeated and unsuccessful attempts to capture them. They have roamed over the country at will, placing no value upon human life, and appropriating the property of ranchmen and travelers without stint. Posses of men have been in hot pursuit of them for weeks, but they succeeded in eluding their pursuers every time. However, the right boys started out, well mounted and heavily armed, and were successful in bagging their game.

YESTERDAY AFTERNOON
the town [of Las Vegas] was thrown into a fever of excitement by the announcement that the "Kid" and other members of his gang of outlaws had been captured, and were nearing the city. The rumor was soon verified by the appearance in town of a squad of men led by Pat Garrett, deputy sheriff of Lincoln county, and Frank Stewart, of the Panhandle country, having in custody the Kid, Dave Rudabaugh, Billy Wilson and Tom Pickett. They were taken at once to the jail, and locked up, and arrangements made to guard the jail against any attempt to take the prisoners out and hang them. Feeling was particularly high against Rudabaugh, who was an accessory to the murder of the Mexican jailor in an attempt to release [inmate, J.J.] Webb some months ago.

THE PURSUIT OF THE GANG.

It will be remembered that Frank Stewart, with a party of men, left Las Vegas on December 14th, to join Pat Garrett and his squad, who were in waiting in Fort Sumner. The boys made a quick trip of it, arriving at the designated place of meeting on the night of the 17th instant. Nothing unusual transpired until the following night, when the Kid's party approached the place, for the purpose of cleaning out Garrett's squad, not knowing that reinforcements had come. Precaution had been taken to place a guard on the outside of the house, and upon hearing

THE CLATTER OF HORSES' HOOFS

in the distance, he warned his companions of the danger and they at once prepared to give the outlaws a warm reception. The night was very dark and foggy and even moving objects could be seen only at a very short distance. The first rider who came in range of the trusty Winchesters was Tom O'Folliard who fell dead from his horse under the unerring aim of a half-dozen frontiersmen. Tom Pickett was following immediately behind, but, after the first volley, he turned his horse and

FLED FOR HIS LIFE.

Pursuit was out of the question, owing to the intense darkness that prevailed and the additional fact that a heavy snowstorm had set in. Dave Rudabaugh's horse was shot but succeeded in carrying his rider a distance of twelve miles before dropping dead. The

PARTY OF PLUCKY PURSUERS

now laid over two days starting forward on the evening of the third day, the 23rd. Promptly at the hour of twelve, they mounted their horses and rode twelve miles to [Brazil-] Wilcox's ranch. Here it was obtained that the Kid and his followers had taken supper there the night before and were at their rendezvous, a vacant stone house, about three miles further on. After a few moments halt the brave pursuers ... put spur to their horses and rode quietly to the house designated as the hiding place of the Kid's men. Upon approaching the premises at about 2 o'clock in the morning, three horses were seen hitched to the front door ready to be mounted

AT A SECOND'S NOTICE.

Garrett and Stewart chose at once surrounded the house, giving their men instructions to lay flat in the snow and await further developments.

JUST AT DAYBREAK

on the morning of the 24th [22nd] a man supposed to be the Kid but afterwards proving to be Charles Bowdre, appeared at the door. His body was pierced by two balls almost in an instant. The signal for the shooting was given immediately upon the appearance of Bowdre, as Kid, who is a sure shot, had often boasted that he would never be taken alive. The only way to capture him was to shoot him down at sight. The killing of Bowdre alarmed those upon the inside of the house and they endeavored to ascertain what party was in pursuit of them; however, their calling elicited no response. Two of the three horses standing at the door were

SHOT DOWN IN THEIR TRACKS,

and the third one was shot in the doorway while the Kid was in the act of getting the animal upon the inside out of the reach of the deadly bullets. The carcass of the dead horse across the threshold prevented the Kid from leaping upon his horse, which was in the room with him, and attempting to escape. About four o'clock in the afternoon, the surrounded party

DISPLAYED A FLAG

and Rudabaugh walked out boldly and said they were willing to surrender, provided they were guaranteed protection. This was promised them and, in turn, "Kid," Billy Wilson and Tom Pickett joined Rudabaugh upon the outside and gave themselves up to their captors, who put their prisoners on horses, doubling up as occasion required, and rode back to [Brazil-]Wilcox's ranch, from which place a wagon was sent back after the arsenal left at the robbers' rendezvous. The captors and their prisoners remained at the ranch all night, starting for Las Vegas on Christmas morning and arriving there before supper last night – very rapid riding.

The party of men **WHO RISKED THEIR LIVES** in the attempt to rid the country of this bloodthirsty gang of robbers and murderers are deserving of unbounded praise and should be rewarded handsomely for their services. **They will undoubtedly obtain the reward of $500 offered by the Governor [Wallace] for the capture of the Kid, and it remains for interested citizens to raise a purse of money and present it to these sixteen men, as they have paid out money and endured hardships in the endeavor to hunt down and bring to justice one of the most desperate gangs of outlaws that ever terrorized the southwest**.

THE PRISONERS.

Kid is about 24 years of age, and has a bold yet pleasant cast of countenance. when interviewed between the bars at the [Las Vegas] jail this morning, he was in a talkative mood, **but said that anything he might say would not be believed by the people**. He laughed heartily when informed that the papers of the Territory had built him up a reputation second only to that of Victorio. **Kid claims never to have had a large number of men with him, and that the few who were with him when captured were employed on a ranch. This is his state-ment and is taken for what it is worth**.

DAVE RUDABAUGH looks and dresses about the same as when in Las Vegas, apparently not having made any raids upon clothing stores ... Rudabaugh inquired somewhat anxiously in regard to the feeling in the community and was told that it was very strong against him ...

TOM PICKETT.

Tom, who once was a policeman in West Las Vegas, greeted everybody with a hearty grip of the hand and seemed reasonably anxious to undergo examination ...

BILLY WILSON, the other occupant of the cell, reclined leisurely on some blankets ....

GREATHOUSE IMPLICATED

There remained no doubt of the fact that James Greathouse was a member of the Kid's marauding party ...

OFF FOR SANTA FE

Billy Kid, Billy Wilson and Dave Rudabaugh, under the escort of Pat Garrett, Frank Stewart, Mr. Cosgrove and one or two others were taken to Santa Fe this afternoon. As the train was ready to leave the depot an unsuccessful attempt was made by [San Miguel County] Sheriff [Desiderio] Romero to secure Rudabaugh and return him to the county jail ... If the sheriff had been as plucky as some of the citizens who urged him forward, the matter would have been settled without any excitement whatever. The prisoner, Rudabaugh, the only one wanted [in Las Vegas], was virtually in the hands of the United States authorities, having been arrested by Deputy United States marshals, and they were in duty bound to deliver him to the authorities in Santa Fe.

On December 28, 1880, Billy was again interviewed for the *Las Vegas Gazette* when still in Las Vegas, but inside the train for departure to the Santa Fe jail. The reporter was either editor "Lute" Wilcox or owner J.H. Koogler, for "Interview with the Kid."

Billy's nonchalant banter reflects his steely self-control when one realizes that, during his interview, his train was being detained by an aggressive mob on the tracks, with unclear intent either to lynch or to rescue him. He joked about his Stinking Springs capture with a silly dime novel escape fantasy about jumping his famous bay mare out of the rock-walled line cabin's doorway, which was obstructed by a dead horse, earlier shot by Pat Garrett. With the mob dispersed and the train finally departing, Billy avoided morbidity by giving the reporter another joke: asking him to visit in Santa Fe. The article stated:

We saw him again at the depot when the crowd presented a really war like appearance. Standing by the car, out of one of the windows from which he was leaning, he talked freely with us of the whole affair:

"I don't blame you for writing of me as you have. You have had to believe others' stories, but then **I don't know as anyone would believe anything good of me, anyway,**" he said. "I really wasn't the leader of any gang. I was for Billy all the time. About that Portales business, I owned the ranch with Charlie Bowdre. I took it up and was holding it because I knew that at some time a stage line would run there, and I wanted to keep it for a station. **But I found that there were certain men who wouldn't let me live in the country and so I was going to leave.**

We had all our grub in the house when they took us in, and we were going to a place six miles away in the morning to cook it and then light out. I haven't stolen any stock. I made my living by gambling, but that was the only way I could live. **They wouldn't let me settle down; if they had I wouldn't be here today,**" and he held up his right arm on which was the bracelet.

"Chisum got me into all this trouble and then wouldn't help me out. I went up to Lincoln to stand my trial on the warrant that was out for me, but the Territory took a change of venue to Dona Ana, and I knew I had no show, and so I skinned out …

If it had not been for the dead horse in the doorway

I wouldn't be here in Las Vegas. I would have ridden out on my bay mare and taken my chances of escaping. But I couldn't ride over that for she would have jumped back **and I would have got it in the head**. We could have stayed in the house but there wouldn't have been anything gained by that for they would have starved us out. I thought it was better to come out and get a square meal - don't you?"

The prospects of a fight exhilarated him, and he bitterly bemoaned being chained.

"If I only had my Winchester, I'd lick the whole crowd" was his confident comment on the strength of the attacking party. He sighed and sighed again for the chance to take a hand in the fight and the burden of his desire was to be set free to fight on the side of his captors as soon as he should smell powder.

As the train rolled out, he lifted his hat and invited us to call and see him in Santa Fe, calling out "*adios.*"

BILLY'S LAST PARDON PLEA LETTERS

Billy never stopped pleading with Lew Wallace for his justified pardon. But his four last request letters - written to Wallace during his almost three month imprisonment in the Santa Fe jail awaiting transport to his Mesilla trial - became demands. His righteous tone likely contributed to guilty Wallace's later pardon obsession of publishing self-serving lying versions.

Wallace was particularly enraged by Billy's March 2, 1881 letter, which he called blackmail; but may have frightened him as referring to now lost letters in which he had apparently put the pardon promise in writing in 1879 to Ira Leonard or to Billy himself. Billy had stated: "*I have some letters which date back two years, and there are Parties who are very anxious to get them but I shall not dispose of them until I see you. that is if you will come immediately.*" Wallace answered none of Billy's jail letters. But he took them with the rest of his Billy communications when he left New Mexico Territory, and carefully preserved them.

And while he was "crucifying" Billy by not responding to his letters, Wallace was solidifying mining investments, basking in accolades for *Ben-Hur: A Tale of the Christ* from President Hayes and Archbishop Lamy; and would soon get his desired appointment as Ambassador to Turkey from President Garfield.

BILLY'S FIRST JAIL LETTER: JANUARY 1, 1881

On January 1, 1881, four days after arriving, Billy wrote:

> *Santa Fe*
> *Jan 1ˢᵗ 1881*
>
> *Gov. Lew Wallace*
> *Dear Sir*
> *I would like to see you for a few moments if You can spare the time.*
> *Yours Respect.*
> *W.HBonney*

BILLY'S SECOND JAIL LETTER: MARCH 2, 1881

On March 2, 1881, Billy sent his second jail letter, about which Wallace would obsess for the next 20 years as "blackmail." Billy wrote:

> *Santa Fe Jail New Mex*
> *March 2ⁿᵈ 1881*
> *Gov. Lew Wallace*
> *Dear Sir*
> *I wish you would come down to the jail to see me. it will be to your interest to come and see me.* **I have some letters which date back two years, and there are Parties who are very anxious to get them but I shall not dispose of them until I see you. that is if you will come immediately**
> *Yours Respect*
> *W<u>m</u> H Bonney*

BILLY'S THIRD JAIL LETTER: MARCH 4, 1881

On March 4, 1881, Billy wrote his third jail letter in tragic confirmation of the pardon's betrayal: "*I have done everything that I promised you I would, and You have done nothing that You promised me.*" Billy wrote:

> Santa Fe. In jail.
> March 4th 1881
> Gov. Lew Wallace
>
> Dear Sir
>
> I wrote You a little note the day before yesterday but have received no annser. I Expect you have forgotten what you promised me, this Month two Years ago. but I have not, and I think You had ought to have come and seen me as I requested you to. **I have done everything that I promised you I would, and You have done nothing that You promised me.**
>
> I think when You think the matter over, You will come down and See me, and I can then Explain Everything to You.
>
> Judge Leonard, Passed through here on his way East, in january and promised to come and See me on his way back. but he did not fulfill his Promise. it looks to me like I am getting left in the Cold. I am not treated right by [U.S. Marshal John] Sherman. he lets Every Stranger that comes to See me through Curiosity in to See me, but will not let a Single one of my friends in, not Even an Attorney.
>
> I guess they mean to Send me up without giving me any Show. but they will have a nice time doing it. I am not entirely without friends.
>
> I shall Expect to See you Sometime today
> Patiently Waiting
> I am Very truly Yours, Respect.
> W<u>m</u> H. Bonney.

BILLY'S FOURTH JAIL LETTER: MARCH 27, 1881

On March 27, 1881, Billy wrote to Wallace for the last time, emphasizing the pardon promise. He may have still hoped that the pardon would be issued at its technically proper time: after his sentencing in the Mesilla trial to come. He wrote:

> Santa Fe New Mexico
> March 27th/81
> Gov Lew Wallace
> Dear Sir
> for the last <u>time</u> I ask: Will you keep Your promise. I start below tomorrow. Send Annser by bearer.
> Yours Respt
> WBonney

CHAPTER 24

BILLY BONNEY'S TRIALS BY THE SANTA FE RING

HANGING TRIALS IN MESILLA

SUMMARY: Billy Bonney's capture left him in the power of the Santa Fe Ring, now able to kill him under the guise of law by hanging in a rigged court. Lew Wallace could have saved him by the pardon, but did not. Loyal Ira Leonard was his defense attorney, until likely threat of assassination made him withdraw. So Billy was left alone with an inevitable outcome. It was the Ring versus Billy the Kid.

Once captured, Billy Bonney faced an inevitable hanging sentence in the Ring-controlled Mesilla court. His added disadvantage was that all defense witnesses - like Justice of the Peace "Squire" Wilson or Juan Patrón - were too terrified to again risk assassination; and Billy's outlaw vilification must have seemed impenetrable to truth.

This was the time for Governor Lew Wallace to issue the pardon. But he did not. Billy's only ally was Ira Leonard, still representing him; until Leonard's unexpected victory in that court elicited an apparent death threat, forcing his abandoning Billy to Ring-biased public defenders appointed by Judge Bristol, and to a certain death sentence.

TRANSPORT TO MESILLA FOR TRIAL

Attorney Ira Leonard bravely and protectively accompanied Billy from Santa Fe on the Atchison, Topeka, and Santa Fe Railroad, whose southward track construction had only reached the Rincón depot. From there, Leonard stayed with him on the stagecoach ride to Las Cruces. With them were guards, including Ringite Tony Neis from Santa Fe. And prisoner, Billy Wilson, was also transported with them to Mesilla. At Las Cruces, a crowd had gathered to see the famous outlaw, Billy the Kid.

A spectator named W.S. Fletcher from Mesilla either asked, or saw someone ask, the group which was "the Kid." Billy's cheeky response was reported in the April 3, 1881 Santa Fe *Daily New Mexican* in: "Something About the Kid." Billy pointed to balding, middle aged Leonard, declaring: "This is the man!" That article also quoted Billy's retaliatory quip: "At least two hundred men have been killed in Lincoln County during the past three years, but I did not kill all of them." The article stated:

Something about the Kid.

An extract of a letter written by W.S. Fletcher from Mesilla to a gentleman in the city reads about as follows: Tony Neis and Francisco Chaves, deputy U.S. Marshals, arrived Thursday night with **Billy, the Kid,** and Billy Wilson. They met an ugly crowd at Rincon, where some threats were made, but Tony's crowd were too much for them. **At Las Cruces an impulsive mob gathered around the coach and someone asked which is "Billy the Kid." The Kid himself answered by placing his hand on Judge Leonard's shoulder and saying "this is the man."** The Kid weakened somewhat at Las Cruces, where he found quite a number of Lincoln County men, who were to appear against him as witnesses.

[AUTHOR'S NOTE: Billy had no defense witnesses. The prosecution had Ringites James Dolan, Saturnino Baca, and Sheriff William Brady's deputy, Billy Matthews; and subpoenaed Lincolnite, Isaac Ellis.]

He says at least two hundred men have been killed in Lincoln County during the past three years, but that he did not kill all of them. I think twenty murders can be charged against him. He was arraigned yesterday (Wednesday) before the United States court for the murder of Roberts, on the Mescalero Apache reservation, in 1878. Judge Leonard was assigned to his defense. Judge Newcomb gave notice that he had three other indictments for murder against him, and it looks as if he had no show to get off. His counsel asked today for time to send to Lincoln, which was granted, so that his trial will not commence for at least ten days. Billy Wilson's case is before the grand jury. He is charged with passing counterfeit money. He has retained Judge Thornton as his counsel. He seems to have friends here while the Kid has none.

No mails between Rincon and Doña Ana for the past week. Mosquitoes and flies abound and weather hot as blazes.

SURPRISE QUASHING OF CATRON'S FEDERAL INDICTMENT

U.S. Attorney Thomas Benton Catron's June 21, 1878 federal indictment, Case No. 411, for Billy Bonney and other Regulators in the Andrew "Buckshot" Roberts Blazer's Mill killing was a trap long set against pardon by any Territorial governor.

On March 30, 1881, under Judge Warren Bristol, it was Billy's first indictment to be heard. The prosecutor was Ringite U.S. Attorney Sidney Barnes, who had replaced Catron. But Attorney Ira Leonard surprised that court. He filed a motion to quash the indictment based on its invalidity!

In the resulting juryless hearing before Judge Bristol, with Prosecutor Barnes present, Leonard argued that Catron's indictment asserted federal jurisdiction by claiming that Blazer's Mill was part of the federally-controlled Mescalero Indian Reservation; where a murder would correctly be under federal jurisdiction. But since Blazer's Mill was, in fact, private a property owned by Dr. Joseph Blazer, and irrelevantly within the Reservation's perimeter, it came under Territorial law for private land. That argument was correct. Bristol was forced to quash the indictment. The Ring had underestimated Leonard after observing his mediocre Dudley Court of Inquiry arguments.

So the Ring reverted to its usual response to opposition: death threat followed by real death. Leonard, having barely survived Ring assassination on April 25, 1879 - only 67 days after Huston Chapman's actual killing - abruptly abandoned Billy's defense. Billy was left with court-appointed Ring-biased public defenders, Attorneys Albert Jennings Fountain and John Bail, for his William Brady and George Hindman murder trials' defense.

And it should be noted that if the Brady and Hindman indictments did not yield a hanging sentence, Bristol could have gotten a Territorial one against Billy for the Roberts killing.

PREJUDICIAL PRESS

To prejudice potential jurymen for the next trial, Ring press spewed out the outlaw myth of Billy the Kid. On April 2, 1881, *Newman's Semi-Weekly*" ran an article titled "The Kid;" stating:

[The Kid] is a notoriously dangerous character, has on several occasions before escaped justice where escape appeared even more improbable than now, and has made his brags that he only wants to get free in order to kill three men – one of them being Governor Wallace. Should he break jail now, there is no doubt that he would immediately proceed to execute his threat ... We expect every day to hear of his escape and hope that legal technicalities may not be permitted to render escape more probable.

TRIAL FOR THE BRADY KILLING

Chosen next for a jury's likely hanging sentence was the murder of the Lincoln County's Sheriff: Case No. 532, New Mexico Territory versus Billy Bonney for the murder of William Brady. Billy was to be defended by Attorneys Albert Jennings Fountain and John Bail. For prosecution was Ringite District Attorney Simon Newcomb, who, with Fountain, had freed Lew Wallace's murderer-rustler captives in Fort Stanton by *habeas corpus* on April 13, 1879 to sabotage his prosecution of Ring criminals.

With likely Ring expurgation, the transcript for that trial is now lost. But under Judge Warren Bristol, and with Ringite prosecution witnesses, like James Dolan, Jacob Basil "Billy" Matthews, and Saturnino Baca - along with subpoenaed terrified Lincoln merchant, Isaac Ellis, and no defense witnesses - Billy had no chance of avoiding conviction.

JUDGE BRISTOL'S BIASED JURY INSTRUCTIONS

Judge Bristol's prejudicial jury instructions still exist, and show that he made first degree murder the necessary verdict - meaning that the only sentence could be hanging. Bristol stated: "*There is no evidence before you showing that the killing of Brady is murder in any degree than the first ... The legislature of this Territory has enacted a law prescribing that the punishment for murder in the 1st degree shall be death.*" And since first degree murder required "*premeditated design,*" Bristol made that inevitable also, stating: "*If the design to kill is completely formed in the mind but for a moment before inflicting the fatal wounds it would be premeditated and in law the effect would be the same as though the design to kill had existed for a long time.*" He stated:

Territory of New Mexico
District Court 3d Judicial
District Doña Ana County
April Term A.D. 1881

                          In the Third Judicial
                       District Court April Term / 1879

Territory of New Mexico	)
vs	)
	) *Murder*
William Bonney alias Kid	) *1st Degree*
Alias William Antrim	)

    Gentlemen of the Jury:
The defendant in this case William Bonney alias Kid alias William Antrim is charged in and by the indictment against him which has been laid before you with having committed in connection with certain other persons the crime of murder in the County of Lincoln in the 3d Judicial District of the Territory of New Mexico in the month of April of the year 1878 by then and there unlawfully killing one William Brady by inflicting upon his body certain fatal gunshot wounds from a premeditated design to effect his death.

    The case is here for trial by a change of venue from the said County of Lincoln.

    The facts alleged in the indictment if true constitute Murder in the 1st and highest degree and whether these allegations are true or not true are for you to determine from the evidence which you have heard and which is now submitted to you for your careful consideration.

    In the matter of determining what your verdict shall be it will be improper for you to consider anything except the evidence before you.

    You as Jurors are the exclusive judges of the weight of the evidence. You are the exclusive judges of the credibility of the witnesses. It is for you to determine whether the testimony of any witnesses whom you have heard is to be believed or not. You are also the exclusive judges whether the evidence is sufficiently clear and strong to satisfy your minds that the defendant is guilty.

    There is no evidence tending to show that the killing of Brady was either justifiable or excusable by law. As a matter of law therefore such killing was unlawful and whoever committed the deed or was present and advised or aided or abetted and consented to such killing committed the crime of murder in some one of the degrees of murder.

There is no evidence before you showing that the killing of Brady is murder in any degree than the first.

Your verdict therefore should be either that the defendant is guilty of the murder in the 1st degree or that he is not guilty at all under this indictment.

Murder in the 1st degree consists in the killing of one human being by another without authority of law and from a premeditated design to affect the death of the person killed.

Every killing of one human being by another that is not justifiable or excusable should be necessarily a killing without authority of law.

As I have already instructed you to consider murder in the 1st degree it is necessary that the killing should have been perpetrated from a premeditated design to effect the death of the person killed.

As to this premeditated design I charge you that to render design to kill premeditated it is not necessary that such design to kill should exist in the mind for any considerable length of time before the killing.

If the design to kill is completely formed in the mind but for a moment before inflicting the fatal wounds it would be premeditated and in law the effect would be the same as though the design to kill had existed for a long time.

In this case in order to justify you in finding this defendant guilty of murder in the 1st degree under the peculiar circumstances as presented by the indictment and the evidence you should be satisfied and believe from the evidence to the exclusion of every reasonable doubt of the truth of several propositions.

1st That the defendant either inflicted one or more of the fatal wounds causing Brady's death or that he was present at the time and place of the killing and encouraged – incited – aided in – abetted – advised or commanded such killing.

2d That such killing was without justification or excuse.

3d That such killing of Brady was caused by inflicting upon his body a fatal gunshot wound.

And 4th that such fatal wound was either inflicted by the defendant upon a premeditated design to effect Brady's death or that he was present at the time and place of the killing of Brady and from a premeditated design to effect his death he then and there encouraged – incited – aided in – abetted – advised or commanded such killing.

If he was so present – encouraging – inciting – aiding in – abetting – advising – or commanding the killing of Brady he is as much guilty as though he fired the fatal shot.

I have charged you that to justify you in finding the defendant guilty of murder in the 1st degree you should be satisfied from the evidence to the exclusion of every reasonable doubt that the defendant is actually guilty.

As to what would be or would not be reasonable doubt of guilt I charge you that belief in the guilt of the defendant to the exclusion of every reasonable doubt does not require you to so believe absolutely and to mathematical certainty – That is to justify a verdict of guilty it is not necessary for you to be as certain that the defendant is guilty as you are that two and two are four or that two and three are five.

Merely a vague conjecture or bare possibility that the defendant my be innocent is not sufficient to raise reasonable doubt of his guilt.

If all the evidence before you which you believe to be true convinces and directs your understanding and satisfies your reason and judgment while acting upon it conscientiously under your oath as jurors and if this evidence leaves in your minds an abiding conviction to a moral certainty that the defendant is guilty of the crime charged against him: then this would be proof of guilt to the exclusion of every reasonable doubt and would justify you in finding the defendant guilty.

You will apply the evidence to this case according to the instructions I have given you and determine whether the defendant is guilty of murder in the 1st degree or not guilty.

Murder in the 1st degree is the greatest crime known to our laws. The legislature of this Territory has enacted a law prescribing that the punishment for murder in the 1st degree shall be death.

This then is the law: No other punishment than death can be imposed – for murder in the 1st degree.

If you believe and are satisfied therefore from the evidence before you to the exclusion of every reasonable doubt that the defendant is guilty of murder in the 1st degree then it will be your duty to find a verdict that the defendant is guilty of murder in that degree naming murder in the 1st degree in your verdict and also saying in your verdict that the defendant shall suffer the punishment of death.

If from the evidence you do not believe to the exclusion of every reasonable doubt that the defendant is guilty of murder in the 1st degree or if you entertain a reasonable doubt as to the guilt of the defendant, then in that case your verdict should be not guilty.

<u>532</u>

Territory
  Vs.) Murder
William Bonney
Alias "Kid" alias
William Antrim

<u>Charge to Trial Jury</u>
     Filed in my office this 9th day of April A.D. 1881.
                             George R. Bowman
                                        Clerk

ATTORNEY ALBERT JENNINGS FOUNTAIN'S BIASED INSTRUCTIONS FOR THE DEFENDANT

Albert Jennings Fountain's sly jury instructions for the defense showed bias against Billy by stymieing jurors: after Bristol *gave no doubt* as to it being 1st degree murder, he said the only ground for acquittal was *to have that doubt*! He stated:

Territory of New Mexico
    vs   *) Murder*
William Bonney alias Kid alias William Antrim

            In the District Court of Doña
            County March 1881 term.

Instructions asked for by Defendants counsel. The Court is asked to instruct the Jury as follows: to wit:
1st Instructions asked –
Under the evidence the Jury must either find the defendant guilty the defendant guilty of Murder in the 1st degree, or acquit him.
2nd Instruction asked –
The jury will not be justified in finding the defendant guilty of Murder in the 1st degree unless they are satisfied, from the evidence, to the exclusion of all reasonable doubt, that the

defendant actually fired the shot that caused the death of the deceased Brady, and that such shot was fired by the defendant with the premeditated design to effect the death of the deceased, or that the defendant was present and actually assisted in firing the fatal shot or shots that caused the death of the deceased, and that he was present in a position to render such assistance and actually rendered assistance from a premeditated design to effect the death of the deceased.

3rd Instruction asked –

If the Jury are satisfied from the evidence to the exclusion of all reasonable doubt that the defendant was present at the time of the firing of the shot or shots that caused the death of the deceased Brady, yet, before they will be justified in finding the defendant guilty, they must be further satisfied from the evidence and the evidence alone, to the exclusion of all reasonable doubt, that the defendant either fired the shots that killed the deceased, or some one of them, or that he assisted in firing said shot or shots, or assisted in firing the same, or assisted the parties who fired the same either by his advice, encouragement procurement or command, from a premeditated design to effect the death of Brady. If the Jury entertains any reasonable doubt upon any of these points they must find a verdict of acquittal.

A.J. Fountain
J.D. Bail

HYPOTHETICAL DEFENSE ARGUMENTS

Though the trial's transcript is lost, one can extrapolate from the Ring-biased instructions of Bristol and Fountain that no correct defense arguments were used for Billy. He, however, was unaware, since he tried to raise money by selling his bay racing mare to pay Fountain to do his appeal. Nevertheless, hypothetical defense arguments are presented here to show that proper evidence and argument could have established reasonable doubt against a 1st degree murder verdict and its hanging penalty.

Bristol and Fountain claimed inevitability of a 1st degree murder verdict based on evidence presented. Bristol stated: "*There is **no evidence before you** showing that the killing of Brady is murder in any degree than the first.*" Fountain stated: "***Under the evidence** [as presented] the Jury must either find the defendant guilty of Murder in the 1st degree, or acquit him.*"

The argument should have been for justifiable homicide for defense of another, as forcing the group of men - including the Defendant - to use deadly force against Brady on April 1, 1878 to stop his murdering of McSween. If the group's response had been to immediate threat - like seeing Brady attacking McSween - it would be a complete defense for exoneration - like self-defense.

But the time gap of about three hours between Brady's killing and McSween's arrival in Lincoln required a mitigating defense based on the Defendant's *certainty* that Brady would then kill McSween. So trial evidence had to show why any reasonable person would think Brady would murder McSween.

Evidence for William Brady as a murderer:

Brady was a known murderer, since his posse had murdered McSween's friend, John Tunstall, just 42 days earlier. And Brady made a death threat to Tunstall in McSween's presence, stating: "I won't shoot you now, you haven't long to run."

Brady was also a rogue lawman, blocking arrest of Tunstall's killers, who were also his deputies and possemen. And he illegally imprisoned the Defendant, on February 20, 1878, to obstruct Defendant's arrest of Tunstall's killers in his capacity as a Deputy Constable appointed by Justice of the Peace John Wilson.

Brady was a known threat to McSween, having harassed him by property attachment for his embezzlement case far in excess of the $8,000 set. And McSween hid because of certainty of Brady's murderous intent, staying in protective custody of Sheriff Adolph Barrier, also certain of McSween's murder risk from Brady. On March 28, 1878, Brady, brought Fort Stanton soldiers to the ranch of John Chisum, in failed attempt to apprehend, and likely kill, McSween. And just four days later - the murder day - McSween would return to Lincoln for his Grand Jury trial.

Importantly, there existed no legal way to stop Brady from killing McSween, since, by a March 9, 1878 illegal Proclamation, then Governor, S.B. Axtell, had removed Justice of the Peace Wilson, stating: "there are no Territorial Officers here to enforce [laws] except Sheriff Brady and his Deputies." And Axtell was subsequently removed for that illegality.

Seeing themselves as McSween's sole protection, citizens, including the Defendant, came to Lincoln on the day of Brady's killing. They saw him and his deputies - accused Tunstall murderers - all heavily armed and positioning themselves for McSween's imminent arrival. Brady's murder intent was obvious.

Evidence for Defendant, Billy Bonney's motive:

As to Defendant's character, he had been a ranch worker for murdered Tunstall, and had been deputized to serve warrants on Tunstall's murderers after Brady refused to do arresting - only losing his deputyship by its illegal removal by Governor Axtell. Defendant's commitment to law and order was further proved by his giving an eye-witness affidavit and a deposition to bring Tunstall's killers to justice.

On the murder day, Defendant was in a citizens' group having sole consensus that McSween would be killed by Brady.

Furthermore, in that group, the Defendant had only a revolver, since Brady had confiscated his carbine; and all others had carbines. Defendant could not attain the 60 yard range to Brady's position, so could not have been Brady's shooter.

The Defendant's intent was to save McSween's life; and killing of Brady was the only possible way to achieve that end.

Other trial variables:

No translator was provided to the Spanish-speaking jury, except for jury instructions. A translator was required.

Defense witnesses should have included Billy himself; and subpoenaed Deputy Adolph Barrier, John Chisum, John Wilson, and Juan Patrón. Prosecution witnesses James Dolan and Jacob B. Matthews should have been impeached as being on Brady's murder posse, and themselves indicted for Tunstall's murder.

Defense argument:

Self-defense murder is legally blameless. So is defense of another from immediate death. The weight of the evidence has shown that the Defendant shared with his companions certainty that Brady was about to kill McSween, and that no recourse existed except to kill Brady to save McSween.

Defendant had no motive to kill Brady except in defense of McSween. To protect another from certain death is noble, and mitigates against a verdict of 1st degree murder, which is wanton and with malice aforethought.

The evidence has shown that after Brady's posse maliciously murdered Tunstall, there was good reason for the Defendant to believe Brady would next kill McSween. It has been shown that McSween and Deputy Barrier likewise believed that Brady would kill McSween. It has been shown that no legal recourse through public officials existed to stop Brady's murderous act.

Furthermore, the Defendant was not Brady's actual killer, since his revolver lacked range. And he was not wanton or malicious, since his intent was to preserve McSween's life.

All the evidence therefore mitigates against a verdict of 1st degree murder, which requires hanging, and should be morally repugnant to declare against a reasonable man acting save the life of another man.

And it is the burden of the Territory, not the Defendant, to prove beyond reasonable doubt that the Defendant *did not* act in defense of another. The prosecution, having used Brady's indicted fellow murderers as witnesses, has failed to do that. So, if you, the jurors, have a reasonable doubt as to whether the defendant acted in defense of another, you cannot find the Defendant guilty of 1st degree murder, and are free to find the defendant not guilty - or, at most, guilty of 2nd degree murder, which spares his life.

VERDICT AND SENTENCE

On April 9, 1881, the jury's inevitable verdict after Bristol's and Fountains prejudicial instructions was murder in the 1st degree for William Brady's murder. On April 13, 1881, Judge Warren Bristol sentenced Billy to hang a month later - on May 13, 1881 - leaving little time to appeal.

BILLY'S RESPONSE TO SENTENCING

Billy wanted to appeal. Two days later, on April 15, 1881, he wrote to Las Vegas attorney, Edgar Caypless, whom he had earlier hired on contingency to file his audacious replevin (rustling) suit for recovery of his bay mare from Pat Garrett's posseman, Frank Stewart, who had stolen her at Billy's Stinking Springs capture. Billy hoped to sell her to pay an appeal lawyer, with grounds that his Spanish-speaking jurymen had been deprived of a translator except for instructions. Caypless prevailed in the replevin case, but only after Billy's death, and kept the mare's sales price as fee. For his last known letter, Billy wrote:

> *Dear Sir. I would have written before this but could get no paper. My United States case was thrown out of court and I was rushed to trial on my Territorial charge. was convicted of murder in the first degree and am to be hanged on the 13th day of May. Mr. A.J. Fountain was appointed to defend me and has done the*

best he could for me. He is willing to carry the case further if I can raise the money to bear his expense. The mare is about all I can depend on at present so hope you will settle the case right away and give him the money you get for her. If you do not settle the matter with Scott Moore [to whom Frank Stewart sold the mare] and have to go to court about it either give him [Fountain] the mare or sell her at auction and give him the money. please do as he wishes in the matter. I know you will do the best you can for me in this. I shall be taken to Lincoln tomorrow. Please write and direct care of Garrett, sheriff. excuse bad writing. I have my handcuffs on. I remain as ever

Yours respectfully,
W.H. Bonney

That same April 15th, for an April 16, 1881 article, Billy, interviewed by the *Mesilla News*, summarized Santa Fe Ring injustice: "I think it hard that I should be the only one to suffer the extreme penalty of the law." He called his court "mob law;" ending with facetious "personal advice": "If mob law is going to rule, better dismiss judge and sheriff and let all take chances alike ... Advise persons never to engage in killing." Asked about Wallace's pardon - showing it was universally known - Billy said curtly: "Don't know that he will do it." The article stated:

Well I had intended at one time not to say a word on my own behalf because persons would say, "Oh he lied." Newman, editor of the *Semi-Weekly*, gave me a rough deal; he created prejudice against me, and is trying to incite a mob to lynch me. He sent me a paper which showed it; I think it a dirty mean advantage to take of me, **considering my situation and knowing that I could not defend myself by word or act. But I suppose he thought he would give me a kick down hill.** Newman came to see me the other day. I refused to talk to him or tell him anything. But I believe the *News* is always willing to give its readers both sides of a question. **If mob law is going to rule, better dismiss judge and sheriff and let all take chances alike.** I expect to be lynched going to Lincoln. **Advise persons never to engage in killing.**

Considering the active part Governor Wallace took on our

side and the friendly relations that existed between him and me, and the promise he made me, I think he ought to pardon me. Don't know that he will do it. When I was arrested for that murder he let me out and gave me freedom of the town, and let me go about with my arms. When I got ready to leave Lincoln in June, 1879, I left. **I think it hard that I should be the only one to suffer the extreme penalty of the law.**

TRANSPORT TO LINCOLN COUNTY COURTHOUSE-JAIL

In darkness, on April 17, 1881, Billy was secretly taken by wagon from the Mesilla jail to prevent rescue attempts on his way to the Lincoln jail and to hanging. Newman's *Semi-Weekly* reported his departure, with Billy, as usual, joking:

On Saturday night about 10 o'clock Deputy U.S. Marshal Robt. Ollinger with Deputy Sheriff David Woods and a posse of five men ... started for Lincoln with Henry Antrim alias the Kid. The fact that they intended to leave at that time had been purposely concealed and the report circulated that they would not leave before the middle of the week in order to avoid any possibility of trouble, it having been rumored that the Kid's band would attempt a rescue. They stopped in front of the Semi-Weekly office while we talked to them, and we handed the Kid an addressed envelope with some paper and he said he would write some things he wanted to make public. **He appeared quite cheerful and remarked that he wanted to stay until their whiskey gave out, anyway.** Said he was sure that his guard would not hurt him unless a rescue should be attempted and he was certain that it would not be done unless perhaps "those fellows at White Oaks come out to take me," meaning to kill him. **It was, he said, about a stand-off whether he was hanged or killed in the wagon.**

CHAPTER 25

BILLY BONNEY'S GREAT ESCAPE AND KILLING

THE GREAT ESCAPE

SUMMARY: With his astounding Lincoln jailbreak, the real Billy Bonney exceeded the outlaw myth of his Ringite press, to enter the realm of legend. And it occurred against the backdrop of non-interference by townspeople, finally winning the Lincoln County War their own way.

On April 21, 1881, Billy arrived from Mesilla with his armed guards to the custody of Lincoln County Sheriff Pat Garrett and to the new Lincoln County courthouse with jail. Symbolizing triumph of the Ring, it was the converted "House," sold by its owner, T.B. Catron to the County. And Billy's two guards, deputized by Garrett, were Bob Olinger - Seven Rivers Ring rustler and murder posseman in killings of Tunstall, MacNab, and Lincoln County War Battle victims; and James Bell - White Oaks posseman and possible friendly-fire killer of Jim Carlyle.

Billy had 23 days till hanging; and no money to appeal. He was arm and leg shackled and chained to the second story jail's floor. Sealing his own heroic legend, on April 28th, his eighth day there, he escaped. He was likely aided by John Tunstall's past cook and current courthouse caretaker, Gottfried Gauss. In the outhouse, Billy was likely left a revolver, and wrist shackle key.

He shot his guard, James Bell, who refused to be tied and attempted escape to get help. To kill Bob Olinger, hated since 1878 as a killer of Regulators, Billy used the man's own Whitney double-barreled shotgun to ambush him from a window. From Gauss, Billy got a miner's pick to break his leg chain.

During the few hours that task required, Lincolnites fought the Ring with silent resistance, clustering on Lincoln's single street, listening to Billy addressing them from the court house-jail's second story balcony, and making no attempt to stop him. Gauss provided a horse. It was recounted that Billy had shouted to the people: "I'm standing pat against the world." He had finally broken free from clinging to Lew Wallace and the pardon.

But in escaping, he defied fate. Only 21 years old, bi-cultural and fluent in Spanish, he could have ridden 150 miles southward for a new life in Mexico. But he refused to leave his Territory home and his love, Paulita Maxwell. So he rode 150 miles northeast, to Fort Sumner. Known to its 200 residents since 1878, he must have realized that, though most were his friends, hiding there from Pat Garrett and death would be impossible. He had 77 days to live.

On April 30, 1881, when Garrett arrived back in Lincoln from collecting White Oaks taxes, he had the humiliating task of reporting his failed assignment to kill "Billy the Kid." He wrote on the back of Billy's court documents:

> *I certify that I rec'd the within named William Bonny [sic] into my custody on the 21st day of April 1881. And I further certify that on April 28th he made his escape by killing his guards James Bell and Robert Olinger in Lincoln Co. N. M. Boarding Prisoner and two Guards 8 days - $40.00. Guarding and transporting from Fort Stanton - $69.00. Returning Writ - $.50. Total: $109.00 [sic].*

BILLY ON THE RUN

Billy's friend, John Meadows, was at his Peñasco River ranch when Billy arrived, still joking. In the 2004 book, *Pat Garrett and Billy the Kid as I Knew Them,* Meadows is quoted:

> Old Man Salazar [Ygenio Salazar, Billy's friend in Las Tablas, on the north side of the Capitan Mountains] let the Kid have a little sorrel horse and a good one, and also a saddle. He hung around for a day or so under cover in the hills and one night, after dark he showed up at Tom Norris' and my ranch ... Tom Norris and I was in the cabin cooking some supper. Kid come up to the corner of the house and seeing there was nobody there but us two, whom he could trust, he stepped to the door and said, "Well, I've got you, haven't I?"
>
> I said, "Well, you have. So what are you going to do with us?"
>
> He said, "I'm going to eat supper with you."

WALLACE OVERTLY REJECTS PARDON

On April 28, 1881, unaware of Billy's jailbreak that day, and believing Billy would be hanged on May 13th, Lew Wallace spoke with the *Las Vegas Gazette's* Ringite owner, J.H. Koogler, in "Interview with Governor Lew Wallace on 'The Kid.'"

Wallace's attempts to keep the pardon bargain secret to enable covert betrayal had failed. Koogler reflected its common knowledge. Wallace was cornered. Technically, the correct time for pardon was right then: after sentencing. And Catron's federal indictment had been quashed by Judge Bristol. Territorial pardon was now possible. So Wallace, nakedly the betrayer, finally emerged, stating: "I can't see how a fellow like him should expect any clemency from me." Koogler wrote:

> The conversation drifted into the sentence of "THE KID."
> "It looks as though he would hang, governor."
> "Yes, the chances seem good that the 13th of May would finish him."
> "He appears to look to you to save his neck."
> "Yes," said Gov. Wallace smiling, "but I can't see how a fellow like him should expect any clemency from me."
> Although not committing himself, the general tenor of the governor's remarks indicated that he would resolutely refuse to grant "the Kid" a pardon. It would seem as though "the Kid" had undertaken to bulldoze the governor, which has not helped his chances in the slightest.

J.H. Koogler had forced out the truth: Pardon was denied. Wallace now stood in the light of history. Only 55 days before, Billy had written to him from the Santa Fe jail on March 4, 1881: *"I have done everything that I promised you I would, and you have done nothing that you promised me."* But Wallace had now lied to the world: "I can't see how a fellow like him should expect any clemency from me." This hypocritical denial of his own blame would yield his obsessive, literary transmogrifying of freedom fighting Billy into unredeemable outlaw, "Billy the Kid."

Up to this moment, Wallace had been covertly sadistic to Billy. Now, with his pardon refusal public, his sadism became overt. He wanted to kill. On April 30, 1881, by then aware of Billy's jailbreak, he wrote out Billy's death warrant for Sheriff Pat

Garrett. And, as will be seen, Wallace would keep this murderous impulse for life, but would project it by reversal onto Billy the Kid as obsessed with killing him! Wallace wrote for Garrett:

To the Sheriff of Lincoln County, New Mexico, Greeting:

At the March term, A.D. 1881 of the District Court for the Third Judicial District of New Mexico, held at La Mesilla in the County of Doña Ana, William Bonney <u>alias</u> Kid, <u>alias</u> William Antrim, was duly convicted of the crime of murder in the First Degree; and on the fifteenth day of said term, the same being the thirteenth day of April, A.D. 1881, the judgment and sentence of said court were pronounced against the said William Bonney, <u>alias</u> Kid, <u>alias</u> William Antrim, upon said conviction according to law: whereby the said William Bonney, <u>alias</u> Kid, <u>alias</u> William Antrim, was adjudged and sentenced to be hanged by the neck until dead, by the Sheriff of the said County of Lincoln, within said county.

Therefore, you the Sheriff of the said county of Lincoln, are hereby commanded that on Friday, the thirteenth day of May, A.D. 1881, pursuant to the said judgment and sentence of the said court, you take the said William Bonney, <u>alias</u> Kid, <u>alias</u> William Antrim, from the county jail of the county of Lincoln where he is now confined, to some safe and convenient place within the said county, and there, between the hours of ten o'clock, A.M. and three o'clock, P.M., of said day, you hang the said William Bonney, <u>alias</u> Kid, <u>alias</u> William Antrim, by the neck until he is dead. And make due return of your acts hereunder:

> *Done at Santa Fe in the Territory of New Mexico, this 30th day of April, A.D. 1881. Witness my hand and the great seal of the Territory.*
> *Lew. Wallace,*
> *Governor New Mexico*

Four days later, on May 3, 1881, Wallace placed his second reward notice; this time fittingly in the Ringite *Santa Fe Daily New Mexican*:

BILLY THE KID.
$500 REWARD.

I will pay $ 500 reward to any person or persons who Will capture William Bonney, alias The Kid, and deliver him to any sheriff of New Mexico. Satisfactory proofs of identity will be required.

    LEW. WALLACE,
    Governor of New Mexico

RING PRESS SWINGS INTO ACTION

On May 4, 1881, Ringite *Santa Fe Daily New Mexican* published an outlaw myth editorial signed "D," titled "More Killing by Kid." It stated:

MORE KILLING BY KID

When But a Short Distance From Lincoln,

He Meets one of His Old Enemies, and Kills Him and His Companion.

Two More Victims.

White Oaks, N.M.
    April 30, 1881.
EDITOR NEW MEXICAN
    Information reaches us tonight, by reliable party, to the effect that the "Kid," while escaping from justice, met Billy Matthews and an unknown party, and killed them both. The tragedy occurred a few miles from Lincoln.

    Matthews was one of Lincoln county's best men, and was always an enemy of the "Kid's" he (Matthews) having shot him through the thigh in the Lincoln County War.   D.

On May 5, 1881, was the *Santa Fe Daily New Mexican*'s untitled item; stating:

    Anything that the imagination can concoct in the way of murders and desperate deeds, may be heard upon the reports now in regard to Billy the Kid: but getting at the truth of the rumors is another thing altogether.

    There was a report ... that the Kid was in Albuquerque, and was bound for Santa Fe. It was also said that he had killed another man near there, but the rumor thus far lacks confirmation.

On May 5, 1881. the *Santa Fe Daily New Mexican* also ran an untitled story that Billy was back in Stinking Springs. It stated:

> Mr. Richard Dunham says that on the second instant he met the Kid at Stinking Springs and had a conversation with him. The Kid said that he was going to Salt Lake, but that he intended doing up Santa Fe on his trip. He desired, he said, to pay his respects to Governor Wallace and U.S. Marshal Sherman, after which he would probably hunt up his old associates in Durango. He thought he would be able to ride over his troubles and make an honest living for the future. He says he has been badly treated and spoke as though he had no particular love to waste on anyone. So the young man thinks he can escape altogether and that after paying his respects to the Governor and the United States Marshal? Well he has enough assurance to carry him through at any rate.

PRESS FAME OF THE GREAT ESCAPE

Unbeknownst to himself, Lew Wallace was no longer in control of Billy's meteoric trajectory of fame. Billy's great escape captured public imagination; and his true daring broke through his outlaw myth. On May 4, 1881, the day after Wallace's reward notice, *Santa Fe Daily New Mexican* excitedly reported Billy's jailbreak:

> The above [account of the escape] is the record of as bold a deed as those versed in the annals of crime can recall. It surpasses anything of which the Kid had been guilty, so far that his past offences lose much of their heinousness in comparison with it, and it effectually settles the question of whether the Kid is a cowardly cut-throat or a thoroughly reckless and fearless man. Never before has he faced death boldly or run any great risk in the perpetration of his bloody deeds. Bob Olinger used to say that he was a cur, and that every man he had killed had been murdered in cold blood and without the slightest chance of defending himself. The Kid displayed no disposition to correct this until this last act of his when he taught Olinger by bitter experience that his theory was anything but correct. (Nolan, *The Lincoln County War*, p. 420)

WALLACE'S FIRST BILLY THE KID OUTLAW MYTH ARTICLE

Lew Wallace likely read the May 4, 1881, adulatory, *Santa Fe Daily New Mexican's* jailbreak story. It may have precipitated his first full-blown Billy the Kid outlaw myth, twelve days later, on May 16th. With Billy still alive to be pardoned, he used the *St. Louis Daily Globe-Democrat* to launch "The Thugs Territory, Stage Robbers and Cut-Throats Have Things Their Own Way in New Mexico, Gen. Lew Wallace Anxious to Punish Crime that is So Prevalent - A Chapter About "Billy the Kid."

Revealing a promised pardon, he lied that it was withheld because Billy refused to reform. But with Billy now on the loose to expose him as a liar, Wallace's panic yielded his paranoid fantasy of Billy wanting to kill him, as well as hysterical defamations: "He stole, murdered, ravished women ... It is claimed he has killed some forty men, and it is positively known that he killed at least five or six in Mexico alone." So Wallace's first tale of the West - with Billy the Kid as its villain and himself as hero - emerged as crazy, dime novel pulp. The article stated:

The Thugs Territory.

Stage Robbers and Cut-Throats Have Things Their Own Way in New Mexico.

Gen. Lew Wallace Anxious to Punish Crime that is So Prevalent – A Chapter About "Billy the Kid" – The Governor has a Narrow Escape from Being Spanked.

Special correspondence of the Globe-Democrat.

DEMING, N.M. May 9, 1881. – Your correspondent visited ... Santa Fe and had a pleasant talk with Governor Lew Wallace ... [T]he Governor gave a very interesting sketch of the life of

"BILLY THE KID,"

the most noted and desperate character in New Mexico, and who was sentenced to be hanged on the 13th inst., but escaped by killing his guards and defying the entire population of Lincoln to take him, and Governor Wallace has offered a reward of $500 for his recapture, and has a posse consisting of seventy-five men on his trail.

"I deem him," said the Governor, "the most dangerous man at large, and I hope I will have the pleasure of seeing him meet his just deserts for the many crimes he has committed."

Billy, he said, was born in the East, and for some years lived in Indianapolis, Ind. He is 21 years of age, and came to New Mexico with his head crammed with dime novel stories. His ambition was to become one of the most noted outlaws he had read so much of. He settled down in Lincoln, and a splendid field was afforded to make his name in the terror of the inhabitants. He stole, murdered, ravished women, and at one time stole a herd of cattle consisting of 300 head, drove them to a station and sold them. He then pocketed the money and went back to Lincoln and defied the authorities to take him. It is claimed he has killed some forty men, and it is positively known that he killed at least five or six in Mexico alone. Some two years ago a murder was committed in New Mexico and Governor Wallace was positive that Billy had a hand in the deed, but was unable to discover his whereabouts. Finally he learned that he was in the mountains a short distance from Santa Fe, and sent a messenger with a note to the outlaw, saying that if he knew anything about the matter and was willing to give his evidence before the Grand Jury, he would grant him a pardon, providing he also led a different life. Billy was to meet him at a certain house in Santa Fe at 12 o'clock on a certain night and date, and the matter would be thoroughly discussed. At the appointed time

GOV. WALLACE

was at the house, and exactly at 12 o'clock a knock was heard at the door and in walked "Billy the Kid." A long talk followed, and it was agreed that the Sheriff should arrest him to protect him from the pals of the murderer. The Governor's idea in granting a pardon to Billy was to capture the leader and break up the gang. On the next day the Sheriff with a posse of men captured Billy and he was brought before the Grand Jury, testified, and two of the men were sentenced to be hanged on Billy's evidence. Since the day Billy received the Governor's letter he has been leading the life of a murderer, stage robber, etc., and felt that the letter would forever shield him from the law should he be captured. At length Billy committed one murder too many, was arrested, and sentenced to be hanged on the 13th inst. at Santa Fe, but escaped by killing two of the guards. While in jail he wrote two letters to the Governor, demanding a pardon, and threatening to expose him should he not do as requested. The Governor remembered the letter, and sent word to Billy's lawyer that he might do him a favor by publishing it. This was too much for the outlaw, and he by letters and words openly avowed that Lew Wallace would die by his hands before he left the Territory. But the Governor does not fear him, and as soon as the outlaw is within two days ride of Santa Fe Wallace himself will start the pursuit. A hundred other frontiersmen are also on the track of Billy, and will capture him if he is within the Territory.

Governor Wallace, since performing the duties of Chief

Executive officer of New Mexico, has done considerable toward
PUTTING DOWN LAWLESSNESS
in the Territory. He is a man of courage, as the people know, and would not hesitate to face and attempt to take the most desperate character in this Territory if it became necessary. An interesting and ludicrous story is told of a recent meeting which was held by stage robbers and cutthroats of the Territory generally. It was resolved that as Governor Wallace had taken such great care in placing a large number of their crowd under arrest, that he should be assassinated when the first opportunity presented itself. Each man was sworn to the agreement in a general celebration and jubilee followed at Lincoln over the action of the meeting. The members, some 300 in number, paraded through the streets with cocked guns and revolvers, and the citizens deemed it best to look on and not in any way molest the gang. Somehow or other, when the boys got pretty full of whiskey, a streak of goodness entered their hearts, and right in the saloon another meeting was called, and it was resolved that Lew Wallace was a brave man, and only doing his duty. As this was the case, the first resolution was reconsidered, and the following notice was sent to Governor Wallace, which is still in his possession:

"At our first meeting we resolved that you should die for interfering with our crowd, but as we think you a brave man and one who fought for the same cause that we did during the war, therefore we have resolved that instead of killing you we will, when the first opportunity presents itself, take off your pants and give you the worst spanking you ever had."

The Governor said that he actually believed that they would carry out their intention and he was very careful that they shouldn't get an opportunity
TO SPANK HIM
if he could help it. A short time after receiving the note he had occasion to cross the country, and he felt that the outlaws would attempt the trick. He felt so certain of this that before he started he gave the driver notice that should any person order the coach to halt, the mules should be whipped into a dead run. As the coach was descending a steep ditch a couple of men jumped out, and before they had time to sing out, the driver gave the mules the whip and away they dashed down the declivity. The Governor here jocosely remarked "that he didn't know which was the worst – running the risk of breaking his neck or getting the spanking." Anyhow, they didn't catch him, and if they do, it must be before the new Governor arrives. Governor Wallace will return to the East in a few weeks, settle up his affairs, then return to New Mexico for the purpose of seeing to his mining interests.

LEW WALLACE EXITS

Not waiting to complete his term, Wallace departed hated New Mexico Territory on May 28, 1881, and was welcomed in Crawfordsville, Indiana, on June 2, 1881. From there, on June 4, he got his longed-for appointment as Ambassador to Turkey from President James Abram Garfield, who, on April 19, 1881, had also written him in praise of *Ben-Hur*: *"With this beautiful and reverent book you have lightened the burden of my daily life."* From "reverent" Wallace's arrival home, Billy had 45 days to live.

KISTLER'S *DAILY OPTIC* OUTLAW MYTH

Russell Kistler's *Las Vegas Daily Optic* of June 15, 1881 published "**The Land of the Petulant Pistol**, "Scenes" where Life and Land are Cheap ... Billy the Kid as a Killer." However, its by-line stated: "Jap Turpen in Indianapolis Saturday Review," making the article a possible submission by Lew Wallace, who was then back in Indiana; and, three days later, published "Billy the Kid, General Wallace Tells Why the Young Desperado of New Mexico Wanted to Kill Him. A Dashing and Daring Career **in the Land of the Petulant Pistol**" in the Crawfordsville *Saturday Evening Journal*. Other clues of Wallace's authorship are that the fictionalized tale has his favorite theme: "The Kid" wanted to kill *him*!" Furthermore, the interview style, which Wallace used for his other articles, erroneously has Lute Wilcox - editor at Koogler's *Las Vegas* Gazette - being editor at Kistler's *Las Vegas Daily Optic*. The outlaw myth article's portion about Billy, stated:

THE LAND OF THE PETULANT PISTOL,

"Scenes" where Life and Land are Cheap ...
"Billy the Kid" as a Killer

Jap Turpen in Indianapolis Saturday Review.

A young man by the name of Lute Wilcox, city editor of the DAILY OPTIC, Las Vegas, New Mexico stopping over for a few hours last Saturday, sought and found and talked to me ... I knew him by his slang, strong modes of expression, and the tales he told. "No," he answered, "the press reports do not give a tithe of the killings ..."Tell me something of 'Billy the Kid.' "

"Of all the killers in that country the "Kid" is the most

successful. He has slain 36, and wants to wind up with Governor Wallace. The Governor has offered a reward of $500 for his apprehension and return to Santa Fe. He was once a bootblack in New York; a great reader of dime novels. He had been in New Mexico about four years. At first he was only a herder, and got his hands in by killing Mexicans. His last triumphant escape was about three months ago. He was under guard. Two officers were on duty, one a deputy United States marshal by the name of Bell, in the room with him. A pistol shot was heard. 'The Kid has tried to escape,' said one of the officers who at the time was upon the street, 'and Bell has shot him.' The room was in the second story of the building. Saying this he opened the door and walked in the house. 'Billy the Kid' stood at the head of the stairs and shot him down. He had worked his bracelet off and snatched the officer's pistol. Billy then walked down stairs and shuffled along the street to a blacksmith shop. The smith cut his irons, and he compelled another man to saddle him a fleet horse. He was a full three-quarters of an hour in getting out of town. He had not ridden far when he was met by two other killers whose friends he had slain, and who had sworn to kill him. Here was a ride of death. They all knew that one or more of them had to die. They rode along watching each other for twelve miles.

"At last 'Billy the Kid' got the drop and killed them both. He is now in the San Juan country, collecting, it is said, a large party of killers. A few days before I left Las Vegas, officer Bill Goodlet, at the insistence of Governor Wallace, started in search of him ..."

"Billy, the Kid" will surrender as placidly as a union depot pickpocket if officer Goodlet gets the drop on him.

WALLACE'S NEXT CERTAIN BILLY THE KID ARTICLE

By June 13, 1881, back home in Indiana only 11 days, Lew Wallace returned to obsessive reworking of his pardon betrayal for an interview with the Crawfordsville *Saturday Evening Journal*, published on June 18, 1881 as "Billy the Kid, General Wallace Tells Why the Young Desperado of New Mexico Wanted to Kill Him. A Dashing and Daring Career in the Land of the Petulant Pistol." This version is more refined than his May 16, 1881, "The Thugs' Territory" article,' and concocts a new version of his pardon denial, with himself as hero. Sprinkled are facts, like Chapman's murder, though with fabricated murderers. And Jesse James is added. It stated:

BILLY THE KID.

General Wallace Tells Why the Young Desperado of New Mexico Wanted to Kill Him.

A Dashing and Daring Career in the Land of the Petulant Pistol.

Late newspaper accounts of the exploits of "Billy the Kid," the New Mexico outlaw, have made him the chief among frontier desperados and familiarized readers with his depredations and murdering. In Crawfordsville additional interest in him is created by the fact that he is the same who swore to kill General Wallace, late Governor of New Mexico. His real name is William Bonne [sic], and he was born in New York, which place he left when a small boy with his widowed mother, for Indiana. He lived for a while in Indianapolis, and then Terre Haute, and four years ago went to the Territory of New Mexico. He had been a close reader of blood-and-thunder literature, and soon succeeded in out doing any of the desperate thugs he had ever read of. He now belongs to Silver City where his mother resides, but lives in the mountains to evade the edicts of the law, he now being under sentence for death for murder. He has killed in all, thirty-nine men, and is still not satisfied. He worked for John Chisum, the cattle dealer, in the late Lincoln county trouble, and claiming he has never received the promised $5 per day for his services, he is hunting down and killing Chisum's herdsmen, and giving their employer credit for $5 for each man killed.

[AUTHOR'S NOTE: Concealing the real Lincoln County War anti-Ring issues, Wallace manufactures anger at Chisum as Billy's motive for killings.]

It is only recently that he killed two guards of the Lincoln county jail, compelled one man to file off his irons, and another to furnish him with a horse and rode away before the eyes of the whole town. It was during this confinement that he swore to kill Governor Wallace. Given in the following narrative which a reporter of THE JOURNAL got from General Wallace, last Monday, is the cause of Billy's anger at the that Governor: A young lawyer named Chapman was murdered in Lincoln county, and for this were arrested four men, among whom was the notorious Jesse James, under one of his many names. The witnesses against the murderers all lied, and the latter were about to be liberated on a writ of habeas corpus. Governor Wallace heard that the "kid" saw the murder, and finding a man who could find Billy, sent him a note requesting a conference with him at midnight at a certain house which was designated. The note assured the "Kid" that if the conference proved that he did not have the necessary information about the murder he would be permitted to leave the city, but if he did and would testify before the grand jury, the note implied that the Governor would pardon him for crimes for which he had been indicted, provided he would leave the Territory for good.

[AUTHOR'S NOTE: This admits reality of pardon promise letters which Billy referred in his jail letter of March 2, 1881, and made Wallace accuse him of blackmailing. And Wallace admits to a pardon bargain; though fabricating the rest of the circumstances.]

Governor Wallace repaired to the meeting place early, and promptly at midnight, a slight knock was heard at the door and upon response in the inside, "Billy the Kid" opened the door and walked in. The Governor found Billy to be a mild-faced young man, 19 years old, small, slender, sloping shoulders, manly head, and an open expression of the face, and a deliberate and pleasant voice. After taking a cigar apiece, and talking over matters in Indiana, (for Billy was proud to say that he was once a Hoosier), Governor Wallace asked Billy to tell what he knew. He proceeded in good language to slowly tell what he knew, which proved to be what the authorities wanted. The Governor asked him if he would go before the grand jury and tell the same thing. Billy's reply was that he would not dare to do it voluntarily, as the criminals' friends would kill him. The Governor suggested that the difficulty might be surmounted by the "Kid" permitting himself to be captured.

[AUTHOR'S NOTE: Lying Wallace, in his decades of reworking this tale, would always undo Billy's courage in contacting him and in suggesting the sham arrest, by claiming he himself instigated both.]

This was agreed upon, and accordingly and by arrangement Billy was surprised at a safe place in the mountains, while asleep, captured, and taken to jail. He went before the grand jury and by his evidence the criminals were indicted for murder. But before the trial in which he was to appear as a witness for the prosecution, he tired of jail life, and one day at dinner, he left his guards and took to the mountains.

[AUTHOR'S NOTE: Wallace admits Billy testified for the pardon bargain, but fabricates that Billy absconded before testifying in a (fabricated) trial; thus, failing his side of the bargain. In later articles, Wallace used the absconding story to make Billy the bargain betrayer. Omitted here, and forever after, is that Billy stayed in jail until June of 1879 to testify also in the Dudley Court of Inquiry to seek justice.]

He then resumed robbing raids and stealing cattle ... until two years later, Pat Garrett, Sheriff of Lincoln County, and the only man now in New Mexico who is not afraid of Billy, got on his track and effected his capture. During this imprisonment the "Kid," who had constantly carried the Governor's note about the convicting of Chapman's murderers, wrote twice to Governor Wallace, threatening to publish the proposition to pardon if he was not liberated. No attention was paid to these and Billy's lawyer then came before the Governor with the same threat. The reply from the executive was that Billy might publish as much as he chose, as the matter had been reported in Washington and there approved.

[AUTHOR'S NOTE: Here is more evidence of a lost pardon promise letter. But Wallace's guilt was so great that he devised this pompous fable of reporting to Washington about "the matter."]

Billy was further informed that he had not complied with all the conditions of the promise. This greatly enraged the young outlaw and he said he would take the life of the Governor. While under sentence of death he swore to kill three men before he died – Governor Wallace, John Chisum, the cattle dealer, and Pat Garrett, the Lincoln County Sheriff. In a short time he gained liberty by killing his two guards as before stated. Although Bonne [sic] was a desperate character, Governor Wallace felt no particular alarm and was more anxious to find Billy than Billy was to find him. He had it so arranged that he would have heard of the young desperado's approach 150 miles from Santa Fe, and other precautions were taken at the Governor's office.

[AUTHOR'S NOTE: This fabricated tale of Billy's murderous vendetta against him, is Wallace's projection of his own murderous feelings against Billy. And it is his conceited method of putting himself in the center of the jailbreak, when, in fact, he was irrelevant by then. But Wallace recycled it in all his future articles.]

Billy was sentenced to be hung, and took desperate chances to escape. He was successful and was in no hurry to come in the way of the law. His success had in his great amount of nerve. He never allowed himself to become excited, and never missed the object he shot at. Before Billy became involved in so many crimes he had one day showing Governor Wallace a specimen of his workmanship. He explained his perfection thus: He never took aim with the revolver, but placed his index finger along the barrel, and as if pointing at the object pulled the trigger with his second finger ... Nevertheless he is ever on the alert guarding against the other fellows getting the "drop."

There was once a three day siege of a house in which were Billy and a party. General Wallace had a report of the maneuvering on the out-side and when Billy was a prisoner had him to tell of the workings on the inside. The besieging party finally succeeded in firing the house and those inside were driven from room to room, and finally to the kitchen. Then, there was but one door of exit and the outside men kept a continual storm of bullets pouring into it. One by one those attacked "took chances" and ran out the door rather than to be burned. Each fell with from four to fourteen bullets in the bodies until the "Kid" who was the last to go rushed out and escaped without a scratch, though his clothing was completely riddled with bullets, and even his necktie was cut at his throat.

[AUTHOR'S NOTE: This rendition indicates that Billy had told Wallace about the Lincoln County War Battle in their meetings; though Wallace obscures the facts and puts himself in the center of the event.]

The "Kid" is a great favorite with Mexican women and does not want for friends, but as hard, bold, and daring as he is, he will doubtless soon meet death at the rope end of the gun's muzzle.

KILLING BILLY IN FORT SUMNER

Pat Garrett fulfilled the desire of Ringites and Lew Wallace by killing Billy Bonney on July 14, 1881 in Fort Sumner, in the mansion bedroom of Peter Maxwell, Paulita Maxwell's traitorous brother, who likely lured him there to the ambush.

For the body of this last killed Lincoln County War hero, the townspeople, who were Billy's friends, made a candlelit night vigil in Fort Sumner's carpenter's shop for his body.

The next morning, on July 15th, the Coroner's Jury met in Fort Sumner. Its President was Ringite Milnor Rudolph, the contested Speaker of the House of Representatives in the 1872 Legislature Revolt, and now Postmaster at nearby Sunnyside. Realizing that no place in the Territory was now safe, the frightened jurymen signed bi-lingual Rudolph's Spanish text; thus, parroting Rudolph's words: *"[O]ur verdict is that the deed of said Garrett was justifiable homicide and we are unanimous in the opinion that the gratitude of all the community is due to the said Garrett for his deed and he is worthy of being rewarded."*

The outlaw lie had become the public cant. And terror silenced a generation about the truth about Billy Bonney.

The Coroner's Jury Report stated:

Greetings:

On this 15th day of July, A.D. 1881, I, the undersigned, Justice of the Peace of the above named precinct, received information that a murder had taken place in Fort Sumner, in said precinct, and immediately upon receiving said information I proceeded to the said place and named Milnor Rudulph, Jose Silva, Antonio Sevedra, Pedro Antonio Lucero, Lorenzo Jaramillo and Sabal Gutierres a jury to investigate the case and the above jury convened in the home of Luz B. Maxwell and proceeded to a room in the said house where they found the body of William Bonney alias "Kid" with a shot in the left breast and having examined the body they examined the evidence of Pedro Maxwell, which evidence is as follows: "I being in my bed in my room, at about midnight on the 14th day of July, Pat F. Garrett came into my room and sat down. William Bonney came in and got close to my bed with a gun in his hand and asked me "who is it" and then Pat F. Garrett fired two shots at the said William Bonney and the said William Bonney fell near my fire place and I went out of the room and when I came in again about three or four minutes after the shots the said William Bonney was dead."

The jury has found the following verdict: We the jury unanimously find that William Bonney has been killed by a shot on the left breast near the region of the heart, the same having been fired with a gun in the hand of Pat F. Garrett and our verdict is that the deed of said Garrett was justifiable homicide and we are unanimous in the opinion that the gratitude of all the community is due to the said Garrett for his deed and he is worthy of being rewarded.

M. Rudulph, President   Anto, Sevedra *(signature)*
Pedro Anto. m. Lucero *(signature)*
Jose Silba *(x)*   Sabal Gutierrez *(x)*
Lorenzo Jaramillo *(x)*

All said information I place to your knowledge.

Alejandro Segura Justice of the Peace

CHAPTER 26

LEW WALLACE'S RING-INSPIRED BILLY THE KID MYTH

THE RING AND WALLACE IN SYNC

SUMMARY: Lew Wallace's excuse of pursuing outlaws merged with the Ring's outlaw myth to yield his literary creation of the outlaw, Billy the Kid. The motive of both was cover-up of the Ring's existence and crimes.

Though Lew Wallace appeared proud of himself for not succumbing to the Santa Fe Ring, in truth, he did. He had yielded to their post-Lincoln County War cover-ups, and had adopted their outlaw myths to deflect from their crimes. With addition of his literary skill, it made him the Ring's ideal mouthpiece. And for the rest of his life, he published outlaw myth articles on desperado Billy the Kid, devoid of the freedom fight and the Ring. They became fodder for future historians and the media.

"LEW WALLACE'S FOE": DECEMBER 10, 1893

Lew Wallace actually had two obsessions connected to the pardon bargain. One was concealing his betrayal, the other was repairing his self-esteem wounded by guilt at that ignoble act. The latter task resulted in his December 10, 1893 *San Francisco Chronicle* self-aggrandizing article titled "Lew Wallace's Foe, Threatened by "Billy the Kid," The Writing of 'Ben-Hur' Interrupted, An Incident of the Soldier-Author's Career in New Mexico." It made himself all good, and Billy all bad. The pardon was left out. It was replaced with a Wallace-ordered capture of outlaw Billy who was "surrounded by overwhelming numbers" of men - likely Wallace's cribbing of Secret Service Agent Azariah Wild's 1880 reports' versions of posses chasing Billy's mythical outlaw gang. Wallace even added snide denigration by calling his "Billy" short - a "diminutive prisoner" - though real Billy was of above average height, and the same as Wallace's. It stated:

LEW WALLACE'S FOE.
Threatened by "Billy the Kid"
The Writing of "Ben-Hur" Interrupted.
An Incident of the Soldier-Author's Career in New Mexico.

General Lew Wallace, best known to the general public by his two great books, "Ben-Hur" and the "Prince of India," is a man of many roles. He has been successful as a soldier, politician, diplomat and author, and some startling experiences have fallen to his lot.

His career on the battlefield, his life in Turkey, When he was Minister to Constantinople, and his later triumphs in the world of literature have all gone to make an eventful record, and they have all been so often recounted in the public prints that it would seem that every incident of his life would be familiar to those who keep themselves posted on the careers of public men. Yet there is one ordeal through which General Wallace has passed, and which he probably will never forget, that has escaped the vigilance of the scribes. It is, probably, not generally remembered that General Wallace was once Governor of the Territory of New Mexico, but it is a fact that in 1880, and for a year or so after that, he occupied the former palace of the Captains-General of Spain, in the historic old town of Santa Fe, N.M. He was the chief executive of the Territory, by appointment of President Garfield [Hayes], and it was during his administration that he fell under the ban of an assassin, and was given very good reason to believe that he would have to look down the ugly barrel of a 45-caliber revolver, and to defend his life as best he might.

The Governor's enemy was no less a personage than the illustrious "Billy the Kid," than whom no man had ever excited more terror on the frontier or given better ground for the dread in which he was held. He had perpetrated murder after murder and there were few crimes of which he was not believed to be capable. He boasted that he had killed more men than he was years of age and would shoot a man if he felt so disposed, "just to see him kick."

After "Billy the Kid" had been carrying things with a high hand for a long time Governor Wallace offered a reward for his capture. It proved a tempting bait to the "gun fighters" and officers of the law in the Territory. There were plenty of men among them who would not shirk from a hunt through the mountain fastnesses, even after such formidable game as this border bully, and the result of the Governor's offer was that after a most exciting pursuit **"Billy the Kid" was surrounded by overwhelming numbers and forced to surrender**. He was taken to Santa Fe and thence to Lincoln County to answer a charge of murder.

Enraged at having been trapped, the outlaw swore that

if he ever regained his liberty he would kill three men. One was a judge who had passed sentence upon him, one was Pat Garrett of Lincoln county, who had been conspicuously active in effecting his capture, and the third was Governor Lew Wallace.

"After I have settled accounts with these three men," said the desperado, "I will be willing to surrender and be hanged. **When I get out I will ride into Santa Fe, hitch my horse in front of the Palace, and walk in and put a bullet through Lew Wallace**.

This seemed idle boasting at the time, because there appeared to be not the remotest possibility of the prisoner's escape. He was in the custody of Sheriff Garrett in the County Jail of Lincoln, and the Sheriff, besides being a cool, courageous and reliable man, had every incentive to be watchful of his charge. It was thought a pretty sure thing that Garrett would never let the "Kid" go, and Governor Wallace felt fairly secure in his office away off in Santa Fe.

Garrett appointed as guards over the "Kid" Bob Ollinger [Olinger] and John [James] Bell. They were his personal friends, both big, burley **six-footers, who towered over their diminutive prisoner**. In addition to this physical superiority over him, they counted themselves as his equals when it came to a fair and square gun-fight. If anyone had told them that the "Kid" would outwit them and escape they would have laughed at the very thought of it.

For months the "Kid" was as docile as a kitten. The guards became used to him, then familiar, and then friendly. He seemed to have forgotten that they had helped to cage him and were his custodians, and as time passed the trio became boon companions. The guards laughed at the "Kid's" stories of his exploits, played cards with him during their long watches and would often remove one of the "cuffs" from his wrist, so that he could manipulate his cards or ply knife and fork at meal times. Whenever this was done both handcuffs were fastened to the right wrist, and thus locked in a cell with one of his stalwart guards the little cut-throat was safe enough.

Ollinger and Bell took turns watching in the jail and relieved each other to go to dinner. One day when Ollinger had gone across the street to a restaurant Bell took the "Kid" from his cell to an up-stairs room in the little two-story adobe jail. He put some food on a table for him and then unfastened the left cuff and locked it on the prisoner's right wrist.

The "Kid" sat down and began to eat without the slightest apparent concern. While he was munching the coarse prison fare Bell strode restlessly up and down the room. He wore no coat and his heavy revolver protruded from the holster attached to his cartridge belt. Each time he walked the room he passed within two feet of where the "Kid" sat, and once when he came within reach the "Kid," with the quickness of a cat, leaped upon his chair and dealt him a rap on the head with the handcuffs. Bell staggered under the blow, and before he could recover the "Kid" had snatched the revolver from the holster and sent a bullet through Bell's body. The guard tottered and fell and in a few moments was dead.

Ollinger was across the street and had, no doubt, heard the shot. The outlaw seized a double-barreled shotgun and ran out on the front balcony. Already Ollinger had crossed the street. He had come on the run, but before his foot struck the steps he fell with a load of buckshot in his heart.

The murderer walked carelessly down the stairs, stepped over Allinger's [Olinger's] prostrate form and strutted down the street with the revolver and shotgun in his hands. A blacksmith was shoeing a horse in a neighboring shop, and "Billy the Kid" easily persuaded him to desist, **then mounted and rode out of town at a walk, saying just before he started: "Now for the Governor."**

The news of the escape quickly reached Santa Fe, and Governor Wallace's friends became very uneasy lest the "Kid" should carry out his threat. The Governor himself was not entirely tranquil in the circumstances. It is one thing to face an enemy in the open field and quite another to have a treacherous one dogging one's footsteps.

Brave as Governor Wallace had shown himself to be, he recognized his danger and prepared to meet it. At that time he had already begun "Ben-Hur," and used to sit for hours in his office each day engaged upon the absorbing work. From the day upon which "Billy the Kid" escaped from the Lincoln County Jail a close observer entering the office might have detected lying on the table, partially hidden among papers and scraps of manuscript, the glint of a pistol, for the Governor was never without one while he knew that his arch-enemy was at large.

The people of Santa Fe were well aware that the head of the Territorial Government was preparing for war for every morning about 7 o'clock the sharp crack of a revolver being fired rapidly resounded from the corral in the rear of the gubernatorial residence. It soon became known that it was Governor Wallace improving himself as a pistol shot preparatory to an impromptu duel with "Billy the Kid." A figure had been marked on the adobe wall of the corral, and the Governor filled it full of holes. He became so expert that he could knock an imaginary eye out of the figure at twenty paces. He made no bones of the matter and, in fact, could be easily seen from the adjoining houses.

During the weeks which elapsed before the termination of this period of suspense Pat

Garrett was in hot pursuit of "Billy the Kid." It was a most remarkable and exciting chase. The whole Territory was deeply intent upon it, and news of the whereabouts of the two men was eagerly looked for. Governor Wallace repeatedly said to the writer: "When these two men meet one or both of them will bite the dust."

He was right. The announcement finally came from Fort Sumner that Garrett had forever rid the country of the "Kid." He had tracked him to the house of Peter Maxwell, near Fort Sumner, and, concealing himself in one of the rooms, had fired one shot at his man. That shot passed through the desperado's heart and he fell dead in his tracks.

Governor Wallace breathed easier, and the next night a reporter found tall, muscular Pat Garrett waltzing with a four-foot Mexican girl in a dance hall of Santa Fe.

"STREET PICKINGS": JANUARY 6, 1894

A month after his violent Billy the Kid fantasy of "Lew Wallace's Foe," on January 6, 1894, Wallace gave a "Billy the Kid" interview to the Weekly *Crawfordsville Review* as "Street Pickings." Still omitting the pardon bargain, it fabricated himself as the object the Kid's vengeful obsession. He also made himself an expert marksman - like real Billy. Wallace was quoted:

Street Pickings

Gen. Lew Wallace is a dead-shot with the pistol. Speaking of how and why he acquired such expert marksmanship, the renowned author-soldier said a few days ago in conversation with a party of friends:

"When I was governor of New Mexico that territory was and had been for years terrorized by bands of daring and murderous outlaws, at the head of whom was the famous border desperado, "Billy the Kid." By virtue of my office I became this man [sic] deadliest enemy. No man ever excited more terror along the frontier or gave better ground for the dread in which he was held than this man. He perpetrated murder and their [sic] were few crimes of which he was not guilty. He had openly boasted that he killed nearly fifty men and enjoyed shooting a man down 'just to see him kick.' I determined to rid the territory of this scourge and offered a large reward for his capture. The offer proved to be a great sensation throughout the territory and a tempting bait to ready shooters and officers of the law. There were in the territory hundreds of men who accepted with great delight this opportunity to take a hunt through the mountains after such formidable game. Well, the result was that after a most exciting chase the outlaw was surrounded by overwhelming numbers and compelled to surrender at the point of fifty guns after shooting down three of his pursuers. He was taken to Lincoln county, away up in the state, to answer an unusually flagrant murder. He was wildly enraged at having been trapped and swore that the moment he got free he would ride clear through to Santa Fe, shoot me down and then gladly hang.

"I knew the character of the man and while never dreaming that he would ever again be at large, I determined in order to be safer, to begin pistol practice in case an impromptu duel should ever take place between us. I got a brace of the best pistols I could find and every morning spent an hour in the corral firing at a mark. In a few weeks I got so I could hit the figure of a man marked out on the wall at twenty paces about every time. And as I became more and more skillful, I felt correspondingly safer and didn't much dread an open meting even with the caged murderer and with my life for the stake.

"Two months dragged along and one day at Santa Fe we got the alarming news that "Billy the Kid" had murdered his two jailors, stolen a horse and had started for Santa Fe with the open threat, 'Now for the governor and then hang.' Then I began practicing several hours every day and for weeks I was in daily expectation of meeting the ruffian. I still went about my duties, but heavily armed with my pistols ever ready. Pat Garrett was the sheriff to whose charge "Billy the Kid" had been entrusted, and when he learned a half-hour afterward and while away from home, that 'Billy the Kid' had escaped, he started in hot pursuit. For weeks there was unbroken suspense during which he heard nothing from the pursuer or pursued. They were both dead shots and there would be killing when they met. It was a most remarkable and exciting chase. The whole territory was deeply intent upon it and news of the whereabouts of both men was eagerly awaited.

"Finally, one day there rode up to my residence a travel-stained six-footer in a wide sombrero hat, mounted on a pony worn out with hard work. He got off, let his pony wander loose and came up to the door. I met him on the front step with my guns ready for instant use and asked him his errand. 'I am Pat Garrett, governor, and have just shot 'Billy the Kid' out here at Ft. Sumner.' And it was true. He had come up with the desperado heading for Santa Fe to end me, had got the drop on him and without a word shot him through the heart. I have still kept up my practice somewhat, but not under as thrilling circumstances."

"GEN. WALLACE'S FEUD WITH BILLY THE KID": JUNE 23, 1900

Lew Wallace, possibly contemplating writing a future Billy the Kid novel, on June 23, 1900, published a novella-like outlaw myth article expanding his tales of the now famous outlaw boy.

For *The Indianapolis Press* on June 23, 1900, he continued his pardon obsession with "Gen. Wallace's Feud with Billy the Kid, When the General Was Governor of New Mexico and Billy Bonne Was the Most Dangerous Western Outlaw, He Was a Waif and was Reared in Indiana." And Wallace settled on a mythical murder tally for the monster he had created: "[H]e killed a man for every one of the twenty-two years he lived." It stated:

GEN. WALLACE'S FEUD WITH BILLY THE KID
When the General Was Governor of New Mexico and Billy Bonne Was the Most Dangerous Western Outlaw
HE WAS A WAIF AND WAS REARED IN INDIANA

(By a Staff Correspondent)
CRAWFORDSVILLE, Ind., June 23. –

"Yes, **he killed a man for every one of the twenty-two years he lived**, and died in his stocking feet – a marvelous, far more than marvelous, career his was – a nightmare of existence."

Gen. Lew Wallace's shaggy brows contracted with a frown as he closed his eyes as though to shut out from his memory unpleasant things. There was a pause. He arose from his chair, and after walking up and down his study in silence, finally said:

"So long as I live, I will never lose the image of Billy the Kid, as I saw him that midnight in old Santa Fe, back in 1879. There he stands in the doorway of the little adobe house, form outlined by moonlight at his back, face illuminated by glow of the little lamp. The clock had made its first stroke of the midnight hour, when by appointment to the second there was a knock at the door that I can hear yet. 'Come in,' I said. The door flew open and there stood the most feared, the most adored, the most reverenced man in New Mexico, hunted by every limb of the law as a criminal, and sought by every Spanish senorita as her lover. The room was covered by a Winchester rifle held in one hand. In the other was a Colt's revolver. It was a musical growl that said, "I was to meet the Governor here at midnight. It is midnight: is he here?"

"I asked him to come in for a conference, and told him that I was the Governor of New Mexico.

"Your note gave me the promise of protection," he said.

"There is no one here but us three," replied I, pointing to the owner of the cottage.

"Billy threw his gun over his arm and came straight to the table near which I sat. I looked at him in wonder. This was the man that had killed his scores: the man whom every officer hunted. I was not expecting to see a stripling, with rounded shoulders, slightly stooping stature, slender, effeminate physique. His face was smooth and soft, and yet character and firmness were shown in every line. His voice was as musical as that of a society belle. Over him, with a majesty, hung the cloak of fearlessness and alertness penetrated only by two eyes that looked deep into every man's intentions."

Reared in Indiana.

The General passed from the thoughtful to the narrative and said: "Billy the Kid, the New Mexican outlaw that attracted the attention of a nation, and under whose fearful vendetta I was placed while Governor of New Mexico, was a New York waif whose name was William Bonne.

[AUTHOR'S NOTE: Inflating his own daring, Wallace makes Billy famous in 1879, and invents Billy's "fearful vendetta" against himself.]

He was brought to Indiana when he was a small boy and was reared in Indianapolis and Terre Haute. He was about 17 years old in 1876, when he went West. During his early years he had been a close reader of blood-and-thunder literature. He outdid in reality the lurid pictures of the literature in which he was schooled.

"It was not long until 'Billy the Kid' became the most daring and notorious of desperadoes. Stories of his crimes, his escapes, his fascinating faculties were the nursery tales of the Territory. He started to grow up with the country by taking employment of John Chisum, who was known as the 'Cattle King,' was a hard taskmaster and disputed Billy's account. The latter swore that he would square matters by killing Chisum's herdsmen: that for each man he killed he would credit the cattleman with $5, but if he killed Chisum himself then the whole account would be wiped out.

[AUTHOR'S NOTE: Wallace makes Chisum Billy's killing motive to hide Lincoln County War issues.]

Midnight Meeting Arranged.

"A young lawyer named Chapman was murdered at Lincoln. Four men were arrested, among them the notorious Jesse James.

[AUTHOR'S NOTE: New Mexico Territory Ringite outlaw, Jessie Evans, whom Wallace had captured, here becomes famous Jesse James!]

The witnesses to the killing were filled with terror and fled the country. Because of the lack of evidence the prisoners were about to be released on a writ of habeas corpus. I had been sent to pacify the country and had realized this was an opportunity I could not let slip. At last I heard that Billy the Kid had witnessed the murder.

[AUTHOR'S NOTE: Wallace hides Billy's pardon bargain to make himself the hero.]

In the outskirts of Santa Fe lived an old 'squire,' who was one of Billy's friends.

[AUTHOR'S NOTE: Wallace omits any hint of his Lincoln humiliation, instead setting the meeting in Santa Fe. This fabrication dispenses with Lincoln County War issues and the Dudley Court of Inquiry.]

I went to him one evening and told him I wanted the young outlaw to meet me promptly at midnight. He professed that he had no connection with the sought-for youth. I ordered pen and ink and wrote a note, and, leaving it, told him that I would expect it to be delivered to Billy. In the note I said I understood he was the only remaining man that had witnessed the murder, and that if he would appear before the Grand Jury and court and convict them I would pardon him for all his crimes.

[AUTHOR'S NOTE: Though reversing roles with Billy as to proposing the pardon, Wallace here admits to it. That would require his later concealing of his betrayal.]

"The midnight meeting was as I have described. When he heard from my lips my proposition he said: 'My God, Governor, they would kill me.' 'But that can be arranged,' I replied.

[AUTHOR'S NOTE: Wallace lies that he devised the sham imprisonment.]

It was decided that Billy was to be taken the next morning while asleep in a cabin back in the mountain. He picked the men that were to capture him. He required me to keep him in irons during confinement, that his reputation not be marred."

[AUTHOR'S NOTE: Wallace hides the Lincoln location of the jail for his lie.]

Billy's Secret in Revolver Shooting.

"It was during this confinement that 'the Kid' gave the most phenomenal exhibition of shooting I have ever witnessed. I sent word to the jail to have him brought to my office.

" 'Billy,' I said, 'I am told you are a phenomenal shot. I wish you would give me an exhibition of your skill.'

" 'With pleasure, Governor. Have my pistols brought.'

" 'Here is a pistol, and a good one.'

" 'A violinist always wants his own bow, though another might be better. I want my own pistol.'

"His pistol was brought and we took him out into the big, open court.

[AUTHOR'S NOTE: Continuing his fabricated location

of Santa Fe, Wallace seems to describe the inner courtyard of the Palace of the Governors, in keeping with the boy being brought to his "office." In fact, the Lincoln demonstration would have been behind jailor Juan Patrón's house.]

I ordered his chains taken from him. The guards whispered to me, 'For God's sake, Governor, do you know that you are giving him your life or his escape?'

[AUTHOR'S NOTE: To hide his pardon bargain, Wallace conceals that jailing was a sham; and that jailor, Juan Patrón, was Billy's loyalist.]

"I know that I was the last man in New Mexico Billy wanted to kill, for I was the only man that could give him a pardon.

[AUTHOR'S NOTE: This shows the sadism that mixed power and pardon in Wallace's troubled psyche.]

"The guards stood with their weapons in their hands, ready to defend themselves from this man with a charmed life. Billy spied a small Boston bean can in the court. He ordered a guard to throw it high as he could. The can sailed in the air. Without taking aim, and seemingly without concern, he fired at it. The bullet passed through the center. As it struck the ground, in the same unconcerned manner, Billy fired at it, and, emptying his revolver, he rolled it along much the same as one can roll a can with the stream from a lawn hose.

" 'Billy,' said I, 'There is a trick in that, and I want to know it.'

" 'Yes,' he replied, 'there is a trick. Ever since you were a child, Governor, you have been doing it unconsciously, every time you have said 'Look at that you have pointed at it with your index finger. Without knowing it, you have become an expert mark – and so has everyone. I put my index finger along the barrel, catch the trigger with my second finger and say, 'Why look at that, Billy,' and, pointing unconsciously at it, pull the trigger. I am not known as a crack shot, Governor – rather a dead shot.'

"He asked for his horse and gun – his own Winchester. Mounting, he started down the court on a dead run, and as he went he shot with his left hand, emptying his magazine into a four-inch sapling that was 200 yards distant. Back he came on a gallop, shooting with the right hand. Every shot took effect.

" 'And what is the trick about that, Billy?'

" 'Oh, General, there is no trick in that rifle. My horse bounds away, I level, I feel it all over, I pull the trigger and the bullet goes straight.

Was Something of a Hypnotist.

"It was a week before the trial. Billy had been taken to dinner in his chains. After the meal he said: "Well, I wish you would tell the Governor that I am tired. Much obliged boys,' and leaving them as though in a trance, he quietly walked across the street, and, unhitching a horse, dashed out of town. There could be no suspicion that the guards had conspired for his release. They were victims of that mysterious something that Billy exerted over men.

[AUTHOR'S NOTE: Here is Wallace's perfidy: hiding Billy's testimony that fulfilled the pardon bargain, substituting a dream-like escape. Besides its lie, it insults by Billy by the quote, "I'm tired;" as if he lacked moral fiber to stick out his pardon deal.]

"Later Billy was arrested for a series of murders.

[AUTHOR'S NOTE: This is a purposeful lie, since Billy's Stinking Springs arrest by Sheriff Pat Garrett was only for the Brady-Hindman-Roberts indictments.]

He had kept my note offering pardon in the affair.

[AUTHOR'S NOTE: This references Billy's jail letter about possessing pardon letters.]

He had been in jail a week when he addressed me: 'Governor, why haven't you come to see me?' I paid no attention to it. A few days later there was a second note: 'Governor, I have some papers you would not want to see displayed. Come to the jail.' I knew what he meant.

[AUTHOR'S NOTE: Here is chilling proof that 19 years after he betrayed Billy, Wallace remembered his jail letters. But here he is reworking their truth, making them seem just a blackmail attempt, which he next triumphantly fabricates as himself thwarting.]

I sent a copy of the old note and the story over to the paper and it was published. I sent him a copy of the paper and drew his fire. It was then that he swore his vendetta on my life and on that of Pat Garrett, the sheriff of Lincoln County.

[AUTHOR'S NOTE: This false "Billy vendetta" against himself is a projection of his hostility to the boy, as well as his unconscious expression of guilt and his own deserved punishment. Wallace's adding of Garrett, reflects his request to Garrett to report back to him after Billy's hanging death, like a compatriot in his murderous plan.]

He was convicted for murder and sentenced to be hanged. When the sentence was read, he arose in court and said:

" 'Judge, that doesn't frighten me the least bit. Billy the Kid was not born to be hung.'

"This young desperado was a thorough fatalist. He believed that for the time he had a charmed life: that he had nothing to fear from the weapons of enemies, and that he would not go 'until his time came,' and the time was not at hand.

"He had gone through many a danger. At one time, surrounded in a Mexican house, 'the Kid' fought nine men. The house was set on fire, and he made a dash for liberty and escaped through all the musketry of the guards. There were a dozen bullet holes in his clothing and his necktie had been cut away at the throat by a bullet, but Billy received not a mark on his skin.

[AUTHOR'S NOTE: This reduction of the Lincoln County War to a "surrounded ... Mexican house" with Billy fighting nine men is Wallace's ongoing shielding of the Santa Fe Ring, years after his governorship. It is made more outrageous by the fact that Wallace himself went through the Dudley Court of Inquiry and faced Ring abuses. But his rewriting of history is his ongoing campaign against admitting his humiliating failures.]

"From his trial," continued General Wallace, "Billy was taken back to jail. He was in no wise disturbed. A day before the execution nine guards were watching him. At dinner time all but one left. Billy was in chains. The guard on duty received a tray that bore Billy's dinner. As the guard stood to place the tray on the floor, Billy the Kid struck him on the head with the handcuffs, crushing the skull. Then he took the guard's revolver, routed all the other guards that appeared, forced a blacksmith near by to break the handcuffs, mounted a good horse near at hand and rode away. He said as he started: 'Tell the Judge that I said that Billy the Kid was not born to be hung.'"

End of Billy the Kid.

"It is needless to touch upon my danger under the vendetta," returned Gen. Wallace. Sufficient it is to say that he started for Santa Fe at once, and, determined to have a shot in return, I started out to meet him, but for some reason he never reached the point.

[AUTHOR'S NOTE: Wallace continues his coat-tailing on Billy's great escape, though, by then, he was likely the last thing on the boy's mind. But at the 1900 date of this article, Billy the Kid was already famous, so Wallace was now also parasitizing that fame for self-aggrandizement.]

Sheriff Pat Garrett was the only man in New Mexico not afraid of Billy and his charmed life. Garrett started out to make his capture, and it was a scout lasting for weeks, each man waiting to get the drop. All New Mexicans had their eyes on the two, and every morning the general question was, 'Has Pat and the Kid met yet?' It was a long siege, but Billy fell through love.

"Pat received information that Billy had gone back to an old fort in the mountains to see his sweetheart. Garrett journeyed there. He lay in wait in the dooryard of Billy's love, and finally saw the door open one night and a man come out in stocking feet. His hat was off; he wore only shirt and trousers. He passed out into the night. Garrett walked in and covered the girl's father with a gun. 'Not a word,' he whispered, as he passed behind the headboard of the bed with gun in hand. The door opened again. Billy seemed to smell danger, as a camel smells rain. He knew by instinct that something was wrong. He cried to the old man in Spanish, 'Who's there? Who's there?' Garrett raised his revolver. There were two reports. Billy the Kid jumped into the air and fell in his tracks. There were two bullet holes through his heart."

[AUTHOR'S NOTE: Lew Wallace also seems to have sought inspiration from his fellow Billy the Kid outlaw myth maker, Pat Garrett, to approximate the scene for Billy's killing from his 1882 *Authentic Life of Billy the Kid*.]

As he concluded the story there was a tremble in Gen. Wallace's voice that indicated that with the horrible picture there was a feeling of admiration for Billy. There was a pause and he said: "And he was only twenty-two."
E.I. LEWIS

[AUTHOR'S NOTE: Did "staff correspondent" E.I. Lewis inadvertently report the physical manifestation of old hypocrite Wallace's guilt, as "a tremble" of Wallace's voice, and as his "admiration for Billy?"]

"GEN. LEW WALLACE WRITES A ROMANCE OF BILLY THE KID": JUNE 8 1902

Twenty-one years after Billy's killing because of his pardon betrayal, and two years after his *The Indianapolis Press's* "Gen. Wallace's Feud with Billy the Kid," Wallace regurgitated his last lies. In *New York World Magazine* on June 8, 1902, with three more years left to live, he published another novella as "General Lew Wallace Writes a Romance of 'Billy the Kid' Most Famous Bandit of the Plains, Thrilling Story of the Midnight Meeting Between Gen. Wallace, Then Governor of New Mexico, and the Notorious Outlaw, in a Lonesome Hut at Santa Fe." In it, Wallace confirmed the pardon bargain as: " 'Testify,' I said ... 'and convict the murderer of Chapman and I will let you go scot-free with a pardon in your pocket.' " As usual, his outlaw Billy the Kid betrays the bargain. This version was incorporated into his *Autobiography*, advertising his life by the boy's far greater fame. It stated:

GENERAL LEW WALLACE WRITES A ROMANCE OF 'BILLY THE KID' MOST FAMOUS BANDIT OF THE PLAINS

Thrilling Story of the Midnight Meeting Between Gen. Wallace, Then Governor of New Mexico, and the Notorious Outlaw, in a Lonesome Hut at Santa Fe.

Gen. LEW WALLACE, author of "Ben Hur," is completing his autobiography, which will be issued in a few weeks.

The most thrilling chapter in this remarkable personal narrative tells of the midnight meeting in a lonely hut between Gen. Wallace, at the time Governor of the Territory of New Mexico, and "Billy the Kid," the most notorious outlaw the far West has ever produced.

From advance sheets of Gen. Wallace's book the following account of this strange rendezvous has been copied and compiled for the Sunday World Magazine. The story has never been printed in any newspaper or magazine before.

The episode occurred in 1879. The outlaw was at the zenith of his wild career. Gen. Wallace conceived the idea that he might gain certain important information by a face-to-face talk with the outlaw. With much difficulty the meeting was finally arranged. It was not without a strong element of danger to both participants, but they trusted each other and the trust was not betrayed.

The Midnight Rendezvous.

On the night of the meeting two men sat, shortly before midnight, silent and expectant, in the hut which had been chosen for the rendezvous, which was on the outskirts of Santa F, N.M.

Their gaze was fastened on the door, and, as the minutes slipped away the tension grew more severe, the silence more oppressive.

One man was the owner of the rude home that stood desolate in the shifting sands of the great mesa.

The other was Gen. Lew Wallace, Governor of New Mexico.

The hands of the clock pointed to 12.

The hush deepened. Suddenly it was broken by the sound of a resolute knock on the door of the cabin.

"Come in," said the Governor of New Mexico.

The door flew open and, standing with his form outlined by the moonlight behind him, was "Billy the Kid." In his left hand he carried a Winchester rifle. In his right was a revolver. The weapons, quick as a flash, covered the two occupants in the room.

"I was to meet the Governor here at midnight. It is midnight: Is the Governor here?"

The light of the candles flickered against a boyish face, yet the man who stood in the doorway was the most notorious desperado in all the West. He had killed scores of men: he was the quarry of every sheriff from the Rio Grande to the bordering foothills that shut in Death Valley.

The Boy Outlaw.

In facial features "Billy the Kid" was a mere stripling. His narrow shoulders were rounded, his posture slightly stooping, his voice low and effeminate. But his eyes were cold and piercing, steady, alert, gray like steel.

Gen. Wallace rose to his feet and held out his hand, inviting the visitor forward for a conference.

"Your note gave the promise of absolute protection," said the outlaw, warily.

"I have been true to my promise," replied the Governor. "This man," pointing to the owner of the cabin, "and myself are the only persons present."

The rifle was slowly lowered, the revolver returned to its leather holster. "Billy" advanced and the two seated themselves at opposite sides of the narrow table.

Gen. Wallace was able to effect an important arrangement with the outlaw, of which he gives the details. In fact, a very friendly understanding was established between the two.

Explaining the purpose of the interview and its result with "Billy," Gen. Wallace says:

"Shortly before I had become Governor of New Mexico, Chapman, a young attorney in Lincoln, had been murdered. Half a dozen men were arrested, accused of the crime. Among them was Jesse James.

While it was more than probable that one or more of the men charged with the murder were guilty, it was impossible to prove the allegation, for the witnesses, filled with terror, fled the country. **When I reached New Mexico it was declared on every hand that "Billy the Kid" had been a witness to the murder. Could he be made to testify?**

"That was a question on the tip of every tongue.

"**I had been sent to the Southwest to pacify the territory; here was an opportunity I could not afford to pass by. Therefore I arranged the meeting by note deposited with one of the outlaw's friends, and at midnight was ready to receive the** desperado should he appear. He was there on time – punctual to the second.

"When 'Billy the Kid' stepped to the chair opposite mine, I lost no time in announcing me proposition.

Agrees to the Plan.

" **'Testify,' I said, 'before the Grand Jury and the trial court and convict the murderer of Chapman and I will let you go scot-free with a pardon in your pocket for all your misdeeds.'**

[AUTHOR'S NOTE: After 23 years, Wallace confirmed the bargain.]

" 'Billy' heard me in silence; he thought several minutes without reply.

" 'Governor,' said he, "if I were to do what you ask they would kill me."

" 'We can prevent that," said I.

"Then I unfolded my plan. 'Billy' was to be seized while he was asleep. To all appearances, his capture was to be genuine. To this he agreed, picking the men who were to effect his capture. He was afraid of hostile bullets and would run no risk. Another stipulation was to the effect that during his confinement he should be kept in irons. 'Billy the Kid' was afraid also of the loss of his reputation as a desperate man."

The plan agreed upon in the cabin on the lonely mesa at midnight was carried out to the letter. "Billy the Kid" was seized the following morning and confined in the Lincoln County jail. It was here that Gen. Wallace, in spite of the fears of the guards, permitted the outlaw to give an exhibition of his skill with the revolver and the rifle. "Billy," standing or riding, using either the one weapon or the other, sent every bullet true to its mark.

"Billy," said the General, "there's some trick to that shooting. How do you do it?"

"Well, General," replied the desperado, "there is a trick to it. When I was a boy I noticed that a man in pointing to anything he wished observed, used his index finger. With long use, unconsciously, the man had learned to point it with unerring aim. When I lift my revolver, I say to myself, 'Point with your finger.' I stretch the finger along the barrel and, unconsciously, it makes the aim certain. There is no failure; I pull the trigger and the bullet goes true to its mark."

"Billy," though at his own request kept in irons, did not remain long confined. One morning the guards led him to breakfast. Returning, the desperado drawled in the feminine voice that was a part and parcel of his character:

"Boys, I'm tired. Tell the Governor I'm tired."

The manacles slipped like magic from his wrists. The guards stood stupefied, and "Billy the Kid," laughing mockingly, walked leisurely from the jail yard, through the gate and across the street. Easily, gracefully, he threw himself into the saddle on the back of a horse standing near at hand and, putting spurs to the animal, dashed away. "Billy" was gone. He had not escaped in the night; he had walked away in the broad light of day, with his guards, heavily armed, standing about him.

"Boys," I'm tired," he said, and looked them straight in the eyes.

They were not in collusion with the desperado; Gen. Wallace satisfied himself of the fact.

But how account for "Billy's" escape?

Hypnotism, some say – hypnotism or that strange something that lurked in the depths of the steel-gray eyes.

The desperado's freedom, however, was not long-lived. He was arrested soon afterward for a series of murders, and was brought again to the Lincoln County Jail. Patrick Garrett was Sheriff. He was probably the one man in New Mexico who did not fear "Billy the Kid." He was his match in every respect – as calm, as desperate, as certain.

Perhaps "Billy" knew this. At any rate he must have considered himself in desperate straits. He sent for Gen. Wallace. The General refused to respond. Then the outlaw sent him a note. The note said:

"Come to the jail. I have some papers you would not want to see displayed."

"I knew what he meant," said Gen. Wallace, reminiscently. "He referred to the note he received from me in response to which he appeared in the hut on the mesa. He was threatening to publish it if I refused to see him. I thwarted his purpose by giving a copy of the latter and a narrative of the circumstances connected with it to the paper published in the town. It was duly printed and upon its appearance a copy was sent to "Billy" in his cell. He had nothing further to say."

Not Daunted By His Sentence.

In the end the desperado was convicted and sentenced to be hanged. When the sentence was read he stood before the trial judge and said:

"Judge, that doesn't frighten me a bit. 'Billy the Kid' was not born to be hung."

He was a thorough fatalist. He believed he bore a charmed life. He believed he would not die until his "time came," and then death was inevitable.

From the court-room "Billy" was led back to the jail. Nine men were put on guard, and he was never allowed a moment from the sight of one of them.

On the day before that set for his execution one man sat in front of Billy while he ate his dinner. During the meal the guard forgot himself and suddenly stooped. "Billy's" quick eye took in the situation in a glance.

With a leap he sprang upon the bending man and dashed his brains out with his handcuffs. He seized the dead guard's revolver and, his steel-gray eyes gleaming, he walked forward deliberately and routed all the other guards, who ran to the assistance of their comrade.

Once more "Billy the Kid" escaped in the full light of day through the doors of the jail. He forced a blacksmith to break the manacle chains, seized a good horse that stood nearby and rode away.

He called back as he spurred the animal into a gallop: "Tell the judge that I said "Billy the Kid' was not born to be hung."

But "Billy" had forgotten one thing; he had not reckoned on the character of the man who was Sheriff of the county. He had forgotten Patrick Garrett. Garrett shut his teeth hard, like a man who is determined to accomplish his purpose, no matter the obstacles presenting themselves. He set out to take "Billy the Kid," dead or alive.

Garrett received information that "Billy" had gone back to an old fort in the mountains to see his sweetheart. Garrett followed. He lay in wait in the dooryard of the home of "Billy's" love, and finally his vigil was rewarded when he saw the door open one night and a man step out into the white light of the moon.

His hat was off, he was in his stocking feet and he wore only shirt and trousers. He passed out into the night.

Garrett crept to the door and passed in.

He covered the girl's father with his gun.

"Not a word," he said, and slid behind the headboard of the bed.

The Death of "Billy the Kid."

The door opened again and "Billy the Kid" entered. He seemed to scent danger as a camel scents rain; instinct taught him that something was wrong. He cried to the cowering old man in Spanish:

"Who's here?" he asked. "Who's here?"

Garrett raised his revolver; two shots rang out on the quiet air and the room filled with smoke. A form tottered, then crashed to the floor. In the nerveless hand was a smoking revolver; for the first and last time the notorious New Mexican outlaw had missed his aim. Garrett escaped unwounded. But there were two bullet wounds in the body of "Billy the Kid" and both pierced the heart. Garrett's aim was unerring.

To-day there is a little lowly heap of earth located in Las Cruces, N.M. [sic – Fort Sumner] To the curious stranger some idle native may, now and again, point out this little grave and explain, with a certain pride, that Las Cruces possesses the final resting place of the worst bad man that ever infested the Southwestern border. An ancient Mexican, who sometimes shows this grave to visitors, once made the cautious remark regarding its occupant that, had he lived, he would probably have turned out to be a bad man.

"And how old was 'Billy' when he died?" asked one curious stranger.

"Twenty-one, senor," replied the ancient. "He died, almost one might say, before he fully began to live."

"You say he was bad?" remarked another stranger.

"He is said to have killed many men."

"How many? How many, amigo, had this man killed at the time he himself died?"

"He had killed," replied the ancient Mexican, "twenty-one men, one for each year of his age, may the saints defend us," said the Mexican.

[AUTHOR'S NOTE: Wallace's 21 men for 21 years is on one of Billy's Fort Sumner gravestones.]

"He was a good man, and very kind to poor people. Yet, had he lived, he might, according to the opinion of some, have turned into a bad man."

Gen. Wallace also tells in his autobiography how and why "Billy the Kid" started on his career of crime:

A Waif of New York City.

"The man whose deeds of blood had drawn upon him the eyes of an entire nation, was born a New York waif. Before he was more than ten years of age he was brought to Indiana, and in Terre Haute and Indianapolis, where he was reared, he was known as William Bonne. In 1876, when he was about seventeen years old, he suddenly left his home, crossed the Mississippi and went to the country of the men of his kind – the frontier of the far West.

"Billy began his career with an oath to kill John Chisum, his first employer when the lad reached the plains. Chisum and the "Kid' had been unable to agree on terms of settlement for a season's work. The result was the lad's fearful vendetta, sworn not only against Chisum, but against all of Chisum's other employees as well.

" 'For each herdsman employed by you whom I kill," Billy sent him word, "I will deduct $5 from our unsquared account. If I kill you,' he added grimly, 'my bill will be receipted in full.'

"Then his bloody career began. It was not long until William Bonne, the waif, reared in the peaceful surroundings of Indiana, became the most feared man in the Southwest. At the same time, he was the most revered, the most adored and the most respected man in the Territory.

"It was the kind of good reward that sometimes comes to bad men."

CHAPTER 27

THE SANTA FE RING REGROUPS

THE SANTA FE RING UNCHECKED

SUMMARY: With Ringite Governor Lionel Sheldon replacing Lew Wallace, the Santa Fe Ring was triumphant after crushing 1870's rebellions. All criminal Ringites were unpunished. The Ring was now the perfect criminal organization: invisible and immune, quashing truth with pseudo-history and making New Mexico Territory a fiefdom.

REINSTATEMENT OF SAMUEL BEACH AXTELL

Symbolizing its now unassailably evil supremacy, was the Ring's restoration to power of its 1870's agent in land-grabs, terror, obstruction of justice, and murders: ousted Governor, Samuel Beach Axtell: their only punished member; albeit by removal rather than deserved criminal prosecution. By 1881, with Lew Wallace departing before completing his term, the Ring moved audaciously to return Axtell in his old job.

Stephen Benton Elkins led the campaign to reinstate Axtell as Governor, notwithstanding Frank Warner Angel's incriminating investigative report of October 3, 1878, and subsequent removal of Axtell from that public office.

On March 17, 1881, Elkins wrote a disingenuous letter to his good friend President James Abram Garfield - arguably beholden to him for his office - garbling facts for public consumption and relying on Garfield's continuation of President Hayes's protection of the Ring. Smarmy Elkins, calling Axtell *"the most popular Governor New Mexico has ever had,"* wrote: *"I beg to state that I think Gov. Wallace was appointed in place of Gov. S.B. Axtell under a misapprehension of the facts and to the injustice of Axtell which I am informed President Hayes after a full understanding of the case regretted very much indeed and expressed his willingness to reappoint Gov. Axtell or give him some other appointment."* In fact, sly Elkins had already met secretly with scheming Garfield the week before. Elkins wrote:

> 115 Broadway
> New York Mar. 17 1881
>
> To the President.
>
> Referring to a conversation had with you last week about the Federal appointees in New Mexico I beg to state that I think Gov. Wallace was appointed in place of Gov. S.B. Axtell under a misapprehension of the facts and to the injustice of Axtell which I am informed President Hayes after a full understanding of the case regretted very much indeed and expressed his willingness to reappoint Gov. Axtell or give him some other appointment. As a matter of justice to **Gov. Axtell who probably was the most popular Governor New Mexico has ever had**, I greatly desire his appointment as Governor. I think it would fully vindicate him and be the proper course to pursue. If however you feel that you cannot appoint him I am glad to concur in the appointment of Lionel Sheldon. I served with him in the House and know him long and favorably and believe he would make a thorough and vigorous Governor. If Lionel Sheldon should be appointed Governor of New Mexico I hope you will not forget Gov. Axtell.
>
> Very truly &c
> S.B. Elkins

Noteworthy is that the Ring's second choice was Ringite Lionel Sheldon, who was ultimately appointed to replace Lew Wallace.

With President Garfield's shooting assassination on July 2, 1881, and death on September 19, 1881, Vice-president Chester A. Arthur became President. By the next year, when New Mexico Territory Chief Justice L. Bradford Prince, resigned, Axtell was put forth to replace him. Review of Axtell was done by the U.S. Senate Judiciary Committee in June of 1882. The new Secretary of the Interior, Henry M. Teller, ignored or suppressed the exposés of Mary McPherson. But the Frank Warner Angel report surfaced. Bradstreet wrote:

> **U.S. SENATE CHAMBER**
>
> **WASHINGTON** 22 June 1882
>
> Sir:
>
> Referring to the nomination of Sam'l B. Axtell of Ohio to be chief justice of the supreme court of New Mexico, now pending before the judiciary committee of the Senate, I am directed by that committee to ask you to please send to them, so that they may have them by next Saturday (the 24th inst.), the report and papers made

by Judge Angell [sic] of New York upon charges made against Axtell while he was governor of that territory, and upon which he is alleged to have been removed by President Hayes.

[AUTHOR'S NOTE: Do not miss the duplicitous "alleged to have been removed" to conceal documented justified removal.]

The committee would also be glad to have any other papers or information in the possession of your department touching said charges, or bearing upon his appointment as chief justice.
Respectfully yours,
Geo P. Bradstreet

That June, Attorney Frank Springer, showing vestigial conscience as a past Colfax County War victim, went to Washington, D.C. to oppose Axtell's appointment. He was ignored.

Axtell was confirmed as Territorial Chief Justice on July 13, 1882. And the *Santa Fe New Mexican* responded with smug thuggery of real Ringite outlaws, including Axtell himself: " 'Chief Justice Axtell' is a bitter pill for the Raton *News and Press*. Don't make a wry face, you've got to swallow it."

As Chief Justice, Axtell also became Judge of the First Judicial District, including Colfax County, where he had earlier tried to murder the Ring's adversaries, and where he had illegally removed their court - in which he now served. Axtell voluntarily retired on May 11, 1885 to pursue business in Santa Fe.

After S.B. Axtell's outrageous reappointment as a major New Mexico Territory public official, there was no further overt protest by anyone. The Ring now ruled by fear and favor.

LEW WALLACE ON CATRON

More than 15 years after he escaped New Mexico Territory, leaving its citizens in the thrall of the Santa Fe Ring by his self-serving cover-ups, and after the restorative experience of his exotic ambassadorship to Turkey, Lew Wallace felt safe enough to speak some truth about Catron and the Ring.

The recipient of his November 6, 1897 letter was his friend, Eugene Fiske, whom Frank Warner Angel had described in his secret notebook of 1878: *"Fiske E.A. Santa Fe, Lawyer - Shrewd - honest reliable - can be of great service to you ... Well posted as to the people and frauds in the Territory."*

To Fiske, Wallace now admitted: "**One of the curious incidents pertaining to Mr. Catron is his astonishing influence over New Mexicans.** I cannot recall one instance in which he did not absolutely submerge and control all persons who came in contact with him."

SANTA FE RING FIGHTER IN THE 20th CENTURY

After a gap of 90 years after the Santa Fe Ring's killing of Billy Bonney, there arose one anti-Ring historian in the 20th century. He was Norman Cleaveland: Mary Tibbles McPherson's great-grandson, Raymond and Ada Morley's grandson, and Agnes Morley Cleaveland's son. In 1971, he published unvarnished truth, tinged with back-country irony, in his book, *The Morleys: Young Upstarts of the Southwest*. He wrote:

> When my grandparents, William Raymond Morley and Ada McPherson Morley, pioneer New Mexicans, were in their twenties they were confronted with an "establishment" known as the Santa Fe Ring. By comparison, present-day establishments would rate rather as societies of butterfly collectors. (Cleaveland, p. viii)

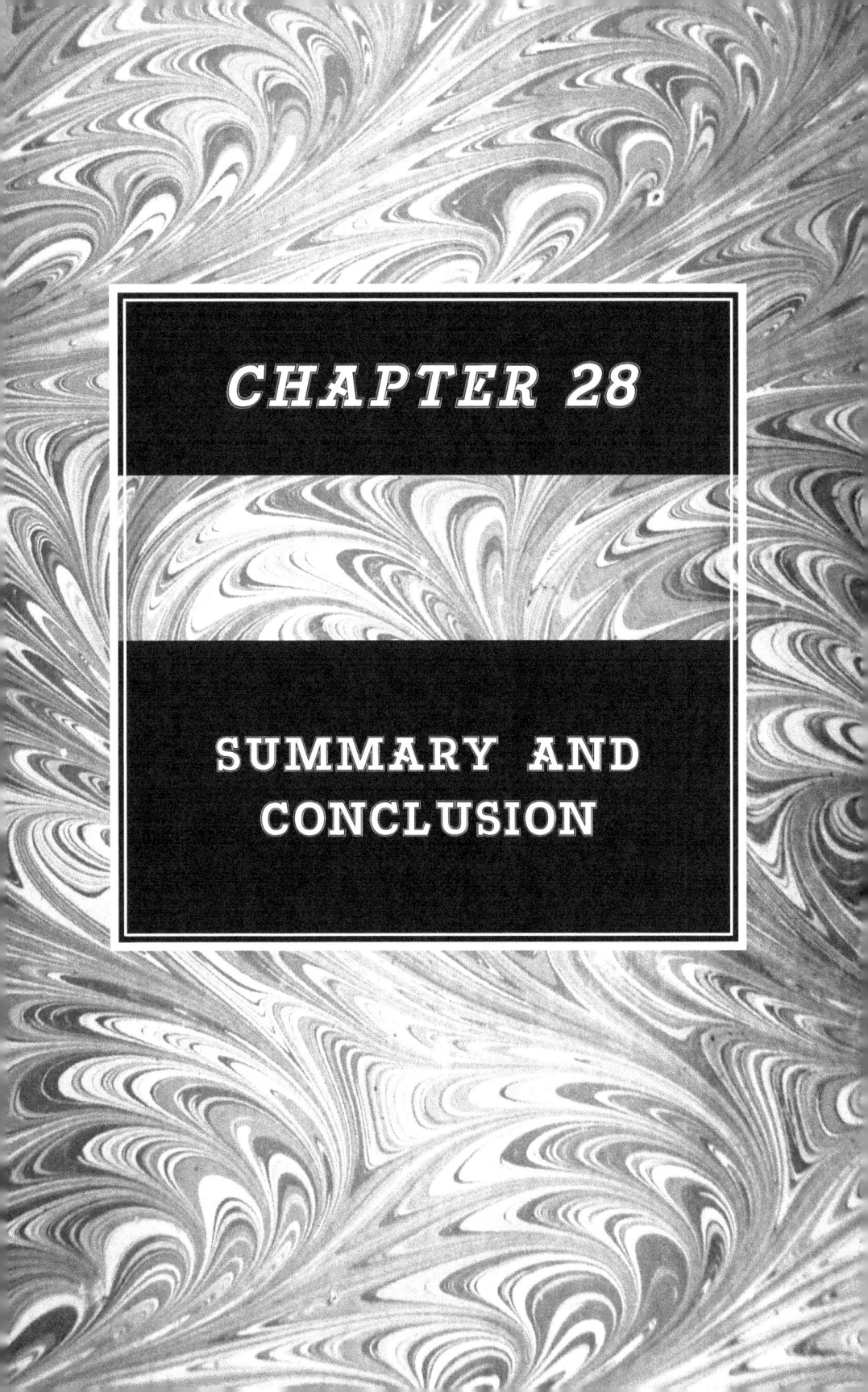

THE SANTA FE RING VERSUS BILLY BONNEY

The missing link in Lincoln County War and Billy the Kid history is the Santa Fe Ring. Without factoring it in, one is left with historian Robert Utley's vapid void: "a war without heroes." Filling that vacuum, from the days of Billy Bonney to the era of Utley's *High Noon in Lincoln*, have been the paralleling outlaw myth lies of the Ring, Investigator Frank Warner Angel, Territorial Governor Lew Wallace, Secret Service Operative Azariah Wild, Lincoln County Sheriff Pat Garrett, and 20th century historians (with exceptions of Norman Cleaveland and Jerry Weddle).

Missing is not just truth, but a magnificent grass-roots uprising against a tyrannical colossus, and a freedom fighting hero: Billy Bonney. Billy summed up that war *with* heroes in his April 16, 1881 *Mesilla News* interview after his hanging sentence, making clear the Regulators' choice of revolution and the malicious prosecution he had faced: "If mob law [of the Ring] is going to rule, better dismiss judge and sheriff and let all take chances alike." And he comprehended that it had been the Santa Fe Ring versus himself all along: "I think it hard that I should be the only one to suffer the extreme penalty of the law." At that moment, he was only 89 days from the Ring's extreme solution of killing.

So in their assault on Billy Bonney, the Santa Fe Ring won in the short run. What Billy did not recognize is that one person can make a difference. What if credible adversary, Frank Springer, had not changed sides? What if Susan McSween had prevailed in military court against past Commander N.A.M. Dudley? What if Investigator Frank Warner Angel had not capitulated? What if Governor Lew Wallace had been willing to fight the Ring? What if Secret Service Agent Azariah Wild had gotten Billy a pardon? What if Ira Leonard had stayed to undo Billy's hanging trials?

But standing alone against the Ring as the last freedom fighter, Billy is the one person who did make a difference. He was a star when alive, and a greater star after death. And in the span of a person's history, which far exceeds a lifetime and can become part of our collective awareness, Billy has remained the gadfly, transcending outlaw mythology by remarkable reality of his own writings, words, and acts; undoing the Ring's cover-ups by the sheer glory of truth. When Billy wins at last, the citizens of New Mexico will finally be free, and Americans will have another proof of democracy's regenerative power.

Billy will tow with him the others who should not be forgotten: Raymond and Ada Morley, Mary Tibbles McPherson, Reverend Franklin Tolby, Oscar McMains, Juan Patrón, John Tunstall, Attorney Alexander McSween, Deputy Sheriff Adolph Barrier, Justice of the Peace John Wilson, Francisco Zamora, Vincente Romero, Susan McSween, Attorney Huston Chapman, Attorney Ira Leonard, Attorney Montegue Leverson, Private James Bush, Sergeant Huston Lusk, Judge Napoleon Bonaparte Laughlin, and the other Ring opponents who gave, or risked their lives and futures, for fellow citizens' freedoms.

As great and wise freedom fighter and champion of the oppressed, Benito Juárez, the 26th President of Mexico, stated: "It is given a man, sir, to attack the rights of others, seize their goods ... make of their virtues crimes, and one's vices a virtue, but there is one thing beyond the reach of such perversity: the tremendous judgment of history."

Billy Bonney has by now long outdistanced his betrayers by international recognition of his ambiguous fame. He is now poised for "the tremendous judgment of history" against the American monster: the Santa Fe Ring, and against its outlaw myth of Billy the Kid. Time has finally turned the tables to bring about Billy the Kid versus the Santa Fe Ring.

SOURCES

ANNOTATED BIBLIOGRAPHY

GENERAL REFERENCES

Nolan, Frederick. *The Lincoln County War: A Documentary History.* Norman: University of Oklahoma Press. 1992.

_____. *The West of Billy the Kid.* Norman: University of Oklahoma Press. 1998.

History of New Mexico: Its Resources and People. Volume 1. Los Angeles: Pacific States Publishing Company. 1907.

HISTORICAL ORGANIZATIONS (PERIOD)

NORTH CAROLINA REGULATORS, 18th CENTURY

HISTORY OF 18th CENTURY REGULATORS

Hudson, Arthur Palmer. "Songs of the Regulators." *William and Mary Quarterly.* No. 4. (1947). Page 146.

Kars, Marjoline. *Breaking Loose Together: The Regulator Rebellion in Pre-Revolutionary North Carolina.* Chapel Hill and London: The University of North Carolina Press. 2002.

Maier, Pauline. *From Resistance to Revolution: Colonial radicals and the development of American opposition to Britain, 1765-1776.* New York and London: W.W. Norton & Company. 1991.

LINCOLN COUNTY REGULATORS, 19th CENTURY

AMERICAN INDEPENDENCE DOCUMENTS

Vincent, Wilson, Jr. *The Book of Great American Documents.* Brookville, Maryland: American History Research Associates. 1993.

DIME NOVELS ON REGULATORS (CONTEMPORARY)

Lody, William F. "Gold Bullet Sport; The Knights of the Overland". *Beadle's Dime New York Library.* 7(83). New York: Beadle & Adams, Publishers. December 17, 1874.

Cooms, Oll. "The Boy Ranger: or, The Heiress of the Golden Horn." *Pocket Series. No. 11.* New York: Beadle & Adams, Publishers. 1874.

Wheeler, Edward L. "The Deadwood Dick Library. A Tale of the Regulators and Road-Agents of the Black Hills. The Double Daggers; or, Deadwood Dick's Defiance." *Beadles Half Dime Library.* No. 20. Cleveland, Ohio: Arthur Westbrook Co. 1877.

_____. "Deadwood Dick, The Prince of the Road: or The Black Rider of the Black Hills". *The Deadwood Dick Library. 1(1).* Cleveland, Ohio: The Arthur Westbrook Co. 1877.

No Author. "The Rover of the Forest." *Munro's Ten Cent Novels.* No. 42. New York: George Munro & Co. 1864.

LINCOLN COUNTY REGULATOR MANIFESTO

Regulator. "Mr. Walz. Sir ..." Letter to Edgar Walz. July 13, 1878. Adjutant General's Office. File 1405 AGO 1878. (Quoted in Maurice Garland Fulton, *History of the Lincoln County War.* Tucson: University of Arizona Press. 1975, Pages 246-247, and Frederick Nolan, *The Lincoln County War: A Documentary History,* Page 310.)

SANTA FE RING, 19th CENTURY

GENERAL BOOKS ON ORGANIZED CRIME

Ackerman, Kenneth D. *Boss Tweed: The Rise and Fall of the Corrupt Pol Who Conceived the Soul of Modern New York*. New York: Carroll & Graff Publishers. 2005.

Critchley, David. *The Origin of Organized Crime in America: The New York Mafia, 1891-1931*. New York, London: Routledge, Taylor & Francis Group. 2009.

Reppetto, Thomas. *American Mafia: A History of Its Rise to Power*. New York: Henry Holt and Company. 2004.

Short, Martin. *The Rise of the Mafia: The Definitive Story of Organized Crime*. London: John Blake Publishing Ltd. 2009.

MODERN SOURCES

Brown, Richard Maxwell. *Strain of Violence: Historical Studies of American Violence and Vigilantism*. New York: Oxford University Press. 1975. (**New Mexico unique for assassination as part of political system**)

Caffey, David L. *Chasing the Santa Fe Ring: Power and Privilege in Territorial New Mexico*. Albuquerque, New Mexico: University of New Mexico Press. 2014.

_____. *Frank Springer and New Mexico: From the Colfax County War to the Emergence of Modern Santa Fe*. Texas A and M. University Press. 2007.

Cleaveland, Agnes Morley. *No Life for a Lady*. Boston: Houghton Mifflin. 1941.

_____. *Satan's Paradise: From Lucien Maxwell to Fred Lambert*. Boston: Houghton Mifflin Company. 1952.

Cleaveland, Norman, *Colfax County's Chronic Murder Mystery*. Santa Fe: New Mexico. The Rydel Press. 1977.

_____. *A Synopsis of the Great New Mexico Cover-up*. Self-printed. 1989.

_____. *Some Comments Norman Cleveland May Make to the Huntington Westerners on Sept. 19, 1987*. Unpublished.

_____. *Some Highlights of William R. Morley's Contribution to the Pioneer Development of the Southwest*. Self-printed. No Date.

_____. *The Great Santa Fe Cover-up*. Based on a Talk given Before the Santa Fe Historical Society on November 1, 1978. Self-printed. 1982.

Cleaveland, Norman and George Fitzpatrick. *The Morleys - Young Upstarts on the Southwest Frontier*. Albuquerque, New Mexico: Calvin Horn Publisher, Inc. 1971.

Klasner, Lilly. Eve Ball. Ed. *My Girlhood Among Outlaws*. Tucson, Arizona: The University of Arizona Press. 1972. Klasner, Lilly. Eve Ball. Ed. *My Girlhood Among Outlaws*. Tucson, Arizona: The University of Arizona Press. 1972. (**John Chisum's in jail write-up about Santa Fe Ring injustices to himself**)

Lamar, Howard Robert N. *The Far Southwest 1846 – 1912: A Territorial History*. New Haven and London: Yale University Press. 1966. (**Chapter 6 covers the Santa Fe Ring**))

Meinig, D. W. *The Shaping of America. A Geographical Perspective on 500 Years of History*. Vol. 3. *Transcontinental America 1850 - 1915*. New Haven and London: Yale University Press. 1998. (**Pages 127 and 132 are on the Santa Fe Ring.**)

Montoya, María E. Translating Property. The Maxwell Land Grant and the Conflict Over Land in the American West, 1840-1900. Berkeley and Los Angeles: University of California Press. 2002.

Naegle, Conrad Keeler. *The History of Silver City, New Mexico 1870-1886*. University of New Mexico Bachelor of Arts thesis. Pages 30-60. Unpublished. 1943. Collection of the Silver City Museum, Silver City, New Mexico. (**Grant County rebellion**)

_____. "The Rebellion of Grant County, New Mexico in 1876." *Arizona and the West: A Quarterly Journal of History*. Autumn, 1968. Volume 10. Number 3. Tucson, Arizona: The University of Arizona Press. 1968. Pages 225-240. (**Grant County rebellion against Santa Fe Ring**)

Newman, Simeon Harrison III. "The Santa Fe Ring." *Arizona and the West*. Volume 12. Autumn 1970. Pages 269-288.

Otero, Miguel A. *My Life on the Frontier, 1882-1897: Incidents and Characters of the period when Kansas, Colorado, and New Mexico were Passing Through the Last of their Wild and Romantic Years*. New York: The Press of the Pioneers. 1935. Pages 232-233. (Quoted by Victor Westphall, *Thomas Benton Catron and His Era*. Page 188) **(Quote: "the 'Santa Fe Ring,' the real machine controlling the political situation in New Mexico.")**

Pearson, Jim Berry. *The Maxwell Land Grant*. Norman: University of Oklahoma Press. 1961.

Taylor, Morris F. *O.P. McMains and the Maxwell Land Grant Conflict*. Tucson, Arizona: The University of Arizona Press. 1979. **(Traces origins of the Santa Fe Ring)**

Theisen, Lee Scott. "Frank Warner Angel's Notes on New Mexico Territory, 1878." *Arizona and the West: A Quarterly Journal of History*. Winter 1976. Volume 18. Number 4. Pages 333-370. **(About the Angel notebook given to Lew Wallace and listing names of Santa Fe Ring members)**

Westphall, Victor. *Thomas Benton Catron and His Era*. Tucson, Arizona: University of Arizona Press. 1973. **(Ring-denier, who cites sources exposing the Ring)**

CONTEMPORARY SOURCES (CHRONOLOGICAL)

No Author. *Diario del Consejo der Territorio de Neuvo Mejico, Session de 1871-1872. Santa Fe New Mexican*. **January 8, 1872**. Santa Fe: A.P. Sullivan. 1872. Pages 144-154. New Mexico Supreme Court Library. Santa Fe, New Mexico. **(A Ring expurgated document, with copy found in 1942 by Conrad Naegle; confirms troops used by Ring to suppress 1872 Legislature Revolt)**

No Author. *Diario del Consejo der Territorio de Neuvo Mejico, Session de 1871-1872*. Las Cruces *Borderer*. **January 24, 1872**. Pages 110-113. **(President of the Council Don Diego Archuleta objects to troops in legislature)**

No Author. *Journal of the House of Representatives of the Territory of New Mexico, Session of 1871-1872*. Santa Fe: A.P. Sullivan. **1872**. Pages 144-154. **(Confirms troops used by Ring to suppress the Legislature Revolt of 1872)**

No Author. "Ring influence [in the Territorial legislature is] being actively used against every measure that tends to do justice" [in Grant and Doña Ana Counties]." *Grant County Herald*. **August 8, 1875**. Quoted by Conrad Keeler Naegle in *The History of Silver City, New Mexico 1870-1886*, doctoral thesis. Page 39.

A.C.L. Editorial. "New Mexico, A Sorry Showing for a Would-be State, Tweed's Disciples Preying on the Populace, How the Territorial Ring is Run, Why the Territory Should Not Be Made a State. **March 13, 1876**. *The Boston Daily Globe*. Volume IX, Number 62. Newspaperarchive.com.

No Author. "A Contemplated Political Change." Grant County *Herald*. **September 16, 1876**. Quoted by Conrad Keeler Naegle in *The History of Silver City, New Mexico 1870-1886* doctoral thesis. Pages 39-40. **(Listing reasons to escape the Ring by annexing to Arizona Territory)**

Wallace, Lew. "Our mutual friend, M. Hinds, who will hand you this ..." Letter to A.H. Markland. **November 14, 1878**. Indiana Historical Society. Lew Wallace Collection. M0292. Box 3. Folder 17. **(Ring tries to remove him as governor)**

Leonard, Ira E. "When you left here I promised to write you concerning events transpiring here ..." Letter to Lew Wallace. **May 20, 1878** [sic - 79]. Indiana Historical Society. Lew Wallace Collection. M0292. Box 4. Folder 10. **(Quote: "Santa Fe ring ... so long an incubus on the government.")**

Wallace, Lew. "I have the honor to inform you that the Legislature of this Territory adjourned ..." **February 16, 1880**. Letter to Carl Schurz. Indiana Historical Society. Lew Wallace Collection. M0292. Box 4. Folder 14. **(Key documentation of Catron as head of the Santa Fe Ring, and Wallace's Ring opposition)**

No Author. "White Cap's Proclamation." *Las Vegas Optic*. March 12, 1880. (**Manifesto against land-grabbing Catron and the Ring**)

No Author. "The Santa Fe Ring is the most corrupt combination that ever cursed any country or community." Las Cruces *Thirty-Four Newspaper*. **October 27, 1880**. From Victor Westphall, *Thomas Benton Catron and His Era*. Page 186. (**Article on Santa Fe Ring abuses urging voters to oppose Ring candidates**)

No Author. "The Ring must soon discover that the time has passed in New Mexico when men can be herded like so many sheep …" *Albuquerque Daily Democrat*. **March 4, 1884**. (Quoted by Victor Westphall, *Thomas Benton Catron and His Era*. Page 191.) (**About Santa Fe Ring control of appointments to legislature**)

No Author. *Santa Fe Weekly New Mexican Review*. **March 13, 1884.** *Santa Fe Weekly New Mexican Review*. (**Accusation of Catron and the Ring of controlling grand juries and** bribery)

No Author. *Albuquerque Daily Democrat*. **March 15, 1884**. (**Oscar P. McMains "Memorial" against land-grabbing Ring**)

Valdez, Jose and Enrique Mares. "Scorching Letter, The Knights of Labor Send a Communication to Powderly! Politicians Arraigned! The Boldest Document Ever Issued in the Territory." **August 18, 1890.** *Las Vegas Democrat*. Volume 1. Center for Southwest Studies. Thomas B. Catron Papers, MSS 29, Series 102, Box 8, Folder 4. (**Gives history of Santa Fe Ring with T.B. Catron as head**)

No Author. *Los Angeles Times*. **1899**. Undated clipping, Laughlin Papers, State Records Center, Santa Fe, New Mexico. Quoted by Victor Westphall, *Thomas Benton Catron and His Era*. Page 285. (**Joking article about the Santa Fe Ring**)

(SEE: Thomas Benton Catron; Stephen Benton Elkins; Raymond Morley, Mary McPherson, Frank Springer, Frank Warner Angel, William B. Sloan, Legislature Revolt, Grant County Rebellion, Colfax County War, Lincoln County War)

SECRET SERVICE, 19th CENTURY

Bowen, Walter S. and Harry Edward Neal. *The United States Secret Service*. Philadelphia and New York: Chilton Company Publishers. 1960.

Brooks, James J. *1877 Report on Secret Service Operatives*. (September 26, 1877). "On Azariah Wild." p.392. Department of the Treasury. United States Secret Service. Washington, D.C.

Johnson, David R. *Illegal Tender. Counterfeiting and the Secret Service in Nineteenth Century America*. Washington and London: Smithsonian Institution Press. 1995.

(SEE: Azariah Wild)

NEW MEXICO TERRITORY REBELLIONS AGAINST THE SANTA FE RING (CHRONOLOGICAL)

LEGISLATURE REVOLT (1872)

No Author. "Our Own Dear Steve, How Elkins Made His Influence Felt in New Mexico – The Ring in Which a Judge Figured – Politics in 1870. *Las Vegas Daily Optic*. **September 2, 1884.** (Reprinted from the *Omaha Herald*) Front Page. Volume V, Number 258, Column 4. Newspaperarchive.com. (**Exposing the Ring in the 1872 Legislature Revolt with Catron's and Elkins's corrupt alliance with Judge Joseph Palen**)

GRANT COUNTY REBELLION (1876)

MODERN SOURCES

Naegle, Conrad Keeler. *The History of Silver City, New Mexico 1870-1886*. University of New Mexico Bachelor of Arts thesis. Pages 30-60. Unpublished. 1943. Collection of the Silver City Museum, Silver City, New Mexico.

_____. "The Rebellion of Grant County, New Mexico in 1876." *Arizona and the West: A Quarterly Journal of History*. Autumn, 1968. Volume 10. Number 3. Tucson, Arizona: The University of Arizona Press. 1968. Pages 225-240. **(Rebellion against Santa Fe Ring)**

CONTEMPORARY SOURCES (CHRONOLOGICAL)

No Author. "Diario del Consejo der Territorio de Neuvo Mejico, Session de 1871-1872." *Santa Fe New Mexican*. **January 8, 1872**. Santa Fe: A.P. Sullivan. 1872. Pages 144-154. New Mexico Supreme Court Library. Santa Fe, New Mexico. **(A Ring expurgated document, with a copy found in 1942 by Conrad Naegle; confirming troops used by Ring to suppress Territorial legislature)**

No Author. "Diario del Consejo der Territorio de Neuvo Mejico, Session de 1871-1872. Las Cruces *Borderer*. **January 24, 1872**. Pages 110-113. **(Don Diego Archuleta, President of the Council, gives speech objecting to troops in legislature)**

No Author. "Ring influence [in the Territorial legislature is] being actively used against every measure that tends to do justice" [in Grant and Doña Ana Counties]." *Grant County Herald*. **August 8, 1875**. Quoted by Conrad Keeler Naegle in *The History of Silver City, New Mexico 1870-1886,* doctoral thesis. Page 39.

No Author. "A Contemplated Political Change." Grant County *Herald*. **September 16, 1876**. Quoted by Conrad Keeler Naegle in *The History of Silver City, New Mexico 1870-1886* doctoral thesis. Pages 39-40. **(Listing reasons to escape the Ring by annexing to Arizona Territory)**

No Author. [Grant County should not] "sort o' wait and hear from Santa Fe ... before taking action." Tucson *Arizona Citizen*. **September 23, 1876**. Quoted by Conrad Keeler Naegle in *The History of Silver City, New Mexico 1870-1886* doctoral thesis. Page 41. **(Arizona encourages escape from Santa Fe Ring)**

No Author. Grant County *Herald*. **September 23, 1876**. **(Need for school system stressed.)**

No Author. Grant County *Herald*. **September 30, 1876**. **("Annexation Meeting" announced)**

No Author. "Proceedings of Grant County Annexation Meeting." Grant County *Herald*. **Saturday October 7, 1876**. Page 2. Columns 1 and 2. Collection of the Silver City, New Mexico, Museum. **(Anti-Santa Fe Ring "Grant County Declaration of Independence" published)**

No Author. Grant County *Herald*. " 'Petition to Remove Judge Bristol. We the undersigned citizens of the Third Judicial District of the Territory of New Mexico, without regard to party, would respectfully request and petition for the removal of Judge Warren Bristol ...' " No date. **1876 or 1877**.(Quoted in "W.B. Matchett and Mary E. McPherson 'Make certain charges against the U.S. Officials in the Territory of New Mexico.' " Letter to President Rutherford B. Hayes. Received and filed May 1, 1877. Interior Department Papers 1850-1907; Appointments Division and Subsequent Actions. Microfilm File Case Number 44-4-8-3. Record Group 48. Microfilm No. M750. Roll 1. National Archives and Records Administration. U.S. Department of Justice. Washington, D.C.) **(Anti-Santa Fe Ring article)**

(SEE: Santa Fe Ring; Thomas Benton Catron; Stephen Benton Elkins; John Simpson Chisum)

COLFAX COUNTY WAR (1877)

MODERN SOURCES

Caffey, David L. *Frank Springer and New Mexico: From the Colfax County War to the Emergence of Modern Santa Fe.* Texas A and M. University Press. 2007.

Cleaveland, Norman. *The Morleys - Young Upstarts on the Southwest Frontier.* Albuquerque, New Mexico: Calvin Horn Publisher, Inc. 1971.

Dunham, Harold H. "New Mexican Land Grants with Special Reference to the Title Papers of the Maxwell Grant." *New Mexico Historical Review.* (January 1955) Vol. 30, No. 1. pp. 1 - 23.

Keleher, William A. *The Maxwell Land Grant. A New Mexico Item.* Albuquerque, New Mexico: University of New Mexico Press. 1964.

Lamar, Howard Roberts. *The Far Southwest 1846 - 1912. A Territorial History.* New Haven and London: Yale University Press. 1966.

Montoya, María E. *Translating Property. The Maxwell Land Grant and the Conflict Over Land in the American West, 1840-1900.* Berkeley and Los Angeles, California: University of California Press. 2002.

Murphy, Lawrence R. *Lucien Bonaparte Maxwell. Napoleon of the Southwest.* Norman: University of Oklahoma Press. 1983.

Pearson, Jim Berry. *The Maxwell Land Grant.* Norman: University of Oklahoma Press. 1961.

Poe, Sophie. *Buckboard Days.* Albuquerque, New Mexico: University of New Mexico Press. 1964.

Taylor, Morris F. *O.P. McMains and the Maxwell Land Grant Conflict.* Tucson, Arizona: The University of Arizona Press. 1979.

CONTEMPORARY SOURCES (CHRONOLOGICAL)

No author. "Anarchy at Cimarron." *Santa Fe Weekly New Mexican.* **November 16, 1875.** (**Ringite backing of Axtell's use of troops in the Colfax County War**)

Dawson, Will. Editorial. *Cimarron News and Press.* **December 31, 1875.** (**Ring-biased editorial by temporary editor blaming citizens for unrest**)

No Author. Report on murder trial for Franklin Tolby. Pueblo, *Colorado Chieftain.* **May 25, 1876.** Quoting *Daily New Mexican*, May 1, 1876. From Morris F. Taylor. *O.P. McMains and the Maxwell Land Grant Conflict.* Tucson, Arizona: The University of Arizona Press. 1979. Page 49. (**Ring-biased jury instructions by Judge Henry Waldo to protect Ring murderers of Tolby**)

No Author. "Rejoicing at Cimarron," "Axtell's Head Falls at Last," "General Lew. Wallace Appointed Governor." *Cimarron News and Press.* **September 6, 1878**.

No Author. *Santa Fe Weekly New Mexican.* **September 21, 1878 and October 19, 1878.** (**Ring-biased accolades for removed Gov. Axtell**)

(SEE: Regulators, Santa Fe Ring; Thomas Benton Catron; Stephen Benton Elkins, William Raymond Morley, Mary Tibbles McPherson, Franklin Tolby, Oscar McMains, Colfax County War, Lincoln County War)

LINCOLN COUNTY WAR (1878)

MODERN SOURCES

Cramer, T. Dudley. *The Pecos Ranchers in the Lincoln County War.* Orinda, California: Branding Iron Press. 1996.

Fulton, Maurice Garland. Robert N. Mullin. Ed. *History of the Lincoln County War.* Tucson, Arizona: The University of Arizona Press. 1997.

Jacobson, Joel. *Such Men as Billy the Kid. The Lincoln County War Reconsidered.* Lincoln and London: University of Nebraska Press. 1994.

Keleher, William A. *The Fabulous Frontier: Twelve New Mexico Items.* Albuquerque, New Mexico: The University of New Mexico Press. 1962.

_____.*Violence in Lincoln County 1869-1881.* Albuquerque, New Mexico: University of New Mexico Press. 1957.

Mullin, Robert N. Re: Frank Warner Angel Meeting with President Hayes. August, 1878. Binder RNM, VI, M. Midland, Texas: Nita Stewart Haley Memorial Library and J. Evetts Haley History Center. (Unpublished).

Nolan, Frederick W. *The Life and Death of John Henry Tunstall.* Albuquerque, New Mexico: The University of New Mexico Press. 1965.

_____. *The Lincoln County War: A Documentary History.* Norman: University of Oklahoma Press. 1992.

_____. *The West of Billy the Kid.* Norman: University of Oklahoma Press. 1998.

Rasch, Philip J. *Gunsmoke in Lincoln County.* Laramie, Wyoming: National Association for Outlaw and Lawmen History, Inc. with University of Wyoming. 1997.

_____. Robert K. DeArment. Ed. *Warriors of Lincoln County.* Laramie: National Association for Outlaw and Lawmen History, Inc. with University of Wyoming. 1998.

Utley, Robert M. *High Noon in Lincoln. Violence on the Western Frontier.* Albuquerque, New Mexico: University of New Mexico Press. 1987.

Wilson, John P. *Merchants, Guns, and Money: The Story of Lincoln County and Its Wars.* Santa Fe, New Mexico: Museum of New Mexico Press. 1987.

No Author. "Disturbances in the Territories, 1878 - 1894. Lawlessness in New Mexico." Senate Documents. 67th Congress. 2nd Session. December 5, 1921 - September 22, 1922. pp. 176 - 187. Washington, D.C.: Government Printing Office. 1922.

CONTEMPORARY SOURCES (CHRONOLOGICAL)

No Author. "Brady Inventory McSween Property." **February, 1878**. Herman B. Weisner Papers, ca. 1957-1992. New Mexico State University Library at Las Cruses. Rio Grande Historical Collections. Accession No. Weisner Ms 0249. Box 10. Folder M15. Folder Name. "Will and Testament A. McSween."

No Author. "Amnesty for Matthews and Long in the Third Judicial Court April Term 1879." **April, 1879**. Herman B. Weisner Papers, ca. 1957-1992. New Mexico State University Library at Las Cruces. Rio Grande Historical Collections. Accession No. Ms 0249. Box 1. Folder 4. Folder Name. "Amnesty."

No Author. "Charges against Jessie Evans and John Kinney." Doña Ana County Civil and Criminal Docket Book. **August 18, 1875 to November 7, 1878**. Herman B. Weisner Papers, ca. 1957-1992. New Mexico State University Library at Las Cruces. Rio Grande Historical Collections. Accession No. Ms 0249. Box 13. Folder V 3. Folder Name. "Venue, Change Of."

No Author. "Dismissal of Cases Against Dolan, Matthews, Peppin, October 1879 District Court." **October, 1879**. Herman B. Weisner Papers, ca. 1957-1992. New Mexico State University Library at Las Cruces. Rio Grande Historical Collections. Accession No. Ms 0249. Box 13. Folder V3. Folder Name: "Venue, Change Of."

No Author. "Killers of Tunstall. February 18, 1879." Herman B. Weisner Papers, ca. 1957-1992. New Mexico State University Library at Las Cruces. Rio Grande Historical Collections. Accession No. Ms 0249. Box 12. Folder T1. Folder Name: "Tunstall, John H."

No Author. "Lincoln County Indictments July 1872 - 1881." Herman B. Weisner Papers, ca. 1957-1992. New Mexico State University Library at Las Cruces. Rio Grande Historical Collections. Accession No. Ms 0249. Box 8. Folder L11. Folder Name. "Lincoln Co. Indictments."

(SEE: William H. Bonney, John Henry Tunstall, Alexander McSween, Frank Warner Angel, Nathan Augustus Monroe Dudley)

ARTICLES (CHRONOLOGICAL)

No author. "Why Axtell Wanted Troops." **July 31, 1878**. Santa Fe. Newspaper unknown. Enclosed in report of Frank Warner Angel: *In the Matter of the Examination of the Causes and Circumstances of the Death of John H. Tunstall a British Subject*. Report filed October 4, 1878. Interior Department Papers 1850-1907; Appointments Division and Subsequent Actions. Microfilm File Case Number 44-4-8-3. Record Group 48. Microfilm No. M750. Roll 1. National Archives and Records Administration. U.S. Department of Justice. Washington, D.C. (**Enclosed with letter to the President, from a John G. Hubbard of August 1, 1878.**).

(SEE: John Henry Tunstall's "A Tax-Payer's Complaint," Alexander McSween Santa Fe Ring; Thomas Benton Catron; Stephen Benton Elkins, Samuel Beach Axtell, Frank Warner Angel)

WHITE CAPS (LAS GORRAS BLANCAS) (1880)

No Author. "White Cap's Proclamation." *Las Vegas Optic*. March 12, 1880. (**Manifesto against land-grabbing Catron and the Ring**)

HISTORICAL FIGURES (PERIOD)

ANGEL, FRANK WARNER

PRESIDENT HAYES MEETING BY

Mullin, Robert N. Re: Frank Warner Angel Meeting With President Hayes August, 1878. Binder RNM, VI, M. (Unpublished). Midland, Texas: Nita Stewart Haley Memorial Library and J. Evetts Haley History Center. (Undated).

LETTERS BY

Angel, Frank Warner. "I am in receipt of your favor of the 12th ..." Letter to Samuel Beach Axtell. **August 13, 1878**. Interior Department Papers 1850-1907; Appointments Division and Subsequent Actions. Microfilm Roll M750. National Archives and Records Administration Record Group 48. Microfilm Case Number 44-4-8-3. U.S. Department of Interior. Washington D.C.

_____. "I enclose copies of letters received by me from Gov Axtell ..." Letter to Secretary of the Interior Carl Schurz. **August 24, 1878**. (Enclosing copy of letter to him from Governor S.B. Axtell of August 12, 1878; and Angel's response to Axtell of August 13, 1878.) Microfilm File Case Number 44-4-8-3. Record Group 48. Microfilm No. M750. Roll 1. National Archives and Records Administration. U.S. Department of Justice. Washington, D.C.

_____. "I have just been favored by a call from W.L. Rynerson ..." Letter to Secretary of Interior Carl Schurz. **September 6, 1878**. Microfilm File Case Number 44-4-8-3. Record Group 48. Microfilm No. M750. Roll 1. National Archives and Records Administration. U.S. Department of Justice. Washington, D.C.

REPORTS BY

Angel, Frank Warner. *Examination of charges against F. C. Godfroy, Indian Agent, Mescalero, N. M.* **October 2, 1878**. (Report 1981, Inspector E.C. Watkins; Cited as Watkins Report). M319-20 and L147, 44-4-8. Record Group 075. National Archives and Records Administration. U.S. Department of Justice. Washington, D. C.

_____. *In the Matter of the Investigation of the Charges Against S.B. Axtell Governor of New Mexico. Report and Testimony.* **October 3, 1878.** Angel Report. Interior Department Papers 1850-1907; Appointments Division and Subsequent Actions. Microfilm Case File No. 44-4-8-3. Record Group 48. Microfilm Roll M750. National Archives and Records Administration. U.S. Department of Interior. Washington, D.C. (**Mentions Santa Fe Ring**)

_____. *In the Matter of the Examination of the Causes and Circumstances of the Death of John H. Tunstall a British Subject.* Report filed **October 4, 1878.** Angel Report. Interior Department Papers 1850-1907; Appointments Division and Subsequent Actions. Microfilm File Case Number 44-4-8-3. Record Group 48. Microfilm No. M750. Roll 1. National Archives and Records Administration. U.S. Department of Justice. Washington, D.C.

_____. *In the Matter of the Lincoln County Troubles. To the Honorable Charles Devens, Attorney General.* **October 4, 1878.** Angel Report. Microfilm Case File No. 44-4-8-3. Record Group 48. Microfilm Roll M750. National Archives and Records Administration. U.S. Department of Justice. Washington, D.C.

NOTEBOOK ON SANTA FE RING MEMBERS BY

Angel, Frank Warner. "To Gov. Lew Wallace / Santa Fe, N. M., 1878." Notebook. **1878.** Indiana Historical Society. Lew Wallace Collection. M0292. Microfilm No. F372. (**Original missing, copy on microfilm; Notebook prepared for Lew Wallace listing names of Santa Fe Ring members**)

Theisen, Lee Scott. "Frank Warner Angel's Notes on New Mexico Territory, 1878." *Arizona and the West: A Quarterly Journal of History.* Winter 1976. Volume 18. Number 4. Pages 333-370. (**About the Angel notebook**)

ASHENFELTER, SINGLETON M.

BIOGRAPHICAL SOURCE

Twitchell, Ralph Emerson. *The Leading Facts of New Mexico History.* Volume III. Cedar Rapids: The Torch Press. 1917.

AXTELL, SAMUEL BEACH

CONTEMPORARY SOURCES (CHRONOLOGICAL)

No author. "Anarchy at Cimarron." *Santa Fe Weekly New Mexico.* **November 16, 1875.** (**Ring-biased article justifying Governor S.B. Axtell calling in troops in the Colfax County War after murder of Reverend Franklin Tolby**)

Axtell, Samuel B. "The Legislature to Assess Property. *Message of Gov. Samuel B. Axtell to the Legislative Assembly of New Mexico, Twenty-second Session.* Page 4. Manderfield & Tucker, Public Printers: Santa Fe, New Mexico. **1875 or 1876**. Interior Department Papers 1850-1907; Appointments Division and Subsequent Actions. Microfilm File Case Number 44-4-8-3. Record Group 48. Microfilm No. M750. Roll 1. National Archives and Records Administration. U.S. Department of Justice. Washington, D.C.

Elkins, Stephen B. "I trouble you to say a word in behalf of Gov. Axtell ..." Letter to President Rutherford B. Hayes. **June 11, 1877**. Interior Department Papers 1850-1907; Appointments Division and Subsequent Actions. Microfilm Roll M750. National Archives and Records Administration Record Group 48. Microfilm Case Number 44-4-8-3. U. S. Department of Interior. Washington D. C. (**Trying to prevent Axtell's removal as governor**)

Axtell, Samuel B. "I have today mailed to you a reply to the charges on file in your Dept against me." Letter to Secretary of the Interior Carl Schurz. **June 15, 1877**. Interior Department Papers 1850-1907; Appointments Division and Subsequent Actions. Microfilm Roll M750. National Archives and Records Administration

Record Group 48. Microfilm Case Number 44-4-8-3 U.S. Department of Interior. Washington D.C. (**Refuting charges made in Colfax County**).

Isaacs, I. and G.N. Coe. "Charges Against S.B. Axtell, Governor of New Mexico." **June 22, 1878**. Interior Department Papers 1850-1907; Appointments Division and Subsequent Actions. Microfilm File Case Number 44-4-8-3. Microfilm No. M750. Roll 1. National Archives and Records Administration. Record Group 48. U.S. Department of Justice. Washington, D.C.

Routt, John C. "I am here on a visit to my daughter and have more by accident than otherwise heard statements ..." Letter to President Rutherford B. Hayes. **August 29, 1878**. Interior Department Papers 1850-1907; Appointments Division and Subsequent Actions. Microfilm File Case Number 44-4-8-3. Microfilm No. M750. Roll 1. National Archives and Records Administration. U.S. Department of Justice. Washington, D.C. (**Ringite letter opposing removal of Governor Axtell and U.S. Attorney Catron.**)

Schurz, Carl. "I transmit herewith an order from the President ..." **September 4, 1878**. Letter to Lew Wallace. Indiana Historical Society. Lew Wallace Collection. M0292. Box 3. Folder 14. (**Suspension of Governor S.B. Axtell and Wallace's appointment as new Governor**)

Elkins, Stephen Benton. "To the President. Referring to a conversation had with you last week ..." Letter to President James Abram Garfield. **March 17, 1881**. (Received Executive Mansion April 6, 1881). Interior Department Papers 1850-1907; Appointments Division and Subsequent Actions. Microfilm Roll M750. National Archives and Records Administration Microfilm Roll M750. National Archives and Records Administration Record Group 48. Microfilm Case Number 44-4-8-3. U.S. Department of Interior. Washington D.C. Microfilm Case Number 44-4-8-3. U.S. Department of Interior. Washington D.C. (**Request for re-appointment of Axtell as Territorial New Mexico Governor**)

Bradstreet, George P. "Referring to the nomination of Sam'l B. Axtell of Ohio to be Chief Justice of the Supreme Court of New Mexico ... he is alleged to have been removed by President Hayes ..." Letter to Judiciary Committee of the U.S. Senate. **June 22, 1882**. Interior Department Papers 1850-1907; Appointments Division and Subsequent Actions. Microfilm Roll M750. National Archives and Records Administration Microfilm Roll M750. National Archives and Records Administration Record Group 48. Microfilm Case Number 44-4-8-3. U.S. Department of Interior. Washington D.C.

No Author. " 'Chief Justice Axtell' is a bitter pill for the Raton *News and Press.*" *Santa Fe New Mexican.* **July 18, 1882**. (**Santa Fe Ring instatement of S.B. Axtell as Chief Justice**)

EXPOSÉS ABOUT

(SEE: William Raymond Morley, Frank Springer, Mary Tibbles McPherson, Frank Warner Angel)

WILLIAM HENRY BONNEY ("BILLY THE KID")

BIOGRAPHICAL SOURCES

Abbott, E.C. ("Teddy Blue") and Helena Huntington Smith. *We Pointed Them North: Recollections of a Cowpuncher.* Norman, Oklahoma: University of Oklahoma Press. 1955. (**Billy the Kid's multi-culturalism, Page 47.**)

Anaya, Paco. *I Buried Billy*. College Station, Texas: Creative Publishing Company. 1991.

Ball, Eve. *Ma'am Jones of the Pecos*. Tucson, Arizona: The University of Arizona Press. 1969.

Bell, Bob Boze. *The Illustrated Life and Times of Billy the Kid*. Cave Creek, Arizona: Boze Books. 1992. (Frank Coe quote about the Kid's cartridge use, Page 45.)

Bell, Bob Boze. *The Illustrated Life and Times of Billy the Kid.* Second Edition. Phoenix, Arizona: Tri Star-Boze Publications, Inc. 1996.

Burns, Walter Noble. *The Saga of Billy the Kid.* Stamford, Connecticut: Longmeadow Press. 1992. (Original printing: 1926, Doubleday.)

_____. *"I also know that the Kid and Paulita were sweethearts."* Unpublished letter to Jim East. June 3, 1926. Robert N. Mullin Collection. File RNM, IV, NM, 116-117. Nita Stewart Haley Memorial Museum, Haley Library. Midland, Texas.

Coe, George with Doyce B. Nunis, Jr. Ed. *Frontier Fighter. The Autobiography of George Coe Who Fought and Rode With Billy the Kid.* Chicago: R. R. Donnelley and Sons Company. 1984.

Cooper, Gale. *Billy the Kid's Writings, Words, and Wit.* Gelcour Books: Albuquerque: New Mexico. 2012.

_____. *Billy and Paulita: A Novel.* Gelcour Books: Albuquerque: New Mexico. 2012.

_____. *The Lost Pardon of Billy the Kid: An Analysis Factoring in the Santa Fe Ring, Governor Lew Wallace's Dilemma, and a Territory in Rebellion.* Gelcour Books: Albuquerque: New Mexico. 2012.

Garrett, Pat F. *The Authentic Life of Billy the Kid The Noted Desperado of the Southwest, Whose Deeds of Daring and Blood Made His Name a Terror in New Mexico, Arizona, and Northern Mexico.* Santa Fe, New Mexico: New Mexico Printing and Publishing Co. 1882. (Reprint used: New York: Indian Head Books. 1994.)

Hendron, J. W. *The Story of Billy the Kid. New Mexico's Number One Desperado.* New York: Indian Head Books. 1994.

Hoyt, Henry. *A Frontier Doctor.* Boston and New York: Houghton Mifflin Company. 1929. (**Describes Billy's superior abilities. Pages 93-94.**)

Jacobsen, Joel. *Such Men as Billy the Kid. The Lincoln County War Reconsidered.* Lincoln and London: University of Nebraska Press. 1994.

Kadlec, Robert F. *They "Knew" Billy the Kid. Interviews with Old-Time New Mexicans.* Santa Fe, New Mexico: Ancient City Press. 1987.

Keleher, William A. *The Fabulous Frontier: Twelve New Mexico Items.* Albuquerque, New Mexico: The University of New Mexico Press. 1962.

_____.*Violence in Lincoln County 1869-1881.* Albuquerque, New Mexico: University of New Mexico Press. 1957. (***Las Vegas Gazette* article of December 28, 1880, "The Kid. Interview with Billy Bonney The Best Known Man in New Mexico": Pages 293-295; *Las Vegas Gazette* article of December 28, 1880. Untitled - at train station. Pages 296-297**)

McFarland, David F. Reverend. *Ledger: Session Records 1867-1874. Marriages in Santa Fe New Mexico. "Mr. William H. Antrim and Mrs. Catherine McCarty." March 1, 1873.* (Unpublished). Santa Fe, New Mexico: First Presbyterian Church of Santa Fe.

Meadows, John P. "Billy the Kid to John P. Meadows on the Peñasco, May 1-2, 1881." *Roswell Daily Record.* February 16, 1931. Page 6.

_____. Ed. John P. Wilson. *Pat Garrett and Billy the Kid as I Knew Them: Reminiscences of John P. Meadows.* Albuquerque: University of New Mexico Press. 2004.

Mullin, Robert N. *The Boyhood of Billy the Kid.* Monograph 17, Southwestern Studies 5(1). El Paso, Texas: Texas Western Press. University of Texas at El Paso. 1967.

Poe, John W. *The Death of Billy the Kid.* (Introduction by Maurice Garland Fulton). Boston and New York: Houghton Mifflin Company. 1933.

_____. "The Killing of Billy the Kid." (a personal letter written at Roswell, New Mexico to Mr. Charles Goodnight, Goodnight P.C., Texas) July 10, 1917. Earle Vandale Collection. 1813-946. No. 2H475. Center for American History. University of Texas at Austin.

Rakocy, Bill. *Billy the Kid.* El Paso, Texas: Bravo Press. 1985.

Rasch, Phillip J. *Trailing Billy the Kid.* Laramie, Wyoming: National Association for Outlaw and Lawman History, Inc. with University of Wyoming. 1995.

Russell, Randy. *Billy the Kid. The Story - The Trial.* Lincoln, New Mexico: The Crystal Press. 1994.

Scanland, John M. (Foreword) using Patrick F. Garrett, Patrick F. *Billy the Kid: The Outlaw. Authentic Story of Billy the Kid by Pat F. Garrett. Greatest Sheriff of the Old Southwest.* New York: Atomic Books Inc. **1946**. Oberlin College Library Special Collections, Pop Culture. Walter F. Tunks Collection. Number 2344. **(Pirated edition of Pat Garrett's *Authentic Life of Billy the Kid* featuring apocryphal outlawry of Billy the Kid)**

Siringo, Charles A. *The History of Billy the Kid.* Santa Fe: New Mexico. Privately Printed. 1920.

Tuska, Jon. *Billy the Kid. His Life and Legend.* Westport, Connecticut: Greenwood Press. 1983.

Utley, Robert M. *High Noon in Lincoln. Violence on the Western Frontier.* Albuquerque, New Mexico: University of New Mexico Press. 1987.

_____. *Billy the Kid. A Short and Violent Life.* Lincoln and London: University of Nebraska Press. 1989.

Weddle, Jerry. *Antrim is My Stepfather's Name. The Boyhood of Billy the Kid.* Monograph 9, Globe, Arizona: Arizona Historical Society. 1993.

No Author. "The Prisoners Who Saw the Kid Kill Olinger." April 28, 1881. Herman B. Weisner Papers, ca. 1957-1992. New Mexico State University Library at Las Cruces. Rio Grande Historical Collections. Accession No. Ms 0249. Box 30 T. Folder 8.

WORDS OF (CHRONOLOGICAL)

HOYT BILL OF SALE

Bonney, W H. "Know all persons by these presents ..." Thursday, **October 24, 1878.** Collection of Panhandle-Plains Historical Museum, Canyon, Texas. Item No. X1974-98/1. (**Hoyt Bill of Sale**)

LETTERS TO LEW WALLACE

Bonney, W H. "I have heard you will give one thousand $ dollars for my body which as I see it means alive ..." **March 13(?), 1879**. Fray Angélico Chávez Historical Library, Santa Fe, New Mexico. Lincoln County Heritage Trust Collection. (AC481).

_____. "I will keep the keep the appointment ..." **March 20, 1879**. Indiana Historical Society. M0292.

_____. "... on the Pecos." ("Billie" letter fragment). **March 24(?), 1879**. Indiana Historical Society. Lew Wallace Collection. M0292. Box 4. Folder 7.

_____. "I noticed in the *Las Vegas* Gazette a piece which stated that 'Billy the Kid' ..." **December 12, 1880**. Indiana Historical Society. Lew Wallace Collection. M0292.

_____. "I would like to see you ..." **January 1, 1881**. Indiana Historical Society. Lew Wallace Collection. M0292.

_____. "I wish you would come down to the jail and see me ..." **March 2, 1881**. Fray Angélico Chávez Historical Library, Santa Fe, New Mexico. Lincoln County Heritage Trust Collection. (AC481).

_____. "I wrote you a little note day before yesterday ..." **March 4, 1881**. Indiana Historical Society. Lew Wallace Collection. M0292.

_____. "For the last time I ask ..." **March 27, 1881**. Indiana Historical Society. Lew Wallace Collection. M0292.

(SEE: Lew Wallace response letters to)

LETTER TO SQUIRE WILSON

Bonney, W H. "Friend Wilson ..." **March 18, 1879**. Indiana Historical Society. Lew Wallace Collection. M0292. (**For pardon negotiation with Lew Wallace**)

LETTER TO EDGAR CAYPLESS

Bonney, W H. "I would have written before ..." **April 15, 1881**. Copy in William Kelleher's *Violence in Lincoln County;* originally reproduced in Griggs *History of the Mesilla Valley*. (**Original lost**)

REGULATOR MANIFESTO LETTER

Regulator. "Mr. Walz. Sir ..." Letter to Edgar Walz. **July 13, 1878**. Adjutant General's Office. File 1405 AGO 1878. (Quoted in Maurice Garland Fulton, *History of the Lincoln County War*. Tucson: University of Arizona Press. 1975. Pages 246-247.)

DEPOSITION OF

Bonney, William Henry. Deposition to Frank Warner Angel. **June 8, 1878**. Frank Warner Angel report, Pages 314-319 from *In the Matter of the Examination of the Causes and Circumstances of the Death of John H. Tunstall a British Subject*. Report filed October 4, 1878. Angel Report. Records of the Justice Department. Record Group 60. Class 44 Litigation Files. Container 21. National Archives and Records Administration. U.S. Department of Justice. Washington, D.C. or Angel Report in Interior Department Papers 1850-1907; Appointments Division and Subsequent Actions. Microfilm File Case Number 44-4-8-3. Record Group 48. Microfilm No. M750. Roll 1. National Archives and Records Administration. U.S. Department of Justice. Washington, D.C.

COURT TESTIMONY OF

Rynerson, William. "The Grand Jurors for the Territory of New Mexico taken from the body of the good and lawful men of the County of Lincoln ..." Indictments of the April, Lincoln County Grand Jury. **April 28, 1879**. Herman B. Weisner Papers, ca. 1957-1992. New Mexico State University Library at Las Cruces. Rio Grande Historical Collection. Accession No. Ms 0249. Box 4/39. Folder E-Z. Folder Name: "Jessie Evans Accessory to Murder." (**Billy's testimony for pardon bargain**)

Bonney, William Henry. Testimony in Court of Inquiry for N.A.M. Dudley. **May 28-29, 1879**. *Proceedings of a Court of Inquiry in the Case of Lt. Col. N.A.M. Dudley (May 2,1879 – July 5, 1879)*. File No. QQ1284. (Boxes 3304, 3305, 3305A); Court Martial Files 1809-1894. Records of the Office of the Judge Advocate General - Army. Record Group 153. Old Military and Civil Branch. National Archives and Records Administration. Washington, D. C.

Waldo, Henry. "Then was brought forward William Bonney, alias "Antrim," alias "the Kid," a known criminal of the worst type ..." Closing argument on Billy Bonney's testimony in Court of Inquiry for N.A.M. Dudley. **July 5, 1879**. *Proceedings of a Court of Inquiry in the Case of Lt. Col. N.A.M. Dudley (May 2,1879 – July 5, 1879)*. File No. QQ1284. (Boxes 3304, 3305, 3305A); Court Martial Files 1809-1894. Records of the Office of the Judge Advocate General – Army. Record Group 153. Old Military and Civil Branch. National Archives and Records Administration. Washington, D. C.

INTERVIEW WITH LEW WALLACE BY

Wallace, Lew. "Statements by Kid, made Sunday night **March 23, 1879**." (Cover sheet reads: "Fort Stanton, March 20, 1879. William Bonney ("Kid") relative to arrangement with him." Indiana Historical Society. Lew Wallace Collection. M0292. Box 4. Folder 6.

NEWSPAPER INTERVIEWS BY

Wilcox, Lucius "Lute" M. (city editor, owner, J.H. Koogler). "The Kid. Interview with Billy Bonney The Best Known Man in New Mexico." *Las Vegas Gazette.* **December 27, 1880. (Has Billy Bonney's quote that "the laugh's on me this time")**

_____. Interview, at train depot. *Las Vegas Gazette.* **December 28, 1880. (Has Billy Bonney's "adios" quote.)**

No Author. "Something About the Kid." Santa Fe *Daily New Mexican.* **April 3, 1881. (With quotes Billy Bonney's "this is the man" and "two hundred men have been killed ... he did not kill all of them.")**

No Author. "I got a rough deal ..." *Mesilla News.* **April 15, 1881.**

Newman, Simon N. Ed. Interview with "The Kid." *Newman's Semi-Weekly.* **April 15, 1881.**

_____. Departure from Mesilla. *Newman's Semi-Weekly.* **April 15, 1881.**

No Author. "Advise persons never to engage in killing." *Mesilla News.* **April 16, 1881. (Billy Bonney's quote)**

FEDERAL INDICTMENT OF

Catron, Thomas Benton. "Case No. 411. The United States vs. Charles Bowdry [Bowdre], Doc Scurlock, Henry Brown, Henry Antrim alias "Kid," John Middleton, Stephen Stevens, John Scroggins, George Coe and Frederick Waite." **June 21, 1878**. Herman B. Weisner Papers, ca. 1957-1992. New Mexico State University Library at Las Cruces. Rio Grande Historical Collections. Accession No. Ms 0249. Box 1. B-Folder 4. Name: Andrew Roberts Indictment. **(Federal murder indictment of Billy Bonney and Regulators)**

GENERAL LETTERS ABOUT

Kimbrell, George. "I have the honor to request that you will furnish me a posse ..." Letter to Lieutenant Millard Filmore Goodwin. **February 20, 1879**. Indiana Historical Society. Lew Wallace Collection. Box 4, Folder 3. **(For pursuit of William Bonney and Yginio Salazar)**

Goodwin, Millard Filmore. ""I have the honor to submit the following report regarding my duties performed ..." Letter to Fort Stanton Post Adjutant John Loud. **February 23, 1879**. Indiana Historical Society. Lew Wallace Collection. Box 4. Folder 3. **(Assisting pursuit of William Bonney and Yginio Salazar)**

Dudley, Nathan Augustus Monroe. "I enclose herewith report of 2nd Lieut. M.F. Goodwin ..." Letter to Acting Assistant Adjutant General at Headquarters. **February 24, 1879**. Indiana Historical Society. Lew Wallace Collection. M0292. Box 4, Folder 3. **(Documents military pursuit of William Bonney)**

Leonard, Ira. "The air is filled tonight with 'rumors of wars ... Letter to Lew Wallace. **April 20, 1879**. Indiana Historical Society. Lew Wallace Collection. M0292. Box 4. Folder 9. **(About District Attorney Rynerson: "He is bent on going for the Kid")**

Hoyt, Henry F. "This time it is me who is apologizing for the long delay in answering ..." (Letter to Lew Wallace Jr.) **April 27, 1927**. Indiana Historical Society. Lew Wallace Collection. M0292. Box 14, Folder 11.

_____. "Copy of a bill of sale written by Wm H. Bonney ..." Letter to Lew Wallace Jr. **April 27, 1927**. Indiana Historical Society. Lew Wallace Collection. M0292. Box 14, Folder 11. **(Calls Billy Bonney "a natural leader of men")**

SECRET SERVICE REPORTS ABOUT

Wild, Azariah F. "Daily Reports of U. S. Secret Service Agents, Azariah F. Wild." Microfilm T-915. Record Group 87. Rolls 306 (June 15, 1877 - December 31, 1877), 307 (January 1,1878 - June 30, 1879), 308 (July 1, 1879 - June 30, 1881), 309

(July 1, 1881 - September 30, 1883), 310 (October 1, 1883 - July 31, 1886). National Archives and Records Department. Department of the Treasury. United States Secret Service. Washington, D. C.

LEW WALLACE WRITINGS TO AND ABOUT

WALLACE'S LETTERS TO (CHRONOLOGICAL)

Wallace, Lew. "Come to the house of Squire Wilson ..." Letter to W H. Bonney. **March 15, 1879**. Indiana Historical Society. Lew Wallace Collection. M0292. Box 4. Folder 6.

_____. "The escape makes no difference in arrangements ..." Letter to W.H. Bonney. **March 20, 1879**. Indiana Historical Society. Lew Wallace Collection. M0292. Box 4. Folder 6.

WALLACE'S LETTERS ABOUT (CHRONOLOGICAL)

Wallace, Lew. "I have just ascertained that 'The Kid' is at a place called Las Tablas ..." Letter to Edward Hatch. **March 6, 1879**. Indiana Historical Society. Lew Wallace Collection. Box 9, Folder 10. (**Written on dead John Tunstall's stationery**)

_____. "I beg to submit to you a list of persons whom it is necessary, in my judgment, to arrest ..." Letter to Henry Carroll. **March 11, 1879**. Indiana Historical Society. Lew Wallace Collection. M0292. Box 4. Folder 5. (**Sherman outlaw list with "The Kid" – William Bonney**)

_____. "I enclose a note for Bonney." Letter to John "Squire" Wilson. **March 20, 1879**. Indiana Historical Society. Lew Wallace Collection. M0292. Box 4. Folder 6.

_____. "My time has been so constantly occupied in getting my work into operation ..." Letter to Carl Schurz. **March 21, 1879**. Indiana Historical Society. Lew Wallace Collection. M0292. Box 4. Folder 7. (**Progress report with multiple enclosures; one listing "The Kid -William Bonney in anti-outlaw campaign of "taking the head off the evil."**)

_____. "To day I forwarded a telegram to you, with another to the President ..." Letter to Carl Schurz. **March 31, 1879**. Indiana Historical Society. Lew Wallace Collection. M0292. Box 4. Folder 7. (**Mention of "precious specimen nicknamed 'The Kid' "**)

REWARD NOTICES FOR

Wallace, Lew. "Be good enough to prepare a draft of proclamation of reward $500 for the capture and delivery of William Bonney, alias the Kid ..." Letter to Territorial Secretary William Ritch. **December 13, 1880**. Herman B. Weisner Papers, ca. 1957-1992. New Mexico State University Library at Las Cruces. Rio Grande Historical Collections. Accession No. Ms 0249. Box W3. Folder 13. Folder Name: "Wallace, Gov. N.M." From Lew Wallace Papers. New Mexico State Records Center. Santa Fe, New Mexico (**Wallace's first reward for Billy the Kid**)

_____. "Billy the Kid: $500 Reward." *Las Vegas Gazette*. **December 22, 1880**.

_____. "Billy the Kid. $500 Reward." **May 3, 1881**. *Daily New Mexican*. Vol. X, No. 33. p. 1, c. 3.

REWARD POSTERS FOR

Greene, Chas. W. "To the New Mexican Printing and Publishing Company." **May 20, 1881**. Indiana Historical Society. Lew Wallace Collection. M0292. Box 4, Folder 17. (**Bill to Lew Wallace for Reward posters for "Kid"**)

_____. "I enclose a bill ..." Letter to Lew Wallace for "Kid" wanted posters. **June 2, 1881**. Indiana Historical Society. Lew Wallace Collection. M0292. Box 4, Folder 18.

DEATH WARRANT FOR

Wallace, Lew. "To the Sheriff of Lincoln County, Greeting ..." **April 30, 1881**. Indiana Historical Society. Lew Wallace Collection. M0292. Box 9, Folder 11.

CORONER'S JURY REPORT FOR

Keleher, William A. *Violence in Lincoln County 1869-1881*. Albuquerque, New Mexico: University of New Mexico Press. 1957. (**Photocopy of Spanish Coroner's Jury Report, Pages 306-308; Kelleher's English translation, Pages 343-344.**)

Rudulph, Milnor, Pedro Lucero, Jose Silba, Sabal Gutierrez, Lorenso Jaramillo. Coroner's Jury Report for William Bonney alias "Kid." Indiana Historical Society. Lew Wallace Collection. M0292. Box 9. Folder 11. (**Photocopy of Spanish Coroner's Jury Report - matches photo in William Kelleher's** *Violence in Lincoln County* **copy except for rodent damage to Kelleher's**)

OUTLAW MYTH ARTICLES ABOUT (CHRONOLOGICAL)

GENERAL ARTICLES (CHRONOLOGICAL)

No Author. Grant County *Herald*. **May 10, 1879**. Results of the Lincoln County Grand Jury. (**Also published in the Mesilla** *Thirty Four*. **Confirmation of the William Bonney testimony and James Dolan and Billy Campbell murder indictments, from Page 224 of William Kelleher,** *Violence in Lincoln County*.)

Koogler, John H. Editorial. "Desperadoe's Stronghold, An Organized Gang Assisted by Nature and Defiantly Reckless, Who Terrorize the Country to the East of Us." *Las Vegas Morning Gazette*. **December 3, 1880**. Volume 2, Number 120. https://chroniclingamerica.loc.gov. (**Calling Billy Bonney an outlaw leader; motivating his denial letter of December 12, 1880 to Governor Lew Wallace.**)

No Author. "Outlaws of New Mexico. The Exploits of a Band Headed by a New York Youth. The Mountain Fastness of the Kid and His Followers - War Against a Gang of Cattle Thieves and Murderers - The Frontier Confederates of Brockway, the Counterfeiter." *The Sun*. New York. **December 22, 1880**. Vol. XLVIII, No. 118, Page 3, Columns 1-2.

No Author. "A Big Haul! Billy Kid, Dave Rudabaugh, Billy Wilson and Tom Pickett in the Clutches of the Law." *The Las Vegas Daily Optic*. Monday, **December 27, 1880**. Volume 2, Number. 45. Page 4, Column 2. https://chroniclingamerica.loc.gov.

No Author. "A Bay-Mare. Everyone who has heard of Billy 'the kid' has heard of his beautiful bay mare." *Las Vegas Morning Gazette*. Tuesday, **January 4, 1881**.

No Author. "The Kid. Billy 'the Kid' and Billy Wilson were on Monday taken to Mesilla for Trial." *Las Vegas Morning Gazette*. Tuesday, **March 15, 1881**.

Newman, Simon. "In the Name of Justice! In the Case of Billy Kid." *Newman's Semi-Weekly*. Saturday, **April 2, 1881**.

No Author. "Billy the Kid. Seems to be having a stormy journey on his trip Southward." *Las Vegas Morning Gazette*. Tuesday, **April 5, 1881**.

No Author. "The Kid." *Santa Fe Daily New Mexican*. **May 1, 1881**. Volume X, Number 32, Page 1, Column 2.

No Author. "Billy Bonney. Advices from Lincoln bring the intelligence of the escape of 'Billy the Kid.'" *Las Vegas Daily Optic*. Monday, **May 2, 1881**.

No Author. "The Kid's Escape." *Santa Fe Daily New Mexican*. Tuesday Morning, **May 3, 1881**. Volume X, Number 33, Page 1, Column 2.

No Author. "The above is the record of as bold a deed ..." *Santa Fe Daily New Mexican*. **May 4, 1881**. (**About Billy's great escape jailbreak**)

No Author. "Dare Devil Desperado. Pursuit of 'Billy the Kid' has been abandoned." *Las Vegas Daily Optic*. **May 4, 1881**.

No Author. "More Killing by Kid, When But a Short Distance From Lincoln, He Meets one of His Old Enemies, and Kills Him and His Companion. Two More Victims." Editorial. *Santa Fe Daily New Mexican*. **May 4, 1881**. Volume X, No. 34, Page 1, Column 2. Newspaperarchive.com. (**Claims Kid killed Billy Matthews**)

No Author. No headline. "Anything that the imagination can concoct ..." *Santa Fe Daily New Mexican*. **May 5, 1881**. Volume X. Page 4, Column 1. Newspaperarchive.com. (**Claims Kid was in Albuquerque**)

No Author. No headline. Mr. Richard Dunham says ..." *Santa Fe Daily New Mexican*, **May 5, 1881**, Volume X. Page 4, Column 3. Newspaperarchive.com. (**Claims Kid was in Stinking Springs**)

No Author. "Richard Dunham's May 2, 1881 encounter with Billy the Kid.", *Santa Fe Daily New Mexican*, **May 5, 1881**, Page 4, Column 3. (private collection)

No Author. "The question if how to deal with desperados who commit murder has but one solution - kill them." *Las Vegas Daily Optic*. Tuesday, **May 10, 1881**.

No Author. "Billy 'the Kid.' " *Las Vegas Gazette*. Thursday, **May 12, 1881**.

No Author. "The Kid was in Chloride City ..." *Santa Fe Daily New Mexican*. **May 13, 1881**. Page 4, Column 3.

No Author. "Billy 'the Kid' is in the vicinity of Sumner." *Las Vegas Gazette*. Sunday, **May 15, 1881**.

No Author. "The Kid is believed to be in the Black Range ..." *Santa Fe Daily New Mexican*. **May 19, 1881**. Page 4, Column 1.

No Author. "Billy the Kid was last seen in Lincoln County ..." *Santa Fe Daily New Mexican*. **May 19, 1881**. Page 4, Column 1.

No Author. (O.L. Houghton's Conversation with Lew Wallace, before May 26, 1881), *The Las Vegas Daily Optic*, **May 26, 1881**, p.4, c.4. Indiana Historical Society. Lew Wallace Collection. M0292.

No Author. " 'Billy the Kid' has been heard from again." *Las Vegas Daily Optic*. Friday, **June 10, 1881**.

No Author. " 'Billy the Kid,' He is Reported to Have Been Seen on Our Streets Saturday Night." *Las Vegas Daily Optic*. Monday Evening, **June 13, 1881**. Vol. 2, No. 188, Page 4, Column 2.

Wilcox, Lute, Ed. "Billy the Kid would make an ideal newspaper-man in that he always endeavors to 'get even' with his enemies." *Las Vegas Daily Optic*. Monday Evening, **June 13, 1881**. Volume 2, Number 188, Page 4, Column 1.

No Author. "Land of the Petulant Pistol, "Scenes" where Life and Land are Cheap ... 'Billy the Kid' as a Killer." *Las Vegas Daily Optic*. Wednesday Evening, **June 15, 1881**. Front Page. 1, Volume 2, Number 190, Columns 1-2. (Possibly contributed to by Lew Wallace, who published with a similar title in the Crawfordsville *Saturday Evening Journal* on June 18, 1881)

No Author. "Barney Mason at Fort Sumner states the 'Kid' is in Local Sheep Camps." *Las Vegas Morning Gazette*. **June 16, 1881**.

No Author. "The Kid." *Santa Fe Daily New Mexican*. **June 16, 1881**. Volume X, Number 90, Page 4, Column 2.

No Author. "Billy the Kid." *Las Vegas Daily Optic*. Thursday, June 28, 1881.

No Author. " 'The Kid' Killed." *Las Vegas Daily Optic*. **July 18. 1881**.

No Author. No title. **Thursday, July 28, 1881**. Pueblo, Colorado, Colo*rado Chieftain*. www.coloradohistoricnewspapers.org. (**Quoting from the New York Tribune on killing of "Tiger in human form known as "Billy the Kid"**)

Gauss, Gottfried. Interview with *Lincoln County Leader*. **November 21, 1889**. (**About Billy Bonney's Lincoln jailbreak**)

LEW WALLACE'S ARTICLES

Koogler, John H. "Interview with Governor Lew Wallace on 'The Kid.'" *Las Vegas Gazette*. **April 28, 1881**.

No Author. "The Thug's Territory. Stage Robbers and Cut-Throats Have Things Their Own Way in New Mexico. Gen. Lew Wallace Anxious to Punish the Crime That is So Prevalent – A Chapter About 'Billy the Kid' – The Governor has a Narrow Escape From Being Spanked." *St. Louis Daily Globe-Democrat.* Monday Morning, **May 16, 1881**. Page 2, Columns 5 and 6. (private collection)

No Author. (Lew Wallace interview) "Billy the Kid. General Wallace Tells Why the Young Desperado of New Mexico Wanted to Kill Him, A Dashing and Daring Career in the Land of the Petulant Pistol." (Lew Wallace interviewed on June 13, 1881), Crawfordsville *Saturday Evening Journal*, **June 18, 1881**. Indiana Historical Society. The Papers of Lew and Susan Wallace. Microfilm Edition. Indianapolis, Indiana: Indiana Historical Society Press. 2008.

No Author. (Lew Wallace interview) "Lew Wallace's Foe. Threatened by 'Billy the Kid.' The Writing of 'Ben Hur' Interrupted. An Incident of the Soldier-Author's Career in New Mexico. *San Francisco Chronicle.* December 10, 1893. Indiana Historical Society. Lew Wallace Collection. M0292. Box 14. Folder 11. (Lew Wallace creating outlaw myth of outlaw Billy the Kid")

No Author. "Street Pickings," Weekly *Crawfordsville Review - Saturday Edition*, **January 6, 1894**. Indiana Historical Society. The Papers of Lew and Susan Wallace. Microfilm Edition. Series I. Reel 27. Indianapolis, Indiana: Indiana Historical Society Press. 2008.

No Author. "An Old Incident Recalled." Crawfordsville *Weekly News-Review*. **December 20, 1901**. Indiana Historical Society. The Papers of Lew and Susan Wallace. Microfilm Edition. Series I. Reel 27. Indianapolis, Indiana: Indiana Historical Society Press. 2008.

Lewis, E.I. "Gen. Wallace's Feud with Billy the Kid, When the General Was Governor of New Mexico and Billy Bonne Was the Most Dangerous Western Outlaw. He Was a Waif and Was Reared in Indiana. *The Indianapolis Press.* Saturday, **June 23, 1900**. Page 7. Lew Wallace Collection. Indiana Historical Society. M0292. Box 14. Folder 11. (photocopy) (Original article is in OMB 23, Box 1. Folder 5) (**Creating self-serving myth of outlaw Billy the Kid"**)

Wallace, Lew. "General Lew Wallace Writes a Romance of 'Billy the Kid' Most Famous Bandit of the Plains: Thrilling Story of the Midnight Meeting Between Gen Wallace, Then Governor of New Mexico, and the Notorious Outlaw, in a Lonesome Hut in Santa Fe." *New York World Magazine.* Sunday, **June 8, 1902**. Lew Wallace Collection. Indiana Historical Society. M0292. . Box 14. Folder 11.

BACA, SATURNINO

BIOGRAPHICAL SOURCES

Charles, Tom. (Edited by Mrs. Tom Charles) "The Father of Lincoln County." *More Tales of Tularosa.* 1961. (unpublished manuscript)

Jonathan (no last name given). "About Saturnino Baca." July 23, 2001. http://www.genealogy.com/forum/surnames/topics/baca/509/

Nolan, Frederick. "New and Updated Biographies." *The Lincoln County War: A Documentary History. Revised Edition.* .Santa Fe: Sunstone Press. 2009.

LETTERS FROM AND ABOUT (CHRONOLOGICAL)

Baca, Saturnino. "When I sent in my bid for the hay contract ..." Letter to Quartermaster Captain A.J. McGonigle. **July 19, 1871.** University of New Mexico Library. Center for Southwest Studies. Thomas B. Catron Papers, MSS 29, Series 803, Box 1, Folder 25. (**About hay contract to Fort Stanton**)

Kantz, August V. "I learn from Col. Fritz that you are under the impression ..." Letter to Quartermaster Captain A.J. McGonigle. **July 20, 1871.** University of New Mexico Library. Center for Southwest Studies. Thomas B. Catron Papers, MSS 29, Series 803, Box 1, Folder 25. (**Emil Fritz pressures Fort Stanton to take** bottom hay - which would make contract for Baca fillable - and Kantz warns that Fritz and Murphy will get hay monopoly)

Carey, A.B. "Letter of Saturnino Baca, dated Fort Stanton ..." Letter to Quartermaster Captain A.J. McGonigle. **July 20, 1871.** University of New Mexico Library. Center for Southwest Studies. Thomas B. Catron Papers, MSS 29, Series 803, Box 1, Folder 25. **(Baca declines his contract to supply grama hay)**

McGonigle, A.J.M. "I have the honor to forward enclosed herewith ..." Letter to Quartermaster General M.C. Meigs. **September 24, 1871.** University of New Mexico Library. Center for Southwest Studies. Thomas B. Catron Papers, MSS 29, Series 803, Box 1, Folder 25. **(Wants Baca barred from hay contracts)**

(SEE: Letter to Thomas Benton Catron)

BAIL, JOHN D.

BIOGRAPHICAL SOURCE

No Author. *Minutes of the New Mexico Bar Association at its Regular Annual Session 1904.* Obituary. Santa Fe: New Mexico Publishing Company. 1904.

LETTERS BY (CHRONOLOGICAL)

Bail, John D. "Did you call Mr. Catron's attention ..." Letter to F.W. Clancy. **June 8, 1889.** University of New Mexico Library. Center for Southwest Studies. Thomas B. Catron Papers, MSS 29, Series 102, Box 1, Folder 2.

_____. "I am in receipt of your letter of 11th inst..." Letter to T.B. Catron. **May 14, 1890.** University of New Mexico Library. Center for Southwest Studies. Thomas B. Catron Papers, MSS 29, Series 102, Box 7, Folder 2.

BLAZER, JOSEPH

No Author. "Dr. Blazer Dead." **November 8, 1898.** *Albuquerque Daily Citizen.* https://chroniclingamerica.loc.gov/.

BOWDRE, CHARLES

CONTEMPORARY SOURCES (CHRONOLOGICAL)

Wallace, Lew. "Please select ten of your Rangers ..." Letter to Juan Patrón. **March 3, 1879.** Indiana Historical Society. Lew Wallace Collection. M0292. Box 4. Folder 4. **(To arrest "Scurlock and Bowdre")**

_____. "I have reliable information that J.G. Scurlock and Charles Bowdre are now at a ranch called Taiban ..." Letter to Edward Hatch. **March 6, 1879.** Indiana Historical Society. Lew Wallace Collection. Box 4, Folder 4.

BRADY, WILLIAM

BIOGRAPHICAL SOURCE

Lavash, Donald R. *Sheriff William Brady. Tragic Hero of the Lincoln County War.* Santa Fe, New Mexico: Sunstone Press. 1986.

CONTEMPORARY SOURCES (CHRONOLOGICAL)

Brady, William. Affidavit of **July 2, 1876** concerning appointment as Administrator for the Emil Fritz Estate. Copied from the original District Court Record. (private collection)

_____. Affidavit of **August 22, 1876** documenting business debts to L. G. Murphy and Co. pertaining to the Emil Fritz Estate. Copied from the original District Court Record. (private collection)

_____. Affidavit of **July _, 1876** of Resignation as Emil Fritz Estate Administrator. Copied from the original District Court Record. (private collection.)

_____. Affidavit of **August 22, 1876** confirming giving Alexander McSween the books of the L.G. Murphy Company for the purpose of making business debt collections. Copied from the original District Court Record. (private collection)

Tunstall, John Henry. "A Taxpayer's Complaint ... January 18, 1878." Mesilla *Independent.* **January 26, 1878.** (**Exposé of William Brady embezzling tax money to buy cattle for "The House;" and Catron then paid that bill**)

Dolan, James J. "Answer to A Taxpayer's Complaint." Mesilla *Independent.* **January 29, 1878.** (**Response to J.H. Tunstall's exposé of tax money embezzling**)

Bristol, Warren. "Action of Assumpsit to command Sheriff Brady of Lincoln County to attach goods of Alexander A. McSween." **February 7, 1878**. District Court Record. (private collection).

_____. Preprinted form for "Writ of Attachment" (Printed and sold at the office of the Mesilla News) filled out to command the Sheriff of Lincoln County to attach goods of Alexander McSween for a suit of damages for ten thousand dollars. **February 7, 1878**. District Court Record. (private collection).

Brady, William. "List of Articles Inventoried by Wm Brady sheriff in the suit of Charles Fritz & Emilie Scholand vs A.A. McSween now in the dwelling house belonging to A.A. McSween." (undated, but in **February of 1878**) (private collection)

BREEDEN, WILLIAM

Speer, William S. and John Henry Brown, eds. *The Encyclopedia of the New West, Containing Fully Authenticated Information of the Agricultural, Mercantile, Commercial, Manufacturing, Mining and Grazing Industries, and Representing the Character, Development, Resources and Present Development of Texas, Arkansas, Colorado, New Mexico and Indian Territory, Also Biographical Sketches of Their Representative Men and Women.* Marshall, Texas: The United States Biographical Publishing Company. **1881**.

Ayer, N.W. and Son. eds. *N.W. Ayer & Son's American Newspaper Annual Containing a Catalogue of American Newspapers.* Philadelphia: N.W. Ayer & Son. **1888**. (**Listing Breeden's and Henry Waldo's New Mexico Printing Company as publishing** *The Santa Fe New Mexican*)

No Author. "Obituary Notes." *The New York Times.* **January 29, 1913**. Page 11, Column 5. Newspaperarchive.com.

BRISTOL, WARREN HENRY

BIOGRAPHICAL SOURCES

Thompson, Mark. "Judge Warren Henry Bristol: A Man of his Time and Place? January 3, 2012. https://www.leg.state.mn.us/archive/LegDB/Articles/11430Essay.

Twitchell, Ralph Emerson. *The Leading Facts of New Mexico History.* Vol. II. Page 420, Note 247. Santa Fe: Sunstone Press. 2007. (Reprinted from 1912 edition)

CONTEMPORARY SOURCES (CHRONOLOGICAL)

Bristol Warren. "From sources of information that I deem perfectly reliable I am satisfied that there are public disorders in Lincoln County ..." Letter to Governor Marsh Giddings. **January 10, 1874**. Herman B. Weisner Papers, ca. 1957-1992. New Mexico State University Library at Las Cruces. Rio Grande Historical Collections. Accession No. Weisner Ms 0249. Box 4/39. Folder D-4. Folder Name: "Judge Bristol's letter." (**Creating Ring's outlaw myth and proposing military intervention**)

_____. "Writ of Embezzlement." **December 21, 1877**. Herman B. Weisner Papers, ca. 1957-1992. New Mexico State University Library at Las Cruces. Rio Grande Historical Collections. Accession No. Ms 0249. Box 10. Folder M-13. Folder Name. "Will and Testament A. McSween." (**Emilie Fritz Scholand's sworn complaint against Alexander McSween**)

_____. "Action of Assumpsit to command Sheriff Brady of Lincoln County to attach goods of Alexander A. McSween." **February 7, 1878**. District Court Record. (private collection).

_____. Preprinted form for "Writ of Attachment" (Printed and sold at the office of the Mesilla News) filled out to command the Sheriff of Lincoln County to attach goods of Alexander McSween for a suit of damages for ten thousand dollars. **February 7, 1878**. District Court Record. (private collection).

_____. "My reasons for not holding October term of Court ..." Telegram to U.S. Marshal John Sherman. **October 4, 1878**. Indiana Historical Society. Lew Wallace Collection. M0292. Box 3. Folder 15.

No Author. "For Delegate Benito Baca. County Ticket Juan C. Armijo." *Albuquerque Review*. **October 5, 1878**. Indiana Historical Society. The Papers of Lew and Susan Wallace. Microfilm Edition. Indianapolis, Indiana: Indiana Historical Society Press. 2008. (**About Lew Wallace's arrival in New Mexico Territory and swearing in by Warren Bristol**)

Bristol, Warren. *Instructions to the Jury*. District Court 3rd Judicial. District Doña Ana. Filed **April 9, 1881**. Writ of Embezzlement. New Mexico State University Library at Las Cruces. Rio Grande Historical Collection. Accession No. Ms 0249. Box 1. Folder 14C. Folder Name: "Billy the Kid Legal Documents."

CATRON, THOMAS BENTON

BIBLIOGRAPHICAL SOURCES

Cleaveland, Norman, *A Synopsis of the Great New Mexico Cover-up*. Self-printed. 1989.

_____. *The Great Santa Fe Cover-up. Based on a Talk given Before the Santa Fe Historical Society on November 1, 1978*. Self-printed. 1982.

_____. *The Morleys - Young Upstarts on the Southwest Frontier*. Albuquerque, New Mexico: Calvin Horn Publisher, Inc. 1971. (**Page 93 gives Catron's vindictive indictment of Cleaveland's grandmother, Ada Morley, for mail theft as revenge denying him use of a Maxwell Land Grant buggy.**

Dodge, Andrew R., and Betty K. Koed, eds. *Biographical Directory of the United States Congress 1774-2005*. Washington, D.C.: United States Government Printing Office. 2005

Dunham, Harold H. "New Mexican Land Grants with Special Reference to the Title Papers of the Maxwell Grant." *New Mexico Historical Review*. (January, 1955) Vol. 70. No. 1. pp. 1 - 23.

Hefferan, Vioalle Clark. *Thomas Benton Catron*. Albuquerque, New Mexico: University of New Mexico. Zimmerman Library. Unpublished Thesis for the Degree of Master of Arts. 1940. .(**In praise of Catron; includes railroad involvement, Page 35; First National Bank stockholder from 1871 to 1907, Page 28**)

Keleher, William A. *The Maxwell Land Grant. A New Mexico Item*. Albuquerque, New Mexico: University of New Mexico Press. 1964.

Klasner, Lilly. Eve Ball. Ed. *My Girlhood Among Outlaws*. Tucson, Arizona: The University of Arizona Press. 1972.

Lamar, Howard Robert N. *The Far Southwest 1846 – 1912: A Territorial History*. New Haven and London: Yale University Press. 1966. (**Chapter 6 covers the Santa Fe Ring**))

Montoya, María E. *Translating Property. The Maxwell Land Grant and the Conflict Over Land in the American West, 1840-1900*. Berkeley and Los Angeles: University of California Press. 2002.

Mullin, Robert N. "A Specimen of Catron's Dirty Work. Sworn Affidavit of Samuel Davis." October 1, 1878. Binder RNM IV, EE. (Unpublished). Midland, Texas: Nita Stewart Haley Memorial Library and J. Evetts Haley Historical Center.

————. "Catron Embarrassed Throughout His Life by an Affliction." (Date Unknown). Binder RNM, IV, M. (Unpublished). Midland, Texas: Nita Stewart Haley Memorial Library and J. Evetts Haley Historical Center. Robert Mullin Papers. Binder RNM IV, EE (Unpublished).

————. "Prior to Lincoln County War Catron Had Defended Colonel Dudley." (No Date). Notes from "Lincoln County War Cast of Characters." Midland, Texas: Nita Stewart Haley Memorial Library and J. Evetts Haley Historical Center.

Murphy, Lawrence R. *Lucien Bonaparte Maxwell. Napoleon of the Southwest.* Norman: University of Oklahoma Press. 1983.

Otero, Miguel A. *My Life on the Frontier, 1882-1897: Incidents and Characters of the period when Kansas, Colorado, and New Mexico were passing through the last of their Wild and Romantic Years.* New York: The Press of the Pioneers. 1935. Pages 232-233. (Quoted by Victor Westphall, *Thomas Benton Catron and His Era.* Page 188*)* (**Quote: "the 'Santa Fe Ring,' the real machine controlling the political situation in New Mexico."**)

Pearson, Jim Berry. *The Maxwell Land Grant.* Norman: University of Oklahoma Press. 1961.

Routt, John C. "I am here on a visit to my daughter and have more by accident than otherwise heard statements ..." Letter to President Rutherford B. Hayes. August 29, 1878. Interior Department Papers 1850-1907; Appointments Division and Subsequent Actions. Microfilm File Case Number 44-4-8-3. Microfilm Roll M750. National Archives and Records Administration Record Group 48. U.S. Department of Interior. Washington D.C. (**In opposition to removal of Governor Axtell and U.S. Attorney Thomas Benton Catron.**)

Sluga, Mary Elizabeth. *Political Life of Thomas Benton Catron 1896-1912.* Albuquerque, New Mexico: University of New Mexico. Zimmerman Library. Unpublished Thesis for the Degree of Master of Arts. 1941. (**Thesis in praise of Catron for an M.A.**)

Taylor, Morris F. *O.P. McMains and the Maxwell Land Grant Conflict.* Tucson, Arizona: The University of Arizona Press. 1979. (**Traces origins of the Santa Fe Ring with T.B. Catron and S.B. Elkins**)

Westphall, Victor. *Thomas Benton Catron and His Era.* Tucson, Arizona: University of Arizona Press. 1973.

————. "Fraud and Implications of Fraud in the Land Grants of New Mexico." *New Mexico Historical Review.* 1974. Vol. XLIX, No. 3. 189 - 218.

Wooden, John Paul. *Thomas Benton Catron and New Mexico Politics 1866-1921.* Albuquerque, New Mexico: University of New Mexico. Zimmerman Library. Unpublished Thesis for the Degree of Master of Arts. 1959. (**M.A. thesis praising Catron**)

CONTEMPORARY EXPOSÉS OF (CHRONOLOGICAL)

Middaugh, Asa F. Deposition. **March 31, 1876.** "Exhibit B" in the August 9, 1878 deposition of Frank Springer to Investigator Frank Warner Angel. Frank Warner Angel report titled *In the Matter of the Investigation of the Charges Against S.B. Axtell Governor of New Mexico.* October 3, 1878. Interior Department Papers 1850-1907; Appointments Division and Subsequent Actions. Microfilm Case File No. 44-4-8-3. Record Group 48. Microfilm Roll M750. National Archives and Records Administration. U.S. Department of Interior. Washington, D.C. (**About Catron's malicious prosecution of Ada McPherson Morley**)

Springer, Frank. Deposition to Investigator Frank Warner Angel. **August 9, 1878**. Frank Warner Angel report titled *In the Matter of the Investigation of the Charges Against S.B. Axtell Governor of New Mexico.* October 3, 1878. Interior Department

Papers 1850-1907; Appointments Division and Subsequent Actions. Microfilm Case File No. 44-4-8-3. Record Group 48. Microfilm Roll M750. National Archives and Records Administration. U.S. Department of Interior. Washington, D.C. (**Mentions Catron, Elkins, and the Santa Fe Ring, and provided Exhibits of letters exposing Catron's evil.**)

No Author. "The Santa Fe Ring is the most corrupt combination that ever cursed any country or community." Las Cruces *Thirty-Four Newspaper*. **October 27, 1880**. From Victor Westphall, *Thomas Benton Catron and His Era*. Page 186. (**Article summarizing Ring abuses in urging voters to oppose Ring candidates**)

No Author. "The Ring must soon discover that the time has passed in New Mexico when men can be herded like so many sheep ..." *Albuquerque Daily Democrat*. **March 4, 1884**. Quoted by Victor Westphall, *Thomas Benton Catron and His Era*. Page 191. (**About Santa Fe Ring control of appointments to legislature**)

Valdez, Jose and Enrique Mares. "Scorching Letter, The Knights of Labor Send a Communication to Powderly! Politicians Arraigned! The Boldest Document Ever Issued in the Territory." **August 18, 1890**. *Las Vegas Democrat*. Volume 1. Center for Southwest Studies. Thomas B. Catron Papers, MSS 29, Series 102, Box 8, Folder 4. (**Gives history of Santa Fe Ring with T.B. Catron as head**)

No Author. "Catron and the Laboring Men." Unknown newspaper. **1892?** University of New Mexico Library. Center for Southwest Studies. Thomas B. Catron Papers, MSS 29, Series 401, Box 1, Folder 3. (**Opposition to Catron as Delegate to Congress as "the biggest corporation man in New Mexico"**)

Victory, John P. "No Consistent Democrat Should Vote for T.B. Catron, John P. Victory in Forcible and Cogent Language Gives Answerable Reasons." —, **1895**. Printed broadside. University of New Mexico Library. Center for Southwest Studies. Thomas B. Catron Papers, MSS 29, Series 409, Box 1, Folder 3.

Wallace, Lew. "I have your several letters, including the last one of the 3rd inst." Letter to Eugene Fiske. **November 6, 1897**. Indiana Historical Society. Lew Wallace Collection. AC233. Box 1. Folder 7. (part of 1981 addition) (**About Catron's control over New Mexicans**)

Cutting, Bronson. "Catron was the boss of the Territory ..." Letter to James Roger Addison. **December 11, 1911**. Cited by Victor Westphall in *Thomas Benton Catron and His Era* from his citation: Lincoln County Manuscripts Division. Box 12. Courtesy of David Stratton. (**Catron as head of the Santa Fe Ring**)

Johnson, E. Dana. "[H]e ruled with a rod of iron ..." Editorial. *Santa Fe New Mexican*. **May 16, 1921**. Catron Papers 801, Box 1. Quoted by Victor Westphall, *Thomas Benton Catron and His Era*. Pages 394-395. (**Tactics of "boss" Catron without using the words Santa Fe Ring**)

(SEE: William Raymond Morley, Mary Tibbles McPherson, Franklin Tolby, Oscar McMains, Frank Warner Angel)

SECRET CIPHER-CODE OF

McSween, Alexander. "Catron being "Grapes ..." **June 6, 1878**. Deposition to Frank Warner Angel. Pages 5-183 of Frank Warner Angel report *In the Matter of the Examination of the Causes and Circumstances of the Death of John H. Tunstall a British Subject*. Report filed **October 4, 1878**. Angel Report. Microfilm File Case Number 44-4-8-3. Record Group 48. Microfilm No. M750. Roll 1. National Archives and Records Administration. U.S. Department of Justice. Washington, D.C. (**Ring code book discovered on February 14, 1878 from John Riley**)

Elkins, Stephen Benton. "Elkins - Telegraph Cipher, Cipher with Catron." Sent to Thomas Benton Catron. —, **1978?** University of New Mexico Library. Center for Southwest Studies. Thomas B. Catron Papers, MSS 29, Series 108, Box 1, Folder 4. (**Code reference to "Angel" dates codes to 1878**)

Catron, Thomas Benton. "Waldo ... Robinson, Newcomb ... Turner ..." To unknown recipient(s). ___, **1881 ?**. University of New Mexico Library. Center for Southwest

Studies. Thomas B. Catron Papers, MSS 29, Series 804, Box 1, stored with T.B. Catron's pocket notebooks dated 1869 to 1886. (**Santa Fe Ring code-cipher key**)

Elkins, Stephen Benton. "Elkins – Telegraph Cipher, Cipher with Catron." Mailing to T.B. Catron. ___ **1878?** University of New Mexico Library. Center for Southwest Studies. Thomas B. Catron Papers, MSS 29, Series 108, Box 1, Folder 4. (**Ring code-cipher key about T.B. Catron's resignation as U.S. Attorney; code reference to "Angel" dates codes to 1878**)

Dame, W.E. "We earnestly request you to give the Honorable T.B. Catron ..." Letter to the President. **May ___, 1905.** University of New Mexico Library. Center for Southwest Studies. Thomas B. Catron Papers, MSS 29, Series 103, Box 22, Folder 5. (**"Dame" was used in a cipher-code message**))

Catron, Thomas Benton. "I have yours of Aug. 1st. I never contributed ..." **August 11, 1908.** Letter to Ralph Emerson Twitchell. University of New Mexico Library. Center for Southwest Studies. Thomas B. Catron Papers, MSS 29, Series 105, Volume 28, Page 9. (**Part of the money transaction continuing to August 14, 1908 apparently using cipher-code**)

_____. "Yours of the 13th at hand ..." **August 14, 1908.** Letter to Ralph Emerson Twitchell. University of New Mexico Library. Center for Southwest Studies. Thomas B. Catron Papers, MSS 29, Series 105, Volume 28, Page 20. (**Part of the money transaction of August 11, 1908 apparently using cipher-code "display of apples"**)

FEDERAL INDICTMENT OF REGULATORS BY

Catron, Thomas Benton. "Case No. 411. The United States vs. Charles Bowdry [Bowdre], Doc Scurlock, Henry Brown, Henry Antrim alias "Kid," John Middleton, Stephen Stevens, John Scroggins, George Coe and Frederick Waite." **June 21, 1878.** Herman B. Weisner Papers, ca. 1957-1992. New Mexico State University Library at Las Cruces. Rio Grande Historical Collections. Accession No. Ms 0249. Box 1. Folder B-4. Folder Name: Andrew Roberts Indictment.

RESIGNATION AS TERRITORIAL U.S. ATTORNEY BY

Elkins, Stephen Benton. "Elkins – Telegraph Cipher, Cipher with Catron." Sent to T.B. Catron. ___ **1878?** University of New Mexico Library. Center for Southwest Studies. Thomas B. Catron Papers, MSS 29, Series 108, Box 1, Folder 4. (**Ring code-cipher key about T.B. Catron's resignation as U.S. Attorney**)

_____. "Asking delay of action upon charges against U.S. Atty. Catron ..." **September 24, 1878.** Angel Report. Microfilm File Case No. 44-4-8-3. Record Group 48. National Records and Archives Administration. Microfilm No. M750. Roll 1. U.S. Department of Justice. Washington, D. C.

_____. "Regarding Attorney General's decision on T.B. Catron." Letter. **September___, 1878.** Angel Report. Microfilm File Case No. 44-4-8-3. Record Group 48. National Records and Archives Administration. Microfilm No. M750. Roll 1. U.S. Department of Justice. Washington, D.C.

Catron, Thomas Benton. "In accordance with a purpose long entertained ...." Letter to Charles Devens. **October 10, 1878.** Angel Report. Microfilm File Case No. 44-4-8-3. Record Group 48. National Records and Archives Administration. Microfilm No. M750. Roll 1. U.S. Department of Justice. Washington, D.C. (**Resignation as U.S. Attorney**)

Devens, Charles. "Your resignation of the office of United States Attorney ..." Letter to T.B. Catron. **October 19, 1878.** Angel Report. Microfilm File Case No. 44-4-8-3. Record Group 48. National Records and Archives Administration. Microfilm No. M750. Roll 1. U.S. Department of Justice. Washington, D. C.

Catron, Thomas Benton. "Please change my resignation ...." **November 4, 1878.** Telegram to Charles Devens. Angel Report. Microfilm File Case No. 44-4-8-3. Record Group 48. National Records and Archives Administration. Microfilm No.

M750. Roll 1. U.S. Department of Justice. Washington, D. C. (**Resignation as U.S. Attorney**)

Devens, Charles. "Your resignation of the office of United States Attorney ..." Letter to T.B. Catron. **November 12, 1878**. Angel Report. Microfilm File Case No. 44-4-8-3. Record Group 48. National Records and Archives Administration. Microfilm No. M750. Roll 1. U.S. Department of Justice. Washington, D.C.

Elkins, Stephen Benton. "Relative to resignation of T. B. Catron U. S. Attorney." Letter to Charles Devens. **November 10, 1878**. Angel Report. Microfilm File Case No. 44-4-8-3. Record Group 48. National Records and Archives Administration. Microfilm No. M750. Roll 1. U.S. Department of Justice. Washington, D.C.

Devens, Charles. "To honorable S. B. Elkins re. T. B. Catron continuing to act as U.S. Attorney ..." Letter to Stephen B. Elkins. **November 12, 1878**. Angel Report. Microfilm File Case No. 44-4-8-3. Record Group 48. National Records and Archives Administration. Microfilm No. M750. Roll 1. U.S. Department of Justice. Washington, D.C.

Barnes, Sidney M.. "I Sidney M. Barnes do solemnly swear ..." Swearing in as U.S. Attorney. **January 20, 1879**. Angel Report. Microfilm File Case No. 44-4-8-3. Record Group 48. National Records and Archives Administration. Microfilm No. M750. Roll 1. U.S. Department of Justice. Washington, D.C. (**Catron replaced by Ringite attorney Sidney Barnes**)

Elkins, Stephen Benton. "I have waited some time to reply to your lengthy letter ..." Letter to T.B. Catron. **August 15, 1879**. West Virginia & Regional History Center. West Virginia University Libraries, Morgantown, W. Va. Stephen B. Elkins Papers (A&M 53). Box 1. Folder 1. (**Reveals he prevented Catron's dismissal and indictment from Angel's report**)

Clancy, Frank W. "From something I have heard ..." Letter to T.B. Catron. **September 20, 1892**. University of New Mexico Library. Center for Southwest Studies. Thomas B. Catron Papers, MSS 29, Series 102, Box 16, Folder 2. (**Warning Catron that opponents are seeking the Angel Report to use against his campaign for Delegate, but Elkins is making obstacles**)

_____. "I am much surprised at what you say in your letter ..." Letter to T.B. Catron. **December 2, 1896**. University of New Mexico Library. Center for Southwest Studies. Thomas B. Catron Papers, MSS 29, Series 106, Box 1, Folder 6. (**Surprise that Catron now wants to be U.S. Attorney again**)

OWNERSHIP FILING ON CARRIZOZO CATTLE COMPANY

Catron, Thomas Benton.. Statement of Sole ownership of Carrizozo Ranch in Tax Dispute Case. No date. Herman B. Weisner Papers, ca. 1957-1992. New Mexico State University Library at Las Cruces. Rio Grande Historical Collections. Accession No. Ms 0249. Box. 2. Folder C-8. Folder Name "T.B. Catron Tax Troubles." (**One of Catron's Lincoln County holdings**)

AZTEC MINE OWNERSHIP OF

Catron, Thomas Benton. "I have disposed of the Aztec mine ..." Letter to Charles C. Catron. **September 30, 1914**. University of New Mexico Library. Center for Southwest Studies. Thomas B. Catron Papers, MSS 29, Series 107, Box 1, Folder 3. (**Sale of Aztec mine reported to son**)

EXPURGATING OFFICE FIRE OF 1888 OF

Smith, Derwent H. "I have a letter from Geo. W. Knaebel; in which he mentions the destruction of your office ..." Letter to Frank W. Clancy. **July 29, 1888**. University of New Mexico Library. Center for Southwest Studies. Thomas B. Catron Papers, MSS 29, Series 102, Box 1, Folder 1. (**Gives the July 20, 1888 date of the record expurgating fire**)

Beatty, Denson & Oatman. "... We have noticed in the papers, with very much concern for yourselves ..." Letter to Catron, Knaebel, and Clancy. **July 30, 1888.** University of New Mexico Library. Center for Southwest Studies. Thomas B. Catron Papers, MSS 29, Series 102, Box 1, Folder 1. (**Provides the July 20, 1888 date of the record-expurgating fire**)

PECOS RIVER COW CAMP OF (CHRONOLOGICAL)

Riley, John H. Letter to N.A.M. Dudley. **May 19, 1878.** (**Fabricated Regulator theft of Catron's cattle from the Dolan Pecos Cow Camp**) Cited by Victor Westphall, Page 87.

Catron, Thomas Benton. Catron letter to Governor S. B. Axtell to intervene in Lincoln County. **May 30, 1878.** Midland, Texas: Nita Stewart Haley Memorial Library and J. Evetts Haley Historical Center. Robert Mullin Papers. Binder RNM IV, EE (Unpublished). (**Fabricated attack of Regulators on his cow camp workers**) Cited by Victor Westphall, Page 89-90.

SELLING AND BUYING LAND BY

Catron, Thomas Benton. Letter to a Don Matais Contreras. **July 30, 1896.** (**On acquiring land grants by bartering attorney's fees**) Cited in John Paul Wooden's unpublished masters thesis, Page 11.

(SEE: Land-grab exposés of Mary McPherson)

POSSIBLE VOTE BUYING AND POLITICAL PAY OFFS BY

Otero, Miguel A. "At the time of the Rep. Convention in this City ..." Letter to T.B. Catron. **October 25, 1888.** University of New Mexico Library. Center for Southwest Studies. Thomas B. Catron Papers, MSS 29, Series 102, Box 1, Folder 5. (**Documents a pay off to remove a candidate for a clerkship**)

Gonzales y Borrego, Francisco. "I have the honor to Report to you that I have two men ..." Letter to T.B. Catron. **July 23, 1890.** University of New Mexico Library. Center for Southwest Studies. Thomas B. Catron Papers, MSS 29, Series 102, Box 8, Folder 2. (**Documents T.B. Catron's vote buying**)

Lucero, Jose A. "the Democrats are making a desperate fight and I been oblige to meet them ..." Letter to T.B. Catron. **October 29, 1890.** University of New Mexico Library. Center for Southwest Studies. Thomas B. Catron Papers, MSS 29, Series 102, Box 9, Folder 3. (**Requests more money for vote apparent buying of Democrats and necessary secrecy about it**)

Carley, R.M. "The following is a list of men that voted ..." Letter to E.L. Bartlett. for T.B. Catron **November 5, 1890.** University of New Mexico Library. Center for Southwest Studies. Thomas B. Catron Papers, MSS 29, Series 102, Box 9, Folder 3. (**Reporting on voters for Catron**)

Martinez, D. "I most heartily have the honor to congratulate you ..." Letter to T.B. Catron. **August 30, 1892.** University of New Mexico Library. Center for Southwest Studies. Thomas B. Catron Papers, MSS 29, Series 102, Box 15, Folder 5. (**Getting voters by paying their poll taxes**)

Santistevan, Juan. "I had delayed the answer to your esteemed favor ..." Letter to T.B. Catron. **April 9, 1892.** University of New Mexico Library. Center for Southwest Studies. Thomas B. Catron Papers, MSS 29, Series 102, Box 14, Folder 3. (**Possible vote fixing**)

Gregg, George W. "I have your letter from parties in this county ..." **October 22, 1892.** Letter to R.E. Twitchell. University of New Mexico Library. Center for Southwest Studies. Thomas B. Catron Papers, MSS 29, Series 401, Box 1, Folder 3. (**Planning possible vote buying for Catron's campaign for Delegate**)

Hunt, Charles F. "I returned from Colfax County yesterday ..." Letter to T.B. Catron. **October 29, 1892.** University of New Mexico Library. Center for Southwest

Studies. Thomas B. Catron Papers, MSS 29, Series 102, Box 16, Folder 5. (**Vote buying by exchange for free naturalization certificates**)

Amires, Jesucita. "I write you a short letter. ..." Letter to T.B. Catron. **November 4, 1892.** University of New Mexico Library. Center for Southwest Studies. Thomas B. Catron Papers, MSS 29, Series 102, Box 16, Folder 5. (**Wants money in exchange for vote-getting**)

Martin, T.P. "Our campaign committee has just arrived from the north ..." — **1896.** Letter to T.B. Catron. University of New Mexico Library. Center for Southwest Studies. Thomas B. Catron Papers, MSS 29, Series 103. Box 11, Folder 4. (**Wants $250 "to buy enough votes ... to carry the county**)

Santistevan, P.J. "I am doing the possible for your Election ..." Letter to T.B. Catron. **October 12, 1896.** University of New Mexico Library. Center for Southwest Studies. Thomas B. Catron Papers, MSS 29, Series 401, Box 1, Folder 7. (**Wants possible vote buying money**)

Catron, Thomas B. "I am entitled to same from a political standpoint ... having made the race paying all the expenses ..." Letter to Joshua S. Reynolds. **December 16, 1897.** Quoted in Mary Elizabeth Sluga's masters thesis, Page 53.

Mills, Melvin W. "There are a few men who are candidates [for Senator] that I guess have some money ..." Letter to T.B. Catron. **September 12, 1911.** Catron Papers 103, Box 37. Quoted by Victor Westphall, *Thomas Benton Catron and His Era.* Page 350. (**Revealing possible bribery for legislators' vote**)

ALLEGED ASSASSINATION ATTEMPT ON

Elkins, Stephen Benton. "I was shocked this morning on reading of the attempted assassination of you ..." Letter to T.B. Catron. **February 7, 1891.** University of New Mexico Library. Center for Southwest Studies. Thomas B. Catron Papers, MSS 29, Series 102, Box 10, Folder 5.

Francolon, J.B. "Please accept my hearty congratulations on your happy narrow escape ..." Letter to T.B. Catron. **February 7, 1891.** University of New Mexico Library. Center for Southwest Studies. Thomas B. Catron Papers, MSS 29, Series 102, Box 10, Folder 4.

Broad, W.E. "Since reading the account of the attempted assassination ..." Letter to T.B. Catron. **January 2, 1891.** University of New Mexico Library. Center for Southwest Studies. Thomas B. Catron Papers, MSS 29, Series 102, Box 10, Folder 3. (**Catron's Ringite agent for the Tierra Amarilla Grant, setting up malicious prosecution of rebellious settlers, primarily Refugio Martinez.**)

_____. "Since reading the account of the attempted assassination ..." Letter to T.B. Catron. **February 9, 1891.** University of New Mexico Library. Center for Southwest Studies. Thomas B. Catron Papers, MSS 29, Series 102, Box 11, Folder 4. (**Catron's Ringite agent for the Tierra Amarilla Grant, setting up malicious prosecution of Refugio Martinez as an alleged White Cap attempted assassin of Catron.**)

Wright, John M.. "Ancheta is talking very hard about Catron ..." Letter to R.E. Twitchell. **September 12, 1892.** University of New Mexico Library. Center for Southwest Studies. Thomas B. Catron Papers, MSS 29, Series 401, Box 1, Folder 11. (**Letter from Silver City operative to Ringite informer Twitchell about rumor that Catron faked the assassination plot**)

TERRITORIAL DELEGATE ELECTIONS RUNNING FOR

Mills, Melvin W. "Yours of recent date at hand." Letter to T.B. Catron. **August 2, 1892.** University of New Mexico Library. Center for Southwest Studies. Thomas B. Catron Papers, MSS 29, Series 102, Box 15, Folder 3. (**Discourages his running for Delegate because of White Cap opposition**)

Catron, Thomas Benton. "A short time since I wrote you with reference to the position of Chief Justice ..." Letter to Stephen Benton Elkins. **August 15, 1892.** University of New Mexico Library. Center for Southwest Studies. Thomas B. Catron Papers, MSS 29, Series 401, Box 1, Folder 3.

No Author. "Catron and the Laboring Men." **September ? __, 1892.** Printed opposition advertisement. Unknown publication. Center for Southwest Studies. Thomas B. Catron Papers, MSS 29, Series 401, Box 1, Folder 3. (**Opposition to Catron as Delegate to Congress as "the biggest corporation man in New Mexico"**)

No Author. "One of the Ablest and Most Brainy Men in New Mexico, He Should Be Elected." **September 8, 1892.** *The Daily New Mexican.* Front Page. Column 3. https://chroniclingamerica.loc.gov/ (**On behalf of Catron for Delegate**)

Clancy, Frank W. "From something I have heard ..." Letter to T.B. Catron. **September 20, 1892.** University of New Mexico Library. Center for Southwest Studies. Thomas B. Catron Papers, MSS 29, Series 102, Box 16, Folder 2. (**Warning Catron that opponents are seeking the Angel Report to use against his campaign for Delegate, but Elkins is making obstacles**)

No Author. *Las Vegas Daily Optic* . **September 30, 1896.** (**Stating Catron had been an incompetent Delegate to Congress**)

Clancy, Frank W. "I am much surprised at what you say in your letter ..." Letter to T.B. Catron. **December 2, 1896.** University of New Mexico Library. Center for Southwest Studies. Thomas B. Catron Papers, MSS 29, Series 106, Box 1, Folder 6. (**Surprise that Catron now wants to be U.S. Attorney again; and that he lost as Delegate because of his enemies**)

BORREGO MURDER CASE BY

Gonzales y Borrego, Francisco. "I have the honor to Report to you that I have two men ..." Letter to T.B. Catron. **July 23, 1890.** University of New Mexico Library. Center for Southwest Studies. Thomas B. Catron Papers, MSS 29, Series 102, Box 8, Folder 2. (**Documents T.B. Catron's vote buying**)

Frost, Max. "Matters are progressing well here ..." Letter to Judge A.L. Morrison. **September 26, 1892.** University of New Mexico Library. Center for Southwest Studies. Thomas B. Catron Papers, MSS 29, Series 401, Box 1, Folder 3. (**States that Catron and Sheriff Charles Conklin are rumored as Francisco Chavez's murderers**)

Chavez, Juliana V. "Mr. Catron, you are not above suspicion of knowing more about the assassination of my son than you have found it convenient to reveal ..." Letter of Juliana Chavez to T.B. Catron. Reprinted in *Santa Fe Weekly New Mexican.* **March 8, 1894.** Quoted in Victor Westphall, *Thomas Benton Catron and his Era.* Page 226. (**Open letter from mother of Francisco Chavez implicating Catron in his murder**)

Hudson, Richard. "In talking with a Santa Fe man a few days ago in regard to the trial of the men whom you are defending ..." Letter to T.B. Catron. **May 14, 1995.** University of New Mexico Library. Center for Southwest Studies. Thomas B. Catron Papers, MSS 29, Series 102, Box 25, Folder 4. (**Feigned warning about Sheriff Cunningham being a danger to the Borrego case defendants by a Ringite lackey**)

Catron, Thomas Benton. "[The Francisco Chavez murder case] has left me more prostrated than any case I have ever had." Letter to wife, Julia Catron. **June 1, 1895.** C.P. 105, Vol. 12. Quoted in Victor Westphall, *Thomas Benton Catron and His Era.* Page 228. (**Catron implicated in political murder**)

Laughlin, Napoleon B. "In the Supreme Court of the Territory of New Mexico, In re Thomas B. Catron and Charles A. Spiess, Dissenting Opinion of Associate Justice N.B. Laughlin." **December 20, 1895.** University of New Mexico Library. Center for Southwest Studies. Thomas B. Catron Papers, MSS 29, Series 801, Box 1, Folder 8. (**Confirms that victim Sheriff Francisco Chavez was a political enemy of Catron's, implying that Catron may have instigated his murder using the Borregos**)

Catron, Thomas Benton. "... I wrote you a short time ago that I thought arrangements ought to be made ..." Letter to Charles A. Spiess. **January 22, 1897.** University of New Mexico Library. Center for Southwest Studies. Thomas B. Catron Papers, MSS 29, Series 103, Box 2, Folder 3. (**Trying to prevent Borregos' hanging by using political favors**)

No Author. "The Borregos Respited. The President Grants a Respite to the Condemned Men Until March 23. Telegram from Attorney-General." ____, **1897.** Unknown newspaper. University of New Mexico Library. Center for Southwest Studies. Thomas B. Catron Papers, MSS 29, Series 103, Box 2, Folder 3.

Catron, Thomas Benton. "Francisco Gonzales y Borrego, Antonio Gonzales y Borrego, Lauriano Alarid and Patricia Valencia are present under sentence of death ..." Letter to President Grover Cleveland. **February 16, 1897.** University of New Mexico Library. Center for Southwest Studies. Thomas B. Catron Papers, MSS 29, Series 106, Box 2, Folder 2. (**Request for commuting to life sentence**)

No Author. "The Borregos Respited, The President Grants a Respite to the Condemned Men Until March 23." — **1897.** Unknown newspaper clipping. University of New Mexico Library. Center for Southwest Studies. Thomas B. Catron Papers, MSS 29, Series 103, Box 2, Folder 3.

Mills, Melvin W. "Up at the Court House today the question of the power of the President to respite the Borregos ..." Letter to T.B. Catron. **February 22, 1897.** University of New Mexico Library. Center for Southwest Studies. Thomas B. Catron Papers, MSS 29, Series 106, Box 2, Folder 4. (**Helping in Borrego case**)

Gortner, Robert C. "I have your letter of Feb. 25th ..." Letter to T.B. Catron. **March 3, 1897.** University of New Mexico Library. Center for Southwest Studies. Thomas B. Catron Papers, MSS 29, Series 106, Box 2, Folder 6. (**Law partner helping in Borrego case**)

Catron, Thomas Benton. "Yours of the 4th instant at hand ..." Letter to Melvin W. Mills. **March 8, 1897.** University of New Mexico Library. Center for Southwest Studies. Thomas B. Catron Papers, MSS 29, Series 106, Box 2, Folder 7. (**Gives political maneuvering connecting to Borrego case**)

DISBARMENT CASE NO. 637 FOR (CHRONOLOGICAL)

Crist, Jacob. "In the Supreme Court of the Territory of New Mexico, at the July Term, A.D. 1895. Case No. 637." **August 20, 1895.** University of New Mexico Library. Center for Southwest Studies. Thomas B. Catron Papers, MSS 29, Series 801, Box 1, Folder 8. (**Filed information about unprofessional conduct**)

Victory, John P. "In the Supreme Court of the Territory of New Mexico, In the matter of the information concerning Thomas B. Catron and Charles A. Spiess." **August 31, 1895.** University of New Mexico Library. Center for Southwest Studies. Thomas B. Catron Papers, MSS 29, Series 801, Box 1, Folder 7. (**Committee appointed by Supreme Court lists misconduct**)

Catron, Thomas Benton. "In the Supreme Court of the Territory of New Mexico, In the matter of Thomas B. Catron and Charles A. Spiess." **July Term, 1895.** University of New Mexico Library. Center for Southwest Studies. Thomas B. Catron Papers, MSS 29, Series 801, Box 1, Folder 7. (**Response to the Supreme Court denying the charges**)

Spiess, Charles A. "In the Supreme Court of the Territory of New Mexico, In the matter of charges and specifications against Charles A. Spiess." **July Term, 1895.** University of New Mexico Library. Center for Southwest Studies. Thomas B. Catron Papers, MSS 29, Series 801, Box 1, Folder 7. (**Response to the Supreme Court denying the charges**)

Committee Appointed by Supreme Court. "In the Supreme Court of the Territory of New Mexico, In the matter of the Information concerning Thomas B. Catron and Charles A. Spiess." **August 31, 1895.** University of New Mexico Library. Center for Southwest Studies. Thomas B. Catron Papers, MSS 29, Series 801, Box 1,

Folder 8. (**Based on information filed by Prosecutor Jacob Crist in the Supreme Court on August 20, 1895 as Case No. 637**)

No author. *Las Vegas Independent Democrat.* ___ **1895**; based on *Las Vegas Optic.* September 2, 1884. (**About disbarring Catron**)

Field, Neil B. "I received this morning papers from Springer ..." **September 7, 1895.** Letter to T.B. Catron. University of New Mexico Library. Center for Southwest Studies. Thomas B. Catron Papers, MSS 29, Series 801, Box 1, Folder 7. (**Sends copies of legal defense answers written by Attorney Frank Springer**)

Elkins, Stephen Benton. "Mr. Catron's prominence in the capital territory and his leadership ..." Letter to Gideon B. Bantz. **September 9, 1895.** Quoted in John Paul Wooden's unpublished thesis, Page 32. (**Corrupt influencing of Supreme Court judge not to disbar Catron**)

No Author. "In the Supreme Court of the Territory of New Mexico, In the matter of the charges and specifications against Thomas B. Catron and Charles A. Spiess – Unprofessional Conduct." Transcript of Supreme Court testimony. **October, 1895.** University of New Mexico Library. Center for Southwest Studies. Thomas B. Catron Papers, MSS 29, Series 801, Box 2, Folder 22. (**With testimony on Catron trying to get false affidavits by having a refusing woman witness beaten**)

Springer, Frank. "In the Matter of Thomas B. Catron and Charles A. Spiess." Response of Respondents. **October, 1895.** University of New Mexico Library. Center for Southwest Studies. Thomas B. Catron Papers, MSS 29, Series 801, Box 1, Folder 7. (**On behalf of Catron and Spiess moves for all evidence given by prosecution witnesses to be stricken from the record based on alleging that they had bad moral and no credibility**)

_____. "In the Matter of Thomas B. Catron and Charles A. Spiess." Moving to find then not guilty. **October, 1895.** University of New Mexico Library. Center for Southwest Studies. Thomas B. Catron Papers, MSS 29, Series 801, Box 1, Folder 7.

Crist, Jacob. "Mr. Crist Speaks Out. Makes a Clean Breast of the Davis Communication – Served as Attorney and Was Paid For it. What's Catron's Case to Do With it? Invites the Bar Association to Investigate." *The Daily New Mexican.* **October 5, 1895.** Letter to the Editor. University of New Mexico Library. Center for Southwest Studies. Thomas B. Catron Papers, MSS 29, Series 801, Box 1, Folder 8. (**Makes clear that testimony to the Supreme Court will support the disbarment charges for the Borrego Case**)

Hamilton, Humphrey B. "In the Supreme Court of the Territory of New Mexico, In the matter of the charges and specifications against Thomas B. Catron and Charles A. Spiess – Unprofessional Conduct." Majority Opinion. **October 25, 1895.** University of New Mexico Library. Center for Southwest Studies. Thomas B. Catron Papers, MSS 29, Series 801, Box 1, Folder 8. (**Corrupt Supreme Court's vindication of Catron and Spiess from disbarment**)

Elkins, Stephen Benton. "We reached home yesterday at noon ..." Letter to T.B. Catron. **October 30, 1895.** University of New Mexico Library. Center for Southwest Studies. Thomas B. Catron Papers, MSS 29, Series 102, Box 26, Folder 2. (**Congratulating on not being disbarred**)

Laughlin, Napoleon B. "In the Supreme Court of the Territory of New Mexico, In re Thomas B. Catron and Charles A. Spiess, Dissenting Opinion of Associate Justice N.B. Laughlin." **December 20, 1895.** University of New Mexico Library. Center for Southwest Studies. Thomas B. Catron Papers, MSS 29, Series 801, Box 1, Folder 8. (**Dissenting opinion: favoring disbarment**)

Keleher, William A. *The Fabulous Frontier: Twelve New Mexico Items.* Pages 128-129. Albuquerque, New Mexico: The University of New Mexico Press. 1962. (**Ring-biased historian's distortion of Catron's disbarment case**)

ALBUQUERQUE DAILY CITIZEN ANONYMOUS LETTER PLOT AGAINST CHIEF JUSTICE THOMAS SMITH TO SABOTAGE DISBARMENT CASE BY

Twitchell, Ralph Emerson. ""I enclose you herewith a letter from Mr. Hughes, the editor of the Citizen ...." **September 26, 1892.** Letter to T.B. Catron. University of New Mexico Library. Center for Southwest Studies. Thomas B. Catron Papers, MSS 29, Series 401, Box 1, Folder 3. (**Advising a pay-off of editor Hughes**)

Catron, Thomas Benton (As "Anonymous"). "Is it honesty or partisanship?" Letter to the Editor, Thomas Hughes. *Albuquerque Daily Citizen*. **October 9, 1895**. Thomas B. Catron Papers. University of New Mexico Center for Southwest Studies. University Library. Center for Southwest Research, University Libraries, University of New Mexico. (Selectively quoted by Victor Westphall, *Thomas Benton Catron and His Era*. Page 246.) (**Catron's defamation of his disbarment Judge Thomas J. Smith to block a disbarment decision**)

_____. "Editor of the Citizen: I have noticed an article in the Citizen of the 9th inst., which seems to reflect on Chief Justice Smith ..." Published letter to Editor of the *Albuquerque Daily Citizen* Thomas Hughes. **October 10, 1895**. Catron Papers 801. Box 1. Folder 8. (Selectively quoted by Victor Westphall, *Thomas Benton Catron and His Era*. Page 248) (**Catron's lying Letter to the Editor to Thomas Hughes to conceal his own authorship of the editorial**)

_____. "The editorial in your paper came to hand today and the democrats and members of the Supreme Court are very indignant ..." Real letter to the Editor, Thomas Hughes. **October 10, 1895**. University of New Mexico Library. Center for Southwest Studies. Thomas B. Catron Papers, MSS 29, Series 801. Box 1, Folder 8. (Selectively quoted by Victor Westphall, *Thomas Benton Catron and His Era*. Page 248.) (**Catron's coercing Hughes not to reveal him as the anonymous "Is it honesty or partisanship?" letter.**)

Hobart, D.C. "As I was returning home yesterday (on the train) ..." Letter to T.B. Catron. **October 14, 1895**. University of New Mexico Library. Center for Southwest Studies. Thomas B. Catron Papers, MSS 29, Series 102, Box 27, Folder 1. (**Warning Catron that he is identified as the *Albuquerque Citizen* anonymous writer, and that editor, Hughes, would be prosecuted**)

Catron, Thomas Benton. "Tom Smith, son of "Extra Billy" Smith, brother of ... the embezzler, who fled from justice in Arizona ..." "[Judge] Hamilton should ... see that the decision is an absolute, complete, unconditional vindication. This is what I ask him." Letter to *Socorro Chieftain* publisher S.W. Williams. **October 25, 1895**. Catron Papers. 105. Vol. 13. Quoted by Victor Westphall, *Thomas Benton Catron and His Era*. Pages 251-254. (**Defamation of his disbarment Chief Judge Thomas Smith; and illegal influence on another judge**)

_____. "[Smith], thank heaven, took the diarrhoea from the article published in the 'Citizen' and was soon after thrown into a congestive chill ..." Letter to Walter C. Hadley. **October 29, 1895.** (**Gloating over his sadistic attack on his disbarment judge, Thomas Smith**) Quoted by Victor Westphall, *Thomas Benton Catron and His Era*. Page 259.

_____. "His skin is so thin that the slightest attack punctures him. I think the papers should now puncture him ..." Letter to T.W. Collier. **November 11, 1895.** Catron Papers. 105. Vol. 13. (**Sadistic attack on his disbarment judge, Thomas Smith**) Quoted by Victor Westphall, *Thomas Benton Catron and His Era*. Page 249.

_____. First National Bank check to T. Hughes for $350.00. **July 11, 1896.** Check to Thomas Hughes. University of New Mexico Library. Center for Southwest Studies. Thomas B. Catron Papers, MSS 29, Series 805, Box 1, Bunch 1. (**Catron's pay-off check to Thomas Hughes**)

(SEE: Thomas Hughes)

CONGRATULATIONS FOR AVOIDING DISBARMENT TO

Helm, T.J. "Will you allow me to extend my harty congratulations ..." **October 28, 1895.** Letter to T.B. Catron. University of New Mexico Library. Center for Southwest Studies. Thomas B. Catron Papers, MSS 29, Series 801, Box 1, Folder 9. (**Decision against disbarment**)

Elkins, Stephen Benton. "We reached home yesterday at noon ..." Letter to T.B. Catron. **October 30, 1895.** University of New Mexico Library. Center for Southwest Studies. Thomas B. Catron Papers, MSS 29, Series 102, Box 26, Folder 2. (**Congratulating on not being disbarred**)

Ashenfelter, Singleton M. "I congratulate you on the result of the Supreme Court Inquiry ..." **November 1, 1895.** Letter to T.B. Catron. University of New Mexico Library. Center for Southwest Studies. Thomas B. Catron Papers, MSS 29, Series 801, Box 1, Folder 9. (**Decision against disbarment**)

Rudulph, Charles. "Allow me to congratulate you on your recent great victory. **November 5, 1895.** Letter to T.B. Catron. University of New Mexico Library. Center for Southwest Studies. Thomas B. Catron Papers, MSS 29, Series 102, Box 27, Folder 2. (**Son of Milnor Rudulph, Billy Bonney's Ringite President of his Coroner's Jury who wrote its Report praising Pat Garrett**)

REVENGE FOR DISBARMENT CASE BY

ATTACKING PROSECUTOR JACOB CRIST BY

Broad, W.E. "Replying to that part of your letter of the 3rd inst ..." Letter to T.B. Catron. **December 6, 1890.** University of New Mexico Library. Center for Southwest Studies. Thomas B. Catron Papers, MSS 29, Series 102, Box 9, Folder 5. (**Ringite agent reporting to Catron about Jacob H. Crist**)

Crist, Jacob. "Mr. Crist Speaks Out. Makes a Clean Breast of the Davis Communication – Served as Attorney and Was Paid For it. What's Catron's Case to Do With it? Invites the Bar Association to Investigate." *The Daily New Mexican.* **October 5, 1895.** Letter to the Editor. University of New Mexico Library. Center for Southwest Studies. Thomas B. Catron Papers, MSS 29, Series 801, Box 1, Folder 8. (**Makes clear that testimony to the Supreme Court will support the disbarment charges for the Borrego Case**)

Johnson, Charles A. "I am in receipt of your favor of 27th ultimo re. Crist matter ..." Letter to T.B. Catron. **October 3, 1895.** University of New Mexico Library. Center for Southwest Studies. Thomas B. Catron Papers, MSS 29, Series 102, Box 27, Folder 1. (**Catron's investigator to find dirt on Jacob H. Crist**)

_____. "I am in receipt of your favor of the 24th ultimo regarding the Crist matter." Letter to T.B. Catron. **November 4, 1895.** University of New Mexico Library. Center for Southwest Studies. Thomas B. Catron Papers, MSS 29, Series 102, Box 27, Folder 3.(**About Catron's revenge pursuit of Crist**)

ATTACKING DISSENTING SUPREME COURT JUDGE NAPOLEON BONAPARTE LAUGHLIN BY

Catron, Thomas Benton. "This man [Judge] Laughlin ... tried to disbar me and when he could not do it he wrote a filthy, dirty, dissenting opinion ..." Letter to William J. Mills. **July 18, 1896.** Catron Papers. 105. Vol. 13. Quoted by Victor Westphall, *Thomas Benton Catron and His Era.* Page 258. (**Trying to destroy reputation of disbarment judge, Napoleon B. Laughlin**)

ALBUQUERQUE CITIZEN ANONYMOUS "POKER BILL" ATTACK ON GOVERNOR WILLIAM THORNTON BY

Catron, Thomas Benton (as Anonymous, "XXX"). "Severe Criticism, Gov. Thornton Charged With Prostituting His Office." *Albuquerque Daily Citizen.*

September 5, 1896. (With reprinted letter dated September 4, 1896) Vol. 10, No. 276. Page 2. Center for Southwest Research Collection, University Libraries, University of New Mexico. Zim CSWR oversize AN2, A411 January – June 1896, July – December 1896. Reprinted September 11, 1896 in the *Santa Fe Daily New Mexican*. University of New Mexico Library. Center for Southwest Studies. Thomas B. Catron Papers, MSS 29, Series 801, Box 2, Folder 13. (**Catron's anonymous attack on Governor William Thornton**)

Thornton, William T. "The following is an extract from a communication from Santa Fé which appeared in last Saturday's issue of the Albuquerque Citizen under the nom de plum of XXXX ..." Letter to T.B. Catron. **September 10, 1896.** University of New Mexico Library. Center for Southwest Studies. Thomas B. Catron Papers, MSS 29, Series 801, Box 2, Folder 13. (**Responding to Catron's anonymous defamatory "Poker Bill" letter published in the** *Albuquerque Daily Citizen*)

_____. "Open Letter to T.B. Catron." *Santa Fe Daily New Mexican*. **September 11, 1896.** Front Page. University of New Mexico Library. Center for Southwest Studies. Thomas B. Catron Papers, MSS 29, Series 801, Box 2, Folder 13. (Quoted by Victor Westphall, *Thomas Benton Catron and His Era*. Page 262.) (**Reprinting his own letter of September 10, 1896 to Catron debunking Catron's anonymous defamatory "Poker Bill" letter of September 4, 1896 to the Editor of the** *Albuquerque Daily Citizen*)

Catron, Thomas Benton. "I am this morning in possession of your communication of the 10th inst., written from the "Office of the Executive" ... Letter to William T. Thornton. **September 16, 1896.** University of New Mexico Library. Center for Southwest Studies. Thomas B. Catron Papers, MSS 29, Series 801, Box 2, Folder 13. (Quoted by Victor Westphall, *Thomas Benton Catron and His Era* Page 263.) (**Catron's paranoid and violent letter against Thornton**)

_____. "You will recognize me as the Delegate from New Mexico ..." Letter to President Grover Cleveland. **September 16, 1896.** University of New Mexico Library. Center for Southwest Studies. Thomas B. Catron Papers, MSS 29, Series 801, Box 2, Folder 13. (Quoted by Victor Westphall, *Thomas Benton Catron and His Era*. Pages 269-270) (**Catron's attempted revenge on Governor William Thornton**)

_____. "Enclosed I send you copies of two letters ..." Letter to Stephen Benton Elkins. **September 16, 1896.** University of New Mexico Library. Center for Southwest Studies. Thomas B. Catron Papers, MSS 29, Series 801, Box 2, Folder 13. (**Denying the "Poker Bill" plot to Elkins**)

Thornton, William T. "Catron Begs the Question – Replies to Gov. Thornton's Open Letter – But Does Not Deny That the Anonymous Screed Emanated from His Office." **September 17, 1896.** *Santa Fe Daily New Mexican*. University of New Mexico Library. Center for Southwest Studies. Thomas B. Catron Papers, MSS 29, Series 106, Box 2, Folder 2.

Catron, Thomas Benton. "Yours of the 18th instant at hand. Thornton's trial came out about as I expected ..." Letter to Max Frost. **February 23, 1897.** University of New Mexico Library. Center for Southwest Studies. Thomas B. Catron Papers, MSS 29, Series 106, Box 2, Folder 4. (**Still denying his anonymous letter plots in the** *Albuquerque Daily Citizen*)

UN-MASONIC BEHAVIOR CHARGE AGAINST

Walker, Addison. "Pursuant to the order of the Grand Lodge of New Mexico..." Letter to T.B. Catron. **February 1, 1897.** University of New Mexico Library. Center for Southwest Studies. Thomas B. Catron Papers, MSS 29, Series 106, Box 2, Folder 2. (**Catron charged with un-Masonic conduct**)

Catron, Thomas Benton. 'I have yours of the 12th instant, and I have also received a copy of the charges ..." Letter to E.L. Bartlett. **February 17, 1897.** University of

New Mexico Library. Center for Southwest Studies. Thomas B. Catron Papers, MSS 29, Series 106, Box 2, Folder 3. (**Denying un-Masonic conduct and blaming William Thornton**)

_____. "Yours of the 18th instant at hand. Thornton's trial came out about as I expected ..." Letter to Max Frost. **February 23, 1897.** University of New Mexico Library. Center for Southwest Studies. Thomas B. Catron Papers, MSS 29, Series 106, Box 2, Folder 4.

PURSUIT OF OLIVER LEE USING PAT GARRETT BY

Bryan, John D. "On yesterday indictments were returned by our Grand Jury against Oliver M. Lee ..." Letter to Thomas Benton Catron. **October 1, 1898.** University of New Mexico Library. Center for Southwest Studies. Thomas B. Catron Papers, MSS 29, Series 103, Box 6, Folder 2. (**Reporting to Catron on malicious prosecution of Oliver Lee**)

Barnes, R.P. "I have spent a couple of days down here on the Fountain cases ..." Letter to T.B. Catron. **May 21, 1899.** University of New Mexico Library. Center for Southwest Studies. Thomas B. Catron Papers, MSS 29, Series 103, Box 7, Folder 5. (**Update on Pat Garrett on the Fountain murder cases to get conviction of Oliver Lee**

CAMPAIGN SPEECH BY

Catron, Thomas Benton. "Speech of Thomas B. Catron, delivered before the Bernalillo County Republican Convention at Albuquerque." **October 26, 1898.** University of New Mexico Library. Center for Southwest Studies. Thomas B. Catron Papers, MSS 29, Series 401, Box 1, Folder 9.

Fergusson, Harvey B. "Speech of H.G. Fergusson, Santa Fe N.M." **October 29, 1898.** University of New Mexico Library. Center for Southwest Studies. Thomas B. Catron Papers, MSS 29, Series 401. Box 1, Folder 9. (**Alluding to Santa Fe Ring tactics in response to Catron's October 26, 1898 speech**)

ATTACKS ON GOVERNOR MIGUEL OTERO BY

Elkins, Stephen Benton. "Your letter from Las Vegas received ..." Letter to T.B. Catron. **June 14, 1901.** University of New Mexico Library. Center for Southwest Studies. Thomas B. Catron Papers, MSS 29, Series 103, Box 13, Folder 1. (**Informing him that Miguel Otero was appointed governor despite his efforts to the contrary**)

Catron, Thomas Benton. "[Otero backers] have made a very villainous, mean ugly fight against me." **September 20, 1902.** Letter to Dave Winters. Catron Papers 105, Volume 20. Quoted by Victor Westphall, *Thomas Benton Catron and His Era.* Pages 291. (**Catron's accusing political rival, Governor Miguel Otero, of his own ring-style criminality**)

Miller, Fred and W.E. Dame. "We earnestly request you to give the Honorable T.B. Catron, formerly Delegate to Congress from New Mexico ..." **May __, 1905.** Letter to Theodore Roosevelt. University of New Mexico Library. Center for Southwest Studies. Thomas B. Catron Papers, MSS 29, Series 103, Box 22, Folder 5. (**"Dame" is a name which appeared in a Catron cipher-code letter**)

MAYOR OF SANTA FE OF

Montenie, L.F. "The City of Santa Fe, Office of the City Clerk, Certificate of Election." **April 3, 1906.** University of New Mexico Library. Center for Southwest Studies. Thomas B. Catron Papers, MSS 29, Series 801, Box 2, Folder 17. (**Election as Mayor**)

SENATORSHIP OF

Mills, Melvin W. "There are a few men who are candidates [for Senator] that I guess have some money ..." Letter to T.B. Catron. **September 12, 1911.** Catron Papers 103, Box 37. Quoted by Victor Westphall, *Thomas Benton Catron and His Era.* Page 350. (**Revealing possible bribery for legislators' vote**)

Catron, Thomas Benton. "I am informed that you have been elected a member of the House Of Representatives ..." Form letter from T.B. Catron to legislators. **November 15, 1911.** University of New Mexico Library. Center for Southwest Studies. Thomas B. Catron Papers, MSS 29, Series 511, Box 1, Folder 5. (**Soliciting votes for himself for Senator**)

LETTERS FROM, TO, ABOUT (CHRONOLOGICAL)
FROM SINGLETON M. ASHENFELTER

Ashenfelter, S.M. "Johnny Riley writes me from Las Cruces ..." Letter to T.B. Catron. **October 26, 1892.** University of New Mexico Library. Center for Southwest Studies. Thomas B. Catron Papers, MSS 29, Series 102, Box 16, Folder 5.

Riley, John H. "I have been away for some days ..." **April 10, 1893.** Letter to S.M. Ashenfelter. University of New Mexico Library. Center for Southwest Studies. Thomas B. Catron Papers, MSS 29, Series 102, Box 18, Folder 3.

_____. "Yours notifying me of having drawn on me ..." **May 13, 1894.** Letter to T.B. Catron. University of New Mexico Library. Center for Southwest Studies. Thomas B. Catron Papers, MSS 29, Series 102, Box 21, Folder 6. (**About Catron's renting newspaper office from Ashenfelter**)

Ashenfelter, S.M. "I congratulate you on the result of the Supreme Court Inquiry ..." **November 1, 1895.** Letter to T.B. Catron. University of New Mexico Library. Center for Southwest Studies. Thomas B. Catron Papers, MSS 29, Series 801, Box 1, Folder 9. (**Decision against disbarment**)

_____. "I do not know whether you are interested in the matter of this grant ..." **April 14, 1898.** Letter to T.B. Catron. University of New Mexico Library. Center for Southwest Studies. Thomas B. Catron Papers, MSS 29, Series 102, Box 5, Folder 1. (**Keeping eye out for land for Catron**)

FROM SATURNINO BACA

Baca, Saturnino. "Which if anything has been done in regard to the claim of Francisco Baca ..." Letter to T.B. Catron. **March 28, 1892.** University of New Mexico Library. Center for Southwest Studies. Thomas B. Catron Papers, MSS 29, Series 102, Box 14, Folder 2.

TO AND FROM JOHN D. BAIL

Catron, Thomas Benton et al. "Can you give us any information in regard to A.M. Connor, whom we are informed is living in Silver City ..." Letter to John D. Bail. **December 28, 1888.** University of New Mexico Library. Center for Southwest Studies. Thomas B. Catron Papers, MSS 29, Series 101, Volume 1, Page 250. (**Using Bail as a spy for his law firm**)

Bail, John H. "Yes I will do so ..." Telegram to T.B. Catron. **August 20, 1889.** University of New Mexico Library. Center for Southwest Studies. Thomas B. Catron Papers, MSS 29, Series 102, Box 4, Folder 5.

_____. "I will attend to the Hughes case ..." Letter to T.B. Catron. **August 21, 1889.** University of New Mexico Library. Center for Southwest Studies. Thomas B. Catron Papers, MSS 29, Series 102, Box 4, Folder 5.

_____. "I send you a print ..." Letter to T.B. Catron. **April 19, 1892.** University of New Mexico Library. Center for Southwest Studies. Thomas B. Catron Papers, MSS 29, Series 102, Box 14, Folder 3.

_____. "I have received your letter..." Letter to T.B. Catron. **February 6, 1893.** University of New Mexico Library. Center for Southwest Studies. Thomas B. Catron Papers, MSS 29, Series 102, Box 17, Folder 4.

Catron, Thomas Benton. First National Bank check to John D. Bail for $250.00 **July 15, 1896.** Check to J.D. Bail. University of New Mexico Library. Center for Southwest Studies. Thomas B. Catron Papers, MSS 29, Series 805, Box 1, Bunch 1. (**Payment to attorney who had been Billy Bonney's court appointed defense lawyer in Mesilla in 1881**)

FROM AND ABOUT JOSEPH BLAZER

Easton, David M. "I am in receipt of a letter from Maj Llewellyn ..." Letter to T.B. Catron. **May 15, 1890.** University of New Mexico Library. Center for Southwest Studies. Thomas B. Catron Papers, MSS 29, Series 102, Box 7, Folder 3. (**Easton in trying to sell all his Mescalero property to Catron, mentions that John Riley and William Rynerson are part owners of Joseph Blazer's mill property in Mescalero**)

FROM CHARLES C. CATRON

Catron, Charles C. "My father probably spent over a million dollars in following up his hobby [of politics]." Letter to Major Harry F. Cameron. **June 3, 1921.** Catron Papers 101, Box 29. Quoted by Victor Westphall, *Thomas Benton Catron and His Era*. Page 387. (**Revealing possible political bribery**)

FROM, TO, ABOUT JAMES J. DOLAN

Dolan, James J. "I want to borrow from you about one thousand dollars ..." Letter to T.B. Catron. **December 14, 1889.** University of New Mexico Library. Center for Southwest Studies. Thomas B. Catron Papers, MSS 29, Series 102, Box 5, Folder 5.

_____. "I wish you would try & carry that note ..." Letter to T.B. Catron. **July 9, 1890**. University of New Mexico Library. Center for Southwest Studies. Thomas B. Catron Papers, MSS 29, Series 102, Box 8, Folder 1.

_____. "Will you do me the kindness to send me a personal letter to S.B. Elkins ..." Letter to T.B. Catron. **October 15, 1891.** University of New Mexico Library. Center for Southwest Studies. Thomas B. Catron Papers, MSS 29, Series 102, Box 12, Folder 2.

_____. "It looks like we may be left ..." Letter to T.B. Catron. **November 26, 1892.** University of New Mexico Library. Center for Southwest Studies. Thomas B. Catron Papers, MSS 29, Series 102, Box 16, Folder 7.

_____. "I met with Curry on the street this Evening ..." Letter to T.B. Catron. **October 6, 1894.** University of New Mexico Library. Center for Southwest Studies. Thomas B. Catron Papers, MSS 29, Series 401, Box 1, Folder 5. (**Dolan as Catron's Lincoln spy**)

_____. "You no doubt have noticed that cowardly slanderous article against me ..." Letter to T.B. Catron. **June 11, 1995.** University of New Mexico Library. Center for Southwest Studies. Thomas B. Catron Papers, MSS 29, Series 102, Box 25, Folder 6. (**Using Catron to prosecute his political enemies**)

Dolan, James J. "Your favor of the 2nd ins't received, I have delayed answering it until after my trip to Lincoln ..." Letter to T.B. Catron. **February 23, 1897.** University of New Mexico Library. Center for Southwest Studies. Thomas B. Catron Papers, MSS 29, Series 106, Box 2, Folder 4. (**Attacking Lincoln County War politician Florencio Gonzales**)

FROM AND ABOUT DAVID M. EASTON AND WIFE

Easton, David M. "While in Santa Fe I several times sought an opportunity to see you ..." Letter to T.B. Catron. **April 8, 1889.** University of New Mexico

Library. Center for Southwest Studies. Thomas B. Catron Papers, MSS 29, Series 102, Box 3, Folder 4. (**About being in debt to Catron and wanting Catron to make him Mescalero Indian Reservation Agent to pay it back; and entanglement with William Rynerson and John Riley**)

_____. "I would like to know about time you can come up ..." Letter to W.H.H. Llewellyn. **April 17, 1890.** University of New Mexico Library. Center for Southwest Studies. Thomas B. Catron Papers, MSS 29, Series 102, Box 7, Folder 2. (**Trying to settle business with Catron**)

_____. "I am in receipt of a letter from Maj Llewellyn ..." Letter to T.B. Catron. **May 15, 1890.** University of New Mexico Library. Center for Southwest Studies. Thomas B. Catron Papers, MSS 29, Series 102, Box 7, Folder 3. (**Easton desperately trying to sell all his property to settle his huge loan to Catron**)

_____. "Maj Llewellyn informed me personally ..." Letter to T.B. Catron. **November 15, 1891.** University of New Mexico Library. Center for Southwest Studies. Thomas B. Catron Papers, MSS 29, Series 102, Box 12, Folder 4. (**Still trying to get an answer of resolving his loan to Catron**)

Easton, Lizzie A. "Mr. Easton is absent from home ..." Letter to T.B. Catron. **April 2, 1894.** University of New Mexico Library. Center for Southwest Studies. Thomas B. Catron Papers, MSS 29, Series 102, Box 21, Folder 4.

Easton, Davin M. "Your letter of the 13th inst in answer ..." Letter to T.B. Catron. **July 24, 1894.** University of New Mexico Library. Center for Southwest Studies. Thomas B. Catron Papers, MSS 29, Series 102, Box 22, Folder 3. (**Catron sadistically toyed with Easton about the land deal**)

_____. "As you have failed to make a legal appraisement ..." Letter to W.H.H. Llewellyn. **July 25, 1894.** University of New Mexico Library. Center for Southwest Studies. Thomas B. Catron Papers, MSS 29, Series 102, Box 22, Folder 3. (**Easton fired appraiser Llewellyn**)

Galleger, __. "I am about to buy the farm of Dave Easton's ..." Letter to T.B. Catron. **April 11, 1898.** University of New Mexico Library. Center for Southwest Studies. Thomas B. Catron Papers, MSS 29, Series 103, Box 5, Folder 1. (**Shows Easton had Catron as mortgage holder**)

FROM AND TO STEPHEN BENTON ELKINS

Elkins, Stephen Benton. "I beg to acknowledge the receipt of yours of the 15th inst. ..." Letter to T.B. Catron. **August 19, 1892.** University of New Mexico Library. Center for Southwest Studies. Thomas B. Catron Papers, MSS 29, Series 102, Box 15, Folder 5. (**Confirming his directing the requested appointment; and advising Catron that becoming Senator was more important than becoming Territorial Delegate**)

_____. "Kerens sent me your letter. Letter to T.B. Catron. **December 4, 1897.** University of New Mexico Library. Center for Southwest Studies. Thomas B. Catron Papers, MSS 29, Series 103, Box 4, Folder 2. (**Tried to influence the President and Attorney General to get Catron appointed U.S. Attorney**)

_____. "Your letter from Las Vegas received ..." Letter to T.B. Catron. **June 14, 1901.** University of New Mexico Library. Center for Southwest Studies. Thomas B. Catron Papers, MSS 29, Series 103, Box 13, Folder 1. (**Informing that Miguel Otero was appointed governor despite Elkins's efforts to the contrary**)

Catron, Thomas Benton. "I understand from the press dispatches last night that the bill for the admission of New Mexico ..." **February 1, 1910.** Letter to S.B. Elkins. University of New Mexico Library. Center for Southwest Studies. Thomas B. Catron Papers, MSS 29, Series 105, Volume 29, Pages 374-376. (**Using Elkins as a Washington insider source to block federal control of New Mexico's public lands and irrigation**)

_____. "I have your letter and am sorry to hear that you are not feeling well ..." **September 19, 1910.** Letter to S.B. Elkins. University of New Mexico Library. Center for Southwest Studies. Thomas B. Catron Papers, MSS 29, Series 105, Volume 30, Page 116. (**Feels his chances for senatorship are good**)

(SEE: Stephen Benton Elkins; Thomas Benton Catron topics on U.S. Attorney resignation, assassination attempt on, disbarment attempt on)

ABOUT BY MARSH GIDDINGS

Giddings, Marsh. "To defeat Catron's confirmation [as U.S. Attorney] a grossly false affidavit [by August Kirchner] has been sent to Senator [Lyman Trumbull]." **Month (?) 1872.** Telegram from Governor Marsh Giddings to Washington, D.C. Attorney General George H. Williams. From Victor Westphall. *Thomas Benton Catron and His Era.* Page 107. (**About the 1872 legislature's actions against Palen and Catron**)

TO JAMES J. HAGERMAN

Catron, Thomas Benton. "[If your son] is to be appointed, I shall be very pleased ... if he will take immediate steps to have the "Augean stables" cleaned ..." Letter to James J. Hagerman. **November 22, 1905.** (**Wanting appointment as Attorney General to maliciously prosecute opponents**) Quoted in Mary Elizabeth Sluga's masters thesis, Pages 87-88.

TO R.C. KERENS

Catron, Thomas Benton. "His administration has been guilty of the most wholesale plunder of the resources of this territory ..." Letter to Richard C. Kerens. **April 4, 1901.** (**Revenge defamation of Governor Miguel A. Otero**) Quoted in Mary Elizabeth Sluga's masters thesis, Pages 66-69.

FROM JOHN H. KOOGLER

Koogler, John H. "I will start for Kansas City to-morrow ..." Letter to T.B. Catron. **July 17, 1889.** University of New Mexico Library. Center for Southwest Studies. Thomas B. Catron Papers, MSS 29, Series 102, Box 4, Folder 3. (**Pleading for money**)

_____. "I wrote you before I left Las Vegas ..." Letter to T.B. Catron. **July 29, 1889.** University of New Mexico Library. Center for Southwest Studies. Thomas B. Catron Papers, MSS 29, Series 102, Box 4, Folder 4. (**Pleading for money**)

_____. "Mr. Gorther in sending me the balance of the testimony in the case of Doloritas Martin ..." Letter to T.B. Catron. **August 14, 1890.** University of New Mexico Library. Center for Southwest Studies. Thomas B. Catron Papers. MSS 29, Series 102, Box 8, Folder 4. (**About fees for legal work for Catron**)

ABOUT ROBERT LONGWILL TO

McComas, Alice Moore. "Will you kindly inform me if Dr. R.H. Longwill is in your city ..." Letter to T.B. Catron. **May 12, 1891.** University of New Mexico Library. Center for Southwest Studies. Thomas B. Catron Papers, MSS 29, Series 102, Box 11, Folder 1.

Roy, W.C. "I would ask you as a favor ..." Letter to Charles Spiess. **April 4, 1995.** University of New Mexico Library. Center for Southwest Studies. Thomas B. Catron Papers, MSS 29, Series 102, Box 25, Folder 2. (**About finding administrator of Robert Longwill's estate**)

FROM JACOB BASIL "BILLY" MATTHEWS

Matthews, Jacob Basil. "I congratulate you upon your nomination ..." Letter to T.B. Catron. **August 30, 1892.** University of New Mexico Library. Center for Southwest Studies. Thomas B. Catron Papers, MSS 29, Series 102, Box 16, Folder 1.

TO MARY McPHERSON COMPLAINT

Catron, Thomas Benton. "Answering Charges of Mary E. McPherson." **February 24, 1877.** Letter to Attorney General Alphonso Taft. Interior Department Papers 1850-1907; Appointments Division and Subsequent Actions. Microfilm File Case Number 44-4-8-3. Record Group 48. Microfilm Roll M750. National Archives and Records Administration. U.S. Department of Justice. Washington, D.C. (**Letter denying McPherson's charges**)

ABOUT LAWRENCE GUSTAV MURPHY

Gilliam, W.J. " I have been told you were administrator of Murphys estate. ..." Letter to T.B. Catron. **April 24, 1895.** University of New Mexico Library. Center for Southwest Studies. Thomas B. Catron Papers, MSS 29, Series 102, Box 25, Folder 3.

FROM MELVIN WHITSON MILLS

Mills, Melvin W. "Would you take a little of the political situation as we have it here ..." Letter to T.B. Catron. **February 1, 1889.** University of New Mexico Library. Center for Southwest Studies. Thomas B. Catron Papers, MSS 29, Series 102, Box 2, Folder 4.

_____. "Yours of recent date at hand." Letter to T.B. Catron. **August 2, 1892.** University of New Mexico Library. Center for Southwest Studies. Thomas B. Catron Papers, MSS 29, Series 102, Box 15, Folder 3. (**Coaching and advising Catron for Delegate election**)

_____. "Will you go over to Mora Court ..." Letter to T.B. Catron. **October 13, 1892.** University of New Mexico Library. Center for Southwest Studies. Thomas B. Catron Papers, MSS 29, Series 102, Box 16, Folder 4. (**Political machinations with Catron and Frank Springer**)

_____. "Up at the Court House today the question of the power of the President to respite the Borregos ..." Letter to T.B. Catron. **February 22, 1897.** University of New Mexico Library. Center for Southwest Studies. Thomas B. Catron Papers, MSS 29, Series 106, Box 2, Folder 4. (**Helping in Borrego case**)

_____."There are a few men who are candidates [for Senator] that I guess have some money ..." Letter to T.B. Catron. **September 12, 1911.** Catron Papers 103, Box 37. Quoted by Victor Westphall, *Thomas Benton Catron and His Era*. Page 350. (**Revealing possible bribery for legislators' vote**)

FROM TONY NEIS

Neis, Tony. "Friend Catron you have seen by this time. ..." Letter to T.B. Catron. **November 12, 1892.** University of New Mexico Library. Center for Southwest Studies. Thomas B. Catron Papers, MSS 29, Series 102, Box 16, Folder 6. (**Giving election results and advising on revenge against adversaries**)

FROM, TO, ABOUT MIGUEL OTERO

Otero, Miguel A. "At the time of the Rep. Convention in this City ..." Letter to T.B. Catron. **October 25, 1888.** University of New Mexico Library. Center for Southwest Studies. Thomas B. Catron Papers, MSS 29, Series 102, Box 1, Folder 5.(**Documents a pay off to remove a candidate for a clerkship**)

Catron, Thomas Benton. "You must see that Otero is not reappointed ..." Letter to Stephen Benton Elkins. **November 11, 1901**. Quoted in Mary Elizabeth Sluga's masters thesis, Page 79.

_____. "[Otero backers] have made a very villainous, mean ugly fight against me." **September 20, 1902**. Letter to Dave Winters. Catron Papers 105, Volume 20. Quoted by Victor Westphall, *Thomas Benton Catron and His Era*. Pages 291. (**Accusing Governor Otero of his own Ring-style criminality**)

FROM, TO, ABOUT JOHN HENRY RILEY

Riley, John H. "Today mailed Senator Edmunds my affidavit corroborated by Dolan against Fiske ..." Letter to T.B Catron. **February 5, 1890**. University of New Mexico Library. Center for Southwest Studies. Thomas B. Catron Papers, MSS 29, Series 102, Box 6, Folder 1.

_____. "Ought you not see to the matter of the Wilson Waddingham tract of land ..." Letter to T.B. Catron. **June 19, 1890**. University of New Mexico Library. Center for Southwest Studies. Thomas B. Catron Papers, MSS 29, Series 102, Box 7, Folder 4. (**Lookout for land for Catron**)

_____. "Rynerson and I wish to talk with you ..." Letter to T.B. Catron. **December 19, 1891**. University of New Mexico Library. Center for Southwest Studies. Thomas B. Catron Papers, MSS 29, Series 102, Box 12, Folder 6.

_____. "I can now recommend to you a foreman ..." Letter to T.B. Catron. **January 27, 1892**. University of New Mexico Library. Center for Southwest Studies. Thomas B. Catron Papers, MSS 29, Series 102, Box 13, Folder 2.

_____. "Rynerson and I called on Hughes (Levi) last night ..." Letter to T.B. Catron. **February 9, 1892**. University of New Mexico Library. Center for Southwest Studies. Thomas B. Catron Papers, MSS 29, Series 102, Box 13, Folder 4.

_____. "Yours notifying me of having drawn on me favor ..." Letter to T.B. Catron. **May 13, 1894**. University of New Mexico Library. Center for Southwest Studies. Thomas B. Catron Papers, MSS 29, Series 102, Box 21, Folder 6.

FROM WILLIAM LOGAN RYNERSON

Rynerson, William. "I notice what you say in relation to having mutual understanding ..." Letter to T.B. Catron. **November 11, 1888**. University of New Mexico Library. Center for Southwest Studies. Thomas B. Catron Papers, MSS 29, Series 102, Box 2, Folder 1.

_____. "I was close after you ..." Letter to T.B. Catron. **December 28, 1888**. University of New Mexico Library. Center for Southwest Studies. Thomas B. Catron Papers, MSS 29, Series 102, Box 2, Folder 3. (**Shoes that Rynerson traveled to Washington for the Ring, meeting Elkins and influencing the** *New York Tribune*)

_____. "Riley is away over at Lincoln ..." Letter to T.B. Catron. **April 13, 1891**. University of New Mexico Library. Center for Southwest Studies. Thomas B. Catron Papers, MSS 29, Series 102, Box 10, Folder 7.

FROM, TO FRANK SPRINGER

Springer, Frank. "From various indications, both in Court and out ..." Letter to Catron, Knaebel, and Clancy. **October 24, 1888**. University of New Mexico Library. Center for Southwest Studies. Thomas B. Catron Papers, MSS 29, Series 102, Box 1, Folder 5. (**Spelling out how to litigate to remove Maxwell Land Grant settlers**)

Clancy, Frank W. "Van der Veer is now in Washington ..." Letter to Frank Springer. **March 14, 1889**. University of New Mexico Library. Center for Southwest Studies. Thomas B. Catron Papers, MSS 29, Series 101, Volume 1. Pages 330-331. (**Key communication from Catron's firm attacking Leonard and Wallace**)

Clancy, Frank W. "Have you done anything about the U.S. Attorney business ..." Letter to Frank Springer. **May 8, 1889.** University of New Mexico Library. Center for Southwest Studies. Thomas B. Catron Papers, MSS 29, Series 101, Volume 1. Page 419. (**Springer as backed by Catron for U.S. Attorney**)

Springer, Frank. "Yours of the 8th received ..." Letter to F.W. Clancy. **May 10, 1889.** University of New Mexico Library. Center for Southwest Studies. Thomas B. Catron Papers, MSS 29, Series 102, Box 3, Folder 5. (**Says he does not want to be U.S. Attorney**)

_____. "I should have answered your letter ..." Letter to F.W. Clancy. **May 30, 1889.** University of New Mexico Library. Center for Southwest Studies. Thomas B. Catron Papers, MSS 29, Series 102, Box 3, Folder 6. (**Says he might run for U.S. Attorney if politically necessary**)

Mills, M.W. "Will you go over to Mora Court ..." **October 13, 1892.** Letter to T.B. Catron. University of New Mexico Library. Center for Southwest Studies. Thomas B. Catron Papers, MSS 29, Series 102, Box 16, Folder 4. (**Springer advising Catron on political machinations**)

SEE: Frank Springer Biographical Entry

FROM AND TO RALPH EMERSON TWITCHELL

Twitchell, Ralph Emerson. "I enclose you herewith a letter from Mr. Hughes, the editor of the Citizen ...." **September 26, 1892.** Letter to T.B. Catron. University of New Mexico Library. Center for Southwest Studies. Thomas B. Catron Papers, MSS 29, Series 401, Box 1, Folder 3. (**Advising a pay-off of press owner Hughes**)

Gregg, George W. "I have your letter from parties in this county ..." **October 22, 1892.** Letter to R.E. Twitchell. University of New Mexico Library. Center for Southwest Studies. Thomas B. Catron Papers, MSS 29, Series 401, Box 1, Folder 3. (**Planning possible vote buying for Catron**)

Riley, John H. "I suggest you get out in Spanish a number of copies of your letter ..." Letter to Ralph E. Twitchell. **October 24, 1907.** University of New Mexico Library. Center for Southwest Studies. Thomas B. Catron Papers, MSS 29, Series 401-409, Box 1, Folder 3. (**Using Twitchell to fix votes for Catron**)

(SEE: Thomas Benton Catron's cipher-code letters to)

FROM EDGAR WALZ

Walz, Edgar. "I have often while in New Mexico heard ..." Letter to T.B. Catron. **June 8, 1897.** University of New Mexico Library. Center for Southwest Studies. Thomas B. Catron Papers, MSS 29, Series 103, Box 3, Folder 1.

ABOUT LEW WALLACE

Catron, Thomas Benton. "He [Lew Wallace] and I were not on friendly terms while he was governor." Letter to Stephen Benton Elkins. **August 4, 1897.** (**About Wallace's opposition to his reappointment as U.S. Attorney**) Quoted in Mary Elizabeth Sluga's masters thesis, Page 50.

OBITUARIES FOR

Johnson, E. Dana. "[H]e ruled with a rod of iron ..." Editorial Obituary. *Santa Fe New Mexican.* **May 16, 1921.** Catron Papers 801, Box 1. Quoted by Victor Westphall, *Thomas Benton Catron and His Era.* Pages 394-395. (**Hinted at tactics of "boss" Catron without using the words Santa Fe Ring**)

Pritchard, George W. "Eulogy." **May 17, 1921.** University of New Mexico Library. Center for Southwest Studies. Thomas B. Catron Papers, MSS 29, Series 104. Box 1, Folder 3. (Quoted by Victor Westphall, *Thomas Benton Catron and His Era.* Pages 393-394.)

(SEE: Stephen Benton Elkins; Santa Fe Ring, Mary Tibbles McPherson, Lincoln County War)

CHAPMAN, HUSTON INGRAM
CONTEMPORARY SOURCES (CHRONOLOGICAL)

Wallace, Lew. "I enclose you a copy of a letter from Las Vegas ..." Letter to Edward Hatch. **October 28, 1878**. Indiana Historical Society. Lew Wallace Collection. M0292. Box 3. Folder 16. (**Forwards Chapman's letter to Hatch**)

_____. "In a communication, dated October 28. inst., I requested, for reasons stated, a safe-guard for Mrs. McSween ..." Letter to Edward Hatch. **November 9, 1878**. Indiana Historical Society. Lew Wallace Collection. M0292. Box 3. Folder 17.

No Author. (signed E.). "Death of Chapman." *Las Vegas Gazette*. **March 1, 1879**. From *Proceedings of a Court of Inquiry in the Case of Lt. Col. N.A.M. Dudley (May 2,1879 – July 5, 1879)*. File No. QQ1284. (Boxes 3304, 3305, 3305A); Court Martial Files 1809-1894. Records of the Office of the Judge Advocate General – Army. Record Group 153. Old Military and Civil Branch. National Archives and Records Administration. Washington, D. C.

No Author. "Wallace and Lincoln County." Grant County *Herald*. **March 1, 1879**. Indiana Historical Society. The Papers of Lew and Susan Wallace. Microfilm Edition. Indianapolis, Indiana: Indiana Historical Society Press. 2008. (**Ridicule about Huston Chapman's murder**)

Chapman, W.W. "Yours of the 1st inst. came ..." Letter to Ira E. Leonard. **March 20, 1879**. Indiana Historical Society. Lew Wallace Collection. M0292. Box 4. Folder 6.

Rynerson, William. "The Grand Jurors for the Territory of New Mexico taken from the body of the good and lawful men of the County of Lincoln ..." Indictments of the April, Lincoln County Grand Jury. **April 28, 1879**. Herman B. Weisner Papers, ca. 1957-1992. New Mexico State University Library at Las Cruces. Rio Grande Historical Collection. Accession No. Ms 0249. Box 4/39. Folder E-Z. Folder Name: "Jessie Evans Accessory to Murder." (**Billy's testimony indicts J.J. Dolan, Billy Campbell, and Jessie Evans fulfilling his pardon bargain**)

Chapman, W.W. "Since receiving yours of the 1st March ..." Letter to Ira Leonard. **May 8, 1879**. Indiana Historical Society. Lew Wallace Collection. M0292. Box 4. Folder 10.

LETTERS BY

Chapman, Huston I. "You will please pardon me for presuming so much upon your kindness ..." Letter to Lew Wallace. **October 24, 1878**. Indiana Historical Society. Lew Wallace Collection. M0292. Box 3. Folder 16. (**Makes clear N.A.M. Dudley's danger to Susan McSween**)

_____. *'You attach much importance to the awe-inspiring influence of the military* ..." Letter to Lew Wallace. **November 25, 1878**. From Frederick Nolan, *The Lincoln County War*, p. 359.

_____. "You must pardon me for so often presuming upon your kindness ..." Letter to Lew Wallace. **November 29, 1878**. Indiana Historical Society. Lew Wallace Collection. M0292. Box 3. Folder 18.

CHISUM, JOHN SIMPSON

Hinton, Harwood P., Jr. "John Simpson Chisum, 1877-84." *New Mexico Historical Review* 31(3) (July 1956): 177 - 205; 31(4) (October 1956): 310 - 337; 32(1) (January 1957): 53 - 65.

Klasner, Lilly. Eve Ball. Ed. *My Girlhood Among Outlaws*. Tucson, Arizona: The University of Arizona Press. 1972. (**Contains John Chisum's in jail write-up about Santa Fe Ring injustices to himself**)

COE FAMILY

BIOGRAPHICAL SOURCES

Coe, George. Doyce B. Nunis, Jr. Ed. *Frontier Fighter. The Autobiography of George Coe Who Fought and Rode With Billy the Kid.* Chicago: R. R. Donnelley and Sons Company. 1984.

Coe, Wilbur. *Ranch on the Ruidoso. The Story of a Pioneer Family in New Mexico, 1871 - 1968.* New York: Alfred A. Knopf. 1968.

CONTEMPORARY SOURCES (CHRONOLOGICAL)

Coe, George. "We are two residents of Lincoln County ..." Letter written with Isaac Ellis to President Rutherford B. Hayes. **June 22, 1878**. In Angel Report papers. Microfilm File Case Number 44-4-8-3. Record Group 48. Microfilm No. M750. Roll 1. National Archives and Records Administration. U.S. Department of Justice. Washington, D.C.

CORBETT, SAMUEL R.

Corbett, Samuel R. "Deposition of Samuel R. Corbett." **March ?, 1879**. Indiana Historical Society, Lew Wallace Collection. M0292. Box 4, Folder 7.

DEDRICK BROTHERS

BIOGRAPHICAL SOURCES

Upham, Elizabeth. (Related by marriage to Daniel Dedrick). Personal interviews. 1998.
Upham, Marquita. (Relative by marriage to Daniel Dedrick). Personal interview. 1998.

CONTEMPORARY SOURCES (CHRONOLOGICAL)

Dedrick, Dan. "I have been under an arrest for six days ..." **April 5, 1879**. Letter to Lew Wallace. Indiana Historical Society. Lew Wallace Collection. M0292. Box 4. Folder 8. (**Says he was not told his arrest charges**)

No Author. "Arrests of Dedricks. Legal Documents." Herman B. Weisner Papers, ca. 1957-1992. New Mexico State University Library at Las Cruces. Rio Grande Historical Collections. Accession No. Ms 0249. Box 1. Folder B-8. Folder Name: "Lincoln County Bonds."

DOLAN, JAMES JOSEPH

BIOGRAPHICAL SOURCE

Slates, Thomas. "The James J. Dolan House, Lincoln New Mexico." *New Mexico Architecture* 11. 8/9 (1969). pp. 17-20.(**With Dolan biography**)

CONTEMPORARY SOURCES BY AND ABOUT (CHRONOLOGICAL)

Tunstall, John Henry. "A Tax-payer's Complaint, Office of John H. Tunstall, Lincoln, Lincoln Co., N.M., January 18, 1878, 'The Present Sheriff of Lincoln County Has Paid Nothing During His Present Term of Office.' Governor's Message for 1878." Mesilla *Independent*. **January 26, 1878**. Volume 1, Number 32. NewspaperArchive.com. (**Exposé of William Brady and John Riley for embezzling tax money to buy cattle; T.B. Catron then paid that bill**)

Dolan, James J. "Answer to A Taxpayer's Complaint." Mesilla *Independent*. **January 29, 1878**. (**Response to J.H. Tunstall's exposé of embezzlement of tax money to buy cattle**)

McSween, Alexander. "It looks as though the agent were the property of J.J. Dolan & J.H. Riley, known here as Dolan & Co." Letter to Secretary of Interior Carl Schurz. **February 11, 1878**. From Frederick Nolan. *The Life and Death of John Henry Tunstall*. Albuquerque, New Mexico: The University of New Mexico Press. 1965. Page 266.

Rynerson, William. "Friends Riley & Dolan, Lincoln N.M. I have just received letters from you mailed 10th inst." **February 14, 1878**. Letter to James Dolan and John Riley. Copy as Exhibit B in June 6, 1878 deposition of Alexander McSween. Frank Warner Angel report. *In the Matter of the Examination of the Causes and Circumstances of the Death of John H. Tunstall a British Subject*. Report filed October 4, 1878. Frank Warner Angel report. Interior Department Papers 1850-1907; Appointments Division and Subsequent Actions. Microfilm File Case Number 44-4-8-3. Record Group 48. Microfilm No. M750. Roll 1. National Archives and Records Administration. U.S. Department of Justice. Washington, D.C. (James J. Dolan Deposition. June 20, 1878. Pages 235-247.) (**Implying planned killing of J.H. Tunstall**)

Wilson, John, George B. Barker, Robert M. Gilbert, John Newcomb, Samuel Smith, Benjamin Ellis. "We the undersigned Justice of the Peace and Coroners Jury who sat upon the inquest held this 19th day of February 1878 on the body of John H. Tunstall ..." Coroner's Jury Report for John Tunstall. **February 19, 1878**. (**Naming as murderers, among others, James Dolan, Frank Baker, Jessie Evans, William Morton, and George Hindman**)

Wallace, Lew. "J.J. Dolan was down here tonight. Arrest him upon his return ..." Letter to Henry Carroll. **March 10, 1879**. Indiana Historical Society. Lew Wallace Collection. M0292. Box 4. Folder 4.

_____. "I beg to submit to you a list of persons whom it is necessary, in my judgment, to arrest speedily ..." Letter to Henry Carroll. **March 11, 1879**. Indiana Historical Society. Lew Wallace Collection. M0292. Box 4. Folder 5. (**Lists James Dolan, "The Kid" – William Bonney, Jessie Evans, Yginio Salazar**)

_____. "Upon reflection, I am of opinion that if Col. Dudley is really going to Fort Union ..." Letter to Henry Carroll. **March 11, 1879**. Indiana Historical Society. Lew Wallace Collection. M0292. Box 4. Folder 5. (**Advises not to send prisoners Evans, Campbell, Matthews, and Dolan to Fort Union because of N.A.M. Dudley being there**)

Rynerson, William. "The Grand Jurors for the Territory of New Mexico taken from the body of the good and lawful men of the County of Lincoln ..." Indictments of the April, Lincoln County Grand Jury. **April 28, 1879**. Herman B. Weisner Papers, ca. 1957-1992. New Mexico State University Library at Las Cruces. Rio Grande Historical Collection. Accession No. Weisner MS 249. Box 4/39. Folder E-Z. Folder Name: "Jessie Evans Accessory to Murder." (**Billy Bonney's testimony indicts J.J. Dolan, Billy Campbell, and Jessie Evans for pardon bargain**)

Purington, George Augustus. "The District Court adjourned on Thursday ..." **May 3, 1879**. Indiana Historical Society. Lew Wallace Collection. M0292. Box 4. Folder 10. (**Letter to Adjutant General on Grand Jury indictments of the Murphy-Dolans - including Dolan for the H.I. Chapman murder - and N.A.M. Dudley; copy sent to Lew Wallace**)

Wild, Azariah F. "Daily Reports of U. S. Secret Service Agents, Azariah F. Wild." Microfilm T-915. Record Group 87. Rolls 307 (January 1,1878 - June 30, 1879) and 308 (**July 1, 1879 - June 30, 1881**). National Archives and Records Department. Department of the Treasury. United States Secret Service. Washington, D. C. (**Dolan as an informer against "the Kid gang"**)

No Author. "J.A. Dolan Missing. A Well Known Lincoln County Politician Said to Have Fled the Country." *Santa Fe Daily New Mexican*. June 3, 1895. Volume 32,

Number 85. Front Page. Column 6. Library of Congress's "Chronicling America" database: https://chroniclingamerica.loc.gov. (**Accidental exposé of Dolan, while garbling him with a missing man**)

No Author. "Not James J. Dolan Missing. Senator Curry Corrects a Misleading Paragraph – James A. Not James J. Dolan Missing ..." *Santa Fe Daily New Mexican.* **June 4, 1895.** Volume 32, Number 85. Page 4. Column 3. https://chroniclingamerica.loc.gov. (**Dolan attempting to set up libel case**)

No Author. "Death of Hon. James J. Dolan. Has Been Engaged in Cattle Business in New Mexico for 30 Years - Faithful to Every Trust His Demise Sincerely Deplored." *Santa Fe New Mexican.* **March 2, 1898.** Volume 33, Number 8. Page 4. http://chroniclingamerica.loc.gov.

LETTERS BY (CHRONOLOGICAL)

LETTERS TO THOMAS BENTON CATRON (SEE THOMAS BENTON CATRON)

LETTERS TO LEW WALLACE

Dolan, James J. "On my arrival at Fort Stanton, I repeated Your Explanation &c to the Comd'g Officer (Gen'l Dudley) ..." Letter to Lew Wallace. **December 31, 1878.** Indiana Historical Society. Lew Wallace Collection. M0292. Box 3. Folder 19.

_____. "Attorney Wilson told me yesterday that 'your life was threatened' ..." Letter to Lew Wallace. **December 31, 1878.** Indiana Historical Society. Lew Wallace Collection. M0292. Box 4. Folder 7.

_____. "I hear from reliable authority that it has been reported to you that I was one of a party ..." Letter to Lew Wallace. **March 14, 1879.** Indiana Historical Society. Lew Wallace Collection. M0292. Box 4. Folder 5.

DUDLEY, NATHAN AUGUSTUS MONROE

BIOGRAPHICAL SOURCES

Heitman, Francis B. *Historical Register and Dictionary of the United States Army, From Its Organization, September 29, 1789, to March 2, 1903.* (Entry for Galusha Pennypacker, Pages 782-7830.) Washington, D.C.: Government Printing Office. 1903.

Kaye, E. Donald. *Nathan Augustus Monroe Dudley: Rogue, Hero, or Both?* Parker, Colorado: Outskirts Press, Inc. 2007.

Oliva, Leo E., *Fort Union and the Frontier Army in the Southwest.* Southwest Cultural Resource Center, Professional Papers No. 41, National Park Service, 1993, Pages 488-489, 550, 574, 624-626, 656-659 are on Dudley. (**Quoted to E. Donald Kaye from the now-lost letter of Amos Kimball: "I guess you heard that Dudley made Colonel. The army bureaucracy is like a giant cesspool, where the biggest chunks rise to the top."**)

POSSE COMITATUS ACT ISSUE FOR

No Author. *Regulations of the Army of the United States,* Washington, D.C.: Government Printing Office. 1891.

No Author. "The Army as a Posse Comitatus." *The Internal Revenue and Customs Journal.* October 14, 1878. New York: C.&F.P. Church. 1878.

MILITARY COURT OF INQUIRY FOR

Leonard, Ira E. *"Charges and specifications against Lieutenant Colonel N.A.M. Dudley, Commander at Fort Stanton, New Mexico."* **March 4, 1879.** Letter to Secretary of War George McCrary. *Proceedings of a Court of Inquiry in the Case of Lt. Col.*

N.A.M. Dudley (May 2,1879 - July 5, 1879). File No. QQ1284. (Boxes 3304, 3305, 3305A); Court Martial Files 1809-1894. Records of the Office of the Judge Advocate General - Army. Record Group 153. Old Military and Civil Branch. National Archives and Records Administration. Washington, D. C. (**Charges against Dudley for murders of A.A. McSween and H.I. Chapman and arson of McSween's house**)

No Author. *Proceedings of a Court of Inquiry in the Case of Lt. Col. N.A.M. Dudley (May 2,1879 – July 5, 1879)*. File No. QQ1284. (Boxes 3304, 3305, 3305A); Court Martial Files 1809-1894. Records of the Office of the Judge Advocate General - Army. Record Group 153. Old Military and Civil Branch. National Archives and Records Administration. Washington, D. C.

OTHER CONTEMPORARY SOURCES FOR (CHRONOLOGICAL)

Dudley, Nathan Augustus Monroe. "I avail myself of the opportunity to send this in advance of the next mail by Mr. Dolan ..." Letter to Assistant Adjutant General of New Mexico. **September 29, 1878**. Indiana Historical Society. Lew Wallace Collection. M0292. Box 3. Folder 14. (**Outlaw propaganda to distract from Ring activity in Lincoln County**)

Loud, John S. "In compliance with instructions of the General Commanding ..." **October 27, 1878**. Letter to N.A.M. Dudley. Indiana Historical Society. Lew Wallace Collection. M0292. Box 3. Folder 16. (**Order for troops to arrest outlaws per the request of the Secretary of War**)

Dudley, Nathan Augustus Monroe. "I am in receipt of a copy of letter written by one H.I. Chapman, calling himself the Attorney ..." **November 9, 1878**. Letter to Lew Wallace. From *Proceedings of a Court of Inquiry in the Case of Lt. Col. N.A.M. Dudley (May 2,1879 – July 5, 1879)*. File No. QQ1284. (Boxes 3304, 3305, 3305A); Court Martial Files 1809-1894. Records of the Office of the Judge Advocate General – Army. Record Group 153. Old Military and Civil Branch. National Archives and Records Administration. Washington, D.C. (**Forwarding the Susan McSween affidavits in answer to the charges made by Chapman**)

Wallace, Lew. "I am in receipt of Col. Dudley's reply to the charges against him ..." Letter to Edward Hatch. **November 14, 1878**. Indiana Historical Society. Lew Wallace Collection. M0292. Box 3. Folder 17. (**Has quote: "the "reply is perfectly satisfactory"**)

_____. "Your favor containing the duplicate accounts of the messenger who posted the President's Proclamation ..." Letter to N.A.M. Dudley. **November 30, 1878**. Indiana Historical Society. Lew Wallace Collection. M0292. Box 3. Folder 18.

_____. "I am constrained to request that Lieut Col. N.A.M. Dudley, Commanding at Fort Stanton, be relieved ..." Letter to Edward Hatch. **December 7, 1878**. Indiana Historical Society. Lew Wallace Collection. M0292. Box 3. Folder 18. (**Removal of Dudley requested**)

Dudley, Nathan Augustus Monroe. "An Open Letter, By Lieut. Col. N.A.M. Dudley, 9th Cavalry, to His Excellency Governor Lew Wallace." Letter to Lew Wallace. Santa Fe *Weekly New Mexican*. **December 14, 1878**. Reprinted in *Mesilla News*. December 21, 1878. As Exhibit 13 from *Proceedings of a Court of Inquiry in the Case of Lt. Col. N.A.M. Dudley (May 2,1879 – July 5, 1879)*. File No. QQ1284. (Boxes 3304, 3305, 3305A); Court Martial Files 1809-1894. Records of the Office of the Judge Advocate General – Army. Record Group 153. Old Military and Civil Branch. National Archives and Records Administration. Washington, D.C. (**Attacks Wallace's Amnesty Proclamation as applying to the military**)

Wallace, Lew. "The public interests with which I am officially charged make it in my judgment ..." **December 16, 1878**. Letter to N.A.M. Dudley and other Fort Stanton officers. Indiana Historical Society. Lew Wallace Collection. M0292. Box 3. Folder 19.

_____. "I have the honor to report that affairs of the Territory are moving on quietly ..." Letter to Carl Schurz. **December 21, 1878**. Indiana Historical Society. Lew Wallace Collection. M0292. Box 3, Folder 19. (**Mentions N.A.M. Dudley's indignation about the Amnesty Proclamation**)

_____. "I have the honor to repeat the request made on a former occasion that Lt. Col. N.A.M. Dudley be relieved of the command ..." Letter to Edward Hatch. **March 7, 1879**. Indiana Historical Society. Lew Wallace Collection. M0292. Box 4, Folder 4.

Hatch, Edward. "Lieutenant Colonel N.A.M. Dudley is hereby relieved from command and duty ..." Special Field Order 2. **March 8, 1879**. Indiana Historical Society. Lew Wallace Collection. M0292. Box 4, Folder 4. (**Wallace succeeds in removing Dudley**)

Wallace, Lew. "I have official information that a court of inquiry for Col. Dudley has been ordered ..." Letter to Carl Schurz. **April 4, 1879**. Indiana Historical Society. Lew Wallace Collection. M0292. Box 4. Folder 8.

Purington, George Augustus. "The District Court adjourned on Thursday ..." **May 3, 1879**. Indiana Historical Society. Lew Wallace Collection. M0292. Box 4. Folder 10. (**Letter to Adjutant General on Grand Jury indictments of the Murphy-Dolans and N.A.M. Dudley; copy sent to Lew Wallace**)

No Author. Verdict on Civil Cause 298 for arson of Susan McSween's house. *Mesilla News*. **December 6, 1879**. Unpublished. personal communication from Frederick Nolan. July 29, 2005. (**Dudley exonerated**)

ELKINS, STEPHEN BENTON

BIOGRAPHICAL SOURCES

Cleaveland, Norman, *A Synopsis of the Great New Mexico Cover-up*. Self-printed. 1989.

_____. *The Great Santa Fe Cover-up. Based on a Talk given Before the Santa Fe Historical Society on November 1, 1978*. Self-printed. 1982.

_____. *The Morleys - Young Upstarts on the Southwest Frontier*. Albuquerque, New Mexico: Calvin Horn Publisher, Inc. 1971.

Dodge, Andrew R. and Betty K. Koed, eds. *Biographical Directory of the United States Congress 1774-2005*. Washington D.C.: United States Printing Office. 2005.

Gates, Merril E. *Men of Mark in America*. Washington D.C.: Men of Mark Publishing Company. 1905. (Pages 315-317)

Lamar, Howard Robert N. *The Far Southwest 1846 – 1912: A Territorial History*. New Haven and London: Yale University Press. 1966. (**Chapter 6 on Santa Fe Ring**))

Lambert, Oscar Doane. *Stephen Benton Elkins. American Foursquare*. Pittsburgh, Pennsylvania: University of Pittsburg Press. 1955.

Montoya, María E. *Translating Property. The Maxwell Land Grant and the Conflict Over Land in the American West, 1840-1900*. Berkeley and Los Angeles: University of California Press. 2002.

Spears, Jae. "Stephen Benton Elkins." e-WV: *The West Virginia Encyclopedia*. January 14, 2016. https://www.wvencyclopedia.org/articles/2199.

Taylor, Morris F. *O.P. McMains and the Maxwell Land Grant Conflict*. Tucson, Arizona: The University of Arizona Press. 1979. (**Traces origins of the Santa Fe Ring with T.B. Catron and S.B. Elkins**)

Westphall, Victor. *Thomas Benton Catron and His Era*. Tucson, Arizona: University of Arizona Press. 1973.

EXPOSÉS OF (SEE: William Raymond Morley, Frank Springer Deposition, Mary Tibbles McPherson)

SECRET CODE WITH CATRON (SEE Thomas Benton Catron)

LETTERS TO, FROM, ABOUT (SEE: Thomas Benton Catron)

TO PRESIDENT RUTHERFORD B. HAYES

Elkins, Stephen Benton. "Axtell Gov. New Mexico: A strong protest against his removal by S.B. Elkins who says the charges against him are vague & irresponsible." To the President. **June 11, 1877.** Microfilm File Case Number 44-4-8-3. Record Group 48. Microfilm No. M750. Roll 1. National Archives and Records Administration. U.S. Department of Justice. Washington, D.C. (**Against removal of Ringite Governor S.B. Axtell**)

_____. "To the President. Referring to a conversation had with you last week ... " Letter to President Rutherford B. Hayes. **March 17, 1881.** (Received Executive Mansion April 6, 1881). Microfilm Roll M750. National Archives and Records Administration. Record Group 48. Microfilm Case File Number 44-4-8-3. U.S. Department of Interior. Washington, D.C. (**Reappointing Axtell**)

FROM JAMES JOSEPH DOLAN

Dolan, James J. "Will you do me the kindness to send me a personal letter to S.B. Elkins ..." Letter to T.B. Catron. **October 15, 1891.** University of New Mexico Library. Center for Southwest Studies. Thomas B. Catron Papers, MSS 29, Series 102, Box 12, Folder 2.

FROM HENRY L. WALDO

Waldo, Henry L. "My most loved friend, Yours under date of ..." **May 9, 18 —.** Letter to S.B. Elkins. West Virginia & Regional History Center. West Virginia University Libraries, Morgantown, West Virginia. Stephen B. Elkins Papers (A&M 53). Box 1, Folder 1.

_____. "My Dear Steve, Yours of July 15th ..." **February 18, 1866.** Letter to S.B. Elkins. West Virginia & Regional History Center. West Virginia University Libraries, Morgantown, West Virginia. Stephen B. Elkins Papers (A&M 53). Box 1, Folder 1. (**Hinting at wanting a law firm position**)

FROM WILLIAM BREEDEN

Breeden, William. "I read your speech yesterday ..." **May 31, 1874.** Letter to S.B. Elkins. West Virginia & Regional History Center. West Virginia University Libraries, Morgantown, West Virginia. Stephen B. Elkins Papers (A&M 53). Box 1, Folder 1.

ACTING FOR ANGEL REPORT AND CATRON'S DISMISSAL BY

Elkins, Stephen Benton. "Asking delay of action upon charges against U.S. Atty. Catron ..." Letter about Angel Report. **September 24, 1878.** Angel Report. Microfilm File Case No. 44-4-8-3. Record Group 48. National Records and Archives Administration. Microfilm No. M750. Roll 1. U.S. Department of Justice. Washington, D. C.

_____. "Regarding Attorney General's decision on T.B. Catron." Letter. **September___, 1878.** Angel Report. Microfilm File Case No. 44-4-8-3. Record Group 48. National Records and Archives Administration. Microfilm No. M750. Roll 1. U.S. Department of Justice. Washington, D.C.

_____. "Relative to resignation of T. B. Catron U. S. Attorney." Letter. **November 10, 1878.** Angel Report. Microfilm File Case No. 44-4-8-3. Record Group 48. National Records and Archives Administration. Microfilm No. M750. Roll 1. U.S. Department of Justice. Washington, D. C.

Devens, Charles. "To honorable S. B. Elkins re. T. B. Catron continuing to act as U.S. Attorney." Letter to Stephen B. Elkins. **November 12, 1878.** Angel Report. Microfilm File Case No. 44-4-8-3. Record Group 48. National Records and Archives Administration. Microfilm No. M750. Roll 1. U.S. Department of Justice. Washington, D. C.

Elkins, Stephen Benton. "I have waited some time to reply to your lengthy letter ..." Letter to T.B. Catron. **August 15, 1879**. West Virginia & Regional History Center. West Virginia University Libraries, Morgantown, W. Va. Stephen B. Elkins Papers (A&M 53). Box 1. Folder 1. (**Reveals he prevented Catron's dismissal and indictment from Angel's report**)

ATTEMPTING REINSTATEMENT OF S.B. AXTELL BY

Elkins, Stephen Benton. "To the President. Referring to a conversation had with you last week ... Hon S. Elkins favors appointment Axtell, Ex Gov. as Gov'r of New Mexico". Letter to President James Abram Garfield. **March 17, 1881**. (Received Executive Mansion April 6, 1881). Interior Department Papers 1850-1907; Appointments Division and Subsequent Actions. Microfilm Roll M750. National Archives and Records Administration Record Group 48. Microfilm Case Number 44-4-8-3. U.S. Department of Interior. Washington D.C. (**Requesting S.B. Axtell reappointment as Territorial New Mexico Governor**)

_____. "I trouble you to say a word in behalf of Gov. Axtell ..." Letter to President Rutherford B. Hayes. **June 11, 1877**. (Referred by direction of President to the Secretary of the Interior June 13, 1877.) Interior Department Papers 1850-1907; Appointments Division and Subsequent Actions. Microfilm File Case No. 44-4-8-3. Record Group 48. National Records and Archives Administration. Microfilm No. M750. Roll 1. U.S. Department of Justice. Washington, D. C.

ARTICLES ABOUT (CHRONOLOGICAL)

No Author. " 'The Territory of Elkins.' Assassination of Supposed Sun Correspondent. The Murder of the Rev. F.J. Tolby in New Mexico. A Probate Judge Accused of Complicity in the Crime. Indignation Meeting." *New York Weekly Sun*. **December 22, 1875**. Interior Department Papers 1850-1907; Appointments Division and Subsequent Actions. Microfilm Roll M750. National Archives and Records Administration. Record Group 48. Microfilm Case File Number 44-4-8-3. U. S. Department of Interior. Washington, D.C. (**In May 1, 1877 complaint to President Hayes as "Mary E. McPherson and W.B. Matchett 'Make certain charges against the U.S. Officials in the Territory of New Mexico.' "**)

No Author. "Elkins would probably have been Garfield's Secretary of the Interior ..." *New York Sun*. **June 13, 1881**. Quoted by Oscar Doane Lambert. *Stephen Benton Elkins: American Foursquare*. Page 89. (**Political influence of**)

No Author. "Our Own Dear Steve, How Elkins Made His Influence Felt in New Mexico – The Ring in Which a Judge Figured – Politics in 1870. *Las Vegas Daily Optic*. **September 2, 1884**. (Reprinted from the *Omaha Herald*) Front Page. Volume V, Number 258, Column 4. Newspaperarchive.com. (**Exposing Elkins, Catron, and Palen in the 1872 Legislature Revolt.**)

Faulkner, C.J. "I will tell you the secret of Elkins' political as well as business success." Baltimore, Maryland *The Sun*. **December 17, 1891**. Quoted by Oscar Doane Lambert. *Stephen Benton Elkins: American Foursquare*. Page 141. (**Elkins's success from loyalty to friends**)

No Author. "T.B. Catron's reputation now being "smirched" by evidence that he was a briber and too dishonest even to practice law ..." *Las Vegas Independent Democrat*. **1895**; quoting from *Las Vegas Optic*. September 2, 1884. From Victor Westphall. *Thomas Benton Catron and His Era*. Pages 105-106. (**About Catron's and Elkins's dishonesty, the Ring, and disbarring Catron**)

No Author. "It seems that Senator Elkins was one of the five stockholders in the North American Commercial Company that had leased from the United States the sea Islands of Alaska." Cincinnati, Ohio *Commercial Tribune*. **June 8, 1897**. Quoted by Oscar Doane Lambert. *Stephen Benton Elkins: American Foursquare*. Pages 224-225. (**Elkins's tax violation cover-up**)

No Author. "He is the biggest man ... the State of West Virginia has ever had in the Senate of the United States." West Virginia *St. Mary's Journal.* **June 22, 1906.** From Oscar Doane Lambert. *Stephen Benton Elkins.* Page 286.

ELLIS, ISAAC

Ellis, Isaac. "We are two residents of Lincoln County ..." Letter written with George Coe to President Rutherford B. Hayes. **June 22, 1878.** In Angel Report papers. Microfilm File Case Number 44-4-8-3. Record Group 48. Microfilm No. M750. Roll 1. National Archives and Records Administration. U.S. Department of Justice. Washington, D.C.

_____. Affidavit of Isaac Ellis. **March ?, 1879.** Indiana Historical Society. Lew Wallace Collection. M0292. Box 4, Folder 7.

EVANS, JESSIE

BIOGRAPHICAL SOURCE

McCright, Grady E. and James H. Powell. *Jessie Evans: Lincoln County Badman.* College Station, Texas: Creative Publishing Company. 1983.

CONTEMPORARY SOURCES (CHRONOLOGICAL)

Wilson, John, George B. Barker, Robert M. Gilbert, John Newcomb, Samuel Smith, Benjamin Ellis. "We the undersigned Justice of the Peace and Coroners Jury who sat upon the inquest held this 19th day of February 1878 on the body of John H. Tunstall ..." Coroner's Jury Report for John Tunstall. **February 19, 1878.** (**Naming as murderers, among others, James Dolan, Frank Baker, Jessie Evans, William Morton, and George Hindman**)

Wallace, Lew. "I have information that William Campbell, J.B. Matthews, and Jesse Evans were of the party engaged in the killing ..." Letter to Edward Hatch. **March 5, 1879.** Indiana Historical Society. Lew Wallace Collection. M0292. Box 4, Folder 4. (**Murder of Huston Chapman**)

_____. "Under the circumstances, particularly in the absence here of suitable cells for safekeeping of Jesse Evans, Jacob B. Matthews and William Campbell ..." Letter to Henry Carroll. **March 10, 1879.** Indiana Historical Society. Lew Wallace Collection. M0292. Box 4. Folder 4.

_____. "Upon reflection, I am of opinion that if Col. Dudley is really going to Fort Union ..." Letter to Henry Carroll. **March 11, 1879.** Indiana Historical Society. Lew Wallace Collection. M0292. Box 4. Folder 5. (**Advises not to send Evans, Campbell, Matthews, and Dolan to Fort Union because of N.A.M. Dudley being there**)

_____. "I beg to submit to you a list of persons whom it is necessary, in my judgment, to arrest ..." Letter to Henry Carroll. **March 11, 1879.** Indiana Historical Society. Lew Wallace Collection. M0292. Box 4. Folder 5. (**Lists Jessie Evans, "The Kid" – William Bonney, Yginio Salazar**)

_____. "Be good enough to send word to all your men to turn out soon as possible ..." Letter to Juan Patrón. **March 19, 1879.** Indiana Historical Society. Lew Wallace Collection. M0292. Box 4. Folder 6. (**Reports escape of Jessie Evans and Billy Campbell from Fort Stanton; $1000 reward**)

_____. "With Evans and Campbell at large ..." Letter to Henry Carroll. **March 19, 1879.** Indiana Historical Society. Lew Wallace Collection. M0292. Box 4. Folder 6.

Rynerson, William. "Indictments of the April, Lincoln County Grand Jury." **April 28, 1879.** Herman B. Weisner Papers, ca. 1957-1992. New Mexico State University Library at Las Cruces. Rio Grande Historical Society Collection. Accession No. Ms 0249. Box 4/39. Folder E-Z. Folder Name: "Jessie Evans Accessory to Murder." (**Billy's testimony indicts Dolan, Campbell, and Evans for his pardon**)

Purington, George Augustus. "The District Court adjourned on Thursday ..." **May 3, 1879**. Indiana Historical Society. Lew Wallace Collection. M0292. Box 4. Folder 10. (**Letter to Adjutant General on Grand Jury indictments of the Murphy-Dolans - including Evans for the H.I. Chapman murder - and N.A.M. Dudley; copy sent to Lew Wallace**)

No Author. "Charges against Jessie Evans and John Kinney." Doña Ana County Criminal Docket Book. **August 18, 1875 to November 7, 1878**. Herman B. Weisner Papers, ca. 1957-1992. New Mexico State University Library at Las Cruces. Rio Grande Historical Collections. Accession No. Ms 0249. Box No. 13. Folder V3. Folder Name: "Venue, Change of."

FOUNTAIN, ALBERT JENNINGS

BIBLIOGRAPHICAL SOURCE

Gibson, A. M. *The Life and Death of Colonel Albert Jennings Fountain.* Norman: University of Oklahoma Press. 1965.

CONTEMPORARY SOURCES (CHRONOLOGICAL)

Fountain, Albert Jennings, Attorney and J.D. Bail. "Instructions Asked for by Defendants Counsel. April 9, 1881. Herman B. Weisner Papers, ca. 1957-1992. New Mexico State University Library at Las Cruces. Rio Grande Historical Society Collection. Accession No. Ms 0249. Box 1. Folder 14-D. Folder Name: "Billy the Kid Legal Documents."

_____. "Please send me this case ..." Telegram to T.B. Catron. **September 16, 1890**. University of New Mexico Library. Center for Southwest Studies. Thomas B. Catron Papers. MSS 29, Series 102, Box 8, Folder 5.

FRITZ FAMILY (EMIL AND CHARLES FRITZ AND EMILIE FRITZ SCHOLAND)

Fritz, Charles. Affidavit of **September 18, 1876** claiming that Emil Fritz had a will. Probate Court Record. (private collection)

_____. Affidavit of **September 26, 1876** Authorizing Alexander McSween to Receive Payments for the Emil Fritz Estate. Probate Court Record. (private collection)

Scholand, Emilie and Charles Fritz. Affidavit of **September 26, 1876** appointing McSween to collect debts for the Emil Fritz Estate. Copied from the original District Court Record. (private collection)

Fritz, Charles. Affidavit of **December 7, 1877** to order Alexander McSween to pay the Emil Fritz insurance policy money. Probate Court Record. (private collection)

Scholand, Emilie. Affidavit of **December 21, 1877** Accusing Alexander McSween of Embezzlement. Copied from the original District Court Record. (private collection)

Bristol Warren. "Writ of Embezzlement." **December 21, 1877**. Herman B. Weisner Papers, ca. 1957-1992. New Mexico State University Library at Las Cruces. Rio Grande Historical Collections. Accession No. Ms 0249. Box 10. Folder M-13. Folder Name. "Will and Testament A. McSween." (**Emilie Fritz Scholand's sworn complaint against Alexander McSween**)

Fritz, Charles. Affidavit sworn before John Crouch, Clerk of Doña Ana District Court, for Writ of Attachment issued against property of Alexander A. McSween. Probate Court Record. **February 6, 1878**. (private collection)

_____ and Emilie Scholand. Attachment Bond sworn before John Crouch, Clerk of Doña Ana District Court, against Alexander A. McSween for indebtedness to them. **February 6, 1878**. (private collection).

No Author. Diagram showing parcels of land to each of the heirs of Emil Fritz. Herman B. Weisner Papers, ca. 1957-1992. New Mexico State University Library at Las Cruces. Rio Grande Historical Collections. Accession No. Ms 0249. Box P1. Folder 11. Folder Name. "Charles Fritz Estate."

GARRETT, PATRICK FLOYD

BIBLIOGRAPHICAL SOURCES

Garrett, Pat F. *The Authentic Life of Billy the Kid The Noted Desperado of the Southwest, Whose Deeds of Daring and Blood Made His Name a Terror in New Mexico, Arizona, and Northern Mexico.* Santa Fe, New Mexico: New Mexico Printing and Publishing Co. 1882.

Metz, Leon C. *Pat Garrett. The Story of a Western Lawman.* Norman: University of Oklahoma Press. 1974.

Mullin, Robert N. "Killing of Joe Briscoe." Letter to Eve Ball. January 31, 1964. (Unpublished). Binder RNM, VI, H. Nita Stewart Haley Memorial Museum. Haley Library. Midland, Texas.

———. "Pat Garrett. Two Forgotten Killings." *Password.* X(2) (Summer 1965). pp. 57 - 65.

———. "Skelton Glen's Manuscript Entitled 'Pat Garrett As I Knew Him on the Buffalo Ranges.'" (Unpublished). Binder RNM, III B, 20. Nita Stewart Haley Memorial Museum. Haley Library. Midland, Texas.

CONTEMPORARY SOURCES (CHRONOLOGICAL)

Wild, Azariah F. "Daily Reports of U. S. Secret Service Agents, Azariah F. Wild." Microfilm T-915. Record Group 87. Rolls 306 (June 15, 1877 - December 31, 1877), 307 (January 1,1878 - June 30, 1879), 308 (**July 1, 1879 - June 30, 1881**), 309 (July 1, 1881 - September 30, 1883), 310 (October 1, 1883 - July 31, 1886). National Archives and Records Department. Department of the Treasury. United States Secret Service. Washington, D. C. (**Aiding Garrett's capture of Billy**)

(SEE: Thomas Benton Catron communications about his pursuit of Oliver Lee)

GAUSS, GOTTFRIED

Gauss, Gottfried. Interview with *Lincoln County Leader*. **November 21, 1889.** (**About Billy Bonney's Lincoln jailbreak**)

GIDDINGS, MARSH

CONTEMPORARY SOURCES (CHRONOLOGICAL)

No Author. *Diario del Consejo der Territorio de Neuvo Mejico, Session de 1871-1872. Santa Fe New Mexican.* **January 8, 1872.** Santa Fe: A.P. Sullivan. 1872. Pages 144-154. New Mexico Supreme Court Library. Santa Fe, New Mexico. (**Confirms Giddings's use of troops for Ring suppression in 1872 Legislature Revolt**)

No Author. *Diario del Consejo der Territorio de Neuvo Mejico, Session de 1871-1872.* Las Cruces *Borderer.* **January 24, 1872.** Pages 110-113. (**President of the Council Don Diego Archuleta gives speech objecting to Giddings's bringing troops into legislature**)

No Author. *Journal of the House of Representatives of the Territory of New Mexico, Session of 1871-1872.* Santa Fe: A.P. Sullivan. **1872.** (**Covers 1872 Legislature Revolt: Pages 86-91 on Giddings's veto of House acts; Pages 144-154 on Giddings's use of troops for suppression**)

Catron, Thomas B., M.A. Breeden, William Breeden, José D. Sena, J.G. Palen, T.F. Conway. "We have just learned that the character of the Adjutant General of New Mexico has been attacked at Washington ..." Letter to Senator Thomas W. Ferry. **March 26, 1873.** Interior Department Papers 1850-1907; Appointments Division and Subsequent Actions. Microfilm File Case Number 44-4-8-3. Record

Group 48. Microfilm No. M750. Roll 1. National Archives and Records Administration. U.S. Department of Justice. Washington, D.C. (**Ringmen supporting Marsh Giddings's appointing his son as Adjutant General**)

Gallegos, Jose M. "My people are extremely anxious to have Governor Giddings removed as Governor ..." Letter to President Ulysses S. Grant. **March 13, 1873**. Interior Department Papers 1850-1907; Appointments Division and Subsequent Actions. Microfilm File Case Number 44-4-8-3. Record Group 48. Microfilm No. M750. Roll 1. National Archives and Records Administration. U.S. Department of Justice. Washington, D.C. (**Movement to remove Governor Marsh Giddings**)

Giddings, Marsh. "A transfer of Territorial officers from the State Dept. to the Dept of the interior ..." Letter to Secretary of the Interior. **April 3, 1873**. Interior Department Papers 1850-1907; Appointments Division and Subsequent Actions. Microfilm File Case Number 44-4-8-3. Record Group 48. Microfilm No. M750. Roll 1. National Archives and Records Administration. U.S. Department of Justice. Washington, D.C. (**Responses to charges against him**)

_____. "By the enactment of these laws in the last two days of the session our securities doubled in value within six months ..." Letter to Secretary of the Interior. **April 20, 1873**. Interior Department Papers 1850-1907; Appointments Division and Subsequent Actions. Microfilm File Case Number 44-4-8-3. Record Group 48. Microfilm No. M750. Roll 1. National Archives and Records Administration. U.S. Department of Justice. Washington, D.C. (**About charges**)

_____. "I have the honor to inform you that ... there have been disturbances between the Mexicans and Texans ..." Letter to Secretary of Interior C. Delano. **January 12, 1874**. Interior Department Papers 1850-1907; Appointments Division and Subsequent Actions. Microfilm File Case Number 44-4-8-3. Record Group 48. Microfilm No. M750. Roll 1. National Archives and Records Administration. U.S. Department of Justice. Washington, D.C. (**Creating outlaw myth to justify military intervention against Ring opponents**)

GILBERT, ROBERT M.

Gilbert, Robert M. Letter to Lew Wallace. **June 1, 1879**. Collection Indiana Historical Society. Lew Wallace Collection. M0292. Box 4, Folder 11.

HAYES, RUTHERFORD BIRCHARD

BIOGRAPHICAL SOURCES

Davison, Kenneth E. *The Presidency of Rutherford B. Hayes*. Westport, Connecticut: Greenwood Press, Inc. 1972.

Hoogenboom, Ari. *Rutherford B. Hayes. Warrior and President*. Lawrence, Kansas: University Press of Kansas. 1995.

Mullin, Robert N. Re: Frank Warner Angel Meeting With President Hayes August, 1878. Binder RNM, VI, M. (Unpublished). Midland, Texas: Nita Stewart Haley Memorial Library and J. Evetts Haley History Center. (Undated).

Williams, Charles Richard. *The Life of Rutherford Birchard Hayes. Nineteenth President of the United States. Vol. I*. Boston and New York: Houghton Mifflin Co. 1914.

_____. The Life of Rutherford Birchard Hayes. Nineteenth President of the United States. Vol. II. Boston and New York: Houghton Mifflin Co. 1914.

PROCLAMATION BY

Hayes, Rutherford B. "By the President of the United States of America: A Proclamation." **October 7, 1878**. Indiana Historical Society. Lew Wallace Collection. OMB 0023. Box 1. Folder 1; and Senate Documents. 67th Congress. 2nd Session. December 5, 1921 - September 22, 1922. Washington: Government Printing Office. 1922.

LETTERS TO

Leverson, Montague R. "His Excellency Rutherford B. Hayes. President of the United States. Excellency! Since my last letter to your Excellency on the state of affairs in this Territory ..." Letter to Rutherford B. Hayes. **March 16, 1878.** Microfilm Roll M750. National Archives and Records Administration. Record Group 60. Microfilm Case No. 44-4-8-3. U.S. Department of Interior. Washington, D.C

Isaacs, J. and J. N. Coe. "We are two residents of Lincoln Co. who after incurring the greatest peril at the hands of thieves and murderers when the Governor and the U.S. troops aided ..." Letter to Rutherford B. Hayes. **June 22, 1878.** Frank Warner Angel File. Microfilm Roll M750. National Archives and Records Administration. Record Group 60. Microfilm Case Number 44-4-8-3. U.S. Department of Interior. Washington, D.C.

McSween, A. A. "The undersigned have the Honor of transmitting you as requested a copy of the proceeds of a meeting held by the Citizens of Lincoln County, N. Mex. relative to the late troubles ..." Letter to Rutherford B. Hayes. **April 26,1878.** Frank Warner Angel File. Microfilm Roll M750. National Archives and Records Administration. Record Group 060. Microfilm Case Number 44-4-8-3. U.S. Department of Interior. Washington, D.C.

Elkins, Stephen B. "To the President referring to a conversation ..." Letter titled "Hon. S. R. Elkins favors appointment Axtell, ExGov. as Gov'r of New Mexico. **March 23, 1881.** (Received Executive Mansion April 6, 1881) Microfilm Roll M750. National Archives and Records Administration. Record Group 60. Microfilm Case File Number 44-4-8-3. U.S. Department of Interior. Washington, D.C.

LETTERS TO AND FROM LEW WALLACE

Wallace, Lew. "I avail myself of your request this morning. It is hardly necessary to give reasons for a preference of the Italian mission ..." Letter to Rutherford B. Hayes. **March 9, 1877.** Indiana Historical Society. Lew Wallace Collection. M0292. Box 3. Folder 13. (**Desired ambassadorships**)

_____. "The feuds recently in Lincoln county, New Mexico, left a large many thieves and murderers, who, with others of like class since added to their number, are now confederated for plunder." Letter to Rutherford B. Hayes. **March 31, 1879.** Indiana Historical Society. Lew Wallace Collection. M0292. Box 4. Folder 7. (**Wants martial law against confederacy of outlaws**)

Hayes, Rutherford B. "We are greatly obliged by your kindness." Letter to Lew Wallace. **January 9, 1881.** Indiana Historical Society. Lew Wallace Collection. M0292. Box 4. Folder 16. (**Thanking for gift of Ben-Hur**)

HOYT, HENRY F.

AUTOBIOGRAPHICAL SOURCE

Hoyt, Henry. *A Frontier Doctor*. Boston and New York: Houghton Mifflin Company. 1929. (**Describes Billy's superior abilities, pp. 93-94.**)

CONTEMPORARY SOURCES (CHRONOLOGICAL)

Bonney, William H. Bill of Sale to Henry Hoyt. **October 24, 1878.** Collection of Panhandle-Plains Historical Museum. Canyon, Texas. (Item No. X1974-98/1)

Hoyt, Henry F. "This time it is me who is apologizing for the long delay in answering ..." Letter to Lew Wallace Jr. (Lew Wallace's grandson) **April 27, 1927.** Indiana Historical Society. Lew Wallace Collection. M0292. Box 14, Folder 11.

_____. "Copy of a bill of sale written by Wm H. Bonney ..." Letter to Lew Wallace Jr. **April 27, 1927.** Indiana Historical Society. Lew Wallace Collection. M0292. Box 14, Folder 11.

HUBBARD, JOHN G.

Hubbard, John G. "Herewith I hand you an extract from one of our N.M. papers relative to Gov Axtell of New Mexico to which I would draw your especial attention ..." Letter to President Rutherford B. Hayes. **August 1, 1878.** In Angel Report papers. Microfilm File Case Number 44-4-8-3. Record Group 48. Microfilm No. M750. Roll 1. National Archives and Records Administration. U.S. Department of Justice. Washington, D.C.

HUGHES, THOMAS

History of New Mexico: Its Resources and People. Volume 1. Pages 471-472. Los Angeles: Pacific States Publishing Company. 1907.

Keleher, William A. *Memoirs: Episodes in New Mexico History 1892-1969.* Pages 29-30. Santa Fe: Sunstone Press. 2008.

JUÁREZ, BENITO

Parkes, Henry Bamford. *A History of Mexico.* Boston: Houghton Mifflin Co. 1969. Page 261. (**Quote about "the tremendous judgment of history"**)

KIMBRELL, GEORGE

Kimbrell, George. "I have the honor to request that you will furnish me a posse ..." Letter to Lieutenant Millard Filmore Goodwin. **February 20, 1879.** Indiana Historical Society. Lew Wallace Collection. Box 4, Folder 3.

KINNEY, JOHN

BIOGRAPHICAL SOURCE

Mullin, Robert N. "Here Lies John Kinney." *Journal of Arizona History.* 14 (Autumn 1973). Pages 223 - 242.

CONTEMPORARY SOURCES (CHRONOLOGICAL)

No Author. "Charges against Jessie Evans and John Kinney." Doña Ana County Criminal Docket Book. **August 18, 1875 to November 7, 1878.** Herman Weisner Collection. New Mexico State University Library at Las Cruces. Rio Grande Historical Collections. Accession No. Ms 0249. Box 13. Folder V-3. Folder Name: "Venue, Change of."

No Author. "Obituary of John Kinney." *Prescott Courier.* **August 30, 1919**. Obituary Section.

No Author. Obituary. "Over the Range Goes Another Pioneer." *Journal Miner.* Tuesday Morning, **August 26, 1919**.

No Author. "Captain Kinney Dead." *The Daily Arizona Silver Belt.* August 29, 1919. Page 2. NewspaperArchive.com.

KISTLER, RUSSELL A.

LETTERS ABOUT

Elston, J.A. "Mr. Kistler of the "Optic" of Las Vegas, your territory, referred me to you ..." Letter to T.B. Catron. **December 16, 1889.** University of New Mexico Library. Center for Southwest Studies. Thomas B. Catron Papers, MSS 29, Series 102, Box 5, Folder 4.

Mills, William J. "Kistler has been in to see me ..." Letter to T.B. Catron. **December 12, 1891.** University of New Mexico Library. Center for Southwest Studies. Thomas B. Catron Papers, MSS 29, Series 102, Box 12, Folder 6. (**About a boycott attempting to have Kistler removed from the *Optic***)

Gould, George T. "Replying to yours of a recent date ..." Letter to T.B. Catron. **August 19, 1899.** University of New Mexico Library. Center for Southwest Studies. Thomas B. Catron Papers, MSS 29, Series 103, Box 8, Folder 3. (**Confirming that Frank Springer, among others, bought Kistler's *Optic***)

BILLY THE KID ARTICLES BY (SEE: William H. Bonney's *Las Vegas Optic* articles)

KOOGLER, JOHN H.
LETTERS ABOUT AND FROM

Koogler, John H. "Affidavit of publication." **March 9, 1876.** University of New Mexico Library. Center for Southwest Studies. Thomas B. Catron Papers, MSS 29, Series 103, Box 26, Folder 2. (**For case with Catron representing the plaintiffs.**)

Wilcox, Lucius "Lute" M. (city editor; owner, J.H. Koogler). "The Kid. Interview with Billy Bonney The Best Known Man in New Mexico." *Las Vegas Gazette.* **December 28, 1880.** (**Has Billy Bonney's quote that "the laugh's on me this time"**)

_____. Interview, at train depot. *Las Vegas Gazette.* **December 28, 1880.** (**Has Billy Bonney's "adios" quote.**)

Catron, Thomas Benton. "Paid Koogler for Paper & advertisement ..." **August 14, 1881.** Pocket notebook kept by T.B. Catron. University of New Mexico Library. Center for Southwest Studies. Thomas B. Catron Papers, MSS 29, Series 804, Box 1. (**Demonstrating Catron's paying *Las Vegas Gazette* editor, J.H. Koogler, who published Ring-biased articles on Billy the Kid**)

Koogler, John H. "I will start for Kansas City to-morrow ..." Letter to T.B. Catron. **July 17, 1889.** University of New Mexico Library. Center for Southwest Studies. Thomas B. Catron Papers, MSS 29, Series 102, Box 4, Folder 3. (**Pleading for money**)

_____. "I wrote you before I left Las Vegas ..." Letter to T.B. Catron. **July 29, 1889.** University of New Mexico Library. Center for Southwest Studies. Thomas B. Catron Papers, MSS 29, Series 102, Box 4, Folder 4. (**Pleading for money**)

_____. "Mr. Gorther in sending me the balance of the testimony in the case of Doloritas Martin ..." Letter to T.B. Catron. **August 14, 1890.** University of New Mexico Library. Center for Southwest Studies. Thomas B. Catron Papers. MSS 29, Series 102, Box 8, Folder 4. (**About fees for legal work for Catron**)

ARTICLES PUBLISHED BY (CHRONOLOGICAL)

No Author. (signed E.). "Death of Chapman." *Las Vegas Gazette.* **March 1, 1879.** From *Proceedings of a Court of Inquiry in the Case of Lt. Col. N.A.M. Dudley (May 2, 1879 – July 5, 1879).* File No. QQ1284. (Boxes 3304, 3305, 3305A); Court Martial Files 1809-1894. Records of the Office of the Judge Advocate General – Army. Record Group 153. Old Military and Civil Branch. National Archives and Records Administration. Washington, D. C.

(SEE: *Las Vegas Gazette* articles under William H. Bonney, William B. Sloan)

LEONARD, IRA E.
BIOGRAPHICAL SOURCE

Nolan, Frederick. Biography and photograph of Ira Leonard. Unpublished. personal communication. July 29, 2005.

ARTICLES ABOUT

No Author. "[He] attracted special commendation by his fearless action in the suppression of disorder..." *St. Louis Globe* of September 7, 1872. Unpublished. Personal communication from Frederick Nolan. July 29, 2005.

No Author. Obituary. **July 6, 1889**. Las Cruces *Rio Grande Republican*. Unpublished. Personal communication from Frederick Nolan. July 29, 2005.

LETTERS FROM HUSTON CHAPMAN'S FATHER TO

Chapman, W.W. "Yours of the 1st inst. came ..." Letter to Ira E. Leonard. March 20, 1879. Indiana Historical Society. Lew Wallace Collection. M0292. Box 4. Folder 6.

_____. "Since receiving yours of the 1st March ..." Letter to Ira Leonard. May 8, 1879. Indiana Historical Society. Lew Wallace Collection. M0292. Box 4. Folder 10.

COURT OF INQUIRY OF N.A.M. DUDLEY BY (SEE: Nathan Augustus Monroe Dudley Court of Inquiry)

LETTERS TO AND FROM

HUSTON CHAPMAN'S FATHER TO

Chapman, W.W. "Yours of the 1st inst. came ..." Letter to Ira E. Leonard. **March 20, 1879**. Indiana Historical Society. Lew Wallace Collection. M0292. Box 4. Folder 6.

_____. "Since receiving yours of the 1st March ..." Letter to Ira Leonard. **May 8, 1879**. Indiana Historical Society. Lew Wallace Collection. M0292. Box 4. Folder 10.

LEW WALLACE TO AND FROM

Leonard, Ira E. "Dear Gov. You have undoubtedly learned ere this of the assassination ..." Letter to Lew Wallace. **February 24, 1879**. Indiana Historical Society. Lew Wallace Collection. M0292. Box 4. Folder 3. (**On Chapman murder.**)

Wallace, Lew. "It is important to take steps to protect the coming court ..." Letter to Ira Leonard. **April 6, 1879**. Indiana Historical Society. Lew Wallace Collection. M0292. Box 4. Folder 8.

Leonard, Ira E. "You may have learned the result of the cattle examination ..." Letter to Lew Wallace. **April 8, 1879**. Indiana Historical Society. Lew Wallace Collection. M0292. Box 4. Folder 8. (**Mentions the ongoing "cruel war"**)

_____. "One Wm Wilson, a saloon keeper ..." Letter to Lew Wallace. **April 9, 1879**. Indiana Historical Society. Lew Wallace Collection. M0292. Box 4. Folder 9.

Wallace, Lew. "Your favors both received." Letter to Ira Leonard. **April 9, 1879**. Indiana Historical Society. Lew Wallace Collection. M0292. Box 4. Folder 9. (**Wallace's "martyr" letter: "all the world against you"**)

_____. "Mr. Howell goes to the Plaza to give bond ..." Letter to Ira Leonard. **April 9, 1879**. Indiana Historical Society. Lew Wallace Collection. M0292. Box 4. Folder 9.

_____. "Referring to the testimony in Mr. Howell's cattle case ..." Letter to Ira Leonard. **April 9, 1879**. Indiana Historical Society. Lew Wallace Collection. M0292. Box 4. Folder 9.

Leonard, Ira. "Yours received it might perhaps be a good idea to surrender the cattle to Mr Howell." Letter to Lew Wallace. **April 9, 1879**. Indiana Historical Society. Lew Wallace Collection. M0292. Box 4. Folder 9.

_____. "... *if the wind does not blow so I can't.*" Letter to Lew Wallace. **April 9, 1879**. Unpublished. Personal communication from Frederick Nolan. July 29, 2005.

_____. "I was disappointed in not seeing you ..." Letter to Lew Wallace. **April 12, 1879**. Indiana Historical Society. Lew Wallace Collection. M0292. Box 4. Folder 9. (**Anxious about hard looking characters coming into Lincoln**)

Wallace, Lew. "Your favor, with the prisoner received." Letter to Ira Leonard. **April 13, 1879**. Indiana Historical Society. Lew Wallace Collection. M0292. Box 4. Folder 9. (**About writs of habeas corpus to free his Fort Stanton prisoners**)

Leonard, Ira. "Yours was received last night ..." **April 13, 1879**. Indiana Historical Society. Lew Wallace Collection. M0292. Box 4. Folder 9. (**Enforcing vagrancy and gun laws in Lincoln**)

_____. "The air is filled tonight with 'rumors of wars ... Letter to Lew Wallace. **April 20, 1879**. Indiana Historical Society. Lew Wallace Collection. M0292. Box 4. Folder 9. (**About District Attorney Rynerson: "He is bent on going for the Kid"**)

_____. "When you left here I promised to write you concerning events transpiring here ..." Letter to Lew Wallace. **May 20, 1878 [sic - 79]**. Indiana Historical Society. Lew Wallace Collection. M0292. Box 4. Folder 10. (**Has quote on the Murphy-Dolan party as: "part and parcel of the Santa Fe ring that has been so long an incubus on the government of this territory."**)

_____. "I write to you with pencil because I am laboring for breath ..." Letter to Lew Wallace. **May 23, 1879**. Indiana Historical Society. Lew Wallace Collection. M0292. Box 4. Folder 11. (**With quote "we are pouring the 'hot shot' into Dudley."**) (**With enclosed letter of May 20, 1879**)

_____. "Dudley commenced on the defense Thursday afternoon ..." Letter to Wallace. **June 6, 1879**, Indiana Historical Society. Lew Wallace Collection. M0292. Box 4. Folder 11. (**About disgust at Court."**)

_____. "Yours of the 7th inst reached me ..." Letter to Lew Wallace. **June 13, 1879**. Indiana Historical Society. Lew Wallace Collection. M0292. Box 4. Folder 11. (**about Court of Inquiry bias**)

_____. About having become impoverished by Lincoln County legal work. Letter to Lew Wallace. **November 26, 1888**. Unpublished. Personal communication from Frederick Nolan. July 29, 2005.

LEVERSON, MONTEGUE
CONTEMPORARY SOURCES (CHRONOLOGICAL)

Leverson, Montegue. "I earnestly entreat you to read the enclosed letter and hand it to the president ..." Letter to Secretary of Interior Carl Schurz. **March 16, 1878**. Part of file of report of October 4, 1878. Angel Report. Microfilm File Case Number 44-4-8-3. Record Group 48. Microfilm No. M750. Roll 1. National Archives and Records Administration. U.S. Department of Justice. Washington, D.C.

_____. "Affairs of Lincoln County." Letter to Secretary of Interior Carl Schurz and President Rutherford B. Hayes. **June 28, 1878**. Part of file of report of October 4, 1878. Angel Report. Microfilm File Case Number 44-4-8-3. Record Group 48. Microfilm No. M750. Roll 1. National Archives and Records Administration. U.S. Department of Justice. Washington, D.C. (**About Santa Fe Ring**)

_____. "I send you herewith a copy of a letter I have published ..." Letter to Secretary of Interior Carl Schurz. **July 12 (?), 1878**. Part of file of report of October 4, 1878. Angel Report. Microfilm File Case Number 44-4-8-3. Record Group 48. Microfilm No. M750. Roll 1. National Archives and Records Administration. U.S. Department of Justice. Washington, D.C. (**About opposing Thomas Benton Catron and the Ring**)

_____. "I enclose you a letter I have just received ..." Letter to President Rutherford B. Hayes. **July 30, 1878**. Part of file of report of October 4, 1878. Angel Report. Microfilm File Case Number 44-4-8-3. Record Group 48. Microfilm No. M750. Roll 1. National Archives and Records Administration. U.S. Department of Justice. Washington, D.C. (**About murder of Alexander McSween and Frank MacNab by the Ring – blaming Hayes**)

LONGWILL, ROBERT H.

CONTEMPORARY SOURCES (CHRONOLOGICAL)

No Author. (Editorial). **May 15, 1876.** *The Daily New Mexican.* Volume 9. http://chroniclingamerica.loc.gov. (**Ringite article covering up guilt of Mills with Robert Longwill in murder of Franklin Tolby as just "rumor"**)

Longwill, Robert H. "R.H. Longwill, M.D. Has moved ..." *Santa Fe Daily New Mexican.* **September 26, 1889.** Page 2, Column 2. (**Advertising services**)

No Author. "Death of Dr. R.H. Longwill." **March 1, 1895.** *Santa Fe Daily New Mexican.* Front Page, Volume 32, Number 8, Column 4. http://chroniclingamerica.loc.gov.

Segale, Blandina. *At the End of the Santa Fe Trail.* Columbus, Ohio: The Columbian Press. **1932.** (**Mentions him as her chief doctor at her Santa Fe hospital**)

MARKLAND, ABSALOM HANKS

BIOGRAPHICAL SOURCE

Perret, Geoffrey. *Ulysses S. Grant: Soldier and President.* New York: Random House. 1997. (**Pages 16, 467, 471**)

CONTEMPORARY SOURCES (CHRONOLOGICAL)

Grant, Ulysses. Presentation of the Grimsby Saddle to Colonel Absalom Markland. **May 19, 1865.** *The Papers of Ulysses S. Grant: May 1-December 31, 1865.* Carbondale, Illinois: Southern Illinois University Press. 1967 - 2009.

Wallace, Lew. "Our mutual friend, M. Hinds, who will hand you this ..." Letter to A.H. Markland. **November 14, 1878.** Indiana Historical Society. Lew Wallace Collection. M0292. Box 3. Folder 17. (**About Santa Fe Ring attempting to remove him as governor**)

MATTHEWS, JACOB BASIL "BILLY"

BIOGRAPHICAL SOURCE

Fleming, Elvis E. *J.B. Matthews. Biography of a Lincoln County Deputy.* Las Cruces, New Mexico: Yucca Tree Press. 1999.

CONTEMPORARY SOURCES (CHRONOLOGICAL)

Wallace, Lew. "Under the circumstances, particularly in the absence here of suitable cells for safekeeping of Jesse Evans, Jacob B. Matthews and William Campbell ..." Letter to Henry Carroll. **March 10, 1879.** Indiana Historical Society. Lew Wallace Collection. M0292. Box 4. Folder 4.

_____. "Upon reflection, I am of opinion that if Col. Dudley is really going to Fort Union ..." Letter to Henry Carroll. **March 11, 1879.** Indiana Historical Society. Lew Wallace Collection. M0292. Box 4. Folder 5. (**Advises not to send Evans, Campbell, Matthews, and Dolan to Fort Union**)

(SEE: Letter to Thomas Benton Catron)

MAXWELL FAMILY

Cleaveland, Agnes Morley. *No Life for a Lady.* Boston: Houghton Mifflin. 1941.

_____. *Satan's Paradise: From Lucien Maxwell to Fred Lambert.* Boston: Houghton Mifflin Company. 1952.

Cleaveland, Norman. *The Morleys - Young Upstarts on the Southwest Frontier.* Albuquerque, New Mexico: Calvin Horn Publisher, Inc. 1971.

Dunham, Harold H. "New Mexican Land Grants with Special Reference to the Title Papers of the Maxwell Grant." *New Mexico Historical Review*. (January 1955) Vol. 30, No. 1. pp. 1 - 23.

Freiberger, Harriet. *Lucien Maxwell: Villain or Visionary*. Santa Fe, New Mexico: Sunstone Press. 1999.

Keleher, William A. *The Maxwell Land Grant. A New Mexico Item*. Albuquerque, New Mexico: University of New Mexico Press. 1964.

Lamar, Howard Roberts. *The Far Southwest 1846 - 1912. A Territorial History*. New Haven and London: Yale University Press. 1966.

Miller, Kenny. Descendant of Lucien Bonaparte Maxwell. Personal communication. 2011 to 2012.

Montoya, María E. *Translating Property. The Maxwell Land Grant and the Conflict Over Land in the American West, 1840-1900*. Berkeley and Los Angeles, California: University of California Press. 2002.

Murphy, Lawrence R. *Lucien Bonaparte Maxwell. Napoleon of the Southwest*. Norman: University of Oklahoma Press. 1983.

Pearson, Jim Berry. *The Maxwell Land Grant*. Norman: University of Oklahoma Press. 1961.

Poe, Sophie. *Buckboard Days*. Albuquerque, New Mexico: University of New Mexico Press. 1964.

Taylor, Morris F. *O. P. McMains and the Maxwell Land Grant Conflict*. Tucson, Arizona: The University of Arizona Press. 1979. (**Origins of Santa Fe Ring**)

No Author. "Mrs. Paula M. Jaramillo, 65 Died Here Tuesday." *The Fort Sumner Leader*. Official Newspaper County of De Baca. December 20, 1929. No. 1158, Page 1, Column 1. (**Death of Paulita Maxwell Jaramillo, Billy Bonney's sweetheart**)

McMAINS, OSCAR P.

BIOGRAPHICAL SOURCES FOR

Cleaveland, Norman. *The Morleys - Young Upstarts on the Southwest Frontier*. Albuquerque, New Mexico: Calvin Horn Publisher, Inc. 1971.

Taylor, Morris F. *O.P. McMains and the Maxwell Land Grant Conflict*. Tucson, Arizona: The University of Arizona Press. 1979. (**Traces origins of the Santa Fe Ring with T.B. Catron and S.B. Elkins**)

CONTEMPORARY SOURCES ABOUT (CHRONOLOGICAL)

Morley, William Raymond and Frank Springer. On Oscar McMains's citizen's Meeting. *Cimarron News and Press*. **November 10, 1875**. In Mary McPherson, Letters and Petitions to President Rutherford B. Hayes re: Removal Governor Axtell and the Santa Fe Ring. 1977. Interior Department Papers 1850-1907; Appointments Division and Subsequent Actions. Microfilm File Case Number 44-4-8-3. **Record Group 48.** Microfilm Roll M750. National Archives and Records Administration. (**Colfax County citizens meeting on F.J. Tolby murder by Santa Fe Ring accusing murderers**.)

No Author. About Santa Fe Ring scapegoating of O.P. McMains by murder indictment. Pueblo, *Colorado Chieftain*. **May 25, 1876**.

Lambert, J.J. "At It Again." Pueblo, Colorado, *Enterprise and Chronicle*. **April 21, 1877**. Interior Department Papers 1850-1907; Appointments Division and Subsequent Actions. Microfilm File Case Number 44-4-8-3. Record Group 48. Microfilm No. M750. Roll 1. National Archives and Records Administration. U.S. Department of Justice. Washington, D.C. (**Description of Santa Fe Ring control of courts and malicious prosecution of opponents like Oscar McMains in the Franklin Tolby murder; used in: "W.B. Matchett and Mary E. McPherson 'Make Certain Charges Against the U.S. Officials in the Territory of New Mexico.' " Letter to President Rutherford B. Hayes.**

Received and filed May 1, 1877. Interior Department Papers 1850-1907; Appointments Division and Subsequent Actions. Microfilm File Case Number 44-4-8-3. Record Group 48. Microfilm No. M750. Roll 1. National Archives and Records Administration. U. S. Department of Justice. Washington, D.C.)

Chaplin, F.B. Obituary of O.P. McMains. No date (but died April 15, 1899). Quoted by Mary McMains to a Robert Fischer. (**Owned by Morris F. Taylor**)

No Author. "O.P. McMains, the agitator, is dead." *Raton Range.* **April 20, 1899.**

(SEE: Mary Tibbles McPherson)

McPHERSON, MARY E. TIBBLES

BIOGRAPHICAL SOURCES

Cleaveland, Agnes Morley. *No Life for a Lady.* Boston: Houghton Mifflin. 1941.

_____. *Satan's Paradise: From Lucien Maxwell to Fred Lambert.* Boston: Houghton Mifflin Company. 1952.

Cleaveland, Norman, *A Synopsis of the Great New Mexico Cover-up.* Self-printed. 1989.

_____. *The Great Santa Fe Cover-up. Based on a Talk given Before the Santa Fe Historical Society on November 1, 1978.* Self-printed. 1982.

_____. *The Morleys - Young Upstarts on the Southwest Frontier.* Albuquerque, New Mexico: Calvin Horn Publisher, Inc. 1971.

Taylor, Morris F. *O.P. McMains and the Maxwell Land Grant Conflict.* Tucson, Arizona: The University of Arizona Press. 1979.

Tibbles, Thomas Henry. Editor Vivian K. Barris. *Buckskin and Blanket Days: Memoirs of a Friend of the Indians.* Written in 1905. Published by Garden City, New York: Doubleday & Company, Inc. in 1957. (**Brother of Mary Tibbles McPherson**)

McPHERSON'S SANTA FE RING EXPOSÉS

McPherson, Mary. "Charges against Thomas B. Catron, U.S. Attorney, and Others." **February 7, 1877.** Letter to Attorney General Alphonso Taft. Interior Department Papers 1850-1907; Appointments Division and Subsequent Actions. Microfilm File Case Number 44-4-8-3. Record Group 48. Microfilm Roll M750. National Archives and Records Administration. U.S. Department of Justice. Washington, D.C.

Catron, Thomas Benton. "Answering Charges of Mary E. McPherson." **February 24, 1877.** Letter to Attorney General Alphonso Taft. Interior Department Papers 1850-1907; Appointments Division and Subsequent Actions. Microfilm File Case Number 44-4-8-3. Record Group 48. Microfilm Roll M750. National Archives and Records Administration. U.S. Department of Justice. Washington, D.C.

Matchett, W.B. and Mary E. McPherson. "W.B. Matchett and Mary E. McPherson 'Make Certain Charges Against the U.S. Officials in the Territory of New Mexico, Together With Corroboration Evidence.' " Letter to President Rutherford B. Hayes. Received and filed **May 1, 1877**. Interior Department Papers 1850-1907; Appointments Division and Subsequent Actions. Microfilm File Case Number 44-4-8-3. Record Group 48. Microfilm No. M750. Roll 1. National Archives and Records Administration. U. S. Department of Justice. Washington, D.C.

McPherson, Mary and W.B. Matchett. "To The President. Please make the enclosed a part of the evidence in the case of "Charges Against New Mexican Officials" Letter to President Rutherford B. Hayes. **May 3, 1877.** McPherson, Mary E. Letters and Petitions to President Rutherford B. Hayes re: Removal Governor Axtell and the Santa Fe Ring. Interior Department Papers 1850-1907; Appointments Division and Subsequent Actions. Microfilm File Case Number 44-4-8-3. Record Group 48. Microfilm Roll M750. National Archives and Records Administration. U.S. Department of Justice. Washington, D. C. (**Addendum to their May, 1877 "Certain Charges Against U.S. Officials in New Mexico Territory."**)

McPherson, Mary and W.B. Matchett. "The Secretary of the Interior, Sir - Accompanying please find copy of charges, &c., against S.B. Axtell, Governor and other New Mexico Officials ..." "Charges Against New Mexican Officials." Letter to Secretary of the Interior Carl Schurz. **May 5, 1877**. McPherson, Mary E. Letters and Petitions to President Rutherford B. Hayes re: Removal Governor Axtell and the Santa Fe Ring. Interior Department Papers 1850-1907; Appointments Division and Subsequent Actions. Microfilm File Case Number 44-4-8-3. Record Group 48. Microfilm Roll M750. National Archives and Records Administration. U.S. Department of Justice. Washington, D. C.

McPherson, Mary and W.B. Matchett. "We have respectfully to request that the following named records, documents, papers, communications and correspondence be supplied ..." Records Request to Secretary of the Interior Carl Schurz. **July 26, 1877**. Interior Department Papers 1850-1907; Appointments Division and Subsequent Actions. Microfilm File Case Number 44-4-8-3. Record Group 48. Microfilm No. M750. Roll 1. National Archives and Records Administration. U.S. Department of Justice. Washington, D.C. (**Requesting records of the Santa Fe Ring, Carton, Elkins, and Axtell**)

McPherson, Mary. "Please place before the Attorney General ..." Letter to President Rutherford B. Hayes. **August 23, 1877**. Interior Department Papers 1850-1907; Appointments Division and Subsequent Actions. Microfilm File Case Number 44-4-8-3. Record Group 48. Microfilm No. M750. Roll 1. National Archives and Records Administration. U. S. Department of Justice. Washington, D.C. (**Requesting that her "Charges" go to the Attorney General.**)

McPherson, Mary and W.B. Matchett. "*In the Matter of Charges vs. Gov. S.B. Axtell and Other New Mexico Officials. Submitted to the Departments of the Interior and Justice.* **August, 1877**. Printed as a 31 page booklet. No publisher listed. Indiana Historical Society. Lew Wallace Collection. M0292. Box 3. Folder 20.

McPherson, Mary. "I desire to know when I can be heard ..." Letter to Secretary of Interior Carl Schurz. **September 30, 1977**. Interior Department Papers 1850-1907; Appointments Division and Subsequent Actions. Microfilm File Case Number 44-4-8-3. Record Group 48. Microfilm No. M750. Roll 1. National Archives and Records Administration. U. S. Department of Justice. Washington, D.C.

CONTEMPORARY SOURCES (CHRONOLOGICAL)

Morley, William Raymond and Frank Springer. On Oscar McMains's citizen's Meeting. *Cimarron News and Press.* **November 10, 1875**. In Mary McPherson, Letters and Petitions to President Rutherford B. Hayes re: Removal Governor Axtell and the Santa Fe Ring. 1977. Interior Department Papers 1850-1907; Appointments Division and Subsequent Actions. Microfilm File Case Number 44-4-8-3. **Record Group 48.** Microfilm Roll M750. National Archives and Records Administration. (**Colfax County citizens meeting on F.J. Tolby murder by Santa Fe Ring**.)

Morley, William Raymond and Frank Springer. " 'The Territory of Elkins.' Assassination of Supposed Sun Correspondent. The Murder of the Rev. F.J. Tolby in New Mexico. A Probate Judge Accused of Complicity in the Crime. Indignation Meeting." *New York Weekly Sun.* **December 22, 1875**. Interior Department Papers 1850-1907; Appointments Division and Subsequent Actions. Microfilm Roll M750. National Archives and Records Administration. Record Group 48. Microfilm Case File Number 44-4-8-3. U.S. Department of Interior. Washington, D. C.(**Submitted to President Hayes in May 1, 1877's "Mary E. McPherson and W.B. Matchett 'Make certain charges against the U.S. Officials."**)

Morley William Raymond. "I was astonished beyond measure at your proceedings, and have fears as to the result ..." Letter to Mary McPherson. **March 6, 1877**. McPherson, Mary E. Letters and Petitions to President Rutherford B. Hayes re: Removal Governor Axtell and the Santa Fe Ring. Interior Department Papers

1850-1907; Appointments Division and Subsequent Actions. Microfilm File Case Number 44-4-8-3. Record Group 48. Microfilm Roll M750. National Archives and Records Administration. U.S. Department of Justice. Washington, D.C. **(Hopes she can help fight against Santa Fe Ring)**

Morley, Ada. "Yes, we have received all your letters at Vermejo here but we have hesitated about replying ..." Letter to Mary McPherson. **March 7, 1877.**

McPherson, Mary E. Letters and Petitions to President Rutherford B. Hayes re: Removal Governor Axtell and the Santa Fe Ring. Interior Department Papers 1850-1907; Appointments Division and Subsequent Actions. Microfilm File Case Number 44-4-8-3. Record Group 48. Microfilm Roll M750. National Archives and Records Administration. U.S. Department of Justice. Washington, D.C. **(Fears about her fight against Santa Fe Ring)**

McSWEEN, ALEXANDER

Bristol Warren. "Writ of Embezzlement." **December 21, 1877.** Writ of Embezzlement. New Mexico State University Library at Las Cruces. Rio Grande Historical Collections. Lincoln County Papers. New Mexico State University Library at Las Cruces. Rio Grande Historical Collections. Accession No. Ms 0249. Box No. 10. Folder M-13. "Will and Testament A. McSween." **(Emilie Fritz Scholand's sworn complaint against Alexander McSween)**

Fritz, Charles. Affidavit sworn before John Crouch, Clerk of Doña Ana District Court, for Writ of Attachment issued against property of Alexander A. McSween. Probate Court Record. **February 6, 1878.** (private collection).

_____. Fritz, Charles and Emilie Scholand. Attachment Bond sworn before John Crouch, Clerk of Doña Ana District Court, against Alexander A. McSween for indebtedness to them. **February 6, 1878.** (private collection).

Bristol, Warren. Action of Assumpsit to command Sheriff of Lincoln County to attach goods of Alexander A. McSween. **February 7, 1878.** District Court Record. (private collection).

_____. Preprinted form in his name for "Writ of Attachment" (Printed and sold at the office of the Mesilla News) filled out to command the Sheriff of Lincoln County to attach goods of Alexander McSween for a suit of damages for ten thousand dollars. **February 7, 1878.** (private collection).

McSween, Alexander. "It looks as though the agent were the property of J.J. Dolan & J.H. Riley, known here as Dolan & Co." Letter to Secretary of Interior Carl Schurz. **February 11, 1878.** From Frederick Nolan. *The Life and Death of John Henry Tunstall.* Albuquerque, New Mexico: The University of New Mexico Press. 1965. Page 266.

_____. "Will and Testament A. McSween." **February 25, 1878.** Herman B. Weisner Papers, ca. 1957-1992. New Mexico State University Library at Las Cruces. Rio Grande Historical Collections. Accession No. Ms 0249. Box 10. Folder M15. Folder Name. "Will and Testament A. McSween."

_____. and B.H. Ellis. Secretaries. "The undersigned have the Honor of transmitting you, as requested, a copy of the proceedings of a meeting held by the citizens of Lincoln County ..." Letter to President Rutherford B. Hayes; with attached proceedings of the April 1878 Lincoln Grand Jury. **April 26, 1878.** Microfilm File Case Number 44-4-8-3. Record Group 48. Microfilm No. M750. Roll 1. National Archives and Records Administration. U.S. Department of Justice. Washington, D.C.

_____. Deposition to Frank Warner Angel. **June 6, 1878.** Pages 5-183 of Frank Warner Angel report *In the Matter of the Examination of the Causes and Circumstances of the Death of John H. Tunstall a British Subject.* Report filed **October 4, 1878.** Angel Report. Microfilm File Case Number 44-4-8-3. Record Group 48. Microfilm No. M750. Roll 1. National Archives and Records Administration. U.S. Department of Justice. Washington, D.C. **(Reports secret**

Angel, Frank Warner. *In the Matter of the Lincoln County Troubles. To the Honorable Charles Devens, Attorney General.* **October 4, 1878**. Angel Report. Microfilm File Case Number 44-4-8-3. Record Group 48. Microfilm No. M750. Roll 1. National Archives and Records Administration. U.S. Department of Justice. Washington, D.C.

McSWEEN, SUSAN
BIOGRAPHICAL SOURCE FOR
Chamberlain, Kathleen P. *In the Shadow of Billy the Kid: Susan McSween and the Lincoln County War.* Albuquerque: University of New Mexico Press. 2013.

CONTEMPORARY SOURCES ABOUT (CHRONOLOGICAL)
Dudley, Nathan Augustus Monroe. "I am in receipt of a copy of letter written by one H.I. Chapman, calling himself the Attorney ..." **November 9, 1878**. Letter to Lew Wallace. From *Proceedings of a Court of Inquiry in the Case of Lt. Col. N.A.M. Dudley (May 2,1879 – July 5, 1879)*. File No. QQ1284. (Boxes 3304, 3305, 3305A); Court Martial Files 1809-1894. Records of the Office of the Judge Advocate General - Army. Record Group 153. Old Military and Civil Branch. National Archives and Records Administration. Washington, D.C. (**Answer to charges, with the Susan McSween defamatory affidavits**)

Wallace, Lew. "In a communication ... I requested for reasons stated, a safe-guard for Mrs. McSween ..." Letter to Edward Hatch. **November 9, 1878**. Indiana Historical Society. Lew Wallace Collection. M0292. Box 3. Folder 17.

McSween, Susan. Testimony in Court of Inquiry for Lieutenant Colonel N.A.M. Dudley. **May 23-24, 26, 1879**. *Proceedings of a Court of Inquiry in the Case of Lt. Col. N.A.M. Dudley (May 2,1879 – July 5, 1879)*. File No. QQ1284. (Boxes 3304, 3305, 3305A); Court Martial Files 1809-1894. Records of the Office of the Judge Advocate General – Army. Record Group 153. Old Military and Civil Branch. National Archives and Records Administration. Washington, D.C.

Waldo, Henry. "Nothing has been accomplished in the least that connects Col. Dudley with anything which transpired in the town of Lincoln on the occasion of his presence there on the 19th..." Closing argument for Dudley Court of Inquiry. **July 5, 1879**. *Proceedings of a Court of Inquiry in the Case of Lt. Col. N.A.M. Dudley (May 2,1879 – July 5, 1879)*. File No. QQ1284. (Boxes 3304, 3305, 3305A); Court Martial Files 1809-1894. Records of the Office of the Judge Advocate General – Army. Record Group 153. Old Military and Civil Branch. National Archives and Records Administration. Washington, D. C.

No Author. Verdict on Civil Cause 298 for arson of Susan McSween's house. *Mesilla News*. **December 6, 1879**. Unpublished. personal communication from Frederick Nolan. July 29, 2005. (**Dudley exonerated**)

MEADOWS, JOHN P.
Meadows, John P. "Billy the Kid to John P. Meadows on the Peñasco, May 1-2, 1881." *Roswell Daily Record*. February 16, 1931. Page 6.

_____. Ed. John P. Wilson. *Pat Garrett and Billy the Kid as I Knew Them: Reminiscences of John P. Meadows*. Albuquerque: University of New Mexico Press. 2004.

MILLS, MELVIN WHITSON
BIOGRAPHICAL SOURCE
Bloom, Lansing B. and Paul A.F. Walter. Eds. "Melvin Witson Mills." *New Mexico Historical Review*. Volume 1. Pages 86-87. Santa Fe: The Museum Press. 1926.

CONTEMPORARY SOURCES (CHRONOLOGICAL)

Mills, Melvin W. "Thought I would write you how things are running." Letter to Robert H. Longwill. **December 5, 1873.** "Exhibit A" in the August 9, 1878 deposition of Frank Springer to Investigator Frank Warner Angel. Frank Warner Angel report titled *In the Matter of the Investigation of the Charges Against S.B. Axtell Governor of New Mexico.* October 3, 1878. Interior Department Papers 1850-1907; Appointments Division and Subsequent Actions. Microfilm Case File No. 44-4-8-3. Record Group 48. Microfilm Roll M750. National Archives and Records Administration. U.S. Department of Interior. Washington, D.C. (**About his Catron and Ring empowerment**)

No Author. (Editorial). **May 15, 1876.** *The Daily New Mexican.* Volume 9. http://chroniclingamerica.loc.gov. (**Cover-up of murderers Mills and Longwill**)

Meadows, John P. Ed. John P. Wilson. *Pat Garrett and Billy the Kid as I Knew Them: Reminiscences of John P. Meadows.* Albuquerque: University of New Mexico Press. 2004.

(SEE: Correspondence with Thomas Benton Catron)

MORLEY, ADA McPHERSON

Morley, Ada. "Yes, we have received all your letters at Vermejo here but we have hesitated about replying ..." Letter to Mary McPherson. **March 7, 1877.** McPherson, Mary E. Letters and Petitions to President Rutherford B. Hayes re: Removal Governor Axtell and the Santa Fe Ring. Interior Department Papers 1850-1907; Appointments Division and Subsequent Actions. Interior Department Papers 1850-1907; Appointments Division and Subsequent Actions. Microfilm File Case Number 44-4-8-3. Record Group 48. Microfilm Roll M750. National Archives and Records Administration. U.S. Department of Justice. Washington, D.C. (**Fears about her mother's fight against Santa Fe Ring as endangering the whole family**)

Middaugh, Asa F. Deposition. **March 31, 1876.** "Exhibit B" in the August 9, 1878 deposition of Frank Springer to Investigator Frank Warner Angel. Frank Warner Angel report titled *In the Matter of the Investigation of the Charges Against S.B. Axtell Governor of New Mexico.* October 3, 1878. Interior Department Papers 1850-1907; Appointments Division and Subsequent Actions. Microfilm Case File No. 44-4-8-3. Record Group 48. Microfilm Roll M750. National Archives and Records Administration. U.S. Department of Interior. Washington, D.C. (**About Catron's malicious prosecution of Ada McPherson Morley for alleged mail theft**)

MORLEY, WILLIAM RAYMOND

BIOGRAPHICAL SOURCES

Caffey, David L. *Frank Springer and New Mexico: From the Colfax County War to the Emergence of Modern Santa Fe.* Texas A and M. University Press. 2007.

Cleaveland, Agnes Morley. *No Life for a Lady.* Boston: Houghton Mifflin. 1941.

_____. *Satan's Paradise: From Lucien Maxwell to Fred Lambert.* Boston: Houghton Mifflin Company. 1952.

Cleaveland, Norman. *The Morleys - Young Upstarts on the Southwest Frontier.* Albuquerque, New Mexico: Calvin Horn Publisher, Inc. 1971.

Taylor, Morris F. *O.P. McMains and the Maxwell Land Grant Conflict.* Tucson, Arizona: The University of Arizona Press. 1979.

WORDS OF (CHRONOLOGICAL)

Morley, William Raymond and Frank Springer. On Oscar McMains's citizen's Meeting. *Cimarron News and Press.* **November 10, 1875.** In Mary McPherson, Letters and Petitions to President Rutherford B. Hayes re: Removal Governor Axtell and the Santa Fe Ring. 1977. Interior Department Papers 1850-1907; Appointments Division and Subsequent Actions. Microfilm File Case Number 44-4-8-3. **Record Group 48.** Microfilm Roll M750. National Archives and Records Administration. (**Colfax County citizens meeting on F.J. Tolby murder by Santa Fe Ring.**)

_____. " 'The Territory of Elkins.' Assassination of Supposed Sun Correspondent. The Murder of the Rev. F.J. Tolby in New Mexico. A Probate Judge Accused of Complicity in the Crime. Indignation Meeting." *New York Weekly Sun.* **December 22, 1875.** Interior Department Papers 1850-1907; Appointments Division and Subsequent Actions. Microfilm Roll M750. National Archives and Records Administration. Record Group 48. Microfilm Case File Number 44-4-8-3. U.S. Department of Interior. Washington, D. C. (**From May 1, 1877 submission to President Rutherford B. Hates as "Mary E. McPherson and W.B. Matchett 'Make certain charges against the U.S. Officials in the Territory of New Mexico.' "**)

_____. "I was astonished beyond measure at your proceedings, and have fears as to the result ..." Letter to Mary McPherson. **March 6, 1877.** McPherson, Mary E. Letters and Petitions to President Rutherford B. Hayes re: Removal Governor Axtell and the Santa Fe Ring. Interior Department Papers 1850-1907; Appointments Division and Subsequent Actions. Microfilm File Case Number 44-4-8-3. Record Group 48. Microfilm Roll M750. National Archives and Records Administration. U.S. Department of Justice. Washington, D.C. (**Hopes she can help fight against Santa Fe Ring**)

_____. "Your letter of the 7th came last night and it was a good long newsy letter ..." Letter to wife, Ada McPherson Morley. **August 15, 1878.** Collection of Norman Cleaveland. Quoted in Norman Cleaveland, *The Morleys: Young Upstarts in the Southwest.* Albuquerque, New Mexico: Calvin Horn Publisher, Inc. 1971. Pages 152-155. (**About possible betrayal by Angel's reports; about the Santa Fe Ring, T.B. Catron, S.B. Elkins, S.B. Axtell, and Henry Waldo; and the Lincoln County War**)

_____. Deposition to Investigator Frank Warner Angel. August 9, 1878. Frank Warner Angel report titled *In the Matter of the Investigation of the Charges Against S.B. Axtell Governor of New Mexico.* **October 3, 1878.** Interior Department Papers 1850-1907; Appointments Division and Subsequent Actions. Microfilm Case File No. 44-4-8-3. Record Group 48. Microfilm Roll M750. National Archives and Records Administration. U.S. Department of Interior. Washington, D.C. (**Mentions Catron, Elkins, and the Santa Fe Ring**)

(SEE: Mary Tibbles McPherson)

MURPHY, LAWRENCE GUSTAV

Gilliam, W. J. "I have been told you were administrator of Murphy's estate ..." Letter to T.B. Catron. **March 18, 1895.** University of New Mexico Library. Center for Southwest Studies. Thomas B. Catron Papers, MSS 29, Series 102, Box 25, Folder 3. (**To Catron as administrator of L.G. Murphy's estate**)

Murphy, Lawrence G. "Will of Lawrence G. Murphy." Herman B. Weisner Papers, ca. 1957-1992. New Mexico State University Library at Las Cruces. Rio Grande Historical Collections. Accession No. Ms 0249. Box 11. Folder P15. Folder Name: "Murphy, Lawrence G."

PATRÓN, JUAN

Wallace, Lew. "Be good enough to send word to all your men to turn out soon as possible ..." Letter to Juan Patrón. **March 19, 1879**. Indiana Historical Society. Lew Wallace Collection. M0292. Box 4. Folder 6. (**Reports escape of Jessie Evans and Billy Campbell from Fort Stanton**)

Patrón, Juan. First letter to Lew Wallace on **March 29, 1879**. Indiana Historical Society. Lew Wallace Collection. M0292. Box 4, Folder 7.

_____. Second letter to Lew Wallace on **March 29, 1879**. Indiana Historical Society. Lew Wallace Collection. M0292. Box 4, Folder 7.

_____. Letter to Rosa. **April 12, 1879**. Indiana Historical Society. Lew Wallace Collection. M0292. Box 4, Folder 9.

PENNYPACKER, GALUSHA

BIOGRAPHICAL SOURCE

Heitman, Francis B. *Historical Register and Dictionary of the United States Army, From Its Organization, September 29, 1789, to March 2, 1903*. (Entry for Galusha Pennypacker, Pages 782-7830.) Washington, D.C.: Government Printing Office. 1903.

CONTEMPORARY SOURCE

No Author. *Proceedings of a Court of Inquiry in the Case of Lt. Col. N.A.M. Dudley (May 2,1879 – July 5, 1879)*. File No. QQ1284. (Boxes 3304, 3305, 3305A); Court Martial Files 1809-1894. Records of the Office of the Judge Advocate General - Army. Record Group 153. Old Military and Civil Branch. National Archives and Records Administration. Washington, D.C. (**Chief Judge in Court of Inquiry**)

PEPPIN, GEORGE

No Author. "Old Citizen Gone." *Capitan News*. **September 23, 1904.** Volume 5. Number 29. Page 4. Center for Southwest Research. Microfilm AN2.L52a.

POE, JOHN WILLIAM

Poe, John W. "The Killing of Billy the Kid." (a personal letter written at Roswell, New Mexico to Mr. Charles Goodnight, Goodnight P.C., Texas) July 10, 1917.

_____. *The Death of Billy the Kid*. (Introduction by Maurice Garland Fulton). Boston and New York: Houghton Mifflin Company. 1933.

Poe, Sophie. *Buckboard Days*. Albuquerque, New Mexico: University of New Mexico Press. 1964.

PURINGTON, GEORGE AUGUSTUS

BIOGRAPHICAL SOURCES

Caldwell, Clifford R. *John Simpson Chisum: Cattle King of the Pecos Revisited*. Santa FE: Sunstone Press. 2010.

Coffey, David. "Hatch, Edward." *Encyclopedia of North American Indian Wars, 1607-1890: A Political, Social, and Military History*. Ed. Spencer C. Tucker. Volume 1. Santa Barbara: ABC-CLIO. 2010.

Trapp, Dan L. *Encyclopedia of Frontier Biography*. Volume 3. Spokane: University of Nebraska Press. 1988.

LETTER TO ADJUTANT GENERAL FROM

Purington, George Augustus. "The District Court adjourned on Thursday ..." **May 3, 1879**. Indiana Historical Society. Lew Wallace Collection. M0292. Box 4. Folder 10. (**Documenting Grand Jury indictments**)

RILEY, JOHN HENRY
CONTEMPORARY SOURCES ABOUT

Tunstall, John Henry. "A Tax-payer's Complaint, Office of John H. Tunstall, Lincoln, Lincoln Co., N.M., January 18, 1878, 'The Present Sheriff of Lincoln County Has Paid Nothing During His Present Term of Office.' Governor's Message for 1878." Mesilla *Independent.* **January 26, 1878.** Volume 1, Number 32. NewspaperArchive.com. **(Exposé of William Brady and John Riley for embezzling tax money to buy cattle; and T.B. Catron then paid that bill)**

Dolan, James J. "Answer to A Taxpayer's Complaint." Mesilla *Independent.* **January 29, 1878.** **(Response to J.H. Tunstall's exposé of embezzlement of tax money to buy cattle)**

McSween, Alexander. "It looks as though the [Indian] agent were the property of J.J. Dolan & J.H. Riley, known here as Dolan & Co." Letter to Secretary of Interior Carl Schurz. **February 11, 1878.** From Frederick Nolan. *The Life and Death of John Henry Tunstall.* Albuquerque, New Mexico: The University of New Mexico Press. 1965. Page 266.

_____. Deposition to Frank Warner Angel. **June 6, 1878.** Pages 5-183 of Frank Warner Angel report *In the Matter of the Examination of the Causes and Circumstances of the Death of John H. Tunstall a British Subject.* Report filed **October 4, 1878.** Angel Report. Microfilm File Case Number 44-4-8-3. Record Group 48. Microfilm No. M750. Roll 1. National Archives and Records Administration. U.S. Department of Justice. Washington, D.C.

No Author. "John Riley Dead." *Deming Graphic.* February 25, 1916. Page 2. Column 1. http://chroniclingamerica.loc.gov.

LETTERS FROM, TO, ABOUT (CHRONOLOGICAL)
TO AND FROM THOMAS BENTON CATRON (SEE: T.B. Catron)
TO N.A.M DUDLEY

Riley, John H. Letter to N.A.M. Dudley. **May 19, 1878. (Fabricated Regulator theft from Catron-Dolan Pecos Cow Camp)** Cited by Victor Westphall, *Thomas Benton Catron and His Era*, Page 87.

FROM WILLIAM L. RYNERSON

Rynerson, William. "Friends Riley & Dolan, Lincoln N.M. I have just received letters from you mailed 10th inst." **February 14, 1878.** Letter to James Dolan and John Riley. Copy as Exhibit B in June 6, 1878 deposition of Alexander McSween. Frank Warner Angel report. *In the Matter of the Examination of the Causes and Circumstances of the Death of John H. Tunstall a British Subject.* Report filed October 4, 1878. Interior Department Papers 1850-1907; Appointments Division and Subsequent Actions. Microfilm File Case Number 44-4-8-3. Record Group 48. Microfilm No. M750. Roll 1. National Archives and Records Administration. U.S. Department of Justice. Washington, D.C. (James J. Dolan Deposition. June 20, 1878. pp. 235-247.) **(Planned killing of J.H. Tunstall)**

RUDULPH, MILNOR

Keleher, William A. *Violence in Lincoln County 1869-1881.* Pages 350-351. Albuquerque, New Mexico: University of New Mexico Press. 1957.

RYNERSON, WILLIAM LOGAN

BIOGRAPHICAL SOURCES

Miller, Darlis A. "William Logan Rynerson in New Mexico. 1862-1893." *New Mexico Historical Review* 48 (April 1973) pp. 101-131.

No Author. "A Brief History of the Rynerson House." Las Cruces: Del Valle Design & Imaging. No copyright. https://delvalleprintinglc.com/rynerson-house/.

CONTEMPORARY SOURCES BY AND ABOUT (CHRONOLOGICAL)

Rynerson, William L "Indictments of the April, Lincoln County Grand Jury." **April 28, 1879**. Herman B. Weisner Papers, ca. 1957-1992. New Mexico State University Library at Las Cruces. Rio Grande Historical Society Collection. Accession No. Ms 0249. Box 4/39. Folder E-Z. Folder Name: "Jessie Evans Accessory to Murder." **(Indictments of Dolan, Campbell, and Evans)**

_____. "Friends Riley & Dolan, Lincoln N M. I have just received letters from you mailed 10th inst." Letter to James Dolan and John Riley. **February 14, 1878**. Copy as Exhibit B in June 6, 1878 deposition of Alexander McSween. Frank Warner Angel report. *In the Matter of the Examination of the Causes and Circumstances of the Death of John H. Tunstall a British Subject*. Report filed October 4, 1878. Interior Department Papers 1850-1907; Appointments Division and Subsequent Actions. Microfilm File Case Number 44-4-8-3. Microfilm No. M750. Roll 1. National Archives and Records Administration. U.S. Department of Justice. Washington, D.C. (James J. Dolan Deposition. June 20, 1878. Pages 235-247.) **(Planned killing of J.H. Tunstall)**

Angel, Frank Warner. "I have just been favored by a call from W.L. Rynerson ..." Letter to Secretary of Interior Carl Schurz. **September 6, 1878**. Microfilm File Case Number 44-4-8-3. Record Group 48. Microfilm No. M750. Roll 1. National Archives and Records Administration. U. S. Department of Justice. Washington, D.C.

Rynerson, William. Venue Change. **April 21, 1879**. Herman B. Weisner Papers, ca. 1957-1992. New Mexico State University Library at Las Cruces. Rio Grande Historical Collection. Accession No. Ms 0249. Box 1. Folder 14-D. Folder Name: "Billy the Kid Legal Documents."

No Author. "Local Items." *Rio Grande Republican*. **September 30, 1893**. Page 1, Column 3. NewspaperArchive.com. **(Death notice)**

(SEE: Letters for Thomas Benton Catron, John H. Riley)

SALAZAR, YGINIO

Kimbrell, George. "I have the honor to request that you will furnish me a posse ..." Letter to Lieutenant Millard Filmore Goodwin. **February 20, 1879**. Indiana Historical Society. Lew Wallace Collection. Box 4, Folder 3. **(For pursuit of Yginio Salazar and William Bonney)**

Goodwin, Millard Filmore. ""I have the honor to submit the following report regarding my duties performed ..." Letter to Fort Stanton Post Adjutant John Loud. **February 23, 1879**. Indiana Historical Society. Lew Wallace Collection. Box 4, Folder 3. **(Assisting pursuit of William Bonney and Yginio Salazar)**

Wallace, Lew. "I beg to submit to you a list of persons ... to arrest ..." Letter to Henry Carroll. **March 11, 1879**. Indiana Historical Society. Lew Wallace Collection. M0292. Box 4. Folder 5. **(Lists Ygenio Salazar and "the Kid)**

Salazar, Joe. (Grandson of Yginio Salazar). Personal Interviews 1999-2001.

SEGALE, BLANDINA

Cooper, Gale. *Blandina Segale, The Nun Who Rode on Billy the Kid: Sleuthing a Foisted Frontier Fable.* Albuquerque, New Mexico: Gelcour Books. 2017.

Segale, Blandina. *At the End of the Santa Fe Trail.* Columbus, Ohio: The Columbian Press. **1932**.

SHERMAN, JOHN

Sherman, John. Letter to Governor Lew Wallace. **October 6, 1878**. Indiana Historical Society. Lew Wallace Collection. M0292. Box 3, Folder 15. (**First reference of "outlaw," Billy Bonney, to Governor Wallace.**)

SHIELD, DAVID

Shield, David. "Your letter of the 23rd inst is at hand and content noted ..." Letter to Montegue Leverson. **July 26, 1878**. Interior Department Papers 1850-1907; Appointments Division and Subsequent Actions. Microfilm File Case Number 44-4-8-3. Record Group 48. Microfilm Roll M750. National Archives and Records Administration. U.S. Department of Justice. Washington, D. C.

(SEE: Letter to Lew Wallace about N.A.M. Dudley's affidavits)

SLOAN, WILLIAM B.

Sloan, William B. "Sam Elkins, Tom Catron, ... Gov. Sheldon ..." List of names in envelope to a Judge W.B. Sloan and list signed W.B.S. **July __, 1884.** University of New Mexico Library. Center for Southwest Studies. Thomas B. Catron Papers, MSS 29, Series 104, Box 1, Folder 2. (**List of Santa Fe Ring members by Sloan**)

_____. "The situation is as follows: The Old S.F. crowd are urging Mariano S. Otero to run ..." Letter to unknown recipient written on Palace Hotel, Santa Fe, letterhead. **[July] 25, [1884]**. University of New Mexico Library. Center for Southwest Studies. Thomas B. Catron Papers, MSS 29, Series 401, Box 1, Folder 7. (**Insider notes about Santa Fe Ring**)

_____. (anonymous, signed "Ithurial") "The Santa Fe Politician, He is Not a Backward Individual in Religion, Politics or Society – The Ring and the Next Delegate to Congress." **July 31, 1884**. *Las Vegas Daily Optic*. Volume V, Number 228. NewspaperArchive.com. (**The anti-Ring "Ithurial" letter; used by the Ring to accuse both L. Bradford Prince and W.B. Sloan of slander**)

Fountain, Albert Jennings. "The 'Ithurial' Letters." **September 27, 1884**. *Rio Grande Republican*. Volume IV, Number 19, Page 2, Column 5. NewspaperArchive.com. (**Ringite accusation of W.B. Sloan and L. Bradford Prince as the anonymous creators of the "Ithurial" letter**)

Sloan, William B. "Commissioner Circular." **September 30, 1885**. Letter to the Editor. *Las Vegas Gazette*. Volume 13, Number 80. https://chroniclingamerica.loc.gov/. (**Seeking railroad exhibits for New Orleans exposition**)

_____. "The New Orleans Exposition. An Important Circular From Commissioner Sloan." **October 15, 1885**. Letter to the Editor. *Las Vegas Daily Gazette*. Volume 13, Number 93. https://chroniclingamerica.loc.gov/.

_____. "Judge W.B. Sloan, a commissioner from New Mexico to the New Orleans exposition." **April 21, 1886**. Notice of travel to announcement. *The Wichita Daily Eagle*. https://chroniclingamerica.loc.gov/. (**Seeking towns to exhibit in New Orleans exposition**)

Anonymous. (W.B. Sloan). "Telegraphic Tidings." **September 14, 1889**. *Las Vegas Daily Optic*. Volume X, Number 270. NewspaperArchive.com. (**Exposé of Ringites in the Republican convention**)

No Author. "Affairs of State ... The Optic Man Barred Out for Misrepresentation." **September 17, 1889.** *Daily New Mexican.* Volume 26, Number 177, Page 4, Column 2. https://chroniclingamerica.loc.gov/. (**Editor fired for printing W.B. Sloan's Ring exposé**)

Sloan, William B. "W.B. Sloan, Lawyer, Notary Public and United States Commissioner ..." **September 26, 1889.** Notice of services. *Santa Fe Daily New Mexican. Volume 26, Number 185.* https://chroniclingamerica.loc.gov/. (**Seeking towns to exhibit in New Orleans exposition**)

_____. "Although not a member of your lodge, yet as a Mason ..." Letter to T.B. Catron. **October 28, 1890.** University of New Mexico Library. Center for Southwest Studies. Thomas B. Catron Papers, MSS 29, Series 102, Box 9, Folder 3.

No Author. No Title. *Las Vegas Daily Optic.* January 9, 1909. Page 1, Column 3. NewspaperArchive.com. (**Death notice**)

SLOUGH, JOHN P.

Roberts, Gary L. *Death Comes For the Chief Justice: The Slough-Rynerson Quarrel and Political Violence in New Mexico.* Denver: University Press of Colorado. 1990. (**William Rynerson's murder of J.P. Slough as political assassination**)

SPRINGER, FRANK

BIBLIOGRAPHICAL SOURCES

Keleher, William A. *The Fabulous Frontier: Twelve New Mexico Items.* Albuquerque, New Mexico: The University of New Mexico Press. 1962. (**States that Springer was part of the original Santa Fe Ring, Page 125**)

Cleaveland, Norman, *A Synopsis of the Great New Mexico Cover-up.* Self-printed. 1989.

_____. *The Great Santa Fe Cover-up. Based on a Talk given Before the Santa Fe Historical Society on November 1, 1978.* Self-printed. 1982.

_____. *The Morleys - Young Upstarts on the Southwest Frontier.* Albuquerque, New Mexico: Calvin Horn Publisher, Inc. 1971.

Taylor, Morris F. *O. P. McMains and the Maxwell Land Grant Conflict.* Tucson, Arizona: The University of Arizona Press. 1979.

Keenan, Lorrena E. Ed. Michael E. Taylor. *A Brief History of Springer, New Mexico.* Springer, New Mexico: Santa Fe Trail Museum of Springer. 1998. (**From manuscript of July 11, 1966**)

Julyan, Robert. "The Place Names of New Mexico." Albuquerque: University of New Mexico Press. 1998. (**About naming of Springer, New Mexico**)

DEPOSITION TO FRANK WARNER ANGEL OF

Springer, Frank. Deposition to Investigator Frank Warner Angel. **August 9, 1878.** Frank Warner Angel report titled *In the Matter of the Investigation of the Charges Against S.B. Axtell Governor of New Mexico.* October 3, 1878. Interior Department Papers 1850-1907; Appointments Division and Subsequent Actions. Microfilm Case File No. 44-4-8-3. Record Group 48. Microfilm Roll M750. National Archives and Records Administration. U.S. Department of Interior. Washington, D.C. (**Mentions Catron, Elkins, and the Santa Fe Ring; with Exhibits of letters, including Asa Middaugh's on Catron's malicious prosecution of Ada Morley; but concludes by covering up Ring involvement in killing John Tunstall and Alexander McSween and in the Lincoln County War**)

CONTEMPORARY SOURCES (CHRONOLOGICAL)

Springer, Frank. "I hope you have received a full account of the Troubles in Lincoln County from your nephew ..." Letter to Senator Rush Clark. **April 9, 1878.** Herman B. Weisner Papers, ca. 1957-1992. New Mexico State University Library at Las Cruces. Rio Grande Historical Collections. Accession No. Ms 0249. Box 4/39. Folder D-6. Folder Name "Frank Springer Letter to Rush Clark." **(Links Santa Fe Ring to murder of J.H. Tunstall)**

_____. "I endorse herewith, directed to the President charges against S.B. Axtell Governor of New Mexico ..." Letter to Secretary of the Interior Carl Schurz. **June 10, 1878.** Microfilm File Case Number 44-4-8-3. Record Group 48. Microfilm No. M750. Roll 1. National Archives and Records Administration. U. S. Department of Justice. Washington, D.C.

_____. "The undersigned, a citizen of the County of Colfax ..." Letter to Rutherford B. Hayes enclosed in letter to Secretary of the Interior Carl Schurz. **June 10, 1878.** Interior Department Papers 1850-1907; Appointments Division and Subsequent Actions. Microfilm File Case Number 44-4-8-3. Record Group 48. Microfilm No. M750. Roll 1. National Archives and Records Administration. U.S. Department of Justice. Washington, D.C.

No Author. "Frank Springer, Pioneer of the State, is Dead, Was Prominent in Early Affairs of New Mexico of Recent Years Followed Scientific Career." **September 23, 1927.** *Albuquerque Journal.* Volume CXCIV, Number 85. Front Page. https://chroniclingamerica.loc.gov.

(SEE: Thomas Benton Catron, and law firm letters to and from)

THORNTON, WILLIAM TAYLOR

(SEE: Thomas Benton Catron letters to and from, and Catron's "Poker Bill" Plot)

TOLBY, FRANKLIN J.

BIOGRAPHICAL SOURCES

Cleaveland, Norman. *The Morleys - Young Upstarts on the Southwest Frontier.* Albuquerque, New Mexico: Calvin Horn Publisher, Inc. 1971.

Taylor, Morris F. *O.P. McMains and the Maxwell Land Grant Conflict.* Tucson, Arizona: The University of Arizona Press. 1979. **(Origins of the Santa Fe Ring)**

CONTEMPORARY SOURCES (CHRONOLOGICAL)

Morley, William Raymond and Frank Springer. On Oscar McMains's citizen's Meeting. *Cimarron News and Press.* **November 10, 1875.** In Mary McPherson, Letters and Petitions to President Rutherford B. Hayes re: Removal Governor Axtell and the Santa Fe Ring. 1977. Interior Department Papers 1850-1907; Appointments Division and Subsequent Actions. Microfilm File Case Number 44-4-8-3. **Record Group 48.** Microfilm Roll M750. National Archives and Records Administration.

_____. " 'The Territory of Elkins.' Assassination of Supposed Sun Correspondent. The Murder of the Rev. F.J. Tolby in New Mexico. A Probate Judge Accused of Complicity in the Crime. Indignation Meeting." New York *Weekly Sun.* **December 22, 1875.** Interior Department Papers 1850-1907; Appointments Division and Subsequent Actions. Microfilm Roll M750. National Archives and Records Administration. Record Group 48. Microfilm Case File Number 44-4-8-3. U.S. Department of Interior. Washington, D. C. **(From May 1, 1877 submission to President Hates as "Mary E. McPherson and W.B. Matchett 'Make certain charges against the U.S. Officials"**)

No Author. Report on murder trial for Franklin Tolby. Pueblo, Colorado *Chieftain*, May 25, 1876 quoting from *Daily New Mexican*, **May 1, 1876**. From Morris F. Taylor. *O.P. McMains and the Maxwell Land Grant Conflict*. Tucson, Arizona: The University of Arizona Press. 1979. Page 49. (**Ring-biased jury instructions by Judge Henry Waldo**)

No Author. (Editorial). **May 15, 1876.** *The Daily New Mexican.* Volume 9. http://chroniclingamerica.loc.gov. (**Ringite article covering up guilt of Mills with Longwill in murder of Franklin Tolby as just "rumor"**)

(SEE: Mary Tibbles McPherson, Oscar McMains)

TUNSTALL, JOHN HENRY

BIOGRAPHICAL SOURCES

Nolan, Frederick W. *The Life and Death of John Henry Tunstall*. Albuquerque, New Mexico: The University of New Mexico Press. 1965.

CONTEMPORARY SOURCES (CHRONOLOGICAL)

Tunstall, John Henry. "A Tax-payer's Complaint, Office of John H. Tunstall, Lincoln, Lincoln Co., N.M., January 18, 1878, 'The Present Sheriff of Lincoln County Has Paid Nothing During His Present Term of Office.' Governor's Message for 1878." Mesilla *Independent.* **January 26, 1878**. Volume 1, Number 32. NewspaperArchive.com. (**Exposé of William Brady and John Riley for embezzling tax money to buy cattle; and T.B. Catron then paid that bill**)

Dolan, James J. "Answer to A Taxpayer's Complaint." Mesilla *Independent.* **January 29, 1878.** (**Response to J.H. Tunstall's exposé of embezzlement of tax money to buy cattle**)

Rynerson, William. "Friends Riley & Dolan, Lincoln N.M. I have just received letters from you mailed 10th inst." Letter to James Dolan and John Riley. **February 14, 1878**. Copy as Exhibit B in June 6, 1878 deposition of Alexander McSween. Frank Warner Angel report. *In the Matter of the Examination of the Causes and Circumstances of the Death of John H. Tunstall a British Subject.* Report filed October 4, 1878. Interior Department Papers 1850-1907; Appointments Division and Subsequent Actions. Microfilm File Case Number 44-4-8-3. Record Group 48. Microfilm No. M750. Roll 1. National Archives and Records Administration. U. S. Department of Justice. Washington, D.C. (James J. Dolan Deposition. June 20, 1878. pp. 235-247.) (**Planned killing of J.H. Tunstall**)

Wilson, John, George B. Barker, Robert M. Gilbert, John Newcomb, Samuel Smith, Benjamin Ellis. "We the undersigned Justice of the Peace and Coroners Jury who sat upon the inquest held this 19th day of February 1878 on the body of John H. Tunstall ..." Coroner's Jury Report for John Tunstall. **February 19, 1878**. (**Naming Tunstall's murderers**)

Springer, Frank. "I hope you have received a full account of the Troubles in Lincoln County from your nephew ..." Letter to Senator Rush Clark. **April 9, 1878**. Herman B. Weisner Papers, ca. 1957-1992. New Mexico State University Library at Las Cruces. Rio Grande Historical Collections. Accession No. Ms 0249. Box 4/39. Folder D-6. Folder Name "Frank Springer Letter to Rush Clark." (**Links Santa Fe Ring to murder of J.H. Tunstall**)

(SEE: Frank Warner Angel)

TWITCHELL, RALPH EMERSON

BOOKS BY

Twitchell, Ralph Emerson. *The Leading Facts of New Mexico History.* Vol. I-II. Santa Fe: Sunstone Press. 2007. (Reprinted from a 1912 edition) (**Ring cover-up historian**)

LETTERS TO, FROM, AND ABOUT (CONTEMPORARY)

Wright, John M. "Ancheta is talking very hard about Catron ..." Letter to Ralph E. Twitchell. **September 12, 1892.** University of New Mexico Library. Center for Southwest Studies. Thomas B. Catron Papers, MSS 29, Series 401, Box 1, Folder 11. (**Twitchell as Catron's political agent**)

Twitchell, Ralph Emerson. "I enclose you herewith a letter from Mr. Hughes, the editor of the Citizen ..." Letter to T.B. Catron. **September 26, 1892.** University of New Mexico Library. Center for Southwest Studies. Thomas B. Catron Papers, MSS 29, Series 401, Box 1, Folder 3.

Frost, Max. "Matters are progressing well here ..." Letter to Ralph E. Twitchell as "Judge". **September 26, 1892.** University of New Mexico Library. Center for Southwest Studies. Thomas B. Catron Papers, MSS 29, Series 401, Box 1, Folder 3.

Twitchell, Ralph Emerson. "I enclose you herewith a letter from Mr. Hughes, the editor of the Citizen ..." Letter to T.B. Catron. **September 26, 1892.** University of New Mexico Library. Center for Southwest Studies. Thomas B. Catron Papers, MSS 29, Series 401-409, Box 1, Folder 3. (**Twitchell involved with Hughes**)

Catron, Thomas Benton. I wired Hughes ..." Letter to Ralph E. Twitchell. **October 16, 1892.** University of New Mexico Library. Center for Southwest Studies. Thomas B. Catron Papers, MSS 29, Series 401, Box 1, Folder 3. (**Catron's campaign**)

Gregg, G.W. "I have your letter from parties in this county ..." Letter to Ralph E. Twitchell. **October 22, 1892.** University of New Mexico Library. Center for Southwest Studies. Thomas B. Catron Papers, MSS 29, Series 401, Box 1, Folder 3.

Riley, John. "I suggest you get out in Spanish a number of copies of your letter ..." Letter to Ralph E. Twitchell. **October 24, 1907.** University of New Mexico Library. Center for Southwest Studies. Thomas B. Catron Papers, MSS 29, Series 401, Box 1, Folder 3.

(SEE: Correspondence with Thomas Benton Catron)

UNDERWOOD (NATHAN) AND NASH (JOSIAH "JOE")

MODERN SOURCES

Armes, George A. *Ups and Downs of an Army Officer.* Washington, D.C. No Publisher listed. 1900. Page 464.

Klasner, Lilly. Eve Ball ed. *My Childhood Among Outlaws.* Tucson: The University of Arizona Press. 1972.

Dearen, Patrick. *A Cowboy of Pecos.* Guilford, Connecticut: Lone Star Books. 2017.

Haley, J. Evetts. J. Phelps White Interview." March 2, 1933. Roswell, New Mexico. Nita Stewart Haley Memorial Library. Midland Texas. Page 101. (**Dates the Underwood and Nash cattle partnership to pre-1875, Page 76**)

"James P. Jones Interview." January 13-14, 1927. Rocky Arroyo, New Mexico. *Notes on the History of Southeastern New Mexico.* Nita Stewart Haley Memorial Library. Midland Texas. Page 101.

"W.R. Owen Interview." March 2, 1933. Carlsbad, New Mexico. Nita Stewart Haley Memorial Library. Midland Texas. Pages 86, 95.

CONTEMPORARY SOURCE

Tunstall, John Henry. "A Tax-payer's Complaint, Office of John H. Tunstall, Lincoln, Lincoln Co., N.M., January 18, 1878, 'The Present Sheriff of Lincoln County Has Paid Nothing During His Present Term of Office.' Governor's Message for 1878." Mesilla *Independent.* **January 26, 1878**. Volume 1, Number 32. NewspaperArchive.com. (**Exposé of William Brady and John Riley for embezzling tax money to buy cattle from Underwood and Nash; T.B. Catron then paid that bill**)

WALDO, HENRY

BIOGRAPHICAL SOURCES

Speer, William S. and John Henry Brown, eds. *The Encyclopedia of the New West, Containing Fully Authenticated Information of the Agricultural, Mercantile, Commercial, Manufacturing, Mining and Grazing Industries, and Representing the Character, Development, Resources and Present Development of Texas, Arkansas, Colorado, New Mexico and Indian Territory, Also Biographical Sketches of Their Representative Men and Women.* Marshall, Texas: The United States Biographical Publishing Company. 1881.

Twitchell, Ralph Emerson. *The Leading Facts of New Mexico History.* Volume III. Cedar Rapids: The Torch Press. 1917.

CONTEMPORARY SOURCES (CHRONOLOGICAL)

Waldo, Henry. *Proceedings of a Court of Inquiry in the Case of Lt. Col. N.A.M. Dudley (May 2, 1879 – July 5, 1879)*. File No. QQ1284. (Boxes 3304, 3305, 3305A); Court Martial Files 1809-1894. Records of the Office of the Judge Advocate General - Army. Record Group 153. Old Military and Civil Branch. National Archives and Records Administration. Washington, D.C. (**Defense attorney for Dudley**)

Ayer, N.W. and Son. eds. *N.W. Ayer & Son's American Newspaper Annual Containing a Catalogue of American Newspapers.* Philadelphia: N.W. Ayer & Son. **1888**. (**Listing Waldo's and Breeden's New Mexico Printing Company as publishing** *The Santa Fe New Mexican*)

Waldo, Henry L. "Yours at hand ..." Letter to T.B. Catron. **December 24, 1890**. University of New Mexico Library. Center for Southwest Studies. Thomas B. Catron Papers, MSS 29, Series 102, Box 10, Folder 1.

No Author. "Death of Judge Waldo." *Santa Fe Magazine.* **August, 1915**. Volume IX, Number 9, Page 50.

(SEE: William Raymond Morley, Mary Tibbles McPherson, N.A.M. Dudley)

WALLACE, LEW

BIOGRAPHICAL SOURCES

Grant, Ulysses S. "General Lew Wallace and General McCook at Shiloh: Memoranda on the Civil War." *Battles and Leaders of the Civil War. Century* magazine. 30 [n.s. 8], 776. August, 1885. Vol. I, Page 468. (**About Shiloh**)

Jones, Oakah L. "Lew Wallace: Hoosier Governor of Territorial New Mexico. 1878-81." *New Mexico Historical Review. 59(1)* (January, l984).

Morsberger, Robert E. and Katherine M. Morsberger. *Lew Wallace: Militant Romantic.* New York: McGraw-Hill Book Company. 1980.

Perret, Geoffrey. *Ulysses S. Grant: Soldier and President.* New York: Random House. 1997. (**Pages 170-171, 185, 188, 191**)

Stephens, Gail. "Shadow of Shiloh: Major General Lew Wallace in the Civil War." Indianapolis: Indiana Historical Society Press. 2010.

Wallace, Lew. *An Autobiography*. Vol. I. New York and London: Harper and Brothers Publishers. 1997.

_____. *An Autobiography*. Vol. II. New York and London: Harper and Brothers Publishers. 1997.

COLLECTED PAPERS OF

Wallace, Lew. Collected Papers. Microfilm Project Sponsored by the National Historical Publications Commission. Microfilm Roll No. 99. Santa Fe, New Mexico: State of New Mexico Records Center and Archives. 1974.

_____. Lew and Susan Wallace Collection. Indiana Historical Society. M0292.

_____. Collected Papers. Lilly Library. Bloomington, Indiana.

SECRET ANGEL NOTEBOOK ON SANTA FE RING FOR

Angel, Frank Warner. "To Gov. Lew Wallace, Santa Fe, N. M., 1878." Notebook. **1878**. Indiana Historical Society. Lew Wallace Collection. M0292. Microfilm No. F372. (**Original missing, copy on microfilm; Notebook prepared for Lew Wallace listing names for Lincoln County and the Santa Fe Ring**)

Theisen, Lee Scott. "Frank Warner Angel's Notes on New Mexico Territory, 1878." *Arizona and the West: A Quarterly Journal of History*. Winter 1976. Volume 18. Number 4. Pages 333-370. (**About the Angel notebook**)

SECRETLY RECEIVED BOOKLET ON SANTA FE RING FOR

McPherson, Mary and W.B. Matchett. "*In the Matter of Charges vs. Gov. S.B. Axtell and Other New Mexico Officials. Submitted to the Departments of the Interior and Justice.* **August, 1877**. Printed as a 31 page booklet. No publisher listed. Indiana Historical Society. Lew Wallace Collection. M0292. Box 3. Folder 20. (**Exposé about Santa Fe Ring, Catron, and Elkins; in Lew Wallace's possession**)

OATH OF OFFICE OF

Wallace, Lew. "Oath of Office, Governor, New Mexico Territory. **October 1, 1878**. Indiana Historical Society. Lew Wallace Collection. DNA; RG 48, M364. [Copy in New Mexico Archives: Records of Secretary of Territory of New Mexico (Acc# 1971-001), Series B-02: Executive Record Book 2, 1867-1882.]

AMNESTY PROCLAMATION OF

Wallace, Lew. "Proclamation by the Governor." **November 13, 1878**. Indiana Historical Society. Lew Wallace Collection. M0292. Box 3. Folder 17. (**Amnesty Proclamation for Lincoln County War fighters**)

PARDONS TO RINGITES ISSUED AS GOVERNOR BY

Wallace, Lew. "Pardon of Jacob B. Matthews, William B. Powell, John Long, and John Hurlie et al." April, 1879 District Court. Filed **May 1, 1879**. (Under Attorneys S.B. Newcomb, Sidney Wilson, and Catron & Thornton). Herman B. Weisner Papers, ca. 1957-1992. New Mexico State University Library at Las Cruces. Rio Grande Historical Society Collection. Accession No. Ms 0249. Box 1. Folder 4. Folder Name: "Amnesty." (**Condoned pardon for Ringites**)

_____. Pardon of Marian Turner. April, 1879 District Court. Filed **May 1, 1879**. (Under Attorneys Catron & Thornton and S.B. Newcomb). Herman B. Weisner Papers, ca. 1957-1992. New Mexico State University Library at Las Cruces. Rio Grande Historical Society Collection. Accession No. Ms 0249. Box 1. Folder 4. Folder Name: "Amnesty." (**Condoned pardon for a Ringman**)

DUDLEY COURT OF INQUIRY TESTIMONY BY

Wallace, Lew. Testimony in Court of Inquiry for Lieutenant Colonel N.A.M. Dudley. **May 12-15, 1879.** *Proceedings of a Court of Inquiry in the Case of Lt. Col. N.A.M. Dudley (May 2,1879 – July 5, 1879).* File No. QQ1284. (Boxes 3304, 3305, 3305A); Court Martial Files 1809-1894. Records of the Office of the Judge Advocate General – Army. Record Group 153. Old Military and Civil Branch. National Archives and Records Administration. Washington, D.C.

INTERVIEW NOTES ON BILLY BONNEY BY (SEE: William H. Bonney)

REWARD NOTICES AND POSTERS FOR WILLIAM BONNEY BY
(SEE: William H. Bonney)

DEATH WARRANT FOR BILLY THE KID BY (SEE: William H. Bonney)
LETTERS BY AND TO

TO AND FROM WILLIAM BONNEY (SEE: William H. Bonney)

TO CAPTAIN HENRY CARROLL

Wallace, Lew. "Under the circumstances, particularly in the absence here of suitable cells for safekeeping of Jesse Evans, Jacob B. Matthews and William Campbell ..." Letter to Henry Carroll. **March 10, 1879.** Indiana Historical Society. Lew Wallace Collection. M0292. Box 4. Folder 4.

_____. "J.J. Dolan was down here tonight. Arrest him upon his return ..." Letter to Henry Carroll. **March 10, 1879.** Indiana Historical Society. Lew Wallace Collection. M0292. Box 4. Folder 4.

_____. "I beg to submit to you a list of persons whom it is necessary, in my judgment, to arrest ..." Letter to Henry Carroll. **March 11, 1879.** Indiana Historical Society. Lew Wallace Collection. M0292. Box 4. Folder 5. (**U.S. Marshal John Sherman's outlaw list, with 14, "The Kid."**)

_____. "I sent you herewith a complete copy of all the cattle brands regularly recorded in the clerk's office of Lincoln County." **March 12, 1879.** Indiana Historical Society. Lew Wallace Collection. M0292. Box 4. Folder 5.

_____. "With Evans and Campbell at large ..." Letter to Henry Carroll. **March 19, 1879.** Indiana Historical Society. Lew Wallace Collection. M0292. Box 4. Folder 6.

FROM, TO, AND ABOUT ATTORNEY HUSTON CHAPMAN

Chapman, Huston I. "You will please pardon me for presuming so much upon your kindness ..." **October 24, 1878.** Indiana Historical Society. Lew Wallace Collection. M0292. Box 3. Folder 16.

Wallace, Lew. "I enclose you a copy of a letter from Las Vegas ..." Letter to Edward Hatch. **October 28, 1878.** Indiana Historical Society. Lew Wallace Collection. M0292. Box 3. Folder 16.

Chapman, Huston I. "You must pardon me for so often presuming upon your kindness ..." **November 29, 1878.** Indiana Historical Society. Lew Wallace Collection. M0292. Box 3. Folder 18.

FROM JAMES JOSEPH DOLAN (SEE: James J. Dolan)

TO AND FROM COMMANDER N.A.M. DUDLEY

Dudley, Nathan Augustus Monroe. "I am in receipt of a copy of letter written by one H.I. Chapman, calling himself the Attorney ..." **November 9, 1878.** Letter to Lew Wallace. From *Proceedings of a Court of Inquiry in the Case of Lt. Col. N.A.M. Dudley (May 2,1879 – July 5, 1879).* File No. QQ1284. (Boxes 3304, 3305, 3305A);

Court Martial Files 1809-1894. Records of the Office of the Judge Advocate General – Army. Record Group 153. Old Military and Civil Branch. National Archives and Records Administration. Washington, D.C. (**Forwarding the Susan McSween affidavits in answer to the charges made by Chapman**)

Wallace, Lew. "Your favor containing the duplicate accounts of the messenger who posted the President's Proclamation ..." Letter to N.A.M. Dudley. **November 30, 1878**. Indiana Historical Society. Lew Wallace Collection. M0292. Box 3. Folder 18.

Dudley, Nathan Augustus Monroe. "An Open Letter, By Lieut. Col. N.A.M. Dudley, 9th Cavalry, to His Excellency Governor Lew Wallace." Letter to Lew Wallace. Santa Fe *Weekly New Mexican*. **December 14, 1878**. Reprinted in *Mesilla News*. December 21, 1878. As Exhibit 13 from *Proceedings of a Court of Inquiry in the Case of Lt. Col. N.A.M. Dudley (May 2, 1879 - July 5, 1879)*. File No. QQ1284. (Boxes 3304, 3305, 3305A); Court Martial Files 1809-1894. Records of the Office of the Judge Advocate General - Army. Record Group 153. Old Military and Civil Branch. National Archives and Records Administration. Washington, D.C. (**Attacks Wallace's Amnesty Proclamation as applying to the military**)

Wallace, Lew. "The public interests with which I am charged make it, in my judgment, exceedingly improper for me to answer publicly your letters in the New Mexican ..." Letter to N.A.M. Dudley and other Fort Stanton officers. **December 16, 1878**. Indiana Historical Society. Lew Wallace Collection. M0292. Box 3. Folder 19.

Dudley, Nathan Augustus Monroe Dudley. "This being regular report day, I respectfully state ..." **March 1, 1879**. Indiana Historical Society. Lew Wallace Collection. M0292. Box 4. Folder 4. (**Blaming Lincoln County "troubles" on rustlers**)

TO ATTORNEY EUGENE A. FISKE

Wallace, Lew. "I have your several letters, including the last one of the 3rd inst." Letter to Eugene Fiske. **November 6, 1897**. Indiana Historical Society. Lew Wallace Collection. AC233. Box 1. Folder 7. (part of 1981 addition) (**About T.B. Catron's control over New Mexicans**)

FROM PRESIDENT JAMES ABRAM GARFIELD

Garfield, James Abram. "I have, this morning, finished reading "Ben-Hur" ...." Letter to Lew Wallace. **April 19, 1881**. Indiana Historical Society. Lew Wallace Collection. M0292. Box 4. Folder 17.

TO SHERIFF PATRICK F. GARRETT

Wallace, Lew. "To the Sheriff of Lincoln County, New Mexico, Greeting ..." **April 30, 1881**. Indiana Historical Society. Lew Wallace Collection. M0292. Box 9. Folder 11. (**Death Warrant for William Bonney**)

TO MESCALERO APACHE AGENT FREDERICK C. GODFROY

Wallace, Lew. "You can be of the greatest possible help to me in the effort now making to catch the thieves and murderers in this part of the Territory ..." **March 12, 1879**. Indiana Historical Society. Lew Wallace Collection. M0292. Box 4. Folder 5. (**Wants Indian "guides"**)

TO AND FROM GENERAL EDWARD HATCH

Wallace, Lew. "I think all that is needed now for the thorough pacification of Lincoln County is ..." Letter to Edward Hatch. **October 26, 1878**. Indiana Historical Society. Lew Wallace Collection. M0292. Box 3. Folder 16.

_____. "In a communication, dated October 28. inst., I requested, for reasons stated, a safe-guard for Mrs. McSween ..." Letter to Edward Hatch. **November 9,**

1878. Indiana Historical Society. Lew Wallace Collection. M0292. Box 3. Folder 17.

_____. "I am in receipt of Col. Dudley's reply to the charges against him ..." Letter to Edward Hatch. **November 14, 1878**. Indiana Historical Society. Lew Wallace Collection. M0292. Box 3, Folder 17. (**Has quote: "the "reply is perfectly satisfactory"**)

_____. "I am constrained to request that Lieut Col. N.A.M. Dudley, Commanding at Fort Stanton, be relieved ..." **December 7, 1878**. Indiana Historical Society. Lew Wallace Collection. M0292. Box 3, Folder 18. (**Removal of Dudley requested**)

_____. "I have the honor to repeat the request made on a former occasion that Lt. Col. N.A.M. Dudley be relieved of the command ..." **March 7, 1879**. Letter to Edward Hatch. Indiana Historical Society. Lew Wallace Collection. M0292. Box 4, Folder 4.

Hatch, Edward. "Lieutenant Colonel N.A.M. Dudley is hereby relieved from command and duty ..." Special Field Order 2. **March 8, 1879**. Indiana Historical Society. Lew Wallace Collection. M0292. Box 4, Folder 4. (**Wallace removes Dudley**)

TO AND FROM PRESIDENT RUTHERFORD B. HAYES

Wallace, Lew. "I avail myself of your request this morning. It is hardly necessary to give reasons for a preference of the Italian mission ..." Letter to Rutherford B. Hayes. **March 9, 1877**. Indiana Historical Society. Lew Wallace Collection. M0292. Box 3. Folder 13. (**Desired ambassadorships**)

_____. "The feuds recently in Lincoln county, New Mexico, left a large many thieves and murderers, who, with others of like class since added to their number, are now confederated for plunder." Letter to Rutherford B. Hayes. **March 31, 1879**. Indiana Historical Society. Lew Wallace Collection. M0292. Box 4. Folder 7. (**Wants martial law against confederacy of outlaws**)

Hayes, Rutherford B. "We are greatly obliged by your kindness." Letter to Lew Wallace. **January 9, 1881**. Indiana Historical Society. Lew Wallace Collection. M0292. Box 4. Folder 16. (**Thanking for gift of *Ben-Hur***)

TO LINCOLN COUNTY SHERIFF GEORGE KIMBRELL

Wallace, Lew. "The duty of keeping the peace in the county and arresting offenders is devolved by the law upon you ..." **April 2, 1879**. Indiana Historical Society. Lew Wallace Collection. Box 4, Folder 8.

TO AND FROM IRA E. LEONARD (SEE: Ira Leonard)

TO COLONEL ABSALOM H. MARKLAND

Wallace, Lew. "Our mutual friend, M. Hinds, who will hand you this ..." Letter to A.H. Markland. **November 14, 1878**. Indiana Historical Society. Lew Wallace Collection. M0292. Box 3. Folder 17. (**Fully aware of the Santa Fe Ring and its attempt to remove him as governor**)

FROM SECRETARY OF WAR GEORGE W. McCRARY

McCrary, George W. "I have the honor to acknowledge the receipt of your letter..." **November 23, 1878**. Indiana Historical Society. Lew Wallace Collection. M0292. Box 3. Folder 17. (**About requesting arms**)

McCrary, George W. "I have the honor to acknowledge the receipt of your letter..." **August 26, 1879**. Indiana Historical Society. Lew Wallace Collection. M0292. Box 4. Folder 12.(**Freeing Wallace from responsibility for Dudley Court of Inquiry outcome**)

TO LINCOLN JAILOR JUAN PATRÓN

Wallace, Lew. "Please select ten of your Rangers ..." Letter to Juan Patrón. **March 3, 1879**. Indiana Historical Society. Lew Wallace Collection. M0292. Box 4. Folder 4. (**To arrest "Scurlock and Bowdre"**)

_____. "Please report to Sheriff Kimbrell ..." Letter to Juan Patrón. **March 3, 1879**. Indiana Historical Society. Lew Wallace Collection. M0292. Box 4. Folder 4.

_____. Wallace, Lew. "Be good enough to send word to all your men to turn out soon as possible ..." Letter to Juan Patrón. **March 19, 1879**. Indiana Historical Society. Lew Wallace Collection. M0292. Box 4. Folder 6. (**Reports escape of Jessie Evans and Billy Campbell from Fort Stanton**)

FROM LIEUTENANT GEORGE PURINGTON

Purington, George Augustus. "The District Court adjourned on Thursday ..." **May 3, 1879**. Indiana Historical Society. Lew Wallace Collection. M0292. Box 4. Folder 10. (**Letter to Adjutant General on Grand Jury indictments of the Murphy-Dolans and N.A.M. Dudley; copy sent to Lew Wallace**)

TO AND FROM SECRETARY OF INTERIOR CARL SCHURZ

Wallace, Lew. "I have the honor to inform you ..." Letter to Carl Schurz. **October 1, 1878**. Indiana Historical Society. Lew Wallace Collection. M0292. Box 3. Folder 15. (**Informing Schurz that he informed Axtell of suspension and that he now qualified as Governor, and wanted "extreme measures"**)

_____. "I have the honor to enclose herewith a requisition ..." **October 4, 1878**. Letter to Carl Schurz. Indiana Historical Society. Lew Wallace Collection. M0292. Box 3. Folder 15. (**About arms from Secretary of War**)

_____. "As the basis of the request which I have to prefer relative to the affairs in the county of Lincoln ..." Letter to Carl Schurz. **October 5, 1878**. Indiana Historical Society. Lew Wallace Collection. M0292. Box 3. Folder 15. (**Requesting President to declare martial law**)

_____. "In further exemplification of affairs in Lincoln county accept extract received ..." Letter to Carl Schurz. **October 5, 1878**. Indiana Historical Society. Lew Wallace Collection. M0292. Box 3. Folder 15. (**N.A.M. Dudley's report of "Wrestlers" raping in Lincoln County**)

No signatures. (But in Lew Wallace's handwriting). "Yesterday, at the request of Governor Wallace the undersigned, physicians ...." Letter to Carl Schurz. **October 23, 1878**. Indiana Historical Society. Lew Wallace Collection. M0292. Box 3. Folder 16. (**Focus on need to refurbish the Palace of the Governors**)

Schurz, Carl. "I acknowledge the receipt of your letter of the 13th instant ..." Letter from Carl Schurz. **November 23, 1878**. Indiana Historical Society. Lew Wallace Collection. M0292. Box 3. Folder 18. (**Amnesty Proclamation, has approval of President**)

_____. "I have received your letter ..." Letter to Lew Wallace. **December 9, 1878**. Indiana Historical Society. Lew Wallace Collection. M0292. Box 3. Folder 19. (**Answer denying he would be removed**)

Wallace, Lew. "I have the honor to report that affairs of the Territory are moving on quietly ..." Letter to Carl Schurz. **December 21, 1878**. Indiana Historical Society. Lew Wallace Collection. M0292. Box 3. Folder 19. (**N.A.M. Dudley's indignation about the Amnesty Proclamation and discrediting H.I. Chapman**)

_____. "One H.I. Chapman, lawyer, was assassinated ...." Letter to Carl Schurz. **February 27, 1879**. Indiana Historical Society. Lew Wallace Collection. M0292. Box 4. Folder 3. (**Reacting to Chapman murder by using troops to track "outlaws" – meaning the Regulators.**)

_____. "My time has been so constantly occupied in getting my work into operation ..." Letter to Carl Schurz. **March 21, 1879**. Indiana Historical Society. Lew Wallace Collection. M0292. Box 4. Folder 7. (**Progress report with enclosure of Sherman's outlaw list with "The Kid," and outlaw myth**)

_____. "To day I forwarded a telegram to you, with another to the President ..." Letter to Carl Schurz. **March 31, 1879**. Indiana Historical Society. Lew Wallace Collection. M0292. Box 4. Folder 7. (**Mention of "precious specimen nicknamed 'The Kid' "**)

_____. "I have official information that a court of inquiry for Col. Dudley has been ordered ..." Letter to Carl Schurz. **April 4, 1879**. Indiana Historical Society. Lew Wallace Collection. M0292. Box 4, Folder 8.

_____. "I have the honor to inform you that affairs in Lincoln County are progressing favorably ..." Letter to Carl Schurz. **April 18, 1879**. Indiana Historical Society. Lew Wallace Collection. M0292. Box 4, Folder 9.

_____. "I have the honor to inform you that all the recent reports, military and otherwise, justify me in saying Lincoln County is enjoying a term of peace." Letter to Carl Schurz. **May 5, 1879**. Indiana Historical Society. Lew Wallace Collection. M0292. Box 4. Folder 10.

_____. "Enclosed please find a copy of the report of the commandant at Fort Stanton." Letter to Carl Schurz. **June 11, 1879**. Indiana Historical Society. Lew Wallace Collection. M0292. Box 4. Folder 11. (**Self-serving progress report of quelling disturbances**)

_____. "The accompanying document received from Fort Stanton which will explain itself." Letter to Carl Schurz. **July 30, 1879**. Indiana Historical Society. Lew Wallace Collection. M0292. Box 4. Folder 12. (**Claims he pacified the Territory**)

_____. "In reply to the communication of Acting Secretary Bell ..." **September 15, 1879**. Letter to Carl Schurz. Indiana Historical Society. Lew Wallace Collection. M0292. Box 4. Folder 13. (**On Bob Olinger killing John Jones; calling Olinger a "bloody ... Bandit of the Pecos."**)

_____. "I have the honor to inform you ..." **February 16, 1880**. Letter to Carl Schurz. Indiana Historical Society. Lew Wallace Collection. M0292. Box 4, Folder 14. (**Reports Catron as head of Ring**)

_____. "From private advices received from Lincoln county ..." **December 7, 1880**. Indiana Historical Society. Lew Wallace Collection. M0292. Box 4. Folder 15. (**Reports pursuit of outlaws by people in Lincoln County**)

_____. "I have private business urgently requiring my presence in New York City ..." Letter to Carl Schurz. **December 14, 1880**. Indiana Historical Society. Lew Wallace Collection. M0292. Box No. 4. Folder 15. (**Mention's - without giving names - the deputy sheriff [Garrett] tracking the "leader of the outlaws" [Billy] for whom Wallace has set a "$500 reward."**)

TO AND FROM ATTORNEY DAVID SHIELD

Shield, David. "It is rumored that 'Eight long Affidavits' are in your possession ..." Letter to Lew Wallace. **February 11, 1879**. Indiana Historical Society. Lew Wallace Collection. M0292. Box 4. Folder 2. (**Commander Dudley's defamatory affidavits about Susan McSween**)

Wallace, Lew. "I am in receipt of your letter of this date requesting inspection ..." Letter to David Shield. **February 19, 1879**. Indiana Historical Society. Lew Wallace Collection. M0292. Box 4. Folder 2. (**Refuses to give copies of Dudley's affidavits about Susan McSween**)

TO AND FROM JUSTICE OF THE PEACE JOHN B. WILSON

Wallace, Lew. "I hasten to acknowledge receipt of your favor of the 11th Jan. ult. ..." **January 18, 1879**. Indiana Historical Society. Lew Wallace Collection.

M0292. Box 4. Folder 1. (**Lincoln County as carrying on a revolution**)

_____. "Your favors are both in hand and place me under renewed obligation. ..." **February 6, 1879.** Indiana Historical Society. Lew Wallace Collection. M0292. Box 4. Folder 2.

Wilson, John B. Letter to Lew Wallace. Unsigned but noted as from "Sqr. Wilson by Wallace. Undated, but likely **March, 1879**. Indiana Historical Society. Lew Wallace Collection. M0292. Box 4, Folder 7. (**On Lady Liberty stationery**)

_____. Affidavit of John Wilson. **March ?, 1879**. Indiana Historical Society. Lew Wallace Collection. M0292. Box 4, Folder 7.

Wallace, Lew. "I understand that affidavits will be filed with you against the prisoners. ..." Letter to John B. Wilson. **March 8, 1879**. Indiana Historical Society. Lew Wallace Collection. M0292. Box 4. Folder 4.

_____. "I enclose a note for Bonney." Letter to John "Squire" Wilson. **March 20, 1879.** Indiana Historical Society. Lew Wallace Collection. M0292. Box 4. Folder 6. (**The pardon negotiation for Billy Bonney**)

Wilson, John B. Signed JBW. **April 8, 1879.** Indiana Historical Society, Lew Wallace Collection. M0292. Box 4, Folder 8. (**Notes on rustling**)

_____. Letter to Lew Wallace. **May 18, 1879.** Indiana Historical Society. Lew Wallace Collection. M0292. Box 4, Folder 5.

ARTICLES ABOUT WILLIAM BONNEY BY (SEE: William H. Bonney)

WALZ, EDGAR A.

No Author. *The American Book of Biography: Men of 1912*. Chicago: American Publishers Association. 1913. Page 614.

No Author. "Edgar A. Walz Dead: Expert on credit, Founder of The Travelers Hotel Credit Corporation – Managed New Mexico Ranch in Youth." *The New York Times*. **April 5, 1935.** Volume LXXXIV, Number 28,195. Page 24.

WILD, AZARIAH

BIOGRAPHICAL SOURCE

Nolan, Frederick. "Biography of Azariah Wild." Unpublished and personal communications, June 11, 2005 and October 9, 2005.

CONTEMPORARY SOURCES (CHRONOLOGICAL)

Brooks, James J. *1877 Report on Secret Service Operatives*. "On Azariah Wild." **September 26, 1877.** Page 392. Department of the Treasury. United States Secret Service. Washington, D.C.

Wild, Azariah F. "Daily Reports of U. S. Secret Service Agents, Azariah F. Wild. Microfilm T-915. Record Group 87. Rolls 306 **(June 15, 1877 - December 31, 1877), 307 (January 1, 1878 - June 30, 1879), 308 (July 1, 1879 - June 30, 1881), 309 (July 1, 1881 - September 30, 1883)**, and 310 **(October 1, 1883 - July 31, 1886)**. National Archives and Records Department. Department of Treasury. United States Secret Service. Washington, D. C.

Wild, Azariah. Telegraph on counterfeit bills. **January 4, 1881.** Herman B. Weisner Papers, ca. 1957-1992. New Mexico State University Library at Las Cruces. Rio Grande Historical Collections. Accession No. Ms 0249. Box 11. Folder O-1. Folder Name: "Olinger, Robert and James W. Bell."

WILSON, JOHN B. "SQUIRE"

CORONER'S JURY REPORT BY

Wilson, John, George B. Barker, Robert M. Gilbert, John Newcomb, Samuel Smith, Benjamin Ellis. "We the undersigned Justice of the Peace and Coroners Jury who sat upon the inquest held this 19th day of February 1878 on the body of John H. Tunstall ..." Coroner's Jury Report for John Tunstall. **February 19, 1878.** (**Naming as murderers, among others, James Dolan, Frank Baker, Jessie Evans, William Morton, and George Hindman**)

(SEE: John Henry Tunstall, James Dolan, Frank Baker, Jessie Evans, William Morton, and George Hindman)

LETTERS FROM

Wilson, John B. Letter to Lew Wallace. Unsigned but noted as from "Sqr. Wilson by Wallace. Undated, but likely **March, 1879**. Indiana Historical Society. Lew Wallace Collection. M0292. Box 4, Folder 7. (**On Lady Liberty stationery**)

_____. Affidavit of John Wilson. **March ?, 1879**. Indiana Historical Society. Lew Wallace Collection. M0292. Box 4, Folder 7.

_____. Signed JBW. **April 8, 1879**. Indiana Historical Society, Lew Wallace Collection. M0292. Box 4, Folder 8. (**Notes on rustling**)

_____. Letter to Lew Wallace. **May 18, 1879**. Indiana Historical Society. Lew Wallace Collection. M0292. Box 4, Folder 5.

LETTERS TO

Bonney, W H. "Friend Wilson ..." **March 18, 1879**. Indiana Historical Society. Lew Wallace Collection. M0292. (**For pardon negotiation with Lew Wallace**)

Wallace, Lew. "I understand that affidavits will be filed with you against the prisoners. ..." Letter to John B. Wilson. **March 8, 1879**. Indiana Historical Society. Lew Wallace Collection. M0292. Box 4. Folder 4.

_____. "I enclose a note for Bonney." Letter to John "Squire" Wilson. **March 20, 1879.** Indiana Historical Society. Lew Wallace Collection. M0292. Box 4. Folder 6. (**The pardon negotiation for Billy Bonney**)

(SEE: William H. Bonney and Lew Wallace)

INDEX

INDEX

Abbott, E.C. "Teddy Blue" – 36
  We Pointed Them North by: 36
Abeytia, Antonio – 68
Addison, James Roger – 60
Alamogordo News – 36
Alarid, Laurencio – 68, 618
Albany Law School – 503
Albuquerque Daily Citizen – 112, 120, 122, 124, 127, 129, 132, 134, 141, 203 (see T.B. Catron for anonymous letter plot with Editor, Thomas Hughes)
Albuquerque Daily Democrat – 56-57, 203
Albuquerque, New Mexico – 66, 68, 84, 112-113, 121, 150, 203-204, 461, 472-473, 624, 689
Albuquerque Review – 471
Allison, Clay – 103, 241, 250, 252-254, 260-262, 267, 304-305, 310, 312, 321, 438, 457; **Catron offer of $700 to kill Franklin Tolby to:** 103, 252; **attempt to catch Tolby murderer Robert Longwill by:** 254, 304; **accused of Cruz Vega lynching:** 253; **murder of Francisco Griego by:** 253, 304-305, 318; **indicted for murders in Taos court:** 267
Amador County, California – 182
American Valley Company ranch – 81, 91-92, 246 (see Catron's American Valley murders)
Amires, Andres – 94
Amires, Jesucita – 94
Amnesty Proclamation (see Lew Wallace)
Angel, Frank Warner – 17, 19-20, 33, 45, 64, 82-83, 86-88, 98, 105, 109, 183, 191, 246, 249-250, 252, 261, 264, 269, 274-276, 289, 295-296, 312-315, 324, 341, 347, 353, 361, 374-375, 380, 389, 416-421, 425, 433, 443-461, 464, 471-475, 480, 483-484, 498, 501, 522, 530, 536, 583, 618, 725-727, 731; **bribery attempt by Ring on:** 64, 416, 420; **in Ring cipher-code as "stick":** 83; **deposition of William Bonney by:** (see William H. Bonney); **deposition of Alexander McSween by:** (see Alexander McSween); **deposition of Frank Springer by:** (see Frank Springer); **secret Ring notebook for Lew Wallace of:** 20, 464; the notebook: 471-475, 480; **likely provider of McPherson exposé to Lew Wallace:** 20, 296, 464; "In the Matter of the Cause and Circumstances of the Death of John H. Tunstall, a British Subject" by: 444-446; "In the Matter of the Lincoln County Troubles" by: 446-448; "In the Matter of the Investigation of the Charges Against S.B. Axtel [Axtell] Governor of New Mexico" by: 448-450; the report: 450-458; "Examination of Charges against F.C. Godfroy, Indian Agent, Mescalero, New Mexico" by: 498, 522; Uña de Gato Land Grant fraud exposed by: 289, 295, 464; **report on Catron by:** 82, 86-89, 314, 458-461, 618; **Ring cover-up by and outlaw myth by:** 19, 274-276, 324, 371, 417, 443-458, 461, 464, 698, 731 (see Thomas Benton Catron)
Angostura Grant – 298
Ann Arbor, Michigan – 206
Antrim, Catherine – 12
Antrim, Henry (see William Henry Bonney)
Antrim, Josie – 12
Antrim, William Henry Harrison – 12
Appel, Daniel – 352, 401, 428, 497-498, 523-524; **fraudulent Tunstall autopsy report by:** 352
Apodaca, Dominga – 105, 110
Archuleta, Diego – 211, 241
Archuleta, Rallos – 97-98 (see White Caps)
Arizona and the West – 54, 211, 215, 233
Arizona Territory – 13, 52, 157, 187, 200, 233-234, 237-238, 326, 360, 542
Arlington National Cemetery – 201
Armijo, Manuel – 243
Arney, William F.M. – 76, 167, 184, 209, 471
Arthur, Chester A. – 726

Ashenfelter, Singleton M. – 129, 203; **biography of:** 203-204
Atchison, Topeka, and Santa Fe Rail Road – 79, 162, 191, 326
Atkins Cantina – 13
Atkinson, Henry M. – 68, 79, 81, 91-92, 246, 471
Atzerodt, George – 469
Axtell, Samuel Beach – 16, 18-20, 45-46, 63-65, 68, 77-78, 85-87, 96, 99, 162, 168-169, 182-185, 189-190, 215, 230, 238, 242, 250, 252, 254, 259, 261-272, 283, 287-310, 312-314, 318-320, 322-323, 325, 331, 336-337, 367-369, 371-372, 377, 379, 385, 388-389, 404, 416-418, 420, 426, 436, 438-439, 443, 447-459, 464, 467, 470, 484, 501, 553, 603, 678-679, 725-727; **biography of:** 182; **Catron Ring bribe of through John Riley:** 80, 182, 331, 433, 455; **belonging to Santa Fe Ring of:** 65, 68-69, 77, 293; "Governor's Message" of 1875: 230; **using troops for suppression in Colfax County by:** 99, 230, 254, 262-263, 322, 438; **front for Uña de Gato Land Grant fraud:** 79, 87, 230, 289, 295, 323, 484; **removing Colfax County courts to shield F.J. Tolby's murderers:** 77, 87, 168-169, 183, 215, 230, 261, 287-288, 303-304, 309, 312, 318, 320, 453, 553 (see Melvin Mills, Robert Longwill); **illegal Taos courts of:** 264-271; **removing Colfax County Sheriff O.K. Chittenden to block arrests:** 263, 320; "Dear Ben plot" to murder Ring opponents by: 87, 168, 196, 250, 261-264, 275, 312, 320-322, 353, 381, 388, 420, 436-437, 439, 457, 501; the Dear Ben telegram: 263-264, 439 (see Benjamin Stevens); **appointing W. Rynerson District Attorney by:** 184, 418; **in exposé of F.J. Tolby:** 252; **in exposés of by Mary McPherson of:** 64, 242, 259, 276, 283, 287-292, 294, 450; **requesting troops in Lincoln County War by:** 16, 18, 77, 87, 183, 185, 189, 230, 263, 336, 367, 369, 385, 388, 404, 415-416, 418, 429, 437-438, 319-320, 336-337, 367-369, 371-372, 377, 379, 404, 415-416, 418, 420, 426, 678-679; **in exposés of Montegue Leverson:** 371-372, 418; **in exposé of A.A. McSween:** 404; **Catron's letter about a fake Regulator attack to:** 388, **obstructing arrest of Tunstall's murderers:** 87, 496; by using troops: 367, 369, 404, 416, 429, 437-438; by removal of Justice of the Peace Wilson by Proclamation of March 9, 1878 and outlawing his deputizings:16, 18, 87, 183, 185, 230, 319-320, 336-337, 368-369, 371-372, 377, 379, 404, 415-416, 418, 420, 426, 678-679; the Proclamation: 368-369; **Proclamation of May 28, 1878 removing Sheriff Copeland by:** 18, 87, 189, 263, 336, 385, 388, 415-416, 418; **assassination attempt against M. Leverson by:** 436; **Frank Warner Reports about:** 183, 389, 447-448; improperly pressured about: 448-450; the Axtell report: 450-458; **scapegoated for Ring by removal as Governor:** 20, 183, 458; **S.B. Elkins's try to save his Governorship:** 311; **made Chief Justice:** 96, 162, 725-727; **outlaw myths by and for:** 87, 182, 230, 294-295, 311, 318, 320, 369, 388
Aztec gold mine – 79, 243, 463 (see Thomas Benton Catron)
Baca, Bernadino – 105
Baca, Epifanio – 92
Baca, Saturnino – 19, 181-182, 378, 409, 422, 426-427, 524, 581, 670, 672; **biography of:** 181; **Baca's ranch of:** 534
Bailhache, W.H. – 68
Bail, John D. – 27, 184, 193-194, 203, 395, 473, 504, 671-672, 677; **biography of:** 193; **loyalty to Catron of:** 27, 193-194; **co-counsel for Billy Bonney's Brady trial:** 27, 184, 504, 671-672; jury instructions by: 677
Baker, Frank – 16, 24, 28, 199, 341, 352, 361-363, 366-367, 385, 397, 400, 404, 539-541
Baldy, Louis H. – 555
Ball, Eve (see Lilly Klasner)
Bantz, Gideon B. – 111-112, 194

823

Barnes, Sidney M. – 87, 89, 145, 171, 461, 614, 619, 623-632, 635, 671; **replacing Catron as U.S. Attorney by:** 461; **defending Dudley in Susan McSween's civil case by:** 87, 89, 614; **working with Secret Service to capture Billy Bonney by:** 623-635; **prosecutor against Billy Bonney for Brady trial by:** 87, 671; **trying to convict Oliver Lee of A.J. Fountain's murder by:** 145

Barrier, Adolph P. – 15-16, 343, 347, 373, 381, 396-398, 403-405, 425, 444, 471, 678-679, 732

Bates, Sebrian – 601

Bartlett, Charles – 471

Batavia, New York – 505

Batavia *Republican Advocate* – 503

Battle of Alamance – 359-360

Battle of Monocacy – 468

Battle of Shiloh – 167, 467-469, 477, 483, 490; **casualties in:** 468

"Battle of the Archives" (see Thomas Benton Catron)

bay mare – 201, 652, 663-664, 680

Beardsley, Ezra I. – 471

Beaubien, Charles Hipolite Trotier "Don Carlos Beaubien" – 243

Beaubien-Miranda Land Grant – 23, 242-243, 291

Beaubien, Narciso – 243

Beaver Smith's Saloon – 23

Beckwith family – 540, 542-542

Beckwith, Henry – 540

Beckwith, John – 197, 477, 540, 542

Beckwith, Robert "Bob" – 249, 429, 540, 542, 590

Bedaraco, Joe – 95

Bell, James W. – 12, 27-28, 639, 685-686; **possible accidental killer of Jim Carlyle:** 685; **made Deputy by Pat Garrett to guard Billy Bonney;** 12, 27, 685, 705; **killed by Billy Bonney:** 12, 28, 685-686

Benedict, Kirby – 158

Benton, Thomas Hart – 75

Bering Sea Fisheries – 163

Bernstein, Morris – 43, 495

Bethany College – 190

"Big Mose" – 539

Billy and Paulita: The Saga of Billy the Kid, Paulita Maxwell, and the Santa Fe Ring – xviii; 44

Billy the Kid (see William H. Bonney)

Billy the Kid Case hoax – xviii

Billy the Kid reward notices (see William H. Bonney)

Billy the Kid's Pretenders: Brushy Bill and John Miller – xxi

Billy the Kid's Writings, Words, and Wit – 529, 539

Bingham, George – 199

"Black Knights" – 521

Blaine, James Gillespie – 160-162, 222, 224

Blalock, George – 195

Blazer, Joseph H. – 181

Blazer's Mill – 17, 27, 144, 330, 373, 387, 411, 543, 633, 671

Bonita, Arizona – 13, 199

Bonito River – 19, 427

Bonney, William Henry "Billy" (William Henry McCarty, Henry Antrim, Billy Bonney, the Kid, Billy the Kid) – 4, 6-8, 11-36, 39-48, 51-65, 70, 77, 80, 83, 85, 87, 90, 109, 130, 136-137, 139, 144-145, 171, 174, 176, 180, 183-186, 188-189, 193-195, 197-199, 201-202, 204-205, 210, 225, 238, 241-243, 245, 250, 252, 264, 268, 287, 292, 319-320, 326, 329, 331-332, 334-337, 341, 360-369, 373-375, 385-387, 390, 408-409, 411-415, 419, 423-424, 427-430, 439-440, 444, 453, 461, 464, 467, 470, 495, 498, 500-501, 503-504, 509, 517-518, 520-522, 526, 529-534, 537-546, 549-558, 561, 571, 573, 578, 586-592, 594, 598-599, 606-608, 614, 617, 620, 625-654, 657-666, 669-682, 685-700, 703-721, 728, 731-732; **biography of:** 11-29; **as William Henry McCarty:** 12; **as Henry Antrim:** 12; **creating William Henry "Billy" Bonney by:** 13, 238, 326; **first mention as "Billy the Kid":** 578; **tintype of:** 17, 24; **contemporary champions of:** 30-36; **bi-culturalism of:** 7, 12, 153, 423, 440; potential to inspire Hispanic revolt by: 18, 21, 90, 153, 360, 500; **Silver City robbing and jailing of:** 13, 334; **killing of Frank "Windy" Cahill by:** 13, 90, 131, 174, 625; **as Tunstall ranch hand:** 3, 336; "Little Casino" **nickname of:** 23; Peñasco River **ranch of:** 13, 332, 351; **Winchester '73 carbine of:** 16,

341, 368; **attempts to murder by J.B. Matthews:** 188; **eye-witness to John Tunstall murder of:** 15, 351-352; **becoming a Regulator by** (see Regulators of 1878); **affidavit on Tunstall murder by:** 360-361; **deposition on Tunstall murder by:** 17, 33, 361-365, 389, 419, 444; the deposition: 362-365; **Lincoln County War in** (see Regulators of 1878, see Lincoln County War); **as deputy and posseman:** 16, 18, 320, 365-366, 453, 529-530; **illegal jailing of by Sheriff Brady:** 367-368; **illegal outlawing of by Governor Axtell:** 16, 87, 368-369; **in Regulator arrest and killing of "Buck" Morton and Frank Baker by:** 16, 24, 28, 367, 385; **in Regulator killing of William Brady and George Hindman:** 16, 24, 28, 185, 373, 385; **in Regulator killing of "Buckshot" Roberts by:** 17, 24, 28, 90, 185, 373-374; **Lincoln County 1878 Grand Jury indictments against for killing of Brady and Hindman:** 20, 27, 361, 375, 381, 385, 408, 411, 495, 529-530, 598, 628, 671; venue change for trials of: 264, 319; **federal indictment No. 411 against for killing of Roberts:** 20, 27, 90, 245, 361, 375, 381, 408, 411-415, 495, 501, 529, 598, 628, 671; the indictment: 412-415; (see Thomas Benton Catron); **David Easton warrant against:** 180, 387; **"Regulator Manifesto" by:** 18, 61, 198, 385, 423-424, 440, 617; text of: 424; **Lincoln County War Battle in** (see Lincoln County War, Battle in); eye-witness of Commander Dudley's troops firing a volley at him and escaping McSweens in: 19, 22, 200, 429, 517, 586-591; **guerrilla rustling by:** 20, 85, 440, 617; **Hoyt Bill of Sale by:** 20, 440; the Bill of Sale: 440; **peace meeting with James Dolan of:** 20-21, 174; 335, 500, 530; **eye-witness to Huston Chapman murder by:** 21, 174, 335, 360, 500, 529; **on John Sherman's outlaw list of:** 478-479 (see John Sherman); **pursued as an "outlaw" by Lew Wallace:** 21, 500, 518, 520-521; **pardon bargain with Lew Wallace of:** 21, 335, 360, 408, 440, 470, 495, 498, 504, 517-518, 521, 526, 529; secret helpers for: 529-530; sham arrest and jailing for: 21, 529; meeting with Lew Wallace about: 21, 532; Lew Wallace's "pardon in your pocket" quote about: 532, 715, 717; interview of by Lew Wallace: 522, 537-539; the interview: 537-539; **pardon bargain letters to Lew Wallace:** 530-534, 564, 645-647, 664-666; Billy's letter of March 13, 1879: 530-531; the letter: 531; Lew Wallace's response to: 531-532; Lew Wallace's response to Billy's March 20, 1879 letter to "Squire" Wilson: 533 (see pardon bargain letter to "Squire" Wilson); the letter: 533; Billy's letter of March 20, 1879: 32, 424, 530, 534; the letter: 534; Billy's "Billie" letter of March 24, 1879: 539-544; the letter: 540; Billy's letter of December 12, 1880: 26, 645-647; the letter: 646-647; Billy's jail letter of January 1, 1881: 665; the letter: 665; Billy's jail letter of March 2, 1881: 664-665; the letter: 665; Billy's jail letter of March 4, 1881: 665-666; the letter: 666; Billy's jail letter of March 27, 1881: 666; the letter: 666; **pardon bargain letter to "Squire" Wilson:** of March 20, 1879: 533; the letter: 533; **departing sham jailing by:** 599; **pardon bargain fulfilled in 1879 Grand Jury testimony by:** 21, 185, 546, 549-553, 594; not indicted himself in: 556-557; venue change given for Brady, Hindman, and Roberts in: 21, 553-555, 571; **Lew Wallace's pardon betrayal of:** 6, 39, 139, 470, 534, 544-545, 558, 647, 669, 687; Wallace's "precious specimen" letter about: 544-545; **testifying in Dudley Court of Inquiry by:** 22, 200, 556, 561, 586-591; the testimony: 587-591; as to three soldiers firing: 587, 589-591; as to firing a volley: 590; as to white soldiers: 591; attacked in Henry Waldo's closing argument: 606-608; **taken as a client by Ira**

Leonard: 22; **return to guerilla rustling by:** 617, 620; **gambling by:** 617; **killing of Joe Grant by:** 24, 617; **Secret Service pursuit in fabricated "Kid gang" of:** 24-25, 87, 90, 331, 461, 620, 625-626, 628-643, 657; (see Azariah Wild, Pat Garrett); **Secret Service pardon for:** 25, 504, 620, 627- 632 (see Azariah Wild); **Lew Wallace reward notices for:** 204, 647-648; 688-689; in *Las Vegas Gazette,* December 22, 1880: 647-648; the notice: 648; in *Daily New Mexican,* May 3, 1881: 204, 688- 689; the notice: 689; **Coyote Spring ambush of:** 25, 639; **Greathouse ranch ambush of:** 26, 639, 641-642; **ambushes by Pat Garrett on:** 195; **Stinking Springs capture of:** 12, 26, 195, 657; **transport to Santa Fe jail of:** 26; **transport to Mesilla jail of:** 189, 198; **trial for Roberts's federal indictment of:** 27, 287, 504, 669, 671; quashing of: 504, 671; **Ira Leonard resigns as attorney of after likely threat:** 504, 669 (see Ira Leonard); **trial for William Brady territorial indictment No. 532 of:** 27, 195, 287, 292, 461, 671-680; Judge Bristol prejudicial jury instructions for: 672-676; A.J. Fountain's prejudicial jury instructions for: 676-677; hypothetical correct defense argument for: 677-680; verdict and sentence: 504, 680; **letter to Edgar Caypless by:** 27, 680-681; the letter: 680-681; *Mesilla News* interview as "only one to suffer the extreme penalty of the law" by: 681-682; **Lew Wallace death warrant for:** 470, 697-688; **transport to Lincoln County jail of:** 682; **jailbreak (great escape) by:** 12, 28, 62, 90, 242, 685, 687; killing in jailbreak of James Bell and Robert Olinger by: 12, 28, 33-34, 685-686; **killing of by Pat Garrett:** 22, 29, 90, 195, 242-243, 699; **Coroner's Jury Report of:** 29, 205, 213, 700 (see Milnor Rudulph); the Report: 700; **outlaw myth of:** 24-25, 29-30, 36, 39-48, 53, 65, 81, 90, 131, 139, 195, 201- 202, 204, 225, 320, 334, 386, 411, 470, 476-478, 500, 520-522, 541, 558, 572, 574-575, 595, 606, 621, 625-626, 632-643, 645, 648, 657, 671-672, 685, 689-699, 703, 709-721, 731; outlaw myth press of the Ring about: 90, 201-202, 643-654, 657-664, 670-672, 682, 685, 687, 689-690; Billy Bonney responds to: 646-647; outlaw myth press of Lew Wallace about: 691-699, 703-721 (see Santa Fe Ring, Lew Wallace, Azariah Wild, Pat Garrett, 20th century historians)

Booth, John Wilkes – 469, 531

Borrego murder trial (see Thomas Benton Catron)

Bosque Grande ranch – 20, 620, 627, 631, 639, 650-651

Bosque Redondo – 23, 172, 244

Boston and New Mexico Cattle Company – 81, 91

Boulder, Colorado – 503

Bowdre, Charles "Charlie" – 12, 16-17, 20, 24, 26-27, 35, 144, 188, 195, 374, 409, 411-412, 423, 428, 477, 617, 625, 632, 634, 644, 646-647, 661; **shot by "Buckshot" Roberts:** 17, 28, 374; **fatally shot "Buckshot" Roberts:** 409; **attempts to murder by J.B. Matthews:** 188; **in federal indictment No. 411:** 27, 411-412, 620; **killed by Pat Garrett:** 16, 23, 26, 144, 195, 646, 661

Bowdre, Manuela – 20

Bowman, George R. – 676

Boyle, Andrew – 197, 471, 477, 598, 606, 608; **Ringite murderer freed on *habeas corpus:*** 598; **indicted Ringite murderer pardoned by Catron's abuse of Amnesty Proclamation:** 21, 197, 557, 594 (see Thomas Benton Catron); **as testifying for N.A.M. Dudley against Billy Bonney:** 606, 608

Brady, William – 14-20, 24, 27-28, 31, 33, 35, 40, 43, 80, 91, 103, 145, 150, 172-173, 181, 185, 187-188, 196-197, 199, 252-253, 263, 317, 320, 330, 332, 336-337, 341-342, 344-347, 349-351, 361, 364-365, 367-369, 372-373, 375, 377, 381, 385-386, 388-389, 392-394, 396-399, 402-406, 411-416, 419, 422, 440, 454, 495-496, 499, 504, 525,

529-530, 606, 634, 670-675, 677-680, 713; **biography of:** 187; **as first Lincoln County Sheriff:** 181; **shielding rustlers of J.S. Chisum's cattle by:** 345; **embezzling tax money by:** 14, 80, 103, 150, 173, 187, 197, 337, 344-346, 393, 398 (see "A Tax-Payer's Complaint"); **assisting jailbreak of Jessie Evans and his boys:** 341, 392-393; **malicious attachments on J.H. Tunstall and A.A. McSween by:** 15, 187, 263, 320, 347, 399, 402, 524; **threatening to shoot Tunstall:** 342, 392; **murder of Tunstall by posse of:** 15, 33, 91, 145, 187-188, 196, 199, 317, 351, 361; **shielding of Tunstall's murderers by:** 16, 33, 103, 253, 365, 369, 496; illegally jailing Bonney, Waite and Martinez to block arrests by: 16, 368, 402; **lethal risk to McSween of:** 15-16, 347, 373, 381, 398-399, 403-405; using soldiers as posse against McSween by: 381, 405, 422; **illegal Axtell Proclamation making him only law enforcer:** 16, 367-369; **killing of by Regulators:** 16, 28, 185, 187-188, 372-373

Brazel, Wayne – 195
Breeden, Marshal A. – 68, 221, 471
Breeden, William – 67-68, 76, 110-111, 167-168, 190, 193, 204, 209, 212, 216, 221, 252, 264, 266-267, 271, 280, 307-308, 310, 316, 618-619; **biography of:** 167-168
Bremen, Martin W. – 301-302
Brewer, Richard M. "Dick" – 16-17, 31, 33, 144, 341, 361-367, 374, 377, 386, 391-392, 399-400, 405, 529; **affidavit for J.H. Tunstall's murder by:** 361, 366; **as Regulator leader:** 16; **deputized by Justice of the Peace J.B. Wilson:** 366, 404; **apprehension and shooting of W. Morton and F. Baker by:** 367; **murdered by "Buckshot" Roberts:** 17, 28, 374, 409
Brinkerhoff, Henry R. – 557, 563
Briscoe, Joe – 22, 194
Bristol, Warren H. – 15, 21-22, 27, 65, 83, 85, 89-90, 183, 185, 197, 225-229, 242, 267, 272, 276, 283, 287, 301-303, 319, 332, 342-343, 346-347, 369-370, 372, 375, 377, 395-397, 402, 470-471, 776, 504, 545-546, 549, 553, 557, 570-574, 596, 598, 614, 638, 669, 671-677, 680, 687; **biography of:** 183; **exposé of:** 276, 296-310, 573-574; **petition to remove:** 183, 283, 287, 301-303; **malicious prosecution of A.A. McSween by:** 15, 183, 267; obstructing bondsmen by: 372, 396-397, 402; **malicious prosecution of J.H. Tunstall by:** 15, 183, 342-343, 346-347, 370, 375, 396-397, 402, 572-573; **malicious prosecution of J.S. Chisum by:** 343; **as co-enforcer with W.H. Brady in Axtell's Proclamation:** 369; **obstructing prosecution of J.H. Tunstall's murderers:** 90, 319; **shielding H.I. Chapman's murderers:** 22, 185; voiding J.J. Dolan's indictment by: 22; **freeing Fort Stanton Ringite prisoners by *habeas corpus*:** 546, 570; **pardoning indicted Ringites by misuse of Wallace's Amnesty Proclamation:** 197, 557, 594; **obstructing Susan McSween's civil trial against N.A.M. Dudley:** 614; **Billy Bonney's hanging trials by:** 27, 90, 183, 185, 669, 671-672, 680; quashing "Buckshot" Roberts indictment by: 671, 687; jury instructions by: 27, 672-677; hanging sentence by: 680; **outlaw myths by:** 225-229, 476; for canceling the Lincoln County October, 1878 Grand Jury: 476

Broad, W.E. – 97
Brockway, William – 649, 652
Brooks, James J. – 24-25, 620-623, 635-636, 638, 640, 642
Brookville, Indiana – 467
Brown, Henry – 27, 33, 363, 400, 411-414, 477, 553-554, 620
Brown, Richard Maxwell – 6; *Strain of Violence: Historical Studies of American Violence and Vigilantism* by: 6
Bryan, John D. – 145

Bryant, Bob "Rustling Bob" – 477
Buell, George – 200
Burns, Walter Noble – 32, 41-42
   The Saga of Billy the Kid by: 32, 41
Bush, James – 592,601, 732
Caffey, David L. – 242, 312; *Frank Springer & New Mexico: From the Colfax County War to the Emergence of Modern Santa Fe* by: 242
Cahill, Frank "Windy" – 13, 16-17, 24, 28, 131, 326, 625; **killed by Billy Bonney:** 13, 16-17, 24, 28, 131, 326, 625; **Coroner's Jury Report of:** 13
Cameron, Harry F. – 152
Campbell, Billy – 21, 199, 500, 518, 520, 532, 534-537, 551-553; **attempted murder of Juan Patrón by:** 500; **murder of H.I. Chapman for N.A.M. Dudley:** 500; **indicted for Chapman's murder:** 500; **escape from Fort Stanton:** 199, 520, 536-537, 551
Camp McDowell –200
Canadian River – 639
Capitan Mountains – 29, 537, 642, 686
Cardenas, Manuel – 169, 171, 196, 253-254, 263-265, 267, 305, 307, 317-318
Carleton, James H. – 172, 184, 188
Carley, R.M. – 93
Carlyle, Jim – 26, 28, 639-640, 642, 646-647, 651-652, 685
Carrizozo Land and Cattle Company (see Thomas Benton Catron)
Carrizozo, New Mexico Territory – 537
Carroll, Henry – 472, 518, 521, 536, 538, 575, 595-596
Carson, Kit – 172, 181, 243
Casey, John P. – 91-92
Casey, Robert – 14, 136, 173, 196, 332
Catron, Charles C. – 152
Catron, Julia Walz – 178
Catron, Thomas Benton – 4-6, 8, 12, 14-15, 17-25, 27, 35-36, 43, 45-46, 48, 51-66, 68-69, 71-72, 75-154, 157-158, 161-164, 167-198, 200-206, 209-210, 212-214, 216-225, 230, 233, 242, 244-252, 254, 256, 262, 267-272, 274-279, 282-283, 285-287, 289, 293, 297-310, 312, 314-316, 319, 323-324, 326, 329-336, 339, 342-343, 345, 347, 349, 351-352, 357, 367, 369, 371-372, 375, 381, 385-386, 387-389, 396, 400, 403, 407-409, 411-420, 422-426, 428, 430, 434-436, 438, 440, 458-461, 471-476, 487-488, 493, 497, 500-501, 517, 520, 532, 541, 543, 545, 557, 593, 599, 603, 614, 617-620, 625, 628-629, 633, 636, 643, 645, 657, 671, 685, 687, 671, 727-728; **biography of:** 75-154; **collected papers of:** 66, 92, 95; **Kettenring family surname of:** 75; **as law partner of S.B. Elkins:** 76;

   CRIMINALITY OF

   as Territorial Ring "boss": 4, 8, 15, 17, 43, 45, 53-55, 59-60, 62, 64, 68, 189, 196, 272, 372, 279, 372, 385, 520, 603, 618; **creating Ring style by:** 53, 75; **land-grabs by:** 12, 23, 36, 51-52, 57, 72, 75-76, 78-79, 85, 96-97, 150, 158-159, 161-162, 210, 221, 242, 244-247, 272, 276, 285-287, 297-300, 306, 322, 326, 329, 358, 422, 725; **got 6 million acres:** 23; **buying Maxwell Land Grant for back taxes by:** 169, 244, 246, 309 (see Maxwell Land Grant, Sierra Mosca Grant, Tierra Amarilla Grant, Santa Teresa Grant); **fear of Hispanic uprising by:** 21, 36, 153; **cipher-codes of:** 4, 72, 81-84, 89, 148, 177, 206; **expurgating 1888 office fire of:** 78, 81, 85, 91, 174, 180-181, 186, 192-194, 372; **destroying Territorial archives by:** 77, 210; **to split public offices by:** 77, 210; **spy system of:** against Mary McPherson: 272; Billy Bonney: 90, 131, 174, 625; against Lew Wallace: 603; against Jacob Crist; 105, 130-131; by Saturnino Baca: 601; by James Dolan: 175; by Tony Neis: 189; by Melvin Mills: 143; by John Bail: 193-194; **vote fixing by:** 56, 77, 92-95, 99, 102, 141, 150, 152, 170, 206, 270, 288; **defamatory affidavits by:** 22, 85, 87, 89, 104, 108-110, 122, 130-131, 145-146, 178, 180, 189, 440, 488-489, 562, 576, 614 (see Susan McSween, William H. Bonney, Alexander McSween, Thomas Smith, Jacob Crist, Mauricio Gonzales, Porfilia Martinez de Strong, Oliver Lee, Eugene Fiske); **malicious**

prosecutions by: 6, 14-16, 46, 63, 71, 75-77, 79, 81, 96-98, 131, 209, 212, 218, 225, 244, 248, 267-268, 275, 323-324, 332, 342-343, 347, 351, 357, 371, 396, 400 (see Ada Morley, Oscar McMains, Alexander McSween, John Tunstall, John Chisum, Pat Coghlan, Jacob Crist, White Caps); **assassinations by** (see John P. Slough, Franklin Tolby, Maxwell Land Grant settlers, John Tunstall, Richard Brewer, Frank MacNab, San Patricio massacre victims, Alexander McSween, Harvey Morris, Vincente Romero, Francisco Zamora, unnamed Lincoln County War fighters, Huston Chapman, Alexis Grossetete, Robert Elsinger, and Francisco Chavez; **attempted assassinations by** (see Raymond Morley, Clay Allison, Henry Porter, Oscar P. McMains, Ira Leonard, Montegue Leverson, Oliver Lee, James Gilliland); **control of press by:** pay-off of T. Hughes by: 203 (see Thomas Hughes); pay-off of S.M. Ashenfelter by" 204 (see Singleton Ashenfelter); pay-off of J.H. Koogler by: 201-202 (see John Koogler); loyalty to R.A. Kistler by: 202 (see Russell Kistler); (see *Santa Fe New Mexican*);

PROFITEERING OF

Maxwell Land Grant and Railroad Company attrney: 245 (see Maxwell Land Grant and Railroad Company); **government beef contracts of:** 80-81, 171-172, 180, 184, 329, 618, 625 (see "The House," Seven Rivers rustlers); **government hay contracts of:** 172, 177; **loans and bribes by:** 80, 95, 171, 331 (see Samuel Beach Axtell, Ralph Emerson Twitchell); **banks of** (see First National Bank of Santa Fe, Second National Bank of Santa Fe); **railroads of:** 23, 52, 79, 161-163, 244; **cattle ranches of:** Pecos River Cow Camp (see below); Carrizozo Land and Cattle Company (see below); Feliz Land and Cattle Company involvement: 81, 185; Boston and New Mexico Cattle Company: 81, 177, 185; Tularosa Land and Cattle Company: 81, 177, 185; American Valley Company Ranch: 81, 177;

POLITICAL POWER OF

as D.A. for Third Judicial District: 76, 167, 184; 209; **as Attorney General:** 76-77, 209-210; **as U.S. (District) Attorney:** 15, 17, 19-20, 27, 43-45, 62, 65, 76-77, 87-88, 90, 217-219, 221-222, 245, 247-248, 252, 267, 269-270, 276, 278-283, 286-287, 293, 297, 307-309, 323, 330, 333, 336, 343, 369, 371-372, 389, 396, 404, 409, 412, 415-416, 436, 459, 461, 501, 557, 618, 620, 671; forced resignation as: 20, 65, 77, 82, 86-88, 461-463, 501 (see Frank Warner Angel report on); in lieu of indictment: 461-462, 501; as arranged by S.B. Elkins: 87, 461-463; replaced by Sidney Barnes as: 149-150; seeking reappointment as: 149-150; **in Territorial legislature:** 95-96; Rump Council against: 96; **as Territorial Delegate to Congress:** 98-101, 141, 174, 189, 193, 205-206 (see vote fixing); **as Mayor of Santa Fe:** 149; **as a first New Mexico Senator:** 23, 75, 151-153; implied vote buying for: 152;

ANTI-RING REVOLTS AGAINST

Legislature Revolt against: 212-214, 217, 219, 222-224, 226; bribing legislators in: 214, 217; take-over of legislature by: 219; **Grant County Rebellion against:** 234; **Colfax County War against:** 242, 244 (see Maxwell Land Grant, Maxwell Land Grant and Railroad Company, Maxwell Land Grant settlers, "Dear Ben" plot); **Lincoln County War against** (see Lincoln County interests of, Regulator Manifesto, Lincoln County War);

LINCOLN COUNTY WAR PERIOD INVOLVEMENT OF

assisting in formation of Lincoln County by: 181; **Lincoln**

County involvement of: 330-332, 386 (see "The House," J.J. Dolan and Company, government beef contracts); **Lincoln County sub-bosses of:** 335-336; **Pecos River Cow Camp of:** 14, 81, 197, 329-331, 351, 367, 541; **Carrizozo Land and Cattle Company of:** 14, 18, 25, 35, 81, 178, 197, 329, 331, 345, 388, 424, 440, 520, 633; **competition with J.H. Tunstall by:** 14, 171, 329, 332-333, 344-345, 347 (see John Tunstall); **"The House" mortgaged to:** 14, 65, 174, 330, 408; **taking possession of "The House" by:** 174, 331, 389, 409, 415-416, 616; **selling "The House" for the county courthouse by:** 685; **repossessing L.G. Murphy's ranch by:** 173; **accused of J.H. Tunstall's murder:** 351; **obstructing A.A. McSween's bondsmen by legal threats by:** 403; **obstructing arrest of John Tunstall's murderers by** (see William Brady, S.B. Axtell); **W. Brady requesting troops through:** 369; **federal indictment No. 411 against Regulators by:** 27, 90, 245, 411-415, 501, 504, 532, 543, 557, 620, 629, 671, 687; **as blocking future Territorial pardon by:** 245, 543, 629; quashed: 27, 504, 629, 671, 687 (see William H. Bonney); the indictment: 412-415; **writing letter for S.B. Axtell about fake Regulator attack on his Pecos Cow Camp:** 375, 387-388; the letter: 388; **"Regulator Manifesto" against:** 18, 35, 61, 198, 385, 423-425, 617 (see William H. Bonney); **link to Lincoln County War Battle posseman John Kinney of:** 198; **role in N.A.M. Dudley's Lincoln County War intervention:** 425-426, 428;

F.W. ANGEL EXPOSING OF

Frank Warner Angel report about: 19, 82, 86-89, 314, 458-461, 618; as covered up by S.B. Elkins: 88, 98, 459-461, 618; **Frank Warner Angel secret notebook exposing:** 471-475;

LINCOLN COUNTY WAR AFTERMATH

H.I. Chapman as risk to: 487 (see Huston Chapman, N.A.M. Dudley); **getting pardons by abusing Lew Wallace's Amnesty Proclamation for Lincoln County War indicted Ringites by:** 188, 197, 557, 593-594 (see Jacob B. Matthews, William B. Powell, John Long, John Hurlie); **past representing of N.A.M. Dudley for court martials by:** 22, 89, 200, 381, 476; **role in Dudley Court of Inquiry by:** 517; **possible role in N.A.M. Dudley's "Open Letter" to Lew Wallace by:** 493; **bringing in Secret Service against Billy Bonney:** 24, 620, 633; **killing of Billy Bonney by** (see William H. Bonney, federal indictment No. 411, Azariah Wild, Pat Garrett, outlaw myth by Santa Fe Ring);

LATER CRIMINALITY

feigned "assassination attempt" on: 96-98; **member of Knights of Liberty:** 92, 102; **Borrego case and trial by:** 92, 99, 101-107, 109-130, 132, 135, 141-143; for murder of Francisco Chavez: 101-105, 132; Catron's offer of $700 for murder of: 103; accused by Chavez's mother of: 104, 132; shielding of Catron by judge: 103, 128; Catron's shielding of accomplices: 103, 139 (see Francisco Chavez); coercing prosecution witnesses in: 111-123; failure to stop hanging of murderers in: 142-143 (see Francisco Gonzales y Borrego); **disbarment trial against:** 105-128, 191, 222; coercion of judges in: 111-112; attack on Chief Justice T. Smith in (see *Albuquerque Daily Citizen* defamation plot, "Extra Billy Smith" plot); outlawing of prosecution witnesses by: 108-109, 111, 124-126; acquittal in: 123-128, 142; dissent of N.B. Laughlin in: 126-128 ***Albuquerque Daily Citizen* defamation plot against Borrego case Chief Justice Thomas J. Smith with complicit Editor Thomas Hughes by:** 112-

122; the anonymous letter by: 112-118; sham response letter as himself by: 118-119; secret plot letter with Hughes by: 120-121; pay-off to Hughes by: 203 (see Thomas Hughes); **"Extra Billy Smith"** *Socorro Chieftain* **plot against Borrego case Chief Justice Thomas J. Smith with complicit Editor W.S. Williams by:** 122-123, 146; **revenge attack against Borrego case prosecutor, Jacob Crist, by:** 130-131; **revenge attack against Borrego case dissenter N.B. Laughlin by:** 131; **revenge "Poker Bill" plot against Governor William T. Thornton of:** 130-137, 203; exposed by Thornton: 134-135, 139-140; **revenge attempt to remove Thornton as Governor by:** 137-139; **un-Masonic charges against:** 140-141; **made President of Bar Association:** 129; **using Pat Garrett to attack Oliver Lee by:** 144-146; "loan" to Pat Garrett by: 196; **attack against M. Otero by:** 146-148; **exposés of** (see Franklin Tolby, William Morley, Mary McPherson, Montegue Leverson, Lew Wallace, William B. Sloan); **outlaw myth by:** 108-109, 111, 124-126, 279, 388, 411 (see outlaw myth, by Ringites)

Caypless, Edgar – 27, 680

Cebolleta, New Mexico Territory – 181

Cerillos Coal and Iron Company – 162

Chaffe, Gerome Bunty – 159, 161, 244-245

Chalk Hill – 146

Chaplin, F.B. – 272

Chapman, Huston I. – 20, 22, 34, 46, 174, 185, 198-200, 318, 360, 439, 470, 480-481, 487-493, 498, 500-506, 509, 512-521, 530-532, 534, 536, 541, 546, 549, 551-553, 561, 564-566, 570-571, 576, 587, 594, 598, 613, 695-696, 698, 710, 715, 717, 732; **letters to Lew Wallace of:** 480-481, 487, 489-490-492; **charges against N.A.M. Dudley by:** 493; **identification of "ring" by:** 491; **outlawing of:** 512, 514; **assassination of:** 21, 174, 199-200, 318, 335, 470, 500, 502, 504, 509, 512-517, 529-530, 535, 546, 553, 565-566, 671, 695, 710

Chapman, W.W. – 505, 513

Chavez, A. – 472

Chavez boys – 538

Chavez, Francisco "Frank" – 92, 99, 101-105, 109-110, 126, 128, 130, 132, 136, 139, 143-144, 205; **political power of:** 101; **assassination fear of:** 101; **assassination of:** 99, 101, 109-110, 126, 130; **Catron accused as murderer of:** 101, 103, 132; Catron's offer of $700 for murder of: 103; accused by Chavez's mother: 104, 132; **shielding of Catron:** 103, 128; **shielding of accomplices:** 103, 139 (see Thomas Benton Catron's Borrego case trial)

Chavez, J. Francisco – 618

Cháves y Cháves, José – 427, 588, 590-591, 607

Chicago Times – 558

Chilcott, George – 244

Childers, W.B. – 106, 113-114, 116, 119

Chisum, John Simpson – 15-17, 43, 62-65, 81, 197, 263, 330, 333-334, 343-345, 369, 373-374, 379, 381, 396, 405, 422, 426, 472, 540-544, 633, 635, 646-647, 663, 678-679, 696, 710, 721; **as president of J.H. Tunstall's bank:** 15, 333, 337; **Ring exposé of:** 63; **malicious prosecution of:** 15, 63, 333, 343, 396; **outlaw myth for:** 333

Chittenden, O.K. – 263

Cimarron News and Press – 103, 191, 242, 248, 251, 253-254, 256, 259-260, 287, 309, 312, 321, 325, 377-378, 438, 457

Cimarron, New Mexico Territory – 8, 94, 171, 228, 244, 248-254256, 258, 261-263, 272, 275, 277, 295, 304, 312, 316-317, 320-321, 323, 381, 439, 455-457, 471, 474, 457

Cimarron Press – 245, 248

Cimarron River – 260

Cincinnati *Commercial Tribune* – 662

cipher-codes (of Santa Fe Ring) – 4, 72, 81-84, 89, 148, 177, 206

Civil War – 6-8, 20, 22, 51-52, 76, 86, 157, 167, 173, 181, 200, 443, 464, 467, 483, 592, 621
Cisneza del Matcho (Mule Spring) – 537
Claiborne Parish, Louisiana – 22, 194
Clancy, Frank W. – 85, 88, 133, 149, 191-192
Clark, Rush – 353
Cleaveland, Agnes Morley – 3, 66, 241, 249, 257, 273-275, 325, 728; *Satan's Paradise* by: 3, 66, 241, 325; *No Life for a Lady* by: 241, 257, 325
Cleaveland, Norman – 159-160, 245-246, 248-250, 254, 265, 275, 295, 728, 731; *The Morleys: Young Upstarts of the Southwest Frontier* by: 159, 241, 250
Clenny, Avery M. – 379
Cleveland, Grover – 57, 128, 137-138, 142-143, 161-162
Cocoran, T. – 400
Coe, Frank – 16-17, 27, 30-31, 386-387, 409-410, 472; **ranch of:** 538
Coe, George – 27, 30-32, 374, 386, 415, 620; **hand mutilated by "Buckshot" Roberts's shot:** 17, 374; **federal indictment No. 411 against:** 27, 411-413, 620
Coghlan, Pat – 20, 81, 440, 472, 618, 620; **malicious prosecution of by Catron:** 81
Colfax County, New Mexico Territory – 11, 63, 77, 87, 92, 94, 103, 168-170, 183, 196, 215, 229-230, 243, 247, 249, 251-252, 254-256, 258-272, 276, 287-290, 295-296, 306-308, 311-315, 317, 319-320, 322-326, 337, 353, 357, 368, 436, 438-439, 443, 452-453, 455-457, 464, 501, 553, 576, 727; **became county in 1869:** 243; **named after Vice-President Schyler Colfax:** 213; **county seat as Elizabethtown:** 243; **county seat as Cimarron:** 247; **county seat as Springer:** 326 (see Colfax County War, Maxwell Land Grant settlers)
"Colfax County Ring" – 253
Colfax County's courts removal (see Samuel Beach Axtell, see Colfax County War)
Colfax County "troubles" – 256
Colfax County War – 56, 61, 79, 85-86, 96, 103, 109, 168, 183, 191, 206, 210, 228, 230, 241-248, 251-252, 257-270, 273-310, 325-326; **assassination of anti-Ring leader** (see Franklin J. Tolby); **attempted assassination of Ring opponents:** (see "Dear Ben plot"); **removal of courts in:** 230, 259-261, 271, 287, 296, 322, 368, 452-453, 553; **Taos courts for:** 264-270; **return of courts:** 272; **exposés in:** 103, 191, 257-259, 273-310 (see Maxwell Land Grant, Samuel Beach Axtell, William R. Morley, Mary McPherson, Frank Springer); **Ring outlaw myth for:** 228-229, 247, 254-256, 261, 272, 279, 309, 320, 326
Colfax, Schyler – 243
Collier, Needham – 112
Collier, T.W. – 123
Collins, "The Prowler" – 538
Collinson, John – 245
Collinson syndicate – 245
Colorado Chieftain – 264, 267
Colorado Springs, Colorado –177
Congressional Compromise of 1850 – 51
Conklin, Carlos (Charles) M. – 101, 103, 107, 139, 213-214
Congress House Resolution 795 –
Connelly, Henry – 157
Contreras, Don Matais – 78
Conway, Thomas (T.F.) – 221, 472
Cooper, Thomas "Tom" – 24, 620, 623-624, 626-627, 630-631, 633, 635, 641
Copeland, John – 17-18, 87, 185, 189, 263, 374-375, 380, 386-388, 408-411, 415-416, 419; **posting bond for A.A. McSween by:** 348; **removal by Governor Axtell of:** 185, 189, 263, 415, 454, 472; **outlaw myth of:** 375
Coralitos, Mexico – 539
Corbin, James – 235
Coroner's Jury Reports – **for "Windy" Cahill:** 13; **for John Tunstall:** 352; **for William Bonney:** 29, 205, 213, 700
Corbet, Sam – 64-65, 525, 538, 567; **"affidavit" of:** 525
Corbin, James – 235
Cortéz, Hernándo – 464
County Cavan, Ireland – 187
County Kerry, Ireland – 177

County Wexford, Ireland – 172
Cox, Jacob D. – 244
Coyote Spring ambush – 25, 640, 651
Cracking the Billy the Kid Case Hoax – xxi
Crawford, Charles "Charlie" – 428
Crawford, C.P. – 415
Crawfordsville, Indiana – 468-469, 694, 696, 709
Crawfordsville *Saturday Evening Journal* – 694-695
Crist, Jacob H. – 103-106, 108, 113, 116, 130-131, 625; **as Borrego case prosecutor:** 103-104; **defamatory affidavits used by Catron against:** 104, 131; **Complaint No. 637 to disbar Catron by:** 105-106
Crouch, John A. – 472
Cunningham, William P. – 103-105, 110, 132-133, 139, 143, 161; **Catron's outlawing of deputies of:** 132, 139, 143
Curry, George – 149, 175-176, 189, 195
Cutting, Bronson – 60
Daily New Mexican – 26, 66, 71, 100-101, 111, 134, 137, 139, 141, 171, 175, 264-265, 267, 386, 670, 688-691
Daily Southwest – 203-204
Dame, W.E. – 84, 148
D+D Ranch – 177
Davis Coal and Coke Company – 161, 163
Davis, George (alias Tom Jones) – 199, 361, 366, 401, 478, 521, 540-541
Davis, Hallie – 160
Davis, Sylvester – 68
Dawson, Will D. – 248, 259-260
"Dear Ben plot" (see Samuel Beach Axtell)
"Declaration of Independence" (1776) – 7, 357-358
Dedrick, Dan – 20, 24-25, 440, 617, 620, 623, 626-627, 630-631, 635, 637, 639-641, 643
Dedrick, Mose – 620, 626, 637, 640
Dedrick, Sam – 620, 626, 637, 639-640
Deer Park, Maryland – 163, 460
Delaney, Cyrus – 82, 367, 407
Delaney, William – 624, 630
Delgado, F. – 472
Delgado, Juan – 618
Deming, New Mexico Territory – 174, 177, 183, 204, 691

Denver *Daily Tribune* – 558
Denver and Rio Grande Railroad Company – 79, 129, 596
Devens, Charles – 87, 267-268, 276, 293, 444, 446, 449, 460-461, 504
DeVours, James – 634, 636
Desert Land Act – 185, 337
"Diario de Consejo" – 211, 215
DNA (collection, records, documents) – xix
Dolan, James A. – 175
Dolan, James Joseph – 14, 16, 18-22, 24-25, 27, 35, 43, 64-65, 80-82, 90-91, 96, 172-174, 177-178, 180, 185, 188, 197, 199, 249, 252, 318, 330-331, 334-336, 341-342, 345-347, 349-302, 361, 363, 366, 375, 387, 389, 391-393, 395-400, 403-409, 411, 415-416, 426-427, 452-454, 472-473, 475-477, 498-500, 504, 515, 518-520, 530-532, 535, 540-542, 546, 549-553, 555-557, 569, 571, 592-593, 597-598, 611, 623-625, 630, 670, 672, 679; **biography of:** 173-174; **attempted murder of James Randlett by:** 173, 335-336; **murder Hilario Jaramillo by:** 173; **Lincoln mercantile monopoly of:** 65, 80, 172-173, 330, 336, 349 (see L.G. Murphy and Company, J.J. Dolan and Company, "The House"); **Catron as backer of:** 65, 330; **as local Ring boss:** 518, 541; **front for Catron's Pecos Cow Camp:** 81, 197, 330, 400, 541; **selling D. Brewer a ranch without title by:** 341; **government contract frauds of:** 333, 348, 498; **fraudulent claim on Fritz estate of $76,000 by:** 342; **response to "A Tax-payer's Complaint" by:** 345-346, 398; **mortgaging "The House" to Catron by:** 174, 331, 389, 409, 415; **assisting jailbreak of Jessie Evans and his boys:** 392-393; **government contract frauds of "The House" by:** 333, 348, 498; **involved in malicious prosecution of A.A. McSween and J.H. Tunstall:** 342, 347; **attempted murder of J.H. Tunstall by:** 397-398; **recipient of "Friends Riley Dolan"**

833

letter: 82, 177, 185, 349-350, 407 (see William L. Rynerson); **obstructing A.A. McSween's bondsmen:** 403; **getting alias warrant against A.A. McSween:** 403-404; **indicted murderer of J.H. Tunstall:** 16, 173, 252, 351-352, 361, 363, 366, 375, 400; **A.A. McSween fearing murder by:** 408; **getting D. Easton's malicious prosecution warrants against A.A. McSween and Billy Bonney:** 180, 387; **in Lincoln County War Battle:** 18-19, 426-427; **take-over of Tunstall's store by:** 22; **letter about silencing H.I. Chapman by:** 498-499; **peace meeting with Billy Bonney of:** 20-21, 173, 335, 530-531; **indicted murderer of H.I. Chapman: 21-22,** 173, 199, 500, 571; indicted for: 549, 552, 556, 571, 598; never tried: 22, 551; **take-over of Tunstall's ranch as Feliz River Land and Cattle Company by:** 22, 81, 91, 174, 177, 185; **possible attempted assassination of I. Leonard by:** 96, 185, 555; **death threats against Lew Wallace reported by:** 518, 520; **arrested by Lew Wallace for Chapman murder:** 318; freed by *habeas corpus*: 546, 598; **claiming counterfeit bill by:** 24-25, 623-625, 630; **testifying for prosecution in Billy Bonney's Brady trial:** 27, 670, 672, 679; **staying in contact with Catron:** 174-177; **Director of Peñasco Reservoir and Irrigation Company:** 188; **in Territorial Senate:** 174 (see Murphy-Dolans)
Doña Ana County, New Mexico Territory – 21, 76, 89, 145, 157-158, 177, 195, 233, 292, 537, 553, 556, 673
Donnell Lawson, and Co. – 375, 394
Donoghue, Florencio – 253-254, 256, 258, 265-267, 270, 304-305, 307, 317-318; **released on bail in Taos 1876 Grand Jury and never prosecuted:** 318;

Dorsey, Stephen Wallace – 79, 272, 288, 295, 298, 323, 472, 484
Dow Brothers Merchants – 375
Dowlin and Delaney – 624
Dowlin, William "Will" – 472, 624, 630
D'Sena, Jose – 472
Dudley Court of Inquiry (see Nathan Augustus Monroe Dudley)
Dudley, Nathan Augustus Monroe – 18-20, 22, 34-35, 43-44, 47, 87, 89, 146, 153, 161, 181, 189-190, 196, 199-201, 247, 249, 254, 262, 269, 330, 375, 379, 381, 385-387, 389, 407, 422-423, 425-430, 439, 461, 469, 470, 472-473, 475-476, 478, 480-481, 487-491, 493-501, 503-504, 509-518, 522-526, 530, 535-536, 541, 544, 546, 549, 552-553, 556-558, 561-592, 597-607, 609-613, 671, 697, 711, 714, 731; **biography of:** 199-201, 381; **past and potential court martials of:** 200, 381, 385, 426, 429, 512, 517, 586, 613; defended by Catron: 200, 381, 426, 517; **Lincoln County War in:** releasing Ringite murderers in Fort Stanton by: 387; attempting capture of A.A. McSween and Billy Bonney by: 387; used by G.W. Peppin in attempted murder of A.A. McSween: 423 (see Lincoln County War Battle); **in Lincoln County War Battle:** 19, 87, 89, 153; , 189, 196, 247, 254, 262, 269, 386, 426-429, 480, 524-525, 541; coercing Justice of the Peace Wilson for false arrest warrants for Regulators by: 387, 426, 522-523; accomplice to murders of A.A. McSween, Harvey Morris, Vincente Romero, Francisco Zamora: 19, 89, 189, 196, 262, 429, 481, 513, 524-525; accomplice to arson: 19, 89, 189, 262, 429, 524-525; accomplice to looting: 189, 430, 525; **indictment by Lincoln County 1879 Grand Jury of:** 552-553, 556; **pardoned in Lew Wallace's Amnesty Proclamation for:** 482, 487, 493, 515; **responses to Lew Wallace by:** 488; "Open Letter" by: 493, 513, 517, 536; **removal requested by Lew Wallace:**

200, 517; **threatening Susan McSween by:** 481, 513-514; **Susan McSween's charges against:** 20, 22, 34, 439, 469, 503-504, 509, 561-562; the charges: 509-512 (see Susan McSween, H.I. Chapman, Ira Leonard); **Court of Inquiry of:** 22, 35, 44, 47, 87, 89, 190, 196, 200, 249, 269, 470, 522, 530, 544, 546, 558, 561-592, 597-614, 671, 697, 711, 714; testimony in: 562-592, 599-602; (see Lew Wallace, Susan McSween, Billy Bonney); defense closing argument: 603-609; prosecution closing argument: 609-611; judgment of Court: 611-613; **Susan McSween's civil case against:** 22, 87, 89, 461, 614; as Cause Numbers 298 and 176: 614; **outlaw myth by:** 476, 478, 501
Dunham, Richard – 690
Durango, Colorado – 130-131, 690
"Dutch Chris" – 538
Ealy, Taylor – 352-353, 374, 400-401, 426, 429, 601; **J.H. Tunstall's autopsy by:** 352-353, 401; **Ealy family of:** 426, 601
Early, Jubal – 468
Easton, David M. – 66, 68-69, 180, 330-331, 349, 387, 410, 424, 427, 429, 511, 579, 625; **as a Ringite:** 66, 68-69; **as Catron's Lincoln County agent:** 180, 330-331, 349, 387; **writing warrants against Regulators:** 180, 331, 387, 427, 429, 410, 427, 429, 579; **resigning as Justice of the Peace invalidating warrants:** 387, 424; **refusing to write defamatory affidavit against Susan McSween:** 511; **Catron communications:** 180; **tricking Azariah Wild that Billy Bonney was a murderous counterfeiter:** 625; **concealing rustling for Ring beef contracts:** 625
Eaton Land Grant – 78
Eckles, William H. – 235
Eddy Argus – 100
Eddy County, New Mexico Territory – 100, 176
Elizabethtown, New Mexico – 169, 210, 243, 247-248, 252-253, 262, 303-304, 317
Elk City, Kansas – 198
Elkins, John T. – 246
Elkins, Stephen Benton – 4, 12, 23-24, 51-53, 57, 64, 68-70, 75-82, 85, 87-89, 91-92, 96, 98, 105, 108, 112, 129, 138-139, 141, 147, 149-152, 157-164, 167-169, 174, 179, 183-184, 187, 190, 206, 209-210, 212, 214, 216, 221-224, 242, 244-248, 252-259, 267, 269-270, 272, 278, 280, 285-287, 293, 295, 297-301, 309, 311, 314-317, 319-320, 323-324, 335, 358, 372, 417, 420, 422, 433, 438, 459-463, 472-474, 483-484, 618, 620, 725, 727; **biography of:** 157-164; **as Washington, D.C. Ring boss:** 4, 75, 105, 157, 159, 161, 287, 372, 453; **land-grab scheme of:** 12, 23, 36, 51-52, 57, 72, 75-76, 78-79, 85, 96-97, 150, 158-159, 161-162, 221, 244-246, 272, 276, 285-287, 306, 322, 326, 329, 358, 422, 725; (see Maxwell Land Grant); **banks of** (see First National Bank of Santa Fe, Second National Bank of Santa Fe); **election rigging by:** 92, 212, 214, 270, 300, 316; **exposés of:** 222, 224, 242, 252, 257-259, 277, 283-310 (see Mary McPherson); **arranging Catron's U.S. Attorney resignation by:** 87, 461-463; **covering up for Catron's Angel report by:** 88, 98, 459-461, 618; **influencing Catron's disbarment judges by:** 112; **influencing as Washington, D.C.-based Ring boss:** 53, 75, 105, 138-139, 147, 149-151, 161, 174, 183, 206, 246, 267, 358, 372, 483-484, 620; **defamatory affidavits by:** 161 (see Santa Fe Ring); **reinstating S.B. Axtell attempts by:** 162, 183, 311, 725-727 (see Santa Fe Ring, Thomas Benton Catron, cipher-code, land-grab)
Elk Garden Coal Company – 163
Ellis, Benjamin "Ben" – 352, 378, 380, 428, 472
Ellis house – 386
Ellis, Isaac – 348, 402, 404, 410-411, 427, 472, 524, 567, 670, 672; **"affidavit" of:** 524-525
Ellison, Sam – 472

835

Elsinger, Robert – 81, 91-92, 98, 136, 144; **Catron accused of murder of:** 81, 91, 136, 144
Elston, Susan Arnold – 468
El Paso and South Western Railroad – 79
Emancipation Proclamation – 7
embezzlement case – (see Alexander McSween)
Emil Fritz insurance policy (see Emil Fritz)
Enterprise and Chronicle – 288
Evans, Jessie – 15-16, 21, 91, 196, 198-199, 316-317, 325, 332, 334, 340-341, 351-352, 361, 366-367, 371, 385, 389, 392, 397, 400-401, 426, 445, 475, 477, 500, 520, 531-532, 539, 541, 549, 552, 710; **biography of:** 198-199; **murder of J.H. Tunstall by:** 71, 196, 198, 252, 317, 351-352, 361, 366, 371, 400-401, 445; **in Lincoln County War Battle:** 426; **escape by:** 250; **indicted for Chapman's murder of:** 549; **2nd degree murder verdict for killing by:** 199
Evarts, William M. – 159, 161, 206, 245, 460, 480, 484; **attorney in Maxwell Land Grant sale:** 245, 460
expurgating fire of 1888 (see Thomas Benton Catron)
Fall, Albert Bacon – 153
Fanning, Edmund – 359
Farmer, Joseph H. – 472
federal indictment No. 411 (see Thomas Benton Catron)
Federalist Papers – 3
Fields, W. – 375
Feliz Land and Cattle Company – 81, 91, 174-176, 178, 185-186
Feliz River (Rio Feliz) – 14, 332, 337, 362, 538, 542
Feliz River Ranch – 15, 33, 177, 185, 351
Fergusson, Harvey B. – 95, 150-151
Ferry, Thomas T. – 216, 220
Field, N.B. – 116
Fields, Westley – 472
First Judicial District – 76, 101, 103, 113, 168, 205, 212, 258, 504, 727
First National Bank of Santa Fe – 43, 45, 65, 80, 122, 159, 171, 178, 244, 330, 339, 344-345, 462 (see Thomas Benton Catron, Stephen Benton Elkins)

Fiske, Eugene A. – 83, 114, 116, 178, 192, 473-474, 618-619, 727-728; **defamatory affidavits against:** 178
Flavey, T.A. – 199
Flint, Robert – 388
Fort Bayard – 80, 184
Fort Bliss – 562
Fort Donnellson – 468
Fort Grant – 13
Fort Griffin – 539
Fort Henry – 468
Fort Marcy – 213-214, 247, 262
Fort Stanton – 14, 18, 80-82, 85, 89, 153, 171-174, 177, 181-182, 187, 197, 199-200, 247, 262, 269, 318, 329-333, 336, 352, 367-368, 373, 375, 379, 381, 387, 389, 402, 406-407, 410, 422-424, 426-428, 433, 454, 472, 474, 488, 492-494, 497, 499, 509-511, 513, 515, 517-518, 520-525, 531-532, 535, 538, 542, 546, 555-557, 561-562, 566, 570, 572, 574-575, 586, 592-593, 595-596, 601-602, 610-611, 613, 621, 623-625, 627, 629-631, 636, 672, 678, 686
Fort Sumner – 11-12, 20, 22-26, 29, 172, 194-195, 201-202, 205, 242, 244, 335, 617, 620, 625, 627, 630-637, 641-647, 649-650, 652, 657, 660, 686, 699-700, 707-708, 720
Fort Union – 17, 200, 247, 254-255, 262-264, 318, 320, 353, 381, 438-439, 456, 521, 526, 602
Fort Wingate – 108
Fountain, Albert Jennings – 27, 70, 83, 144-146, 185-186, 195, 395, 618, 676-677, 680-681; **court-appointed for William H. Bonney's Brady trial:** 27, 70, 185-186, 193, 504, 546, 671-672; **jury instructions for Brady trial:** 676-677, 680; **murder of: prosecuting Oliver Lee with Catron by:** 144; **murder of:** 144, 195
Fountain, Henry – 144-145
Fowler State and National Law School – 183
Francolon, J.B. – 98
Franklin College – 184
Franklin County, Ohio – 182
French, James – 498-499, 511-514, 516

836

French, Jim "Frenchie" – 16-18, 27, 373, 427, 440, 477, 578, 620, 634
"Friends Riley and Dolan" letter (see William L. Rynerson)
Fritz, Charles – 174, 177, 342, 386, 393-396, 399, 599
Fritz, Emil Christian Adolf – 14-15, 43, 80, 172-173, 176, 181, 187, 330, 335, 341-343, 350, 376, 390, 393-395, 436; **biography of:** 172; **life insurance policy of:** 14-15, 173, 176, 341, 343, 350, 376, 390, 393-394, 436; **heirs of:** 15, 342, 393-395; **L.G. Murphy and Company debt of $23, 276.10 to the Fritz estate:** 394; **fraudulent debt of $76,000 of Fritz estate to L.G. Murphy claimed by J.J. Dolan:** 395 (see L.G. Murphy and Company)
Fritz, Emil (son of Charles Fritz) –175, 177
Frost, Max – 68, 101, 141, 185
Fulton, Maurice Garland – 65, 423
Gadsden Purchase – 51
Gallegos, José – 215
Gallegos, Juan – 103
Gallegos, Pantaleon – 361, 392, 401
Garcia, Roman – 107
Garfield, James Abran – 160-161, 417, 470, 664, 694, 704, 725-726
Garrett, Patrick Floyd "Pat" – 11-12, 22-29, 40-42, 47, 65, 80, 90, 137, 144-145, 198, 202, 205, 213, 242-243, 470, 504, 614, 617, 621, 637-643, 646-648, 651, 657-658, 660-663, 680-681, 685-686, 688, 697-700, 705, 707-708, 713-715, 718-720, 731; **biography of:** 22-25, 194-195, 637-638; **possible murder of a black man by:** 194; **murder of Joe Briscoe by:** 22, 194; **"Big Casino" nickname of:** 23; **election as Lincoln County Sheriff of:** 24-25, 90, 195, 637-638, 640; **working with Secret Service to capture Billy Bonney:** 25-26, 29, 617, 621, 633, 638-640, 648, 657; **made Deputy U.S. Marshal by Azariah Wild:** 621; **murder of Tom O'Folliard by:** 12, 23, 26, 195, 646; **murder of Charlie Bowdre by:** 12, 23, 6, 195, 646; **capturing Billy Bonney by:** 12, 26, 90, 195, 504, 657-658; **reporting jailbreak of Billy Bonney:** 686; **killing Billy Bonney by:** 11, 26, 29, 90, 242-243, 699; **made Doña County Sheriff:** 195; **pursuing Oliver Lee by:** 144-146, 195; **"loan" from Catron for:** 196; **killing of Norman Newman by:** 195; **murder of:** 195-196; *The Authentic Life of Billy the Kid* **by:** 24, 40, 65, 195, 638, 715; **outlaw myth of Billy the Kid by:** 40-42, 47, 65, 195, 638, 731
Gatling gun – 19, 153, 429, 510, 524, 577, 611
Gauss, Gottfried – 28, 33, 363-364, 685 **interview by:** 33-34; **aiding Billy Bonney's jailbreak by:** 28, 685
Genesee County, New York – 503
Giddings, William M. "Marsh" – 77, 139, 159, 168, 182, 209-221, 225, 227-229, 238, 247, 261-262, 304, 357, 422; **in Legislature Revolt:** 210-221, 225; **using troops against civilians by:** 214-215, 247, 262; **gerrymandering by:** 215, 238, 261; **outlaw myth by:** 227-230; **death in office of:** 210, 230
Gilbert, Robert M. – 352, 374, 405, 522, 593
Gildey, Gus – 477, 538
Gilliland, James – 144-146, 195
Ginn, John M. – 235
Gladstone, William – 433
Gobles, Reese – 538
Godfroy, Frederick C. – 65, 82, 173, 180-181, 330, 333, 349, 377, 388-389, 398, 407, 472-473, 498, 522, 543
Gold Hill – 175-176
Gonzales, Florencio – 176, 378, 380, 402, 473; **attacked by James Dolan:** 176
Gonzales, Ignacio – 18, 427
Gonzales, Mauricio – 106, 108, 125; **false affidavit from forced by Catron:** 108
Gonzales y Borrego, Antonio – 99, 102-103, 110, 132-135, 142-143; **murdering F. Chavez by:** 99; **Presidential respite for:** 143; **hanging of:** 143
Gonzales y Borrego, Francisco (Frank) – 92-93, 99, 101-103, 107, 110, 132-135, 142-143, 205; **vote**

buying for Catron by: 92-93; Knights of Liberty member: 92; past murders by: 102; murdering Francisco Chavez by: 99; Presidential respite for: 143; hanging for murder of Francisco Chavez of: 143

Goodwin, Millard Filmore – 410, 424, 490, 498, 501, 520, 524, 534, 606-607; **as testifying for N.A.M. Dudley against Billy Bonney:** 606, 608

Gonzales, Luiz – 105, 125

Gonzales, Muricio – 125

Gonzales, Muricio – 125

Gonzales y Baca, Rosa – 105, 108

Gortner, Robert C. – 133, 143

Grace, Fred – 473

Grand Juries – **Colfax County 1875 Grand Jury:** 304; acquittal of F. Griego in: 304; **Taos County 1876 Grand Jury:** 250, 262, 264-265, 267, 280, 305-307, 312, 316, 318; prejudicial jury instructions by H. Waldo in: 264-265; Ada Morley indicted in: 250, 280; acquittal of M. Mills and R. Longwill, murderers of F.J. Tolby in: 262, 264-265, 305, 312, 316, 318; F. Donoghue released on bail: 318; Clay Allison indicted in: 267; O.P. McMains indicted in: 267; **Taos County 1877 Grand Jury:** 268, 271; O.P. McMains tried: 271; **Grant County Grand Jury:** 302; **Lincoln County April, 1878 Grand Jury:** 15-17, 185, 188, 349, 351, 361, 373, 375-377, 380-381, 387, 397, 402-403, 407, 423, 572-573, 634, 678; W. Bristol's prejudicial jury instructions for: 572-573; J. Dolan and J. Matthews indicted for Tunstall murder in: 185, 375, 408; Billy Bonney indicted for Brady and Hindman in: 185, 361, 375, 634; trial venues changed: 185; A.A. McSween acquitted in: 17, 375, 387, 407, 423 (explaining the Ring's urgency to kill him before it: 351, 375); refusal of W. Rynerson to arrest indicted Ringites from: 380-381, 408; **Lincoln County October, 1878 Grand Jury:** 476; canceled by W. Bristol to block Lincoln County War indictments of Ringites: 476;

Lincoln County April, 1879 Grand Jury: 21, 34-35, 185, 188, 197, 509, 529-530, 532, 546, 549-550, 552-558, 561, 565-566, 570-571, 583, 594, 692, 697, 711, 717; Billy Bonney testifies for pardon bargain in and indicts Chapman's murderers: 21, 34, 529-530, 532, 549-550, 552-553, 561 (J. Dolan, B. Campbell, and J. Evans indicted in: 556); N.A.M. Dudley and G. Peppin indicted in: 197; venue change for Billy Bonney and Ringites in: 553-555; pardon of indicted Ringites by Amnesty Proclamation in: 188, 197, 557; G. Purington reports indictments in: **556-557**; Lew Wallace reports indictments in: 594; **Doña Ana County 1879 Grand Jury:** 614; Susan McSween's case against N.A.M. Dudley lost in: 614; **Doña Ana County 1880 Grand Jury:** 670; Billy Wilson tried: 670; **Doña Ana County 1898 Grand Jury:** 145; **Oliver Lee indicted in:** 145

Granger, Gorden – 213, 224

"Grant County Declaration of Independence" (see Grant County Rebellion)

Grant County Herald – 203-204, 234-237, 287, 300, 502, 552

Grant County, New Mexico Territory – 63, 80, 176, 184, 211, h233-235, 237-238, 273, 287, 372, 502

Grant County Rebellion – 54, 85, 206, 210-211, 230, 233-238, 251, 270, 273; **Grant County Annexation Meeting in:** 235-237; "**Grant County Declaration of Independence**" in: 233, 235-238

Grant, Joe – 24, 28

Grant, Ulysses S. – 44, 77, 86, 159-160, 182-182, 190, 203, 209-210, 216, 222, 230, 233, 243, 247, 268, 434-435, 467-468

Graves, Peter – 235

Greathouse, Jim "Whiskey Jim" –26, 646-647, 651-652, 662

Greathouse ranch – 26, 639-642, 647, 650-651; **ambush of Billy Bonney there:** 26, 646-647

Green, Tom – 366, 401

Gregg, George W. – 94, 206

Gregg, John J. – 228

Griego, Francisco "Pancho" – 171, 248,

253, 258, 264, 267, 304-305, 316-318; election rigging for M. Mills and R. Longwill by: 171, 252; **murder of soldiers by:** 248, 252, 304, 316; **murder of F.J. Tolby by:** 253, 258, 304, 317; **killed by Clay Allison:** 253
Griffin, W.W. – 68, 473
Grossetete, Alexis – 81, 91-92, 98, 136, 144; **Catron accused of murder of:** 81, 91, 136, 144
Grove, Jesse A. – 200
Guadalupe Mountains – 539
Gutierrez, Apolinaria – 23
Gutierrez, Celsa – 23, 29
Gutierrez, Jose M. – 538
Gutierrez, Juanita – 23
Gutierrez, Saval (Sabal) – 23, 29, 700
habeas corpus (for freeing Ring prisoners)– 213-214, 256, 318, 546, 550, 555, 570, 598, 672; **in Legislature Revolt:** 213-214; **in Colfax County War:** 256, 318; **after Lincoln County War:** 546, 550, 555, 570, 598, 672
Hadley, Walter C. – 129
Hagerman, Herbert J. – 148-149
Hagerman, James J. – 148
Hallborough, North Carolina – 359
Hallborough skirmish – 359
Hall, Caleb (alias Collins) – 477
Halliehurst – 163, 461-462
Hamilton, Humphrey B. – 104, 111, 115, 117, 123-126, 133-135, 176; **biased Supreme Court Opinion of:** 124-126
Hargrove's Saloon – 23-24, 194, 617
Harper's Weekly – 5
Harrison, Benjamin – 141, 161-162, 175, 187, 192
Harrison, Russell B. – 162
Hatch, Edward – 200, 263, 367, 417, 426, 438-439, 472-474, 480, 487-489, 493, 495, 498, 509, 517-518, 521, 535-536, 563-564, 566, 602, 620, 650; **removes Commander N.A.M. Dudley:** 517
Hayes, Rutherford B. – 6, 8, 17, 20, 46, 53, 85-87, 159-161, 183, 206, 237-238, 241, 245-246, 267-270, 272, 274-276, 278, 283, 286-287, 289, 292, 309, 311, 313, 329, 357, 369, 357, 369-371, 375, 378, 385, 389, 415, 417, 419, 421, 434-435, 437; **Florida election fraud accusation of:** 6, 237;

Proclamation of October 7, 1878 by: 478-479
Hayward, C.B. – 68
Hefferan, Vioalle Clark – 153
Helm, T.J. – 129
Herold, David – 469
Hill, John – 473
Hill, Joseph (alias Joseph Olney) – 478, 539
Hill, Thomas "Tom" (alias Tom Chelson) – 149, 342, 352, 362-363, 366, 392, 398-399, 401, 445, 540-541
Hindman, George – 16, 20, 24, 27-28, 185, 199, 361-362, 366, 372-373, 375, 377, 381, 385-386, 401, 406, 408, 411, 495, 529-530, 671, 713; **murder of John Tunstall by:** 352, 361, 366, 385, 401; **killing by Regulators:** 372-373, 385, 406, 408, 495
historians of 20th century – **outlaw myth of Billy the Kid by:** 41-48, 731
Historical Society of New Mexico – 206
Hobart, D.C. – 121-122
Hockradle, Jerrie – 473
Homestead Act – 13, 30, 542
Hondo River – 332
howitzer cannon – 19, 153, 428-429, 524, 577, 601, 611
Hoyt, Henry – 20, 35, 440; **Billy Bonney's bill of sale to:** 440; *A Frontier Doctor* **by**: 35
Howe, Albert – 473
Hubbard, John G. – 437
Hudgens, William "Will" – 533, 640, 642
Hudson, Richard – 104
Hughes, Thomas –112-122, 132, 203; **biography of:** 203; **early Catron bribe of:** 112; *Albuquerque Daily Citizen* **plot against Thomas Smith with Catron of:** (see Thomas Benton Catron); **jailing for perjury about plot:** 203; *Albuquerque Daily Citizen* **"Poker Bill" plot against William Thornton with Catron of:** (see Thomas Benton Catron)
Humphreys, Henry H. –562-563, 565-566, 576, 579-584, 602, 609; **closing argument in Dudley Court of Inquiry by:** 609-611
Hunt, Charles R. – 94
Hurlie (Hurley), John – 21, 197, 473,

557, 593-594; **indicted Ringite murderer pardoned by Catron's abuse of Amnesty Proclamation:** 21, 197, 557, 594 (see Thomas Benton Catron); **as testifying for N.A.M. Dudley against Billy Bonney:** 608
Husband, Herman – 359
Hyson, James – 477
I. Ellis & Sons – 374, 410, 525
Indiana Volunteers – 468
Indianapolis, Indiana – 691, 696, 710, 721
Indianapolis Saturday Review – 694
Ione City, California –191
Irvin, James – 538
"Ithurial" (see William B. Sloan)
Isaacs, J. – 415-417
Jacobs, Sarah – 158
Jacobson, Joel –47-48; *Such Men as Billy the Kid* by: 47
Jackson County, Missouri – 190
James, Jesse – 621, 695-696, 710, 717
Jamarillo, Hilario – 173
Jaramillo, Lorenzo – 700
Jefferson, Thomas – 7
Jicarillo Mountains – 534
Johnson, Andrew – 159, 167, 469
Johnson, E. Dana – 154
Johnson, Hezekiah S. – 214
Johnson, Charles A. – 130-131
Johnson, E. Dana – 154
Johnston Riot Act – 360
J.J. Dolan and Company (see James Dolan)
Jones, A.A. – 106, 116
Jones, Bill – 197, 478, 521
Jones family – 539, 542
Jones, Heiskell – 478
Jones, Jim – 197, 478, 521, 539
Jones, John –197, 478, 521, 539, 588, 590, 614
Jones, Tom (see George Davis)
Joseph, Antonio – 71, 94, 100, 175, 185, 193, 206
"Journal of the House of Representatives" – 211-212
Juárez, Benito – 468, 732
Kansas Pacific Railroad – 244
Kantz, August V. – 181-182
Kars, Marjoline – 358-360; *Breaking Loose Together: The Regulator Rebellion in Pre-Revolutionary North Carolina* by: 358
Kefauver, Estes – 5
Keokuk, Iowa – 167

Kingman, Lewis – 295
Kaye, Donald E. – 199; *Nathan Augustus Monroe Dudley, 1825-1910: Rogue, Hero, or Both?* by: 199
Keleher, William – 43-45, 128, 170, 191, 211, 213; *The Fabulous Frontier* by: 43, 128, 170, 191; *The Maxwell Land Grant: A New Mexico Item* by: 242; *Violence in Lincoln County 1869-1881* by: 211, 213-214
Kerens, Richard C. – 141, 146, 151, 161
Kimbrell, George – 20, 25, 501, 515, 518, 521-522, 529, 533-534, 556, 571, 630, 633, 635, 637-638
Kinney, John – 18, 43, 61, 188-189, 196, 198-199, 316, 332-333, 385-386, 423-424, 426-427, 447, 475, 492, 501, 579, 639; **biography of:** 198; **connection to Catron of:** 198; **murder of Frank MacNab by:** 386; **massacre at San Patricio by:** 18, 189, 423, 501; **Murphy-Kinney party of:** 61, 385; **in Lincoln County War Battle:** 18, 188, 196, 426-427; **murder of Alexander McSween by:** 454; **looting of Tunstall store by:** 454; **made Deputy U.S. Marshal by Azariah Wild:** 639
Kirchner, August – 212, 214, 222, 224
Kistler, Russell A. – 187, 202-203, 659, 694
Klasner, Lilly – 62-63; *My Girlhood Among Outlaws* by: 62
Knaebel, George W. – 116
Knaebel, John H. – 85
Knights of Labor – 57-60, 102
Knights of Liberty – 92, 102, 205
Knodt, Max – 105, 107-108
Koogler, John H. – 201-202, 643-646, 663, 687, 694
Kriling, Charles – 473
Kruling, Charles "Dutch Charlie" – 197, 386-387
Ladbessor, Chris – 538
Lamar, Howard R. – 44-45; *The Far Southwest 1846-1912* by: 44
Lambert, J.J. – 270, 288
Lambert, Oscar Doane – 157-164; *Stephen Benton Elkins: American Foursquare* by: 157
Las Cruces *Borderer* – 234
Las Cruces Masonic Cemetery – 186

Las Cruces, New Mexico ("Cruces") – 68-70, 76, 145, 174, 177, 184-186, 195-196, 198, 204, 345, 350, 380, 474-475, 539, 669-670, 720

Las Cruces *Thirty-Four Newspaper* – 55, 552

Las Cruces *Rio Grande Republican* – 70, 185, 505

Las Gorras Blancas (see White Caps)

Las Vegas Daily Gazette – 26, 657 (see John H. Koogler)

Las Vegas Daily Optic – 66, 71-72, 141, 202-203, 222, 659; **bought by F. Springer:** 203

Las Vegas Democrat – 57, 222

Las Vegas Gazette – 39, 48, 201, 325, 471, 509, 512, 643, 645-647, 663, 687, 694 (see John H. Koogler)

Las Vegas Independent Democrat – 144

Las Vegas jail – 62-63, 333, 343, 654, 662

Las Vegas, New Mexico – 15, 22, 26, 58, 68, 100, 122, 131, 192-193, 202, 373, 396, 403, 425, 432-433, 439, 471-474, 480, 493, 500, 504, 513-515, 570, 604, 617, 632, 644, 649, 652, 657, 660, 662-663, 680, 694-695

Las Vegas Optic – 67-68, 70-71, 96-97, 187, 202-203, 214 (see Russell A. Kistler)

Las Tablas, New Mexico – 29, 686

Laughlin, Napoleon Bonaparte – 101, 103, 105, 108, 111, 126-128, 130-131, 732; **Supreme Court dissenting opinion in favor of Catron's disbarment:** 126-128; **Catron's revenge against:** 131

Legislature Revolt of 1872 – 52, 85, 205-206, 209-225, 230, 233-234, 247, 251-252, 261-262, 422, 443, 699; **outlaw myth for:** 210, 212, 216, 218, 225

Lee, Oliver Milton –144-146, 195-196; **outlaw myth for:** 144-146; **defamatory affidavits for:** 145-146; **attempted killing of:** 195

Lee, William – 473

L.G. Murphy and Company – 85, 171-173, 177, 330-335, 390-391, 393-395, 401, 446; **sutler store of:** 80, 85, 171-173, 181-182, 187, 330-331, 336 (see Emil Fritz and Lawrence Murphy)

Lemon, John – 185

Leonard, Ira E. – 22, 25, 27, 34-35, 89, 96, 136, 174, 185, 193, 439, 503-505, 508-511, 516, 518-520, 537, 549-550; 557, 561-562, 568-576, 592-593, 596-599, 604, 609-611, 613-614, 618, 621, 624, 627-632, 637, 646, 664, 666, 669-671, 731-732; **biography of:** 34, 503-505; **asthma of:** 504-505, 562, 568; **assisting 1879 Lincoln County Grand Jury prosecutions:** 546; **assassination attempt on:** 22, 35, 136, 174, 518, 520, 555-556, 568, 571; **representing Susan McSween against N.A.M. Dudley:** 22, 503, 614; charges against: 508-511, 561-562; for Court of Inquiry: 89, 508, 561-563, 576, 579, 583, 592, 596, 598, 604, 609, 613, 610-611; **letters to Lew Wallace by:** 519, 549-550, 568-569; 570-575 (exposing Santa Fe Ring as "incubus on the government": 569, 574); 592-593, 596-598; **assisting Billy Bonney's Wallace pardon:** 34-35, 549, 646, 664; **attempting Billy Bonney's Secret Service pardon:** 22, 25, 599, 621, 627-632; **representing Billy Bonney in "Buckshot" Roberts trial:** 27, 646, 669-671; **withdrawing as Billy Bonney's attorney:** 27, 35, 185, 193, 669, 671; **defamatory affidavits against:** 505 (see Dudley Court of Inquiry)

Leverson, Montegue R. – 64, 369-370, 372-373, 375, 415, 417, 421, 432-433-437, 732; **major exposés of S.B. Axtell, Catron, and Santa Fe Ring by:** 369-372, 417-421, 433-437; **assassination attempt by Catron and Axtell on:** 436

Lexington Masonic College – 167

Lexington, Massachusetts – 199

Lexington, Missouri – 167

Lima Seminary – 183

Lincoln, Abraham – 7, 20, 157, 464, 468

Lincoln County Bank (see J.H. Tunstall)

Lincoln County Commissioners – 17, 368, 375, 416, 419, 454

Lincoln County courthouse-jail – 33, 90, 198, 685, 688, 696, 705-706, 718

Lincoln County Farmers Club – 173

Lincoln County Grand Juries (see grand juries)
Lincoln County Justice of the Peace (see John "Squire" Wilson)
Lincoln County Leader – 33
Lincoln County, New Mexico Territory – 4, 8, 14, 16, 19, 21, 24-25, 27, 33-34, 40-45, 61, 69, 80, 82, 89, 109, 144, 171, 175, 177-178, 180-183, 189, 197-198, 204, 215, 225-227, 252, 259, 263-264, 267, 308-309, 317-320, 329-338, 340-341, 344-345, 348, 352-253, 357-358, 361-362, 365-366, 368-370, 374, 377-379, 381, 385-386, 390-391, 395-398, 402, 406-410, 415, 422-423, 425, 430, 433, 438, 440, 444, 446-448, 450-453, 470-471, 477, 479-482, 484, 488, 490-492, 494-498, 502-505, 510-515, 517, 522, 524-525, 534, 541, 544-546, 551, 554-555, 558, 561, 564-565, 567, 570, 585, 593-595, 599, 603-605, 610-614, 623-627, 634, 636, 642, 644, 648, 651, 653, 660, 670, 688-689, 696-697, 704-705, 708, 713;
description of: 329, 570-571;
involvement of Catron in: 4, 27, 329-332
Lincoln County Sheriff (see William Brady, John Copeland, George Peppin, George Kimbrell, Pat Garrett)
Lincoln County "troubles" (disturbances) – 20, 22, 36, 47, 198, 227, 314, 332-333, 353, 379, 389, 391, 404, 417, 443, 446, 448, 450-451, 453, 455, 459, 472, 475, 484, 497, 515, 542, 554, 579, 595, 696;
Angel Report on: 446-448, 451, 455, 472
Lincoln County War – 4, 8, 11-12, 14, 16, 21, 23, 25, 27-28, 31-33, 39-40, 43-48, 52-53, 63, 65, 77, 81, 85, 89, 91, 102, 105, 109, 130, 134, 144-145, 149, 153, 159, 167, 171, 173-174, 177-178, 180-184, 187-188, 190-191, 197-200, 206, 215, 229-230, 241-242, 249, 254, 263, 269, 287, 296, 313, 318-319, 322, 325-326, 330-331, 334-335, 360, 365, 385-386, 422-423, 425, 430, 436, 440, 469, 520, 522, 529-531, 536-537, 539, 541-542, 544, 556, 562, 572-573, 575, 587, 614, 623, 632, 637, 644, 685, 689, 696, 703, 710-711, 714, 731; **Battle in:** 7, 18, 20, 30, 32, 35, 39, 90, 188-189, 196-200, 227, 247, 254, 262, 273, 275-276, 287, 314, 353, 357, 385-386, 417, 423, 425-429, 432, 454, 464, 476, 493, 498, 524, 541, 561-5624, 639, 685, 699; **deaths in:** 573, 670; **as a freedom fight:** 8, 11, 30-31, 39, 44, 46, 48, 53, 188, 247, 276, 318, 385, 425, 430, 446, 505, 536, 558, 705; **as an Hispanic uprising:** 423; **outlaw myth for:** 225-229, 331, 333-334, 361, 365, 369, 375, 377, 385-386, 388, 411, 428, 430, 443, 446, 495 (see "Regulator Manifesto," Posse Comitatus Act, N.A.M. Dudley); freedom fighter deaths in (see A.A. McSween, Vincente Romero, Francisco Zamora, Harvey Morris)
Lincoln Grand Jury (see Grand Jury)
Lincoln, New Mexico Territory – 8, 14-16, 19-21, 24, 27-28, 31-33, 41, 44, 82, 90, 95, 153, 174, 176, 181, 186, 188-189, 201-202, 204, 332-333, 335-337, 342-344, 347, 350-353, 361-370, 373-375, 380, 386-387, 389, 394, 396-401, 403-406, 409-411, 422-423, 425-429, 433, 439, 445, 447, 464, 470, 472-475, 480-482, 487-488, 490, 492, 498-504, 509-515- 517-518, 521, 523-524, 529, 531-532, 535, 537, 544, 546, 549, 553, 555, 558, 562-563, 565-567, 569-572, 575-576, 581, 584, 586-587, 597-602, 604-605, 610-614, 620-621, 3-624, 626-627, 632-639, 642, 646-647, 653, 663, 670, 672, 678, 681-682, 685-686, 689, 691-693, 710-712, 717
Lincoln pit jail – 16, 341, 368, 392
Llewellyn, W.H.H. – 68, 147
Lockport, New York – 183
Logan, John A. – 161
Long, Jack (John) – 197, 373, 426-427, 553, 557, 580, 585-586, 588, 594; **indicted Ringite murderer pardoned by Catron's abuse of Amnesty Proclamation:** 21, 197, 557, 593-594 (see Thomas Benton Catron)
Longhrea County, Galway, Ireland – 173
Longwill, Robert H. – 43, 68, 91, 169, 171, 191, 193, 196, 249-250, 252-254, 266-267, 270, 287, 304-305,

307, 315-316, 318, 320-324, 326; in Santa Fe Ring: 43, 68, 170, 191, 248, 315, 473; election fixing for: 252, 316; accused murderer of F.J. Tolby: 91, 169, 193, 196, 245, 250-251, 253, 255, 258, 265-267, 270, 287, 304, 307, 318, 322; obituary of: 171
Lopes, Paulin – 93
Lopes, Rafael – 93
Lopez, Lorenzo – 92
Loud, John S. – 420, 473, 480
Lovato, María Paula – 243
Lucero, Jose Anado – 93
Lucero, Pedro Antonio – 700
Lujan, Jesus – 78
Luna, Tranquilano – 56
Lusk, Huston – 592, 601, 732
Mackie, John – 13
MacNab, Frank – 16, 18, 28, 144, 174, 198, 386-387, 409-411, 425, 427, 434, 509, 520, 553, 685; as Regulator leader: 386, 541; murder of: 18, 28, 144, 174, 198, 386-387, 410-411, 425, 433-434, 520, 553, 685
Madison, James – 37, 167
Mafia (American) – 4-6
Maier, Pauline – 538; *From Resistance to Revolution* by: 538
Maingay, J.B. – 245
manifest destiny – 75, 157
Markland, Absalom H. – 483-484, 603
martial law – 469, 475-478, 481, 502, 544-545, 595
Martin, T.P. – 95
Martinez, Atanacio – 16, 366-367, 401, 453
Martinez, D. – 93
Martinez de Strong, Porfilia –105-106, 109, 124-125; false affidavit induced from by Catron: 109-110
Martinez, Refugio – 97 (see White Caps)
Martinez, Romulo – 171
Martz, Martin "Dutch Martin" – 33, 363-364, 400, 538
Mason, Barney – 24, 29, 202, 639, 641
Matchett, W.B. – 270, 274, 282-283, 287, 289, 291-293, 296
Matterson, M. – 473
Matthews, Jacob Basil "Billy" – 17, 22, 187-188, 318, 332, 362-364, 366, 373, 387, 399-401, 406, 410, 473, 477, 500, 518, 532, 535, 546, 553,

557, 606, 670, 672, 679, 689; biography of: 187; in malicious prosecution of J.H. Tunstall: 362-363, 399-400; as Chief Deputy in Tunstall murder posse: 363-364, 366, 399-401, 406, 679; at Brady's ambush: 188, 373; shot Billy Bonney in it: 17, 373, 689; other attempts to kill Billy Bonney by: 17, 188; indicted for Tunstall murder: 375, 553; attempts to kill A.A. McSween by: 406; swearing out D. Easton warrant against Regulators by: 387, 410; as Lincoln County War indicted murderer: 188; at murder of H.I. Chapman: 500; arrested by Lew Wallace: 518, 532, 535; freed by *habeas corpus*: 318, 546; indicted Ringite murderer pardoned by Catron's abuse of Amnesty Proclamation: 21, 88, 197, 557, 593-594 (see Thomas Benton Catron); testified for N.A.M. Dudley: 606; testified against Billy Bonney in Brady trial: 670, 672, 679; as "enemy" of "the Kid": 689; Ring reward of Peñasco River Ranch: 188; Peñasco Cattle Company of: 188; as Director of Peñasco Reservoir and Irrigation Company: 188; contact with Catron of: 188
Maxwell, Deluvina – 11
Maxwell family – 12, 23 29, 52, 242, 336
Maxwell family cemetery – 23
Maxwell Land Grant – 12, 23, 52-53, 79, 91, 159, 169, 191, 242-244, 246-248, 274, 295, 298-299, 309, 325-326; bought for back taxes by Catron: 169, 244, 246; settlers of: 79, 144, 170, 191-192, 210, 228, 241, 247-248, 275, 326; surveying fraud for: 246-247
Maxwell Land Grant and Railroad Company – 191, 241, 244-246, 253, 261, 270, 272, 277; Catron as attorney for: 245; S.B. Elkins as President of Board of: 245
Maxwell Land Grant settlers – outlaw myth for as "squatters" and anarchists: 79, 192, 247, 255-257

Maxwell, Lucien Bonaparte – 11, 23, 79-80, 158-159, 169, 242, 295, 460

Maxwell, Luz Trotier de Beaubien – 23, 242, 335, 700

Maxwell mansion – **in Cimarron:** 243, 245, 253; **in Fort Sumner:** 11, 242, 244, 699

Maxwell, Paulita – 11-12, 23, 29, 242-243, 335, 646, 686, 699

Maxwell, Peter "Pete" – 11, 24, 29, 194, 639, 648-649, 699-700, 707

McCandleis, Charles – 474

McCarty, William Henry (see William H. Bonney)

McCloskey, William – 33, 363-364, 367

McComas, C.C. – 68

McCormick, Richard C. – 157, 187

McCrary, George – 476, 483, 498, 512, 561, 614

McCreight, William T. – 120-122, 203

McCullich, John B. – 248, 280-281

McDaniels, Jim – 473, 539

McGonigle, A.J. – 181-182

McKinley, William – 104, 143, 146-147, 162-163

McKinney, Thomas "Kip" – 24, 29, 194

McKnight, William L. – 216

McMains, Oscar P. – 56-57, 96, 136, 242, 252-255, 258, 260-261, 264-265, 267-268, 270-272; **pursuit of F.J. Tolby's murderers by:** 253-255, 258, 265; **indicted for Cruz Vega murder:** 267-268; **trials of:** 271-272, 308; **outlaw myth for:** 272

McMullen, William – 474

McNew, William – 144-145

McPherson, Mary Tibbles – 8, 86, 242, 248-249, 254, 256-257, 259-260, 264, 268, 270, 272, 275-310, 312, 314, 325, 370, 372, 389, 439, 450, 460, 464, 473, 573-574, 726, 728, 732; **public records request by:** 292-293; **exposé of Catron by:** 276-278; **response by Catron to:** 278-282; **exposés of other Ringites by:** 46, 86, 242, 256-257, 259-260, 264, 270, 275-310, 314, 372, 389, 450, 464, 573-574, 726

McSween, Alexander A. – 8, 14-19, 21, 28, 43, 46-47, 62, 64-65, 82, 89, 109, 131, 136, 144, 172, 174, 180, 183, 185, 187-189, 196, 200, 225, 250, 263, 267-268, 287, 320, 329, 331, 333-334, 336-338, 341-344, 346-350, 352-353, 357, 362, 366-367, 372-375, 378-381, 385-411, 415, 422-423, 425-430, 433-434, 436, 440, 444-447, 453-454, 457, 474-476, 481, 488, 491, 498, 501, 504, 509-511, 513-515, 517, 520-521, 523, 525, 530, 538, 540-542, 544, 562-563, 566, 572-573, 575-577, 580-581, 583, 585, 587, 589-590, 597, 600, 602, 606, 611-612, 678-679, 732; **as counsel to "The House":** 14, 333; **bringing J.H. Tunstall to Lincoln:** 336, 338; **Ring code-name "Diablo" for:** 82, 407; **exposing government contract frauds of "The House" and Catron:** 333, 349, 498; **Fritz life insurance proceeds pursuit:** 14-15, 172-173, 176, 341, 343, 350, 376, 390, 393-394, 436; **protecting heirs of:** 15, 342, 393-395; **malicious prosecution by fake embezzlement case for:** 15, 46, 172, 174, 177, 180, 183, 267, 287, 331, 334, 342-343, 346-347, 350, 436, 572-573, 611, 678; **bail of:** 15, 347; **obstructed bondsmen for:** 347-348, 372, 403; **fraudulent property attachment for:** 15, 263, 347, 362, 678; **in "A Tax-Payer's Complaint":** 344; **getting T. Ealy's Tunstall autopsy by:** 352; **getting warrant for hay theft against W. Brady by:** 367; **filing Tunstall murder complaint with British Ambassador by:** 17, 366; **exposing the Santa Fe Ring by:** 62; **complaint to President Hayes by:** 378-380; **in likely assassination plots against by W. Brady:** 16, 28, 187-188, 263, 320, 347, 372-373, 422, 678-679; **Grand Jury exoneration of:** 17, 375, 387, 573; **deposition to Frank Warner Angel by:** 82, 389-111; **outlaw myth about:** 43, 331, 333-334, 566; **accusatory affidavits against for David Easton warrants:** 180, 387; **assassination attempts against by G.W. Peppin:** 200, 375, 385, 423, 501; **hiding out to avoid murder of:** 16, 18, 678 (see Adolph Barrier); **in Lincoln County War:** 357, 386-388; **as leader:** 357, malicious prosecution warrant against by David Easton: 180, 387;

844

in Lincoln County War Battle of: 18-19, 423, 425-430, 521, 577-578, 580-581, 583, 585, 587-589, 590-591; coerced Wilson warrant against: 19, 387, 428, 523, 600, 602, 612; **murder of:** 19, 89, 136, 144, 174, 189, 196, 225, 268, 366, 429, 432-434, 454, 457, 476, 491, 501, 510, 513-515, 517, 520, 523, 525, 542, 563, 566, 575, 583, 585, 590, 611-612, 678; N.A.M. Dudley as responsible (see Nathan Augustus Monroe Dudley); **arson of house of:** 19, 89, 425, 476, 523, 525, 539, 540, 542, 583, 585, 612; **outlaw myth for:** 43, 333

McSween party (faction, side, alliance, McSweens) – 18-19, 144, 331, 447, 471-472, 474, 498, 515, 517, 524, 541, 556, 562-563, 565-566, 572-574, 579, 597, 600, 611-612, 699

McSween, Susan – 8, 18, 20, 22, 34, 87, 89, 96, 109, 146, 189, 273, 337, 343, 375, 426, 428-430, 432, 439-440, 461, 469, 480, 487-489, 495, 498, 500, 503-504, 509, 561-562, 565-566, 576-587, 732; **Grand Jury testifying by:** 509; **defamatory affidavits against:** 22, 89, 146, 189, 440, 488-489, 562, 576, 614 (see her civil case against N.A,M. Dudley for libel); **case against N.A.M. Dudley by:** 20, 22, 34, 89, 432, 469, 503-504, 509, 561; testimony in military Court of Inquiry: 576-586, 645-656; civil cases against (Numbers 298, 176): 22, 87, 89, 461, 614 (see Nathan Augustus Monroe Dudley)

Meadows, John P. – 36, 440, 686
Pat Garrett and Billy the Kid as I Knew Them by: 36

Meinig, D.W. – 52; *The Shaping of America* by: 52

Mercer County, Kentucky – 183

Merchants Life Insurance Company – 393

Mescalero Indian Reservation – 14, 17, 27, 41, 80-81, 90, 172-173, 177, 180-181, 197, 329-330, 333, 335, 349, 373, 377, 389, 398, 409, 411-413, 498, 522, 542-543, 625, 670-671; **as "the Agency":** 540, 543

Mesilla Independent – 345, 378, 471-472

Mesilla jail – 27, 682

Mesilla Land Grant – 184

Mesilla (La Mesilla), New Mexico Territory – 15, 18, 22, 26-27, 35, 69, 76, 89-90, 144, 157, 184-185, 188-189, 193, 195, 198, 201, 203, 264, 287, 319, 333, 346-347, 386, 396, 398, 403-405, 423, 426, 454, 460-461, 471-475, 504, 537, 546, 553, 557, 614, 621, 664, 666, 669-670, 682, 685, 688

Mesilla News – 471, 493, 614, 681, 731

Mesilla Riot of 1871 – 184

Mesilla Valley – 51

Merchants National Bank of New Bedford Massachusetts – 626

Metcalf, Robert – 235

Metz, Leon – 144-145, 196; *Pat Garrett: The Story of a Western Lawman* by: 144, 196

Mexican-American War – 51, 193, 243, 468

Michigan State University – 168

Middaugh, Asa F. – 250-251; **deposition of:** 251

Middleton, John – 16-17, 27, 33, 361, 363-365, 400, 409, 411-414, 477, 553-554, 620

Miller, Fred – 148

Mills, A. Ham – 361

Mills, Melvin Whitson – 91, 98-99, 143, 152, 168-171, 193, 196, 245-246, 248-254, 256, 258, 264-267, 270, 278, 282, 287, 304-305, 307, 312, 315-316, 318, 323-324, 326; **biography of:** 168-169; **a Director of Maxwell Land Grant and Railway Co.:** 245, 248; **election fixing for:** 171, 252, 316; **accused F.J. Tolby murderer:** 91, 98, 152, 169, 171, 193, 196, 245, 251, 253-254, 256, 258, 264-267, 278, 282, 287, 304-305, 307, 312, 318; **trial of:** 264, 312; **buying Maxwell Land Grant for Catron:** 169, 246, 309, 316; **Catron's confidant and business manager:** 98-99, 143, 152, 168-171, 193

Mills, Sam F. – 415

Mills, William J. – 131, 149, 202

Miranda, Guadalupe – 243

Missouri State University – 190

845

Mitchell, Robert Byington. – 76, 181, 209
Montaño Jose – 374, 378-379, 402-403, 523, 601
Moore, F. – 438
Moore, Scott – 681
Moore, William – 361
Mora County, New Mexico Territory – 63, 76-77, 99, 170-171, 271, 300
Mora Land Grant – 60, 79
Morley, Ada McPherson – 242, 245, 248-251, 254, 256-257, 260, 264, 268, 270, 272-276, 282, 310, 323-325, 464, 576, 728, 732; **buggy incident of:** 250-251, 276-277, 281; **malicious prosecution by Catron of:** 248-250, 256, 264, 268, 275-276, 310, 323-324; **terrified letter by:** 272-274, 282
Morley, William Raymond – 87, 136, 191, 241-242, 245-248, 250-251, 254, 256-264, 268-270, 272, 275, 277, 279, 281, 292, 295, 308, 310, , 321-325, 439, 464, 728, 732; **Santa Fe Ring exposé by:** 246, 257-259; 268-270, 464; **blackmailed by Ring attempting to stop exposés:** 323; **forced flight of:** 191, 325; **shot dead in Mexico:** 269, 325 (see *Cimarron News and Press*, "Dear Ben plot," Ada Morley, Mary McPherson)
Mormon City (Mimbres) – 539
Mormon colonization – 285
Mormon War – 200
Morsberger, Katherine – 467
Morsberger, Robert – 467
Morris, Harvey – 18-19, 21, 136, 144, 189, 196, 337, 426, 429, 476, 509, 520, 525, 590-591
Morton, Oliver P. – 468
Morton, William "Buck" – 16, 24, 28, 197, 199, 351-352, 361, 366-367, 385, 400-401, 404-405, 445, 541
Moten, Chris – 540-541, 543
Mora County, New Mexico Territory – 63, 271, 300
Mount Baldy – 243
Mullen, James – 235
Murphy-Dolans (Murphy-Dolan cause Dolan outfit, Dolan party) – 18, 329, 334, 540-541, 544, 556, 574, 594 (see Lawrence Murphy, James Dolan)
Murphy party – 424, 447, 464, 472-475, 582 (see Lawrence Murphy)

Murphy-Kinney party – 61, 198, 385, 424 (see Lawrence Murphy, John Kinney)
Murphy, Lawrence Gustav – 14, 172-173, 181-182, 187, 196, 198, 329-336, 341-342, 385, 389-396, 398-402, 404-409, 411, 415-416, 424, 446-447, 452-454, 464; **biography of:** 172-173; **possible assassination of Robert Casey by:** 14, 173, 196, 332; **attack on Captain Randlett by:** 336; **embezzlement of Lincoln County taxes by:** 173; **selling R.M. Brewer ranch without title:** 341; **store of as monopoly:** 390, 408, 446; **store connected to Catron of** (see sutler store, L.G. Murphy and Company, "The House"); **taking settlers' land by:** 390-391; **debt to Emil Fritz estate of $23,376.10:** 394; **trying to get A.A. McSween killed:** 408; **store taken over by Catron:** 14, 173, 331, 409, 415-416; **Lincoln County War** (see Murphy-Dolans, Murphy party, Murphy-Kinney party)
Naegle, Conrad Keeler – 54, 211-215, 233-235, 237-238
Nast, Thomas – 5, 60, 75
Nash, Josiah "Joe" H. –197, 344-345, 606, 608 **as testifying for N.A.M. Dudley against Billy Bonney:** 606, 608
National Archives – 88, 272, 276, 423
Navajo Wars – 172
Neis, Tony – 189, 669-670
Newcomb, John – 352, 401-402
Newcomb, Simon B. – 83, 106, 116, 185, 395, 546, 557, 618, 670, 672; **prosecutor in Billy Bonney's Brady trial:** 185, 546, 672; **freeing imprisoned Ringites by:** 546, 672; **getting pardon for indicted Ringites by:** 557
Newman's Semi-Weekly – 66, 621-622, 628-629, 643, 657
New Mexican Printing and Publishing Company – 168
New Mexico and Arizona Railroad Company – 190
New Mexico Bar Association – xix; 57, 113, 115-116, 118, 129, 193, 205; **electing Catron President of:** 129

New Mexico Territory – 3-8, 11-13, 20, 22, 36, 39, 51-53, 75-76, 92, 144, 157, 161-163, 167, 169, 172, 177-178, 182-183, 187-188, 193-195, 198, 203, 205, 233, 238, 242, 245, 296, 325-326, 345, 358, 360, 369, 372, 389, 422, 437, 443-444, 467, 469, 542, 620-623, 643, 664, 672, 694, 710, 725-727; **Compromise of 1850 for:** 51; **Gadsden Purchase for:** 51 (see Treaty of Guadalupe Hidalgo)

New Orleans, Louisiana – 66, 621-622, 628-629, 643, 657

New Southwest – 203-204

New York Times – 6, 168, 178

New York Tribune – 187

New York Sun – 25, 248, 252, 257, 259-260, 287, 648

New York Weekly Sun – 259, 309

New York World Magazine – 532, 715

Nolan, Frederick – 45-47, 61-62, 64-65, 336-341, 345-346, 349, 490, 690; *The Life and Death of John Henry Tunstall* by: 61, 336-337; *The Lincoln County War: A Documentary History* by: 45

Norris, Tom – 686

North American Commercial Company – 163

Nowell, Ike – 105-106, 110-111, 124

Oberlin College – 182

O'Brien, James – 5

O'Brien, Gus – 110, 133, 142

O'Folliard, Tom – 12, 18, 20-21, 23-26, 35, 144, 195, 427, 553, 617, 625, 632, 635, 646, 660

Ojo Caliente Grant – 298

Olinger, Robert "Bob" – 12, 27-28, 33-34, 62, 189, 197, 540, 543, 598, 606, 608, 614, 632, 639, 641, 685-686, 690, 705-706; **as Seven Rivers rustler and Lincoln County War murderer:** 28, 197, 540, 543; **Ringite murderer freed on *habeas corpus*:** 598; **testifying for N.A.M. Dudley against Billy Bonney:** 606, 608; **indicted Ringite murderer pardoned by Catron's abuse of Amnesty Proclamation:** 21, 197, 557, 594 (see Thomas Benton Catron); **killing of John Jones by:** 614; Olinger, Wallace – 197, 540, 543, 598; **made U.S. Marshal by Secret Service to track Billy Bonney:** 189, 197, 632, 639, 641; **made Deputy by Pat Garrett to guard Billy Bonney;** 12, 27, 614, 685, 705; **killed by Billy Bonney:** 12, 28, 685-686, 690

Olney, Joe (see alias Joseph Hill)

Omaha, Nebraska *Daily Herald* – 275

O'Phallier, Tom (see Tom O'Folliard)

Osborne, Nathan W. – 557, 562

Ortiz y Salazar, Antonio – 68

Otero, Mariano S. – 68

Otero, Miguel A. – 56, 84, 92, 146-149; **Catron's attack on:** 146-148

outlaw myth – 24-25, 29-30, 36, 39-40, 42, 45, 47-48, 86, 90, 96, 130-131, 139, 145, 195, 201, 204, 218, 225, 229-230, 261, 272, 309, 320, 326, 333, 385-386, 388, 411, 428, 430, 446-448, 458-459, 469-470, 475-476, 490, 495-500, 509, 535, 544-545, 572, 574-575, 593, 595, 619, 621, 625-626, 633-654, 657, 669, 671-672, 685, 689-699, 703, 709-721, 731-732; **by Warren Bristol** (see Warren Bristol); **by Marsh Giddings** (see Marsh Giddings); **by S.B. Axtell** (see Samuel Beach Axtell); **by Frank Warner Angel:** 446-448, 731; **Sherman's outlaw list for** (see John Sherman); **by Lew Wallace** (see Lew Wallace); **by N.A.M. Dudley** (see Nathan Augustus Monroe Dudley); **by Azariah Wild** (see Azariah Wild); **by Pat Garrett** (see Patrick Garrett); **by 20th century historians** (see historians of 20th century); **against Legislature Revolt opponents** (see Legislature Revolt of 1872); **against Colfax County War fighters** (see Colfax County War, Maxwell Land grant settlers); **against Mary McPherson:** 279; **against J.H. Tunstall** (see John Tunstall); **against Lincoln County War fighters** (see Lincoln County War); **against A.A. McSween** (see Alexander McSween); **against J.S. Chisum** (see John Chisum); **against John Copeland** (see John Copeland); **against Billy Bonney** (see William H. Bonney); (see Santa Fe Ring); **against Oliver Lee** (see Oliver Lee)

Owatanna, Minnesota – 178
Owens, Jake – 477, 538
Owens-Wheeler outfit – 538
Palace of the Governors – 223, 469, 480, 704, 712
Pallen, John – 415
Palen, Joseph G. – 77, 99, 209, 212-214, 216-218, 220-224, 252, 258-259, 262, 264, 276, 301, 304, 315, 317; **in Legislature Revolt:** 212-214; **conflict with Franklin Tolby:** 252
Pague, Sam – 498
Panhandle Cattlemen's Association – 650
Panhandle Transportation Company – 650 (see Panhandle Cattlemen's Association)
pardon bargain with Lew Wallace (see William H. Bonney)
pardon bargain with Secret Service (see William H. Bonney)
pardon of indicted Tunstall murderers and Lincoln County War Ringites – 21, 188, 197, 552-553, 556-557, 593-594 (see Jacob B. Matthews, William B. Powell, John Long, John Hurlie, Marion Turner, Thomas Benton Catron, Lew Wallace)
Partition Act – 286
Patrón, Juan – 8, 14, 21, 177, 332, 350, 367, 370, 427, 500, 515, 518, 521, 529, 537, 539, 599, 669, 679, 712, 732; **attempted murder of by J. Riley:** 14, 177; **attempted murder of by B. Campbell:** 500
Paxton, Louis – 197, 345, 540, 543
Pearson, Jim Berry – 241;
The Maxwell Land Grant by: 241
Pecos River – 23, 197, 332-333, 404, 440, 651
Pecos River Cow Camp (see Thomas Benton Catron)
Peñasco Reservoir and Irrigation Company – 188
Peñasco River – 13, 332, 337, 351, 542, 686
Peñasco River Ranch – 187-188, 347; **as Billy Bonney's ranch:** 13, 22
Pennypacker, Galusha – 526, 557, 562, 582-583, 611
Peppin, George Warden – 18-20, 87, 173, 185, 188-189, 196, 198-200, 330, 336, 373, 375, 385, 387-389, 406, 410, 415-416, 419-420, 423, 426-430, 447, 454-455, 474, 490-492, 499, 501, 509, 523-525, 538, 540, 542-543, 552-553,556-557, 576-578, 581, 584-587, 589, 592, 599, 601-602, 606-608, 639; **biography of:** 188-189; **builder of "The House":** 173, 188, 330, 336; **married wife of murdered Hilario Jaramillo:** 173; **Deputy of Sheriff Brady:** 373; **made Sheriff by illegal Governor Axtell proclamation:** 415-416, 419-420, 447, 454-455; **leader of murder posse for Frank MacNab:** 198; **likely assassination plot against A.A. McSween by:** 375, 385, 423; **leader of raid on San Patricio:** 200, 423, 501; **leader of San Patricio massacre:** 18, 189, 198, 501, 639; **Sheriff in Lincoln County War Battle:** 18-19, 189, 196, 198-199, 387, 423, 426-429, 454, 524-525, 542, 577-578, 584-587, 589-592, 601-602, 606-607; **enabler of looting of Tunstall's store:** 430, 454, 525, 581; **indicted for Lincoln County War murder and arson:** 419, 491, 509, 552-553, 556-557
Perea, Pedro – 95, 150
Perry County, Ohio – 157
Perry, S.R. – 474
Picacho, New Mexico Territory – 18, 357, 423, 425, 427, 501, 521
Pickett, Tom – 25-26, 202, 617, 620, 658-662
Phillips, C.M. – 68
Pierce, Milo – 197, 345, 540, 543, 598, 606; **Ringite murderer freed on *habeas corpus*:** 598; **indicted Ringite murderer pardoned by Catron's abuse of Amnesty Proclamation:** 21, 197, 557, 594 (see Thomas Benton Catron); **as testifying for N.A.M. Dudley against Billy Bonney:** 606
Pile, William Anderson – 77, 79, 184, 209-210, 245, 247, 293; **with Catron in "Battle of the Archives:** 210; **using troops to suppress settlers:** 247
Pino, Nicholas – 78
pit jail – 16, 341, 368, 392
Poe, John William – 22, 29, 137-139; **recommended for Governor by Catron:** 137-139

Portales, New Mexico Territory – 39, 644, 646-647, 649-651, 663
"Poker Bill" plot (see Thomas Benton Catron, William Thornton)
Pope, John – 494, 498, 515-516

Porter, Henry M. – 245, 250, 261-263, 312, 321-322, 439 (see "Dear Ben plot")
Portland, Oregon – 439, 513
Posse Comitatus Act – 19, 22, 200, 422-423, 426-429, 487, 567, 576, 602, 609
Potawatomis Indians – 467
Powell, Lewis – 469
Powell, William "Buck" – 188, 197, 478, 557, 594, 598; **Ringite murderer freed on *habeas corpus*:** 598; **indicted Ringite murderer pardoned by Catron's abuse of Amnesty Proclamation:** 21, 197, 557, 593-594 (see Thomas Benton Catron)
Pratt, John – 213-214, 277, 281, 324
"precious specimen" quote (see Lew Wallace)
Priest, E.C. – 538
Prince, Bradford L. – 66, 70-71, 169, 185, 272, 619, 726
Pritchard, George W. – 153
Puerto de Luna – 647
Purington, George – 200, 332, 367-368, 375, 381, 386, 389, 406, 417, 428, 474, 520, 523-524, 556-557, 593, 596, 598, 606; **as testifying for N.A.M. Dudley against Billy Bonney:** 606
Racketeer Influenced and Corrupt Organizations Act (RICO) – 5
Randlett, James F. – 173, 335-336
Rasch, Philip J. – 43, 180; *Gunsmoke in Lincoln County* by: 180
Raton, New Mexico Territory – 94, 191
Raton News and Press – 727
Raton pass – 242, 245, 326
Rayado, New Mexico Territory – 243
Raymers, Jim – 540
Raymond, Numa – 185
Rea, D.B. – 235
Read, Bert M. – 68
redistricting – 68
Regulators of 1771 – 8, 16, 358-360
Regulators of 1878 – 16-21, 27-28, 30, 35, 39, 43, 45-46, 77, 90, 97, 139, 174, 180, 183, 185, 187-189, 199, 245, 250, 253, 268-269, 357, 361, 373, 375, 380, 385-387, 408-409, 415, 425, 430, 469-470, 476, 501, 511, 518, 520-521, 541, 592, 620-621, 623, 632, 634-635, 671, 685, 731

"Regulator Manifesto" (see William H. Bonney)
removal of courts (see Samuel Beach Axtell)
Republican Advocate – 503
Revolutionary War – 8, 16, 358
Riley, John – 14, 22, 43, 64, 80-82, 146, 173-174, 177, 180, 182, 185-186, 204, 252, 330-332, 336, 344-345, 349-351, 375, 387-389, 391-392, 394-396, 398-409, 411, 426, 452-455, 474-475, 540, 542, 611, 624; **biography of:** 177-178; **as J.J. Dolan and Company partner:** 330-331, 336, 349, 401, 540, 542; **as Ring sub-boss:** 173, 336, 389; **attempted assassination of Juan Patrón by:** 14, 332; **assisting bribe of Governor Axtell by:** 182, 331, 453; **helping recruit Sheriff Brady's Tunstall murder posse:** 400; **codebook of:** 82, 407; **as Catron agent:** 177-178, 186, 204, 206, 331, 426, 474; **reporting fake Regulator attack of May 30, 1878:** 375, 387-388, 425; **in Lincoln County War:** 426, 452-454; **Feliz Land and Cattle Company of:** 22, 174, 177, 185; **"A Tax-Payer's Complaint" about:** 344-345, 393; **Tularosa Land and Cattle Company of:** 81, 185; **American Cattle Company of:** 177; **D+D Ranch of:** 177; **Terra Amarilla Land Grant with Catron of:** 177; **Santa Teresa Land Grant with Catron of:** 177 (see J.J. Dolan and Company, "The House")
Rinconada Bonita – 534
Rincón, New Mexico Territory – 670
Rio Ariba County, New Mexico Territory – 76, 98, 300
Rio Feliz Land and Cattle Company – 81, 91, 185
Rio Grande, Mexico and Pacific Railroad Company – 190

Rio Grande Republican – 70, 185, 505
Ritch, William G. – 68, 474, 483, 503, 647
Rivera, Emiterio – 95
Rivers, Frank – 361-362, 397, 478
Rock Corral – 540, 543
Rocky Arroyo – 540, 543
Rocky Mountain News – 211
Roberts, Andrew "Buckshot" – 17, 24, 27-28, 90, 245, 366, 373-374, 385, 411, 424, 529, 543, 606, 620, 628-629, 633, 671; **murderer of J.H. Tunstall:** 366; **self-defense Regulator killing of:** 17, 24, 373-374, 385, 529, 543 (see federal indictment No. 411 for murder of)
Roberts, Oliver "Brushy Bill" – xviii-xix; (see *Billy the Kid's Pretenders, Brushy Bill and John Miller*)
Robinson, Berry – 19, 387, 428-429, 523, 579
Robinson, George – 405
Rodey, P.S. – 106
Romero, J. – 474
Romero, R. – 474
Romero, Vincente – 18-19, 21, 136, 144, 189, 196, 427, 429, 476, 520, 525, 588, 732
Romero y Valencia, Francisco – 348
Romney, West Virginia – 468
Roosevelt, Theodore – 146-148, 163, 195
Ross County, Ohio – 193
Ross, Edmund G. – 57, 169, 204
Roswell Daily Record – 36
Roswell, New Mexico Territory – 24, 36, 175, 188, 475, 538, 621, 640-642
Rough Rider – 147
Routt, John C. – 458-459
Roxbury, Massachusetts – 201
"Roxey" – 474
Roy, W.C. – 171
Rudabaugh, Dave "Dirty Dave" – 24-26, 202, 649, 651, 653-654, 658-662
Rudolph, Charles – 129
Rudolph, Milnor – 29, 205, 213-214, 218, 224, 699-700; **biography of:** 205; **Legislature Revolt against:** 29, 213-214, 218, 224, 699; **Billy Bonney's Coroner's Jury President:** 29, 205, 213, 699-700
"Rump Council" – 96
"Rustling Bob" – 538
Rynerson, William Logan – 15, 21, 35, 43, 46, 66-71, 81-82, 90-91, 112, 145, 174, 177-178, 180, 183-186, 198, 249, 319, 332, 342, 347-351, 370, 372, 375, 377, 380-381, 389, 396-397, 400, 402-404, 407-408, 418, 449-450, 455, 474, 546, 549-552, 554-555, 598; **biography of:** 183-186; **murderer of John P. Slough:** 112, 184, 349, 418; **Mesilla Riot about:** 184; **exposed as Ringite by W.B. Sloan:** 66-70, 185; **getting county seat moved to Las Cruces to profit personally:** 185; **removal of sought:** 372; **malicious prosecution of A.A. McSween and J.H. Tunstall by:** 46, 145, 183, 342, 347, 396-397, 400, 404; **obstructing McSween's bondsmen by:** 15, 347-348, 372, 403; **"Friends Riley and Dolan" letter by:** 82, 177, 185, 349-350, 407; **letter:** 350; **involved in Tunstall murder:** 351, 370; **obstructing of Tunstall's murderers' prosecution by:** 46, 90, 185, 319, 380-381, 408; **changing Billy Bonney's trial venue by:** 21, 319, 554-555; **recruiting John Kinney's gang for Lincoln County War by:** 198; **attempted shielding of S.B. Axtell from Angel investigation by:** 449-450; **obstructing arrest of H.I. Chapman's murderers by:** 185, 551-552, 598; **attacking Billy Bonney in 1879 Grand Jury by:** 35, 185, 549-550; **threat to Ira Leonard by:** 546; **assisting in Billy Bonney's Brady trial by:** 185; **Feliz River Land and Cattle Company of:** 81, 185; **Feliz River Land and Cattle Company of:** 22, 81, 91, 174, 177, 185; **Tularosa Land and Cattle Company of:** 81, 185; **working politically with Catron:** 178, 186-187;
Safford, A.P.K. – 237
Salazar, Yginio – 32, 429, 500, 686
Salisbury, Robert Gascoyne-Cecil – 433
Sampson, C. – 375
San Bernadino, California – 505
San Carlos Indian Reservation – 81
Sanchez, Pancho – 538
Sanders, James – 409
Sandy Creek Manifesto – 358
San Francisco Chronicle – 703

850

San Miguel County, New Mexico Territory – 25, 343, 396, 636, 644-645, 658, 662
San Nicholas Spring – 539
San Patricio, New Mexico Territory – 16, 18, 144, 189, 198, 200, 250, 357, 387, 404, 422-423, 425, 427, 476, 501, 520, 533-534, 639; **massacre at:** 18, 144, 189, 198, 422-423, 476, 501, 515, 639
Santa Fe Daily New Mexican – 66, 111, 134, 137, 139, 171, 175, 267, 386
Santa Fe Archives – 77, 85 (see Battle of the Archives)
Santa Fe County – 101, 103, 162, 168, 213-214, 504
Santa Fe jail –26, 189, 663-665, 687
Santa Fe, New Mexico Territory – 63-64, 66-67, 69-70, 76, 79-80, 97, 104, 106, 116, 161, 168, 171, 180, 183, 186, 190, 223, 227, 229, 246, 261, 277-278, 280-281, 289-290, 295, 316, 318, 323, 326, 339, 345, 370, 393, 396, 400, 409, 420, 426, 469, 473-475, 480, 492, 509, 513-514, 546, 626-627, 631, 641, 643, 659, 662, 666, 669, 688, 690-692, 704, 706, 708, 711, 714
Santa Fe New Mexican – 55, 103, 154, 168, 174-175, 190, 204, 471, 727
Santa Fe News – 471
Santa Fe Post – 212
Santa Fe Ring (the Ring) – 3-8, 12-13, 20, 23, 29-30, 36, 39-48, 51-57, 61-72, 75, 77, 79-80, 85-86, 89, 91, 96, 128, 152, 157-160, 164, 167, 170, 182-183, 191, 199, 205-206, 209-218, 221-223, 225, 227-230, 233-235, 237-238, 241-264, 267-276, 278-289, 292-297, 299-301, 303-326, 329-345, 347, 351, 353, 357-358, 360, 365-373, 375, 378-381, 385-389, 408, 417, 419-420, 422-423, 425-428, 430, 433, 435-440, 443-444, 449-450, 452, 454-461, 464, 467, 469-473, 475-476, 478, 480, 483-484, 487-490, 493, 495, 497-498, 500-501, 504, 518, 520-521, 529-530, 533, 540-542, 544, 546, 550, 553, 555, 557, 561-563, 565, 568-569, 573-576, 578, 586-587, 594-595, 599, 601, 603, 605-606, 614, 617-621, 623-625, 627, 629-630, 632, 634, 636-637, 640, 642-646, 648, 657, 659, 669, 671-672, 677, 681, 685, 703, 714, 725-728, 731-732; **as organized crime:** 4-8, 51, 154, 249, 283-284; **as perfect crime of:** 6-7; **existence of:** 60-70; **formula of:** 72, 276; **land-grab scheme of:** 36, 51, 72, 75-76, 85, 96, 150, 160, 221, 244, 246, 272, 276, 285-287, 306, 322, 326, 329, 358, 422, 725; **terrorism of:** 4, 8, 14, 29, 53, 91, 143, 164, 182, 184, 206, 211, 230, 242, 254, 272, 354, 419, 430, 480, 521, 535, 669, 725; **defamatory affidavits by:** 22, 85, 89, 104, 122, 131, 145, 161, 178, 440, 488-489, 562, 576, 614 (see Thomas Benton Catron and victims Susan McSween, Ira Leonard, Thomas J. Smith, Jacob Crist, Eugene Fiske, Oliver Lee); **malicious prosecutions by:** 4, 6-7, 46, 51, 63, 71-72, 75-77, 79, 81, 85, 91, 96-97, 130-131, 143-145, 148, 172, 174, 180, 182-184, 187, 197, 209, 212, 218, 222, 225, 241, 247-248, 251, 255-256, 260, 268, 273, 275-276, 287, 308, 310, 323, 325-326, 331-334, 342-343, 347, 351-357, 428, 430, 436 (see Ada Morley, A.A. McSween, J.H. Tunstall, J.S. Chisum, Jacob Crist, Oliver Lee) **outlawing opponents by** (see outlaw myth); **military suppression by:** 8, 13, 51, 85, 99, 153, 211, 214, 218, 225-227, 251, 255, 262, 314, 318, 353, 358, 367, 386-387, 415, 425, 430, 436, 438-439, 454, 480, 491, 513, 515, 575; **assassinations and attempted assassinations by:** (see F.J. Tolby, Robert Casey, O.P. McMains, J.H. Tunstall, A.A. McSween, Harvey Morris, Francisco Zamora, Vincente Romero, Ygenio Salazar, Ira Leonard, Susan McSween, Alexis Grossetete, Robert Elsinger, Francisco Chavez, Oliver Lee) **obstruction of justice by:** 85, 111, 255, 264, 269, 341, 347, 352, 557, 725 (see shielded killers of J.T. Tolby, J.H. Tunstall, A.A. McSween, Harvey Morris, Francisco Zamora, Vincente Romero, Francisco Chavez; *habeas corpus* (used to free Ringite prisoners)); **exposés of** (see

851

W. Morley, Mary McPherson, Ira Leonard, M. Leverson, W. B. Sloan, Lew Wallace, Frank Warner Angel)
Santa Fe Sentinel – 558
Santa Fe Trail – 157, 326
Santa Fe Weekly New Mexican – 96, 103-104, 132, 256
Santa Fe Weekly New Mexican Review – 96
Santa Fe Weekly Sun – 103
Santa Teresa Land Grant – 177 (see Thomas Benton Catron)
San Juan County Index – 100
Santistevan, P.Y. – 141
Scholand, Emilie – 342-343, 393-395, 399
Schurz, Carl – 64, 161, 206, 246, 269, 275-276, 282, 292, 294, 313, 329, 349, 370, 417, 434-435, 443, 448-450, 459, 460, 470, 476-478, 480, 484, 498, 501, 504, 518, 534-536, 544, 546, 557-558, 561, 593, 596, 603, 614, 617-619, 639, 645, 648
Scroggins, John – 411-414
Scurlock, Josiah "Doc" – 18, 21, 27, 31, 411-414, 427, 477, 521, 530, 556-557, 620, 632, 634
Second Judicial District – 94, 168, 262, 320, 505
Second National Bank of Santa Fe – 80, 168 (see Thomas Benton Catron, Stephen Benton Elkins)
Secret Service – 24, 29, 39, 47, 81, 87, 90, 131, 139, 153, 195, 197, 202, 331, 461, 504, 617, 620-623, 627, 634, 638, 646, 648, 657, 703, 731 (see Azariah Wild)
Secret Service pardon (see Azariah Wild)
Segale, Blandina – 42, 171; *At the End of the Santa Fe Trial* by: 42; *Blandina Segale, The Nun Who Rode on Billy the Kid* about: 42
Segura, Alejandro – 700
Selman alias "Tom Cat" – 477, 521
Selman, John – 477, 538
Sena, José D. – 221
Sevedra, Antonio – 700
Seven Rivers, New Mexico Territory – 197, 331, 344, 392, 534, 538, 540, 542-543, 596
Seven Rivers rustlers (boys, outlaws, murderers) – 18, 27-28, 81, 174, 188-189, 196-197, 318, 332, 334, 344-345, 351, 385-387, 392, 411, 426-429, 75, 492, 518, 521, 533, 541-544, 546, 570, 579, 596, 614, 632, 639, 686; **as posse in Lincoln County War Battle:** 427-429, 544, 579; **freed from Fort Stanton custody by** *habeas corpus*: 318, 546
Seward, F.W. – 479
Shedd's Ranch – 397, 539, 541
Sheldon, Lionel – 68, 90, 168-169, 725-726
Sherman, John E. – 65, 470, 474-477, 500, 520-521, 534, 536, 606, 622-624, 666, 690; **Sherman's outlaw list by:** 470, 475, 477-478, 500, 520-521, 534, 536, 606; the list: 477-478; **working with Secret Service:** 622-624 (see outlaw myth)
Sherman's outlaw list (see John Sherman)
Shield, David – 64, 337, 347-348, 374-375, 378, 380, 395, 397, 406, 426, 433-434, 439, 504
Shield, Elizabeth – 377, 426, 432
Shield family – 426, 432, 439
Sierra Mosca Grant – 298
Silba (Silva), Jose – 700
Silver City, New Mexico Territory – 12-13, 54, 68, 80, 98, 213-215, 233-235, 238, 334, 360, 502, 538-539, 696
Slaughter, John – 477
Sloan, William B. – 66-72; **"Ithurial" letter by:** 66-70
Slough, John Potts – 69, 112, 144, 184, 349, 418; **murder by William Rynerson:** 69, 112, 184
Sluga, Mary Elizabeth – 141, 148
Smith, Charles F. – 468
Smith, G.A. – 474
Smith, George W. – 406, 410, 497, 519
Smith, G.G. – 475
Smith, John – 520
Smith, Kirby – 468
Smith, Samuel – 352
Smithsonian Museum – 199
Smith, Thomas J. – 111-123, 127-130, 132, 134, 146, 203; **Catron's** *Albuquerque Daily Citizen* **plot against:** 113-121, 127, 129, 132, 134, 203; **Catron's "Extra Billy Smith"** *Socorro chieftain* **plot against:** 122-123, 146; **defamatory affidavits against:** 122
Smith, Thomas W. – 251

Socorro Chieftain – 111, 122, 130, 146
Socorro County, New Mexico Territory – 557, 598
Socorro, New Mexico Territory – 68, 473, 504, 553, 571
Socorro Sun – 504
Sons of Liberty of 1765 – 358
sorrel horse – 20, 35, 440
south foothills (see Lincoln County War Battle)
Southern Pacific Railroad – 79, 99, 175, 190, 194, 236
South Spring River Ranch – 373, 405-406, 422, 426
Spanish-American War – 153
Sparta, Ontario – 168
Speaks, Robert – 477
Spencerian handwriting – 12, 21, 530
Spiegelberg Brothers of Santa Fe – 43, 79, 331, 393, 474
Spiegelberg, Lehman – 79
Spiegelberg, Levi – 393-394
Spiess, Charles A. – 102, 104-111, 115-116, 122-123, 125-128, 142-143, 191; **in Knights of Liberty:** 102; **Borrego case disbarment charges and trial of:** 105-111, 115-116, 123, 126-128, 191; represented by Frank Springer in: 109, 191; corrupt vindication in: 123; dissenting opinion against: 126-128 (see Thomas Benton Catron)
Springer, Frank – 43, 71, 83, 109, 116, 127, 136, 169-170, 191-193, 203, 241-242, 247, 249-250, 252, 256, 259-264, 268, 271, 288, 295, 312-324, 353-354, 439, 443-444, 473-475, 497, 618, 727, 731; **biography of:** 91, 247-248, 312; **deposition of:** 191, 250, 252, 264, 314-324; **newspapers of** (see *Cimarron News and Press* and *Las Vegas Optic*); **trying to save Colfax County courts:** 261; **intervening in Ada Morley's buggy incident by:** 281; **scapegoating S.B. Axtell by:** 313-314, 474; **defending Oscar P. McMains:** 268, 271; **as turncoat:** 109, 191, 264; **town of Springer as pay-off for:** 94, 99, 169, 191, 353; **defending Melvin Mills for F.J. Tolby murder:** 264; **defending Catron and C.A. Spiess against disbarment:** 109, 111, 127; **working for Catron:** 191-193 (see "Dear Ben plot")
Springer, New Mexico Territory (see Frank Springer)
Springfield, Illinois – 193
Staab, Adolph – 43, 170, 191
Staab Z and Brother of Santa Fe – 474
Stafford, New York – 183
Stam and Ruggles Attorneys – 394
Stamp Act – 358
Stanley, Stephen – 391, 408, 474
Stanley house of: 608
statehood of New Mexico – 23, 138, 151-152, 210
Stevens, Benjamin "Ben" – 168, 250, 262, 312, 320-321; **as "Dear Ben plot" accomplice:** 168, 250, 262, 312, 320-321; **"Dear Ben" telegraph to:** 263, 439 (see "Dear Ben plot")
Stevens, I.N. – 235
Stevens, R.S. – 238
Stevens, Stephen – 411-414
Stewart, Frank – 27, 651, 658, 660, 662, 681; **stealing of Billy Bonney's bay mare by:** 681; **replevin suit against:** 27, 680
Stewart, Isaac S. – 216
Stinking Springs, New Mexico Territory – 12, 26-27, 195, 204, 646, 657, 663, 680, 690, 713
St. James Hotel – 248, 253, 262
St. Louis Daily Globe Democrat – 691
St. Louis, Missouri – 15, 193, 209, 343, 394-396, 503, 691
Stowe, Harriett Beecher – 505
Uncle Tom's Cabin by: 505
St. Patrick's College – 172
St. Paul, Minnesota *Dispatch* –
Strachen, W.J. – 475
Stuttgart, Germany – 172
Sullivan, Alexander P. – 212
Sunnyside, New Mexico Territory – 29, 205, 699
Surratt, Mary – 469, 531
sutler store – 80, 85, 171-173, 181-182, 187, 330-331, 336 (see Fort Stanton; see "The House")
Taft, Alfonso – 86, 276, 278
Tafoya, Santos – 538
Taggart, Moses – 503
Tammany Hall (see William Tweed)
Taos Grand Jury (see Grand Jury)
Taos Rebellion – 243
Tascosa, Texas – 20, 35, 440, 617
Taylor, George – 555
Taylor, John L. – 288

853

Taylor, Morris F. – 241, 252, 265, 268; *O.P. McMains and the Maxwell Land Grant Conflict* by: 241
Teller, Henry M. – 726
Terre Haute, Indiana – 696, 710, 721
"Texas Jack" – 520
Thayer, Charles B. – 475
Thayer, Fred – 107, 124
The Daily Arizona Silver Belt –198
The Deming Graphic – 177
The Hotel Men's Confidential Agency – 179
"The House" – 14-15, 33, 44, 79-81, 90, 95, 146, 172-174, 176-178, 197, 199, 329-333, 335, 337, 342, 345, 349, 367, 374, 381, 389, 393, 401-402, 408-409, 424, 427-428, 522, 685; **usurious credit of:** 14; **government contracts of:** 14, 80-81, 173, 177, 181-182, 197, 330-331, 337-338, 350, 393, 522, 542-543, 552, 618, 625; **as Catron's front:** 197, 331; **Catron's possession of:** 174, 331, 389, 409, 415-416, 616; (see L.G. Murphy and Company, J.J. Dolan and Company, Thomas Benton Catron)
The Independent – 344, 471
The Indianapolis Press – 409, 415
The Lost Pardon of Billy the Kid – xxii, 85, 467
The Mesilla Valley Independent – 197, 344-345, 378, 471-472
The Oregonian – 439, 505
"The Pilgrim" – 477
The Santa Fe Magazine – 190
"The Rustlers" – 538
The Santa Fe Sentinel – 471
"The Wrestlers" – 476, 478, 520
Third Judicial District – 76, 158, 167, 183-184, 204, 209, 212, 226, 242, 301, 343, 347, 369-370, 399, 412-414, 504, 554, 688
Thornton, Edward – 366, 389, 443
Thornton, William Taylor 89, 103, 105, 130, 132-141, 143, 145-146, 194, 198, 200, 203, 246, 331, 420, 424, 475, 557; **lawyer in Maxwell Land Grant's patent:** 246; **lawyer in Catron's take-over of "The House":** 331; **assisted in Dudley Court of Inquiry:** 89; **Catron's "Poker Bill" plot against:** 132-137, 139-140; **Catron's attempt to remove as Governor:** 137-139

Three Rivers, New Mexico Territory – 81, 440, 617
Tibbles, Thomas Henry – 275
Tidwell, Silas – 301-302
Tierra Amarilla Grant – 79, 97, 162, 169, 177
Tilden, Samuel J. – 6, 237, 469
tintype (see William H. Bonney)
Tolby, Franklin J. – 56, 63, 77, 87, 91, 98, 103, 136, 143, 152, 168-169, 171, 193, 196, 241, 245, 248-262, 264-267, 270, 275-276, 278, 282-282, 287-288, 290, 296, 303-310, 312, 317-319, 321, 323, 326, 337, 349, 351-352, 368, 381, 438, 456, 501, 553, 732; **assassination of:** 56, 63, 77, 91, 168-169, 196, 241, 249, 251-252, 257, 259, 265, 275, 296, 303-310, 312, 317, 319, 321, 323, 326, 349, 351-352, 381, 438, 456, 501, 553; **obstructing prosecution of murderers of:** 261-262, 264-265, 268, 278, 290, 312, 317, 349, 368 (see Oscar P. McMains, Robert Longwill, Melvin Mills, Manuel Cardenas, Cruz Vega)
Tompkins, R.H. – 475
Treaty of Guadalupe Hidalgo – 51, 58, 243, 291, 299, 306
Trinidad, Colorado – 502
Trujillo, Gregorio – 387
Trujillo, Juan – 538
Trujillo, Lorenzo – 538
Trumball, Lyman – 222
Tryon, William – 358-360; **Tryon's Palace for:** 359
Tularosa Land and Cattle Company – 81, 150, 177-178, 185-186
Tunstall, Emily Frances – 337
Tunstall, Emily Ramie – 337
Tunstall, John Henry – 8, 11, 13-17, 21-22, 28, 30-31, 33, 41, 43, 45-46, 61-62, 64-65, 80-82, 86-87, 90-91, 103, 109, 136, 144, 171-174, 177, 183, 185, 187-188, 191, 196-199, 225, 246, 250, 252, 255, 263, 268, 287, 317, 319-320, 322, 329-342, 344-347, 349-354, 357, 360-368, 370-375, 377-378, 380-381, 385-386, 388-392, 397-402, 404, 406-409, 411, 416-417, 419, 423-428, 432, 436, 443-446, 454, 457-458, 495-496, 498, 500-501, 504, 509-510, 514, 520, 522, 525, 529, 531, 535, 538, 541-542, 544, 551, 553, 562,

576, 581, 584, 586-587, 589-590, 601-602, 607-608, 612, 632, 646, 678-679, 685, 732; **biography of:** 336-337; **store of:** 14, 16, 22, 332, 337, 340, 367, 375, 391, 426-427, 501, 584, 587, 589-590, 602, 607-608, 612; looting of: 430, 439, 454, 508-509, 524, 562, 581, 584, 601; **ranches of:** 14, 22, 33, 187, 332, 340, 391; **Lincoln County Bank of:** 14-15, 332-333, 337, 347, 373, 378, 430; **Ring competition of:** 14-15, 81, 173-174, 330-333, 337, 339, 541-542; **letters home of:** 61, 337-342, 346; **employer of Billy Bonney:** 13, 31, 33, 199, 332, 334; gave Peñasco River ranch to Bonney: 188, 362; **horse and mule theft of:** 392; **exposing Ring tax embezzling by:** 80, 187, 197, 344-346, 398-399; "A Tax-payer's Complaint" by: 197, 344-345; **malicious prosecution of:** 14-15, 46, 173, 183, 263, 287, 320, 334, 342-343, 347, 399, 436, 457; **J.J. Dolan's attempted murder of:** 397-398; **Sheriff Brady's death threat to:** 342, 392, 678; **assassination of:** 14-15, 21-22, 33, 81, 91, 188, 196, 252, 255, 349, 351-352, 357, 361-365, 374, 401, 417, 443-446, 541, 361-365; **autopsy reports of:** 351, 353, 401, 428; **shielding of murderers of:** 16, 20-21, 46, 86-87, 103, 174, 185, 246, 253, 255, 319, 331, 351, 354, 380-381, 385, 389, 408, 415-417, 425, 529, 551, 678; cover-up by Frank Warner Angel: 389, 444-446; **federal investigation for murder of:** 366, 380, 389, 443-446, 501; cover-up by Frank Warner Angel: 389, 444-446; **taking ranches of:** 81, 91, 174, 177, 185, 322; **taking store of:** 322; **stealing cattle of:** 424, 436, 538; **outlaw myth for:** 43, 45, 334
Tunstall, John Partridge – 62, 337, 433
Tunstall, Lilian – 337
Tunstall, Mabel – 337
Turkey Springs – 400
Turner, Beeton and Tunstall – 337
Turner, Marion – 197, 478, 521, 539, 553-555, 557, 593-594, 598; **Ringite murderer freed on** *habeas corpus:* 598; **indicted Ringite murderer pardoned by Catron's abuse of Amnesty Proclamation:** 21, 197, 557, 594 (see Thomas Benton Catron); **as testifying for N.A.M. Dudley against Billy Bonney:** 606
Tweed, William Magear "Boss" – 5-6, 55, 60, 86, 160, 237, 419; **Tammany Hall of:** 5-6, 60, 237
Twitchell, Ralph Emerson – 41-42, 80, 84, 94, 98, 112, 170, 183, 190, 205-205; **biography of:** 205-206; **Catron loan for embezzled money by:** 80; **cipher-code with Catron by:** 84; *Leading Facts in New Mexico History* by: 41, 80, 183, 205
Uña de Gato Land Grant – 288, 295
Underwood and Nash – 197, 344; **subject of "A Tax-Payer's Complaint":** 344
Underwood, Nathan – 197, 344-345
Upson, Marshall Ashmun "Ash" –
Utley, Robert – 42, 44-45, 731; *High Noon in Lincoln* by: 42,44
Uvalde, Texas – 195
Valdez, Pedro – 160, 300
Valencia County, New Mexico Territory – 181, 300
Valencia, Patricio – 102-104, 132, 134-135, 142
Vega, Cruz – 169, 171, 196, 253-255, 263, 267, 270-271, 304, 307
Victorio – 200, 662
Victory, J.P. – 106
Vigil, Hipolito – 102
volley – 19, 22, 200, 429, 586, 590-591, 602, 608, 660
Waddingham, Wilson – 245, 288
Wade, Edward C. – 197
Wade, James F. – 263
Wagner, John – 541
Waite, Fred Tecumseh – 13, 16-17, 27, 347, 362-368, 400-402, 411-414, 453, 477, 452, 620
Wakefiels, E.H. – 475
Waldo, Henry L. – 22, 83, 89, 146, 161, 168, 170, 190-192, 200, 204-205, 242, 249, 254, 259, 264-265, 267, 269, 271-272, 274, 276, 278, 282-283, 297, 300-301, 305-308, 310, 470, 475, 517, 522, 550, 563-564, 566-567, 579, 582-583, 585-586, 593, 597-598, 601-609; **biography of:** 190; **in Catron's law firm:** 22,

146, 255, 260; **as Taos County judge:** 264-265, 267, 271; **Colfax County charges against:** 283, 297, 301, 305-307, 310; **law partner with William Breeden:** 168; **defense for N.A.M. Dudley's Court of Inquiry:** 89, 200, 249, 254, 269, 517, 522, 563-564, 566-567, 579, 582-583, 585-586, 598-599, 601-602; closing argument for: 587, 603-609; **publishing Santa Fe New Mexican by:** 204

Wallace, David – 467-468

Wallace, Henry – 468

Wallace, Lew – 6, 12, 20-22, 26, 32, 34-35, 39, 44, 52, 87, 90, 139, 150, 167-169, 176, 183, 188, 191-192, 197, 199-201, 204, 270, 296, 318, 335, 360, 375, 385, 424, 430, 440, 443, 464, 467-481, 483-484, 487, 489-490, 493-503, 505, 509, 511, 513, 515, 517-522, 524-526, 529-539, 541-546, 549, 553, 555-558, 561-576, 586-587, 592-596, 599, 601, 603, 617-621, 632, 637, -640, 642-643, 653, 657, 662, 664-666, 669, 672, 681, 687, 689-699, 703-721, 725-727, 731; **biography of:** 20, 467-470; **Shiloh Battle's humiliation of:** 167, 467-469, 477, 490, 561, 603 (see Battle of Shiloh) **helping R.B. Hayes win Presidency:** 6, 469; **made Governor of New Mexico Territory:** 6, 270; **secret Frank Warner Angel notebook on Ring of:** 20, 471-475; **Mary McPherson's exposé owned by:** 296; **confirming existence of Angel's Catron report:** 459; **seeking troops and martial law by:** 480, 501, 595; **Amnesty Proclamation by:** 20, 188, 197, 360, 481, 489; **condemned by Grant County:** 502-503; **Ring removal rumors about:** 484; **H.I. Chapman murder forcing response by** (see H.I. Chapman); **arresting Chapman's murderers by:** 199, 318, 518; **pardon bargain with Billy Bonney by** (see William H. Bonney); **pardoning indicted Ringites by allowing abuse of Amnesty Proclamation:** 21, 188, 197, 556-557, 594 (see Jacob B. Matthews, William B. Powell, John Long, John Hurlie, Marion Turner, Thomas Benton Catron, Amnesty Proclamation); **conflict with N.A.M. Dudley of:** 22, 200, 487, 489, 493-498, 509, 511, 513, 515, 517, 526, 562-568, 574, 601, 603-605, 609, 614, 621, 627-628; Court of Inquiry prosecution testimony in: 562-568, 574; attack on by defense lawyer Henry Waldo: 603-605, 609; **pardon bargain betrayal by:** 12, 21, 26, 39, 470, 544-545 ("precious specimen" quote: 545), 549, 553, 587, 617, 647-648, 669, 687; **reward notices for Billy Bonney by** (see William H. Bonney); **death warrant for Billy Bonney by** (see William H. Bonney); **exposing Catron and the Santa Fe Ring by:** 483-484, 603, 617-619, 727-728; **coordinating with Secret Service operative Azariah Wild to capture Billy Bonney:** 621, 657; **departing governorship early by:** 725; **ambassadorship to Turkey for:** 20, 470, 664, 694, 704; **books by:** *The Man at Arms* by: 468; *The Fair God* by: 469; *Ben-Hur: A Tale of the Christ* by: 20, 464, 469-470, 617, 648, 664, 694, 703-704, 706, 716; *The Prince of India* by: 470; *Lew Wallace: An Autobiography* by: 467, 470, 715-716, 720; **outlaw myth by:** 469, 475-478, 488, 509, 520-522, 534, 536, 544-545, 558, 572, 574-575, 593-595, 619, 621, 703; **outlaw myth of Billy the Kid by:** 39, 202, 476-478, 500, 520-522, 541, 545, 558, 572, 574-575, 595, 621, 632, 637, 640, 645, 648, 657, 687; Billy the Kid as outlaw leader by: 648; (see Sherman's outlaw list); Billy the Kid outlaw myth articles by: 657, 691-693, 695-699, 703-721, 731 (see William H. Bonney; see outlaw myth)

Wallace, Susan Arnold Elston – 468, 470

Walz, Edgar – 25, 35, 61, 81, 178-179, 198, 331, 385, 409, 423-424, 430, 475, 500, 598, 624-625, 630, 633-634, 636

Wapello, Iowa – 191

Ward, Artemeus – 67

Washington, George (of Lincoln) – 44, 181, 400
Washington Times – 36, 153
Watertown, Wisconsin – 503
Watkins, E.C. – 333
Watts, John S. – 475
Weddle, Jerry – xxiii, 40, 731; *Antrim is My Stepfather's Name* by: 40
Weekly *Crawfordsville Review* – 707
"West Harden Gang" – 539
West, James – 348, 626, 630, 641
West, Joseph – 475
West Virginia Coal Company – 163
Westphall, Victor – 48, 57-57, 60, 71, 75-82, 84-89, 91-92, 96-97, 102-105, 108-109, 111-113, 122-124, 128-131, 136-137, 141, 146-154, 157, 198, 210-214, 222, 225, 241, 245-249, 256, 262, 267-268, 276, 329-334, 342-343, 345, 347, 351, 369, 375, 386-388, 425-426, 430, 440, 461; *Thomas Benton Catron and His Era* by: 48, 54, 75, 211, 242
Wetter, Henry – 212
Wheeler, Edward L. – 357
Wheeler, Frank – 477,538
White Caps – 96-97; **Proclamation of:** 97
Whitehill, Harvey – 13
White Oaks Eagle – 175
White Oaks livery – 20, 24-25, 440, 620, 626, 639-640
White Oaks, New Mexico Territory – 20, 24-29, 176, 440, 504, 620-621, 623-624, 626-627, 630-631, 633, 635, 637-641, 645-646, 651, 653, 682, 685-686, 689
White Oaks posse (rangers) – 28, 640, 646, 651, 685
White Sands, New Mexico Territory – 195
Widenmann, Robert A. – 33, 64, 350, 362-365, 400, 406, 475
Wigham, Henry – 475
Wild, Azariah – 24-26, 29, 87, 131, 195, 461, 504, 620-643, 645, 648, 657, 703, 731; **biography of:** 621; **backing of Pat Garrett by:** 26, 195, 621, 637-638; **tracking Billy Bonney by:** 87, 620, 625; **Secret Service pardon offer to Billy Bonney by:** 621, 627-632, 645, 731; **reports of stolen by Billy Bonney:** 632-633, 635; **meeting with Lew Wallace by:** 657; **outlaw myth for Billy Bonney by:** 131, 621, 625-626, 633-643, 648, 657, 703, 731
Williams, W.S. – 111
Wilson, Andrew – 475
Wilson, Aurelius – 415
Wilson Collegiate Institute – 183
Wilson, Robert B. – 301
Wilson, William "Billy" – 24-26, 201-202, 617, 620, 623-627, 630-632, 634, 638-642, 649, 653, 658-662, 669-670
Wilson, Willie – 196, 332
Wilson, John B. "Squire" – 16, 18-1921, 109, 237, 319-320, 341, 347-348, 350, 352, 360-361, 365-368, 371, 373-374, 377, 387, 397, 401-402, 404-405, 426, 429, 453, 475, 510, 512, 518, 521-522, 529-530, 532-533, 542, 562, 567, 579, 585, 600, 608, 669, 678-679, 732; **arrest warrants for J.H. Tunstall's murderers by:** 361, 365, 371, 401, 404; **deputizings to serve warrants by:** 365-366, 453; **illegal removal by Governor Axtell's Proclamation of:** 367-369, 377, 387, 404-405, 678; **N.A.M. Dudley's coerced warrants by:** 387, 426, 429, 510, 562, 567, 579 **"affidavit" of:** 522-524; **assisting of Billy Bonney's pardon by:** 518, 529-530, 532-533, 542
Wilson, Robert B. – 301
Wildy Well – 145
Wirz, Henry – 469
Wise, Lola – 538
Wright, John M. – 98
Yates Academy – 183
Zamora, Francisco – 18-19, 21, 136, 144, 189, 196, 427, 429, 476, 520, 525, 588, 590-591, 732
Zuber, Hugo – 647

www.ingramcontent.com/pod-product-compliance
Lightning Source LLC
Chambersburg PA
CBHW051122230426
43670CB00007B/641